Y0-BSN-095

APA Handbook of

Psychology, Religion, and Spirituality

APA Handbooks in Psychology

APA Handbook of Psychology, Religion, and Spirituality

VOLUME 2

An Applied Psychology of Religion and Spirituality

Kenneth I. Pargament, *Editor-in-Chief*

Annette Mahoney and Edward P. Shafranske, *Associate Editors*

American Psychological Association • Washington, DC

Published by
American Psychological Association
750 First Street, NE
Washington, DC 20002-4242
www.apa.org

To order
APA Order Department
P.O. Box 92984
Washington, DC 20090-2984
Tel: (800) 374-2721; Direct: (202) 336-5510
Fax: (202) 336-5502; TDD/TTY: (202) 336-6123
Online: www.apa.org/pubs/books/
E-mail: order@apa.org

In the U.K., Europe, Africa, and the Middle East, copies may be ordered from
American Psychological Association
3 Henrietta Street
Covent Garden, London
WC2E 8LU England

AMERICAN PSYCHOLOGICAL ASSOCIATION STAFF
Gary R. VandenBos, PhD, *Publisher*
Julia Frank-McNeil, *Senior Director, APA Books*
Theodore J. Baroody, *Director, Reference, APA Books*

Typeset in Berkeley by Cenveo Publisher Services, Columbia, MD

Printer: United Book Press, Baltimore, MD
Cover Designer: Naylor Design, Washington, DC

Library of Congress Cataloging-in-Publication Data

APA handbook of psychology, religion, and spirituality / editor, Kenneth I. Pargament.
v. ; cm. — (APA Handbooks in Psychology)
Includes bibliographical references and index.
ISBN 978-1-4338-1077-0 — ISBN 1-4338-1077-8
1. Psychology and religion. 2. Psychology, Religious. 3. Adjustment (Psychology)—Religious aspects. 4. Spirituality. I. Pargament, Kenneth I. (Kenneth Ira), 1950– II. Title: Handbook of psychology, religion, and spirituality.
BF51.A53 2013
201′.615—dc23
2012015189

British Library Cataloguing-in-Publication Data
A CIP record is available from the British Library.

Printed in the United States of America
First Edition

DOI: 10.1037/14046-000

To psychologists of religion and spirituality,
past, present, and future—
pioneers and partners exploring the deepest dimensions of life.

Contents

Volume 2: An Applied Psychology of Religion and Spirituality

Editorial Board

Part I

INTRODUCTION TO AN APPLIED PSYCHOLOGY OF RELIGION AND SPIRITUALITY

CHAPTER 1

FROM RESEARCH TO PRACTICE: TOWARD AN APPLIED PSYCHOLOGY OF RELIGION AND SPIRITUALITY

Kenneth I. Pargament, Annette Mahoney, Edward P. Shafranske, Julie J. Exline, and James W. Jones

An important shift in our field is now under way—the psychology of religion and spirituality is extending beyond research to encompass practice. Consider the following examples:

- Women with eating disorders in an inpatient setting who take part in a spirituality group improve more than those who participate in an emotional support group and a cognitive group (Richards, Berrett, Hardman, & Eggett, 2006).
- A psychologist of religion regularly lectures to police and the Federal Bureau of Investigation on the religious and spiritual roots of terrorism.
- A group of oncologists is trained to integrate questions about religion and spirituality as part of the initial patient interview; the program is associated with greater satisfaction with physician care (Kristeller, Rhodes, Cripe, & Sheets, 2005).
- Pastors from African American churches are involved in a program to encourage their members to engage in healthier eating, with positive results (Resnicow et al., 2004).
- Public school teachers and administrators participate in a 2-year spiritually based program that helps them nourish and rejuvenate themselves personally and professionally (Palmer, Jackson, Jackson, & Sluyter, 2001).
- A faith-based community organization program in Camden, New Jersey, results in a 25% drop in drug-related crime in areas in which vacant housing is targeted (Speer et al., 2003).
- Health professionals who participate in a program using spiritually based self-management tools experience significant improvements in mental health and stress levels over a 19-week follow-up period (Oman, Hedberg, & Thoresen, 2006).

Each of these programs targets some aspect of religion or spirituality to promote the health and well-being of individuals, families, institutions, or communities, and each one draws upon psychological theory, research, or professionals.

The movement from research to application is, in part, an outgrowth of the success the field is achieving as a basic science. The first volume of this *APA Handbook of Psychology, Religion, and Spirituality* documents the tremendous growth in knowledge about religion and spirituality that has taken place over the past 50 years. We have begun to shed new light on some of the deepest and most elusive dimensions of human functioning. We are learning about the rich variety of religious and spiritual forms and functions, their intricate links to individual, social, and community life, and their double-sided capacity to ameliorate and add to human suffering. True, questions continue to far outnumber answers in the field. Nevertheless, we have made significant progress toward three of the basic goals of any area of psychology: description, explanation, and prediction. These advances have made possible the pursuit of a fourth and vital goal of the discipline—putting the knowledge from research and scholarship into practice.

In the second volume of this handbook, we introduce our readers to many of the exciting steps that are being taken toward an empirically based applied

DOI: 10.1037/14046-001
APA Handbook of Psychology, Religion, and Spirituality: Vol. 2. An Applied Psychology of Religion and Spirituality, K. I. Pargament (Editor-in-Chief)

psychology of religion and spirituality. This chapter sets the stage for the chapters to follow. We begin with a discussion of the tensions in the field of psychology generally and in the psychology of religion and spirituality more specifically that make the integration of research and practice particularly challenging. We then present a rationale for why it is so important to conceptualize the psychology of religion and spirituality as an applied field. We conclude by offering a vision for an applied psychology of religion and spirituality that draws on the integrative paradigm that was introduced in the first volume (see Volume 1, Chapter 1, this handbook).

An applied psychology of religion and spirituality is not the exclusive province of clinical or counseling psychology; and it does not focus exclusively on psychotherapy. To date, the majority of the applied work in the field has occurred in the clinical realm. Yet, as the examples above attest, there are many potential applications of the psychology of religion and spirituality that extend well beyond psychotherapy and call on the skills of many kinds of psychologists, health care professionals, educators, and social scientists, including those who see themselves as predominantly theorists and researchers. An applied psychology of religion and spirituality, as we envision it, simply highlights the importance of putting knowledge into practice in ways that benefit individuals, families, institutions, and society. Every psychologist of religion and spirituality has a stake in this goal.

As noble as the goal of putting research into practice may sound, the process is anything but simple and straightforward. Why might that be?

TENSIONS BETWEEN RESEARCH AND PRACTICE IN THE PSYCHOLOGY OF RELIGION AND SPIRITUALITY

The movement from research to practice in the realm of religion and spirituality is complicated in part by the long-standing schism between the goals of research and practice that has run through the discipline of psychology as a whole. The rift runs deep, manifesting itself in several ways. First, the professional roles of researcher and practitioner are sharply distinguished from each other. Although many psychologists were trained in the scientist–practitioner model, relatively few psychologists are fully engaged in both science and practice (Kazdin, 2008). In fact, according to one survey of clinical and counseling psychologists who had graduated on average 18 years earlier, the modal and median number of journal articles, chapters, and books generated by these individuals was zero (Brems, Johnson, & Galluci, 1996). Conversely, research-oriented psychologists generally have limited applied experience. Second, researchers and practitioners weigh potential sources of knowledge quite differently. Researchers lend the greatest credence to well-controlled, quantitative studies of samples of the larger population, which are designed to yield generalizable rules and principles of human functioning. Practitioners, in contrast, are less concerned about general rules than the particular case—individual, couple, family, institution, or community. More relevant and convincing to the practitioner are case studies, narrative accounts, and qualitative analyses of specific people grappling with particular problems. Third, our institutions of higher education in psychology and the field of psychology itself have restructured themselves into research or academic and applied camps. In the past 30 years, the number of applied or professional schools of psychology awarding the practice-oriented doctorate of psychology degree (PsyD) has increased dramatically. One indicator of this change is that the number of clinical PsyD graduates has outpaced the number of clinical PhD graduates since 2003 (Finno, 2010). Research-oriented psychologists have reacted with concern to this shift in the field. For example, the American Psychological Society was founded in 1988 by academic psychologists in response to the perception that the American Psychological Association (APA) was overly responsive to the interests of practitioners (Pickens & Fowler, 2003).

The rift between science and practice in psychology runs especially deep in the domain of religion and spirituality. Although psychologists have treaded carefully around the scientific study of religion and spirituality for many years, they have been particularly reluctant to integrate religion and spirituality into the practice of psychology.

Their reluctance has several roots. To establish itself as a hard science, the discipline of psychology avoided anything that hinted of superstition or magic (Wulff, 1997). Religion with its appeals to the supernatural as a cause of human behavior and a remedy to human problems was off-limits. Admittedly, the picture has begun to change in the 21st century. Psychologists have started to turn their attention to practices that are deeply rooted in religious traditions, such as meditation and the virtues of forgiveness and gratitude, but they continue to tiptoe gingerly around the underlying religious and spiritual meanings of these practices (Kristeller, 2010; Walsh & Shapiro, 2006).

It is also true that psychologists as a group are considerably more skeptical about the ontological validity of a sacred dimension than the general population in the United States. Although more than 90% of Americans report that they believe in God, only 24% of clinical and counseling psychologists do so (Shafranske, 2001; see also Chapter 2 in this volume). Perhaps as a result of their skepticism, psychologists tend to underestimate the significance of religion and spirituality in people's lives. Rather than treat these phenomena as legitimate and distinctive aspects of human functioning, they shift their focus to psychological, social, and physical processes that are presumably more basic and more "real." There is, from this point of view, no need to focus on religion and spirituality in practice.

Some leading psychological figures, such as Freud and Skinner, go beyond skepticism to antagonism toward religion and spirituality, equating religious practices with pathology and discouraging psychologists from supporting this purportedly defensive way of life. Albert Ellis (1986), founder of Rational Emotive Therapy, had this to say: "Obviously, the sane effective psychotherapist should not . . . go along with the patient's religious orientation, for this is equivalent to trying to help them live successfully with their emotional illness" (p. 15). Ellis (2000), however, did soften his uniformly antagonistic position toward religion in his later writings.

Perhaps for these reasons, psychologists are generally ill informed about religion and spirituality, lacking the training to integrate these domains into practice, even if they were inclined to do so (see Chapter 33 in this volume). In a survey of directors of clinical psychology training programs in the United States and Canada, only 13% reported that they offered a course in the area of religion and spirituality (Brawer, Handal, Fabricatore, Roberts, & Wajda-Johnson, 2002). Similarly, only 46% of a national sample of counseling educators felt that they were prepared or very prepared to integrate religious and spiritual issues into their teaching and supervision activities (Young, Cashwell, Wiggins-Frame, & Belaire, 2002). We doubt that the situation is much different in other applied areas of psychology, although data are lacking. In any case, the lack of training may translate into religious and spiritual neglect in practice. For example, most clinicians do not routinely assess the client's religion and spirituality as part of treatment (Hathaway, Scott, & Garver, 2004).

Skepticism, antagonism, and spiritual illiteracy are hardly ideal qualities for the practice of psychology with individuals, families, institutions, and communities that attach deep value to matters of faith. A clear separation between religion, spirituality, and the science and practice of psychological is not problematic for everyone. As one psychologist commented, "We have no business sticking our noses into matters of personal faith." According to this perspective, psychology should maintain strict and clear boundaries from religion and spirituality, akin to the separation of church and state, lest the field try to manipulate or use religion as a tool to promote a particular agenda, be it secular or religious.

In sum, there are significant forces that work against a psychology of religion and spirituality that is inclusive of both research and practice. These forces have to be taken seriously and addressed directly in any effort to apply the knowledge generated from research.

A RATIONALE FOR AN EMPIRICALLY BASED APPLIED PSYCHOLOGY OF RELIGION AND SPIRITUALITY

There are several reasons why it makes good sense to view the psychology of religion and spirituality as not only a science but also an empirically based applied field.

Religion and Spirituality Are Embedded in U.S. Culture

Consider the following statistical indicators:

- More than 147 million people are members of religious congregations, and there are approximately 335,000 congregations in the United States (Lindner, 2010).
- According to the U.S. Religious Landscape Survey (Pew Forum on Religion and Public Life, 2008),
  - 58% of Americans report that they pray daily,
  - 74% believe in life after death,
  - 68% believe in angels and demons,
  - 59% believe in hell, and
  - 57% agree that it is necessary to believe in God to be moral and have good values.
- Four of the top-10 most admired people of the 20th century were religious: Mother Teresa, Martin Luther King Jr., Billy Graham, and Pope John Paul II (Gallup Poll, 1999).
- Despite the value of separation of church and state in the United States, there is a strong relationship between the religious beliefs of members of the U.S. Congress and their voting behavior on significant issues (Benson & Williams, 1982).

Taken as a whole, these indictors make an important point—religion and spirituality are "cultural facts" in the United States (Shafranske & Malony, 1996). Our experience has been that many psychologists are surprised by these figures, perhaps because they themselves tend to be less religious and spiritual than the general population (see Chapter 2 in this volume). Yet regardless of psychologists' personal religious and spiritual orientations, the reality is that religion and spirituality are a part of the lives of the majority of Americans. Shafranske (2002) put it this way:

> The religious beliefs that people hold, the rituals they use to signify human milestones such as birth and death, their expression of faith in private and public prayer, and the religiously-derived moral prescriptions and proscriptions they follow, as well as other spiritual practices, suggest the important influence of religion and spirituality. (p. 2)

In short, many people see the world through a sacred lens, speak the language of religion and spirituality, and traverse well-established religious pathways over the course of their lives. Practitioners can ill afford to overlook the role of religion and spirituality, given their place in the lives of most Americans. This is more than good sense. The APA (2002) has underscored psychologists' ethical obligation to attend to religion and spirituality as contributors to human diversity. Principle E of the APA Ethics Code states that "psychologists are aware of and respect cultural, individual, and role differences," including religion, and "consider these factors when working with members of such groups" (p. 1063).

Religion and Spirituality Can Be a Source of Solutions to Problems

Religion and spirituality are not only cultural facts; many people also regard them as significant sources of solutions to problems. In times of greatest stress, people often turn first and foremost to their faith for help. For instance, following the September 11 terrorist attacks, 90% of a random sample of people drawn from across the United States said they coped with these attacks by turning to religion (Schuster, Stein, & Jaycox, 2001). This finding is not unusual. Studies of combat veterans, divorcees, widows, physically abused spouses, parents of children with disabilities, and the medically ill consistently show that people frequently seek and find help from their religion in coping (Pargament, 2011; see also Volume 1, Chapter 19, this handbook). More rigorous studies have yielded positive links between religion and spirituality with physical and mental health (see Part III in this volume). In the most extensive review of this literature to date, Koenig, King, and Carson (2012) found that in the majority of studies, religious involvement was associated with a number of indicators of better mental health, including life satisfaction, marital stability, happiness, social support, less depression and anxiety, lower rates of suicide, and lower rates of substance abuse. In the physical health domain, they concluded that religious and spiritual people are on average "physically healthier (less cardiovascular diseases, better immune and endocrine functioning, perhaps less cancer and better prognosis, and greater longevity overall)" (pp. 601–602).

It could be argued that religious and spiritual resources are merely manifestations of more basic secular resources clothed in sacred garb. From this perspective, the support individuals feel from God is simply an expression of social support, religious beliefs are just another way of making meaning out of life, and religious and spiritual coping is only one among many ways to deal with the crises of living. Because religion and spirituality are not in any way distinctive, the argument goes, there is no need to pay particular attention to them in efforts to understand or improve the human condition.

In contrast to this argument, there is evidence that religion and spirituality represent distinctive resources at multiple levels—individual, institutional, and community (Volume 1, Chapter 14, this handbook). For example, empirical studies have shown that various religious and spiritual beliefs and practices, such as support from God and congregation members, contribute to individual health and well-being even after the effects of general social support and coping activities are taken into account (Gall, 2006; Krause, 2006). At the institutional level, religious congregations have a distinctive access to minority, marginalized, and disadvantaged groups. Furthermore, the average citizen is more likely to look to help from clergy than from other professionals, including physicians, psychologists, social services agencies, attorneys, and marriage counselors (Chalfant et al., 1990). These are good reasons to locate health prevention and promotion programs within settings or to collaborate with religious communities in this kind of programming (see Chapters 23, 26, and 32 in this volume). Communities also benefit from the special power of religiously based philanthropy. On average, the most secular one fifth of Americans gave $1,000 to charity annually; the most religious one fifth of Americans gave $3,000 to charity annually (Putnam & Campbell, 2010).

What makes religious and spiritual resources special? We suggest that the distinctiveness of these resources grows out of their sacred character. Religion and spirituality are vitally concerned about the sacred as an ultimate end in life and as a pathway to reach this destination (see Volume 1, Chapter 1, this handbook). With respect to the ultimate goals of living, religion and spirituality provide many people with an overarching, organizing vision for their lives. This vision often takes the form of a set of virtues and vices that prescribes what people should and should not strive for, who they should and should not be. These virtues and vices are not simply a set of moral standards; imbued with divine significance and qualities they become sacred, set apart, and elevated above other values. And empirical studies suggest that people who have a stronger sacred vision for their lives experience the benefits of greater purpose and meaning, fewer goal-related conflicts within themselves, and greater investment in the pursuit of their strivings (Emmons, Cheung, & Tehrani, 1998; Mahoney et al., 2005).

Religion and spirituality also offer people a set of pathways or tools to reach their destinations, tools that are especially tailored to the struggle with human limitations and finitude. As anthropologist Clifford Geertz (1968) wrote, "The events through which we live are forever outrunning the power of our ordinary, everyday moral, emotional and intellectual concepts to construct them, leaving us, as a Javanese image has it, like a water buffalo listening to an orchestra" (p. 101). Although U.S. psychology tends to respond to these events by encouraging a greater sense of control, religion and spirituality suggest a different set of solutions to problems that push us beyond our limits. These solutions involve a lexicon relatively unfamiliar to psychologists until recently (Pargament, 1997). We hear words such as *suffering*, *surrender*, *transcendence*, *transformation*, *love*, *compassion*, and *forgiveness* that speak more to acceptance and hope than mastery and control. The value of this way of thinking about people, problems, and solutions is borne out by research studies that have shown that religious and spiritual involvement is especially helpful to people with limited resources (e.g., minorities, elderly, impoverished) dealing with uncontrollable life situations (e.g., major illness, death of loved ones, accidents, natural disasters; Pargament, 1997, 2011). There is no need to choose between solutions that emphasize control and those that emphasize acceptance and forbearance. Problems in living generally contain elements of both controllability and uncontrollability. With their focus on human frailty and finitude, religious and spiritual resources provide an important complement to those control-oriented strategies often advocated by the larger field of psychology. It is encouraging to see that the field has begun to expand its focus to include religiously and spiritually based constructs, as witnessed in the rise of positive psychology, mindfulness, meditation, and acceptance-based psychotherapies (Shafranske, 2002). A great deal more work is needed, however, to integrate religious and spiritual resources more fully into our attempts to foster health and well-being.

Religion and Spirituality Can Be a Source of Problems

In the past, psychologists have stereotyped religion and spirituality as defensive, head-in-the-sand approaches to dealing with the world, fueled by the desire to avoid the painful confrontation with reality. Empirical studies, however, have indicated that these stereotypes are just that, stereotypes (Pargament & Park, 1995). Certainly we can find examples of religious and spiritually based defensiveness and passivity, but more often than not, religion and spirituality are tied to active problem solving and engagement with the world.

Nevertheless, it is true that religion and spirituality can be problematic at times. As psychologist Paul Pruyser (1977) noted, there is a "seamy" side to religion. Extremism, interpersonal conflict, prejudice, hypocrisy, dependence, guilt, passivity, denial, depression, and anxiety all have their religious and spiritual roots (see Chapter 4 in this volume). Moreover, religion and spirituality can create their own special brand of tensions and conflicts, including struggles over sacred matters with God, with other people, and within oneself (see Volume 1, Chapter 25, this handbook). The American Psychiatric Association recognized religious and spiritual problems in the 1994 fourth edition of the *Diagnostic and Statistical Manual of Mental Disorders*, which introduced "Religious or Spiritual Problem" as a new V code, "including distressing experiences that involve loss or questioning of faith, problems associated with conversion to a new faith, or questioning of other spiritual values which may not necessarily be related to an organized church or religious institution" (American Psychiatric Association, 1994, p. 685).

Religious and spiritual problems are not rampant, but they are not uncommon either. According to a survey of 5,000 university students, 25% reported that they had experienced considerable distress related to religious or spiritual concerns (Johnson & Hayes, 2003). In another study of medically ill patients, 20% described moderate to high levels of religious and spiritual struggle, marked by feelings of anger, abandonment, or punishment in relation to God (Fitchett et al., 2004).

Religious and spiritual problems are important, in part, because they can lead to other psychological, social, and physical problems. One of the largest areas of study relevant to this topic involves religious and spiritual struggles (for a review, see Volume 1, Chapter 25, this handbook). Struggles have emerged as predictors of increases in distress and emotional problems and declines in physical health status. Religious and spiritual struggles have even been tied to greater risk of mortality among medically ill elderly patients (Pargament, Koenig, Tarakeshwar, & Hahn, 2001). Many of these effects are robust across various subgroups (e.g., race, socioeconomic status, gender). Furthermore, religious and spiritual struggles are typically stronger predictors of distress than standard measures of religiousness, such as frequency of church attendance and prayer (Ellison & Lee, 2010).

Religious and spiritual problems are also important in and of themselves to many people. Hathaway, Scott, and Garver (2004) argued persuasively that problems in the religious and spiritual domain are clinically relevant and coined the term *clinically significant religious or spiritual impairment* to describe "a reduced ability to perform religious/spiritual activities, achieve religious/spiritual goals, or experience religious/spiritual states because of a psychological disorder" (p. 97). In this vein, McConnell, Pargament, Ellison, and Flannelly (2006) examined the links between various forms of psychopathology and religious and spiritual struggles through a national survey, and found that several indicators of serious psychological problems (anxiety, phobic anxiety, depression, paranoid ideation, obsessive–compulsiveness, somatization) were associated with higher levels of spiritual struggle after controlling for religious and demographic variables.

Although the findings can be interpreted in different ways, McConnell et al. noted that "like a physical illness, psychological symptomatology may challenge the individual's spiritual worldview, resulting in significant turmoil about spiritual matters" (2006, p. 1480).

Religious and spiritual problems are not restricted to individuals. Religious and spiritual tensions and conflicts occur between as well as within people. Moreover, these conflicts within couples, family members, institutions, communities, and cultures are all-too-often marked by exceptional power and passion. Perhaps this should not be altogether surprising; these conflicts are, in part, about sacred matters, values of deepest importance to people. Unfortunately, the sacred dimension of interpersonal conflicts has been frequently overlooked. This is a big oversight. In his book evocatively entitled *Blood That Cries Out From the Earth: The Psychology of Religious Terrorism*, Jones (2008) argued that we are unlikely to arrive at an effective response to this problem of our age until we develop a deeper understanding of "what is at stake religiously and spiritually" (p. 6) for groups involved in terrorism.

Whatever their form, religious and spiritual problems are a source of significant personal, social, and cultural pain and suffering in the world in the 21st century. These problems call for a response, one that should be informed by research and practice in the psychology of religion and spirituality.

People Are Interested in Spiritually Integrated Approaches to Improving the Human Condition

The lack of attention to religion and spirituality in psychological efforts to create change does not appear to stem from widespread disinterest on the part of the people psychologists serve. According to the 2000 National Survey of Americans on their attitudes toward spiritual values and beliefs in treatment, 83% reported that spiritual faith and religious beliefs are closely tied to their state of mental and emotional health, and 75% said it is important to see professional counselors who integrate their values and beliefs into counseling (American Association of Pastoral Counselors, 2000). Conversely, concerns about the openness of mental health professionals to spirituality was the second most common reason for not seeking help from this group; 15% said that they "fear that [their] spiritual values and beliefs may not be respected and taken seriously." These fears were especially pronounced among African Americans and devout Evangelicals. Other surveys of individuals dealing with physical and emotional problems point to the same conclusion—a majority of people would like to see religion and spirituality integrated into their treatment in a sensitive and respectful fashion (e.g., Lindgren, & Coursey, 1995; Stanley et al., 2011).

Going beyond the realm of counseling and health care, are people interested in a more spiritually integrated approach to other areas of life? Data are lacking, but there are signs of growing interest, many of them documented in the chapters in this second volume. New attention is being given to how institutions of higher education help students address the bigger questions of life (see Chapter 30 in this volume), how correctional institutions can draw on the religious and spiritual needs and interests of inmates to promote change (see Chapter 28 in this volume), and how work settings can become more religiously and spiritually sensitive to an increasingly diverse workforce (see Chapter 31 in this volume). It appears that many groups within many contexts would welcome an applied psychology of religion and spirituality.

Spiritually Integrated Interventions Have Shown Promising Results

In this age of evidence-based care, the question arises whether spiritually integrated interventions are, in fact, effective. Although research relevant to this question is still in its early stages of development, the findings suggest that spiritually integrated treatments are more effective than control conditions and as effective as other secular treatments (see Paukert, Phillips, Cully, Romero, & Stanley, 2011; T. B. Smith, Bartz, & Richards, 2007; see also Chapter 34 in this volume). To take one example, Avants, Beitel, and Margolin (2005) developed and evaluated Spiritual Self-Schema (3-S) therapy to help drug-dependent and HIV-at risk people access their higher "spiritual self" through the development of spiritual and religious resources rooted in

Buddhist principles. Working with treatment-resistant cocaine and opiate-dependent clients, they found that 3-S therapy was tied to significant decreases in the use of illicit drugs, according to both self-report and drug-free urines, and shifts from an "addict self" to "spiritual self" schema, as measured by a computerized reaction time task.

Spiritually integrated treatments have outperformed secular therapies in some instances (e.g., Azhar & Varma, 1995; Wachholtz & Pargament, 2008). For example, Richards, Berrett, Hardman, and Eggett (2006) studied women with eating disorders in an inpatient setting and compared the effectiveness of a spirituality group with a cognitive–behavioral group and emotional support group. Although all three groups showed positive changes over the course of treatment, the spiritual group manifested significantly more improvement in eating attitudes and spiritual well-being, and significant greater reductions in symptom distress, social role conflict, and relational distress. In comparison with secular treatments, spiritually integrated therapy generally results in more gains on spiritual outcomes (Worthington, Hook, Davis, & McDaniel, 2011).

The distinction between a spiritual and secular intervention can become murky. A finding by Rye et al. (2005) is relevant here. They compared the effectiveness of religious and secular forgiveness groups and found that the two groups were equally effective in fostering forgiveness among former spouses. When the participants were asked about the resources that helped them move to forgiveness, two of the three most common resources *among secular group members* were spiritual in nature (e.g., "I asked God for help and/or support as I was trying to forgive.") The secular intervention was not, in fact, purely secular. Religious beliefs and practices were at play in the background. This phenomenon may be operative in other secular treatments, a point supported by a few evaluative studies in which secular therapies have resulted in changes in religious and spiritual outcomes (e.g., Tisdale et al., 1997). Findings such as these raise the intriguing, but as yet untested, possibility that spiritual factors are an active ingredient in the change that takes place in secular treatments.

Psychotherapy is not the only tool of applied psychology. Looking at interventions outside the realm of psychotherapy, however, evaluative research pertinent to religion and spirituality is relatively meager. There is at least some evidence, however, that psychosocial approaches to change are equally or more effective when they are spiritually integrated. For instance, Maton and Seibert (1991) evaluated a community-based program, Raising Ambition Instills Self Esteem (RAISE), designed to provide academic and social support and mentoring to inner-city youth over a 7-year period. The researchers compared the effectiveness of church-based mentors with that of mentors from other community organizations and found that church-based mentors were more likely than nonchurch mentors to maintain a longer term relationship with their students. Furthermore, students served by church mentors manifested greater academic improvements. A few studies have shown that health education and physical illness prevention programs implemented in African American churches are more effective when the messages and resources in the programs are spiritually integrated (see Chapter 23 in this volume).

In short, there are some solid empirically based reasons why the psychology of religion and spirituality has begun to move beyond research to include practice: religion and spirituality are cultural facts; they are sources of solutions to problems and at times problems in and of themselves; people are looking for spiritually integrated approaches to change; and, evaluations of spiritually integrated interventions are showing promising results. As Shafranske (2005) has noted, this "confluence of developments is leading to the emergence of an applied psychology of religion and spirituality" (p. 496). In the next section, we envision this applied field through the lens of our integrative paradigm that was introduced in the first volume (see Volume 1, Chapter 1, this handbook).

ENVISIONING AN APPLIED PSYCHOLOGY OF RELIGION AND SPIRITUALITY

Linking Theory, Research, and Practice

Psychologists are not the only group interested in bettering the world. Police, clergy, real estate agents, wait staff, and hair stylists are just a few of the many other occupations that serve others. What distinguishes the practice of psychology from other approaches to change is its grounding in the methods of science. By *science*, we are referring to a set of methods that provide some degree of check on our personal biases, allow for the possibility of disconfirmation of our expectations, and are systematic enough to enable others to follow in our footsteps and replicate our work. Forrest Tyler, one of our mentors, once said that other people can be every bit as sensitive, compassionate, wise and helpful as psychologists in the work they do. But only psychologists can tell you how to do what they do. Only psychologists can tell you how they got there (personal communication, 1997). It follows that when the practice of psychology is disconnected from its scientific foundations, it becomes less a distinctively *psychological* approach to change. And an applied psychology that has lost its scientific moorings is particularly problematic in the context of the rising demand for evidence-based approaches to psychological care (APA, 2006).

Research and practice, in fact, can inform and enhance each other. On the one hand, empirical studies can lead directly to much-needed programs in the community. Aten, Topping, Denney, and Hosey (2011) provided a nice illustration of this point in their participatory research program with African American clergy in south Mississippi 1 year after Hurricane Katrina. The researchers conducted qualitative interviews with the clergy to assess their needs for training in disaster mental health. These interviews were systematically analyzed using grounded theory and the constant comparative method of Glaser and Strauss (1967). The findings led to the development of outreach and training programs to help clergy, leaders, and congregation members identify signs of psychological distress, provide psychological support, develop self-care methods, and access local and national mental health resources. In addition, the findings spurred the development of a website to prepare religious leaders and religious communities to respond to the spiritual and mental health needs of the community in times of disaster.

On the other hand, psychological practice can facilitate theory and research. Arguably the most significant theoretical contributions to 20th-century psychology—those of Freud and Piaget—did not grow out of empirical research but rather out of keen observations of individuals. Observation, case studies, and interviews continue to be rich sources of questions, ideas, and information that can translate directly into more systematic study. For example, a number of empirically useful measures of religion and spirituality have been generated not from larger theories, but inductively (i.e., "bottom-up") from interviews with various groups, including elders (Krause, 2008), ethnic minorities (Krause & Bastida, 2009), and people coping with major life stressors (Pargament, Koenig, & Perez, 2000).

There is, in short, a vital link between research and practice. In fact, it has been argued that some forms of research are a type of practice—a way of responding to community needs, a way of solving personal problems, a tool for social action, a way of enhancing the decision-making process, and a way to give greater voice to people (Price & Cherniss, 1977).

The psychology of religion and spirituality has work to do before it realizes this more integrated vision of theory, research, and practice. To progress in this direction, theory must be understood as not simply an end in itself but rather as a means of ultimately advancing the human condition. Theorists who give some consideration to the practical implications of their conceptual work are more likely to produce practically relevant theories (see Volume 1, this handbook, for illustrations). Researchers for their part could take several steps to increase the likelihood that their findings will be applied: (a) move beyond general studies of religion and spirituality to focused studies of specific forms of religion and spirituality as they relate to specific aspects of human functioning within specific cultures and contexts; (b) broaden the repertoire of research methodologies to encompass approaches that can be easily translated into practice, such as needs assessments, program evaluation, *N* of 1 designs, idiographic methods, and qualitative designs; and (c) disseminate research findings beyond professional journals by translating this knowledge into user-friendly language and channeling it back to the larger community through general media and public forums. Finally, practitioners should recognize the critical role they can play in the research enterprise. By virtue of their grassroots experiences, they are uniquely positioned to generate hypotheses that can be put to more formal empirical test. Practitioners are also in the best place to field test the findings gleaned from scientific study. And practitioners can also engage in important empirical research of their own through *N* of 1 designs and qualitative methods (see Chapter 17 in this volume).

Building Bridges With Mainstream Science and Practice

In spite of the advances that have been made in the field, the psychology of religion and spirituality remains marginalized within the social sciences and applied psychology. The integrative paradigm underscores the importance of creating stronger linkages between the psychology of religion and spirituality and mainstream social science and practice (see Hill & Gibson, 2008). Promising work is under way in this direction. A number of theorists have elaborated on the practical therapeutic implications of mainstream psychological theories for religion and spirituality. The two volumes of this handbook highlight many of these theories, including social learning theory (see Volume 1, Chapter 10, this handbook), psychodynamic theory (see Chapters 6 and 7 in this volume), cognitive–behavioral theory (see Chapter 8 in this volume), family systems theory (see Chapter 9 in this volume), and stress and coping theory (see Chapter 19 in this volume). Practitioners have also begun to apply mainstream models of intervention that go beyond traditional psychological treatment. These innovations include applications of premarital education to Christian and Jewish couples (Markman, Renick, Floyd, Stanley, & Clements, 1993), motivational interviewing methods to improve the dietary habits of Black church members (Resnicow et al., 2001), organizational–development theory for congregational development (Pargament et al., 1991), and empowerment theory for substance abuse prevention programs within churches (Roberts & Thorsheim, 1987).

The relationship between mainstream social science and the psychology of religion and spirituality should be a two-way street. Although our field has much to gain by integrating the contributions from mainstream social science, the psychology of religion and spirituality can make significant contributions to theory and practice in mainstream science. It is difficult to imagine how psychologists could achieve a comprehensive understanding of many of the most important topics of our time—from terrorism; trauma; and resilience to virtues, consciousness, and community—without attending to religion and spirituality. In fact, we believe that any psychological perspective on these phenomena that overlooks religion and spirituality is incomplete.

In some instances, the psychology of religion and spirituality can extend or even correct mainstream psychological theory and research. Research in the area of locus of control provides a case in point. Classic theory in this domain has distinguished between two loci of control (e.g., Rotter, 1990): internal control in which individuals perceive themselves as the authors of their own lives, and external control in which people perceive themselves as shaped by outside forces, such as luck or powerful others. A substantial body of research has pointed to the health benefits of an internal over an external locus of control. Research from the psychology of religion and spirituality, however, suggests that the distinction between control by self and control by external forces overlooks a third possibility—control through a relationship. This latter type of "interactional control" is nicely illustrated by the individual's perceived relationship with the divine. Empirical studies have pointed to important mental health advantages among people who feel that their lives are shaped through a partnership with God in which both the individual and God *share* control (Pargament et al., 1988). Similarly, as stated, the psychology of religion and spirituality provides needed balance to the emphasis in Western psychology on mastery, self-determination, and control by highlighting human processes that help people come to terms with their limitations and finitude (see Volume 1, Chapters 22 and 23, this handbook; see also Chapters 15 and 25 in this volume).

More practically, many applications of religious and spiritual knowledge could broaden and deepen psychological approaches to change. For example, Murray-Swank has developed a spiritually integrated approach to treating women who have experienced sexual abuse (Chapter 17 in this volume). Her work rests on the recognition that sexual abuse victims are often profoundly shaken spiritually. No longer can they assume that their world is safe, that others are trustworthy, that good behavior is invariably rewarded, and that they can count on a divine being for protection. Murray-Swank has addressed these spiritual injuries directly and has initiated a process of repair by drawing on their psychological, social, and spiritual resources. Practitioners have begun to apply religious and spiritual knowledge in other domains as well, such as training oncologists to conduct spiritual assessments in their diagnostic interviews (Kristeller, Rhodes, Cripe, & Sheets, 2005).

Exciting as these programs are, the jury is still out on their effectiveness. As noted, a few studies have demonstrated the "value-added benefits" of integrating a religious and spiritual dimension into practical interventions, but research on this vital topic is just beginning. It will be important to evaluate whether spiritually integrated approaches enhance outcomes defined not only by traditional psychological, social, and physical measures but also by the willingness of participants to engage in and remain in these programs (see Martinez, Smith, & Barlow, 2007).

Attending to the Varieties of Religion and Spirituality

The integrative paradigm underscores the rich, varied character of religious and spiritual life. As we noted in the first volume (see Volume 1, Chapter 1, this handbook), religion and spirituality are varied in three important respects. First, they are multidimensional. Part of the power of these phenomena lies in their capacity to respond selectively to the needs and temperaments of different people. Through religion and spirituality, people can opt to follow or construct many pathways—traditional and nontraditional—to many significant destinations. Those who prefer an intellectual pathway can engage in scriptural study or scientific research. Those who prefer an action-oriented pathway can take part in traditional ritual practices or creative expressions, such as writing poetry or quilting. People drawn to an experiential pathway can engage in mantra meditation or seek out transcendence in the quiet solitude of nature. And those who prefer a relational pathway can find satisfaction from shared worship or loving ties with families and friends.

Second, religion and spirituality are multivalent. On the one hand, they provide people with sources of strength, resilience, and solutions to problems. On the other hand, they can be sources of problems in and of themselves, adding to human pain and suffering.

Third, religion and spirituality are multilevel. Even though the vast majority of work in the psychology of religion and spirituality has focused on individuals, these processes are also expressed by couples, families, institutions, communities, and cultures. Each of these levels of expression, as well as the links between them, deserve attention.

The multidimensional, multivalent, and multilevel nature of religion and spirituality create a tremendous number of possibilities for change, possibilities that include but go well beyond traditional individual psychotherapy. Consider a few of the examples drawn from a fascinating array of new programs, some described in greater detail in this volume.

- Rosmarin et al. (2010) implemented a novel, spiritually integrated Internet-based treatment for subclinical anxiety among individuals in the Jewish community. The 2-week program drew on classic Jewish sources to facilitate trust in God among participants. Those in the spiritually integrated treatment reported large to moderate improvements in stress, worry, intolerance of uncertainty, positive religious coping, and mistrust in God. Moreover, participants in the spiritually integrated treatment showed greater improvements overall than those in progressive muscle relaxation and waiting list control groups.
- Fincham, Lambert, and Beach (2010; see also Chapter 24 in this volume) conducted a well-designed set of studies on the effects of prayer on infidelity among couples in romantic relationships. Couples who prayed for each other were less likely to engage in emotional and physical infidelity, even after controlling for baseline infidelity and relationship satisfaction. Furthermore,

praying for one's partner had stronger effects on infidelity than undirected prayers and thinking positive thoughts about one's partner. The effects of praying for partners were mediated by perceptions that the romantic relationship was sacred.

- As part of the U.S. Army's Comprehensive Soldier Fitness program, Pargament and Sweeney (2011) developed an educational, computer-based program designed to enhance the spiritual resilience of soldiers *before* they encounter serious problems. The Spiritual Fitness initiative focuses specifically on cultivating the human spirit through such resources as rituals, spiritual support, meaning making, and contemplation or meditation. The program is unusual in its strength-building, preventive focus and its ambitious effort to create cultural change in the Army.

These are a few of the exciting possibilities for prevention, education, and treatment that grow out of an appreciation for the rich and varied character of religion and spirituality. Although this area of work is early in its development, two types of spiritually integrated interventions appear to be emerging: spiritually integrated efforts that are geared to the needs of specific religious groups (i.e., religiously accommodative programs), and spiritually integrated efforts that are designed to appeal to people with diverse religious and spiritual backgrounds and orientations (i.e., spiritually generalized programs). Each type of intervention may have its own strengths and limitations, but both are likely to have an important place in the applied psychology of religion and spirituality.

Attending to the Sacred Dimension of Clients, Change Agents, Change Process, and Context of Change

Our integrative paradigm underscores the distinctive potential of religion and spirituality for efforts to advance the human condition. After all, no other human phenomena have the sacred as their central focus. Within an applied psychology of religion and spirituality, researchers and practitioners must attend to the ways the sacred dimension can be a part of each of the basic building blocks of change, or the "four Cs": clients, change agents, change process, and change context. Because we have already emphasized the varieties of sacred expressions among potential clients, we focus on the latter three Cs in the following sections.

Change agent. Psychologists and other helping professionals are rarely neutral when it comes to religion and spirituality. Atheists may have feelings about religion that are every bit as impassioned as those of the most devout believer. This does not disqualify the atheist from working effectively with religious or spiritual clients, just as deep religious commitment does not disqualify the psychologist from working with clients who are atheists. In this vein, Propst, Ostrom, Watkins, Dean, and Mashburn (1992) studied the efficacy of religious and nonreligious cognitive–behavioral therapy for religious people who were clinically depressed. Interestingly, the greatest improvement was shown by patients treated by nonreligious therapists offering religious cognitive–behavioral therapy. A modest degree of value dissimilarity, Propst et al. (1992) suggested, may in fact facilitate treatment.

What is unacceptable on the part of change agents is spiritual intolerance (see Chapter 3 in this volume). Intolerance can manifest itself through an attitude of rejectionism to any expression of religiousness and spirituality (Pargament, 2007). One therapist revealed this attitude in response to a bereaved mother who described a visitation by her dead child: "Well, you've healed enough that you don't need that any more" (Brotherson & Soderquist, 2002, p. 77). Intolerance also can be shown through an attitude of exclusivism that rejects all expressions of religion and spirituality other than those the change agent holds to be ultimately true. It is important to add that exclusivism is not restricted to any particular stance toward religion; the nontraditional spiritually oriented therapist can be as exclusivist as the traditional religious therapist. Both forms of intolerance, rejectionism, and exclusivism, are inconsistent with the APA's *Guidelines for Providers of Psychological Services to Ethnic, Linguistic, and Culturally Diverse Populations*: "Psychologists [should] respect clients' religious and/or spiritual beliefs and values, including attributions and taboos, since they affect world view, psychosocial functioning, and expressions of distress" (APA, 1993, p. 46).

Equally unacceptable is spiritual illiteracy by the change agent. Earlier, we noted that only a small percentage of psychologists receive any formal training in the area of religion and spirituality (e.g., Brawer et al., 2002). Thus, many change agents may be unaware of the diversity of religious and spiritual pathways and destinations, unappreciative of diverse religious traditions, and unfamiliar with the extensive empirical literature in the psychology of religion and spirituality. Although practitioners do not have to be experts in this area, they should be aware of their own limitations, knowledgeable about external resources, and willing to seek additional education and training (see Chapter 33 in this volume).

In the place of intolerance and illiteracy, applied psychologists of religion and spirituality should demonstrate openness, authenticity, and self-awareness (Pargament, 2007). Practitioners must communicate a genuine respect for the variety of ways people understand and approach the sacred. This is not to say that every religious and spiritual pathway and destination should be affirmed. As we have stressed, not all pathways and destinations are created equal; some are clearly destructive and have to be addressed. This conversation, however, should unfold within a larger milieu of sensitivity and respect for the client's core values and ultimate right to choose his or her own direction in life, even if those choices would not be those of the change agent. The challenge for change agents is to deal with the tension between the need to affirm diverse ways of being human and the need to live consistently and authentically within one's own system of values. Self-awareness is a prerequisite to dealing successfully with this tension. The ability to identify one's own blind spots, vulnerabilities, biases, strengths, and values in the religious and spiritual realm offer some protection against the twin dangers of coerciveness and inauthenticity. In preliminary practice guidelines, the APA's Division 36 (Society for the Psychology of Religion and Spirituality) has underscored the need for self-awareness among change agents:

> Psychologists strive to be self-aware of their own perspective, attitudes, history, and self-understandings of religion and spirituality. Psychologists should be mindful of how their own background on religious/spiritual matters might bias their response and approach to clients of differing background. (Hathaway & Ripley, 2009, p. 48)

Change process. There is a spiritual dimension to the relationship between client and change agent, whether or not it is recognized and articulated in treatment (Pargament, 2007). The partners in this relationship meet not only as psychological, social, and physical beings but also as spiritual beings. And through the process of change, spirituality can be affected, even when it is not an explicit focus of the intervention. For example, Tisdale et al. (1997) evaluated the effectiveness of a secular inpatient treatment that included individual, group, milieu, and psychotropic interventions. As expected, the treatment program produced improvements in measures of personal adjustment. Surprisingly, however, the program also resulted in more positive images of God among the patients. Similarly, in a study of women undergoing treatment for eating disorders in an inpatient program, improvements in spiritual well-being went hand in hand with improvements in body image, better attitudes toward eating, and reductions in psychological symptoms and relational conflict (F. T. Smith, Hardman, Richards, & Fischer, 2003).

The process of change takes on a sacred character in many ways: When religious and spiritual resources are accessed in treatment, when the conversation focuses on religious and spiritual problems, concerns, and struggles, and when the relationship between client and change agent itself becomes imbued with sacred qualities. This latter notion that the relationship between client and practitioner can become sacred may sound a bit strange, and yet clinicians have used sacred language, akin to Martin Buber's (1996) I–Thou relationship, to describe their connection with clients. They have talked about the feeling that a moment in treatment is transcendent or extraordinary, the experience of a deep interconnectedness or a "meeting of souls" between client and practitioner, a sense of being part of something larger than oneself in the helping relationship, feelings of inspiration and grace in the relationship, and the experience of moving beyond the surface to a deeper more ultimate truth (Lomax, Kripal, & Pargament, 2011; O'Grady & Richards, 2010; West, 2000).

Studies of the spiritual dimension of the helping relationship represent a promising direction for further research. Empirical studies have shown that the helping alliance may account for as much as 50% of the variance for treatment effects (Horvath, 2001). Perhaps the spiritual dimension of this professional relationship represents a vital contributor to these effects.

Context of change. Clients do not seek help as isolated beings. They carry a larger context along with them into the helping relationship. The context consists of many ingredients—gender, ethnicity, age, family, friends, congregation, community, and culture (see Volume 1, Part IV, this handbook). Religion and spirituality are a part of this context as well, adding distinctive character and flavor.

This larger context is relevant to everyone, even those who define themselves as "spiritual not religious." It has been argued that 21st-century spirituality has emerged from a cultural context that encourages the privatization of spiritual experience (Wuthnow, 1998). Spirituality unfolds in this field of larger forces; this point holds true even for clients who are unaware of these forces or explicitly reject them. A context that has been rejected by a client plays as critical a role in spirituality as the context that is accepted.

An appreciation for context by change agents is vital because the same religious and spiritual beliefs and practices can have very different meanings when set against different contextual backgrounds. For instance, commitment to a conservative Christian religious worldview and community will be experienced quite differently by heterosexuals than by gays and lesbians (see Volume 1, Chapter 34, this handbook). Whether Protestants, Jews, and Catholics grow up in neighborhoods in which they are part of a religious majority or minority can color the development of their identity and self-esteem in distinctive ways; high school students raised in religiously dissonant neighborhoods report lower levels of self-esteem and greater anxiety and depressive affect than those reared in religiously consonant neighborhoods (Rosenberg, 1962). A conversion experience may unfold very differently for men and women (Mahoney & Pargament, 2004); both genders reorganize their lives around the sacred, but the transformation for men may be more likely to involve a shift away from pride, whereas conversion for women may involve a shift away from self-abnegation.

These contexts are as rich and diverse as individuals. For example, although religious traditions shape people in varying ways, it is a misnomer to speak of "the" Christian, "the" Jewish, or the "Hindu" client, for there is remarkable contextual diversity within each of these and other major faiths (Lovinger, 1996).

Efforts to help clients that overlook their larger context are unlikely to be successful. For example, mental health professionals occasionally face difficult diagnostic questions about clients who present with unusual beliefs and perceptions. Are the clients experiencing delusions and hallucinations signaling serious psychopathology, or are they expressing religiously or culturally based beliefs and perceptions (Gellerman & Lu, 2011)? What may appear to be a disturbed way of thinking or perceiving the world to an outsider may turn out to be quite ordinary within a particular religious subgroup. In this vein, Miller and Kelley (2005) noted, "in some African communities, a person would be considered insane *not* to believe that the spirits of the dead actively influence an individual's life" (p. 471). The critical diagnostic questions here cannot be answered by appealing to ontological criteria; after all, psychologists are not in a privileged position to speak to the ultimate truth of any set of religious beliefs or practices. Rather, assessment is made in part by evaluating the client's beliefs and perceptions against the backdrop of his or her larger social, cultural, and religious context.

Similarly, practitioners interested in reaching out to religious congregations and their members are likely to be far more effective when they build sensitivity to the larger context into their interventions. In fact, congregational support is a prerequisite for psychological programs geared toward members of religious communities (Winett, Anderson, Wojcik, Winett, & Bowden, 2007). Furthermore, programs designed to encourage better health practices in religious congregations have proven to be more effective when the interventions are tailored to the distinctive needs and resources of the congregations, leaders, and members (see Chapters 23 and 32 in this volume). These findings highlight the need for programs that are sensitive to the context of change. It is especially important to recognize that religious institutions are not social service agencies or mental health centers. Although they serve their members in many ways—psychologically, socially, and physically—religious systems are first and foremost oriented toward the sacred; as such, they have missions, structures, theologies, resources, and histories that distinguish them from any other setting (Rappaport, 1981). As Scheie, Markham, Mayer, Slettom, and Williams (1991) put it, "They [religious systems] have institutional memories that go back hundreds or thousands of years, and a future vision that stretches to eternity" (p. 75).

FUTURE DIRECTIONS, FUTURE CHALLENGES

In this chapter, we have presented a rationale for an applied psychology of religion and spirituality. In fact, our field is making important strides in this direction, and is now arguably approaching the necessary and sufficient conditions for an applied psychology of religion and spirituality articulated by Shafranske (2002): demonstrations of significant ties between religion or spirituality and health, evidence of the practical efficacy of spiritually integrated interventions, theoretical breadth, and education and training activities. We have suggested that an applied field will move forward with greater coherence and effectiveness if it is guided by an integrative paradigm that (a) links theory, research, and practice; (b) builds bridges with mainstream theory and practice; (c) recognizes the varieties of religion and spirituality; and (d) attends to the sacred dimension of clients, change agent, and the process and context of change. There are, however, several challenges we will face as the field moves from research to practice.

First, perhaps more than any other domain of human functioning, religion and spirituality are deeply emotional topics. This should come as no surprise. We are, after all, talking about sacred matters, issues of greatest value to people. As we have stressed, it is hard find anyone who is neutral about religion and spirituality, including those who have disengaged from these spheres of life, including researchers and practitioners themselves. Newcomers to this area of study and practice should be aware of the tremendous emotionality of the field they are entering. They should be ready to face misunderstanding, stereotypes, and strong reactions among not only the general public but also fellow psychologists, social scientists, and health care professionals. To work effectively in this area, researchers and practitioners have to cultivate an exquisite sensitivity to the place of religion and spirituality in people's lives. For psychologists interested in collaborating with religious and spiritual individuals and communities to study and promote health and well-being, it is particularly important to remember that, for many people, religion and spirituality are not simply ways to attain greater meaning, peace, comfort, connectedness, and health; they are values in and of themselves, values of profound significance that supersede all other goals.

Second, when moving from research to practice, psychologists will have to grapple with the complexities of religion and spirituality. These are multidimensional, multilevel, and multivalent phenomena that can be a part of every aspect of change. Difficult value issues are commonplace in efforts to integrate greater sensitivity to religion and spirituality into an applied psychology (see Chapter 3 in this volume). For example, challenges are likely to arise in the application of both types of spiritually integrated interventions: religious accommodative treatments and spiritually generalized treatments. In the case of religious accommodative therapy, the therapist is explicit about working within a particular religious frame of reference to facilitate change. What happens, however, if the client wants to explore other religious groups, switch faith commitments, or disengage from religious pursuits altogether? The questions can become even more difficult if the therapist is employed by a religiously based institution.
Who then does the therapist work for? How does the therapist balance concerns for the values of the client, those of the larger religious context, and those of the therapist him- or herself? How are

potential conflicts among these multiple commitments best approached and resolved? With respect to spiritually generalized treatments, the therapist must be alert to the different meanings the intervention may have for clients who come from different religious backgrounds. In addition, the therapist must be ready to respond to potentially difficult questions. How does the treatment fit with a client's particular religious commitments? What are the underlying spiritual and religious values embedded in the intervention? How can the intervention be integrated into the client's own religious worldview? We offer no easy answers here. We are simply illustrating the kinds of thorny questions that will need to be addressed in the field's movement toward an applied discipline. An ability to tolerate ambiguity may be a prerequisite for people entering this field as they encounter these challenging issues.

Third, because this area of work is likely to be so complex and fraught with emotion, it is particularly important to work together with others in pluralistic, multidisciplinary teams. Few, if any, among us have all of the tools and resources that are needed to be effective as applied psychologists of religion and spirituality. Through collaboration with others inside and outside of psychology, researchers and practitioners can address their own biases and limitations, multiply their own resources, and support each other in the process. Although this kind of collaboration contrasts with traditional training models that create "lone scientists," it is already showing promising results. A number of universities and medical centers have developed multidisciplinary research and practice groups in the area of religion and spirituality that have been successful in developing, evaluating, and disseminating spiritually integrated interventions. Multidisciplinary, multicenter research projects that cut across geographic locales represent another promising direction for work in this area (see Chapter 34 in this volume).

Finally, the applied psychology of religion and spirituality is in its infancy; questions far outnumber answers. For this field to progress, it will be vital for practitioners to receive training in this area through formal graduate and postgraduate programs and supervision. Institutional changes in the academy will be required to accommodate these educational needs (see Chapters 2 and 33 in this volume). Formal training limited to one time of life will not be sufficient, however; education in this sphere might be better understood as lifelong. Although some of this training can come from continuing education and supervision, much of the learning in this domain is likely to come from doing; a kind of learning that grows out of trial and error, interactions with colleagues, and an openness to being taught, challenged, and surprised by those we try to help and change.

There are then, significant challenges as our field moves from research to practice. None of these challenges, however, is insurmountable. Our integrative paradigm for an applied psychology of religion and spirituality does not represent an alternative approach to understanding and fostering health and well-being. For instance, spiritually integrated psychotherapy has not been introduced as a competitor to other models of psychotherapy, such as cognitive–behavioral, dialectical–behavioral, psychodynamic, interpersonal, or acceptance and commitment therapies. Rather, it has the potential to broaden and deepen any approach to treatment and change. The same point holds true for other applications of theory and research on religion and spirituality. Greater attention to the religious and spiritual dimension, we firmly believe, can enrich and vitalize our efforts to understand and enhance the human condition. In the chapters that follow, we illustrate the promise and potential of an applied psychology of religion and spirituality.

References

American Association of Pastoral Counselors. (2000, November 8). *Samaritan Institute report.* Washington, DC: Greenberg Quinlan Research.

American Psychiatric Association. (1994). *Diagnostic and statistical manual of mental disorders* (4th ed.). Washington, DC: Author.

American Psychological Association. (1993). Guidelines for providers of psychological services to ethnic, linguistic, and culturally diverse populations. *American Psychologist, 48*, 45–48.

American Psychological Association. (2002). Ethical principles of psychologists and code of conduct. *American Psychologist, 57*, 1060–1073. doi:10.1037/0003-066X.57.12.1060

American Psychological Association. (2006). Evidence-based practice in psychology. *American Psychologist, 61*, 271–285. doi:10.1037/0003-066X.61.4.271

Aten, J. D., Topping, S., Denney, R. M., & Hosey, J. M. (2011). Helping African American clergy and churches address minority disaster mental health disparities: Training needs, model, and example. *Psychology of Religion and Spirituality, 3*, 15–23. doi:10.1037/a0020497

Avants, S. K., Beitel, M., & Margolin, A. (2005). Making the shift from "addict self" to "spiritual self": Results from a Stage I study of spiritual self-schema (3-S) therapy for the treatment of addiction and HIV risk behavior. *Mental Health, Religion, and Culture, 8*, 167–177. doi:10.1080/13694670500138924

Azhar, M. Z., & Varma, S. I. (1995). Religious psychotherapy in depressive patients. *Psychotherapy and Psychosomatics, 63*, 165–168. doi:10.1159/000288954

Benson, P. L., & Williams, D. L. (1982). *Religion on Capitol Hill: Myths and realities.* New York, NY: Harper & Row.

Brawer, P. A., Handal, P. J., Fabricatore, A. N., Roberts, R., & Wajda-Johnston, V. A. (2002). Training and education in religion/spirituality within APA-accredited clinical psychology programs. *Professional Psychology: Research and Practice, 33*, 203–206. doi:10.1037/0735-7028.33.2.203

Brems, C., Johnson, M. E., & Galluci, P. (1996). Publication productivity of clinical and counseling psychologists. *Journal of Clinical Psychology, 52*, 723–725. doi:10.1002/(SICI)1097-4679(199611)52:6<723::AID-JCLP15>3.0.CO;2-O

Brotherson, S. E., & Soderquist, J. (2002). Coping with a child's death: Spiritual issues and therapeutic implications. *Journal of Family Psychotherapy, 13*, 53–86. doi:10.1300/J085v13n01_04

Buber, M. (1996). *I and thou* (W. Kaufmann, Trans.). New York, NY: Simon & Schuster. (Original work published 1923)

Chalfant, H. P., Heller, P. L., Roberts, A., Briones, D., Acquirre-Hochbaum, S., & Farr, W. (1990). The clergy as a resource for those encountering psychological distress. *Review of Religious Research, 31*, 305–313. doi:10.2307/3511620

Ellis, A. (1986). *The case against religion: A psychotherapist's view and the case against religiosity.* Austin, TX: American Atheist Press.

Ellis, A. (2000). Can rational emotive behavior therapy (REBT) be effectively used with people who have devout beliefs in God and religion? *Professional Psychology: Research and Practice, 31*, 29–33. doi:10.1037/0735-7028.31.1.29

Ellison, C. G., & Lee, J. (2010). Spiritual struggles and psychological distress: Is there a dark side of religion? *Social Indicators Research, 98*, 501–517. doi:10.1007/s11205-009-9553-3

Emmons, R. A., Cheung, C., & Tehrani, K. (1998). Assessing spirituality through personal goals: Implications for research on religion and subjective well-being. *Social Indicators Research, 45*, 391–422. doi:10.1023/A:1006926720976

Fincham, F. D., Lambert, N. M., & Beach, S. R. H. (2010). Faith and unfaithfulness: Can praying for your partner reduce infidelity? *Journal of Personality and Social Psychology, 99*, 649–659. doi:10.1037/a0019628

Finno, D. (2010, April). *Educational and workforce trends in psychology: Debt, financial support, and salary data.* Paper presented at the Annual Convention of the Rocky Mountain Psychological Association, Denver, CO.

Fitchett, G., Murphy, P., Kim, J., Gibbons, J. L., Cameron, J., & Davis, J. A. (2004). Religious struggle: Prevalence, correlates and mental health risks in diabetic, congestive heart failure, and oncology patients. *Journal of Counseling Psychology, 44*, 1–22.

Gall, T. L. (2006). Spirituality and coping with life stress among adult survivors of childhood sexual abuse. *Child Abuse and Neglect, 30*, 829–844. doi:10.1016/j.chiabu.2006.01.003

Gallup Poll. (1999). *Mother Teresa voted by American people as most admired person of the century.* Retrieved from http://www.gallup.com/poll/3367/mother-teresa-voted-american-people-most-admired-person-century.aspx

Geertz, C. (1968). *Islam observed: Religious developments in Morocco and Indonesia.* New Haven, CT: Yale University Press.

Gellerman, D. M., & Lu, F. G. (2011). Religious and spiritual issues in the outline for cultural formation. In J. R. Peteet, F. G. Lu, & W. E. Narrow (Eds.), *Religious and spiritual issues in psychiatric diagnosis: A research agenda for* DSM–V (pp. 207–220). Arlington, VA: American Psychiatric Association.

Glaser, B., & Strauss, A. (1967). *The discovery of grounded theory: Strategies for qualitative research.* Chicago, IL: Aldine.

Hathaway, W. L., & Ripley, J. S. (2009). Ethical concerns around spirituality and religion in clinical practice. In J. D. Aten & M. M. Leach (Eds.), *Spirituality and the therapeutic process: A comprehensive resource from intake to termination* (pp. 25–52). Washington, DC: American Psychological Association. doi:10.1037/11853-002

Hathaway, W. L., Scott, S. Y., & Garver, S. A. (2004). Assessing religious/spiritual functioning: A neglected domain in clinical practice. *Professional Psychology: Research and Practice, 35*, 97–104. doi:10.1037/0735-7028.35.1.97

Hill, P. C., & Gibson, N. J. S. (2008). Whither the roots? Achieving conceptual depth in psychology of religion. *Archive for the Psychology of Religion, 30*, 19–35.

Horvath, A. O. (2001). The alliance. *Psychotherapy: Theory, Research, Practice, Training, 38*, 365–372. doi:10.1037/0033-3204.38.4.365

Johnson, C. V., & Hayes, J. A. (2003). Troubled spirits: Prevalence and predictors of religious and spiritual concerns among university students and counseling center clients. *Journal of Counseling Psychology, 50*, 409–419. doi:10.1037/0022-0167.50.4.409

Jones, J. (2008). *Blood that cries out from the earth: The psychology of religious terrorism.* New York, NY: Oxford University Press. doi:10.1093/acprof:oso/9780195335972.001.0001

Kazdin, A. E. (2008). Evidence-based treatment and practice: New opportunities to bridge clinical research and practice, enhance the knowledge base, and improve patient care. *American Psychologist, 63*, 146–159. doi:10.1037/0003-066X.63.3.146

Koenig, H. G., King, D., & Carson, V. B. (2012). *Handbook of religion and health* (2nd ed.). New York, NY: Oxford University Press.

Krause, N. (2006). Exploring the stress-buffering effects of church-based and secular social support on self-rated health in late life. *The Journals of Gerontology, Series B: Psychological Sciences and Social Sciences, 61*, S35–S43. doi:10.1093/geronb/61.1.S35

Krause, N. (2008). *Aging in the church: How social relationships affect health.* West Conshohocken, PA: Templeton Foundation Press.

Krause, N., & Bastida, E. (2009). Religion, suffering, and health among older Mexican Americans. *Journal of Aging Studies, 23*, 114–123. doi:10.1016/j.jaging.2008.11.002

Kristeller, J. L. (2010). Spiritual engagement as a mechanism of change in mindfulness- and acceptance-based therapies. In R. A. Baer (Ed.), *Assessing mindfulness and acceptance processes in clients* (pp. 155–184). Oakland, CA: New Harbinger.

Kristeller, J. L., Rhodes, M., Cripe, L. D., & Sheets, V. (2005). Oncologist Assisted Intervention Study (OASIS): Patient acceptability and initial evidence of effects. *International Journal of Psychiatry in Medicine, 35*, 329–347.

Lindgren, K. N., & Coursey, R. D. (1995). Spirituality and serious mental illness: A two-part study. *Psychosocial Rehabilitation Journal, 18*, 93–111.

Lindner, E. W. (2010). *Yearbook of American and Canadian churches 2010.* Nashville, TN: Abingdon Press.

Lomax, J. W., Kripal, J. J., & Pargament, K. I. (2011). Perspective on "sacred moments" in psychotherapy. *American Journal of Psychiatry, 168*, 12–18. doi:10.1176/appi.ajp.2010.10050739

Lovinger, R. J. (1996). Considering the religious dimension in assessment and treatment. In E. P. Shafranske (Ed.), *Religion and the clinical practice of psychology* (pp. 327–364). Washington, DC: American Psychological Association. doi:10.1037/10199-012

Mahoney, A., & Pargament, K. I. (2004). Sacred changes: Spirituality conversion and transformation. *In Session: Psychotherapy in Practice, 60*, 481–492.

Mahoney, A., Pargament, K. I., Cole, B., Jewell, T., Magyar-Russell, G., Tarakeshwar, N., . . . Phillips, R. (2005). A higher purpose: The sanctification of strivings in a community sample. *The International Journal for the Psychology of Religion, 15*, 239–262. doi:10.1207/s15327582ijpr1503_4

Markman, H. J., Renick, M. J., Floyd, F. J., Stanley, S. M., & Clements, M. (1993). Preventing marital distress through communication and conflict-management training: A four and five year follow-up. *Journal of Consulting and Clinical Psychology, 62*, 1–8.

Martinez, J. S., Smith, T. B., & Barlow, S. H. (2007). Spiritual interventions in psychotherapy: Evaluations by highly religious clients. *Journal of Clinical Psychology, 63*, 943–960. doi:10.1002/jclp.20399

Maton, K. I., & Seibert, M. (1991, December). *Third year evaluation of Project RAISE: Unpublished evaluation report.* University of Maryland, Baltimore County.

McConnell, K. M., Pargament, K. I., Ellison, C. G., & Flannelly, K. J. (2006). Examining the links between spiritual struggles and symptoms of psychopathology in a national sample. *Journal of Clinical Psychology, 62*, 1469–1484. doi:10.1002/jclp.20325

Miller, L., & Kelley, B. S. (2005). Relationships of religiosity and spirituality with mental health and psychopathology. In R. F. Paloutzian & C. L. Park (Eds.), *Handbook of the psychology of religion and spirituality* (pp. 460–478). New York, NY: Guilford Press.

O'Grady, K. A., & Richards, P. S. (2010). The role of inspiration in the helping professions. *Psychology of Religion and Spirituality, 2*, 57–66. doi:10.1037/a0018551

Oman, D., Hedberg, J., & Thoresen, C. E. (2006). Passage meditation reduces perceived stress in health professionals: A randomized, controlled trial. *Journal of Consulting and Clinical Psychology, 74*, 714–719. doi:10.1037/0022-006X.74.4.714

Palmer, P. J., Jackson, M., Jackson, R., & Sluyter, D. (2001). The courage to teach: A program for teacher renewal. In L. Lantieri (Ed.), *Schools with spirit: Nurturing the inner lives of children and teachers* (pp. 132–147). Boston, MA: Beacon Press.

Pargament, K. I. (1997). *The psychology of religion and coping: Theory, research, practice.* New York, NY: Guilford Press.

Pargament, K. I. (2007). *Spiritually integrated psychotherapy: Understanding and addressing the sacred.* New York, NY: Guilford Press.

Pargament, K. I. (2011). Religion and coping: The current state of knowledge. In S. Folkman (Ed.), *Oxford handbook of stress, health, and coping* (pp. 269–288). New York, NY: Oxford University Press.

Pargament, K. I., Ensing, D. S., Falgout, K., Olsen, H., Reilly, B., Van Haitsma, K., . . . Warren, R. (1991). The congregation development program: Data-based consulation with churches and synagogues. *Professional Psychology: Research and Practice, 22,* 393–404. doi:10.1037/0735-7028.22.5.393

Pargament, K. I., Kennell, J., Hathaway, W., Grevengoed, N., Newman, J., & Jones, W. (1988). Religion and the problem-solving process: Three styles of coping. *Journal for the Scientific Study of Religion, 27,* 90–104. doi:10.2307/1387404

Pargament, K. I., Koenig, H. G., & Perez, L. (2000). The many methods of religious coping: Development and initial validation of the RCOPE. *Journal of Clinical Psychology, 56,* 519–543. doi:10.1002/(SICI)1097-4679(200004)56:4<519::AID-JCLP6>3.0.CO;2-1

Pargament, K. I., Koenig, H. G., Tarakeshwar, N., & Hahn, J. (2001). Religious struggle as a predictor of mortality among medically ill elderly patients: A two-year longitudinal study. *Archives of Internal Medicine, 161,* 1881–1885. doi:10.1001/archinte.161.15.1881

Pargament, K. I., & Park, C. (1995). Merely a defense? The variety of religious means and ends. *Journal of Social Issues, 51,* 13–32. doi:10.1111/j.1540-4560.1995.tb01321.x

Pargament, K. I., & Sweeney, P. J. (2011). Building spiritual fitness in the Army: An innovative approach to a vital aspect of human development. *American Psychologist, 66,* 58–64. doi:10.1037/a0021657

Paukert, A. L., Phillips, L. L., Cully, J. A., Romero, C., & Stanley, M. A. (2011). Systematic review of religion-accommodative psychotherapy for depression and anxiety. *Journal of Contemporary Psychotherapy, 41,* 99–108. doi:10.1007/s10879-010-9154-0

Pew Forum on Religion and Public Life. (2008). *U.S. Religious Landscape Survey.* Washington, DC: Pew Research Center.

Pickens, W. G., & Fowler, R. D. (2003). Professional organizations. In I. B. Weiner & D. Freedheim (Eds.), *Handbook of psychology: Vol. 1. History of psychology* (pp. 535–544). New York, NY: Wiley.

Price, R. H., & Cherniss, C. (1977). Training for a new profession: Research as social action. *Professional Psychology, 8,* 222–231. doi:10.1037/0735-7028.8.2.222

Propst, L. R., Ostrom, R., Watkins, P., Dean, T., & Mashburn, D. (1992). Comparative efficacy of religious and nonreligious cognitive–behavioral therapy for the treatment of clinical depression in religious individuals. *Journal of Consulting and Clinical Psychology, 60,* 94–103. doi:10.1037/0022-006X.60.1.94

Pruyser, P. W. (1977). The seamy side of current religious beliefs. *Bulletin of the Menninger Clinic, 41,* 329–348.

Putnam, R. D., & Campbell, D. E. (2010). *American grace: How religion divides and unites us.* New York, NY: Simon & Schuster.

Rappaport, J. (1981). In praise of paradox: A social policy of empowerment over prevention. *American Journal of Community Psychology, 9,* 1–25. doi:10.1007/BF00896357

Resnicow, K., Campbell, M. K., Carr, C., McCarty, F., Wang, T., Periasamy, S., . . . Stables, G. (2004). Body and Soul. A dietary intervention conducted through African-American churches. *American Journal of Preventive Medicine, 27,* 97–105. doi:10.1016/j.amepre.2004.04.009

Resnicow, K., Jackson, A., Wang, T., De, A. K., McCarty, F., Dudley, W. N., & Baranowski, T. (2001). A motivational interviewing intervention to increase fruit and vegetable intake through Black churches: Results of the Eat for Life trial. *American Journal of Public Health, 91,* 1686–1693. doi:10.2105/AJPH.91.10.1686

Richards, P. S., Berrett, M. E., Hardman, R. K., & Eggett, D. L. (2006). Comparative efficacy of spirituality, cognitive, and emotional support groups for treating eating disorder inpatients. *Eating Disorders, 14,* 401–415. doi:10.1080/10640260600952548

Roberts, B., & Thorsheim, H. (1987). A partnership approach to consultation: The process and results of a major primary prevention field experiment. In J. Kelly & R. Hess (Eds.), *The ecology of prevention: Illustrating mental health consultation* (pp. 151–186). New York, NY: Haworth Press.

Rosenberg, M. (1962). The dissonant religious context and emotional disturbance. *American Journal of Sociology, 68,* 1–10. doi:10.1086/223261

Rosmarin, D. H., Pargament, K. I., Pirutinsky, S., & Mahoney, A. (2010). A randomized controlled evaluation of a spiritually integrated treatment for subclinical anxiety in the Jewish community, delivered via the Internet. *Journal of Anxiety Disorders, 24,* 799–808. doi:10.1016/j.janxdis.2010.05.014

Rotter, J. B. (1990). Internal versus external control of reinforcement: A case history of a variable. *American*

Psychologist, 45, 489–493. doi:10.1037/0003-066X.45.4.489

Rye, M. S., Pargament, K. I., Wei, P., Yingling, D. W., Shogren, K. A., & Ito, M. (2005). Can group interventions facilitate forgiveness of an ex-spouse? A randomized clinical trial. *Journal of Consulting and Clinical Psychology, 73*, 880–892. doi:10.1037/0022-006X.73.5.880

Scheie, D. M., Markham, J., Mayer, S. E., Slettom, J., & Williams, T. (1991). *Religious partners as partners in community based program development: Findings from year one of the Lilly Endowment Program.* Minneapolis, MN: Rainbow Research Program.

Schuster, M. A., Stein, B. D., & Jaycox, L. H. (2001). A national survey of stress reactions after the September 11, 2001 terrorist attacks. *New England Journal of Medicine, 345*, 1507–1512. doi:10.1056/NEJM200111153452024

Shafranske, E. P. (2001). The religious dimension of patient care within rehabilitation medicine: The role of religious attitudes, beliefs, and personal and professional practices. In T. G. Plante & A. C. Sherman (Eds.), *Faith and health: Psychological perspectives* (pp. 311–338). New York, NY: Guilford Press.

Shafranske, E. P. (2002). The necessary and sufficient conditions for an applied psychology of religion. *Psychology of Religion Newsletter, 27*(4), 1–12.

Shafranske, E. P. (2005). The psychology of religion in clinical and counseling psychology. In R. F. Paloutzian & C. L. Park (Eds.), *Handbook of the psychology of religion and spirituality* (pp. 496–514). New York, NY: Guilford Press.

Shafranske, E. P., & Malony, H. N. (1996). Religion and the clinical practice of psychology: A case for inclusion. In E. P. Shafranske (Ed.), *Religion and the clinical practice of psychology* (pp. 561–586). Washington, DC: American Psychological Association. doi:10.1037/10199-041

Smith, F. T., Hardman, R. K., Richards, P. S., & Fischer, L. (2003). Intrinsic religiosity and spiritual well-being as predictors of treatment outcome among women with eating disorders. *Eating Disorders, 11*, 15–26. doi:10.1080/10640260390167456-2199

Smith, T. B., Bartz, J. D., & Richards, P. S. (2007). Outcomes of religious and spiritual adaptations to psychotherapy: A meta-analytic review. *Psychotherapy Research, 17*, 643–655. doi:10.1080/10503300701250347

Speer, P. W., Ontkush, M., Schmitt, B., Raman, P., Jackson, C., Rengert, K., & Peterson, N. A. (2003). The intentional exercise of power: Community organizing in Camden, NJ. *Journal of Community and Applied Social Psychology, 13*, 399–408. doi:10.1002/casp.745

Stanley, M. A., Bush, A. L., Camp, M. E., Jameson, J. P., Phillips, L. L., Barber, C. B., . . . Cully, J. A. (2011). Older preferences for religion/spirituality in treatment for anxiety and depression. *Aging and Mental Health, 15*, 334–343. doi:10.1080/13607863.2010.519326

Tisdale, T. C., Keys, T. L., Edwards, K. J., Brokaw, B. F., Kemperman, S. R., Cloud, H., . . . Okamoto, T. (1997). Impact of treatment on God image and personal adjustment, and correlations of God image to personal adjustment and object relations adjustment. *Journal of Psychology and Theology, 25*, 227–239.

Wachholtz, A. B., & Pargament, K. I. (2008). Migraines and meditation: Does spirituality matter? *Journal of Behavioral Medicine, 31*, 351–366. doi:10.1007/s10865-008-9159-2

Walsh, R., & Shapiro, S. L. (2006). The meeting of meditative disciplines and western psychology: A mutually enriching dialogue. *American Psychologist, 61*, 227–239. doi:10.1037/0003-066X.61.3.227

West, W. (2000). *Psychotherapy and spirituality: Crossing the line between therapy and religion.* Thousand Oaks, CA: Sage.

Winett, R. A., Anderson, E. S., Wojcik, J. R., Winett, S. G., & Bowden, T. (2007). Guide to Health: Nutrition and physical activity outcomes of a group-randomized trial of an internet-based intervention in churches. *Annals of Behavioral Medicine, 33*, 251–261. doi:10.1007/BF02879907

Worthington, E. L., Jr., Hook, J. N., Davis, D. E., & McDaniel, M. A. (2011). Religion and spirituality. In J. Norcross (Ed.), *Psychotherapy relationships that work* (2nd ed., pp. 402–420). New York, NY: Oxford University Press. doi:10.1093/acprof:oso/9780199737208.003.0020

Wulff, D. M. (1997). *Psychology of religion: Classic and contemporary* (2nd ed.). New York, NY: Wiley.

Wuthnow, R. (1998). *After heaven: Spirituality in America since the 1950's.* Berkeley: University of California Press.

Young, J. S., Cashwell, C., Wiggins-Frame, M., & Belaire, C. (2002). Spiritual and religious competencies: A national survey of CACREP-accredited programs. *Counseling and Values, 47*, 22–33. doi:10.1002/j.2161-007X.2002.tb00221.x

CHAPTER 2

RELIGIOUS AND SPIRITUAL BELIEFS, AFFILIATIONS, AND PRACTICES OF PSYCHOLOGISTS

Edward P. Shafranske and Jeremy P. Cummings

A rapidly growing body of empirical evidence suggests that religiousness and spirituality have the power to affect health and well-being in significant ways (see Volume 1, Chapter 1, this handbook) and that the inclusion of spiritually oriented therapeutic approaches and resources may have particular benefits for clients for whom religion and spirituality (R/S) are personally meaningful (see Chapter 1 in this volume). Furthermore, clinician sensitivity and responsiveness to client R/S may influence the formation of the therapeutic relationship, which has a well-established role in the change process and outcome (Norcross, 2010). Also, the ethical requirement to integrate a multicultural perspective in treatment (American Psychological Association [APA], 2010) extends to considering R/S because (a) they are features of culture (APA, 2003) and (b) clinicians as well as clients may hold important loyalties and attachments to their R/S worldviews and communities (Fowers, 2001). Given these considerations, it is surprising that less is known about practitioners' own R/S and how these factors influence their work in contrast to other clinical and cultural factors that affect treatment. Our focus in this chapter is on reviewing the literature about psychologists' R/S beliefs, affiliations, and practices; the nature of their professional training; and their attitudes and practices relevant to the integration of R/S resources and interventions in psychotherapy. Although we intentionally delimit this review to psychologists (and with emphasis on clinicians), the implications and recommendations we present are likely relevant for many mental health professions, such as psychiatry and social work, in addition to a wide range of professional activities concerned with individual, family, corporate, and social change, including treatment, consultation, public policy, and applied research.

This review has several objectives. First, reviewing the R/S beliefs, attitudes, commitments, and practices of mental health professionals and comparing these professionals to the population base of their clients can give us insight into potential areas of similarity and dissimilarity, which in turn may affect clinical understanding, clients' experiences of empathy, and the therapeutic relationship. Furthermore, such a comparison is useful to better understand the roles and dynamics of R/S in helping relationships. The second goal is to describe the degree to which R/S resources are currently integrated into treatment by presenting data on professionals' attitudes toward and use of R/S interventions. Third, by examining research on graduate education and training pertaining to R/S, we can evaluate the adequacy of professionals' preparation for addressing R/S in practice and offer recommendations to the training community. Finally, we hope that the data presented in this chapter will encourage the reader to reflect on his or her own stance toward R/S both personally and professionally.

We begin by considering the degree to which psychologists rate R/S as important in their own lives and comparing psychologists to the general population of the United States in terms of these variables. Next, we discuss the prevalence of typical

DOI: 10.1037/14046-002
APA Handbook of Psychology, Religion, and Spirituality: Vol. 2. An Applied Psychology of Religion and Spirituality, K. I. Pargament (Editor-in-Chief)

R/S beliefs in samples of psychologists, followed by a consideration of the religious affiliations and spiritual practices of psychologists. Then, we present data on psychologists' attitudes toward and use of R/S interventions. We also review the amount and kinds of training psychologists receive in graduate school, clinical supervision, and during their clinical internship. In light of this information, we discuss implications for clinical practice, training, and research.

IMPORTANCE OF RELIGION AND SPIRITUALITY

"How important is religion in your life?" This question (and a parallel form for spirituality) is one of the most common ways that researchers assess R/S. It is straightforward and relatively easy to answer, but it is based on the assumption that researchers know how respondents define R/S. Zinnbauer et al. (1997) sought to shed light on this issue by studying individuals' definitions of these terms. They found a discrepancy between self-ratings, with respondents' ratings of their spirituality significantly higher than their religiousness; some subsamples showed greater discrepancies than others. In response to open-ended questions, participants' definitions of spirituality generally included a sense of connectedness with God, a Higher Power, Nature, or some transcendent reality or personal beliefs about sacred entities. Whereas definitions of religiousness also occasionally included references to personal beliefs, the themes of participation in organized practices, commitment to organized beliefs, and integrating personal values or God's will into one's life distinguished religiousness from spirituality. As we consider the research presented in this section, it is important to keep in mind that the public tends to see spirituality as a personal, experiential, free-form phenomenon, whereas religion is perceived as more communal and codified.

How do psychologists and other mental health professionals compare with the general population in terms of religious salience? Nationally representative studies have consistently found that a large majority of Americans say religion is very or fairly important to them (Gallup, 1994, 1999; Newport, 2007; see Table 2.1). In contrast, samples drawn from the APA and the American Psychiatric Association are substantially less likely to consider religion personally salient, with gaps ranging from 18% to 40% (Delaney, Miller, & Bisonó, 2007; McMinn,

TABLE 2.1

Importance of Religion

Sample	Very important (%)	Fairly important (%)	Not very important (%)	No opinion (%)
National sample 1993[a]	59	29	12	< 1
National sample 1999[b]	58	30	11	1
National sample 2007[c]	56	24	17	–
Psychiatrists[d]	38	19	42	2
Psychologists/rehabilitation[e]	41	29	29	1
Psychologists/clinical–counseling[f]	26	22	51	0
Psychologists/clinical–counseling[g]	21	31	48	0
Psychologists/APA leaders[h,i]	21	25	54	0

[a]Gallup Poll (Gallup, 1994). [b]Gallup Poll (Gallup, 1999). [c]Gallup Poll (Newport, 2007). [d]Random sample of members of the American Psychiatric Association (*N* = 105; Shafranske, 2000). [e]Random sample of American Psychological Association, Division 22 (Rehabilitation Psychology) members (*N* = 242; Shafranske, 2001). [f]Random sample of American Psychological Association members listing degrees in Clinical Psychology or Counseling Psychology (*N* = 253; Shafranske, 1996). [g]Random sample of members from multiple American Psychological Association divisions associated with clinical work (*N* = 258; Delaney et al., 2007). [h]Entire leadership of American Psychological Association contacted (*N* = 63; McMinn et al., 2009). [i]This question differed from the others and used a five-point Likert-type scale ranging from 1 (*not at all important; I have no religion*) to 5 (*highly important; it is the center of my life*). We classified responses of 1 and 2 as "not very important," 3 as "fairly important," and 4 and 5 as "very important."

Hathaway, Woods, & Snow, 2009; Shafranske, 1996, 2000, 2001). Even so, many mental health professionals report that religion is at least fairly important to them. Religious salience appears to vary across samples of different disciplines and specializations. Psychologists specializing in rehabilitation have indicated the highest levels of religious salience (Shafranske, 2001), whereas general samples of clinically oriented psychologists have reported notably lower levels of religious salience (Delaney et al., 2007; Shafranske, 1996). Because response rates for these studies (Delaney et al., 2007; McMinn et al., 2009; Shafranske, 1996, 2000, 2001) are typically low, the findings may not accurately represent the salience of religion to all psychologists. When researchers have compared the characteristics of psychologists who do and do not respond to surveys about religiousness, the former group reports greater religious salience than the latter group, possibly because respondents are more willing to spend time answering these questions because of the higher value they place on religion (Shafranske, 2001; Shafranske & Malony, 1990).

Researchers have also assessed the importance of religion by asking about the practical impact of religion on one's lifestyle. Many mental health professionals (65%–70%) agree that they "try hard to live according to [their] religious beliefs" (Bergin & Jensen, 1990; Delaney et al., 2007; see Table 2.2), but they are less likely to endorse this statement than the public (84%; Gallup, 2002). The gap is even greater when the question is whether "[their] whole approach to life is based on [their] religion." Participants in a 1999 Gallup Poll (Gallup & Lindsay, 1999) were more than twice as likely to respond affirmatively than were mental health workers (72% vs. 33%–35%; Bergin & Jensen, 1990; Delaney et al., 2007).

Compared with religion, psychologists are much more enthusiastic about spirituality. In Table 2.2, spiritual salience is uniformly high across four study samples (McMinn et al., 2009; Shafranske, 1996, 2000, 2001; there are unfortunately no directly comparable data on this topic in national samples). Furthermore, each sample shows marked gaps between religious and spiritual salience. Rehabilitation psychologists report the smallest discrepancy (Shafranske, 2001). The discrepancy is greatest for APA leaders, with spiritual salience leading religious salience by 36 points (McMinn et al., 2009).

In light of popular distinctions between religion and spirituality (Zinnbauer et al., 1997), the findings reported in this section may mean that mental health professionals favor more individualistic expressions of connectedness with the sacred instead of more traditional, institutionalized forms. Furthermore, although many mental health professionals state that they try to integrate their faith into their daily life, most deny that it is the sole or most important influence on their approach to life. One potential reason is that they may view faith and religious belief to be antithetical to science, and furthermore, that conclusions drawn from science or from

TABLE 2.2

Importance of Spirituality

Sample	Very important (%)	Fairly important (%)	Not very important (%)	No opinion (%)
Psychiatrists[a]	56	25	18	1
Psychologists/rehabilitation[b]	50	30	19	1
Psychologists/clinical–counseling[c]	48	25	26	0
APA leaders[d,e]	61	21	18	0

[a]Random sample of members of the American Psychiatric Association (N = 105; Shafranske, 2000). [b]Random sample of American Psychological Association Division 22 (Rehabilitation Psychology) members (N = 242; Shafranske, 2001). [c]Random sample of American Psychological Association members listing degrees in Clinical Psychology or Counseling Psychology (N = 253; Shafranske, 1996). [d]Entire leadership of American Psychological Association contacted (N = 63; McMinn et al., 2009). [e]This question differed from the others and used a five-point Likert-type scale ranging from 1 (*not at all important; I have no religion*) to 5 (*highly important; it is the center of my life*). We classified responses of 1 and 2 as "not very important," 3 as "fairly important," and 4 and 5 as "very important."

TABLE 2.3

Ideological Orientations

Ideological statement	1990[a] (%)	1995[b] (%)	1998[c] (%)
There is a personal God of transcendent existence and power whose purposes will ultimately be worked out in human history.	30	24	36
There is a transcendent aspect of human experience which some persons call God but who is not immanently involved in the events of the world and human history.	10	14	11
There is a transcendent or divine dimension that is unique and specific to the human self.	9	7	10
There is a transcendent or divine dimension found in all manifestations of nature.	21	31	27
The notions of God or the transcendent are illusory products of human imagination; however, they are meaningful aspects of human existence.	26	24	16
The notions of God or the transcendent are illusory products of human imagination; therefore, they are irrelevant to the real world.	2	1	0
No response.	2	0	0

Note. From *Faith and Health: Psychological Perspectives* (p. 322), by T. G. Plante and A. C. Sherman (Eds.), 2001, New York, NY: Guilford Press. Copyright 2001 by The Guilford Press. Adapted with permission.
[a]Random sample of American Psychological Association Division 12 (Clinical Psychology) members (*N* = 409; Shafranske & Malony, 1990). [b]Random sample of American Psychological Association members listing degrees in clinical psychology or counseling psychology (*N* = 253; Shafranske, 1996). [c]Random sample of American Psychological Association Division 22 (Rehabilitation Psychology) members (*N* = 242; Shafranske, 2001).

psychology as a profession may conflict with the authority of religious texts, church teachings, and traditions. Although full discussion of this issue is beyond the scope of this chapter, we suggest that embedded within psychology's dominant epistemology is skepticism, if not antipathy, toward approaches deviating from the accepted canons of positivistic science. Although some have called for a postmaterialistic, spiritual psychology (L. Miller, 2010), dissonance is likely when considering approaches outside of the paradigmatic positivistic mainstream. Skinner (1987) may have perfectly captured the prevailing sentiment among psychologists: "Science, not religion, has taught me my most useful values, among them intellectual honesty. It is better to go without answers than to accept those which merely resolve puzzlement" (pp. 12–13).

For others, intuitive self-direction may be preferable to religious teachings. Carl Rogers expressed this opinion concisely: "Neither the Bible nor the prophets—neither Freud nor research—neither the revelations of God nor man—can take precedence over my own direct experience" (1961, p. 24).

Concluding that such sentiments are more common among psychologists than the public (solely on the basis of self-reported religious and spiritual salience) could be premature. As we will see, however, other approaches to studying psychologists' R/S have yielded findings that are in line with trends we have already observed.

Religious Beliefs

Freud (1927/1961) famously asserted that belief in God was nothing more than faith in an illusion, a form of projection, aimed to humanize the impersonal forces of nature and to counter one's helplessness in the face of those forces. Although we do not know their rationale, we do know that psychologists are more likely than the general public to deny the existence of a transcendent God. In Ragan, Malony, and Beit-Hallahmi's (1980) sample of APA members, 35% denied any belief in God or a higher power. More recent studies (Shafranske, 1996, 2001; Shafranske & Malony, 1990; see Table 2.4), restricted to clinical and counseling psychologists, have continued to find that psychologists are more likely to report not believing in any divine entity than the rest of the United States, insofar as only 5% of a national sample denied belief in God or a Universal Spirit (Gallup, 1999). The study conducted by Delaney et al. (2007) framed this

TABLE 2.4

Religious Affiliations

Sample	Protestant (%)	Jewish (%)	Catholic (%)	Other (%)	None (%)
National sample[a]	51	2	24	3	16
Various mental health professionals[b]	38	18	15	9	19
Psychologists/clinical[c]	25	16	14	16	30
Childhood affiliation[c]	45	20	22	10	3
Psychologists/clinical–counseling[d]	28	23	18	15	16

[a]The Pew Forum on Religion and Public Life, 2008 (*N* = 35,556). [b]Sample of clinical psychologists, psychiatrists, social workers, and marriage and family therapists (*N* = 425; Bergin & Jensen, 1990). [c]Random sample of members of American Psychological Association Division 12 (Shafranske & Malony, 1990). [d]Random sample of members from multiple American Psychological Association divisions associated with clinical work (*N* = 258; Delaney et al., 2007).

TABLE 2.5

Degree of Involvement in Organized Religion

Involvement	1990[a] (%)	1991[b] (%)	1992[c] (%)	1995[d] (%)
Active participation, high level of involvement	18	12	11	16
Regular participation, some involvement	23	23	24	21
Identification with religious very limited, or no involvement	30	34	37	29
No identification, participation, or involvement with religion	22	20	22	21
Somewhat negative reaction to religion	–	9	5	9
Disdain or very negative reaction to religion	7	3	1	4

[a]Random sample of member of American Psychological Association, Division 12 (Clinical Psychology; *N* = 409; Shafranske & Malony, 1990). [b]Random sample of members of American Psychological Association, Division 29 (Psychotherapy; *N* = 270; Derr, 1991). [c]Random sample of training directors listed in the 1990–1991 directory published by the Association of Psychology Internship Centers (*N* = 79; Lannert, 1992). [d]Random sample of American Psychological Association members listing degrees in clinical psychology or counseling psychology (*N* = 253; Shafranske, 1996).

question differently but still found one quarter of their sample did not believe in God or was unsure about their beliefs. Interestingly, the same percentage said they used to believe in God but no longer did. Their sample was more than 6 times more likely to have stopped believing in God at some point in the past than the sample in the National Opinion Research Center–General Social Survey of 1998 and 2004 (NORC-GSS, 2005).

Psychologists who indicate some form of belief in the divine display variety in their views (Shafranske, 1996, 2001; Shafranske & Malony, 1990). Many believe in a transcendent God involved in human affairs (theism). One fifth to nearly a third of participants in these samples said nature itself is divine (pantheism), outnumbering theists in one study (Shafranske, 1996). Others reported deistic views (God as a creative power no longer involved in human affairs) or the belief that humanity is divine. These findings confirm what we have suggested thus far, namely that many psychologists' beliefs about the divine diverge from those that have traditionally characterized R/S in the United States.

Religious Affiliations and Practices

Most Americans self-identify as either Protestant Christian or Roman Catholic (Pew Forum on Religion and Public Life, 2008). As in national samples, Protestants are usually the majority in psychologist samples; however, Protestants were underrepresented in every study of psychologists included in Table 2.5 (Bergin & Jensen, 1990; Delaney et al.,

2007; Shafranske & Malony, 1990). Similarly, there were fewer Catholics in studies of psychologists compared with the national sample. The proportions of Jewish respondents and members of other religions were consistently and substantially higher than in the national sample, but the evidence for a higher than average number of psychologists with no R/S affiliation was mixed.

Possible explanations are that the field of psychology is especially attractive to people from non-Christian upbringings on the basis of sociocultural and historical factors, or that the profession offers a privileging of diverse perspectives and individual decision making that may have an appeal for people who have switched to a non-Christian affiliation or hold to noninstitutional forms of spirituality. On the other hand, psychologists may turn away from Christianity or religious institutions in general as a result of their psychological education and training. Psychology professors are among the least religious in the academy; 61% of psychology faculty members are atheistic or agnostic (Gross & Simmons, 2007) and social science faculty are less likely to be spiritual compared with university faculty in general (Lindholm & Astin, 2006). Although the impact of psychology graduate education and training on spirituality and religious affiliation has not been prospectively studied, it may be that subtle attitudes about R/S belief and affiliation are communicated during doctoral education. In a recent exploratory study, however, 71% of psychology interns reported that the attitudes or opinions of faculty members resulted in no change in their R/S and 15% reported a strengthening of their R/S (Francis, 2011). Although we do not know the specific impacts of training or professional practice on religious affiliations and practices, we do know that it is not uncommon for psychologists to change their R/S commitments. The data from Shafranske and Malony's (1990) study regarding psychologists' childhood affiliations do not directly test these impacts, but they do suggest that many psychologists have switched their affiliation at some point in life. Comparing the present affiliations of psychologists with their childhood affiliations, there was a 44% drop in Protestant affiliation as well as a decrease of 36% for Catholicism and 20% for Judaism. In contrast, the number of religious "nones" increased tenfold, from 3% to 30%; membership in other religions increased by 60%. These findings suggest psychologists have a strong tendency to shift toward having no affiliation or toward non-Judeo–Christian affiliations. These findings, although dramatic, parallel a general trend in which the percentage of Americans claiming no religion is on the increase. "Nones" represented 8.2% of the U.S. population in 1990 and now account for 15%; the majority switched to the status of "none" having previously held a religious preference (Kosmin, Keysar, Cragun, & Navarro-Rivera, 2009).

Claiming an affiliation and actually investing one's time and energy in R/S pursuits are two different matters. Four studies reported that between one third and two fifths of psychologists describe themselves as actively or regularly participating in organized religion (Derr, 1991; Lannert, 1992; Shafranske, 1996; Shafranske & Malony, 1990; see Table 2.5). Beyond being less involved, a sizable minority of psychologists in these studies indicated having a somewhat or very negative reaction to religion. Delaney et al. (2007) asked about psychologists' frequency of R/S behaviors more specifically. Using data from the Gallup Poll (Gallup & Lindsay, 1999) for comparison, the researchers found that psychologists were more likely to attend religious services never or rarely (55% vs. 40%) and once or twice a month (22% vs. 13%) but were less likely to attend weekly or more (23% vs. 47%). Similarly, although 90% of Americans prayed once a week or more, only 54% of psychologists reported praying as frequently. The contrast is more striking when it is considered that 75% of Americans said they prayed once a day or more, but only 19% of psychologists prayed daily. These numbers indicate a significant gap between the R/S activities of psychologists and the general public. In other respects, however, psychologists appear to be generally similar or may even demonstrate greater interest in religion when compared with the U. S. population. For example, 36% of psychologists said they read or study R/S materials at least once per week (Delaney et al., 2007), whereas 21% of religiously affiliated Americans read books (other than Scripture) or visit websites about their religion (Pew Forum on Religion and Public Life, 2010) at least once per week (note, however, that a clear comparison cannot be drawn because of differences in question format and inability to control for education level). Additional research is required to more fully understand the points of similarity and difference between psychologists and the clients they serve, but this review suggests that striking differences do exist, particularly in respect to affiliation with and participation in religion.

PSYCHOLOGISTS' RELIGIOUSNESS AND SPIRITUALITY IN THE CONTEXT OF CURRENT U.S. TRENDS

It is clear that, relative to other Americans, psychologists typically have moderate to low levels of religiousness. For the past few decades, however, U.S. religiousness and spirituality have changed in ways that may bring them closer to perspectives common among psychologists. For instance, Roof (1999) has argued that the baby boomer generation by and large approached R/S as an open-ended, self-directed quest more than earlier generations. Guided by personal preferences and exposed to a greater range of options because of globalization and mass media, many boomers shopped around for R/S products that would help them in their search for self-expression, inner peace, and meaning in life. They were more skeptical of institutionalized faith, questioning the value of traditional doctrines and church attendance. In a similar vein, Wuthnow (2007) has noted that the generation following the baby boomers attends church less frequently and is less likely to have a religious affiliation. Wuthnow described this generation as "spiritual tinkerers" who blend beliefs and practices from multiple sources, such as orthodox creeds, texts from different traditions, conversations with friends, popular music, and personal reflection.

It seems that a growing proportion of younger adults, like many psychologists, may reject organized religion or at least refuse to follow prescribed forms of spirituality. Although this trend can promote a greater sense of personal autonomy and choice, it may bring with it ambivalence and uncertainty. To illustrate, 42% of college freshmen characterize their current views about R/S matters as confident, but 23% are seeking, 15% conflicted, 10% doubting, and 15% uninterested (Higher Education Research Institute, 2004, p. 6). This research does not provide a longitudinal perspective to assess a trend; however, it does suggest possible impacts when a sustaining spiritual perspective is not in place. Pargament (2007) suggested that established R/S traditions often have breadth and depth that result from centuries of wrestling with the human condition; in picking and choosing only the elements that are most immediately appealing, modern tinkerers may miss out on other important, if less obviously palatable, elements. If these individuals seek mental health services, they may present with spiritual orienting systems that lack crucial resources that would relieve suffering or, even worse, systems that actively contribute to dysfunction. Another potential problem is that the public may feel bewildered by the abundance of R/S options and yet alienated from the institutions that have historically offered guidance for the most critical moments in life. Instead of consulting R/S leaders, people increasingly may turn to secular professionals to resolve existential or even spiritual issues and to conserve or transform their spirituality, or they may seek psychotherapy as a spiritual quest (Shafranske & Sperry, 2005), or they may not even recognize the spiritual nature of their concerns. How will practitioners respond in such cases? Will they be prepared? Will they even be willing to integrate R/S into the services they provide? In the remainder of this chapter, we will describe research on the state of training and practice in one applied area, spiritually integrated psychotherapy, and discuss how our field might rise to these challenges (see also Chapter 33 in this volume).

RELIGIOUS AND SPIRITUAL ISSUES IN PROFESSIONAL PRACTICE

The past few decades have seen an explosion of evidence for the importance of addressing R/S issues in clinical work. One argument in favor of spiritually integrated psychotherapy is that R/S difficulties are very common. A large study of college students found that 19% of students receiving services at university counseling centers reported moderate to extreme distress related to R/S problems (Johnson &

Hayes, 2003). In a smaller study, 200 psychologists, participating in a real-time behavior sampling investigation, reported that spirituality was involved in both the problem and the solution in 26% of their cases (APA, Practice Directorate, 2003). Furthermore, many therapy clients believe it is appropriate to discuss R/S in therapy and want to do so (Rose, Westefeld, & Ansley, 2001); this is especially true for highly R/S clients (J. S. Martinez, Smith, & Barlow, 2007; Worthington & Sandage, 2001). In fact, therapists' use of R/S interventions may help highly R/S Christian clients feel closer to their therapist and benefit more from therapy (Wade, Worthington, & Vogel, 2007). Additionally, R/S resources such as prayer and participation in a faith community can promote psychological well-being (Pargament, Murray-Swank, & Tarakeshwar, 2005). In the interest of integrating R/S into treatment more effectively, researchers have developed interventions that incorporate R/S concepts and practices. A recent review found that spiritually integrated interventions were typically equally or more effective than comparison treatments (Post & Wade, 2009). In fact, using conventional standards to determine treatment efficacy, Hook et al. (2010) were able to identify several efficacious and possibly efficacious R/S treatments. With respect to these research developments, it is important to determine how well clinicians' attitudes and practices are keeping up.

In general, psychologists tend to view R/S as significant and relevant parts of their clients' lives. Hathaway, Scott, and Garver (2004) reported that half of their national sample of therapists strongly agreed that R/S functioning is a significant and important domain of human adjustment, and only about 1 in 10 disagreed. Multiple studies have asked psychologists to estimate the prevalence of R/S issues in treatment. In one study, the average reported prevalence of clients who discussed R/S issues was 30% (Frazier & Hansen, 2009). The vast majority of psychologists in recent studies have indicated that R/S is at least sometimes relevant to their clinical work (Delaney et al., 2007; Shafranske, 2001). Moreover, 82% of the psychologists in the sample collected by Delaney et al. (2007) stated that religion is positively related to mental health. This figure, higher than the 53% who viewed religious beliefs as desirable for people in general in Shafranske and Malony's (1990) study, may reflect greater awareness of research on links between R/S and mental health.

When it comes to addressing R/S actively in treatment, therapists' attitudes and practices are mixed. Whereas members of the APA tended to view R/S integration as only slightly important for therapeutic competence (Frazier & Hansen, 2009), the majority of a sample of American Counseling Association members agreed that the R/S competencies specified by that organization (e.g., use the client's spiritual beliefs in the pursuit of the client's therapeutic goals) were important (Young, Wiggins-Frame, & Cashwell, 2007). Nearly two thirds of a sample of rehabilitation psychologists indicated that psychologists should not provide R/S resources unless the client initiates a conversation about such matters (Shafranske, 2001). In the same sample, 38% disagreed with the position that psychologists should use specific, empirically supported R/S interventions regardless of their personal beliefs, and another 18% were undecided.

Shafranske (1996; 2001) and Frazier and Hansen (2009) noted that psychologists' reported approval of R/S integration in therapy is often significantly higher than the degree to which they actually address these issues in their clinical work on a regular basis. Although a meta-analysis of studies of R/S integration in therapy found that approximately two thirds of therapists had used prayer or R/S language, metaphors, and concepts in therapy at some point during their career (Walker, Gorsuch, & Tan, 2004), the frequency of such interventions may be quite low. On average, psychologists report integrating R/S into treatment between "rarely" and "sometimes" (Frazier & Hansen, 2009). Most psychologists say they address R/S at least sometimes through general, basic therapy behaviors, such as assessing their clients' R/S beliefs and practices (Delaney et al., 2007) and communicating respect for their clients' R/S beliefs (Frazier & Hansen, 2009). It appears less common, however, for psychologists to use active interventions that deal with R/S more explicitly, such as prayer and citing religious texts (Frazier & Hansen, 2009; Shafranske, 1996, 2001). Therapists who explicitly identify themselves as religious may use active interventions more frequently. One study found religious psychologists discussed scripture and biblical concepts in 39% of their therapy cases (Walker et al., 2004). On a related note, O'Grady and Richards (2010) reported that 86.6% of mental health practitioners answered on a survey that they believed that "God may inspire helping professionals as they work with clients" and 74.7% indicated that they had "personally felt God's inspiration in their professional practice" (p. 60). These findings suggest that personal faith may play a more significant role in the conduct of psychotherapy than had been reported previously.

Naturally, researchers have been interested in learning what factors are related to psychologists' attitudes toward and use of R/S interventions. One common finding is that clinicians who are personally more R/S report integrating R/S into treatment to a greater extent, whereas those who have more negative past experiences with R/S are less favorable toward integration (Frazier & Hansen, 2009; Shafranske & Malony, 1990; Walker et al., 2004). In addition to these personal factors, training in working with R/S issues may promote integration. Walker, Gorsuch, and Tan (2005) found that explicitly Christian counselors who received general clinical training with R/S clients or training in specific R/S interventions were more likely to use R/S interventions. In contrast, although obtaining continuing education about R/S was linked to greater use of R/S interventions in Frazier and Hansen's (2009) study, classroom education and supervision involving R/S issues were unrelated to integration.

Psychologists often can serve their clients and communities best by working in tandem with R/S leaders. McMinn, Chaddock, Edwards, Lim, and Campbell (1998) asked members of APA divisions devoted to the psychology of R/S and clinical psychology how common it is for psychologists and R/S leaders to collaborate. On average, psychologists reported engaging in each of 12 specific collaborative activities "sometimes" or less frequently. The most common (although still infrequent) kinds of collaboration included working with R/S leaders on community service, taking referrals from R/S leaders, presenting a seminar to an R/S community, and providing consultation to R/S leaders. Because this sample disproportionately consisted of psychologists interested in the psychology of R/S, these results may overestimate the prevalence of such collaboration in the general population of psychologists. McMinn et al. (1998) also identified several obstacles to collaboration, such as perceptions that psychologists and R/S leaders do not need each other, differences in worldviews associated with the two professions, and a lack of awareness of available resources.

According to Hathaway (2003), the mental health field's neglect of R/S is also evident in how we diagnose mental disorders. He has noted that the *Diagnostic and Statistical Manual of Mental Disorders* (4th ed., text revision; American Psychiatric Association, 2000) includes clinically significant impairment in life domains, such as social and occupational functioning, as a criterion for the diagnosis of a mental disorder. Hathaway has argued that R/S functioning is an important life domain for many people and that mental disorders may make it more difficult to maintain or develop R/S beliefs, practices, and emotions. Unfortunately, more than half of a national sample of APA members said they rarely or never assess how their clients' psychological conditions affect their R/S functioning (Hathaway, Scott, & Garver, 2004). Moreover, even though psychologists frequently help clients improve their social and occupational functioning, most of this sample reported rarely or never including R/S goals in their treatment plans (Hathaway et al., 2004).

Why do so many psychologists overlook such an important aspect of their clients' lives? There are two related explanations for this phenomenon. First, as we have noted, psychologists are often less R/S than the population they serve. If R/S do not play as much of a role in how psychologists view the world and make personal decisions, it may be difficult for them to truly understand how impactful R/S can be for their clients, regardless of psychologists' claims that they believe R/S are important aspects of human functioning. The fact that psychologists who are less R/S report less approval for integrating R/S into treatment fits with this conjecture (Frazier & Hansen, 2009; Shafranske & Malony, 1990; Walker et al., 2004). A second explanation is that psychologists are unprepared for this kind of work. After all, if professional psychologists are not inclined to address R/S in therapy and psychology professors are among the least religious in the professorate (Gross & Simmons, 2007; Politics of the Professorate, 1991), those who are responsible for training future psychologists may have a similar blind spot when it comes to providing education about R/S. Fortunately, we can evaluate this explanation by reviewing research on how much training psychologists receive on R/S issues.

EDUCATION AND TRAINING IN RELIGIOUS AND SPIRITUAL ISSUES

Psychology graduate education and training have historically given little or no consideration to R/S issues in clinical work (Shafranske, 1996). Two decades ago, psychologists seemed to be split in their opinions on the desirability of teaching psychologists in training about the psychology of R/S and providing clinical supervision on R/S issues in clinical work (Shafranske & Malony, 1990). More recent surveys of directors of clinical training in clinical and counseling psychology programs have investigated the coursework and supervision these programs provide regarding R/S (Brawer, Handal, Fabricatore, Roberts, & Wajda-Johnston, 2002; Schulte, Skinner, & Claiborn, 2002; see also Chapter 33 in this volume). A minority of programs (between one in 10 and one in five) offered specific courses on R/S, but more than three in five reportedly addressed R/S in other courses (Brawer et al., 2002; Schulte et al., 2002). In clinical psychology programs, discussions of R/S were most likely to take place in courses on cultural diversity and cross-cultural psychology (57%) or ethics and professional issues (41%); addressing R/S was rarer in more clinically relevant courses on psychotherapy (32%), psychopathology (19%), or assessment (13%; Brawer et al., 2002). Although these reports may suggest that there is coverage of R/S during graduate education, a recent survey found that more than 50% of clinical and counseling psychology interns reported that R/S issues were presented and discussed rarely or never in their academic coursework (Francis, 2011).

Training programs may believe that supervision and clinical experiences involving R/S issues compensate when coursework is lacking. In fact, supervision is the most commonly reported training component in which students might learn about R/S issues in treatment. More than three fourths of programs indicated that their students had access to supervisors who could guide them in conceptualizing and working with R/S (Brawer et al., 2002; Schulte et al., 2002). These figures, however, do not speak to how frequently students actually receive training about R/S issues in supervision. Such training may, in practice, be sporadic and unsystematic (Bishop, Avila-Juarbe, & Thumme, 2003). Considering both coursework and supervision, graduate education in clinical, counseling, and rehabilitation psychology does not consistently prepare students to work with R/S issues (Hage, 2006).

When psychologists are asked about their own training and competency with respect to R/S, a few interesting findings emerge. In Frazier and Hansen's (2009) stratified random sample of professional psychologists in the APA, participants reported a wide range of hours spent in classroom instruction ($M = 14$, $SD = 38$), supervision ($M = 67$, $SD = 431$ [sic]), and continuing education on R/S issues ($M = 13$, $SD = 35$). Most psychologists fall on the lower end of this range. For instance, 82% of the rehabilitation psychologists in Shafranske's (2001) study said R/S issues were rarely or never discussed in their clinical training, and 78% viewed their training in R/S as inadequate. More than half stated that psychologists are generally not well prepared to offer R/S resources to their clients. Their lack of training not withstanding, 73% indicated that they were comfortable discussing R/S with their clients. Finally, in Young et al.'s (2007) survey of members of the American Counseling Association, 47% reported having coursework on R/S, but 68% said they felt prepared to counsel clients with R/S issues. These findings suggest that even though training about R/S is spotty, most mental health professionals are open to and confident about addressing these topics in therapy.

The capstone training experience for professional psychologists is the clinical internship; if students do not learn about R/S issues in their graduate programs, perhaps they do so during this year of intensive clinical work. Two studies have surveyed training directors in internship programs regarding training in R/S. According to Lannert (1992), most training directors said that their programs addressed R/S value issues in clinical case presentations (76%) and initial intake evaluations (60%). Russell and Yarhouse (2006) reported a pattern similar to that found in studies of graduate programs. Although the majority (91%) of internship programs said they discussed R/S in supervision, significantly fewer (35%) offered didactic training on R/S on at least an occasional basis. It was unclear how regularly R/S was discussed in supervision. Only 4% had rotations dedicated to R/S issues, and 2% had access to R/S training materials. Here again, psychological training generally does not seem to address R/S explicitly and systematically.

In the foregoing discussion, we have hinted at concerns about relying on supervision as the primary source of training in R/S. Graduate programs and internships may assume that supervision is adequate in and of itself for producing psychologists competent to work with clients on R/S issues. However, the amount of supervision psychologists receive regarding R/S is extremely variable (Frazier & Hansen, 2009). Bishop et al. (2003) argued that the quantity and quality of supervision on R/S varies greatly because the field has not developed a standardized approach for training therapists to integrate R/S into treatment. They also pointed out that relatively little has been written about how to incorporate discussions of R/S in supervision. Supervisors, therefore, may lack comfort, confidence, or competency in this area.

Qualitative studies of mental health professionals who do integrate R/S into their clinical work have highlighted potential difficulties in supervision. One such difficulty is the disconnect between spiritually integrative clinicians and their supervisors. The former may be particularly sensitive to disparaging comments about R/S (S. Martinez & Baker, 2000) and may worry that their supervisors would react negatively to their use of R/S interventions (Gubi, 2007). Such dynamics discourage open discussions about R/S and are not conducive to developing competence with R/S issues. A participant in S. Martinez and Baker's (2000) study commented on negative religious stereotypes evident in his or her training program:

> I was being invalidated at times—I had to justify myself to people in training who had no idea except their own religious presuppositions that didn't allow them to hear what I had to say. . . . The trainers knew it was happening, joined in or did nothing. (p. 262)

Another risk is that if supervisees think their R/S interventions are going well, they may not bring them up in supervision (Gubi, 2007). Regarding her tendency not to discuss in-session prayer in supervision, one counselor said:

> I don't see that [prayer] as an issue at all. It just blends very well with what I'm doing. I suppose I focus [in supervision] on things that are challenges for me . . . points of tension rather than points of flow.

Supervisors who do not encourage discussing R/S interventions regardless of their perceived utility may miss out on opportunities to ensure their supervisees are practicing competently and ethically. These are just two examples of issues involving R/S that may arise in supervision. Even so, they represent significant challenges that need to be addressed.

DISCUSSION

In spite of cultural changes in the United States, the research presented in this chapter shows that psychologists remain in many ways less R/S than other Americans. Furthermore, psychologists' training in the psychology of R/S and in how to incorporate R/S into treatment is generally inadequate. In light of these two factors, it is not surprising that psychologists are largely reluctant to practice spiritually integrated psychotherapy. Perhaps it is prudent that most clinicians, given the lack of formal education and training they receive in such approaches, refrain from offering such forms of treatment. Considering the value that R/S has for the majority of the U.S. population and the benefits that can be obtained, however, we believe that the mental health field needs to have an ongoing conversation about these findings and their implications for our work. In the following section, we outline a few points worth further consideration.

The Impact of Practitioners' Beliefs and Values on Services

Perhaps the most fundamental issue raised by these findings is that mental health professionals may not be prepared to recognize and privilege the R/S perspectives of their clients. The differences in R/S commitments between clients and clinicians may pose unique therapeutic challenges. For example, some therapists may find themselves clashing with their clients about their understanding of the presenting problem and treatment goals, thereby negatively affecting the therapeutic alliance. Or, they may be unaware of the role that R/S may play as a stressor or as a resource, limiting the effectiveness of the treatment. Furthermore, some clinicians may not fully appreciate or respect the R/S values that shape clients' perspectives or assume that their clients similarly accept the secular values and moral positions that many psychologists hold. Clinicians may not be sensitive to the fact that values are embedded in the psychological theories they employ or that their notions about psychological health inevitably include judgments about the meaning and purpose of life (issues about which religions and spiritual communities have a lot to say). Although most professionals would never intentionally disrespect a client's R/S beliefs and commitments, they may nevertheless challenge the legitimacy of a client's faith or subtly influence their clients' R/S bearings. One approach to address these potential therapeutic challenges has been to pay close attention to client–therapist match. Consider the following case example.

> **Case Example 1**
>
> Lily, a 36-year-old woman, has been working with her therapist, Jane, for several weeks. Lily's parents were severely emotionally abusive to her when she was growing up, and Jane has focused on helping her develop a more positive self-image. Lily has made progress, which Jane attributes in part to the fact that Lily has not spoken to her parents for some time. Lately, Lily has reported thinking about her faith's teachings on forgiveness and feels that she may be violating her own values by completely cutting ties with her parents. Jane is not very R/S, but she does not want to impose her own values. She avoids directly contradicting Lily's beliefs by not really responding to any of Lily's statements about R/S. Whenever Lily brings up forgiveness, Jane reminds her of the pain caused by her parents and the progress she has made while refusing to talk to them. Although this approach successfully steers the conversation in a direction Jane finds more beneficial, Lily remains confused about what she should do.

In this example, the conflict between Jane's and Lily's R/S perspectives has a direct and potentially negative impact on Lily's treatment. How might Jane have dealt with this issue differently? One consistent recommendation in the literature is for clinicians to examine their own R/S beliefs and values as well as any prejudices they may have regarding R/S (Serlin, 2004; Yarhouse & VanOrman, 1999). Jane may not intentionally or explicitly impose her values, but greater self-awareness might help her rethink her approach to working with Lily. She might explore Lily's R/S beliefs about forgiveness in session and encourage Lily to talk more with her own R/S leader and community. In addition, Jane could research Lily's R/S and consult the psychological literature on forgiveness.

Another way Jane could have prevented this situation is if she had given Lily basic information about her own values and R/S perspectives at the outset of treatment (S. Martinez & Baker, 2000; Yarhouse & VanOrman, 1999; see also Chapter 3 in this volume). Yarhouse and VarOrman (1999) have argued that this information assists clients in making informed decisions about the care they receive. In the case example, Jane could have told Lily that her main priority is to help Lily overcome her pain and that although she is not personally R/S, she respects Lily's R/S beliefs. Jane could explain that if she thinks Lily's beliefs may impede her emotional recovery, she will openly communicate that concern and they can discuss it. With this knowledge, Lily is better able to decide whether she can work with

Jane; when conflicts arise, Lily may also feel freer to disagree with Jane because she recognizes that Jane's input is shaped by personal values rather than purely objective and authoritative.

Practitioners who are more R/S also have to deal with the issue of values in their work, as depicted in the following case example.

Case Example 2

Joseph routinely tells his clients that he is a Southern Baptist. He states that his job is to help clients learn about problematic thoughts and behaviors that prevent them from living their ideal life, not to convert them. However, he adds that sometimes clients have treatment goals that are against his R/S values. When this happens, Joseph says he is happy to work with them on other goals or to help them find another therapist. The purpose of this conversation is to make clients aware of the possibility of value conflicts and describe clients' options.

Although Joseph's approach may seem to be a reasonable and ethical approach, we are aware that some therapists may consider such disclosure and refusal to work with a client to attain their expressed goals to be inappropriate. Matching clients with practitioners who adhere to similar R/S convictions before the professional relationship is fully established is also a possible solution for value conflicts. If a client's and his or her therapist's values are too different, they may be unable to work together effectively (Worthington & Aten, 2009). Like many highly R/S clients, Lily could have sought out a value-similar therapist (Worthington & Sandage, 2001). Alternatively, if Jane was familiar with therapists from a range of R/S perspectives, she could have presented Lily with some screening questions about values and beliefs before her first office visit and then referred her to a therapist who more closely shared her perspective. There is, however, only mixed evidence for the benefits of client–therapist matching on R/S (Worthington & Sandage, 2001). Beyond the issue of match, these case examples point to the importance of developing self-awareness and thoughtful self-reflection (starting in graduate school and throughout one's career) regarding the impacts of a psychologist's personal faith perspectives on clients and on the therapeutic process.

Pursuing Religious and Spiritual Competence

Even when practitioners are cognizant of their own values and want to integrate R/S into their work, the prospect of developing competence in this area may seem daunting. Saunders, Miller, and Bright (2010) suggested that therapists think of this work in terms of a continuum of approaches. On one extreme, the *spiritually avoidant* approach entails refusing to discuss R/S at all with clients. *Spiritually directive* care is the other extreme, in which R/S is the primary focus for the therapist. Saunders et al. proposed that most psychologists should operate within one of the two middle-ground approaches. If the therapist has developed competence in working with R/S and the client is open to this work, *spiritually integrative* care—mobilizing the client's R/S framework to promote psychological well-being—may be the most beneficial option. According to Saunders et al., therapists without sufficient competence for spiritually integrative care should offer *spiritually conscious* care. This approach requires respectfully assessing clients' R/S as a routine part of the initial interview and as needed during therapy to understand its role(s) in the client's life and presenting problem. Saunders et al. provided a list of questions that may help the therapist gather this information. With a little effort, the ability to provide spiritually conscious care is within reach for all psychologists.

Reviewing recommendations for addressing R/S in therapy is beyond the scope of this chapter, but we offer a few points to consider. Those who are interested in empirically supported interventions that incorporate R/S might wish to read recent literature reviews on the subject (e.g., Hook et al., 2010; Post & Wade, 2009; Smith, Bartz, & Richards, 2007; Wade et al., 2007). Clinicians should note, however, that R/S clients may vary in their view of the most appropriate and helpful kinds of interventions (J. S. Martinez et al., 2007). For this reason, therapists must have open conversations with their clients to develop a mutually satisfactory approach for including R/S in treatment. Finally, McMinn, Vogel, and Heyne (2010) have encouraged psychologists to develop professional relationships with R/S leaders from diverse traditions. They stated that doing so helps psychologists become more familiar with the resources that faith communities can provide. Furthermore, it opens up the possibility of consultation about clients with challenging R/S issues; similarly, psychologists can share their expertise with R/S leaders (McMinn et al., 2010). Clinicians and R/S leaders can make referrals to each other when appropriate (McMinn et al., 2010). In the past, collaboration between mental health and R/S professionals has largely consisted of the latter sending their congregation members to the former (McMinn et al., 1998). McMinn et al. (1998) argued that collaboration needs to be bidirectional to provide the best care.

Ethical Considerations in Spiritually Sensitive Services

A thorough understanding and deep commitment to ethical principles is essential for integrating R/S into treatment. Suppose our hypothetical client, Lily, were to seek treatment from Joseph, who is personally religious. Joseph has never had any training in spiritually integrated therapy, but he knows that he and Lily come from similar R/S backgrounds. So, Joseph talks with her about forgiving her parents and refers to specific Bible verses on the subject. He also prays with her about whether she should contact her parents, and afterward tells her that he thinks God would want her to do so. Lily still has doubts, but she cannot tell Joseph because she does not want to disagree with what God told him.

This scenario touches on some of the ethical issues identified by Plante (2007) and Yarhouse and VanOrman (1999; see also Hathaway, 2011; Chapter 3 in this volume). For example, Joseph seems to assume that his personal faith makes him competent to conduct psychospiritual interventions (Plante, 2007). Most ethical standards state that professional competence develops through education and training in specific domains of practice. If Joseph wants to conduct spiritually integrated therapy, he should learn about validated measures of R/S functioning and empirically supported R/S interventions (Yarhouse & VanOrman, 1999). On a related note, Joseph must be mindful of the distinctions between his role as a mental health professional and the roles of R/S leaders (Plante, 2007). He is not professionally qualified to give R/S guidance, and his recommendation may be a disguised attempt to impose his own values on Lily. Furthermore, should Joseph believe that he has received divine inspiration in his work with Lily, he should proceed cautiously, remaining open to the possibility that other factors may be influencing his judgment (O'Grady & Richards, 2010). Whereas Joseph may be tempted to cross boundaries because of his R/S beliefs, nonreligious and nonspiritual therapists like Jane are at risk for undervaluing their clients' faith by thinking the only purpose of R/S is to serve other psychological functions, such as tension reduction and social connection (Yarhouse & VanOrman, 1999). Instead, they should try to understand the intrinsic significance R/S may have for clients (Yarhouse & VanOrman, 1999).

Education and Training in Religion and Spirituality as Clinically Relevant Variables

The best way to ensure that psychologists are aware of value issues in therapy and can address R/S in treatment competently and ethically is to be intentional about providing adequate education and training on these subjects (McMinn, Worthington, & Aten, 2011; Shafranske & Malony, 1996; Worthington et al., 2009). As previously discussed, it appears that graduate programs do not currently address R/S as consistently or adequately as other forms of diversity (Brawer et al., 2002). As awareness of the importance of R/S in therapy continues to grow, programs should adjust their curricula to prepare their students better to work with R/S. Yarhouse and Fisher (2002) delineated three models of training from which programs might choose. In the integration–incorporation model, R/S is discussed throughout many preexisting courses, such as multicultural competence, ethics, personality and social psychology, psychopathology, and evidence-based practice. This model is likely the most feasible to implement and offers students broad exposure to the ways in which R/S intersects with psychological theory, research, and practice. The certificate-minor model entails developing a specialization track with courses and clinical experiences that focus on R/S. This elective track can assist interested students in developing expertise in this area. For programs associated with a particular R/S tradition, the religious distinctive model—in which an R/S perspective informs and underlies all instruction and clinical experiences—may be a good fit.

Bowman (1998); Larson, Lu, and Swyers (1996; as related to psychiatric residency training); McMinn et al. (2011); Pargament (2007); Shafranske and Malony (1996); Shafranske and Sperry (2005); and Worthington et al. (2009) and others have opined a general orientation to education and training and have provided descriptions of the content that should be covered in graduate programs, some of which we will present here. First and foremost, students need to learn about R/S, including (a) definitions for each, (b) what we understand about R/S from the perspective of psychology as a science and scholarly discipline, and (c) the prevalence and salience of R/S in the general population. Beyond consideration of the scientific literature, students should engage in a process of personal exploration to identify their core beliefs and commitments through the use of a spiritual autobiography (Pargament, 2007) and reflect on areas of potential conflict. Another critical education component is familiarity with literature on the functions of R/S in daily life, links between R/S and mental health, and R/S coping and struggles. Students should understand how R/S emerges in and contributes to the therapeutic process, including the possible reluctance of their clients to bring up R/S in therapy (Bowman, 1998), so that they will take the initiative to discuss these topics. By the end of their training, students should understand R/S to be important clinical variables and aspects of multicultural identities and should know how to gather and interpret information regarding the client's R/S history as well as the impacts of current beliefs, affiliations, and practices. They should be able to assess R/S resources (e.g., positive coping mechanisms and social support) and problems (Serlin, 2004) and spiritual struggles (see Volume 1, Chapter 25, this handbook). Students should be given instruction in approaches to address R/S in psychotherapy, including empirically supported R/S interventions. In keeping with graduate education, opportunities to apply knowledge should be provided through clinical training and supervision.

Supervision is a key element of psychological training and, as such, should promote competence in working with R/S issues. Supervisors might benefit from reviewing Polanski's (2003) recommendations on incorporating R/S into supervision. For instance, Polanski (2003) encouraged supervisors to teach their supervisees how to formulate questions and reflections that explore the role of R/S in the client's life. Furthermore, she stated that supervisees need guidance in determining what information from the client's R/S history is most important and identifying therapeutically relevant R/S themes. Supervisors should teach R/S interventions and give supervisees opportunities to rehearse those interventions, observe themselves on tape, and evaluate their performance (Polanski, 2003). One other valuable function of supervision is to foster the supervisee's reflection on his/her own R/S beliefs and values and how they influence treatment (Polanski, 2003). Supervisors and training directors may wish to administer the Spiritual Issues in Supervision Scale to students and interns to assess how and to what extent supervision addresses R/S; they can then use that information to improve supervision (M. M. Miller, Korinek, & Ivey, 2006).

Future Research

Many questions remain about psychologists' R/S and its impact on their work. We still do not know why psychologists are less religious than the general public or why they show a preference for more individual expression in the form of spirituality. A related question is what are the factors that influence psychologists' R/S and possibly result in their becoming less religious after entering their field? One interesting approach to this question involves the selective attraction hypothesis, which holds that psychology is especially appealing to those who are or are becoming less religious. Alternatively, interactions with nonreligious colleagues (e.g., psychology professors) may socialize psychologists to become less religious over time. A third possibility is that the knowledge psychologists gain through their studies is at odds with religious tenets or with positions of religious authority. Longitudinal studies, ideally beginning during undergraduate education, could give us more insight into the validity of these hypotheses. We need to better understand the role of psychology as a career on the personal R/S of the clinician.

It is important to continue to investigate R/S issues in practice. Among the many topics worthy of examination, researchers could gather data from client–therapist dyads to see whether an R/S match between the client and therapist is associated with empathy, alliance, agreement regarding R/S contributions to problem conceptualization and treatment goals, or the use of R/S resources. Investigations of the effectiveness of graduate education, clinical training, and continuing education programs designed to enhance understanding of R/S as clinical variables and the use of R/S resources are needed to ensure professional preparation. These are just a few examples of areas in which research inform practice.

CONCLUSION

As a profession tasked with analyzing the inner workings of the human mind, we need to engage in our own self-reflection—in this case, about our readiness as mental health professionals to fully, openly, and competently address R/S as clinically relevant variables and potential therapeutic resources. We have attempted to stimulate reflection by presenting and summarizing research on psychologists' R/S perspectives and how R/S matters are addressed in psychologists' education and practice. This chapter was intended to promote a better understanding of the R/S similarities and differences between mental health professionals and those we serve as well as to highlight the gap between our clients' need for spiritually integrated treatment and the current state of training and practice in these kinds of services. We hope this knowledge will inspire greater commitment to treating R/S with both respect and an approach based in empirical evidence. Significant improvements have been made during the past 3 decades, but we believe it is vital that efforts be continued to more fully address religiousness and spirituality in the clinical practice of psychology.

References

American Psychiatric Association. (2000). *Diagnostic and statistical manual of mental disorders* (4th ed., text revision). Washington, DC: Author.

American Psychological Association. (2003). *Guidelines on multicultural education, training, research, practice, and organizational change for psychologists.* Retrieved from http://www.apapracticecentral.org/ce/guidelines/multicultural.pdf

American Psychological Association. (2010). *Ethical principles of psychologists and code of conduct (2002, Amended June 1, 2010)*. Retrieved from http://www.apa.org/ethics/code/index.aspx

American Psychological Association, Practice Directorate. (2003). *PracticeNet survey: Clinical practice patterns.* Retrieved from http://www.apapracticenet/results/Summer2003/2.asp

Bergin, A. E., & Jensen, J. P. (1990). Religiosity of psychotherapists: A national survey. *Psychotherapy: Theory, Research, Practice, Training, 27*, 3–7. doi:10.1037/0033-3204.27.1.3

Bishop, D. R., Avila-Juarbe, E., & Thumme, B. (2003). Recognizing spirituality as an important factor in counselor supervision. *Counseling and Values, 48*, 34–46. doi:10.1002/j.2161-007X.2003.tb00273.x

Bowman, E. S. (1998). Integrating religion into the education of mental health professionals. In H. G. Koenig (Ed.), *Handbook of religion and mental health* (pp. 367–378). San Diego, CA: Academic Press. doi:10.1016/B978-012417645-4/50092-4

Brawer, P. A., Handal, P. J., Fabricatore, A. N., Roberts, R., & Wajda-Johnston, V. A. (2002). Training and education in religion/spirituality within APA-accredited clinical psychology programs. *Professional Psychology: Research and Practice, 33*, 203–206. doi:10.1037/0735-7028.33.2.203

Delaney, H. D., Miller, W. R., & Bisonó, A. M. (2007). Religiosity and spirituality among psychologists: A survey of clinician members of the American Psychological Association. *Professional Psychology: Research and Practice, 38*, 538–546. doi:10.1037/0735-7028.38.5.538

Derr, K. (1991). *Religious issues in psychotherapy: Factors associated with the selection of clinical interventions.* Unpublished doctoral dissertation, University of Southern California, Los Angeles.

Fowers, B. J. (2001). Culture, identity, and loyalty: New pathways for a culturally aware psychotherapy. In B. D. Slife, R. N. Williams, & S. H. Barlow (Eds.),

Critical issues in psychotherapy (pp. 263–280). Thousand Oaks, CA: Sage.

Francis, J. (2011). *Religious and spiritual beliefs, practices, professional attitudes, and behaviors of clinical and counseling psychology interns* (Doctoral dissertation). Retrieved from Proquest (Publication No. AAT 3466394).

Frazier, R. E., & Hansen, N. D. (2009). Religious/spiritual psychotherapy behaviors: Do we do what we believe to be important? *Professional Psychology: Research and Practice, 40*, 81–87. doi:10:1037/a0011671

Freud, S. (1961). *The future of an illusion* (J. Strachey, Trans.). New York, NY: Norton. (Original work published 1927)

Gallup, G. H., Jr. (1994). *The Gallup poll: Public opinion 1993.* Wilmington, DE: Scholarly Resources.

Gallup, G. H., Jr. (1999). *Americans celebrate Easter, 1999.* Princeton, NJ: Gallup Organization.

Gallup, G. H., Jr. (2002). *The Gallup poll: Public opinion 2001.* Wilmington, DE: Scholarly Resources.

Gallup, G. H., Jr., & Lindsay, D. M. (1999). *Surveying the religious landscape: Trends in U.S. beliefs.* Harrisburg, PA: Morehouse.

Gross, N., & Simmons, S. (2007, February 6). *How religious are America's college and university professors?* Social Science Research Council. Retrieved from http://religion.ssrc.org/reforum/Gross_Simmons.pdf

Gubi, P. M. (2007). Exploring the supervision experience of some mainstream counselors who integrate prayer in counseling. *Counselling and Psychotherapy Research, 7*, 114–121. doi:10.1080/14733140701342544

Hage, S. M. (2006). A closer look at the role of spirituality in psychology training programs. *Professional Psychology: Research and Practice, 37*, 303–310. doi:10.1037/0735-7028.37.3.303

Hathaway, W. L. (2003). Clinically significant religious impairment. *Mental Health, Religion, and Culture, 6*, 113–129. doi:10.1080/1367467021000038174

Hathaway, W. L. (2011). Ethical guidelines for using spiritually oriented interventions. In J. D. Aten, M. R. McMinn, & E. L. Worthington Jr. (Eds.), *Spiritually oriented interventions for counseling and psychotherapy* (pp. 65–81). Washington, DC: American Psychological Association. doi:10.1037/12313-003

Hathaway, W. L., Scott, S. Y., & Garver, S. A. (2004). Assessing religious/spiritual functioning: A neglected domain in clinical practice. *Professional Psychology: Research and Practice, 35*, 97–104. doi:10.1037/0735-7028.35.1.97

Higher Education Research Institute. (2004). *The spiritual life of college students: A national study of college students' search for meaning and purpose.* Los Angeles, CA: University of California, Los Angeles.

Hook, J. N., Worthington, E. L., Jr., Davis, D. E., Jennings, D. J., II, Gartner, A. L., & Hook, J. P. (2010). Empirically supported religious and spiritual therapies. *Journal of Clinical Psychology, 66*, 46–72. doi:10.1002/jclp.20626

Johnson, C. V., & Hayes, J. A. (2003). Troubled spirits: Prevalence and predictors of religious and spiritual concerns among university students and counseling center clients. *Journal of Counseling Psychology, 50*, 409–419. doi:10.1037/0022-0167.50.4.409

Kosmin, B. A., Keysar, A., Cragun, R., & Navarro-Rivera, J. (2009). *American Nones: The profile of the no religion population.* Hartford, CT: Program on Public Values, Trinity College.

Lannert, J. L. (1992). *Spiritual and religious attitudes, beliefs, and practices of clinical training directors and their internship sites.* Unpublished doctoral dissertation, University of Southern California, Los Angeles.

Larson, D. B., Lu, F. G., & Swyers, M. A. (Eds.). (1996). *Model curriculum for psychiatry residency training programs: Religion and spirituality in clinical practice.* Rockville, MD: National Institute for Healthcare Research.

Lindholm, J. A., & Astin, H. S. (2006). Understanding the "interior" life" of faculty: How important is spirituality? *Religious Education, 33*(2), 64–90.

Martinez, J. S., Smith, T. B., & Barlow, S. H. (2007). Spiritual interventions in psychotherapy: Evaluations by highly religious clients. *Journal of Clinical Psychology, 63*, 943–960. doi:10.1002/jclp.20399

Martinez, S., & Baker, M. (2000). "Psychodynamic and religious?" Religiously committed psychodynamic counselors, in training and practice. *Counselling Psychology Quarterly, 13*, 259–264. doi:10.1080/09515070010027607

McMinn, M. R., Chaddock, T. P., Edwards, L. C., Lim, B. R. K. B., & Campbell, C. D. (1998). Psychologists collaborating with clergy. *Professional Psychology: Research and Practice, 29*, 564–570. doi:10.1037/0735-7028.29.6.564

McMinn, M. R., Hathaway, W. L., Woods, S. W., & Snow, K. N. (2009). What American Psychological Association leasers have to say about *Psychology of Religion and Spirituality. Psychology of Religion and Spirituality, 1*, 3–13. doi:10.1037/a0014991

McMinn, M. R., Vogel, M. J., & Heyne, L. K. (2010). A place for the church within professional psychology. *Journal of Psychology and Theology, 38*, 267–274.

McMinn, M. R., Worthington, E. L., Jr., & Aten, J. D. (2011). Spiritually oriented interventions: Future directions in training and research. In J. D. Aten, M. R. McMinn, & E. L. Worthington Jr. (Eds.), *Spiritually oriented interventions for counseling and psychotherapy* (pp. 345–351). Washington, DC: American Psychological Association. doi:10.1037/12313-014

Miller, L. (2010). Watching for light: Spiritual psychology beyond materialism. *Psychology of Religion and Spirituality*, 2, 35–36. doi:10.1037/a0018554

Miller, M. M., Korinek, A. W., & Ivey, D. C. (2006). Integrating spirituality into training: The Spiritual Issues in Supervision Scale. *American Journal of Family Therapy, 34*, 355–372. doi:10.1080/01926180600553811

Newport, F. (2007, December). *Questions and answers about Americans' religion.* Retrieved from http://www.gallup.com/poll/103459/Questions-Answers-About-Americans-Religion.aspx#3

National Opinion Research Center–General Social Survey. (2005). *NORC-GSS cumulative data file, 1972–2004* (Version 1) [Data file]. Storrs, CT: Roper Center for Public Opinion Research.

Norcross, J. C. (2010). The therapeutic relationship. In B. L. Duncan, S. D. Miller, B. E. Wampold, & M. A. Hubble (Eds.), *The heart and soul of change* (2nd ed., pp. 113–141). Washington, DC: American Psychological Association.

O'Grady, K. A., & Richards, P. S. (2010). The role of inspiration in the helping professions. *Psychology of Religion and Spirituality*, 2, 57–66. doi:10.1037/a0018551

Pargament, K. I. (2007). *Spiritually integrated psychotherapy: Understanding and addressing the sacred.* New York, NY: Guilford Press.

Pargament, K. I., Murray-Swank, N. A., & Tarakeshwar, N. (2005). Editorial: An empirically-based rationale for a spiritually-integrated psychotherapy. *Mental Health, Religion, and Culture, 8*, 155–165. doi:10.1080/13694670500138940

Pew Forum on Religion and Public Life. (2008). *U.S. religious landscape survey*. Washington, DC: Author.

Pew Forum on Religion and Public Life. (2010). *U.S. religious knowledge survey*. Washington, DC: Author.

Plante, T. G. (2007). Integrating spirituality and psychotherapy: Ethical issues and principles to consider. *Journal of Clinical Psychology, 63*, 891–902. doi:10.1002/jclp.20383

Polanski, P. J. (2003). Spirituality in supervision. *Counseling and Values, 47*, 131–141. doi:10.1002/j.2161-007X.2003.tb00230.x

Politics of the professorate. (1991, July–August). *The Public Perspective*, pp. 86–87.

Post, B. C., & Wade, N. (2009). Religion and spirituality in psychotherapy: A practice-friendly review. *Journal of Clinical Psychology, 65*, 131–146. doi:10.1002/jclp.20563

Ragan, C., Malony, H. N., & Beit-Hallahmi, B. (1980). Psychologists and religion: Professional factors associated with personal beliefs. *Review of Religious Research, 21*, 208–217. doi:10.2307/3509885

Rogers, C. R. (1961). *On becoming a person: A therapist's view of psychotherapy*. Boston, MA: Houghton Mifflin.

Roof, W. C. (1999). *Spiritual marketplace: Baby boomers and the remaking of American religion*. Princeton, NJ: Princeton University Press.

Rose, E. M., Westefeld, J. S., & Ansley, T. N. (2001). Spiritual issues in counseling: Clients' beliefs and preferences. *Journal of Counseling Psychology, 48*, 61–71. doi:10.1037/0022-0167.48.1.61

Russell, S. R., & Yarhouse, M. A. (2006). Training in religion/spirituality within APA-accredited psychology predoctoral internships. *Professional Psychology: Research and Practice, 37*, 430–436. doi:10.1037/0735-7028.37.4.430

Saunders, S. M., Miller, M. L., & Bright, M. M. (2010). Spiritually conscious psychological care. *Professional Psychology: Research and Practice, 41*, 355–362. doi:10.1037/a0020953

Schulte, P., Skinner, T., & Claiborn, C. (2002). Religious and spiritual issues in counseling psychology training. *The Counseling Psychologist, 30*, 118–134. doi:10.1177/0011000002301009

Serlin, I. (2004). Spiritual diversity and clinical practice. In J. L. Chin (Ed.), *The psychology of prejudice and discrimination: Vol. 4. Disability, religion, physique, and other traits* (pp. 27–49). Westport, CT: Praeger.

Shafranske, E. P. (1996). Religious beliefs, affiliations, and practices of clinical psychologists. In E. Shafranske (Ed.), *Religion and the clinical practice of psychology* (pp. 149–162). Washington, DC: American Psychological Association. doi:10.1037/10199-005

Shafranske, E. P. (2000). Religious involvement and professional practices of psychiatrists and other mental health professionals. *Psychiatric Annals, 30*, 525–532.

Shafranske, E. P. (2001). The religious dimension of patient care within rehabilitation medicine. The role of religious beliefs, attitudes, and personal and professional practices. In T. G. Plante & A. C. Sherman (Eds.), *Faith and health: Psychological perspectives* (pp. 311–335). New York, NY: Guilford Press.

Shafranske, E. P., & Malony, H. N. (1990). Clinical psychologists' religious and spiritual orientations and their practice of psychotherapy. *Psychotherapy: Theory, Research, Practice, Training, 27*, 72–78. doi:10.1037/0033-3204.27.1.72

Shafranske, E. P., & Malony, H. N. (1996). Religion and the clinical practice of psychology: A case for inclusion. In E. P. Shafranske (Ed.), *Religion and the clinical practice of psychology* (pp. 561–586). Washington, DC: American Psychological Association. doi:10.1037/10199-041

Shafranske, E. P., & Sperry, L. (2005). Future directions: Opportunities and challenges. In L. Sperry & E. P. Shafranske (Eds.), *Spiritually oriented psychotherapy* (pp. 351–354). Washington, DC: American Psychological Association.

Skinner, B. F. (1987). What religion means to me. *Free Inquiry (Buffalo, N. Y.)*, *7*, 12–13.

Smith, T. B., Bartz, J., & Richards, P. S. (2007). Outcomes of religious and spiritual adaptations to psychotherapy: A meta-analytic review. *Psychotherapy Research*, *17*, 643–655. doi:10.1080/10503300701250347

Wade, N. G., Worthington, E. L., Jr., & Vogel, D. L. (2007). Effectiveness of religiously tailored interventions in Christian therapy. *Psychotherapy Research*, *17*, 91–105. doi:10.1080/10503300500497388

Walker, D. F., Gorsuch, R. L., & Tan, S.-Y. (2004). Therapists' integration of religion and spirituality in counseling: A meta-analysis. *Counseling and Values*, *49*, 69–80. doi:10.1002/j.2161-007X.2004.tb00254.x

Walker, D. F., Gorsuch, R. L., & Tan, S.-Y. (2005). Therapists' use of religious and spiritual interventions in Christian counseling: A preliminary report. *Counseling and Values*, *49*, 107–119. doi:10.1002/j.2161-007X.2005.tb00257.x

Worthington, E. L., Jr., & Aten, J. D. (2009). Psychotherapy with religious and spiritual clients: An introduction. *Journal of Clinical Psychology*, *65*, 123–130. doi:10.1002/jclp.20561

Worthington, E. L., Jr., & Sandage, S. J. (2001). Religion and spirituality. *Psychotherapy: Theory, Research, Practice, Training*, *38*, 473–478. doi:10.1037/0033-3204.38.4.473

Worthington, E. L., Jr., Sandage, S. J., Davis, D. E., Hook, J. N., Miller, A. J., Hall, M. E., & Hall, T. W. (2009). Training therapists to address spiritual concerns in clinical practice and research. In J. D. Aten & M. M. Leach (Eds.), *Spirituality and the therapeutic process* (pp. 267–292). Washington, DC: American Psychological Association.

Wuthnow, R. (2007). *After the baby boomers: How twenty- and thirty-somethings are shaping the future of American religion*. Princeton, NJ: Princeton University Press.

Yarhouse, M. A., & VanOrman, B. T. (1999). When psychologists work with religious clients: Applications of the general principles of ethical conduct. *Professional Psychology: Research and Practice*, *30*, 557–562. doi:10.1037/0735-7028.30.6.557

Yarhouse, M. A., & Fisher, W. (2002). Levels of training to address religion in clinical practice. *Psychotherapy: Theory, Research, Practice, Training*, *39*, 171–176. doi:10.1037/0033-3204.39.2.171

Young, J. S., Wiggins-Frame, M., & Cashwell, C. S. (2007). Spirituality and counselor competence: A national survey of American Counseling Association members. *Journal of Counseling and Development*, *85*, 47–52. doi:10.1002/j.1556-6678.2007.tb00443.x

Zinnbauer, B. J., Pargament, K. I., Cole, B., Rye, M. S., Butter, E. M., Belavich, T. G., . . . Kadar, J. L. (1997). Religion and spirituality: Unfuzzying the fuzzy. *Journal for the Scientific Study of Religion*, *36*, 549–564. doi:10.2307/1387689

CHAPTER 3

VALUE AND ETHICAL ISSUES: THE INTERFACE BETWEEN PSYCHOLOGY AND RELIGION

Mark A. Yarhouse and Veronica Johnson

Inherent in the clinical practice of psychologists are personal beliefs, values, and assumptive frameworks that interact with professional ethical considerations. These personal beliefs and values often reflect or are related to religious or spiritual assumptive frameworks. This chapter examines psychology as a value-laden profession and discusses the value dimensions inherent in clinical practice, which affect informed consent and self-disclosure, assessment and diagnosis, psychological interventions, and the therapeutic relationship. Particular emphasis is given to the interface between these value-laden aspects of applied practice, the science of psychology, and the ethics set within the profession.

CONTEXT

Value conflicts and ethical dilemmas are among the issues that influence the course of treatment and can be particularly difficult paths to navigate. When client religious or spiritual beliefs, commitments, or practices emerge as clinically salient features, the paths become even more complex and ethically challenging. This is because psychology and religion and spirituality approach meaning from significantly different perspectives. To begin, psychology is based in a naturalistic worldview, whereas most major religions operate within a theistic worldview. Differing worldviews entail different assumptive frameworks, epistemological bases, language, and values that can create dissonance in therapeutic relationships and have led some to wonder whether the two are in fact incompatible (Slife & Reber, 2009).

Differing assumptive frameworks and commitments can lead to seemingly insurmountable division. For example, there are some clinical theorists (e.g., Gonsiorek, Richards, Pargament, & McMinn, 2009; Plante, 2009) that advocate a dichotomous approach to psychological roles and religious or spiritual roles. That is, when one is working as a psychologist, she or he is to operate solely within a naturalistic worldview and may speak only out of scientific knowledge. Yet, others might say that this is a false dichotomy. A professional holding a theistic worldview might approach all of life as religious or spiritual, and embed his or her role as a psychologist within this religious or spiritual understanding. It might be undesirable or impossible for that psychologist to vacate his or her convictions when stepping into a psychologist role. One can clearly see the dilemmas that arise when differing assumptive frameworks are at hand. Even within similar assumptive frameworks, personal beliefs and values may conflict among professionals as well as between professionals and those they serve. The division seems irreconcilable, and yet it must be resolved. For example, a psychologist might work with a woman suffering from an anxiety disorder in which she feels compelled to pray numerous times before going to bed to offset the fear that she will die in her sleep. One psychologist might treat her obsessive–compulsive presentation with little regard for the place of prayer in her life (and her beliefs about the sacred and about God who she believes cares about her and responds to her prayers) beyond the symptom presentation. Another psychologist who holds a

DOI: 10.1037/14046-003
APA Handbook of Psychology, Religion, and Spirituality: Vol. 2. An Applied Psychology of Religion and Spirituality, K. I. Pargament (Editor-in-Chief)

theistic worldview might work with the same client to retain the capacity to pray in meaningful ways to foster her relationship with the sacred while also intervening to treat the obsessive–compulsive symptoms.

Those who advocate a separation between the scientific and religious aspects of the field have cited the differences in epistemologies as a primary reason (American Psychological Association [APA], 2007; Gonsiorek et al., 2009). Psychology is based on a modern scientific model of knowing, whereas religious and spiritual realities are based on a classical realist method of obtaining knowledge, which is informed by tradition, experience, and revelation (Coe & Hall, 2010). Whereas psychology's practitioners offer the public scientific knowledge that has been objectively tested and understood with reason, their methods offer no means to admit religious and spiritual knowledge because such understanding cannot be objectively known or empirically proven. When stated as such, it can be presumed that such knowledge is not able to be studied, and therefore should not be studied within the field of psychology. Yet each epistemological approach—the modern scientific approach or religious and spiritual approaches based on classical realism—has limitations; a working model is necessary to use each approach well and for the benefit of the client.

Language can become a source of confusion when professionals approach their work from a naturalistic worldview while those receiving services are operating out of a theistic worldview, or vice versa. For example, a researcher who has integrated psychology and religion or spirituality might include questions on a survey about "sacrifice," with the implicit understanding that sacrifice is inherently honorable, positive, and even necessary for healthy relationships. Respondents with feminist understandings, however, might endorse the items with the understanding that sacrifice is inherently detrimental and an artifact of patriarchal oppression. These responses could be misunderstood and devalued when analyzing the data and making conclusions. Psychologists use language to develop, measure, and communicate constructs, but values are embedded within language. Even the fact that this chapter is written by authors holding a particular worldview limits the scope of language used and topics discussed. Holding a limited language framework can lead to unintentional prejudice against others who think differently. Again, the interface between psychology, religion, and spirituality presents a special concern for value conflicts.

In addition to the impact of differing worldviews on the complexity of value and ethical issues, there are significant differences of opinion as to how psychology and religion ought to be integrated, if at all, within professional practice. The challenge in answering this question is complicated by the fact that there are a variety of philosophies and models of integration as well as numerous categorizations of these philosophies and models (Carter & Narramore, 1979; Eck, 1996; Johnson & Jones, 2000). For example, Carter and Narramore offered one of the earliest attempts to categorize the relationship between psychology and theology by offering four broad approaches. To broaden the discussion, we will frame these as the relationship between psychology and religion or spirituality to include those traditions that do not have an explicit theological dimension. The four approaches are as follows: (a) a conflictual relationship between psychology and religion or spirituality (the *against* model), (b) the study of religion by psychology (the *of* model), (c) the view that psychology and religion or spirituality are both important and valid but run parallel to each other and cannot be integrated (the *parallels* model), and (d) the study of congruence between religion or spirituality and psychology as both seek truth and assume that there is a unity that characterizes truth (the *integrates* model). Within these approaches, various subtypes are proposed. More recent categorizations reflect similar considerations and expand the discussion somewhat (cf. Johnson, 2010, for five "views" of the relationship between psychology and Christianity, although the approaches could arguably be expanded to other religions or spiritual considerations).

Notably, there seems to be little discussion, much less consensus, as to which models are most ethically sound. This relates to how one might integrate theistic and psychological understandings of what it means to be human and healthy while maintaining the aspirational principles that the psychological field sets forth, such as promoting beneficence; relating to others and practicing with fidelity, integrity, and justice; and demonstrating respect for people's rights and dignity (APA, 2002). Some approaches may lend themselves more easily to abiding by these principles than others. For example, psychologists following an approach that integrates psychology with religion or spirituality may be more likely to remain aware of their "scientific responsibilities to society" (APA, 2002, Principle B), than those following an approach that assumes conflict between psychology and religious belief or theology. For example, the psychologist who frames the relationship between religion and psychology as one in which religion is against psychology may feel justified in foregoing informed consent for the use of prayer or the use of sacred texts in therapy. In contrast, the psychologist who integrates psychology with religion may be more inclined to review the empirical research on the benefits of prayer or reading sacred texts in the process of obtaining informed consent to religiously accommodative treatment.

Resolving values conflicts becomes exponentially complex when we realize the depths to which religious and spiritual convictions can be held. Discussing a cultural value difference (e.g., the preeminence of the community vs. individual) can be as simple as acknowledging the difference and respecting the implications. But differences among religious beliefs and values can carry moral, even life and death implications. In light of the significant role that belief and values commitments make in human motivation and behavior, it is vital to understand how to respect value differences within the interface of psychology and religion.

An example of the complexity within this interface is a recent resolution adopted by the APA (2007) on religious, religion-based, and/or religion-derived prejudice. The resolution noted that psychology "has no legitimate function in arbitrating" (p. 2) matters concerned with religion and vice versa; yet within that document, the APA "condemns prejudice . . . derived from . . . religious or spiritual beliefs" (p. 3). Notwithstanding the condemnation of prejudice per se, by stating it so, the APA went beyond its self-imposed limit and arbitrated religious and spiritual beliefs when it declared understanding of religion-based prejudice. Even when making a concerted effort to resolve ethical and value issues within psychology, there are inherent complexities as values exert influence at multiple levels, for example, between individual beliefs, political advocacy, organizational policies, and so on.

Pargament (as cited in Gonsiorek et al., 2009) wrote, "Dealing with religious and spiritual issues in psychotherapy is inherently messy. Why? In part, because religion and science are not totally separable" (Gonsiorek et al., 2009, p. 391). Both religion and science (in the form of psychology) have an interest in helping people live better lives. As we shall discuss in the following sections, the applied dimension of psychology makes assumptions about how people ought to live in light of various theories of personality. Efforts to facilitate how people can improve their lives reflect values much the way religious and spiritual beliefs reflect values. The inherent mess therefore necessitates explicit discussion of values and value conflicts for the field (and its clinicians) to proceed in an ethical manner. We agree with Jones (1994) who wrote that "psychology could be enriched by a more explicit exploration of the interface of religion with its scientific and applied activities" (p. 197). Although it would be ideal to clearly delineate the necessary steps to resolve value or ethical issues within the interface between psychology and religion, this hope is unrealistic. Our hope is to acknowledge commonly cited issues, explore meanings and ramifications of these issues, and offer guidelines on how academic and applied psychologists and other mental health professionals might proceed with professional and personal integrity. Furthermore, we hope to encourage the explicit discussion of value conflicts among educational programs, training sites, professional agencies, and psychological associations.

This chapter (a) describes psychological practice as inherently value laden, (b) explores particular ethical issues that arise in the interface of psychology and religion or spirituality, and (c) offers ethical guidelines to resolving value conflicts. We offer only one contribution in this longstanding effort to reconcile the fields of psychology and religion, and this chapter is designed to reach a wider audience and in a way that intends to be sensitive to diverse religious traditions. It is our hope that this handbook will inspire more psychologists to engage in the establishment of a psychology–religion interface filled with integrity and respect.

DEFINITIONS

In any discussion of ethics, values, and the interface between psychology and religion, it is important to define key terms. Although wading through definitions and theory can become a bit cumbersome, such an examination is essential for professional discussion. We begin with a case example to clarify how ethics and values can be defined and influence the therapeutic process and relationship.

> **Case Example 1**
>
> Jenny, a 38-year-old Latino woman with three children under 14 years of age, explains to her therapist that she wants a divorce from her husband of 16 years. She is seeking therapy to increase her assertiveness and guidance in making difficult decisions related to the divorce. During the initial intake, her therapist finds out that Jenny attends a church with her husband and children. When asked how the divorce would affect her church involvement, Jenny reports that her pastor does not support the divorce and that she would probably have to leave the church, presuming her husband would continue taking their children to church. Thinking of Jenny's goals and unaware of how a therapist's questions may have an impact on how Jenny thinks about ethical and moral considerations, the therapist probed about this potential loss of support. Jenny replies, "I know I'm losing everything, maybe even my faith, but I'm dying inside. And I think God would want me to be happy."

In considering the issues Jenny is facing, it is important to acknowledge the backdrop of ethics and moral considerations. Ethics is understood as a field within philosophy that addresses moral issues and moral judgments (Koocher & Keith-Spiegel, 2008). One draws upon ethical systems of thought to evaluate behavior. When we look at the case of Jenny, ethics is concerned with what is right or wrong in terms of evaluating behavior. Examples of ethical systems of thought include deontological, teleological, and aretaic ethics. A deontological ethical system is concerned with whether a behavior is right or wrong with reference to a rule that guides behavior. For example, the claim that it is wrong to break a promise might be relevant to Jenny as she reflects on the commitment she made to her husband when they were first married.

Deontological ethics is often contrasted with a teleological ethical system in which behavior is determined to be right or wrong on the basis of the consequences of the action. The decision to leave her husband appears to bring with it many potential negative consequences for Jenny, including the loss of community and her sense of her religious faith. At the same time, Jenny may also weigh the consequences of staying in a marriage in which she feels she is "dying inside."

These two kinds of ethical systems—deontological and teleological—can be contrasted with aretaic ethics in which the character of the person considering a course of action is the focus of interest. If Jenny were to reflect on this approach, she would be less concerned with rules that guide her behavior (it is wrong to break a promise) or with the consequences per se (the impact of divorce on her community or children); rather, she would be reflecting on the kind of person she is and the kind of person she hopes to become in terms of her own character and virtue. For example, Jenny might imagine looking back on her life and want to say to herself, "I persevered through difficult times, and I was faithful."

In addition to being mindful of these ethical systems, psychologists are also held to professional ethics. When we think of the ethical behavior of psychologists, we are actually referring to that which conforms to established professional ethical principles or guidelines. Toward that end, codes of ethics "guide the professional conduct of those in a given profession" (Freeman, 2000, p. 17). In that sense, we are still discussing right and wrong behavior with reference not explicitly to an ethical system of thought, such as deontological, teleological, or aretaic ethics, but rather to ethical codes of conduct delineating the kinds of behaviors, principles, and standards that are thought to characterize the profession of psychology. Ethics codes, then can function as "moral guides to self-regulation, reflecting the normative values of the profession" (Freeman, 2000, p. 17). From this point of view, the focus is not on the ethical system Jenny identifies with in making a decision about the future of her marriage. Rather, the focus is on the conduct of the psychologist in terms of her clinical practice, which might include *competence* in working with someone making a decision about the future of her marriage in light of the impact it would have on her faith, *integrity* in terms of communicating relevant research on divorce to someone making that decision, and *respect for autonomy* in terms of respecting Jenny's self-determination with respect to making her own decision in this regard.

In this context, it is helpful to distinguish between clinical psychologists functioning as ethicists and moralists. An *ethicist* is "a person who reflects on, has convictions about, and/or attempts to influence others about ethical questions and issues" (Tjeltveit, 1999, p. 35). A *moralist*, in contrast, is someone who attempts "to impose values on others" (Tjeltveit, 1999, p. 35). The concern raised by some psychologists is that discussions of religion or the integration of religion into the clinical practice of psychology bring with them a greater risk for imposing values on clients. However relevant, this concern should not be limited to discussion of religion. Religion functions as an organized way of understanding reality that informs a worldview, but all people have and act on a worldview whether or not they are religious. So to limit our concern of imposition to when religion is a salient part of clinical practice is to focus on the wrong sorts of things. It brings the focus on religion rather than worldviews. One safeguard in this discussion of psychologists' worldviews and the impact of these on clients is the distinction made between psychologists as ethicists and moralists.

In clinical practice, the psychotherapist can function as an ethicist, and some would argue that is the proper function and role of a discerning clinician (Tjeltveit, 1999). Psychotherapists do this in many ways, including through instruction about moral dilemmas, modeling of decision-making considerations and appropriate self-disclosure that models decision-making strategies, coaching clients to reach their potential in navigating difficult decisions, and so on (Tjeltveit, 1999). With respect to Jenny, the psychologist who functions as an ethicist would have thought extensively about ethical matters, received training in ethics, and been prepared to create a clinical space for Jenny to reflect well on ethics and values—in particular how her own decisions are made with reference to various ethical systems of thought. In contrast, a moralist might impose her values on Jenny by instructing her on a course of action the psychologist believes Jenny should follow. The weight of the psychologist's authority might influence Jenny to one course of action over another. This type of moralism, with or without religiosity, fails to respect the autonomy and self-determination of the client. A clinician who functions as an ethicist, however, is providing clinical services in a way that maximizes client autonomy and self-determination by creating a safe and informed clinical space for decision making. This distinction is especially important in the applied clinical psychology of religion because religion and spirituality touch on beliefs and values in ways that organize a client's understanding of their own behavior and identity. In this chapter, we offer ways to act as an ethicist, not a moralist.

PSYCHOLOGICAL PRACTICE AS INHERENTLY VALUE LADEN

Psychological practice draws first on theory and research; all good research is based on sound theory. The practice of psychology is then based on clinically relevant information and evidence of what has been demonstrated to be helpful (APA Presidential Task Force on Evidence-Based Practice, 2006). Personality theories, however, are neither neutral nor objective (e.g., Browning, 1987, 2004; Jones & Butman, 1991; Roberts, 1993; Tjeltveit, 1999). Rather, they reflect implicit values about what it means to be human, what it means to be well functioning, what constitutes dysfunction, and suggestions for how to resolve concerns related to well-being. In all of these areas, we can expect intelligent, good-hearted people to disagree. The following section delineates three aspects of personality theories and how each is related to values.

Personality Theories

In a discussion of the differences among psychological perspectives and between psychology and religion or spirituality, Vitz (1997) recognized three levels of personality theory. The first level consists of the categories tied to clinical observation that provide criteria for making diagnoses in treatment. Take, for example, the various psychopathologies in the *Diagnostic and Statistical Manual of Mental Disorders* (4th ed., text revision; *DSM–IV–TR*; American Psychiatric Association, 2000). The diagnostic criteria are not typically tied to theoretical orientations and thus are not linked to the values within that particular orientation. Rather, they are primarily observable behaviors that are described in a way that facilitates greater uniformity in making diagnosis. The criteria for obsessive–compulsive disorder, for example, cover "recurrent and persistent thoughts, impulses or images" (American Psychiatric Association, 2000, p. 462) as well as "repetitive behaviors" (p. 462) without committing the clinician to one theoretical way to conceptualize a case. These criteria are presumably supported by research and are intended to increase diagnostic reliability and to enhance professional communication. This category is the least likely to be directly affected by values, at least in an *explicit* way.

Many, however, would say that the choice of categories to be included in the *DSM–IV–TR* as a *disorder* is imbued with great meaning and significance to various stakeholders, thus revealing the fact that values are involved. Consider the debates on whether to continue to include gender identity disorder in the fifth edition of the *DSM*. What is included in the *DSM–IV–TR* implies values.

The second level of personality theories describes the concepts that distinguish between specific theories. Whereas the first level focuses on observable behaviors or symptoms, the second level focuses on understanding the processes that lead to behaviors. For example, the concepts of automatic thoughts and schema distinguish cognitive theory from psychoanalytic theory, with its emphasis on the Oedipal complex or a Jungian model with its central emphasis on archetypes (Vitz, 1997). According to Vitz (1997), research support may be lacking for these concepts—they are usually understood or interpreted in the context of private therapy sessions in which the careful observation of behavior in that context provides evidence to support the theory. As such, they seem to generally find support among subscribers of a particular theory, which may be in part because those who subscribe to a theory may choose that approach or orientation precisely because they value what the orientation values, such as cognitions rather than relationships, an emphasis on the present rather than the past, and so on.

These first two levels—that is, (a) the current criteria for making diagnoses and (b) concepts that distinguish specific theories—rely less on values. Or perhaps it is more accurate that the reliance on values in these first two levels is more indirect and implicit. The third level, however, points to the general presuppositions that function at an assumptive level in the theory of personality. These are metaphysical or ethical; indeed, they are "applied philosophies of life" (Vitz, 1997, p. 21) or what Browning (1987) has referred to as "systems of practical moral philosophy" (p. 238). They often begin with shared assumptions that contrast sharply with some claims in several of the major world religions. What these applied philosophies of life, these theories of personality, hold in common are assumed or implicit moral and metaphysical assertions. One such assertion is atheism: "The rejection or omission of God, and the omission of religious life, is crucial for any personality theory" (Browning, 1987, p. 23). For Browning, the modern psychologies reject or omit God's existence and even the salience of religion in the lives of human beings (whether or not God exists) in their personality theories. Although this may be overstated—we can envision a theory of personality that neither rejects nor omits God's existence—we agree that few personality theorists address theistic concerns in the 21st century.

Consider, for example, assumptions held within Rogerian theory. As Vitz (1997) observed, Rogers's book *On Becoming a Person* (1961) is misleading in that his is a theory about becoming not a person but an individual, "an autonomous, self-actualizing, independent individual" (Vitz, 1997, p. 32). Such an individual develops over time by "separating from others, by concentrating psychological thought, energy, and emotion on the self instead of on God and other people" (Vitz, 1997, p. 32). Consider even more the fundamental assumption within Rogerian theory of self-actualization and an organic model predicated on growth. Self-actualization is not just considered an observation on or hypothesis about what can happen in the life of a human being; rather, self-actualization becomes a moral imperative, one that helps a human being solve other and more complex moral dilemmas (Browning, 1987). Indeed, the implicit and explicit claim made in Rogerian theory (and humanistic psychology more broadly) is that "the self-actualizing tendency is a trustworthy guide to decision making in all aspects of life, including those that are normally called moral" (Browning, 1987, p. 69).

Contrast the Rogerian or humanistic vision with that found in rational emotive therapy (RET) or rational emotive behavioral therapy (REBT). The primary emphasis in RET is that situations or circumstances do not make people upset or depressed or anxious; rather, what a person believes about that event is critical in causing negative emotions. As Roberts (1993) put it, "the truth is that nothing is horrible or awful, and the world owes us nothing. If we can get these truths into our heads, most of our severe emotional problems will be over" (p. 41). Negative emotions can be the result of irrational or false beliefs about ourselves, other people, and our circumstances. What is recommended is greater rationality, transparency, self-acceptance, and mutuality in relationships (Roberts, 1993). In practice, however, the self-acceptance found in RET translates into independence from others, which is an implicit value and one that may be at odds with various religious beliefs about community and interdependence in relationships (Roberts, 1993). Similar concerns have been raised about other foundational concepts, such as RET equanimity and self-acceptance (with its emphasis on how one thinks about oneself). These concepts are quite at odds with some of the beliefs and values found within some religions that define the terms differently. For example, little is written about how one thinks about oneself in Jewish sacred texts or the Christian scriptures; emphasis is on how one thinks about God and others, or how God thinks about the individual, which significantly alters the sense for how central self-acceptance may be (Roberts, 1993). More recent efforts have been made to integrate RET concepts into religiously accommodative frameworks (e.g., Nielson, Johnson, & Ellis, 2001), and Ellis himself made more of an accommodation with the potential positive impacts of religion later in his career (e.g., Ellis, 1994).

An even greater contrast can be found between either a Rogerian or REBT approach and a theologically integrated model of personality. Recent examples of Christian models include tntegrative psychotherapy (McMinn & Campbell, 2007) and transformational psychology (Coe & Hall, 2010). Although integrative psychotherapy is more cognitively based and transformational psychology is more depth-oriented, both share a common Christian theory of personality that incorporates what it means to be created "in the image of God" (McMinn & Campbell, 2007, p. 26), to be made for relationships (that mirrors relationships found within a trinitarian view of God), to address the reality of the fall into sin as both a state or condition of existence and as something reflected in actions and inaction, and to live in a place of redemption that provides people with their "fundamental identity" (Coe & Hall, 2010, p. 35). Such an understanding leads to important departures away from RET and Rogerian understandings of self-acceptance or certain cognitions toward a more specific understanding of a Christian view of the self and of cognitions. For example, Roberts (1993) argued that an RET self-acceptance is premised on avoiding "all terms of self-evaluation so that the only feeling of self-acceptance left is whatever precognitive self-esteem one possesses" (p. 52). When one incorporates a Christian worldview, self-acceptance may still involve removing unhelpful and inaccurate self-evaluations, but it will offer "some global self-conceptualizations to promote that will be central to the formation of self-acceptance in the client" (p. 52). Other religions and spiritual perspectives might offer specific self-conceptualizations that are meant to inform self-evaluation and self-acceptance.

Again, at this third level of analysis, theories of personality are clearly seeped in value assumptions. Far from being the objective theories of personality that are derived from science, the theories of personality function as "practical moral philosophies" that contrast sharply with what we might think of as "scientific psychologies" because they are not morally neutral (Browning, 1987, p. 8).

We encourage clinical psychologists to acknowledge and become increasingly aware of the values held herein. We have begun to see some of these philosophies of life being critiqued from specific religious frameworks (e.g., Jones & Butman, 1991; Yarhouse & Sells, 2008) as well as models of psychopathology (e.g., Coe & Hall, 2010; Yarhouse, Butman, & McRay, 2005) and emerging models of religion or spirituality based approaches to psychology (e.g., Coe & Hall, 2010; McMinn & Campbell, 2007; Pargament, 2007; Richards & Bergin, 1997; see also Chapters 6, 7, 8, 9, and 10 in this volume). Furthermore, we hope for continued development of personality theories that integrate a variety of religious and spiritual beliefs. Such development is critical in developing multicultural competence in all areas of professional practice (e.g., research, advocacy, clinical practice, and so on).

Well-Being

In particular, the definitions of health and well-being offered by personality theories will likely differ depending on whether the definition is provided from a mental health perspective or from a religious or spiritual perspective. Indeed, recent scholarship suggests that modernist psychology limits its understanding of health and well-being significantly to merely describing events and not offering clear statements about values associated with health and well-being (Coe & Hall, 2010). For example, the biopsychosocial model of health draws on biological explanations, psychological accounts, and social factors (Engel, 1977). Although this model is a helpful corrective to more reductionistic approaches found in any one of the three explanatory frameworks (e.g., biological reductionism), each of the three aspects of the model describes phenomena but offers little by way of explicit, normative views about health and well-being. A biopsychosocial–spiritual model might bring in a spiritual dimension for consideration, and many may see that as an improvement by at least opening up a discussion of the sacred.

Without consensus regarding how to live rightly, psychology developed and adopted language for what does not work, for dysfunction (Coe & Hall, 2010). Even in discussions of dysfunction, there is significant latitude for how people live, and the mental health field has tried to remove from its discourse any mention of morality or reference to a right or preferred way to live.

Ultimately, the attempt by some clinicians to pursue moral neutrality in practice has led to a valuing of client autonomy about how they will choose to live and about what they will ultimately value. According to Coe and Hall (2010), the preference by those who value and pursue moral neutrality instead led to the elevation of ways to increase client autonomy—as important as it may be—to a higher moral good and to safeguard the individual's right to pursue their own subjective sense of the good life:

> Modernist psychology was much more reticent to discuss psychological health insofar as this clearly appeared to go beyond the bounds of a purely descriptive science. Furthermore, modernist therapists also thought moral guidance regarding the flourishing life seemed to be a violation of their patients' human autonomy and freedom that modernity so prized and that the new approaches to therapy were so intent on opening to its clients. In general, claims about human health and virtue and vice seemed to be a violation of the very ethos of modernity, which so ardently strove to free western civilization from the moralizing shackles evident in the Roman Catholic hierarchy, in natural law theory and in the conservative Protestant approach to Scripture and faith. (p. 308)

What is the result of this development? In the 21st century, we are left with an ethic in which there

> is no objective view of the good or bad life (good or bad values) or virtue or vice (good or bad character) insofar as science is merely descriptive and does not provide such information (and science is the language of objective knowledge). (Coe & Hall, 2010, p. 309)

Instead, "the good life, good and bad values, and character are determined by the individual and/or society," with one caveat: a "minimal morality" that protects the right of the individual to pursue the good life "as long as it does not violate the freedoms of others" (Coe & Hall, 2010, p. 309). The upside of this evolution is a strong regard for client autonomy and self-determination; the downside has been significant ambiguity around the meaning and place of other values in mental health practice. An exception may be found in recent work within positive psychology (see Volume 1, Chapter 23, this handbook, and Chapter 25, this volume); however, such advances may reflect essentially religious and spiritual categories removed from their original religious meanings and foundations. In other words, it is not that psychology is always incapable of discussing values, but it does so at a minimum and without much intentional regard for the religious and spiritual foundations from which many values historically have been understood.

At a practical level, we can imagine a psychologist emphasizing self-report of improved quality of life in the workplace and in relationships, decreased symptoms of depression or anxiety, and so on, whereas a religious or spiritual faith tradition might emphasize growing in spiritual maturity characterized by love, kindness, faithfulness, joy, and other emotions that come to function as character traits (Roberts, 1993). These two ways of understanding health and well-being may at times be compatible with one another. A Jewish woman suffering from depression may want to work toward a reduction in depressive symptomatology while also growing in her experience of joy in her work and family relationships, particularly if she understands these spheres of work and family as vocational and as a way to honor G-d in her responsibilities. But we can also envision times when a client may emphasize one over the other in ways that a psychologist may not fully appreciate. A Mormon husband who experiences same-sex attraction may choose to stay in a mixed-sexual orientation marriage in which he struggles with the stress and strain associated with that commitment for the purpose of remaining faithful to his commitments to his spouse and children. Some psychologists may understand this decision, whereas others might wonder whether this kind of limitation is really in the best interest of the client's health and well-being.

There are differences in understandings of health and well-being not only between psychological or mental health and religious or spiritual perspectives but also within theoretical orientations in psychology (on the basis of assumptions about personality) and within religions and spiritual traditions. Buddhism, Hinduism, Judaism, and Christianity say different things about what it means to be healthy and whole. At the risk of oversimplifying complex and diverse expressions of various world religions, a Judeo-Christian understanding sees sin and the potential for good and evil as important dimensions of human nature that can lead to suffering and must be understood to foster personal health and wholeness (Miller, 2005). A devout Hindu would speak less of a Judeo-Christian concept of sin but more of ignorance (not understanding the consequences of our behaviors) and karma (Sharma, 2000). Buddhist understandings of health and wholeness may be related to how a person experiences suffering and expectations of permanence in a life that is transitory and impermanent (Finn & Rubin, 2000). Moreover, there is diversity in understandings of health and well-being within these world religions, among individuals who belong to each of these religious traditions, and within theoretical orientations. According to Tjeltveit (1999),

> Given ethical diversity and the aspiration that therapy should be a universal, cross-culturally valid type of healing relationship, codes of professional ethics are necessarily built on consensus. A minimalist ethics results in asking that

> therapists treat "moral strangers" justly and with respect. (p. 266)

The rest of the chapter attempts to find ways to practice psychology well among "moral strangers."

Objections to the View of Applied Psychology as Value Laden

Applied psychologists have tried to respond to or resolve the value issues or concerns we have raised in a number of ways. One way is to argue that the practice of psychology is not inherently value laden or, if it is, then it is resolvable by appealing to the nature of therapy (that it is client-directed) or to the ways that therapeutic interventions are derived (through scientific research). Tjeltveit (1999) discussed several possible responses to the claim that psychological practice is inherently value laden. The most common objections are that (a) therapy involves only mental health values, (b) clients alone should choose therapy values, (c) science rather than values should determine ethical practice, and (d) allowing religious or spiritual values in psychological practice will lead the field to become fractious and ineffective.

Therapy involves only mental health values. One way psychologists respond to the claim that clinical practice is inherently value laden is to say that therapy is really only dealing with mental health values. What are mental health values? Tjeltveit (1999) noted that some have put forth values like client autonomy and self-determination as examples of mental health values (e.g., Strupp, 1980). The challenge for those who make this claim is that they have to make a distinction between essential mental health values and other values, and this distinction has to make sense to both the clinician and the client and transfer over into clinical practice. They would also have to explain how to respond to various other (nonessential) values and whether they understand them to play a role in the selection of therapeutic goals—not just the self-determination of the person in selecting those goals but also the various goals themselves, goals that are available to a client and how those goals are selected and who else is affected by those goals (e.g., family members, third-party payers, employers). So the decision to pursue divorce or to continue to work on a marriage; the decision to set limits with an adolescent or not to do so; the decision to work through forgiveness for an offense by one's parent or not are all goals tied to values. As Tjeltviet (1999) asserted, "any therapeutic goal held by therapists, clients, or third parties (e.g., insurance companies or government funding sources) represents a commitment (implicit or explicit, limited or extensive) to some value(s) and some working ethical theory" (p. 6).

Clients alone should choose therapy values. Another way psychologists object to the claim that clinical practice is value laden is by asserting that only clients should make choices about therapy values (Tjeltveit, 1999). There is a concession here that therapy probably does involve values, perhaps even a range of values, but that these values should be chosen by the client and not the therapist. A related point is that what is essential to good clinical practice is that the therapist become aware of her own values and keep those values from having an influence on the course of therapy. Objections to the claim that clients alone determine therapy values is that it completely ignores other stakeholders, such as third-party payers, employers, and others who have a vested interest in the therapeutic goals and often shape the scope of therapeutic care. Also, it does not account for inappropriate client-chosen therapeutic goals. Tjeltveit offered two examples: (a) the client who wants to feel better but does not want to make any changes to accomplish that goal, and (b) the client who wants the therapist to tell them what to do.

Science rather than values should determine ethical practice. A third common objection to the claim that clinical practice is value laden is to state that values are essentially irrelevant and that only science should determine clinical practice. From this perspective, clinical practice is a scientific practice, one characterized by findings about "diagnosis, etiology, empirically validated behavioral interventions, efficacious treatments," and so on (Tjeltveit, 1999, p. 9). In response to this assertion, Tjeltveit (1999) noted that science does not currently provide us with "unequivocal empirical findings that . . . permit definitive prescriptions for therapist behavior regarding values and other therapeutic techniques"

(p. 9). Even if it did, we would still be left with value-laden questions about outcome measures—about what is meant by "functioning optimally," "proper functioning," or "improved mental health." And we would still need to address client values and preferences, which may themselves vary considerably when applied to questions of what constitutes success in treatment (see APA Presidential Task Force on Evidence-Based Practice, 2006).

Allowing religious or spiritual values in psychological practice will lead the field to fractiousness and ineffectiveness. In addition, it is important to recognize that respect for religion involves not only respecting the religion or spirituality of clients but also respecting what religion and spirituality mean to the practice of psychology. Currently, the practice of psychology is quite diverse and far-reaching. In part because of the zeitgeist that existed during the birth of psychology as a science, however, much of psychology is premised on models that essentially reflect secular humanism in their assumptive frameworks (Hergenhahn, 2005). But it is also possible to derive psychologies from religious assumptive frameworks, and some professionals are doing just that. For example, it is possible to conceive of models developed from a Christian framework—as well as a Judaic framework and an Islamic framework—insofar as the conceptualizations and assumptive frameworks inform what it means to be human, how difficulties arise, and how they might be resolved.

Critics might raise the concern that this will lead to a Balkanization of psychology (Gonsiorek et al., 2009). More specifically, the concern is that different communities might offer different expressions of psychology and, as a result, prevent the field from functioning as a coherent science and practice. It is one thing to protect the field and the public from an incoherent science and practice, and it is another thing to deny that different psychologies in a sense already exist because they have derived from the relationship between various religious and spiritual traditions and the practice of psychology. There is a need to balance etic and emic considerations. This distinction originated from the study of linguistics and has been applied to discussions in multicultural and community psychology. *Etic* originally referred to an outsider perspective, and it has come to reflect an understanding of a topic on the basis of more universal claims. In contrast, *emic* refers to insider perspectives. It looks at what is meaningful to those within the group being studied from the standpoint of those within the group (the insiders).

Gonsiorek et al. (2009) represented a view that values etic distinctions in psychology, that is, what distinguishes psychology as a scientific endeavor is what can be measured and taught in a particular way. These are universal claims of what is helpful for people in terms of clinical intervention. This can be balanced by emic considerations or within-a-community considerations that reflect how a specific community, culture, or religious faith community experiences issues or concerns. It is important to consider ways in which psychology functions as a coherent science and practice. The etic perspective reflects this concern and fosters an appreciation for scientific observation and universal claims that lend themselves to a more coherent scientific and professional identity. It is also important to look at religion from an emic perspective that takes seriously the insider experience of the religion under study. For example, many religious traditions have an established approach to the person, to values, to morality, and to health and well-being that might well be referred to as a psychology. Also, many religious traditions also have their own understanding of various topics, such as marriage, divorce, sexuality and sexual ethics, and so on. An emic perspective highlights the importance of appreciating various religious and spiritual communities and experiences. To overlook emic considerations will undoubtedly be a setback in developing a multiculturally competent psychology.

ETHICS OF PRACTICING PSYCHOLOGY

The developers of the APA's *Ethical Principles of Psychologists and Code of Conduct* (the Ethics Code; APA, 2002) hoped to offer psychologists "a set of values and practical techniques for identifying and resolving moral problems" (Fisher, 2003, p. 3). Ethics guide professional behavior in aspirational and regulatory ways. This section highlights some ways that ethical guidelines are especially relevant within the psychology of religion and spirituality.

Beneficence and Nonmaleficence

The principle of beneficence guides psychologists to "strive to benefit those with whom they work and take care to do no harm" (APA, 2002, p. 1062). This ethical principle is about safeguarding "the welfare and rights of those with whom [psychologists] interact professionally" (p. 1062). Considering that a majority of the U.S. public acknowledges spirituality as an important aspect of their lives, all applied psychologists can reflect on how they attempt to benefit their clientele in the realm of spirituality. To take this aspirational principle seriously, training programs would do well to reflect on how their curriculum represents the domain of religion and spirituality (see Chapter 33 in this volume). Survey research of APA-accredited clinical psychology programs suggests that few programs systematically include training in religion or spirituality (Brawer, Handal, Fabricatore, Roberts, & Wajda-Johnston, 2002). Similar findings have been reported for training in religion and spirituality among APA-accredited predoctoral psychology internship sites, where much of the guidance that is received is in the context of supervision of cases rather than intentional or systematic training (Russell & Yarhouse, 2006).

When it comes to improving training in religion and spirituality, Brawer et al. (2002) have offered several recommendations, including increasing sensitivity to the topic itself, adding or modifying curriculum in existing courses and including it regularly as a topic in supervision, increasing knowledge of various religious traditions and relevant assessment measures, informing students of conferences and seminars on religion and spirituality, and so on. Similar recommendations are offered by Russell and Yarhouse (2006) for internship sites.

We recommend that program administrators carefully evaluate their programs' approach to and coverage of the religion and spirituality as clinically relevant factors in mental health. The following questions may be used to facilitate such a review:

- Would graduates from your training program be able to name some of the benefits that religion and spirituality offers to the population at large? For example, studies within the psychology of religion can inform professionals of ways religion benefits those involved, such as increased marital satisfaction (Mahoney, Pargament, Tarakeshwar, & Swank, 2001; Wilson & Filsinger, 1986) and improved physical health (Oman & Thoresen, 2005).
- Would graduates also be able to speak more specifically to particular religious groups or ethnic groups?
- Do the graduates have a nuanced and informed understanding of the risks and harm associated with religion and spirituality?
- Have graduates been exposed to content in courses such as psychology of religion that includes perspectives of those from outside of a religious tradition (e.g., Freud, 1927) as well as those from within a religious tradition (e.g., Stevenson, Eck, & Hill, 2007)?
- Have graduates been exposed to personality theories taught within the curriculum from both a naturalistic worldview and from a theistic worldview?

Fidelity and Responsibility

The principles of fidelity and responsibility reflect the idea of establishing trust in professional relationships. This principle also refers to obtaining appropriate consultations and making referrals "to the extent needed to serve the best interests of those with whom they work" (APA, 2002, p. 1062). It would be consistent with this principle for psychologists to be aware of community resources for religious and spiritual clients. These resources would include places of worship, such as churches, synagogues, and mosques, youth groups, faith-based mutual aid support groups, prayer groups, and fellowship groups (Tan, 1996).

It is equally consistent with this aspirational principle for religious or spiritual clinicians to withhold the promotion of religious and spiritual resources to resolve nonspiritual struggles or problems. Those seeking psychological services ought to be offered psychological resolutions when possible. The division between psychological and religious struggles and resources are not as dichotomized as one might think. Marital tension, for example, blurs the edges of these domains. Imagine a wife distraught over the discovery of her husband's use of pornography and a husband unwilling to reduce his use. Psychological resolutions supported by research include initially attempting to change the immediate situation, then shifting focus to acceptance (on the part of the wife) of the offending husband. After working to improve communication and problem-solving skills, what might acceptance look like for the wife? A religious or spiritual clinician might ask her what it looks like to trust God in her situation. How might her faith help her accept her husband despite his behavior? We see ethical concerns in this situation if

- the client is not religious or spiritual;
- the client does not view his or her marriage (or committed relationship) as sacred or important in religious or spiritual ways; or
- the client did not give informed consent for the clinician to use religious or spiritual resources.

Integrity

With respect to the ethical principle of integrity, psychologists are to "promote accuracy, honesty, and truthfulness in the science, teaching, and practice of psychology" (APA, 2002, p. 1062). What are the implications of this principle for addressing religion and spirituality? In his discussion of the ethical principle of integrity, Plante (2009) suggested that psychologists "monitor professional and personal boundaries, which can be easily blurred when religion–spirituality is integrated into psychological services" (p. 107). This would involve reflecting intentionally on the role of the psychologist, who is a mental health professional licensed by his or her state to provide psychological care. In this role, a religiously affiliated psychologist does not function as clergy, theologian, or other religious leader even in cases in which the specific psychologist actually may have both sets of credentials (Plante, 2009).

The principle of integrity within the domain of religion and spirituality also applies to psychologists' roles in the realm of research. From the initial conceptualization of a research endeavor, to the organizations funding specific projects, to the reading of and response to journal articles, integrity may be a growth area for the field of psychology (Jones, 1994). Are psychologists (religious or not) as skeptical in the domain of religious and spiritual research as they are in other areas? Are there as many funding sources available for research questions posed from a theistic worldview as there are from a naturalistic worldview? Is a researcher's article as likely to be published if her conclusions question rather than support an evolutionary theory? The principle of integrity can be lived out among practicing psychologists only if all aspects of a topic are available for inquiry.

Another dimension of integrity has to do with presenting scientific knowledge accurately. The concern has been raised by some (e.g., Cummings, O'Donohue, & Cummings, 2009; Wright & Cummings, 2005) that APA's public positions have not always reflected the state of the scientific research. The examples provided in these resources that are directly tied to religious and spiritual considerations have to do with research on sex education, same-sex marriage and parenting, marriage and cohabitation, and postabortion negative emotional sequelae (Yarhouse, 2009). Although this is a challenging issue for any professional organization, we can acknowledge that it is an area of potential conflict and strain that is likely intrinsic to a discussion about values and how they might affect the scientific process in light of specific political and social contexts.

Justice

The principle of justice reflects a high regard for fairness in which psychologists "entitle all persons to access to and benefit from the contributions of psychology and to equal quality in the processes, procedures, and services being conducted by psychologists" (APA, 2002, p. 1062). The Ethics Code elaborates that psychologists "ensure that their potential biases, the boundaries of their competence, and the limitations of their expertise do not lead to or condone unjust practices" (p. 1063). How might this concern for justice overlap with religion and spirituality?

Certainly religious and spiritual considerations can compel a psychologist to be an advocate for religious interests and for an accurate portrayal of religion and spirituality in the media, entertainment, and other public venues. However, conflicts may arise when a psychologist's religious and spiritual commitments contrast with what the APA or other mental health organizations decide are important issues for advocacy. Recent scholarship (e.g., Cummings et al., 2009; Wright & Cummings, 2005) has noted several potential points of tension, including sex education approaches, same-sex marriage and parenting, and issues related to abortion and negative emotional sequelae.

Lillis, O'Donohue, Cucciare, and Lillis (2005) have argued that social justice approaches in psychology raise both practical and conceptual questions about what it means to be "disadvantaged" and may promote a "politics of victimization" (p. 289) that may have unintended negative consequences. Along these lines, Redding (2005) has made the observation that the lack of sociopolitical diversity in psychology may limit what mental health organizations identify as viable advocacy topics. Some would argue that expanding sociopolitical diversity would increase opportunities for advocacy in more diverse forums. For example, major psychology organizations have recently aligned solely with a subset of the gay, lesbian, bisexual (GLB) community, whether it is advocating for same-sex marriage or adoption, or another issue. It is not so much that advocacy is directly for or against religious or spiritual issues but that religious perspectives often form a framework for understanding a topic. The topic of marriage, for example, is deeply rooted in religious constructs and institutions, and current positions "for" one group (e.g., some within the GLB community) can be viewed as "against" another group (e.g., conventionally religious community, a subset of those who are religious or spiritual), both of which are to be valued within the field of psychology. Others (e.g., Yarhouse, 2009) have called for psychology as a science to make scientific data available to policy makers without taking steps to advocate for specific political positions. Another option would be to more clearly articulate how multiple stakeholders might be affected by public policies by attempting to explain the effects from various perspectives.

Respect for People's Rights and Dignity

The last major ethical principle in the APA Ethics Code deals with respect for people's rights and dignity: "Psychologists respect the dignity and worth of all people, and the rights of individuals to privacy, confidentiality, and self-determination" (APA, 2002, p. 1063). Psychologists are reminded of individual, cultural, and role differences that include religion as well as age, culture, national origin, and other differences. It is in this context that psychologists are exhorted to "try to eliminate the effect on their work of biases based on these factors" (p. 1063).

Perhaps the greatest and broadest challenge for psychologists is safeguarding the self-determination of clients who hold to different religious beliefs than those held by the psychologists (or who hold to religious beliefs if the psychologists are not religious). This challenge can present a conflict between what a psychologist views as beneficent for the client and the client's autonomy. There are at least two relevant issues here. The first is the impact of the beliefs and value commitments that are implicit in psychology as a science and as a profession, particularly as expressed (explicitly or implicitly) in theories of psychological health, psychotherapy processes, and assumptions about human nature in general.

The second issue is the impact of personal beliefs and value commitments on the part of the clinician as they pertain to treatment. There is great potential value in clinicians being increasingly aware of their own beliefs and value commitments so that they can look at when those values may need to be "bracketed" to provide good clinical services. Such a time may arise when there are possible value conflicts with a client. It also may be important to bracket beliefs and value commitments even when the therapist and client share assumptive frameworks, when it is possible that similar worldviews could lead to a shared blind spot around decisions that may need to be considered from a different perspective.

For example, consider a highly religious single woman with depression who is seeking therapy from a religiously or spiritually oriented psychologist recommended by her pastor. The client is attempting to support herself in a professional career that has contributed to a sense of isolation, feelings of inadequacy, and chronic financial struggles. When the psychologist asks about her choice of profession, the client describes with great detail how she has felt called by God to do this particular work. She tells stories of God's provision, relationally and monetarily, that increase her faith that this work is part of God's purpose for her life. The psychologist accepts her explanation as an act of faith, even admiring the client's willingness to sacrifice a more fulfilling work experience.

In doing so, however, this psychologist may be allowing her own beliefs and values (e.g., God has a purpose for every person's life, and God provides) to get in the way of a more thorough clinical evaluation. Clinicians holding a different assumptive framework could evaluate the client's choice of profession and tenacious faith as fear of success, sabotaging behaviors, or a defense against autonomy. In this example, it is possible that the shared assumptive framework led to a mutual decision to not challenge the beliefs and values that keep the woman in a problematic situation. On the other hand, clinicians from different assumptive frameworks also need to allow the client her faithful decisions, despite their seeming pathology, to maintain this ethical principle.

There are no easy answers on how to live out these aspirational principles within the psychology of religion and spirituality. In reviewing them, our hope is to raise awareness and understanding of the issues and challenges associated with practicing in accord with these aspirational principles. The next section more specifically addresses the ethical requirements to integrate spiritually oriented interventions within psychological practice.

ETHICAL GUIDELINES FOR SPIRITUALLY INTEGRATED INTERVENTIONS

Psychologists have begun to describe what it means to provide competent psychological services to religious clients (e.g., Aten & Worthington, 2009; Pargament, 1997; Richards & Bergin, 1997; Yarhouse & Van-Orman, 1999). These are becoming known as integration competencies. Although there is no one list of such competencies—no consensus per se—it can be helpful to identify several integration competencies that have been identified in multiple resources.

Self-Awareness

A place to begin with establishing integration competencies is to reflect on one's own presuppositions, beliefs, values, and biases around religion and spirituality (Richards & Bergin, 2000). Not only is religion and spirituality an area of diversity training in psychology, but also self-awareness in religion and spirituality increases psychologists' abilities in the competencies discussed in this section. Increasing self-awareness can allow a psychologist to intentionally monitor and manage natural blind spots he or she might have in regards to religion and spirituality. Without an understanding of one's own internal framework, psychologists can unintentionally operate in ways that denigrate or deny aspects that clients deem important to their well-being.

Generally speaking, a psychologist can reflect on his or her beliefs about religion and spirituality as a whole. Following are some questions on which to reflect:

- What function do I see religion and spirituality playing (in an individual's life, in culture, etc.)?
- What benefits do I believe can come out of religious or spiritual involvement?
- What risks do I believe can come out of religious or spiritual involvement?
- What is the valence of my emotional reactions when religiosity and spirituality is a topic of conversation?
- How do I understand religion and spirituality's role in psychology?

In addition to looking at one's perception of religion and spirituality from the outside, it is equally important to increase awareness of one's own experience with religion and spirituality. Some points on which to ponder are the following:

- What is the role of religion or spirituality in my own life?
- What are positive and negative experiences I have had with religion or spirituality?
- How does my worldview affect how I view the supernatural?
- Do I believe religion and spirituality can help my client, consultee, trainee, or participant?
- What are my thoughts and emotions about sacred texts?

Consider the following examples in which self-awareness is lacking for psychologists working with a religious client.

Case Example 2

While staffing cases, an intern presented about a client who was involved in a bondage-domination-sado-masochistic (BDSM) culture. This client typically chose the submissive position in her sexual encounters. There was some discussion around the BDSM culture, and one clinician noted that the submissive partner actually had more power in the relationship. Another clinician cautioned the group of clinicians and trainees to be sure their prejudices about her behavior would not get in the way of their input on diagnostic considerations and treatment planning. The clinicians diligently worked to speak only of the client's presenting problem, carefully omitting their biases as well as most discussion around her BDSM involvement.

Case Example 3

Shortly thereafter, another case was presented that involved a couple from a religious culture that endorsed the practice of male headship and female submission. As the clinician detailed the client history, several members of the group gave nonverbal feedback that denoted their disapproval of the patriarchal practice. The case conceptualization included the wife's submissive behaviors as a causal and maintaining factor of the presenting problem. The clinician's proposed treatment plan sought to reduce the husband's controlling behaviors and increase the wife's assertiveness.

Examining one's own biases and assumptions about working with various religious or spiritual clients may go far in identifying appropriate limits of practice. For example, not every clinician will be able to work with every client or presenting concern. Some of this is a matter of competence, and some of this may be the result of biases and assumptions that will make it more difficult to provide professional services.

This concern for personal bias also touches on ethical issues in overlooking or ignoring potential spiritual struggles or resources. Several ethical topics are relevant here, including what it means to promote the welfare of the client whose spiritual struggles are affecting his or her welfare, respect for religious and spiritual issues that may be important to the client, and basic multicultural competence that includes religious identity and expression.

These issues of competence can be seen when a psychologist fails to identify helpful resources within the client's religious tradition (e.g., use of prayer, social support) because of a failure to ask about religion and spirituality. This may prolong the work of therapy by not tapping into the multiple resources that may be available to the client.

Another clinician might overlook existing resources that have been adapted for religious clients, such as the use of religious imagery in basic imagery exercises. A psychologist could miss opportunities to draw on distinctively religious concepts (e.g., forgiveness) in therapy that might be particularly meaningful to religious clients. Learning to view religion and spirituality as common, normal, and salient experiences of many in the U.S. population is important. The awareness that we are describing lends itself to the use of religious concepts as appropriate, which is in keeping with the competency movement in which self-awareness or self-reflection in practice is essential (Ecclestone, 1996).

Training to improve competence can be attained through continuing education in religion and spirituality as well as through consultations with professionals who have expertise in this area. But each of these suggestions presumes self-awareness that can be fostered in the context of graduate training and internship training as well as indirectly through the development of practice guidelines to enhance professional competence.

Religious and Spiritually Affirming Environment

Relevant to the self-evaluation of "minimal competency," Richards (2009, p. 389) asked the key question: Do clinicians have "the ability to create a spiritually safe and affirming therapeutic environment" for their clients?

Part of creating a "spiritually safe and affirming" environment is being able to discuss religion and spirituality. This means having some familiarity with categories of thinking and behaving that are tied to particular religious traditions. In the Judeo-Christian tradition, for example, repentance, forgiveness, and sanctification are words that carry meaning to some religious clients (Yarhouse & VanOrman, 1999). Depending on how "normative the client's religious/spiritual life is for the client's religious reference group" (APA Division 36 Preliminary Practice Guideline A-5, cited in Hathaway & Ripley, 2009, p. 44), it can be helpful to be familiar with these words and to talk with clients about what they mean to them in light of their presenting concerns. Although this seems obvious, this conversation can be difficult when one's primary theoretical orientation defines these constructs in ways antithetical to a religious or spiritual perspective.

Take, for example, the following transcript in which the clinician is drawing primarily on her understanding of "guilt" from a rational emotive behavioral therapy theoretical orientation:

Client: I just worry that God will . . . disapprove of me. I mean, I need to make a decision, but I don't hear anything from him. I could really screw it up. I want to get his guidance, but I can't . . . I guess I feel guilty—like it's my fault I can't hear him.

Therapist: It sounds like you are "shoulding" on yourself.

Client: (Confused)

Therapist: The reason you feel guilty about not hearing God is because you believe you *should* hear him, no matter what the situation is. Where do you think you learned that?

Client: Well . . . it seems like the people in my church can hear God when they need to. All growing up, I'd hear, "God told me . . ."

Therapist: Hm-mm. It seems like the problem isn't that you aren't hearing God as much as you believe that you should hear from him whenever you want. If we can tackle that irrational belief (that you should always hear God), then maybe you can stop feeling so guilty. Maybe you could experience some freedom in your decisions.

Client: But what if I really ought to be hearing from God? Maybe I really am guilty for not listening when—or how—I should.

Therapist: It sounds like you might be "shoulding" again.

In addition to discussing religion and spirituality topics, creating an affirming environment requires the psychologist to be respectful of the sacred. Aside from knowledge about religions, knowledge about oneself, and knowledge about integrated interventions, the therapist must be able to deeply appreciate that which the client perceives as deeply meaningful, regardless of the therapist's own religious or spiritual understanding. The therapist does not have to hold as reverent that which the client holds as reverent, but the therapist can come to appreciate that the client holds an experience, concept, ritual, tradition, belief, or value as reverent. Although some spiritual encounters can sound ridiculous to an outsider, they are extremely significant to those who experienced them. Joining a client can be difficult when there is a great discrepancy between what they are hearing and the therapist's own religious or spiritual experiences and attitudes.

Recognize Limits of Competence

Competence is determined by education, training, and supervised clinical experience. Although personal religious affiliation may predispose a clinician to recognize the salience of religious or spiritual matters as they pertain to presenting concerns, personal religious affiliation does not substitute for competence to work with religious clients (Gonsiorek et al., 2009). Consider the following case example in which the limits of competence appear to have been reached.

Case Example 4

A clinician who worships in a Conservative Jewish synagogue began seeing a male client from a similar Jewish tradition. This client was experiencing anxiety, much of which seemed sourced in his relationship with his aging parents. Though physically ailing, neither his

> mother nor father would consent to moving to a nursing home to receive necessary care. The client was also unable to house and care for them. He worried constantly for their safety, their well-being, and about their forthcoming deaths. As the client wrestled with the anxiety, he asked one question repeatedly, "What does the Torah really say about honoring my parents?" Though familiar with the Torah, the clinician felt that his understanding of rabbinic commentary on this commandment would be insufficient for his client's needs. He suggested that his client speak with his rabbi about this particular text to come to some understanding. In addition, the clinician also pursued further study on this passage to gain knowledge in this specific area of Jewish law.

Clinicians can enhance integration competencies through continuing education. This might involve attending workshops on religion and clinical practice, including assessment, and learning about various religious traditions and how religious beliefs and values can be best understood in the context of the psychologist's professional role. In exploring various religious traditions, it must be recognized that there are more and less religiously committed adherents of any religion and that degree of adherence likely affects the salience of religious beliefs and values in relation to a client's clinical presentation (Yarhouse & VanOrman, 1999).

In this context, it might be helpful to join an alliance of professional colleagues who have a greater familiarity with religion and spirituality in clinical practice. These might include members of professional organizations, such as the Christian Association for Psychological Studies, the Society for Christian Psychology, the International Association of Muslim Psychologists, the Mormon Social Science Association, or the Sufism and Psychology Forum (Russell & Yarhouse, 2006).

Part of recognizing one's limits is realizing when psychological practice risks undermining the authority of faith communities and their leaders. One strategy for guarding against such practice is to be in ongoing and mutually supportive relationships with clergy, chaplains, and pastoral counselors; such relationships can foster a greater sense of the roles and responsibilities of the different sources of support for clients.

Richards (2009) requested information from pastoral professionals on the kinds of circumstances in which they would like a therapist to contact them for consultation or consider a referral. He identified the following:

> (a) You are struggling to understand or feel confused by the religious beliefs or thought world of a religious client.
> (b) You are wondering whether a religious client's religious beliefs are healthy and normative or unhealthy and idiosyncratic.
> (c) You believe a client's religious beliefs may be keeping him or her emotionally stuck.
> (d) A client expresses feelings of guilt that seem to originate in violations of his or her religious beliefs and values.
> (e) A client expresses a desire to reconnect with previously held religious beliefs and community.
> (f) A client raises questions about God, or a higher power, or other sources of hope.
> (g) A client expresses a desire to participate in or experience a religious ritual, or inquires about spiritual–religious resources.
> (h) A religious client is severely depressed and socially isolated.
> (i) A religious client is suffering from serious illness, loss, or grief. (pp. 390–391)

These recommendations are easy to write about, but when they arise in real life, dilemmas often accompany them. Consider the man with eight children under 14 who is unemployed and severely depressed but who will not use birth control because of the religious beliefs he and his wife hold. Would you feel comfortable referring him to his pastor who teaches these beliefs? Or perhaps you are a religious or spiritual clinician and your atheist client who lives in a rural area begins asking you about God. After referring him to the one church in his area, he says that he would never attend that church on account of the pastor's personality, well known in the community for being unfriendly. Would you insist that he get his information about God elsewhere or would you explore the topic in session? What if his presenting problem seems best conceptualized existentially? What are the ethical risks involved?

Awareness of Relevant Resources

In addition to self-awareness about personal beliefs and professional competence, it is important to be aware of relevant resources in the areas of religion and spirituality. These include assessment methods for religious clients, and religiously congruent interventions, including religious imagery in meditation and interventions aligned with religious constructs, such as forgiveness (e.g., Enright, 2001).

Practitioners should be aware of various tools for assessing religiousness and spirituality in treatment. For example, Hall, Tisdale, and Brokaw (1994) reviewed selected instruments and organized them in the following categories: (a) measures of religious orientation, (b) measures of religiosity and spirituality, (c) measures of function and use of personal faith, (d) measures of God concept, (e) measures of personal experience of God, and (f) additional measures of interest (see Chapter 5 in this volume). The measures in each category vary in their clinical relevance. They also suffer from a lack of norms for diverse populations. Indeed, Aten and Worthington (2009) called for more sophistication in clinically useful spiritual assessments. Many assessments, however, can provide clinically meaningful information (e.g., the Spiritual Well-Being Scale; Ellison, 1983; the God Questionnaire; Rizzuto, 1979; Fetzer Institute, National Institute on Aging Working Group, 1999). Regardless of the assessments chosen, the interpretations made will be laced with the values of the interpreter. Assessment often is conducted to guide treatment strategies, such as therapeutic goals or psychopharmacology. Consider the following case example.

Case Example 5

As part of a diagnostic interview with a Muslim client, a psychologist asked about her client's spirituality. The client, having displayed several depressive symptoms, reported that spiritual matters were of great importance to her. Having read about a correlation between spiritual meaning and depression (Mascaro, 2008), she administered the Spiritual Meaning Scale (Mascaro, Rosen, & Morey, 2004). From the results, she determined that a lack of meaning was contributing to her client's depression. In preparation for treatment, she consulted with a local Islamic temple to discover various passages of the Qur'an that could increase her client's sense of meaning. In addition to including these passages in her treatment plan, she also inquired about the religion's views on medications for the treatment of depression. In this way she prepared for what responses the client might have to her suggestion about medication. Finally, the psychologist allowed space for the client to discuss religious topics that were pertinent to develop a sense of spiritual meaning to help reduce her depression.

Psychologists can consider ways to draw on religion and spirituality in terms of clinical interventions with religious or spiritual clients (Shafranske, 1996; Smith, Bartz, & Richards, 2007). This might include conducting implicit or explicit spiritual assessment (Pargament, 2007) as well as drawing on important religious constructs in clinical practice, such as forgiveness protocols (e.g., Worthington, 2006), religious coping practices (e.g., Pargament, 1997), and the use of God image resources to address a person's emotional experience of God (e.g., Moriarty, 2006). Other religious techniques discussed in the literature include the use of prayer, meditation, the reading of sacred texts, and referrals to religious communities or organizations, such as religiously affiliated prayer groups, youth groups, and religiously oriented self-help or mutual aid recovery groups (Richards & Bergin, 1997; Richards & Potts, 1995; Tan, 1996).

When using less structured religious or spiritual interventions, the clinician should stay closely in tune with the literature on such interventions. Knowing what those in the field recommend as well as what they caution against can be invaluable. Theorists and practitioners in this area have grappled with many religious and spiritual interventions over the years and can offer rich information to help psychologists weigh the risks and benefits associated with a potential course of therapeutic action. For example, Gubi (2009) discussed potential concerns when using prayer as a clinical intervention, including the use of prayer when uncertain about the direction of therapy and its impact on therapist–client dynamics.

The religiously competent clinician can consult and collaborate with as well as refer to religious leaders, such as pastors, elders, and others (Richards, 2009). In the following case example, the psychologist makes constructive use of a consultative resource.

Case Example 6

A community psychologist developed a program for friends and family of those struggling with substance dependence. Because recovery programs often have a spiritual aspect woven throughout, this psychologist felt it was very important to also include aspects of the divine in the friends and family program. By doing so, he felt all members of the system could remain on relatively equal spiritual footing as they progressed. However, this particular psychologist did not ascribe to a particular faith. After learning about the "higher power" construct presented by Alcoholics Anonymous, the psychologist decided to consult with a local New Age shaman as he felt her understanding and description would be broad enough to incorporate people of many faiths. The psychologist arranged to meet with this expert once a week for 2 months, explaining his program to her and learning how he might address the divine within the curriculum.

Support Client Autonomy and Self-Determination

As discussed, one of the hallmarks of contemporary psychological practice is a high regard for individual autonomy and self-determination (APA, 2002, Ethical Principle E). An integration competency involves being able to respect how religious and spiritual considerations, beliefs, and values can guide a client in decision making in ways that may not be in accord with the psychologist's beliefs and values.

An ethical concern related to Principle E is the possibility of psychologists imposing their values onto clients. To impose is to apply by authority or to force on another. Yet it is often implicitly asserted that having different values implies imposition. Consider Marecek's (1987) recommendation for clinicians working with teenaged girls with problem pregnancies:

> Some counselors are wholly opposed to abortion, whereas others are equally opposed to "children having children." Individuals with such absolutist views or with moral convictions that proscribe certain choices should not undertake to counsel clients with problem pregnancies. The imposition of counselors' personal beliefs on clients is inconsistent with clients' rights to self-determination. Putting forth such beliefs as scientific fact is a form of misrepresentation that violates psychologist's duty to preserve their clients' autonomy. (p. 92)

It is interesting that Marecek (1987) disqualified a significant portion of individuals from engaging with a population on the basis of merely holding a particular belief or moral conviction. Could it be possible that a psychologist can practice ethically while retaining his or her values? Marecek noted in the preceding quote that it is the imposition of such beliefs (not the holding of them), and the act of "putting forth such beliefs as scientific fact" that is problematic.

We have seen some models that reflect greater sensitivity to the ways in which values are a part of the clinical practice. For example, Doherty (1999) discussed an approach that functions like "moral consultation" and he identified levels that reflect the degree to which a topic is overtly a discussion of beliefs and values. The degrees of intensity are as follows:

1. Acknowledge the client's spontaneous statements of spiritual beliefs.
2. Inquire about the client's spiritual beliefs and practice.
3. Inquire about how the client connects the spiritual, clinical, and moral dimensions of his or her life or problems.
4. Express agreement with the client's spiritual beliefs or sensibilities when such self-disclosure could be therapeutic.
5. Articulate the client's dilemma without giving your own position.
6. Point out the contradictions between the client's spiritual beliefs, or between spiritual beliefs and clinical realities or moral issues.
7. Challenge the client's way of handling spiritual beliefs on the basis of your own spiritual beliefs, your moral beliefs, or your clinical beliefs. (Doherty, 1999, pp. 189–190)

There is much about this approach that we appreciate, particularly as it recognizes the different degrees of intensity and relies upon that which is considered therapeutic, particularly in deciding whether to express agreement with a client's spiritual beliefs. The last level is likely the most potentially problematic as it calls for challenging a client's spiritual beliefs on the basis of one's own spiritual beliefs. It would be important, again, to consider what is therapeutic on the basis of the presenting concern, stage of therapy, quality of therapeutic relationship, benefit to the care of the client, and other considerations before directly challenging a client's spiritual beliefs on the basis of one's own spiritual beliefs.

Provide Religious and Spiritual Interventions in the Context of Psychological Case Conceptualization and Treatment Plan

Psychologists who incorporate religion and spirituality in clinical practice should do so in a way that fits into an overall case conceptualization and treatment plan (McMinn, 2009). In the following case example, the clinician emphasizes religious considerations but fails to anchor them in a broader treatment plan.

Case Example 7

A student in a graduate psychology training program has been reading about religious interventions in clinical practice and has been interested in the use of prayer as a result of her own positive experience with prayer. In her work with a conventionally religious client, the student asks whether the client would like to open or close their sessions with a brief prayer. The client says that she would like to do that, and the student begins to open the session with prayer, asking God for guidance in their work together. This practice begins to significantly shape decisions about what they discuss and how each session develops as well as how the sessions are seen in light of the larger treatment plan. The student attends supervision and is asked to provide an update on the larger treatment plan. The student replies, "While I keep the treatment plan in view, I have been focusing more on what I feel I receive in prayer as what we should focus on in the session that day. So I would have to say that the treatment plan isn't the focus as much as what I feel I should do for the client that day."

This use (misuse) of a religious intervention is perhaps a greater risk for a new clinician learning how to incorporate religion in therapy. Rather than use prayer to enhance services, prayer can become a way to manage a case when a student is unsure where to go next and how each session is best tied into a comprehensive case conceptualization and treatment plan. Despite this risk, a line of research suggests that prayer or inspiration has been and can continue to be a part of enhancing clinical work (e.g., O'Grady & Richards, 2010).

In addition, McMinn (2009) has recommended that psychologists document religious and spiritual interventions and activities, reflecting on how they would be perceived by their peer group and by a third-party payer of psychological services. A question to ask here includes, "How would my peer group understand my practice?" *Peer group* refers not to a group of religious peers, but rather to a group of psychologists. The benefit of such an exercise is that it helps the psychologist monitor how his or her practice is conducted, which may mean translating religious or spiritual interests into language that is more accessible to nonreligious peers. For example, a clinician who uses prayer in session might accurately represent such a practice as religiously accommodative rather than use words or phrases that might be inaccessible to nonreligious peers. Furthermore, an additional question to aid in ethical practice is, "Does my documentation accurately reflect my practice?" This is another area in which the clinician can describe what occurs in session in ways that accurately reflect clinical practice but still make sense to those who may not themselves be particularly religious or spiritual.

Ethical Model of Resolving Value Conflicts

Value conflicts have long been recognized as inevitable in clinical practice. Clinicians will work with clients who have different values than they have. A clinician who is a life-long Democrat may work with a client who is a life-long Republican or vice versa. A mother who homeschools may seek the professional services of a female psychologist whose children went through public school. A feminist psychologist may provide services to an evangelical Christian couple. A gay psychologist may treat an anxiety disorder in a conservative Mormon. In this section, we focus on value conflicts that involve religious or spiritual beliefs or values, addressing the ethical considerations that sometimes guide and sometimes complicate clinical practice.

In the midst of a potential value conflict, the clinician typically engages in an introspective process. Williams and Levitt (2007) acknowledged that the "decision making process about when to challenge clients' constructions of the world is rarely discussed overtly in the psychotherapy literature" (p. 172). To help clinicians organize their inner process, we offer an ethical decision-making model for addressing value conflicts that reflects religious or spiritual considerations.

Step 1: Identify the value conflict and determine whether it is substantive and meaningful. It is not uncommon to experience value conflicts in therapeutic or educational settings. In other words, some differences are differences in preference or taste; they might reflect different understanding of political issues or religious or spiritual preferences, but they do not rise to the level of a substantive or meaningful value conflict. Perhaps a client holds strong political views that differ from the psychologist's, but these may have little if any bearing on case conceptualization or treatment planning. In this case, it is best simply to recognize that differences exist but to function as a psychologist within the realm of mental health considerations that are not being shaped by the different approaches to politics, religion, or other issues. It is important, however, to consider whether the conflict rises to the level of affecting client well-being or therapist–educator integrity and when the conflicts are also relevant to the clinical services being provided.

Step 2: Identify the various individuals or organizations that have a stake in the concern. In cases in which value conflicts exist and are substantive and meaningful, psychologists can reflect further on the client's perspective by trying to see and understand the issue in light of that client's religious or spiritual background and current commitments. Such an approach is a step toward multicultural competence because religious and spiritual considerations can be an important and salient dimension in the lives of many people in society even if they do not function that way in the life of the psychologist. Although much of contemporary psychological practice is limited to individuals working with individuals, other approaches include working with couples or families, providing consultations to organizations with multiple stakeholders, and so on. Even in instances in which an individual client is requesting services, that person's request for assistance is not limited to themselves. Stakeholders include other family members, employers, third-party payers, religious organizations, and others.

Step 3: Delineate the origins of the contrasting values. After coming to a better understanding of the values of the various stakeholders, attempt to delineate where each stakeholder's underlying values and beliefs are embedded. To what extent are they derived from empirical findings, a religious or spiritual framework, experience, or other sources of influence? An equally important step for the psychologist—once there is increased empathy and insight into the client's religious and spiritual worldview, beliefs, and commitments—is to reflect well on the psychologist's own values and beliefs. If a psychologist is not explicitly religious or spiritual, that does not mean he or she is not committed to a worldview. He or she may be deeply committed to modernist assumptions, naturalism, humanism, secularism, or any combination of commitments that he or she may be largely unaware of without taking the intentional step to reflect on them.

Step 4: Consult with colleagues to identify implications of the value conflict. How would psychologists' values show themselves in how they conduct therapy, in treatment planning, in how they view the client, and in the (in)congruence they experience with the client? In light of our focus on the interface between psychology and religion, it is important to consult on decisions with colleagues and other relevant individuals, such as clergy or other religious leaders or representatives of a particular faith tradition. When it comes to identifying colleagues, it may be helpful to contact those who have a greater personal or professional familiarity with religion and spirituality.

Step 5: Consider whether to discuss the value conflict with the client. Discussions of values within therapy allow for actual client autonomy. Whether or not we state it, our values and beliefs are apparent to those around us. When we withhold information about a substantive value conflict, our clients may intuit our incongruence and be influenced by it in ways we would not have intended. Being forthright and professional about the concerns, acknowledging it as a difference, and clearly stating the client's freedom to choose is more in line with ethical practice. This discussion might involve exploring options to expand possibilities, being explicit about the role of the psychologist, or being explicit about the psychologist's values.

For example, if a psychologist were to explore other options in decision making, this would necessitate offering more than what his or her own value system would recommend. This has the benefit of allowing clients expanded alternatives and rests on the assumption that clients are free to choose among options, some of which they may not fully appreciate at the time.

Another consideration is to explain that the psychologist's role might dictate certain values. For example, a psychologist working with a couple in marital therapy might create a therapeutic space for each person to make an informed decision about the future of their marriage. The role of the psychologist in this instance might be framed as providing (a) a safe therapeutic space for decision making, (b) skill-building techniques to enhance relationship satisfaction, (c) relevant information about marriage and possible consequences of both divorce and staying together, and (d) the impact of that decision on others.

Finally, it is important to recognize that one's biases might limit what is seen as desirable in a given decision. Psychologists have preferences, and these preferences come from many possible sources. For example, a psychologist working with a couple in marital therapy might have a strong bias toward salvaging that particular marriage as well as a strong bias against divorce. Some of that can be conveyed in empirical terms, in the sense that the data on the effects of divorce on children might lead to a discussion of how a decision to divorce might be detrimental to their children. Whether and how data on the effects of divorce is conveyed, however, might be the result of a number of factors, including one's personal beliefs and experiences with divorce, and the potential for bias may be helpful and honest to acknowledge. It is also important to obtain a comprehensive understanding of the empirical literature to prevent bias in the selection of which studies to highlight and the tendency to ignore disconfirming evidence.

Step 6: Restate that the life decisions the clients make are the client's decisions. This restatement is good practice for everyone involved. The psychologist puts information into the hands of the consumer who makes decisions about his or her life. Some decisions may be beyond the psychologist's ability to work competently. A psychologist might struggle with keeping his or her biases from negatively affecting the course of therapy. In such cases, a referral may be appropriate.

Let us look at this decisional-making model in light of a specific case example.

Case Example 8

Jake and Emma are a Caucasian couple in their mid 40s. They identify themselves as Christians. They have been married now for 19 years and have three children. Emma shares that she has experienced attraction to women since she was in her teens. She was involved in two long-term same-sex relationships in college. She met Jake in her senior year. She and Jake dated off and on for the next 2 years, during which time she was also involved in a faith-based ministry that she found helpful in terms of managing her attraction to the same sex. Over time, she and Jake committed to the relationship and a life together. Although Emma has been aware of some attraction to the same sex over the years, it has not really bothered her that much, at least not until recently. For the past 4 months, she has had very strong feelings of attraction for a coworker. She has made excuses to stay at work late and to spend extra time with her coworker. She has also been honest with Jake about what appears to be a reemergence of feelings that she thought had largely been "dealt with" years ago. Emma shares that the experience of healing years ago is something she can continue to address. She shares that they are involved in a local Christian church that offers a ministry to people who experience "sexual brokenness," and she plans to attend.

Psychologists can follow the steps in managing value conflicts. First, identify the value conflict and determine whether it is substantive and meaningful. A psychologist working with Emma might have strong opinions about her experience of same-sex attraction, her experience in faith-based ministry, and her decision to stay in the marriage. Does a substantive or meaningful value conflict exist here? Only the psychologist can answer this question. Some psychologists might experience a conflict with the way Emma is reporting her experience and discussing her options. If the psychologist believed that such faith-based ministries are unhelpful or potentially harmful, he or she might strongly react to the client's past experience of reported benefit and the anticipated future involvement in these ministries to address same-sex attraction.

Second, identify the various individuals or organizations that have a stake in the concern. Stakeholders in this case include Emma and Jake and the clinician providing services, although other family members who have a stake in their marriage undoubtedly also exist but are not mentioned in the case example. It may be helpful to understand each of the stakeholder's religious and spiritual considerations as multicultural considerations. To take an emic perspective, understanding the faith commitments from a "within group" perspective, the psychologist could talk further with Emma about her beliefs and values, how they were formed, what they mean to her, and how they are informing what she sees as viable options at this point.

The third step is to delineate the origins of the contrasting values. This involves reflecting on the origins of Emma and Jake's values as well as others who have a stake in decision making. The psychologist should reflect on his or her values. A psychologist who is having a strong reaction to Emma's religious beliefs and values might benefit from reflecting on his or her own underlying values and beliefs. The psychologist might view Emma's same-sex attractions as signaling a lesbian sexuality and identity that has been suppressed in favor of conventional identity labels that ultimately are doing more harm than good. These values might come from contemporary humanistic assumptions about what attractions signal about a person in terms of identity and personhood. They might also fit into different models of sexual identity development and the challenges sexual minorities face in forming a sexual identity in light of religious doctrine and identity commitments.

Fourth, consult with colleagues to identify implications of the value conflict. The psychologist can contact colleagues who may have greater familiarity with the worldview held by Emma and Jake. This involves recognizing that there are persons of faith who organize their understanding of sexuality and relationships in ways that are similar to what both Emma and Jake appear to value. This discussion not only confirms the importance and relevance of this worldview to these particular clients but also provides an opportunity to reflect on how the psychologist's beliefs and values might keep appropriate services from being provided.

Fifth, consider whether to discuss the value conflict with the client. In the decision-making model, we noted that this might entail expanding options, explaining the role of the psychologist, or being explicit about biases. If the psychologist's values indicate that Emma should come to terms with her same-sex sexuality as a reliable guide in making decisions about who she is (as identity) and what will make her happy, then one option is for Emma to consider where following her attractions-as-identity would take her. But the point of this recommendation is to have the psychologist also offer more than his or her own value system in terms of exploring viable options. This approach would include exploring what it would mean for the client to stay in her marriage and follow her religious beliefs and values that are guiding her toward faithfulness to her prior commitments to Jake and her children.

The psychologist working with Emma can explain that his or her role is to work with Emma on what is in her best interest. If the psychologist saw Jake and Emma as the client, then a different discussion might develop, as some psychologists would then see the marriage as the client, with each individual making decisions to support that relationship. In working with Emma, the psychologist likely would have the role of creating a therapeutic space for her to make an informed decision about the future of her marriage as well as how to respond to her experiences of same-sex attraction in light of her other commitments and relationships.

The psychologist could explain that his or her own biases might limit what he or she sees as desirable in a given decision. Although most psychologists might be neutral in thinking through the options, some may have strong opinions steeped in assumptive frameworks that may make it difficult to see options.

The sixth and final step is to restate that the life decisions the clients make are the client's. The psychologist working with Emma provides her with information in the context of a safe and supportive therapeutic relationship. If the psychologist is unable to do so because of lack of competence with mixed–sexual orientation couples or because of a strong bias that is likely to negatively affect the course of therapy, then a referral should be made.

CONCLUSION

Informed consent has been regarded as one way to prevent potential value conflicts. After all, clients who are aware of some of the assumptive frameworks of the clinician in advance are in a better position to decide whether the clinician is well suited to help them reach their goals. Yet this process is not without ethical implications. A clinician's self-disclosure can affect a client's future actions and decisions.

In sum, the clinical practice of psychology is inherently value laden. These values are often though not always informed by religion or spirituality. This chapter addresses ways in which personality theories are not objective accounts of persons but rather reflect implicit values about what it means to be human, often connected to religious or spiritual beliefs and values. In addition, there are many practical implications of the ways in which these values influence clinical practice with all clients, including those who are religious or spiritual. Competency is a major consideration for those who practice within the interface of psychology and religion. Finally, we offered guidelines to resolve value conflicts. Overall, we believe that the more explicitly we discuss the values inherent in the practice of psychology and religion, the more practicing psychologists will be able to adhere to ethical guidelines and personal integrity. The ability and willingness to explicitly acknowledge the value ladeness of clinical practice is predicated on our capacity within the field to adequately educate and train students. It is from our training that we increase awareness and, ultimately, the competence to work ethically with the value dimensions of professional psychology, including those values that are explicitly and implicitly tied to religion and spirituality.

References

American Psychiatric Association. (2000). *Diagnostic and statistical manual of mental disorders* (4th ed., text revision). Washington, DC: Author.

American Psychological Association. (2002). Ethical principles of psychologists and code of conduct. *American Psychologist, 57*, 1060–1073. doi:10.1037/0003-066X.57.12.1060

American Psychological Association. (2007). *Resolution on religious, religion-based and/or religion-derived prejudice*. Retrieved from http://www.apa.org/about/policy/religious-descrimination.pdf

American Psychological Association Presidential Task Force on Evidence-Based Practice. (2006). Evidence-based practice in psychology. *American Psychologist, 61*, 271–285. doi:10.1037/0003-066X.61.4.271

Aten, J. D., & Worthington, E. L. (2009). Next steps for clinicians in religious and spiritual therapy: An end-piece. *Journal of Clinical Psychology, 65*, 224–229. doi:10.1002/jclp.20562

Brawer, P. A., Handal, P. J., Fabricatore, A. N., Roberts, R., & Wajda-Johnston, V. A. (2002). Training and education in religion/spirituality within APA-accredited clinical psychology programs. *Professional Psychology: Research and Practice, 33*, 203–206. doi:10.1037/0735-7028.33.2.203

Browning, D. S. (1987). *Religious thought and the modern psychologies: A critical conversation in the theology of culture*. Philadelphia, PA: Fortress Press.

Browning, D. S. (2004). *Religious thought and the modern psychologies: A critical conversation in the theology of culture* (2nd ed.). Philadelphia, PA: Fortress Press.

Carter, J., & Narramore, B. (1979). *The integration of psychology and theology*. Grand Rapids, MI: Eerdmans.

Coe, J. H., & Hall, T. W. (2010). *Psychology in the Spirit: Contours of a transformational psychology*. Downers Grove, IL: InterVarsity Press Academic.

Cummings, N., O'Donohue, W., & Cummings, J. (Eds.). (2009). *Psychology's war on religion*. Phoenix, AZ: Zeig, Tucker & Theisen.

Doherty, W. J. (1999). Morality and spirituality in therapy. In F. Walsh (Ed.), *Spiritual resources in family therapy* (pp. 179–192). New York, NY: Guilford Press.

Ecclestone, K. (1996). The reflective practitioner: Mantra or model for emancipation? *Studies in the Education of Adults, 28*, 146–161.

Eck, B. E. (1996). Integrating the integrators: An organizing framework for a multifaceted process of integration. *Journal of Psychology and Christianity, 15*, 101–115.

Ellison, C. W. (1983). Spiritual well-being: Conceptualization and measurement. *Journal of Psychology and Theology, 11*, 330–340.

Engel, G. L. (1977). The need for a new medical model: A challenge for biomedicine. *Science* 196:129–136. doi:10.1126/science. 847460

Enright, R. D. (2001). *Forgiveness is a choice: A step-by-step process for resolving anger and restoring hope*. Washington, DC: American Psychological Association.

Fetzer Institute, National Institute on Aging Working Group. (1999). *Multidimensional measurement of religiousness/spirituality for use in health research. A report of the Fetzer Institute/National Institute on Aging Working Group*. Kalamazoo, MI: Fetzer Institute.

Finn, M., & Rubin, J. B. (2000). Psychotherapy with Hindus. In P. S. Richards & A. E. Bergin (Eds.), *Handbook of psychotherapy and religious diversity* (pp. 317–340). Washington, DC: American Psychological Association. doi:10.1037/10347-013

Freeman, S. J. (2000). *Ethics: An introduction to philosophy and practice*. Belmont, CA: Wadsworth Press.

Freud, S. (1927). *The future of an illusion*. Honolulu, HI: Hogarth Press.

Gonsiorek, J. C., Richards, P. S., Pargament, K. I., & McMinn, M. R. (2009). Ethical challenges and opportunities on the edge: Incorporating spirituality and religion into psychotherapy. *Professional Psychology: Research and Practice, 40*, 385–395. doi:10.1037/a0016488

Gubi, P. M. (2009). A qualitative exploration into how the use of prayer in counselling and psychotherapy might be ethically problematic. *Counselling and Psychotherapy Research, 9*, 115–121. doi:10.1080/14733140802685312

Hall, T. W., Tisdale, T. C., & Brokaw, B. F. (1994). Assessment of religious dimensions in Christian clients: A review of selected instruments for research and clinical use. *Journal of Psychology and Theology, 22*, 395–421.

Hathaway, W. L., & Ripley, J. S. (2009). Ethical concerns around spirituality and religion in clinical practice. In J. D. Aten & M. M. Leach (Eds.), *Spirituality and the therapeutic process: A comprehensive resource from intake to termination* (pp. 25–52). Washington, DC: American Psychological Association. doi:10.1037/11853-002

Johnson, E. L. (2010). *Psychology and Christianity: Five views*. Downers Grove, IL: InterVarsity Press.

Johnson, E. L., & Jones, S. L. (2000). *Psychology and Christianity: Four views*. Downers Grove, IL: InterVarsity Press.

Jones, S. L. (1994). A constructive relationship for religion with the science and profession of psychology: Perhaps the boldest model yet. *American Psychologist, 49*, 184–199. doi:10.1037/0003-066X.49.3.184

Jones, S. L., & Butman, R. E. (1991). *Modern psychotherapies: A comprehensive Christian appraisal*. Downers Grove, IL: InterVarsity Press.

Koocher, G. P., & Keith-Spiegel, P. (2008). *Ethics in psychology: Professional standards and cases* (2nd ed.). New York, NY: Oxford University Press.

Lillis, J., O'Donohue, W. T., Cucciare, M., & Lillis, E. (2005). Social justice in community psychology. In R. H. Wright & N. A. Cummings (Eds.), *Destructive trends in mental health: The well-intentioned path to harm* (pp. 283–302). New York, NY: Routledge.

Mahoney, A., Pargament, K. I., Tarakeshwar, N., & Swank, A. (2001). Religion in the home in the 1980s and 90s: A meta-analytic review and conceptual analysis of religion, marriage, and parenting. *Journal of Family Psychology, 15*, 559–596. doi:10.1037/0893-3200.15.4.559

Marecek, J. (1987). Counseling adolescents with problem pregnancies. *American Psychologist, 42*, 89–93. doi:10.1037/0003-066X.42.1.89

Mascaro, N. (2008). Assessment of existential meaning and its longitudinal relations with depressive symptoms. *Journal of Social and Clinical Psychology, 27*, 576–599. doi:10.1521/jscp.2008.27.6.576

Mascaro, N., Rosen, D. H., & Morey, L. C. (2004). The development, construct validity, and clinical utility of the spiritual meaning scale. *Personality and Individual Differences, 37*, 845–860. doi:10.1016/j.paid.2003.12.011

McMinn, M. R. (2009). Ethical considerations with spiritually oriented interventions. *Professional Psychology: Research and Practice, 40*, 393–394.

Miller, W. R. (2005). What is human nature? In W. R. Miller & H. D. Delaney (Eds.), *Judeo-Christian perspectives on psychology: Human nature, motivation, and change* (pp. 11–29). Washington, DC: American Psychological Association. doi:10.1037/10859-001

Moriarty, G. (2006). *Pastoral care of depression: Helping clients heal their relationship with God*. Binghamton, NY: Haworth Press.

O'Grady, K. A., & Richards, P. S. (2010). The role of inspiration in the helping professions. *Psychology of Religion and Spirituality, 2*, 57–66. doi:10.1037/a0018551

Oman, D., & Thoresen, C. E. (2005). Do religion and spirituality influence health? In R. F. Paloutzian & C. L. Park (Eds.), *Handbook of the psychology of religion and spirituality* (pp. 435–459). New York, NY: Guilford Press.

Pargament, K. I. (1997). *The psychology of religion and coping: Theory, research, practice*. New York, NY: Guilford Press.

Pargament, K. I. (2007). *Spiritually integrated psychotherapy: Understanding and addressing the sacred*. New York, NY: Guilford Press.

Plante, T. G. (2009). Religion–spirituality in the practice and science of psychology. In T. G. Plante (Ed.), *Spiritual practices in psychotherapy: Thirteen tools for enhancing psychological health* (pp. 9–28). Washington, DC: American Psychological Association. doi:10.1037/11872-001

Redding, R. E. (2005). Sociopolitical diversity in psychology: The case for pluralism. In R. H. Wright & A. N. Cummings (Eds.), *Destructive trends in mental health: The well-intentioned path to harm* (pp. 303–324). New York, NY: Routledge.

Richards, P. S. (2009). Toward religious and spiritual competence for psychologists: Some reflections and recommendations. *Professional Psychology: Research and Practice, 40*, 389–391.

Richards, P. S., & Bergin, A. E. (1997). *A spiritual strategy for counseling and psychotherapy*. Washington, DC: American Psychological Association. doi:10.1037/10241-000

Richards, P. S., & Bergin, A. E. (2000). Toward religious and spiritual competency for mental health professionals. In P. S. Richards & A. E. Bergin (Eds.), *Handbook of psychotherapy and religious diversity* (pp. 3–26). Washington, DC: American Psychological Association. doi:10.1037/10347-001

Richards, P. S., & Potts, R. W. (1995). Using spiritual interventions in psychotherapy: Practices, successes, failures, and ethical concerns of Mormon psychotherapists. *Professional Psychology: Research and Practice, 26*, 163–170. doi:10.1037/0735-7028.26.2.163

Rizzuto, A. (1979). *The birth of the living God*. Chicago, IL: University of Chicago Press.

Roberts, R. C. (1993). *Taking the word to heart: Self and other in an age of therapies*. Grand Rapids, MI: Eerdmans.

Russell, S. R., & Yarhouse, M. A. (2006). Training in religion/spirituality within APA-accredited psychology pre-doctoral internships. *Professional Psychology: Research and Practice, 37*, 430–436. doi:10.1037/0735-7028.37.4.430

Shafranske, E. P. (Ed.). (1996). *Religion and the clinical practice of psychology*. Washington, DC: American Psychological Association. doi:10.1037/10199-000

Sharma, A. R. (2000). Psychotherapy with Hindus. In P. S. Richards & A. E. Bergin (Eds.), *Handbook of psychotherapy and religious diversity* (pp. 341–365). Washington, DC: American Psychological Association. doi:10.1037/10347-014

Slife, B. D., & Reber, J. S. (2009). Is there a pervasive implicit bias against theism in psychology? *Journal of Theoretical and Philosophical Psychology, 29*, 63–79. doi:10.1037/a0016985

Smith, T. B., Bartz, J., & Richards, P. S. (2007). Outcomes of religious and spiritual adaptations to psychotherapy: A meta-analytic review. *Psychotherapy Research, 17*, 643–655.

Stevenson, D. H., Eck, B. E., & Hill, P. C. (Eds.). (2007). *Psychology and Christianity integration: Seminal works that shaped the movement.* Batavia, IL: Christian Association for Psychological Studies.

Tan, S. Y. (1996). Religion in clinical practice: Implicit and explicit integration. In E. P. Shafranske (Ed.), *Religion and the clinical practice of psychology* (pp. 365–387). Washington, DC: American Psychological Association. doi:10.1037/10199-013

Tjeltveit, A. C. (1999). *Ethics and values in psychotherapy*. New York, NY: Routledge. doi:10.4324/978020 3360453

Williams, D. C., & Levitt, H. M. (2007). A qualitative investigation of eminent therapists' values within psychotherapy: Developing integrative principles for moment-to-moment psychotherapy practice. *Journal of Psychotherapy Integration, 17*, 159–184. doi:10.1037/1053-0479.17.2.159

Wilson, M. R., & Filsinger, E. E. (1986). Religiosity and marital adjustment: Multidimensional interrelationships. *Journal of Marriage and the Family, 48*, 147–151. doi:10.2307/352238

Worthington, E. L., Jr. (2006). *Forgiveness and reconciliation: Theory and application*. New York, NY: Routledge.

Wright, R. H., & Cummings, N. A. (Eds.). (2005). *Destructive trends in mental health: The well-intentioned path to harm.* New York, NY: Routledge.

Yarhouse, M. A. (2009). The battle over sexuality. In N. Cummings, W. O'Donohue, & J. Cummings (Eds.), *Psychology's war on religion* (pp. 63–94). Phoenix, AZ: Zeig, Tucker & Theisen.

Yarhouse, M. A., & VanOrman, B. T. (1999). When psychologists work with religious clients: Applications of the general principles of ethical conduct. *Professional Psychology: Research and Practice, 30*, 557–562. doi:10.1037/0735-7028.30.6.557

CHAPTER 4

MODELS OF HEALTHY AND UNHEALTHY RELIGION AND SPIRITUALITY

Brian J. Zinnbauer

It is clear from even a casual glance through the mental health literature that religiousness and spirituality have been the focus of much writing and research in the past few decades. Proposed methods of including religious and spiritual phenomena within psychological study and practice have been plentiful and varied, and such professional organizations as the American Psychological Association (APA), American Counseling Association (ACA), and American Medical Association (AMA) have made respect for religious and spiritual beliefs and traditions an ethical directive (ACA, 2005; APA, 2003; see also Hathaway & Ripley, 2009). Overall, religious and spiritual diversity is now often included within the broad cultural umbrella of human individual and cultural diversity.

One controversy inherent in the process of integrating religiousness, spirituality, and psychology lies in the domain of evaluation. The clinician or researcher who is interested in descriptions of faith has a much easier task than the one who attempts to differentiate healthy from unhealthy religiousness, or mature from immature spirituality. In fact, to even suggest that another's worldviews, sacred beliefs, or traditions are "healthy" or "unhealthy" is akin to wading into a social, political, and cultural minefield. One misstep and an explosion of controversy and criticisms is triggered: "Who gets to make those judgments?"; "From what perspective?"; "In what context?"; "With what groups or individuals?"; and "With what consequences?"

In response, it is tempting to sidestep—to place religiousness and spirituality apart from psychology and science and to suggest that the magisteria are nonoverlapping (Gould, 1997). This solution, however, is severely restrictive to psychologists (Pargament, 1997) and has been criticized by scholars in other sciences (e.g., Dawkins, 1997; Lineweaver, 2008). Complicating matters, evaluation must proceed within a context of adequate description. Judging spirituality as positive or negative requires some initial understanding of spirituality, health, and dysfunction. The stance "I have no idea what it is, but I know I don't like it" is no more an intelligible scientific position than "it's bad because I disagree with it" or even "it's good because my questionnaire says so." Ultimately, the ways in which a phenomenon is conceptualized will have implications for the process of evaluation and can reveal the intended or unintended confluence of an investigator's scientific inquiry with his or her personal values and faith commitments.

This chapter addresses not whether we *should* distinguish healthy from unhealthy forms of religiousness and spirituality but rather *how* to do so in a psychological, ethical, effective, and sensitive manner. And rather than attempt a herculean critique of every psychological interpretation of spirituality, the goal is to present an ethical and effective framework for evaluation consistent with the integrative paradigm presented in this handbook. Once outlined, this process is used to critique several current and past models of spiritual health within psychology. To keep this discussion sharply focused, the term *spirituality* is used because its concern, the search for the sacred, represents the core phenomenon of

DOI: 10.1037/14046-004
APA Handbook of Psychology, Religion, and Spirituality: Vol. 2. An Applied Psychology of Religion and Spirituality, K. I. Pargament (Editor-in-Chief)

interest here. The terms *healthy* and *unhealthy* are used broadly to represent the various evaluative descriptors applied to mental and spiritual psychopathology and wellness.

CONCEPTUALIZING THE SACRED

The nature of the sacred remains an active area of inquiry within the psychology of spirituality (Emmons & Paloutzian, 2003; Hill et al., 2000; Moberg, 2002; Zinnbauer, Pargament, & Scott, 1999); for a more thorough discussion of the pitfalls and possibilities of current conceptions, the reader is referred to Zinnbauer and Pargament (2005) and Hill et al. (2000; see also Volume 1, Chapters 1 and 14, this handbook). The need for consensus among researchers, scholars, and clinicians regarding definitions of spirituality is clear. Progress within any field of inquiry rests on a certain amount of agreement as to what is to be studied and what constitutes knowledge. Otherwise, information from one study to the next cannot be compared and contrasted, knowledge does not accumulate, and the field itself loses focus and boundaries (Zinnbauer et al., 1997). For the psychology of spirituality, it makes no sense as a field to gauge differences between healthy and unhealthy faith if no two professionals hold the same conceptions of the terms *healthy*, *unhealthy*, or *spirituality*.

Consistent with the integrative paradigm of this handbook (see Volume 1, Chapter 1, this handbook), spirituality is considered a personal or group search for the sacred, and religiousness involves a personal or group search for the sacred and other significant goals that unfolds within a traditional sacred context (see also Zinnbauer & Pargament, 2005). The advantages of these definitions include recognition of the sacred core of both religiousness and spirituality, continuity with common usage of the terms among believers and other professionals, and preservation of the popular association between religiousness and tradition (Zinnbauer et al., 1997).

Alas, universal conceptions of health, and by extension healthy spirituality, are not as easily given. The process of conceptualizing health is complex, and views of health have changed dramatically over the course of Western history.

CONCEPTUALIZING MENTAL HEALTH

Health is not a static concept. Rather, it has changed over time (Manderscheid et al., 2010) and reflected the values and worldviews of a given culture (Fabrega, 2002). Descriptions of health are not isolated; they are interrelated with language, advances in the physical sciences, and changing models of human functioning (Kirmayer, 2001; Maddux, Gosselin, & Winstead, 2012). Constructs within Western psychology and psychiatry are no exceptions. Views about the nature of mental health and illness have changed as cultural beliefs about human nature, selfhood, morality, and behavior have changed (McHugh & Slavney, 1998). By extension, evaluations of healthy and unhealthy spirituality are similarly embedded within context and worldview. A brief examination of the evolution of thought within psychology and psychiatry regarding the nature of mental health and illness can inform our efforts to distinguish healthy from unhealthy spirituality.

As discussed by various authors (Dueck & Parsons, 2004; Fabrega, 2002, 2008; Gergen, 2001; Laugharne & Laugharne, 2002; Lewis, 2000; McHugh & Slavney, 1998; Westheafer, 2004; Wilber, 1998), the history of modern Western thought may be divided into three chronological periods or movements: the premodern, the modern, and the postmodern. Each of these three is distinguished by different conceptions of reality (metaphysics) and by different theories of knowledge (epistemology). A summary of these eras can be seen in Table 4.1. A full historical discussion of these periods is precluded here, but the reader is directed to works such as Harvey (1989); Hoffman, Hoffman, Robison, and Lawrence (2005); McHugh and Slavney (1998); Richards and Bergin (1997); and Wilber (1998, 2001) for more thorough treatments.

Premodernity is considered to be the general period that extends from ancient history up to the 17th century. Knowledge during this era was embedded within the prevailing cultural worldviews of the time. Greco-Roman philosophy and the humoral theory of medicine informed early conceptions of abnormal physical functioning, mental experience, and behavior. Later in the medieval period, Christianity heavily influenced Western

TABLE 4.1

Comparison of Premodern, Modern, Postmodern, and Integrative Perspectives in Western Thought

Dimension	Premodern	Modern	Postmodern	Integrative
Ultimate truth	Knowable	Knowable	No such thing	Multiple truths across multiple dimensions
Epistemology	Divine revelation	Rationalism and empiricism; scientific method	Equality of local truths constructed through multiple methods	Multiple methods, local and universal truths
Knowledge	Universal, revelatory	Universal, objective, rational	Relative, contextual, and political	Half-life of knowledge
Authority	Church, aristocracy	Science, philosophy	To be distrusted	Multiple contextual authorities
Good defined as	Determined by authority	Promotes equality, freedom, justice	Pragmatic, internally coherent	Flexible, both universal and local good
Goal of life	Spiritual progress	Material social progress and emancipation	Respect for others, relative gains and losses	Defined by point of view

perspectives on truth, madness, spirituality, and sin (Alexander & Selesnick, 1995; Fabrega, 2002; Richards & Bergin, 1997). Knowledge of the world for many thus became synonymous with religious knowledge. Ultimate truths were gleaned through divine revelation or inspiration, and the Christian church maintained and interpreted these spiritual truths (Hoffman et al., 2005). Broadly defined, the goal of life for many was synonymous with spiritual progress or religious adherence.

This era predates the fields of psychiatry and psychology. Under the influence of Christianity, mental health was often synonymous with spiritual health and therefore conditions associated with mental illness were interpreted as spiritual maladies (Alexander & Selesnick, 1995). This position was not incompatible with the slowly advancing materialist understanding of the human body. Punishment from God for spiritual transgressions or attack by evil spiritual forces were considered the ultimate causes of psychological problems, and these manifested through the physical mechanisms of the human body. Treatments were accordingly both spiritual and physical in nature. Confession, penance, exorcism, and a renewal of faith were prescribed along with bloodletting and later trepanning. Among the laity, superstitions about the nature of aberrant behavior were prevalent, and the use of magical charms and religious relics to treat physical and mental problems was common (Roffe & Roffe, 1995).

The dawn of modernity, traced roughly to the mid-1600s, is associated with the rise of empirical and rational methods of inquiry, the questioning of religious authority, the rejection of superstition, the public accessibility of truth, and a focus on improving social conditions through reason (McHugh & Slavney, 1998). As a reaction to the power of the aristocracy and the revealed truths of the Christian Church, sources of authority were expanded to include the academic and scientific. In this period, objective reality was considered knowable, and universal truths were thought to be discoverable through reason, observation, and measurement (Hoffman et al., 2005). The goals of modernity were progress, improving social conditions, and the liberation of inquiry from tradition and religion. This intent was also reflected in the emergence of universalist cultural values of equality, freedom, governance, and justice (Wilber, 1998).

The Enlightenment period in particular is credited with the first emergence of modern psychological and psychiatric perspectives (Laugharne & Laugharne, 2002; McHugh & Slavney, 1998; Wilber, 1998). Mental illnesses as disease entities began to be separated from religious and moral conceptions, and a naturalistic, materialistic, and deterministic worldview rose in influence. The quest to find universal aspects of psychiatric conditions led to the development of early classification and diagnostic systems (Widiger, 2012). Enlightenment thinkers hoped to improve psychological functioning and public health through the discovery of universal causal laws for human experience and behavior. Thus for early psychologists and physicians, legitimacy and social intervention were sought through science and the scientific method.

The genesis of the postmodern era in Europe and the United States is often traced to the 1950s. As each new era is often a polemic to its predecessor, the postmodern was a refutation of the modern (Harvey, 1989; Hoffman et al., 2005). For postmodernists, the central Enlightenment notion of objective or Ultimate Truth is false and potentially dangerous. The proposed replacement is a metaphysics of local and contextual truths generated through multiple methods. As such, truth is constructed and not discovered (Held, 1995), and objective truth claims may reveal the means by which groups in power control, marginalize, or oppress others. Also, as described by Lewis (2000), all metanarratives or overarching cross-contextual frames are considered suspect, including the modernist ideals of progress and emancipation.

Postmodernist psychologists and psychiatrists are therefore critical of Establishment systems of mental health care (Fabrega, 2008; Foucault, 1980) and consider them means of exerting cultural power to support capitalist and oppressive authority structures. Traditional attempts to explain mental health or illness as cross-contextual universals are therefore rejected. For radical postmodernists, diagnostic labeling is considered an act of oppression or marginalization. All modernist conceptual frames and theories about mental health are considered value laden, relative, biased, and narrow. For the postmodernist psychologist or psychiatrist, there are multiple truths known through multiple methods. No truth or method is privileged, for all statements about reality are caught in the same relativistic language trap (see Watson, 2008). For the radical postmodernist, the scientist's conclusions about depression are not inherently more correct than the poet's. The clinician's beliefs about depression are not more accurate than those of the depressed individual.

THE INTEGRATIVE MODEL

As is obvious from the previous discussion, the worldviews associated with each era from the premodern to the postmodern produce different psychological perspectives on health and illness. Furthermore, all three perspectives exist side by side in our current cultural dialogue. Clashes of worldview can be seen in present-day arguments over such topics as abortion, civil rights, stem cell research, and evolution.

Extrapolating from the previous section on this history of mental illness, views about the merits of spirituality are dependent on the assumptions and worldview of the evaluator. A premodern thinker may judge the health or merit of faith on the basis of correspondence with approved theology. A modern thinker might deny the reality of all nonmaterial aspects of faith, and judge spirituality in terms of its rationality, empirical outcomes, and observable qualities. And a postmodern thinker could view spirituality as a context-bound cultural narrative to be considered in terms of its internal coherence, pragmatic usefulness, and relationship to social systems and power hierarchies. Each perspective has merit, but each perspective is also limited (Wilber, 1998, 2001). Consistent with the integrative intent of Ken Wilber (1998, 2001), Dueck and Parsons (2004) and Morris, Leung, Ames, and Lickel (1999) suggested that the route to more ethical and effective evaluation may lie in the integration of these different belief systems. An integrated, "integral" (Wilber, 1998, 1999), or "broad science" approach (Westheafer, 2004) thus would attempt to maintain the best of each era without including its limitations or baggage. To fully evaluate spirituality, it will be necessary to consider the insider's view of believers and spiritual experts, objective rational and empirical criteria, and the larger framework of culture, power, and privilege. The following is one such integrative attempt that distills frames from these three movements.

Premodern Frames

For our current purposes, what we can borrow from premodernity is a focus on the cultural insider's perspective. That is, evaluation starts with a description from the point of view of the spiritual adherent or group and reflects an emic orientation to inquiry. Borrowed from anthropology and linguistics (Pike, 1967), emic descriptive accounts and evaluations are analyses consistent with the subjective perspectives of a given individual, group, or culture. Emic knowledge is evaluated according to the consensual perceptions of cultural insiders (Lett, 1996, 1990), and emic researchers often assume that belief systems and cultures are best understood holistically as interconnected systems (Morris et al., 1999).

Within this frame, the health of spiritual beliefs is evaluated within a given spiritual system at the level of the individual adherent, in the community of the faithful, and by spiritual experts or authorities. Belief and behavior can thus be compared with formal doctrine, the lives and examples of spiritual paragons (e.g., "what would Jesus do"), or formal spiritual prescriptions interpreted through the prism of traditional religious systems. Other related subcultural communities may provide in-group evaluative criteria for spirituality, including groupings by gender, sexuality, race, age, and ethnicity (Winstead & Sanchez-Hucles, 2012).

The benefits of this frame include accurate description, a wealth of detail, and understanding spiritual beliefs and cultural meanings on their own terms (Morris et al., 1999). This approach is consistent with some qualitative research approaches, such as phenomenology and hermeneutics, as well as anthropological ethnographic fieldwork. It is attuned to the native worldviews, values, and beliefs of spiritual adherents, but it has its limitations. Emic approaches used alone have been criticized as producing strings of incomparable unique cases (Bourguignon, 1989), vulnerable to biased interpretations by researchers, and unable to decipher key concepts or relevant information from large amounts of gathered data (Morris et al., 1999). Furthermore, in the absence of any shared system of beliefs, community of believers, or spiritual authority, evaluation is limited to the quasi-solipsism of individual spiritual opinion.

Modern Frames

The bulk of work in the psychology of spirituality has been conducted within a modernist framework. Rational theory building and empirical analysis have generated a substantial body of knowledge about spiritual belief, behavior, emotion, experience, and values. As such, this endeavor generally falls within the range of etic approaches to inquiry. Etic constructs are developed in accordance with the scientific method, and thus must be objective, replicable, falsifiable, comprehensive, and precise (Lett, 1996, 1990). In contrast to the emic insider's perspective, the etic researcher may use abstracted descriptions, cross-cultural constructs, publicly debated data gathering and interpretation, and causal inferences that are not contained within nor constrained by the believer's worldview. This has the potential to provide common ground for researchers and clinicians interested in spirituality and to distill common factors across individual spiritual belief and experience. Data gathering is observational, data manipulation and analysis are largely mathematical, and etic results are interpreted logically.

Much of the research cited in the volume is modernist in design. The health of spiritual systems is determined through rational and empirical assessment. Healthy spirituality is presumably that which makes internal logical sense and which is related to positive indexes of adaptive functioning and well-being. Examples of this include developmental models of spirituality (e.g., Benson, 2004; Fowler, 1981; Reich, 1993; Richards & Bergin, 1997), correlations of spirituality with secular health outcomes (see Gartner, 1996; Koenig, 2008; Pargament, 1997), religious coping research (Pargament, 1997), and psychological models of spiritual health, such as those reviewed later in this chapter.

The benefits of the modernist approach are clear. Advances in the basic and applied sciences are ubiquitously obvious, and nearly every aspect of Western life has been affected by modernist knowledge and resultant technology. Etic approaches do hold the promise of generalizable and cumulative knowledge, and applied sciences based on etic data can provide interventions to the widest range of individuals. Etic approaches, however, also have their limitations.

Much of the tension between faith and science can be traced to the worldview clashes generated through emic and etic stances. Conflicts between religious traditions and modernistic metaphysics and epistemology have been well documented by both spiritual advocates (e.g., Richards & Bergin, 1997; Watson, 2008) and atheistic polemicists (e.g., Dawkins, 2006; Dennett, 2006; Harris, 2004). With regard to the latter, the criticisms of faith given by the "new atheists" are indeed coherent refutations of premodern faith from the point of view of modernism. If you accept the premises of modernistic science, including naturalistic, reductionistic, mechanistic, and positivistic assumptions (Richards & Bergin, 1997), then you are logically constrained to accept the conclusions that premodern faith is largely irrational and based on historical myth (Stenger, 2007). In contrast, if you accept a solely premodern worldview and an emic position of inquiry, then arguments that reduce one's sacred beliefs to evolutionary epiphenomenon, cultural artifacts, or mass hysteria are at best incendiary fighting words, and at worst, nefarious spiritual threats.

Neither of these stances alone is adequate for our present purposes. To leave the evaluation of spiritual health solely to local or insiders' perspectives disqualifies the psychology of spirituality as a science and threatens the field itself with regression to pre-Enlightenment inquiry (Helminiak, 2010). To adopt a fully etic stance or modernist metaphysics and epistemology risks losing nuances of meaning, overlooking contextual or local truths, or neglecting other sociopolitical factors that influence the process of inquiry itself. In essence, modernist evaluations of spirituality can clash with the fundamental core of spirituality itself and with the substantive center of the psychology of spirituality: the human experience of the sacred.

Postmodern Frames

Postmodernism for our purposes enlarges the frame of evaluation beyond the modernist to include the social and cultural processes of investigation. As the modernist frame expands inquiry beyond local or authority-driven truth, the postmodernist expands inquiry to include multiple truths, multiple methods of investigation, and an examination of the very sociopolitical processes in which inquiry is conducted. Context is therefore considered critical to inquiry. Two current scholarly contributions illustrate the value of this postmodernist concern.

As postmodernists question the validity of universal truths and posit local truths that are relative to one another in value and veracity, the challenge becomes how to translate concepts and knowledge across these local truth communities. Watson (2008) has presented the model of the "ideological surround" as one such solution and as a check against subtle prejudice against spirituality in some modernist research. A combination of the emic and the etic, Watson's approach is sensitive to contextual meaning and is consistent with epistemic pluralism (Hood, Hill, & Spilka, 2009).

According to Watson (2008), all human activity takes place within context, and the meaning system of a given context can be described as an ideological surround. He suggested that all systems of thought are ideological, including the premodern, modern, and postmodern worldviews. When two disparate ideologies come into contact and pursue dialogue (e.g., the modernist researcher and the spiritual believer), a bridge must be built that accounts for ideological differences, permits understanding, and preserves meaning. Travel across this bridge goes in both directions. The etic researcher may desire to effectively and empirically examine human activity that takes place within various other ideological surrounds, and the spiritual believer may desire to bring spiritual concepts to other ideological groups.

Two methods presented by Watson (2008) are the empirical translation scheme and comparative rationality analysis. As discussed by Watson and also summarized by Hood et al. (2009), empirical translation schemes are used to determine whether translation is possible between two ideological surrounds. Statements from one ideological surround are translated into the language and concepts of the other with the goal of finding positive correlations between the two different expressions of the same central idea. Direct rational analysis is used to determine whether one ideological group has constructed a biased or prejudicial depiction of another ideological group. Examples of this latter method can be found in Watson (1993, 2008) and Watson et al.'s (2003) examination of Christian and humanistic conceptions of self-actualization as measured by secular questionnaire and Christian college students' responses on measures of homophobia and tolerance for ambiguity. Watson et al. administered these scales to university students who identified themselves as Christians and to students at a Christian college, and then they deconstructed and analyzed the scales. They found that supposedly neutral and "objective" social science research can be influenced in complex and subtle ways by ideology. Instead of discovering truth, these modernist research attempts were found to contain antireligious ideological surrounds as well as prejudicial, overgeneralized conclusions about some Christian's beliefs and attitudes. As concluded by Watson (2008), "all research programs—Christian, anti-Christian, and otherwise—will invariably be framed within the norms of inclusion and exclusion that define an ideological surround, and those norms can promote the creation of misleading empirical findings" (p. 16).

Another example of a postmodernist trend in inquiry comes from a journalistic summary of the cross-cultural effects of Western mental health diagnostic practices (Watters, 2010). As discussed by Widiger (2012), the original driving force in the development of a universal diagnostic nomenclature within psychiatry was the "the crippling confusion generated by its absence" (p. 64). A common language and conceptual scheme is a fully modernist project: It promotes research, knowledge accumulation and dissemination, and public debate and criticism. The current diagnostic systems, most notably the *Diagnostic and Statistical Manual of Mental Disorders* (American Psychiatric Association, 2000) and ICD-10 (World Health Organization, 2003), are crowning modernist achievements. As such, they are clear improvements over premodern psychiatric practices.

As documented by Watters (2010; see also Horwitz, 2002), however, the Western psychological diagnostic system may not be as "objective" and culture-free as the modernist enterprise would suggest. Watters documented four separate effects of Western psychiatry on foreign cultures and concluded that as the West has exported Western psychological culture to the rest of the world, it has actually shaped the form and experience of mental illness. From the rise of Western-style anorexia in Hong Kong, to the influx of Western traumatologists into posttsunami Sri Lanka, to the experience of schizophrenia in Zanzibar, to the direct marketing of Western conceptions of depression to Japan (followed, of course, by antidepressants to cure it), the conclusion is an uncomfortable one. Watters argued that Western conceptions of mental illness actually shape and create certain symptoms among members of other cultures. As one ideological surround invades another, it reframes and changes certain views of health, illness, and language.

Watters's (2010) discussion of anorexia in Hong Kong questioned whether psychiatrists "discover" or "construct" psychiatric disorders. His arguments focused on extensive observations and professional articles by psychiatrist Sing Lee, who observed a rapid change in presented symptoms of anorexia from a unique and rare symptom cluster to a much more prevalent American version. The confluence of changing professional conceptions of anorexia, media coverage, cultural shifts, and patients' suggestibility all reportedly produced a significant change in anorexic symptoms over a relatively brief amount of time. The conclusion Watters and Lee drew from this observation was not that enlightened professionals "discovered" preexisting but overlooked eating disorders in Hong Kong, but they actually participated in the construction of that reality as Western ideology infected Hong Kong culture.

Describing the work of historian Edward Shorter (1992, 1994), Watters suggested that throughout history there have been various psychosomatic symptoms among individuals and populations that are amenable to influence by various cultural and interpersonal factors. In essence, a portion of the distress and impairment associated with mental illness constitutes a "symptom pool" that is defined as the acceptable or expected expression of distress according to a given culture at a given point in history. As psychology and psychiatry settle on names, causes, and symptoms for a given disease, they are not merely discovering truths in the objective world. For that portion of mental illnesses that fall within the psychosomatic spectrum, professionals essentially define the symptom pool. They help shape the experience of distress for their patients, define the nature of the cure, and promote the cultural acceptance of a given ideology. This perspective does not suggest that all mental illnesses are simply cultural artifacts, but it does suggest that one side effect of professional and media attention given to certain forms of pathology is the entry of those symptoms into the cultural symptom pool. In essence, professionals who are working to eradicate mental illness can at times be part of a cultural disease vector that transmits the illnesses to others (Watters, 2010).

What the work of Watson and Watters suggests is that naive realist perspectives of psychological work and study are inadequate and potentially undesirable. Culture and ideology are often intimately intertwined with the collection, interpretation, and promulgation of research (Bergin, 1993). The hope that the world can be deciphered solely through the use of objective rational and empirical methods is short-sighted and particularly problematic as inquiry moves from the physical to the social sciences. The process of inquiry takes place within ideological surrounds, and ethical psychologists have to account for the power, politics, and social influence in their work. Ideological differences between groups, and the impact of power differentials between groups, are variables to be examined rather than factors assumed a priori to be either absent or ubiquitous. Failure to include this in social scientific inquiry renders certain groups and cultures vulnerable to oppression and a Western cultural hegemony.

Integrative Frames

The elements of an integrative frame can be seen in the final column of Table 4.1 and serve as our template to critique current and past models of spiritual health within psychology. This perspective recognizes the possibility of multiple truths across multiple dimensions, multiple methods of inquiry, the power of context, and a flexible approach to evaluating outcome. Some of these elements have already been gathered from the survey of premodern, modern, and postmodern perspectives. Additional elements, such as the need to specify point of view and the "half life" of knowledge, will complete the integrative frame.

The principle of multiple truths holds that multiple perspectives in metaphysics and epistemology must be honored in ethical inquiry. Thus, both emic and etic analyses of spirituality can be conducted and integrated (Richards & Bergin, 1997). As indicated earlier, the emic question for this chapter is whether cultural or spiritual insiders deem a given spirituality to be unhealthy.

We cannot be satisfied solely with emic answers. A brief reflection on destructive spiritual groups—such as the cults of Jonestown, the Branch Davidians, Heaven's Gate, Aum Shinrikyo, or the Solar Temple—shows the potential limits of relying solely on insider's evaluative accounts. Etic research programs complement the emic by revealing relationships among various spiritual beliefs, attitudes, behavior, and health outcomes. These outcomes can range from universally accepted values in the Western world (e.g., justice and freedom) to pragmatic local outcomes specific to certain research questions or cultural groups. Causal links are also determined through experimental manipulation and causal modeling.

Integrative inquiry need not focus on single dimensions but on multiple dimensions that vary in their horizontal breadth and vertical span (Wilber, 1995; Zinnbauer & Pargament, 2005). Horizontal breadth refers to the multidimensionality of spirituality (Emmons & Paloutzian, 2003) for a given individual. Because spirituality can be described along various psychological dimensions, such as biology, sensation, affect, cognition, behavior, identity, meaning, morality, creativity, personality, and self-awareness, it also can be evaluated along those same dimensions. Explicating one's dimensional point of focus when etically evaluating spirituality is critical; spiritual activities that can be distressing along one dimension, such as physical pain from vision quests or fasting, may prove beneficial along others, such as identity, spiritual insight, and self-awareness.

Vertical span refers to the concept of levels of analysis (see Wilber, 1995; Zinnbauer & Pargament, 2005). According to Wilber (1995) human phenomena can be examined along a progression of increasing complexity and emergent properties from the microscopic to the macroscopic: subatomic particles, atoms, molecules, cells, tissues, organ systems, person, family, community, culture or subculture, society or nation, and biosphere and beyond. Fundamental levels are described as necessary but not sufficient for the organization of higher levels. For example, groups contain various individuals, but a group's organization and processes are not captured by examining any single person's behavior within the group. When evaluating spirituality, it is again necessary to specify point of view with respect to levels of analysis. For example, individual spiritual conversion experiences may have multiple effects. A new convert might quit poor health habits such as smoking or excessive drinking to the benefit of her tissues and organ systems. She might also experience a new identity and purpose in life, reflected in healthy gains for her individual psychology. She might, however, conflict with her husband and family members over her changes in belief and behavior to the detriment of her relational functioning. If she lives in a social or political context that represses spiritual expression, she might also find herself at odds with authorities and power structures in her environment. Evaluators may privilege any of these perspectives (e.g., the physical health perspective, the family perspective, or the political authority perspective) as long they are explicit about taking those positions and ethically consider the various potential impacts of inquiry. Of note, psychologists generally privilege psychological criteria of well-being over criteria that may be more central to spiritually minded people themselves. Given the value-laden nature of psychotherapy and counseling (e.g., Zinnbauer & Pargament, 2000), this contrast of values can be potentially problematic.

The "half-life" of truth concept adds the dimension of time to the validation of psychological truths. In addition to subjective truths, objective truths, and contextual truths, we must add temporal or historical truths. As seen in medical research, the truth status of medical findings can be considered to have a validity half-life that changes as expertise advances. For example, surgical knowledge and medical knowledge about adult cirrhosis and hepatitis are considered to have a half-life of 45 years (Poynard et al., 2002). For medicine, advances in etic knowledge likely account for the revision of medical truths.

This notion is extended when applied to psychological and spiritual inquiry. Psychological truths change as etic knowledge advances, but they are also related to various levels of analysis, and elements of those levels can change at different rates. For example, knowledge about psychobiological aspects of spirituality will change as ongoing research expands professional understanding. It also will change much more slowly as environmental and evolutionary forces change the human body. In contrast, research on the sociopolitical beliefs of spiritual adherents is likely to fluctuate more rapidly as the protean social and political landscapes change over time.

In summary, the integrative frame borrows elements of the premodern, modern, and postmodern worldviews and emphasizes explicating points of view and change processes. Questions to consider when generating models of spiritual health thus include the following:

- Are subjective, objective, contextual, and temporal truths examined?
- Is the point of view specified?
- Does the model include horizontal breadth and vertical span?
- Are inquiries open to multiple methods and means of inquiry?
- Are change processes accounted for within the model?

CURRENT AND PAST PSYCHOLOGICAL MODELS OF SPIRITUAL HEALTH

With the framework now explicated, we can examine several past and present psychological conceptions of spiritual health. This section presents a sample of models that have been popular within the psychology of religion and spirituality. This section concludes with a focus on two current frameworks that incorporate most elements of the integrative frame, and the use of a case example to illustrate integrative elements found in each of the discussed models.

William James

The father of American psychology can be credited with one of the earliest psychological examinations of religion. Drawn from his classic work, *The Varieties of Religious Experience*, James (1902/1961) distinguished the "healthy minded" temperament from the "sick souled."

> The healthy minded are those who are perpetually optimistic. They see only good around them, refuse to think ill of life, and refuse to acknowledge or experience evil. Whether as a voluntary pursuit or a reflexive unconscious defense, the healthy minded individual's . . . soul is of this sky-blue tint, whose affinities are rather with flowers and birds and all enchanting innocencies than with dark human passions, who can think no ill of man or God, and in whom religious gladness, being in possession from the outset, needs no deliverance from any antecedent burden. (pp. 79–80)

In contrast, according to James (1902/1961), the sick souled are those who view evil, sin, and suffering as essential parts of humanity. These "morbid-minded" individuals are sensitive to discord to the point of pathological melancholia and often perceive humanity as fundamentally flawed or rooted in failure. For James, this pessimism "keeps us from our real good" (p. 143) and must be renounced to enter into the spiritual life. The sick souled are thus the "twice born" that must come to spirituality through surrender and conversion.

Because his method of description is categorical, James's (1902/1961) method of evaluation is essentially a pragmatic one (Pargament, 2007). What is good or true is simply that which works. As stated by Pargament (2007), "Rather than focus on the roots of religion, [James] proposed, consider its fruits" (p. 131).

It may seem awkward to evaluate the adequacy of a century-old psychological model of spirituality using contemporary criteria, but James's (1902/1961) presentation does have several strong elements. He used firsthand accounts to bolster his descriptions of the two types, and it is likely that those who are described by these constructs would recognize their experience, if not actually the labels that summarize them, in James's descriptions. Furthermore, the two temperaments are linked to religious movements and social attitudes prevalent in James's time, and the process of change from the sick-souled, divided self to the integrated spiritual self through conversion is explicated. Finally, the use of pragmatic evaluation rises above mere emic perspectives and is applicable across a variety of etic methods of inquiry.

Questions posed by the integrative frame are relevant to James's (1902/1961) descriptive accounts and method of evaluation. To be adequate as a line of research, the healthy-minded and the sick-souled constructs would need to be operationalized then greatly expanded to address issues of horizontal breadth and vertical span and investigated across numerous contexts. Failing to do so reduces the multidimensions of spiritual life to just one aspect of its horizontal breadth. It is also unlikely that James proposed these two categories with populations in mind other than early 20th-century Caucasian Christians. Are they reliable and valid depictions for other identifiable groups, other cultural contexts, and believers in the 21st century? Also, in what ways are these spiritual temperaments different from related constructs, such as optimism, dysthymia, depression, and neuroticism?

Postmodernist concerns about point of view and cultural value judgments are also relevant in this context. What are the cultural value judgments at work in labeling one group "healthy" and another group "sick" or "morbid"? Also, who determines what "works"? Pragmatic outcomes may vary widely depending on the use of emic, etic, contextual, or historical criteria. What may be viewed as spiritually useful to a clinician or academician may diverge from the perspectives of the believer, the spiritual expert, or the atheist. In essence, James (1902/1961) remains a relevant voice in the current work to understand spirituality, but his approach of categorical description and pragmatic evaluation does not escape problems of ideology and the need to specify context.

Gordon Allport

From James (1902/1961), we move forward 50 years to Allport (1950). When Allport published his classic work *The Individual and His Religion* in 1950, and he presented six differences between "mature" and "immature" religious sentiment. First, mature religious sentiment is "differentiated" or complex, rich, open to criticism and revision, and flexibly maintained. Immature religious sentiment in contrast is uncritically accepted, exclusionary, self-centered, and prejudicial. Second, mature religious sentiment has a "derivate and dynamic nature," which refers to the process by which basic psychoanalytic drives develop into functionally autonomous and transformational motives or values. In contrast, immaturity refers to religious sentiment that is fanatical, impulsive, or primitive. Third, maturity is directive in that it produces consistent effects in an individual's life. Immaturity refers to a lack of such influence on a person's beliefs, conduct, or values. Fourth, mature religious sentiment is comprehensive. It provides a philosophy of life, existential meaning, and tolerance for a diversity of meaning and value. In contrast, immature religious sentiment is intolerant, incomplete, and an inadequate response to existential questions. Fifth, maturity is defined as integral. By this, Allport suggested that beliefs about faith and science must be woven together into a "harmonious tapestry" (p. 79), and issues of freedom, determination, and evil must be realistically integrated. Allport contrasted immaturity on this dimension as that spirituality that is internally conflicted, inconsistent, or regressive to prescientific or antiscientific stances. Finally, the heuristic or tentative character of mature sentiment is contrasted with an inability to tolerate ambiguity, experience uncertainty, or revise one's beliefs when necessary.

These distinctions were later developed into one of the most influential and investigated sets of constructs in the psychology of religion: intrinsic and extrinsic religiousness. These dimensions have been related to a number of phenomena, such as prejudice, authoritarianism, altruism, mysticism, and self-esteem (see Hood et al., 2009), and these were further refined by Batson, Schoenrade, and Ventis (1993). The adequacy of these constructs has been evaluated elsewhere (e.g., Hood, 1998), and so the focus in this section will remain on Allport's larger conceptions.

From an integrative perspective, Allport's (1950) distinctions between mature and immature faith are rich in description and evaluative dimensions. They are thorough and encompass a great deal of personal belief, psychological development, and psychological functioning. In this form, however, they do not lend themselves easily to integrative inquiry.

There is little emic investigation within this framework, and it is not clear to what extent Allport's (1950 criticism of faith is consistent with insider's beliefs or those of spiritual experts. For example, Allport took to task spirituality that is uncritically accepted, intolerant of uncertainty, or nonrevisable. Many spiritual believers, however, may find virtue in unshakable faith, certainty in worldview, and resistance to temptations that would erode spiritual belief or commitment.

Furthermore, the ideological surround of this conception contains elements consistent with psychodynamic theory. This position is not qualified as Allport's point of view, or even presented with explicit description of psychodynamic assumptions, but rather asserted as truth. As such, the potential for prejudicial labeling increases. Given their widely differing views of human functioning, much work would need to be done to bridge the ideological surrounds of psychodynamic theory and spiritual belief.

Finally, using an integrative framework that posits multiple truths and multiple methods is daunting enough given the difficulty of the task. This gets exponentially harder when applied to the complexity of Allport's (1950) descriptions. To fully capture his model, it would be necessary to emically and etically measure the degree to which faith provides such things as a philosophy of life, transformational values, integration of beliefs about science and spirit, and flexible adaptation to one's internal and external worlds. Once measured, it would be even more challenging to determine the local or universal nature of the findings. As a practical point for the practicing clinician, Allport's model may best be used as a set of heuristics that might guide psychotherapy or assessment rather than as a basis for empirical research. In essence, Allport's descriptions are rich and intellectually compelling but do not include insider's perspectives or clear means to measure several of the proposed dimensions of maturity and immaturity.

Paul Pruyser

Pruyser's contributions to the psychology of spirituality are considerable. A clinical psychologist at the

Menninger Clinic, Pruyser (1968) wrote about spirituality from a psychodynamic perspective. In his article "The Seamy Side of Current Religious Beliefs" (1977/1991), he identified several elements of neurotic behavior and then used them to distinguish neurotic from healthy spirituality. This seamy side of faith was described as a function of individual belief as well as a reflection of the popular culture. First, unhealthy spirituality requires a "sacrifice of the intellect" to maintain blind faith, private delusions, and an "eagerness to be deceived." Similarly, this spirituality can involve an anti-intellectual idealization of primitive cultures in a "dabbling with archaisms."

A second characteristic is "wishful compromise," which refers to the poor trade-offs associated with reconciling deeply held neurotic fantasies with reality. Pruyser (1977/1991) here presented the psychodynamic conflict between the reality principle and the pleasure principle in religious terms. Unhealthy spirituality can be observed in libidinal fantasies of paradise or heaven, aggressive fantasies such as visions of enemies vanquished and judged, or wishful apocalyptic or eschatological fantasies. Pruyser described the third feature of unhealthy spirituality as an inability or unwillingness to tolerate freedom. Such an authoritarian faith insists on the surrender of personal and intellectual freedom as a form of thought control. In a similar vein, Pruyser described unhealthy faith as promoting regressive hyperemotionalism and a surrender of personal agency.

Pruyser (1977/1991) also detailed ways in which neurotic coping styles can manifest through spiritual belief and behavior. As defenses against aggression, one's spirituality can reflect dissociation, denial, and counterphobic behavior observed in such activity as snake handling. As displacement of psychic conflict onto the body, spirituality may manifest as martyrdom, self-punishment, or asceticism. As a means of magically controlling external dangers, spirituality may promote rituals and symbols that are regressive and lead to obsessions or compulsions. And as frozen or habitual coping mechanisms, spirituality may reinforce character pathology, including chronic deception and fraudulence, extreme attitudes toward sexuality, or avoidance of aggression through mystical states or bouts of intense spiritual ideation. Taken together, these neurotic coping styles "shrink personal freedom, reduce the vision of the world's richness, and curb human potentialities" (p. 64).

To his credit, Pruyser (1977/1991) updated psychoanalytic conceptions about spirituality from the frankly pejorative writings of Freud (1927/1961; see also Zinnbauer & Pargament, 2000), but in light of the integrative frame, this conception has several missing elements. First, Pruyser wrote from an explicitly psychoanalytic perspective that did not lend itself to etic or empirical inquiry. Second, his writings contained little emic inquiry that would illuminate whether insiders share similar conceptions about unhealthy spiritual beliefs or practices.

Similar to Allport (1950), it is difficult to determine how one would measure and study some of the phenomena identified by Pruyser (1977/1991). The challenge of capturing psychological defenses at work, the process of regression, and libidinal fantasies with questionnaires or even qualitative research are considerable. The degree to which these phenomena are a product of historically bound philosophy and culture is also unknown.

In essence, the value of Pruyser's (1977/1991) approach lies in the revision of negative psychoanalytic conceptions of spirituality and the rich description of psychological functioning. Like Allport's (1950) framework, however, its value lies in organizing and interpreting clinical observations rather than guiding an empirical integrative line of inquiry.

Scott Richards and Allen Bergin

More recently, Richards and Bergin (1997, 2000) have actively and comprehensively presented a theistic spiritual approach to assessment and psychotherapy. In their 1997 work, they present a survey of several different historical models of healthy spirituality, including one adapted from Bergin (1993) that contrasts a wide range of adaptive and healthy spiritual values, behaviors, lifestyle dimensions, personality factors, and identity issues with related maladaptive and unhealthy ones. Described as an assessment, an interview guide, and a means of measuring therapeutic gains over time, this model distinguishes positive intrinsic, actualizing, renewing, interpersonal, nurturing, reconciling, and inspiring spirituality from their opposites: extrinsic, perfectionist, authoritarian, narcissistic, aggressive, dependent, and hyperspiritual faith. These authors also presented models for healthy personality functioning and development, healthy spiritual identity, and degree of congruence between one's values and lifestyle.

More important, however, is the framework in which Richards and Bergin (1997, 2000) presented their conceptions of mental and spiritual health. To their credit, they embraced a multicultural perspective and methodologically pluralistic approach to inquiry. This includes qualitative research designed to capture "clients' inner subjective worlds . . . or 'lived experience' thereby enabling them to understand and empathize with them more fully" (Richards & Bergin, 1997, p. 327) as well as traditional etic research models. Their method of assessing elements of health or pathology within a psychotherapy or counseling context consists of a two-step strategy that reflects both emic and etic approaches. The first step includes emic inquiry in which clients' worldviews and beliefs are gathered. If this assessment reveals relevant religious and spiritual issues or information, a level-two assessment is conducted. This type of assessment is etic in that it may include information or measures outside of client's conceptions and experiences.

In their writings, Richards and Bergin (2000) have been explicit about taking a theistic point of view and have encouraged other faith-based approaches consistent with the worldviews and cultures of other religious traditions. Their spiritual strategy also addressed the issues of horizontal breadth and vertical span. Spirituality is related to various intrapsychic phenomena as well as vertically related to various levels of analysis anchored ultimately in a conception of God.

From an integrative perspective, this approach could benefit from a discussion of the larger historical, power, and cultural contexts that frame theistic spiritual approaches. The ideological surrounds of theistic religious organizations and traditions have implications for individual belief, political stances and allegiances, and social issues. Furthermore, researchers' spirituality, or rejection thereof, can influence the process and content of inquiry. It is critical when conducting research for investigators to disclose their biases and for the stakeholders of that research to be recognized and included. Just as medical researchers must disclose ties to pharmaceutical companies, so too should researchers in the psychology of spirituality disclosure their ties to religious or spiritual organizations and traditions. For example, in research articles the first page footnote that describes a researcher's contact information and institutional affiliation might also include his or her self-reported religious and spiritual status.

Finally, as proponents of diversity run into paradoxes when the range of perspectives they champion include antidiversity worldviews, one wonders how far a diversity of views can be extended within a theistic strategy before some of those views contradict core assumptions of that framework? In essence, because the ultimate arbiter of inquiry for Richards and Bergin (1997, 2000) lies in God and scripture, what guidelines do they take from empirically supported research? On issues such as dietary restrictions, celibacy, and divorce, is the ultimate arbiter of truth empirical research, contextual inquiry, or theological tenet?

Kenneth Pargament

Pargament has detailed a thorough treatment of spiritual issues in research (1997) and psychotherapy (2007). He divided psychological models of healthy or unhealthy spirituality into three groups on the basis of their evaluative criteria: truth based, pragmatic, or process. These three groups correspond roughly to the three eras of inquiry discussed in this chapter. Those who judge spirituality using truth criteria are similar to premodern or emic approaches, those who favor pragmatic criteria are consistent with many modern research methods, and those who use process criteria evaluations share elements in common with postmodern methods.

Pargament (2007) identified his own evaluative scheme as largely a process method in which quality is emphasized over outcome or truth status. In his words, the highest levels of spirituality are described "in terms of balance, dynamism, comprehensiveness, flexibility, and interconnectedness" (Pargament, 2007, p. 133). Consistent with a postmodernist approach, Pargament emphasized the coherence and consistency of spiritual components and the degree to which that system of belief and behavior is integrated within the larger sociocultural context. In his words,

> At its best, spirituality is defined by pathways that are broad and deep, responsive to life's situations, nurtured by the larger social context, capable of flexibility and continuity, and oriented toward a sacred destination that is large enough to encompass the full range of human potential and luminous to provide the individual with a powerful guiding vision. At its worst, spirituality is dis-integrated, defined by pathways that lack scope and depth, fail to meet the challenges and demands of life events, clash and collide with the surrounding social system, change and shift too easily or not at all, and misdirect the individual in the pursuit of spiritual value. (Pargament, 2007, p. 136)

From this description, Pargament (2007) further elucidated the ends and means of spiritual disintegration. He identified problematic spiritual destinations such as insufficient spiritual understandings (i.e., small gods), worship or pursuit of nonsacred objects (i.e., false gods), and the problem of internal spiritual conflict. He also described problematic spiritual pathways, such as insufficient spiritual breadth and depth, problems of continuity and change, and problems of fit. The latter includes conflicts between spiritual pathways and destinations, spiritual pathways and situations, and individuals with their social and cultural context.

From the perspective of the integrative frame, Pargament (1997) has met most of the demands of an integrative frame. He included case examples and emic descriptions, an etic body of research detailing spiritual paths and destinations (see Pargament, 1997), attention to context and change, explication of horizontal breadth, integration criteria along the vertical span, methods of assessment that enable practitioners to evaluate spiritual integration and disintegration, and process criteria by which to judge the internal adequacy of spiritual constructions. Pargament is refreshingly transparent about his own history and personal perspectives.

An additional consideration for this process model would include the need to specify point of view in inquiry and to explicitly discuss the value judgments inherent in describing and evaluating spiritual pathways, destinations, and integrations. These issues are apparent when reviewing the case examples provided by Pargament (2007). Whether an individual is in distress as the result of having small gods, false gods, or no god, that diagnosis is highly value laden. In a clinical context, is this spiritual evaluation generated by the consumer, the professional, or both in the process of narrative construction or dialogue? Every therapeutic encounter requires a bridge of ideologies. Sometimes this is a small bridge between two complementary worldviews. Other times it is a huge structure spanning a wide gap between two divergent belief systems. Specifying point of view (e.g., individual believer, spiritual expert, empirical researcher, religious group, popular culture, etc.) in this situation may not assist in the modernist project of uncovering universal or cross-contextual truths, but it may yield more valid contextual understandings. Overall, however, Pargament has provided a thorough and nuanced approach to evaluating the sacred.

Illustrative Case Example

The following case example illustrates the use of integrative frames and relates these frames to integrative elements found in the models discussed in this section.

> **Case Example**
>
> Rich Daekins is a 44-year-old, married, father of one son. He was referred to the Behavioral Health Corporation by his wife who "insisted he see someone."
>
> Mr. Daekins described himself over the phone as a "card carrying atheist" until a recent experience during a fishing trip. He described waking up one morning before dawn and watching the sun rise over the lake. All at once, he felt "alive" and connected to "the entire universe." Since that time, he has been "obsessed" with reading about mysticism and trying to find groups in his area

> with which to discuss his excitement and experiences. He stated that his wife finds him "annoying" now and has stated several times that he needs to "knock it off" and "rejoin his bowling league." When she has tried to question him about his beliefs, she reportedly complained that he is rigid about his new faith and talks "like he has answers to everything."
>
> During the intake interview, Mr. Daekins further shared that he is now more hopeful and "positive" than he has ever been in his life. He frequently daydreams about heaven and is considering a quitting his job at the paint store to pursue a year of prayer, celibacy, and fasting. At the end of the session Mr. Daekins asked the clinician if therapy could explore his faith and find ways to bring his wife "into the fold."

Consistent with emic inquiry, the first task of the clinician is to fully understand Mr. Daekins's subjective spiritual world. His recent spiritual experience must be fully explored, and the effects of his spiritual change must be explicated. As this inquiry proceeds, the first evaluation is taken from the point of view of the client. In this case, Mr. Daekins has welcomed the spiritual change and is more than content with his current spiritual status.

The next level of evaluation is from the point of view of other similar spiritually minded people. The clinician can compare Mr. Daekins's report to his or her own spiritual experiences or to other clients treated in the past. If this spiritual change is a novel phenomenon to the clinician, information must be gathered from other analogous spiritual individuals or experts within the same worldview.

Consistent with etic inquiry, the clinician can strive to understand Mr. Daekins's report from the point of view of empirical research (e.g., Pargament, 1997, 2007), theoretical models of spiritual change (e.g., James, 1902/1961), spiritual health (e.g., Richards & Bergin, 1997, 2000), and the clinician's own psychotherapeutic orientation (e.g., Allport, 1950; Pruyser, 1968, 1977/1991). This can certainly yield conclusions that contrast with those of the emic inquiry. Thus, the task becomes bridge-building between the ideological surrounds of the clinician and Mr. Daekins. Common language must be negotiated and the meaning of certain concepts verified, much as psychological scales that are translated into a foreign languages are then retranslated back to the original to verify the consistency of meaning across both tongues. If both clinician and client are alike, care is taken to ensure that actual differences are not overlooked because of assumed similarity (Zinnbauer & Pargament, 2000). If clinician and client are widely divergent in ideological surround, care is taken to ensure that the clinician and client understand each other fully and accurately.

Finally, the horizontal breadth and vertical span of Mr. Daekins's spiritual change and current functioning are examined. Changes in the client's mood, identity, behavior, morality, meaning, values, and personality are explicated from the point of view of both clinician and client. Of note, in the course of treatment, Mr. Daekins will be invited to more fully understand himself and his point of view, whereas the clinician must understand both the client's perspective as well as his or her own professional viewpoint. The clinician may later decide when, where, and if to share that viewpoint with Mr. Daekins in a therapeutic manner.

Potential causes and effects of the client's spiritual change can be considered along the levels of analysis. Phenomena that could account for Mr. Daekins's spiritual change such as changes in biochemistry, recent head injury, central nervous system damage, psychotic processes, stress reactions, personal growth, psychospiritual maturation, social influences, global movements, and transcendent connections may be entertained or discarded. Post-change effects can be examined, including changes in health behaviors, new social connections, marital changes, family stress and system dynamics, and relationships with social or cultural norms and currents. Clearly Mr. Daekins's relationship with his wife has shifted, and her reactions to his newfound faith must be considered.

With this information in hand, the clinician can turn to setting the therapeutic agenda and establishing the goals for treatment (e.g., see Zinnbauer & Barrett, 2008). This may involve a process of negotiation if the clinician and Mr. Daekins disagree about the potential targets of therapeutic intervention. It is unlikely that a clinician would pencil in "convert spouse to client's spiritual view" onto the clinic treatment plan or insurance form no matter how invested the client is in that goal. Treatment could potentially take place in an individual, marital, family, or group setting. If Mr. Daekins is content with his life and functioning and his presentation does not fall in an extreme range of psychopathology requiring acute psychiatric intervention, therapy could end with the intake interview.

The psychospiritual jury is still out for Mr. Daekins. The models used by the treating clinician, however, may be helpful or harmful to him depending on the ways in which his self-report and observed functioning are interpreted by the clinician. Clients in therapy often are asked to transform the implicit into the explicit, the assumed into the critically evaluated, and the automatic into the mindfully chosen. Integrative clinicians and researchers are obligated to do no less.

CONCLUSION

All methods of evaluating religiousness and spirituality are not created equal. The assumptions made about faith and the ideologies used to evaluate the sacred have clear implications for psychology as a discipline. Psychological evaluation has the potential to clarify the paths, destinations, and integrity of the sacred, but it also has the potential to insult, pathologize, and oppress. Metanarratives of health and maturity must be broad enough to include a wide range of human spiritual diversity, but specific enough to be pragmatically useful, intellectually illuminating, and empirically accurate. Furthermore, they must be open to debate. For phenomena as complex as spiritual beliefs and behavior, we must leave room for multiple approaches of inquiry and the possibility of local and universal truths. No psychological map of spiritual or religious maturity is fully complete; each attempt must be subject to revision as new knowledge is discovered, as the terrain of human diversity changes and shifts, and as the cultural context of evaluation is revised. Evaluative programs such as those of Pargament (1997, 2007) and of Richards and Bergin (1997, 2000) are steps in this integrative direction.

Ultimately, the fundamental query for this chapter—is spirituality healthy?—is a nonsense question. The more illuminating and integrative inquiry asks, For whom is spirituality healthy, in what context, by which outcome, from which point of view, and at what point in time?

References

Alexander, F., & Selesnick, S. T. (1995). The history of psychiatry: An evaluation of psychiatric thought and practice from prehistoric times to the present. Northvale, NJ: Aronson.

Allport, G. W. (1950). *The individual and his religion: A psychological interpretation.* Oxford, England: Macmillan.

American Counseling Association. (2005). *Bylaws.* Retrieved from http://www.counseling.org/AboutUs/ByLaws/TP/Home/CT2.aspx

American Psychiatric Association. (2000). *Diagnostic and statistical manual of mental disorders* (4th ed., text revision). Washington, DC: Author.

American Psychological Association. (2003). Guidelines on multicultural education, training, research, practice, and organizational change for psychologists. *American Psychologist, 58*, 377–402. doi:10.1037/0003-066X.58.5.377

Batson, C. D., Schoenrade, P., & Ventis, L. (1993). *Religion and the individual.* New York, NY: Oxford University Press.

Benson, P. L. (2004). Emerging themes in research on adolescent spiritual and religious development. *Applied Developmental Science, 8*, 47–50. doi:10.1207/S1532480XADS0801_6

Bergin, A. E. (1993). *Adaptive/healthy versus maladaptive/unhealthy religious lifestyles.* Unpublished manuscript, Brigham Young University, Provo, UT.

Bourguignon, E. (1989). Trance and shamanism: What's in a name? *Journal of Psychoactive Drugs, 21*, 9–15. doi:10.1080/02791072.1989.10472138

Dawkins, R. (1997). Obscurantism to the rescue. *Quarterly Review of Biology, 72*, 397–399. doi:10.1086/419951

Dawkins, R. (2006). *The god delusion.* London, England: Bantam.

Dennett, D. C. (2006). *Breaking the spell: Religion as a natural phenomenon.* New York, NY: Penguin.

Dueck, A., & Parsons, T. D. (2004). Integration discourse: Modern and postmodern. *Journal of Psychology and Theology, 32*, 232–247.

Emmons, R. A., & Paloutzian, R. F. (2003). The psychology of religion. *Annual Review of Psychology, 54*, 377–402. doi:10.1146/annurev.psych.54.101601.145024

Fabrega, H. (2002). Evolutionary theory, culture and psychiatric diagnosis. In M. Maj, W. Gaebel, J. Jose Lopez-Ibor, & N. Satorius (Eds.), *Psychiatric diagnosis and classification* (pp. 107–135). New York, NY: Wiley.

Fabrega, H. (2008). On the postmodernist critique and reformation of psychiatry. *Psychiatry: Interpersonal and Biological Processes, 71*, 183–196. doi:10.1521/psyc.2008.71.2.183

Foucault, M. (1980). Prison talk. In C. Gordon (Ed.), *Power/knowledge: Selected interviews and other writings, 1972–1977* (pp. 37–54). New York, NY: Pantheon.

Fowler, J. W. (1981). *Stages of faith: The psychology of human development and the quest for meaning.* San Francisco, CA: HarperCollins.

Freud, S. (1961). The future of an illusion. In J. Strachey (Ed. & Trans.), *The standard edition of the complete psychological works of Sigmund Freud* (Vol. 11, pp. 5–56). London, England: Hogarth Press. (Original work published 1927)

Gartner, J. (1996). Religious commitment, mental health, and prosocial behavior: A review of the empirical literature. In E. P. Shafranske (Ed.), *Religion and the clinical practice of psychology* (pp. 187–214). Washington, DC: American Psychological Association. doi:10.1037/10199-007

Gergen, K. J. (2001). Psychological science in a postmodern context. *American Psychologist, 56*, 803–813. doi:10.1037/0003-066X.56.10.803

Gould, S. J. (1997). Nonoverlapping magisteria. *Natural History, 106*, 16–22.

Harris, S. (2004). *The end of faith.* New York, NY: Knopf.

Harvey, D. (1989). *The condition of postmodernity: An enquiry into the origins of cultural change.* New York, NY: Blackwell.

Hathaway, W., & Ripley, J. S. (2009). Ethical concerns around spirituality and religion in clinical practice. In J. Aten & M. Leach (Eds.), *Spirituality and the therapeutic process: A comprehensive resource from intake to termination* (pp. 25–52). Washington, DC: American Psychological Association. doi:10.1037/11853-002

Held, B. S. (1995). *Back to reality: A critique of postmodern theory in psychotherapy.* New York, NY: Norton.

Helminiak, D. (2010). Theistic psychology and psychotherapy: A theological and scientific critique. *Zygon, 45*, 47–74. doi:10.1111/j.1467-9744.2010.01058.x

Hill, P. C., Pargament, K. I., Hood, R. W., McCullough, M. E., Swyers, J. P., Larson, D. B., & Zinnbauer, B. J. (2000). Conceptualizing religion and spirituality: Points of commonality, points of departure. *Journal for the Theory of Social Behaviour, 30*, 51–77. doi:10.1111/1468-5914.00119

Hoffman, L., Hoffman, J. L., Robison, B., & Lawrence, K. (2005, April). *Modern and postmodern ways of knowing: Implications for therapy and integration.* Paper presented at the Christian Association for Psychological Studies International Conference, Dallas, TX.

Hood, R. W. (1998). Intrinsic–extrinsic religiosity. In W. H. Swantos (Ed.), *Encyclopedia of religion and society.* Walnut Creek, CA: AltaMira Press. Retrieved from http://hirr.hartsem.edu/ency/Intrinsic-Extrinsic.htm

Hood, R. W., Hill, P. C., & Spilka, B. (2009). *The psychology of religion: An empirical approach* (4th ed.). New York, NY: Guilford Press.

Horwitz, A. V. (2002). *Creating mental illness.* Chicago, IL: University of Chicago Press.

James, W. (1961). *The varieties of religious experience.* New York, NY: Collier Books. (Original work published 1902)

Kirmayer, L. J. (2001). Cultural variations in the clinical presentation of depression and anxiety: Implications for diagnosis and treatment. *Journal of Clinical Psychiatry, 62*, 22–28.

Koenig, H. G. (2008). *Medicine, religion, and health: Where science and spirituality meet.* West Conshohocken, PA: Templeton Foundation Press.

Laugharne, R., & Laugharne, J. (2002). Psychiatry, postmodernism and postnormal science. *Journal of the Royal Society of Medicine, 95*, 207–210. doi:10.1258/jrsm.95.4.207

Lett, J. (1990). Emics and etics: Notes on the epistemology of anthropology. In T. Headland, K. Pike, & M. Harris (Eds.), *Emics and etics: The insider/outsider debate* (pp. 127–142). Newbury Park, CA: Sage.

Lett, J. (1996). Emic/etic distinctions. In D. Levinson & M. Ember (Eds.), *Encyclopedia of cultural anthropology* (pp. 382–383). New York, NY: Holt.

Lewis, B. (2000). Psychiatry and postmodern theory. *Journal of Medical Humanities, 21*, 71–84. doi:10.1023/A:1009018429802

Lineweaver, C. H. (2008). Increasingly overlapping magisterial of science and religion. In R. Gordon & J. Seckbach (Eds.), *Divine action and natural selection: Questions of science and faith in biological evolution* (pp. 154–181). Singapore: World Scientific. doi:10.1142/9789812834355_0010

Maddux, J. E., Gosselin, J. T., & Winstead, B. A. (2012). Conceptions of psychopathology: A social constructionist perspective. In J. E. Maddux & B. A. Winstead (Eds.), *Psychopathology: Foundations for a contemporary understanding* (3rd ed., pp. 3–22). New York, NY: Routledge.

Manderscheid, R. W., Ryff, C. D., Freeman, E. J., McKnight-Eily, L. R., Dhingra, S., & Strine, T. W. (2010). Evolving definitions of mental illness and wellness. *Preventing Chronic Disease, 7*, A19.

McHugh, P. R., & Slavney, P. R. (1998). *The perspectives of psychiatry*. Baltimore, MD: Johns Hopkins University Press. doi:10.1007/978-3-642-70922-7

Moberg, D. O. (2002). Assessing and measuring spirituality: Confronting dilemmas of universal and particular evaluative criteria. *Journal of Adult Development, 9*, 47–60. doi:10.1023/A:1013877201375

Morris, M. W., Leung, K., Ames, D., & Lickel, B. (1999). Views from inside and outside: Integrating emic and etic insights about culture and justice judgment. *Academy of Management Review* 24, 781–796.

Pargament, K. I. (1997). *The psychology of religion and coping: Theory, research, practice*. New York, NY: Guilford Press.

Pargament, K. I. (2007). *Spiritually integrated psychotherapy: Understanding and addressing the sacred*. New York, NY: Guilford Press.

Pike, K. L. (1967). *Language in relation to a unified theory of the structure of human behavior* (2nd ed.). The Hague, the Netherlands: Mouton.

Poynard, T., Munteanu, M., Ratziu, V., Benhamou, Y., Di Martino, V., Taieb, J., & Opolon, P. (2002). Truth survival in clinical research: An evidence-based requiem. *Annals of Internal Medicine, 136*, 888–895.

Pruyser, P. W. (1968). *A dynamic psychology of religion*. New York, NY: Harper & Row.

Pruyser, P. W. (1991). The seamy side of current religious beliefs. In H. N. Malony & B. Spilka (Eds.), *Religion in psychodynamic perspective: The contributions of Paul W. Pruyser* (pp. 47–65). Oxford, England: Oxford University Press. (Original work published 1977)

Reich, K. H. (1993). Cognitive-developmental approaches to religiousness: Which version for which purpose? *The International Journal for the Psychology of Religion, 3*, 145–171. doi:10.1207/s15327582ijpr0303_1

Richards, P. S., & Bergin, A. E. (1997). *A spiritual strategy for counseling and psychotherapy*. Washington, DC: American Psychological Association. doi:10.1037/10241-000

Richards, P. S., & Bergin, A. E. (Eds.). (2000). *Handbook of psychotherapy and religious diversity*. Washington, DC: American Psychological Association. doi:10.1037/10347-000

Roffe, D., & Roffe, C. (1995). Madness and care in the community: A Medieval perspective. *British Medical Journal, 311*, 1708–1712. doi:10.1136/bmj.311.7021.1708

Shorter, E. (1992). *From paralysis to fatigue: A history of psychosomatic illness in the modern era*. New York, NY: Free Press.

Shorter, E. (1994). *From the mind into the body: The cultural origins of psychosomatic symptoms*. New York, NY: Free Press.

Stenger, V. J. (2007). *God: The failed hypothesis: How science shows that God does not exist*. New York, NY: Prometheus Books.

Watson, P. J. (1993). Apologetics and ethnocentrism: Psychology and religion within an ideological surround. *The International Journal for the Psychology of Religion, 3*, 1–20. doi:10.1207/s15327582ijpr0301_1

Watson, P. J. (2008). Faithful translation and postmodernism: Norms and linguistic relativity within a Christian ideological surround. *Edification, 2*, 5–18.

Watson, P. J., Sawyers, P., Morris, R. J., Carpenter, M., Jimenez, R. S., Jonas, K. A., & Robinson, D. L. (2003). Reanalysis within a Christian ideological surround: Relationships of intrinsic religious orientation with fundamentalism and right-wing authoritarianism. *Journal of Psychology and Theology, 31*, 315–328.

Watters, E. (2010). *Crazy like us: The globalization of the American psyche*. New York, NY: Free Press.

Westheafer, C. (2004). Wilber's "broad science": A cure for postmodernism? *Australian and New Zealand Journal of Family Therapy, 25*, 106–112.

Widiger, T. A. (2012). Classification and diagnosis: Historical development and contemporary issues. In J. E. Maddux & B. A. Winstead (Eds.), *Psychopathology: Foundations for a contemporary understanding* (3rd ed., pp. 101–120). New York, NY: Routledge.

Wilber, K. (1995). *Sex, ecology, spirituality: The spirit of evolution*. Boston, MA: Shambhala.

Wilber, K. (1998). *The marriage of sense and soul: Integrating science and religion*. New York, NY: Pimlico-Random House.

Wilber, K. (1999). Integral psychology. In *The collected works of Ken Wilber* (Vol. 4, pp. 423–717). Boston, MA: Shambhala.

Wilber, K. (2001). *A theory of everything*. Boston, MA: Shambhala.

Winstead, B. A., & Sanchez-Hucles, J. (2012). The role of gender, race, and class in psychopathology. In J. E. Maddux & B. A. Winstead (Eds.), *Psychopathology: Foundations for a contemporary understanding* (3rd ed., pp. 69–100). New York, NY: Routledge.

World Health Organization. (2003). *The ICD-10 classification of mental and behavioural disorders*. Geneva, Switzerland: Author.

Zinnbauer, B. J., & Barrett, J. J. (2008). Spirituality and treatment planning. In M. Leach & J. D. Aten (Eds.), *Spirituality and the therapeutic process: A guide for mental health professionals* (pp. 143–166). Washington, DC: American Psychological Association.

Zinnbauer, B. J., & Pargament, K. I. (2000). Working with the sacred: Four approaches to working with religious and spiritual issues in counseling. *Journal of Counseling and Development, 78*, 162–171. doi:10.1002/j.1556-6676.2000.tb02574.x

Zinnbauer, B. J., & Pargament, K. I. (2005). Spirituality and religiousness. In R. F. Paloutzian & C. L. Park (Eds.), *Handbook of the psychology of religion* (pp. 21–42). New York, NY: Guilford Press.

Zinnbauer, B. J., Pargament, K. I., Cole, B., Rye, M. S., Butter, E. M., Belavich, T. G., . . . Kadar, J. L. (1997). Religion and spirituality: Unfuzzying the fuzzy. *Journal for the Scientific Study of Religion, 36*, 549–564. doi:10.2307/1387689

Zinnbauer, B. J., Pargament, K. I., & Scott, A. B. (1999). The emerging meanings of religiousness and spirituality: Problems and prospects. *Journal of Personality, 67*, 889–919. doi:10.1111/1467-6494.00077

PART II

RELIGION AND SPIRITUALITY FROM THE PERSPECTIVE OF MAJOR ORIENTATIONS TO CHANGE

CHAPTER 5

ASSESSING SPIRITUALITY AND RELIGION IN THE CONTEXT OF COUNSELING AND PSYCHOTHERAPY

David R. Hodge

Assessment plays a critical role in psychological treatment. Successful therapeutic outcomes are typically predicated on developing a comprehensive understanding of clinically relevant information. In a manner analogous to the biological, psychological, and social dimensions of existence, spirituality and religion are linked to mental health and wellness (Koenig, King, & Carson, 2012). Accordingly, assessing spirituality and religion—as part of a larger biopsychosocial–spiritual evaluation—provides a more complete, holistic understanding of clients' existential realities.

Spiritual and religious assessment can be defined as the process of gathering, analyzing, and synthesizing information about these two interrelated constructs into a framework that provides the basis for practice decisions (Hodge, 2001a). The process is organized around understanding how spirituality and religion shape functioning (Shafranske, 2005). In other words, the assessment process aims not to determine the correctness of clients' beliefs, values, and practices, but rather how they influence functioning related to clients' problems. For instance, understanding how religion enhances psychological coping can provide the basis for subsequent practice strategies designed to ameliorate problems.

Although spirituality and religion are defined in different ways, it is helpful to view them as distinctive constructs that are both oriented toward the sacred (see Pargament, 2007; see also Volume 1, Chapter 1, in this handbook). This understanding facilitates the assessment process in two key ways. First, it respects clients' views of the sacred. Spirituality and religion are seen as natural, normal, and unique aspects of existence (Pargament, 2007). By conceptualizing these constructs in a manner that is congruent with clients' lived realities, practitioners implicitly communicate respect for clients themselves.

Second, it captures the diverse range of clients' experiences (Hill & Pargament, 2008). The sacred refers to people's conceptions of God and manifestations of the transcendent and extends to any aspect of life that takes on divine character by virtue of its association with divinity. Essentially any aspect of life can be considered sacred by virtue of being embedded in a transcendent narrative. For example, marriage, work, and recreational activities can all be considered spiritual activities as a result of being endowed with sacred meaning (Crisp, 2010; Mahoney, Pargament, & Hernandez, in press; Pargament & Mahoney, 2005).

For many people, their experience of the sacred is a fundamental component of their identity. These features of self-experience do not exist in isolation because other aspects of diversity (e.g., race, gender, class), shape and influence how the search for the sacred is expressed, as can be seen by those who attend services in predominantly White and Black Baptist churches. This can have important implications for addressing spirituality in practice. For example, spirituality and religion are often highly salient to many African Americans (Newport, 2006; Taylor, Chatters, & Jackson, 2007). Yet, when working with European American therapists, African American clients may be hesitant to discuss the topic because of culturally

DOI: 10.1037/14046-005
APA Handbook of Psychology, Religion, and Spirituality: Vol. 2. An Applied Psychology of Religion and Spirituality, K. I. Pargament (Editor-in-Chief)

animated mistrust (Sue & Sue, 2008; Whaley, 2001; Wintersteen, Mensinger, & Diamond, 2005). Thus, it is important to bear in mind the holistic, multidimensional nature of human existence when considering an assessment of spirituality and religion.

The assessment process is perhaps best operationalized using a constructivist theoretical framework. Constructivism posits that no one, including the therapist, has a completely objective understanding of the world (Raskin, 2002). Rather, humans, individually and corporately as social groups, tend to construct their realities. The search for the sacred is one avenue that people use to create constructions of reality.

These spiritually animated reality constructions include cognitive, affective, and volitional dimensions. People construct individual worldviews on the basis of multiple knowledge sources (Pargament, 2007). Cognitive considerations, emotional encounters, and volitional commitments—experienced individually and corporately—help individuals construct their own unique understandings of reality.

Assessment focuses on understanding these sacred reality constructions or worldviews as they intersect service provision. In keeping with constructivist theory, the goal is not to determine the accuracy of clients' worldviews. Rather, exploration is focused on the *viability*, as opposed to the *validity*, of clients' worldviews.

This chapter presents a two-stage assessment model consisting of a brief preliminary assessment that may be followed, if necessary, by a more extensive comprehensive assessment. Guidelines are presented to help practitioners decide whether the comprehensive assessment is warranted. The strengths and limitations of four comprehensive assessment approaches are presented to assist practitioners in selecting a reliable and valid approach. The chapter concludes by (a) highlighting two key precepts to facilitate a successful assessment and (b) discussing the concept of an implicit spiritual assessment for use with clients for whom traditional spiritual and religious language does not resonate. Before discussing the two-stage assessment model, I review rationales that underscore the importance of conducting a spiritual and religious assessment.

RATIONALES FOR CONDUCTING A SPIRITUAL AND RELIGIOUS ASSESSMENT

The following six aspects of clinical practice provide a basis for conducting an assessment of spirituality and religion in practice: professional ethics, client autonomy, knowledge of clients' worldviews, the identification of spiritual and religious strengths, the identification of problems related to spirituality and religion, and agency and accrediting requirements. Rationales derived from these areas of practice often overlap and reinforce one another.

Ethics

Although professional ethics codes are designed for many purposes, a primary function is to guide practitioners' conduct (Freeman, 2000; Hathaway & Ripley, 2009; see also Chapter 3 in this volume). Take, for instance, the American Psychological Association's (APA'S) *Ethical Principles of Psychologists and Code of Conduct* (the Ethics Code; APA, 2002). The general principles set forth aspirational goals and the ethical standards delineate specific rules that, together, serve to guide conduct in work-related settings.

The Ethics Code (APA, 2002) directly mentions religion in four locations. Perhaps the most salient of these occurs in Principle E. After noting the importance of respecting people's dignity, worth, and self-determination, the Ethics Code states that "psychologists are aware of and respect cultural, individual, and role differences, including those based on . . . religion" (APA, 2002) and consider religious factors when working with members of religious groups. The Code goes on to state that psychologists try to eliminate religious biases that affect their work, a sentiment that appears in later standards that prohibit discriminatory, harassing, or demeaning behaviors based on religion (3.01, 3.03). Religion is also mentioned as an area in which psychologists must take steps to ensure the competency of the services they provide (2.01b). These principles were largely reiterated in the APA Council of Representatives' (2007) resolution on spirituality and religion.

The APA's ethical principles regarding religion are echoed in the ethics codes of allied professions

(G. Miller, 2003). Similar standards are articulated in the American Association of Marriage and Family Therapy's Code of Ethics, the American Counseling Association's Code of Ethics and Standards of Practice, the American Psychiatric Association's Principles of Medical Ethics with Annotations Especially Applicable to Psychiatry, and the National Association of Social Workers' Code of Ethics. This suggests that ethical guidelines about religion are not relegated to a single profession but that some type of broad ethical consensus exists concerning how practitioners should approach religion in clinical settings.

Clinicians who operationalize the APA Ethics Code's (2002) injunctions regarding religion should conduct an assessment of spirituality and religion as part of routine practice (Hodge, 2004b). Such an assessment provides the information necessary to help ensure ethical compliance (Plante, 2009). For instance, to consider religious factors in work with clients, it is necessary to obtain some information about those factors. Similarly, to avoid inadvertently discriminating or demeaning religious clients, it is frequently necessary to have some understanding of clients' spiritual and religious narratives (Richards & Bergin, 2000; Van Hook, Hugen, & Aguilar, 2001). In short, conducting a spiritual and religious assessment plays a foundational role in assisting practitioners conform to professional ethics.

Client Autonomy

Exhibiting respect for client self-determination is a central practice tenet. The importance of client preference is underscored in APA's 2006 policy (APA Presidential Task Force on Evidence-Based Practice, 2006), which set evidence-based practice as the standard for professional practice as a psychologist. This requires that psychologists consider client preferences, including those based on worldviews and values (Hodge, 2011). Effective therapy is predicated on a noncoercive therapeutic atmosphere in which clients' desires are valued (Richards & Bergin, 2005).

Many people want to have their spiritual and religious values integrated into the therapeutic dialogue. According to Gallup data reported by Bart (1998), 81% of the public would prefer to have their spiritual values and beliefs integrated into the counseling process. Similar views have emerged in studies of various client populations (Arnold, Avants, Margolin, & Marcotte, 2002; Larimore, Parker, & Crowther, 2002; Mathai & North, 2003; Rose, Westefeld, & Ansley, 2001, 2008; Solhkhah, Galanter, Dermatis, Daly, & Bunt, 2008). In these studies, a majority of clients typically report interest in incorporating their spiritual and religious values into therapy. For instance, in one therapeutic community devoted to helping clients overcome alcoholism and other types of chemical dependency, the authors found that 84% of all clients surveyed ($N = 322$) wanted more emphasis on spirituality in treatment (Dermatis, Guschwan, Galanter, & Bunt, 2004).

Practitioners have an ethical obligation to respond to clients' desires to integrate their spiritual and religious values into therapy (APA, 2002; APA Presidential Task Force on Evidence-Based Practice, 2006). A spiritual and religious assessment provides a forum for identifying clinically relevant beliefs and practices. In other words, it demonstrates responsiveness to clients' desire to integrate spirituality and religion into therapy (Leach, Aten, Wade, & Hernandez, 2009).

Knowledge of Clients' Worldviews

It is increasingly recognized that successful therapy is contingent on practitioners' knowledge of clients' cultural worldviews (Sue & Sue, 2008). Understanding how clients experience reality assists in building therapeutic rapport, using culturally sensitive interventions that are more likely to be adopted, and avoiding interactions that place the therapeutic relationship at risk. Interactions that are congruent with clients' worldviews can enhance client buy-in and facilitate positive outcomes (Cross, 2002; Gone, 2007).

For many people, religion provides an interpretive framework for understanding reality that informs adherents of who they are and how they should live (Pargament, 2007). These religious worldviews can affect attitudes in many areas of potential significance to practitioners, including views about animals, burial practices, child care, communication styles, coping practices, death, diet, finances, grieving, marital relations, medical care, military participation, recreation, and schooling (Hodge, 2004b). Put differently, for many individuals, the search for the sacred is expressed in distinct religious cultures (Koenig, 1998; Richards & Bergin, 2000; Van Hook et al., 2001). For instance, evangelical Christians, Latter Day Saints, and traditional Catholics have all developed subcultures in keeping with their unique value systems. These value systems often differ from those affirmed in the wider secular culture as well as those affirmed by other religious groups, both within and outside of Christianity (Hodge, 2009).

The United States is perhaps the most religiously diverse nation in the world (Eck, 2001). Over the course of the past few decades, the nation's existing religious traditions have been supplemented with a growing number of Asian Muslims, Hispanic Catholics, Indian Hindus, Korean Presbyterians, Latino Pentecostals, Punjabi Sikhs, and Soviet Jews (Melton, 2009; T. W. Smith, 2002). Although religion is important to people across all populations, it is often particularly important among traditionally disadvantaged populations, including women, racial and ethnic minorities, the elderly, and people who are poor (Newport, 2006; Taylor et al., 2007).

A spiritual and religious assessment provides a window into these culturally unique worldviews (Richards & Bergin, 2005). Learning how clients construct their world helps practitioners develop an empathetic understanding of clients' beliefs and values (Frame, 2003). Administering a spiritual and religious assessment creates a space to gather the information necessary for building rapport and designing strategies that clients may be more inclined to implement. By suggesting interventions that are congruent with, and even resonate with, clients' spiritual worldviews, clients' sense of ownership is enhanced, increasing the likelihood that clients will implement and follow through with treatment recommendations and processes (Sue & Sue, 2008; Wolf, 1978). This dynamic may be even more likely to occur if interventions are based on clients' spiritual and religious strengths.

Identifying Spiritual and Religious Strengths

Identifying clients' assets, resources, and strengths is an important part of the assessment process (Saleebey, 2009; E. J. Smith, 2006). Ascertaining "what works" is often fundamental to promoting wellness (Lopez & Snyder, 2003). Areas of strength can be built on to facilitate the resources that ameliorate problems.

Spirituality and religion are often salient strengths in clients' lives. A relatively large and growing body of research has linked spirituality and religion with a wide variety of positive health outcomes (Ano & Vasconcelles, 2005; Koenig, McCullough, & Larson, 2001; Koenig et al., 2012; Pargament & Abu-Raiya, 2007; see also Volume 1, Chapter 19, this handbook). In addition, a number of studies have examined the outcomes of interventions that incorporate clients' spiritual and religious values into therapy (e.g., cognitive–behavioral therapy [CBT] that has been modified to incorporate clients' spiritual beliefs and practices). Reviews of this literature indicate that psychospiritual interventions can effectively address problems (Hodge, 2006a; Hook et al., 2010; Kaplar, Wachholtz, & O'Brien, 2004; T. B. Smith, Bartz, & Richards, 2007; see also Chapters 8 and 34 in this volume).

The importance of spiritual and religious assets may become more pronounced during times of stress or difficulty, which may help explain why these variables tend to play a more significant role among disenfranchised populations for which limited sources of support are available. Research suggests that spiritual and religious coping resources are more salient in the face of difficult situations (Pargament, 1997; Pargament, 2007; see also Volume 1, Chapter 19, this handbook). This is important because practitioners typically encounter people when they are wrestling with problems.

A spiritual and religious assessment provides a mechanism for identifying important resources that otherwise may lie dormant. Clients often assume therapists are secular and, consequently, may be inclined to avoid discussing spirituality and religion (Lewis, 2001; Lyles, 1992; Richards & Bergin, 2000). A spiritual assessment helps legitimate the topic by implicitly sending the message that spirituality is an important and valued resource that can be used to address problems.

Identifying Problems Related to Spirituality and Religion

Spiritual and religious dimensions are typically intertwined with other dimensions of life, including life challenges. For example, problems can impair salutary religious functioning (Hathaway, Scott, & Garver, 2004). The onset of a problem (e.g., depression) might interfere with client's personal spiritual practices or participation in a religious community that has traditionally served as a source of support.

Alternatively, spirituality and religion may contribute to difficulties or be problems in and of themselves. Although spirituality and religion are typically strengths, this is not universally the case (Koenig et al., 2001; Chapter 4 in this volume). Congregations can be sources of conflict and tension instead of support and assistance (Exline & Rose, 2005). Coping styles can be detrimental rather than helpful (Pargament, 2007). Spirituality and religion can be sources of struggle and strain (see Volume 1, Chapter 25, this handbook). To assist clients, it is necessary to understand the relationship between spirituality and religion and clients' presenting challenges. A spiritual and religious assessment can help practitioners unravel the complex interplay between these variables (Richards & Bergin, 2005).

Agency and Accrediting Requirements

In keeping with the importance of spirituality and religion in treatment (Canda & Furman, 2010; Koenig et al., 2001; W. R. Miller & Thoresen, 2003), some agencies and accrediting bodies have instituted policies requiring the administration of an assessment to optimize client care. Thus, in some work settings, practitioners may be required to conduct a spiritual and religious assessment as a matter of organizational policy.

Perhaps the most notable example involves formal requirements of the Joint Commission, formerly known as the Joint Commission on Accreditation of Healthcare Organizations (Hodge, 2006b). The Joint Commission is the largest health care accrediting body in the United States, accrediting most of the nation's hospitals as well as thousands of other health care organizations (Koenig, 2007). Since approximately the turn of the century, the Joint Commission has required a spiritual and religious assessment in hospitals, agencies providing addiction treatment, and other settings where mental health services are delivered. In keeping with widespread practice, the Joint Commission recommends the use of a two-stage assessment process (Hodge, 2006b).

TWO-STAGE ASSESSMENT PROCESS

It is helpful to conceptualize a spiritual and religious assessment as a process consisting of two stages: a brief preliminary assessment and an extensive comprehensive assessment (Shafranske, 2005). The purpose of the preliminary assessment is to determine the clinical relevance of spirituality and religion and to ascertain whether a comprehensive assessment is needed.

According to national survey data, nearly all Americans have reported some level of spiritual or religious belief or behavior. Approximately 90% of Americans believe in God, 85% have reported a denominational preference, 80% pray daily, and more than 30% have attended a religious service at least weekly (Davis, Smith, & Marsden, 2006). Approximately 60% have reported that religion is "very important" in their lives and an additional 26% have reported that it is "fairly important" (Newport, 2006). The prevalence of religious belief, in tandem with the salience attributed to religion, underscores the importance of conducting an assessment.

Concurrently, it should be noted that spirituality and religion may play limited or marginal roles in clients' lives or be peripheral to presenting problems. In such instances, a brief assessment may be all that is required. Indeed, as soon as it becomes clear that spirituality and religion are unrelated to the presenting problem, practitioners should consider redirecting their attention toward more clinically relevant content (Plante, 2009). The following section discusses one method of conducting a preliminary assessment that may assist practitioners in determining the clinical relevance of spirituality and religion and, correspondingly, whether a comprehensive assessment is required.

Preliminary Assessment

Time is limited during the initial intake session to determine psychological and psychiatric functioning and treatment goals. Many issues must be explored during this timeframe, including the nature of the presenting problem; mental, psychological, and social histories; risk factors; and treatment goals (Pargament & Krumrei, 2009). Although it is important not to overlook spirituality and religion during this process, they are just two variables that should be explored during the initial assessment (Leach et al., 2009).

A number of brief question sets have been provided to assist practitioners in conducting a preliminary spiritual assessment (Hodge, 2004a; Koenig & Pritchett, 1998; Pargament & Krumrei, 2009; Plante, 2009; Richards & Bergin, 2005; Shafranske, 2005). Table 5.1 presents one set of questions that practitioners may find useful. The table depicts four questions along with the general aim the question is designed to address. It is important to tailor the language to fit the client's value system to operationalize the aim in a culturally appropriate manner.

The first question of the preliminary assessment determines significance: "I was wondering how important spirituality or religion is to you?" This item may provide information on the importance or relevance of spirituality and religion in the client's life. Tentative language is often helpful in creating a neutral environment that allows clients the freedom to respond in diverse ways. To flesh out the degree of importance, prompts and follow-up questions may be used (Shafranske, 2005).

The second question explores the larger religious context: "Do you happen to attend a church or some other type of spiritual or religious community?" Initially, it is often helpful to use common terms to aid understanding (e.g., church) followed with a broad term or terms to ensure as much inclusivity as possible. Naturally, if the first question revealed that the client was affiliated with a certain religion (e.g., Islam), the second question would employ the culturally appropriate terminology (mosque). Affiliation with a specific religion, in tandem with regular participation, raises the possibility that clients may see the world through a distinct cultural lens (Koenig, 1998; Richards & Bergin, 2000; Van Hook et al., 2001). It is also important to discern if clients have rejected a particular faith tradition or are experiencing spiritual struggles related to their faith community (Pargament & Krumrei, 2009; see also Volume 1, Chapters 25 and 40, this handbook).

The third question investigates clients' strengths: "Are there certain spiritual or religious beliefs and practices that you find particularly helpful in dealing with difficulties?" This item provides insight into the use of spirituality and religion as a means to cope with problems. Clients can become overwhelmed by their present challenges and overlook pertinent resources (Saleebey, 2009). If clients have used spiritual and religious assets previously to help them deal with problems, practitioners may be able to help clients leverage strategies used in the past to address present problems.

The final item examines how spirituality and religion may be related to the presenting problem: "I was also wondering if your present problem has affected you spiritually or religiously?" This query provides insight into clients' understanding of the relationship between their presenting problem and their expression of spirituality and religion. Practitioners should be alert for signs of impaired religious functioning (Hathaway et al., 2004), spiritual and religious struggles, and other clinically relevant issues. For example, clients may feel abandoned by

TABLE 5.1

Questions for Conducting a Preliminary Spiritual and Religious Assessment

General aim	Question to operationalize aim
1. Importance	I was wondering how important spirituality or religion is to you?
2. Affiliation	Do you happen to attend a church or some other type of spiritual or religious community?
3. Resources	Are there certain spiritual or religious beliefs and practices that you find particularly helpful in dealing with difficulties?
4. Relationship to problem	I was also wondering if your present problem has affected you spiritually or religiously?

Note. Questions adapted from Hodge (2004a), Pargament and Krumrei (2009), Plante (2009), and Shafranske (2005).

God and may be wrestling with spiritual doubts, a status that may contribute to clients' psychological difficulties (Exline, Park, Smyth, & Carey, 2011; Pargament, 2007; see also Volume 1, Chapter 25, this handbook).

These questions may be asked together in a loose sequential manner (Richards & Bergin, 2005; Plante, 2009). Alternatively, they may be integrated into other domains covered during the intake process. For example, the first two questions on importance and affiliation might be integrated into other content areas examining clients' roles and identities (e.g., occupation, family status). The third question on assets could be woven into content areas exploring clients' strengths, and the fourth question on problems might be incorporated into content exploring the impact of the presenting problem on other psychological, social, and physical systems (Pargament & Krumrei, 2009; Saleebey, 2009; E. J. Smith, 2006).

Regardless of their placement in the intake assessment, the overall aim of these questions is to determine whether a comprehensive assessment is warranted (Shafranske, 2005). As noted, the preliminary assessment may suggest that spirituality and religion are not clinically relevant. Conversely, the preliminary assessment may imply that spirituality and religion are related to service provision; in which case, a comprehensive assessment would be necessary. The following principles may be helpful in determining whether to proceed with a comprehensive assessment.

Guidelines for Moving to a Comprehensive Assessment

At least four factors may bear on the decision to move from a preliminary to a comprehensive assessment (Hodge, 2006b). These four guidelines are often held in tension with, and inform, one another. In brief, these four principles are related to clients' openness, practitioners' level of cultural competence with respect to spirituality and religion, the salience clients attribute to spirituality and religion, and the degree to which clients' spiritual and religious values intersect service provision.

Client openness. It is important to ascertain clients' openness to the idea of moving to a comprehensive assessment. Although research indicates that many, if not most, clients want to integrate their spiritual and religious values into therapy, these same studies also reveal that some clients believe discussing spirituality and religion in clinical settings is inappropriate (Arnold et al., 2002; Dermatis et al., 2004; Larimore et al., 2002; Mathai & North, 2003; Rose et al., 2001, 2008; Solhkhah et al., 2008). Furthermore, because of the intensely personal nature of spirituality and religion, other clients may be hesitant to trust practitioners with such a personal dimension of their being (Richards & Bergin, 2000).

Although many clients may be willing to answer the relatively few questions involved in a preliminary assessment, informed consent should be obtained again before proceeding with a comprehensive assessment. Indeed, it is perhaps best to view informed consent as an ongoing process in which practitioners continuously monitor clients' responses to ensure that they remain fully supportive of the continuing dialogue. Practitioners should be alert throughout the assessment process to verbal and nonverbal cues so that clients remain comfortable with the therapeutic conversation. Clients may, for example, initially agree to a comprehensive assessment but later reconsider their consent if practitioners exhibit culturally insensitive behaviors. Conversely, clients may be unwilling to discuss these topics until they have determined their therapist is trustworthy. Thus, therapists should remain open to the possibility of a comprehensive assessment throughout the therapy process even if the initial assessment suggests clients are uninterested in spirituality and religion.

Cultural competence. A second factor to consider is practitioners' level of cultural competence with the client's religious culture and its associated value system (Yarhouse & VanOrman, 1999). Given the difference in worldviews between many practitioners and religious clients, it is important to consider one's ability to work with a culturally different worldview in an ethical and professional manner (Shafranske, 2001; Sheridan, 2009). Interactions that are incongruent with clients' worldviews can damage the therapeutic relationship and, in some instances, even cause harm to clients (Cross, 2002; Gone, 2007).

For instance, asking Native American clients about certain religious rituals or ceremonies is culturally inappropriate and can even cause further negative effect (Hodge & Limb, 2010a; see also Volume 1, Chapter 31, this handbook). In some tribal cultures, religious rituals are understood to be instrumental to health and wellness; but they can be discussed only with other tribal members. Inquiring about such rituals, even in the context of a therapeutic relationship, is often experienced as stressful by clients and can result in clients terminating therapy.

Practitioners should consider their ability to work with the client in a culturally competent manner in light of the information obtained in the preliminary assessment. In contexts in which sufficient levels of competency do not exist, consultation or referral should be considered (APA, 2002). In other contexts, strategies might be implemented to help counter marginal levels of competency. For instance, practitioners might acknowledge that spiritual beliefs and practices are personal, explain why it is helpful to gather spiritual and religious information, indicate how the information will be used, proactively ask forgiveness for asking questions that might inadvertently be offensive, and clarify that clients are free to refuse to answer any or all questions (Hodge & Limb, 2010a).

To follow up on the example regarding Native American ceremonies, practitioners might recognize the sensitive nature of the topic, ask for permission to address it, and create an environment that allows clients to share according to their comfort level (e.g., "While you may not be able to share the details of a ceremony, are there some ceremonies that help you cope with difficulties?"). In keeping with this goal, another option is to use open-ended, implicit questions that do not explicitly address potentially private matters or call for a direct response, but leave the option of how to respond with the client. A different approach is to ask clients to visualize potentially health-enhancing ceremonies. Clients identify ceremonies in their mind but do not verbalize them. Once identified, treatment plans can be developed that incorporate the (unspecified) practices (Hodge & Limb, 2010a). For example, if the client identified a certain ceremony as salutary, the therapist and client might brainstorm about ways in which the client might participate (e.g., arranging for the use of a private room so that elders can perform the ceremony in secrecy, a trip back to tribal homelands).

Spiritual and religious salience. The importance attributed to spirituality and religion is also a crucial factor (Shafranske, 2005). If clients are highly committed, then the potential for worldview conflicts is likely accentuated. Devout Muslims, for instance, may be more uncomfortable receiving services—particularly those that address sexual or other intimate issues—from practitioners of the opposite gender than less committed adherents of Islam (J. I. Smith, 1999). Similarly, relatively committed clients may be disproportionately likely to draw on their spiritual and religious beliefs and practices to help them deal with challenges (Azhar & Varma, 2000; D'Souza & Rodrigo, 2004; Pargament, 2002).

During the preliminary assessment process, it is helpful to look for concrete indicators of spiritual and religious salience. For example, one possible indicator is the degree to which clients practice the norms of their faith tradition. Catholics who attend mass weekly, Hindus who perform morning *puja* each day, and Muslims who practice the "five pillars" are likely more spiritually committed than their less engaged peers. Another possibility is to use a short, culturally appropriate, quantitative instrument to assess clients' degree of religious motivation (Gorsuch & McPherson, 1989) or commitment (Worthington et al., 2003). Regardless of the method used, if the initial assessment suggests that spirituality functions as an organizing principle in the client's life, a more extensive assessment is likely appropriate.

A couple of caveats should be mentioned. Spiritual and religious issues may be salient among clients who are uninvolved or disengaged. These clients may be experiencing spiritual struggles that are central to their psychological problems (Exline et al., 2011). Conversely, for some devout clients, spirituality and religion may not be related to their problems and, in some cases, solutions. The degree to which spirituality and religion are utilized to help solve problems within the context of psychotherapy also will be affected by practitioners' theoretical orientation. For example, therapists who adhere to solution-focused, strengths-based, or brief therapeutic modalities typically will benefit from exploring how the spiritual and religious assets of devout clients can be operationalized to ameliorate problems. Similarly, within the context of CBT, a comprehensive assessment can help practitioners identify salient spiritual precepts and practices that can be incorporated into CBT protocols (Hodge & Nadir, 2008; Nielsen, 2004).

Intersection of spiritual and religious values with service provision. The final factor that should be considered is the degree to which the norms of the client's religious tradition intersect with service provision (Hathaway & Ripley, 2009). In many instances, clients' spiritual and religious values relate directly to the presenting problem. The *Diagnostic and Statistical Manual of Mental Disorders* (American Psychiatric Association, 2000) acknowledges that symptoms of psychopathology are often culturally contingent. Beliefs, experiences, and practices that are normative in religious cultures, when seen from the vantage point of Western secular culture, can be understood as indicators of pathology.

For instance, in many tribal cultures, hearing the Creator's voice is a normative experience, as opposed to an indicator of mental illness. Likewise, the Hindu emphasis on selflessness, detachment, and dharma may result in some Hindu clients appearing to have an "underdeveloped ego" from a psychodynamic perspective (Roland, 1997). During the initial assessment, practitioners should be alert to various indicators that might suggest a connection between clients' spiritual and religious values and their presenting problems. In such cases, a comprehensive assessment may be necessary to determine whether clients' values (e.g., hearing the voice of the Creator) represent a manifestation of mental illness or are conventional expressions of faith. When these values are related to clients' problems, then an extensive spiritual and religious assessment may be appropriate. In the next section, various options for conducting such assessments are presented.

COMPREHENSIVE ASSESSMENT TOOLS

The goals of a comprehensive spiritual and religious assessment are to obtain a more detailed understanding of (a) clients' spiritual and religious beliefs, practices, and experiences and (b) how these variables are related to clients' problems and solutions (Pargament & Krumrei, 2009). This includes determining (a) how normative clients' spiritual and religious lives are in comparison to their religious reference group, (b) the degree to which psychological problems are impairing clients' spiritual and religious functioning, and (c) exploring how clients' spiritual and religious beliefs and practices function as resources to ameliorate problems or constitute constraints to treatment (Hathaway & Ripley, 2009).

Toward these ends, a number of unique comprehensive spiritual and religious assessment approaches or tools have been developed. Both clients and practitioners have a variety of needs and interests. The amount of time available for assessment, the nature of the presenting problem, the client's communication style and cultural background, and similar factors vary from case to case. Ideally, therapists should select the approach that provides the best fit for each clinical setting.

In this section, four conceptually distinct comprehensive assessment tools are discussed. Each tool is reviewed conceptually, an example is provided to operationalize the concept, and each tool's respective strengths and limitations are discussed. Understanding the respective strengths and limitations of each assessment tool helps practitioners select the most appropriate approach. Developing an assessment toolbox allows practitioners to provide more client-centered, clinically effective services in the same way that developing a degree of familiarity with various quantitative instruments equips practitioners to select the instrument that best addresses a given client's therapeutic needs. The four assessment tools are spiritual and religious histories—a completely verbally based approach—and three diagrammatic approaches: spiritual and religious lifemaps, genograms, and eco-maps.

Spiritual and Religious Histories

Perhaps the most widely used method of conducting a comprehensive assessment is a spiritual and religious history. This method is analogous to conducting a family history. A series of open-ended questions are commonly used to flesh out clients' spiritual and religious stories in the course of a therapeutic conversation.

A number of question sets have been proposed to assist practitioners in the process of unpacking clients' spiritual and religious narratives (Canda & Furman, 2010; Fitchett, 1993; Hodge, 2001a; Pargament, 2007; Pargament & Krumrei, 2009). Exhibit 5.1 features one approach drawn from the work of Pargament. As is the general case with all qualitative approaches, the questions are not meant to be asked in a rote, sequential word-for-word manner. Rather, the questions should be adapted to fit the client's cultural worldview and integrated into the general flow of the discussion in a natural, conversational manner.

As can be seen in Exhibit 5.1, a number of question sets are used to guide the conversation (Pargament & Krumrei, 2009). In broad relief, these questions provide practitioners with some possible options to help clients tell their spiritual stories, typically moving from childhood through to the present and into the future. The first primary set,

Exhibit 5.1
Questions for Conducting a Spiritual and Religious History

Past spirituality

Describe the spiritual/religious tradition you grew up in. How did your family express its spirituality?
When did you first personally discover or learn about the sacred?
How did you conceptualize spirituality when you were younger?
How did you express your spirituality?
What sort of spiritual experiences stood out for you when you were growing up?
What spiritual milestones have you experienced during your journey?

Present spirituality

Conceptualizations of the sacred

What do you hold sacred in your life?
How has your understanding or experience of the sacred changed since you were a child?
How have your spiritual beliefs and practices changed since you were a child?
Why are you involved in spirituality?
What do you feel God wants from you?
What do you imagine God feels when he sees you going through this difficult time?
Have there been times where you felt the sacred was absent in your life?
Do you ever experience a different side of the sacred than you are experiencing now? What is that like?
Do you ever have mixed thoughts and feelings about the sacred? What are they like?

Expression and experience of spirituality

How would you describe your current spiritual orientation?
How do you experience the sacred in your life?
What has helped nurture your spirituality?
What has damaged or hindered your spirituality?
When/where do you feel most connected to the sacred?
When/where do you feel the sacred is not present?
What spiritual beliefs do you find especially meaningful?
What spiritual rituals or practices are particularly important to you?
What aspects of your spirituality are particularly uplifting?
When/where do you feel closest to God?
How have your present challenges affected your relationship with God?

Spiritual efficacy
How has your spirituality changed your life for the better?
How has your spirituality changed your life for the worse?
To what degree has your spirituality been a source of strength? Pleasure? Meaning? Joy? Intimacy? Connectedness to others? Closeness with God? Hope for the future? Confidence in yourself? Compassion for others?
To what degree has your spirituality been a source of pain? Frustration? Guilt? Anger? Confusion and doubt? Anxiety? Fear? Feelings of personal insignificance? Feelings of alienation from others?
In what ways has your spirituality helped you understand or cope with your problems?
In what ways has your spirituality hindered your ability to understand or cope with problems?

Spiritual environment
Who supports you spiritually? How so?
Who does not support you spiritually? How so?
In what ways has your religious community been a source of assistance and encouragement?
In what ways has your religious community been a source of difficulties and problems?

Future spirituality
How do you see yourself changing spiritually in the future?
In what ways do you want to grow spiritually?
How does your spirituality relate to your goals in life?
How does your relationship with God affect your future life plans?

Note. Questions adapted from Hodge (2003), Pargament (2007), and Pargament and Krumrei (2009).

past spirituality, is designed to explore the role spirituality played in clients' past, and perhaps particularly, their family of origin. Understanding how spirituality functioned in the past provides the context for understanding how the sacred functions in clients' current existential situation.

The second primary set, *present spirituality*, deals with clients' present experience of the sacred and includes three secondary question sets. The first, *expressions and experiences of spirituality*, examines current understandings of spirituality and how those understandings may have changed and matured since childhood. The second set, *spiritual efficacy*, examines the functionality of spirituality. These questions reflect the assumption that spirituality can, at least in some cases, have both beneficial and detrimental effects. The final set of questions, *spiritual environment*, examines the role that people and communities play in fostering or hindering clients' spirituality. Clients typically express their spirituality in community settings with others who hold similar views of the sacred. These religious communities can be traditional (e.g., the Catholic Church) or nontraditional (the syncretistic spirituality or new age movement). Although these communities are typically perceived to be assets or strengths, in some cases they can be a source of difficulties.

The third primary question set, *future spirituality*, explores the role that spirituality plays in future plans. Future aspirations are also a part of clients' sacred narratives. In the same way that past and present beliefs can shape current beliefs and practices, clients' views regarding their future can also shape present functioning. Accordingly, an exploration of future plans, goals, dreams, and expectations can provide important therapeutic insights.

It is important to emphasize that there is no single correct format for asking these questions in clinical settings (Pargament, 2007). Assessment is a complex, multilevel process. Spirituality and religion are intertwined with the biological, psychological, and social dimensions of existence. Spirituality and religion, separately or in some combination with these dimensions, may play a role in the development, maintenance, and solution of psychological difficulties.

Practitioners should be alert to the many ways in which spirituality and religion can be related to problems and solutions. Specifically, these constructs can be (a) related to the problem but not related to the solution, (b) not related to the problem but related to the solution, (c) not related to the problem or the solution, or (d) related to both the problem and the solution. Because these various relationships can surface at essentially any time, practitioners should be ready to explore this nexus throughout the course of therapy, a topic that will be covered in more depth in the section on conducting an implicit spiritual assessment later in this chapter.

Pargament (2007) illustrated the importance of being ready to integrate assessment questions into the therapeutic conversation with the story of Agnes, a 50-year-old European American woman recently released from an inpatient psychiatric unit where she had voluntarily committed herself after considering committing suicide or murdering her husband. During the course of one session, Agnes commented that she felt "soulless." Following up on this reference to the sacred led to an illuminating conversation about how Agnes had lost her soul. Over the course of her married life, she had sacrificed all she held sacred—her art, her cello, her musical and career aspirations—for her husband who, in turn, had been unsupportive of Agnes financially, emotionally, and spiritually. Agnes had responded by coming uncomfortably close to murdering her husband, the idol who had accepted her sacrifice but had failed to care for her in return. She had also come close to killing herself to end the emptiness she felt. Although the sacred was related to the problem, it was also part of the solution as Agnes reconnected with manifestations of the sacred that nourished her soul. As Agnes's impromptu comment implied, she was essentially engaged in a spiritual struggle for her soul, with which she had lost contact as a result of sacrificing everything that was sacred to her. With the help of her therapist, she was able to identify the false gods and work toward developing a more fulfilling spirituality characterized by creativity and beauty. Facilitating Agnes's spiritual transformation toward a more personally authentic spirituality that nurtured her soul became a central focus of therapy.

Strengths and Limitations

The most prominent strength of spiritual and religious histories may be their appeal to more verbally oriented people who are comfortable with the direct exploration of spirituality and religion. Similarly, it may represent a good fit for clients from cultures that value oral storytelling (Hodge & Limb, 2010b). In addition, the relatively nonstructured, nonlinear format allows clients to relate their stories in a straightforward manner, without having to adapt their narratives to fit a particular diagrammatic format. For example, whereas spiritual and religious genograms require clients to circumscribe their stories to fit the parameters of a generational chart, spiritual and religious histories allow clients to express themselves in a manner that is unique to their own experience. Spiritual and religious histories are easy to conduct, the assessment method is relatively easy to communicate to clients, the verbal format is conducive to building a therapeutic alliance, and the questions used to conduct spiritual and religious histories can readily be integrated into a broader assessment of clients' psychosocial functioning.

In terms of limitations, it is important to note that not all clients are verbally oriented or comfortable with the direct exploration of their spiritual and religious narratives. The use of spiritual and religious histories may be contraindicated with individuals who are more reserved, introverted, or uncomfortable sharing personal information in a face-to-face setting, perhaps because of cultural norms that favor indirect communication patterns (Hodge, 2005a). Some of these individuals may prefer the pictorial assessment approaches discussed in the section Spiritual and Religious Lifemaps. Individuals who are nervous about sharing what is often a highly sensitive personal topic may desire a diagrammatic approach that deflects attention from themselves onto an inanimate object. Some clients prefer having a specific framework around which to organize their thoughts, such as a spiritual and religious eco-map. Similarly, the process of conceptualizing and pictorially depicting one's spiritual and religious journey may help to identify assets, which can then be discussed and marshaled to address problems. Another limitation is the time spent exploring portions of the client's spiritual history that may have limited utility in terms of addressing the client's presenting problem. In addition, more artistic clients may desire an assessment approach—such as spiritual and religious lifemaps—that allows for a more creative expression of their narratives. Regardless of the approach adopted to conduct a comprehensive assessment, however, the purpose of the assessment is not to collect spiritual information for its own sake, but rather to collect information that is relevant to helping clients ameliorate problems.

Spiritual and Religious Lifemaps

Spiritual and religious lifemaps represent a diagrammatic alternative to verbally based histories (Hodge, 2005d). More specifically, lifemaps are a pictorial delineation of a client's spiritual and religious journey. In a manner analogous to a spiritual autobiography, lifemaps represent an illustrated account of the client's relationship with God or the sacred over time (Faiver, Ingersoll, O'Brien, & McNally, 2001; Wiggins, 2009). Much like road maps, lifemaps tell us where we have come from, where we are now, and where we are going.

At its most basic level, drawing instruments are used to sketch various spiritually and religious significant life events on a large sheet of paper. Such events are depicted on a path, a roadway, or a single line that represents clients' sojourn. Typically, the path proceeds chronologically, from birth to the present. Frequently, the path continues on to death and the client's transition to the afterlife. Hand-drawn symbols, cutout pictures, and other media can be used to mark key events along the journey. In keeping with the tenets of many faith traditions, which conceive material existence to be an extension of the sacred, it is common to depict important "secular" events on the lifemap (e.g., marriage, death, loss of a job). Hills, bumps and potholes, rain, clouds, and lightning are some of the ways to portray difficult life situations. To fully operationalize the potential of the method, it is important to ask clients to incorporate the various trials they have faced into their lifemaps along with the spiritual and religious resources they have used to overcome those trials. Delineating successful coping strategies clients have used in the past—strategies that are often overlooked because of the overwhelming nature of existing problems—frequently suggests options for overcoming present struggles.

Figure 5.1 provides an example of a lifemap. It features the journey of a 42-year-old African American male, Tyrone, who was recently diagnosed with terminal cancer and given 6 months to live. He sought counseling to address existential concerns about the shortness and meaninglessness of his life. The map depicts his idyllic childhood, his parents' divorce at 18 and resulting personal confusion, conversion and rededication, loss of employment, struggles and strengths, and his current shock and despair related to his cancer diagnosis. His therapist used the lifemap to help Tyrone reflect on his life, his pit and peak experiences, the lessons he had learned, and the people who had assisted him. Tyrone began to see that his life had meaning and purpose, and he identified key people that would support him through his present illness. The process of creating the lifemap helped Tyrone clarify the goals he still wanted to accomplish, such as mentoring some young boys in church who were growing up in single-parent homes. In addition, viewing his life in a broader spiritual context resulted in Tyrone adding another page to his lifemap in which his journey ended in heaven, rather than cancer and death. This exercise, supplemented by scriptural passages he identified with his therapist, helped instill a sense of hope for the future as his illness progressed.

Strengths and Limitations

As Tyrone's example suggests, spiritual and religious lifemaps are often useful when clients are dealing with existential concerns (Bushfield, 2009). Lifemaps also fit well with interventions drawn from existential therapy that emphasize the brevity of life. More generally, they are particularly suitable for creative or artistically oriented clients, increasing client buy-in through an approach that is perceived to be more personally authentic. In addition, the visual depiction of clients' journeys may elicit fresh insights, allowing clients to identify previously overlooked

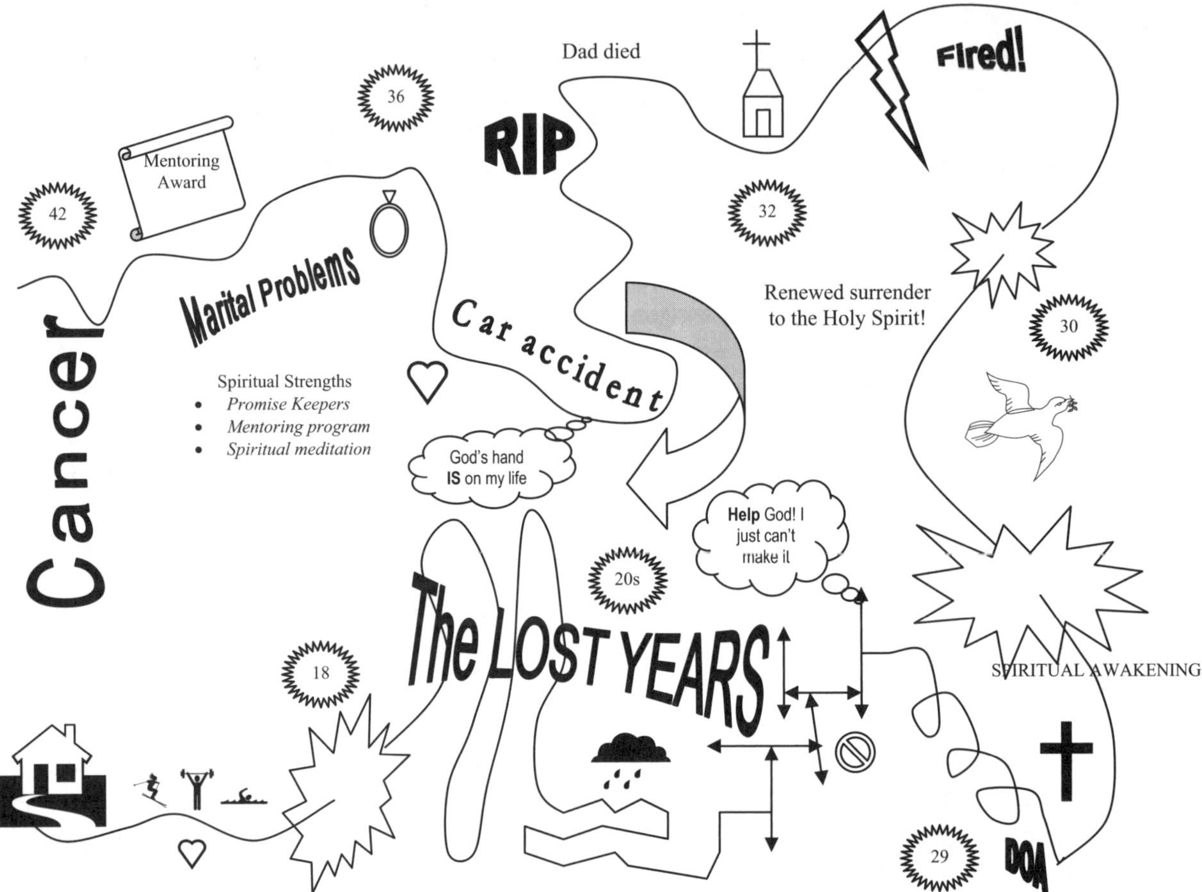

FIGURE 5.1. Spiritual and religious lifemap. From *Spiritual Assessment: A Handbook for Helping Professionals* (p. 39), by D. R. Hodge, 2003, Botsford, CT: North American Association of Christians in Social Work. Copyright 2003 by the National American Association of Christians in Social Work. Adapted with permission.

strengths or to understand spiritual or religious problems in new ways (e.g., as part of a larger narrative). For clients for whom spirituality is a highly sensitive and significant area, lifemaps provide a means of shifting the focus from the client to a more neutral object, a process that may help set clients at ease (Hodge, 2005a).

Of the four comprehensive assessment methods reviewed, lifemaps are perhaps the most client directed. The relatively secondary role that practitioners play during assessment offers important advantages. Individuals who are not verbally oriented may find pictorial expression more conducive to their personal communication styles (Hodge & Limb, 2010b). In addition, less risk exists that practitioners will jeopardize the therapeutic relationship through comments that are inadvertently offensive, an important consideration given that many practitioners report receiving minimal, if any, training in spirituality and religion (Carlson, Kirkpatrick, Hecker, & Killmer, 2002; Shafranske, 2001; Sheridan, 2009). The pictorial lifemap affords practitioners the opportunity to learn more about a client's worldview while focusing on building therapeutic rapport by providing an atmosphere that is accepting, nonjudgmental, and supportive during assessment. Placing a client-constructed media at the center of the assessment process implicitly communicates important therapeutic messages, namely that clients are competent, proactive, self-directed, fully engaged participants in the therapeutic process. Finally, they are particularly amenable to being assigned as counseling homework, which can conserve valuable therapeutic time.

A primary limitation of spiritual and religious lifemaps is related to clients' levels of artistic ability.

For clients who see themselves as lacking such ability, or who are uninterested in drawing, the use of lifemaps may actually increase anxiety and stress, particularly if practitioners do not adequately explain the assessment tool and its purpose (Hodge & Limb, 2010b). In addition, some practitioners may feel so removed from the process that this assessment approach makes poor use of their time. Furthermore, clients who prefer more direct practitioner–client involvement or more verbal interaction may find the use of a largely nonverbal, pictorial method to be a poor fit with their needs. In other situations, it may be important to understand the effects of spirituality and religion in greater breadth (i.e., across the wider family system) or in greater depth (i.e., back through the generations). In such settings, spiritual and religious genograms may be used.

Spiritual and Religious Genograms

Spiritual and religious genograms, much like spiritual and religious histories, have often been recommended as a method of comprehensive assessment (Frame, 2003; Hodge, 2001b; McGoldrick, Gerson, & Petry, 2008; Wiggins, 2009). This approach provides a graphic representation of spirituality and religion across at least three generations. Through the use of what is essentially a family tree that has been modified to incorporate spiritual and religious information, genograms help both practitioners and clients understand the flow of historically rooted patterns through time. In short, spiritual and religious genograms present a "color snapshot" of complex intergenerational interactions related to spirituality and religion.

The basic family system is delineated in keeping with standard genogram conventions (McGoldrick et al., 2008). Nonstandard geometric shapes (e.g., triangles) are used to designate individuals who have played major roles but are not members of the immediate biological family (e.g., "Ruth" in Figure 5.2). To indicate clients' religion, colored drawing pencils are used to shade in the circles and squares (Frame, 2003). Various colors are used to signify religious affiliation. A change in an

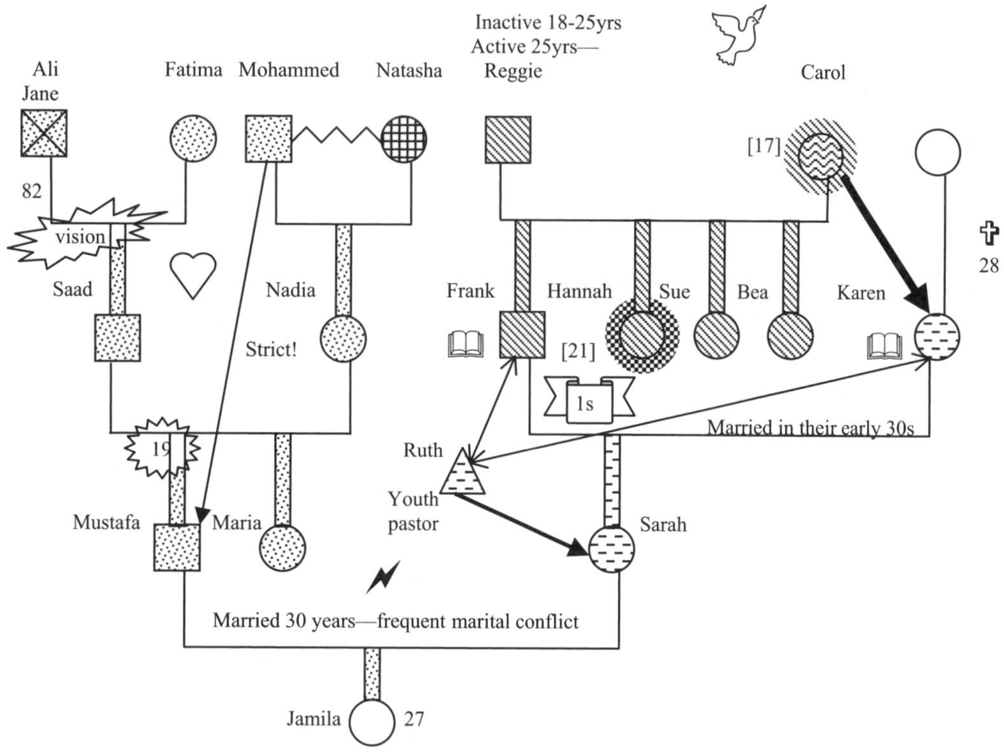

FIGURE 5.2. Spiritual and religious genogram. From *Spiritual Assessment: A Handbook for Helping Professionals* (p. 84), by D. R. Hodge, 2003, Botsford, CT: North American Association of Christians in Social Work. Copyright 2003 by the National American Association of Christians in Social Work. Adapted with permission.

adult's affiliation can be signified by listing the date of the change beside a circle, which is drawn outside the figure, and filling in the space between the circle and the figure with the appropriate color, a procedure that indicates the stability or fluidity of the person's beliefs over time. Using a similar approach, changes in affiliation from one's family of origin can be noted by coloring the vertical segment connecting the child with the parents. Symbols drawn from the client's worldview can be used to signify meaningful events, such as water and spirit baptisms, confirmations, church memberships, and bar mitzvahs. It is also possible to incorporate relational information using the guidelines featured in Exhibit 5.2.

Figure 5.2 depicts a relatively straightforward genogram for Jamila, a 27-year-old female of mixed Arab European American descent who sought counseling because she was feeling mildly depressed, lonely, and increasingly discontent. She had achieved many of her career goals and wanted to get married but noticed that she had a tendency to sabotage relationships prematurely. Given her religiously diverse background, Jamila's therapist decided to administer a spiritual and religious genogram. Jamila's father was a Muslim and her mother was a Christian. Although they stayed together for 30 years, their marriage was characterized by frequent conflict, much of which was related to the differing religious beliefs that characterized their respective family systems. As their only child, Jamila was often triangulated into family conflicts. The genogram helped Jamila clarify the source of her ambivalence about marriage.

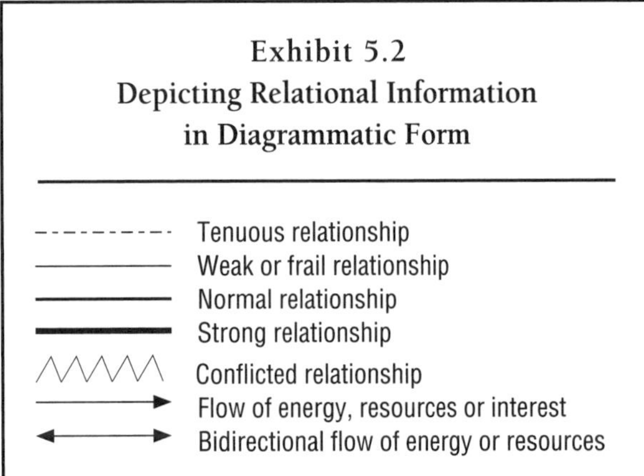

Exhibit 5.2
Depicting Relational Information in Diagrammatic Form

Namely, she had avoided making choices about her own spirituality in an attempt to remain "neutral" in her family's religious conflicts. In addition, she recalled making a vow in her late teens never to marry someone with different religious values, as her parents had done. With these new insights, Jamila was able to identify some productive strategies to help her address these issues, including developing a series of projects with her therapist to come to terms with her own religious beliefs.

Strengths and Limitations

Spiritual and religious genograms may be particularly advantageous when the family system plays a significant role in the client's life (McGoldrick et al., 2008; see Chapter 9 in this volume). Problems involving family members or family of origin issues may be effectively explored with this approach (Frame, 2003). As illustrated in Jamila's example, genograms are helpful when working with clients who are differentiating from their family of origin, and in so doing, choosing different spiritual beliefs or practices. If this spiritual change is producing family conflict or estrangement, a genogram is particularly salient (Hodge, 2005a). Spiritual and religious genograms may also appeal to clients who prefer a structured assessment approach. In some instances, they may be useful with members of cultures that value tradition and the wider family system, such as Latinos (Poole, 1998) and Muslims (Daneshpour, 1998).

In terms of their limitations, spiritual and religious genograms place some constraints on how clients relate their spiritual and religious stories, and they often require a fair degree of practitioner involvement to explain and administer the assessment (Hodge & Limb, 2010b). They are also relatively complicated and time consuming to construct. These latter problems are compounded when working with more diverse, nonnuclear family structures (McGoldrick et al., 2008). In situations in which the family system or historical influences are of minor importance, spiritual genograms may have limited utility. Furthermore, because many clients do not connect past events with current difficulties, some clients may view genogram construction as an inefficient use of time (Kuehl, 1995). With such clients, it may be more appropriate to use a more present-oriented assessment approach, such as spiritual and religious eco-maps.

Spiritual and Religious Eco-Maps

In contrast with the assessment tools discussed thus far, spiritual and religious eco-maps focus on clients' current relationships to spiritual and religious systems in their environment (Hodge, 2000). Religious and spiritual histories, lifemaps, and genograms are similar in the sense that they are all designed to tap some portion of clients' stories as they unfold through time. These assessment approaches typically cover a timeframe ranging from one to three generations. Conversely, eco-maps focus on clients' present, existential relationships with spiritual and religious systems.

In the center of a sheet of paper, an individual is depicted using traditional genogram conventions (Hodge & Williams, 2002). On the outskirts of the paper, surrounding the individual system, significant spiritual and religious systems are depicted as circles, along with other relevant systems (e.g., work, recreation, significant others). The heart of the spiritual eco-map illustrates the relationships between the individual (or family) system and the spiritual and religious systems. In keeping with the conventions listed in Exhibit 5.2, these relationships are represented with various types of lines and arrows that convey information about the content and character of the relational connection between these systems (Hodge, 2003; Hodge & Limb, 2009). As is the case with the other diagrammatic approaches, short, descriptive encapsulations, significant dates, or other creative depictions can be incorporated onto the eco-map to provide more information about relational dynamics.

Figure 5.3 depicts an eco-map for Miguel, a 42-year-old Latino male who presented for alcohol treatment after his devout wife, Amy, asked for a separation upon learning that Miguel had recently received his second arrest for driving while intoxicated. The therapist used the eco-map to help Miguel identify positive and negative relationships with significant systems in his environment, particularly those that fostered or inhibited his drinking. Miguel, a popular and well-respected engineer, enjoyed his job tremendously. His work relationships, however, often resulted in after-hours socialization at local bars. Similarly, his relationships with St. Mary's, the church he attended with Amy, also drained his emotional batteries, prepping him for socializing after work. The eco-map helped Miguel see these detrimental relationships while concurrently helping him identify assets that might help him overcome his alcoholism, such as José, his cousin who was a recovering alcoholic who could sponsor his recovery. The physical depiction of the positive and negative energy flows helped Miguel decide to leave St. Mary's, in favor of St. Peter's, where he would receive support from José and attend the weekly Alcoholics Anonymous (AA) meetings in the basement. The relational patterns delineated on the map enabled Miguel and his therapist to identify settings and emotional triggers that precipitated decisions to use alcohol, develop strategies to counter such triggers (e.g., spend more time engaged in hobbies and in prayerful self-examination), and build on the precepts he was learning in AA. In addition, the therapist used eco-maps to track changes in Miguel's relationships by administering eco-maps over the course of treatment, an exercise that reinforced the progress that occurred in therapy as Miguel saw the changes over time.

Strengths and Limitations

Spiritual and religious eco-maps are relatively easy to grasp conceptually, quick to construct and, perhaps most important, focus on clients' current, existential relationships. This assessment approach may be ideal for operationalizing clients' spiritual and religious assets (or identifying problems) in a timely fashion because the time spent in assessment is focused on exploring clients' relationship to spiritual and religious systems in their present environment (Hodge, 2005a). Like spiritual and religious histories, they can be readily adapted to a broader assessment of psychosocial functioning by adding relevant environmental systems to the map.

As is the case with all diagrammatic methods, eco-maps provide an object that can serve as the focal point of discussion, which can be an important consideration for clients hesitant to discuss spirituality, personal problems such as alcoholism, and

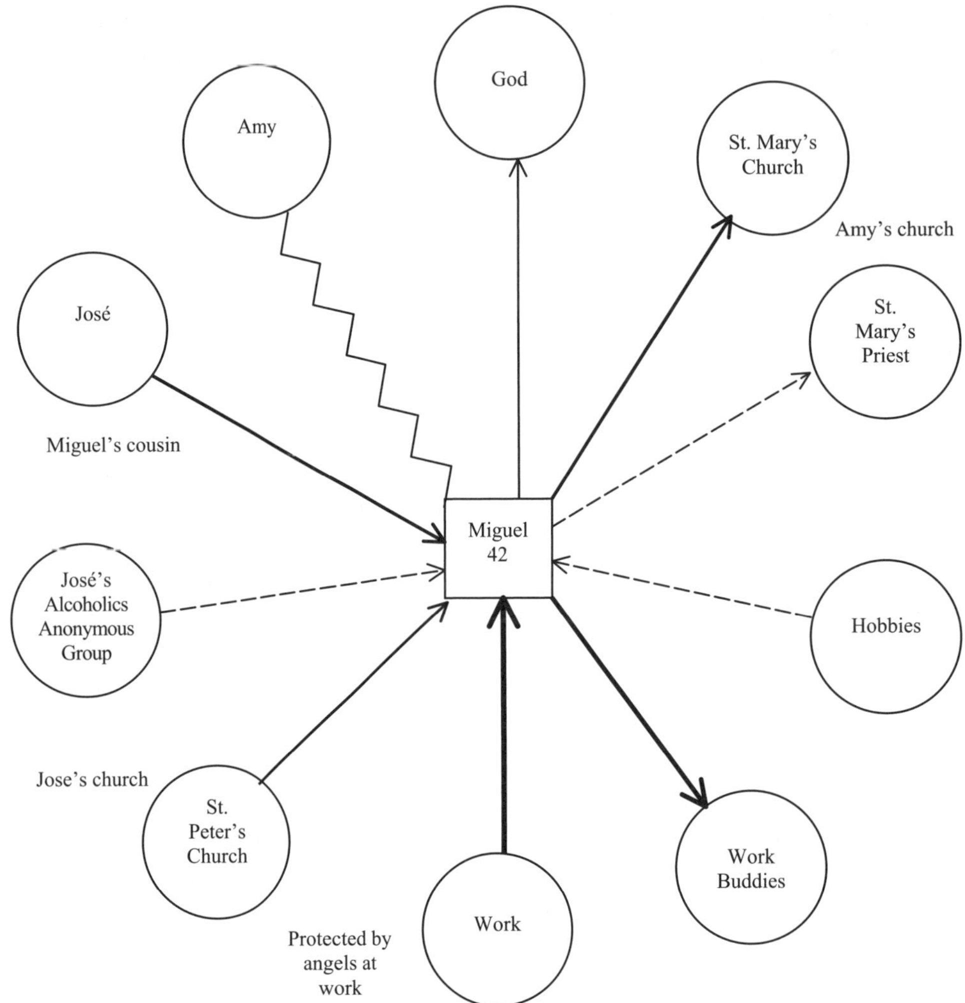

FIGURE 5.3. Spiritual and religious eco-map. From *Spiritual Assessment: A Handbook for Helping Professionals* (p. 70), by D. R. Hodge, 2003, Botsford, CT: North American Association of Christians in Social Work. Copyright 2003 by the National American Association of Christians in Social Work. Adapted with permission.

other sensitive topics. By virtue of their design, eco-maps may be particularly helpful in transferring attention from the client to the concrete, diagrammatic assessment tool because they focus on environmental systems rather than, for example, clients' problems. Although other approaches may implicitly emphasize the client, eco-maps explicitly stress the systems in clients' environments (Hartman, 1995). Thus, this approach may be particularly useful with clients who would benefit from a comprehensive assessment but are reluctant to proceed because of the sensitive nature of the subject matter.

Spiritual and religious eco-maps suffer from the same limitations as other diagrammatic approaches relative to verbally based spiritual and religious histories. In other words, a diagrammatic approach may hold relatively little appeal to clients who thrive on direct, face-to-face verbal interaction. Although relatively fast and easy to construct, eco-maps may not appeal to more creative individuals, although to some extent, this concern can be mitigated by encouraging clients to express their creativity by adding symbols and other material to the eco-map. Finally, in some situations, the focus on the client's current, existential relationships to spiritual assets may result in a limited assessment that overlooks important historical factors.

Although all four comprehensive assessment approaches are illustrated with individual clients, they also can be used with couples and families. For instance, each member of a family might complete a separate lifemap or eco-map and then review the results with their therapist. Alternatively, a couple might depict their respective spiritual stories on a single genogram or eco-map (see Hodge, 2001b and Hodge, 2000, respectively, for examples). Practitioners might also conduct a joint spiritual and religious history or have a couple construct a spiritual and religious lifemap that depicts their spiritual journey as a couple (for further discussion of the role of spirituality and religion in couples or family treatment, see Volume 1, Chapter 20, this handbook and Chapter 9 in this volume).

Tables 5.2 and 5.3 summarize the strengths and limitations, respectively, of the four comprehensive approaches (Hodge, 2005a; Hodge, & Limb, 2010b). These strengths and limitations are not necessary relevant to all clients. Some people, for example, may readily understand spiritual and religious genograms and be able to construct their own genograms as homework, whereas others may have trouble grasping the concept of a spiritual and religious eco-map. Accordingly, it is perhaps most helpful to understand the characteristics listed in these two tables in a more malleable sense, as areas of potential strengths and limitations that may be relevant to specific, individual clients. Developing a working familiarity with these strengths and limitations can help in the process of selecting an assessment approach by alerting practitioners to pertinent areas to explore with clients. In the following section, some additional considerations are discussed that may be helpful in this process.

SELECTING AN ASSESSMENT APPROACH

No clear-cut rules exist for selecting among comprehensive assessment approaches. A number of intertwined factors are typically considered—such as practitioners' theoretical orientation, available time, and training, along with clients' presenting problem, cultural influences, and personal preferences—in tandem with each approach's strengths and limitations. In weighing various factors, it is important to select an approach that results in a reliable and valid assessment.

Figure 5.4 depicts an assessment decision tree organized by time (Hodge, 2005c). The first decision is to determine whether a comprehensive assessment is warranted after taking into account the four guidelines

TABLE 5.2

Strengths of Comprehensive Assessment Approaches

Approach	Strengths
History	Appeals to highly verbal people who enjoy face-to-face interaction
	Congruent with cultures that value story-telling/oral transmission of knowledge
	Nonstructured, nonlinear approach to assessment
	Client centered/directed
	Conducive to building a therapeutic alliance
	Relatively easy to conduct and explain to clients
	Possible to integrate concepts into a broader psychosocial assessment
Lifemap	Allows for creativity and artistic expression
	Honors nonverbal talents and strengths
	Congruent with cultures that value the use of symbols to convey information
	Diagrammatic focus may help ease concerns about discussing sensitive topics
	Visual depiction of life history can foster new insights (e.g., untapped strengths)
	Approach readily understood by clients
	Client constructed (implicitly communicates important competencies)
	Client controls level of intrusiveness/vulnerability
	Preparation process may be cathartic or healing
	Secondary role of therapists allows time to acclimate to clients' worldview
	Possible to assign as therapeutic homework
Genogram	Identifies spiritual and religious patterns across generations
	Explores family of origin issues
	Depicts problems rooted in differing family systems (interfaith couples)
	Implicitly communicates respect for extended family members
Eco-map	Quick and easy to construct
	Highlights relational strengths (and problems) to environmental systems
	Approach readily understood by clients
	Relational focus can mitigate client concerns about discussing sensitive topics
	Ability to depict often complex relationships in a diagrammatic format
	Possible to integrate concepts into a broader psychosocial assessment

TABLE 5.3

Limitations of Comprehensive Assessment Approaches

Approach	Limitations
History	Minimal appeal for people who are relatively nonverbal Face-to-face interaction may increase nervousness about sensitive topics Amount of time required to conduct a spiritual history appropriately Some clients may prefer a more structured or concrete format
Lifemap	Client concern over perceived lack of artistic skills and/or dislike of drawing Clients may feel uncomfortable drawing some aspects of their journeys Potential poor use of practitioners' time Can be time intensive to construct Lacks generational information
Genogram	Complex (can be difficult to explain and construct) Time-consuming to construct Highly structured Speaking of those who have passed on is forbidden in many indigenous cultures Clients may not connect exploration of past functioning with present problems May explore dimensions of clients' stories unrelated to presenting problem
Eco-map	Overlooks important generational information May oversimplify complex, multifaceted relationships Like other diagrammatic approaches, clients who thrive on face-to-face verbal interaction may find spiritual and religious eco-maps a poor fit

and any other relevant contextual information. Assuming a comprehensive assessment is warranted, the next consideration is the saliency of historical influences. In many situations, intergenerational or historical factors will tend to drive the decision-making process. For example, individuals seeking to understand or break with established religious patterns, or interfaith couples experiencing conflicts stemming from differing family histories, might find spiritual and religious genograms to be an appropriate choice (Frame, 2003; McGoldrick et al., 2008).

If more present-oriented factors are of primary therapeutic importance, then spiritual and religious histories, lifemaps, or eco-maps might be considered. To decide among these three methods, consideration might be given to the relevance of present relationships versus life history. In situations in which present relationships are of primary importance in addressing the presenting problem, eco-maps might be considered because they focus on clients' relationships to current relationships, are quick to construct, relatively easy to grasp conceptually, and, if needed, can be integrated into a broader general assessment. As noted, clients generally understand the need to explore present relationships to ameliorate problems that they are experiencing (McGoldrick et al., 2008), an understanding that can enhance the validity of information obtained during the assessment.

If the initial assessment suggests that some degree of life history is important, then either lifemaps or histories might be used. At one level, this represents a choice between a diagrammatic method and a more verbal approach. As the strengths and limitations tables suggest, however, other factors should be considered as well.

During the comprehensive assessment, the accuracy and consistency of the information obtained should be evaluated. A number of criteria have been proposed to evaluate the trustworthiness of information obtained during the assessment (Franklin & Jordan, 1995; Pargament & Krumrei, 2009). These criteria involve attending to clients' words, feelings, and actions. These observations are integrated with information obtained through other aspects of the broader, overall assessment of psychosocial functioning.

Attention should be given to the degree to which metaphors, pictures, and patterns elicited during the assessment make sense as a part of a coherent story. If clients' narratives are coherent within the context of their associated worldviews, then the trustworthiness of the information is enhanced. Other items to consider include the extent to which collaboration occurred with the client in the discussion and interpretation of the problem, and the degree to which attempts are made to falsify preconceived initial interpretations. Regarding this latter process, quantitative instruments can be useful.

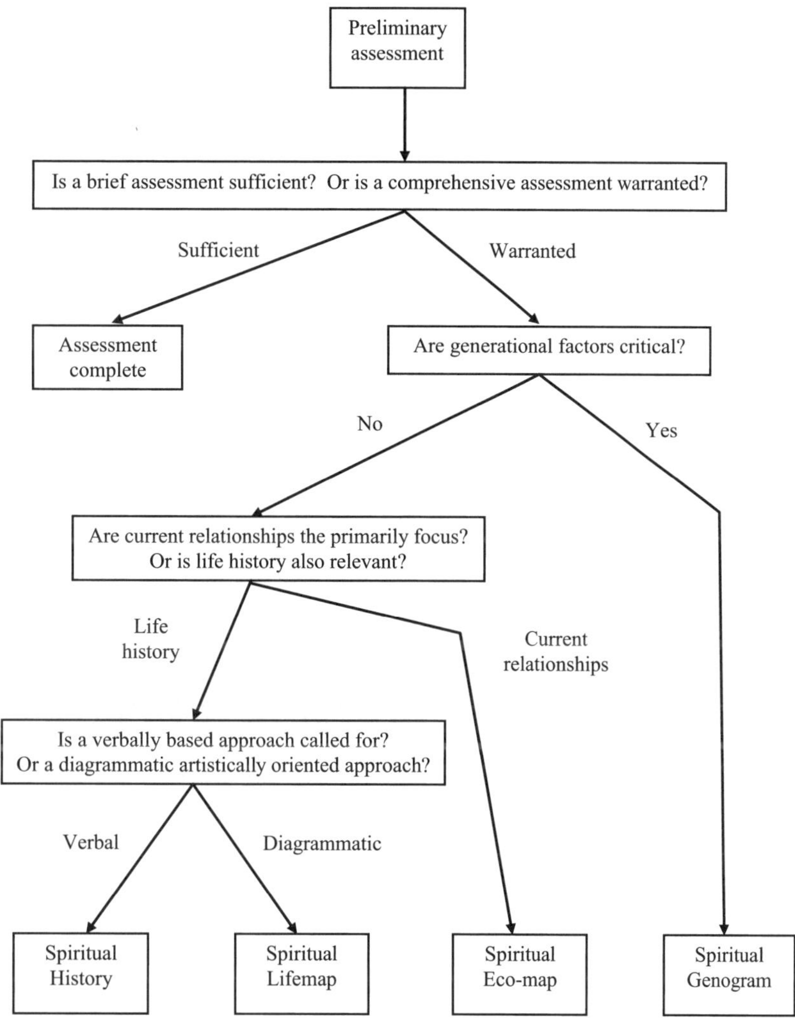

FIGURE 5.4. **Assessment decision tree.**

QUANTITATIVE SPIRITUAL AND RELIGIOUS ASSESSMENT

Quantitative instruments can provide an important supplementary source of information. More than 100 instruments have been developed to measure various dimensions of spirituality and religion (Hill & Hood, 1999), although few of these instruments have been standardized for use in clinical situations (Shafranske, 2005). When considering quantitative instruments, it is important to assess their reliability and validity with a given client population (Hill, 2005; see also Volume 1, Chapter 3, this handbook). Every instrument reflects a certain set of culturally based suppositions about the nature of existence (see Chapter 4 in this volume). To obtain an accurate assessment, the values of the instrument's designers and those of the client's must be congruent.

Many instruments were developed within a Christian theological framework, limiting their utility with other groups (Hill & Pargament, 2008; see also Volume 1, Chapter 3, this handbook). Conversely, it should not be assumed that a given measure provides valid results with all Christians (Slater, Hall, & Edwards, 2001). Take, for instance, a measure that operationalized spirituality with such items as "I exercise regularly" and "I feel sexually fulfilled" (Whitfield, 1984). Such an instrument may have limited validity with a devout Catholic sister who foregoes a systematic exercise program to spend more time in prayer and service to the poor. Consequently, each instrument should be carefully examined to ensure it accurately measures the construct it purports to measure with the client at hand.

Given these cautions, practitioners may find a number of instruments useful with some clients. Table 5.4 lists five widely used, publicly available instruments. These instruments measure various aspects of the sacred, including coping methods (Pargament, Smith, Koenig, & Perez, 1998), motivation (Gorsuch & McPherson, 1989), commitment (Worthington et al., 2003), and well-being (Paloutzian & Ellison, 1982). In addition, the Brief Multidimensional Measure of Religiousness/Spirituality—developed by the Fetzer Institute (1999) in collaboration with the National Institute on Aging—consists of 10 measures that tap various dimensions or pathways that are theoretically related to health and wellness (Idler et al., 2003). Although none of these instruments has been normed with clinical samples, they are generally held to provide reliable and valid information, and they can be administered quickly.

These measures potentially can be used to check biases, confirm hypotheses, evaluate the efficacy of treatment, and monitor changes over time (Pargament & Krumrei, 2009). For example, practitioners might ask clients to complete the brief Religious Coping Inventory (RCOPE; Pargament et al., 1998) in the context of the primary stressor that is driving their psychological distress. The resulting information helps confirm therapists' assumptions regarding clients' use of positive or negative coping methods. Alternatively, the measure might be administered at various intervals to monitor changes in coping patterns over the course of treatment (Pargament, 2007). This might help assess the effectiveness of a psychospiritual intervention, such as spiritually

TABLE 5.4

Instruments for Assessing Various Dimensions of Spirituality and Religion

Construct, measure, and subscales	Illustrative item
Religious coping methods	
Brief RCOPE ($N = 14$; Pargament et al., 1998)	
Positive coping	"Looked for a stronger connection with God"
Negative coping	"Wondered what I did for God to punish me"
Religious motivation	
Intrinsic/Extrinsic–Revised ($N = 14$; Gorsuch & McPherson, 1989)	
Intrinsic	"My whole approach to life is based upon my religion"
Extrinsic	"I go to church mainly because I enjoy seeing people I know there"
Religious commitment	
Religious Commitment Inventory ($N = 10$; Worthington et al., 2003)	"I enjoy working in the activities of my religious organization"
Spiritual well-being	
Spiritual Well-Being Scale ($N = 20$; Paloutzian & Ellison, 1982)	
Religious well-being	"I believe that God loves me and cares about me"
Existential well-being	"I feel good about my future"
Spiritual and religious pathways	
Brief Multidimensional Measure of Religiousness/Spirituality ($N = 33$; Fetzer Institute, 1999)	
Public religious activities	Religious service attendance
Private religious activities	Private prayer
Congregational benefits	Congregation helps with illness
Congregational problems	Congregation is critical
Positive religious coping	Work with God as a partner
Negative religious coping	Feel that God is punishing
Religious intensity	Religious person
Forgiveness	Forgiven others
Daily spiritual experiences	Feel God's love
Beliefs and values	God watches over me

modified CBT, in ameliorating problems (Hodge & Nadir, 2008; Nielsen, 2004). In short, quantitative measures can add richness to a comprehensive qualitative assessment and enhance its validity by providing an important source of additional data.

CONDUCTING A SPIRITUAL AND RELIGIOUS ASSESSMENT

A successful assessment is predicated on the creation of a safe, open, and respectful therapeutic climate (Nielsen, Johnson & Ellis, 2001). Many devout clients—individuals for whom an assessment may be highly germane—are suspicious of therapists (Richards & Bergin, 2005). Psychology's long history of attempting to pathologize religious belief is well documented as is the disproportionally secular value systems affirmed by psychologists (Plante, 2009). As noted at the beginning of this chapter, clients' concerns are often compounded by differences between therapists and clients related to race, gender, and class (Sue & Sue, 2008; Whaley, 2001; Wintersteen et al., 2005). To at least partially address such concerns, it is important to develop competence with commonly encountered faith traditions and practice within the parameters of one's professional training.

Spiritual and Religious Competence

Spiritual and religious competence on the part of the therapist can be conceptualized as a continuous, life-long process characterized by (a) a growing awareness of one's own value-informed worldview and its assumptions, limitations, and biases; (b) an empathetic understanding of the client's spiritual or religious worldview; and (c) the ability to design and implement interventions that resonate with clients' spiritual and religious worldviews (Hodge & Bushfield, 2006; Sue & Sue, 2008). Thus, spiritual and religious competence is a dynamic set of attitudes, knowledge, and skills regarding various faith traditions, which is developed over time.

Awareness of one's worldview plays an important role in managing spiritual and religious countertransference (Genia, 2000; Wiggins, 2009). When encountering culturally different worldviews, unresolved personal issues may unconsciously affect interactions. For instance, therapists who have rejected their family of origin's religion may consciously or unconsciously react when encountering clients who affirm that particular belief system. Subtle expressions of disapproval can damage the practitioner's relationship with clients.

Similarly, effective assessment is contingent on developing an empathetic understanding of the internal logic of alternative cultural worldviews. Take, for instance, Islam, likely the second-largest theistic population in the United States (Husain & Ross-Sheriff, 2011). From within the vantage point of the Western secular worldview, it can appear that some Islamic values engender the oppression of women (Hodge, 2005b). Conversely, from within the vantage point of an Islamic worldview, many women believe that it is Western secular values that lead to the oppression of women by, for example, fostering debilitating eating disorders, treating women as sexual commodities, perpetuating high levels of physical violence against women, and producing popular music that extols the humiliation of women. Different vantage points lead to different understandings of the oppression of women.

It is not necessary to personally affirm the values of culturally different worldviews (Husain & Ross-Sheriff, 2011). It is essential, however, to understand and appreciate clients' value systems as legitimate constructions of reality. The ongoing development of an empathetic stance toward commonly encountered worldviews is implicitly communicated to clients, helping to create a positive environment for the administration of the assessment.

Professional Competence

Working within the boundaries of one's areas of professional competence is an ethical requirement (APA, 2002). For most practitioners, engaging in religious roles falls outside the parameters of their professional training. Therapists are not, for example, typically trained to assess the theological veracity of clients' religious beliefs. In addition, clients are often sensitive to interactions that undermine, displace, or usurp the role of their religious leaders (G. Miller, 2003; Nielsen et al., 2001).

It can be difficult to respect these boundaries during the assessment process because of the similarities that exist between psychotherapy and spiritual direction (Sperry, 2005; see also Chapter 11 in this volume). Consequently, when conducting a comprehensive assessment, it is easy to inadvertently fall into the latter role, perhaps especially if the practitioner is devout and shares the same spiritual perspective as the client. A central distinction to bear in mind is that the overarching aim of a comprehensive assessment is to elicit information about spirituality and religion only to the extent that such information is clinically relevant to clients' presenting problems (Hathaway & Ripley, 2009). The content elicited during assessment should be related to addressing the challenges that precipitated the decision to seek assistance.

As experts on spirituality and religion, clergy are an important resource (Plante, 2009). Clergy and other types of spiritual leaders are often open to forming collaborative relationships (McMinn, Aikins, & Lish, 2003; Oppenheimer, Flannelly, & Weaver, 2004). Collaborations with such leaders can be helpful in determining the normative status of clients' beliefs and behaviors while fostering spiritual and religious competence. Incorporating clients' religious leaders into the therapeutic conversation (with the client's permission) can be helpful in the selection and implementation of spiritual and religious strategies designed to cope with or ameliorate problems. In short, forming collaborative relationships with clergy can enhance service provision to clients (Richards & Bergin, 2005).

IMPLICIT SPIRITUAL ASSESSMENT

An implicit spiritual assessment consists of two key components: listening for implied spiritual content in clients' narratives and asking questions that hint at the possibility of spiritual experiences (Pargament & Krumrei, 2009). This type of assessment might be used with clients who are hesitant to discuss spirituality, perhaps because of concerns about the therapists' level of spiritual and religious competence, along with clients for whom explicitly spiritual and religious language does not resonate. For such clients, an implicit approach provides a mechanism through which to invite clients to explore sacred issues.

Listening for implied spiritual content involves attending to clients' language and emotions (Pargament, 2007). Practitioners should listen carefully for terms and phrases that signal the presence of spiritual issues below the surface. Clients often describe thoughts, experiences, and feelings that parallel the spiritual. For example, self-described atheists might express anger toward images that function as a type of hypothetical God (Exline et al., 2011).

Attending to emotions is an important part of the assessment process because many people experience the sacred primarily through their feelings (Pargament & Krumrei, 2009). Spiritual experiences can produce especially strong emotions. Understanding what elicits excitement, joy, meaning, hope, and purpose, as well as despair, discouragement, and regret, can provide important insights into what clients hold sacred. Listening for implicit spiritual language, asking implicit spiritual questions, and attending to emotions can lead to therapeutic breakthroughs. For example, Ava, a 43-year-old European American lesbian, sought counseling for persistent feelings of fatigue, depression, and disinterest in life. Although she continued to experience considerable professional success, approximately 5 years ago she reported hitting an emotional wall. With each succeeding year, her motivation to carry on seemed to dissipate, even as she continued climbing the corporate ladder. A preliminary assessment revealed no current affiliation or interest in spirituality or religion. She shared that she had been raised in the Metropolitan Community Church but left the church in her early 20s after feeling rejected for holding libertarian beliefs. As a result, she became hostile toward the faith community in which she had participated in her youth. Although she still harbored a degree of resentment for how she had been treated, she considered this to be "old business" and not relevant to her current difficulties. Her therapist took her lead and did not inquire further about the alienation she encountered with her religion 20 years before. Nevertheless, therapy produced little improvement. That changed, however, when the therapist asked Ava how she had celebrated accomplishments during various times in her life journey. When Ava described how she used to reward herself by spending extended periods of time gardening, the tenor of her voice changed and a sparkle appeared in her eyes. Subsequent exploration revealed that gardening—working the soil with her hands, seeing new life emerge—was a sacred experience for Ava. In her drive for professional success, she had neglected a sacred activity that helped animate her life. Sensitivity to the spiritual dimension allowed both Ava and her therapist to better understand how the spiritual struggles she encountered within her faith community had created a vacuum and how it was through gardening that she reconnected with the sacred. Ava shared later in therapy that the opportunity to talk even briefly about the alienation she had experienced from her church and about how her spirituality was transformed helped her to feel more at peace.

Exhibit 5.3 features questions that can be used to indirectly explore the role of spirituality in clients' lives. The questions cover the same basic domains as those used to conduct a spiritual and religious history. As the case with any qualitative assessment, however, the questions should be adapted and integrated into the therapeutic conversation in a way that makes sense in the context of clients' value systems (Griffith & Griffith, 2002). For instance, in Ava's case, a therapist might use a spiritual and religious lifemap to help identify various sources of strength, comfort, and inspiration over the course of her life, or an eco-map to identify entities in her life that both charged and drained her emotional batteries. To orient Ava toward these tools, they might be explained using the implicit spiritual language exemplified in Exhibit 5.3.

In a certain sense, assessment is an ongoing process. Throughout the course of therapy, practitioners' spiritual radar should always be operating. As implied in the example of Agnes's impromptu comments about her lost soul (Pargament, 2007), it is important to be alert to the possibility that spirituality may be clinically relevant at any time and to ask questions that invite a deeper exploration of spirituality when clients' words or emotions allude to the presence of the sacred.

CONCLUSION

Spirituality and religion are distinct motivations. Like other human motivations, the search for the sacred contributes to health in unique ways (Pargament, 2007). Consequently, it is necessary to understand these pathways to optimize service provision. A biopsychosocial–spiritual assessment provides the foundation for effective treatment decisions.

To explore the spiritual and religious dimensions of existence, this chapter presented a two-stage assessment model: a brief preliminary assessment followed, if clinically warranted, by an extensive comprehensive assessment. Four conceptually distinct comprehensive approaches were discussed along with their associated strengths and limitations. Selecting an approach that clients perceive to be relevant to their beliefs and values contributes to the trustworthiness of the assessment.

Similarly, when using quantitative instruments to supplement the information obtained with qualitative tools, it is imperative to consider a given instrument's cultural fit to ensure that valid information is obtained. To negotiate these decisions successfully requires developing some degree of spiritual and religious competence with faith traditions that are commonly encountered in therapy and collaborating with clergy when necessary. Finally, an implicit spiritual assessment model was presented to elicit sacred content with clients who do not use traditional spiritual or religion language or who may be uncertain about discussing these topics with therapists.

Ultimately, the most important variable in the assessment process is the relational context in which it occurs. The relationship between the practitioner and the client must be characterized by mutual trust and respect for clients to enter into a discussion of the sacred realities that are explicitly or implicitly embedded in their personal narratives. Attending to these relational dynamics will help ensure a successful assessment that, in turn, lays a foundation for practice decisions that promote clients' health and wellness.

Exhibit 5.3
Questions for Conducting an Implicit Spiritual Assessment

Past spirituality
What gave you joy growing up?
When were you happiest?
When you think back on your younger years, what things gave you a sense of meaning? A sense of purpose? Hope for the future?
What sort of experiences stood out for you when you were growing up?
How did you cope with challenging situations?
Over the course of your life, what accomplishments are you particularly proud of?

Present spirituality
Conceptualizations of the sacred
Who/what do you put your hope in?
Who/what gives you a sense of purpose and meaning in life?
Who/what do you rely on most in life?
For what are you deeply grateful?
To whom/what are you most devoted?
To whom/what do you most freely express love?
What things are you most passionate about in life?
What causes you the greatest despair/suffering?
Expression and experience of spirituality
When have you felt most deeply and fully alive?
Where do you find peace?
At the deepest levels, what nurtures or strengthens you?
What pulls you down and discourages you?
What kinds of experiences provide you with the deepest sense of meaning in life?
What rituals or practices are especially important to you?
How do you commemorate special occasions and accomplishments?
When in your life have you experienced forgiveness?
What are your deepest regrets?
Spiritual efficacy
What sustains you in the midst of your troubles?
From what sources do you draw the strength or courage to go on?
When you are afraid or in pain, how do you find comfort and solace?
How have difficult situations changed your life for the better? The worse?
What gives you the strength to carry on day after day?
What would you like to be able to let go of in your life?
What has this experience taught you that you wish you had never known?
What have you discovered about yourself that you find most disturbing?
Spiritual environment
Who truly understands your situation?
Who supports you in difficult times? How so?
Who does not support you in difficult times? How so?

Future spirituality
What are you striving for in your life?
If you only had a year to live, what things are the most important things you would like to accomplish?
Why is it important that you are here in this world?
What legacy would you like to leave behind in your life?
How would you like people to remember you when you are gone?

Note. Questions adapted from Griffith and Griffith (2002), Pargament (2007), and Pargament and Krumrei (2009).

References

American Psychiatric Association. (2000). *Diagnostic and statistical manual of mental disorders* (4th ed., text revision). Washington, DC: Author.

American Psychological Association. (2002). *Ethical principles of psychologists and code of conduct.* Retrieved from http://www.apa.org/ethics/code/index.aspx

American Psychological Association Council of Representatives. (2007). *Resolution on religious, religion-based and/or religion-derived prejudice.* Retrieved from http://www.apa.org/about/governance/council/policy/religious-discrimination.pdf

American Psychological Association, Presidential Task Force on Evidence-Based Practice. (2006). Evidence-based practice in psychology. *American Psychologist, 61*, 271–285.

Ano, G. G., & Vasconcelles, E. B. (2005). Religious coping and psychological adjustment to stress: A meta-analysis. *Journal of Clinical Psychology, 61*, 461–480. doi:10.1002/jclp.20049

Arnold, R. M., Avants, S. K., Margolin, A. M., & Marcotte, D. (2002). Patient attitudes concerning the inclusion of spirituality into addiction treatment. *Journal of Substance Abuse Treatment, 23*, 319–326. doi:10.1016/S0740-5472(02)00282-9

Azhar, M. Z., & Varma, S. L. (2000). Mental illness and its treatment in Malaysia. In I. Al-Issa (Ed.), *Al-Junun: Mental illness in the Islamic world* (pp. 163–186). Madison, CT: International Universities Press.

Bart, M. (1998). Spirituality in counseling finding believers. *Counseling Today, 41*(6), 1–6.

Bushfield, S. Y. (2009, November 20). *Use of spiritual lifemaps in a hospice setting.* Paper presented the 62nd Annual Meeting of the Gerontological Society of America, Atlanta, GA.

Canda, E. R., & Furman, L. D. (2010). *Spiritual diversity in social work practice: The heart of helping* (2nd ed.). New York, NY: Oxford University Press.

Carlson, T. D., Kirkpatrick, D., Hecker, L., & Killmer, M. (2002). Religion, spirituality, and marriage and family therapy: A study on family therapists' beliefs about the appropriateness of addressing religious and spiritual issues in therapy. *American Journal of Family Therapy, 30*, 157–171. doi:10.1080/019261802753573867

Crisp, B. R. (2010). *Spirituality and social work.* Surrey, England: Ashgate.

Cross, T. (2002). Spirituality and mental health: A Native American perspective. *Focal Point, 16*(1), 22–24.

Daneshpour, M. (1998). Muslim families and family therapy. *Journal of Marital and Family Therapy, 24*, 355–368. doi:10.1111/j.1752-0606.1998.tb01090.x

Davis, J. A., Smith, T. W., & Marsden, P. V. (2006). *The General Social Surveys, 1972–2006: Cumulative codebook.* Chicago, IL: National Opinion Research Center.

Dermatis, H., Guschwan, M. T., Galanter, M., & Bunt, G. (2004). Orientation toward spirituality and self-help approaches in the therapeutic community. *Journal of Addictive Diseases, 23*, 39–54. doi:10.1300/J069v23n01_04

D'Souza, R. F., & Rodrigo, A. (2004). Spiritually augmented cognitive behavioral therapy. *Australasian Psychiatry, 12*(2), 148–152.

Eck, D. L. (2001). *A new religious America.* New York, NY: HarperCollins.

Exline, J. J., Park, C. L., Smyth, J. M., & Carey, M. P. (2011). Anger toward God: Social–cognitive predictors, prevalence, and links with adjustment to bereavement and cancer. *Journal of Personality and Social Psychology, 100*, 129–148. doi:10.1037/a0021716

Exline, J. J., & Rose, E. (2005). Religious and spiritual struggles. In R. F. Paloutzian & C. L. Park (Eds.), *Handbook of the psychology of religion and spirituality* (pp. 315–330). New York, NY: Guilford Press.

Faiver, C., Ingersoll, R. E., O'Brien, E., & McNally, C. (2001). *Explorations in counseling and spirituality.* Belmont, CA: Brooks/Cole.

Fetzer Institute. (1999). *Multidimensional measurement of religiousness/spirituality for use in health research.* Retrieved from http://www.fetzer.org/component/content/article/18-main/248-dses

Fitchett, G. (1993). *Assessing spiritual needs: A guide for caregivers.* Minneapolis, MN: Augsburg Fortress.

Frame, M. W. (2003). *Integrating religion and spirituality into counseling.* Pacific Grove, CA: Brooks/Cole.

Franklin, C., & Jordan, C. (1995). Qualitative assessment: A methodological review. *Families in Society, 76*(5), 281–295.

Freeman, S. J. (2000). *Ethics: An introduction to philosophy and practice.* Belmont, CA: Wadsworth.

Genia, V. (2000). Religious issues in secularly based psychotherapy. *Counseling and Values, 44*, 213–221. doi:10.1002/j.2161-007X.2000.tb00173.x

Gone, J. P. (2007). "We never was happy living like a whiteman": Mental health disparities and the postcolonial predicament in American Indian communities. *American Journal of Community Psychology, 40*, 290–300. doi:10.1007/s10464-007-9136-x

Gorsuch, R. L., & McPherson, S. E. (1989). Intrinsic/extrinsic measurement: I/E-revised and single item scales. *Journal for the Scientific Study of Religion, 28*, 348–354. doi:10.2307/1386745

Griffith, J. L., & Griffith, M. E. (2002). *Encountering the sacred in psychotherapy*. New York, NY: Guilford Press.

Hartman, A. (1995). Diagrammatic assessment of family relationships. *Families in Society*, *76*(2), 111–122.

Hathaway, W. L., & Ripley, J. S. (2009). Ethical concerns around spirituality and religion in clinical practice. In J. D. Aten & M. M. Leach (Eds.), *Spirituality and the therapeutic process: A comprehensive resource from intake to termination* (pp. 25–52). Washington, DC: American Psychological Association. doi:10.1037/11853-002

Hathaway, W. L., Scott, S. Y., & Garver, S. A. (2004). Assessing religious/spiritual functioning: A neglected domain in clinical practice? *Professional Psychology: Research and Practice*, *35*, 97–104. doi:10.1037/0735-7028.35.1.97

Hill, P. C. (2005). Measurement in the psychology of religion and spirituality: Current status and evaluation. In R. F. Paloutzian & C. L. Park (Eds.), *Handbook of the psychology of religion and spirituality* (pp. 43–61). New York, NY: Guilford Press.

Hill, P. C., & Hood, R. W. (1999). *Measures of religiosity*. Birmingham, AL: Religious Education Press.

Hill, P. C., & Pargament, K. I. (2008). Advances in the conceptualization and measurement of religion and spirituality: Implications for physical and mental health research. *Psychology of Religion and Spirituality*, *S*(1), 3–17.

Hodge, D. R. (2000). Spiritual ecomaps: A new diagrammatic tool for assessing marital and family spirituality. *Journal of Marital and Family Therapy*, *26*, 217–228. doi:10.1111/j.1752-0606.2000.tb00291.x

Hodge, D. R. (2001a). Spiritual assessment: A review of major qualitative methods and a new framework for assessing spirituality. *Social Work*, *46*, 203–214. doi:10.1093/sw/46.3.203

Hodge, D. R. (2001b). Spiritual genograms: A generational approach to assessing spirituality. *Families in Society*, *82*(1), 35–48.

Hodge, D. R. (2003). *Spiritual assessment: A handbook for helping professionals*. Botsford, CT: North American Association of Christians in Social Work.

Hodge, D. R. (2004a). Spirituality and people with mental illness: Developing spiritual competency in assessment and intervention. *Families in Society*, *85*(1), 36–44.

Hodge, D. R. (2004b). Why conduct a spiritual assessment? A theoretical rationale for assessment. *Advances in Social Work*, *5*(2), 183–196.

Hodge, D. R. (2005a). Developing a spiritual assessment toolbox: A discussion of the strengths and limitations of five different assessment methods. *Health and Social Work*, *30*, 314–323. doi:10.1093/hsw/30.4.314

Hodge, D. R. (2005b). Social work and the house of Islam: Orienting practitioners to the beliefs and values of Muslims in the United States. *Social Work*, *50*, 162–173. doi:10.1093/sw/50.2.162

Hodge, D. R. (2005c). Spiritual assessment in marital and family therapy: A methodological framework for selecting between six qualitative assessment tools. *Journal of Marital and Family Therapy*, *31*, 341–356. doi:10.1111/j.1752-0606.2005.tb01575.x

Hodge, D. R. (2005d). Spiritual life maps: A client-centered pictorial instrument for spiritual assessment, planning, and intervention. *Social Work*, *50*, 77–87. doi:10.1093/sw/50.1.77

Hodge, D. R. (2006a). Spiritually modified cognitive therapy: A review of the literature. *Social Work*, *51*, 157–166. doi:10.1093/sw/51.2.157

Hodge, D. R. (2006b). A template for spiritual assessment: A review of the JCAHO requirements and guidelines for implementation. *Social Work*, *51*, 317–326. doi:10.1093/sw/51.4.317

Hodge, D. R. (2009). Secular privilege: Deconstructing the invisible rose-tinted sunglasses. *Journal of Religion and Spirituality in Social Work*, *28*(1–2), 8–34.

Hodge, D. R. (2011). Using spiritual interventions in practice: Developing some guidelines from evidence-based practice. *Social Work*, *56*, 149–158. doi:10.1093/sw/56.2.149

Hodge, D. R., & Bushfield, S. (2006). Developing spiritual competence in practice. *Journal of Ethnic and Cultural Diversity in Social Work*, *15*, 101–127. doi:10.1300/J051v15n03_05

Hodge, D. R., & Limb, G. E. (2009). Establishing the preliminary validity of spiritual eco-maps with Native Americans. *Clinical Social Work Journal*, *37*, 320–331. doi:10.1007/s10615-009-0203-7

Hodge, D. R., & Limb, G. E. (2010a). Conducting spiritual assessments with Native Americans: Enhancing cultural competence in social work practice courses. *Journal of Social Work Education*, *46*, 265–284. doi:10.5175/JSWE.2010.200800084

Hodge, D. R., & Limb, G. E. (2010b). A Native American perspective on spiritual assessment: The strengths and limitations of a complementary set of assessment tools. *Health and Social Work*, *35*, 121–131. doi:10.1093/hsw/35.2.121

Hodge, D. R., & Nadir, A. (2008). Moving toward culturally competent practice with Muslims: Modifying cognitive therapy with Islamic tenets. *Social Work*, *53*, 31–41. doi:10.1093/sw/53.1.31

Hodge, D. R., & Williams, T. R. (2002). Assessing African American spirituality with spiritual eco-maps. *Families in Society*, *83*, 585–595.

Hook, J. N., Worthington, E. L., Davis, D. E., Jennings, D. J., Gartner, A. L., & Hook, J. P. (2010). Empirically supported religious and spiritual therapies. *Journal of Clinical Psychology*, *66*, 46–72.

Husain, A., & Ross-Sheriff, F. (2011). Cultural competence with Muslim Americans. In D. Lum (Ed.), *Culturally competent practice: A framework for understanding diverse groups and justice issues* (4th ed., pp. 358–389). Belmont, CA: Brooks/Cole.

Idler, E. L., Musick, M. A., Ellison, C. G., George, L. K., Krause, N., Ory, M. G., . . . Williams, D. R. (2003). Measuring multiple dimensions of religion and spirituality for health research. *Research on Aging*, *25*, 327–365. doi:10.1177/0164027503025004001

Kaplar, M. E., Wachholtz, A. B., & O'Brien, W. H. (2004). The effect of religious and spiritual interventions on the biological, psychological, and spiritual outcomes of oncology patients: A meta-analytic review. *Journal of Psychosocial Oncology*, 22, 39–49. doi:10.1300/J077v22n01_03

Koenig, H. G. (Ed.). (1998). *Handbook of religion and mental health.* New York, NY: Academic Press.

Koenig, H. G. (2007). *Spirituality in patient care* (2nd ed.). Philadelphia, PA: Templeton Press.

Koenig, H. G., King, D., & Carson, V. B. (2012). *Handbook of religion and health* (2nd ed.). New York, NY: Oxford University Press.

Koenig, H. G., McCullough, M. E., & Larson, D. B. (2001). *Handbook of religion and health.* New York, NY: Oxford University Press. doi:10.1093/acprof:oso/9780195118667.001.0001

Koenig, H. G., & Pritchett, J. (1998). Religion and psychotherapy. In H. G. Koenig (Ed.), *Handbook of religion and mental health* (pp. 323–336). New York, NY: Academic Press. doi:10.1016/B978-012417645-4/50089-4

Kuehl, B. P. (1995). The solution-oriented genogram: A collaborative approach. *Journal of Marital and Family Therapy*, *21*, 239–250. doi:10.1111/j.1752-0606.1995.tb00159.x

Larimore, W. L., Parker, M., & Crowther, M. (2002). Should clinicians incorporate positive spirituality into their practices? What does the evidence say? *Annals of Behavioral Medicine*, *24*, 69–73. doi:10.1207/S15324796ABM2401_08

Leach, M. M., Aten, J. D., Wade, N. G., & Hernandez, B. C. (2009). Noting the importance of spirituality during the clinical intake. In J. D. Aten & M. M. Leach (Eds.), *Spirituality and the therapeutic process: A comprehensive resource from intake to termination* (pp. 75–92). Washington, DC: American Psychological Association. doi:10.1037/11853-004

Lewis, M. M. (2001). Spirituality, counseling, and the elderly: An introduction to the spiritual life review. *Journal of Adult Development*, *8*, 231–240. doi:10.1023/A:1011390528828

Lopez, S. J., & Snyder, C. R. (Eds.). (2003). *Positive psychological assessment: A handbook of models and measures.* Washington, DC: American Psychological Association. doi:10.1037/10612-000

Lyles, M. R. (1992). Mental health perceptions of black pastors: Implications for psychotherapy with black patients. *Journal of Psychology and Christianity*, *11*, 368–377.

Mahoney, A., Pargament, K. I., & Hernandez, K. (in press). The beneficial effects of sanctification on individual and interpersonal well-being. In J. Henry (Ed.), *Oxford handbook of happiness.* New York, NY: Oxford University Press.

Mathai, J., & North, A. (2003). Spiritual history of parents of children attending a child and adolescent mental health service. *Australasian Psychiatry*, *11*, 172–174. doi:10.1046/j.1039-8562.2003.00511.x

McGoldrick, M., Gerson, R., & Petry, S. S. (2008). *Genograms: Assessment and intervention* (3rd ed.). New York, NY: Norton.

McMinn, M. R., Aikins, D. C., & Lish, R. A. (2003). Basic and advanced competence in collaborating with clergy. *Professional Psychology: Research and Practice*, *34*, 197–202. doi:10.1037/0735-7028.34.2.197

Melton, J. G. (2009). *The encyclopedia of American religions* (8th ed.). Detroit, MI: Gale Research.

Miller, G. (2003). *Incorporating spirituality in counseling and psychotherapy.* Hoboken, NJ: Wiley.

Miller, W. R., & Thoresen, C. E. (2003). Spirituality, religion, and health: An emerging research field. *American Psychologist*, *58*, 24–35. doi:10.1037/0003-066X.58.1.24

Newport, F. (2006). *Religion most important to Blacks, women, and older Americans.* Retrieved from http://www.gallup.com/poll/25585/religion-most-important-blacks-women-older-americans.aspx.

Nielsen, S. L. (2004). A Mormon rational emotive behavior therapist attempts Qur'anic rational emotive behavior therapy. In P. S. Richards & A. E. Bergin (Eds.), *Casebook for a spiritual strategy in counseling and psychotherapy* (pp. 213–230). Washington, DC: American Psychological Association. doi:10.1037/10652-013

Nielsen, S. L., Johnson, W. B., & Ellis, A. (2001). *Counseling and psychotherapy with religious clients: A rationale emotive behavior therapy approach.* Mahwah, NJ: Erlbaum.

Oppenheimer, J. E., Flannelly, K. J., & Weaver, A. J. (2004). A comparative analysis of the psychological literature on collaboration between clergy and mental-health professionals—perspectives from secular and religious journals: 1970–1999. *Pastoral Psychology*, *53*, 153–162. doi:10.1023/B:PASP.0000046826.29719.8d

Paloutzian, R. F., & Ellison, C. W. (1982). Loneliness, spiritual well-being and quality of life. In L. A. Peplau & D. Perlman (Eds.), *Loneliness: A sourcebook of current theory, research and therapy* (pp. 224–237). New York, NY: Wiley InterScience.

Pargament, K. I. (1997). *The psychology of religion and coping*. New York, NY: Guilford Press.

Pargament, K. I. (2002). The bitter and the sweet: An evaluation of the costs and benefits of religiousness. *Psychological Inquiry, 13*, 168–181. doi:10.1207/S15327965PLI1303_02

Pargament, K. I. (2007). *Spiritually integrated psychotherapy: Understanding and addressing the sacred.* New York, NY: Guilford Press.

Pargament, K. I., & Abu-Raiya, H. A. (2007). A decade of research on the psychology of coping. *Psyke and Logos, 28*, 742–766.

Pargament, K. I., & Krumrei, E. J. (2009). Clinical assessment of clients' spirituality. In J. D. Aten & M. M. Leach (Eds.), *Spirituality and the therapeutic process: A comprehensive resource from intake to termination* (pp. 93–120). Washington, DC: American Psychological Association. doi:10.1037/11853-005

Pargament, K. I., & Mahoney, A. (2005). Sacred matters: Sanctification as a vital topic for the psychology of religion. *The International Journal for the Psychology of Religion, 15*, 179–198. doi:10.1207/s15327582ijpr1503_1

Pargament, K. I., Smith, B. W., Koenig, H. G., & Perez, L. (1998). Patterns of positive and negative coping with major life stressors. *Journal for the Scientific Study of Religion, 37*, 710–724. doi:10.2307/1388152

Plante, T. G. (2009). *Spiritual practices in psychotherapy*. Washington, DC: American Psychological Association.

Poole, D. L. (1998). Politically correct or culturally competent? *Health and Social Work, 23*, 163–166. doi:10.1093/hsw/23.3.163

Raskin, J. D. (2002). Constructivism in psychology: Personal construct psychology, radical constructivism, and social constructionism. *American Communication Journal, 5*(3), 1–17.

Richards, P. S., & Bergin, A. E. (Eds.). (2000). *Handbook of psychotherapy and religious diversity*. Washington, DC: American Psychological Association. doi:10.1037/10347-000

Richards, P. S., & Bergin, A. E. (2005). *A spiritual strategy for counseling and psychotherapy* (2nd ed.). Washington, DC: American Psychological Association. doi:10.1037/11214-000

Roland, A. (1997). How universal is psychoanalysis? The self in India, Japan, and the United States. In D. Allen (Ed.), *Culture and self* (pp. 27–39). Boulder, CO: Westview Press.

Rose, E. M., Westefeld, J. S., & Ansley, T. N. (2001). Spiritual issues in counseling: Clients' beliefs and preferences. *Journal of Counseling Psychology, 48*, 61–71.

Rose, E. M., Westefeld, J. S., & Ansley, T. N. (2008). Spiritual issues in counseling: Clients' beliefs and preferences. *Psychology of Religion and Spirituality, S*(1), 18–33. doi:10.1037/1941-1022.S.1.18

Saleebey, D. (2009). *The strengths perspective in social work practice* (5th ed.). Boston, MA: Pearson/Allyn & Bacon.

Shafranske, E. P. (2001). The religious dimension of patient care within rehabilitation medicine: The role of religious attitudes, beliefs, and professional practice. In T. G. Plante & A. C. Sherman (Eds.), *Faith and health* (pp. 311–335). New York, NY: Guilford Press.

Shafranske, E. P. (2005). The psychology of religion in clinical and counseling psychology. In R. F. Paloutzian & C. L. Park (Eds.), *Handbook of the psychology of religion and spirituality* (pp. 496–514). New York, NY: Guilford Press.

Sheridan, M. (2009). Ethical issues in the use of spiritually based interventions in social work practice: What we are doing and why. *Journal of Religion and Spirituality in Social Work, 28*(1–2), 99–126.

Slater, W., Hall, T. W., & Edwards, K. J. (2001). Measuring religion and spirituality: Where are we and where are we going? *Journal of Psychology and Theology, 29*, 4–21.

Smith, E. J. (2006). The strength-based counseling model. *The Counseling Psychologist, 34*, 13–79. doi:10.1177/0011000005277018

Smith, J. I. (1999). *Islam in America.* New York, NY: Columbia University Press.

Smith, T. B., Bartz, J., & Richards, P. S. (2007). Outcomes of religious and spiritual adaptations to psychotherapy: A meta-analytic review. *Psychotherapy Research, 17*, 643–655. doi:10.1080/10503300701250347

Smith, T. W. (2002). Religious diversity in America: The emergence of Muslims, Buddhists, Hindus, and others. *Journal for the Scientific Study of Religion, 41*, 577–585. doi:10.1111/1468-5906.00138

Solhkhah, R., Galanter, M., Dermatis, H., Daly, J., & Bunt, G. (2008). Spiritual orientation among adolescents in a drug-free residential therapeutic community. *Journal of Child and Adolescent Substance Abuse, 18*, 57–71. doi:10.1080/154706 50802541129

Sperry, L. (2005). Integrative spiritually oriented psychotherapy. In L. Sperry & E. P. Shafranske (Eds.), *Spiritually oriented psychotherapy* (pp. 307–329). Washington, DC: American Psychological Association. doi:10.1037/10886-013

Sue, D. W., & Sue, D. (2008). *Counseling the culturally diverse: Theory and practice* (5th ed.). Hoboken, NJ: Wiley.

Taylor, R. J., Chatters, L. M., & Jackson, J. S. (2007). Religious and spiritual involvement among older African Americans, Caribbean Blacks, and non-Hispanic Whites: Findings from the National Survey of American Life. *The Journals of Gerontology, Series B: Psychological Sciences and Social Sciences, 62,* S238–S250. doi:10.1093/geronb/62.4.S238

Van Hook, M., Hugen, B., & Aguilar, M. A. (2001). *Spirituality within religious traditions in social work practice.* Pacific Grove, CA: Brooks/Cole.

Whaley, A. L. (2001). Cultural mistrust and mental health services for African Americans: A review and meta-analysis. *The Counseling Psychologist, 29,* 513–531. doi:10.1177/0011000001294003

Whitfield, C. L. (1984). Stress management and spirituality during recovery: A transpersonal approach. Part 1: Becoming. *Alcoholism Treatment Quarterly, 1,* 3–54. doi:10.1300/J020V01N01_02

Wiggins, M. I. (2009). Therapist self-awareness of spirituality. In J. D. Aten & M. M. Leach (Eds.), *Spirituality and the therapeutic process: A comprehensive resource from intake to termination* (pp. 53–74). Washington, DC: American Psychological Association. doi:10.1037/11853-003

Wintersteen, M. B., Mensinger, J. L., & Diamond, G. S. (2005). Do gender and racial differences between patient and therapist affect therapeutic alliance and treatment retention in adolescents? *Professional Psychology: Research and Practice, 36,* 400–408. doi:10.1037/0735-7028.36.4.400

Wolf, M. M. (1978). Social validity: The case for subjective measurement. *Journal of Applied Behavior Analysis, 11,* 203–214. doi:10.1901/jaba.1978.11-203

Worthington, E. L., Wade, N. G., Hight, T. L., Ripley, J. S., McCullough, M. E., Berry, J. W., . . . O'Connor, L. (2003). The religious commitment inventory–10: Development, refinement, and validation of a brief scale for research and counseling. *Journal of Counseling Psychology, 50,* 84–96. doi:10.1037/0022-0167.50.1.84

Yarhouse, M. A., & VanOrman, B. T. (1999). When psychologists work with religious clients: Applications of general principles of ethical conduct. *Professional Psychology: Research and Practice, 30,* 557–562. doi:10.1037/0735-7028.30.6.557

CHAPTER 6

ADDRESSING RELIGION AND SPIRITUALITY IN TREATMENT FROM A PSYCHODYNAMIC PERSPECTIVE

Ana-María Rizzuto and Edward P. Shafranske

People strive to make sense of their lives. Indeed, this activity may be the defining characteristic of human existence. We cannot help but make meaning of our experiences, whether they are commonplace or life changing (see Volume 1, Chapter 8, this handbook). As clinicians, we observe firsthand that our patients do not exist in a vacuum of meaning and that such a state appears to be abhorrent (Frank & Frank, 1991), if not impossible. As Freud (1915/1961) discovered, we are never devoid of meaning; unbeknownst to ourselves, we have already tried to answer the fundamental questions about life's origins, purpose, and final destination (Lear, 1990/1998; Rizzuto, 2002). As children, we form conceptions of the universe and our place within it and strive to locate our personal experiences within the surrounding familial, historical, and cultural systems of meaning that are available to us, including the grand metanarratives, which religions supply, linking the believer to a universe or a God that transcends the individual (Rizzuto, 2005). Indeed, religion is the cultural manifestation of humankind's efforts to give meaning to life (Rizzuto, 2002, p. 184) in addition to its other functions, for example, in coping, providing opportunities for social affiliation, or in self-regulation. For many people, as discussed in this handbook, religion and spirituality furnish important pathways upon which significance is constructed. Although much of the discussion has examined the role of conscious beliefs, attributions, and behaviors, consideration of unconscious factors, what William James (1902) referred to as the "hither side" of religion, provides a necessary and complementary viewpoint. In this chapter we take up this issue, with a clinical perspective in mind, and focus attention on religious and spiritual (R/S) experience as it appears, is understood, and is addressed within psychoanalytic treatment.

PREFACE: AN ORIENTATION TO THE PSYCHOANALYTIC PERSPECTIVE

A foundational psychoanalytic perspective is that early experience teaches us important lessons about our nature and worth, whether engagement with others is safe, and the extent to which the world we inhabit is benevolent and approachable. We are biologically driven to attach to those who are entrusted with our care and, as a consequence, our basic ways of relating to others bear the unconscious imprint of these early relationships. We also learn about desire, its expression and frustration, and we become familiar with the complex emotional states that form our subjective experience and arouse our motivation to seek satisfaction. Based on the sum of our experiences, our minds develop tendencies or principles, which structure, or more accurately, prime the ways in which we make meaning of the events that constitute our lives, relate to others and to ourselves, and form compromises between the expression of impulses and other psychological motivations. These organizing principles, which are usually outside of conscious awareness, literally shape our experience and are quite resistant to change (Atwood & Stolorow, 1984). In contrast to

DOI: 10.1037/14046-006
APA Handbook of Psychology, Religion, and Spirituality: Vol. 2. An Applied Psychology of Religion and Spirituality, K. I. Pargament (Editor-in-Chief)

approaches that primarily focus on conscious attributions, personal constructs, or representations that contribute to global and situational meaning making (Park, 2010; see also Volume 1, Chapter 8, this handbook), psychoanalysis views meaning making as unconscious cognitive and affective processing that involves memory, fantasy, and the rapid use of defense in situations of intrapsychic anxiety or external threat. Whereas conscious meaning making often results in conclusions about the significance or impact of an event in a person's life, the consequences of unconscious mental processing are more commonly found in the patient's ability to respond in an emotionally engaged manner while expressing their needs within a relationship.

Psychoanalytic clinicians are particularly interested in the relationships, personal experiences, and fantasies that originally contributed to the formation of these unconscious principles, how they are maintained, and how they influence a patient's current experience and give rise to symptoms. Gaining insight into the nature of a patient's relationships (both historically and developmentally and in current relationships, including the patient's relationship with the psychotherapist) is considered essential in the therapeutic process. An analyst is always curious (and hopes to engender the same curiosity in her patient) about the often subtle yet pervasive influence of these unconscious organizing principles in a patient's life. To illustrate, when a young woman meets an acquaintance for dinner, does she enter the foyer with excited anticipation or hesitate at the door's threshold? Does she expect a warm embrace, cold criticism, or dangerous (or exciting) seduction? Or does she have no thoughts at all, just vague feelings of comfort, arousal, apprehension, or nausea? And what does she make of her experience? Can she think of it at all? And from the analyst's perspective, what are the forces, fantasies, and experiences that have colored her unconscious expectations and determined to some degree her experience? Psychoanalytic treatment focuses attention on the gradual uncovering and exploration of meaning (both conscious and unconscious) that shapes psychological experience and influences behavior. Although in this chapter we place emphasis on illuminating unconscious meaning, psychoanalytic treatment in practice assists the patient in making improvements in a number of interrelated psychological capabilities. Through the course of treatment, patients improve their ability to recognize their mental states and those of others, which Fonagy (1991) referred to as *mentalization*, as well as to better tolerate painful or dysregulating emotional experiences. Gains are also made in the ability to engage intimately with others as well as to manage states of desire and resolve intrapsychic conflict with less employment of defenses. Each of these advances results in a decrease in psychiatric symptoms and leads to increased personal and interpersonal effectiveness.

Should a woman who repeatedly expects criticism or danger or who experiences somatic symptoms in meeting an acquaintance seek psychoanalytic treatment (as alluded to earlier in this chapter), she would be gently encouraged and given the "psychological space" to explore, by means of free association, the meanings of her reactions and behavior. Her therapist would also consider how past experiences continue to exert influence on her current relationships, including her relationship with her analyst. With insight and important newer and safer experiences gained within the treatment, she would be enabled to live more fully in meaningful relationships, with less psychological conflict, better attuned to her needs and consistent with her values.

How does this relate to religion and spirituality? To begin with, the psychotherapist would (or should) assume the same stance of curiosity and interest in her patient's reactions to entering a church or synagogue, her recounting a moment of prayer, or her descriptions of spiritual inspiration as when she described her reactions to other meaningful events. Since analysts believe that each moment of experience reflects in some way the patient's history and psychological compromises, reporting of religious associations are seen to also express important personal meaning. Memories and associations that arise in treatment, including associations to R/S contents, have particular significance because they are coming to mind within the context of the therapeutic relationship. To put it clearly, psychoanalysis approaches R/S beliefs, symbols, experiences, sentiments, associations, practices, and identifications in a similar manner and with the same aim as it would for any content disclosed in treatment: to assist the patient to better understand the meanings that shape personal experience, motivation, and behavior. A patient's religious ideas and feelings (no more than sexuality, work, professional interest, and family relationships) should not be discarded from the psychoanalytic endeavor (Vergote, 2002)—the "analyst owes the patient a full analytic experience in which his [or her] private religious world is explored with the same attentiveness and respectful exploration as the rest of his [or her] psychic life" (Rizzuto, 2002, p. 202). Just as conflict, arrested development, and maladjustment are addressed in other aspects of human life (e.g., in sexual intimacy), psychoanalytic treatment aims to resolve conflicts associated with R/S experiences to enable patients to more fully engage in the transcendent dimension as they choose. R/S contents should neither be ignored nor placed on a pedestal; rather, they should be considered vital expressions of the patient's psychological life. In maintaining such a measured response, the clinician looks for the salience in the patient's associations, history, and present conflicts. It has been our experience that the emergence and discussion of R/S associations are important given the role of religion and spirituality in articulating the fundamental (and teleological) relationships between the individual and the world and transcendent realities. Lessons learned through religious training and by example may silently shape meaning and disposition towards R/S experiences, outside of conscious awareness.

In the following sections, we present the ways in which psychoanalytic theory and technique are applied to address the "religious and spiritual" as emergent in the mind of the patient. We begin with an overview of psychoanalytic treatment, examine historical and contemporary contexts, and introduce assumptions and theories that are applied when addressing religion and spirituality. We then present clinical material from a composite case to illustrate how theory informs technique.

PRINCIPLES OF PSYCHOANALYTIC TREATMENT

Although it is challenging to arrive at a description of psychoanalytic treatment that is inclusive given the diverse theoretical positions and schools in psychoanalysis and the different forms of treatment in which psychoanalytic principles are applied, one unifying construct is readily identified and will serve as a starting point: the unconscious. The concept of unconscious mental functioning is considered one of the definers of the field; indeed, it was central to Freud's (1915/1961) early investigations and shaped his thinking throughout his work. In the 21st century, exploration of unconscious mental functioning animates the rapprochement between psychoanalytic clinicians and neuroscientists (the journal *Neuro-Psychoanalysis* serves as an example of collaborative scientific efforts to bridge the two disciplines). Simply put, psychoanalysts (as well as most cognitive scientists) believe that unconscious (or nonconscious) mentation underlies conscious experience, including affective states, motivation, and behavior. Bearing this in mind, symptoms also involve unconscious mentation and, from a psychoanalytic perspective, reflect unconscious conflict, which is the root cause of psychological distress and maladjustment. In light of its centrality in the psychoanalytic model, more needs to be said about what is known about unconscious mental functioning.

The formation of meaning is initiated in unconscious mental processing, albeit referred to as fantasy, which is expressed in associations, states of mind, actions, and symptoms. A large body of scientific evidence points to the ubiquity (Bargh, 2007) and the adaptive advantages of information processing (Dijksterhuis, 2004; Dijksterhuis & Nordgren, 2006) that does not require consciousness. Research in automaticity (e.g., studies on social behavior and close relationships) demonstrates that unconscious schemas, originating in previous emotion-arousing interpersonal experiences, prime and shape future experience. Subliminal exposure to relevant triggering cues preconsciously activates knowledge structures that determine the subject's experience.

Furthermore, it has been demonstrated that highly accessible knowledge structures influence perception without the necessity of a trigger—a finding that is consistent with the analytic notion of unconscious organizing principles. Chen, Fitzsimons, and Anderson (2007), following their review of the literature (including their own studies), concluded that "in the case of chronically accessible knowledge structures, perceivers typically do not consciously intend, nor are they aware of, the activation of these highly accessible structures and the consequent meaning they impart" (p. 135). Similarly, experimental research in social cognition has found that internal working models of relationship, originally identified by Bowlby (1969) and central to attachment research, can be understood to function as chronically accessible knowledge structures that are activated outside of conscious awareness. This body of research has also provided support for the psychoanalytic construct of transference (Berk & Anderson, 2000) in which the patient's perception of the psychotherapist is influenced by other emotionally salient relationships through the mechanism of projection. These findings are consistent with the core principles in psychoanalytic theory concerning unconscious mental functioning, fantasy, and psychic determination. In daily life, in therapeutic relationships, as well as in the lab, it appears that experience is determined to a great extent, if not altogether, by unconscious mental processes. What is unique in psychoanalytic theory, however, is the proposition that not only are most mental contents unconscious but also psychodynamic forces occlude conscious recognition.

To return to the earlier example, the young woman's psychological experience at the threshold of the dining room (no matter what it might have been) can be understood to be the result of the activation of a specific unconscious (and possibly chronically accessible) knowledge structure, which in psychoanalytic jargon, corresponds to fantasy. Her ability to become aware of the meanings associated with the unconscious fantasy that gave rise to her subjective experience will be determined in part by the degree of defense employed to manage unconscious anxiety.

We suggest that deeply held religious or spiritual symbols, stories, and rituals (and possibly beliefs themselves) involve a distinctive type of unconscious knowledge structure and likely trigger other associated knowledge structures (e.g., those structures related to human attachment). Religious and spiritual experiences include the activation of unconscious mental processes, which shape subjective experience. For example, we posit that a person's sense of awe while praying in church involves the evocation of an unconscious knowledge structure, which was formed through countless experiences beginning in childhood as well as conscious beliefs and attributions. The origins of such "religious" sentiment may not be fully accessible to conscious awareness given the nature of implicit mental functioning, which from a psychoanalytic perspective may involve the use of unconscious defenses. Similar to the psychodynamics discussed in the clinical illustration, religious and spiritual experiences may be influenced by unresolved unconscious conflict, which may be addressed in psychoanalytic treatment.

Psychoanalytic Technique: An Overview

The psychoanalytic process is intended to bring into awareness the mind's unconscious organizing tendencies, or to put it another way, to assist the patient in becoming familiar with his or her preconscious knowledge structures and modes of experiencing reality. Psychoanalysis aims to elucidate not only unconscious cognition but also its influence on the ways in which the patient relates to him- or herself and others. It does so through the use of free association, paying close attention to meanings constructed between patient and analyst (i.e., transference and countertransference), dreams, affects, actions, and enactments. Psychoanalysts pay close attention to the emotional experiences of their patients (Blagys & Hilsenroth, 2000; Diener, Hilsenroth, & Weinberger, 2007) and monitor their own affects (as well as cognitions) spontaneously arising during the course of a clinical session. Attunement to such psychological states contributes to therapist empathy as well as supports the process of vicarious introspection (Kohut, 1959) by which the clinician grasps the subjective experiences of her patient. Psychoanalysts also focus attention on the patient's avoidance of distressing thoughts and feelings, their use of defenses, and the recurring patterns that dominate their relationships, particularly as these trends become evident within the therapeutic relationship. In fact, it is through elucidating and working with these intersubjective dynamics in the here and now—in the in vivo setting of treatment (involving transference, countertransference, enactment)—that psychoanalysis finds its unique therapeutic effectiveness and transformative potential.

A number of factors (including the psychotherapist's empathic understanding of the patient's conflicts, gains in insight, and engagement in and resolution of transference) contribute to the therapeutic process in which the patient gradually initiates less constricted ways of relating to her- or himself and with others. Often changes first occur within the therapeutic relationship, and then generalize to other relationships through trial action. Although each school of psychoanalysis (e.g., ego psychology, object relations, self-psychology) has its own unique perspective or emphasis on the determinants of psychological conflict and suffering and clinical technique (Wallerstein, 1988), there is agreement that the focus of treatment is on the resolution of unconscious conflict, rather than on the narrowly defined alleviation of the symptoms (Rangell, 2007).

Psychoanalysis and Psychodynamic Psychotherapy

We conclude this introduction with a brief discussion of the continuum of psychological treatments in which psychoanalytic principles and selected techniques are applied (see Table 6.1). In psychoanalysis and long-term psychodynamic psychotherapy,

TABLE 6.1

The Continuum of Psychoanalytic Treatment

Psychotherapy integration	Psychoanalytic informed or supportive psychotherapy	Brief psychodynamic psychotherapy	Psychodynamic psychotherapy	Psychoanalysis
Integration of principles and techniques derived from psychoanalysis with other treatment approaches	Psychoanalytic theory informs clinical understanding and technique; however, interventions are aimed at support and present-oriented problem solving rather than on modification of personality functioning	Psychoanalytic theory informs clinical understanding; however, techniques are modified to accommodate brief treatment	Psychoanalytic theory and technique are employed with attention directed to the analysis of intrapsychic conflict, modification of defenses, and relationship patterns, with modifications in session frequency and primary use of face-to-face interaction	Psychoanalytic theory and technique are employed with attention directed to the analysis of intrapsychic conflict, modification of defenses, and relationship patterns, particularly as expressed within the context of transference
Focus: specific problem alleviation	Focus: improvement in problem solving, adjustment, and coping	Focus: modification in one area in the patient's psychological functioning	Focus: improved psychological functioning and adaptation in multiple areas	Focus: modification in core psychological structure leading to significant improvement in psychological functioning
Frequency of sessions: variable based on treatment goals	Frequency of sessions: variable based on treatment goals and patient mental health status	Frequency of sessions: one time per week, variable length based on specific approach use (12–36 sessions)	Frequency of sessions: one or two times per week often for a period of years	Frequency of sessions: four or five times per week for a period of years

emphasis is placed on exploration and the resolution of intrapsychic conflict, including the use of transference interpretation. Other forms of psychoanalytic-informed therapy, such as intensive short-term dynamic psychotherapy (Davanloo, 1995), make modifications in technique (e.g., active confrontation of defense) to meet the needs of particular patient populations and consider economic and practice constraints that affect the nature of service that can be offered. In actuality, many treatments include a mixture of exploration and support and, in some instances, integrate psychopharmacologic intervention or approaches derived from other theoretical systems, for example, dialectical behavior therapy (DBT).

The Effectiveness of Psychoanalytic Treatment

It is difficult to empirically study the efficacy of psychoanalytic treatment given its complexity, variability, and length; however, a growing body of empirical literature (Levy, Ablon, & Kachele, 2012; see also Leuzinger-Bohleber, 2010) has demonstrated the effectiveness of various forms of psychoanalytic or psychodynamic treatment (Shedler, 2010a, 2010b). Leichsenring and Rabung (2008) found long-term psychodynamic psychotherapy to be, "an effective treatment for complex mental disorders" (p. 1551), such as personality disorders and complex depressive and anxiety disorders. A randomly controlled trial conducted by Huber, Gastner, Henrich, and Klug (2008) demonstrated psychoanalysis and psychodynamic psychotherapy to be efficacious at termination and follow-up in the treatment of depression and that these forms of treatment produced character change. Several reviews and meta-analyses of the empirical evidence conclude that psychodynamic therapies are efficacious or possibly efficacious (Abbass, Hancock, Henderson, & Kisely, 2006; Connolly Gibbons, Crits-Christoph, & Hearon, 2008; de Maat, de Jonghe, Schoevers, & Dekker, 2009; Leichsenring & Rabung, 2008; Leichsenring, Rabung, & Leibing, 2004; Shedler, 2010a). Clarkin, Levy, Lezenweger, and Kernberg (2007) reported positive outcomes for patients with borderline personality disorder using transference-focused psychodynamic psychotherapy. Bateman and Fonagy (2008, 2012a) reported similar results employing mentalization-based psychotherapy (which draws in part from a psychoanalytic and attachment-focused understanding of mentalization) as well as in the treatment of other disorders (Bateman & Fonagy, 2012b). Although numerous case studies (e.g., Rizzuto, 2001, 2009; Shafranske, 2005, 2009; Stålsett, Engedal, & Austad, 2010) have been published that examine the means by which religion and spirituality can be integrated in psychodynamic treatment, no randomly controlled studies have been conducted to date, which would unequivocally establish the therapeutic effectiveness of an explicit spiritually oriented psychoanalytic treatment protocol.

Assumptions When Addressing Religion and Spirituality in Psychoanalytic Treatment

Before we discuss contemporary psychoanalytic assumptions, it is important to acknowledge the historic role that Freud's (1915/1961) personal attitudes and seminal theorizing had on the early psychoanalytic understanding of religion. As is well known, Freud considered himself a "godless Jew," and as Gay (1978) put it, he "advertised his unbelief every time he could find, or make, an opportunity" (p. 3). For Freud, religion was a parcel of illusion that stood in opposition to reality and therefore served as an obstacle to scientific progress; however, it is clear from the available scholarship (Rizzuto, 1998) that the origins of Freud's disbelief were not solely born out of professional or academic interest, but rather that they ran deep into his personal history and psychodynamics. Nevertheless, the ghost of Freud made the full exploration of religion and spirituality a taboo in the minds of many analysts (Sorenson, 2004). Fortunately, that perspective is changing in both contemporary psychoanalytic theory building (e.g., Hoffman, 2011; Rizzuto, 2009; Spero & Cohen, 2009) and in practice. For example, in discussing the results of her study of U.S. training analysts, Bartoli (2003) noted changes in attitudes since Freud's time and concluded that the majority of the participants were "quite appreciative of the patient's religious involvement when it allowed for flexibility in its theological tenets and when it was growth-promoting for their patients" (p. 364). These attitudes, we suggest, are similar to those of most psychotherapists. We turn now to a number of assumptions that provide an orientation to apprehend and address religion and spirituality in psychoanalysis and psychodynamic psychotherapy.

Understanding obtained from psychoanalytic treatment has no bearing on the veridical status of the religious and spiritual beliefs of a patient. The first assumption when addressing religion and spirituality is that the exploration of an individual's faith, including those psychological factors that may have contributed to the creation of the sacred objects of a patient's faith (e.g., as found in God representations), has no relevance to the veridical status of a deity or transcendent reality. Psychoanalysis cannot answer (and should not attempt to answer) the question of the truth of the claims contained in theological tenets or expressed in spiritual traditions; however, exploration of a patient's certainty or doubt is acceptable as related to the goals of treatment. Psychoanalysis can only examine the psychological processes through which a patient apprehends sacred transcendent realities, which constitute acts of personal faith. One must respectfully hold what Ricoeur (1970) coined as the "double possibility," that the patient's God exists or the patient's God does not exist. Psychotherapists (or others) are not in the privileged position to assert a singular possibility. Furthermore, as Jones (1995) commented, "religious symbols are reappropriated not to give us dubious information about the world of space and time but point us to realities that elude those whose nets only troll the waters of the physical world" (p. 19). Such a perspective is consistent with the view of psychoanalysis (and its clinical application) as a *historical–hermeneutical* science, which has as its primary concern meaning, rather than as a *natural* science (Habermas, 1971), which aims to examine verifiable reality. Although it is unquestioned that psychoanalysis focuses on unconscious meaning, it is important to consider that psychoanalytic observations are empirical and based on a theory of developmental structures and their integration with the personal and nonreplicable history of each individual. The introduction of the question of truth (i.e., objective standing) of a patient's religious faith, however, violates the fundamental philosophical underpinnings of the discipline. From a clinical perspective, psychotherapists should not call into question the truth claims of a patient's beliefs, assume a positivistic stance to objects of faith, or reduce a patient's religion or spirituality into purely psychological categories. The means by which a patient forms belief or the exploration of the psychological and cultural influences that have informed faith or its functions certainly may and should be explored, but such examination is essentially different from a clinician assuming the stance of an arbiter of truth.

R/S associations are unique to the setting in which they occur. For example, the emergence of thoughts involving R/S content during treatment are distinct from thoughts that occur when the patient is participating in a formal religious ritual or any religious activity outside the therapeutic setting. Although the manifest content of the thoughts may be similar, the unconscious meanings associated are different because of the differences in the psychological and social contexts in which the thoughts emerged—that is, psychoanalytic treatment in contrast to a religious worship or spiritual observance and practice. To amplify the point, religious thinking in the context of a religious observance is influenced by the ongoing participation in a community of believers in which personal, idiosyncratic, and private meanings are conjoined with communally held beliefs, history, and shared experience. Religious associations conjured out of the immediate engagement of communal worship, involving the experience of being together with others in praise of a transcendent Deity, under a sacred canopy in which similar beliefs and meanings are shared, are certainly different from religious associations emerging within the privacy of psychoanalytic treatment in which an intimate professional relationship and therapeutic process are the focus. R/S associations (i.e., thoughts, memories, experiences) are unique phenomena and bear the influence of the intrapsychic, interpersonal, cultural, and intentional structures in which they are formed. An important clinical starting point is the recognition that religious or spiritual associations in psychoanalysis primarily serve the functions of an analysis—to understand the person—rather than to foster or enhance religious or spiritual practices per se.

Processes specific to psychoanalysis and psychodynamic psychotherapy provide unique opportunities for the exploration of R/S sources of meaning. The psychoanalytic situation is intended to create a unique *"affectively accepting analytic space"* (Rizzuto, 2009, p. 188) through which conscious and unconscious R/S associations, memories, and God representations in connection with the sum of the patient's subjective experience may be elicited, shared in the presence of an other, understood, and explored. It is through the living encounter with an analyst and her empathic, interpretive, and respectful stance that an analytic space is created and may be further transformed into a "sacred space" in which the patient is able to more fully come into genuine relationship, first with the analyst and then with others, including the patient's God or what the patient considers transcendent reality (Rizzuto, 2009). In addition to the nonjudgmental, affectively attuned stance of the therapist, the emphasis on free association as the primary activity in treatment and the use of the couch (in psychoanalysis) encourages the emergence of a broad range of associations and memories, including those with R/S contents. Furthermore, such experiences are not primarily or solely "religious" but rather are constructions drawing on religious motifs and memories for the purpose of representing and narrating self-experience. This particular function of religious narrative may be seen most clearly within psychoanalytic treatment as the patient struggles to find language to articulate his or her subjective experience. The thesis offered is that the essential character of the associations emerges out of the psychoanalytic process and that such expression differs from religious associations occurring within the setting of a religious observance or in any other interpersonal and sociocultural situation. Such associations are located within the treatment and bear its unique teleology, which concerns the resolution of psychic conflict and human suffering.

R/S experiences are influenced by ever-present psychodynamics in ways similar to other complex psychological phenomena. Religious experiences such as found in prayer may reflect wishes (e.g., the desire to be fully known and loved by an all-accepting God) or conflicts (e.g., a conflict between striving for religious piety and satisfaction of self-centered physical desire). Furthermore, such experiences may involve psychological compromises, which involve the use of defenses and are influenced by an individual's history. For example, a person striving to be virtuous may draw on early life experiences and religious teaching in forming conceptions of holiness that proscribe expression of anger or require harsh punishment. Contemporary analysts consider the multiple functions of R/S experiences within the psychological life of the individual. Unlike Freud (1915/1961), they do not define such experiences a priori to be manifestations of neurosis; rather multiple possibilities exist, including enhanced psychological functioning.

R/S experiences reflect a multiplicity of meaning and psychological functions. For example, particular beliefs may not only answer fundamental religious, spiritual, or existential questions but also may establish relationship with others to counter conditions of isolation, to inspire confidence by "knowing the truth," to provide moral scaffolding to manage dysregulating impulses, or to obtain the self-consolidating benefits found in twinship self–object relating, in which identification with another person's experience leads to a sense of connection (Kohut, 1984). In the clinical setting, an association to a frightening experience of confession may reflect the patient's unconscious fear that the therapist will condemn the patient for the "sinful" fantasies or experiences that he or she reveals. The analyst is mindful to not precipitously close the exploration of meaning or to quickly interpret but rather encourages further free association. This provides the patient with the opportunity to more fully explore the underlying psychological dynamics, which are embedded in their associations.

These assumptions shape the process of treatment, encouraging disclosure and fostering understanding of the ways in which religion and spirituality contribute to the patient's psychological functioning. Psychoanalysts do not collapse the patient's experience into preset categories or arbitrarily dismiss religion or spirituality as irrelevant to psychoanalytic inquiry, but rather they offer an opportunity to patients to more fully realize the importance and multifaceted nature of their R/S beliefs, commitments, and experiences through the process of exploration.

In each of these assumptions, there is an implicit appeal to the psychotherapist (and patient) to maintain an open stance of discovery, which privileges the patient's R/S worldview. Each school of psychoanalysis offers a particular perspective on the nature of the mind and psychological functioning, motivation, and conflict. These theories, when applied to an understanding of R/S phenomena, guide the inquiry regarding the psychological functions served by them. Table 6.2 presents selected examples of perspectives drawn from psychoanalytic theory. We now turn to a discussion of two important and interrelated contributions of psychoanalytic theory to the psychology of religion and spirituality that have particular import for psychotherapy: the distinction between religious ideas and God representations and the transitional modes of experience as found in religion and spirituality.

RELIGIOUS IDEAS, GOD REPRESENTATIONS, AND THE TRANSITIONAL REALM OF EXPERIENCE

Ideas culled from a variety of religious sources contribute to the formation of beliefs and attributions that bring coherence to experience and establish in part a foundation of global life meaning. Freud (1915/1961) considered religious ideas and God imagoes to be fixed by their origins in phylogeny (i.e., developmental history of the species over time) and shaped by ontogeny (i.e., one's personal history), which primarily served the function of wish fulfillment. In the 21st century, notions of

TABLE 6.2

Examples of Psychoanalytic Approaches to Understanding Religion and Spirituality

Freudian theory	Contemporary ego psychology	Object relations	Self-psychology	Attachment theory
God imagoes are derived from parental figures under the influence of unconscious fantasy	God representations are dynamically created from parents and other sources	God representations reflect internalizations of relational events between the self and other under the influence of phantasy	Experiences of God reflect particular forms of self–object functioning	The nature of a patient's relationship with God reflects his or her internal working models of relationship
R/S contributes to psychic conflict and poor adjustment to reality	R/S plays an instrumental role in conflict as well as compromise formation	R/S serves as a container of projections, which may then be re-introjected	R/S experiences may support consolidation by serving self–object functions or conversely evoke terror and disintegration anxiety	R/S experiences not only reflect internal working models of relationship but also may offer alternative, compensatory models of relationship
R/S as regressive	R/S is involved in complex psychological functions, which may serve adaptation or reflect psychic conflict	R/S reflects psychological processes involving projection; R/S provides the means to symbolize psychic experience	R/S often provides a means to obtain self–object functions	R/S may provide experiences of secure attachment or reinforce forms of insecure attachment

biological inheritance have been rejected and replaced by a more expansive understanding of the roles of individual development and psychodynamics, including familial and cultural influences as well as fantasy. The formation of R/S thoughts and mental representations involve complex psychological and neurological processes, dynamically incorporating perception, memory, affects, and fantasy, influenced by priming effects, emotions, state and trait (genetic and constitutional) factors, contexts, and defenses. Religious ideas bear unique qualities in that they emerge out of psychocultural contexts and are born within developmental periods in which transitional modes of thinking dominate.

The transitional realm of experience is neither internally generated fantasy nor external perception; rather, it constitutes a third, intermediate area of experiencing (Winnicott, 1971). Ideas and representations formed within this context remain as an enduring presence of the sacred within a person's life and maintain the ability to produce powerful emotional and motivational states. Of particular interest to psychoanalysts are God representations. An important distinction is made within psychoanalysis between God concepts and God representations. A God concept is an intellectual *idea*, whereas a God representation serves as a *psychological object* and not only involves a cognitive representation but also effects emotions, motivation, and a full range of psychological experiences. For example, a person in prayer does not pray to a theological concept or religious idea, rather he or she enters into an emotionally rich human engagement with God, in which the experience of being understood or comforted may ensue. Similarly, a person's fear of punishment from God for a transgression is not experienced as an abstract principle, rather their fear is tangible and draws on previous interpersonal experiences of judgment and punishment.

Furthermore, a God representation is not simply the learned notion of the sacred, which corresponds to culturally given depictions of God (drawn from organized religion), but rather it is a dynamically created psychological object (Jones, 1991, 1996, 2002; Meissner, 1984; Rizzuto, 1979, 2001, 2005; Shafranske, 1992, 2002, 2005; Vergote, 2002).

Although the God imago or representation draws on religious sources and experiences of powerful others, such as one's parents, it is "a *new* original representation which, because it is new, may have the varied components that serve to soothe and comfort, provide inspiration and courage—or terror and dread—far beyond that inspired by actual parents" (Rizzuto, 1979, p. 46). God representations, involving reciprocal processes of internalization and projection (in which interpersonal experience and fantasy simultaneously contribute), are influenced by current psychodynamics and conditions of safety or threat. God representations are no longer delimited to pre-Oedipal dynamics—that is, belief in God as rooted in a child's helpless dependency (as proposed by Freud, 1915/1961)—but rather serve multiple psychological functions (see Table 6.2). For example, the nature of attachment and the quality of object relations influence the quality and functions of God representations (Granqvist & Hagekull, 1999; Jones, 2002; Kirkpatrick, 1997, 1998, 1999; Tisdale et al., 1997; see also Volume 1, Chapter 7, this handbook). God representations, as we will see in the clinical illustration, play a vital role in psychological functioning and adaptation, and offer alternative objects and models of relationship, which may compensate for pathological interpersonal experiences. Contemporary Jungian approaches complement current psychoanalytic thinking in suggesting that religious complexes emerge out of innate capacities (archetypes) to form images, reflecting deep structures or processes in the psyche, which draw on memories, fantasies, and images of interactions, and their emotional tone, to produce stable intrapsychic structures (Corbett & Stein, 2005; see also Chapter 7 in this volume).

Our discussion to this point has emphasized the psychological, cultural, developmental, and dynamic aspects (i.e., role of defense, conflict) that contribute to the formation of a God representation. Some have criticized what has been perceived to be an exclusive focus on the human (or anthropocentric) contributions in the formation of God representations to the exclusion of the role of the transcendent. We briefly comment on this issue.

Spero (1992), in his critique of what he considers to be an exclusive anthropocentric view of God representations, proposed the inclusion into theory of a deocentric dimension in which an actual deity or

God is afforded the status of reality within a positivistic framework. From this theoretical vantage, a God representation reflects in part the internalization of the interaction of the believer with an actual God. This proposed revision places within analytic conceptualization an objective "God"; however, such a modification neglects the fundamental principle that all experience is mediated through human psychological processes and violates Ricoeur's (1970) previously mentioned "double possibility." In our view, the anthropocentric view, which Spero named and considered to be limited, does not preclude the contributions of a transcendent God in the life of an individual, but rather it acknowledges that all that we can come to understand are in fact the psychological processes and subjective experiences of our patients.

For the practicing clinician, contemporary psychoanalytic theory provides an orientation to religious ideas and God representations, which account for the influences of development, family, religion, and culture and point to the dynamic functions which religion and spirituality serve in an individual's psychology. Also, clinical exploration of a patient's God representations provides an additional portal into the unconscious schemas that reflect relationship. This is because God representations always involve a representation of the self in relationship with the sacred. In this sense, religion itself might be viewed as "the personal to the *nth* degree" (Guntrip, 1969, p. 324). Hence it is useful to place emphasis on the relationship that is expressed in the representation rather than on a static conception of the God object in the psyche (McDargh, 1983; Sorenson, 2004). God representations are not static, rather they are dynamic in their creation and are multifacted. Psychoanalysis offers an approach that considers "an infinite range of possibilities [in] assigning new meaning to the personal and universal, immanent and transcendental experience of contact with a God whom we simultaneously create and discover" (de Mello Franco, 1998, p. 128). Religion also can be seen to offer alternative models and experiences of relationship, narratives through which life experiences can be represented, images of sanctification through which experience can be made holy and placed within an ontological context, and cohesiveness through experiences which provide mirroring (i.e., the experience of being empathically understood), idealizing (i.e., the experience of being with an other who has the capacity to comfort and provide strength in the face of anxiety), and twinship (i.e., the self-bolstering experience of being part of the human community; Kohut, 1984; Rector, 2000; Strozier, 1997).

The application of our understanding of God representations is necessarily delimited to theistic forms of religious expression. Although beyond the scope of this chapter, other psychoanalytic models have been developed that address nontheistic forms of spirituality, for example, Buddhism (Epstein, 1995; Safran, 2003), as well as conceptualizations that concern transcendence without reference to spirituality per se (e.g., Bion's explorations of "O"; Grotstein, 2007). Additionally, R/S practices can produce alterations in psychological functioning that can bring about adaptive regressions in the service of the ego (Fauteux, 1994) and ultimately can strengthen a person's self. Similarly, mystical states, rather than simply regressive phenomena (Finn, 1992; Kakar, 1991; Parsons, 1999; see also Volume 1, Chapter 21, this handbook) can lead to progression and enhancement of psychological functioning.

Psychoanalytic theory provides the clinician with unique perspectives to understand the contributions of religion and spirituality to psychological functioning and adaptation. General knowledge about the major religious traditions, including beliefs and practices, contribute as well to psychotherapist's understanding of the client. We turn now to excerpts from a clinical case example,[1] that illustrate many of the concepts and perspectives we have described. In particular, the case provides an opportunity to examine the dynamic functions of religious faith and spiritual experience through the lens of psychoanalysis and highlights the role of religious narrative to give language to psychological as well as spiritual experience. Although the case is unique, we find that it illustrates a host of psychological dynamics that may be common when working with

[1]Aspects of the case have been altered to protect patient confidentiality.

R/S beliefs and experiences within psychodynamic treatment.

CLINICAL CASE EXAMPLE: RELIGIOUS EXPERIENCE AND NARRATIVE AND THE EXPRESSION OF TRAUMA[2]

> There was a palpable quality of anxiety when M, a religious sister in her late 30s from a Roman Catholic church missionary order, entered my office. She was clearly nervous about speaking with me because she had never before consulted a psychotherapist; however, the feeling state was more than simply the initial discomfort that patients sometimes feel. It was as if there was terror lying beneath the surface, which informed our initial meeting. M told me that she was having difficulty sleeping and that her physician as well as her superior recommended that she speak with someone. She said that she felt some relief in coming to see me, although she observed and made the point to me that she twice missed the turnoff to my office. Gradually, in the sessions that followed, M began to describe feelings of anxiety that would surface at different times during the day, often when in chapel or when performing solitary duties, and particularly when she was trying to go to sleep at night. "It's like I begin to feel unsafe, as if something terrible is about to happen, although I don't know what it is. I have nothing to be afraid of but there are times when I just feel afraid of *being*." Her sleep was also disturbed by nightmares in which she would awaken, terrified from images of running to escape from physical attacks. Although she did not report a history of anxiety or panic attacks, the more I learned of her life—growing up in rural poverty, her father's alcoholism and abusive behavior, the chaos in her religiously devout Hispanic family, and her caring but mostly ineffectual mother—the more apparent the background of chronic anxiety and complex trauma appeared. What also emerged was the powerful influence religious faith had in offering an alternative image of relationship and of human possibility.

Psychoanalytic treatment provides a process in which the meaning of symptoms takes precedence over the eradication of symptoms. Free association was the primary model of interaction and the therapist's interventions focused on facilitating such a process. In the initial phase of treatment, the patient settled into (although not without anxiety and at times with discomfort) greater freedom in associations. Her religious faith, vocation, and experiences were certainly of interest, but their relevance was left to their own natural emergence in her associations.

> We wondered together about the timing of the appearance of her symptoms and over time began to piece together the dynamics giving rise to them. Although her desired self-perception was that she was a well-adjusted, optimistic person who was generally asymptomatic, upon reflection and with increasing trust in me, she revealed that she had always felt a bit uneasy around people and as a child found it difficult at times to go to sleep (particularly when hearing her parents arguing). She tried hard to fit in with others and to present an accepting, calm, "spiritual" demeanor. It appeared that her religious faith and the daily prayers and rituals observed within her community were sources of tranquility, which she looked forward to. Upon further inquiry, she shared that she did not feel comfortable in the local community to which she had recently been assigned and that the move to California from Mexico had been upsetting, although she accepted it as the "will of God." Although the other sisters were inviting to her and she had

[2]Aspects of this case and its analysis were previously discussed in "The Psychoanalytic Meaning of Religious Experience" by E. P. Shafranske, 2002, in M. Arieti & F. De Nardi (Eds.), *Psychoanalisi e religione* (pp. 227–258). Torino, Italy: Centro Scientifico Editore.

lived with a few of them before and knew them quite well, the house nevertheless felt cold to her. She fell silent and then commented that she was disconnected from the others and felt like she was just "occupying space." In the silence and in the instant of telling me her association, I felt an emotional vacancy in the room. Although I was interested in what she was saying and cognitively experienced thoughts of compassion, I was momentarily emotionless, almost disengaged, which then gave way to a profound sense of emptiness. Initially confused by my own reactions, I gathered my thoughts (and feelings). Notions of vicarious introspection and projective identification came to mind—as if my unusual reactions alerted me that I was experiencing in some manner *her* inner state of emptiness and isolation and through my associations I was beginning to "mentalize" experiences of which she could not yet speak. We sat in silence for a few moments and I attempted to reflect the feelings of sadness and isolation that her association of "occupying space" aroused in me. She sat silently in front of me. She began to chat about life in the community and reassured me that this was a normal period of adjustment; then her voice trailed off, the momentary elevation in affect evaporated, and she again fell silent and a blanket of sadness covered the room.

Psychoanalytic clinicians pay close attention to their own subjective experiences when conducting treatment and view such experiences as vital in the understanding of the patient. Rather than stopping their own free associations, many analysts invite or are receptive to experiences of reverie (Ogden, 1997). In retrospect, the experiences in the session marked an important shift and deepening in the patient's trust of the therapist and of the therapist's experience of the patient.

Over the weeks and months that followed, M gradually shared more about the emotional pain in her life and her sense of isolation and anxiety, particularly during childhood. She painfully recalled a memory when as a little girl she had upset her father, who while intoxicated flew into a rage; her mother, overwhelmed by the prospect of another fight and concerned for her daughter, locked her in a closet, simultaneously "protecting" her while admonishing her to be quiet and reminding her that she should have known not to anger her father. Terrified by the darkness, the suffocating dead air, the shouting outside, and not knowing when she could leave her sequestered hiding place, she recalled wanting to "not exist"—she went to "another place" in her mind and "patiently" waited out the storm. This experience unfortunately was not an isolated event but rather depicted the quality of apprehension and abuse that filled her family home. Although her mother clearly loved and attempted to protect her children, she was also prone (although rarely) to emotional outbursts; one time, when angry at M's disobeying her, she picked up M and put her in the garbage can. Although a flash of emotion registered initially on her face, she lowered her head and her voice became quiet as she recalled the memory. She reported that although she became better at recognizing the signs of impending danger in the house, safety was at best momentary and always precarious. As the treatment progressed, there were signs that I was not an entirely benign and caring figure in her mind. When telling me the aforementioned story, she momentarily appeared to be filled with rage (which she later reported); however, she immediately showed alarm, and her presentation shifted as she slumped on the couch with her head down, overwhelmed with feelings of shame. Her mood changed as she voiced self-criticism for making "a big deal" of such a long-suppressed

> secret. It appeared as if a rapid succession of unconscious transference configurations had just taken place that resulted in M attempting through self-depreciation (also, with transference implications) to undo the feelings and impulses (anger and shame) she had expressed. I pointed out the shifts in her affect and interpreted her need to deprecate herself as a defense against the expression of feelings of anger toward her mother. She responded initially by becoming silent. After a few moments, she calmly noted that her mother wasn't being abusive; rather, she was only trying to get her point across about misbehavior. I inquired as to her initial silence, following my comment, and how my remark had affected her. Again, she was silent but then said that she had felt criticized.

It appeared that my defense interpretation had the impact of placing her once again in the garbage can and her explicit statement of defense of her mother was a similar attempt within the transference to exculpate the therapist, as I was also only trying to get my point across. The therapy was marked by similar interactions, as she struggled to express her affects, while maintaining intrapsychic and interpersonal safety. These moments may be seen as enactments, which provide opportunities not only for understanding interpersonal and intrapsychic dynamics but also for her experiencing along with the analyst emotional moments that would help her revise her past affective experiences and ways of relating.

It seemed that her personality functioning was oriented toward defensive processes aimed at forestalling danger from the outside world and maintaining rigid control of the dangers within, that is, the expression of her emotions and impulses. From a structural perspective, her ego functioning was closely aligned with a harsh superego; she was not only wary of external objects but also of inner objects and self-experiences of affects and impulses, which threatened the safety she was attempting to secure. The attempt to obtain safety may further be understood as motivated by the need to maintain cohesion of the self and to ward off disintegration (Kohut, 1984). Her dominant self-representations involved schemas of worthlessness and core beliefs that she was defective, bad, and responsible for others' abusive behavior toward her, and her objects were superior and critical. These experiences are reflective of the nature of unconscious, invariant, organizing principles discussed earlier (Stolorow, Brandchaft, & Atwood, 1987). An important aim of treatment is for the patient to gain insight into these principles, their consequences for his or her well-being, and their origins, which will prepare for their gradual modification.

> She lived in a persistent state of vigilance, so interwoven into her psychological functioning as to be initially imperceptible. As I came to learn, only in moments of prayer, spiritual reverie, or contemplation did she suspend to some extent her heightened state of vigilance. These were associated with moments of positive object relating, gained in interactions with her maternal grandmother (who always had a big smile and a hug when she visited) and her teachers (who, although demanding, seemed to like her and want to help her) and culled from religious stories (Jesus as the good shepherd) and Catholic rituals. In these moments she could imagine that she was a nice person and valued "child of God"; however, these were insufficient to counter the dominating effects of the fear-inducing traumas (both direct and vicarious) on her object world and interpersonal schemas.

In addition to the potential benefits of affiliation with a faith community, religious stories, perspectives, beliefs, and experiences can provide important experiences of relationship and self-worth and, for some persons, can provide alternative ways of viewing themselves in the world. We are not minimizing the harmful experiences that persons have experienced as well within the context of R/S involvement or the nature of spiritual struggles that can affect psychological health and well-being. Clinicians need to be mindful of the impacts of R/S involvement on their patients both at present and in the past.

We turn now to the selective elements of this case example, which involve specific religious experiences as well as religious narrative, which served to express highly personal, ineffable states of mind.

> Religion played a crucial role throughout M's life. No matter the difficulties at home, her Catholic parish and religious faith served as unwavering sources of stability and offered alternative experiences and conceptions of relationship.
>
> Gradually she began to speak of her spiritual experiences and to begin to link the spiritual and psychological dimensions of these experiences. In experiences of prayer, she visualized Jesus reaching out to her, listening with a comforting heart. Her representation of Jesus reflected relational qualities of consistency, tenderness, patience, understanding, and love—indeed, characteristics of a good object from whence security could be divined.

Drawing on attachment theory, it could be posited that her ability to construct such a stable relationship was based on a foundation of secure attachment and benign object and self representations originating in very early life with her mother and other caregivers, before the traumas and neglect of later childhood. Her experience of Jesus reflected a form of attachment in which the neglect she suffered as a child was compensated in her relationship with a gracious and understanding Savior. Her associations also illustrate the ability of prayer, particularly as understood as involving transitional experience (Winnicott, 1971), to provide psychological nurturance.

> When M thought of God, she immediately thought of Jesus or the Spirit of God animating life itself, not God the father. This religious concept posed a psychological conflict as she was challenged to reconcile her God concept (which was influenced by what she had been taught as a child and later studied in scripture and theology) and her God representation of father (which was in part culled from her family history of trauma). Her compromise had been to put this conflict out of mind and to focus solely on Jesus. When disappointments occurred, however, such as her transfer to a new community in a remote country, it was God as father who was responsible; Jesus served as the understanding intercessory in her prayers. As she began working through the traumas, which she had endured as a child, her view of her father began to change or rather became increasingly multifaceted. She recalled moments when he was delighted to see her as well or "would push me on the swing as many times as I wanted." Memories came to mind about the burdens that she saw as contributing to his alcoholism. "He worked all of these hours, sometimes two shifts, and odd jobs on weekends. He could never make enough money, never could keep up with the bills with all of the kids, and then he'd just start drinking. He couldn't stand us being poor, not having the kind of house his brother had. He really hadn't a chance; I guess his life unraveled at times." Although subtle, there appeared to be greater willingness to think about God as father. "I don't really know about God actually—I mean I know what I believe—I really know Jesus, but I don't really know God."

In keeping with contemporary theory, M's God representations were not static but rather were dynamically created in the moment, reflecting multiple sources of input—religious training, scripture, and religious experiences, as well as internalizations of human relationships. Her spiritual life involved motivations related to dependency, as Freud (1915/1961) proposed; however, contrary to Freudian theory, her religious faith appeared to strengthen rather than compromise her ego functioning and gave form to a self-definition, which encouraged her engagement in the world (cf. Meissner, 1984). The process of constructing representations involved drawing on a multiverse of associations, memories, and fantasies serving multiple purposes of expression, defense, and compromise formation, in keeping with all psychological functioning.

M's spiritual life was well developed and benefited from structured and ongoing formation provided within her religious congregation. The impact of spirituality was manifest in her vocation and she derived personal significance from her religious beliefs, prayers, and practices. The qualities of her experiences of prayer were of particular note both clinically and for our purposes.

She described moments in prayer in which she felt oneness in the love of Jesus, which also evinced other qualities, such as gratitude, awe, and compassion. These experiences animated her personal beliefs and illustrate Geertz's view of religion's ability to establish "powerful, persuasive, and long-lasting moods and motivations" (Geertz, 1966/1973, p. 90). These experiences were characterized by a timeless quality of transcendence and peace, which infused meaning and sanctified her life. "I can feel Christ's love and his suffering for us completely. We are so blessed, so loved . . . no matter what happens in this life . . . we are loved so completely." When she shared this experience, it was as if she was transformed in front of my eyes, she spoke with conviction, without anxiety, and resonated with confidence. In contrast to Otto's *mysterium tremendum* (1958), M was not so much overwhelmed by "the Holy" or drawn into a defensive overidealization leading to splitting the world into the sacred and profane (Jones, 2002); rather, she was drawn to participate in the world through experiences of a God who transforms (Bollas, 1987; Shafranske, 1992).

> These experiences intensified when she began to address the suffering she had endured as a child. As our work together deepened, vague memories began to surface involving incest with a relative outside of her immediate family, who from a child's vantage, had initially taken a benign special interest in her. With these memories were associations to sexuality in general, which revealed the conflicts she had been attempting to hold at bay. States of sexual arousal, initially animated through cordial contact with a visiting chaplain, brought about apprehension and danger, associated to earlier trauma. Such arousal was always matched with a shading of paranoia and an exacerbation of symptoms—she began double checking the lock on the door to her room and dreaded going to sleep. I considered the impacts of my understanding and relating to her and the pressures the therapeutic process was having on her both consciously and unconsciously—to what extent was I an object to be desired as well as to be feared?
>
> M reported that her prayer life was being affected, which she hoped I could help her understand. She was troubled by particular episodes, when kneeling before the Blessed Sacrament. She winced with embarrassment as she discussed her overwhelming sense of love and gratitude to Jesus. She felt a visceral identification with the suffering Christ; however, she worried that such identification with Christ bordered on the sacrilegious. She felt so passionate that her body was almost reaching an orgasmic state. She wondered whether these experiences were similar to the vivid states of communion with God that St. Teresa of Avila described. She visualized Jesus as the suffering Christ, alone on the cross. This identification with Christ's suffering appeared to provide a context for her to integrate her own experiences of suffering. Her memories of abuse triggered associations to Christ's suffering (and perhaps her identification with Jesus offered hope for resurrection).

The religious motif of Christ's death and resurrection provided a language to formulate her emerging affective experience and to make meaningful experiences of arousal, betrayal, injury, and humiliation. Were these experiences primarily defensive reactions, deflecting the full impact of the abuse and sublimating desires for retaliation through identification with Jesus' forgiveness? These motives cannot be ruled out; however, the impact was not a sealing off of emotion or a defensive pseudotranscendence of suffering; rather, these experiences in prayer appeared to provide a meaningful context to sustain her self-cohesion in the face of the potentially self-disintegrating effects involved in the "recovery" of memories of trauma (as evidenced by the dysregulation of her sleep and intrusion of anxiety). The ability to self-represent affective experience involves higher order cognitive processing and results in the possibility of greater integration of trauma, serving adaptation in contrast to maintaining repression or use of more regressive operations, such as dissociation. These experiences of prayer and communion and identification with Jesus could be seen as providing a modicum of safety to work through the traumas she had suffered. From the perspective of self-psychology, identification with Christ may have offered sustaining twinship as well as mirroring self–object experiences. These experiences of prayer took form within the transitional realm of psychological functioning, the wellspring of religion (Winnicott, 1971), in which reductive distinctions between objective and subjective reality are suspended and illusion is valued (Meissner, 1984; Rizzuto, 1979), in part for its potential to represent dimensions that transcend empirical categories. In apprehending M's experience, it was neither necessary nor actually clinically relevant to ask whether these experiences were real or imaginary—rather it was important to appreciate the meaning these spiritual reveries had for M. Bringing her religious beliefs and experiences into unmediated contact with the emergence of past trauma offered a therapeutic opportunity to integrate existing representations and their affects with emerging experiences in treatment (cf. Rizzuto, 2005, p. 38). Although the ecstatic and sexualized quality appearing in her spiritual reverie was also of importance, further explication of the dynamics is beyond the scope of this chapter. It seemed as if Christ became an object of desire in light of her subjective experience in prayer of exquisite understanding and intimacy as well as in light of identification with Christ's suffering.

For many months, therapy consisted of the working through of fear and anxieties associated with early life experience as well as exploring the impacts of these experiences on her ways of being in the world, particularly of how she entered into relationships. Over time her symptoms abated and she began to become more assertive as well as receptive to enhancing her relationships within the community. She continued to struggle with the direct expression of her affects, and we had only begun in earnest to explore her range of feelings toward me, when the therapy was abruptly brought to an end. Although we were both aware that at some point she would be reassigned and would need to leave the area, it came as a shock to learn that a decision had been made and within the month she would be moving and her therapy with me would need to come to a close. Our attention shifted to processing her reactions to the move and to the ending of treatment. With poignancy, she was able to express her gratitude and to express feelings of loss. I made arrangements to provide her with referrals in the city where she would be moving; several months after our last session, I received a card of thanks and a note that she was doing well and that I was in her prayers. Had she continued in treatment, our work would have encouraged further development in her capacity to experience more fully her emotional life; to engage with others more deeply; to integrate all of the features of her spirituality, including resolving conflicts related to the image of God as Father; and to find more complete fulfillment in her vocation and support and affiliation in her religious community.

Discussion

Among the many salient features of this case, the transformative power of the sacred in her prayer life and her use of religious narrative to articulate her suffering (as well as hope) stand out as particularly relevant. These features illustrate the potency of religious and spiritual experiences in a person's efforts to heal. As seen in this case, religion and spirituality can serve as a foundation for the healthy appreciation of the self and for the resolution of psychic pain and trauma.

Psychoanalytic theory as applied in this case illuminates the role of culture, religious education and training, processes of internalization of interpersonal interactions, fantasy, and ever-present psychodynamics that undoubtedly influenced her experiences in prayer and God representations. The clinical material provided examples of how God representations are formed by the self as well as how experiences in prayer may serve self–object functions and reflect secure attachment. Although needs for security were expressed in these experiences, so too were experiences of awe and compassion. In the transitional space, the theology of her beliefs came to life—in that space the suffering Jesus could minister to her directly.

M's use of culturally given religious narratives conveyed the meaning of her experiences of trauma far more effectively than a simple reporting of the actual events. It is through speech that psychic experience is articulated to support processes of healing and conflict resolution (Rizzuto, 2003). Religious narrative furnished points of reference, a language, and a teleology for ascribing meaning and a means to incorporate and to transform the suffering she had endured as a child. Although religious devotion was not sufficient to heal M, religious narrative augmented processes of remembering and working through—and ultimately of bringing into consciousness—the origins of her suffering that were producing her symptoms of anxiety. In our view, religious leitmotifs served the process of representing ineffable states of mind associated with trauma. Her vivid descriptions of the aloneness and suffering that Christ felt in the garden and the agony of his anticipation of his crucifixion and humiliation brought expression to her quiet suffering. Her experiences were projected onto her Christ and were born by Him in her experience. These leitmotifs were not endpoints but rather served as intermediary constructions supporting the gradual process of de-repression and abreaction leading to working through her psychological experiences and psychic pain. Her experiences in spiritual reverie, not unlike the reports of St. Teresa of Avila, reflect the mind's infinite symbolizing capacity for using metaphor to express psychic realities (Milner, 1987). Simultaneously, her experience of trauma in some ways animated the religious text and mediated and enlivened the mythic story of death and resurrection. To value the symbolizing capacity of the mind does not diminish the fact that the language we employ is itself a product of psychodynamics and necessarily involves both expression and defense. To understand a patient's communication requires the interpretation of both expressive and defensive uses of narrative. Identification with Christ and His forgiveness of those responsible for His death provided for M a model of response in which her long-standing defenses against the expression of aggression were maintained. Religious ideas, in keeping with the character of all ideation, simultaneously serve multiple functions.

Religious narrative provides a means to articulate self-experience, drawing on stories and metaphors commonly understood within a given culture. The figure of the suffering Christ articulated something quite meaningful to M and, in fact, may have furnished the means to represent and to communicate experiences that otherwise would have remained formless and perhaps unspoken. This representation of her experience to herself through identification opened the door to her emerging capacity to suffer. The Christ of her prayers and her narrative involved not only a personal relationship with Jesus and a personal figure for identification but also served as a signifier of her experience. In the use of religious signification, M was able to locate her personal subjectivity within a cultural context in which modes of signification were unconsciously and consciously expressed. Her use of linguistic and symbolic resources found within her religious tradition (see DiCenso, 1999) provided a means of representation, which led to transformation. Furthermore, M addressed the larger ontological problem of human evil through her use of religious narrative. Additionally, processes of sanctification (Pargament & Mahoney, 2005), that is, viewing life through a sacred lens, not only supported M's working through of her trauma but also enabled her to see others in the world from a perspective transcending her early experiences of abuse and offered a possibility of viewing persons and relationships in a positive way. And this process of sanctification led her to gradually appreciate herself as a valued child of God.

CONCLUSION

Clinical psychoanalysis provides a unique aperture to glimpse at the myriad ways that R/S experiences contribute to psychological functioning, including conflict and its resolution. In practice, psychoanalytic forms of treatment create unique opportunities for understanding and transforming personality functioning, which for some patients may involve exploring and transforming deeply held religious beliefs and God and self-representations. Clinicians uphold their responsibilities to their patients by providing a psychological space and personal and professional responsiveness that deeply respects the individual R/S experiences of their patients (including the multiverse of R/S expression and communal and institutional forms), recognizes the multiple functions that religion and spirituality serve, understands R/S ideation and experiences as emergent in treatment as clinical phenomena, and inspires openness and curiosity in their patients to fully appreciate the role of religion and spirituality in their lives.

References

Abbass, A. A., Hancock, J. T., Henderson, J., & Kisely, S. (2006). Short term psychodynamic psychotherapies for common mental disorders. *Cochrane Database of Systematic Reviews, 4*, CD004687.

Atwood, G. E., & Stolorow, G. E. (1984). *Structures of subjectivity: Explorations in psychoanalytic phenomenology*. Hillsdale, NJ: Analytic Press.

Bargh, J. A. (Ed.). (2007). *Social psychology and the unconscious*. New York, NY: Psychology Press.

Bartoli, E. (2003). Psychoanalytic practice and the religious patient: A current perspective. *Bulletin of the Menninger Clinic, 67*, 347–366. doi:10.1521/bumc.67.4.347.26984

Bateman, A., & Fonagy, P. (2008). Eight-year follow-up of patients treated for borderline personality disorder: Mentalization-based treatment versus treatment as usual. *American Journal of Psychiatry, 165*, 631–638. doi:10.1176/appi.ajp.2007.07040636

Bateman, A. W., & Fonagy, P. (2012a). Borderline personality disorder. In A. W. Bateman & P. Fonagy (Eds.), *Handbook of mentalizing in mental health practice* (pp. 273–288). Washington, DC: American Psychiatric Publishing.

Bateman, A. W., & Fonagy, P. (Eds.). (2012b). *Handbook of mentalizing in mental health practice*. Washington, DC: American Psychiatric Publishing.

Berk, M. S., & Anderson, S. M. (2000). The impact of past relationships in interpersonal behavior: Confirmation in the social–cognitive process of transference. *Journal of Personality and Social Psychology, 79*, 546–562. doi:10.1037/0022-3514.79.4.546

Blagys, M. D., & Hilsenroth, M. J. (2000). Distinctive features of short-term psychodynamic-interpersonal psychotherapy: A review of the comparative psychotherapy process literature. *Clinical Psychology: Science and Practice, 7*, 167–188.

Bollas, C. (1987). *The shadow of the object: Psychoanalysis of the unthought known*. New York, NY: Columbia University Press.

Bowlby, J. (1969). *Attachment and loss: Vol. 1. Attachment.* New York, NY: Basic Books.

Chen, S., Fitzsimons, G. M., & Anderson, S. M. (2007). Automaticity in close relationships. In J. A. Bargh (Ed.), *Social psychology and the unconscious* (pp. 133–172). New York, NY: Psychology Press.

Clarkin, J. F., Levy, K. N., Lezenweger, M. F., & Kernberg, O. F. (2007). Evaluating three treatments for borderline personality disorder: A multiwave study. *American Journal of Psychiatry, 164*, 922–928. doi:10.1176/appi.ajp.164.6.922

Connolly Gibbons, M. B., Crits-Christoph, P., & Hearon, B. (2008). The empirical status of psychodynamic therapies. *Annual Review of Clinical Psychology, 4*, 93–108. doi:10.1146/annurev.clinpsy.4.022007.141252

Corbett, L., & Stein, M. (2005). Contemporary Jungian approaches to spiritually oriented psychotherapy. In L. Sperry & E. P. Shafranske (Eds.), *Spiritually oriented psychotherapy: Contemporary approaches* (pp. 51–73). Washington, DC: American Psychological Association. doi:10.1037/10886-003

Davanloo, H. (1995). *Unlocking the unconscious*. New York, NY: Wiley.

de Maat, S., de Jonghe, F., Schoevers, R., & Dekker, J. (2009). The effectiveness of long-term psychoanalytic therapy: A systematic review of empirical studies. *Harvard Review of Psychiatry, 17*, 1–23. doi:10.1080/10673220902742476

de Mello Franco, O. (1998). Religious experience and psychoanalysis: From man-as-God to man-with-God. *International Journal of Psychoanalysis, 79*, 113–131.

DiCenso, J. J. (1999). *The other Freud: Religion, culture, and psychoanalysis*. London, England: Routledge.

Diener, M. J., Hilsenroth, M. J., & Weinberger, J. (2007). Therapist affect focus and patient outcomes in psychodynamic psychotherapy: A meta-analysis. *American Journal of Psychiatry, 164*, 936–941. doi:10.1176/appi.ajp.164.6.936

Dijksterhuis, A. (2004). Think different: The merits of unconscious thought in preference development and decision making. *Journal of Personality and Social Psychology, 87*, 586–598. doi:10.1037/0022-3514.87.5.586

Dijksterhuis, A., & Nordgren, L. F. (2006). A theory of unconscious thought. *Perspectives on Psychological Science, 1*, 95–109. doi:10.1111/j.1745-6916.2006.00007.x

Epstein, M. (1995). *Thoughts without a thinker: Psychotherapy from a Buddhist perspective.* New York, NY: Basic Books.

Fauteux, K. (1994). *The recovery of the self. Regression and redemption in religious experience.* Mahwah, NJ: Paulist Press.

Finn, M. (1992). Transitional space and Tibetan Buddhism: The object relations of meditation. In J. Gartner & M. Finn (Eds.), *Object relations theory and religion* (pp. 109–118). Westport, CT: Praeger.

Fonagy, P. (1991). Thinking about thinking: Some clinical and theoretical considerations in the treatment of a borderline patient. *International Journal of Psychoanalysis, 72*, 639–656.

Frank, J. D. H., & Frank, J. B. (1991). *Persuasion and healing* (3rd ed.). Baltimore, MD: Johns Hopkins University Press.

Freud, S. (1961). The unconscious. In J. Strachey (Ed. & Trans.), *The standard edition of the complete psychological works of Sigmund Freud* (Vol. 14, pp. 166–215). London, England: Hogarth Press. (Original work published 1915)

Gay, P. (1978). *A godless Jew.* New Haven, CT: Yale University Press.

Granqvist, P., & Hagekull, B. (1999). Religiousness and perceived childhood attachment: Profiling socialized correspondence and emotional compensation. *Journal for the Scientific Study of Religion, 38*, 254–273. doi:10.2307/1387793

Grotstein, J. S. (2007). *A beam of intense darkness.* London, England: Karnac.

Guntrip, H. (1969). Religion in relation to personal integration. *British Journal of Medical Psychology, 42*, 323–333. doi:10.1111/j.2044-8341.1969.tb02086.x

Habermas, J. (1971). *Knowledge and human interests* (J. J. Shapiro, Trans.). Boston, MA: Beacon Press. (Original work published 1968)

Hoffman, M. T. (2011). *Toward mutual recognition.* New York, NY: Routledge.

Huber, D., Gastner, J., Henrich, G., & Klug, G. (2008, June). *Munich Psychotherapy Study (MPS): Interpersonal and intrapsychic change.* Presentation at the 39th International Meeting SPR, Barcelona, Spain.

James, W. (1902). *The varieties of religious experience.* New York, NY: Collier. doi:10.1037/10004-000

Jones, J. W. (1991). *Contemporary psychoanalysis and religion: Transference and transcendence.* New Haven, CT: Yale University Press.

Jones, J. W. (1995). *In the middle of the road we call our life.* New York, NY: HarperCollins.

Jones, J. W. (1996). *Religion and psychology in transition: Psychoanalysis, feminism, and theology.* New Haven, CT: Yale University Press.

Jones, J. W. (2002). *Terror and transformation.* East Sussex, England: Brunner-Routledge.

Kakar, S. (1991). *The analyst and the mystic.* Chicago, IL: University of Chicago Press.

Kirkpatrick, L. A. (1997). A longitudinal study of changes in religious belief and behavior as a function of individual differences in adult attachment style. *Journal for the Scientific Study of Religion, 36*, 207–217. doi:10.2307/1387553

Kirkpatrick, L. A. (1998). God as a substitute attachment figure: A longitudinal study of adult attachment style and religious change in college students. *Personality and Social Psychology Bulletin, 24*, 961–973. doi:10.1177/0146167298249004

Kirkpatrick, L. A. (1999). Attachment and religious representations and behavior. In J. Cassidy and P. R. Shaver (Eds.), *Handbook of attachment: Theory, research, and clinical applications* (pp. 803–822). New York, NY: Guilford Press.

Kohut, H. (1959). Introspection, empathy, and psychoanalysis. *Journal of the American Psychoanalytic Association, 7*, 459–483. doi:10.1177/000306515900700304

Kohut, H. (1984). *How does analysis cure?* Chicago, IL: University of Chicago Press.

Lear, J. (1998). *Love and its place in nature: A philosophical interpretation of Freudian psychoanalysis.* New Haven, CT: Yale University Press. (Original work published 1990)

Leichsenring, F., & Rabung, S. (2008). Effectiveness of long-term psychodynamic psychotherapy. A meta-analysis. *JAMA, 300*, 1551–1565. doi:10.1001/jama.300.13.1551

Leichsenring, F., Rabung, S., & Leibing, E. (2004). The efficacy of short-term psychodynamic psychotherapy in specific psychiatric disorders: A meta-analysis. *Archives of General Psychiatry, 61*, 1208–1216. doi:10.1001/archpsyc.61.12.1208

Leuzinger-Bohleber, M. (2010, March). *Psychoanalysis as a "science of the unconscious."* Paper presented at the Centenary of the International Psychoanalytical Association, London, England.

Levy, R. A., Ablon, J. S., & Kachele, H. (2012). *Psychodynamic psychotherapy research: Evidence-based practice and practice-based evidence.* New York, NY: Humana Press.

McDargh, J. (1983). *Psychoanalytic object relations theory and the study of religion.* Washington, DC: University Press of America.

Meissner, W. W. (1984). *Psychoanalysis and religion.* New Haven, CT: Yale University Press.

Milner, M. (1987). *The suppressed madness of sane men: Forty-four years of Exploring Psychoanalysis.* London, England: Routledge.

Ogden, T. (1997). Reverie and metaphor: Some thoughts on how I work as a psychoanalyst. *International Journal of Psychoanalysis, 78,* 719–732.

Pargament, K. I., & Mahoney, A. (2005). Sacred matters: Sanctification as a vital topic for the psychology of religion. *The International Journal for the Psychology of Religion, 15,* 179–198. doi:10.1207/s15327582ijpr1503_1

Park, C. L. (2010). Making sense of the meaning literature: An integrative review of meaning making and its effects on adjustment to stressful life events. *Psychological Bulletin, 136,* 257–301. doi:10.1037/a0018301

Parsons, W. B. (1999). *The enigma of the oceanic feeling: Revisioning the psychoanalytic theory of mysticism.* New York, NY: Oxford University Press.

Rangell, L. (2007). *The road to unity in psychoanalytic theory.* Plymouth, England: Rowman & Littlefield.

Rector, L. J. (2000). Developmental aspects of the twinship self-object need and religious experience. In A. I. Goldberg (Ed.), *Progress in self psychology* (Vol. 16, pp. 257–276). Hillsdale, NJ: Analytic Press.

Ricoeur, P. (1970). *Freud and philosophy: An essay on interpretation* (D. Savage, Trans.). New Haven, CT: Yale University Press.

Rizzuto, A.-M. (1979). *The birth of the living God.* Chicago, IL: University of Chicago Press.

Rizzuto, A.-M. (1998). *Why did Freud reject God?* New Haven, CT: Yale University Press.

Rizzuto, A.-M. (2001). Vicissitudes of self, object, and God representations during psychoanalysis. In M. Aletti & G. Rossi (Eds.), *L'Illusione religiosa: Rive e derive* (pp. 26–55). Torino, Italy: Centro Scientifico Editore.

Rizzuto, A.-M. (2002). Technical approach to religious issues in psychoanalysis. In M. Aletti & G. Rossi (Eds.), *Psicoanalisi e Religione: Nuove prospettive clinico-ermeneutiche* (pp. 184–215). Torino, Italy: Centro Scientifico Editore.

Rizzuto, A.-M. (2003). Psychoanalysis: The transformation of the subject by the spoken word. *Psychoanalytic Quarterly, 72,* 287–323.

Rizzuto, A.-M. (2005). Psychoanalytic considerations about spiritually-oriented psychotherapy. In L. Sperry & E. P. Shafranske (Eds.), *Spiritually oriented psychotherapy: Contemporary approaches* (pp. 31–50). Washington, DC: American Psychological Association. doi:10.1037/10886-002

Rizzuto, A.-M. (2009). Sacred space, analytic space, the self, and God. *Journal of the American Academy of Psychoanalysis and Dynamic Psychiatry, 37,* 175–188. doi:10.1521/jaap.2009.37.1.175

Safran, J. D. (Ed.). (2003). *Psychoanalysis and Buddhism: An unfolding dialogue.* Somerville, MA: Wisdom Publications.

Shafranske, E. P. (1992). God-representation as the transformational object. In M. Finn & J. Gartner (Eds.), *Object relations theory and religion* (pp. 57–72). Westport, CT: Praeger.

Shafranske, E. P. (2002). The psychoanalytic meaning of religious experience. In M. Arieti & F. De Nardi (Eds.), *Psychoanalisi e religione* (pp. 227–258). Torino, Italy: Centro Scientifico Editore.

Shafranske, E. P. (2005). A psychoanalytic approach to spiritually oriented psychotherapy. In L. Sperry & E. P. Shafranske (Eds.), *Spiritually oriented psychotherapy: Contemporary approaches* (pp. 105–130). Washington, DC: American Psychological Association. doi:10.1037/10886-005

Shafranske, E. P. (2009). Spiritually oriented psychodynamic psychotherapy. *Journal of Clinical Psychology, 65,* 147–157. doi:10.1002/jclp.20565

Shedler, J. (2010a). The efficacy of psychodynamic psychotherapy. *American Psychologist, 65,* 98–109. doi:10.1037/a0018378

Shedler, J. (2010b, November–December). Getting to know me. *Scientific American, 21*(5), 53–57.

Sorenson, R. L. (2004). *Minding spirituality: Perspectives from relational psychoanalytic theory, clinical practice, and empirical research.* Hillsdale, NJ: Analytic Press.

Spero, M. H. (1992). *Religious objects as psychological structures.* Chicago, IL: University of Chicago Press.

Spero, M. H., & Cohen, M. (2009). Introduction to a symposium: The God representation in the psychoanalytic relationship. When is three a crowd? *Journal of the American Academy of Psychoanalysis and Dynamic Psychiatry, 37,* 1–20. doi:10.1521/jaap.2009.37.1.1

Stålsett, G., Engedal, L., & Austad, A. (2010). Reflections on Olav's therapy: The roles of religious experience, self psychology, and mentalization. *Pragmatic Case Studies in Psychotherapy, 6*(2). Retrieved from http://www2.scc.rutgers.edu/journals/index.php/pcsp/article/view/1028/2424

Stolorow, R. D., Brandchaft, B., & Atwood, G. E. (1987). *Psychoanalytic treatment: An intersubjective approach.* Hillsdale, NJ: Analytic Press.

Strozier, C. B. (1997). Heinz Kohut's struggles with religion, ethnicity and God. In J. L. Jacobs & D. Capps (Eds.), *Religion, society, and psychoanalysis* (pp. 165–180). Boulder, CO: Westview Press.

Tisdale, T. C., Key, T. L., Edwards, K. J., Brokaw, B. F., Kemperman, S. R., Cloud, H., . . . Okamotom, T. (1997). Impact of treatment on God image and personal adjustment, and correlations of God image to personal adjustment and object relations development. *Journal of Psychology and Theology, 25*, 227–239.

Vergote, A. (2002). At the crossroads of the personal word. In M. Arieti & F. De Nardi (Eds.), *Psychoanalisi e religione* (pp. 4–34). Torino, Italy: Centro Scientifico Editore.

Wallerstein, R. S. (1988). One psychoanalysis or many? *International Journal of Psychoanalysis, 69*, 5–21.

Winnicott, D. W. (1971). *Playing and reality*. New York, NY: Basic Books.

CHAPTER 7

JUNG'S APPROACH TO SPIRITUALITY AND RELIGION

Lionel Corbett

Jungian psychology has always stressed the importance of spirituality and religion to mental health — and indeed, their inseparability from mental health. In fact, this emphasis is one of the historical reasons that Jungian thought has been marginalized in the psychotherapy community. In the 21st century, however, because it is now clear that a spiritual life benefits physical and mental health and is important in the lives of many people (Hill & Pargament, 2003), the value of Jung's approach is becoming more obvious. Perhaps related to the contemporary movement in psychotherapy toward treatments that tend to ignore spirituality and the unconscious, there is now a groundswell of grassroots interest in Jung, as evidenced by the existence of many local community organizations in the United States and overseas that study Jungian psychology. Most of these are education programs for laypeople. I believe this interest results from the fact that Jungian psychology offers a spiritual approach to the development of the personality and to psychotherapy, thus filling a cultural need.

Religion is so much a part of Jung's writing that this focus has become one of the critical points of agreement or disagreement with his approach to the psyche. Throughout his work, one has the constant sense that he is aware of the presence of a spiritual reality behind what is conscious. For Jung's detractors, this emphasis oversteps the bounds of psychology, but Jungian psychotherapists find that his approach contributes a unique perspective; it allows us to work spiritually and psychologically at the same time. Jungians do not work in any standardized way, partly because, as Jung put it, each patient requires his or her own theory, and partly because in the last analysis, the personality of the therapist is the main therapeutic instrument.

Broadly speaking, Jung's approach is a depth psychology that places great emphasis on the unconscious, especially its transpersonal or archetypal levels. When dealing with personal material, most Jungians marry Jung's classical approach with some form of contemporary psychoanalytic theory. In the United Kingdom, many Jungians appropriate Kleinian theory, whereas in the United States, object relations theory and psychoanalytic self psychology are popular, and we find that many aspects of traditional Jungian analysis are similar to recent developments in relational psychoanalysis (Giannoni, 2009). In spite of these differences, there are important features of the Jungian approach common to all practitioners, among which we find a spiritual approach to the psyche.

This chapter outlines some of the ways in which Jungian psychotherapy allows the psychotherapist to view the psyche and the process of psychotherapy from a spiritual as well as a clinical perspective. For the clinician, Jung's approach has various advantages; it does not compartmentalize the patient's spiritual and psychological lives, it allows the development of a spirituality that is not based on any traditional religious institution, and it allows an organic God image to emerge that has not been dictated by any specific theology (Corbett, 1996, 2007). Because Jungian treatment is tailored to the unique needs and dynamics of the patient and the personality and theoretical

DOI: 10.1037/14046-007
APA Handbook of Psychology, Religion, and Spirituality: Vol. 2. An Applied Psychology of Religion and Spirituality, K. I. Pargament (Editor-in-Chief)

preferences of the clinician, this approach does not lend itself to a standardized or "manualized" format. Rather, foundational theoretical principles drawn from Jung inform clinical understanding, which, in turn, influences the therapist's interventions and interpretations. This chapter presents these fundamental principles, which can be incorporated into different forms of depth psychotherapy.

THE SELF AS AN INTRAPSYCHIC GOD IMAGE

Jung's approach assumes the presence of an a priori God image in the psyche, which he referred to as the Self. The Self is an intrapsychic ordering principle that depicts itself by means of imagery that arises from the unconscious. Because the unconscious is regarded as a source of wisdom and healing, Jungian therapists pay a great deal of attention to dreams and other manifestations of the Self, which is thought to be in dialogue with consciousness. As the therapeutic process opens up more and more of the unconscious, the individual's true God image—rather than what was learned in Sunday school—becomes conscious and transforms. We see this "transformation of God" in the person's dreams (Jung, 1975b, p. 314; see also Edinger, 1992). For example, early on in her therapeutic work, a woman dreams that while lying in bed a large hook descends from above, transfixes her through the chest, and suspends her helplessly in midair. Below she sees a white-robed old man who fires at her from a cannon—she realizes that the figure is God. Her psychological work includes her attempt to deal with her tyrannical father, whose qualities she had unconsciously projected onto her punitive God image, a dynamic well documented by Rizzuto (1981). Eventually, as her father problem softens, she dreams that she is led around a large room that contains images and icons of all the world's religious traditions. She is told that she can choose any of them; she decides on a statue of the laughing Buddha, an image of joyful spirituality quite unlike the gloomy spirituality in which she was raised. Her psychotherapeutic work leads to a concomitant change in her spirituality.

As another example, consider a patient who complains of life-long anxiety. Her parents were extremely critical, insensitive, anxious, and unable to soothe her. They made her feel that the world is dangerous and offered no sense of protection. She was raised to be a devout Christian, and she was told that she was cared for by a loving God, who would at the same time be punitive and angry if she misbehaved. Her inability to trust this God, and her fear of him, cause guilt and confusion; it is difficult for her to understand how she can constantly feel so afraid while also being protected by God. Her relationship to God is as important to her as any other relationship, and she wants to address it at its own level, but her image of God cannot be separated from psychotherapeutic work on her anxiety. The content of her innate potential to experience the divine has been filled in by personal experience; her God image has been colored by the projection of her parental imagoes and her religious training. Rather than treat her anxiety and her religious difficulty as two separate problems, which would require her to obtain advice from a minister of religion as well as a psychotherapist, for the Jungian therapist, psychotherapeutic work proceeds *pari passu* on both her God image and her early object relations. She is encouraged to examine her God image through the use of free association and open-ended questions. Such exploration makes her conscious of the connections between her God image and her early family dynamics, a process that frees her to develop a more mature relationship to the divine.

GOD IMAGES AND RELIGIONS

For Jung, the specific contents of collective God images are culturally and historically determined projections. Christ, Zeus, Yahweh, Odin, or any of the other names of God are local names for the Self, which is a transpersonal, intrapsychic principle, which Jung (1953/1977b) believed to be empirically demonstrable and universally present (Heisig, 1979). The Self is depicted symbolically in myths and religions and (crucially for this approach) also appears within the individual's dream imagery. Jung made an important distinction between such images of God and the divine itself. Although there are many images of God, we cannot, as psychologists, say anything about their source; psychology can only speak of the intrapsychic representations of the divine. The "original beyond the images" is psychologically inaccessible (Jung, 1950/1976c, p. 706). Jung never said that the God image we experience is *only* psychological, but he believed that the question of the existence of a transcendent God beyond the psyche is a problem for theologians and not psychologists.

Jung (1921/1971, 1958/1977c) suggested that one's real God image is whatever is of the highest value or the greatest power in the psyche; this may be money, science, power, sex, or wherever a person becomes absolute. One's actual God image (rather than what one was told to believe) is often unconscious, so that the God image people outwardly profess may not correspond to their subjective image of God. A Christian may believe in the sacred figures without actually experiencing the divine as a personal experience. Such a Christian's motives and behavior, according to Jung (1953/1977b), "do not spring from the sphere of Christianity but from the unconscious and undeveloped psyche, which is as pagan and archaic as ever . . . his soul is out of key with his external beliefs" (pp. 11–12). Thus, Ulanov (1986) reported a dream in which a man is "ardently, sincerely, deeply engaged in an act of worship, but the worship was of a giant pig" (p. 164). As Hall (1993) put it, our religious concerns may go underground, into the unconscious, and return in dreams. For this reason, Jungian therapists place a great deal of emphasis on the exploration of dreams. Dreams provide a window into unconscious mental processes in which religious and psychological contents are often meaningfully intertwined. For example, Jung (1958/1977c, p. 346) reported the case of a woman who had lost any interest in religion. In a dream that had a major emotional impact on her, the analyst is a giant, standing in an enormous field of wheat through which the wind (an ancient image of the spirit) was blowing, making the wheat flow in waves. The analyst holds the patient in his arms and rocks her, while she felt she was in the arms of a god. At the personal level, this dream depicts an idealizing transference and, at the same time, it suggests that she is projecting onto the analyst not the Judeo–Christian image of God but rather a pagan god of nature or vegetation. Jungian therapists are similarly attuned to both the individual and cultural sources of meaning conveyed in dreams.

THE SELF

In Jungian clinical practice, the Self or the *imago dei* is a centrally important idea. The Self is typically thought of as another, transcendent consciousness to which the ego relates. For Jung (1973), "everything essential happens in the Self and the ego functions as a receiver, spectator, and transmitter" (p. 236). As Edinger (1992) put it, "the ego is the seat of subjective identity while the Self is the seat of objective identity" (p. 3). The Self is the true center of gravity of the personality, which it organizes and unifies. The relationship between ego and Self is referred to as the ego–Self axis because these two are thought to be in a dialogical relationship with each other. For example, the Self is considered to be the source of dreams, and psychotherapeutic work on dreams leads to further dreams in a reciprocal sequence. The idea of the ego–Self axis corresponds to a devotional or dualistic form of spirituality of the kind found in monotheistic traditions; the ego level represents the individual human being in relation to the divine, the two being quite distinct from each other. Jung also spoke of the Self as the totality of the psyche, which means that the ego is a part of the Self, suggesting a form of nondual spirituality akin to that found in many mystical traditions. For nondual philosophers, reality is an undivided unity, so that for theistic Eastern traditions the divine and the human are not two separate entities. Nondual approaches to psychotherapy are just beginning to appear in the literature (Prendergast & Bradford, 2007); examples are found in Buddhist psychology and emerging mindfulness-based psychotherapies (see Chapter 10 in this volume). This perspective not only offers the therapist multiple ways to understand the patient's relationship with the divine but also shapes his or her understanding of the therapeutic process as one in which a firm division between psychological and spiritual growth dissolves. Jungian therapists believe that psychotherapy is carried out within the supraordinate field of the transpersonal Self, which is a third presence in the room. At this nondual level, the consciousness of the therapist and that of the patient are not truly separate, so it is not surprising that synchronistically the patient may bring in some aspect of the therapist's own material. For Jungians, the theory of synchronicity (which refers to an outer event that meaningfully coincides in time with intrapsychic material) expresses the deep symmetry between the realms of psyche and world, which are not separate. The psychotherapeutic implications of a nondual approach to the Self, however, have not been developed in the Jungian literature (Corbett, 2011b), although the notion of the Self as the totality of the psyche remains heuristically and philosophically important.

Symbols of the Self occur spontaneously in dreams, and they are recognizable by their numinous or spiritual quality—they arouse emotions of awe and mystery. One might dream of a well-known God image such as Christ, or dreams may produce previously unknown images of the Self in a way that is particularly relevant to the subject. The Self may appear in an abstract form, commonly as a mandala shape (Jung, 1959/1977a). A *mandala* (the Sanskrit word for circle) is a symmetrical geometrical figure usually consisting of some combination of squares, circles, or triangles, often with a focus on the center. In Eastern religious traditions, these diagrams are used as an aid to meditation. They usually have a four-fold symmetry; the number four is an ancient symbol of wholeness and stability. The level of organization or disorganization of mandalas that appear within a person's spontaneous paintings may reflect the degree of integration or order in the individual's psyche, so that some Jungian clinicians encourage artwork not only for its expressive value but also to monitor the course of the treatment. In dreams, mandalas take such forms as symmetrical cities with streets or rivers radiating from a center, or wheels, circular flowers, and so on. Symmetrical mandala imagery tends to appear in dreams when the dreamer's life is going through a period of disorganization, because the psyche, like the body, tends to be self-regulating. When the personality is out of balance, the psyche tries to correct itself by producing images of order and structure. At other times, in an attempt to resolve internal conflict, the Self depicts itself in the form of dream imagery that unites apparent opposites, such as a snake with wings or a figure that is both young and old or both male and female. These qualities, which the dreamer in his conscious life believes to be in opposition to each other, are then shown to be complementary, part of a unified whole. They tend to appear when the dreamer has overidentified with one pole of a conflict. For example, a man in conflict between aggression and passivity dreams of a wild animal and a lamb coexisting. The Self may also appear as a spectacular natural phenomenon, such an enormous golden animal, perhaps referring to an instinctual level of the psyche, or to a great tree, referring to the psyche's vegetative aspect. Each of these images refers only to a particular aspect of the Self, depending on the dreamer's need. These images may be quite novel, with no connection to any religious tradition, recognizable only by their numinosity. This attitude is the antithesis of approaches that insist on only one dogmatically correct God image, such as traditional Christianity, which projects the Self onto Christ. Because the transpersonal level of the psyche is autonomous, the individual has no control over the way in which the Self may appear. Images of the Self therefore may contradict received doctrine. A man dreamed that a gigantic unidentified flying object (UFO) descended from the sky and hovered a short distance above his head. The base of the UFO was studded with eyes, from each of which a bright beam of light shone down onto the dreamer as if the craft was looking at him. The affect in the dream was one of awe and wonder. Although a UFO is not a Judeo–Christian image of the divine, for Jung, the numinosity of the dream and the mandala shape of the vessel qualify it as a Self-symbol. Additionally, one of the dreamer's developmental difficulties resulted from growing up in a family in which he was not seen; the dream directly addresses this complex and opens the door to psychotherapeutic exploration of this difficulty. In addition to the obvious relational or transference dynamic that the dream may imply, the therapist could add that the patient is seen by the Self, or even by the eye of God. The beneficial psychological effects of this experience are obvious.

Jung believed that although he could demonstrate the existence of the Self as a psychological function, to do so did not "take the place of God" or prove the existence of God in the metaphysical sense (1964/1978b, p. 463). Nevertheless, it is clear that Jung located the *experience* of the divine within human subjectivity, without committing himself to the question of whether images of God in the psyche are exactly the same as, or only correspond to, the transcendent God of traditional theism. He believed there is a consistent psychological relationship between the divine itself and its intrapsychic images, but speaking as a psychologist, he could not say whether or not these are the same thing. Nevertheless, in clinical practice, the Self has become a de facto God term; many Jungian psychotherapists tacitly think of the experience of the Self as an experience of the God who is referred to in traditional theism, although this practice is not strictly faithful to Jung's technical definition. At the same time, we are careful not to import theological ideas into our psychological work, because the Self may appear in completely novel ways that may conflict with the imagery of the subject's religious tradition. A scientist with a traditional masculine image of God dreamed of an enormous, luminous female figure sitting on him. As she did so, "we merged and it felt as though she was entering each and every one of my body's cells." Only a splinter of a personal self remained, which gave the dreamer a sense of scale, "as though I were no bigger than a tiny spider." This experience was humbling and transformative. The dream could be reduced by explaining it in terms of an overwhelming mother or some similar interpretation of the dreamer's personal life. Even if this were correct, the Jungian therapist would also point out that this was a numinous experience of the feminine aspects of the divine, or the Self in its feminine aspects, which has important implications for the individual's spiritual development. Pointing this out would make him conscious of the limitations of his overly masculine, traditional God image. At the same time he would become aware that, like all men, he has a feminine element within his psyche (what Jung called the *anima*), which is valuable to understand and relate to. This new awareness would foster his individuation process, which requires this kind of increasing assimilation of, and relationship with, the unconscious.

THE SELF AND THE GOD IMAGE

The Self in Jung's work is a kind of psychological version of the Atman of the Hindu tradition. He said that "what is meant by the Self is not only in me but in all beings," (Jung, 1964/1978b, p. 463), which corresponds to a similar statement in the *Bhagavad Gita* (IX, 20). Jung's belief that there can be no exclusive God image is also in agreement with the *Gita* (V, 21) that the Self can be worshiped in any form. The idea that the Self may appear in many different forms contributed to the discomfort of Christian theologians with Jung's theory, because traditional Christianity was committed to a Christology and a God image that it held to be supreme.

Because a God image exists in the psyche, Jung was able to speak of the "relativity of God," meaning that for him God was not absolute, existing beyond the human realm, but in a way depended on the consciousness of humanity, so that there is a "reciprocal and essential relation between man and God, whereby man can be understood as a function of God and God as a function of man" (1921/1971, p. 243). In this context, Jung quoted the 17th-century mystic Angelus Silesius, who said of God, "He cannot live without me, nor I without him" (Jung, 1958/1977c, p. 190). That is, it takes a person to know that God is God. Jung's God image is therefore relative rather than transcendent. In this context, it is noteworthy that the subtitle of an exhibit of Jung's *The Red Book* at New York's Rubin Museum of Art was "Creation of a New Cosmology." Dourley (1995) suggested that Jung has introduced a radically new cosmology in which divinity and humanity are intimately involved in a unitary process of mutual redemption. The idea of human–divine mutual cocreation is found in various religious texts, again including the *Bhagavad Gita* (III, 11). In support of this idea, Jung also invoked the 14th-century Meister Eckhart's notion that God is born continuously in the soul, which for Jung was synonymous with the psyche (Jung, 1921/1971). Jung's notion of an innate God image in the soul continued Eckhart's line of thought. Jung also made use of Eckhart's distinction between God, which we can name, and the Godhead, which is beyond our experience. For Jung, what Eckhart meant by God is a function of the psyche, whereas traditional Christianity sees God as "absolute, existing in himself" (Jung, 1921/1971, p. 243).

Here I should distinguish Jung's notion of the relativity of God from the work of Feuerbach, for whom human ideas, feelings, and imagination have been transformed into a divine being, so that religious doctrine is the objectification of some aspect of human nature. For Jung, the Self and the archetypal level of the psyche are autonomous, objective realities that radically transcend the ego; they are not something we make up, and they are distinct from human nature. Because Jung believed that the ego and Self affect each other mutually, some contemporary process theologians believe that Jung's approach is consistent with theirs (Griffin, 1990). In this process context, Jung believed that the Self is an undivided unity that differentiates itself within human consciousness, and the gradual expansion of our consciousness is a central human task (Jaffe, 1983). Accordingly, because psychotherapeutic work expands consciousness, psychotherapy has an important collective as well as personal function; it allows the Self to differentiate itself, for example, by becoming more conscious of opposing principles within itself. I take up this metaphysical idea further in Jung's discussion of the story of Job (*vide infra*).

ARCHETYPES AND COMPLEXES

The archetype, one of Jung's most controversial ideas, is an organizing principle in the psyche that provides an innate disposition for typical human experiences. Archetypal processes can be thought of as the psychological analogues to the laws that physicists use to describe the material world, which act as restrictions on the way physicists formulate their theories. Similarly, the psyche operates according to deep structures and processes that govern the organization of experience and our way of describing it. The idea of invariant principles in the psyche and the concept of intrinsic psychological structures are now taken seriously among evolutionary psychologists and are implicit or explicit in Piaget's approach to cognitive development, Chomsky's linguistics, Lévi-Strauss's structural anthropology, and ethological descriptions of innate release mechanisms (Stevens, 1982). The image–schemata of cognitive psychology also come to mind. The usual misunderstanding of the notion of the archetype is to dismiss it as a stereotype; in fact, it is a pure potential whose specific content is filled in by the individual's experience and culture.

Jung (1921/1971) had no good explanation for the origin of the archetypes. In his early writing, when he was concerned to find a physiological substrate for the idea, he suggested that the archetypes are the inherited residues of the repeated experiences of humanity, which for millennia found itself in similar situations, leaving indelible traces in the brain (Jung, 1921/1971). This idea was criticized as Lamarkian, although Jung always insisted that the specific contents of the archetypes are not inherited—the archetypes only represent the potentials for certain types of experience. Gradually, he realized that an explanation in terms of inheritance puts the problem of the origin of the archetypes back into prehistory without solving it. Therefore, in his later work, Jung (1964) said that the origin of the archetypes is unknown, and even the question of whether they "originated" at all is an unanswerable metaphysical problem; they appear with the appearance of the psyche, whose origin is itself a mystery (Jung, 1959/1977a). They enter into the picture "with life itself" (Jung, 1958/1977c, p. 149).

Jung (1964) believed that the archetypal level of the psyche is common to all of humanity because he found similar religious and mythological motifs across cultures and historical periods. For example, all religions and mythological systems represent the Great Mother, the goddess, or the feminine aspects of the divine, who is given different names in different cultures. The Blessed Virgin Mary, Kali, Isis, or Demeter are local aspects of the same archetypal structure that is irreducible and only known symbolically. This perspective has clinical implications; to understand those archetypal images that are dominant in the individual psyche reveals the organizing principles that affect the person's spiritual beliefs and also his or her core psychological functioning. At the human level, the mother archetype, which includes the potential to be and to experience a mother, may be expressed in many ways. The human details of mothering vary from culture to culture and family to family, so the mother complex consists of this archetypal potential filled in with experiences of one's actual mother, leading to the development of a mother complex. Complexes are affectively toned, enduring, intrapsychic structures consisting of groups of related associations, memories, and images that cluster around an archetypal core. For Jungian analysts, theories such as object relations theory and psychoanalytic self-psychology are descriptions of the ways in which the human level of the complex is formed. Depending on the behavior of one's early caregivers, the emotional tone of one's complexes may be positive or negative; the negative complex—for example, the result of a traumatic selfobject milieu—leads to psychopathology. The Oedipus complex is one of many possible complexes in a person's mind and is not necessarily central.

Jung (1975b) believed that the archetypes are spiritual principles in the psyche; he referred to them as "organs" or "tools" of God (p. 130). (Here he was clearly referring to the God of the theologians.) Because the archetypes form the core of complexes, the Jungian therapist is always aware that the individual's suffering has a spiritual ground as well as a human level. The archetypal core of the complex may be represented in a dream. For example, a woman dreams that the severed head of her mother is chasing her; instead of hair, the head is covered in snakes like the head of the mythic Medusa, who turned people to stone. This image graphically illustrates the effect the mother had on the dreamer, and the mythic association suggests the quality of the archetypal core of her mother complex.

The archetypes are represented mythologically in the form of the gods and goddesses of antiquity, which Jung (1959/1977a) considered to be contents of the psyche that were "extrapolated in metaphysical space and hypostasized" (p. 59). By giving their deities names and personalities, the ancients personified what Jung now refers to as archetypal processes. This mythopoetic level of the psyche is autonomous; the ego has no control over its function, as we see, for example, when we fall in love—an archetypal process that in antiquity was attributed to the goddess Aphrodite. The archetype can manifest itself either negatively or positively, depending on the behavior of one's early caretakers because they "humanize" the experience of the archetype and bring it into time and space. A man whose father was domineering and punitive suffers from a negative father complex that renders him terrified of male authority figures. The human level of such a complex could be described by various psychological theories. What Jung added is to point to the archetypal core of the complex; this man's father behaved like the mythological Sky Father gods, such as Zeus, who demanded to be obeyed and who punished mortals for disobedience. Another father was an Apollo type of man, a remote perfectionist preoccupied with rational thought, logic, and order. The only way his son could escape this internalized critic was by means of altered states of consciousness; he turned to a Dionysian escape in drugs, music, and sensuality. (Dionysus was the god of ecstasy, wine, and madness.) The psychological processes represented by such mythological deities are still present in us, but now, in Jung's words, "the gods have become diseases" (Jung, 1967/1976a, p. 37)—we see them in our pathologies.

ARCHETYPES AND THE THERAPEUTIC PROCESS

An added value for the therapist to recognize such archetypal elements in the individual's material is the acknowledgment of their numinous gripping power. When struggling with a complex, it is as if one is struggling with a force that seems to be more than human. This recognition puts the patient's difficulty in a larger perspective than is possible with a more limited view of the problem. The patient can locate his or her situation within the storehouse of human experience depicted in mythology and religion, and thereby not feel so isolated. After any negative transference is worked out, the therapeutic relationship evokes the positive side of the archetype because this is always present as a potential, so that the benefits of psychotherapy are only in part the result of the therapist's efforts. In addition to the intersubjective field between the participants, a third presence, the archetypal Self, participates in the therapeutic process, an awareness that produces a certain humility in the Jungian therapist.

In addition to awareness of the personal interaction that is operating in the therapy room, the Jungian therapist is also conscious that there are archetypal dimensions of the therapeutic field that can be described metaphorically using mythic imagery. For example, Winnicott (1971) described the analytic space as an intermediate area between the reality of the therapist and the patient's fantasies, a space that offers the possibility of experiencing new meanings. In an evolution of this idea, Ogden (2004) described a cocreated "analytic third" to which the individual subjectivities of analyst and analysand are subordinated; this level takes on a life of its own within the interpersonal field and is experienced as barely perceptible background reverie in the therapist's mind. Ogden believed that his reverie informed him of what was happening unconsciously between himself and the patient. Within this ambiguous, nonlinear, "in-between" space, communication not only goes on at the human level but can also be represented mythologically as the presence of Mercurius–Hermes. In antiquity, he was a guide of souls, a wily, elusive, and sometimes deceitful god of communication and revelation who was impossible to pin down. Mercurius therefore can be thought of metaphorically as an archetypal aspect of the process that lies between the participants and is thus a way of talking about the intangible spirit of relationship, transformation, and the slippery processes of the unconscious. It is therefore important for the therapist to pay attention to his or her internal imagery, thoughts, feelings, and body sensations, which cannot be dismissed as irrelevant primary process thinking but can be recognized as the presence of a mercurial field, a form of communication from the unconscious that is directly relevant to the work (Schaverien, 2007). Jungians find that consciousness of such an archetypal dimension adds further depth of meaning to the therapeutic process. Clinicians therefore pay close attention to their subjective experiences when conducting therapy as well as to their associations and dreams about the patient outside of the session, as these phenomena help us to understand the patient and the archetypal level of the therapeutic relationship.

SPIRITUAL DIMENSIONS OF THE THERAPEUTIC RELATIONSHIP

Jung described the archetypal or spiritual level of the therapeutic relationship using the metaphor of the sacred marriage, which leads to the sense that the therapeutic couple belongs to a family. Jung (1954/1975a) depicted this level of the transference as an intrapsychic *coniunctio* or union, a term borrowed from the medieval alchemists. He believed not only that the ancient practice of alchemy was the antecedent to modern chemistry but also that the alchemists projected transformative intrapsychic processes into the material operations of the laboratory. Therefore, what the alchemists were doing was psychological as well as material. At least among the spiritual alchemists, what was described as the search for literal gold was actually a search for spiritual gold, the Self, or for the spiritual transformation of leaden personality traits. Jung found many parallels between alchemical imagery and psychotherapy, so that alchemy seems to offer metaphorical representations of unconscious processes. (Here it is important to recall Lakoff's, 1993, suggestion that metaphor is a fundamental mode of thought.) The therapist can sometimes see analogies between alchemical imagery and a process that is going on in the patient, which is helpful if it allows one to see that the patient's experience is part of an archetypal or transpersonal pattern. For example, the alchemists conducted their experiments in a *vas bene clausum*, or a well-sealed vessel, which is regarded as analogous to the container, the holding environment, or the frame of psychotherapy. Within this vessel, the elements separated and recombined to form alchemical "gold," or the emergence of the Self. The alchemists used the term *nigredo,* or blackness, to describe the initial, dark state of the material with which they worked, which corresponds to the patient's state of mind at the beginning of the work—the alchemical *prima materia.* Gradually, a series of color changes occurred in the alchemical vessel, which were said to end in the production of gold; these colors follow a particular sequence (black, white, yellow, and red) that sometimes can be seen in patient's dream imagery, indicating stages of the work. Edinger (1991) has provided a list of similar parallels between the operations of the alchemists and various processes of psychotherapy, indicating ways in which the alchemists, like the therapist, separated, analyzed, and then synthesized and consolidated new material. The discovery of an analogous archetypal process reflected in a historical tradition far removed from 21st-century depth psychology adds to the Jungian therapist's sense that the patient's suffering is purposeful and not random. For Jungian therapists, symptoms such as anxiety and depression cannot be fully understood by looking at childhood developmental factors; symptoms also have a prospective or forward-looking function. Jungian therapists understand such symptoms as a kind of wake-up call from the Self to greater consciousness (Jung, 1964/1978b), as if it were intending to move the patient in a particular direction. The symptom is at the same time an experience of the dark side of the Self and an important aspect of the patient's ongoing development. The therapeutic task includes helping the individual discover the new direction that the symptom is taking him by looking into the ways in which his life has been changed by the problem.

Jung found that many of the people who consulted him for psychotherapy were not suffering from a clinically definable disorder. They suffered from a sense of futility, the lack of a spiritual connection, and the lack of a believable myth, a sacred story by which they could live. One of Jung's early criticisms of Freud was that an exclusive concern with the drives does not satisfy the patient's spiritual needs and does not add meaning to life. For Jung, a neurosis can be understood as "the suffering of a human being who has not discovered what life means for him." Spiritual stagnation causes suffering, and the psychotherapeutic problem is to find "the meaning that quickens" (Jung, 1958/1977c, p. 331). Reason and science will not supply what is needed; the patient is ill because "he has failed to read the meaning of his own existence" (Jung, 1933/2005, pp. 230–231). The patient's religious problem is therefore relevant to his emotional problem and may even be the cause of it (Jung, 1933/2005, p. 239). Jung believed that the major problems of our lives are not so much solved as outgrown, meaning that we find a larger perspective so that the problem loses its urgency even if it is not solved on its own terms. He found that for patients dealing with existential questions of meaning and purpose, especially those in the second half of life, it is essential to find a religious outlook on life. This does not necessarily mean adherence to a traditional religion, although it may do so; it means the recovery of a personal connection to the sacred dimension. Jung (1960/1978c) believed that the therapist's recognition of the spiritual factors within a patient's struggle is vitally important. If a patient found that a traditional religion was still alive, Jung felt that a satisfactory outcome of psychotherapy would be for the patient to return to his or her church. Like many contemporary psychotherapists, however, Jung saw many patients who had no faith, people for whom God was dead. In this situation, when the church fails, the psychotherapist may be called on to act in a capacity that used to be the role of the priest or spiritual director (Jung, 1958/1977c). For Jung, the recovery of a spiritual attitude implied paying attention to the manifestations of the unconscious because God acts out of the unconscious (Jung, 1958/1977c, p. 468). Part of the value of attending to dreams is that paradoxically, although the source of emotional suffering may be in the unconscious (in the form of a complex), we also look to the unconscious for help.

Approaches to psychotherapy such as psychoanalytic self-psychology clarify the human level of psychotherapy but not the archetypal or spiritual level. For example, Kohut (1984) stressed the importance of mirroring in psychotherapy; in brief, this means to respond in an attuned manner to the person's affective state and to affirm his or her worth. This is particularly important for patients who were never responded to in an empathic manner in childhood, who therefore remain hungry for responsiveness. For Jungian therapists, one then responds not only to the human level but also to the presence of the Self as a divine child, the prepersonal or transpersonal level of the child that was always present but never recognized. This archetypal level of the child is seen in the mythology of child gods, such as the baby Jesus, the baby Krishna, and so on. Kohut also described a developmental need to idealize, to merge psychologically with a source of strength and soothing. This role is projected upon the therapist when the patient suffers a defect along this developmental line. When one sees another person in an idealized light, somehow perfect and wise, one is projecting the Self onto that person or unconsciously seeking the divine in the other.

INDIVIDUATION AS A SPIRITUAL PROCESS

Jung believed he could discern a teleological process, which he termed *individuation*, meaning the full and unique development of the personality. For individuation to occur, consciousness must relate to the unconscious but not be overwhelmed by it. Individuation requires the gradual widening of ego consciousness so that unconscious contents, including painful and dark material, are gradually acknowledged and integrated. We have no idea what the result of this process will look like or what it will require in terms of suffering; the result cannot be imagined by the ego—it takes time to discover who one really is, but the urge to live out one's uniqueness is an ineluctable natural law (Jung, 1959/1977a). The individuation process can be difficult because it is guided by the Self and, as Jung put it, "the experience of the Self is always a defeat for the ego" (1963/1976b, p. 546). Gradually, "the individuated ego senses itself as the object of an unknown and supraordinate subject" (Jung, 1952/1976d, p. 240)—that is, I realize that the Self is aware of me. This statement should not be understood to imply the presence of the transcendent deity of traditional monotheism; within Jung's paradigm, all religious experience is intrapsychic. For him, "transcendence" was a function of an immanent power in the psyche that transcends the possibility of conscious expression; nothing can be known beyond the boundaries of the psyche (Dourley, 2001). Early in life one is not conscious of the presence of the Self, but one gradually becomes aware of the presence of a *spiritus rector* (a ruling spirit) within the personality that guides its development (Jung, 1959/1978a, p. 167). Like any spiritual path, this process is not easy; it exposes one to the demands of the unconscious—the traditional perils of the soul.

Individuation involves a life-long process of the incarnation of specific potentials of the Self into an empirical personality. For Jung, the life of Christ is an example of individuation, because He lived His life as fully as possible in spite of the suffering this incurred (Edinger, 1987; Jung, 1958/1977c), but Jung believed that we can now become conscious of this incarnation in ourselves rather than load everything onto Christ (McGuire & Hull, 1987, pp. 97–98). Individuation may happen unconsciously, in which case one simply lives one's life and development occurs naturally, or one enhances the process by becoming conscious of it (Jung, 1959/1977a), which is one function of psychotherapy.

Individuation does not mean egocentricity; individuation means that although one is not alienated from or in opposition to collective norms, one is oriented to them differently. One does not ignore the world but rather "gathers the world to oneself" (Jung, 1960/1978c, p. 226). One differentiates oneself as much as possible from family and culture, but paradoxically the more one individuates the more one is led to relationships rather than isolation (Jung, 1921/1971). Eventually, one experiences the Self as a new center of consciousness. All religious traditions offer paths toward individuation, but one may also individuate outside a religious tradition by paying attention to the manifestations of the Self (the phenomenology of the spirit) within one's soul.

THE RELIGIOUS FUNCTION OF THE PSYCHE

This section describes what may be the core of Jung's psychology—his notion that the psyche has an intrinsic religious function, a natural, spontaneous tendency to produce religious experience. Jung believed that an experience of the archetypal level of the unconscious, or direct contact with the Self, produces numinous or mystical experiences. Here, Jung was influenced by Rudolf Otto's (1958) concept of the numinous, although there are some differences of perspective between their uses of this term. Otto described numinous experience as an encounter with the *mysterium tremendum et fascinans*—a fascinating and tremendous mystery. Biblical examples included Moses being addressed by God at the burning bush (Exod. 3), or Saul on the road to Damascus, who heard Jesus' voice saying, "Why do you persecute me?" (Acts 9:3–9). Faced with such an experience, the subject is awestruck, producing the "speechless humility" of a creature in the presence of an inexpressible mystery (Otto, 1958, p. 13). These experiences produce astonishment, dread, and a sense of the uncanny. They are also fascinating, promising divine love, forgiveness, or grace, although at times they may produce horror and terror. Numinous experience cannot be brought about intentionally and cannot be controlled; it has to be suffered without being understood.

Like Otto (1958), Jung (1964/1978b) believed that numinous experiences are irreducible experiences of the holy, but whereas Otto linked numinous experience with the Christian God image, for Jung, a numinous experience does not carry traditional theistic overtones and may appear in any form. For Otto the *numinosum* is "wholly other," whereas for Jung, there is a God image located within the psyche, so the divine is more "in here" than "out there." Unlike Otto, Jung (1965) did not believe that one must totally submit to numinous experience; he believed that it is important for the ego to take a stand in relation to transpersonal experience. Jung (1967/1976a) recognized that in spite of its importance, a numinous experience may cause fragmentation of the personality, so he believed one should maintain some distance from it rather than be totally overwhelmed by it, which may produce a psychosis. Jungian therapists encourage the subject to try to relate to the experience, rather than identify with it, and to find a way to express it through a medium such as painting, writing, or dance.

Jung believed that whatever form numinous experiences take, they may have a healing effect—indeed, he noted that "the approach to the numinous is the real therapy" (Jung, 1973, p. 377). For example, a woman whose mother was devaluing, withholding, and critical of her and her body had the following dream:

> I am in a glass elevator which, with no visible cables, is heading straight up in the middle of a vast, open space. The sky is clear blue and I can see for hundreds of miles. I realize I am pressed up against a group of beautiful, other-worldly women who are swaying and singing a mesmerizing melody. We are naked. I am lifted up by them, they hold me, stroke me, and embrace me. Their song is one of love, compassion, and forgiveness. There is a feeling of intimacy. At one point they begin dripping honey on me; it feels loving and sweet; I am filled with incredible peace and joy, beyond words or description.

This numinous dream directly addressed the woman's emotional difficulties and had a powerfully healing effect. It also meets Otto's (1958) criteria—it is mysterious, tremendous, and fascinating—but the imagery has no particular relation to the Judeo–Christian tradition. These kinds of numinous experience are affectively powerful, which is why they are helpful, because "the thing that cures a neurosis must be as convincing as the neurosis, and since the latter is only too real, the helpful experience must be equally real" (Jung, 1958/1977c, p. 105).

Jung (1953/1977b) believed that the Enlightenment spirit of our times has alienated us from the depths of the psyche, from which such numinous experience emanates. Jung was concerned that for many moderns, "everything is to be found outside . . . in Church and Bible—but never inside. . . . Too few people have experienced the divine image as the innermost possession of their own souls" (1953/1977b, p. 12). Rationalists meet the numinous contents of the unconscious with a materialistic prejudice by reducing or ignoring imagery that has great symbolic meaning to the soul. In contrast, Jung (1958/1977c) believed that numinous experiences are a treasure that provides us with a source of life, meaning, and beauty: "And if such experience helps to make your life healthier, more beautiful, more complete and more satisfactory to yourself and to those who love you, you may safely say: 'This was the grace of God'" (pp. 113–114). Numinous experiences can be reduced by dismissing them as hallucinatory or hysterical or as the products of an overheated imagination, but in the absence of other evidence of overt psychological disorder, Jungian therapists are inclined to take such experiences at face value, as direct experience of the holy. When the experience is self-authenticating because of its emotional power, the therapist only needs to affirm or mirror the patient's appreciation of the experience. Occasionally one may need to explain to a bewildered patient what it is that he or she has experienced. The therapeutic task is to help the person assimilate the meaning of the experience and its effects on his or her life. Jung believed that the psyche is by its nature religious and that it spontaneously produces numinous experiences, which for Jung were a form of continuing revelation occurring within the individual psyche. For him, revelation is not confined to a particular event in a religious tradition's sacred history. Revelation may appear to the individual in a way that does not necessarily coincide with traditional scriptures or their elaboration by the churches. Traditional religions that focus largely on worship, Bible study, and preaching often do not stress direct experience of the numinosum, but for Jung "it is pointless to praise the light and preach it if nobody can see it" (1953/1977b, p. 13); the problem is to teach people the art of seeing because people do not realize that numinous imagery lies within the psyche. Traditional churches, however, often mistrust direct mystical experience because it may contravene their theology. Jung gave the example of the 15th-century Nicholas von Flüe, who experienced a frightening numinous vision. He struggled to make sense of this experience in the light of his theology and did so by deciding he must have "gazed upon the Holy Trinity itself," even though the original experience was not at all Trinitarian. It required a long struggle to get the experience into a form von Flüe could understand, using dogma to transform "something horribly alive into the beautiful abstraction of the Trinity idea," a transformation which saved him from the stake (Jung, 1959/1977a, pp. 9–13). For Jung, this is an example of the way in which dogma protects the person at the price of changing the meaning of a genuinely numinous experience. Jung (1958/1977c) even said that it is the function of the church to oppose original forms of religious experience when they are unorthodox. He believed that the church tried to suppress gnosticism because it contained mythological motifs and irrational elements that Christianity could not incorporate.

NUMINOUS EXPERIENCE: CLINICAL IMPLICATIONS

Numinous imagery often contradicts the teaching of a patient's childhood religion, and these experiences are often related to the patient's emotional difficulties. A woman with a raging, abusive father grew up in a fundamentalist family in which she was taught that she was a sinful person in grave danger of eternal punishment from an angry God. In a dream, she is in a library (a place of safety for her) in which Jesus is reading a book to a small child. The dreamer is delighted to be in his presence; she walks over and leans against him. He puts his arm around the dreamer, whereupon "my whole being felt flooded with acceptance, love, and peace." She understood this to mean, "If I am beloved by Jesus, then I must be good." This dream not only felt sacramental, it had a profoundly healing effect; because it was a direct experience of the sacred, it assuaged her fears of eternal damnation in a way that would have been difficult to achieve by psychotherapeutic means alone.

Jung frequently warned that numinous experiences are not without danger; they can possess people and inspire them to believe they are prophets. Identification with the numinous then leads to a dangerous inflation. Therefore, if one has had such a powerful experience, it is critical that one overcome the temptation to set oneself up as a world redeemer (Jung, 1953/1977d). Ironically, in spite of his frequent warnings about these dangers, Jung's detractors often accused him of these very excesses (Corbett, 2011a).

For the psychotherapist, it is important to note that a numinous experience may or may not have a traditional Judeo–Christian content—only its affective quality is important. We usually find that the experience addresses a particular aspect of the subject's life, such as a psychological difficulty or an existential problem. The experience may occur in one of several modes: as a dream, as a waking vision, through the body, in the natural world, in the course of creative work, or as a synchronistic event

(Corbett, 1996, 2000a, 2000b, 2006). Jungians pay particular attention to dreams, which are thought to be produced by the Self, following a long biblical tradition of dreams sent by God (Jung, 1964/1978b). As Dourley (1981) pointed out, because the *numinosum* manifests itself within the psyche, the psyche is sacramental. For Jung (1953/1977b), the relationship between the psyche and God was like that between the eye and the sun, and "it would be blasphemy to assert that God can manifest himself everywhere save only in the human soul" (p. 10).

In clinical practice, we sometimes find that numinous experiences speak for themselves and need no interpretation, but at other times very puzzling or frightening numinous imagery erupts into consciousness, as the following dream as described by a patient indicates. For the dreamer this imagery was deeply mysterious, very powerful, and fascinating at the same time:

> I was in a chemistry laboratory. I felt a tiny movement in my left ear, and with my finger I scooped out a tiny snake with the wings of a bird. I dropped the snake into a flask, and immediately there was a beautiful, lush forest in the flask. This happened again with a second flask. Suddenly, a much larger winged snake flew out of my left ear, followed closely by a second one just like it. Blood came from my ear. Then my skin started to shed, and a huge winged snake came up through my throat and burst out of my mouth as my face fell backwards and began to slide down over the body of the emerging snake. It felt as if I would die, since this snake was much bigger than my body. I woke up afraid before my body had been completely shed.

This kind of numinous dream is sometimes considered to be demonic by traditional ministers of religion (such an interpretation was given to a patient of mine by her minister when she told him that she had dreamed of Jesus as a woman). Given the numinosity of this dream of a winged snake, Jungian therapists would not judge its origin in that way. We would try to understand the imagery in terms of the person's life story, taking into account her development, personality structure, and her cultural setting. It is also important to discern the prospective importance of the dream, the direction in which it is moving the dreamer. In this case, given the dreamer's lack of personal associations, the dream could not be understood in purely personal terms. Nor can it be explained only in terms of the Judeo–Christian tradition; it requires an excursion into the larger mythic history of humanity for its full significance to be grasped. The snake is an enormously complex symbol—it is not simply phallic or demonic. The winged snake is a mythological image of the harmony between heaven and Earth, or the union of chthonic matter and spirit. The snake may represent primordial life energy, or the primitive instinctual level of the psyche, and because it sheds its skin, it also implies the capacity for renewal. In antiquity, the snake was associated with the Great Mother or the goddess and many other deities, including Aesculapius, the divine healer. The dream therefore represents a tremendous activation of such archetypal forces within the unconscious of the dreamer. It is common for numinous dream imagery to take a form that is quite different than the dreamer's own religious tradition. In such a case, the therapist tries to help the person find the meaning of the experience, if necessary by locating its imagery within religions or mythologies with which the dreamer may not be familiar. Because symbolic material from any mythological or religious tradition may appear in a patient's dream, Jungian therapists try to be familiar with as many such traditions as possible.

Because numinous phenomena are intrapsychic and of great subjective importance, Jung believed they are the appropriate province of psychology. Because of Kant's influence, which denies the possibility of knowing anything definite about the metaphysical realm, Jung eschewed speculation about the source of numinous experience and made no ontological claims about the transcendent God of traditional religion. He insisted he was unable to make any statement about the divine itself, as this is the province of theology. He could only speak of the God image that appears in the psyche. This insistence, however, did not protect him from criticism by both psychologists and theologians.

Fromm (1959) complained that Jung elevated the unconscious to the status of a religious phenomenon. Buber (1952) objected that to speak of the Self as an intrapsychic image of the divine reduces God to something psychological and therefore not transcendent, whereas for Buber the divine was an "absolute Other" (p. 68), an ontological reality beyond the psyche and independent of the human being.

Jung (1958/1977c) responded to such critics by pointing out that the psyche is real, so an intrapsychic God image is real. Furthermore, we can only experience the world or God by means of the psyche, and the psychologist cannot say what lies beyond it. He insisted that he was merely pointing out the empirical fact that the divine mystery chooses to manifest itself by means of the psyche, a claim that does not exclude the possibility of a transcendent level of divinity—it simply means that speculation about that level is not the province of psychology. For Jung, Buber's (1952) Other is actually the transpersonal level of the psyche, with which the ego is in a relationship. Jung trenchantly pointed out that Buber's divine Thou would be defined in one way by Buber and in another by the advocates of other traditions. It must be acknowledged, however, that if Jung is correct, the value of prayer and ritual are called into question: Do these have an objective referent? Perhaps they are simply an expression of the ego–Self axis. Dourley (2002) suggested that there is no common ground between Jung and Buber because the differences between traditional monotheism and Jung's approach are foundational and irresolvable.

For Jung (1958/1977c), when we experience the *numinosum*, we cannot distinguish whether these actions emanate from God or from the unconscious: "We cannot tell whether God and the unconscious are two different entities. Both are borderline concepts for transcendental contents" (p. 468). Jung did not fully commit himself about whether what we call God is synonymous with the unconscious or whether the unconscious is simply a medium of divine expression; he believed that empirically we cannot distinguish between these possibilities. Here is it important to mention what Jung meant by the unconscious. He insisted that we have no idea about the nature of the unconscious, which is only a posit, not an independent entity whose metaphysical essence we understand (Jung, 1961/1979). The unconscious "designates only my *unknowing*" (Jung, 1973, p. 411). According to Jung (1958/1977c), "the concept of the unconscious is an assumption for the sake of convenience" (p. 39). Jung viewed the unconscious as a kind of consciousness in its own right; he noted that perception, thinking, feeling, volition, and intention go on in the unconscious as though a subject were present (Jung, 1960/1978c). The unconscious cannot be hypostasized; it contains many centers of consciousness, it is not an entity and should not be thought of as "an encapsulated personal system" (Jung, 1959/1977a, p. 22).

Some of the resistance to the idea that the psyche plays a part in the production of numinous experience seems to originate in a prejudice that wants to make religion the province only of the sublime and the transcendent, thus splitting off everyday psychological realities and psychopathology, which are seen as somehow inferior to religious realities. As Schaer (1950, p. 60) pointed out, this is partly why Freud's contemporaries were so outraged at his linking religion and ordinary human psychology. Some of the same concern still seems to apply to theologians who criticize Jung's approach to religion because he linked it so intimately with the structures of the psyche. Thus, redolent of the Jung–Buber debate, when Edinger (1984) rather daringly suggested that a depth psychological approach to spirituality (of the kind described in this chapter) might be an emerging form of divine dispensation, he was accused of confusing theological and psychological discourse.

JUNG ON THE SOUL

Jung published his *Modern Man in Search of a Soul* in 1933, at a time when many behaviorists and psychoanalysts were denying the very existence of the soul and would eschew the use of such language because it sounded too theological. Jungians use the term *soul* in a variety of ways, all of which are distinct from its traditional theological usage. For Jungians in general, *soul* is synonymous with *psyche*. At times, the soul is also spoken of as if it were a kind of psychological "organ" that allows us to bridge to spirit by casting that experience into images and affects that we can experience intelligibly. (Here, *spirit* is used to mean the transpersonal level of the psyche, rather than in its traditional sense as the power and presence of God.) The word *soul* is also used to convey a sense of depth, fullness, meaning, and the deepest subjectivity of the individual as distinct from everyday ego concerns (Corbett, 2009).

Most important for Jung (1964/1978b, 1960/1978c), the soul or the psyche is the sine qua non of all experience and is a domain in its own right; the soul is not reducible to the functioning of the brain. This question is as controversial among Jungians as it is in the larger community of psychologists and philosophers. Some contemporary Jungians have pointed out a variety of ways in which contemporary neuroscience is compatible with Jung's theories. The archetypes have been seen as emergent functions of the developing right brain, and Jung's emphasis on the unconscious and the Self system is seen to be consistent with contemporary understanding of the highest levels of the nonverbal right hemisphere (Wilkinson, 2006). For many of us, however, this approach is too close to physicalism or materialistic monism, which would make the psyche an epiphenomenon of brain. Brain functioning might explain the emergence of a personal self but not the presence of the transpersonal Self when it is understood as the God within. Given our present state of knowledge, it seems preferable to tolerate the tension raised by the mind–brain question without an attempt at premature closure.

JUNG'S EPISTEMOLOGY

Jung's emphasis on the reality of the psyche is crucial to understanding his theoretical standpoint, which has important clinical implications. For him, the psyche is real because it has real effects. It seems to have its own purposes and it must be approached on its own terms (Jung, 1960/1978c). Jung's psychological standpoint avoided extreme realism (*esse in re*) and extreme idealism (*esse in intellectu*). He called his epistemological position *esse in anima*, which recognizes that there is an outer world but holds that the psyche is the indispensable link between our subjective experience of the world and the world itself (Jung, 1921/1971). In defense of this position, Kotsch (2000) has argued that Jung's nonobjectivist epistemology is consistent with that held by many contemporary cognitive scientists. Nonobjectivist psychology contrasts vividly with traditional objectivism, which holds that the mind is a passive reflection of the world of real objects and that concepts are meaningful to the extent they correspond to known objects—that is, order and meaning are assumed to be external to human experience. Some psychologists and philosophers of science now believe that this perspective cannot be correct, given the discovery of the "cognitive unconscious" and the importance of tacit knowledge on conscious thought. These writers have suggested that the relationship between subject and object is essentially psychological, dependent on human mental and social processes. Jung's emphasis on the reality of the psyche and his epistemological position mediated between the forced choice of objectivist and relativist accounts of knowledge. In Jung's interactionist epistemology, a mental image is not a simple copy of an object in the outer world but rather is in part generated by the psyche's own predispositions. Jung's emphasis on the reality of the psyche means that the physical world is not the only reality; we can trust our intuition that there is a spiritual level not detectable by the senses. The imagination has its own reality, and for the clinician, the patient's psychological contents, no matter how bizarre, can never be dismissed as meaningless fabrications; they are a living reality that have real effects. A fear of ghosts is as real as a fear of fire.

JUNG ON RELIGION, DOGMA, AND DOCTRINE

Jung (1958/1977c) used the term *religion* in one of its traditional etymological senses—from the Latin *relegere*, religion means careful attention to whatever is numinous. For Jung, religion was so important that far from being regressive or neurotic, the lack of a spiritual connection is a potential source of neurosis. According to Jung (1950/1976c), religious institutions act as psychotherapeutic systems. They allow the believer to feel part of a whole and to find help when suffering; they provide spiritual teachings and an answer to life's dilemmas. At the same time, Jung (1975b) emphasized direct experience of the sacred in contrast to purely faith-based approaches to religion, which he felt invariably produce concomitant doubt, at least unconsciously, which has to be repressed. Jung, therefore, was ambivalent about belief in traditional dogma and doctrine. He believed that dogma, symbols (such as the cross), and rituals all originate in the archetypal level of the psyche, so that religions allow this level of the unconscious to be experienced in a contained manner. An individual experience of the *numinosum* was followed by faith in the experience and then its institutionalization in the form of dogma (Jung, 1953/1977b). Dogmas such as the God-man, the Virgin Birth, and the Trinity are archetypal images of the divine, which are also found in several pre-Christian, pagan religions (Jung, 1958/1977c). Therefore, because they are archetypal, when dogmas such as these are alive for a person, they provide indirect contact with the unconscious, albeit at the price of a connection to his or her own psyche. For religion to be authentic, faith must be connected to personal experiences that correspond to the tenets of the tradition. Institutional religion is only helpful if its symbols are alive and meaningful for the individual; otherwise, belief in a creed can substitute for real spirituality because it tells the individual what to believe, which may make direct experience of the sacred more difficult to attain and thus stand in the way of spiritual development. Adherence to an institutional creed may protect the person from immediate numinous experience, which may be an important safeguard for people who cannot tolerate the affective intensity of numinous experience and for those who need certainty and external structure. Belief without direct experience of the holy, however, may fade under the onslaught of painful life events, whereas direct experience of the *numinosum* produces faith and knowledge that are self-authenticating and do not require belief because of the power of the experience (Jung, 1958/1977c). To approach the sacred in terms of personal experience avoids the problem of deciding which of the competing theological claims of traditional religions are correct.

In the spiritual crisis produced by the demise of traditional Judeo–Christian symbols, Jung recommended a turn to the personal experience of the autonomous psyche, which produces primordial religious experience, a turn that he believed can restore faith. The psyche's numinous imagery bridges consciousness and the unconscious. These images become personal symbols that may have no meaning to others, but because they are numinous, they allow the development of a personal as distinct from a collective spirituality. For example, I reported the dream of a Roman Catholic priest in which a huge figure of the Venus of Willendorf appeared above him; from her breast, a stream of milk poured into a chalice he was holding (Corbett, 2007). This dream represents an archetypal image of the goddess in a pre-Christian form, telling the dreamer that the nourishment of the divine feminine is sacramental to him. This numinous image compensates for an overly masculine image of the divine. The affective intensity of this dream makes this figure a true religious symbol for him, although it would not be considered so in his Church—an example of the way in which the autonomous psyche cannot be Christianized. The unconscious produces symbolic material from any religious pantheon that may be heretical to the individual's tradition but that is nevertheless of great personal significance. Needless to say, most established traditions would balk at the idea of accepting such a manifestation of the unconscious as an authentic revelation of the sacred, but for the Jungian therapist, the emotional quality of this dream does meet Otto's (1958) criteria of numinosity. One can understand the anxiety that this approach might produce because it could open the door to pathological material being accepted as spiritually valid, a concern that probably further contributed to the theologian's distaste for Jung's approach. Jungians would respond by pointing out that the dangers of facing unconscious material is not different than the dangers of religious experience in general—as the New Testament puts it, "It is a fearful thing to fall into the hands of the living God" (Hebrews 10:13). Numinous imagery of this kind often appears when the individual is in a life crisis—certainly this is likely in the case of people in psychotherapy. Typically, Jungian therapists find that such experience tends to produce a new attitude regarding the person's symptoms, even if they are not alleviated.

JUNG AS AN EMPIRICIST AND PHENOMENOLOGIST

Jung was commonly accused of practicing metaphysics, to which he typically replied that he repudiated metaphysical speculation and only reported empirical observations. He claimed to work phenomenologically, asserting that he was concerned only with the phenomena of religion and avoided speculation about the source and nature of religious experience. The Jungian clinician tries to understand the psychological meaning of numinous experience without interpreting it in terms of preexisting doctrines and without making ontological claims about the source of the experience.

JUNG'S CRITIQUE OF THE CHRISTIAN GOD IMAGE

A Jungian approach to the dominant God image is helpful to many contemporary people for whom the Christian God image is no longer meaningful. Jung believed that the Christian God image was overly masculine and too exclusively light. It was therefore important to him that in 1950 the Pope pronounced the dogma that the Blessed Virgin Mary had been assumed into heaven body and soul, as this finally integrated the feminine aspects of the divine into the official Christian God image (Jung, 1973, p. 567). More controversially, Jung believed that because the Self is a totality, it must contain all the opposites, and thus it must have both a light and a dark side. The dark side of the God image of the Hebrew Bible is apparent for example in Isaiah 45:7, which says that God makes both evil and peace, and in Amos 3:6, which says that evil does not befall a city unless the Lord wills it. Christian writers, however, prefer to project evil onto the figure of Satan or the anti-Christ and stress God as love. Thus, 1 John 1:5 says that "God is light, and in him there is no darkness at all." (The apocalyptic book of Revelation is an exception to this benevolent God image.) Jung (1959/1978a), however, felt that to exclude evil from our image of the divine does not accord with such events as the Holocaust and detonating the nuclear bomb. He believed that St. Augustine's notion that evil is the *privatio boni*, the absence of good, does not do justice to the power and presence of evil in the world (Jung, 1959/1978a). Although Jung's criticism does not do justice to Augustine's idea, Jung was concerned that the idea of "all good from God, all evil from man" creates an inflation in us, a "Luciferian vanity" that gives "monstrous importance to the soul" without mentioning that God created the serpent in the Garden of Eden (1973, p. 540). Jung (1975b) therefore objected to the medieval notion of God as the *summum bonum* (the highest good), because our image of ultimate reality must represent all the qualities of its creation, both benevolent and malevolent. For some patients in psychotherapy, the notion that the divine has both a dark side and a feminine aspect is very helpful; it allows them to maintain a relationship with the divine that is not beholden to the traditional God image.

For Jung, an important example of the dark side of the traditional God image is found in the book of Job. In Jung's *Answer to Job* (1958/1977c), he suggested that in this story the figure of Yahweh is initially unconscious of his atrocious treatment of Job, but because Job maintains his integrity in the face of God's injustice, Yahweh is forced to become conscious of his dark side. Job thereby acts as a reflecting consciousness for the divine, who has to catch up with the moral development of humanity, represented by Job, as a result of which the canonical God image has to change. Thus, the answer to Job is the incarnation in Christ because the God image of the Hebrew Bible now becomes a God of love who lives and suffers among human beings. In this discussion, Jung insisted that he was only talking about the anthropomorphic God image found in the book of Job (Jung, 1975b), and if we take him at his word, Jung was not talking about the darkness of the divine itself. Because this text repeatedly uses the words *God* or *Yahweh*, and rarely the term *God image*, many interpreters believe that Jung was accusing the divine itself of behaving unconsciously. Jung can be read this way because he suggested that since the divine is an undivided totality, the opposing principles within the divine nature (e.g., Yahweh as both persecutor and helper) can only separate into their constituent opposites when they are experienced within human consciousness, so that we become "vessels full of divine conflict" (1958/1977c, p. 416). Some Jungian therapists therefore believe that human beings act as a reflecting consciousness for divinity itself. Applied to the practice of psychotherapy, this means that the more conscious we become, the more we render the divine a service by allowing it to differentiate and become conscious of itself within the human psyche. As Jung put it, "God becomes manifest in the human act of reflection" (1958/1977c, p. 161)—another example of the traditional idea that the divine potential only achieves form within its creation.

CONTEMPORARY TRENDS IN JUNGIAN PRACTICE

The Jungian therapeutic community is currently concerned with many of the same problems that engage the larger field of psychotherapy. There is debate about the place of the body in psychotherapy, the correlation of Jungian ideas and neurobiology, affect theory, trauma, addiction, gender identity, dynamic systems theory, complexity, and the nature of the self. At the same time, there are some research questions such as synchronicity and its relationship to the quantum mechanical notion of nonlocality that are specifically tied to Jungian theory. Cambray (2010) has attempted to tie Jung's notion of the Self to contemporary theories of emergence. Jung's typology (Beebe, 2006) is widely used in the form of the Myers–Briggs Type Indicator, now a popular psychological instrument.

Jung (1967/1976a) wished to develop his psychology as a science of subjectivity, a way of studying the mystery of personality. He was most concerned with the scientific status of psychology in the face of the "personal equation"—the consciousness of the researcher. He believed that psychology straddles the natural and the human sciences, and he collaborated with the quantum physicist Wolfgang Pauli in this area. The standard academic critique of Jung is the lack of empirical evidence for his ideas, but Jung in turn criticized the experimental and statistical approach of mainstream academic psychology on the grounds that these approaches impose conditions on nature that force it to answer in a way that is oriented to the human question and thus limits nature's possible responses. He felt this produces a prejudiced and partial view, leaving out unique, nonrepeatable, or rare aspects of the world that cannot be approached statistically (Jung, 1960/1978c). (Numinous experiences are a good example of the latter type of experience.) In response to critics of his theory of the archetypes and the objective psyche, which is still dismissed by positivist scientists, Jung (1975b) defended the heuristic value and empirical status of these concepts, which he believed gave a satisfactory explanation for his observations. He pointed out that the way we prove a fact is different in different disciplines, raising the contemporary question of the nature of evidence. Jung realized that his work had left many loose ends, and he suggested several areas of potential research, most of which, however, have been ignored by contemporary Jungian scholars (Shamdasani, 2003). One of the problems with the field is that many Jungians are content with Jung's ideas in a rather complacent and parochial way, and they do not reach out to the academic community. This reticence may be the result of a fear that teaching Jung in the university may lead to an external, intellectualized approach to the psyche rather than a personal encounter with the transpersonal unconscious. Jung himself accused universities of "sterile rationalism" and a lack of vision. Tacey (1997) has pointed out that Jung's neo-Platonic approach to knowledge is a challenge to the Aristotelian, heroic bent of the academy, which values logic and rationality. Jung spoke of unseen, spiritual forces in the psyche that do not lend themselves to quantification, an approach that is viewed with suspicion by hard-core empirical researchers who view him (unfairly, because this was not his intention) as the founder of New Age speculation. These critics believe that because Jung's ideas "cannot" be true according to their materialistic worldview, his ideas "must not" be true.

Almost all the Jungian literature is qualitative, phenomenological, and hermeneutic rather than empirical, quantitative, or statistical; the research tends to focus on individual case studies, the process of psychotherapy, archetypal imagery, typology, mythology, religion, and the humanities. For most Jungian clinicians, positivist–physicalist models of proof do not seem appropriate for this kind of material, especially given the important differences between the ontological assumptions of materialistic science and Jungian psychology. The dearth of empirical research in this field may be attributable to the type of personality that is attracted to Jungian psychology. Most Jungians are introverted and intuitive, with a Romantic and religious outlook on life, preoccupied with their own individuation process and not drawn to quantitative research. These factors contribute to the alienation of Jungian psychology from the mainstream of academic psychology, which views Jungians as too soft-headed. Jungians in turn view the academy as too soulless and ignorant of the transpersonal levels of the psyche, perhaps even defended against it. Jung's break with Freud, and Freud's bitter denunciation of Jung, have had a surprisingly lingering effect, so that mainstream psychoanalysis has ignored Jung's contributions, many of which have been rediscovered by Freudian analysts without attribution (Beebe, Cambray, & Kirsch, 2001). Jung's alleged and much-debated anti-Semitism (Maidenbaum, 2003) has been a contributory factor in this estrangement, although the work of Heidegger and Wagner, known for their dubious politics and racism, has been embraced by the academy. In many academic circles and textbooks, there is a high level of misrepresentation of Jung and his thought, which Shamdasani (2003) called "History Lite" (p. 27) or evidence-free history.

In spite of the failure of Jungian psychology to integrate into mainstream psychology, 53 established analytic training programs exist around the world, and 22 groups are developing, under the aegis of the International Association of Analytical Psychology. Needless to say, the field is divided by typical institutional conflicts and there are several schools of Jungian thought. Various models of Jungian training have been described by Casement (2010). I believe clinicians who come to this field are drawn to it by Jung's religious approach to the psyche and the reverent attitude toward it, which develops during Jungian analysis. Although few universities teach Jung, a possible sign that the field may gradually integrate with the mainstream is the development of a few graduate programs that do teach Jungian psychology, such as Pacifica Graduate Institute in Santa Barbara, Texas A&M University, and the University of Essex in England.

CONCLUSION

Jungian psychology is by its nature a spiritual approach to the psyche because Jung postulated both a personal and a spiritual or transpersonal level to the psyche. Both of these participate in the structures of the personality, including its psychopathology. These levels of the psyche are inextricably interwoven, and because they always work in tandem, the practice of Jungian psychotherapy is an intrinsically spiritual pursuit (Corbett, 2011b; Corbett & Stein, 2005). Because Jung did not categorically separate psyche and spirit, one cannot definitively state either that Jungian psychotherapy is a spiritual approach with psychological aspects or a psychological approach with a spiritual coloring; his psychology and his spirituality were synonymous. Jung wanted religion to be a living reality, and he saw depth psychology and psychotherapy as vehicles for this possibility. His approach is helpful for those of us who retain a sense of the sacred even though we are alienated from traditional religious institutions. We find that personal contact with the transpersonal psyche helps us avoid the danger of remaining unconsciously trapped in the particular collective myth into which we were born, which may prevent us from discovering our personal connection to the sacred. If Jung was correct, a new myth of God and a new God image (Edinger, 1996) are arising both individually and collectively; if this approach flowers, it could ameliorate the religious conflicts that threaten our civilization. Psychotherapists can contribute to the emergence of the new God image by becoming conscious of it in our own material and that of our patients. Meanwhile, it is worth remembering the inscription that stood over the front door of Jung's house: *Vocatus atque non vocatus, Deus aderit* (Called or not called, God will be present).

References

Beebe, J. (2006). Psychological types. In R. K. Papadopolous (Ed.), *The handbook of Jungian psychology* (pp. 130–152). New York, NY: Routledge.

Beebe, J., Cambray, J., & Kirsch, T. B. (2001). What Freudians can learn from Jung. *Psychoanalytic Psychology, 18*, 213–242. doi:10.1037/0736-9735.18.2.213

Buber, M. (1952). *Eclipse of God*. New York, NY: Harper & Row.

Cambray, J. (2010). Emergence and the Self. In M. Stein (Ed.), *Jungian psychoanalysis* (pp. 53–66). Chicago, IL: Open Court.

Casement, A. (2010). Training programs. In M. Stein (Ed.), *Jungian psychoanalysis* (pp. 362–377). Chicago, IL: Open Court.

Corbett, L. (1996). *The religious function of the psyche*. New York, NY: Routledge. doi:10.4324/9780203130179

Corbett, L. (2000a). A depth psychological approach to the sacred. In D. Slattery & L. Corbett (Eds.), *Depth psychology: Meditations in the field* (pp. 73–86). Einsiedeln, Switzerland: Daimon.

Corbett, L. (2000b). Jung's approach to the phenomenology of religious experience. In R. Brooke (Ed.), *Pathways into the Jungian world* (pp. 105–120). New York, NY: Brunner-Routledge.

Corbett, L. (2006). Varieties of numinous experience. In A. Casement (Ed.), *The idea of the numinou* (pp. 53–67). New York, NY: Brunner-Routledge.

Corbett, L. (2007). *Psyche and the sacred*. New Orleans, LA: Spring.

Corbett, L. (2009). Soul: A depth psychological approach. In D. Leeming, K. Madden, & S. Marlan (Eds.), *The encyclopedia of psychology and religion* (pp. 866–868). New York, NY: Springer.

Corbett, L. (2011a). Jung's *Red Book* dialogues with the soul: Herald of a new religion? *Jung Journal: Culture and Psyche, 53*, 63–77.

Corbett, L. (2011b). *The sacred cauldron: Psychotherapy as a spiritual practice*. Wilmette, IL: Chiron.

Corbett, L., & Stein, M. (2005). Contemporary Jungian approaches to spiritually oriented psychotherapy. In L. Sperry & E. P. Shafranske (Eds.), *Spiritually oriented psychotherapy* (pp. 51–73). Washington, DC: American Psychological Association. doi:10.1037/10886-003

Dourley, J. (1981). *Psyche as sacrament: A comparative study of C. G. Jung and Paul Tillich*. Toronto, Ontario, Canada: Inner City Books.

Dourley, J. (1995). The religious implications of Jung's psychology. *Journal of Analytical Psychology, 40*, 177–203. doi:10.1111/j.1465-5922.1995.00177.x

Dourley, J. (2001). Response to Barbara Stephen's "The Martin Buber–Carl Jung Disputations." *Journal of Analytical Psychology, 46*, 455–491.

Dourley, J. (2002). Responses: The importance of the issues. *Journal of Analytical Psychology, 47*, 479–492.

Edinger, E. F. (1984). *The creation of consciousness: Jung's myth for modern man*. Toronto, Ontario, Canada: Inner City Books.

Edinger, E. F. (1987). *The Christian archetype: A Jungian commentary on the life of Christ*. Toronto, Ontario, Canada: Inner City Books.

Edinger, E. F. (1991). *The anatomy of the psyche: Alchemical symbolism in psychotherapy*. La Salle, IL: Open Court.

Edinger, E. F. (1992). *Transformation of the God-image: An elucidation of Jung's Answer to Job*. Toronto, Ontario, Canada: Inner City Books.

Edinger, E. F. (1996). *The new God-image: A study of Jung's key letters concerning the evolution of the Western God-image*. Wilmette, IL: Chiron.

Fromm, E. (1959). *Psychoanalysis and religion*. New Haven, CT: Yale University Press.

Giannoni, M. (2009). The session of the two dreams. *Journal of Analytical Psychology, 54*, 103–115. doi:10.1111/j.1468-5922.2008.01760.x

Griffin, D. R. (Ed.). (1990). *Archetypal process: Self and divine in Whitehead, Jung, and Hillman*. Evanston, IL: Northwestern University Press.

Hall, J. (1993). *The unconscious Christian*. Mahwah, NJ: Paulist Press.

Heisig, J. W. (1979). *Imago Dei: A study of C. G. Jung's psychology of religion*. London, England: Associated Universities Press.

Hill, P. C., & Pargament, K. I. (2003). Advances in the conceptualization and measurement of religion and spirituality: Implications for physical and mental health research. *American Psychologist, 58*, 64–74. doi:10.1037/0003-066X.58.1.64

Jaffe, A. (1983). *The myth of meaning in the work of C. G. Jung*. Zurich, Switzerland: Daimon Verlag.

Jung, C. G. (1964). *Man and his symbols*. New York, NY: Doubleday.

Jung, C. G. (1965). *Memories, dreams, reflections*. New York, NY: Vintage Books.

Jung, C. G. (1971). *The collected works of C. G. Jung: Vol. 6. Psychological types*. Princeton, NJ: Princeton University Press. (Original work published 1921)

Jung, C. G. (1973). *Letters: Vol. 1* (G. Adler & A. Jaffé, Eds.; R. F. C. Hull, Trans.). Princeton, NJ: Princeton University Press.

Jung, C. G. (1975a). *The collected works of C. G. Jung: Vol. 16. The practice of psychotherapy*. Princeton, NJ: Princeton University Press. (Original work published 1954)

Jung, C. G. (1975b). *Letters: Vol. 2* (G. Adler & A. Jaffé, Eds.; R. F. C. Hull, Trans.). Princeton, NJ: Princeton University Press.

Jung, C. G. (1976a). *The collected works of C. G. Jung: Vol. 13. Alchemical studies*. Princeton, NJ: Princeton University Press. (Original work published 1967)

Jung, C. G. (1976b). *The collected works of C. G. Jung: Vol. 14. Mysterium coniunctionis*. Princeton, NJ: Princeton University Press. (Original work published 1963)

Jung, C. G. (1976c). *The collected works of C. G. Jung: Vol. 18. The symbolic life*. Princeton, NJ: Princeton University Press. (Original work published 1950)

Jung, C. G. (1976d). *The collected works of C. G. Jung: Vol. 5. Symbols of transformation*. Princeton, NJ: Princeton University Press. (Original work published 1952)

Jung, C. G. (1977a). *The collected works of C. G. Jung: Vol. 9.i. The archetypes and the collective unconscious*. Princeton, NJ: Princeton University Press. (Original work published 1959)

Jung, C. G. (1977b). *The collected works of C. G. Jung: Vol. 12. Psychology and alchemy*. Princeton, NJ: Princeton University Press. (Original work published 1953)

Jung, C. G. (1977c). *The collected works of C. G. Jung: Vol. 11. Psychology and religion: West and East*. Princeton, NJ: Princeton University Press. (Original work published 1958)

Jung, C. G. (1977d). *The collected works of C. G. Jung: Vol. 7. Two essays on analytical psychology*. Princeton, NJ: Princeton University Press. (Original work published 1953)

Jung, C. G. (1978a). *The collected works of C. G. Jung: Vol. 9.ii. Aion: Researches into the phenomenology of the self*. Princeton, NJ: Princeton University Press. (Original work published in 1959)

Jung, C. G. (1978b). *The collected works of C. G. Jung: Vol. 10. Civilization in transition*. Princeton, NJ: Princeton University Press. (Original work published 1964)

Jung, C. G. (1978c). *The collected works of C. G. Jung: Vol. 8. The structure and dynamics of the psyche*. Princeton, NJ: Princeton University Press. (Original work published 1960)

Jung, C. G. (1979). *The collected works of C. G. Jung: Vol. 4. Freud and psychoanalysis*. Princeton, NJ: Princeton University Press. (Original work published 1961)

Jung, C. G. (2005). *Modern man in search of a soul*. New York, NY: Routledge. (Original work published 1933)

Kohut, H. (1984). *How does analysis cure?* Chicago, IL: University of Chicago Press.

Kotsch, W. E. (2000). Jung's mediatory science as a psychology beyond objectivism. *Journal of Analytical Psychology, 45*, 217–244. doi:10.1111/1465-5922.00153

Lakoff, G. (1993). The contemporary theory of metaphor. In A. Ortony (Ed.), *Metaphor and thought* (pp. 202–251). New York, NY: Cambridge University Press.

Maidenbaum, A. (Ed.). (2003). *Jung and the shadow of anti-Semitism*. York Beach, ME: Nicholas Hays.

McGuire, W., & Hull, R. F. C. (1987). *C. G. Jung speaking*. Princeton, NJ: Princeton University Press.

Ogden, T. H. (2004). The analytic third: Implications for psychoanalytic theory and technique. *Psychoanalytic Quarterly, 73*, 167–195.

Otto, R. (1958). *The idea of the holy*. New York, NY: Oxford University Press.

Prendergast, J. J., & Bradford, G. K. (Eds.). (2007). *Listening from the heart of silence: Nondual wisdom and psychotherapy*. St. Paul, MN: Paragon House.

Rizzuto, A.-M. (1981). *The birth of the living God: A psychoanalytic study*. Chicago, IL: University of Chicago Press.

Schaer, H. (1950). *Religion and the cure of souls in Jung's psychology* (R. F. C. Hull, Trans.). New York, NY: Pantheon Books.

Schaverien, J. (2007). Countertransference as active imagination: Imaginative experiences of the analyst. *Journal of Analytical Psychology, 52*, 413–431. doi:10.1111/j.1468-5922.2007.00674.x

Shamdasani, S. (2003). *Jung and the making of modern psychology*. New York, NY: Cambridge University Press. doi:10.1017/CBO9780511490095

Stevens, A. (1982). *Archetypes: A natural history of the self*. New York, NY: Morrow.

Tacey, D. (1997). Jung in the academy: Devotions and resistances. *Journal of Analytical Psychology, 42*, 269–283. doi:10.1111/j.1465-5922.1997.00269.x

Ulanov, A. B. (1986). *Picturing God*. Salt Lake City, UT: Cowley.

Wilkinson, M. (2006). *Coming into mind*. New York, NY: Routledge.

Winnicott, D. W. (1971). *Playing and reality*. London, England: Routledge.

CHAPTER 8

ADDRESSING RELIGION AND SPIRITUALITY FROM A COGNITIVE–BEHAVIORAL PERSPECTIVE

Siang-Yang Tan

Historically, tensions have existed between secular cognitive–behavioral therapy (CBT) and religion and spirituality. A well-known example involved the late Albert Ellis, the founder of rational emotive behavior therapy (REBT), a major approach to CBT. Ellis was initially antireligious (Ellis, 1960, 1971, 1980) but over the years, he became relatively more open to integrating REBT and religion and spirituality in working with religious clients while favoring a nonsectarian approach to religion (e.g., see Ellis, 2000; Nielsen, Johnson, & Ellis, 2001). CBT in general has undergone significant changes and expanded its traditional approaches to incorporate more spiritually oriented and religious forms of CBT, especially in the past two decades or so (e.g., see Tan, 2007; Tan & Johnson, 2005). This chapter addresses religion and spirituality from a cognitive–behavioral perspective or CBT framework.

Following the definitional criteria used in this handbook the terms *spirituality* and *religion* are used together, in this chapter, to refer to both traditionally based and nontraditionally based beliefs, practices, relationships, or experiences having to do with the sacred or to refer to the full range of functions (psychological, social, physical, and spiritual) that are linked to beliefs, practices, relationships, or experiences having to do with the sacred. This chapter therefore assumes and affirms the integrative paradigm for the psychology of religion and spirituality that attempts to pull together into a more coherent whole the diverse elements that make up this subdiscipline of psychology. This integrative paradigm also supports the ethical and competent integration of religion and spirituality with psychotherapy, including CBT, that is the focus of this chapter.

RECENT DEVELOPMENTS IN CONTEMPORARY CBT

CBT has its roots in behavior therapy. Historically, behavior therapy has been described as consisting of three major generations or waves (Hayes, Luoma, Bond, Masuda, & Lillis, 2006). The first wave of traditional behavior therapy that occurred in the late 1950s and 1960s and early 1970s was based mainly on so-called modern learning theories, including classical conditioning (e.g., Pavlov), operant conditioning (e.g., Skinner), and modeling or observational learning (e.g., Bandura). The second wave of CBT that emerged in the late 1970s went beyond the narrow behavioral focus on environmental factors to include the thinking or cognitions of clients in the assessment and treatment of psychological disorders, and more recently even mindfulness and acceptance (see Hayes, Follette, & Linehan, 2004). The third wave in contemporary CBT that occurred in the 1990s and 2000s incorporates contextualistic approaches, with mindfulness and acceptance as central emphases (see Hayes et al., 2004; Roemer & Orsillo, 2009), and this wave encompasses acceptance and commitment therapy (ACT; Hayes, Strosahl, & Wilson, 1999; see also Luoma, Hayes, & Walser, 2007), mindfulness-based cognitive therapy (MBCT; Segal, Williams, & Teasdale, 2002; see also Williams, Teasdale, Segal, & Kabat-Zinn, 2007), and

DOI: 10.1037/14046-008
APA Handbook of Psychology, Religion, and Spirituality: Vol. 2. An Applied Psychology of Religion and Spirituality, K. I. Pargament (Editor-in-Chief)

dialectical behavior therapy (DBT; Linehan, 1993; see also Dimeff & Koerner, 2007). A somewhat related contemporary approach that expands traditional CBT is metacognitive therapy for anxiety and depression (Wells, 2009), which emphasizes the process rather than the specific contents of thinking, including the use of detached mindfulness techniques.

Another recent development in CBT, and the focus of this chapter, involves explicitly religious and spiritual (R/S) approaches to CBT. The terminology that researchers use to capture this movement varies and is evolving. For the purpose of this chapter, I use the term *spiritually oriented CBT* to refer to CBT interventions that directly address R/S issues. In contrast, some scholars use the term *R/S therapies* to refer to interventions that draw on traditional religious resources, such as prayer and sacred scriptures (e.g., the Qur'an for Muslims and the Bible for Christians), to help clients cope with mental health problems, such as anxiety and depression. Furthermore, the term *religiously accommodative treatments* has been used to discuss CBT interventions tailored to appeal to clients committed to a particular and often conservative religious subculture, such as evangelical Christian or orthodox Jewish or Muslim groups (see Hook et al., 2010; Worthington et al., 2011; see also Chapter 34 in this volume). I use the term *spiritually oriented CBT* here because it encompasses people who hold traditional and nontraditional (i.e., highly individualized spiritualities) religious orientations. In sum, this chapter will describe in more detail CBT approaches that incorporate R/S content into interventions.

Before proceeding, note that mindfulness and acceptance-based approaches to contemporary CBT have some spiritual roots in Zen Buddhism (see Chapter 10 in this volume) or other contemplative and meditative spiritual or religious traditions, such as Christian or Roman Catholic. Yet, although these approaches can be seen broadly as somewhat spiritually oriented, they are only spiritual in a very general or generic sense and certainly not necessarily religious (see Volume 1, Chapter 17, this handbook and Chapter 10, this volume). In fact, Bishop et al. (2004) have proposed the following operational definition of mindfulness in a general sense that does not have to be spiritually or religiously based:

> We propose a two-component model of mindfulness. The first component involves the self-regulation of attention so that it is maintained on immediate experience, thereby allowing for increased recognition of mental events in the present moment. The second component involves adopting a particular orientation that is characterized by curiosity, openness, and acceptance. (p. 232)

Thus, I cover very briefly the mindfulness- and acceptance-based approaches to CBT that are only somewhat, rather than explicitly, spiritually oriented.

THEORETICAL AND EMPIRICAL FOUNDATIONS FOR ADDRESSING RELIGION AND SPIRITUALITY IN CBT

Theoretical Foundations

CBT has been defined as "a more purposeful attempt to preserve the demonstrated efficiencies of behavior modification within a less doctrinaire context, and to incorporate the cognitive activities of the client in the efforts to produce therapeutic change" (Kendall & Hollon, 1979, p. 1). Historically, CBT has included three major approaches: cognitive therapy (CT) founded by Aaron Beck (1976), REBT (previously known as rational emotive therapy or RET) founded by Albert Ellis (1962), and cognitive behavior modification (CBM) including stress inoculation training (SIT) developed by Donald Meichenbaum (1977).

Beck's (1976) CT approach focuses on how maladaptive and dysfunctional thinking affects feelings and behavior. Clients are helped in CT to overcome emotional problems, such as experiencing excessive anxiety, depression, or anger, by learning to identify, challenge, and correct cognitive distortions or errors in thinking. Examples of cognitive dysfunction include overgeneralization to all cases from only one specific instance, or catastrophizing by concluding that things are so horrible and it is the end of the world when they are not that bad. Ellis (1962) similarly developed REBT to actively and "directively" help clients to identify and change their fundamental irrational beliefs that are seen as the basic cause or root of emotional problems. Meichenbaum's (1977) CBM and SIT approach focuses on helping clients learn calming self-talk and other coping skills to better manage stress and other emotional difficulties.

CBT incorporates many approaches and interventions (e.g., see D. Dobson & Dobson, 2009; K. S. Dobson, 2010; Leahy, 2003, 2004), but they all usually share the following six basic tenets or theoretical assumptions (Kendall & Bemis, 1983):

> (1) the human organism responds primarily to cognitive representations of its environments rather than to these environments per se; (2) most human learning is cognitively mediated; (3) thoughts, feelings, and behaviors are causally interrelated; (4) attitudes, expectancies, attributions, and other cognitive activities are central to producing, predicting, and understanding psychopathological behavior and the effects of therapeutic interventions; (5) cognitive processes can be cast into testable formulations that are easily integrated with behavioral paradigms, and it is possible and desirable to combine cognitive treatment strategies with enactive techniques and behavioral contingency management; and (6) the task of the cognitive–behavioral therapist is to act as diagnostician, educator, and technical consultant who assesses maladaptive cognitive processes and works with the client to design learning experiences that may remediate these dysfunctional cognitions and the behavioral and affective patterns with which they correlate. (pp. 565–566)

CBT has become the most popular and fastest-growing approach to psychotherapy as well as the most empirically researched (together with behavior therapy) of all of the current major schools of counseling and psychotherapy (see Tan, 2011). As secular CBT has grown tremendously, spiritually oriented CBT (Tan & Johnson, 2005) has also been developing in significant ways since the 1980s. Spiritually oriented CBT accommodates CBT to the worldviews, values, and spiritual experiences of religious and spiritually oriented clients. Because CBT is belief oriented, using a directive and psychoeducational approach, it is often appealing and easily adaptable to religious clients.

Spiritually oriented CBT usually includes several specific interventions with religious clients, such as the use of sacred scriptures or writings in cognitive restructuring of maladaptive, dysfunctional thinking; the use of religious imagery to reduce tension and anxiety and to deepen relaxation; and the use of prayer or scripture reading in session and as homework to help clients cope more effectively with emotional problems like anxiety, depression, and anger.

Although Christian and Muslim versions of spiritually oriented CBT have been the most common and well developed and researched so far (Tan & Johnson, 2005), more recently, other R/S approaches to spiritually oriented CBT have been described and researched, including Jewish, Taoist, Buddhist, and general spiritual versions (see Worthington, Hook, Davis, & McDaniel, 2011). Spiritually oriented CBT can include the use of mindfulness and acceptance in more passive ways of coping with dysfunctional thoughts, instead of relying only on vigorous cognitive disputation of irrational beliefs based on religious perspectives and sacred scriptures. Mindfulness and more passive acceptance methods in spiritually oriented CBT, however, usually are conducted in a more religiously and spiritually explicit context, such as Buddhism or Taoism, in contrast to the recent contextualistic approaches to CBT, including ACT, MBCT, and DBT. Advances are being made in mindfulness and acceptance-based therapies, including growing empirical support for their efficacy over a widening range of psychological disorders (e.g., see Öst, 2008; Shapiro & Carlson, 2009). Although these are exciting developments in the field, this chapter will not cover these therapies any further because they are not explicitly R/S therapies (see Pargament, 2007).

Empirical Foundations

The empirical evidence available in support of the efficacy or effectiveness of CBT in general is substantial and well-known. CBT is not only the most empirically researched of all the contemporary psychotherapies but also one of the most empirically supported treatments for a wide range of problems (Chambless & Ollendick, 2001; see also Butler, Chapman, Forman & Beck, 2006; Nathan & Gorman, 2007). In a review of 16 methodologically rigorous meta-analyses (with a total of 332 studies and 9,995 subjects) on the outcomes of CBT, for a wide variety of psychiatric disorders, the following findings were reported (Butler et al., 2006):

> (1) Large effect sizes were obtained for CBT for unipolar depression, generalized anxiety disorder, panic disorder with or without agoraphobia, social phobia, posttraumatic stress disorder or PTSD, and childhood depressive and anxiety disorders; (2) Effect sizes in the moderate range were found for CBT of marital distress, anger, childhood somatic disorders, and chronic pain; (3) CBT was somewhat better than antidepressants in the treatment of depression in adults; (4) CBT was as effective as behavior therapy in the treatment of depression and obsessive-compulsive disorder or OCD in adults; (5) Large uncontrolled effect sizes were obtained for CBT for bulimia nervosa and schizophrenia. (p. 17)

Despite the limitations inherent in using meta-analysis as a statistical method, Butler et al. (2006) concluded from their review of these 16 meta-analyses that there is empirical support for the efficacy or effectiveness of CBT for many psychiatric disorders. In a randomized placebo-controlled trial with adults with severe depression, however, behavioral activation was found to be more efficacious than cognitive therapy and as efficacious as antidepressant medication (paroxetine; Dimidjian et al., 2006).

Empirical Foundations of Spiritually Oriented CBT

The empirical evidence for the efficacy or effectiveness of spiritually oriented CBT has grown in the past few years. In an initial qualitative review of the literature that focused on spiritually modified cognitive therapy or spiritually oriented CBT, Hodge (2006) examined 14 CBT outcome studies with varying levels of methodological sophistication. Eight outcome studies were on depression, and there was one outcome study on each of the following disorders: anxiety disorder, neurosis, obsessive–compulsive disorder (OCD), perfectionism, schizophrenia, and stress. Hodge concluded that only in the area of depression can spiritually modified cognitive therapy or CBT be classified as an empirically validated or supported treatment. This review, however, is dated and limited. Its conclusion needs to be revised in light of more recent and better research covered in other reviews of the empirical evidence on the efficacy or effectiveness of spiritually oriented CBT.

In 2007, Smith, Bartz, and Richards conducted a meta-analytic review of the outcomes of R/S adaptations to psychotherapy, with a total of 31 outcome studies (from 1984 to 2005) and 1,845 clients. Eighteen studies (58%) involved true experimental designs, six (19%) were quasi-experimental designs, and seven (22%) involved only single-group pre- to posttest designs. They found a random-effects weighted average effect size of 0.56 across the 31 studies, which provided some empirical support for the efficacy or effectiveness of spiritually oriented psychotherapy approaches for individuals with particular psychological problems, such as depression, anxiety, stress, and eating disorders. Fifteen of the 31 outcome studies were on spiritually oriented CBT. Clients from the 31 studies were primarily Christian (73%) and Muslim (24%), according to the authors. More and better research is still needed and there are obvious limitations of this meta-analytic review.

In a more recent review of empirically supported R/S therapies, using criteria from Chambless and Hollon (1998), Hook et al. (2010) evaluated 24 outcome studies (as of December 15, 2008) that were randomized clinical trials (RCTs) for only mental health problems (i.e., eight studies on depression, six studies on anxiety, three studies on unforgiveness, two studies on eating disorders, one study on schizophrenia, one study on alcoholism, one study on anger, one study on marital issues, and one study on general psychological problems). There were

11 Christian studies, seven Muslim studies, one Taoist study, one Buddhist study, and four general spirituality studies, totaling 24 studies. Eighteen studies focused more specifically on R/S or spiritually oriented CBT (five Christian studies on depression, three Muslim studies on depression, three Muslim studies on anxiety, one Christian study on anxiety, one Taoist study on anxiety, one Christian study on marital issues, one Buddhist study on anger, one spiritual group study on anxiety, one Muslim study on schizophrenia, and one Christian study on eating disorders).

Hook et al. (2010) concluded that Christian accommodative cognitive therapy or CBT for depression, 12-step facilitation for alcoholism, and Muslim CBT for depression as well as for anxiety were efficacious when combined with medication. The following R/S therapies were deemed possibly efficacious: Christian devotional meditation for anxiety, Taoist cognitive therapy for anxiety, Christian accommodative group treatment for unforgiveness, spiritual group treatment for unforgiveness, Christian accommodative group CBT for marital discord, Christian lay counseling for general psychological problems, spiritual group therapy for eating disorders when combined with existing inpatient treatment, and Buddhist accommodative cognitive therapy for anger in a prison setting. There was no evidence for the efficacy of the following R/S therapies: spiritual group cognitive therapy for anxiety, Muslim accommodative CBT for schizophrenia, and Christian accommodative group CBT for eating disorders.

Hook et al. (2010) concluded that R/S therapies may be effective in the treatment of psychological problems for R/S clients, working as well as, and in some instances, better than comparable secular therapies. The empirical evidence, however, is not substantial enough to support the superiority of R/S therapies over comparable secular therapies. Hook et al. therefore suggested that the use of a particular R/S therapy may depend more on client preference and therapist comfort at this time.

In an even more recent and larger meta-analytic review of outcome studies on R/S therapies (from 1980 until December 1, 2009), Worthington et al. (2011) used a total of 51 samples from 46 separate studies that evaluated the efficacy of R/S therapies, involving 3,290 participants or clients. Twenty-four samples (from 21 separate studies) specifically evaluated the efficacy of spiritually oriented CBT (three Muslim samples on depression, four Muslim samples on anxiety, seven Christian samples on depression, one Christian sample on marital issues, one Christian sample on breast cancer, one Christian sample on eating disorders, one Jewish sample on subclinical anxiety, two Buddhist samples on drug use, one general spirituality sample on stress, two general spirituality samples on depression, and one Taoist sample on anxiety). Their overall meta-analytic review found that R/S therapies were generally more effective than no treatment control conditions on both psychological (d = .45) and spiritual (d = .51) outcomes, and R/S therapies generally also did better than alternate psychotherapies on both psychological (d = .26) and spiritual (d = .41) outcomes. When R/S therapies were compared to alternate treatments with the same theoretical orientation and treatment duration in studies that employed a dismantling design, there was little difference between them on psychological outcomes (d = .13), but R/S therapies did better than comparable alternate treatments on spiritual outcomes (d = .33). These are encouraging findings that generally support the efficacy or effectiveness of R/S therapies that included spiritually oriented CBT. There are methodological limitations of a meta-analytic review, however, and therefore there is still a need for more and better controlled outcome research on R/S therapies and spiritually oriented CBT.

At least two other outcome studies on spiritually oriented CBT were not included in any of these recent reviews. Pargament (2007, pp. 326–327) briefly mentioned that there is preliminary evidence for the greater effectiveness of spiritually augmented CBT over supportive case management with patients with depression (D'Souza, Rich, Diamond, Godfery, & Gleeson, 2002) and patients with schizophrenia (D'Souza, Rich, Diamond, & Godfery, 2002) in Australia. At least 26 controlled outcome studies have been conducted on spiritually oriented CBT, and this number will continue to increase significantly in the coming years.

Wade, Worthington, and Vogel (2007) also found evidence for the effectiveness of religiously tailored interventions in Christian therapy in actual clinical settings. They reported that clients who had high religious commitment experienced greater closeness with their therapists and more improvement in their presenting concern when receiving religious interventions compared with clients who had low religious commitment. It therefore may be important to assess a client's level of religious commitment before using explicitly R/S interventions in spiritually oriented psychotherapy, including Christian CBT.

ADDRESSING THE SALIENCE AND ROLE OF RELIGION AND SPIRITUALITY IN CBT: ASSESSMENT

Spiritually oriented CBT approaches assessment in an active and directive way and as an ongoing process throughout therapy (Tan & Johnson, 2005). In the first session or intake interview, a spiritually oriented CBT therapist will conduct an initial spiritual and religious assessment, in addition to the usual CBT assessment that includes history taking, problem listing, and goal setting (Tan, 2007) as well as the possible use of psychological measures (see Tan & Johnson, 2005). The initial R/S assessment will involve at least asking the client about his or her R/S background or denomination, if any, and whether the client would like to discuss or deal with R/S issues directly and use R/S resources such as prayer and scripture or sacred writings in therapy (Tan, 2007).

More specifically, Pargament (2007) has suggested the use of the following questions that would be helpful in spiritually oriented CBT:

> (1) *Do you see yourself as a religious or spiritual person? If so, in what way?* (to assess the salience of spirituality to the client);
> (2) *Are you affiliated with a religious or spiritual denomination or community? If so, which one?* (to assess the salience of a religious affiliation to the client);
> (3) *Has your problem affected you religiously or spiritually? If so, in what way?* (to assess the salience of spirituality to the problem); and
> (4) *Has your religion or spirituality been involved in the way you have coped with your problem? If so, in what way?* (to assess the salience of spirituality to the solution). (p. 211)

If the client responds by saying that religion and spirituality are very important or important to him or her, and he or she is definitely interested in discussing R/S issues openly and using spiritual resources such as prayer and scripture or sacred writings in therapy, then the therapist can obtain informed consent from the client, preferably in written form, to engage in spiritually oriented CBT with the client in an explicit way. If the client is not interested in such an explicit approach, then the therapist should not proceed to use explicit spiritually oriented CBT. It is crucial to obtain client informed consent before any spiritually oriented CBT is explicitly conducted with the client (see Tan, 2007; Tan & Johnson, 2005).

There are two major models of integration of religion and spirituality into psychotherapy, including CBT: implicit and explicit integration, as two ends of a continuum. Tan (1996) has described implicit and explicit integration in therapy thus:

> *Implicit integration* . . . refers to a more covert approach that does not initiate the discussion of religious or spiritual issues and does not openly, directly or systematically use spiritual resources . . . *Explicit integration* . . . refers to a more overt approach that directly and systematically deals with spiritual or religious issues in therapy, and uses spiritual resources like prayer, Scripture or sacred texts, referrals to church or other religious groups or lay counselors, and other religious practices (p. 368).

If a therapist is not familiar with the religion or spirituality of a particular client, it is important for the therapist to ask open-ended questions in an authentic and empathic manner that is sensitive to the client, such as, "I'm not overly familiar with that form of Buddhism (or Christianity, or Judaism), could you tell me more about it and your experience of it?" or "How do you see your faith relating to your most pressing concerns?" (Post & Wade, 2009, p. 143).

Even if a therapist is familiar with a client's R/S background, it is crucial for the therapist to avoid making overarching assumptions about the religiousness or spirituality of the client on the basis of the client's religious affiliation or spiritual orientation. There are significant within-group differences in beliefs and practices even among religious groups such as Christians, Muslims, Jews, Buddhists, and Hindus (see Volume 1, this handbook), especially along a liberal-to-conservative continuum and denominational distinctions. It is crucial for the spiritually oriented CBT therapist to take an idiographic or individually tailored approach to each client, with adequate assessment of the client's unique R/S beliefs and practices as well as experiences, so that appropriately sensitive interventions are provided for a particular client.

For example, a more liberal Christian client from a mainline denomination may be offended by a conservative Christian CBT therapist who takes a more literal interpretation of the Bible that is not in line with the client's own understanding of the Bible, such as women's ordination or role in the church. Conversely, a more conservative Christian client may be offended by a more liberal Christian CBT therapist who assumes and takes a more liberal interpretation of the Bible. The therapist therefore needs to be careful not to impose his or her own interpretations of scripture or values onto the client.

Several promising psychological measures or instruments for explicit spiritual and religious assessment in psychotherapy can be useful in spiritually oriented CBT. Pargament (2007) has listed and briefly described at least 26 of them, including measures of spiritual pathways, spiritual destinations, sacred loss and desecration, spiritual coping, spiritual struggles, spiritual transformation and disengagement, and spiritual efficacy, including spiritual well-being (see pp. 234–236).

Plante (2009) recently listed and briefly described five primary selected measures of religion and spirituality that are relatively brief and easy to use, with adequate reliability and validity: (a) the Brief Multidimensional Measure of Religiousness/Spirituality (Fetzer Institute/National Institute of Aging Working Group, 1999) assesses "denominational affiliation, organizational religiousness, private and public religious practices, religious coping and social support, moral values, time and money donated to religious causes and organizations, spiritual experiences, and self-reported measures of religious-spiritual activities and interests" (p. 63); (b) the Santa Clara Strength of Religious Faith Questionnaire (SCSORF; Plante & Boccaccini, 1997; Plante, Vallaeys, Sherman, & Wallston, 2002) is a 10-item (or 5-item brief version) measure that assesses "general religiousness in any faith tradition as well as lack of involvement in religious-spiritual behaviors or traditions" (p. 63); (c) the Duke University Religious Index (DUREL; Koenig, Meador, & Parkerson, 1997) is a five-item measure that assesses "three dimensions of religious engagement: organizational or public religious expression (e.g., church attendance), private religious expression (e.g., prayer, meditation), and intrinsic religiosity (e.g., incorporation of religious convictions into one's daily life)" (p. 63); (d) the Religious Commitment Inventory-10 (Worthington et al., 2003) is a 10 item measure that assesses "how committed the respondent is to his or her religious beliefs, and practices" (p. 63); and (e) the Religious Coping Inventory (RCOPE; Pargament, Koenig, & Perez, 2000) that assesses "17 factor-derived religious coping strategies (e.g., benevolent religious reappraisal, seeking spiritual support, religious purification/forgiveness)" (p. 64). The RCOPE has 105 items, but a 14-item version (the Brief RCOPE; Pargament, Smith, Koenig, & Perez, 1998) is available, with two main, global dimensions: positive religious coping and negative religious coping (see p. 64).

Another instrument that has often been used as an outcome measure of spiritual well-being is the Spiritual Well-Being Scale (SWB; Ellison, 1983). In actual clinical practice, a spiritually oriented CBT therapist may use only a couple of these measures, such as the Brief RCOPE or the Religious Commitment Inventory-10, and the SWB as an outcome measure, which are relatively short and easy to administer. Many of the assessment measures of religion and spirituality mentioned in this chapter have not been normed with clinical populations or specific ethnically diverse groups.

Religion and spirituality can have both positive and negative effects on clients (e.g., see Griffith, 2010). On the positive side, religion and spirituality in terms of specific beliefs and practices can be a potent resource, helping clients to cope more effectively with the stresses and difficulties in their lives (Pargament, 1997). On the negative side, religion and spirituality can be a source of problems for clients, for example, when they experience anger toward God, face conflicts with their R/S leaders and communities, and struggle with spiritual doubts and confusion (e.g., see Exline & Rose, 2005; see also Volume 1, Chapter 25, this handbook). A crucial area for assessment from a CBT perspective is in the specific R/S beliefs or thoughts of clients, which in turn are foundations of meaning making in their worldviews affecting their coping for better or for worse (see Park & Slattery, 2009; see also Volume 1, Chapter 8, this handbook).

It is important therefore to ask clients who are religiously or spiritually oriented, and who are willing to explore their spiritual issues, what specific thoughts and beliefs they have when they struggle with particular psychological problems, such as anxiety, depression, anger, marital problems, and addictions, or physical problems, such as pain and chronic illnesses. Some clients may have rigidly held spiritual or religious beliefs and deeper underlying schemas that may contribute to their psychological and physical suffering. Pargament (2007) has provided several examples such as, "I am a worthless sinner," "Suffering is a sure sign of spiritual purity," "The Bible says I have to be perfect," "I shouldn't need anyone but God," and "It is sinful for me to focus on myself" (p. 304). Other common examples include "It's wrong for me to feel angry anytime. The Bible says that anger is sinful"; "I should never feel down or sad because if I have enough faith in God I should be happy or joyful all the time"; "My suffering must be a punishment for my past wrongs"; and "If I have enough faith, I will be healed of my illness." Assessment of these rigid and maladaptive or even irrational beliefs can then lead to cognitive restructuring of such beliefs by identifying, challenging, correcting, and replacing them with more adaptive and reasonable beliefs within the client's own particular R/S contexts. The use of scripture or sacred texts may be especially helpful in spiritually oriented CBT with clients who are interested in openly discussing their religious or spiritual beliefs.

Avants and Margolin (2004) described how a client's deeper level self-schema can be habitually activated and lead to destructive or high-risk behavior. They developed a spiritual self-schema (3-S) therapy for the treatment of addictive and HIV high-risk behavior that integrated CBT with Buddhist psychology. They pointed out that a client's addict self-schema that is habitually activated leading to HIV high-risk behavior and drug use usually include self-beliefs, such as "I can handle this; no big deal," "Relief from distress is external," "I'm not responsible for others," and "I don't have anything to lose" (Avants & Margolin, 2004, p. 263). Their Buddhist version of spiritually oriented CBT (3-S therapy) incorporates cognitive restructuring of this addict self-schema to transform it to a 3-S through Buddhist teachings and techniques (e.g., meditation, visualization, and mindfulness) as well as standard CBT strategies. The 3-S, based on Buddhist teachings and sacred writings, includes such self-beliefs as, "This situation is dangerous," "Relief from distress lies within," "I care about myself and others," and "My life has meaning and purpose" (Avants & Margolin, 2004, p. 263). The 3-S can then help the client to engage in HIV-preventive behavior instead of HIV high-risk behavior that has been habitually connected with the previous addict self-schema. Addict self-schemas are therefore identified and clarified in the assessment phase of 3-S therapy.

A PRACTICAL EXAMPLE OF SPIRITUALLY ORIENTED CBT ASSESSMENT WITH A CONSERVATIVE CHRISTIAN CLIENT

The following is a brief hypothetical transcript of a spiritually oriented CBT therapist conducting an assessment of a conservative Christian client's R/S beliefs associated with the client's struggle with depression:

Client: I'm struggling with feeling depressed or down quite often. I don't have much energy, and I don't feel like doing anything because I don't seem to enjoy anything . . . in case you are wondering, I do not have any thoughts of suicide or taking my own life.

Therapist: Can you tell me what usually goes through your mind, what you're thinking about or saying to yourself whenever you feel down or depressed like this?

Client: Well . . . I hate feeling this way but I often wonder why God is allowing me to suffer this depression for a couple of months or so now . . . and I sometimes think that God may be punishing me for my faults or sins.

Therapist: In what sense or in what ways?

Client: Well . . . I have not been attending church as regularly and also because of the poor economy and having my hours cut to half-time at work, I have not been tithing or giving 10% of my gross income to church. Perhaps God is punishing me as a result of my disobedience. Or maybe I just don't have enough faith in God to heal me. I believe that with enough faith I should be healed, and I should be joyful as a believer and not feel down like this . . . it does not glorify God!

Therapist: So let me see if I'm understanding you correctly. As you feel depressed, you are saying to yourself that God may be punishing you for not being regular in your church attendance and giving or tithing, and that if you have enough faith you should be healed by now. Also, as a good believer you should be joyful all the time and not feel depressed because depression does not glorify or honor God. Am I tracking with you here?

Client: Yes! That's exactly how I think and feel.

Building on this assessment of rigid, maladaptive, and religiously inaccurate thinking within the client's Christian belief system, the spiritually oriented CBT therapist will move to the intervention stage of therapy and conduct cognitive restructuring. The next section will deal with intervention or addressing and integrating religion and spirituality in psychotherapy, and more specifically CBT.

ADDRESSING AND INTEGRATING RELIGION AND SPIRITUALITY IN CBT: INTERVENTION

There are many religious and spiritual interventions that can be used to address and integrate religion and spirituality in psychotherapy, including CBT (e.g., see Aten & Leach, 2009; Aten, McMinn, & Worthington, 2011; McMinn & Campbell, 2007; Pargament, 1997, 2007; Plante, 2009; Plante & Sherman, 2001; Richards & Bergin, 2000, 2005; Sperry & Shafranske, 2005; Tan, 1996, 2007, 2011; Tan & Johnson, 2005; Worthington et al., 2011; see also Abu-Raiya & Pargament, 2010; Avants & Margolin, 2004; Rosmarin, Pargament, Pirutinsky, & Mahoney, 2010; Zhang et al., 2002). For example, Plante (2009) recently listed and described the following 13 spiritual practices or tools for enhancing psychological health that are also consistent with a spiritually oriented CBT perspective: prayer; meditation; meaning, purpose, and calling in life; bibliotherapy; attending community services and rituals; volunteerism and charity; ethical values and behavior; forgiveness, gratitude, and kindness; social justice; learning from spiritual models; acceptance of self and others (even with faults); being part of something larger than oneself; and appreciating the sacredness of life.

More specific versions of spiritually oriented CBT include those developed within particular religions, for example, Christian, Muslim, Buddhist, Jewish, and Taoist (Worthington et al., 2011) as well as more general but still spiritual approaches that relate directly to the sacred (see Hook et al., 2010; Pargament, 2007). Some examples of more explicitly religious versions of spiritually oriented CBT will now be provided.

Approaches to CBT designed primarily for clients who belong to conservative branches of Christianity have been around for quite a while and outcome studies have been conducted to evaluate their efficacy since the early 1980s (see Tan & Johnson, 2005; Worthington & Sandage, 2001). Conservatively oriented Christian CBT, with eight controlled outcome studies, has been found to be efficacious for depression and possibly efficacious for anxiety and marital discord (Hook et al., 2010). Such Christian CBT approaches appear to rest on relatively conservative theological assumptions about biblical interpretations and to involve cognitive restructuring or disputation of unbiblical or maladaptive, dysfunctional thoughts and deeper schemas using (a) scripture or the Bible, (b) religious imagery to reduce tension and anxiety and to deepen rest and peace, and (c) prayer in session as well as out of session as part of homework assignments that may also include scripture reading, study, and meditation. Consistent with the theological orientation of the researchers who have designed nearly all currently published versions of Christian CBT for conservative Christian clients, the treatment protocols explicitly affirm the ultimate authority of the Bible as God's inspired Word so that conservative interpretations of biblical truth takes precedence over rational, empirical, or relativistic values in conducting cognitive restructuring of maladaptive thinking and schemas (see Tan, 1987). A recent attempt to integrate CBT and interpersonal therapy within a conservative Christian religious or theological framework has been described as *integrative psychotherapy* by McMinn and Campbell (2007).

A specific type of prayer that can be used in Christian CBT is inner healing prayer or the healing of memories (see Garzon & Burkett, 2002), which helps clients process and resolve painful memories from the past and cognitively and experientially restructure deep-seated schemas (whether self-beliefs or beliefs about God). Tan (2007) has developed and described the following seven steps for inner healing prayer for clients who adhere to a moderate to conservative orientation to Christianity: (a) Begin with prayer for protection and for the Holy Spirit to take control of the session; (b) guide the client into a state of deep relaxation by using brief relaxation techniques (e.g., slow, deep breathing, calming self-talk, pleasant imagery, prayer, and biblical imagery); (c) guide the client to recall in imagery, as clearly as possible, a painful past event or memory, and to deeply feel the hurt, anger, fear, or other painful emotions connected with the memory; (d) pray for the presence of Jesus or of God to minister comfort, love, and grace to the client in whatever way the client needs, without any directive or specific suggestions from the therapist; (e) wait quietly upon Jesus or God to minister healing grace and truth to the client (during this time, the therapist will ask the client from time to time, "What's happening? What are you experiencing or feeling now?"); (f) close in prayer with the client; and (g) debrief and discuss the inner healing prayer experience with the client and assign homework inner healing prayer to the client, if appropriate. This seven-step model can be adapted or modified, even shortened if need be (see Tan, 2007, pp. 105–108). The use of such inner healing prayer may not be appropriate for clients with more severe psychological disorders, such as psychotic clients, severely depressed or bipolar clients, and those with a lack of ego strength and boundaries. Also, Christian clients who are struggling in their faith or who are experiencing rebellion or anger at God and therefore are not interested in prayer or scripture interventions at this time may find such interventions problematic and may benefit from alternative strategies that acknowledge and reframe their spiritual suffering in ways that help them transform and reestablish a different sense of connection to the sacred (Pargament, 2007).

The following is a hypothetical transcript of part of an inner healing prayer session in Christian CBT with a client who expressed a desire to remain embedded in his conservative Christian frame of reference that was consistent with his upbringing and which he viewed as a resource. Furthermore, this transcript reflects the willingness and comfort of a therapist to convey to the client that the therapist also personally holds a conservative Christian orientation:

Therapist: Are you ready today to enter into the seven-step inner healing prayer intervention that we discussed last week and that you've read about? (see Tan & Ortberg, 2004, pp. 64–71)

Client (John): Yes.

Therapist: Okay. Let's begin with prayer as I lead. Please close your eyes and remain in a receptive, prayerful mode to receive whatever the Lord wants to graciously minister to you today. "Dear Jesus, we pray that You will protect us from evil, and come in the presence and power of the Holy Spirit, to minister Your healing grace and truth to John and his painful memory. Thank you for Your love, and presence with us. Amen." Now keep your eyes closed as I guide you on to the second step.

Client: Okay.

Therapist: John, I would like you now to use the brief relaxation techniques that you have learned to help you to relax as deeply as possible . . . (after guiding John through slow, deep breathing, calming self-talk, and pleasant imagery) . . . How are you feeling now John?

Client: Pretty good, pretty calm and relaxed.

Therapist: Good . . . Now I would like you to change the focus of your attention to something else not as pleasant . . . Go back in your imagination to recall and relive the painful memory you previously discussed with me . . . try to see yourself as a young boy, when you were only 8 years old and in Grade 3 . . . when you had to switch to a new school because your parents had to move . . . can you see yourself in this new school and classroom, all alone, with no friends yet, and lonely and afraid?

Client: Yes . . . it's quite clear and I am feeling the emotional pain of the isolation and fear of my strange and new environment in this class . . . and the teacher is not nice but is pretty gruff and strict . . .

Therapist: Keep on with the classroom scene . . . tell me what is happening with the teacher.

Client: The teacher comes right up to me and sees me cowering in the corner where I am sitting, and he yells at me for not paying attention and accuses me of falling asleep which is not true . . . this is really painful [*with tears*] . . .

Therapist: Hang in there . . . tell me what else is happening . . . what are you experiencing or feeling?

Client: I am feeling very alone and hurt and scared, and so ashamed to be scolded before the whole class . . .

Therapist: [*After some time has passed.*] John, are you ready for us to move on to the fourth step and ask Jesus to walk into that painful situation and memory, and to minister to you?

Client: Yes . . . please . . .

Therapist: "Dear Jesus, I pray that You will now, by the power of the Holy Spirit, come and minister Your love, comfort, and grace, as well as truth to John as you walk into that classroom with John. Touch him and bless him in whatever way You know he needs. Thank you, in Your Name, Amen." Now John continue to be in a receptive prayerful mode, being open to whatever Jesus wants to do with you and for you . . . just allow Him to minister His healing grace and loving presence to you.

Client: Okay.

Therapist: [*After a few moments have passed.*] John, please tell me what is going on . . . what is happening and how are you feeling?

Client: I'm beginning to feel comforted and protected as I sense Jesus being with me, and telling me not to fear, that He is with me and He understands because He too suffered ridicule and scorn from others . . . I even see a tear or two from His eyes as He holds me gently and tenderly . . . this is really touching me and releasing me from the pain and fear of the classroom situation and memory.

Therapist: Good . . . just continue to let Jesus minister to you with His healing grace and truth.

Client: Okay.

Therapist: [*After some more time has gone by.*] Is there anything else you want to share with me before we close?

Client: Not really . . . I'm just enjoying the presence of Jesus with me and I am no longer afraid of the teacher or the other students in the classroom.

Therapist: Good . . . shall we close in prayer now?

Client: Yes, please,

Therapist: Why don't you start in prayer and I will close in prayer, okay?

Client: Yes . . . "Dear Jesus, thank you so much for touching me with Your tender love and healing words of grace and comfort, and for walking back into this painful classroom memory with me. I no longer feel stuck there or afraid or hurt or ashamed . . . or angry at the teacher . . . in fact I feel ready to forgive him. Thank you Jesus, Amen."

Therapist: "Yes, thank you so much Jesus for ministering so tenderly and deeply to John today, with Your inner healing grace and truth. Please continue to deepen this work of healing and wholeness in John's life and bless him as he goes. In Jesus' Name, Amen." John, before you go, let's debrief and discuss your experience of inner healing prayer today. Any comments or questions?

Client: Thank you for guiding me through this inner healing prayer experience. I was deeply touched and blessed!

Therapist: Do you think you may want to try praying for further inner healing on your own, in your daily personal prayer time?
Client: Yes, I think it would be helpful.
Therapist: Okay. I'll check in with you next week when we meet again. Take care!

Inner healing prayer does not always proceed so smoothly, and it is not a panacea for all painful memories. However, it can be a helpful intervention in more conservative Christian CBT for facilitating deeper levels of cognitive change and emotional processing. It also involves a more contemplative and receptive prayerful mode on the part of both the client and the therapist, and this is consistent with mindfulness and acceptance-based versions of contemporary CBT in general. More research is needed specifically evaluating the efficacy of inner healing prayer interventions in spiritually oriented CBT (Garzon & Burkett, 2002; Tan, 2007).

Another key intervention in Christian CBT is cognitive restructuring based on scripture. Standard CBT usually uses the following questions in conducting cognitive restructuring of dysfunctional thinking: "On what basis do you say this?"; "Where's the evidence for your view or conclusion?"; "Is there another way of looking at this?"; and "What if this view of yours is true, what does it mean to you?" In Christian CBT, the therapist usually asks further questions to cognitively restructure what are presumed to be unbiblical or inaccurate beliefs based on conservative Christian views about the Bible or God, such as the following: "What does God have to say about this?"; "What do you think the Bible has to say about this?"; and "What does your faith tradition or church or denomination have to say about this?" (see Tan, 2007, p. 108).

To return to the examples of rigidly held spiritual or religious beliefs that can be negative or dysfunctional, the following are a couple of possible therapeutic responses that Pargament (2007) provided to help orthodox Christian clients adopt alternative interpretations of suffering, sin, faith, the Bible, the nature of God, or other religiously based beliefs that appear to be having a negative impact on an individual's psychological or spiritual well-being. For example, when a client says, "Suffering is a sign of spiritual purity," the therapist may respond with, "Why did Jesus spend so much time healing people of various afflictions (physical and emotional) if suffering were so beneficial?" And if a client says, "It is sinful for me to focus on myself," the therapist can say in response, "In fact, Matthew 22:39 says, 'You shall love your neighbor *as* yourself,' not *instead* of yourself" (Pargament, 2007, p. 304). For the client in the hypothetical transcript who believes that if he has enough faith in God he will be fully healed of his depression, the therapist can respond with, "What do you think the Bible has to say about this? Is healing always guaranteed if one has enough faith?"

Muslim CBT approaches primarily designed to help conservative or orthodox Muslim clients have become more well known and have received some empirical support for their efficacy in recent years (see Abu-Raiya & Pargament, 2010). As an example, in such conservative Muslim CBT for anxiety, the therapist would use standard CBT techniques but also add specific Muslim religious or spiritual interventions to help Muslim clients. Muslim CBT interventions include using the Qur'an and Hadith (sayings and customs of the Prophet) in cognitive restructuring of negative thoughts and beliefs that lead to anxiety and encouraging clients to pray and read the Qur'an daily and frequently to reduce tension and to develop deeper feelings of closeness to Allah (e.g., see Razali, Aminah, & Khan, 2002). Six controlled outcome studies have shown that Muslim CBT is an efficacious treatment for anxiety and depression when used in combination with medication (Hook et al., 2010).

Buddhist approaches to CBT have also been developed and researched (see Avants & Margolin, 2004; Margolin, Beitel, Schuman-Olivier, & Avants, 2006; Margolin et al., 2007). As mentioned, 3-S (or 3-S+) therapy is a manual-guided specific version of Buddhist CBT that integrates standard CBT techniques with Buddhist principles or teachings (e.g., the Four Noble Truths and the Noble Eightfold Path) and practices (e.g., training in wisdom with right understanding and right intention; training in ethics with right speech, right behavior, and right livelihood; and training in gaining mastery over the mind with right effort, right mindfulness, and right concentration). Self-schema therapy aims at helping clients to transform their addict self-schema to a spiritual self-schema that is related to mindfulness, compassion, and doing no harm to self or others and hence to less drug use and impulsivity and greater HIV preventive behavior. Two controlled outcome studies have shown support for its efficacy (Margolin et al., 2006, 2007). Avants and Margolin (2004) pointed out that the Buddhist path is clearly not a passive one. Although it involves meditation and mindfulness, it also emphasizes effort and concentration to be more aware of automatic maladaptive thoughts, to reduce and cease such automaticity of thoughts, and to switch to a more spiritual self-schema. Another Buddhist version of CBT involves integrating CBT techniques for anger management with Buddhist teachings and meditation practices to help reduce anger and increase patience, compassion, and kindness. This Buddhist CBT for anger has been found to be possibly efficacious with incarcerated adult males in a prison setting (Vannoy & Hoyt, 2004).

A Jewish CBT approach has been recently developed to specifically treat subclinical anxiety (i.e., stress and worry) for members of Orthodox branches of the Jewish community through the Internet, with some empirical support for its efficacy with religious Jewish clients (Rosmarin et al., 2010). This spiritually integrated treatment was based on input from ultra-Orthodox Jewish rabbis that resulted in two major categories of strategies for coping with stress and worry: cognitive (e.g., reading passages and stories from Jewish religious literature that were inspiring) and behavioral (e.g., engaging in specific spiritual exercises aimed at increasing gratitude, and praying for help in increasing trust in God). It was designed to help Orthodox Jewish clients increase trust (rather than mistrust) in God (who is completely knowing, powerful, kind, and loving, and who will take care of their best interests) so that they can cope better with stress and worry or subclinical anxiety.

Another example of a spiritually oriented CBT is a Taoist approach to CBT that integrates cognitive therapy techniques into Taoist philosophy and teachings that emphasize letting go of excessive control, flexibility in developing one's personality, and yielding to natural laws. This Taoist CBT approach aims at regulating negative affect, changing maladaptive behavior, and modifying particular patterns of thinking and coping (Zhang et al., 2002). It has been used to treat generalized anxiety disorder, with some empirical support for it being a possibly efficacious treatment for anxiety (Hook et al., 2010).

Spiritually oriented CBT that is not as narrowly focused as the religiously accommodative approaches described thus far is also available for clients who are less religiously conservative or who are nonsectarian or for those who describe themselves as spiritual but not religious. The following is a hypothetical example of more broad-based spiritually oriented CBT with a nonsectarian client struggling with spiritual doubts and the search for deeper meaning in life.

Therapist: Tell me more about your spiritual doubts.

Client: I grew up in a very legalistic and fundamentalist church that I left years ago. I have not attended church since then. However, I still struggle with spiritual doubts about whether there is a God and how I can connect with the sacred. I long for deeper meaning in my life, which seems to be empty and depressing at times.

Therapist: What have you done or tried so far, to connect more deeply with the sacred, in your search for more meaning in your life?

Client: Not much . . . and I certainly do not want to return to the oppressive and legalistic church that I grew up in.

Therapist: Umm-hmmm . . .

Client: Yet I still yearn for the connection with God or the sacred that I sometimes experienced in that church despite feeling oppressed and beat up most of the time by the harsh and condemning sermons I often heard. I would describe myself now as nonsectarian spiritual but not religious. I am not interested in churches or organized religion.

Therapist: I understand . . . I wonder if you have had any spiritual experiences that made you feel a bit more connected to the sacred since you left that church years ago?

Client: Well . . . I can recall a couple of times . . . once when I was taking a long walk in the woods . . . and another when I was watching a beautiful sunset . . . I felt some comfort and a sense of a Sacred presence with me for a few moments.

Therapist: I wonder if being in nature such as the woods and watching sunsets, may be especially meaningful for you, in connecting more to a sense of the sacred in your life . . .

Client: I guess so, come to think of it. Perhaps I should intentionally spend some prolonged periods of time, like taking a personal retreat, in a log cabin in the woods, and go on more long reflective walks and watch more sunsets . . .

Therapist: Sounds like a good idea! What do you think?

Client: Yeah, I think it may help me to develop my own sense of spirituality, of having a deeper connection with God or the sacred again. At least I'm willing to try because there is a deep longing or yearning in me to have this connection or deeper experience.

Therapist: Would you like to plan this sometime soon in your schedule?

Client: Yes! I think I can plan a weekend in the next couple of weeks or so, to be at a log cabin not that far away.

In this example, the spiritually oriented CBT therapist empathetically listens to the client and helps the client to come up with a concrete plan to use the client's own way of connecting more with a sense of the sacred presence by spending more time in nature and taking a personal retreat. This may help the client to overcome deepening feelings of emptiness and depression.

ETHICAL GUIDELINES AND ISSUES

Ethical guidelines and issues pertaining to the practice of spiritually oriented CBT will only be briefly dealt with here (see Gonsiorek, Richards, Pargament, & McMinn, 2009; Plante, 2007, 2009; Tan, 1994, 1996, 2003; Tan & Johnson, 2005; see also Chapter 3 in this volume). Relevant ethical guidelines include respect, responsibility, integrity, competence, and concern (Plante, 2007, 2009). The necessity of obtaining informed consent from the client is particularly crucial in spiritually oriented CBT or any religious and spiritual therapy (Tan, 1994, 1996, 2003). It is also essential for therapists not to impose their values or religious beliefs on clients, especially in cognitive restructuring interventions that include challenging maladaptive religious and spiritual beliefs or schemas. Clients should have their freedom to choose their own beliefs and values protected. Therapists may need to refer certain clients to other therapists who may be more familiar with the R/S beliefs of such clients, if they are not comfortable in working with them and their beliefs and problems.

More specific ethical challenges or issues relevant to integrating religion and spirituality into psychotherapy (and CBT) include competence, bias, maintaining traditions and standards of psychology, and integrity in labeling clinical services for third-party insurance reimbursement (Gonsiorek et al., 2009; see also Chapter 3 in this volume).

OPPORTUNITIES, CHALLENGES, AND FUTURE DIRECTIONS: RECOMMENDATIONS FOR FUTURE TRAINING, PRACTICE, AND RESEARCH

Spiritually oriented CBT addresses religion and spirituality from a cognitive–behavioral perspective that focuses on the thoughts and beliefs of the client because maladaptive and dysfunctional thinking can lead to emotional and behavioral problems. Such thinking can also include specific R/S beliefs or schemas that may be maladaptive and distorted even within a client's particular R/S framework. Two major approaches to dealing with these dysfunctional thoughts from a spiritually oriented CBT perspective are now well developed: (a) direct disputation or cognitive restructuring of irrational beliefs or maladaptive thoughts and schemas, which is the more traditional CBT way, and (b) the more recent mindfulness and acceptance-based CBT approaches that emphasize being aware of the present moment and here-and-now experiencing with openness and acceptance instead of judgment, thus letting painful and dysfunctional thoughts come and go more passively and mindfully. Mindfulness and acceptance-based strategies have been incorporated into more explicitly R/S therapies, such as Buddhist and Taoist approaches to spiritually oriented CBT.

Even in these more explicitly R/S therapies, some will emphasize both passive and active components—for example, Buddhist-oriented 3-S therapy and Christian CBT that focuses on both directly challenging maladaptive, unbiblical thinking as well as more passively letting go and letting God take control of such thoughts—whereas others may emphasize more passive acceptance and mindfulness—for example, some Taoist and other Buddhist versions of CBT. Mindfulness and acceptance-based therapies, although often rooted in Buddhist traditions, can also be incorporated into other contemplative and meditative religious and spiritual traditions such as Christian ones (e.g., Roman Catholic and Greek Orthodox; see Tan, 2007). They can also be incorporated into other more general spiritual approaches to therapy and even secular, nonreligious therapies (see Shapiro & Carlson, 2009).

Opportunities therefore exist for the future development of both more explicit spiritually oriented CBT as well as more generic, somewhat spiritual but not specifically religious approaches to CBT such as ACT, DBT, and MBCT. There are also challenges having to do with more clearly differentiating such approaches, so that more and better outcome research can be conducted on the efficacy of these therapies as well as effectiveness in real-life clinical settings (e.g., see Hook et al., 2010; Smith, Bartz, & Richards, 2007; Worthington et al., 2011; see also Wade et al., 2007; Chapter 34 in this volume). A specific need in future research is to use more dismantling designs in RCTs to further determine which specific aspects of a spiritually oriented CBT may be more efficacious or effective (see also Richards & Worthington, 2010).

The training of future therapists who are skilled in conducting spiritually oriented CBT in a professionally competent, clinically sensitive, and ethically responsible and appropriate way is a real need and serious challenge to the mental health professional field (see Chapter 33 in this volume). Biases against religion are still present, although psychologists seem to be more open to spirituality in general (see Chapter 2 in this volume). In a survey of 258 clinician members of the American Psychological Association (APA), Delaney, Miller, and Bisono (2007) found that the psychologists surveyed were no more or less religious than those surveyed two decades ago, but they are still much less religious than the general population of the United States. Nevertheless, the majority of the psychologists surveyed believed religion to be beneficial (82%) rather than harmful (7%) to mental health (see Post & Wade, 2009, p. 133). This does not mean, however, that professional psychologists are adequately trained or able to conduct therapy effectively with religious clients. In fact, only 13% of program leaders and training directors reported having one course specifically on religion/spirituality and psychology, 17% reported that the topic is dealt with systematically, and 16% reported that the topic is not addressed at all in their APA-accredited clinical psychology programs (Brawer, Handal, Fabricatore, Roberts, & Wajda-Johnston, 2002).

Worthington et al. (2009) have made some helpful recommendations for training therapists to deal with spiritual concerns in clinical practice and research. They have suggested several steps for training programs to take to increase their focus on R/S issues and to help their students become more competent in spiritually oriented therapy, including CBT. For example, a program must make a firm decision to train its students in knowing how to deal with R/S issues in therapy and directly encourage faculty, clinical supervisors, and students to openly discuss such issues.

Pargament (2007) has similarly offered six recommendations for formal training in spiritually integrated therapy (including CBT): (a) a seminar at the graduate level in the psychology of religion and spirituality; (b) a comparative religion course, covering the major world religions; (c) a course in spiritually integrated therapy (or more specifically in spiritually oriented CBT) covering both the positive and negative aspects of religion and spirituality; (d) integration of spiritual and religious issues in other courses, such as assessment, psychopathology, therapy approaches, supervision, and consultation; (e) clinical supervision of cases in a spiritually and religiously sensitive way; and (f) continuing education on religious and spiritual issues in therapy so that clinicians can remain updated in this area (see p. 334). Pargament concluded by asserting that there is now "no need to whisper" (p. 342) or be reticent and afraid about integrating religion and spirituality into psychotherapy, including CBT. He affirmed how doing so can transform the work of psychotherapy into a more sacred experience that can deepen the transformative moments that occur at times in the therapeutic process for both the client and the therapist. This is also true for spiritually oriented CBT.

References

Abu-Raiya, H., & Pargament, K. I. (2010). Religiously integrated psychotherapy with Muslim clients: From research to practice. *Professional Psychology: Research and Practice, 41*, 181–188. doi:10.1037/a0017988

Aten, J. D., & Leach, M. M. (Eds.). (2009). *Spirituality and the therapeutic process: A comprehensive resource from intake to termination.* Washington, DC: American Psychological Association. doi:10.1037/11853-000

Aten, J. D., McMinn, M. R., & Worthington, E. L., Jr., (Eds.). (2011). *Spiritually oriented interventions for counseling and psychotherapy*. Washington, DC: American Psychological Association. doi:10.1037/12313-000

Avants, S. K., & Margolin, A. (2004). Development of spiritual self-schema (3-S) therapy for the treatment of addictive and HIV risk behavior: A convergence of cognitive and Buddhist psychology. *Journal of Psychotherapy Integration, 14*, 253–289. doi:10.1037/1053-0479.14.3.253

Beck, A. T. (1976). *Cognitive therapy and the emotional disorders.* New York, NY: International Universities Press.

Bishop, S. R., Lau, M., Shapiro, S., Carlson, L., Anderson, N. D., Carmody, J., . . . Devins, G. (2004). Mindfulness: A proposed operational definition. *Clinical Psychology: Science and Practice, 11*, 230–241. doi:10.1093/clipsy.bph077

Brawer, P. A., Handal, P. J., Fabricatore, A. N., Roberts, R., & Wajda-Johnston, V. A. (2002). Training and education in religion/spirituality within APA-accredited clinical psychology programs. *Professional Psychology: Research and Practice, 33*, 203–206. doi:10.1037/0735-7028.33.2.203

Butler, A. C., Chapman, J. E., Forman, E. M., & Beck, A. T. (2006). The empirical status of cognitive–behavioral therapy: A review of meta-analyses. *Clinical Psychology Review, 26*, 17–31. doi:10.1016/j.cpr.2005.07.003

Chambless, D. L., & Hollon, S. D. (1998). Defining empirically supported therapies. *Journal of Consulting and Clinical Psychology, 66*, 7–18. doi:10.1037/0022-006X.66.1.7

Chambless, D. L., & Ollendick, T. H. (2001). Empirically supported psychological interventions: Controversies and evidence. *Annual Review of Psychology, 52*, 685–716. doi:10.1146/annurev.psych.52.1.685

Delaney, H. D., Miller, W. R., & Bisono, A. M. (2007). Religiosity and spirituality among psychologists: A survey of clinician members of the American Psychological Association. *Professional Psychology: Research and Practice, 38*, 538–546. doi:10.1037/0735-7028.38.5.538

Dimeff, L. A., & Koerner, K. (Eds.). (2007). *Dialectical behavior therapy in clinical practice: Applications across disorders and settings.* New York, NY: Guilford Press.

Dimidjian, S., Hollon, S. D., Dobson, K. S., Schmaling, K. B., Kohlenberg, R. J., Addis, M. E., . . . Jacobson, N. S. (2006). Randomized trial of behavioral activation, cognitive therapy, and antidepressant medication in the acute treatment of adults with major depression. *Journal of Consulting and Clinical Psychology, 74*, 658–670. doi:10.1037/0022-006X.74.4.658

Dobson, D., & Dobson, K. S. (2009). *Evidence-based practice of cognitive–behavioral therapy*. New York, NY: Guilford Press.

Dobson, K. S. (Ed.). (2010). *Handbook of cognitive–behavioral therapies* (3rd ed.). New York, NY: Guilford Press.

D'Souza, R., Rich, D., Diamond, I., & Godfery, K. (2002). An open randomized controlled trial using a spiritually augmented cognitive behavioral therapy for demoralization and treatment adherence in patients with schizophrenia. *Proceedings of the 37th Royal Australian and New Zealand College of Psychiatrists and Congress,* 36(Suppl.), A9.

D'Souza, R., Rich, D., Diamond, I., Godfery, K., & Gleeson, D. (2002). An open randomized controlled trial of a spiritually augmented cognitive behavior therapy in patients with depression and hopelessness. *Proceedings of the 37th Royal Australian and New Zealand College of Psychiatrists and Congress,* 36(Suppl.), A9.

Ellis, A. (1960). There is no place for the concept of sin in psychotherapy. *Journal of Counseling Psychology, 7*, 188–192. doi:10.1037/h0048184

Ellis, A. (1962). *Reason and emotion in psychotherapy.* New York, NY: Lyle Stuart.

Ellis, A. (1971). *The case against religion: A psychotherapist's view.* New York, NY: Institute for Rational Living.

Ellis, A. (1980). Psychotherapy and atheistic values: A response to A. E. Bergin's "Psychotherapy and religious values." *Journal of Consulting and Clinical Psychology, 48*, 635–639. doi:10.1037/0022-006X.48.5.635

Ellis, A. (2000). Can rational emotive behavior therapy (REBT) be effectively used with people who have devout beliefs in God and religion? *Professional Psychology: Research and Practice, 31*, 29–33. doi:10.1037/0735-7028.31.1.29

Ellison, C. W. (1983). Spiritual well-being: Conceptualization and measurement. *Journal of Psychology and Theology, 11*, 330–340.

Exline, J. J., & Rose, E. (2005). Religious and spiritual struggles. In R. F. Paloutzian & C. L. Park (Eds.), *Handbook of the psychology of religion and spirituality* (pp. 315–330). New York, NY: Guilford Press.

Fetzer Institute/National Institute of Aging Working Group. (1999). *Multidimensional measurement of religiousness/spirituality for use in health research: A report of the Fetzer Institute/National Institute on Aging Working Group*. Kalamazoo, MI: John E. Fetzer Institute.

Garzon, F., & Burkett, L. (2002). Healing of memories: Models, research, future directions. *Journal of Psychology and Christianity, 21*, 42–49.

Gonsiorek, J. C., Richards, P. S., Pargament, K. I., & McMinn, M. R. (2009). Ethical challenges and opportunities at the edge: Incorporating spirituality and religion into psychotherapy. *Professional Psychology: Research and Practice, 40*, 385–395. doi:10.1037/a0016488

Griffith, J. L. (2010). *Religion that heals, religion that harms: A guide for clinical practice*. New York, NY: Guilford Press.

Hayes, S. C., Follette, V. M., & Linehan, M. M. (Eds.). (2004). *Mindfulness and acceptance: Expanding the cognitive behavioral tradition*. New York, NY: Guilford Press.

Hayes, S. C., Luoma, J. B., Bond, F. W., Masuda, A. L., & Lillis, J. (2006). Acceptance and commitment therapy: Model, processes, and outcomes. *Behaviour Research and Therapy, 44*, 1–25. doi:10.1016/j.brat.2005.06.006

Hayes, S. C., Strosahl, K. D., & Wilson, K. G. (1999). *Acceptance and commitment therapy: An experiential approach to behavior change*. New York, NY: Guilford Press.

Hodge, D. R. (2006). Spiritually modified cognitive therapy: A review of the literature. *Social Work, 51*, 157–166. doi:10.1093/sw/51.2.157

Hook, J. N., Worthington, E. L., Jr., Davis, D. E., Jennings, D. J., II, Gartner, A. L., & Hook, J. N. (2010). Empirically supported religious and spiritual therapies. *Journal of Clinical Psychology, 66*, 46–72.

Kendall, P. C., & Bemis, K. M. (1983). Thought and action in psychotherapy: The cognitive-behavioral approaches. In M. Hersen, A. E. Kazdin, & A. S. Bellack (Eds.), *The clinical psychology handbook* (pp. 565–592). New York, NY: Pergamon.

Kendall, P. C., & Hollon, S. D. (Eds.). (1979). *Cognitive-behavioral interventions: Theory, research, and procedures*. New York, NY: Academic Press.

Koenig, H., Meador, K., & Parkerson, G. (1997). Religion Index for Psychiatric Research: A 5-item measure for use in health outcome studies [Letter to the editor]. *American Journal of Psychiatry, 154*, 885–886.

Leahy, R. L. (2003). *Cognitive therapy techniques: A practitioner's guide*. New York, NY: Guilford Press.

Leahy, R. L. (2004). *Contemporary cognitive therapy: Theory, research, and practice*. New York, NY: Guilford Press.

Linehan, M. M. (1993). *Cognitive–behavioral treatment of borderline personality disorder*. New York, NY: Guilford Press.

Luoma, J. B., Hayes, S. C., & Walser, R. D. (2007). *Learning ACT: An acceptance and commitment therapy skills-training manual for therapists*. Oakland, CA: New Harbinger.

Margolin, A., Beitel, M., Schuman-Olivier, Z., & Avants, S. K. (2006). A controlled study of a spiritually-focused intervention for increasing motivation for HIV prevention among drug users. *AIDS Education and Prevention, 18*, 311–322. doi:10.1521/aeap.2006.18.4.311

Margolin, A., Schuman-Olivier, Z., Beitel, M., Arnold, R. M., Fulwiler, C. E., & Avants, S. K. (2007). A preliminary study of spiritual self-schema (3-S+) therapy for reducing impulsivity in HIV-positive drug users. *Journal of Clinical Psychology, 63*, 979–999. doi:10.1002/jclp.20407

McMinn, M. R., & Campbell, C. D. (2007). *Integrative psychotherapy: Toward a comprehensive Christian approach*. Downers Grove, IL: IVP Academic.

Meichenbaum, D. (1977). *Cognitive-behavior modification: An integrative approach*. New York, NY: Plenum Press.

Nathan, P. E., & Gorman, J. M. (Eds.). (2007). *A guide to treatments that work* (3rd ed.). New York, NY: Oxford University Press.

Nielsen, S. L., Johnson, W. B., & Ellis, A. (2001). *Counseling and psychotherapy with religious persons: A rational emotive behavior therapy approach*. Mahwah, NJ: Erlbaum.

Öst, L. G. (2008). Efficacy of the third wave of behavioral therapies: A systematic review and meta-analysis. *Behaviour Research and Therapy, 46*, 296–321. doi:10.1016/j.brat.2007.12.005

Pargament, K. I. (1997). *The psychology of religion and coping: Theory, research, practice*. New York, NY: Guilford Press.

Pargament, K. I. (2007). *Spiritually integrated psychotherapy: Understanding and addressing the sacred*. New York, NY: Guilford Press.

Pargament, K. I., Koenig, H. G., & Perez, L. (2000). The many methods of religious coping: Initial development and validation of the RCOPE. *Journal of Clinical Psychology, 56*, 519–543. doi:10.1002/(SICI)1097-4679(200004)56:4<519::AID-JCLP6>3.0.CO;2-1

Pargament, K. I., Smith, B. W., Koenig, H. G., & Perez, L. (1998). Patterns of positive and negative religious coping with major life stressors. *Journal for the Scientific Study of Religion, 37*, 710–724. doi:10.2307/1388152

Park, C. L., & Slattery, J. M. (2009). Including spirituality in case conceptualizations: A meaning-systems approach. In J. D. Aten & M. M. Leach (Eds.), *Spirituality and the therapeutic process: A comprehensive resource from intake to termination* (pp. 121–142). Washington, DC: American Psychological Association. doi:10.1037/11853-006

Plante, T. G. (2007). Integrating spirituality and psychotherapy: Ethical issues and principles to consider. *Journal of Clinical Psychology, 63*, 891–902. doi:10.1002/jclp.20383

Plante, T. G. (2009). *Spiritual practices in psychotherapy: Thirteen tools for enhancing psychological health.* Washington, DC: American Psychological Association. doi:10.1037/11872-000

Plante, T. G., & Boccaccini, B. F. (1997). The Santa Clara Strength of Religious Faith Questionnaire. *Pastoral Psychology, 45*, 375–387. doi:10.1007/BF02230993

Plante, T. G., & Sherman, A. C. (Eds.). (2001). *Faith and health: Psychological perspectives.* New York, NY: Guilford Press.

Plante, T. G., Vallaeys, C. L., Sherman, A. C., & Wallston, K. A. (2002). The development of a brief version of the Santa Clara Strength of Religious Faith Questionnaire. *Pastoral Psychology, 50*, 359–368.

Post, B. C., & Wade, N. G. (2009). Religion and spirituality: A practice-friendly review of research. *Journal of Clinical Psychology, 65*, 131–146. doi:10.1002/jclp.20563

Razali, S. M., Aminah, K., & Khan, U. A. (2002). Religious–cultural psychotherapy in the management of anxiety patients. *Transcultural Psychiatry, 39*, 130–136. doi:10.1177/136346150203900106

Richards, P. S., & Bergin, A. E. (2005). *A spiritual strategy for counseling and psychotherapy* (2nd ed.). Washington, DC: American Psychological Association. doi:10.1037/11214-000

Richards, P. S., & Bergin, A. E. (Eds.). (2000). *Handbook of psychotherapy and religious diversity.* Washington, DC: American Psychological Association. doi:10.1037/10347-000

Richards, P. S., & Worthington, E. L., Jr. (2010). The need for evidence-based spiritually oriented psychotherapies. *Professional Psychology: Research and Practice, 41*, 363–370. doi:10.1037/a0019469

Roemer, L., & Orsillo, S. M. (2009). *Mindfulness- and acceptance-based behavioral therapies in practice.* New York, NY: Guilford Press.

Rosmarin, D. H., Pargament, K. I., Pirutinsky, S., & Mahoney, A. (2010). A randomized controlled evaluation of spiritually integrated treatment for subclinical anxiety in the Jewish community, delivered via the Internet. *Journal of Anxiety Disorders, 24*, 799–808. doi:10.1016/j.janxdis.2010.05.014

Segal, Z. V., Williams, J. M. G., & Teasdale, J. D. (2002). *Mindfulness-based cognitive therapy for depression: A new approach for preventing relapse.* New York, NY: Guilford Press.

Shapiro, S. L., & Carlson, L. E. (2009). *The art and science of mindfulness: Integrating mindfulness into psychology and the helping professions.* Washington, DC: American Psychological Association. doi:10.1037/11885-000

Smith, T. B., Bartz, J., & Richards, P. S. (2007). Outcomes of religious and spiritual adaptations to psychotherapy: A meta-analytic review. *Psychotherapy Research, 17*, 643–655. doi:10.1080/10503300701250347

Sperry, L., & Shafranske, E. P. (Eds.). (2005). *Spiritually oriented psychotherapy: Contemporary approaches.* Washington, DC: American Psychological Association. doi:10.1037/10886-000

Tan, S. Y. (1987). Cognitive-behavior therapy: A biblical approach and critique. *Journal of Psychology and Theology, 15*, 103–112.

Tan, S. Y. (1994). Ethical considerations in religious psychotherapy: Potential pitfalls and unique resources. *Journal of Psychology and Theology, 22*, 389–394.

Tan, S. Y. (1996). Religion in clinical practice: Implicit and explicit integration. In E. P. Shafranske (Ed.), *Religion and the clinical practice of psychology* (pp. 365–387). Washington, DC: American Psychological Association. doi:10.1037/10199-013

Tan, S. Y. (2003). Integrating spiritual direction into psychotherapy: Ethical issues and guidelines. *Journal of Psychology and Theology, 31*, 14–23.

Tan, S. Y. (2007). Use of prayer and scripture in cognitive–behavioral therapy. *Journal of Psychology and Christianity, 26*, 101–111.

Tan, S. Y. (2011). *Counseling and psychotherapy: A Christian perspective.* Grand Rapids, MI: Baker Academic.

Tan, S. Y., & Johnson, W. B. (2005). Spiritually oriented cognitive–behavioral therapy. In L. Sperry & E. P. Shafranske (Eds.), *Spiritually oriented psychotherapy: Contemporary approaches* (pp. 77–103). Washington, DC: American Psychological Association. doi:10.1037/10886-004

Tan, S. Y., & Ortberg, J. (2004). *Coping with depression* (2nd ed.). Grand Rapids, MI: Baker.

Vannoy, S. D., & Hoyt, W. T. (2004). Evaluation of an anger therapy intervention for incarcerated adult males. *Journal of Offender Rehabilitation, 39*, 39–57. doi:10.1300/J076v39n02_03

Wade, N. G., Worthington, E. L., Jr., & Vogel, D. L. (2007). Effectiveness of religiously tailored interventions in Christian therapy. *Psychotherapy Research, 17*, 91–105. doi:10.1080/10503300500497388

Wells, A. (2009). *Metacognitive therapy for anxiety and depression*. New York, NY: Guilford Press.

Williams, M., Teasdale, J., Segal, Z., & Kabat-Zinn, J. (2007). *The mindful way through depression: Freeing yourself from chronic unhappiness*. New York, NY: Guilford Press.

Worthington, E. L., Jr., Hook, J. N., Davis, D. E., & McDaniel, M. A. (2011). Religion and spirituality. In J. C. Norcross (Ed.), *Psychotherapy relationships that work* (2nd ed., pp. 402–420). New York, NY: Oxford University Press. doi:10.1093/acprof:oso/9780199737208.003.0020

Worthington, E. L., Jr., & Sandage, S. J. (2001). Religion and spirituality. *Psychotherapy: Theory, Research, Practice, Training, 38*, 473–478. doi:10.1037/0033-3204.38.4.473

Worthington, E. L., Jr., Sandage, S. J., Davis, D. E., Hook, J. N., Miller, A. J., Hall, M. E. L., & Hall, T. W. (2009). Training therapists to address spiritual concerns in clinical practice and research. In J. D. Aten & M. M. Leach (Eds.), *Spirituality and the therapeutic process: A comprehensive resource from intake to termination* (pp. 267–292). Washington, DC: American Psychological Association.

Worthington, E. L., Jr., Wade, N. G., Hight, T. L., Ripley, J. S., McCullough, M. E., Berry, J. W., . . . O'Connor, L. (2003). The Religious Commitment Inventory-10: Development, refinement, and validation of a brief scale for research and counseling. *Journal of Counseling Psychology, 50*, 84–96. doi:10.1037/0022-0167.50.1.84

Zhang, Y., Young, D., Lee, S., Li, L., Zhang, H., Xiao, Z., . . . Chang, D. F. (2002). Chinese Taoist cognitive psychotherapy in the treatment of generalized anxiety disorder in contemporary China. *Transcultural Psychiatry, 39*, 115–129. doi:10.1177/136346150203900105

CHAPTER 9

RELIGION AND SPIRITUALITY: A FAMILY SYSTEMS PERSPECTIVE IN CLINICAL PRACTICE

Froma Walsh

Spiritual resources can strengthen family bonds and foster resilience in dealing with adversity (Walsh, 2006, 2009a). Spiritual concerns and differences, comingled with family dynamics, can fuel relational strife and tear loved ones apart. Therefore, in working with families, clinicians need to attend to the spiritual dimension of family life to understand members' needs and suffering and to facilitate their healing and growth. This chapter first presents a family systems perspective for clinical practice to address the role of religion and spirituality in family relationships and in sociocultural and developmental contexts. A brief overview of principles for assessment and intervention is provided. Several ways are described for family practitioners to tap spiritual resources toward therapeutic aims, fitting clients' values and preferences. Spiritual sources of distress are then addressed, with particular attention to three areas of concern that commonly arise in family practice: spiritually driven relational wounds, profound spiritual challenges with death and loss, and conflicts in multifaith families.

RELIGION AND SPIRITUALITY: A FAMILY SYSTEMS ORIENTATION

As discussed in Volume 1, Chapter 1, this handbook, the concepts of *religion* and *spirituality* often have been mistakenly polarized or conflated in research and public discourse. Consistent with the perspective of this volume, *religion* here refers to organized, institutionalized faith systems, with shared traditions, beliefs, practices, and communities. *Spirituality*, a broad overarching construct, refers to an active personal investment in transcendent values and practices lived out in daily life and relationships, either within or outside organized religion.

From a systems orientation, spirituality is viewed as a dimension of human experience (Walsh, 2009a). A systems perspective is holistic because it encompasses biological, psychological, social, and spiritual domains. Family systems therapists attend to the interplay of these influences in suffering, healing, and resilience (Wright, 2009). Like other sociocultural influences, spirituality involves streams of experience that flow through all aspects of life, from multigenerational heritage to shared belief systems and their expression in ongoing transactions, spiritual practices, relational conduct, and responses to adversity. Spirituality can foster a sense of meaning, wholeness, harmony, and connection with others—from the most intimate bonds, to extended kinship and community networks, to a unity with all life, nature, and the universe. Like other domains of influence, spiritual beliefs and practices can be hurtful, destructive, and divisive. Thus, spirituality can be seen as inherently relational, with the potential to nourish or to harm.

FAMILY SPIRITUALITY IN SOCIOCULTURAL CONTEXT

Over recent decades, societal dislocations, growing cultural diversity, and family structural transformations have contributed to the changing landscape of religion and spirituality in the United States, as in

DOI: 10.1037/14046-009
APA Handbook of Psychology, Religion, and Spirituality: Vol. 2. An Applied Psychology of Religion and Spirituality, K. I. Pargament (Editor-in-Chief)

other rapidly changing societies (Pew Forum on Religion and Public Life, 2008, 2009). Americans are increasingly independent in their spiritual lives, selecting aspects of their faith traditions and other spiritual pathways to fit their lives and relationships. Interfaith couples and multifaith families are increasingly common. These trends present complexity and challenges in family life and intergenerational relations.

Religious conservatives and scholars have tended to focus on a traditional essentialist model of "the good family" and proper gender roles that does not fit the lives and spiritual needs of most contemporary families (Edgell, 2005; Mahoney, 2010). Despite concerns that "nontraditional" family forms damage children, a large body of research has clearly established that most children fare well and can thrive in a variety of kinship arrangements, with stable, caring, committed bonds and financial security (Cherlin, 2010; Walsh, 2012a).

Most families, in their diversity, value a spiritual dimension in their lives that fosters personal and relational well-being, positive growth, and concern for others. Relationships are oriented by principles of fairness, decency, generosity, and compassion and are marked by giving and forgiving (Anderson, 2009; Doherty, 2009). Some contemporary values break with traditions, such as gender equality and flexible roles in family life. Yet, most families uphold traditional values of commitment, responsibility, and investment in raising healthy children (Gallup & Lindsay, 2000). Of interest, most survey respondents have ranked "family ties, loyalty, and traditions" as the primary factors thought to strengthen the family; next were "moral and spiritual values," which far outranked "family counseling" and "parent training classes."

SPIRITUALITY IN FAMILY DEVELOPMENTAL CONTEXT

Spirituality is intertwined with family development through dynamic processes that ebb and flow, shifting in salience and meaning over the family life course and across the generations (Walsh, 2009b). With a developmental systemic perspective, therapists attend to the interaction of individual, couple, parent–child, and extended family influences over time (Walsh, 2012b). Family systems are meaning-making communities with directionality and a life of their own (Anderson, 2009). Rooted in cultural, spiritual, and multigenerational traditions, each family constructs its own spirituality, which is transmitted and altered through ongoing transactions. Spiritual considerations arise with each family life phase and major transitions: in marital bonds, parenting roles, and childrearing decisions; with divorce and remarriage; and with illness, caregiving, death, and loss (Walsh, 2012b). Critical events and relationship changes may heighten the importance of spirituality or spark new directions.

Spirituality in many families involves a lifelong faithful adherence to their religious tradition. Yet, increasingly, religion is less often a given that people are born into and accept unquestioningly. Recent surveys find that 44% of Americans do not follow the faith tradition of their upbringing; yet most value some expression of spirituality (Pew Forum on Religion and Public Life, 2008, 2009). As adults and their children are increasingly likely to live in varied family configurations over a lengthening life course (Walsh, 2012a), their spiritual pathways may become more complex as they seek meaning and connection in life pursuits and significant relationships. Therefore, clinicians need to explore both continuities and changes over time and across the generations, helping families respect differences and attempt to blend them. Some of these clinical issues will be considered in the next section.

RESEARCH ON RELIGION AND SPIRITUALITY IN FAMILY LIFE

A growing body of research has been examining the influences of spiritual beliefs, practices, and congregational involvement on family functioning, parenting styles, family dynamics, and intergenerational bonds (e.g., Bailey, 2002; Dollahite & Marks, 2009; V. King, 2003; Lambert & Dollahite, 2006; Mahoney, 2005; Mahoney, Pargament, Tarakeshwar, & Swank, 2001; Mahoney & Tarakeshwar, 2005; Marks, 2006; Snarey & Dollahite, 2001; Snider, Clements, & Vazsonyi, 2004; for a critical review, see Mahoney, 2010). Studies of highly religious families are exploring the role of religion in couple conflict (Lambert & Dollahite, 2006; Marsh & Dallos, 2001) and parent–child interactions (Marks, 2004). In general, studies suggest positive benefits of religion for the quality and stability of relationships in traditional and nontraditional family structures.

Limitations of the empirical research to date should be noted (see Mahoney, 2010). Most studies are cross-sectional, do not permit causal associations, and are based on the self-report of one family member. Few studies directly examine links between parental religiousness and child adjustment; most focus on adolescent reports of religiousness and prosocial or risky and antisocial conduct. Most quantitative studies use only one or two items to measure religious variables (e.g., affiliation, attendance, self-rated importance, and biblical conservatism), whereas most qualitative studies focus on highly religious, intact two-parent families. More in-depth research is needed to address the broad diversity of families and their spiritual approaches. Studies need to expand from the predominant focus on Christian families to Jewish (Meyerstein, 2006), Muslim (Daneshpour, 1998), and others. Too often studies lump remarried stepfamilies together with intact married couple households as "two-parent families," not taking into account the more complex family dynamics within and across households. Finally, most studies involve national or community samples in which families are not clinically distressed (Mahoney, 2010). To better inform clinical practice, studies need to illuminate how specific religious and spiritual beliefs and practices can help or hinder family relationships—and how family dynamics interact with spirituality—especially when family functioning is impaired and under stressful conditions.

ADDRESSING THE SPIRITUAL DIMENSION IN FAMILY THERAPY

Spiritual beliefs and practices influence the ways that families deal with adversity, their experience of suffering, and the meaning of symptoms. They also influence how family members communicate about their problems, their causal assumptions and future expectations, their attitudes toward helpers (physicians, therapists, clergy, or faith healers), and their preferred pathways in recovery. It is important to explore the spiritual values, practices, and concerns of each family, intertwined with psychosocial and cultural aspects of their lives.

Assessment and Intervention Guidelines

In clinical assessment, family genograms (McGoldrick, Gerson, & Petry, 2008) and spiritually oriented assessment tools (Hodge, 2005; see also Chapter 5 in this volume) can be valuable tools used to gather important information about religion and spirituality in family life. With growing cultural and spiritual diversity, it is crucial not to make assumptions about faith beliefs and practices on the basis of the client's religious identification or family upbringing. It is important to explore the dynamic nature and significance of spirituality in their lives and relationships over time. A timeline is useful to track their spiritual journey and changes with crisis events or life transitions, such as marriage, divorce, or remarriage. If a family upbringing has not been followed, how has that affected relationships? Most important is to understand clients' lived experience of their faith and how they express core spiritual beliefs in their relationships. The following clinical practice guidelines can be helpful.

- Inquire respectfully about the meaning and significance of religious or spiritual beliefs and practices in family life and in relation to presenting problems, coping, and mastery.
- Identify spiritual resources (current, past, and potential) that might contribute to coping, healing, and resilience. Encourage families to draw on those that fit their values and preferences, including the following:
  - shared contemplative practices and meaningful rituals,
  - involvement in faith community and pastoral guidance,
  - spiritual connectedness with nature and through expressive/creative arts, and
  - community service and social activism.
- Explore any spiritual concerns that contribute to suffering or block healing and relational well-being (e.g., relational injustices/oppressive or

abusive practices; doctrine on family gender roles or sexual orientation; worry about guilt, sin, punishment; alienation from faith and family).

- Facilitate communication, understanding, and mutual respect among family members around religious or spiritual differences and conflicts.
- Facilitate compassion and possibilities for forgiveness and reconciliation in wounded relationships, drawing on clients' faith beliefs to support efforts.

In strengths-based systemic practice, appreciative inquiry is used to explore each family's values and practices for a meaningful life and strong relationships. Therapists offer compassionate listening to each family's struggles, open possibilities for change, and facilitate constructive communication among members to address their concerns and to strengthen and repair their bonds. A collaborative approach is essential, focusing on family spiritual issues, taking care not to impose therapists' own values, and reflecting power back (Walsh, 2006). Because clinicians inescapably bring their personal, family of origin, and societal values into the therapeutic encounter (see Chapter 3 in this volume), they need to explore their own childhood upbringing and spiritual journey, examining their faith beliefs and issues just as they would other family or cultural influences. Links with pastoral care professionals are also important through mutual referral, consultation, and collaboration (see Chapter 11 in this volume).

Attunement to Family and Faith Diversity and Complexity

The increasing diversity and complexity of families and their spiritual life requires a broadly inclusive, nonjudgmental perspective for practitioners to be attuned to their multifaceted relational and spiritual needs (Walsh, 2010). With the growing gap between personal faith and adherence to institutionalized religious systems, clinicians should not assume that particular families, or all members, follow all doctrines of their faith. Most Americans regard decisions such as birth control, abortion, divorce, and assisted dying as a personal matter between them, their loved ones, and their faith. Those with a family member or friend who is gay are twice as likely to be supportive of gay rights. Therefore, clinicians need to explore each family's convictions, lived experience, and any conflicts among members.

Family systems therapists also consider the broader social and cultural context of all family patterns to understand the interweaving of influences in their spiritual experience. Spiritual beliefs and practices vary greatly across and within ethnic groups, and with social class, education, and urban–rural variables. Intergenerational differences can create tensions. Religious, cultural, and racial discrimination in the larger society can lead family members to suppress identification or marry out to assimilate.

Families in impoverished communities, disproportionately African American and Latino, tend to be strong in their faith and congregational involvement to counter despair at blighted conditions and injustices (Boyd-Franklin & Lockwood, 2009; Pew Hispanic Project, 2007; see also Volume 1, Chapters 30 and 33, this handbook). Aponte (2009) has contended that those who have lost hope and faith in their chances for a better life suffer at the core a wounding of the soul. He urged therapists to attend to spiritual as well as practical needs to help marginalized youth and their families reach for meaning, purpose, and connection.

Recent immigrant families, particularly those from Latin America, Asia, and Africa, often combine traditional spiritual beliefs and practices with Christianity. It is important to respectfully explore indigenous healing approaches for physical, emotional, and relational problems often used alongside Western medicine and psychotherapy (Falicov, 2009; Kamya, 2009). Therapists also need to understand beliefs, such as spirit possession, that may contribute to distress or block treatment.

Drawing on Spiritual Resources in Family Life

In therapeutic practice, distressed families can be encouraged to draw on spiritual beliefs and practices as a resource to strengthen family functioning, deepen bonds, and support the positive growth of members. Some questions to open a conversation along these lines might be as follows: How do you find fulfillment, purpose, and connection in your life and important relationships? When overstressed or depleted, are there spiritual resources that might replenish your energies and bonds? When going through hard times, how do you find strength and courage? What beliefs and practices could support your resilience, bolster your family's best efforts, and strengthen your bonds (see Pargament, 2007)? With each question, past and potential resources can be considered.

Spiritual Sources of Resilience in Dealing With Adversity

Serious crises, trauma, loss, or a pile-up of stressful life challenges can affect family functioning, with reverberations for all members and their relationships. Spiritual resources can be wellsprings for resilience (Walsh, 2009a; see also Volume 1, Chapter 19, this handbook). Clinicians can identify and encourage shared spiritual beliefs and practices that enable the family system to rally, buffer stress, reduce the risk of dysfunction, and support optimal adaptation for all members, from small children to frail elders. Family belief systems come to the fore in times of adversity and suffering; they can facilitate or constrain positive adaptation. Powerful beliefs for resilience—meaning making, hope, courage, perseverance, and transcendence—can all be enhanced by spirituality (Walsh, 2003, 2006). Faith can support the family's shared conviction that they can master challenges and accept what is beyond comprehension or control. Resilience-oriented family therapy helps members integrate the full experience of adversity—the suffering, struggle, and strengths that were gained—into their individual and shared life passage (Walsh, 2006).

Abundant research documents the influence of faith beliefs, practices, and congregational involvement for individual well-being, recovery from trauma and loss, coping and positive growth with serious life challenges, and more meaningful relationships and life pursuits (Pargament, 2011; see also Volume 1, Chapter 19, this handbook). A serious crisis can also be an epiphany, opening or deepening a spiritual dimension, as has been found in studies of posttraumatic growth (Tedeschi & Calhoun, 2004). The experience can crystallize important matters and spark reappraisal and redirection of life priorities and pursuits as well as greater investment in meaningful relationships.

Strong religious commitment can support fragile marital bonds through times of conflict (Lambert & Dollahite, 2006). Spouses who are similar in religious affiliation, beliefs, and practices report greater personal well-being and relationship satisfaction, less conflict and abuse, and lower likelihood of divorce than those who differ (Myers, 2006; for an in-depth focus on couples and spirituality, see Volume 1, Chapter 20, this handbook).

In childrearing, individuals from highly religious families report a beneficial role of faith in parent–child interactions, emphasizing that what matters most is that parents practice what they preach (Marks, 2004). When parents are congruent in transmitting and following their spiritual values in parenting their children and when they engage in meaningful spiritual practices together, children are more likely to internalize similar beliefs and practices, to find them a resource, and to feel more positive about their relationships. Children and adolescents most value spiritual practices that are shared and integrated into family life, as in family prayer, rituals and holidays, community service, and attendance at worship services (Bartkowski, Xu, & Levin, 2008). Most adolescents report strong interest in discussing faith issues, life's meaning, and moral decisions (Gallup & Lindsay, 2000), underscoring the importance of open communication and exploration of spiritual matters between parents and youth (Brelsford & Mahoney, 2008; Dollahite & Thatcher, 2008; Smith, 2005). However, "triangulating" God into the middle of family conflicts—to invoke authority, wrath, or divine punishment—worsens relationships.

Studies of low-income families, disproportionately single-parent and minority, suggest that religion may facilitate positive parenting in stressful conditions associated with poverty (Mahoney, 2010). Greater religious attendance and personal salience of God or spirituality has been linked to more maternal satisfaction, efficacy, authoritativeness, and consistency as well as less parental distress. Involvement in religious communities is a strong protective factor for at-risk adolescent single mothers and their children, with lower depression and child maltreatment and with higher socioemotional adjustment and education and job attainment (Carothers, Borkowski, Lefever, & Whitman, 2005). Data from the National Longitudinal Study of Adolescent Health (Pearce & Haynie, 2004) point to lower youth delinquency when mothers and their adolescents both consider religion important and attend religious services together. Here again, religion tends to be protective through shared beliefs and practices.

Families can find spiritual expression and nourishment in varied ways, within or outside organized religion. Clinicians can encourage family members to share involvement in spiritual practices that fit their values and preferences. Resources might include shared contemplative practices and healing rituals, involvement in nature or the creative arts, reconnection with family spiritual roots, meaning and purpose through community service and social activism, or facilitating forgiveness and reconciliation.

Therapeutic use of contemplative practices and rituals. Families can find spiritual nourishment through shared contemplative practices, most often rooted in spirituality or religion and centered in the home. Such resources may involve prayer or meditative practices, sacred or inspirational texts, or expression in music or art. Although prayer serves many functions, almost all pray for the health and well-being of loved ones. As one parent reported, "We talk to God to help our family get through hard times. We pray for strength when we suffer illness or money problems or when my children get into trouble."

Contemplative practices can be of value in couple and family therapy, in or between sessions, to facilitate relationship enhancement, conflict resolution, and reconciliation of relational wounds. Shared meditative experiences with loved ones can facilitate genuine, empathic communication, reduce defensive reactivity, and deepen bonds (Barnes, Brown, Krusemark, Campbell, & Rogge, 2007; Carson, Carson, Gil, & Baucom, 2004; Fincham et al., 2008, see also Chapter 24 in this volume). In couple and family sessions, therapists can lead interactive mindfulness exercises from Buddhist teachings for mutual understanding and more meaningful dialogue in couple and parent–child interactions (Gale, 2009). Reflective moments at the start of a family session or in the midst of conflict can shift attention from petty annoyances to deeper interpersonal concern and connection. Compassionate witnessing of a loved one's suffering decreases isolation, generates shared hope, and builds relational resilience in dealing with problems (Walsh, 2007). Therapists can also encourage client meditation before stressful encounters with extended family members, to facilitate coaching work for constructive changes in conflictual or estranged relationships, and for deeper connection with families of origin and cultural roots.

Rituals and ceremonies connect individuals with their families, communities, shared history, and future course. Couple relationships are enhanced by sharing meaningful spiritual rituals (Fiese & Tomcho, 2001). In work with families, the observance, blending, and invention of meaningful rituals can be encouraged to support therapeutic aims (Imber-Black, Roberts, & Whiting, 2003). They can celebrate or commemorate important events and milestones in family life. They provide guidance through life passage and times of adversity, facilitate unfamiliar or painful transitions, script family actions, and comfort those who are suffering, dying, or bereaved (see Volume 1, Chapter 18, this handbook). Rituals can transcend a particular family's joy or tragedy, connecting it with all human experience.

Reconnecting with family spiritual roots. Therapists trained to look to family-of-origin history for sources of current difficulties need to search also for spiritual resources. Faith may have been a powerful source of resilience in weathering past adversities. Restoring vital bonds with a family's religious heritage can be healing and empowering in therapeutic work, especially in situations in which experiences of oppression, forced migration, and assimilation have shattered a coherent sense of identity and severed vital bonds with ancestors and cultural heritage. For instance, reconnecting North American Native families and youth with their spiritual roots counters high risks of substance abuse and suicide (Kirmayer, Dandeneau, Marshall, Phillips, & Williamson, 2011).

Finding purpose in community service and social activism. Suffering and struggle can increase compassion for the plight of others. Many families, in the course of therapeutic work, transcend their own suffering and find new purpose through service to others in need, efforts to spare other families from similar tragedies, or social activism to change harmful or unjust conditions (Perry & Rolland, 2009). In turn, that initiative and ongoing dedication furthers their own healing. One family was seen in therapy after their beloved daughter, suffering with bipolar disorder, committed suicide. At the first anniversary of her death, the parents determined to forge something positive from the tragedy to honor her life and make a difference for others. They organized an annual community forum, through their faith community, to advocate for mental health research, raise public understanding of mental illness, and reduce the stigma and risk of suicide. In practice, clinicians can listen for and support those sparks of new purpose (Walsh, 2006).

Facilitating forgiveness and reconciliation. The role of forgiveness in marital and family therapy is receiving increased attention (Fincham, Hall, & Beach, 2006; Legaree, Turner, & Lollis, 2007). Spiritual beliefs can support therapeutic efforts to heal relational wounds from trauma, harm, and injustice. Compassion, forgiveness, and reconciliation are central in the teachings of all major religions (see Volume 1, Chapter 23, this handbook and Chapter 25, this volume). Hargrave, Froeschle, and Castillo (2009) have developed a relational model to facilitate forgiveness and reconciliation in couple and family-of-origin relationships, drawing on faith convictions of clients. In cases in which clients cannot forgive a parental transgression or choose not to reconcile, family systems therapists help them to gain a larger perspective and compassion for the life struggles of the parent while not excusing the hurtful actions (Fishbane, 2009; Walsh, 2006).

Forgiveness can also facilitate family healing from a traumatic loss as well as catalyze a process for restorative justice, as in the following case (Walsh, 2006, 2007).

> **Case Example 1**
>
> Mrs. Young, overcome by grief after the tragic shooting death of her oldest son, tapped back into her childhood Catholic religious teachings, leading her to decide she needed to forgive the youth who shot him. As she said: "I struggled to forgive him even more for myself and my family—I know my Bible and what unforgiveness does—it destroys the body, the mind, and the spirit. It eats away the marrow of the bones and causes decay." Although her husband couldn't forgive to the extent she did, it was crucial for their marriage that he respected her efforts. He forged his own healing pathway through social activism, taking leadership in community efforts to stop gun violence. The youth offender, with the support of his priest and members of his parish, left his gang and affiliated with a Christian group in prison. He sought Mrs. Young's forgiveness and, with her continuing encouragement and the involvement of his parish, he made every effort to turn his life around.

The paradox of resilience is that the worst of times can bring out the best in the human spirit. A life-threatening crisis or devastating loss can lead to transformation and growth in unforeseen directions. In facing life's challenges, the struggle can lead to spiritual growth. In turn, spiritual beliefs and practices strengthen the ability to endure and to transcend adversity. When family members are encouraged to share core values and spiritual practices, their relationships are enhanced and their spirituality deepened.

ADDRESSING SPIRITUAL SOURCES OF RELATIONAL DISTRESS

Many families who suffer emotional or relational problems are also in spiritual distress. To address spirituality in its clinical complexities, its potential for harm as well as healing should be considered (Elliott Griffith & Griffith, 2002).

Addressing Spiritually Driven Relational Wounds

Religious or spiritual beliefs and practices can become harmful, intentionally or not, if employed too narrowly, rigidly, or punitively (see Pargament, 2007). A spiritually based relational wound can block coping, mastery, and the ability to invest life with meaning.

Religious ideations or experiences fostering guilt, shame, or worthlessness can contribute to addictions, destructive behavior, or social isolation and breed conflict and alienation in family relationships. The two examples offered in this section concern spiritually based family violence and condemnation of sexual orientation.

Addressing spiritual justifications for family violence. Patriarchal family norms—ancient cultural patterns embedded in traditional religions—have been shifting to more egalitarian partnerships in the couple and parenting values and practices of most contemporary families as both women and men increasingly share workplace, homemaking, and childrearing responsibilities (Anderson, 2009; Walsh, 2012a). Even in many conservative Protestant families, traditional gender norms are moderating, with fathers becoming less authoritarian and more engaged with children, a pattern Wilcox (2004) termed "soft Patriarchs."

Yet tragically, patriarchal religious precepts have also been used to justify the denigration, abuse, and killing of wives and daughters as well as excessively harsh discipline of children (Bottoms, Shaver, Goodman, & Qin, 1995; Ellison & Anderson, 2001; Gunnoe, Hetherington, & Reiss, 2006). Some studies have suggested that higher levels of religiousness are tied to lower risk of domestic violence and child physical abuse in nondistressed families (Mahoney, 2010), yet some strong conservative Christian convictions are predictive of greater corporal punishment (Murray-Swank, Mahoney, & Pargament, 2006). Surprisingly, no published studies directly examine the role between religion and child physical abuse (Mahoney, 2010). Harmful patterns of abuse lead youth to flee their families of origin and, increasingly, women to leave their marriages (Walsh, 2012b). Clinicians should be alert to cases in which devout wives stay in abusive situations, adhering to religious precepts to keep their families intact. Some blame themselves, such as one mother who said that her husband was right to beat her when she challenged his harsh discipline of their children. She agreed with him that she needed to be more submissive, to be a "good wife" in accord with their fundamentalist religious teachings. It is crucial for clinicians to explore faith convictions about a "good husband" (and father) as well as a "good wife" (and mother) and to disentangle abusive practices that are not condoned by any major religion.

Family psychologists have an ethical responsibility to protect all family members from violence and to address harmful practices, whether rooted in family, ethnic, or religious beliefs and traditions. Therapists can affirm transcendent relational values common across faiths, condemning violence and espousing loving kindness, justice, and mutual spousal respect while honoring the dignity and worth of loved ones. Issues of parental authority can be addressed in family therapy, encouraging nonabusive means that foster positive child development and parent–child bonds (Walsh, 2006). (For a discussion of couple relationships see Volume 1, Chapter 20, this handbook.)

Addressing religious issues of sexual orientation in family relationships. The condemnation of homosexuality in religious doctrine can create deeply wounding conflicts and estrangement for gay, lesbian, bisexual, and transgendered persons (see Volume 1, Chapter 34, this handbook). Some denominations have adopted a loving acceptance of gay persons while preaching the immorality of homosexual practice and opposition to same-sex marriage and gay parenting. This dualistic position ("Hate the sin but love the sinner") perpetuates stigma, shame, and heartache for all family members. When the sexual orientation of a family member is a source of pain or cutoff in families that hold more conservative religious views, therapists can facilitate greater understanding, tolerance of differences, and loving acceptance. Sharing relevant research may allay some concerns, such as the abundant evidence that children raised by gay or lesbian parents are not damaged but are as healthy as those raised by heterosexual parents (Green, 2012). For most gay persons and their loved ones, religious challenges have not undermined the importance of their spirituality (Tan, 2005). Many same-sex couples report that their union has divine significance and meaning (Rostosky, Riggle, Brodnicki, & Olson, 2008), although it may be problematic for their relations with their families and faith community. By taking a broadly inclusive position, clinicians can encourage gay couples and parents to forge a more personal expression of spirituality in their relationships and, where desired, to seek out a welcoming faith community.

Addressing Family Spiritual Complications With End of Life and Death

Coming to terms with the death of a loved one, the most difficult challenge families confront, involves multiple losses, including each unique relationship for various members, the position and role function in the family, and shattered hopes and dreams. A significant loss affects family functioning, with reverberations for all members and their relationships (Walsh & McGoldrick, 2004). Family therapists facilitate the ability of family members to make meaning of their loss experience, to share their grief, to reorganize functional and relational patterns, and to reconstruct their lives and love fully beyond loss. Therapists need to help family members understand and respect each other's varied responses and adaptational pathways.

Spiritual matters come to the forefront with end-of-life challenges and loss. Death ends a life but not relationships, which are transformed from physical presence to ongoing spiritual connections, sustained through memory, dreams, rituals, conversations, stories, and legacies (Walsh, 2009c). Shared spiritual beliefs, practices, and support of a faith community can facilitate family adaptation. In some cases, spiritual convictions and concerns about death can complicate adaptation and tear families apart. Because these situations arise commonly in clinical practice and the spiritual aspects are often not addressed, several examples will be discussed.

Death of a child: Sense of injustice. A child's death reverses the natural order in the family life cycle, commonly causing deep spiritual distress for surviving parents. The untimely death of an "innocent" child is often viewed as unjust and can affect the spiritual life of the bereaved (Walsh, 2009c). Some draw closer to their faith, whereas others question or turn away from it. Deep anguish can precipitate a family or marital crisis. It is important for clinicians to explore varied reactions with sensitivity to all family members.

One couple was referred for counseling after the stillbirth of their first child. The birth had been eagerly anticipated by their entire kinship network, as the first son of the first son in a large Greek Orthodox family. When the therapist asked the couple if their faith offered them comfort, the wife said she now went daily to church, but alone, because her husband refused to go. The husband pounded his fist on the table, shouting, "I want no more of the church! I'm too angry at God!" As the therapist gently explored his anguish and the meaning of the loss for him, he sobbed,

> I believe that when something happens there's always a reason. I just can't fathom what the reason is here. We did everything right, by the book: The pregnancy was normal and the doctors did all they could—I don't blame them. God took our son! How could a loving God do this? It's too unfair—I don't mean for me, but to my son. He never had a chance at life.

His sense of injustice shattered his belief in God, alienating him from his church and his wife. As the therapist explored the wife's meaning making of their painful loss, she affirmed her strong belief in God's goodness, even when tragic events were beyond human comprehension. Unable to tolerate her abiding conviction, he withdrew from her at the very time they most needed one another.

Profound grief, such as this, requires compassionate listening to both partners, exploring the multiple meanings and the impact of the loss for each one and for their relationship, their extended family, and their shattered hopes and dreams. Most crucial in this situation is to facilitate mutual support in their bereavement and recovery. A consultation with the hospital chaplain was helpful in addressing the husband's spiritual crisis more in depth.

It was also important in therapy to address the shockwaves rippling through the extended family. Well-intentioned relatives, devastated by the loss, urged the couple to move on quickly and try to conceive another child. This common response, minimizing perinatal loss and urging precipitous replacement, can complicate mourning processes and future relationships, particularly with a birth so significant in meaning for the entire family (Walsh & McGoldrick, 2004). The therapist encouraged the couple to plan a memorial service and burial, including relatives and friends. These religious rites, honoring the birth, death, and loss, were enormously healing for all and helped the husband find consolation, congregational support, and renewal of his faith.

Stigmatized death: Suicide. Suicide is morally condemned by tradition in Jewish, Christian, and Islamic religions; final rites and cemetery burial may not be allowed. These spiritual issues complicate an already agonizing death and loss for the entire family (Walsh, 2009c). Secrecy and cover-up of suicide, not uncommon, can have long-term reverberations.

One young woman came for therapy, distraught upon overhearing relatives talk about her mother's death, 10 years earlier, as a suicide. She was enraged at her father for covering up the circumstances of the death and lying to her and her brothers. Family therapy sessions opened discussion of that tragic event, enabling all three siblings to better understand their mother's depression and the despair that had led her to end her life. The father shared his own devastation, self-blame, and confusion about how to deal with it all. A devout Christian, he had confided in his pastor, who told him that "if" it were a deliberate suicide, her soul would be morally condemned for eternity. Furthermore, she could not be buried in the family cemetery plot, where the couple had always planned to be buried together. Overwhelmed by this religious dimension of the tragedy, he convinced authorities that her death had been accidental and covered up the circumstances to his children to protect them from all the haunting questions and ramifications. He distanced from his religious congregation and carried a heavy burden in his heart that he shared with no one. The secret-keeping became a barrier in relations with his children over the years, with infrequent contact and only superficial communication.

The family sessions strengthened relational bonds as they facilitated the children's deeper understanding of their mother and compassion for their father's painful loss and spiritual dilemma. The therapist encouraged them to visit the mother's grave together—which they had never done—and to consider a fitting memorial that might best honor her life and memory.

End-of-life spiritual concerns. When families face end-of-life challenges, it is important for clinicians to explore spiritual concerns that weigh heavily on life-and-death decisions. Now that medical life support technology calls into question just what is a "natural death," families face morally complicated options and may grapple with religious prohibitions against hastening or assisting death (Walsh, 2009c). Those who are highly religious tend to oppose any actions, seen as interfering with "God's will." Yet, viewpoints vary within families, influenced by their own situations (Pew Forum on Religion and Public Life, 2008). For gay persons and their families, issues are likely to surface around religious death rites in denominations that condemn homosexuality or that do not permit burial of same-sex partners together.

Such profound dilemmas can spark intense relational conflict, which reverberates throughout the kinship network and can affect their relationships for years to come. Too often, patients and their loved ones wait until a medical crisis to broach these matters, when distress is most intense. A physician may only speak directly with a spouse or primary caregiver, leaving a family member unsure how to discuss such fraught issues with others. A series of family consultations is helpful, with planning ahead and prioritizing the wishes of the dying person. The involvement of hospital chaplains can be valuable.

Therapists can best help families by facilitating their discussions to work through complicated beliefs, feelings, and differences. Loved ones can be helped to face loss by encouraging their presence and active involvement through the dying process, drawing comfort and strength from each other and from their faith. Buddhist teachings, in particular, emphasize the healing power for the dying and the bereaved in sharing this precious time with openhearted, genuine communication (Walsh, 2006).

Exploring conceptions of death and afterlife. It is important to explore varying conceptions of death and afterlife among family members and how they concern or comfort the dying and the bereaved. Whether or not they are religious, death and dying bring to the fore questions about the meaning and significance of their lives and relationships (Walsh, 2010; see also Volume 1, Chapter 29, this handbook). These are, in essence, spiritual concerns. In reflecting on their lives, commonly there is heightened focus on relational bonds—past, present, and future—with more openness and urgency to repair past grievances. Clinicians can facilitate strivings to gain "family integrity" (D. A. King & Wynne, 2004), involving efforts to enhance meaning, connection, and continuity within the multigenerational family system. This process can generate a deep and abiding sense of peace and satisfaction with past, present, and future family relationships. A conjoint family life review can facilitate the sharing of varied perspectives, greater mutual understanding, a more balanced integration, and acceptance of family life as it has been lived (Walsh, 2011).

It is important to explore conceptions of afterlife for believers. The anticipation of one's death—or that of a loved one—can be agonizing for those who fear hell and damnation for their sins or lapsed faith. Most believers find consolation in anticipating that they will go to heaven or paradise (of varying conceptions) and contemplating reunion with deceased loved ones and ancestors (Pew Forum on Religion & Public Life, 2009). Many believe they can be in contact with the deceased or receive visitation from spirits, particularly in times of need, to offer reassurance to the bereft or when a serious wrong has not been attended to. The deceased may haunt as ghosts or become guardian angels and inspire as guiding spirits.

The spiritual dimension of death and loss for children is often neglected in clinical practice. Even a young child who does not yet fully comprehend death may pray for a deceased loved one or a pet and imagine them in heaven. When well-intentioned families try to protect children from the reality of death, it can exacerbate anxiety and confusion, as in the following case.

Case Example 2

Jim sought counseling for help with his sons, ages 3 and 5, several months after their mother's death. Although the boys had been aware of her illness and hospitalization, he had not wanted to upset them by telling them she had died and he did not take them to the funeral. As they continually asked about her, he took them weekly to the cemetery to visit her grave, where, he told them, she was sleeping peacefully. As winter approached, the boys became increasingly anxious about their mother's well-being in the cold ground.

The therapist explored the family's faith beliefs concerning what happens with death. The father replied that as Christians, they believed in heaven. He pictured his wife there, lovely and serene after the ordeal of her cancer. When asked if the boys had any notion of heaven, he reflected that from saying prayers together, they imagined heaven as a beautiful place where Jesus lived with God and angels looked down to protect them. The father realized it would comfort the boys to think of their mother in heaven, not sleeping in the cold ground. When the boys were brought into the session, he took them in his arms and told them with great tenderness about their mother's death and how she was now at peace, forever, in heaven. The boys, although very sad, were relieved to know she wouldn't suffer any more. They talked about heaven, that beautiful place where she would be with Jesus and the angels and where she would always watch over them. Their father assured them that they could still take flowers to her grave to honor her.

Often, when the spiritual dimension is opened in therapy, parents who have been blocked are able to handle difficult situations with surprising wisdom and clarity. Parents should be encouraged to follow up such conversations and invite children to discuss any questions or concerns that may arise. Artwork is helpful for children to express ideas and feelings about abstract notions of "spirit" and heaven.

Addressing Complications With Interfaith Marriage

Interfaith marriage, traditionally prohibited by many religions, has become increasingly widespread and accepted with the support of interfaith movements and the blurring of racial and ethnic barriers (Sherkat, 2004). Most often this choice is a natural outgrowth of broader social contacts in our multicultural society. For some, it may also be a way to differentiate from their family of origin. Parents may interpret such actions as rejection of them and their heritage. In some cases, this choice may express a deeper alienation from religious or parental upbringing or rebellion from authority that was experienced as oppressive. Family disapproval of interfaith marriage can have long-lasting reverberations in intergenerational relations. These intertwined dynamics fueled a longstanding cutoff in the following case.

Case Example 3

Mark was suffering an agitated depression as his mother's terminal illness worsened. He had angrily cut off all contact with his father for several years since his father, an observant Jew, refused to accept his marriage to Betsy, who came from a Protestant family. Yet over time, Betsy often took their children to visit their grandparents. Now, Mark felt profound sadness that his mother would die without his reconciliation with his father. Yet he insisted that his father was too self-righteous to ever apologize, but he gradually acknowledged his own "pigheadedness." The therapist suggested that his mother's critical condition made this a precious moment to act and encouraged him to seize the initiative. Mark agreed to try and left a voice message for his father, but before receiving a reply, his mother died.

Mark was in anguish about the unfinished business. He would have to see his father at the funeral and, without his mother as a conduit, relate to him thereafter about his declining health and a myriad of issues. To his amazement, at the funeral his father immediately approached him, hugged him, and thanked him for his message. Mark's call had prompted his father's last bedside vow to his wife to apologize and make amends. They agreed to meet together with the therapist to heal their estrangement. In that session, Mark's father expressed his profound regret for not having accepted the marriage and for his standoff with Mark. As the therapist facilitated a healing conversation, Mark acknowledged his own issues with authority yet also his respect for his father and desire to reconcile. The father revealed that his own parents had forbidden him even from dating non-Jewish girls, but he came to realize that times had changed and to appreciate through his grandchildren what fine parents Mark and Betsy were.

In this case, despite different religious upbringings, the couple shared secular humanist values and created meaningful family rituals and nature-oriented spiritual practices in their childrearing. In interfaith marriage in which partners continue to follow separate religions, strong faith differences can complicate ordinary relationship issues and intensify discord (Curtis & Ellison, 2002). Under stress, tolerance can erode, particularly if one religious approach is upheld as right, true, or morally superior.

Interfaith complications with childrearing. In raising children, interfaith couples may attempt to combine faith approaches or postpone decisions to let children choose their spiritual path as they develop. Differences that initially attracted partners or seemed unimportant often become contentious, particularly if families of origin exert pressures for the spiritual development of grandchildren. Couples who have viewed religion as unimportant in their lives may find that one or both partners care deeply about their children's religious upbringing. Interfaith conflicts commonly arise in early parenthood over decisions regarding rituals, such as circumcision, christening, or baptism. For one couple, submerged religious convictions unexpectedly surfaced with the death of their second child.

Case Example 4

Beth's mother-in-law referred her for therapy, worried about her inconsolable grief many months after the stillbirth of the couple's second child. Beth had withdrawn from her husband and was taking their 4-year-old son daily to the grave. The therapist's exploration revealed her deep spiritual distress, guilt, and self-doubt. Beth, who had immigrated alone from Eastern Europe, had drifted from her childhood Catholic upbringing. Her husband, Ben, who was close to his family, no longer followed their observance of Judaism. Deeply in love, they had married in a civil ceremony, believing religion unimportant to them. When they had their first child, they simply chose not to bring him up in either faith. However, the stillbirth of their second child struck Beth "like a thunderbolt" as God's punishment for not having baptized her son. She had not told her husband or in-laws of her religious turmoil, fearing their upset.

It was important to combine individual and couple sessions to help Beth share her faith concerns with her husband. It was also crucial to explore how Ben's religious views had evolved with parenthood and how they were affected by the loss. The therapist facilitated open communication and mutual support, which strengthened their bond through their shared grief. As they grappled with decisions about religious upbringing for their son and future children, they were referred for consultation with a pastoral counselor who dealt with their interfaith issues. A life crisis can be a spiritual awakening; here, it sparked the wife's realization of the importance of her faith tradition, which also connected her to her family and community left behind in immigration. In couple sessions, she shared the unexpected emergence of these deep connections with her husband and he lovingly encouraged her to return to her faith and assured her of his openness if she wanted to baptize their son and any future children. He also fully supported her decisions in dealings with his own family.

Interfaith complications with divorce and custody issues. With a bitter divorce, faith differences can become entangled with relational hurts, retaliation, and control issues. The noncustodial parent typically has visitation rights on weekends when most religious education and worship take place. In one interfaith marriage, the Catholic husband had agreed to raise children in the wife's Jewish faith. When the couple divorced, the mother gained sole custody and the right to determine their 3-year-old daughter's continued religious upbringing. On his weekend visitation with the child, the father had her baptized and sent photos of the baptism to his ex-wife to spite her. He contended that he worried constantly that if a tragedy took their daughter's life and she had not been baptized she would not have gone to heaven. The mother, enraged, took out a court order against him, which he defied, continuing to take the child weekly to Catholic mass. Legal battles escalated the conflict, with the child caught in the middle through lengthy court appeals. Family therapy or divorce mediation, refused in this case, can be of utmost value in such situations to untangle genuine faith concerns from marital conflict and to avoid protracted triangulation of a child, which can have serious complications for her emotional, relational, and spiritual development.

Interfaith complications with death and dying. With spiritual differences within families, conflicting religious approaches to death and last rites can arise. Planning and discussion are strongly advised. Some who have drifted from the faith of their family of origin may feel spiritually bereft at this time. Members who are religious may hold that for a "proper" death and favorable afterlife, all prescribed rituals from their tradition must be followed, including last rites and burial or cremation. Such matters can be highly contentious in interfaith families, as in the following case.

Case Example 5

Rachel, who practiced Reform Judaism, faced unexpected challenges with her husband's terminal illness. An Ethiopian immigrant, he had left the Orthodox Christian Church of his upbringing and regarded himself as a secular humanist. He wanted only a simple nonreligious memorial service at his death and burial where his wife could one day be buried at his side. His brothers, who had moved to the United States, had not visited in many years but now suddenly appeared. They insisted to Rachel that he must have traditional funeral rites with an Orthodox priest or else suffer eternal damnation. As Rachel vehemently challenged their strong pressure, the conflict intensified.

Rachel's therapist encouraged her to invite her brothers-in-law for a consultation and to bring photo albums of family life with her husband and children. The therapist facilitated discussion to build mutual understanding, with respect for both positions. It was important to listen respectfully to the brothers' faith convictions and to appreciate their loving concern for their brother. Because they had not had contact in many years, the therapist encouraged Rachel to share stories about her husband, his career in social work, and their family life. This helped them gain appreciation of his strong values in raising their children and in his dedication to humanitarian work. Rachel was then better able to convey her husband's last wishes while respecting their faith and loving concern for him. In a following session with Rachel, her husband participated via Skype from his hospital bed. They came up with the idea to seek out the interfaith chaplain who had married them at the college where they had met as students. Now retired, he was most pleased to conduct the service in the campus interfaith chapel.

In arranging burial, Rachel faced another challenge as she learned that non-Jews could not be buried in the Jewish cemetery near their home. Fortunately, she found another cemetery with an interfaith section in a lovely hillside setting. Bringing enormous comfort, the arch at the entrance bore the words *Beit Olam*, which has the same meaning in Hebrew and in her husband's native language, Amharic: "At home in the world."

Beyond respecting spiritual diversity, therapists can encourage a spiritual pluralism within multifaith families (Walsh, 2010). With respect—more than tolerance—for differences, pluralism celebrates both distinctions and commonalities (Eck, 2006). Within families, members who follow different pathways can strengthen bonds by engaging in dialogue, with respect and mutual understanding, and by coalescing around shared values and practices (McCarthy, 2007). Family therapists can nurture these constructive processes for the well-being and connectedness of all family members.

CONCLUSION

The growing diversity and complexity of contemporary families and their approach to religion and spirituality require a broadly inclusive, multifaith perspective in clinical practice. In clinical assessment and research, more attention is needed to the experience of spirituality in the broad spectrum of family structures and in sociocultural and developmental contexts. Furthermore, more nuanced consideration is needed to potential benefits and harm of spiritual beliefs and practices in family life: how they can be a resource and how they can cause distress. Despite differences of faith perspective, the overarching aim of spirituality is to be open to the transcendent dimension of life and all relationships, both in everyday practice and in overcoming adversity. Holding a pluralistic perspective, therapists respect the dignity, worth, and potential of all family members and support their spiritual journey seeking greater meaning and connection as they move forward in their lives.

References

Anderson, H. (2009). A spirituality for family living. In F. Walsh (Ed.), *Spiritual resources in family therapy* (2nd ed., pp. 194–211). New York, NY: Guilford Press.

Aponte, H. (2009). The stresses of poverty and the comfort of spirituality. In F. Walsh (Ed.), *Spiritual resources in family therapy* (2nd ed., pp. 125–140). New York, NY: Guilford Press.

Bailey, C. E. (2002). The effects of spiritual beliefs and practices on family functioning: A qualitative study. *Journal of Family Psychotherapy, 13*, 127–144. doi:10.1300/J085v13n01_07

Barnes, S., Brown, K. W., Krusemark, E., Campbell, W. K., & Rogge, R. D. (2007). The role of mindfulness in romantic relationship satisfaction and responses to relationship stress. *Journal of Marital and Family Therapy, 33*, 482–500. doi:10.1111/j.1752-0606.2007.00033.x

Bartkowski, J. P., Xu, X. H., & Levin, M. L. (2008). Religion and child development: Evidence from the early childhood longitudinal study. *Social Science Research, 37*, 18–36. doi:10.1016/j.ssresearch.2007.02.001

Bottoms, B. L., Shaver, P. R., Goodman, G. S., & Qin, J. (1995). In the name of God: A profile of religion-related child abuse. *Journal of Social Issues, 51*, 85–111. doi:10.1111/j.1540-4560.1995.tb01325.x

Boyd-Franklin, N., & Lockwood, T. W. (2009). Spirituality and religion: Implications for therapy with African American families. In F. Walsh (Ed.), *Spiritual resources in family therapy* (2nd ed., pp. 141–155). New York, NY: Guilford Press.

Brelsford, G. M., & Mahoney, A. (2008). Spiritual disclosure between older adolescents and their mothers. *Journal of Family Psychology, 22*, 62–70. doi:10.1037/0893-3200.22.1.62

Carothers, S. S., Borkowski, J. G., Lefever, J. B., & Whitman, T. L. (2005). Religiosity and the socio-emotional adjustment of adolescent mothers and their children. *Journal of Family Psychology, 19*, 263–275. doi:10.1037/0893-3200.19.2.263

Carson, J. W., Carson, K. M., Gil, K. M., & Baucom, D. H. (2004). Mindfulness-based relationship enhancement. *Behavior Therapy, 35*, 471–494. doi:10.1016/S0005-7894(04)80028-5

Cherlin, A. (2010). Demographic trends in the United States: A review of research in the 2000s. *Journal of Marriage and Family, 72*, 403–419. doi:10.1111/j.1741-3737.2010.00710.x

Curtis, K. T., & Ellison, C. G. (2002). Religious heterogamy and marital conflict—Findings from the national survey of families and households. *Journal of Family Issues, 23*, 551–576. doi:10.1177/0192513X02023004005

Daneshpour, M. (1998). Muslim families and family therapy. *Journal of Marital and Family Therapy, 24*, 355–368. doi:10.1111/j.1752-0606.1998.tb01090.x

Doherty, W. J. (2009). Morality and spirituality in therapy. In F. Walsh (Ed.), *Spiritual resources in family therapy* (2nd ed., pp. 215–228). New York, NY: Guilford Press.

Dollahite, D. C., & Marks, L. D. (2009). A conceptual model of family and religious processes in a diverse, national sample of highly religious families. *Review of Religious Research, 50*, 373–391.

Dollahite, D. C., & Thatcher, J. Y. (2008). Talking about religion: How religious youth and parents discuss their faith. *Journal of Adolescent Research, 23*, 611–641. doi:10.1177/0743558408322141

Eck, D. (2006). *On common ground: World religions in America*. New York, NY: Columbia University Press.

Edgell, P. (2005). *Religion and family in a changing society*. Princeton, NJ: Princeton University Press.

Elliott Griffith, M., & Griffith, J. (2002). Addressing spirituality in its clinical complexities: Its potential for healing, its potential for harm. *Journal of Family Psychotherapy, 13*, 167–194. doi:10.1300/J085v13n01_09

Ellison, C. G., & Anderson, K. L. (2001). Religious involvement and domestic violence among U.S. couples. *Journal for the Scientific Study of Religion, 40*, 269–286. doi:10.1111/0021-8294.00055

Falicov, C. J. (2009). Religion and spiritual traditions in immigrant families: Significance for Latino health and mental health. In F. Walsh (Ed.), *Spiritual resources in family therapy* (2nd ed., pp. 156–173). New York, NY: Guilford Press.

Fiese, B. H., & Tomcho, T. J. (2001). Finding meaning in religious practices: The relation between holiday rituals and marital satisfaction. *Journal of Family Psychology, 15*, 597–609. doi:10.1037/0893-3200.15.4.597

Fincham, F. D., Beach, S. R., Lambert, N. M., Stillman, T., & Braithwaite, S. (2008). Spiritual behaviors and relationship satisfaction: A critical analysis of the role of prayer. *Journal of Social and Clinical Psychology, 27*, 362–388. doi:10.1521/jscp.2008.27.4.362

Fincham, F. D., Hall, J., & Beach, S. (2006). Forgiveness in marriage: Current status and future directions. *Family Relations, 55*, 415–427. doi:10.1111/j.1741-3729.2005.callf.x-i1

Fishbane, M. (2009). Honor your mother and your father. In F. Walsh (Ed.), *Spiritual resources in family therapy* (2nd ed., pp. 174–193). New York, NY: Guilford Press.

Gale, J. (2009). Meditation and relational connectedness: Practices for couples and families. In F. Walsh (Ed.), *Spiritual resources in family therapy* (2nd ed., pp. 247–266). New York, NY: Guilford Press.

Gallup, G., Jr., & Lindsay, D. M. (2000). *Surveying the religious landscape: Trends in U.S. beliefs*. Harrisburg, PA: Morehouse.

Green, R.-J. (2012). Gay and lesbian family life: Risk, resilience, and rising expectations. In F. Walsh (Ed.), *Normal family processes: Diversity and complexity* (4th ed., pp. 172–195). New York, NY: Guilford Press.

Gunnoe, M. L., Hetherington, E. M., & Reiss, D. (2006). Differential impact of fathers' authoritarian parenting on early adolescent adjustment in conservative protestant versus other families. *Journal of Family Psychology, 20*, 589–596. doi:10.1037/0893-3200.20.4.589

Hargrave, T., Froeschle, J., & Castillo, Y. (2009). Forgiveness and spirituality: Elements of healing. In F. Walsh (Ed.), *Spiritual resources in family therapy* (2nd ed., pp. 301–322). New York, NY: Guilford Press.

Hodge, D. R. (2005). Spiritual assessment in marital and family therapy: A methodological framework for selecting from among six qualitative assessment tools. *Journal of Marital and Family Therapy, 31*, 341–356. doi:10.1111/j.1752-0606.2005.tb01575.x

Imber-Black, E., Roberts, J., & Whiting, R. (Eds.). (2003). *Rituals in families and family therapy* (2nd ed.). New York, NY: Norton.

Kamya, H. (2009). Healing from refugee trauma. In F. Walsh (Ed.), *Spiritual resources in family therapy* (2nd ed., pp. 286–300). New York, NY: Guilford Press.

King, D. A., & Wynne, L. C. (2004). The emergence of "family integrity" in later life. *Family Process, 43*, 7–21. doi:10.1111/j.1545-5300.2004.04301003.x

King, V. (2003). The influence of religion on fathers' relationships with their children. *Journal of Marriage and Family, 65*, 382–395. doi:10.1111/j.1741-3737.2003.00382.x

Kirmayer, L. J., Dandeneau, S., Marshall, E., Phillips, M. K., & Williamson, K. J. (2011). Rethinking resilience from indigenous perspectives. *Canadian Journal of Psychiatry, 56*(2), 84–91.

Lambert, N. M., & Dollahite, D. C. (2006). How religiosity helps couples prevent, resolve, and overcome marital conflict. *Family Relations, 55*, 439–449. doi:10.1111/j.1741-3729.2006.00413.x

Legaree, T-A., Turner, J., & Lollis, S. (2007). Forgiveness and therapy: A critical review of conceptualizations, practices, and values found in the literature. *Journal of Marital and Family Therapy, 33*, 192–213. doi:10.1111/j.1752-0606.2007.00016.x

Mahoney, A. (2005). Religion and conflict in marital and parent-child relationships. *Journal of Social Issues, 61*, 689–706. doi:10.1111/j.1540-4560.2005.00427.x

Mahoney, A. (2010). Religion in the home 1999 to 2009: A relational spirituality perspective. *Journal of Marriage and Family, 72*, 805–827. doi:10.1111/j.1741-3737.2010.00732.x

Mahoney, A., Pargament, K. I., Tarakeshwar, N., & Swank, A. (2001). Religion in the home in the 1980s and 1990s: A meta-analytic review and conceptual analysis of links between religion, marriage, and parenting. *Journal of Family Psychology, 15*, 559–596. doi:10.1037/0893-3200.15.4.559

Mahoney, A., & Tarakeshwar, N. (2005). Religion's role in marriage and parenting in daily life and during family crises. In R. F. Paloutzian & C. L. Park (Eds.), *Handbook of the psychology of religion and spirituality* (pp. 177–195). New York, NY: Guilford Press.

Marks, L. (2004). Sacred practices in highly religious families: Christian, Jewish, Mormon and Islamic perspectives. *Family Process, 43*, 217–231. doi:10.1111/j.1545-5300.2004.04302007.x

Marks, L. (2006). Religion and family relational health: Overview and conceptual model. *Journal of Religion and Health, 45*, 603–618. doi:10.1007/s10943-006-9064-3

Marsh, R., & Dallos, R. (2001). Roman Catholic couples: Wrath and religion. *Family Process, 40*, 343–360. doi:10.1111/j.1545-5300.2001.4030100343.x

McCarthy, K. (2007). Pluralist family values: Domestic strategies for living with religious difference. *Annals of the American Academy of Political and Social Science, 612*, 187–208. doi:10.1177/0002716207301196

McGoldrick, M., Gerson, R., & Petry, S. (2008). *Genograms: Assessment and intervention* (3rd ed.). New York, NY: Norton.

Meyerstein, I. (2006). Spiritually sensitive counseling with Jewish clients and families. In K. Helmeke & K. Sori (Eds.), *The therapist's notebook for integrating spirituality in counseling* (pp. 141–155). Binghamton, NY: Haworth.

Murray-Swank, A., Mahoney, A., & Pargament, K. I. (2006). Sanctification of parenting: Influences on corporal punishment and warmth by liberal and conservative Christian mothers. *The International Journal for the Psychology of Religion, 16*, 271–287. doi:10.1207/s15327582ijpr1604_3

Myers, S. (2006). Religious homogamy and marital quality: Historical and generational patterns. *Journal of Marriage and Family, 68*, 292–304. doi:10.1111/j.1741-3737.2006.00253.x

Pargament, K. I. (2007). *Spiritually integrated psychotherapy*. New York, NY: Guilford Press.

Pargament, K. I. (2011). Religion and coping: The current state of knowledge. In S. Folkman (Ed.), *Handbook of coping* (pp. 269–288). New York, NY: Oxford University Press.

Pearce, L. D., & Haynie, D. L. (2004). Intergenerational religious dynamics and adolescent delinquency. *Social Forces, 82*, 1553–1572. doi:10.1353/sof.2004.0089

Perry, A. de, V., & Rolland, J. S. (2009). Therapeutic benefits of a justice-seeking spirituality: Empowerment, healing, and hope. In F. Walsh (Ed.), *Spiritual resources in family therapy* (2nd ed., pp. 379–396). New York, NY: Guilford Press.

Pew Forum on Religion and Public Life. (2008). *U.S. religious landscape survey*. Retrieved from http://religions.pewforum.org/pdf/report2-religious-landscape-study-full.pdf

Pew Forum on Religion and Public Life. (2009, December). *Many Americans mix multiple faiths: Eastern, new age beliefs widespread.* Retrieved from http://www.pewforum.org/Other-Beliefs-and-Practices/Many-Americans-Mix-Multiple-Faiths.aspx

Pew Hispanic Project. (2007, April) *Changing faiths: Latinos and the transformation of American religion.* Retrieved from http://www.pewforum.org/Changing-Faiths-Latinos-and-the-Transformation-of-American-Religion.aspx

Rostosky, S. S., Riggle, E. B., Brodnicki, C., & Olson, A. (2008). An exploration of lived religion in same-sex couples from Judeo-Christian traditions. *Family Process, 47*, 389–403. doi:10.1111/j.1545-5300.2008.00260.x

Sherkat, D. (2004). Religious intermarriage in the United States: Trends, patterns, and predictors. *Social Science Research, 33*, 606–625. doi:10.1016/j.ssresearch.2003.11.001

Smith, C. (with Denton, M. L.). (2005). *Soul searching: The religious and spiritual lives of American teenagers.* New York, NY: Oxford University Press.

Snarey, J. R., & Dollahite, D. C. (2001). Varieties of religion–family linkages. *Journal of Family Psychology, 15*, 646–651. doi:10.1037/0893-3200.15.4.646

Snider, J. B., Clements, A., & Vazsonyi, A. T. (2004). Late adolescent perceptions of parent religiosity and parenting processes. *Family Process, 43*, 489–502. doi:10.1111/j.1545-5300.2004.00036.x

Tan, P. P. (2005). The importance of spirituality among gay and lesbian individuals. *Journal of Homosexuality, 49*, 135–144. doi:10.1300/J082v49n02_08

Tedeschi, R. G., & Calhoun, L. G. (2004). Posttraumatic growth: Conceptual foundations and empirical evidence. *Psychological Inquiry, 15*, 1–18. doi:10.1207/s15327965pli1501_01

Walsh, F. (2003). Family resilience: Framework for clinical practice. *Family Process, 42*, 1–18. doi:10.1111/j.1545-5300.2003.00001.x

Walsh, F. (2006). *Strengthening family resilience* (2nd ed.). New York, NY: Guilford Press.

Walsh, F. (2007). Traumatic loss and major disasters: Strengthening family and community resilience. *Family Process, 46*, 207–227. doi:10.1111/j.1545-5300.2007.00205.x

Walsh, F. (2009a). Integrating spirituality in family therapy. In F. Walsh (Ed.), *Spiritual resources in family therapy* (2nd ed., pp. 31–61). New York, NY: Guilford Press.

Walsh, F. (2009b). Religion and spirituality in couple and family relationships. In J. Bray & M. Stanton (Eds.), *Handbook of family psychology* (pp. 600–612). Boston, MA: Wiley-Blackwell. doi:10.1002/9781444310238.ch42

Walsh, F. (2009c). Spiritual resources in family adaptation to death and loss. In F. Walsh (Ed.), *Spiritual resources in family therapy* (2nd ed., pp. 81–102). New York, NY: Guilford Press.

Walsh, F. (2010). Spiritual diversity: Multifaith perspectives in family therapy. *Family Process, 49*, 330–348. doi:10.1111/j.1545-5300.2010.01326.x

Walsh, F. (2011). Families in later life: Challenges, opportunities, and resilience. In M. McGoldrick, B. Carter, & N. Garcia-Preto (Eds.), *The expanded family life cycle* (4th ed., pp. 261–277). Needham Heights, MA: Allyn & Bacon.

Walsh, F. (Ed.). (2012a). *Normal family processes: Growing diversity and complexity* (4th ed.). New York, NY: Guilford Press.

Walsh, F. (2012b). The spiritual dimension of family life. In F. Walsh (Ed.), *Normal family processes: Growing diversity and complexity* (4th ed., pp. 347–374). New York, NY: Guilford Press.

Walsh, F., & McGoldrick, M. (2004). *Living beyond loss: Death in the family* (2nd ed.). New York, NY: Norton.

Wilcox, W. B. (2004). *Soft patriarchs, new men: How Christianity shapes fathers and husbands.* Chicago, IL: University of Chicago Press.

Wright, L. (2009). Spirituality, suffering, and beliefs: The soul of healing with families. In F. Walsh (Ed.), *Spiritual resources in family therapy* (2nd ed., pp. 65–80). New York, NY: Guilford Press.

CHAPTER 10

MINDFUL AWARENESS, SPIRITUALITY, AND PSYCHOTHERAPY

Eric R. Bergemann, Madeleine W. Siegel, Marvin G. Belzer, Daniel J. Siegel, and Margaret Feuille

The clinical application of the practice of mindfulness meditation derived from the Buddhist tradition has served as a focus of intensive study in recent research (see Davidson et al., 2003; Kabat-Zinn, 1993, 2005). These studies covering a range of clinical situations, from medical conditions, such as psoriasis and chronic pain, to psychiatric populations with disturbances of mood or anxiety, provide preliminary support for the effectiveness of the application of mindfulness meditation skills in therapeutic settings. Although researchers have theorized and begun testing a number of hypotheses about the active ingredients of mindfulness, the field of psychology has done little so far to explore the relationship between spirituality and mindfulness (Kristeller, 2007; Shapiro, Walsh, & Britton, 2003). This is in spite of the fact that mindfulness interventions grew out of a tradition—Buddhism—that many would consider spiritual or religious.

In light of this gap, this chapter provides an overview of mindfulness-based therapies with a particular emphasis on the ways in which the spiritual underpinnings of Buddhist mindfulness may influence, if subtly, aspects of the psychotherapeutic use of mindfulness in its current manifestations. We begin with a discussion of mindfulness in its Buddhist context. Next we provide an overview of Western therapeutic mindfulness-based therapies, including mindfulness-based stress reduction (MBSR), mindfulness-based cognitive therapy (MBCT), acceptance and commitment therapy (ACT), and dialectic behavior therapy (DBT). We conclude with a discussion of one particular conceptualization of mindfulness—mindsight—as potentially useful in understanding how mindfulness may cultivate deeper spiritual connection.

In this chapter we use Pargament's definition of *spirituality* as a "search for the sacred," where the sacred is characterized by three qualities: (a) *transcendence*, which refers to the felt presence of a reality or a being that is wholly different from our ordinary experience; (b) *boundlessness*, meaning having no limits in space or time—lasting forever or pervading the entire universe; and (c) *ultimacy*, referring to the experience of something as fundamental to the nature of reality, at the heart of the mystery of the universe and of all human experience (Pargament, 2007). Also, as we discuss later in the chapter, a fourth quality may be added to this list of three qualities that define the sacred: interconnectedness—that is, there may be something inherently sacred about allowing the boundaries of the self to dissolve and feeling a corresponding increase in a sense of unity with others and the world around us. For the purposes of this chapter, then, components of mindfulness training may be recognized as spiritual when they explicitly engage concepts that practitioners would experience as transcendent, boundless, ultimate, and unifying. For instance, nirvana, the presence of God, and even the notion of soul may be considered spiritual concepts, whereas well-being, clearer thinking, and personal values lie more toward the nonspiritual side of the spectrum. Using boundlessness, ultimacy, transcendence, and interconnectedness as indicators of the sacred, let us turn first to the ways in which

DOI: 10.1037/14046-010
APA Handbook of Psychology, Religion, and Spirituality: Vol. 2. An Applied Psychology of Religion and Spirituality, K. I. Pargament (Editor-in-Chief)

mindfulness as a Buddhist concept may be considered spiritual or nonspiritual.

MINDFULNESS IN ITS BUDDHIST CONTEXT

In many ways, scholars in this research domain see the 2,500-year-old practice of Buddhism as a form of study of the nature of the mind (Lutz, Dunne, & Davidson, 2006) rather than as a theistic tradition. Secularization of many core Buddhist practices is possible because of the nontheistic orientation of Buddhism in which little emphasis is given to endorsement of an abstract creed. It is highly possible to practice Buddhist-derived meditation and subscribe to the psychological view from this perspective while maintaining one's beliefs and membership in other religious traditions, or in no religious tradition at all.

Because mindfulness practice itself, even in a Buddhist context, may be considered a form of the study of mind, as noted, and does not require religious belief or religious adherence, specific issues about religiousness and spirituality do not arise here in the same way they might arise with practices drawn from other religions. Likewise, there is ample room for varying methods of mindfulness practice that are not drawn specifically from Buddhist traditions (see Volume 1, Chapter 17, this handbook).

As much of the research on the application of mindful awareness in psychotherapy is related to a secular use of practices originally derived from the Buddhist tradition (see Davidson & Kabat-Zinn, 2004), here we will offer an overview of some of the specific aspects of contemplative practice from that tradition with its use in clinical settings.

The Buddhist emphasis is on experiential practice in response to the universal problem facing human beings: the reality of suffering in actual experience. This should not be confused with what is known as the problem of suffering, or the problem of evil, in Western religions, which presents itself as a potential abstract challenge to the goodness of a deity. On the contrary, the Buddhist conceptualization of suffering is the problem faced in actual daily life by ordinary human beings, the ways in which one's grasping or resistance to various emotional experiences creates psychological distress.

Current mindfulness instructions (as they are offered in clinical applications) are often drawn directly from the Buddhist practices that are centered on the question of how to deal skillfully and successfully with suffering. The core teachings of Buddhism are called the Four Noble Truths. But Buddhist practice itself does not essentially involve belief in these truths, which is why it is possible to argue, as has Stephen Batchelor (1997), that Buddhist practice does not involve endorsement of beliefs. The Four Noble Truths are as follows:

1. Suffering is a fact of ordinary human life.
2. There are specific causes of suffering.
3. The causes of suffering can be removed so that suffering is dealt with successfully.
4. The methods for removing the causes of suffering involve eight forms of skillful mental and physical activity (the Eightfold Path), which are traditionally divided into three groups: (a) morality (right speech, right action, right livelihood), (b) meditation (right concentration, right effort, right mindfulness), and (c) wisdom (right aim, right understanding).

The causes of suffering in this model are mental dispositions or psychological tendencies, such as aversion and greed. Suffering is said to arise because of the reactions that tend to take place automatically in ordinary experience in response to painful and to pleasant stimuli. In response to pain, we tend to resist. Conversely, in response to pleasure, we tend to grasp. These resisting and grasping reactions are considered to be the root of suffering. Traditionally, Buddhist teachings are optimistic about the capacity of human beings to develop minds that do not suffer in reaction to any form of experience. With training, such a state can be achieved, called "Enlightenment." In this model, a sharp distinction is drawn between pain and suffering: whereas physical and emotional pain is inevitable in any life, suffering is not necessary. For example, if an injury to the knee is sustained, having the thought "I should not have injured my leg, I am such a klutz" will create a high degree of suffering beyond what the physical pain of the injury itself might entail. In this way, our own mental processes—our prejudicial ideas, expectations, and lack of tolerance for the imperfection of being human—create unnecessary suffering in our lives. Within this model, suffering also is generated by the usual reaction to pleasure as the mind attempts to "grasp" that pleasure, trying to hold onto something that cannot in fact be seized. The purpose of practicing the Eightfold Path is to develop the enlightened frame of mind in which suffering does not take place.

"Right mindfulness" is one of the three elements of the "meditation" component of the Eightfold Path, but "mindfulness" as it is taught in current clinical applications actually includes both of the other elements of that group, that is, concentration and effort. One develops concentration by focusing attention on a more or less neutral part of experience (*neutral* meaning neither pleasant or painful, such as the breath) and by sustaining the attention there for some time. The breath is by far the most widely used such focus for this activity, but dozens of other objects of awareness can be used for this purpose, such as sensations in other parts of the body, silently repeating a series of thoughts (mantra), visualizations, and so forth. To do this successfully, one must make some effort (because the ordinary mind will tend to wander away from the neutral focus, being drawn by more stimulating aspects of experience)—but it is a subtle effort and one easily can try too hard. One of the basic difficulties for most people is to truly embrace the radical simplicity of the activity and with practice to find the right amount of effort that is effective. Using the neutral focus as home base, one then brings attention to whatever is most predominant in one's experience.

In contemplative mindful practice, one focuses the mind in specific ways to develop a more rigorous form of present-moment awareness that can directly alleviate some of the suffering in one's life. Modern application of the general concept of mindfulness has built on the traditional skills of meditation and has also developed unique nonmeditative approaches to this process of being mindful.

Most of the clinical applications of mindfulness focus on problematic states (physical pain and difficult emotions), encouraging curiosity in and acceptance of actual experience rather than resistance to it. As noted, this focus is coherent with the general Buddhist concern with dealing skillfully with suffering. On the other hand, the Buddhist teaching that suffering also arises from the tendency to attempt to "grasp" changing pleasurable states has not yet been integrated as deeply into Western medicine. Contemporary applications of these teachings often do not include the ways in which the transience of experience, especially of emotional events we enjoy and treasure, are held onto with an intensity that can become a rigid and automatic clinging in a nonconscious attempt to deny life's uncertainty and temporary nature. Moreover, there may be other ways in which the effects of mindfulness might be magnified by integrating it more fully with the other nonmeditational aspects of the basic Buddhist teachings, including the "virtue" and "wisdom" components of the Eightfold Path.

For example, concerning "virtue" (or "morality"), the Buddhist orientation is radically empirical, emphasizing the importance of paying attention to how actions and habit patterns actually work out in experience rather than specifying a top-down code of ethics, together with the serious intention to live morally. One is instructed to bring evaluative attention to desires, plans, and intentions with the question, "Is this desire or contemplated action likely to be beneficial or harmful?" (and if harmful, to revise plans) as well as to actions and consequences with the question, "Was this action beneficial or harmful to me and others?" If it is seen to have been harmful, one learns from mistakes and attempts to make restitution. Cultivation of virtue in this way could be included in clinical applications, for example, in dealing with troubling habit patterns, as an informal practice outside of formal meditation.

Likewise, there are Buddhist "mind trainings" that develop and cultivate positive states of mind, including gratitude, kindness, compassion, forgiveness, joy, equanimity, and others. These practices may link with the cultivation of virtues in contemporary positive psychology (Seligman et al., 2005). Current research programs in mindfulness do not normally include these practices, but mindfulness instruction routinely includes them as valuable complementary practices (Salzberg, 1995).

The "wisdom" components of the Buddhist Eightfold Path are right aim and right understanding. The relevant "aims" include both kindness and renunciation, which is a concept that is rarely employed in clinical settings because of its associations with austere religions. Yet these negative associations can be undercut because consciously turning one's attention away from an incessant pursuit of sensual pleasure is essential for the cultivation of concentration and mindfulness (it can be as simple in practice as turning off the television to practice meditation, or making the necessary effort to forgo a desired course of action that one sees as harmful). As the benefits of these practices become more widely known, it may become increasingly important to emphasize the importance of consciously making room for them in the midst of busy lives, and this ineluctably requires some sacrifice if one is going to change in a positive way.

Right understanding, on the other hand, pertains to insight into the reality of suffering (rather than, for example, living in optimistic naïve delusion), the reality of impermanence, and the ultimate lack of personal ownership over any of the people or objects one treasures. In traditional Buddhist teachings, these insights are not conceptual tenets taken on faith; on the contrary, they are said to arise naturally out of mindfulness meditation (Pandita, 2006).

All the same, discussion of the traditional ideas may provide a helpful context for interpretation of meditative experiences and development. In turn, to the extent that these traditional ideas may be seen as spiritual, mindfulness training that incorporates these ideas may be considered spiritual as well. For this reason, not all scholars agree that Buddhism is best understood as nonspiritual or even nontheistic. To support their view, such scholars often point out that Buddha is revered as the embodiment of transcendent qualities and even may take on divine attributes (particularly in Mahayana Buddhism; Stace, 1960; Wallace, 1999). Veneration of the Buddha and pilgrimages to the sites of his birth and enlightenment (along with eight other locations at which key events in the Buddha's life occurred) are encouraged in some of the oldest sutras as compatible with mindfulness practice (e.g., Maha-satipatthana Sutta, 2011). Also, nirvana may be seen as representing the eternal as opposed to the temporal (Stace, 1960), and some Buddhist practices aim to induce the reverence and awe associated with spiritual practices and contexts (Emmons, 2005), often by referencing sacred concepts (such as the Buddha, Buddha nature, and nirvana).

Likewise, a number of researchers conceptualize spiritual belief as compatible with mindfulness or at least leave room for spirituality as an active ingredient in mindfulness training (e.g., Kristeller, 2010; Leary & Tate, 2007; Rosch, 2007). In particular, Rosch (2007) argued that mindfulness training does more than simply cultivate a certain kind of attention, but also instructs trainees as to the focus and content of that attention. That is, although there is an emphasis in Buddhism on empiricism rather than faith, mindfulness training may involve more than simply watching the mind and one's experience to discover whatever is there. As explained, classically Buddhism focuses on these three truths—that all is suffering, all is impermanent, and all is devoid of self. These truths are less apparently spiritual than the truths emphasized by other traditions—such as the existence of a loving all-powerful God. Nevertheless, these truths can take on a spiritual flavor because of their ultimacy and universality (Pargament, 2007) and their understood origination with wisdom the Buddha gained through his enlightenment. Also, other teachings in Buddhism are more explicitly spiritual than this. For instance, Buddhist teachers often posit that mindfulness allows practitioners to access the pure loving core—or Buddha nature—that is humankind's true nature (Gunaratana, 1992; Hart, 1987). Mindfulness training, which harnesses these spiritual concepts to guide practitioners and shape their experience, may then be considered spiritual as well, even though the emphasis may be on personal experience rather than acceptance of dogma.

Incorporation of devotional practices is another way that mindfulness in its Buddhist context may take on a spiritual quality (Rosch, 2007). To illustrate, Buddhist teachers and texts often suggest starting a meditation session by reciting the Threefold Refuge, in which the practitioner reminds him- or herself to "take refuge" in the Triple Gem—the Buddha, the Sangha (spiritual community), and the Dharma (teachings; e.g., Buddhaghosa, 1979; Nyanaponika, 1973). As another example, modern U.S. Buddhist teachers Goldstein and Kornfield (1987) recommended choosing one ordinary activity to focus on for several weeks as an opportunity to infuse daily living with mindfulness:

> Even the simplest acts can be a powerful reminder to bring a sense of presence and grace. If you choose the opening of doors throughout the day, you can open each door as if the Buddha himself were to pass through with you. If you choose the act of making tea or coffee, you can do it as if it were a gracious Japanese tea ceremony. (p. 185)

It appears that the tradition of Buddhism is broad enough to accommodate spiritual and secular interpretations. Likewise, mindfulness training and the construct of mindfulness appear sufficiently flexible to accommodate a secular and spiritual orientation. Further research may illuminate the degree to which spirituality is relevant to Buddhist mindfulness practitioners and to address whether spiritual aspects of Buddhist mindfulness training help shape a trainee's experience.

THERAPEUTIC APPROACHES TO INTEGRATING MINDFULNESS IN TREATMENT

Several mindfulness-based interventions for a wide range of populations and disorders are supported by a growing empirical literature base (Baer, 2003). The most popular of these treatments include MBSR (Grossman et al., 2004; Kabat-Zinn, 1990), MBCT (Segal, Williams, & Teasdale, 2002), ACT (Hayes, 1987, 2004), and DBT (Linehan, 1993; Robins & Chapman, 2004). As a group, these therapies have been described as a "third wave" of the cognitive–behavioral tradition (Hayes, 2004, p. 639) because they link cognitive–behavioral methods with increasing focus on emotions, emotional regulation, and contextual and experiential strategies, including mindfulness (Lykins & Baer, 2009). The most intensive formal meditation training is offered by MBSR and MBCT, whereas ACT and DBT use applications of mindfulness skills. After a brief general overview of the clinical application of mindfulness, each of these treatments will be briefly discussed in turn.

A functional view is that mindfulness consists of the important dimensions of the self-regulation of attention and of a certain orientation needed to experience, as Bishop et al. (2004) have proposed, (a) "the self-regulation of attention so that it is maintained on immediate experience, thereby allowing for increased recognition of mental events in the present moment" and (b) "a particular orientation toward one's experiences in the present moment, an orientation that is characterized by curiosity, openness, and acceptance" (p. 232). In the DBT approach, mindfulness has been described as the intentional process of observing, describing, and participating in reality, nonjudgmentally, in the moment, and with effectiveness (Dimidjian & Linehan, 2003). Bishop et al., among other authors, have acknowledged that mindfulness may also result in outcomes such as patience, nonreactivity, self-compassion, and wisdom. In ACT, mindfulness

> can be understood as a collection of related processes that function to undermine the dominance of verbal networks, especially involving temporal and evaluative relations. These processes include acceptance, defusion, contact with the present moment, and the transcendent sense of self. (Fletcher & Hayes, 2005, p. 315)

The following example may serve as an illustration of the way that these definitions of mindfulness may be translated into interventions for one clinical problem in particular—chronic pain. In this intervention, a chronic pain patient is instructed to find one aspect of his or her experience that is not painful and try to rest the attention there. If the entire body seems wracked with pain, one can use ambient sounds or a mantra. As one tries to sustain the attention on the neutral focus, the bodily pain by its nature will tend to draw attention toward itself. When that happens, the individual yields—one actually brings the attention gently right into the midst of the pain, noticing the actual sensations in that part of the body from which it originates. One is not *thinking* about the pain; on the contrary, one is trying to sense the "raw sensations," as it were, underlying the concept "pain." The individual is encouraged to not analyze or try to keep track of the sensations; one simply is noticing the actual sensations as they occur moment by moment. Here we see the concept and actual practice of "acceptance" of things as they are. When the sensations seem overwhelming, the individual returns attention to the neutral focus again; and when drawn back to the pain, one gently returns to give it the focus of attention. This practice, over time, thus involves "pendulating" back and forth in this way, moving the focus of attention between the neutral focus and the actual sensations taking place in the painful region of the body.

This activity may be effective in reducing the pain; however, even when the pain is not eliminated, the capacity for "managing" the pain is increased. This clinically observed result generally is coherent with the traditional Buddhist teachings. As noted, the claim that suffering can be eliminated is not the claim that pain is avoidable in life. Both physical and emotional pain are facts of life, whereas suffering is generated by the individual's reaction to the painful sensation that typically involves resistance to the pain. This resistance increases the subjective experience of suffering. And it is this resistance that can be released with practice—and the subjective units of distress significantly diminished. By attending to the actual sensations, one tends to undercut the resistance to the pain and, in so doing, suffers less.

The same underlying principles illustrated here shape DBT's approach to the management of difficult emotions as well as ACT's approach to persistent maladaptive cognitions. This particular intervention, however, is derived from protocols of Kabat-Zinn's (1990) MBSR, which we review in more detail in the following section.

Mindfulness-Based Stress Reduction

In 1979, MBSR was developed by Jon Kabat-Zinn (1990) as a treatment for sufferers of chronic pain. The scope of MBSR has since widened significantly to include treatment of a wide range of physical and mental disorders. The effectiveness of MBSR has been studied in a variety of populations, including breast cancer patients, nurses, prison inmates, teachers, working adults, healthy people, caregivers of children with chronic conditions, and patients suffering from social anxiety disorder, depression, and heart disease (Chiesa & Serretti, 2009; Gold et al., 2010; Goldin & Gross, 2010; Klatt et al., 2009; Minor et al., 2006; Poulin, 2003; Samuelson et al., 2007; Shapiro, 2003; Tacón, McComb, Caldera, & Randolph, 2003).

MBSR is a highly structured program that teaches mindfulness-based meditation in an 8-week course. It has at its core a practice of carefully focusing attention. Participants are given 45-min daily practice assignments in meditation and yoga to increase their observational powers. One such assignment is a body scan during which attention is first focused on the breath and then on sequential parts of the body. Participants are taught to observe and intentionally relax each body part to which they bring their attention. Sitting meditation is also taught, during which participants are guided to focus their mind on the present moment and repeatedly urged to bring their awareness back to the present with compassion and nonjudgment when it inevitably drifts. Participants are instructed to begin to make the routine activities in their daily lives a meditative practice, such as bringing awareness back to the breath to decrease cognitive rumination over a fight with a spouse.

Brain studies of MBSR participants have shown an increase in the baseline electrical activity of the left frontal area of the brain after MBSR training (Davidson et al., 2003). This "left-shift" is thought to reflect an "approach state," moving toward rather than away from challenging external situations or internal emotional states. This approach state has been thought of as the neural basis for resilience (Siegel, 2010c). Urry et al. (2004) suggested that the neural changes associated with mindful awareness practice as established in the MBSR programs are consistent with a eudemonic view of well-being in which the individual finds connection, meaning, and resilience in the face of stress. MBSR has been shown to improve immune system functioning. MBSR studies have shown that patients feel an internal sense of stability and clarity after the treatment (Davidson & Kabat-Zinn, 2004). Farb et al. (2007) found that subjects were able to alter their brain function in distinguishing internal narrative chatter from the ongoing sensory flow of here-and-now experience after participating in an 8-week MBSR program. This type of discernment may be a crucial step for patients to disentangle their minds from ruminative thoughts, repetitive destructive emotions, and impulsive and addictive behaviors (Siegel, 2010c).

Mindfulness-Based Cognitive Therapy

MBCT (Segal, Williams, & Teasdale, 2002) is a manualized, group-based skills training program designed to enable patients to learn skills that prevent the recurrence of depression. It is developed from MBSR (Kabat-Zinn, 1990) and CBT (Beck et al., 1979). MBCT is structured to help participants learn to become more aware of their thoughts, feelings, and bodily sensations associated with depression relapses and to relate in a more constructive manner to those experiences. Its theoretical and empirical underpinnings are based on research that relates depressive relapse to reinstated automatic modes of counterproductive thinking, feeling, and behaving (Lau, Segal, & Williams, 2004). In an 8-week program, participants learn to recognize negative thoughts and difficult emotions through a process of mindfulness training during the first half of the program. The second half of the program teaches participants to apply mindfulness by stepping out of automatic pilot modes and responding in healthier ways, such as decentering from negative thoughts and feelings, learning to view these phenomena as mental events that come and go rather than as the only accepted truth or reality. Other ways of applying mindfulness include accepting difficulties using self-compassion and using bodily awareness to ground experience in the present moment of sensation. Finally, participants develop an action plan setting out strategies for responding when early warning signs of potential relapse occur.

In one study (Kuyken et al., 2008) of 123 patients with recurrent depression, MBCT with tapering and discontinuing antidepressant medication was found to be more effective than maintenance antidepressant medication alone. Relapse rates at 15-month follow-ups were 47% in MBCT versus 60% in the medication group. MBCT was found to be more effective than medication alone in reducing depressive symptoms and in improving quality of life. Rates of medication usage were reduced in the MBCT group, with 75% of the MBCT patients completely discontinuing their medication.

Acceptance and Commitment Therapy

ACT (Hayes, 1987, 2004) utilizes mindfulness to help patients clarify what really matters in their lives—their core values—and to use these core values to guide and inspire behavioral change through mindful action. ACT is based on an underlying basic research program in language and cognition, relational frame theory (RFT; Hayes, Barnes-Holmes, & Roche, 2001), which emphasizes how language and cognition trap people into behaving in ways that increase or maintain their suffering. The implication of this research is that avoidance of unwanted thoughts and emotions drives psychopathology (Chapman, 2006). ACT has been described as existential humanistic CBT based in the tradition of empirical science (Harris, 2009). The treatment teaches patients to accept what is outside personal control and to take action that enriches their lives to create a full and meaningful life while accepting its inevitable pain.

ACT breaks mindfulness down in the following four ways: defusion, acceptance, present moment contact, and spacious awareness. Summarizing these skills, *defusion* seeks to distance oneself from and let go of negative thoughts, beliefs, memories, and cognitions. *Acceptance* makes room for painful urges, feelings, and sensations, allowing them to move through one's mind without a struggle. *Present moment contact* uses an attitude of curiosity and openness to fully engage with the experience of here and now. *Spacious awareness* establishes an observing self to be conscious of thoughts and feelings as passing experiences but to not identify with them.

These skills have been shown to reduce anxiety and depressive symptoms. In one study example (Forman et al., 2007), 101 outpatients reporting moderate to severe levels of anxiety or depression were randomly assigned to traditional cognitive therapy (CT) or ACT. Equivalent significant improvements in depression, anxiety, and quality of life were found in both groups, but the mechanism of change appeared to differ. Changes in "observing" and "describing" experiences appeared to affect outcomes for the CT group relative to the ACT group, whereas "experiential avoidance," "acting with awareness," and "acceptance" mediated changes for the ACT group. The difference in the two groups was in how the subjects were able to describe their changes narratively. The authors concluded that ACT is a viable treatment comparable to CT, with distinct mechanisms of action.

This finding is validated by at least nine other studies comparing ACT with traditional CT methods (Hayes, 2008). ACT has been most thoroughly studied with anxiety disorders (Eifert & Forsyth, 2005), but the treatment also has been found to be efficacious in treating depression, diabetes, workplace stress, some forms of psychosis, polysubstance use, and chronic pain (Vowles, 2009).

Dialectical Behavior Therapy

DBT (Linehan, 1993) was originally developed as a treatment for suicidal women, many of whom met the criteria for borderline personality disorder (BPD). Because many of these patients often reacted negatively to the emphasis on cognitive and behavioral change in traditional CBT models and dropped out of treatment, Linehan incorporated elements of mindfulness from Zen practice in developing DBT, including acceptance and attention to the present moment. DBT is organized into four stages, each with its particular outcome goal (Linehan, 1998). Stage I goals are to decrease life-threatening behaviors and to increase connections to those people who can help. Stage II goals are to begin to understand the effect of emotional trauma on patients' lives. Stage III goals involve addressing self-respect and self-trust issues. The capacity for sustained joy, along with expanded awareness and spiritual fulfillment are goals of Stage IV.

DBT places great emphasis on the therapeutic relationship, particularly in the areas of acceptance and change. The therapist is continually balancing and modeling for the patient the opposing forces of acceptance and change. In this way, mindfulness becomes a key component of DBT for both the therapist and the patient. Therapeutic strategies are used to help the patient become aware of reality as it is in the present moment. These strategies include observing, describing, and participating. Observing involves noticing the experience of breathing and other sensations of the present moment. Describing involves putting words to what is observed. Participating involves actively engaging with the present moment with whatever arises in sensation, without judgment, and becoming "one" with these experiences. In this way, distress tolerance skills are developed (Chapman, 2006).

The treatment efficacy of DBT for suicidal behavior and BPD has been well documented. One randomized controlled study (Linehan et al., 2006) followed 101 suicidal and self-injurious women in an outpatient clinic setting for 1 year of DBT versus community-based expert treatment, with follow-up measures 1 year later. Women receiving DBT were half as likely to attempt suicide during the 2-year period, required less hospitalization, and had lower medical risk than the community-based treatment group. DBT subjects were also less likely to drop out of treatment and had fewer psychiatric emergency department visits. The authors concluded that DBT was uniquely effective in reducing suicide attempts and other behaviors consistent with BPD.

Is Therapeutic Mindfulness Spiritual?

These treatment descriptions demonstrate the ways in which Buddhist mindfulness has been recontextualized and modified for use in therapeutic settings, often through the removal of overt spiritual references. In these mindfulness-based therapies, references to the Buddha are few, and devotional practices are absent. Also, although Western therapeutic forms of mindfulness often focus on modest goals like improving well-being and cultivating active engagement in present-moment experience, the Buddhist context construes mindfulness as the means to achieve ultimate enlightenment, or nirvana (Goleman, 1984).

At the same time, contrasts between Western "secularized" mindfulness and Buddhist mindfulness training may be overdrawn. That is, spiritual elements addressed in Buddhist contexts may not be not entirely absent from Western therapeutic mindfulness training programs. For instance, the concept of "Buddha nature" is present to some extent even in the "secularized" mindfulness training of MBSR. In *Full Catastrophe Living*, meant to capture for readers the experience of patients attending MBSR at his stress clinic, Kabat-Zinn (1990) echoed Buddhist teachings on the Buddha nature when he discussed a concept he called *wholeness*:

> No matter how many scars we carry about from what we have gone through and suffered in the past, our intrinsic wholeness is still here: what else contains the scars? None of us has to be a helpless victim of what was done to us or what was not done for us in the past, nor do we have to be helpless in the face of what we may be suffering now. We are also what was present before the scarring, our original wholeness, what was born whole. And we can reconnect up with our intrinsic wholeness at any time because its very nature is that it is always present. So when we make contact with the domain of being in the meditation practice, we are already beyond the scarring, beyond the isolation and fragmentation and suffering we may be experiencing. This means that it will always be possible to transcend fragmentation, fear, vulnerability, and insecurity, even despair, if you come to see differently, to see with eyes of wholeness. (p. 161)

Just as in Buddhist mindfulness training, mindfulness as taught in MBSR may be more than just observing experience to find and accept whatever is there, and instead, it is oriented toward a specific aim or intention—the realization of wholeness.

Subtly spiritual language such as this suggests that it is still appropriate to be curious about the spiritual components of these interventions, despite efforts to secularize them, Also, practices promoting the direct experiencing of the present moment have been described as a fundamental part of Christian, Hindu, Islamic, Jewish, and Taoist teachings (Armstrong, 1993; Goleman, 1988). Christian centering prayer (Fitzpatrick-Hopler, 2006; Keating, 2005) may be an especially important example given that it represents one way to reintegrate spirituality into mindfulness training in a manner that is appropriate for the largely Christian population of the United States. It remains to be seen whether integrating spirituality in this way is as helpful or more helpful than the nonspiritual or implicitly spiritual approaches of "secular" therapeutic mindfulness. Given mindfulness teachers' suggestions that the spiritual elements of practice may improve adherence or directly contribute to a mindful state of consciousness (Kabat-Zinn, 1990), we have good reason to wonder whether enhancing the spiritual components of mindfulness training may increase its efficacy.

MINDSIGHT AND SPIRITUALITY

Thus far in the chapter we have been using concepts suggestive of the ultimate or transcendent, such as Buddha nature and nirvana, as cues to aspects of mindfulness training that may be spiritual. In this next section, we explore another possibility, that a sense of connection to the sacred may be fostered through *undoing* concepts. In this account, as we will see, it is thought that concepts (including spiritual ones) by and large isolate people from each other and the world around them, and that people achieve greater connection—to other people, to the larger world, and to the sacred—by getting past those concepts. This paradox (present to some extent in other spiritual traditions, but given particular emphasis in Theravadan Buddhism; Stace, 1960) is that one comes into contact with the sacred only by letting go of all attempts to define, capture, or seek the sacred. Mindfulness, then, becomes spiritual insofar as it allows one to encounter bare *reality*—a reality that affirms our ultimate interconnectedness with other people and the world around us. The particular approach to mindfulness we discuss here is called *mindsight*, which was developed within the framework of interpersonal neurobiology. We therefore turn next to a review of interpersonal neurobiology before looking again at the relationship between spirituality and mindfulness.

Interpersonal Neurobiology

Although the mind is rarely defined in mental health, or even in philosophy and various sciences, this interpersonal neurobiology view places the mind as an emergent property of both bodily and relational processes. In this view (see Siegel, 1999, 2010b), a working definition of a core aspect of the mind is offered as "an embodied and relational process that regulates the flow of energy and information," in which regulation consists of the two related capacities of both monitoring and modifying that which is being regulated. The mind monitors energy and information flow through the focus of attention.

As one could guess from the name, interpersonal neurobiology emphasizes that energy and information flows not only within our own brains but also through the communication we have within our relationships with others. That is, the mind is both embodied and relational. In fact, people may often use their relational interactions to help regulate patterns in energy and information flow. This is how the mind emerges not just from within the body and its neural circuits but also within our patterns of communication with one another. This is the origin of the term *interpersonal neurobiology*.

No one knows how the physical property of neurons' firing and the subjective experience of mental life are truly interrelated. How the substance and function of matter and the essence of our subjective experience of mind influence one another is a fundamental question yet to be answered. We do know, however, something about the neural correlations that accompany mental activity. When we imagine an image, for example, the posterior part of the brain becomes active. But the directionality of these influences appears to be in both vectors; neural firing may "create" mental activity as much as mental activity may stimulate neural firing. When we imagine something, we can induce that part of the brain to fire. Just imagine the Golden Gate Bridge to gain a sense of how imagery generated here may lead to neural activations. And, with practice, imaging the playing of basketball or even musical scales can induce not only changes in brain function but also long-term changes in brain structure (see Begley, 2007; Doidge, 2007). In this way, the mind can change both the activity and the structural connections of the brain. From the relational side of mental life, our typing the words for the Golden Gate Bridge in San Francisco was sent by us and received by your eyes. This communication is interpersonal and engaged the transmission of energy and information flow from author to reader. The flow, initiated within a relationship, directly shapes the activity and perhaps (if you remember this chapter) the structure of your brain.

A Model of Mindsight

In this model, energy flow in mental life would be the smell of a rose within awareness; the information flow would be naming the flower a "rose." Mental activity's utilization of prior experience to symbolize the element in the focus of the attention can be called "top-down." In our human brains, most of what comes in from the "bottom-up" in the form of energy patterns from incoming stimuli—like the scent of the rose—is also filtered by neural firing patterns shaped by related prior experience. This is the way top-down is activated in response to bottom up. The result of the "crashing" of these two streams of energy or information flow within the cortex yields how we become aware of what is happening right now. This is how perception is created.

Figure 10.1 reveals a schematic drawing of the six-layered cortex and how this interaction of bottom-up and top-down flow across a range of cortical columns may be depicted. In this view, basic sensory data streams bottom-up from the lower layers 6 to 5 to 4. Almost simultaneously, this bottom-up stream activates a related flow from the upper most layers as a categorical, prior-experience shaped response begins to move from layers 1 to 2 to 3. The interaction of these two streams occurs between layers 4 and 3 and can be seen as the origin of conscious experience in the present moment. With a dominance of top-down flow of "rose" during an experience, for example, it is possible to not "stop and smell the roses" on a stroll through the garden.

Working within this model of the mind, Siegel (2007a, 2010a) has proposed that mindful awareness is an active process by which these two streams of bottom-up versus top-down sensory flow are differentiated from one another (for further exploration of the notion of a sensory and an observing, narrating set of neural circuits, see also Farb et al., 2007; Siegel, 2007b). With this ability to notice when top-down thinking is preventing one from experiencing present-moment sensation using bottom-up thinking, individuals are able to modulate this imbalance and intentionally create a state of being aware of bottom-up without being swept up by top-down. As alluded

Layer	Top-Down	Top-Down Dominance	Top-Down
1	⇓	⇓⇓⇓	⇓
2	⇓	⇓⇓⇓	⇓
3	⇓	⇓⇓⇓	⇓
AWARENESS	⇒→⇒→	→⇒⇒⇒	⇒→→→→→
4	↑	↑	↑↑↑↑↑
5	↑	↑	↑↑↑↑↑
6	↑	↑	↑↑↑↑↑
	Bottom-Up	Bottom-Up	Bottom-Up Dominance

FIGURE 10.1. A schematic of the six-layered neocortex and the bottom-up and top-down flow of information. Information from sensation flows "bottom-up" from the lower layers of the cortex streaming from layers 6 to 5 to 4. Information from prior learning, called "top-down," streams from layers 1 to 2 to 3. Awareness is thought to emerge by the comingling of these two streams. In the first condition, bottom-up and top-down are balanced and the resultant awareness blends the two streams. In the second condition, top-down input is dominant and prior expectations and categorizations overshadow incoming sensory streams within awareness. In the third condition, sensory input in the here-and-now is dominant and awareness reflects a predominance of input from this sensory flow. Mindfulness may enable layer (e.g., 3 and 4) intermingling to disentangle these two streams by at first practicing enhancement of the bottom-up flow of present sensory experience. From *The Mindful Therapist: A Clinician's Guide to Mindsight and Neural Integration* (p. 105), by D. J. Siegel, 2010, New York, NY: Norton. Copyright 2010 by Mind Your Brain, Inc. Used with permission.

to in the previous paragraph, one could then postulate that the spiritual dimension of mindful practice may emanate in part from the liberation of excessive "private self" top-down flow that constrains the capacity of an individual to be aware of a larger sense of an "interconnected self" that could emerge from bottom-up sensory flow. By contrast, one might conceptualize cultural and familial practices reinforcing the experience of a "separate" or "private" self as isolating. Mindfulness, then, may bring about spiritual awakening by diminishing top-down thinking that emphasizes a private, bodily-defined limit to an individual "self" and by enhancing the clear-headedness and mental flexibility provided by a bottom-up stream that may cultivate awareness of a "self" that is fully embedded in a much broader, interconnected world. In this way, mindfulness may permit access to a way of defining the self that is imbued with deeper meaning than that of the isolated top-down self.

INTEGRATION AND MINDFULNESS

Mindful awareness can be considered a form of "internal attunement" that leads to shifts in the internal state of integration in the brain (see Siegel, 2007a). Integration—the linkage of differentiated elements to one another—is proposed in the field of interpersonal neurobiology to be at the heart of a state of well-being. With integration, a system moves in a fluid, flexible, vitalizing flow, like a choir singing in harmony. Without integration, a system tends toward rigidity, chaos, or both.

An array of research studies suggests that the integrative regions of the brain are those that are harnessed in mindfulness practice. This proposal parallels the work in interpersonal neurobiology, which suggests that secure child–parent attachment relationships involve a form of interpersonal attunement that stimulate the growth of the integrative fibers of the brain (see Cozolino, 2008; Siegel, 1999; see also the independent but relevant work of Teicher, 2002). Recent studies of fundamental processes of a default system in the brain independently suggest that neural integration may indeed be at the heart of healthy neural states of functioning (see Raichle, 2010).

When one examines the integrative regions of the prefrontal cortex located just behind the forehead, nine functions can be revealed to emanate from their coordinated functioning (see Siegel, 2007a, 2010b). This list has fascinating implications for an understanding of mindfulness and psychotherapy. The nine middle prefrontal functions are: body regulation, attuned communication, emotional balance, response flexibility, fear modulation, insight, empathy, morality, and intuition.

This list is a compilation of what thousands of surveyed mental health professionals have deemed as a description of the essential components of mental health (Siegel, 2010b, 2012a). In attachment research, the first eight of these nine functions have emerged from the outcome studies of parent–child relationships assessed as secure that had nothing to do with evaluating brain function or structure (Siegel, 2007a, 2012a). Secure attachment is based on the interpersonal attunement of the parent to the child in which the caregiver "tunes in" to the internal state of the child in an open and accepting way. In presenting this list to Kabat-Zinn (Ackerman, Kabat-Zinn, & Siegel, 2005), it became clear that all nine of these functions could be seen as both the outcome of mindfulness research and the process of living mindfully. Subsequent studies at Harvard (Lazar et al., 2005) and at the University of California—Los Angeles (Luders et al., 2009) have revealed that aspects of these middle prefrontal areas, including the orbitofrontal and insula regions, become thicker in long-term meditators. Functional studies of mindful awareness of the breath reveal that these regions, along with the superior temporal cortex, become active during breath-awareness practice.

The key issue is that these middle prefrontal regions link highly separated regions to each other. They connect cortical, limbic, brainstem, visceral, and even social input to one another. This is a highly integrative region of the brain. With integration emerges coordination and balance in the nervous system.

Here is the basic proposal: Attunement, either interpersonal in the case of secure attachment relationships or internal in the case of mindful awareness, promotes the activation and therefore growth of the integrative fibers of the brain. The subjective side of integration is to feel connected to oneself, to others, and perhaps to the larger world, making integration a spiritual process. On the personal level, attunement activates what Porges (2009) has called the social engagement system, yielding a state of openness and receptivity. For mindfulness, the parallel might also include a "self-engagement system" (Siegel, 2007a) in which the individual feels open and attuned to a deep sense of freedom of the self. For many individuals, this state of inner coherence has been described in such terms as being at ease, with peace, open, free, expansive, and "coming home." Why would mindfulness practice, attunement, and the integrative fibers in the brain participate in the creation of such states? To address this question, we turn now to a speculation of how mind and matter interact and its relationship to a sense of spirituality and the creation of health.

OPPORTUNITIES, CHALLENGES, AND FUTURE DIRECTIONS

In interpersonal neurobiology, the term *mindsight* is used to refer to the capacity to sense energy and information flow as it moves through the structure of the brain, is shared in relationships, and is regulated by the mind itself (Siegel, 2010b). With mindsight, individuals are given the capacity to also modify this flow toward integrative states. A triangle of mind, brain, and relationships (see Figure 10.2) reveals a pictorial depiction of the interconnections of these elements of mindsight. Ultimately, this triangle of well-being allows the energy and information flow to move toward integration.

When mindful awareness is seen as an integrative process, mindful practice can be viewed as enabling *states* to become *traits*. With regular intentional practice, the mind (regulating energy and information flow) drives the activation of neural circuits in the brain. With repeated activation of states of mindful awareness, synaptic growth occurs by the principles of neuroplasticity: Neurons that fire together wire together. With this long-term change in synaptic connections, intentionally created states can become traits with practice.

What are these long-term changes seen with mindfulness practice? One outcome is enhanced empathy (see Shapiro, Schwartz, & Bonner, 1998). Why would internal reflection result in an increased capacity to perceive and make sense of the internal states of others? When the neural correlates of

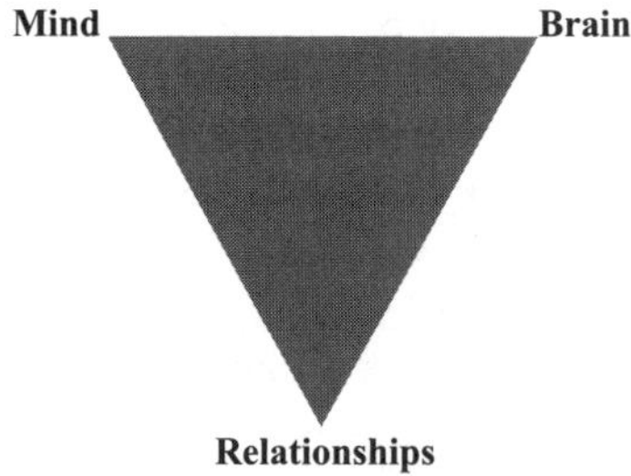

FIGURE 10.2. The triangle of well-being. The harmony of integration is revealed as empathic relationships, coherent mind, and integrated brain. Brain is the mechanism of energy and information flow throughout the extended nervous system distributed throughout the entire body; relationships are the sharing of this flow; mind is the embodied and relational process that regulates the flow of energy and information. From *The Mindful Therapist: A Clinician's Guide to Mindsight and Neural Integration* (p. 121), by D. J. Siegel, 2010, New York, NY: Norton. Copyright 2010 by Mind Your Brain, Inc. Used with permission.

empathy are illuminated as discussed in this chapter (also see Carr et al., 2003), we can see that a focus on the internal flow of the sensations of the body—called interoception—leads to the activation of areas such as the insula and anterior cingulate cortex. These areas of the middle prefrontal regions are a fundamental part of self-awareness. It turns out that these are also the exact circuits of creating maps of the internal world of others—the circuits of empathy.

Here we can see the utility of the concept of mindsight. When we learn to sense our own internal states of energy and information flow, we use overlapping mindsight-enabling circuits of the middle prefrontal region to have empathy for others. Mindsight may be the fundamental mechanism beneath both social and emotional forms of intelligence (see Goleman, 1996, 2006). If educational programs throughout the life span could offer developmentally appropriate mindfulness practice, one could predict that children, adolescents, and adults would emerge with more resilience, enhanced medical and mental health, improved relationships, and a deeper spiritual sense of meaning and connections with themselves and others. In a larger sense, mindsight can be understood as one of the foundations of a larger integration among biological, psychological, social, and spiritual dimensions of life.

CONCLUSION

In this chapter, we have considered the spiritual dimension of mindfulness. We have presented two different approaches to understanding the role of spirituality in therapeutic mindfulness interventions—one that emphasizes sacred concepts as spiritually significant and another that emphasizes *undoing* concepts as a path to spiritual connection. Through this review, we hope to stimulate a more careful and thoughtful conversation about the ways spirituality may or may not be relevant to mindfulness-based therapies as well as accelerating and focusing research efforts to understand the relationship between spirituality and mindfulness.

References

Ackerman, D., Kabat-Zinn, J., & Siegel, D. J. (2005, March). [Panel discussion]. Presented at the Psychotherapy Networker Symposium, Washington, DC.

Armstrong, K. (1993). *A history of God.* New York, NY: Ballantine Books.

Baer, R. A. (2003). Mindfulness training as a clinical intervention: A conceptual and empirical review. *Clinical Psychology: Science and Practice, 10,* 125–143. doi:10.1093/clipsy.bpg015

Batchelor, S. (1997). *Buddhism without beliefs: A contemporary guide to awakening.* New York, NY: Riverhead.

Beck, A., Rush, A., Shaw, B., & Emery, G. (1979). *Cognitive therapy of depression.* New York, NY: Guilford Press.

Begley, S. (2007). *Train your mind, change your brain.* New York, NY: Ballantine Books.

Bishop, S., Lau, M., Shapiro, S., Carlson, L., Anderson, N., Carmody, J., . . . Devins, G. (2004). Mindfulness: A proposed operational definition. *Clinical Psychology: Science and Practice, 11,* 230–241. doi:10.1093/clipsy.bph077

Buddhaghosa, B. (1979). *The path of purification (Visuddhimaga)* (4th ed.; B. Nanamoli, Trans.). Kandy, Sri Lanka: Buddhist Publication Society.

Carr, L., Iacoboni, M., Dubeau, M.-C., Maziotta, J. C., & Lenzi, L. G. (2003). Neural mechanisms of empathy in humans: A relay from neural systems for imitation to limbic areas. *Proceedings of the National Academy of Sciences of the United States of America, 100,* 5497–5502. doi:10.1073/pnas.0935845100

Chapman, A. (2006). Acceptance and mindfulness in behavior therapy: A comparison of dialectical behavior therapy and acceptance and commitment therapy. *International Journal of Behavioral and Consultation Therapy, 2,* 308–313.

Chiesa, A., & Serretti, A. (2009). Mindfulness-based stress reduction for stress management in healthy people: A review and meta-analysis. *Journal of Alternative and Complementary Medicine, 15*, 593–600. doi:10.1089/acm.2008.0495

Cozolino, L. (2008). *The neuroscience of human relationships: Attachment and the developing social brain.* New York, NY: Norton.

Davidson, R. J., & Kabat-Zinn, J. (2004). Alterations in brain and immune function produced by mindfulness meditation: Three caveats. Comment. Response to letter by J. Smith. *Psychosomatic Medicine, 66*, 149–152.

Davidson, R. J., Kabat-Zinn, J., Schumacher, J., Rosenkranz, M., Muller, D., Santorelli, S., . . . Sheridan, J. (2003). Alterations in brain and immune function produced by mindfulness meditation. *Psychosomatic Medicine, 65*, 564–570. doi:10.1097/01.PSY.0000077505.67574.E3

Dimidjian, S., & Linehan, M. (2003). Defining an agenda for future research on the clinical application of mindfulness practice. *Clinical Psychology: Science and Practice, 10*, 166–171. doi:10.1093/clipsy.bpg019

Doidge, N. (2007). *The brain that changes itself: Stories of personal triumph from the frontiers of brain science.* New York, NY: Penguin.

Eifert, G., & Forsyth, J. (2005). *Acceptance and commitment therapy for anxiety disorders: A practitioner's guide to using mindfulness, acceptance, and values-based behavior change strategies.* Oakland, CA: New Harbinger.

Emmons, R. A. (2005). Emotion and religion. In R. Paloutzian & C. Parks (Eds.), *Handbook of psychology and religion* (pp. 235–252). New York, NY: Guilford Press.

Farb, N. A., Segal, Z., Mayberg, H., Bean, J., McKeon, D., Fatima, Z., & Anderson, A. (2007). Attending to the present: Mindfulness meditation reveals distinct neural modes of self-reference. *Social Cognitive and Affective Neuroscience*, 2, 313–322. doi:10.1093/scan/nsm030

Fitzpatrick-Hopler, G. (2006, June). *Christian contemplative practice: Centering prayer.* Paper presented at the Mind and Life Summer Research Institute, Garrison, NY.

Fletcher, L., & Hayes, S. (2005). Relational frame theory, acceptance and commitment therapy, and a functional analytic definition of mindfulness. *Journal of Rational-Emotive and Cognitive Behavior Therapy*, *23*, 315–336. doi:10.1007/s10942-005-0017-7

Forman, E. M., Herbert, J., Moitra, E., Yeomans, P., & Geller, P. (2007). A randomized controlled effectiveness trial of acceptance and commitment therapy and cognitive therapy for anxiety and depression. *Behavior Modification, 31*, 772–799. doi:10.1177/0145445507302202

Gold, E., Smith, A., Hopper, I., Herne, D., Tansey, G., & Hulland, C. (2010). Mindfulness-based stress reduction (MBSR) for primary school teachers. *Journal of Child and Family Studies, 19*, 184–189. doi:10.1007/s10826-009-9344-0

Goldin, P. R., & Gross, J. (2010). Effects of mindfulness-based stress reduction (MBSR) on emotion regulation in social anxiety disorder. *Emotion, 10*, 83–91. doi:10.1037/a0018441

Goldstein, J., & Kornfield, J. (1987). *Seeking the heart of wisdom.* Boston, MA: Shambhala.

Goleman, D. (1984). The Buddha on meditation and states of consciousness. In D. H. Shapiro & R. N. Walsh (Eds.), *Meditation: Classical and contemporary perspectives* (pp. 317–360). New York, NY: Aldine.

Goleman, D. (1988). *The meditative mind: The varieties of meditative experience.* New York, NY: Tarcher/Putnam Books.

Goleman, D. (1996). *Emotional intelligence.* New York, NY: Bantam/Random House.

Goleman, D. (2006). *Social intelligence.* New York, NY: Bantam/Random House.

Grossman, P., Niemann, L., Schmidt, S., & Walach, H. (2004). Mindfulness-based stress reduction and health benefits: A meta-analysis. *Journal of Psychosomatic Research, 57*, 35–43. doi:10.1016/S0022-3999(03)00573-7

Gunaratana, H. (1992). *Mindfulness in plain English.* Somerville, MA: Wisdom.

Harris, R. (2009). Mindfulness without meditation. *Healthcare Counseling and Psychotherapy Journal*, 9(4), 21–24.

Hart, W. (1987). *The art of living: Vipassana meditation as taught by S. N. Goenka.* New York, NY: HarperCollins.

Hayes, S. (1987). A contextual approach to therapeutic change. In N. Jacobson (Ed.), *Psychotherapists in clinical practice: Cognitive and behavioral perspectives* (pp. 327–387). New York, NY: Guilford Press.

Hayes, S. (2004). Acceptance and commitment therapy, relational frame theory, and the third wave of behavioral and cognitive therapies. *Behavior Therapy, 35*, 639–665. doi:10.1016/S0005-7894(04)80013-3

Hayes, S. (2008). Climbing our hills: A beginning conversation on the comparison of acceptance and commitment therapy and traditional cognitive behavioral therapy. *Clinical Psychology: Science and Practice, 15*, 286–295. doi:10.1111/j.1468-2850.2008.00139.x

Hayes, S., Barnes-Holmes, D., & Roche, B. (Eds.). (2001). *Relational frame theory: A post-Skinnerian account of human language and cognition.* New York, NY: Plenum Press.

Kabat-Zinn, J. (1990). *Full catastrophe living: Using the wisdom of your body and mind to face stress, pain, and illness.* New York, NY: Delacorte Press.

Kabat-Zinn, J. (1993). Mindfulness meditation: Health benefits of an ancient Buddhist practice. In D. Goleman & J. Gurin (Eds.), *Mind/body medicine* (pp. 259–275). Yonkers, NY: Consumer Reports.

Kabat-Zinn, J. (2005). *Coming to our senses.* New York, NY: Hyperion.

Keating, T. (2005, November). *The orthodoxy of centering prayer.* Paper presented at the 13th Annual Investigating the Mind: Science and Clinical Applications in Meditation Meeting, Washington, DC.

Klatt, M. D., Buckworth, J., & Malarkey, W. (2009). Effects of low-dose mindfulness-based stress reduction (MBSR-ld) on working adults. *Health Education and Behavior, 36,* 601–614. doi:10.1177/1090198108317627

Kristeller, J. L. (2007). Mindfulness meditation. In P. Lehrer, R. L. Woolfolk, & W. E. Simes (Eds.), *Principles and practice of stress management* (3rd ed., pp. 393–427). New York, NY: Guilford Press.

Kristeller, J. L. (2010). Spiritual engagement as a mechanism of change in mindfulness- and acceptance-based therapies. In R. A. Baer (Ed.), *Assessing mindfulness and acceptance processes in clients: Illuminating the theory and practice of change* (pp. 155–184). Oakland, CA: New Harbinger.

Kuyken, W., Byford, S., Taylor, R., Watkins, E., Holden, E., White, K., . . . Teasdale, J. D. (2008). Mindfulness-based cognitive therapy to prevent relapse in recurrent depression. *Journal of Consulting and Clinical Psychology, 76,* 966–978. doi:10.1037/a0013786

Lau, M. A., Segal, Z. V., & Williams, J. M. (2004). Teasdale's differential activation hypothesis: Implications for mechanisms of depressive relapse and suicidal behaviour. *Behaviour Research and Therapy, 42,* 1001–1017. doi:10.1016/j.brat.2004.03.003

Lazar, S. W., Kerr, C. E., Wasserman, R. H., Gray, J. R., Greve, D. N., Treadway, M. T., . . . Fischl, B. (2005). Meditation experience is associated with increased cortical thickness. *NeuroReport, 16,* 1893–1897. doi:10.1097/01.wnr.0000186598.66243.19

Leary, M. R., & Tate, E. B. (2007). The multi-faceted nature of mindfulness. *Psychological Inquiry, 18,* 251–255. doi:10.1080/10478400701598355

Linehan, M. (1993). *Cognitive-behavioral treatment of borderline personality disorder.* New York, NY: Guilford Press.

Linehan, M. (1998, November). Dialectical behavioral therapy for borderline personality disorder. *Clinician's Research Digest,* pp. 1–2.

Linehan, M., Comtois, K. A., Murray, A., Brown, M., Gallop, R., Heard, H., . . . Lindenboim, N. (2006). Two-year randomized controlled trial and follow-up of dialectical behavioral therapy vs therapy by experts for suicidal behaviors and borderline personality disorder. *Archives of General Psychiatry, 63,* 757–766. doi:10.1001/archpsyc.63.7.757

Luders, E., Toga, A., Lepore, N., & Gaser, C. (2009). The underlying anatomical correlates of long-term meditation: Larger hippocampal and frontal volumes of gray matter. *NeuroImage, 45,* 672–678. doi:10.1016/j.neuroimage.2008.12.061

Lutz, A., Dunne, J., & Davidson, R. (2006). Meditation and the neuroscience of consciousness. In P. Zelazo, M. Moscovitch, & E. Thompson (Eds.), *The Cambridge handbook of consciousness* (pp. 497–549). Cambridge, England: Cambridge University Press.

Lykins, E., & Baer, R. (2009). Psychological functioning in a sample of long-term practitioners of mindfulness meditation. *Journal of Cognitive Psychotherapy, 23,* 226–241.

Maha-satipatthana Sutta: The great frames of reference (DN 22: T. Bhikkhu, Trans.). (2011, October 15). Retrieved from http://www.accesstoinsight.org/tipitaka/dn/dn.22.0.than.html

Minor, H. G., Carlson, L., Mackenzie, M., Zernicke, K., & Jones, L. (2006). Evaluation of a mindfulness-based stress reduction (MBSR) program for caregivers of children with chronic conditions. *Social Work in Health Care, 43,* 91–109. doi:10.1300/J010v43n01_06

Nyanaponika, T. (1973). *The heart of Buddhist meditation.* New York, NY: Weiser.

Pandita, S. U. (2006). *The state of mind called beautiful.* Somerville, MA: Wisdom.

Pargament, K. I. (2007). *Spiritually integrated psychotherapy: Understanding and addressing the sacred.* New York, NY: Guilford Press.

Porges, S. (2009). Reciprocal influences between body and brain in the perception and expression of affect: A polyvagal perspective. In D. Fosha, D. Siegel, & M. Solomon (Eds.), *The healing power of emotion* (pp. 27–54). New York, NY: Norton.

Poulin, P. (2003, August). *Evaluation of a mindfulness-based stress reduction program for nurses.* Paper presented at the 111th Annual Convention of the American Psychological Association, Toronto, Ontario, Canada.

Raichle, M. E. (2010). The dark energy of the brain. Scientific American, March. *Scientific American, 302,* 44–49. doi:10.1038/scientificamerican0310-44

Robins, C. J., & Chapman, A. (2004). Dialectical behavior therapy: Current status, recent developments, and future directions. *Journal of Personality Disorders, 18,* 73–89. doi:10.1521/pedi.18.1.73.32771

Rosch, E. (2007). More than mindfulness: When you have a tiger by the tail, let it eat you. *Psychological Inquiry, 18,* 258–264. doi:10.1080/10478400701598371

Salzberg, S. (1995). *Lovingkindness: The revolutionary art of happiness.* Boston, MA: Shambhala.

Samuelson, M., Carmody, J., Kabat-Zinn, J., & Bratt, M. (2007, November). Mindfulness-based stress reduction is feasible and effective with inmates. *Clinician's Research Digest,* p. 3.

Segal, Z., Williams, J., & Teasdale, J. (2002). *Mindfulness-based cognitive therapy for depression: A new approach to preventing relapse.* New York, NY: Guilford Press.

Seligman, M. E. P., Park, N., Peterson, C., & Steen, T. A. (2005). Positive psychology progress: Empirical validation of interventions. *American Psychologist, 60,* 410–421. doi:10.1037/0003-066X.60.5.410

Shapiro, S. L. (2003, August). *Mindfulness-based interventions for breast cancer: Challenges of a randomized trial.* Paper presented at the 111th Annual Convention of the American Psychological Association, Toronto, Ontario, Canada.

Shapiro, S. L., Schwartz, G., & Bonner, G. (1998). Effects of mindfulness-based stress reduction on medical and premedical students. *Journal of Behavioral Medicine, 21,* 581–599. doi:10.1023/A:1018700829825

Shapiro, S. L., Walsh, R., & Britton, W. B. (2003). An analysis of recent meditation research and suggestions for future directions. *Journal for Meditation and Meditation Research, 3,* 69–90.

Siegel, D. J. (1999). *The developing mind: How relationships and the brain interact to shape who we are.* New York, NY: Guilford Press.

Siegel, D. J. (2007a). *The mindful brain: Reflection and attunement in the cultivation of well-being.* New York, NY: Norton.

Siegel, D. J. (2007b). Mindfulness training and neural integration: Differentiation of distinct streams of awareness and the cultivation of well-being. *Social Cognitive and Affective Neuroscience, 2,* 259–263. doi:10.1093/scan/nsm034

Siegel, D. J. (2010a). *The mindful therapist: A clinician's guide to mindsight and neural integration.* New York, NY: Norton.

Siegel, D. J. (2010b). *Mindsight: The new science of personal transformation.* New York, NY: Bantam Books.

Siegel, D. J. (2010c). The science of mindfulness. *Shambhala Sun, 18*(4), 66–69.

Siegel, D. J. (2012a). *The developing mind: How relationships and the brain interact to shape who we are* (2nd ed.). New York, NY: Guilford Press.

Siegel, D. J. (2012b). *Pocket guide to interpersonal neurobiology: An integrative handbook of the mind.* New York, NY: Norton.

Stace, W. T. (1960). *Mysticism and philosophy.* Philadelphia, PA: Lippincott.

Tacón, A. M., McComb, J., Caldera, Y., & Randolph, P. (2003). Mindfulness meditation, anxiety reduction, and heart disease. A pilot study. *Family and Community Health, 26,* 25–33.

Teicher, M. H. (2002). Scars that won't heal: The neurobiology of child abuse. *Scientific American, 286,* 68–75. doi:10.1038/scientificamerican0302-68

Urry, H. L., Nitschke, J., Dolski, I., Jackson, D., Dalton, K., Mueller, C., . . . Davidson, R. (2004). Making a life worth living: Neural correlates of well-being. *Psychological Science, 15,* 367–372. doi:10.1111/j.0956-7976.2004.00686.x

Vowles, K. (2009, January). Acceptance and commitment therapy for chronic pain. *Clinician's Research Digest,* p. 2.

Wallace, B. A. (1999, November). *Is Buddhism really nontheistic?* Paper presented at the National Conference of the American Academy of Religion, Boston, MA.

CHAPTER 11

DISTINCTIVE APPROACHES TO RELIGION AND SPIRITUALITY: PASTORAL COUNSELING, SPIRITUAL DIRECTION, AND SPIRITUALLY INTEGRATED PSYCHOTHERAPY

Len Sperry

Increasingly, Americans believe that spirituality is vital for growth and essential for dealing with life's problems (Lesser, 1999). As a result, many are pursuing a journey of spiritual growth. Those who pursue this journey may encounter spiritual and psychological roadblocks to growth or discover the need for guidance and counsel. In the past, these individuals were likely to approach religious institutions (i.e., churches or synagogues) for help with these concerns. In the 21st century, however, these individuals are more likely to turn to pastoral counseling, spiritual direction, and, increasingly, psychotherapy—particularly spiritually integrated psychotherapy—for such help.

So what are the differences between these approaches? What are the advantages of each? What are the professional qualifications of these practitioners? Can psychotherapists expand their practice to include spiritual direction or pastoral counseling? What are the criteria for referring individuals to the appropriate approach? This chapter attempts to address these questions. It begins by presenting a reasonably detailed description of pastoral counseling, spiritual direction, and spiritually integrated psychotherapy. Case examples are included to capture the uniqueness of each of these approaches. Next, the approaches are compared, followed by descriptions of training and credentialing for each specialization. I then describe how the three approaches are practiced across various religious traditions. This description is followed by a discussion of some criteria to guide treatment selection. Finally, various ethical and legal issues involved in practice, particularly of spiritually integrated psychotherapy, are considered.

It may be useful to begin this chapter with a brief overview of these three similar but very different approaches. Basically, clients typically come to pastoral counseling, spiritual direction, or spiritually integrated psychotherapy with similar concerns: struggles and suffering, spiritual growth, or both. Although all three approaches can address these concerns, their emphasis differs. Pastoral counseling and spiritual direction primarily emphasize religious or spiritual change, whereas spiritually integrated psychotherapy emphasizes psychological change. Specifically, individuals in spiritually integrated psychotherapy are helped to draw on spiritual resources and address spiritual problems or struggles, which leads to the goal of reducing psychological and relational problems. Although spiritually integrated psychotherapy can foster spiritual growth, such growth represents a by-product of treatment. Thus, it differs from pastoral counseling and spiritual direction wherein spiritual growth tends to be the central goal. Pastoral counseling and spiritual direction also differ from spiritually integrated psychotherapy in the way their practitioners function. Pastoral counselors and spiritual directors are more likely to offer spiritual resources or advice that is rooted in a particular religious or institutional framework, whereas spiritually oriented psychotherapists are more likely

DOI: 10.1037/14046-011
APA Handbook of Psychology, Religion, and Spirituality: Vol. 2. An Applied Psychology of Religion and Spirituality, K. I. Pargament (Editor-in-Chief)

to be noncommittal about a particular religious solution. The following sections elaborate these similarities and differences.

PASTORAL COUNSELING

For centuries clergy have provided pastoral care to believers interested in religious or spiritual change and also to those facing personal problems and crises. Some clergy have also provided pastoral care to those with mental illness. Aside from pastoral care provided by clergy, pastoral counseling is rooted in clinical pastoral education and chaplaincy. Yet, it it has been recognized that additional professional training is necessary to effectively treat some believers (Stone, 1999).

The identity of pastoral counselors as professional counselors with specialized training in theology, pastoral care, and psychology was crystalized with the founding of the American Association of Pastoral Counseling (AAPC) in 1963. Pastoral counseling was often viewed as an alternative to conventional psychotherapy as well as to spiritual direction for many Protestants and Jews. The primary intent and function of pastoral counseling is to assist in coping with physical, emotional, or moral stressors as well as coping with a crisis of meaning. A basic assumption of pastoral counseling is that addressing spiritual or religious needs is essential in effectively dealing with personal problems and crises, particularly for believers.

In the past, *pastoral care* and *pastoral counseling* were often used synonymously, but now they are distinguished (Montgomery, 2010). *Pastoral care* refers to pastoral communication that helps and nurtures individuals and interpersonal relationships in supportive ministries, such as visitation of the sick. It may involve the use of counseling skills, but it does so in a briefer and less therapeutically complex manner than in pastoral counseling. As such it could be considered a form of precounseling that takes place outside a formal counseling context. By contrast, *pastoral counseling* is a more structured and complex form of pastoral communication involving an articulated request for help that occurs within a formal counseling context. Furthermore, specific arrangements for formal sessions, times, and fees are mutually negotiated in pastoral counseling similar to traditional psychotherapy.

Clergy and other ministry personnel with training in pastoral care and counseling provide the majority of short-term pastoral counseling. Ministry personnel and others with formal supervised training in psychotherapy, however, can be certified and licensed to practice what has come to be called pastoral psychotherapy (Wise, 1980).

Currently, three forms of pastoral counseling are practiced: (a) a brief situational form of counseling of a single session; (b) a time-limited form that uses problem-solving or solution-focused methods and that typically lasts two to five sessions; and (c) a long-term form, called *pastoral psychotherapy*, that is often psychoanalytically oriented and focuses on personality change (Montgomery, 2010; Stone, 1999). Clientele for pastoral counseling are typically troubled individuals presenting with life transitions; emotional or relational crises; or guilt, abuse, addictions, or low self-esteem (Benner, 2003; Stone, 1999). Pastoral counseling is well suited to such crises and concerns, and it is a unique form of counseling that uses religious and spiritual resources as well as psychological understanding for healing and growth. In addition to spiritual growth, its goals include problem resolution and restoration of psychological health. In contrast, personality change may be seen as a goal in pastoral psychotherapy—however variously defined (Wise, 1980)—which involves long-term therapy and may be difficult to distinguish from conventional long-term psychotherapy.

As in psychotherapy, the relationship between pastoral counselor and client is important, and maintaining some measure of clinical distance is useful in diagnosis and therapeutic change. Nevertheless, many recently trained pastoral counselors advocate a collaborative relationship with the client (Benner, 2003). A pastoral assessment may be conducted to identify the specific needs and resources of the client and the goals of the counseling. The dimensions of such an assessment include awareness of God, acceptance of God's grace, repentance and responsibility, and the nature of the client's involvement in her or his faith community (Benner, 2003). Treatment interventions usually include active listening and other problem-solving or solution-focused counseling methods. These interventions also may include advice on religious or spiritual matters (i.e., forgiveness) as well as the resources of the client's faith community. Furthermore, pastoral counselors are likely to refer clients with certain presentations for secular or pastoral psychotherapy.

Case Example 1

Maria is a 34-year-old single Hispanic female who sought counseling at a pastoral counseling center in her community. She was referred to the center by the pastor of her church. Maria was concerned about her temporary job layoff, depression, insomnia, and future. She became tearful as she recounted that a year ago she had an abortion and that her guilt, which had been minimal at that time, seemed to be increasing lately. In their first meeting, her Hispanic male pastoral counselor completed a brief developmental history, which included her image of God. They met for four additional sessions during which the matter of her image of God as a judge who was punishing her for her abortion was processed. They also focused on how behavioral activation could reduce her depression, improve her sleep, and help her get ready for a return to her job. At their last meeting, Maria had largely resolved her guilt feelings, was asymptomatic, had grown spiritually, had developed a more positive image of God, and felt the counseling "had worked." The understanding was that a follow-up session could be scheduled if Maria thought it would be helpful. Although the emphasis on Maria's negative God image is not uncommon in pastoral counseling, it is very unlikely to have been the focus of secular counseling or psychotherapy.

SPIRITUAL DIRECTION

Spiritual direction is also known as *spiritual guidance*, *spiritual friendship*, and *spiritual companionship* (Lesser, 1999). Its roots extend from the 3rd century when it was practiced primarily by monks, priests, and other religious, but it has been rediscovered and has evolved; it is now practiced in various forms in nearly all spiritual traditions (Edwards, 1980, 2001). In the 21st century, spiritual direction in the United States is primarily associated with the Catholic tradition, although it is practiced in several Protestant denominations, including Episcopal, Lutheran, and Methodist, among others (Leech, 1977) as well as in Judaism and in Buddhism (Bhikku, 2003).

The primary emphasis in spiritual direction is to facilitate spiritual growth (Barry & Connolly, 2009; Gratton, 1992), whereas its secondary emphasis is psychological change. A basic assumption of spiritual direction is that spiritual growth is fostered by a reflective process with another who guides and models this process (Ruffing, 2000).

Spiritual direction can be described as the art of spiritual listening, which focuses on movement of the divine (in theistic traditions) within another's life story (Stairs, 2000). It involves a trained director who guides or companions others, called directees. Although spiritual direction can occur in a group setting, it is most commonly practiced in the context of a one-on-one trusting relationship. Although a candle, a Bible, or some other nonverbal symbol representing the holy may be incorporated in the setting, spiritual direction always occurs in the context of prayer.

Discernment is central to spiritual direction and usually involves recognizing the spiritual or ultimate meaning of events and circumstances in the directee's life (Barry & Connolly, 1982, 2009). The relationship between director and directee is one of mutual engagement based on the recognition that both are walking the same spiritual journey. The role of faith in the spiritual dimension and one's relationship to a faith community is central to Christian spiritual direction (Gratton, 1992). In addition, spiritual direction involves spiritual conversion, in that it is attentive to the "dynamics of change through conversion, the radical transformation. . . . [and] a relational, personal surrender to a personal, living God" (Galindo, 1997, p. 400).

Spiritual direction focuses on the maintenance and development of spiritual health and well-being. This approach assumes that the person is already whole but has not yet fully embraced this truth for themselves. Thus, spiritual direction is not for everyone because it presumes a moderate degree of psychological health and well-being, the relative absence of psychopathology, and moderate to high psychological functioning (Sperry, 2002).

Interventions in spiritual direction include instruction in prayer and the prescription of rituals and other spiritual practices. A focus on developing and monitoring the directee's prayer life, including meditation or contemplation, is central to spiritual direction. When indicated, spiritual directors may refer directees with certain psychological problems for concurrent psychotherapy or will suspend spiritual direction until the course of therapy is completed (Culligan, 1983). Whether one professional can effectively and appropriately provide both spiritual direction and either psychotherapy or pastoral counseling is a matter of considerable debate (May, 1992).

Case Example 2

Martha is a 59-year-old married Caucasian female and college professor who sought spiritual direction to "put more balance in my spiritual life." She was Catholic and had successfully raised and "launched" three children with her husband and now "wanted to focus a little more on my own growth." Her spiritual director was a 34-year-old Catholic lay woman with a master's degree in spirituality and 2 years of supervision in spiritual direction. After their first meeting, Martha was asked to complete a five-page spiritual history form that asked her to describe her spiritual practices and key historical events and their psychological and spiritual meaning for her. In their next meeting, 3 weeks later, the director and Martha reviewed the form. For each key event, the director asked Martha where God was in the event and then about what she had learned about herself spiritually in her response to the event. Because one of Martha's expectations for direction was to develop her prayer life, the director provided instruction in mantra-based meditation and mindfulness living and reviewed her progress in subsequent meetings. Learning to meditate and engage in mindfulness while eating, walking, and exercising were particularly useful in Martha's spiritual as well as personal development. They continued to meet monthly for the next 3 years after which Martha and her husband, who had just retired, moved to be closer to their children and grandchildren. Martha's evaluation of her spiritual direction experience was positive, and she looked forward to entering into direction after they settled into their new community.

SPIRITUALLY INTEGRATED PSYCHOTHERAPY

Spiritually integrated psychotherapy is the most recent of the three approaches, and unlike the other two, it has its roots in psychological theory and research (Pargament, 2007). Its primary emphasis is psychological change, while its secondary emphasis is religious or spiritual change or growth. Development in this form of psychotherapy stems from both theoretical (Pargament, 2007), research (Hook et al., 2010), and clinical (Sperry & Shafranske, 2005) considerations.

Theoretically, humanistic psychology and psychotherapies have long recognized the importance of self-actualization and transformation. Renewed interest in Jung's individuation therapy in part fostered the development of transpersonal psychotherapy (Cortright, 1997) and spiritually focused versions of mainstream psychotherapeutic approaches (Sperry & Shafranske, 2005) as well as Eastern-oriented approaches such as mindfulness and other Buddhist practices (Bhikku, 2003).

There has also been a dramatic increase of research in the spirituality relevant to psychotherapy. Among other things, it has documented the robust link between religion and physical and mental health. It has also set the stage for the development of new interventions as well as evidence-based professional practice. In addition, research in this area has highlighted the value of meditation and Eastern philosophies as well as shifts in cognitive–behavioral therapy (CBT) to include internal states, as in acceptance commitment therapy (Hayes & Plumb, 2007). Clinically, the expressed interest of clients to have their spiritual values and issues recognized in therapy represented another important factor in the development of spiritually integrated psychotherapy.

With regard to the intent and functions of spiritually integrated psychotherapy, three clinical situations have been identified in which religious and spiritual issues surface in the context of psychotherapy: those in which spirituality offers a key resource for coping with serious problems; traumatic situations that may lead to spiritual struggles, such as a crisis of faith or meaning in life; or the quest for increased well-being and spiritual growth (Shafranske & Sperry, 2005; Sperry, 2010; see also Volume 1, Chapter 25, this handbook). Although a focus on spiritual growth may seem more consistent with traditional spiritual direction, clients increasingly are seeking out psychotherapists rather than ministers and other spiritual guides to foster their spiritual growth and development.

Spiritually integrated psychotherapy is a term that broadly characterizes a variety of psychotherapeutic approaches that are sensitive to the spiritual dimension. These approaches range from non-Christian approaches and transpersonal psychotherapies (Cortright, 1997; Karasu, 1999) to theistic (Richards & Bergin, 1997) and various Christian approaches (Sperry, 1998, 2001, 2002, 2005; Steere, 1997), including Christian counseling and evidence-based religious accommodative forms of psychotherapy (see Chapter 34 in this volume). Despite considerable variability among these approaches, it is possible to make some general observations about typical clientele, goals and purposes, the nature of the relationship with the professional, and the type of interventions utilized in spiritually integrated psychotherapy. Individuals seeking explicitly spiritually integrated psychotherapy range from relatively healthy spiritual seekers to disordered clients presenting with symptomatic distress or impairment in one or more areas of life functioning (Sperry, 2002).

As noted, spiritually integrated psychotherapy is distinct from pastoral counseling and spiritual direction in its emphasis and treatment focus. It draws on spiritual resources in addressing spiritual issues and struggles to resolve psychological and relational problems. Although it can also foster spiritual change and growth, spiritually integrated psychotherapy accomplishes this growth as a by-product that accompanies psychological change. Unlike pastoral counselors and spiritual directors who offer spiritual resources and advice rooted in a particular religious framework, spiritually integrated therapists tend to be less focused on such religious frameworks because spiritually integrated therapies are not restricted to particular religious frameworks.

The goals of treatment vary according to client presentation and need. They may include help with spiritual struggles and emergencies, spiritual growth, increased psychological well-being, self-fulfillment or individuation, or the reduction of symptomatic distress and the restoration of baseline functioning (Sperry, 2002). The therapeutic relationship typically involves collaboration. Not surprisingly, those practicing spiritually integrated psychotherapy presumably demonstrate respect for the client's spiritual values and concerns.

Various psychotherapeutic and psychospiritual interventions are utilized depending on client need and indication (Miller, 1999). If indicated, referral for a psychiatric evaluation for medication or hospitalization may occur. Spiritual interventions are also involved. These include spiritual practices, such as prayer and meditation, and when indicated, collaboration with or referral to clergy or chaplain (Sperry 2001).

Case Example 3

Jessie is a 39-year-old married Caucasian male who sought therapy for his compulsive work pattern and because "I'm basically an angry workaholic." Jessie could be easily angered and was often critical, perfectionistic, and pessimistic. Although he was successful at his job as senior accountant and was in line to become a partner in his firm, his promotion depended on his ability to meet the other partners' expectation that he would become "easier to work with." This work success came at the big price of spending 80 or more hours in the office and relatively few hours with his wife and children. His wife felt cheated by his absence, especially during tax season, and their increasing conflict when they were together. She demanded that he change or she would leave him. Jessie also disliked how his life was going and wished to be "more the person I was meant to be." Thus, he had both external and internal motivation to change. Although he had tried CBT to modify his anger and workaholism, "it didn't work," and he stopped after five sessions. A friend referred him to a psychologist who blended spirituality and psychotherapy. Viewing himself as a spiritual but not religious person, Jessie began spiritually integrated therapy hopeful that things would change.

An integrative diagnostic evaluation found that Jessie did meet criteria for obsessive compulsive personality disorder and barely met those for dysthymic disorder (American Psychiatric Association, 2000), that his image of God was demanding and vengeful, and that his constant negative rumination compounded his condition. A spiritually sensitive case conceptualization and treatment plan were developed. Spiritual aspects of his compulsivity, pessimism, and perfectionism were identified. For example, his pessimistic outlook was related to his stated belief that "God does not really care about me." Treatment focused on three targets: reducing compulsivity and pessimism, replacing worrisome ruminations with mindfulness, and shifting from perfectionism to perfectibility. Specific interventions—including psychological, psychospiritual, and spiritual—were identified and implemented.

Weekly sessions focused on all three targets simultaneously, utilizing a variety of cognitive–behavioral, psychospiritual, and spiritual interventions. Spiritual interventions included guided imagery, inner healing, meditation, and mindfulness. Mindfulness practice was at first difficult and challenging for Jessie, but as he mastered the practice his negative ruminations and critical–pessimistic attitude began to recede. Yet, the most challenging change was to shift from perfectionism to perfectibility, that is, the adaptive pursuit of perfection that is considered a virtue (Chang, 2003). As this shift came about, Jessie's self-view and worldview shifted from his worth depending on achievement and the high flown demands of others to one in which he was worthwhile just as he was. Not surprisingly, in this process, his image of God shifted from one that was harsh, demanding, and judgmental to one that was more caring and concerned. Over a period of some 18 months all treatment targets were achieved.

COMPARISON OF THE THREE APPROACHES

Although there are commonalities among pastoral counseling, spiritual direction, and spiritually integrated psychotherapy, there are also a number of differences. (See Table 11.1 for a summary of the history, development, and features of pastoral counseling, spiritual direction, and spiritually integrated psychotherapy.) This section compares these three approaches according to the client or user's perspective, access to care, the expertise and versatility of its practitioners, treatment goals, nature of the relationship with the practitioner, and interventions.

Unlike data on membership in professional spiritual direction and pastoral counseling organizations, there are no firm estimates on the number of professionals practicing spiritually oriented psychotherapy. There are approximately 500,000 practicing

TABLE 11.1

Comparison of History and Features of Pastoral Counseling, Spiritual Direction, and Spiritually Integrated Psychotherapy

	Pastoral counseling	Spiritual direction	Spiritually integrated psychotherapy
History	Arose as an alternative to spiritual direction for Protestant, Jews and others seeking help	Long history as a spiritual activity for monks, priests, and religious; rediscovered recently by spiritual seekers from all walks of life and religious faiths, including Buddhism	Arose from expectation of clients to have their spiritual values and issues recognized in therapy; alternative to pastoral counseling and spiritual direction
Emphasis	Primarily religious or spiritual change, secondarily psychological change	Primarily spiritual change, secondarily psychological change	Primarily psychological change, secondarily religious or spiritual change or growth
Intent and function	Coping with a physical, emotional, or spiritual stressor, struggles, or a crisis of meaning; personality change (in pastoral psychotherapy)	Facilitating spiritual growth, may include coping with spiritual struggles or emotional problems	Coping with a serious physical or emotional stressor; resolving psychological symptoms; dealing with a crisis of meaning or spiritual struggle; or facilitating spiritual growth with spiritual resources
Practice pattern	Brief situational (one session), or short term (two to five sessions) versus long term (1 year or longer and referred to as *pastoral psychotherapy*)	Usually monthly sessions ongoing for years	Usually weekly sessions for short term or long term
Typical clientele	Troubled individuals often concerned with moral concerns or religious issues; clients often from same denomination as counselor	Usually relatively healthy spiritual seekers	Varies from relatively healthy spiritual seekers to troubled or disordered individuals with emotional, religious, or spiritual concerns

psychotherapists representing all the mental health disciplines in the United States (Lesser, 1999). If even a small number (say, 1%) of these psychotherapists practice some form of spiritually integrated psychotherapy, they would outnumber available spiritual directors by 100-fold and available pastoral counselors by even more. This suggests the need for more mental health professionals to practice spiritually integrated psychotherapy.

The phenomenon of "spiritual homelessness"—the feeling of not being at home in a religious institution (Stairs, 2000)—may further limit individuals from seeking spiritual guidance from spiritual directors with religious institutional ties. Even if pastors, rabbis, or imams were to embrace the role of spiritual counselor wholeheartedly (Stairs, 2000), it is unlikely that such spiritual counselors could be expected to deal adequately with complex spiritual matters involving psychological features.

Accordingly, individuals seeking spiritual advice are likely to have greater access to spiritually integrative psychotherapists than to spiritual directors or counselors, and they can expect that psychotherapists who are sensitive to spiritual issues will have more specialized training in dealing with complex psychological problems that have spiritual aspects than do most spiritual directors. Persons presenting with certain issues such as significant trauma, psychopathology, or substance or drug histories require assistance from those with specialized training, some of which is more regularly obtained in training in clinical psychology, psychiatry, or clinical social work.

Table 11.2 indicates the treatment goals, nature of the relationship with the practitioner, and

TABLE 11.2

Comparison of Goals, Relationships, and Interventions in Pastoral Counseling, Spiritual Direction, and Spiritually Integrated Psychotherapy

	Pastoral counseling	Spiritual direction	Spiritually integrated psychotherapy
Goals	Primarily problem resolution; can include personality change, if long term	Primarily spiritual growth, with a focus on prayer and enhanced relationship with God	Includes reduction of symptom and impairment, resolution of spiritual emergencies, or spiritual growth; often involves personality change
Relationship with provider	Varies from counselor as expert to collaboration	Usually collaboration with the recognition that God is the actual director	Usually collaboration; respectful of spiritual values and concerns
Interventions	Active listening Pastoral assessment Counseling strategies	Active listening Spiritual assessment	Active listening Empathic attunement Assessment and case conceptualization incorporating the spiritual
	Advice giving	Instruction in prayer	Psychotherapeutic strategies and interventions
	Forgiveness Moral guidance Spiritual practices Referral for psychotherapy	Spiritual practices Referral for psychotherapy	Psychospiritual interventions Spiritual interventions Spiritual practices Referral to clergy, religious leader, or spiritual guide

common interventions for all three approaches. The reader will note that active listening and the use of spiritual practices are common to all three approaches.

TRAINING AND CREDENTIALING

There is considerable variation in education, specialized training, supervision, experience, and credentialing requirements for pastoral counseling, spiritual direction, and spiritually integrated psychotherapy. This section briefly discusses these factors and considerations.

Pastoral Counseling

Pastoral counseling is currently very much concerned with becoming a recognized profession. This means that issues of training, certification, and professional identity are central concerns (Sperry, 2002). An increasing number of pastoral counselors are licensed to practice, usually in one of the mental health specialties (i.e., licensed professional counselor), and certification is available from the AAPC. This professional organization represents about 4,000 pastoral counselors and is actively exploring ways of incorporating a focus on spiritual concerns and spiritual direction methods into the practice of pastoral counseling. AAPC certifies pastoral counselors, accredits pastoral counseling centers, and approves training programs. It is an interfaith organization representing more than 80 faith groups, including the Protestant, Catholic, and Jewish faiths. As a nonsectarian professional organization, it respects the spiritual and religious traditions of those who seek assistance without imposition of counselor beliefs.

Recently, some have advocated that pastoral counseling extend its scope of practice to include spiritual guidance or direction. Despite differences in epistemological perspectives and praxis stances between the two fields, there is increasing support for this extension (Galindo, 1997). The identity of pastoral counseling has been significantly affected by such forces as managed behavioral health care and the increasing numbers of spiritual directors and mental health counselors who compete for many of the same clients as pastoral counselors (Stone, 1999).

How are pastoral counselors trained and how do they practice? Pastoral counselors are often psychologically as well as theologically trained, and it is not uncommon for the pastoral counselor or psychotherapist to possess graduate degrees in ministry and in pastoral counseling. An increasing number are licensed to practice, usually in a mental health specialty. This form of counseling usually centers on the client but may include the client's spouse or even the family (Sperry, 2002). Sessions are usually scheduled weekly, more likely in a counseling clinic rather than in a church or synagogue community.

Spiritual Direction

How are spiritual directors trained and how is spiritual direction usually practiced? There are no set requirements to practice spiritual direction. Some contend that it is a vocation rather than a profession; a special calling for which formal coursework and supervision are not essential. Others contend that specialized training in selected areas of theology and psychology are helpful or essential (Lescher, 1997; Sperry, 2002). Currently, there are a number of formal graduate training institutes and programs in spiritual direction but no universally recognized certification or licensure for spiritual directors. A professional organization called Spiritual Directors International claims a worldwide membership, and compared with pastoral counseling and spiritually integrated psychotherapy, it has the least restrictive membership requirements. It appears that anyone interested in spiritual direction can join the Spiritual Directors International global learning community. This organization promulgates its own code of professional ethics for its members.

Spiritual direction is customarily provided in a one-on-one format and usually on a monthly basis, although spiritual direction also occurs in small group settings. Some spiritual directors and guides charge a fee or request a free-will offering, whereas others do not.

Spiritually Integrated Psychotherapy

How are those who practice spiritually integrated psychotherapy trained, and how is spiritually integrated psychotherapy usually practiced? Currently, the training of spiritually integrated psychotherapists is not formalized nor regulated, despite the fact that several recommendations have been offered for training psychologists to address spiritual concerns in the context of psychotherapy (Pargament, 2007; Russell & Yarhouse, 2006; Worthington, 1988; Yarhouse & Fisher, 2002). Although there are a few psychology doctoral programs that are religiously oriented (e.g., Fuller Theological Seminary), the majority of programs that attempt to incorporate spirituality are secular. Yarhouse and Fisher (2002) have identified three training models for incorporating spirituality into such training programs: integration–incorporation, certificate minor, and religious distinctive models (see Chapter 33 in this volume). More recently, Worthington et al. (2009) have challenged such programs to more explicitly train students in spiritual and religious issues. Table 11.3 highlights these key issues regarding training and credentialing for pastoral counseling, spiritual direction, and spiritually integrated psychotherapy.

PRACTICE OF THE THREE APPROACHES ACROSS RELIGIOUS TRADITIONS

Because Protestants make up approximately 50% of the U.S. population and Catholics account for another 25% (Lesser, 2000), it is not surprising that many books, book chapters, and article about pastoral counseling, spiritual direction, and spiritually integrated psychotherapy are largely addressed to those two religious traditions. Nevertheless, there is a growing literature that specifically addresses other faith traditions as discussed in the following subsections.

Pastoral Counseling

Pastoral counseling originated in the United States and has largely remained a North American phenomenon, practiced primarily with clients from Protestant denominations as well as with Jewish clients. Relatively little has been written about ways it can be adapted to other religious cultures. Nevertheless, at least two notable books on cross-cultural pastoral counseling (i.e., Augsburger, 1987; Van

TABLE 11.3

Comparison of Training and Credentialing in Pastoral Counseling, Spiritual Direction, and Spiritually Integrated Psychotherapy

	Pastoral counseling and psychotherapy	Spiritual direction	Spiritually integrated psychotherapy
Education	Master's degree or doctorate in theology or pastoral counseling	Usually a master's degree in spirituality, psychology, etc.	Doctorate in psychology
Specialized training	500 hr (375 + 125) supervised experience; 3 years in ministry; religious body endorsement; one unit of Clinical Pastoral Education	Usually some formal training and supervised experience	(Under consideration)
Sponsoring organization	American Association of Pastoral Counseling (AAPC)	Spiritual Directors International (SDI)	American Psychological Association (APA) Society for the Psychology of Religion and Spirituality (Division 36)
Credentialing	Certified Pastoral Counselor Fellow, AAPC Diploma, AAPC	(None currently)	Fellow: APA (Division 36)
Ethical code or guidelines	AAPC Code of Ethics	Guidelines for Ethical Conduct in Spiritual Direction	Ethical Principles of Psychologists and Code of Conduct; Division 36: "Preliminary Practice Guidelines for Working with Religious and Spiritual Issues"
Licensure/ certification	Certified pastoral counselor plus licensure as LMHC, MSW, MFT, and so on	(None currently)	Licensed psychologist

Note. LMHC = licensed mental health counselor; MSW = master of social work; MFT = marriage and family therapist.

Beek, 1996) offer a more inclusive consideration of the approach.

Spiritual Direction

A recent book compiles the practice of spiritual direction in Buddhist, Sufi, Hindu, and Jewish traditions in addition to Benedictine, Carmelite, Ignatian, and Evangelical Christian traditions (Vest, 2003). As the Buddhist tradition and its related practice of mindfulness have become increasingly known in the United States (see Volume 1, Chapter 35, this handbook and Chapter 10, this volume), this section will briefly describe the practice of spiritual direction in that tradition. There is no term within the Buddhist tradition that describes spiritual direction as it is understood in the West; however, there is a correspondence between the Christian Orthodox tradition and the Buddhist practice with regard to spiritual guidance. Finding a suitable elder, *thera*, is essential to spiritual growth within Buddhism. The role of thera is to serve as guide and mirror for the student being directed. The focus is on wisdom, compassion, and love rather than formal training:

> Watching, observing, interacting, and being with the student are seen as essential elements in giving real direction. The director or thera is one who can look into the heart and mind of the student in order to encourage him to see for himself. (Bhikku, 2003, p. 6)

The relationship between the two is unequal in terms of power and authority; however, students are encouraged to find their own power and authority. Direction is not about gaining knowledge from the thera, but rather about "being in a living relationship with one who is knowing, which makes possible the end of all *dukkha* (suffering and unsatisfactoriness) and fosters the experience of real liberation of heart and mind" (Bhikku, 2003, p. 6). Furthermore, spiritual direction in the Buddhist tradition is largely embedded within a story or narrative that is relational, usually nondirective, nontheoretical, and focused on the here and now.

Spiritually Integrated Psychotherapy

A plethora of psychological and psychospiritual interventions as well as spiritual resources are available to those practicing spiritually integrated psychotherapy. These include compendiums of various intervention (Miller, 1999) and therapeutic strategies (Aten & Leach, 2009). The need to practice psychotherapy sensitive to various religious traditions is addressed in a compendium by Richards and Begin (2000).

TREATMENT SELECTION

On what basis does one determine whether to refer a person for spiritually integrated psychotherapy, pastoral counseling, or spiritual direction? In answering this question, it is important to consider the individual's needs, level of functioning, and expectations. For individuals with moderate to high functioning, who are not in crisis, and who seek or expect to work on spiritual growth, spiritual direction is likely to be the best fit. For individuals with moderate to high functioning, who are in crisis, and who expect treatment of symptoms or problem resolution within a religious or denominational context, pastoral counseling is likely to be the best fit. For individuals with low to moderate functioning—who seek a resolution to their psychological problems as well as a resolution to spiritual struggles and potential spiritual growth—spiritually integrated psychotherapy may be the best fit.

RESEARCH AND THE THREE APPROACHES

Although there have been considerable developments in the clinical practice pastoral counseling, spiritual direction, and spiritually integrated psychotherapy, there has not been corresponding research on these approaches. A few studies have been published on aspects of pastoral counseling, such as differences in the counseling practices of pastoral counselors and parish-based clergy (Mollica, Streets, Boscarino, & Redlich, 1986) and the religiosity and preferences of male and female clients for religious interventions in pastoral counseling (Schaffner & Dixon, 2003). The lack of research in this area is attributable in part to the reluctance of pastoral counselors to undertake such research and the lack of training in this area. In fact, the first chapter in a book dedicated to research methods in pastoral counseling (Vande Creek, Bender, & Jordan, 2008) is devoted to the various reasons this research is avoided. Similarly, research on the effectiveness of spiritual direction is almost nonexistent.

On the other hand, there is a rapidly expanding research literature in spiritually integrated psychotherapy. Summaries of such research are also increasing (Hook et al., 2010; Martinez, Smith, & Barlow, 2007), including research on empirically supported treatments (see Chapter 34 in this volume).

Some commonly researched topics include forgiveness, God image, and spiritually oriented CBT. This section briefly reviews these three areas.

The utilization of forgiveness has become increasingly common as an adjunctive approach among pastoral counselors and spiritually integrated psychotherapists. There is an expanding literature on forgiveness (Enright, 2001; Worthington, 2005; see also Volume 1, Chapter 23, this handbook and Chapter 25, this volume).

God image is commonly assessed in pastoral counseling, spiritual direction, and spiritually integrated psychotherapy (see Volume 1, Chapter 15, this handbook). It is also a focus of intervention as well as a relatively sensitive indicator of change among these approaches. A recent dissertation study reported on a national survey of Christian psychotherapists, pastoral counselors, and spiritual directors and their experience with God image issues with their respective clientele. All practitioners surveyed indicated that nearly half of their clients experience problems with their God image, and a majority reported positive God image changes as a result of treatment (Allmond, 2009).

Spiritually oriented CBT is an adaptation of CBT that uses cognitive disputation through scriptural and other religious evidence to combat irrational beliefs (Tan & Johnson, 2005). Because CBT is the most researched and empirically supported therapy, it is not surprising that versions that are sensitive to religious and spiritual issues have received considerable empirical attention and initial support (Tan & Johnson, 2005; see also Chapter 8 in this volume).

RECOMMENDATIONS FOR ETHICAL PRACTICE

This section discusses a variety of ethical issues and considerations involving the provision of spiritually oriented services (see also Chapter 3 in this volume). Included are ethics codes and key ethical considerations with a particular emphasis on role conflicts and multiple relationships, informed consent, and practitioner competence and scope of practice. This section concludes with a discussion of the competencies basic to each approach.

Codes of Ethics and Exemplar Guidance

The main professional organizations representing both spiritual directors (Spiritual Directors International) and pastoral counselors (AAPC) have specified codes of ethics. At the present time, therapists providing spiritually integrated psychotherapy have no specific code of ethics, beyond the ethical codes of their particular discipline: psychology, counseling, marital and family therapy, and so on.

There are, however, two notable developments to aid professional counselors and psychologists. The Association for Spiritual, Ethical, and Religious Values in Counseling (ASERVIC), a division of the American Counseling Association (ACA), has published a list of competencies for spiritually oriented counseling (Cashwell & Young, 2005), which was recently revised (ASERVIC, 2009). The American Psychological Association's (APA's) Division 36 (Society for the Psychology of Religion and Spirituality) has developed some preliminary guidelines ("Preliminary Practice Guidelines for Working With Religious and Spiritual Issues") that focus on assessment, therapy, and diversity considerations in the practice of spiritually oriented psychotherapy (cf. Hathaway & Ripley, 2009, Appendix 2.1; see Chapter 3 in this volume). Although these guidelines have not been formally adopted by APA, they "represent the sorts of common best practice recommendations from exemplar clinicians who specialize in addressing religious and spiritual issues in practice" (Hathaway & Ripley, 2009, p. 33). Table 11.3 identifies the particular ethical guidelines or codes for each of the three approaches.

Ethical Considerations

The various ethical issues arising in professional practice can be subsumed beneath five core areas: confidentiality, informed consent, conflict of interests, dual or multiple relationships, and competency (Sperry, 2007). Because of the contexts in which spiritually focused services are often provided, dual or multiple relationships can present complex ethical considerations in addition to informed consent—and so, too, can practitioner competence and scope of practice issues, particularly for psychologists. These three ethical considerations are briefly considered here.

Potential role conflicts and multiple relationships. In contrast to psychotherapists who provide spiritually integrated psychotherapy, ministry personnel such as priests, pastors, rabbis, and others who offer pastoral counseling or spiritual direction often experience potential role conflicts—referred to as dual or multiple relationships—with clients who may also be members of their congregations. Although the APA's *Ethical Principles of Psychologists and Code of Conduct* (the Ethics Code; APA, 2002) exhorts psychologists to avoid such relationships, dual and multiple relationships are often an expected part of the job duties for ministry personnel. For example, a pastor who also functions as a pastoral counselor or spiritual director may preach to his or her parishioners about religious values, exhort them to virtue, raise money from them, and counsel them on marital concerns. As long as reasonable boundaries are maintained, managing such multiple roles is possible albeit somewhat challenging.

Informed consent. The imposition of therapists' values of religious beliefs on clients can pose an ethical problem in all three approaches. It is unethical because it undermines the client's autonomy and right to decide about the specifics of treatment (Sperry, 2007). Value imposition can be less a concern for clients seeking spiritual direction or pastoral counseling because these clients have opted for spiritually oriented care. The situation can be considerably different for clients seeking psychotherapy because they may not be seeking spiritually integrated therapy. Consequently, numerous complaints have been filed by clients, or their guardians, to state licensing boards or professional organizations about spiritually oriented treatment that had not been sought or wanted (Bullis, 1996). Case law contains a number of cases in which psychotherapists have been fired for providing unwanted spiritual treatment to clients (Bullis, 1996). Accordingly, therapists would do well to elicit client expectations for treatment and to engage in mutually based treatment decision making so that informed consent is achieved.

Practitioner competence and scope of practice. Although ethical codes for spiritual directors and pastoral counselors directly address practitioner competence and scope of practice, the Ethics Code (APA, 2002) does not deal directly with these considerations for psychologists practicing spiritually integrated psychotherapy. The Ethics Code speaks of "scope of practice" in general terms indicating that psychologists should have sufficient formal training, supervision, and experience in a specialized area.

Scope of practice involves the extent to which an activity is considered to be an acceptable professional practice by a profession or by statute. Questions such as the following arise: Can a psychologist offer spiritual direction in the course of psychotherapy when spiritual direction is outside the legally defined scope of practice for psychology in a given state? Can spiritually integrated psychotherapy be offered in a government-funded community mental health center? What constitutes "sufficient" training, supervision, and experience to practice spiritually integrated psychotherapy? Although space limitations prevent these and related issues from being fully addressed in this chapter, as a starting point, it is essential for psychologists to articulate how they identify and describe spiritually integrated therapy practice. In this chapter, spiritually integrated psychotherapy has been delineated by its primary emphasis on psychological change with spiritual change as a secondary emphasis, and as a by-product accompanying psychological change. Furthermore, a therapeutic approach limited to psychological and psychospiritual techniques and methods is more consistent with the scope of practice of psychotherapy than with the scope of practice of spiritual direction, pastoral counseling, or chaplaincy. It is important for psychologists to carefully consider the issue of professional accountability and communicate with their licensing board regarding the matter of scope of practice (McMinn, 2009).

Core Competencies in the Three Approaches

In professional psychology there is currently no consensus on either competencies or ethical guidelines for practice in which religious or spiritual perspectives and resources are explicitly integrated. Nevertheless, Richards (2009) has offered some preliminary considerations for psychologists who endeavor to practice spiritually integrated psychotherapy. Others have also articulated competencies and ethical guidelines for the practice of spiritually integrated psychotherapy (Gonsiorek, Richards, Pargament, & McMinn, 2009). This lack of consensus on competencies and codes, however, leaves a void for psychologists practicing in this area. Clear guidelines are needed to help this specialty field develop and mature. Central to consideration of professional ethics is the area of professional competence.

As noted, ASERVIC specified and articulated a set of such competencies (Cashwell & Young, 2005) and offered a revision "Competencies for Addressing Spiritual and Religious Issues in Counseling" (ASERVIC, 2009). The revised document includes 14 competencies, of which the first six are cognitive competencies—for example, "can describe the similarities and differences between spirituality and religion"—and the last five are clinical competencies. These competencies involve assessment, diagnosis, goal setting, and the utilization of spiritually sensitive treatment interventions. Further development is required to articulate competencies and to establish clear standards for practice in each of the approaches presented in this chapter. Table 11.4 provides a tentative list of competencies for each approach. The tentative competencies for pastoral counseling were derived from Benner (2003), the

TABLE 11.4

Tentative Competencies of Pastoral Counseling, Spiritual Direction, and Spiritually Integrated Psychotherapy

Pastoral counseling (short term)	Spiritual direction	Spiritually integrated psychotherapy
Join client and set boundaries	Foster a triadic relationship (directee–God–director)	Develop a therapeutic alliance sensitive to spiritual dimension
Explore client's central concerns and history; conduct pastoral assessment	Deal with disturbances in directee–director relationship	Maintain a therapeutic alliance and deal with spiritual transference–countertransference and resistance
Achieve mutually agreeable	Evaluate the directee's spiritual experiences	Assess and diagnose, including the spiritual dimension
Counseling focus	Assist directee to notice and share spiritual experiences	Include spirituality in the case conceptualization
Process the problems and identify resources for coping and change	Foster a contemplative attitude	Include spirituality in treatment planning and mutual goal setting
Evaluate progress and assess		Implement spiritual and psychological interventions
Address remaining concerns (referral if indicated)		Referral to spiritual resource if indicated
		Monitor and evaluate overall treatment progress and outcomes
Terminate		Incorporate spiritual dimension in termination process

tentative competencies for spiritual direction were derived from Barry and Connolly (2009) and the tentative competencies for spiritually integrated psychotherapy were derived from Aten and Leach (2009).

CONCLUSION

This chapter has provided an overview and comparison of three distinctive spiritual approaches. Each of the three has arisen for widely different reasons and in different contexts; each has a different emphasis, intent, and function; and each targets different clientele. As noted, pastoral counseling and spiritual direction primarily emphasize religious or spiritual change. In contrast, spiritually integrated psychotherapy emphasizes psychological change with spiritual change or growth as a secondary goal. Furthermore, pastoral counselors and spiritual directors tend to offer spiritual resources or advice that is rooted in a particular religious or institutional framework. Spiritually oriented psychotherapists are more likely to be noncommittal about a particular religious or spiritual solution. Although it may appear that spiritually integrated psychotherapy simply subsumes the intent and functions of both pastoral counseling and spiritual direction, it typically targets a clientele with more difficult issues and complex dynamics than either pastoral counseling or spiritual direction.

Even though spiritual direction and pastoral counseling have been around for a long time, spiritually integrated psychotherapy is still in its infancy (Pargament, 2007). Additional model development and research demonstrating the effectiveness of spiritually integrated psychotherapy are necessary for the field to come of age. Finally, formal training must become more available for this form of therapy to be practiced more widely.

References

Allmond, J. (2009). *God images in Christian psychology, spiritual direction, and pastoral counseling.* (Doctoral dissertation). Available from Pro Quest Dissertation and Theses detabase. (Publication No. AAT 3370134)

American Psychiatric Association. (2000). *Diagnostic and statistical manual of mental disorders* (4th ed., text revision). Washington, DC: Author.

American Psychological Association. (2002). *Ethical principles of psychologists and code of conduct.*

Retrieved from http://www.apa.org/ethics/code/index.aspx

Association for Spiritual, Ethical, and Religious Values in Counseling. (2009). Competencies for addressing spiritual and religious issues in counseling. *Interaction, 10*(10), 3.

Aten, J., & Leach, M. (Eds.). (2009). *Spirituality and the therapeutic process: A comprehensive resource from intake to termination.* Washington, DC: American Psychological Association. doi:10.1037/11853-000

Augsburger, D. (1987). *Pastoral counseling across cultures.* New York, NY: Westminster-John Knox.

Barry, W., & Connolly, W. (1982). *The practice of spiritual direction.* New York, NY: Seabury.

Barry, W., & Connolly, W. (2009). *The practice of spiritual direction* (2nd ed.). New York, NY: Seabury.

Benner, D. (2003). *Strategic pastoral counseling: A short-term structured model* (2nd ed.). Grand Rapids, MI: Baker Academic.

Bhikku, T. (2003). Making a cup of tea: Some aspects of spiritual direction within a living Buddhist tradition. In N. Vest (Ed.), *Tending the holy: Spiritual direction across traditions* (pp. 3–18). New York, NY: Morehouse.

Bullis, R. (1996). *Spirituality in social work practice.* Washington, DC: Taylor & Francis.

Cashwell, C., & Young, S. (2005). *Integrating spiritual and religion into counseling: A guide to competent practice.* Alexandria, VA: American Counseling Association.

Chang, E. (2003). On the perfectibility of the individual: Going beyond the dialectic of good versus evil. In E. Chang & L. Sanna (Eds.), *Virtue, vice, and personality: The complexity of behavior* (pp. 125–144). Washington, DC: American Psychological Association. doi:10.1037/10614-008

Cortright, R. (1997). *Psychotherapy and spirit: Theory and practice in transpersonal psychotherapy.* Albany: State University of New York Press.

Culligan, K. (1983). The counseling ministry and spiritual direction. In B. Estadt (Ed.), *Pastoral counseling* (pp. 37–49). Englewood Cliffs, NJ: Prentice-Hall.

Edwards, T. (1980). *Spiritual friend: Reclaiming the gift of spiritual direction.* New York, NY: Paulist Press.

Edwards, T. (2001). *Spiritual director, spiritual companion.* New York, NY: Paulist Press.

Enright, R. (2001). *Forgiveness is a choice: A step-by-step process for resolving anger and restoring hope.* Washington, DC: American Psychological Association.

Galindo, I. (1997). Spiritual direction and pastoral counseling. *Journal of Pastoral Care, 51,* 395–402.

Gonsiorek, J. C., Richards, P. S., Pargament, K. I., & McMinn, M. R. (2009). Ethical challenges and opportunities at the edge: Incorporating spiritual and religion into psychotherapy. *Professional Psychology: Research and Practice, 40,* 385–395. doi:10.1037/a0016488

Gratton, C. (1992). *The art of spiritual guidance.* New York, NY: Crossroad.

Hathaway, W., & Ripley, J. (2009). Ethical concerns around spiritual and religion in clinical practice. In J. Aten & M. Leach (Eds.), *Spirituality and the therapeutic process: A comprehensive resource from intake to termination* (pp. 25–52). Washington, DC: American Psychological Association. doi:10.1037/11853-002

Hayes, S. C., & Plumb, J. C. (2007). Mindfulness from the bottom up: Providing an inductive framework for understanding mindfulness processes and their application to human suffering. *Psychological Inquiry, 18,* 242–248. doi:10.1080/10478400701598314

Hook, J. N., Worthington, E., Davis, D., Jennings, D., Gartner, A., & Hook, J. (2010). Empirically supported religious and spiritual therapies. *Journal of Clinical Psychology, 66,* 46–72.

Karasu, T. B. (1999). Spiritual psychotherapy. *American Journal of Psychotherapy, 53,* 143–162.

Leech, K. (1977). *Soul friend.* San Francisco, CA: Harper & Row.

Lescher, B. (1997). The professionalization of spiritual direction: Promise and peril. *Listening, 32,* 81–90.

Lesser, E. (1999). *The new American spirituality: A seeker's guide.* New York, NY: Random House.

Lesser, E. (2000). Insider's guide to 21st-century spirituality. *Spirituality and Health: The Soul/Body Connection, Spring,* 46–51.

May, G. (1992). *Care of mind, care of soul.* San Francisco, CA: HarperCollins.

McMinn, M. (2009). Ethical considerations with spiritually oriented interventions. *Professional Psychology: Research and Practice, 40,* 393–395.

Miller, W. (Ed.). (1999). *Integrating spirituality into treatment: Resources for practitioners.* Washington, DC: American Psychological Association. doi:10.1037/10327-000

Mollica, R. F., Streets, F., Boscarino, J., & Redlich, F. (1986). A community study of formal counseling activities of the clergy. *American Journal of Psychiatry, 143,* 323–328.

Montgomery, D. (2010). *Pastoral counseling and coaching.* Monticello, CA: Compass Works.

Pargament, K. (2007). *Spiritually integrated psychotherapy: Understanding and addressing the sacred.* New York, NY: Guilford Press.

Richards, P., & Bergin, A. (1997). *A spiritual strategy for counseling and psychotherapy*. Washington, DC: American Psychological Association. doi:10.1037/10241-000

Richards, P. S. (2009). Toward religious and spiritual competence for psychologists: Some reflections and recommendations. *Professional Psychology: Research and Practice, 40*, 389–391.

Richards, P. S., & Bergin, A. (Eds.). (2000). *Handbook of psychotherapy and religious diversity*. Washington, DC: American Psychological Association. doi:10.1037/10347-000

Ruffing, J. (2000). *Spiritual direction: Beyond the beginnings*. New York, NY: Paulist Press.

Russell, S., & Yarhouse, M. (2006). Training in religion/spirituality within APA-accredited psychology predoctoral internships. *Professional Psychology: Research and Practice, 37*, 430–436. doi:10.1037/0735-7028.37.4.430

Schaffner, A., & Dixon, D. (2003). Religiosity, gender and preference for religious interventions in counseling: A preliminary study. *Counseling and Values, 48*, 24–33. doi:10.1002/j.2161-007X.2003.tb00272.x

Shafranske, E., & Sperry, L. (2005). Addressing the spiritual dimension in psychotherapy: Introduction and overview. In L. Sperry & E. Shafranske (Eds.), *Spiritually oriented psychotherapy: Contemporary approaches* (pp. 11–29). Washington, DC: American Psychological Association. doi:10.1037/10886-001

Sperry, L. (1998). Spiritual counseling and the process of conversion. *Journal of Christian Healing, 20*(3–4), 37–54.

Sperry, L. (2001). *Spirituality in clinical practice: Incorporating the spiritual dimension in psychotherapy and counseling*. New York, NY: Brunner-Routledge.

Sperry, L. (2002). *Transforming self and community: Revisioning pastoral counseling and spiritual direction*. Collegeville, MN: Liturgical Press.

Sperry, L. (2005). Integrative spiritually oriented psychotherapy. In L. Sperry & E. Shafranske (Eds.), *Spiritually oriented psychotherapy: Contemporary approaches* (pp. 307–329). Washington, DC: American Psychological Association. doi:10.1037/10886-013

Sperry, L. (2007). *The ethical and professional practice of counseling and psychotherapy*. Boston, MA: Allyn & Bacon.

Sperry, L. (2010). Psychotherapy sensitive to spiritual issues: A post-materialist psychology perspective and developmental approach. *Psychology of Religion and Spirituality, 2*, 46–56. doi:10.1037/a0018549

Sperry, L., & Shafranske, E. (Eds.). (2005). *Spiritually oriented psychotherapy: Contemporary approaches*. Washington, DC: American Psychological Association. doi:10.1037/10886-000

Stairs, J. (2000). *Listening for the soul: Pastoral care and spiritual direction*. Minneapolis, MN: Fortress.

Steere, D. (1997). *Spiritual presence in psychotherapy: A guide for caregivers*. New York, NY: Brunner/Mazel.

Stone, H. (1999). Pastoral counseling and the changing times. *Journal of Pastoral Care, 53*, 47–56.

Tan, S., & Johnson, B. (2005). Spiritually oriented cognitive-behavioral therapy. In L. Sperry & E. Shafranske (Eds.), *Spiritually oriented psycho therapy: Contemporary approaches* (pp. 77–103). Washington, DC: American Psychological Association. doi:10.1037/10886-004

Van Beek, A. (1996). *Cross-cultural counseling*. Minneapolis, MN: Augsburg Fortress.

Vande Creek, L., Bender, H., & Jordan, M. (2008). *Research in pastoral care and counseling: Quantitative and qualitative approaches*. New York, NY: Wipf & Stock.

Vest, N. (Ed.). (2003). *Tending the holy: Spiritual direction across traditions*. New York, NY: Morehouse.

Wise, C. (1980). *Pastoral psychotherapy*. New York, NY: Jason Aronson.

Worthington, E. (1988). Understanding the values of religious clients: A model and its application to counseling. *Journal of Counseling Psychology, 35*, 166–174. doi:10.1037/0022-0167.35.2.166

Worthington, E. (2005). *Handbook of forgiveness*. New York, NY: Brunner-Routledge.

Worthington, E., Sandage, S., Davis, D., Hook, J., Miller, A., Hall, L., & Hall, T. (2009). Training therapists to address spiritual concerns in clinical practice and research. In J. Aten & M. Leach (Eds.), *Spirituality and the therapeutic process: A comprehensive resource from intake to termination* (pp. 267–292). Washington, DC: American Psychological Association. doi:10.1037/11853-012

Yarhouse, M., & Fisher, W. (2002). Levels of training to address religion in clinical practice. *Psychotherapy: Theory, Research, Practice, Training, 39*, 171–176. doi:10.1037/0033-3204.39.2.171

Part III

RELIGION AND SPIRITUALITY APPLIED TO SPECIFIC PROBLEMS

CHAPTER 12

RELIGION, SPIRITUALITY, DEPRESSION, AND ANXIETY: THEORY, RESEARCH, AND PRACTICE

Simon Dein

I have written this chapter from the perspective of a Jewish psychiatrist who works in a predominantly White area outside London, England, and who treats clients from a range of religious backgrounds: Christian, Jewish, and Muslim. I employ religious and spiritual interventions with clients suffering from depression and anxiety who endorse a spiritual perspective in their lives. Along with other readings, three books have in particular informed my work in this area: Kenneth Pargament's (2007) *Spiritually Integrated Psychotherapy: Understanding and Addressing the Sacred*; Christopher Williams, Paul Richards, and Ingrid Whitton's (2002) *I'm Not Supposed to Feel Like This: A Christian Approach to Depression and Anxiety*; and Stevan Nielson, W. Brad Johnson, and Albert Ellis's (2001) *Counseling and Psychotherapy With Religious Persons: A Rational Emotive Behaviour Therapy Approach*. I begin with two case examples.

Case Example 1[1]

I first met Peter after he was referred to my office by his general practitioner. Married with three children and an accountant by profession, he had a long history of depression and his symptoms had intensified over several weeks. On my first meeting with him, he was low in mood and preoccupied with thoughts of suicide. Very soon into therapy he told me that he was a practicing Catholic and believed that he had committed an unforgivable sin, which would result in him going to hell for eternity. With his permission I explored these ideas further to find that he had stopped going to Mass for several weeks and had neglected both prayer and confession. Both of these "failures" would result in God punishing him, so he believed.

He described a childhood devoid of love in which his mother was frequently physically and emotionally abusive. His father was passive and appeared to do little in the face of his mother's intimidation. He was bullied by both his brothers and by his peers at school. At the age of 18 he left home and shortly afterward joined an order of Benedictine monks in the hope that religious life would bring him some solace. The experience of living in the monastery, however, only intensified his feelings of inadequacy and his low self-image and perpetuated the idea that God would judge him harshly—something he recollected from his childhood days at a Catholic boarding school, where his teachers had instilled the idea of a God who would severely punish any sins.

My psychotherapeutic work with him deployed a number of strategies: addressing the problem of a small God (see the section Clinical Implications of

[1]The details in the five clinical case examples in this chapter have been significantly altered and disguised to protect anonymity.

DOI: 10.1037/14046-012
APA Handbook of Psychology, Religion, and Spirituality: Vol. 2. An Applied Psychology of Religion and Spirituality, K. I. Pargament (Editor-in-Chief)

Religious Coping in Depression and Anxiety later in this chapter), cognitive reframing regarding biblical interpretations, and referral and encouragement to seek support from a religious professional. First, I addressed his belief in a highly judgmental God who would punish him for every misdemeanor and consign him to Hell. I explained that his expectations that he should be perfect were unrealistic; in Christian teachings, only Jesus is held to be perfect and untainted by sin. To illustrate this point I asked him to search through the Bible and to show me where this expectation was stated. He was unable to find statements of this kind. Over a number of sessions, we spoke about how his conceptualization of a punitive God reflected his early attitudes toward his abusive mother. Slowly, he came to reconceptualize his image of God. As his mood lifted and he felt less angry toward his mother, he began to see God in a more benevolent way.

Another theme that recurrently arose was guilt associated with anger toward his parents. He felt that he had not heeded the commandment, "Thou should honor thy father and mother." I explained that he had a very literal understanding of this commandment and there was some flexibility in its interpretation. We discussed that it would be understandable for him to be angry with his mother and important that he acknowledge his anger, at least to himself, and explore ways to resolve these feelings. I felt that he was ready to look at the possibility of forgiving her using religious resources that were familiar to him.

In addition to my work with him, I encouraged him to speak to his priest, who was able to offer him support and help him understand God's role in his past. By encouraging Peter to read the Bible, the priest helped him reformulate his image of God from harsh and punitive to one who was compassionate and loving—in the priest's words, "a proper image of God." Through discussions with this priest, Peter came to understand that God was helping him to come to terms with his childhood and adolescent suffering and that God had not deserted him. The priest emphasized the fact that like any other human, Christ had suffered on the cross and was present in Peter's suffering. Peter felt that his relationship with the priest had allowed him to work through issues of theodicy and had strengthened his faith. In addition, through joint prayer with the priest, Peter felt closer to God. Finally, the opportunity to confess his sins via the Sacrament of Reconciliation allowed Peter to undergo a process whereby, not only did he feel forgiven by God, but he was also able to forgive himself.

Case Example 2

Clive, a 50-year-old man, suffered with a bipolar illness and attended my clinic on a regular basis. He was a friendly outgoing man who lived alone and had been unemployed for a number of years. Although his mood had been stable for about a year, he came across as disillusioned. He described himself as a "lapsed Jew," someone who grew up *frum* (religious) but after developing bipolar illness lost interest in religion. For 20 years or so he had never entered a synagogue and had largely lost contact with his family who apparently were still practicing Jews. At one appointment, he unexpectedly asked me if I believed in God. When I replied that I was unsure, he continued to tell me that he used to believe in God, but having suffered highs and lows for many years had lost this belief; after all if God existed, why did he suffer so much? Clive admitted that these questions intensified during his darkest moments when he felt most depressed and that on many occasions, he felt that God had abandoned him.

He expressed some surprise that I, as a clinician, should take these concerns seriously. After all, he asked, "Aren't all psychiatrists atheists?" He felt more at ease when I told him that I considered religion and spirituality to be essential for understanding clients' problems and I was keen to find out more about his views. I explained that religious doubts were "normal" and occurred in both deeply religious people and those who were less religious. I shared my belief with him that if there was a God, we cannot, as humans, necessarily understand his ways and offered to refer him to a Jewish chaplain. I suggested to him that although he was seeking answers to "ultimate" questions, he could be better spiritually well informed to answer them. He refused the offer of speaking to a rabbi stating that it was too late and that he would never change his mind about God.

These case studies raise several issues in relation to clinical practice. Should health professionals discuss religious and spiritual issues with their clients? How should religious and spiritual conflicts be addressed? What are the respective roles of health and religious professionals when working with clients with spiritual issues? How do the therapist's own values and beliefs affect spiritually oriented therapy? Both of these cases illustrate the ways in which religious struggles may contribute to, or exacerbate, the experience of depression: In the first instance, a supportive relationship with a priest ameliorated the experience of depression. In the second instance, the client's angry feelings toward God appeared to exacerbate his depression, but he was not open to further religious discussion.

In my own clinical work, I have found that religious and spiritual issues are both common and important among the clients who consult me, both as problems and as solutions. Moreover, many clients are indeed keen and thankful for the opportunity to discuss such issues. Surveys indicate that a significant percentage of clients with psychological problems want spiritually sensitive care (Lindgren & Coursey, 1995; Rose, Westfeld, & Ansley, 2001; Schulte, Skinner, & Claiborn, 2002). Through asking about religious and spiritual issues, clinicians come to understand how patients understand and give meaning to their illness and deal with adversity. Acknowledging and respecting religious coping reinforces this behavior and increases its effectiveness in the long run and helps to consolidate the therapist–client relationship. Consequently I am open to discussing spiritual issues. Furthermore, I argue that it is essential to take account of these issues as part of the therapy process and concur with Bergin and Payne (1991), who wrote: "Ignorance of spiritual constructs and experience predispose a therapist to misjudge, misinterpret, misunderstand, mismanage or neglect important segments of a client's life which may impact significantly on adjustment or growth" (p. 201).

Depression and anxiety raise issues of ultimate meaning. As the renown 20th-century Protestant theologian Paul Tillich (1952) stated, both syndromes are "ultimate anxieties." Related to death, meaningless, and suffering, depression and anxiety raise significant questions about our place in the world, underscore our limited powers, and beg for a spiritual response. C. Williams et al. (2002) pointed out that anxiety and depression can lead individuals to feel cut off from God, guilty, bad, and unloved. Religious–spiritual coping strategies may provide sufferers with a sense of meaning and control and enable them to see their lives from a deeper perspective. But sometimes spiritual solutions are not suited to the problem and even then may become spiritual problems. Thus, this chapter is broadly divided into two areas: (a) aspects of religion and spirituality that may trigger or exacerbate symptoms of depression and anxiety or that may impede recovery when stressful life events trigger emotional distress; and (b) resources that religion and spirituality could offer to reduce depression and anxiety symptoms exhibited by vulnerable individuals or to prevent relapse following recovery. In short, in accordance with the integrative paradigm of these volumes, I consider ways religion can be both as helpful and harmful to people with depression and anxiety as well as discuss the relationship between research, theory, and practice.

My approach to defining religiousness and spirituality is also consistent with the integrative paradigm of this handbook (see Volume 1, Chapter 1). By *religiousness* I refer to beliefs, practices, relationships, or experiences having to do with the sacred that are explicitly and historically rooted in established institutionalized systems. By *spirituality* I refer to beliefs, practices, relationships, or experiences having to do with the sacred that are not necessarily linked to established institutionalized systems. I begin by briefly reviewing the literature on religious coping, depression, and anxiety.

RELIGION, DEPRESSION, ANXIETY, AND COPING

Research on the relationships between religiousness and mental health has burgeoned in the past 20 years. Studies employing surveys in nonclinical general population and community samples reveal fairly consistent inverse relationships between global indexes of religion (such as frequency of church attendance and self-rated religiousness) and depressive disorders (Koenig, McCullough, & Larson, 2001; McCullough & Larson, 1999; Smith, McCullough, & Poll, 2003). Additionally there are fewer suicides, or more negative attitudes toward suicide, among the more religious (Koenig et al., 2001; Rasic et al., 2008). The relationships between anxiety and religious involvement appear to be complex, with some studies reporting less anxiety among the more religious (Koenig, Ford, George, Blazer, & Meador, 1993; Koenig et al., 2001; D. R. Williams, Larson, Buckler, Heckmann, & Pyle, 1991), others demonstrating increased anxiety (Tapanya, Nicki, & Jarusawad, 1997), and yet others finding no relation between religion and anxiety (Krause & Van Tran, 1989).

Surveys in nonclinical samples, although important, say relatively little about the specific ways in which religion is involved in exacerbating or reducing emotional problems in clinically distressed individuals. Furthermore, Hill and Pargament (2003) have underscored the fact that most studies of religion and health (physical and mental) have employed some sort of global index of religious involvement, most notably, denominational affiliation or frequency of church attendance. By relying so heavily on global religion and spirituality indexes, researchers have underestimated the complex nature of religion and spirituality variables, and have overlooked the possibility that something inherent within the religious and spiritual experience itself contributes to or detracts from physical and mental health. To better understand what it is about religion that relates to mental health, we must consider religious coping, moving researchers from the abstract to the concrete to examine how people face life problems in their everyday lives.

Religion and spirituality for many people are overarching frameworks made up of established beliefs, practices, attitudes, goals, and values that orient them to the world, provide direction and meaning, and provide access to a wide array of religious coping strategies, such as spiritual support, meditation, appraisals, and rites of passage. Religious coping happens when events, goals, and the means used to reach them are actively interpreted in relation to the sacred (Pargament, 1997) and serves five main functions: finding meaning, gaining control, gaining comfort from and closeness to God, finding intimacy with others and life transformation. Pargament's (1997, 2007) religious coping model offers an in-depth, complex and dynamic picture of the role of religion in mental health and is one that has direct implications for clinical practice. Whereas dispositional religiousness denotes religious involvement in general, religious coping focuses on the ways in which patients specifically draw on religion in difficult situations (Pargament, 1997; Sherman & Simonton, 2001). As Pargament, Koenig, and Perez (2000) asserted: "It is not enough to know that the individual prays, attends church or watches religious television. Measures of religious coping should specify how the individual is making use of religion to understand and deal with stressors" (p. 521). Thus, an exploration of religious coping provides information about functional religious aspects that may be more or less distinct from dispositional religiousness. Several studies indicate that religious coping methods predict outcomes more strongly than global measures of religion (Loewenthal, MacLeod, Goldblatt, Lubitsh, & Valentine, 2000; Nooney & Woodrum, 2002; Roesch & Ano, 2003).

Religious coping methods can be classified into two broad overarching patterns: positive and negative religious coping (Pargament, Smith, Koenig, & Perez, 1998). Positive religious coping strategies, those that reflect a confident and constructive turning to religion for support, tend to be beneficial for people undergoing stressful life events: religious coping strategies—such as giving and receiving spiritual support, benevolent reappraisal of a stressful situation, and collaborative coping style—have been positively and persistently associated with desirable mental health outcomes (Ano & Vasconcelles, 2005; Koenig et al., 2001). In contrast, negative religious coping strategies, those involving religious struggle and doubt, are generally more maladaptive (Exline & Rose, 2005). Although studies in this area have been predominantly cross-sectional, the few longitudinal studies indicate that religious coping leads to some relatively long-lasting alterations in mental health (Ai, Dunkle, Peterson, & Bolling, 1998; Loewenthal et al., 2000).

Specifically in relation to depression, in a study of older, severely ill, medical patients, those who sought a connection with a benevolent God, as well as support from clergy and faith group members, were less depressed and rated their quality of life as higher, even after taking into account the severity of their illness (Koenig, Pargament, & Nielsen, 1998). Activities such as prayer and reading the Bible have been found to be prevalent in individuals with severe enduring mental illnesses, including those with major depressive illnesses, and may be associated with reduced symptoms (Rogers, Poey, Reger, Tepper, & Coleman, 2002; Tepper, Rogers, Coleman, & Malony, 2001). In a longitudinal study of elderly patients with depression, Bosworth, Park, McQuoid, Hays, and Steffens, (2003) found positive religious coping to be negatively associated with depression above and beyond social support, demographic variables and clinical variables.

In contrast, negative religious coping strategies, such as a deferring religious coping style, negative appraisals of an event and spiritual discontent are associated with an increased prevalence of depressive symptoms (Harrison, Koenig, Hays, Eme-Akwari, & Pargament, 2001). The literature suggests that depression has been associated with perceptions of sacred loss, spiritual self-degradation, and feelings of alienation from, punishment by, and anger toward God (Elkins, 1998; Exline, Yali, & Sanderson, 2000; Fitchett, Murphy, Kim, Gibbons, Cameron, & Davis, 2004; Pargament, Koenig, Tarakeshwar, & Hahn, 2004; Smith et al., 2003). There are fewer studies of anxiety and negative religious coping. Greater anxiety has been linked to spiritual confusion and doubt, an insecure relationship with God, spirituality and narrowness, as well as the perception of a God who expects perfection (Greenberg & Wiztum, 2001; Kooistra & Pargament, 1999; Nielsen et al., 2001). In one study of religious conflict in individuals with panic disorder, people suffered more from panic disorder if they felt more religious guilt and were more unable to meet religious expectations (Trenholm, Trent, & Compton, 1998).

As Pargament et al. (2004) speculated, it appears that those who are unable to solve their struggles over time are at greater risk of poorer mental and physical health, whereas people who experience these struggles temporarily do not face the same risk. The impact of religious struggles may also depend on their social acceptability. In religious groups in which such struggles are unacceptable, individuals may experience feelings of alienation and loneliness resulting in the development of depression. The effects of religious struggles are not always negative; in some instances, they may lead to deepened spirituality. "The dark night of the soul" is an expression describing phases in a person's spiritual life associated with a crisis of faith or spiritual concerns about the relationship with God, which have the potential to lead to spiritual growth.

Recent studies have noted that religious coping takes different forms in different religious groups and the relevance of different facets of religiousness to mental health might be influenced by doctrinal specific values (see Cohen & Hill, 2007; Exline, 2002; see also Volume 1, Chapters 25 and 37, this handbook). The study of religious coping has recently moved beyond the characteristic focus on Christianity to examine coping in Islam (see Abu-Raiya, Pargament, Mahoney, & Stein, 2008; see also Volume 1, Chapter 38, this handbook) and Hinduism (see Tarakeshwar, Pargament, & Mahoney, 2003; see also Volume 1, Chapter 36, this handbook). Within Judaism, specific beliefs such as God's benevolence and trust in God have been found to be important predictors of lower levels of anxiety and depression (Rosmarin, Pargament, Krumrei, & Flannelly, 2009; Rosmarin, Pargament, & Mahoney, 2009; Rosmarin, Pirutinsky, Pargament, & Krumrei, 2009).

CLINICAL IMPLICATIONS OF RELIGIOUS COPING IN DEPRESSION AND ANXIETY

Although many would argue that psychological therapy and religion should be separate entities, or in other words, "Priests should stay out of therapy and therapists should stay out of spirituality" (Prest & Keller, 1993, p. 139), I maintain that under certain circumstances clinicians may address religious or spiritual issues directly. Mental health professionals, however, need to exercise caution in addressing the spiritual needs of patients especially if advanced interventions are being considered (see Meador & Koenig, 2000, for a cogent discussion).

Despite the fact that empirical research has not so far provided conclusive evidence that interventions that integrate religious components are more effective than traditional psychological interventions, psychotherapists are beginning to incorporate spiritual and religious elements into their work with promising results. Some randomized trials have indicated that religious interventions among religious patients enhance recovery from anxiety and depression although the results may be short term (among Christians, see Propst, 1980; Propst, Ostrom, Watkins, Dean, & Mashburn, 1992; among Muslims, see Azhar & Varma, 1995; Razali, Aminah, & Khan, 2002; among Taoists, see Zhang et al., 2002). Smith, Bartz, and Richards (2007) reported a meta-analysis of 31 outcome studies of spiritual therapies (teaching spiritual principles, prayer, meditation, reading religious texts) conducted from 1984 to 2005, which provides some empirical evidence that spiritually oriented psychotherapy approaches may be beneficial to individuals with depression and anxiety. Prayer appears to be a helpful activity in improving depressive symptoms. In one study of depressed individuals, 33% felt that prayer improved their depressive symptomatology (Astin, Harkness, & Ernst, 2000).

In my clinical practice, I routinely inquire whether faith is important in a person's life. With their consent I gently encourage clients to express their spiritual perspectives on life, and we gradually focus on the role of spirituality in their illness and the ways that they deploy religiously based coping with the current illness and in past crises and on discrepancies between the two. In particular, I seek out religious strategies that they might draw on in their current situation and the ways that religious conflicts affect their illness experiences. Occasionally, clients enquire about my own spiritual perspective, and I will then disclose that I have a Jewish background. In some instances, I am willing to discuss my religious views, but only if I consider that this will be therapeutic and facilitate client choice. I do not attempt to impose a particular religious framework on my clients or to be judgmental. The spiritual issues that clients with depression and anxiety raise with me that tend to exacerbate their emotional distress can generally be divided into five types:

- Theodicy—why God has allowed them to become ill and associated anger.
- Feeling that God has deserted them.
- Feelings of guilt and beliefs about sin and punishment.
- Search for a miracle—too much emphasis on deferring coping. The deferral of responsibility for problem solving to God is not generally an effective method of coping because most problems warrant a certain degree of human action.
- Limited perspective on spirituality. What Pargament (2007) referred to as "small gods"—limited conceptualizations of the sacred that are not suited to the complexities of adult life.

I next discuss the ways in which religious and spiritual coping may exacerbate depression and anxiety and explore a number of spiritual strategies to address and replace maladaptive expressions of religion and spirituality with more helpful spiritual strategies to reduce depression and anxiety. These include prayer, benign spiritual reframing, gratitude, the use of religious texts, and referral to religious professionals drawing on strategies discussed in Nielsen et al. (2001), Pargament (2007), and C. Williams et al. (2002). Numerous other strategies are described in the literature. In relation to potentially maladaptive forms of coping, I deploy a standard two-step process of cognitive–behavioral therapy (CBT): identifying maladaptive cognitions and replacing these cognitions with more adaptive cognitions.

I frequently enquire about the content of clients' prayers to learn more about their perceptions of God, their expectations of God, and how prayer has helped with past crises. I sometimes encourage clients to pray as a way of providing hope and enhancing their coping, particularly with depression and anxiety. I recommend that clients explore which prayers are best suited to their needs. Although the efficacy of prayer in psychotherapy remains under-researched, one study has suggested that prayer among older adults may be useful for minor depression and subsyndromal anxiety (Rajagopal, Mackenzie, Bailey, & Lavizzo-Mourey, 2002).

At times I will ask clients to read religious texts as a way of illustrating certain points (e.g., inconsistencies between idiosyncratic religious beliefs and what is taught in religious texts), to reduce inflexibility, and to provide role models as to how they should treat themselves. Recommending books from the client's own tradition might help believers to recognize multiple levels of meaning with the possibility that truth can be found at each of these levels (Brown, 2000; Pargament, 2007).

From a Christian perspective, C. Williams et al. (2002) pointed out that two major problems in depression and anxiety are "false" guilt and low self-esteem. They recommended specific biblical readings that might ameliorate these experiences by focusing on God's love for humankind and his power of forgiveness. For example, they suggested Romans 5:6, 8 "For while we were still weak, at the right time Christ died for the ungodly . . . But God proves his love for us in that while we still were sinners Christ died for us." These verses exemplify the fact that we are forgiven through the atonement of Christ and that God loves us as we *are* rather than as how we *would like* to be. In addition, they point out the importance of reading Psalms that express a wide range of feelings, from elation to despair, from joy to sadness at sin. Typical examples include Psalm 13: praying for relief from despair; Psalm 4: God's protection and peace; and Psalm 139: God is always with us and knows us intimately.

Through spiritual reframing, I attempt to place negative life events in a larger, more meaningful and benign context. I find this technique useful in two situations. In those who have experienced adversity, I will attempt to reformulate the event as one of spiritual growth or increasing faith, by drawing on specific religious teachings and texts. For those who hold an excessively punitive image of God, religious reframing can help them adopt an image that is more benevolent and compassionate. Although empirical work on spiritual reframing is limited, there is some evidence that religious framing may help people to gain a sense of meaning and closure on traumatic situations (Exline, Gregory, Hockemeyer, Tulloch, & Smyth, 2005). One program among abused women utilizing prayer, writing exercises, and visualization facilitated a process of change from a harsh male-dominated image of God to one that was less punitive and more benevolent (Murray-Swank & Pargament, 2005).

I have found that getting clients to express their gratitude to God for the positive things in their life can help to elevate mood in those who are depressed. In many religious traditions, gratitude has been seen as integral to health and well-being. Although the effects of expressing gratitude on clinically depressed samples has not been formally examined, in one study, among undergraduate students, those who kept gratitude journals on a weekly basis exercised more regularly, reported fewer physical symptoms, felt better about their lives as a whole, and were more optimistic about the upcoming week compared with those who recorded hassles or neutral life events (Emmons & McCullough, 2003).

On occasion I will refer clients to clergy who are sympathetic to psychotherapy, especially if the presentation involves a degree of religious inflexibility, if conflicts arise during therapy that I do not feel confident to deal with, when religious issues are mixed with psychopathology and impede progress, or as a way of helping clients to enhance their religious coping. Unlike in pastoral counseling, I do not discuss religious truths or offer sacraments; rather, I help clients understand the ways in which spirituality affect their lives and how they can draw on spiritual resources in facilitating coping with life problems (see Chapter 11 in this volume).

Nielsen et al. (2001), in their discussion of the use of rational emotive therapy with religious clients, discussed the impact of absolutistic evaluations: Individuals with depression or anxiety often have unrealistic expectations regarding religious practices and hold that they "should," "must," or "ought to" be able to perform them. In my own practice, I emphasize the importance of setting realistic targets for bible reading or prayer: Excessive expectations may evoke a sense of failure, enhance guilt, and worsen mood.

I now present several case studies that exemplify (a) helping clients give up maladaptive forms of religiousness or spirituality that may cause or exacerbate depression or anxiety and (b) helping clients identify and use adaptive religious resources to cope effectively with depression and anxiety. Details have been changed to protect anonymity. Reflecting my caseload, these cases portray highly orthodox or conservative clients. I shall not discuss here "the lightly churched," or spiritual seekers who are uninvolved in or reject organized religion (for a number of such examples, see Pargament, 2007).

Case Example 3: A Sunni Muslim

Jasmin was a 30-year-old married woman with two young children. Born in Pakistan, she came to live in the United Kingdom at the age of 15 and had been a devout Muslim for all of her adult life. Her general practitioner referred her to my clinic because of marital problems, feelings of depression, and frequent suicidal ideation. She attended her first visit together with her sister and her youngest child Ahmad who was crying in the background. I remember being struck by the fact that Jasmin was almost silent when she first met me. Her sister did all the speaking until after about an hour when Jasmin spoke up. She recounted the following story.

She had a happy childhood in Pakistan and moved to the United Kingdom during adolescence with her family because of her father's job. Although she initially felt unsettled in London, she soon adapted and made some friends. At the age of 18 she entered an arranged marriage to her husband Mohammed, and this is when her problems started. Her husband was nearly 15 years older than her. She quickly found that he held a very traditional attitude toward women. He was very controlling and critical toward her and was extremely reluctant to allow her to go out of the house by herself. This fact caused immense friction between the couple and soon she felt trapped. At times, she stated, he became very angry toward her, and although she was reluctant to discuss this, he had hit her on several occasions. She felt ashamed and guilty that she could not be a perfect wife, for this is what she felt Islam expected of her.

She attended the mosque and regularly prayed to Allah. I enquired about the content of her prayers. Predominantly, they had focused on asking God to make her husband more accepting toward her and that he should change his personality. She felt unable to discuss her marital distress with her husband and hoped that God would miraculously change their relationship. She stated on several occasions that what Allah did, he did for the best. Her trust in God meant that it was not necessary for her to try anything else and she was extremely reluctant to engage in any form of counseling with her spouse. Furthermore, she maintained that divorce was sinful in Islam and that Allah did not favor divorce and encouraged the continuation of marriage at any costs.

Following advice from an imam, I explained that from a Muslim perspective even though Allah was held to be in control of everything, individuals were still expected to seek help for their problems and that it was acceptable from an Islamic perspective to undergo couple counseling. After several sessions of individual therapy her confidence increased, and she was finally able to confront her husband about their relationship. An imam in her Mosque arranged to meet with the couple to discuss their marriage.

There were two aspects of this case that concerned me. First, I believed that her coping style of deferring responsibility to God was not helping the problem or was even exacerbating it. Through therapy, I attempted to give her a sense of agency in her life. Second, she had a limited understanding of the rights of women in Islam. I attempted to facilitate a process by which she could come to understand that humans have a responsibility to take some action in the world to change their lives and not to defer all responsibility to God and to help her understand that Islam teaches the importance of mutual respect in marriage.

Case Example 4: An Evangelical Christian

Alison, a 32-year-old Evangelical Christian woman of Irish descent, was referred to me with a long history of recurrent depressive illness associated with persecutory delusions. She lived with her grandfather and her 10-year-old son and had not worked for a number of years. She was a rather overweight woman with dyed red hair, tattoos on her arms, and lesbian fantasies, and I first met her while she was a psychiatric inpatient partly because of her perception that a fight was going on in her mind between herself and the Devil. These cognitions never reached the stage at which she believed that the Devil had actually overtaken her, but they caused her immense anxiety, and on several occasions, she cut herself to obtain emotional relief. For a period of time, she was so agitated that she required high doses of antipsychotic medication to calm her, and for most of this time, I was unable to initiate any meaningful discussion with her.

It was only when she was in the recovery phase that I was able to discuss spiritual issues with her. A number of factors appeared to exacerbate her depressive illness. First, although she had attended church regularly when well, during her illness her attendance ceased because she thought that members of her congregation were judging her critically. She began to feel guilty and maintained that she had let God down, subsequently intensifying her depressive feelings. Second, she attributed her illness to the fact that her religious participation had lapsed, thus allowing the Devil to influence her. Finally she considered her attraction to women to be sinful in the eyes of God, and as a result, she experienced extreme guilt feelings. She had never come to terms with her sexual orientation.

My psychotherapeutic work concentrated on two themes: the demonic conflict and her feelings of having let God down. When she was severely depressed, I considered it too dangerous to broach these issues because any mention of religious themes to her appeared to exacerbate her feelings of agitation and the possibility of self-harm. Over several months, I came to recognize that this demonic conflict represented a chronic "war" between the good and evil parts of herself that intensified during her illness and to which she gave a religious label. Since adolescence she had felt self-hatred in part for having sexual feelings toward women; this self-hatred was personified during her depressive experience as a demonic influence.

I addressed her fears that she had let God down in the following way. First I asked her what God had expected of her. She replied that as a Christian it was "sinful" to become depressed. In response I asked her to how she came to believe that the Bible says depression was related to sin. She was unable to find direct evidence of such a belief in the Bible, and I told her that my understanding was that her belief was not based on standard biblical doctrine. Furthermore, I explained that in both the Old and the New Testaments there were well-known individuals who had at some time let God down and that the classic Christian stance is that no one was free from sin except Christ. She seemed reassured by this. I asked her to read C. Williams et al.'s (2002) *I'm Not Supposed to Feel Like This: A Christian Approach to*

Depression and Anxiety, which offers one contemporary Christian perspective of depression that supported these revisions to her spiritual beliefs. I encouraged her to pray that God would protect her because she herself held that God's presence would "keep the Devil away." There is some evidence that prayer might be useful in helping clients deal with their demonic struggles (Jacobson, 2003). Finally, I attempted to change her illness attribution away from one emphasizing sin and demonic influence to one that focused on biochemical changes in her brain. Although I did not directly address her issues concerning sexual orientation, there are theologically grounded resources available to educate people about progressive or liberal Christian theological systems of belief that frame human sexuality differently from the traditional Christian perspective (see Volume 1, Chapter 34, this handbook).

According to Alison, her pastor largely reinforced much of what we had discussed in therapy. He emphasized that Jesus loved her and was with her in her suffering. He encouraged her to read the Lord's Prayer with him and gave her daily readings from the New Testament recounting Jesus's healing powers, including Luke 6:19: "And the whole multitude sought to touch Him: for there went virtue out of Him, and healed them all." She slowly resumed her religious attendance, although for many months she found this anxiety provoking. After her illness remitted, she came to see her religious community as actually having been very supportive during her illness.

This case study illustrates a number of points. When clients are seriously depressed, they may not be receptive to spiritual interventions that, at times, may exacerbate symptoms. Second, it is important to explore ideas about demonic influence in some detail and to attempt to facilitate understanding from the client's perspective. Referral to clergy is often necessary for additional help, such as deliverance, if the individual holds that the devil has possessed them. Third, her feelings of having let God down exacerbated her experience of depression. For Christians, pointing out that no one is without sin apart from Christ can be a useful therapeutic intervention, and this can be reinforced through bibliotherapy. Finally, clients may be helped through a process of reattribution, and clinicians need to be able to integrate biomedical and spiritual attributions of her illness. C. Williams et al. (2002) noted that depression could be viewed in the church in many ways, including a lack of faith, sin, or as a result of demonic activity. These authors posited that although there are always spiritual aspects to anxiety and depression for Christians, these are a secondary consequence of the emotional distress that derives from depression. Thus, strong claims that all depression is spiritual in origin are unhelpful because they overlook the biological factors that contribute to anxiety and depression.

In a recent study of Pentecostal Christians, Trice and Bjorck (2006) found that although Pentecostalists attributed depression to demonic oppression or spiritual failures, many other explanations were endorsed, including relational problems, financial problems, and biological factors. Religious clients may be willing to explore multiple and alternative explanations for their illness as long as their spiritual beliefs are respected.

Case Example 5: A Hasidic Jew

Hasidism is a branch of Orthodox Judaism that promotes spirituality and joy through the popularization and internalization of Jewish mysticism as the fundamental aspects of the Jewish faith. Among Hasidic Jews depression is generally seen in a negative light. The founder of Hasidism, the Ba'al Shem Tov, taught that joy was very important in having a good relationship with God; depression was something that was negative and altered the communication that is needed between Jews and the Creator. Lubavitcher Hasidim depend on their key text titled *Tanya*, a compilation of moral philosophy and metaphysical foundations, for spiritual guidance. *Tanya* states, "Despondency is out of place . . . a stumbling block in the service of God" (see *Tanya*, 1952, Chapter 25 cited in Mindel, 1998, pp. 42–43). This text offers a number of strategies for dealing with poor mood: encouraging *bitachon* (trust in divine providence that all will be good), optimism, and a spiritual perspective on worldly troubles. The efficacy of many of these strategies are now beginning to be empirically supported. For example, among a large Jewish community sample, Rosmarin, Pargament, and Mahoney (2009) found that trust in God was associated with decreased levels of worry, stress, anxiety and depression, and increased levels of happiness. Mistrust in God was associated with increased levels of worry, stress, anxiety and depression, and decreased happiness. Blind trust without any room for doubt, however, may potentially be problematic.

Helen was a 45-year-old woman whom I visited at home. She was a member of Lubavitch and lived with her husband and six children. Brought up as a nonobservant Jew she adopted a more orthodox religious stance after encountering Lubavitchers at a Passover seder. She consulted me about a long history of anxiety and depression, which at times had made her feel suicidal. Her panic attacks were so intense that much of the time she was unable to go out of the house. On my first visit she expressed extreme concern about seeing a psychiatrist. Within her community, as she explained, a history of mental illness was highly stigmatized and negatively affected marriage prospects for her children. Furthermore, she considered psychologists and psychiatrists to generally be irreligious and therefore they would not understand her religious views. As Loewenthal (2006) discussed, there is a generalized mistrust of psychotherapy and psychiatry among Hasidim deriving from a conflict between traditional religious values and secular knowledge.

Initially, Helen was preoccupied with the fact that she had let God down by being depressed. After all, he had created the world and there was much for which she should be joyful. I encouraged her to move away from this cognition and instead focused on her perceptions of God as a healer. She recounted that God had indeed helped her cope with anxiety in the past and I therefore recommended that she pray to God for help with her anxiety. I discussed how she might thank God for the good things in her life, a strategy that she found particularly helpful and is consistent with the literature suggesting inverse relationships between depression and gratitude (Emmons & McCullough, 2004; see also Volume 1, Chapters 23 and 25, this handbook).

As is usual among members of this community, she wrote to the Lubavitcher Rebbe who stated the importance of being joyful and asked that she check her *mezuzot* (a small case in which a handwritten scroll of parchment is placed that is usually fastened to the door frame of one's home). Additionally, he emphasized the importance of affirming trust and faith in God, the value of repeating or studying passages that affirmed this, and the significance of improving spiritually. She found prayers related to God's benevolent support to be helpful alongside the recitation of *tehillim* (psalms). Helen's perceived failure to fulfill religious expectations appeared to exacerbate her experience of depression. Changing her focus onto the positive attributes of God, gratitude, appeal to her Rebbe for constructive support, and the use of prayer and psalms proved particularly helpful in raising her mood.

HOW DEPRESSION AND ANXIETY AFFECT RELIGIOUS AND SPIRITUAL LIVES

Although the literature has predominantly focused on the effects of both positive and negative forms religiousness on mental health, some recent attention has been paid to the impact of psychopathology on religious and spiritual functioning because of growing evidence that religious functioning is an important adaptive domain in its own right. Functionally, religious and spiritual thought and practice are related to the sense of meaning in life, maintaining a sense of purpose and hope, coping with life's difficulties, and dealing with one's own mortality. Substantively, people around the globe value the search for the sacred for its own sake and value mystical experience or a felt connection to God and spiritual insights beyond any psychosocial benefits this journey provides. Therefore, clinicians should routinely consider any possible ways that depression or anxiety may create clinically significant impairments in religious patient's lives (Hathaway, 2003; see Chapter 5 in this volume). For instance, people with depression may have ruminations of past transgressions and lose their sense of connection with their higher power or feel eternally damned (Hathaway, Scott, & Garver, 2004). Aggressive treatment of depression and anxiety may be required to restore religious functioning to the previous level.

IMPLICATIONS FOR MENTAL HEALTH PROFESSIONALS

I have discussed how I work with religious issues in my own clinical practice. What can mental health professionals learn from this to become more receptive and effective in dealing with spiritual issues and concerns? Paramount in working with religious and spiritual issues among clients with depression and anxiety is having sufficient spiritual literacy, not just in terms of the core beliefs and experiences of the different religious traditions but also in terms of knowing how to readily access spiritual resources and address spiritual problems. There is a need for mental health professionals to be aware of their own values and biases and of the limitations in their knowledge that might necessitate referral to religious professionals. I propose that working with spiritual concerns involves a number of elements.

First, professionals need to learn how to perform a spiritual assessment. The purpose of the spiritual assessment is to understand a client's spiritual experiences and spiritual orientation and how these affect their illness. Ask useful probing questions such as, "Is religion or spirituality important in your life? In what ways?" Although I do not routinely employ assessment tools in my clinical practice, there are many described in the literature (see Chapter 5 in this volume).

Second, there is a need to learn how to differentiate spiritual experience from psychopathology. The spiritual journey is sometimes associated with unusual and troubling spiritual experiences, and clinicians are faced with the prospects of differentiating such spiritual experiences from major psychopathology (see Dein, 2004; Greenberg & Wiztum, 2001; see also Chapter 4 in this volume).

Third, practitioners must be aware of the significance of positive and negative religious coping on their client's lives and how they can work with these in therapy. In relation to negative religious coping, they need to learn to recognize "red flags" in religious coping and their impact on the experience of anxiety and depression. Conversely, they must also learn how they can facilitate their clients' positive religious coping strategies.

Finally, effective work with religious issues among religious clients calls for close reciprocal working relationships between mental health professionals and clergy. Just as mental health professionals need to be informed about the role of spirituality in their clients' lives, so too do religious professionals need to be educated about mental health issues.

References

Abu-Raiya, H., Pargament, K. I., Mahoney, A., & Stein, C. (2008). A psychological measure of Islamic religiousness: Development and evidence for reliability and validity. *The International Journal for the Psychology of Religion*, *18*, 291–315. doi:10.1080/105086 10802229270

Ai, A. L., Dunkle, R. E., Peterson, C., & Bolling, S. F. (1998). The role of private prayer in psychological recovery among midlife and aged patients following cardiac surgery. *The Gerontologist, 38*, 591–601. doi:10.1093/geront/38.5.591

Ano, G. G., & Vasconcelles, E. B. (2005). Religious coping and psychological adjustment to stress: A meta-analysis. *Journal of Clinical Psychology, 61*, 461–480. doi:10.1002/jclp.20049

Astin, J. A., Harkness, E. F., & Ernst, E. (2000). The efficacy of "distant healing": A systematic review of randomized trials. *Annals of Internal Medicine, 132*, 903–910.

Azhar, M. Z., & Varma, S. L. (1995). Religious psychotherapy in depressive patients. *Psychotherapy and Psychosomatics, 63*, 165–168. doi:10.1159/000288954

Bergin, A. E., & Payne, I. R. (1991). Proposed agenda for a spiritual strategy in personality and psychotherapy. *Journal of Psychology and Christianity, 10*, 197–210.

Bosworth, H. B., Park, K. S., McQuoid, D. R., Hays, J. C., & Steffens, D. C. (2003). The impact of religious practice and religious coping on geriatric depression. *International Journal of Geriatric Psychiatry, 18*, 905–914. doi:10.1002/gps.945

Brown, M. (2000). *What they don't tell you: A survivor's guide to biblical studies*. Louisville, KY: Westminster John Knox Press.

Cohen, A. B., & Hill, P. C. (2007). Religion as culture: Religious individualism and collectivism among American Catholics, Jews, and Protestants. *Journal of Personality, 75*, 709–742. doi:10.1111/j.1467-6494.2007.00454.x

Dein, S. (2004). Working with patients with religious beliefs. *Advances in Psychiatric Treatment, 10*, 287–294. doi:10.1192/apt.10.4.287

Elkins, D. N. (1998). *Beyond religion: 8 alternative paths to the sacred*. Wheaton, IL: Quest Books.

Emmons, R. A., & McCullough, M. E. (2003). Counting blessings versus burdens: Experimental studies of gratitude and subjective well-being. *Journal of Personality and Social Psychology, 84*, 377–389.

Emmons, R. A., & McCullough, M. E. (2004). *The psychology of gratitude*. New York, NY: Oxford University Press. doi:10.1093/acprof:oso/9780195150100.001.0001

Exline, J. J. (2002). The picture is getting clearer, but is the scope too limited? Three overlooked questions in the psychology of religion. *Psychological Inquiry, 13*, 245–247. doi:10.1207/S15327965PLI1303_07

Exline, J. J., Gregory, J., Hockemeyer, J., Tulloch, H., & Smyth, J. M. (2005). Religious framing by PTSD patients when writing about traumatic experiences. *The International Journal for the Psychology of Religion, 15*, 17–33. doi:10.1207/s15327582ijpr1501_2

Exline, J. J., & Rose, E. (2005). Religious and spiritual struggles. In R. F. Paloutzian, and C. L. Park, C. L. (Eds.), *Handbook of the psychology of religion and spirituality* (pp. 315–330). New York, NY: Guilford Press.

Exline, J. J., Yali, A. M., & Sanderson, W. C. (2000). Guilt, discord, and alienation: The role of religious strain in depression and suicidality. *Journal of Clinical Psychology, 56*, 1481–1496. doi:10.1002/1097-4679(200012)56:12<1481::AID-1>3.0.CO;2-A

Fitchett, G., Murphy, P. E., Kim, J., Gibbons, J. L., Cameron, J. R., & Davis, J. A. (2004). Religious struggle: Prevalence, correlates and mental health risks in diabetic, congestive heart failure, and oncology patients. *International Journal of Psychiatry in Medicine, 34*, 179–196. doi:10.2190/UCJ9-DP4M-9C0X-835M

Greenberg, D., & Wiztum, E. (2001). *Sanity and sanctity: Mental health work among the Ultra Orthodox in Jerusalem*. New Haven, CT: Yale University Press.

Harrison, M. O., Koenig, H. G., Hays, J. C., Eme-Akwari, A. G., & Pargament, K. I. (2001). The epidemiology of religious coping: A review of recent literature. *International Review of Psychiatry, 13*, 86–93. doi:10.1080/09540260120037317

Hathaway, W. (2003). Clinically significant religious impairment. *Mental Health, Religion, and Culture, 6*, 113–129. doi:10.1080/1367467021000038174

Hathaway, W. L., Scott, S. Y., & Garver, S. A. (2004). Assessing religious/spiritual functioning: A neglected domain in clinical practice? *Professional Psychology: Research and Practice, 35*, 97–104. doi:10.1037/0735-7028.35.1.97

Hill, P. C., & Pargament, K. I. (2003). Advances in the conceptualization and measurement of religion and spirituality: Implications for physical and mental health research. *American Psychologist, 58*, 64–74. doi:10.1037/0003-066X.58.1.64

Jacobson, C. J., Jr. (2003). "Espiritus? No. Pero la malad existe": Supernaturalism, religious change and the problem of evil in Puerto Rican folk religion. *Ethics, 31*, 1–30.

Koenig, H. G., Ford, S. M., George, L. K., Blazer, D. G., & Meador, K. G. (1993). Religion and anxiety disorder: An examination and comparison of associations in young, middle-aged and elderly adults. *Journal of Anxiety Disorders, 7*, 321–342. doi:10.1016/0887-6185(93)90028-J

Koenig, H. G., McCullough, M. E., & Larson, D. B. (2001). *Handbook of religion and health*. New York, NY: Oxford University Press. doi:10.1093/acprof:oso/9780195118667.001.0001

Koenig, H. G., Pargament, K. I., & Nielsen, J. (1998). Religious coping and mental health outcomes in medically ill hospitalized older adults. *Journal of Nervous and Mental Disease, 186*, 513–521. doi:10.1097/00005053-199809000-00001

Kooistra, W. P., & Pargament, K. I. (1999). Religious doubting in parochial school adolescents. *Journal of Psychology and Theology, 27*, 33–42.

Krause, N., & Van Tran, T. (1989). Stress and religious involvement among older Blacks. *The Journals of Gerontology, Series B: Psychological Sciences and Social Sciences, 44*, S4–S13.

Lindgren, K. N., & Coursey, R. D. (1995). Spirituality and serious mental illness: A two-part study. *Psychosocial Rehabilitation Journal, 18*(3), 93–111.

Loewenthal, K. (2006). Strictly orthodox Jews and their relations with psychotherapy and psychiatry. *WCPRR, July/Oct*, 128–132.

Loewenthal, K., MacLeod, A. K., Goldblatt, V., Lubitsh, G., & Valentine, J. D. (2000). Comfort and joy? Religion, cognition and mood in Protestants and Jews under stress. *Cognition and Emotion, 14*, 355–374. doi:10.1080/026999300378879

McCullough, M. E., & Larson, D. B. (1999). Religion and depression: A review of the literature. *Twin Research*, 2, 126–136. doi:10.1375/136905299320565997

Meador, K. G., & Koenig, H. G. (2000). Spirituality and religion in psychiatric practice: Parameters and implications. *Psychiatric Annals, 30*, 549–555.

Mindel, N. (1998). *The philosophy of Chabad: Rabbi Schneur Zalman of Liadi.* New York, NY: Kehot Publications Society.

Murray-Swank, N. A., & Pargament, K. I. (2005). God, where are you? Evaluating a spiritually-integrated intervention for sexual abuse. *Mental Health, Religion, and Culture, 8*, 191–203. doi:10.1080/13694670500138866

Nielsen, S., Johnson, W., & Ellis, A. (2001). *Counseling and psychotherapy with religious persons: A rational emotive behaviour therapy approach.* Mahwah, NJ: Erlbaum.

Nooney, J., & Woodrum, E. (2002). Religious coping and church-based social support as predictors of mental health outcomes: Testing a conceptual model. *Journal for the Scientific Study of Religion, 41*, 359–368. doi:10.1111/1468-5906.00122

Pargament, K. I. (1997). *The psychology of religion and coping: Theory, research, practice.* New York, NY: Guilford Press.

Pargament, K. I. (2007). *Spiritually integrated psychotherapy: Understanding and addressing the sacred.* New York, NY: Guilford Press.

Pargament, K. I., Koenig, H. G., & Perez, L. M. (2000). The many methods of religious coping: Development and initial validation of the RCOPE. *Journal of Clinical Psychology, 56*, 519–543. doi:10.1002/(SICI)1097-4679(200004)56:4<519::AID-JCLP6>3.0.CO;2-1

Pargament, K. I., Koenig, H. G., Tarakeshwar, N., & Hahn, J. (2004). Religious coping methods as predictors of psychological, physical and spiritual outcomes among medically ill elderly patients: A two-year longitudinal study. *Journal of Health Psychology, 9*, 713–730. doi:10.1177/1359105304045366

Pargament, K. I., Smith, B. W., Koenig, H. G., & Perez, L. (1998). Patterns of positive and negative religious coping with major life stressors. *Journal for the Scientific Study of Religion, 37*, 710–724. doi:10.2307/1388152

Prest, L. A., & Keller, J. F. (1993). Spirituality and family therapy: Spiritual beliefs, myths, and metaphors. *Journal of Marital and Family Therapy, 19*, 137–148. doi:10.1111/j.1752-0606.1993.tb00973.x

Propst, R. L. (1980). The comparative efficacy of religious and nonreligious imagery for the treatment of mild depression in religious individuals. *Cognitive Therapy and Research, 4*, 167–178. doi:10.1007/BF01173648

Propst, L. R., Ostrom, R., Watkins, P., Dean, T., & Mashburn, D. (1992). Comparative efficacy of religious and nonreligious cognitive–behavioral therapy for the treatment of clinical depression in religious individuals. *Journal of Consulting and Clinical Psychology, 60*, 94–103. doi:10.1037/0022-006X.60.1.94

Rajagopal, D., Mackenzie, E., Bailey, C., & Lavizzo-Mourey, R. (2002). The effectiveness of a spiritually-based intervention to alleviate subsyndromal anxiety and minor depression among older adults. *Journal of Religion and Health, 41*, 153–166. doi:10.1023/A:1015854226937

Rasic, D. T., Belic, S. L., Elias, B., Katz, L. Y., Enns, M., & Sareen, J. (2008). Swampy Cree Suicide Prevention Team. Spirituality, religion, and suicidal behavior in a nationally representative sample. *Journal of Affective Disorders, 114*, 32–40. doi:10.1016/j.jad.2008.08.007

Razali, S. M., Aminah, K., & Khan, U. A. (2002). Religious-cultural psychotherapy in the management of anxiety patients. *Transcultural Psychiatry, 39*, 130–136. doi:10.1177/136346150203900106

Roesch, S. C., & Ano, G. (2003). Testing an attribution and coping model of stress: Religion as an orienting system. *Journal of Psychology and Christianity, 22*, 197–209.

Rogers, S. A., Poey, E. L., Reger, G. M., Tepper, L., & Coleman, E. M. (2002). Religious coping among those with persistent mental illness. *The International Journal for the Psychology of Religion, 12*, 161–175. doi:10.1207/S15327582IJPR1203_03

Rose, E. M., Westfeld, J. S., & Ansley, T. N. (2001). Spiritual issues in counseling: Clients' beliefs and preferences. *Journal of Counseling Psychology, 48*, 61–71. doi:10.1037/0022-0167.48.1.61

Rosmarin, D. H., Pargament, K. I., Krumrei, E. J., & Flannelly, K. J. (2009). Religious coping among Jews: Development and initial validation of the

JCOPE. *Journal of Clinical Psychology*, *65*, 670–683. doi:10.1002/jclp.20574

Rosmarin, D. H., Pargament, K. I., & Mahoney, A. (2009). The role of religiousness in anxiety, depression and happiness in a Jewish community sample: A preliminary investigation. *Mental Health, Religion, and Culture*, *12*, 97–113. doi:10.1080/13674670802321933

Rosmarin, D. H., Pirutinsky, S., Pargament, K. I., & Krumrei, E. J. (2009). Are religious beliefs relevant to mental health among Jews? *Psychology of Religion and Spirituality*, *1*, 180–190. doi:10.1037/a0016728

Schulte, D. L., Skinner, T. A., & Claiborn, C. D. (2002). Religious and spiritual issues in counseling psychology training. *The Counseling Psychologist, 30*, 118–134. doi:10.1177/0011000002301009

Sherman, A. C., & Simonton, S. (2001). Assessment of religiousness and spirituality in health research. In T. G. Plante & A. C. Sherman (Eds.), *Faith and health: Psychological perspectives* (pp. 139–163). New York, NY: Guilford Press.

Smith, T. B., Bartz, J., & Richards, P. S. (2007). Outcomes of religious and spiritual adaptations to psychotherapy: A meta-analytic review. *Psychotherapy Research, 17*, 643–655. doi:10.1080/10503300701250347

Smith, T. B., McCullough, M. E., & Poll, J. (2003). Religiousness and depression: Evidence for a main effect and the moderating influence of stressful life events. *Psychological Bulletin*, *129*, 614–636. doi:10.1037/0033-2909.129.4.614

Tapanya, S., Nicki, R., & Jarusawad, O. (1997). Worry and intrinsic/extrinsic religious orientation among Buddhist (Thai) and Christian (Canadian) elderly persons. *International Journal of Aging and Human Development, 44*, 73–83.

Tarakeshwar, N., Pargament, K. I., & Mahoney, A. (2003). Measures of Hindu pathways: Development and preliminary evidence of reliability and validity. *Cultural Diversity and Ethnic Minority Psychology, 9*, 316–332. doi:10.1037/1099-9809.9.4.316

Tepper, L., Rogers, S. A., Coleman, E. M., & Malony, H. N. (2001). The prevalence of religious coping among persons with persistent mental illness. *Psychiatric Services, 52*, 660–665. doi:10.1176/appi.ps.52.5.660

Tillich, P. (1952). *The courage to be.* New Haven, CT: Yale University Press.

Trenholm, P., Trent, J., & Compton, W. (1998). Negative religious conflict as a predictor of panic disorder. *Journal of Clinical Psychology, 54*, 59–65. doi:10.1002/(SICI)1097-4679(199801)54:1<59::AID-JCLP7>3.0.CO;2-P

Trice, P. D., & Bjorck, J. P. (2006). Pentecostal perspectives on causes and cures of depression. *Professional Psychology: Research and Practice, 37*, 283–294. doi:10.1037/0735-7028.37.3.283

Williams, C., Richards, P., & Whitton, I. (2002). *I'm not supposed to feel like this: A Christian self-help approach to depression and anxiety*. London, England: Hodder & Stoughton.

Williams, D. R., Larson, D. B., Buckler, R. E., Heckmann, R. C., & Pyle, C. M. (1991). Religion and psychological distress in a community sample. *Social Science and Medicine, 32*, 1257–1262. doi:10.1016/0277-9536(91)90040-J

Zhang, Y., Young, D., Lee, S., Li, L., Zhang, H., Xiao, Z., . . . Chang, D. F. (2002). Chinese Taoist cognitive psychotherapy in the treatment of generalized anxiety disorder in contemporary China. *Transcultural Psychiatry*, *39*, 115–129. doi:10.1177/1363461 50203900105

CHAPTER 13

RELIGION, SPIRITUALITY, AND SEVERE MENTAL DISORDER: FROM RESEARCH TO CLINICAL PRACTICE

Sylvia Mohr

According to the National Institute of Mental Health (NIMH), severe mental illnesses (SMI) are mental, behavioral, or emotional disorders (excluding developmental and substance uses disorders) of sufficient duration to meet diagnostic criteria specified within the *Diagnostic and Statistical Manual of Mental Disorders* (4th ed., text revision; *DSM–IV–TR*; American Psychiatric Association, 2000), resulting in serious functional impairment, which substantially interferes with one or more major life activities. The overall prevalence of SMI among U.S. adults in 2008 was 4.5% (U.S. Substance Abuse and Mental Health Services Administration, 2011). In addition to the personal impacts of these disorders, there are significant costs to society. To illustrate, during the year 2002, estimated costs of SMI totaled $317.6 billion, including direct costs of care, such as medication, clinic visits, or hospitalization (32%); indirect costs of disability benefits (8%); and loss of earning (60%). Those costs are in fact underestimated, as costs associated with comorbid physical conditions, incarceration, and homelessness were not taken into account (Insel, 2008). Furthermore, not only are such disorders acute but also the course of these illnesses is often persistent, leading to longstanding individual and societal impacts. When applying an expanded definition of SMI that includes a duration of psychiatric care of 2 years, psychotic disorders represent more than half of all patients (Parabiaghi, Bonetto, Ruggeri, Lasalvia, & Leese, 2006). The impact is striking, considering that lifetime prevalence of psychotic disorders exceeds 3% (Perala et al., 2007) and the 1-year prevalence rate of schizophrenia is about 1% in the United States (Narrow, Rae, Robins, & Regier, 2002). In restricting the definition of SMI to psychotic disorders, such as schizophrenia and bipolar disorders, it is important to note that treatment of these disorders is further complicated by other coexisting conditions—for example, 21% of people with SMI also have a diagnosis of substance abuse or dependence (Buckley & Brown, 2006). Such prevalence, the devastating personal and familial impacts, and the economic burden of SMIs underline the necessity of providing effective mental health care for those patients. Are religion and spirituality (R/S) relevant to that end?

DIAGNOSIS AND TREATMENT OF SEVERE MENTAL DISORDER

According to the *DSM–IV–TR* (American Psychiatric Association, 2000), psychosis is defined by reality distortion (delusions and hallucinations) and severe disorganization (disorganized speech). Characteristic symptoms of schizophrenia also include grossly abnormal psychomotor behavior and negatives symptoms (i.e., restricted affect, or avolition and asociality). To establish the diagnosis of schizophrenia two (or more) of those symptoms have to be present for a significant portion of time associated with the disturbance and have to persist for at least 6 months in one or more major areas of functioning, such as learning, work, interpersonal relations, self-care, and living skills. The proposed revision to be included in *DSM–V* (American Psychiatric Association, 2011) introduces a major change of important clinical value, that is, assessment of severity on the

DOI: 10.1037/14046-013
APA Handbook of Psychology, Religion, and Spirituality: Vol. 2. An Applied Psychology of Religion and Spirituality, K. I. Pargament (Editor-in-Chief)

basis of the past month in the psychopathological domains of hallucinations, delusions, disorganization, abnormal psychomotor behavior, restricted emotional expression, avolition, impaired cognition, depression, and mania. Although this disorder is marked by great heterogeneity across individuals and variability within individuals over time, certain clinical trends have been reliably observed—for example, the onset of schizophrenia typically occurs during early adulthood and is often associated with substance misuse (33%), suicide attempts (40%), and suicide (10%; Herz et al., 2000).

In recent years, the World Psychiatric Association, especially sensitive to cultural factors, introduced the concept of "Psychiatry for the Person," which involves a person-centered diagnosis of disorders and helps to provide a treatment in accordance with the needs and values of the person in his or her context (Mezzich, 2007). Such a diagnosis includes both illness aspects (clinical disorders, disabilities, and risk factors) and positive health status features (remission or recovery, functioning, and protective factors). In the diagnostic process, the personal narrative of the illness experience (including topics such as suffering, values, and the cultural context of illness and care) and of the experience of health (including topics such as quality of life, values, and cultural formulation of identity and context) are central (Salloum & Mezzich, 2011). This approach shifts the mental health professional's focus from treating mental illness to caring for people who manage their mental illness.

In this context, *recovery* has been recognized as an organizing principle for the systems of psychiatric services (Sowers, 2005). Psychological recovery differs from cure, which means a return to a previous level of health and functioning after illness. Recovery is a process of change and growth, highly personal, and ongoing throughout the person's life. A stage model of psychological recovery based on qualitative studies identified five phases: (a) moratorium (withdrawal, hopelessness, and a negative sense of identity), (b) awareness (hope and an awareness of intact aspects of the self), (c) preparation (the examination of core values and the implementation of internal and external resources), (d) rebuilding (taking steps toward meaningful goals), and (e) growth (living a fulfilling life and looking toward a positive future; Andresen, Oades, & Caputi, 2003). Psychological recovery is indicated by the development of a fulfilling life and a positive sense of identity founded on hopefulness and self-determination, beyond the disability.

Practice guidelines for the treatment of patients with schizophrenia are based on the recovery construct and are marked by the following qualities: self-direction, individualized and person-centered, empowerment, holism, nonlinearity, strengths-oriented, peer support, respect, responsibility, and hope. Treatment includes pharmacotherapy (antipsychotic medications) and psychosocial treatments to help these patients deal with the everyday challenges of the illness, such as difficulty with communication, self-care, work, and forming and keeping relationships. Psychosocial treatments include family psychoeducation, assertive community treatment, supported employment, cognitive–behavioral therapy, social skills training, cognitive remediation, peer support and peer-delivered services, weight management, and integrated treatment for substance use disorders (NIMH, 2009). This model of treatment takes into account biological, social, and psychological factors but not explicitly religion or spirituality (R/S), although in some local mental health systems, R/S has been included.

Many of the first mental hospitals were created by religious institutions. Religion was believed to have a positive influence on patients. Then, influenced by prestigious psychiatrists and psychologists, such as Freud (1927/1971) and Ellis (1980), mental health professionals tended to pathologize the R/S dimensions of life. As a consequence, R/S issues were neglected over several decades in research and training of psychiatrists and psychologists. The neglect of R/S issues in psychiatry and psychology may also have been influenced by the underrepresentation of religiously involved mental health professionals in these fields. Indeed, they are less involved in R/S than the general population, both in North America and in Europe (Borras et al., 2010; Neeleman & King, 1993; Shafranske, 1996; see also Chapter 2 in this volume). A growing body of scientific research, however, suggests that religion may be resources for health, and this research has prompted a shift in the attitude toward religion in the mental health field, as illustrated by more frequent inclusion of training in R/S for psychiatrists and psychologists (Brawer, Handal, Shafer, & Ubinger, 2002).

DELUSIONS AND HALLUCINATIONS WITH RELIGIOUS CONTENT

For many years, studies of religion and schizophrenia mainly focused on religious delusions and hallucinations with religious content because these symptoms may lead to violent behavior. For example, homicides have been perpetrated by patients who featured religious delusions (Kraya & Patrick, 1997), religiously deluded people have taken statements literally in the Bible as a prod to pluck out offending eyes or cut off offending body parts (Field & Waldfogel, 1995; Waugh, 1986), and anti-Christ delusions have led to violent behaviors toward others (Silva, Leong, & Weinstock, 1997) or suicide (Reeves & Liberto, 2006). A number of factors, including the role of culture, contribute to the manifestation of these symptoms involving religious content. The prevalence of delusions and hallucinations with religious content varies between cultures as well as varies over time. Some studies compared the prevalence of religious delusions among different populations (Azhar, Varma, & Hakim, 1995; Kim et al., 2001; Ndetei & Vadher, 1984; Suhail, 2003). The prevalence rate for inpatients with religious delusions varied from 6% in Pakistan and 7% in Japan to 20% in Italy, 21% in Germany, 21% in Austria, and to 36% in North America (Appelbaum, Robbins, & Roth, 1999; Raja, Azzoni, & Lubich, 2000; Stompe et al., 1999; Tateyama, Asai, Hashimoto, Bartels, & Kasper, 1998). These studies show the role of culture in interpreting the experience of psychosis. For example, in the case of paranoid delusion, Christians, in contrast to Muslims and Buddhists, were more likely to view the persecutors as supernatural beings. Variances were also found on the basis of changes in culture over time. For example, in Egypt the fluctuations in the frequency of religious delusions over a period of 20 years have been linked to changing patterns of religious emphasis in this country (Atallah, El-Dosoky, Coker, Nabil, & El-Islam, 2001). Also, religious practices have been associated with a higher rate of religious delusions (Getz, Fleck, & Strakowski, 2001; Peters, Day, McKenna, & Orbach, 1999; Siddle, Haddock, Tarrier, & Faragher, 2002); however, religiosity is not necessary for the development of religious delusions (Drinnan & Lavender, 2006; Siddle et al., 2002). All these studies show the important influence of culture on the content of delusions.

The cultural context influences not only the content of delusions but also the understanding of the experience. Explanatory models contain beliefs about the name, nature, cause, expected course, and desired treatment for an episode of illness. Such models are influenced by the culture, and they also vary among individuals of the same cultural background. Indeed, explanatory models are ways of organizing reality that shift over time (Weiss & Somma, 2010). The Western explanatory models of mental illness are not universal. Beliefs that malignant spiritual forces can cause psychiatric illness are likely found in all cultures. Such beliefs influence patterns of help seeking and adherence to treatment. According to research on the availability and cost-effectiveness of spiritual healings, up to 70% of patients use one or more spiritual healings before seeking professional help (Loewenthal, 2010). A naturalistic 3-year follow-up study showed that R/S explanatory models of psychiatric illness often change over time (Huguelet, Mohr, Gillieron, Brandt, & Borras, 2010). Complicating matters further, multiple models may coexist, evolve, and be influenced by the larger social context (Loewenthal, 2010). Moreover, it is difficult to disentangle positive symptoms from spiritual experiences (e.g., hearing of voices, visions, ecstatic states, trances), especially for people with schizophrenia. Some religious coping behavior may be misdiagnosed as symptomatic of psychopathology (Menezes & Moreira-Almeida, 2010). Delusions with religious content may coexist with R/S coping. In a study among 236 outpatients, 16% had delusions with religious content (being persecuted by malevolent spiritual entities, being controlled by spiritual entities, delusions of guilt, sin, or grandiose delusion), yet R/S coping was positive for almost half of them (45%; Mohr, Borras, Betrisey, et al., 2010).

RECOVERY

Recently, the role of religion as a coping mechanism and in the recovery process of patients with SMI has begun to receive growing interest. As of 2011, nearly 10% of Americans believed in God, 54% considered religion as very important in their own life, 55% attended to their religious community at least once a month, and 58% believed that religion can answer all or most of today's problems (Gallup, 2011). Spirituality and religious coping practices are encouraged by religions all over the world, including nontheistic religions (Menezes & Moreira-Almeida, 2010; Huang, Shang, Shieh, Lin, & Su, 2011; Shah et al., 2011). The relevance of R/S to people with SMI is even greater. In a study of 52 psychiatric inpatients in Minnesota, 94% believed in God, 67% in the devil, 53% prayed or consulted the Bible, and 51% attended church weekly (Kroll & Sheehan, 1989). In a study of 406 psychiatric outpatients with SMI in Los Angeles, more than 80% indicated that they used religion to cope; the majority of patients spent nearly half of their total coping time in religious activities (prayer, attending religious services, worshipping God, meditation, reading scriptures, meeting with a spiritual leader); and 65% reported that religion helped them to lessen symptom severity (Tepper, Rogers, Coleman, & Malony, 2001). In an Internet survey on alternative health practices used by persons with SMIs, the most frequently reported practices were R/S activities (50%) and meditation (40%; Russinova, Wewiorski, & Dane, 2002). High prevalence rates of R/S in patients with psychosis have also been reported in Europe. In a comparison of psychiatric patients and a nonpsychiatric control group, the psychiatric patients reported a larger number of religious beliefs and practices that offered comfort during stressful life experiences (Neeleman & Lewis, 1994). In a study of 52 patients with psychosis, 61% were using religion to cope with their illness. Those patients reported greater insight into their illness and greater adherence to medication. Moreover, 30% indicated an increase in religious faith after the onset of their illness (Kirov, Kemp, Kirov, & David, 1998). In a study of 118 patients in a Protestant mental hospital in the Netherlands, 92% were regularly involved in private religious activities and attended religious services. For them, general religiousness and religious coping were associated with better existential and psychological well-being (Pieper, 2004).

The role of R/S in coping with the illness and in the recovery process, however, is not always positive. The *DSM–IV–TR* (American Psychiatric Association, 2000) acknowledged for the first time that distressing religious and spiritual experiences are nonpathological problems and may motivate treatment. R/S problems include loss or questioning of faith, intensification of adherence to beliefs and practices, conversion to a new faith, new religious movements, mystical experience, near-death experience, spiritual emergence or emergency, and medical or terminal illness (Lukoff, Lu, & Turner, 1995). Indeed R/S life is not always a source of joy, hope, and peace. R/S problems may coexist with a mental disorder. Moreover, a severe mental disorder that interferes with major areas of functioning also may produce a "clinically significant religious impairment" defined as "a reduced ability to perform religious activities, achieve religious goals, or to experience religious states" (Hathaway, 2003, p. 114).

According to Pargament (1997), major life events including SMI can threaten or harm many objects of significance. R/S offers specific coping methods for conserving these objects of significance, or if that is no longer possible, transforming these objects of significance. R/S coping methods can serve different purposes (e.g., control, meaning, comfort). Religious coping may be adaptive or not. Helpful forms of specific R/S coping include spiritual support and collaborative religious coping, congregational support, and benevolent religious reframing. Harmful forms of religious coping include discontent with congregation and God, and negative religious reframing. Religious rituals and religious deferral versus self-directed coping may have positive or negative outcomes (Pargament & Brant, 1998). For example, in a study of R/S methods to gain control and recovery among 151 patients with SMI, the collaborative and active surrender methods were associated with greater involvement in recovery-enhancing activities and empowerment, whereas passive religious deferral, pleading, and self-directed methods were inversely associated with recovery (Yangarber-Hicks, 2004). Pargament has argued, however, that no one religious coping strategy is always effective or ineffective. Instead, he maintained, it is important to consider the degree to which spirituality is well integrated, as illustrated by the coordination of spiritual means and ends and the integration of the individual in his or her larger social context (Butter & Pargament, 2003).

In recovery narratives, many people report that R/S is a resource for finding meaning and hope (Corin, 1998; Fallot, 1998, 2007; Kelly & Gamble, 2005; Sullivan, 1998). In a study on faith and recovery among 58 patients with SMIs, 71% reported that their spirituality played a significant role in their recovery by providing them with a definite sense of purpose, peace, and comfort (Bussema & Bussema, 2007). About half of the participants reported that, at times, their R/S fostered negative symptoms, including a strong personal sense of inadequacy engendering feelings of guilt and hopelessness, and feelings of being ignored, judged, or condemned by their religious community. Moreover, most patients indicated that their symptoms occasionally interfered with their spiritual lives.

According to the key R/S themes that emerge in recovery narratives, R/S concerns may become part of the problem as well as part of the recovery. The recovery process is hindered when organized religion is experienced as a source of pain, guilt, or oppression; when the faith community is experienced as stigmatizing and rejecting; when spiritual activities are experienced as a burden; and when spirituality leads to disappointment and demoralization. Conversely, the recovery process is facilitated when spirituality lies at the core of identity; when spirituality is a long-term and effortful journey; when spirituality provides hope for continuing recovery; when divine and human loving relationships are experienced; when spirituality comes with the wisdom to accept human limitations and the courage to overcome obstacles; and when R/S provides meaningful activities of a faith community, such as prayer, meditation, lecture, music, and rituals (Fallot, 1998).

POSITIVE AND NEGATIVE ASPECTS OF R/S COPING AMONG PEOPLE WITH SCHIZOPHRENIA AND OTHER SERIOUS MENTAL ILLNESSES

In a study conducted in Geneva (Switzerland), among 115 outpatients with schizophrenia or schizoaffective disorders, R/S was important in the lives of 85%; moreover, for nearly half of the patients (45%), religion was the most important element in their lives (Mohr, Brandt, Borras, Gillieron, & Huguelet, 2006). R/S was more salient for patients than for the general population and for practitioners (Huguelet, Mohr, Borras, Gillieron, & Brandt, 2006). These results are in line with the high prevalence of R/S in people with SMI found in United States (Kroll & Sheehan, 1989; Tepper et al., 2001), in Europe (Kirov et al., 1998; Neeleman & Lewis, 1994), and Asia (Shah et al., 2011). In the study by Mohr et al. (2006), R/S was elicited through a semistructured clinical interview adapted to a variety of spiritual beliefs and various types of R/S coping. On the basis of several questionnaires (John E. Fetzer Institute, 1999; Koenig, Parkerson, et al., 1997; Pargament, Koenig, & Perez, 2000), the open-ended questions were designed to explore the R/S history of patients, their spiritual beliefs, their private and communal religious activities, the importance of R/S in their daily lives, the importance of R/S as a means of coping with their illness and its consequences, and the synergy versus incompatibility of R/S with psychiatric care. In addition, the salience of those dimensions was quantified by the patient by means of a visual analog scale (Mohr, Gillieron, Borras, Brandt, & Huguelet, 2007).

A qualitative content analysis of all interviews elicited three global R/S coping profiles: positive (71% of patients), negative (14% of patients), and no R/S (15% of patients; Mohr et al., 2006). For patients with positive R/S coping, R/S served several functions, including hope, comfort, meaning of life, enjoyment of life, love, compassion, self-respect, and self-confidence. Two thirds of these patients reported that R/S gave meaning to their illness and fostered an acceptance of the illness or a mobilization of religious resources to cope with their symptoms. In 54% of cases, R/S coping reportedly lessened positive, negative, or general symptoms. Interestingly, only one third of the patients in the positive coping group reported that they actually received social support from a religious community. Some did not receive any support from their communities because of their symptoms (impaired social skills, delusion of persecution) or because they avoided asking for support because of shame. More often, symptoms hindered religious patients from practicing in their religious communities (hallucinations and delusions, lack of motivation).

For patients with negative R/S coping, R/S reportedly contributed to a negative sense of self, including feelings of despair, suffering, fear, anger, and guilt. Some patients felt despair after the failure of the spiritual healing they had sought. In 10% of cases, patients indicated that their religious coping increased delusions, depression, suicide risk, and substance use.

R/S also played positive (14% of cases) and negative (3% of cases) roles in substance misuse, a problem frequently associated with schizophrenia. Patients with a history of substance abuse were particularly likely to use positive R/S coping to deal with their substance abuse. R/S provided them with guidelines for living a sober life, an alternative coping strategy to replace substance use, or even a point of anchorage to completely reorganize their lives around R/S. Some patients, however, turned to drugs and alcohol to cope with their spiritual distress after losing their religious communities (Huguelet, Borras, Gillieron, Brandt, & Mohr, 2009). R/S offered protection against suicidal attempts (in 33% of cases) by giving meaning in life, R/S coping with despair, ethical condemnations of suicide, and R/S experiences. However, R/S was also a risk factor for suicide attempts (in 10% of cases) through loss of faith, anger against God, or break with one's religious community, the wish to live another life after death, and delusions or hallucinations with religious contents (Huguelet et al., 2007). R/S can also play a role in decreasing (15%) or increasing (16%) adherence to psychiatric medication and supportive therapy (Borras et al., 2007). Similar results were obtained in Canada (Borras et al., 2010).

In our cohort of 115 outpatients in Geneva, R/S positive coping was predictive of a better outcome at 3 years for negative symptoms, social adaptation, and quality of life (Mohr et al., 2011). At the 3-year follow-up, 37% of the patients showed significant positive transformations as demonstrated through increased positive R/S coping or shifts from negative to positive R/S coping. Seventeen percent reported negative transformations—that is, declines in positive R/S coping or shifts from positive to negative R/S coping (Mohr, Borras, Rieben, et al., 2010).

We have seen the prevalence and the economic burden of SMIs, the evolution of the mental health field to a holistic view that considers both illness and positive health in diagnosis and treatment, the prevalence of hallucinations and delusions with religious contents, the recovery model, and R/S as a resource as well as a burden in the recovery process. Now, it is time to reflect on ways to integrate all of this knowledge on R/S into more effective care for people with SMI.

CLINICAL IMPLICATIONS

First we consider the clinician's beliefs and attitudes, and then the importance of conducting a spiritual assessment. We also examine R/S issues in psychotherapy for people with psychosis, with a special emphasis on delusions and hallucinations with religious content as well as relationships with religious professionals and communities.

My Professional Spiritual Journey

The clinician does not need to be religious to address R/S issues in psychotherapy. Neither must the practitioner share the same religious affiliation as the patient. It is vital, however, that the clinician demonstrate respect, openness, and interest in the worldview of his or her patient, including the role of R/S in his/her life. It is also important for the practitioner to be aware of his or her own R/S history and orientation. It is appropriate at this point to say a few words about my R/S journey.

My interest in research and practice on the roles of R/S in the lives of people living with SMI was triggered 15 years ago by an unforeseen discovery. I was involved in a 5-year longitudinal study of schizophrenia and found that one third of patients and their families were highly involved in a religious community. At that time, consistent with my training,

I assumed that their involvement in religion was likely an expression of their psychopathology. I thought we might best help these patients by encouraging them to discontinue their involvement in these religious groups. The results of the study were contrary to this assumption: Not only did religious patients display no more symptoms than others, but they also manifested better social adaptation and less substance abuse (Huguelet, Binyet-Vogel, Gonzalez, Favre, & McQuillan, 1997).

My prejudice against religion was revealed, and despite personally being an atheist, my curiosity was triggered. I began to study the effects of R/S within this clinical population. I, however, encountered opposition from other researchers and practitioners who held antireligious prejudices of their own.

Coincidently, during that time, I converted to Christianity and began to attend an evangelical church where ironically I witnessed another kind of prejudice against parishioners with SMI: demonization of psychiatry and advice-giving to quit medication. I felt anger that people with severe mental disorders were being victimized by a double stigmatization: a reduction of R/S to pathology by professionals at the psychiatric hospital and a failure to recognize the need for psychiatric care by their church. Unrecognized by both mental health professionals and religious professionals was the important interface between religion, particularly religious coping, and mental health.

The theory of religious coping, which recognized both positive and negative religious coping with stress (Pargament, 1997), opened the door to my research to better understand the role of religious coping among persons suffering from SMI. Fortunately, I found support from colleagues who also were aware of the antagonism between religion and psychiatric care and were open to the inclusion of R/S to promote the quality of life and social integration of people with severe mental disorders. We collaborated in the development of a clinical instrument to assess R/S coping in European patients with schizophrenia (Mohr et al., 2007), and I began to learn how central R/S were to the lives of many patients. A surprising result was that for nearly half the patients, spirituality and religion were the most important element in their lives, with benevolent as well harmful consequences (Mohr et al., 2006).

My meetings with hundreds of patients brought about deep changes in my comprehension of the relationships among religion, spirituality, and schizophrenia as well as in my own spiritual journey. Indeed, I did not expect to encounter someone who considered his schizophrenia to be a grace—a turning point that led him to fully engage in a spiritual journey. Many patients described how their spiritual identity helped restore their wounded sense of themselves. I learned that people are much more than their mental illness (see also Kehoe, 2009).

My colleagues and I began then to move from research to the integration of R/S into clinical care. We offered training to resident psychiatrists on how to conduct a spiritual assessment. Even though patients appraised this assessment positively, it was not followed by any integration of R/S in psychiatrists' practices (Huguelet et al., 2011). We therefore implemented a Spirituality and Recovery Group for people with severe mental disorder in our ambulatory consultation work (Mohr, 2011). This group was not indicated for some patients who required more tailored individual psychotherapy to meet their special needs.

I also discovered that mental illness as well as its treatment present different kinds of theological challenges to different religious traditions. These challenges are relevant because the integration of spirituality into treatment at times requires collaboration with the chaplaincy service or other relevant religious people. Religious professionals are not mental health professionals (see Chapter 11 in this volume), and they usually see their primary mission as one to help their communities' members to know God. Religious professionals, like mental health professionals, share the same commitment toward alleviation of patients' suffering, however, and each should be encouraged to demonstrate mutual respect for the distinctive resources each partner brings to the helping process (Shuman, 2009). In light of this perspective, we actively developed collaborative relationships with chaplains. The integration of spirituality into the care of people with SMI is just beginning, and I (like the field itself) am continuing to grow and learn through this process.

R/S Assessment

The first step of integration of R/S into mental health care is a systematic inclusion of a R/S assessment into the diagnostic process, treatment, and case management (see Wallace, Lecomte, Wilde, & Liberman, 2001; Chapter 5 in this volume). An initial assessment should consider several aspects of R/S: the importance of R/S in life and in coping with the illness, the patient's involvement in a religious community, and the spiritual needs of the patient and how the patient wants those needs to be addressed (Sims, 2007).

In spite of its importance, R/S assessment often falls short of the ideal. In a study evaluating the concordance between a psychiatric rehabilitation program and patients' goals, Lecomte, Wallace, Perreault, and Caron (2005) reported that 22% of patients set R/S goals for the ongoing year, yet they perceived that their services were insufficient toward supporting those goals. A Swedish study of immigrants with psychosis showed that the greatest differences among health care staff, patients, and families involved religious issues (Hultsjö, Bertero, Arvidsson, & Hjelm, 2011).

R/S may be significant to clinical care even among those patients who attach little current importance to R/S. Indeed, R/S can be conceptualized as a lifelong journey involving processes of discovery, conservation, struggle with, and transformation of the sacred (Murray-Swank & Pargament, 2011). Viewed from this perspective, loss of faith may be temporary or may reflect a clinically significant religious impairment leading to hopelessness and despair. Therefore, it is important to gather a R/S history that includes family background and religious education as well as changes in spirituality and religiousness.

Once patients express spiritual interests, resources, concerns, or wishes to discuss them with the clinician, a more extensive assessment is appropriate. Numerous scales have been developed to assess the multiple dimensions of R/S (Hill & Hood, 1999; Hill & Kilian, 2003; John E. Fetzer Institute, 1999; Koenig, Parkerson, & Meador, 1997; Pargament et al., 2000). Although these scales were designed for research purposes, they may be used as probes to identify R/S topics of special interests and concerns among patients.

Training is needed to help professionals integrate spiritual assessment into psychiatric care. As noted earlier, we offer training to resident psychiatrists on how to conduct a spiritual assessment. According to an evaluation of this program, R/S assessment was well accepted by psychiatric patients. It elicited major spiritual themes that could be integrated into care: supporting of positive coping; working on identity and values; differentiating delusions from faith; linking the patient with clergy, chaplains, or a religious community; addressing negative religious coping; and considering representations of psychiatric disorder and treatment from a religious perspective (Huguelet et al., 2011). Effective training for mental health professionals should also include the facilitation of spiritual groups, supervision and lectures (Galanter, Dermatis, Talbot, McMahon, & Alexander, 2011).

R/S Issues in Psychotherapy for People With Psychosis

The Spirituality and Recovery Group highlighted some of the important issues that arise in psychotherapy among people with severe mental disorders. Sensitive to our sociocultural context (a secular psychiatric service in an international and multicultural city), the group is interfaith, with specific rules, including the guideline to respect other people's spiritual beliefs and to not proselytize (Kehoe, 2007). The group is designed to address R/S issues of clinical significance identified through our research: the roles of positive and negative R/S coping with psychopathology, psychosocial functioning, and adherence to psychiatric treatment; the reciprocal influences of the illness and the spiritual journey; and the part spirituality plays in recovery (Borras et al., 2007; Huguelet et al., 2007, 2009, 2011; Mohr et al., 2006; Mohr & Huguelet, 2004). The group also draws on the work of other R/S groups for people with SMI (Galanter et al., 2011; Goodman & Manierre, 2008; Harris et al., 2011; Kehoe, 2007; Murray-Swank & Pargament, 2005; Phillips, Lakin, & Pargament, 2002; Revheim & Greenberg, 2007; Wong-McDonald, 2007).

Although group psychotherapies provide patients with unique opportunities to share their experiences, some patients are too fearful of social relationships to attend a group or find R/S too personal to be shared in a group. These patients need a more individualized approach.

Several key R/S issues emerge from the Spirituality and Recovery Group; some of which are specific to psychosis while others are not. These issues include the importance of disentangling R/S from psychotic symptoms; discerning the spiritual meaning of the illness and psychiatric care; understanding the interrelations between spiritual history and mental illness; identifying helpful and harmful forms of R/S coping with the symptoms of the illness; addressing supportive versus harmful relationships with religious community members and religious professionals; considering the relationships between R/S and self-identity; recognizing and dealing with stigmatization because of R/S and mental illness; articulating representations and emotional relationships with God and other spiritual figures; and identifying existential issues about the meaning of life and death, sexuality, suffering, theodicy, forgiveness, sin, and guilt. Two issues in particular deserve elaboration: delusions and hallucinations with religious content and impairment in relationships with religious communities.

Psychotherapy of Delusions and Hallucinations With Religious Content

According to the *DSM–IV–TR* (American Psychiatric Association, 2000), the pathological characteristic of a delusion is a fundamental break with reality, with widespread clinical reliability (Bell, Halligan, & Ellis, 2006). The contents of delusions can be categorized into three distinct subtypes: delusions of persecution, delusions of self-significance (grandiose, guilt/sin, reference), and delusions of influence (Kimhy, Goetz, Yale, Corcoran, & Malaspina, 2005). R/S contents fit in this classification: The agents of persecution and of influence may be spiritual entities; in self-significant delusions, people believe that they are a special spiritual being, have special spiritual powers, or have committed unpardonable sins. The qualitative difference between a delusion and a belief, however, cannot be based solely on the content. Epidemiological studies have demonstrated the presence of delusions and hallucinations in the general population without psychiatric disorders (Nuevo et al., 2010). Consequently, delusions are considered to be multidimensional phenomena rather than discrete discontinuous entities. The most commonly retained dimensions of delusions involve (a) the degree of conviction (from doubt to absolute conviction), (b) the degree of preoccupation (from a transient belief to an overwhelming belief), (c) the degree of pervasiveness (limited to one domain or extended to all life domains), (d) negative emotionality (level of anger, anxiety, or distress associated with the belief); and (e) action–inaction (behaviors associated with the belief; Combs et al., 2006). Often, people experience both delusions and hallucinations (i.e., a perception in the absence of external stimuli that have qualities of real perception). The meaning people give to their unusual experience leads to adaptive or nonadaptive emotional and behavioral reactions (Romme & Escher, 2000).

Case Example 1

A 42-year-old man with paranoid schizophrenia identified himself as Protestant yet reported believing in the Madonna. Before receiving psychiatric treatment, he heard voices telling him to kill himself and took refuge in a Catholic Church. During his prayers, he had a vision of the Virgin, and the voices disappeared. His vision of the Madonna gave him comfort and a feeling of protection, opening him up to a world of love and peace. When he felt too anxious, he prayed to her for protection and felt her presence. He made a clear distinction between hallucinations (malevolent voices) and his vision. Because of pervasive delusion of persecution, this man lived an isolated life, without any communal religious involvement. Over the course of time, he stopped praying to the Madonna for comfort and his anxieties worsened.

With the dimensional approach in mind, this man's vision of the Virgin would not be considered a symptom because the patient is convinced of the reality of the apparition of the Madonna, is not preoccupied by this vision, prays to her when needed, and looks to her for comfort and help in relieving his fears; additionally, the vision does not lead to maladaptive behaviors. The only preoccupation the patient has about his vision is a fear that his psychiatrist will dismiss his experience as a hallucination, give him more antipsychotics, or even hospitalize him. Therefore, he avoids the subject of his vision in treatment.

Over time, the same repetitive voice, expressing the same content, may evolve from a very distressing and dangerous experience to a more benign phenomenon, as in the following case example.

> **Case Example 2**
>
> A 20-year-old man with paranoid schizophrenia reported that he feels that other people can control his behavior at a distance and that he hears their voices. As a result of this influence, he became very anxious and even tried to kill himself several times. In trying to make sense of his experience, he met a Buddhist monk who taught him meditation and that his experience was only an illusion, without any reality. Every morning, he practices loving meditation, and he is no longer bothered by his psychotic symptoms. Instead, he can let them pass. He finds in Buddhism a way to liberate himself from suffering.

Malevolent voices can even be experienced as positive, as in the following example:

> **Case Example 3**
>
> A 26-year-old man with schizoaffective disorder reframed his experience of hearing malevolent voices. In the past he was disturbed by a voice insulting him, belittling him, and telling him to commit suicide. Currently, however, he views the voice as a positive experience, a way of fostering his consciousness that something is going wrong in the present situation, a problem he has to handle.

In conclusion, a belief cannot be considered as a delusion solely on the basis of its content; the belief needs to be distressing and dysfunctional. Clinical and R/S assessment should help the practitioner grasp the interactions between psychotic symptoms and R/S. The job of the clinician is not to impose his or her own explanation, but rather to be open to the patient's inner experience and to consider how the belief is constructive or destructive.

Cognitive–behavioral therapy is recommended in the guidelines of treatment for schizophrenia (NIMH, 2009). This model of therapy may be used for delusions and hallucinations, with sensitivity to R/S in the patient's life. According to Beck, Rector, Stolar, and Grant (2009b), the formation and maintenance of delusions are based on cognitive deficits and cognitive bias in the treatment of information that limits the ability of the person to cope with psychosocial stressors. These deficits and biases lead the person to mistake his or her dysfunctional beliefs about the self, others, and the future for reality. Moreover, the intense emotions associated with delusions, such as fear, activate automatic information processing and lead to protective behaviors. As a result, it takes active and effortful process to redefine the delusion as a belief rather than as the reality. Hallucinations are based on the same cognitive deficits, cognitive bias, and dysfunctional beliefs. Delusions and hallucinations therefore reinforce each other (Beck et al., 2009b; Beck, Rector, Stolar, & Grant, 2009a).

To disentangle R/S from psychotic symptoms, it is important to treat symptoms as symptoms, even when they have R/S content. It is also necessary to support and affirm the value of a R/S dimension in a patient's live to avoid stigmatization. The clinician must be able to tolerate some ambiguity in the relationship between R/S and symptoms. The practitioner also must recognize that these issues are complex and require time, effort, and patience in treatment.

> **Case Example 4**
>
> A 50-year-old woman with schizoaffective disorder had hallucinations and

delusions of persecution, self-reference, and control. She denied her illness, refused medication, and was reluctant to enter therapy because she preferred to rely only on Buddhist practices to cope with her symptoms. Her R/S coping strategies, however, were ineffective in preventing emotional distress or non-adaptive behaviors. Yet, totally convinced about the reality of her delusions, she entered therapy with a hidden agenda: to convert me to Buddhism. I encouraged her to view her beliefs as hypotheses about reality (e.g., was her friend bothering her or was she hearing a demon?), to use her R/S coping strategies more effectively (e.g., praying aloud in order not to hear voices), and to question her delusional beliefs. I also encouraged her to find meaning in a voice accusing her of killing her father and suggested that the voice may reflect her own guilt rather than a demon's voice. These activities raised the possibility of an alternative explanation: Her experiences may be symptoms of an illness, one that may be deserved in the context of her belief in karma. This woman began to take medication. She also consulted a monk, who gave her a prayer that protects against demons and illness. This prayer was a turning point. Unsure whether her voices were symptoms or demons, she began to doubt her other delusional beliefs and to test them in reality. She accepted that other people can think in a different way than her and stopped trying to convert me to Buddhism. To ameliorate her karma, she decided to engage in charity acts, which encompassed not harming others, not imposing her thoughts on others, and accepting her situation. This change allowed her to lessen her guilt, reduce her isolation, and use both medication and reality-testing of her beliefs (as well as R/S coping) to deal successfully with her various delusions.

Thus, treating people with religious delusions and hallucinations is challenging work. It is important to address the dysfunctionality and distress associated with these delusions and hallucinations while avoiding the prima facie inaccurate characterization of R/S as a manifestation of pathology.

Relationships With Religious Community Members and Religious Professionals

Despite the salience of spirituality in patients' lives, they are less involved in religious communities than comparable healthy people, either due to their symptoms or rejection by religious communities (Huguelet et al., 2006). Working specifically on symptoms that hinder social adjustment may help patients reintegrate themselves within their religious community. Religious communities may then foster the patient's spiritual life through social interaction and support, and encourage patients to draw on their positive religious coping resources that may have declined over time (Mohr, Borras, Rieben, et al., 2010). People with mental illness often suffer from stigma, rejection, and exclusion. For them, religious communities may be the only source of social connections (Fallot, 1998). In this vein, attendance at religious congregations appears to be a key factor in the spiritual well-being of people with psychiatric disabilities (Fukui, Starnino, & Nelson-Becker, 2011).

To facilitate reintegration into a religious community, clinicians must address the patient's disappointment with and rejection by religious communities or religious professionals. These experiences are especially painful for people with SMI, as they add a profound and often unexpected source of distress to the many other losses in their lives. Anger and disappointment with the religious community may lead to loss of faith, substance misuse, and suicide attempts (Huguelet et al., 2007, 2009). In these cases, the discontent with religious members or professionals may be overgeneralized to God, the spiritual worldview of the community, or religious communities as a whole. It can be important here to help patients achieve a greater acceptance of human limitations and failures, including the limitations of members of religious communities and religious professionals. Through this process, patients may be able to restore confidence in the value of spiritual life, move to a more benevolent understanding of the divine, and reengage in human relationships within a religious community.

Case Example 5

A 43-year-old woman with schizoaffective disorder reported that she was highly involved in a Pentecostal religious community. For years, she engaged in the activities of her religious community every day, had friends only inside her community, and described her friends as her family. When she became depressed, the whole community prayed for her and the pastor engaged in a ministry of deliverance. Following a psychotic episode and hospitalization for several months, she became very angry with her church because no one from her community, including her pastor, visited her at the hospital. Following discharge, she found herself alone and without any activities, and yet she was unwilling to go back to her church. She stayed angry and depressed for months and felt that her faith had vanished. Treatment focused on helping her acknowledge her suffering, accept human limitations, enter into a process of forgiving, reengage in relationships with her religious community, and reinvest in her spiritual life.

Sometimes, patients exclude themselves from their religious communities as a result of the shame they feel for their misbehaviors. This is a self-stigmatization process.

Case Example 6

A 38-year-old man with schizoaffective disorder reported that he was highly involved in a meditation center and the study of Buddhism for years. During a manic episode, he became aggressive, insulting his friends at the meditation center. Afterward, he was so ashamed that he never returned. He became very anxious, suffered from his isolation, and lost direction in his life. He did, however, continue his meditation practices. Therapy addressed his sense of shame by helping him differentiate his true self from his manic symptoms and by restoring a positive sense of self.

In our spiritual group, patients with delusions or hallucinations with religious content often report one of two attitudes by religious professionals they had consulted for spiritual healing: rejection or spiritual support. Patients felt rejected when the religious professionals referred them to a psychiatrist, without further religious or spiritual care by the religious professionals themselves. The patients felt stigmatized and often intensely angry or distressed. Those reactions highlight the need to take R/S into account in mental health care. Referrals to religious professionals should be carefully considered when patients express R/S issues, for not all religious professionals know how to deal with issues of mental illness. Of course, patients may feel the same sense of rejection of their R/S by the psychiatrist or psychologist, and again they may feel that they are not being treated as a whole person. On the other hand, some patients report that their religious professionals offer both spiritual support and encouragement to work with mental health professionals.

Case Example 7

A 24-year-old man with paranoid schizophrenia reported that he was hearing different voices, one telling him that he was Jesus and another pretending to be Lucifer telling him to sell his soul. He was very afraid, refused psychiatric care, and consulted a priest to be exorcized. The priest was able to bring the patient comfort and peacefulness. He never exorcized him, but instead prayed for him and offered him spiritual support by teaching him the gospel and forgiveness, and integrated him in his congregation. The priest enabled the man to accept his illness and psychiatric care.

Religious professionals are regularly confronted with people with SMI and may feel overwhelmed, underskilled, and fearful of contact. To overcome this problem, some churches have developed programs of training and supervision for pastors, promoting spiritual support and adherence to mental health care. For example, Pathways to Promise (2001) offers assistance and resources to many faith groups to develop their capacity to support individuals and families facing serious mental health issues.

In a person-centered approach, the clinician develops relationships with important members of the social network of the patient (family, work, housing authorities). This approach has to be extended to key religious professionals when appropriate, including chaplains working in psychiatric services who often are of great help to the patient and the clinician.

CONCLUSION

R/S has important roles to play in providing effective mental health care for patients with severe mental disorders. Indeed, patients with mental illness appear to be more involved in R/S than the general population, lean on R/S to cope with symptoms, and find that R/S is often instrumental in the recovery process. R/S coping, however, is not always positive; the illness may produce clinically significant religious impairment. In short, R/S may be both a resource and a burden in patients' lives.

It follows that treatment that overlooks the R/S dimension is likely to be less effective. In this work, clinicians must consider the cultural context of the patient, for it shapes the patient's R/S and his or her explanatory models of mental disorders and treatment. Furthermore, the clinician needs to be aware of his or her own R/S history, attitudes, and orientation to avoid imposing his or her view of R/S on the patient and to convey a sense of respectfulness and openness to the patient's worldview (see Chapter 3 in this volume). To achieve this task, clinicians need training in R/S issues, clinical practice, and supervision (see Chapter 33 in this volume). Although work in the area of R/S and severe mental disorder is still in its early stages, it offers the promise of providing people with a more holistic and effective approach to their care.

References

Andresen, R., Oades, L., & Caputi, P. (2003). The experience of recovery from schizophrenia: Towards an empirically validated stage model. *Australian and New Zealand Journal of Psychiatry, 37*, 586–594. doi:10.1046/j.1440-1614.2003.01234.x

American Psychiatric Association. (2000). *Diagnostic and statistical manual of mental disorders* (4th ed., text revision). Washington, DC: Author.

American Psychiatric Association. (2011). *Diagnostic and statistical manual of mental disorders* (DSM–V). Retrieved from http://www.dsm5.org

Appelbaum, P. S., Robbins, P. C., & Roth, L. H. (1999). Dimensional approach to delusions: Comparison across types and diagnoses. *American Journal of Psychiatry, 156*, 1938–1943.

Atallah, S. F., El-Dosoky, A. R., Coker, E. M., Nabil, K. M., & El-Islam, M. F. (2001). A 22-year retrospective analysis of the changing frequency and patterns of religious symptoms among inpatients with psychotic illness in Egypt. *Social Psychiatry and Psychiatric Epidemiology, 36*, 407–415. doi:10.1007/s001270170031

Azhar, M. Z., Varma, S. L., & Hakim, H. R. (1995). Phenomenological differences of delusions between schizophrenic patients of two cultures of Malaysia. *Singapore Medical Journal, 36*, 273–275.

Beck, A. T., Rector, N. A., Stolar, N., & Grant, P. (2009a). A cognitive conceptualization of auditory hallucinations. In A. T. Beck, N. A. Rector, N. Stolar, & P. Grant (Eds.), *Schizophrenia: Cognitive theory, research and therapy* (pp. 102–141). New York, NY: Guilford Press.

Beck, A. T., Rector, N. A., Stolar, N., & Grant, P. (2009b). A cognitive conceptualization of delusions. In A. T. Beck, N. A. Rector, N. Stolar, & P. Grant (Eds.), *Schizophrenia: Cognitive theory, research and therapy* (pp. 62–101). New York, NY: Guilford Press.

Bell, V., Halligan, P. W., & Ellis, H. D. (2006). Explaining delusions: A cognitive perspective. *Trends in Cognitive Sciences, 10*, 219–226. doi:10.1016/j.tics.2006.03.004

Borras, L., Mohr, S., Brandt, P. Y., Gillieron, C., Eytan, A., & Huguelet, P. (2007). Religious beliefs in schizophrenia: Their relevance for adherence to treatment. *Schizophrenia Bulletin, 33*, 1238–1246. doi:10.1093/schbul/sbl070

Borras, L., Mohr, S., Gillieron, C., Brandt, P. Y., Rieben, I., Leclerc, C., & Huguelet, P. (2010). Religion and spirituality: How clinicians in Quebec and Geneva cope with the issue when faced with patients suffering from chronic psychosis. *Community Mental Health Journal, 46*, 77–86. doi:10.1007/s10597-009-9247-y

Brawer, P. A., Handal, P. J., Shafer, R. M., & Ubinger, M. (2002). Training and education in religion/spirituality within APA-accredited clinical psychology programs. *Professional Psychology: Research and Practice, 33*, 203–206. doi:10.1037/0735-7028.33.2.203

Buckley, P. F., & Brown, E. S. (2006). Prevalence and consequences of dual diagnosis. *Journal of Clinical Psychiatry, 67*(7), e01.

Bussema, E. F., & Bussema, K. E. (2007). Gilead revisited: Faith and recovery. *Psychiatric Rehabilitation Journal, 30*, 301–305. doi:10.2975/30.4.2007.301.305

Butter, E. M., & Pargament, K. I. (2003). Development of a model for clinical assessment of religious coping: Initial validation of the Process Evaluation Model. *Mental Health, Religion, and Culture, 6*, 175–194. doi:10.1080/1367467021000038183

Combs, D. R., Adams, S., Michael, C., Penn, D., Basso, M., & Gouvier, W. (2006). The conviction of delusional beliefs scale: Reliability and validity. *Schizophrenia Research, 86*, 80–88. doi:10.1016/j.schres.2006.06.023

Corin, E. (1998). The thickness of being: Intentional worlds, strategies of identity, and experience among schizophrenics. *Psychiatry: Interpersonal and Biological Processes, 61*, 133–146.

Drinnan, A., & Lavender, T. (2006). Deconstructing delusions: A qualitative study examining the relationship between religious beliefs and religious delusions. *Mental Health, Religion, and Culture, 9*, 317–331. doi:10.1080/13694670500071711

Ellis, A. (1980). Psychotherapy and atheistic values: A response to A. E. Bergin's "Psychotherapy and Religious Values." *Journal of Consulting and Clinical Psychology, 48*, 635–639. doi:10.1037/0022-006X.48.5.635

Fallot, R. D. (1998). Spiritual and religious dimensions of mental illness recovery narratives. *New Directions for Mental Health Services, 80*, 35–44. doi:10.1002/yd.23319988006

Fallot, R. D. (2007). Spirituality and religion in recovery: Some current issues. *Psychiatric Rehabilitation Journal, 30*, 261–270. doi:10.2975/30.4.2007.261.270

Field, H. L., & Waldfogel, S. (1995). Severe ocular self-injury. *General Hospital Psychiatry, 17*, 224–227. doi:10.1016/0163-8343(95)00031-L

Freud, S. (1971). *L'avenir d'une illusion.* [The future of an illusion] Paris: Presses Universitaires de France. (Original work published 1927)

Fukui, S., Starnino, V. R., & Nelson-Becker, H. B. (2011). Spiritual well-being of people with psychiatric disabilities: The role of religious attendance, social network size and sense of control. *Community Mental Health Journal, 48*, 202–211. doi:10.1007/s10597-011-9375-z

Galanter, M., Dermatis, H., Talbot, N., McMahon, C., & Alexander, M. J. (2011). Introducing spirituality into psychiatric care. *Journal of Religion and Health, 50*, 81–91. doi:10.1007/s10943-009-9282-6

Gallup. (2011). *Religion.* Retrieved from http://www.gallup.com/poll/1690/Religion.aspx#2

Getz, G. E., Fleck, D. E., & Strakowski, S. M. (2001). Frequency and severity of religious delusions in Christian patients with psychosis. *Psychiatry Research, 103*, 87–91. doi:10.1016/S0165-1781(01)00262-1

Goodman, G., & Manierre, A. (2008). Representations of God uncovered in a spirituality group of borderline inpatients. *International Journal of Group Psychotherapy, 58*, 1–15. doi:10.1521/ijgp.2008.58.1.1

Harris, J. I., Erbes, C. R., Engdahl, B. E., Thuras, P., Murray-Swank, N., Grace, D., . . . Le, T. (2011). The effectiveness of a trauma focused spiritually integrated intervention for veterans exposed to trauma. *Journal of Clinical Psychology, 67*, 425–438. doi:10.1002/jclp.20777

Hathaway, W. (2003). Clinically significant religious impairment: Introduction to special issue. *Mental Health, Religion, and Culture, 6*, 113–129. doi:10.1080/1367467021000038165

Hill, P., & Hood, R. (1999). *Measures of religiosity.* Birmingham, AL: Religious Education Press.

Hill, P., & Kilian, M. (2003). Assessing clinically significant religious impairment in clients: Applications from measures in the psychology of religion and spirituality. *Mental Health, Religion, and Culture, 6*, 149–160. doi:10.1080/1367467021000038192

Huang, C. L., Shang, C. Y., Shieh, M. S., Lin, H. N., & Su, J. C. (2011). The interactions between religion, religiosity, religious delusion/hallucination, and treatment-seeking behavior among schizophrenic patients in Taiwan. *Psychiatry Research, 187*, 347–353. doi:10.1016/j.psychres.2010.07.014

Huguelet, P., Binyet-Vogel, S., Gonzalez, C., Favre, S., & McQuillan, A. (1997). Follow-up study of 67 first episode schizophrenic patients and their involvement in religious activities. *European Psychiatry, 12*, 279–283. doi:10.1016/S0924-9338(97)84786-4

Huguelet, P., Borras, L., Gillieron, C., Brandt, P. Y., & Mohr, S. (2009). Influence of spirituality and religiousness on substance misuse in patients with schizophrenia or schizo-affective disorder. *Substance Use and Misuse, 44*, 502–513. doi:10.1080/10826080802344872

Huguelet, P., Mohr, S., Betrisey, C., Borras, L., Gillieron, C., Marie, A. M., . . . Brandt, P. Y. (2011). A randomized trial of spiritual assessment of outpatients with schizophrenia: Patients' and clinicians' experience. *Psychiatric Services, 62*, 79–86.

Huguelet, P., Mohr, S., Borras, L., Gillieron, C., & Brandt, P. Y. (2006). Spirituality and religious practices among outpatients with schizophrenia and their clinicians. *Psychiatric Services*, *57*, 366–372. doi:10.1176/appi.ps.57.3.366

Huguelet, P., Mohr, S., Gillieron, C., Brandt, P. Y., & Borras, L. (2010). Religious explanatory models in patients with psychosis: A three-year follow-up study. *Psychopathology*, *43*, 230–239. doi:10.1159/000313521

Huguelet, P., Mohr, S., Jung, V., Gillieron, C., Brandt, P. Y., & Borras, L. (2007). Effect of religion on suicide attempts in outpatients with schizophrenia or schizo-affective disorders compared with inpatients with non-psychotic disorders. *European Psychiatry*, *22*, 188–194. doi:10.1016/j.eurpsy.2006.08.001

Hultsjö, S., Bertero, C., Arvidsson, H., & Hjelm, K. (2011). Core components in the care of immigrants with psychoses: A Delphi survey of patients, families, and health-care staff. *International Journal of Mental Health Nursing*, *20*, 174–184. doi:10.1111/j.1447-0349.2010.00720.x

Insel, T. R. (2008). Assessing the economic costs of serious mental illness. *American Journal of Psychiatry*, *165*, 663–665. doi:10.1176/appi.ajp.2008.08030366

John E. Fetzer Institute. (1999). *Multidimensional Measurement of Religiousness/Spirituality for Use in Health Research*. Kalamazoo, MI: Author.

Kehoe, N. (2007). Spirituality groups in serious mental illness. *Southern Medical Journal*, *100*, 647–648. doi:10.1097/SMJ.0b013e31806006dc

Kehoe, N. (2009). *Wrestling with our inner angels. Faith, mental illness, and the journey to wholeness*. San Francisco, CA: Jossey-Bass.

Kelly, M., & Gamble, C. (2005). Exploring the concept of recovery in schizophrenia. *Journal of Psychiatric and Mental Health Nursing*, *12*, 245–251. doi:10.1111/j.1365-2850.2005.00828.x

Kim, K., Hwu, H., Zhang, L. D., Lu, M. K., Park, K. K., Hwang, T. J., . . . Park, Y.-C. (2001). Schizophrenic delusions in Seoul, Shanghai and Taipei: A transcultural study. *Journal of Korean Medical Science*, *16*, 88–94.

Kimhy, D., Goetz, R., Yale, S., Corcoran, C., & Malaspina, D. (2005). Delusions in individuals with schizophrenia: Factor structure, clinical correlates, and putative neurobiology. *Psychopathology*, *38*, 338–344. doi:10.1159/000089455

Kirov, G., Kemp, R., Kirov, K., & David, A. S. (1998). Religious faith after psychotic illness. *Psychopathology*, *31*, 234–245. doi:10.1159/000029045

Koenig, H., Parkerson, G. R., Jr., & Meador, K. G. (1997). Religion index for psychiatric research. *American Journal of Psychiatry*, *154*, 885–886.

Kraya, N. A., & Patrick, C. (1997). Folie a deux in forensic setting. *Australian and New Zealand Journal of Psychiatry*, *31*, 883–888. doi:10.3109/0004867 9709065518

Kroll, J., & Sheehan, W. (1989). Religious beliefs and practices among 52 psychiatric inpatients in Minnesota. *American Journal of Psychiatry*, *146*, 67–72.

Lecomte, T., Wallace, C. J., Perreault, M., & Caron, J. (2005). Consumers' goals in psychiatric rehabilitation and their concordance with existing services. *Psychiatric Services*, *56*, 209–211. doi:10.1176/appi.ps.56.2.209

Loewenthal, K. M. (2010). Spirituality and cultural psychiatry. In D. Bhugra & K. Bhui (Eds.), *Textbook of cultural psychiatry* (pp. 59–71). Cambridge, England: Cambridge University Press.

Lukoff, D., Lu, F. G., & Turner, R. (1995). Cultural considerations in the assessment and treatment of religious and spiritual problems. *Psychiatric Clinics of North America*, *18*, 467–485.

Menezes, A., Jr., & Moreira-Almeida, A. (2010). Religion, spirituality, and psychosis. *Current Psychiatry Reports*, *12*, 174–179. doi:10.1007/s11920-010-0117-7

Mezzich, J. E. (2007). Psychiatry for the Person: Articulating medicine's science and humanism. *World Psychiatry*, *6*(2), 65–67.

Mohr, S. (2011). Integration of spirituality and religion in the care of patients with severe mental disorders. *Religions*, *2*, 549–565. doi:10.3390/rel2040549

Mohr, S., Borras, L., Betrisey, C., Brandt, P.-Y., Gillieron, C., & Huguelet, P. (2010). Delusions with religious content in patients with psychosis: How they interact with spiritual coping. *Psychiatry: Interpersonal and Biological Processes*, *73*, 158–172. doi:10.1521/psyc.2010.73.2.158

Mohr, S., Borras, L., Rieben, I., Betrisey, C., Gillieron, C., Brandt, P. Y., . . . Huguelet, P. (2010). Evolution of spirituality and religiousness in chronic schizophrenia or schizo-affective disorders: A 3-years follow-up study. *Social Psychiatry and Psychiatric Epidemiology*, *45*, 1095–1103. doi:10.1007/s00127-009-0151-0

Mohr, S., Brandt, P. Y., Borras, L., Gillieron, C., & Huguelet, P. (2006). Toward an integration of religiousness and spirituality into the psychosocial dimension of schizophrenia. *American Journal of Psychiatry*, *163*, 1952–1959. doi:10.1176/appi.ajp.163.11.1952

Mohr, S., Gillieron, C., Borras, L., Brandt, P. Y., & Huguelet, P. (2007). The assessment of spirituality and religiousness in schizophrenia. *Journal of Nervous and Mental Disease*, *195*, 247–253. doi:10.1097/01.nmd.0000258230.94304.6b

Mohr, S., & Huguelet, P. (2004). The relationship between schizophrenia and religion and its implications for care. *Swiss Medical Weekly*, *134*, 369–376.

Mohr, S., Perroud, N., Gillièron, C., Brandt, P. Y., Rieben, I., Borras, L., & Huguelet, P. (2011). Spirituality and religiousness as predictive factors of outcome in schizophrenia and schizo-affective disorders. *Psychiatry Research, 186*, 177–182.

Murray-Swank, N. A., & Pargament, K. I. (2005). God, where are you? Evaluating a spiritually-integrated intervention for sexual abuse. *Mental Health, Religion, and Culture, 8*, 191–203. doi:10.1080/13694670500138866

Murray-Swank, N. A., & Pargament, K. I. (2011). Seeking the sacred: The assessment of spirituality in the therapy process. In J. Aten, M. R. McMinn, & E. L. Worthington Jr. (Eds.), *Spiritually oriented interventions for counseling and psychotherapy* (pp. 107–135). Washington, DC: American Psychological Association. doi:10.1037/12313-005

Narrow, W. E., Rae, D. S., Robins, N. L., & Regier, D. A. (2002). Revised prevalence estimates of mental disorders in the United States: Using a clinical significance criterion to reconcile 2 surveys' estimates. *Archives of General Psychiatry, 59*, 115–123. doi:10.1001/archpsyc.59.2.115

National Institute of Mental Health. (2009). *Schizophrenia.* Retrieved from http://www.nimh.nih.gov/health/publications/schizophrenia/how-is-schizophrenia-treated.shtml

Ndetei, D. M., & Vadher, A. (1984). Frequency and clinical significance of delusions across cultures. *Acta Psychiatrica Scandinavica, 70*, 73–76. doi:10.1111/j.1600-0447.1984.tb01184.x

Neeleman, J., & King, M. B. (1993). Psychiatrists' religious attitudes in relation to their clinical practice: A survey of 231 psychiatrists. *Acta Psychiatrica Scandinavica, 88*, 420–424. doi:10.1111/j.1600-0447.1993.tb03484.x

Neeleman, J., & Lewis, G. (1994). Religious identity and comfort beliefs in three groups of psychiatric patients and a group of medical controls. *International Journal of Social Psychiatry, 40*, 124–134. doi:10.1177/002076409404000204

Nuevo, R., Chatterji, S., Verdes, E., Naidoo, N., Arango, C., & Ayuso-Mateos, J. L. (2010). The continuum of psychotic symptoms in the general population: A cross-national study. *Schizophrenia Bulletin, 38*, 475–485.

Parabiaghi, A., Bonetto, C., Ruggeri, M., Lasalvia, A., & Leese, M. (2006). Severe and persistent mental illness: A useful definition for prioritizing community-based mental health service interventions. *Social Psychiatry and Psychiatric Epidemiology, 41*, 457–463. doi:10.1007/s00127-006-0048-0

Pargament, K. I. (1997). *The psychology of religion and coping: Theory, research, practice.* New York, NY: Guilford Press.

Pargament, K. I., & Brant, C. (1998). Religion and coping. In H. Koenig (Ed.), *Handbook of religion and mental health* (pp. 111–128). San Diego, CA: Academic Press. doi:10.1016/B978-012417645-4/50075-4

Pargament, K. I., Koenig, H. G., & Perez, L. M. (2000). The many methods of religious coping: Development and initial validation of the RCOPE. *Journal of Clinical Psychology, 56*, 519–543. doi:10.1002/(SICI)1097-4679(200004)56:4<519::AID-JCLP6>3.0.CO;2-1

Pathways to Promise. (2001). *Ministry and mental illness.* Retrieved from http://www.pathways2promise.org/crisis/index.htm

Perala, J., Suvisaari, J., Saarni, S. I., Kuoppasalmi, K., Isometsä, E., Pirkola, S., . . . Lönnqvist, J. (2007). Lifetime prevalence of psychotic and bipolar I disorders in a general population. *Archives of General Psychiatry, 64*, 19–28. doi:10.1001/archpsyc.64.1.19

Peters, E., Day, S., McKenna, J., & Orbach, G. (1999). Delusional ideation in religious and psychotic populations. *British Journal of Clinical Psychology, 38*, 83–96. doi:10.1348/014466599162683

Phillips, R. E., III, Lakin, R., & Pargament, K. I. (2002). Development and implementation of a spiritual issues psychoeducational group for those with serious mental illness. *Community Mental Health Journal, 38*, 487–495. doi:10.1023/A:1020832218607

Pieper, J. Z. T. (2004). Religious coping in highly religious psychiatric inpatients. *Mental Health, Religion, and Culture, 7*, 349–363. doi:10.1080/136746704100 01719805

Raja, M., Azzoni, A., & Lubich, L. (2000). Religious delusion: An observational study of religious delusion in a population of 313 acute psychiatric inpatients. *Schweizer Archiv für Neurologie und Psychiatrie, 151*, 22–29.

Reeves, R. R., & Liberto, V. (2006). Suicide associated with the Antichrist delusion. *Journal of Forensic Sciences, 51*, 411–412. doi:10.1111/j.1556-4029.2006.00079.x

Revheim, N., & Greenberg, W. M. (2007). Spirituality matters: Creating a time and place for hope. *Psychiatric Rehabilitation Journal, 30*, 307–310. doi:10.2975/30.4.2007.307.310

Romme, M., & Escher, S. (2000). *Making sense of voices.* London, England: Mind.

Russinova, Z., Wewiorski, N. J., & Dane, C. (2002). Use of alternative health care practices by persons with serious mental illness: Perceived benefits. *American Journal of Public Health, 92*, 1600–1603. doi:10.2105/AJPH.92.10.1600

Salloum, I. M., & Mezzich, J. E. (2011). Outlining the bases of person-centered integrative diagnosis. *Journal of Evaluation in Clinical Practice, 17*, 354–356. doi:10.1111/j.1365-2753.2010.01581.x

Shafranske, E. P. (1996). Religious beliefs, affiliations, and practices of clinical psychologists. In E. P. Shafranske (Ed.), *Religion and the clinical practice of psychology* (pp. 149–162). Washington, DC: American Psychological Association. doi:10.1037/10199-005

Shah, R., Kulhara, P., Grover, S., Kumar, S., Malhotra, R., & Tyagi, S. (2011). Relationship between spirituality/religiousness and coping in patients with residual schizophrenia. *Quality of Life Research, 20*, 1053–1060. doi:10.1007/s11136-010-9839-6

Shuman, J. J. (2009). Theological perspectives on the care of patients with psychiatric disorders. In P. Huguelet & H. Koenig (Eds.), *Religion and spirituality in psychiatry* (pp. 19–30). New York, NY: Cambridge University Press. doi:10.1017/CBO9780511576843.003

Siddle, R., Haddock, G., Tarrier, N., & Faragher, E. B. (2002). Religious delusions in patients admitted to hospital with schizophrenia. *Social Psychiatry and Psychiatric Epidemiology, 37*, 130–138. doi:10.1007/s001270200005

Silva, J. A., Leong, G. B., & Weinstock, R. (1997). Violent behaviors associated with the antichrist delusion. *Journal of Forensic Sciences, 42*, 1058–1061.

Sims, A. (2007). Spiritual aspects of management. In D. Bhugra & K. Bhui (Eds.), *Textbook of cultural psychiatry* (pp. 434–444). Cambridge, England: Cambridge University Press. doi:10.1017/CBO9780511543609.035

Sowers, W. (2005). Transforming systems of care: The American Association of Community Psychiatrists guidelines for recovery oriented services. *Community Mental Health Journal, 41*, 757–774. doi:10.1007/s10597-005-6433-4

Stompe, T., Friedman, A., Ortwein, G., Strobl, R., Chaudhry, H. R., Najam, N., & Chaudhry, M. R. (1999). Comparison of delusions among schizophrenics in Austria and in Pakistan. *Psychopathology, 32*, 225–234. doi:10.1159/000029094

Suhail, K. (2003). Phenomenology of delusions in Pakistani patients: Effect of gender and social class. *Psychopathology, 36*, 195–199. doi:10.1159/000072789

Sullivan, W. P. (1998). Recoiling, regrouping, and recovering: First-person accounts of the role of spirituality in the course of serious mental illness. *New Directions for Mental Health Services, 1998*(80), 25–33. doi:10.1002/yd.23319988005

Tateyama, M., Asai, M., Hashimoto, M., Bartels, M., & Kasper, S. T. (1998). Transcultural study of schizophrenic delusions. Tokyo versus Vienna and Tubingen (Germany). *Psychopathology, 31*, 59–68. doi:10.1159/000029025

Tepper, L., Rogers, S. A., Coleman, E. M., & Malony, H. N. (2001). The prevalence of religious coping among persons with persistent mental illness. *Psychiatric Services, 52*, 660–665. doi:10.1176/appi.ps.52.5.660

U.S. Substance Abuse and Mental Health Services Administration. (2011). *Prevalence of serious mental illness among U.S. adults by age, sex, and race.* Retrieved from http://www.nimh.nih.gov/statistics/SMI_AASR.shtml

Wallace, C. J., Lecomte, T., Wilde, J., & Liberman, R. P. (2001). CASIG: A consumer-centered assessment for planning individualized treatment and evaluating program outcomes. *Schizophrenia Research, 50*, 105–119. doi:10.1016/S0920-9964(00)00068-2

Waugh, A. C. (1986). Autocastration and biblical delusions in schizophrenia. *British Journal of Psychiatry, 149*, 656–658. doi:10.1192/bjp.149.5.656

Weiss, M. G., & Somma, D. (2010). Explanatory models in psychiatry. In D. Bhugra & K. Bhui (Eds.), *Textbook of cultural psychiatry* (pp. 127–140). Cambridge, England: Cambridge University Press.

Wong-McDonald, A. (2007). Spirituality and psychosocial rehabilitation: Empowering persons with serious psychiatric disabilities at an inner-city community program. *Psychiatric Rehabilitation Journal, 30*, 295–300. doi:10.2975/30.4.2007.295.300

Yangarber-Hicks, N. (2004). Religious coping styles and recovery from serious mental illnesses. *Journal of Psychology and Theology, 32*, 305–317.

CHAPTER 14

RELIGION AND SPIRITUALITY IN COPING WITH ACUTE AND CHRONIC ILLNESS

Harold G. Koenig

In this chapter, I examine the role that religion/spirituality (R/S) plays in how people with acute and chronic illness cope with their medical conditions (i.e., R/S coping). Physical illness, particularly that which is disabling, painful, and does not quickly resolve, poses enormous challenges to the individual. Such illness influences a person's family life, work, hobbies, and recreational activities, and causes fear and uncertainty about what the future may bring. Although secular coping resources may be very helpful in adapting to these changes, R/S beliefs and practices can further facilitate this process and are widely used for this purpose.

IMPACT OF MEDICAL ILLNESS

Physical illness, especially when chronic and disabling, affects at least four major health domains in a person's life: physical, mental, social, and spiritual (Koenig, King, & Carson, 2011).

Physical Health

Illness is often accompanied by loss of energy and increase in fatigue. The sick person experiences a loss of vigor and may feel weak and have difficulty performing simple tasks, even those involving self-care (bathing, dressing, walking, climbing stairs, etc.). Even more distressing, however, are the physical symptoms that medical illness may bring on, including pain, trouble breathing, nausea and vomiting, diarrhea or constipation, incontinence of urine or feces, chills or sweating from fever, disorientation and inability to concentrate from delirium, and the effects that these symptoms have on eating and sleeping. As physical symptoms begin to interfere with functioning, the person's independence is threatened and he or she may need care from others to survive, especially family members who may need to take over the work that the sick person used to perform. On top of that, the sick person may require medical care that consumes extensive time in traveling to doctor's appointments, waiting in office, and so forth; that is expensive and siphons off scarce resources during trying economic times; and that is inconvenient for family or friends who may need to take time off from jobs to provide transportation or many other services. Clearly, physical illness causes tremendous disruptions in both the sick person's life and the lives of family and close friends. When illness is chronic, all of the effects are magnified as they begin to accumulate over time, exhausting resources and wearing out support systems.

Mental Health

The physical changes just described present enormous psychological challenges for the sick person. First, physical illness often forces people to confront their own mortality, which may have been easily denied or repressed before becoming ill. This confrontation may produce anxiety and fear, which if not dealt with appropriately, may be channeled into inappropriate behaviors destructive to self or others. Second, physical illness can interfere with a person's roles at work, within the family, and within the broader social community. Loss in ability to perform usual roles, especially when others have to compensate

DOI: 10.1037/14046-014
APA Handbook of Psychology, Religion, and Spirituality: Vol. 2. An Applied Psychology of Religion and Spirituality, K. I. Pargament (Editor-in-Chief)

by taking on these roles, often results in loss of power and social status. Third, inability to perform usual roles results in loss of both the ability and the opportunity to be productive and contribute to the lives of others. The sick person, especially when illness is chronic, may soon begin to feel that he is no longer useful, either to himself or others. Fourth, medical illness may interfere with a person's ability to meet important and valued life goals, perhaps eliminating altogether the possibility of achieving them. Fifth, physical illness and disability may lead to the person feeling that she can no longer make a difference—a positive difference in the world. In fact, the opposite may become only too evident. The difference she is making is a negative one that interferes with the lives of loved ones and uses up family resources. This leads to the sixth challenge and perhaps the most devastating. The sick person loses his sense of purpose and meaning in life, feeling that he is simply a burden, no longer sees any possibility of pleasure or enjoyment, and begins to question his reason for being. This loss of hope leads quickly to a downward spiral of giving up, a decline in self-care activities, an increased burden on others—all of which reinforce a sense of hopelessness and futility.

Depending on the person's psychological makeup, defense mechanisms will be mobilized to deal with the psychological pain—including unhealthy ones such as denial and repression—resulting in counterproductive "acting out" behaviors (excessive use of alcohol, inappropriate drug use, etc.). Another response may be a living in the past, wishing that things were like they were and avoiding the realities of the present. A third response may be a dwelling on the negative and complaining or rehearsing woes, either privately within the mind or externally to family and friends, who quickly become bored and lose interest. Alternatively, the sick person may simply withdraw from involvement with others (physically, socially, or psychologically). Such behaviors should be seen in the context of the patient's attempts to cope (no matter how ineffective). Use of such defenses are not in resistance or opposition to coping but rather are ineffective attempts to deal with their challenges.

Social Health

The sick person's and their loved ones' reactions often lead to profound isolation. Chronic illness often leads to a deep sense of loneliness. The person with chronic illness may not have the physical ability, the energy, or the desire to continue to engage in social activities, resulting in a loss of friends and withering relationships with family that must be maintained through effort and attention. If relocation is required because of inability to care for self, or because of financial stresses, then the chronically ill person may be forced to make new friends or become overly dependent on children or other family members, who ultimately may resent this need for attention. Making new friends can also be a challenge, especially if mobility is an issue, hearing is a problem, or the circle of social contacts becomes constricted.

Should the chronically ill person require a lot of assistance, then he will begin to feel like he is a burden on others. This may in fact be true, and depending on the quality of previous relationships with family and friends, these people may come to view the sick person as a burden and sometimes, in subtle or not so subtle ways, communicate this. The sick person may respond in different ways. As noted, one response is to withdraw. Another is to become angry and blame or otherwise display outward aggression toward others, often caretakers. The sick person may even grow to resent the good health of others, adding to his or her anger and irritability.

Spiritual Health

It is not surprising that the effects of chronic illness on physical, mental, and social health can adversely affect spiritual health as well. Unfortunately, health professionals and researchers generally have neglected the spiritual impact of illness. Physically, medical illness can interfere with participation in the religious community, influencing the ability and desire to attend religious services. Physical and emotional symptoms of chronic illness can adversely affect concentration, making it difficult to pray or read religious scriptures or inspirational literature. When chronic illness, disability, and distressing symptoms continue for long periods without relief, despite sincere and persistent prayer by self and loved ones, it is easy to begin to feel abandoned even by God. God may feel distant and appear unconcerned about the painful struggles that the person may be experiencing. Members of the faith community, while calling and visiting faithfully during periods of acute medical illness, may stop coming when illness drags on for months and months or years. This can lead to feelings of abandonment not only by God but also by the religious community.

The sick person may try to make sense of the painful situation, which seems resistant to prayer and other spiritual strategies, by concluding that God must be punishing her for past sins. Why else would God allow the illness and symptoms to continue? Nothing else makes sense. Finally, in pain and frustration, the person may become angry and lash out at God—challenging God's ability to make a difference, God's love for her, or even the goodness of God, and may decide to turn completely away from God, sometimes losing belief in God's existence entirely.

Consequences

A common result of these many losses and challenges is that the chronically ill disabled person begins to suffer from anxiety, depression, despair, or attempts to escape through drugs or alcohol (and even suicide in some cases). In studies of depression in hospitalized patients with medical illness, we and others have found that around 45% (nearly one half) experience depressive disorders that interfere with social, occupational, or recreational functioning (Kitchell, Barnes, & Veith, 1982; Koenig, George, Peterson, & Pieper, 1997). Sadly, depression is even more common in younger persons than in older adults; chronic, disabling illnesses are more expected in later life and considered "on time," whereas those that occur during young adulthood or middle age are not (Koenig et al., 1991).

Although such a long list of negative effects of medical illness can provoke anxiety or be disheartening, even to the readers of this chapter, my objective is to tell it like it is—both from personal experience with chronic illness and nearly three decades of my clinical experience first as a nurse and then as a family physician, geriatrician, and psychiatrist. Many health care professionals are not aware of the tremendous burden that those with chronic illnesses face in multiple areas of life and may wonder why a sick person is irritable, impatient, or ungrateful.

I have emphasized the losses that many but not all persons with chronic illness experience. Yet humans are remarkable creatures capable of adapting to the most difficult of life circumstances, especially if those circumstances come about slowly and if they have the psychological and social resources to deal with them. Likewise, family members and friends can be heroically understanding and supportive even over the long haul to those with chronic illness. Although nearly half of those with chronic illness and disability experience significant depression, we should not forget that systematic studies find that the remainder (more than half) cope impressively well with illness and remain positive, optimistic, and socially involved. The reality, however, is that many do not overcome these losses so gracefully, and because we often encounter such persons in the health care system, some empathy is needed of what these persons may be experiencing.

Nevertheless, there is hope, and one solid reason for hope lies squarely in the religious faith many medically ill persons turn to for comfort and meaning, a faith that remains available to them as long as they are conscious. Although religion may not lead to a cure or even always lead to comfort, extensive evidence from individual testimonies and systematic research shows religion can help people cope better even with the worst circumstances imaginable. Before explaining how this might occur, and whether it does indeed occur, I will define the terms used in this chapter.

DEFINITIONS

I use the terms *religion* and *spirituality* largely interchangeably here. My view, however, is that they have distinct meanings and are also distinguished from secular ways of understanding and coping (for a sense of how this approach fits with the handbook overall, see Volume 1, Chapter 1, this handbook).

Religion and Spirituality

From my perspective, religion involves beliefs, practices, and rituals related to the transcendent or the divine. Religion is often organized and practiced within a community, but it also can be practiced alone and outside of an institution. Religion, then, is not limited to an institutional form only, but includes private forms of expression (Koenig et al., 2011).

In contrast to recent evolutions in ways that some scholars define spirituality (see Volume 1, Chapter 1, this handbook), I approach spirituality using a classic or traditional definition (Koenig, 2008a). Specifically, I define as spiritual those individuals who are deeply religious, whose lives are informed and directed by their religious beliefs, and so are distinguished from the nonreligious and from those who are religious but not deeply so. The spiritual are often those who have dedicated their lives to religion, such as the clergy or deeply committed religious leaders (Gandhi, the Buddha, Confucius, Jesus, Mother Teresa, etc.), although need not be. Spiritual persons would include all those who are sincerely seeking to develop a religious view and way of life that affect their relationships with others, themselves, and world around them.

The Secular

I distinguish the *secular* from both religion and spirituality. The secular approach is a way of viewing human existence and behavior that does not involve religion, that is, the transcendent. The focus is on the rational self (or human community) as the ultimate source of power and meaning.

From here out, I will usually use the term religion or R/S coping, as this is what much of the research has examined—at least the research that has not used measures contaminated with the mental health outcomes being examined (Koenig, 2008a; Tsuang & Simpson, 2008).

R/S Coping

Finally, I use the term *R/S coping* to mean the use of religious beliefs or practices as a way of adapting to the physical, psychological, and social challenges caused by medical illness. For example, in Western religious traditions, religious coping may involve praying to God for strength and comfort, wisdom and direction, health or healing, or help for loved ones (see Pargament, 1997; see also Volume 1, Chapter 19, this handbook). It may involve reading inspirational materials, such as the holy scriptures (Torah, Christian Bible, or Holy Qur'an) or reading popular books or magazines on religious topics. R/S coping may involve getting together with members of one's faith tradition for worship services, singing hymns, prayer, or scripture study. It also may involve the practice of religious rituals related to health and healing, such as lighting candles or participating in sacraments, such as the Eucharist or Confession, or the practice of immersion in a *mikveh* or wearing of *tefillin*. R/S coping may involve asking others to pray for oneself, praying for others, seeking religious counseling, providing religious support to others, or participating in religious rituals focused on healing.

RELIGION AND COPING WITH MEDICAL ILLNESS

Religious beliefs and practices are often mobilized in response to medical illness, and they serve unique roles and diverse functions in the coping process. Three of the major ways that religion does so is by providing emotional support (from others or from a divine being), by giving meaning and purpose to the suffering and by influencing health behaviors and other ways of coping (Koenig, 1998; Koenig, Pargament, & Nielsen, 1998; Pargament, 1997).

Emotional Support

Religious beliefs and practices can provide the emotional support that chronically ill persons need to help them recover. As noted, support can come either directly from having a personal relationship with God, in which case the divine is experienced as a loving presence that is comforting and supportive, or from a faith community whose members represent God in human form. The quality of that support may depend on how well developed the relationship with God is and to what extent the person was involved in their faith community before they got sick. It may depend on how open people are to receiving support from the faith community, either their own faith community or a faith community in which they were not previously involved. Unfortunately, faith communities vary considerably in their ability to provide such support and, if not effective, can actually worsen the sick person's suffering and increase the person's isolation (i.e., by indicating that the person did something that caused the illness, or by insisting on religious healing in preference to medical treatments; Biebel & Koenig, 2004). Fortunately, this is more the exception than the rule, but it needs to be recognized because of the traumatic consequences.

Meaning Making

A primary mechanism by which religious belief can help a person cope with chronic medical illness is by giving the illness meaning and viewing it as serving some greater purpose (see Volume 1, Chapter 8, this handbook). Such beliefs help chronically ill persons to cognitively reframe their situations in a more positive light, and this relieves suffering. Victor Frankl (1946/2006) in *Man's Search for Meaning* indicated that most of those in World War II German concentration camps who retained their sense of purpose and meaning were able to survive, whereas those who lost purpose and meaning ended up giving up and dying. It is amazing what can be endured when the experience has meaning and purpose that leads to something good. Religious beliefs—from Christian beliefs about enduring physical suffering to contribute to God's salvation of the world or about deriving a sense of compassion and solidarity with Jesus who also suffered physically to Hindu beliefs that patience in suffering can improve karma and the next life—provide a perspective on pain and disability that allows it to be endured better. Likewise, the belief that physical illness may help one grow closer to God, or the belief that this present suffering represents a special calling from God, can transform physical or emotional pain into an opportunity rather than an uncontrollable and senseless disaster.

Influences on Health Practices

Religion provides many resources for managing illness, including those that help persons to adapt to illness in healthy ways rather than engage in self-destructive behaviors. Religious beliefs may facilitate the discontinuation of cigarette smoking or unhealthy drinking or drug use and instead provide the motivation to exercise, reduce weight, or engage in healthier eating practices. Understanding that the body is the "temple of the spirit" may help religious persons make these changes. Religious beliefs also provide guidance on how to respond to chronic illness, helping one to avoid temptations that offer temporary relief but at a cost that involves greater problems in the future (i.e., addiction to alcohol, drugs, etc.).

Case Example

Tim, age 57, was having problems urinating, which he attributed to an enlarged prostate, something he thought he inherited from his father. When he went to the doctor for a routine physical, his physician told him he had an elevated PSA (prostate specific antigen) indicating the possibility of prostate cancer, and thought he should see a urologist and have a biopsy done. This news made him feel very anxious. The anxiety increased after the biopsy indicated that he had prostate cancer. Tim was soon scheduled for a radical prostatectomy with pelvic lymph node dissection and partial bladder removal.

Before surgery, members of Tim's faith community rallied around him, visiting and starting a prayer chain that involved hundreds of people praying for a successful surgery. In fact, his minister and several church friends came numerous times to his house to pray with him in person. Knowing that he was not alone and that there were hundreds of others offering up prayers on his behalf brought him comfort.

Tim's anxiety also caused him to turn to personal prayer. Although never much of a prayer person in the past, he realized his need for it now. Shortly after his diagnosis, he began to set aside a regular time each morning to ask God to guide him during the day and help him through the challenges he would face. He prayed that God would heal his prostate cancer and guide the doctors during the surgery. However, he also prayed that "God's will" would be done and acknowledged that only God knew what the best outcome would be for him, and so sought to place his trust in God regardless of outcome.

Tim also began reading the scriptures for the first time, purchasing a Living Bible that made the passages easier to understand. Although he used to use alcohol to help his anxiety in the past (a life-long problem), he realized from his scripture reading that using alcohol in this way was not the right thing to do. Instead, he turned to reading the psalms, which helped calm his nerves without leaving him with a hangover.

Surrounded by his family, minister, and several close friends from his faith community, Tim arrived at the hospital for surgery. The surgery involved some complications, but he got through it and recovered rapidly. While still having to deal with the possibility that the cancer might return despite the surgery, he continued to deal with this fear by involving himself in his faith community and maintaining a regular time each day for prayer and scripture reading. In looking back, Tim realized that the dread and fear caused by the cancer had contributed to his spiritual growth and was continuing to do so.

RESEARCH ON RELIGIOUS COPING WITH MEDICAL ILLNESS

Although Tim certainly benefited from using religion to cope, how often does this actually occur? Is Tim's case rare or unusual? I now examine results from systematic research that have examined relationships between religion and coping in clients with medical illness. Before doing so, however, a brief discussion is indicated on how R/S coping is usually measured (see also Volume 1, Chapter 19, this handbook).

Assessment of R/S Coping

There are at least two approaches to measuring the degree to which persons rely on religion to cope—assessment of overall R/S coping and assessment of specific ways that people use religion to cope. An example of the first approach is the Religious Coping Index (Koenig et al., 1992). This three-item measure combines qualitative and quantitative methods to assess overall R/S coping and must be administered by an interviewer. The first item is an open-ended question that simply asks how the person copes; the interviewer does not mention religion and thus subjects can report whatever they rely on most to help them cope (out of the entire universe of possible coping behaviors). If a religious response is given spontaneously to this question (i.e., God, prayer, church, etc.), then the response is given a score of 10; if not, then a score of 0 is given. Next, persons are asked to rate on a 0-to-10 visual analogue scale to what extent they use religion to cope. In the third and final question, the interviewer asks how the person uses religion to cope and requests that the person give specific examples of how religion was recently used to cope. The interviewer writes down exactly what the subject says and then gives an overall rating from 0 to 10 on the extent to which the person relies on religion to cope. Adding up the three items yields an overall quantitative score ranging from 0 to 30. This score can then be correlated with other quantitative mental and physical health outcomes.

The second approach, developed by Ken Pargament, identifies specific ways that people use religion to cope. Several instruments of varying length have been developed for this purpose, ranging from the14-item brief RCOPE (Pargament et al., 1998) to the 105-item full RCOPE (Pargament et al., 2000). Using this method, two basic types of coping have been differentiated: positive and negative R/ S coping. Positive R/S coping involves, for example, strengthening one's relationship with God, working together with God as a partner, or viewing the stressful situation as an opportunity for spiritual growth. Negative R/S coping (also described as *religious struggle*) involves, for example, questioning God's power, questioning God's commitment to the individual, or seeking to explain the stressful situation as resulting from abandonment from God or from the individual's lack of devotion to God.

Prevalence

Studies have documented the prevalence of R/S coping in a wide range of medical illnesses and in different regions of the world. The prevalence is largely determined by how religious the people are in that particular country or section of the country, and the severity of the health condition. For example, in the Southeastern United States, 90% of patients hospitalized with acute or chronic medical illness rely on religion to cope, and more than 40% indicate that it is the most important factor that keeps them going (Koenig, 1998). This is quite different, however, in northern Europe, where religious involvement is much lower than in the United States and where the use of religion in coping is also much less prevalent (e.g., 2% in Sweden; Cederblad, Dahlin, & Hagnell, 1995). In fact, Ringdal, Gotestam, Kaasa, Kvinnslaud, and Ringdal (1996) reported that even a large percentage of patients with terminal cancer in Norway did not believe in God (43%) and reported they received no comfort from religious beliefs (45%).

Relationship to Mental Health

More than 400 studies have now examined R/S coping in a variety of settings, including medically ill patients (Koenig et al., 2011; Koenig, McCullough, & Larson, 2001). The majority of research in those with disabling medical illness has found better adjustment and better mental health in persons using religion to cope, compared with those relying on other ways of coping. Adjustment or successful coping is often reflected by level of depressive symptoms or presence of depressive disorder, which often occurs when the person is overwhelmed by circumstances and methods of coping fail. In a series of systematic quantitative studies involving hospitalized medically ill patients, Koenig and colleagues found that religious beliefs and practices used in coping were associated with lower rates of depression and faster recovery from depression (Koenig, 2007a, 2007b; Koenig et al., 1992; Koenig, George, & Peterson, 1998). For example, we diagnosed depressive disorder in 1,000 medically ill hospitalized patients with congestive heart failure or chronic lung disease, and then followed 839 of these patients for up to 6 months to assess baseline predictors of depression outcome. We found that the 14% of patients who attended religious services weekly or more, prayed at least daily, read religious scriptures at least three times per week, and scored high on a measure of intrinsic religiosity recovered from depression 53% faster than other patients, independent of multiple psychological, social, and physical health controls (hazard ratio = 1.53, 95% CI 1.20–1.94; Koenig, 2007b).

Relationship to Social Health

Already discussed are ways that R/S coping may facilitate the development and maintenance of supportive relationships (both human and divine), serving to buffer psychological and situational stressors arising from medical illness. Many studies have found a positive association between R/S coping and social support, including those that involved medical patients (for rheumatoid arthritis, see Keefe et al., 2001; for advanced cancer patients, see Tarakeshwar et al., 2006; for cardiac surgery patients, see Ai, Park, Huang, Rodgers, & Tice, 2007). Importantly, social support from religious sources appears to be more durable over time, when physical illness strikes (Krause, 2008). In other words, faith communities continue to support members long after physically ill members can no longer return that support. The reason for this may be because the support is not as much based on the "exchange" principle as nonreligious sources of support are. The religious have an additional reason for providing support—that is, their religious beliefs emphasize the importance of helping others in need whether or not they feel like it and whether or not someone can reciprocate (i.e., love thy neighbor as thyself).

Nevertheless, much further research is needed to better understand this relationship. More studies are needed to determine how the religiousness of those who provide support influences how long they continue to give support when physical illness prevents reciprocation. Likewise, studies are needed to determine how the sick person's religiousness or R/S coping behavior influences the perceived quality of social support. In other words, at any given level of objective support in terms of number of meetings attended, telephone calls from friends, and frequency of getting together with friends and relatives, do those who depend on religion to cope actually report a higher quality of support or greater satisfaction with the level of support provided? Is this different when that support comes from religious sources (vs. secular sources)? Research by Krause (2006) has suggested that religious support adds a distinctive dimension to outcomes beyond the effects of secular support.

Relationship to Functional Health

Research suggests that individuals who turn to religion for comfort and strength when facing medical problems may actually perceive themselves to be less disabled than they really are on the basis of objectives measures of physical illness severity. For example, Idler (1987) examined the relationship between religious involvement, chronic illness, and disability in 2,811 elderly residents of New Haven, Connecticut. Private religiousness was measured by self-rated religiousness and religion as source of strength and comfort. Among men, multivariate analysis revealed that at any given level of objective chronic illness, those who received a great deal of comfort from religion reported less disability compared with those reporting no such comfort from religion. Perceptions of disability are apparently influenced by more than just the actual physical illness itself because a person's sense of self (and how disabled one is) can be affected by many other factors, including attitudes and beliefs (Idler, 1995). By providing a more positive outlook on chronic health conditions, religious belief may enable sick persons to see themselves as less disabled than they really are. Alternatively, the person who is depressed, hopeless, and feels life has little meaning because of physical suffering is going to experience that illness as much more disabling and paralyzing than the person who is hopeful and optimistic about the illness. Religious support and positive cognitions mobilized by R/S coping can influence such uplifting attitudes. Following up on this research, Idler and Kasl (1997) also found in a prospective study that religious involvement delayed the development of physical disability with increasing age, a finding that has been replicated by several other research teams (Benjamins, 2004; N. S. Park et al., 2008; Reyes-Ortiz et al., 2006).

RELIGIOUS RESOURCES FOR PREVENTION OF ILLNESS

Besides helping persons to adapt to medical illness in healthy ways versus engaging in self-destructive behaviors involving alcohol and drugs or seeking high-risk alternative medical treatments, religious beliefs and activities may also help in other ways. For example, religious involvement may facilitate the identification of an illness early or identification of other medical illnesses that may be present (see Chapter 23 in this volume). Likewise, rather than lead to a delay of medical care, religious activity may lead to more timely medical care and better compliance with treatments.

Disease Screening

Participation in a religious community has been shown to increase information exchange, including information related to disease screening. As a result, religious involvement is related to higher rates of mammography (Bowen, Singal, Eng, Crystal, & Burke, 2003; Bowie, Wells, Juon, Sydnor, & Rodriguez, 2008; Holt, Lukwago, & Kreuter, 2003; Mitchell, Lannin, Mathews, & Swanson, 2002; Steele-Moses et al., 2009), pap smears (Benjamins, 2006), HIV testing (Latkin, Tobin, & Gilbert, 2002), blood pressure checks (Aaron, Levine, & Burstin, 2003; Benjamins, 2007), cholesterol monitoring (Benjamins, 2005; Benjamins & Brown, 2004), prostate examinations (Benjamins & Brown, 2004; Holt, Wynn, & Darrington, 2009; Holt, Wynn, Litaker, et al., 2009), blood sugar checks (Benjamins, 2007; Boltri et al., 2008), and well-person physical and dental exams (Hill, Burdette, Ellison, & Musick, 2006). Religiousness has also been correlated with being more likely to see the same medical practitioners on a regular basis over time (King & Pearson, 2003). The result is that diseases may be detected at an early stage when treatment is more effective.

Medical Compliance

Because religious doctrines encourage people to act responsibly, it should not be surprising that religious persons are more likely to comply with their medications. This has been shown for hypertension

(Koenig, George, Hays, et al., 1998), HIV/AIDS (Ironson & Kremer, 2009; Kemppainen, Kim-Godwin, Reynolds, & Spencer, 2008; Mellins et al., 2009), and congestive heart failure (C. L. Park, Moehl, Fenster, Suresh, & Bliss, 2008), to mention just a few. The result is a reduction in the risk of relapse and increased likelihood of effective medical treatment, improving medical outcomes and reducing disease-associated psychological stress.

EXACERBATION OF HEALTH PROBLEMS

Although the vast majority of research suggests that religion is helpful in coping with medical illness, are there circumstances in which religious beliefs and practices might interfere with coping or impede recovery from illness (see Chapter 4 in this volume)?

Avoidance of Medical Care

The person using religion to cope may decide that medical care is not needed, believing that prayer is all that is necessary for healing. Interest in faith healing has grown tremendously in the past few decades. Even mainline Protestant churches now regularly have healing services for members with acute and chronic medical problems. Religious healers in the past (Oral Roberts, Kathryn Kuhlman) attracted hundreds of thousands to their healing crusades, and others (Benny Hinn, Reinhart Bonnke) continue to do so. People suffering with illnesses for which there is no cure are often willing to try anything that promises a chance of relief, regardless of the financial cost or medical risks. Although some faith healers are completely genuine in what they do, others are not so honest and take advantage of the desperation that drives many that come to them for healing.

Dependence on religion to cure rather than to cope also can interfere with medical care when religious convictions conflict with traditional medical treatments. Those attending a healing service may wish to prove that they have the faith to be healed by stopping medication or foregoing conventional treatments. The results can be disastrous, particularly for diabetics who stop their insulin, epileptics who stop seizures medications, cardiac patients who stop antiarrhythmic drugs, and so on. People with diseases that have a lot of fear associated with them, such as cancer, may be especially vulnerable to risky religious rationalizations. A woman who finds a hard lump in her breast may be terrified and use her belief that only God cures cancer to justify a lack of effort to seek medical care that may confirm her worst fears (Lannin et al., 1998). Even when an illness is diagnosed, medical treatments may be refused in preference for religious approaches (Talbot, 1983), a decision that becomes particularly controversial when children are involved (Asser & Swan, 1998).

Avoidance of Mental Health Care

If depression or severe anxiety develops in the chronically ill, the religious person may try to depend entirely on faith or religious practices to cope, rather than seek necessary mental health care. Symptoms may worsen in severity and result in suicide, a situation often escalated by the attitude of mental health professionals toward religion (see Chapters 2 and 6 in this volume). For more than a century, conflict has characterized the relationship between religion and mental health care, exacerbated by Freud's description of religion as "the universal obsessional neurosis" (Freud, 1927/1962). There is open resistance to consideration of religious beliefs in mental health care, resistance that became clear in a recent discussion among British psychiatrists (see e-letters in response to two articles in *The Psychiatrist* by Koenig, 2008b, and Dein, Cook, Powell, and Eagger, 2010). Negative attitudes toward religion by mental health professionals are not limited to Great Britain. A systematic review of the religious content of the *Diagnostic and Statistical Manual of Mental Disorders* (3rd ed., rev.; *DSM–III–R;* American Psychiatric Association, 1987) found that nearly one quarter of all cases of mental illness involved religious examples (Larson et al., 1993). More recent publications by mental health professionals continue to reinforce a lack of concern for patients' religious beliefs (Jones, 2007; Watters, 1992) and a recent national survey of U.S. psychiatrists found that 56% never, rarely, or only sometimes inquire about R/S issues in patients with depression or anxiety (Curlin et al., 2007).

Given the long-standing antagonistic relationship between the mental health professionals and the faith community, the seeking of professional mental health care or taking of psychiatric medications may be opposed both by the patient and by the patient's religious support system. Medically ill religious persons with mental health problems often receive their first treatment by clergy or other counselors within the faith community (Weaver, 1995). On the basis of the generally neglectful (and at times disparaging) attitude of many mental health professionals toward religion, clergy may be reluctant to refer members of the congregation to mental health professionals, especially for psychotherapy. Failure of clergy to refer may prevent many from receiving adequate treatment. Furthermore, if the client belongs to a faith community and that community does not support (or counteracts) the gains made in psychotherapy, then those gains may not last.

Unrealistic Expectations

The client with medical illness and family members may cope by praying for a miraculous cure. When such miracles do not happen, then there may be disappointment, mental distress, and even a turning away from a supportive religious faith. Praying for a miracle may also foster unrealistic expectations concerning the aggressiveness by which medical interventions should be sought, especially in terminal illnesses. At least one major study (Phelps et al., 2009) has found that those using religion to cope are more likely to want expensive, high-tech medical interventions—even when death is imminent, unavoidable, and medical treatment is futile—resulting in the overuse of expensive technology that otherwise could be used for those with reversible medical problems. This is an issue that will require increasing attention as growing medical costs limit the availability of medical services for all. Recent research by the same research team that found a link between R/S coping and increased use of life-prolonging treatments, however, indicated that inappropriate use of such treatments occurred only when clients' spiritual needs were not being met (Balboni et al., 2010). The implications are that addressing patients' spiritual needs toward the end of life (or any time, for that matter) might result in a reduction of inappropriate use of expensive and futile technologies.

Excessive Religious Activity

In a frantic attempt to "change God's mind," medical clients may throw themselves into so much religious activity that they fail to pay adequate attention to family members, engage in self-care activities, or seek medical treatments that could relieve the illness. For example, a person with a serious diagnosis may volunteer at church for so many tasks that little time is left for meeting the emotional needs of spouse or children. Likewise, prayer or scripture reading may become so time-consuming that little or no time is left for physical rehabilitation necessary for recovery. The faith community may admire such persons as deeply spiritual, not knowing that their activities are driven by anxiety (not devotion) that may cause a worsening of a medical condition or relationships with loved ones who depend on them.

Negative R/S Coping

As noted, a common and normal response to a serious medical diagnosis or a persistent chronic illness, is to ask questions such as, "Why me?" "Why am I not healed, despite all my acts of religious devotion?" "Why did this illness come about in the first place, when I took good care of myself and lived right?" "All of my friends are healthy—why have I been selected out for this disease?" Frustration and anger may be the result. Most religious individuals go through such a questioning stage, work through negative emotions about the illness, and then turn to their religious faith to cope with the illness. Others, however, may remain "stuck" in their anger at God and religion. Some persons, not previously religious, may have turned to religion specifically in response to the medical illness because no other alternatives were available. Having turned to God only to get their health back, when health does not return, the need for God disappears. The pleading and bargaining for health, in some cases, may be turned into anger at God. This can be expressed in terms of God punishing them, God not having the power to make a difference, or anger at their faith community for not supporting them at the level expected. These individuals may turn away from religion entirely, stop praying, and disengage from the religious community. Many studies have found that "negative R/S coping" (also referred to as *spiritual struggle*) is an independent predictor of worse health outcomes and greater mortality in medical patients with a range of acute and chronic medical conditions (Ai et al., 2009; Hebert, Zdaniuk, Schulz, & Scheier, 2009; McConnell, Pargament, Ellison, & Flannelly, 2006; Pargament, Koenig, Tarakeshwar, & Hahn, 2001; Zwingmann, Muller, Korber, & Murken, 2008; see also Volume 1, Chapter 25, this handbook).

RELIGIOUS AND SPIRITUAL NEEDS

Religious methods of coping address many of the R/S needs that come up when people experience medical illness, especially when it is chronic and disabling. The effectiveness of R/S coping will influence the extent to which those needs are met. I next describe R/S needs commonly found in those with medical illness who come from a Judeo-Christian background, the religious framework with which I am most familiar. The reader should note that R/S needs are likely to vary from person to person, and the particular needs I describe are not based on any research or empirical studies but rather on my nearly 30 years of clinical practice treating patients with chronic illness and on what I have learned from having to struggle with a chronic illness for about that same period of time. These needs are also colored by my biblical view of Christianity, which many patients and therapists may not share. The important point is that these R/S needs should not be viewed as prescriptive but rather as a starting place for a dialogue with the patient.

Certainty About the Nature of God

R/S coping behaviors are likely to be less effective to the degree that the person becomes confused and less certain of the nature of God. For maximum benefit from R/S coping, many with chronic illness may need to sustain their preexisting beliefs that God really and truly exists and is not imaginary. Others may benefit by renewing or gaining a more clear and meaningful understanding of God's nature within the context of suffering. Conversely, the onset or intensification of uncertainty or confusion about God's nature can create ambivalence about the power of R/S coping strategies, which in turn can undermine the ability of religious activities such as prayer to make a difference in the situation. Certain belief that God exists, that God can make a difference, and that God cares and wants to make a difference (i.e., to find a way through the pain) can increase the sense that the situation is under control and that good outcomes are possible. Admittedly, certainty of God's ability to control medical outcomes is pretty hard to come by and those who are deeply spiritual, but who have grown comfortable with forces being outside of God's control as a core feature of their faith, may be less dependent on certainty in this element of God's powers; however, R/S coping behaviors ought to be more effective to the extent that people have a sense of clarity about what kind of help God can provide in the context of chronic illness.

Belief That God Is on Their Side

Medically ill people also need to believe that God is for them, not against them. The kind of God that one believes in will influence the effectiveness of R/S coping. A God who is distant; has more important things to do; is primarily interested in punishing people for sins, spoiling fun, or seeking retribution; or is weak, not in control, and unable to make a difference is not a God who can be depended on when life and well-being are at stake. An all-powerful, ever-present God who is intensely concerned with, deeply loves, and desires the person's very best, whether in this life or the next, is the kind of God who can be trusted, relied on, and is worthy of the person's time and attention.

Experience of God's Presence

More than just believing in God and mouthing scripted prayers, those with chronic illness need to experience God's loving presence in their lives. Experience of God's presence has the power to melt away the fear, anxiety, and hopelessness that could otherwise overwhelm. Unfortunately, the chronically ill who are experiencing distressing physical and emotional symptoms often have difficulty feeling God's presence, which is drowned out by their pain. Sometimes that pain can be affected by the disappointment felt by those who firmly believe that God will take away the illness and bring about a bodily cure. This is when other people are needed to represent God's love and care for that person. Christian biblical scriptures emphasize that God identifies with those who are sick and suffering, so much so that those people who demonstrate care and love for the suffering are actually caring for God. Thus, often, it is God's servants who provide the sick person with God's presence that will encourage and give hope.

Experience of God's Unconditional Love

The chronically ill need to feel loved unconditionally by God. Like everyone else, the sick have done things that they are not proud of and react in ways that are far less than perfect. Those with disabling health conditions are carrying a heavy burden that tests their patience, understanding, and love for others and themselves. Rash decisions may be made or destructive behaviors engaged in while suffering intolerable physical or emotional symptoms. These persons need to know that God loves them anyway and understands better and more completely than either they or others could possibly imagine. This sense of being unconditionally loved can help the person endure and overcome.

Prayer

The chronically ill need to pray alone, with others, and for others. Prayers need to be said alone and with no one else present. Although prayer can and should be directed at obtaining relief from symptoms and circumstances, the real purpose of prayer is to communicate with and develop a person's relationship with God. Prayers said alone help to develop an intimacy with God that allows a change in the person and his or her attitude toward the circumstances. This is often what provides emotional relief, whether or not the external circumstances are changed. Prayers also need to be said together with other people, as this provides the human contact necessary for emotional healing and for enabling the faith community to be the kind of community it needs to be.

Finally, there is a need to pray for people other than oneself. Others also have problems and some of those problems may even be greater than those the person with medical illness is facing (e.g., caregivers). Supporting others and asking God for relief and comfort for them will help to distract the person's attention away from his or her own problems, help put those problems into perspective, and counter the natural tendency of those with chronic illness to withdraw into and focus on themselves.

Inspiration From Religious Scriptures

Those with chronic illness need direction and inspiration. The holy scriptures of all religious traditions contain certain pieces of wisdom and advice that have been distilled over thousands of years and proven to help people cope successfully with difficult problems. The scriptures also contain promises of assurance and comfort, based on the ultimate authority, and promises of future reward for faithful living. The chronically ill also need to be inspired by examples of people who have overcome their circumstances and have triumphed over them through patience and faith. The Christian biblical scriptures are filled with such examples. Take the book of Job in the Bible, for example. Job was a righteous individual who did everything correctly, worshiped God, and cared for others. Yet he was stricken with major losses in his life, which were followed by both physical illness (boils) and emotional illness (depression) and spiritual struggles (anger at God). In the end, though, through persistence and a direct experience of God's presence, Job obtained healing and his life became even better than it had been before.

Worship

Those with chronic illness need an opportunity to worship God, both alone and with others. Worship is the natural result that occurs from spending time alone with God in prayer and developing a deep understanding of and relationship with God. Worship involves acknowledging God and God's greatness, and expressing thanks and gratitude for what one has been given—even gratitude for one's medical illness, without which such a deep intimacy with God may not have been possible. Worship with others is also necessary because God is perhaps experienced most completely within the faith community (which in Christian terms is the "body of Christ"). Joy, peace, and hope are the fruits that result from private and communal worship—fruits that neutralize feelings of depression, worry, and loneliness.

Service to Others

To experience a full life, all persons—including those with chronic disabling medical illnesses—need to serve God by serving others. Caregivers and health care professionals need to give those with medical illness an opportunity to serve and to encourage them to do so. There are many altruistic acts that the chronically ill can perform, although they may need help identifying what those activities are and how to use their existing abilities to perform them (Koenig, Lamar, & Lamar, 1997). The dependent, disabled person has many opportunities in which they can serve others in dependency—for example, expressing gratefulness to those who provide care, making an effort to relieve caregiver burden by doing as much self-care as possible or otherwise assisting caregivers, praying for caregivers, encouraging other sick people nearby (or by telephone) with similar problems, or gratefully receiving expressions of care and love offered by others, even when wanting to reject that care. Indeed, there are many ways in which the medically ill can serve others, and they need to do so (just like everybody else needs to).

Expression of Anger

Sometimes, circumstances are really bad and suffering continues on and on and on. A natural response to such pain is frustration and anger, and expression of that anger toward the one in ultimate control who is responsible for allowing it to take place, that is, God, and sometimes anyone representing God. Those with chronic illness need to express that anger just like Job expressed his anger, and they need to be able to do so without feeling guilty or feeling like such expression severs their relationship with God or makes God love them any less. If chaplains and other religious caregivers truly understand this, then they will be able to more patiently endure these expressions of anger, often directed at them, and help the chronically ill person work through this normal and expected reaction. Unless they are helped to work through this anger, the consequences may be devastating (see the section on religious struggles).

Expression of Forgiveness

Those with chronic illness need to both receive forgiveness and give it to others. In trying to figure out why they became ill and why the illness continues to persist, medically ill persons sometime blame themselves for bringing on the condition. Sometimes this blame is correctly placed. A careless or unhealthy lifestyle may have contributed to a condition that is now past the treatment stage. Sometimes this is not the case, and the person is simply trying to make sense of the circumstances. Whether self-blame is accurate or imagined, chronically ill people need to forgive themselves and accept the forgiveness that God readily offers (often assisted by various religious rituals). Likewise, there may be others to blame for the medically ill person's circumstances (accurately or imagined) and such lack of forgiveness could create resentment that delays recovery and responses to treatment. Just as the medically ill need to forgive themselves, they also need to forgive others—all others (including God)—and will probably need help in doing so.

IMPLICATIONS

The considerations raised in this chapter have important implications for the way patients with medical illness (and their caretakers) cope with illness and for the health professionals who treat them.

Patients

Those with medical illness should recognize that their religious beliefs and practices can help them to cope better, prevent the development of depression, and indirectly affect the course of physical illness by promoting potentially helpful emotional, cognitive, social, and behavioral processes. Religious clients, that is, nearly two thirds of those seeking medical care in the United States (Gallup Poll, 2009; Pew Forum, 2007), should seek out religious resources to help bolster their R/S coping. Patients who utilize religious belief to cope should alert their physicians and other caretakers that this is important to them and request that religious resources be provided or the health care environment altered to support their R/S coping.

Caretakers

Caretakers should recognize the role that religion may be playing in enabling their loved ones to cope with medical illness and should be encouraged to support healthy religious beliefs and practices that are a source of strength and well-being. R/S coping may be supported by providing inspirational reading materials, giving rides to religious services, or engaging in R/S coping activities with loved ones such as prayer (if desired). Furthermore, caregivers should be made aware of research showing that R/S coping is not only beneficial to loved ones but also to caregivers themselves. Studies show that religious beliefs and activities predict better adjustment to the caregiver role and may prevent the development of depression (Hebert, Dang, & Schulz, 2007; Rabins, Fitting, Eastham, & Fetting, 1990; Rabins, Fitting, Eastham, & Zabora, 1990). In addition, religious motivations may infuse caregiver activities with meaning and purpose that may help relieve stress and improve caregiver burden (Koenig, 2002).

Health Professionals

Health professionals, too, need to be aware of the role that religious beliefs and practices play in the medical client's coping, either as a cause of comfort or a source of stress. Taking a spiritual history may identify both positive and negative R/S coping behaviors that could either work for or against the medical treatments that are prescribed (see Chapter 5 in this volume). Unfortunately, fewer than 10% of physicians regularly take a spiritual history or inquire about spiritual issues (Curlin, Chin, Sellergren, Roach, & Lantos, 2006), and although the role that religion plays in health and well-being is increasingly being addressed in medical schools (Koenig, Hooten, Lindsay-Calkins, & Meador, 2010), it will be years before the medical profession fully appreciates the role that religious involvement plays in health. Discussions concerning the impact of clients' religious beliefs on coping and medical care desired may enhance the likelihood that medical decisions are respectful of and consistent with their faith tradition. There is also evidence that when health professionals address these issues, the result is an improvement in the clinician–patient relationship, a reduction in depressive symptoms, and an increase in functional well-being (Kristeller, Rhodes, Cripe, & Sheets, 2005). In addition, such communications may help to form realistic expectations by clients of what the medical profession can and cannot do as well as clarify what religion can and cannot do (Balboni et al., 2010; Phelps et al., 2009).

ACCESSING RELIGIOUS RESOURCES IN COUNSELING AND PSYCHOTHERAPY

Clinicians who treat anxiety and depressive disorders in persons with chronic medical illness should realize clients' religious beliefs and practices are usually healthy resources for support. Thus, rather than ignore or avoid religious issues, it may be useful to integrate them into therapy. First, clinicians need to conduct a thorough spiritual assessment that determines whether religious resources exist and whether they are positive or negative. Is religion important to the client and how does this play out in day-to-day life?

If the client indicates that this is not a significant aspect of his life or how he copes with illness, then the topic may be dropped for the time being. Later on, however, the therapist may wish to return to the subject after firmly establishing a therapeutic alliance. At that time, gentle inquiry about whether religion has ever been important to the client and what kinds of experiences turned him off to religion are probably worth exploring. Much may be learned from such inquiries.

Alternatively, if the client acknowledges that religion is important, then additional questions should identify how the client expresses religion. Does the client pray, and does she find this comforting? Are their any special prayers or hymns that are particularly meaningful to her (and why)? Does she read religious scriptures or inspirational literature, and how is this helpful or not helpful in coping with the medical illness? Are there particularly rituals that are especially important to her, and how might the therapist assist her to overcome physical barriers resulting from medical illness so that sacred rituals can be practiced? Is the client a member of a religious community and how supportive is that community? If the faith community is supportive, but the client is not currently involved because of health problems, the therapist might inquire if the client wishes to participate in the faith community and, if so, brainstorm on how this could be arranged. Finally, does the client's clergy person or other members of the congregation visit, and is this visitation perceived as helpful and comforting, or alternatively, as anxiety or guilt provoking?

After obtaining a solid understanding of the role of religion and the availability of preferred religious resources, and depending on how important religion is to the client, the therapist may choose to integrate religious resources into therapy or determine how religious beliefs may facilitate the goals of therapy. Some knowledge about the client's faith tradition is needed to do this, and training in pastoral counseling would be especially helpful. Nevertheless, in-depth expertise in religion or religious counseling is not always necessary, and even therapists with little or no religious beliefs can effectively integrate religion into therapy with a little training (Post & Wade, 2009; Propst, 1980; Propst, Ostrom, Watkins, Dean, & Mashburn, 1992).

Having completed the assessment, the therapist may now consider ways to utilize the client's religious faith as a resource in counseling. If the client has become reclusive and socially isolated, then the therapist might encourage him to become more involved in his religious community, especially if this was something he enjoyed previously. The client could be helped to identify friends within the religious community and encouraged to reestablish contact with them. If the client is struggling with low self-esteem, then religious scriptures may be utilized to point out how valuable he is to God. If hopeless and discouraged over the medical condition, religious scriptures may be emphasized that stress that nothing is impossible and that all things, even a painful illness, can be transformed into something good through faith and persistence. If the client is struggling with disability that interferes with purpose and meaning in life, then reframing the situation in religious terms may help him see ways in which the illness and even the suffering associated with the illness may be used to achieve something meaningful or a greater good.

If the client's focus is continually on the negative, the therapist may utilize religious beliefs to help her focus on the positive, expressing gratitude and thanksgiving for the good things in her life. If she is struggling with resentment toward others because of a disabling illness, then help her to forgive others (perhaps by exploring her feeling of being forgiven by God) to enable her to release the bitterness and free her of this burden. If the client has become introverted and focused on himself, religious beliefs may be emphasized that encourage the offering of love and support to others and engagement in altruistic activities to increase an external focus. These are just a few of the ways that religious resources may be used to facilitate emotional healing in those with chronic disabling medical illnesses.

Alternatively, if religious beliefs are being used in an unhealthy way to deny or suppress issues that need to be dealt with or to justify rigid ways of thinking that interfere with healthy relationships, then this should be noted and a plan should be developed to addresses these issues that is gentle and respectful. Challenging unhealthy religious beliefs requires considerably more expertise than supporting healthy religious beliefs or encouraging religious activities in which the client is already engaged. Consultation with clergy or pastoral counselors who are familiar with the client's beliefs may be necessary, or referral of clients to those with sufficient expertise should be considered. This is especially important when the client is stuck in a negative R/S coping style, feeling punished or abandoned by God or the faith community, and supportive listening has not been sufficient to get the client through this stage.

In the Case Example, Tim had plenty of religious and social resources to help him through the anxiety over his prostrate cancer, and the course of his illness was not protracted or associated with severe disability or pain. Not all patients are so fortunate. The occurrence of a life-threatening illness that is progressive, disabling, and painful without relief can challenge those with even the strongest personal faith. I recall a patient of mine, Bob (fictitious name), from a devout religious background who developed a chronic pain syndrome after falling off of a truck at work. In his early 40s at the time of the accident and caring for a family of five, Bob lost his job and required multiple back surgeries in attempts to control his pain from several fractured vertebrae. Soon the family's financial resources were gone, and

Bob, who could not work, was in chronic, severe pain that could not be relieved by conventional means without intolerable side effects. Understandably, he fell into a deep depression, which was exacerbated by his belief that God was punishing him for his past sins, and he reached the verge of suicide despite his strong religious beliefs and a supportive faith community. Bob simply could not imagine any other explanation for why this had happened to him.

After prescribing an antidepressant and doing what I could to control his chronic pain with analgesics, most of our sessions were spent with my just listening to him talk about his anguish and frustration, as he winced when jolting pains shot into his leg from his back. I did not challenge his belief that God was punishing him but let him ventilate this and other feelings related to his feeling helpless and out of control. I told him at the end of each visit that I would be praying for him, as we were of the same faith tradition, and he agreed that I could do this for him. I also let him know I was committed to being there for him day or night if he needed me and that I would work with him to find the right doctors to treat his pain and do what I could to help him get the financial assistance he needed. A time or two, I admitted Bob to the hospital because suicidal thoughts were getting the best of him. Throughout this time, he continued to practice his faith, praying and reading the scriptures and attending and participating in his faith community as an elder. After nearly 10 years, Bob continues to wonder what he did to deserve a life like this, and he hopes that some day a miracle will free him of the pain that he carries with him 24 hours a day, which he has told me is the only hope that sustains him. I pray for that miracle, too, and try to let him know that I will be there for him until that miracle happens even if it is not until the next life that it occurs.

R/S INTEGRATED PSYCHOTHERAPIES

Specific therapies have been developed that integrate R/S beliefs into psychotherapy. The two major therapies that I will address here are spiritually integrated psychotherapy (SIP) and religious cognitive–behavioral therapy (religious CBT), both of which can be used to treat emotional disorders in those with acute or chronic medical illness.

Spiritually Integrated Psychotherapy

Developed by Pargament (2007) on the basis of his vast experience with R/S coping styles, SIP seeks to utilize clients' spiritual beliefs in the treatment of anxiety and depressive disorders or adjustment problems. The underlying premise is that spirituality cannot be separated from psychotherapy. At the heart of SIP is creating a spiritual dialogue between client and therapist, assessing spirituality not only as part of the solution to clients' problems but also as part of those problems, and helping clients to draw on positive spiritual resources in times of stress. SIP is one of the few therapies developed that directly addresses negative forms of R/S coping or religious struggles, which are so common in those with chronic medical illness. This therapy is conducted from a nonsectarian perspective, addressing spirituality from both traditional and nontraditional approaches, and can be used with religious and nonreligious clients alike. In conducting SIP, Pargament noted, clinicians should be careful to avoid trivializing spirituality as simply a tool for mental health, reducing spirituality to more basic motivations and drives, imposing spiritual values on clients, and overstating the importance of spirituality. Research shows that forms of SIP are effective for the treatment of anxiety in persons of all ages (Pargament, 2007; Rosmarin et al., 2010), although more research is needed specifically in medical populations (e.g., Cole, 2005; Tarakeshwar, Pearce, & Sikkema, 2005).

Religious CBT

Religious CBT follows largely the same process as conventional CBT. Conventional CBT helps clients recover from emotional disorders by helping them understand the links between thoughts, emotions, and behavior. It uses guided discovery, Socratic questioning, and challenge of automatic negative thoughts to help clients identify and appraise their cognitions and determine problematic behaviors. Interventions include activity scheduling, along with "practice assignments," in which clients test out ideas and behaviors discussed during sessions. Conventional CBT does not typically utilize the religious beliefs of clients.

In religious CBT, the therapist is open to and brings into therapy the clients' thoughts about their religion or faith (see Chapter 8 in this volume). For example, clients may have obsessive guilt about sin or punishment, report religious doubt, or want to discuss the cognitive and emotional elements of their faith. In religious CBT, all those issues are considered fully acceptable as part of therapy. Religious CBT uses religious rationales and religious arguments consistent with the client's faith tradition to counter irrational thoughts, and utilizes religious behaviors, such as involvement in the religious community, to increase supportive relationships. The underlying philosophy is that religious clients often already have the tools and the motivation to change their negative thinking, although they may not realize this. Religious CBT teaches clients to use religious teachings, doctrines, and behaviors to help change maladaptive beliefs, values, and behaviors to transform their worldview into one that is meaningful, hopeful, and optimistic, which is incompatible with emotional distress. Religious CBT seeks to change dysfunctional beliefs and behaviors (related to self-preoccupation) that may be rooted in values that have created a negative worldview based on physical illness and disability. It seeks to bolster powerful religious beliefs that promote such behaviors as forgiveness, gratitude, generosity, and altruism by focusing on others and on God instead of self to generate meaning and purpose, optimism, and hope, which neutralize anxiety and depressive symptoms.

Research suggests that religious CBT is at least as effective, if not more effective, than conventional CBT in religious clients. Rebecca Propst and colleagues have demonstrated the effectiveness of religious CBT in two studies. In the first, Propst (1980) compared the effects of CBT plus religious imagery versus CBT and nonreligious imagery in 44 religious subjects with depression who received twice-weekly 1-hour sessions for 4 weeks. Outcomes were assessed immediately following the treatment and at the 6-week follow-up. Subjects receiving the religious imagery had a significantly greater response on the Beck Depression Inventory (BDI; 14% with BDI > 9) compared with those receiving nonreligious CBT (60%). In the second study, Propst et al. (1992) conducted a larger randomized clinical trial of religious CBT versus conventional CBT in 59 religious patients with depressive disorders. Subjects were randomized to religious CBT ($n = 19$), conventional CBT ($n = 20$), or two control groups ($n = 21$; pastoral counseling or a wait-list control group [WLC]). A total of 18–20 one-hour sessions were delivered over 12 weeks and outcomes were assessed at completion of treatment, at 3-month follow-up, and at 2-year follow-up. Results indicated that only subjects receiving the religious CBT reported significantly lower posttreatment BDI scores than did the WLC group ($p < .001$), whereas those receiving conventional CBT showed only a nonsignificant trend in that direction. Likewise, only religious CBT showed a clinically meaningful change on the BDI score compared with the WLC group (68% vs. 27%). There has been progress in the area of empirically supportive religious and spiritual therapies (Hook et al., 2010; also see Chapter 34 in this volume), which build on Propst's initial research and is a more contemporary review. Like SIP, religious CBT has not yet been tested in clients with disabling medical illnesses, although plans for such a study are currently under development (Koenig et al., 2010).

CONCLUSION

Religious beliefs and practices are widely utilized by clients with acute and chronic illness to help them to cope. The greatest challenge to coping is presented by chronic disabling medical illnesses accompanied by distressing physical symptoms and interfering with the ability to function. Such illness affects physical, psychological, social, and spiritual domains in life, and is associated with a wide range of spiritual needs. Research has shown that religious involvement, and R/S coping in particular, is associated with better mental health in clients with chronic medical illness and predicts faster recovery from depression. Religious beliefs can also interfere with coping and adversely affect medical outcomes, especially when they conflict with conventional treatments. Nevertheless, there are many reasons why religious resources may help to prevent medical illness, diagnose it earlier, and improve recovery from it as well as help people to cope better with the condition. Several types of counseling and psychotherapy now exist that have promise in treating emotional disorders in those with medical illness, although none have yet been subject to systematic scientific examination in this population.

References

Aaron, K. F., Levine, D., & Burstin, H. R. (2003). African American church participation and health care practices. *Journal of General Internal Medicine, 18,* 908–913. doi:10.1046/j.1525-1497.2003.20936.x

Ai, A. L., Park, C. L., Huang, B., Rodgers, W., & Tice, T. N. (2007). Psychosocial mediation of religious coping styles: A study of short-term psychological distress following cardiac surgery. *Personality and Social Psychology Bulletin, 33,* 867–882. doi:10.1177/0146167207301008

Ai, A. L., Seymour, E. M., Tice, N., Kronfol, Z., Appel, H., & Bolling, S. F. (2009). Spiritual struggle related to plasma interleukin-6 prior to cardiac surgery. *Psychology of Religion and Spirituality, 1,* 112–128. doi:10.1037/a0015775

American Psychiatric Association. (1987). *Diagnostic and statistical manual of mental disorders* (3rd ed., rev.). Washington, DC: Author.

Asser, S. M., & Swan, R. (1998). Child fatalities from religion-motivated medical neglect. *Pediatrics, 101,* 625–629. doi:10.1542/peds.101.4.625

Balboni, T. A., Paul, M. E., Balboni, M. J., Phelps, A. C., Loggers, E. T., Wright, A. A., . . . Prigerson, H. G. (2010). Provision of spiritual care to patients with advanced cancer; Associations with medical care and quality of life near death. *Journal of Clinical Oncology, 28,* 445–452. doi:10.1200/JCO.2009.24.8005

Benjamins, M. R. (2004). Religion and functional health among the elderly: Is there a relationship and is it constant? *Journal of Aging and Health, 16,* 355–374. doi:10.1177/0898264304264204

Benjamins, M. R. (2005). Social determinants of preventive service utilization: How religion influences the use of cholesterol screening in older adults. *Research on Aging, 27,* 475–497. doi:10.1177/0164027505276048

Benjamins, M. R. (2006). Religious influences on preventive health care use in a nationally representative sample of middle-age women. *Journal of Behavioral Medicine, 29,* 1–16. doi:10.1007/s10865-005-9035-2

Benjamins, M. R. (2007). Predictors of preventive health care use among middle-aged and older adults in Mexico: The role of religion. *Journal of Cross-Cultural Gerontology, 22,* 221–234. doi:10.1007/s10823-007-9036-4

Benjamins, M. R., & Brown, C. (2004). Religion and preventative health care utilization among the elderly. *Social Science and Medicine, 58,* 109–118. doi:10.1016/S0277-9536(03)00152-7

Biebel, D., & Koenig, H. G. (2004). *New light on depression: Help and hope for the depressed and those who love them.* New York, NY: Zondervan/HarperCollins.

Boltri, J. M., Davis-Smith, Y. M., Seale, J. P., Shellenberger, S., Okosun, I. S., & Cornelius, M. E. (2008). Diabetes prevention in a faith-based setting: Results of translational research. *Journal of Public Health Management and Practice, 14,* 29–32.

Bowen, D. J., Singal, R., Eng, E., Crystal, S., & Burke, W. (2003). Jewish identity and intentions to obtain breast cancer screening. *Cultural Diversity and Ethnic Minority Psychology, 9,* 79–87. doi:10.1037/1099-9809.9.1.79

Bowie, J. V., Wells, A. M., Juon, H. S., Sydnor, K. D., & Rodriguez, E. M. (2008). How old are African American women when they receive their first mammogram? Results from a church-based study. *Journal of Community Health, 33,* 183–191. doi:10.1007/s10900-008-9092-x

Cederblad, M., Dahlin, L., & Hagnell, O. (1995). Coping with life span crises in a group at risk of mental and behavioral disorders: From the Lundby study. *Acta Psychiatrica Scandinavica, 91,* 322–330. doi:10.1111/j.1600-0447.1995.tb09789.x

Cole, B. S. (2005). Spiritually-focused psychotherapy for people diagnosed with cancer: A pilot outcome study. *Mental Health, Religion, and Culture, 8,* 217–226. doi:10.1080/13694670500138916

Curlin, F. A., Chin, M. H., Sellergren, S. A., Roach, C. J., & Lantos, J. D. (2006). The association of physicians' religious characteristics with their attitudes and self-reported behaviors regarding religion and spirituality in the clinical encounter. *Medical Care, 44,* 446–453. doi:10.1097/01.mlr.0000207434.12450.ef

Curlin, F. A., Lawrence, R. E., Odell, S., Chin, M. H., Lantos, J. D., Koenig, H. G., & Meador, K. G. (2007). Religion, spirituality, and medicine: Psychiatrists' and other physicians' differing observations, interpretations, and clinical approaches. *American Journal of Psychiatry, 164,* 1825–1831. doi:10.1176/appi.ajp.2007.06122088

Dein, S., Cook, C. C. H., Powell, A., & Eagger, S. (2010). Religion, spirituality and mental health. *The Psychiatrist, 34,* 63–64. Retrieved from http://pb.rcpsych.org/cgi/eletters/34/2/63#9946

Frankl, V. E. (2006). *Man's search for meaning.* Boston, MA: Beacon Press. (Original work published 1946)

Freud, S. (1962). Future of an illusion. In J. Strachey (Ed. & Trans.), *Standard edition of the complete psychological works of Sigmund Freud* (p. 43). London, England: Hogarth Press. (Original work published 1962)

Gallup Poll. (2009). *State of the states: Importance of religion.* Retrieved from http://www.gallup.com/poll/114022/state-states-importance-religion.aspx

Hebert, R. S., Dang, Q., & Schulz, R. (2007). Religious beliefs and practices are associated with better mental health in family caregivers of patients with dementia: Findings from the REACH study. *American Journal of Geriatric Psychiatry, 15,* 292–300. doi:10.1097/01.JGP.0000247160.11769.ab

Hebert, R. S., Zdaniuk, B., Schulz, R., & Scheier, M. (2009). Positive and negative religious coping and well-being in women with breast cancer. *Journal of Palliative Medicine, 12,* 537–545. doi:10.1089/jpm.2008.0250

Hill, T. D., Burdette, A. M., Ellison, C. G., & Musick, M. A. (2006). Religious attendance and the health behaviors of Texas adults. *Preventive Medicine, 42,* 309–312. doi:10.1016/j.ypmed.2005.12.005

Holt, C. L., Lukwago, S. N., & Kreuter, M. W. (2003). Spirituality, breast cancer beliefs and mammography utilization among urban African American women. *Journal of Health Psychology, 8,* 383–396. doi:10.1177/13591053030083008

Holt, C. L., Wynn, T. A., & Darrington, J. (2009). Religious involvement and prostate cancer screening behaviors among southeastern African American men. *American Journal of Men's Health, 3,* 214–223. doi:10.1177/1557988308318686

Holt, C. L., Wynn, T. A., Litaker, M. S., Southward, P., Jeames, S., & Schulz, E. (2009). A comparison of a spiritually based and non-spiritually based educational intervention for informed decision making for prostate cancer screening among church-attending African-American men. *Urologic Nursing, 29,* 249–258.

Hook, J. N., Worthington, E. L., Jr., Davis, D. E., Jennings, D. J., 2nd, Gartner, A. L., & Hook, J. P. (2010). Empirically supported religious and spiritual therapies. *Journal of Clinical Psychology, 66,* 46–72.

Idler, E. L. (1987). Religious involvement and the health of the elderly: Some hypotheses and an initial test. *Social Forces, 66,* 226–238.

Idler, E. L. (1995). Religion, health, and nonphysical senses of self. *Social Forces, 74,* 683–704.

Idler, E. L., & Kasl, S. V. (1997). Religion among disabled and nondisabled persons II: Attendance at religious services as a predictor of the course of disability. *The Journals of Gerontology, Series B: Psychological Sciences and Social Sciences, 52,* S306–S316. doi:10.1093/geronb/52B.6.S306

Ironson, G., & Kremer, H. (2009). Spiritual transformation, psychological well-being, health, and survival in people with HIV. *International Journal of Psychiatry in Medicine, 39,* 263–281. doi:10.2190/PM.39.3.d

Jones, H. E. (2007). *Religion: The etiology of mental illness.* Oakdale, CA: Mental Health Education Press.

Keefe, F. J., Affleck, G., Lefebvre, J., Underwood, L., Caldwell, D. S., & Drew, J. (2001). Living with rheumatoid arthritis: The role of daily spirituality and daily religious and spiritual coping. *Journal of Pain, 2,* 101–110. doi:10.1054/jpai.2001.19296

Kemppainen, J., Kim-Godwin, Y. S., Reynolds, N. R., & Spencer, V. S. (2008). Beliefs about HIV disease and medication adherence in persons living with HIV/AIDS in rural southeastern North Carolina. *Journal of the Association of Nurses in AIDS Care, 19,* 127–136. doi:10.1016/j.jana.2007.08.006

King, D. E., & Pearson, W. S. (2003). Religious attendance and continuity of care. *International Journal of Psychiatry in Medicine, 33,* 377–389. doi:10.2190/F5DY-5GAB-K298-EMEK

Kitchell, M. A., Barnes, R. F., & Veith, R. C. (1982). Screening for depression in hospitalized geriatric medical patients. *Journal of the American Geriatrics Society, 30,* 174–177.

Koenig, H. G. (1998). Religious beliefs and practices of hospitalized medically ill older adults. *International Journal of Geriatric Psychiatry, 13,* 213–224. doi:10.1002/(SICI)1099-1166(199804)13:4<213::AID-GPS755>3.0.CO;2-5

Koenig, H. G. (2002). *Purpose and power in retirement: New opportunities for significance and meaning.* Philadelphia, PA: Templeton Foundation Press.

Koenig, H. G. (2007a). Religion and depression in older medical inpatients. *American Journal of Geriatric Psychiatry, 15,* 282–291. doi:10.1097/01.JGP.0000246875.93674.0c

Koenig, H. G. (2007b). Religion and remission of depression in medical inpatients with heart failure/pulmonary disease. *Journal of Nervous and Mental Disease, 195,* 389–395.

Koenig, H. G. (2008a). Concerns about measuring "spirituality" in research. *Journal of Nervous and Mental Disease, 196,* 349–355. doi:10.1097/NMD.0b013e31816ff796

Koenig, H. G. (2008b). Religion and mental health: What are psychiatrists doing and should do? *Psychiatric Bulletin (Royal College of Psychiatrists), 32,* 201–203. Retrieved from http://pb.rcpsych.org/cgi/eletters/32/6/201

Koenig, H. G., Cohen, H. J., Blazer, D. G., Pieper, C., Meador, K. G., Shelp, F., . . . DiPasquale, R. (1992). Religious coping and depression in elderly hospitalized medically ill men. *American Journal of Psychiatry, 149,* 1693–1700.

Koenig, H. G., George, L. K., Hays, J. C., Larson, D. B., Cohen, H. J., & Blazer, D. G. (1998). The relationship between religious activities and blood pressure in older adults. *International Journal of Psychiatry in Medicine, 28,* 189–213. doi:10.2190/75JM-J234-5JKN-4DQD

Koenig, H. G., George, L. K., & Peterson, B. L. (1998). Religiosity and remission from depression in medically ill older patients. *American Journal of Psychiatry, 155*, 536–542.

Koenig, H. G., George, L. K., Peterson, B. L., & Pieper, C. F. (1997). Depression in medically ill hospitalized older adults: Prevalence, correlates, and course of symptoms based on six diagnostic schemes. *American Journal of Psychiatry, 154*, 1376–1383.

Koenig, H. G., Hooten, E. G., Lindsay-Calkins, E., & Meador, K. G. (2010). Spirituality in medical school curricula: Findings from a national survey. *International Journal of Psychiatry in Medicine, 40*, 391–398. doi:10.2190/PM.40.4.c

Koenig, H. G., King, D. E., & Carson, V. B. (2011). *Handbook of religion and health* (2nd ed.). New York, NY: Oxford University Press.

Koenig, H. G., King, M. B., Robins, C. J., Ciarrocchi, J., Dolor, R., deLeon, D., . . . Cohen, H. J. (2010). *Conventional vs. religious psychotherapy for major depression in patients with chronic illness.* Unpublished manuscript, Center for Spirituality, Theology, and Health, Durham, NC.

Koenig, H. G., Lamar, T., & Lamar, B. (1997). *A gospel for the mature years: Finding fulfullment by knowing and using your gift.* Binghamton, NY: Haworth Press.

Koenig, H. G., McCullough, M. E., & Larson, D. B. (2001). *Handbook of religion and health.* New York, NY: Oxford University Press. doi:10.1093/acprof:oso/9780195118667.001.0001

Koenig, H. G., Meador, K. G., Shelp, F., Goli, V., Cohen, H. J., & Blazer, D. G. (1991). Depressive disorders in hospitalized medically ill patients: A comparison of young and elderly men. *Journal of the American Geriatrics Society, 39*, 881–890.

Koenig, H. G., Pargament, K. I., & Nielsen, J. (1998). Religious coping and health outcomes in medically ill hospitalized older adults. *Journal of Nervous and Mental Disease, 186*, 513–521. doi:10.1097/00005053-199809000-00001

Krause, N. (2006). Exploring the stress-buffering effects of church-based and secular social support on self-rated health in late life. *Journal of Gerontology: Social Sciences, 61B*, S35–S43.

Krause, N. (2008). *The kingdom of heaven is in the midst of you: Reflections on social relationships in the church and health in late life.* Philadelphia, PA: Templeton Foundation Press.

Kristeller, J. L., Rhodes, M., Cripe, L. D., & Sheets, V. (2005). Oncologist Assisted Spiritual Intervention Study (OASIS): Patient acceptability and initial evidence of effects. *International Journal of Psychiatry in Medicine, 35*, 329–347. doi:10.2190/8AE4-F01C-60M0-85C8

Lannin, D. R., Mathews, H. F., Mitchell, J., Swanson, M. S., Swanson, F. H., & Edwards, M. S. (1998). Influences of socioeconomic and cultural factors on racial differences in late-stage presentation of breast cancer. *JAMA, 279*, 1801–1807. doi:10.1001/jama.279.22.1801

Larson, D. B., Thielman, S. B., Greenwold, M. A., Lyons, J. S., Post, S. G., Sherrill, K. A., . . . Larson, S. S. (1993). Religious content in the DSM-III-R glossary of technical terms. *American Journal of Psychiatry, 150*, 1884–1885.

Latkin, C. A., Tobin, K. E., & Gilbert, S. H. (2002). Shun or support: The role of religious behaviors and HIV-related health care among drug users in Baltimore, Maryland. *AIDS and Behavior, 6*, 321–329. doi:10.1023/A:1021196528795

McConnell, K. M., Pargament, K. I., Ellison, C. G., & Flannelly, K. J. (2006). Examining the links between spiritual struggles and symptoms of psychopathology in a national sample. *Journal of Clinical Psychology, 62*, 1469–1484. doi:10.1002/jclp.20325

Mellins, C. A., Havens, J. F., McDonnell, C., Lichtenstein, C., Udall, K., & Chesney, M. (2009). Adherence to antiretroviral medications and medical care in HIV-infected adults diagnosed with mental and substance abuse disorders. *AIDS Care, 21*, 168–177. doi:10.1080/09540120802001705

Mitchell, J., Lannin, D. R., Mathews, H. F., & Swanson, M. S. (2002). Religious beliefs and breast cancer screening. *Journal of Women's Health, 11*, 907–915. doi:10.1089/154099902762203740

Pargament, K. I. (1997). *The psychology of religion and coping.* New York, NY: Guilford Press.

Pargament, K. I. (2007). *Spiritually integrated psychotherapy: Understanding and addressing the sacred.* New York, NY: Guilford Press.

Pargament, K. I., Koenig, H. G., & Perez, L. M. (2000). The many methods of religious coping: Development and initial validation of the RCOPE. *Journal of Clinical Psychology, 56*, 519–543. doi:10.1002/(SICI)1097-4679(200004)56:4<519::AID-JCLP6>3.0.CO;2-1

Pargament, K. I., Koenig, H. G., Tarakeshwar, N., & Hahn, J. (2001). Religious struggle as a predictor of mortality among medically ill elderly patients: A two-year longitudinal study. *Archives of Internal Medicine, 161*, 1881–1885. doi:10.1001/archinte.161.15.1881

Pargament, K. I., Smith, B. W., Koenig, H. G., & Perez, L. (1998). Patterns of positive and negative religious coping with major life stressors. *Journal for the Scientific Study of Religion, 37*, 710–724. doi:10.2307/1388152

Park, C. L., Moehl, B., Fenster, J. R., Suresh, D., & Bliss, D. (2008). Religiousness and treatment adherence in congestive heart failure patients. *Journal of Religion, Spirituality, and Aging, 20*, 249–266. doi:10.1080/15528030802232270

Park, N. S., Klemmack, D. L., Roff, L. L., Parker, M. W., Koenig, H. G., & Sawyer, P. (2008). Religiousness and longitudinal trajectories in elders' functional status. *Research on Aging, 30*, 279–298. doi:10.1177/0164027507313001

Pew Forum. (2007). *U.S. religious landscape survey*. Retrieved from http://religions.pewforum.org

Phelps, A. C., Maciejewski, P. K., Nilsson, M., Balboni, T. A., Wright, A. A., Paulk, E., . . . Prigerson, H. G. (2009). Religious coping and use of intensive life-prolonging care near death in patients with advanced cancer. *JAMA, 301*, 1140–1147. doi:10.1001/jama.2009.341

Post, B. C., & Wade, N. G. (2009). Religion and spirituality in psychotherapy: A practice-friendly review of research. *Journal of Clinical Psychology, 65*, 131–146. doi:10.1002/jclp.20563

Propst, L. R. (1980). The comparative efficacy of religious and nonreligious imagery for the treatment of mild depression in religious individuals. *Cognitive Therapy and Research, 4*, 167–178. doi:10.1007/BF01173648

Propst, L. R., Ostrom, R., Watkins, P., Dean, T., & Mashburn, D. (1992). Comparative efficacy of religious and nonreligious cognitive-behavior therapy for the treatment of clinical depression in religious individuals. *Journal of Consulting and Clinical Psychology, 60*, 94–103. doi:10.1037/0022-006X.60.1.94

Rabins, P. V., Fitting, M. D., Eastham, J., & Fetting, J. (1990). The emotional impact of caring for the chronically ill. *Psychosomatics, 31*, 331–336. doi:10.1016/S0033-3182(90)72171-8

Rabins, P. V., Fitting, M. D., Eastham, J., & Zabora, J. (1990). Emotional adaptation over time in caregivers for chronically ill elderly people. *Age and Ageing, 19*, 185–190. doi:10.1093/ageing/19.3.185

Reyes-Ortiz, C. A., Ayele, H., Mulligan, T., Espino, D. V., Berges, I. M., & Markides, K. S. (2006). Higher church attendance predicts lower fear of falling in older Mexican-Americans. *Aging and Mental Health, 10*, 13–18. doi:10.1080/13607860500307787

Ringdal, G. I., Gotestam, K., Kaasa, S., Kvinnslaud, S., & Ringdal, K. (1996). Prognostic factors and survival in a heterogeneous sample of cancer patients. *British Journal of Cancer, 73*, 1594–1599. doi:10.1038/bjc.1996.300

Rosmarin, D. H., Pargament, K. I., Pirutinsky, S., & Mahoney, A. (2010). A randomized controlled evaluation of a spiritually integrated treatment for subclinical anxiety in the Jewish community, delivered via the Internet. *Journal of Anxiety Disorders, 24*, 799–808. doi:10.1016/j.janxdis.2010.05.014

Steele-Moses, S. K., Russell, K. M., Kreuter, M., Monahan, P., Bourff, S., & Champion, V. L. (2009). Cultural constructs, stage of change, and adherence to mammography among low-income African American women. *Journal of Health Care for the Poor and Underserved, 20*, 257–273. doi:10.1353/hpu.0.0123

Talbot, N. A. (1983). The position of the Christian Science Church. *New England Journal of Medicine* 309, 1639–1644.

Tarakeshwar, N., Pearce, M. J., & Sikkema, K. J. (2005). Development and implementation of a spiritual coping group intervention for adults with HIV/AIDS: A pilot study. *Mental Health, Religion, and Culture, 8*, 179–190.

Tarakeshwar, N., Vanderwerker, L. C., Paulk, E., Pearce, M. J., Kasl, S. V., & Prigerson, H. G. (2006). Religious coping is associated with the quality of life of patients with advanced cancer. *Journal of Palliative Medicine, 9*, 646–657. doi:10.1089/jpm.2006.9.646

Tsuang, M. T., & Simpson, J. C. (2008). Commentary on Koenig (2008). "Concerns about measuring 'spirituality' in research." *Journal of Nervous and Mental Disease, 196*, 647–649. doi:10.1097/NMD.0b013e3181813570

Watters, W. (1992). *Deadly doctrine: Health, illness, and Christian God-talk*. Buffalo, NY: Prometheus Books.

Weaver, A. J. (1995). Has there been a failure to prepare and support-based clergy in their role as front-line community mental health workers? A review. *Journal of Pastoral Care, 49*, 129–147.

Zwingmann, C., Muller, C., Korber, J., & Murken, S. (2008). Religious commitment, religious coping and anxiety: A study in German patients with breast cancer. *European Journal of Cancer Care, 17*, 361–370. doi:10.1111/j.1365-2354.2007.00867.x

CHAPTER 15

ADDICTION AND THE SEARCH FOR THE SACRED: RELIGION, SPIRITUALITY, AND THE ORIGINS AND TREATMENT OF SUBSTANCE USE DISORDERS

Thomas J. Johnson

More than 20 years ago as a clinical psychology graduate student, I began working with a client who I felt had a problem with alcohol. When I approached my supervisor for advice, he told me to send the client to Alcoholics Anonymous (AA). When I asked what to do if the client did not want to go, I was told to have him keep trying meetings until he found one he liked. That was all the discussion we had about the issue. My experience is probably not unique. Spirituality is a core component of the AA program. Spirituality and addiction are both areas many psychologists have historically avoided or viewed as the domain of other professionals (DeAngelis, 2001; Pargament, 2007). The relationship between religiousness and spirituality (R/S), however, and the use or abuse of psychoactive substances has, as Ebbinghaus famously said of psychology, "a long past but a short history." Drugs have been used in religious ceremonies for thousands of years. Texts of world religions offer both celebrations of alcohol and warnings against excessive use. Religious groups were at the forefront of the Temperance Movement and among the first to offer treatment for inebriates in the 18th and 19th centuries. Over the past 70-odd years, spirituality has been at the conceptual core of the cultural phenomenon that is AA. Numerous studies have reported inverse relationships between R/S and substance use, but programmatic research aimed at understanding those relationships is comparatively recent (Calhoun, 2007).

This chapter begins with brief overviews of contemporary scientific understandings of substance use and addiction and religious views and practices regarding psychoactive substances. These are followed by a summary of findings from empirical research on R/S and substance use. Finally, I offer an overview of treatment and mutual-help programs involving R/S, findings about the efficacy and mechanisms of action of such programs, and suggestions as to how practitioners might integrate R/S into the assessment and treatment of addictive behaviors.

UNDERSTANDING SUBSTANCE USE DISORDERS—CONTEMPORARY SCIENTIFIC PERSPECTIVES

For much of the 20th century, the addiction field was a battleground of competing ideologies, including secular and religious worldviews, leading McGrady (cited in Bishop, 1995) to quip, "The alcoholism field delights in periodic fits of internecine warfare" (p. 157). In the early 1900s, those who viewed alcoholics as sinners vied with those who saw the problem as alcohol itself. The first perspective incorporated a specifically spiritual and individualistic perspective, and the latter secular view led to the great experiment of Prohibition. After Prohibition, alcoholism was thought of as a medical illness and a spiritual disease. During the last quarter of the 20th century, debates raged about the efficacy of AA, abstinence versus controlled drinking,

DOI: 10.1037/14046-015
APA Handbook of Psychology, Religion, and Spirituality: Vol. 2. An Applied Psychology of Religion and Spirituality, K. I. Pargament (Editor-in-Chief)

disease models of addiction, and numerous other contentious constructs (Doweiko, 2012; Thombs, 2006). Passionate arguments were made on both sides, with some voices becoming strident in their polemics. Some years ago, I attended a workshop on addiction treatment sponsored by a local mental health center and found a similar state of affairs. After expounding at length on why addiction was a disease, the speaker offered that if anyone disagreed with him, he would be happy to go out and settle it in the parking lot.

Such extreme positions resemble what Pargament (2007) called devotion to "small gods" (p. 137). Worshipers of small gods are "committed to the belief that they hold exclusive claim to ultimate truth" (p. 138). Historically, belief in small gods has been used to justify violence in the name of "truth." As more is learned about addiction, it becomes harder to defend extreme positions. Hopefully the future will see more productive cooperation and less ideological "warfare." In this chapter, I hope to maintain some humility about the state of our knowledge while tracing the implications of what we do know from theory and research for clinicians.

TERMINOLOGY

Research often distinguishes between use of a substance, which may or may not be problematic, and use resulting in negative consequences, typically referred to as abuse, dependence, or addiction. Although this chapter focuses on chemical addictions, contemporary thinking is that similar basic processes also underlie alcoholism and behavioral addictions (e.g., compulsive gambling). Donovan (2005) defined *addiction* as

> a process whereby a behavior that can function both to produce pleasure and to provide escape from internal discomfort is employed in a pattern characterized by (1) recurrent failure to control the behavior and (2) continuation of the behavior despite significant negative consequences. (p. 2)

Alcoholic and *addict* are imprecise terms and, although they have been adopted by 12-step groups, such labels still carry stigma in society at large. Therefore, most professionals in the addictions field have used terms like abuse and dependence, even though the line between abuse and dependence is somewhat arbitrary. To add to the complexity, substance problems develop gradually over time and show different trajectories in different individuals. Thus, such problems occur on a continuum rather than as a disease state that is either present or absent (Miller & Carroll, 2006). It is likely that in *DSM–V*, the separate categories of abuse and dependence will be replaced by the single term Substance Use Disorder (SUD) under the more general heading of Addictions and Related Disorders (O'Brien, 2011).

PERSPECTIVES ON SUDS

Theorists have attempted to understand SUDs via numerous biological, psychological, sociocultural, and spiritual perspectives. Each perspective includes multiple individual theories, often presented in deliberate opposition to other views. If there is any emerging consensus in the field, it is one consistent with the overarching theme of this handbook—that multiple levels of analysis (e.g., biological, psychological, cultural, spiritual, etc.) need not be in competition, but rather they offer important pieces of a comprehensive understanding.

Miller and Carroll (2006) offered an integrative summary of the current state of addiction science. People initially choose to use drugs for specific effects or to meet important goals (having fun, socializing, escaping from pain, etc.). Drug use is but one of many behavioral options people use to affect their moods and behaviors, but over time, "addictive behaviors take on a life of their own" (p. 296). The National Institute on Drug Abuse (NIDA; 2009) has emphasized that "drug induced changes in brain function" (p. 7) are involved in the continuum of moving from use to addiction. Changes occur in regions "involved in reward and motivation, learning and memory, and inhibitory control over behavior" (NIDA, 2009, p. v). In addition, availability of alternative sources of reinforcement, developmental issues, family and larger social contexts, personal motivations and goals, and other risk and protective factors contribute to the maintenance of SUDs

(Miller & Carroll, 2006). Miller and Carroll stressed that "it may be important to understand for each individual what is maintaining the pattern of drug use, and, more important, which components need to be addressed to produce stable change" (p. 296). In other words, there is more than one path into and out of the forest of addiction, and those in the woods travel at different speeds and encounter different obstacles. We turn now to a discussion of religion's influence on substance use and spiritual perspectives on the pathway and meaning of addiction.

Understanding SUDs—Religious and Spiritual Perspectives

World religions offer a wide variety of positions on use of intoxicants. Buddhism discourages use of all intoxicants. Islamic texts contain prohibitions against alcohol and other substances, but levels of use among Muslims vary across different countries (Michalak & Trocki, 2006). Alcohol is used in Jewish sacraments, but Jewish culture tends to discourage heavy drinking (Spiegel & Kravitz, 2001). Some Native Americans use tobacco in rituals. The Native American Church uses peyote in ritual, but it discourages use of alcohol.

Among Christian denominations, Catholics, Episcopalians, and some Lutherans use alcohol in the Eucharist, whereas Latter Day Saints (LDS; Mormons), Pentecostals, some Baptists, Churches of Christ, and other denominations require complete abstinence. Nonetheless, national surveys reveal that varying percentages of members of such denominations are aware of proscriptions on alcohol and similarly varying percentages actually drink (Michalak, Trocki, & Bond, 2007). Michalek et al. (2007) found that 95.5% of Mormons in a national survey reported that the LDS church proscribed alcohol use, but only 82.1% reported abstinence in the past year. Other denominations with high percentages of abstainers were Assembly of God (92.9%), Seventh Day Adventists (89.7%), Church of God (80.2%), Muslim (75.6%), and Baptist (69.4%). Catholics and individuals who reported no religion had the lowest rates of abstinence (28.7% and 25.1%, respectively) and highest rates of frequent heavy drinking (6% and 9.9%). Muslims, members of the Assembly of God, and Seventh Day Adventists "had no recorded cases of alcohol abuse in the sample" (Michalek et al., 2007, p. 272).

Several reviewers (Dyslin, 2008; Rivers, 1994) concluded "that when individuals with Protestant backgrounds of strict abstinence drink, there is a relatively high likelihood that they will become problem drinkers" (Rivers, 1994, p. 174). Data from Michalek et al. (2007), however, suggested that this does not hold true in all denominations that proscribe alcohol and that members' perceptions of their individual denomination's position on alcohol is the most important predictor of behavior. For example, in a prospective sample of college students, my colleagues and I found that patterns of change in drinking levels after entering college varied by denomination, with the biggest increases occurring for Catholics and members of the Church of Christ (Johnson, Carlisle, Sheets, & Kristeller, 2008). One practical implication is that clinicians should ask religiously affiliated clients for their personal understanding of their denominations' position on alcohol as well as the impact of this stance on the client's views and behavior.

According to Belcher (2006), conservative Christian denominations tend to view all alcohol use as a sin rather than an illness, whereas many liberal or mainline Protestant bodies view addiction as an illness that separates the person from God. The former stress repentance and may discourage AA involvement, whereas the latter often recommend professional help and perhaps AA. Across all denominations in the United States, 94% of clergy believe that addiction is a crucial issue for their congregations (National Center on Addiction and Substance Abuse at Columbia University [CASA], 2001). Relatively few clergy (36.5%), however, preach about addiction more than once a year and fewer have any training in the area (12.5%).

Theological explanations of addiction are as diverse as the scientific models mentioned thus far. Drug use has been viewed as an attempt to cope with a lack of meaning and purpose in life (Doweiko, 2012) or a lack of perceived connection to God (Mercadante, 1996). Miller (1998) noted that in many traditions addiction can be called idolatry, placing something before God. In Buddhism, addiction is a not-unexpected result of peoples' vain attempts to avoid suffering. Some view addiction as a spiritual quest gone wrong or an attempt to find God in a bottle (Nelson, 2004), but this is only one of the ways in which R/S and SUDs may be related.

Substance Use and the Search for the Sacred

Pargament (2007) described the search for the sacred as a process, implying that there are many ways that people's sacred journeys may intersect with their path through addiction. A vivid illustration of varying spiritual paths connected with drug use is found in Turner's (2006) story of the individual and collective spiritual searches of the Beatles as they went from amphetamines and debauchery in Hamburg to peace, laughter, and smoking marijuana to inner exploration via LSD (lysergic acid diethylamide) to discovering meditation. For many years, John Lennon continued to be troubled and experiment with drugs, whereas George Harrison left drugs entirely behind in favor of the spiritual life. Paul McCartney became a vegetarian and continued to use marijuana, while Ringo Starr was, well, Ringo (and current reports are that he lives a sober lifestyle). The next sections attempt to provide a clinically useful way of thinking about different ways that SUDs can be related to R/S via Pargament's (2007; see also Volume 1, Chapter 14, this handbook) model of the search for the sacred.

Discovery. In Pargament's (2007) model, an individual's first encounter with the sacred is referred to as *discovery*. People discover the sacred in a myriad of ways, including in nature, relationships, or even art, but traditionally the primary goal of most religions is to help members connect to the sacred. Some of the same experiences that are risk factors for the development of SUDs, including lack of involvement in religion, lack of attachment to traditional social norms, and history of physical abuse (Thombs, 2006), are also likely to hinder the discovery of the sacred. Thus, some people with addiction problems may have never discovered the sacred.

Some case histories are suggestive of a person searching for the sacred though drugs (see Pargament, 2007, pp. 56–58). People often begin using drugs for reasons unrelated to the sacred, however. Pathways to addiction in clients I have worked with include joining a fraternity, being prescribed pain medication after an injury, trying to stay awake while working an overnight job and going to college, and dealing drugs and then sampling the merchandise. Quite often, people simply discover that drugs make them feel really good, at least for a short time. Regardless of the reason people start to use, they can develop a SUD because drugs powerfully activate the brain's reward centers and because a lack of external reinforcement (among other things) can increase this effect. For such individuals, substances may not be part of a spiritual search, at least initially, but SUDs could interfere with their ability to discover a connection to the sacred.

It is possible that some individuals are not engaged in a search for the sacred. Many of the men I worked with as a part-time clinician at a super–maximum security prison had life stories that were a series of negative experiences, including physical or sexual abuse, fights, problems in school and relationships, and heavy drug use. Such a background might make it hard to conceive of the existence of the sacred, much less search for it. Alternatively, it could be proposed that these men had given themselves to "false gods" (Pargament, 2007) by sanctifying concepts such as power, dominance over others, or even drug use itself. Several authors have suggested that individuals from troubled backgrounds who become involved with drug use may be vulnerable to making sudden conversions to cults or sects that demand total involvement in the group, separate members from the outside world, and often feature a charismatic leader (Myers, 1991). For more on the potential adaptive and maladaptive aspects of cults and charismatic groups, see Galanter (1990, 1996; see also Volume 1, Chapter 41, this handbook).

Conservation. After people discover the sacred, they generally try to maintain a connection to it, often through practices learned in a religious tradition. People may attempt to conserve their connection with the sacred through substances, or an SUD may interfere with their ability to conserve their spirituality. In either case, treatment should include help in conservational spiritual coping (Pargament, 2007).

Hypothetically, people might use substances in maladaptive attempts to conserve their spirituality. Generally, higher levels of personal importance of religion predict lower levels of drinking. Michalak et al. (2007), however, found in their national sample that in Lutherans, higher levels of personal religious commitment actually predicted more drinking. This could be related to attitudes toward alcohol based in Lutheran tradition, or more general cultural factors, such as German ancestry of some Lutherans.

Gorsuch (1995) suggested that punitive religious experiences can be causally related to substance abuse. Two studies (Drerup, 2005; Kendler et al., 2003) found a relationship between belief in a punitive God and substance abuse problems. Given the connection between SUDs and holding a punishing concept of God, some individuals may only be able to conserve their belief by chemically numbing themselves against the guilt, shame, fear, or anger that such a concept of God might engender. Traumatic religious experiences (e.g., clergy sexual abuse) might also impair victims' abilities to conserve their connection to the sacred using the standard methods and practices of their faith tradition (e.g., someone abused by a priest might be understandably reluctant to attend confession).

Spiritual struggle. A variety of factors may lead to religious or spiritual struggles, including trauma, loss, or unsuccessful efforts at conservation (Pargament, 2007). Religious struggle could be both a cause and a consequence of an SUD. People experiencing spiritual struggles may not be effectively using religious or spiritual forms of coping and thus turn to substances as a coping mechanism. My colleagues and I found support for this in a longitudinal path analytic study of college students (Johnson et al., 2007). Higher levels of spiritual struggles before entering college predicted lower spiritual well-being during the freshman year and higher motives to use alcohol as a coping device in their sophomore year.

Alternatively, individuals raised in a religion that proscribes alcohol use might be especially vulnerable to religious struggles if they begin to drink or develop an SUD. Johnson et al. (2008) reported that in Baptist college students, an increase in alcohol problems between the summer before college and the end of the freshman year was followed by an increase in negative religious support from the end of the freshman year to the end of the sophomore year. Baptist students may have received criticism from members of their faith related to their drinking. In contrast, in Catholic students, an increase in alcohol problems was followed by a decrease in both intrapersonal struggle (negative religious coping) and interpersonal struggle (negative religious support). Perhaps Catholic students were able to successfully conserve their faith via congregational support or using other methods of religious coping. In summary, clinicians should explore with religious clients how their denomination or congregation has responded to their substance use as well as how their substance use might be related to their own spiritual struggles.

Transformation. If spiritual struggles are prolonged, conservational coping is not working, or exceptionally powerful stressors are unfolding (including continued struggle with a SUD), spiritual transformation may occur. Transformation can involve "fundamental changes in the place . . . or the character of the sacred" or "in the pathways the individual takes to the sacred" (Pargament, 2007). Positive transformations can lead to rediscovery of the sacred, whereas negative transformations can lead to disengagement. If an SUD has interfered with conservational coping, an individual might turn to drugs in search of transformation. Alternatively, some find their first experiences with a particular drug to be spiritually transforming. LSD users, including, as previously noted, the Beatles, often reported this in the 1960s and 1970s. AA cofounder Bill W. took LSD, at least in part out of an interest in determining whether spiritual experiences induced by LSD could be beneficial in fostering a spiritual awakening in alcoholics (Kurtz, 1979). However, psychedelics have not been effective components of treatment (Miller et al., 2003). More recently MDMA (3,4-methylenedioxymethamphetamine), especially in the context of rave dancing, has been described in spiritual terms (Sylvan, 2005).

Although Sylvan related stories of positive transformation, MDMA is not a completely benign drug (NIDA, 2006), and studies suggest that the rave scenes now involve the use of a wide variety of substances in addition to MDMA (e.g., Weir, 2000). AA aims to produce a "spiritual awakening," although individual members differ in how important they feel the spiritual aspects of the program are. Even so, "transformational turning points . . . are common among people who resolve drug problems" (Miller & Carroll, 2006 p. 297) even if these do not always involve the sacred. Niclaus (2009) noted that when his 10-year-old son said, "Dad, you're a drunkard, aren't you?" (p. xiii), this started him on the path that led him to help found Lifering Secular Recovery. Motivational interviewing (MI), a collaborative therapeutic process exploring motivation to change, can facilitate motivational transformations that can lead to profound life changes. Individuals do not have to hit bottom to realize they need to change, but it helps to have some goal that makes change worthwhile.

Disengagement. Unresolved spiritual struggles can lead to a disengagement from the sacred. Mullen, Williams, and Hunt (1996) suggested that some denominations may be more likely than others to retain members who drink or develop an SUD. Clients who have disengaged from a relationship with the sacred may prefer secular mutual help or have a strong negative reaction to 12-step groups, which affirm a Higher Power. Although the therapist may believe that such a client might benefit from a reconnection with their spiritual self, this should not be undertaken without the clients' knowledge and consent. It is worth remembering that disengaged clients may have an entirely different perspective on spirituality after they make progress in managing their SUD.

RESEARCH ON R/S AND SUDS

Hundreds of studies have reported inverse relationships between R/S and substance use (Gorsuch, 1995), but only recently have studies begun to measure multiple dimensions of R/S, to look for mediators and moderators of the relationship between R/S and SUDs, and to test whether some aspects of R/S might increase risk for SUDs (Johnson & Bennett, 2009; Miller, 1998). Inverse relationships between R/S and addiction could be due to third variables, such as personality or affect; however, several studies have reported effects of R/S following control for personality traits and psychological distress as covariates (Johnson, Sheets, & Kristeller, 2008a, 2008b). Recent studies have statistically tested for mediation of the relationship between R/S and substance use. The mediators with the most empirical support are beliefs or attitudes about substances (Bachman et al., 2002; Johnson et al., 2008b) and various types of social influences, including perceived norms, peer modeling, and being offered substances (Burkett, 1993; Johnson et al., 2008b).

Gorsuch (1995) suggested that religious involvement might help individuals meet basic needs, including dealing with suffering, and thus reduce motivation for substance use. Two studies found that religiousness may increase experiences of meaning and inner peace and thus reduce the motive to use alcohol as a coping mechanism (Drerup, Johnson, & Bindl, 2011; Johnson et al., 2008b). Religiousness also reduced the motive to use alcohol for the chemical buzz and the motive to use alcohol to facilitate social interaction.

R/S might also decrease substance use by providing sources of meaning or purpose in life. Studies have connected addiction to low levels of meaning in life and recovery to increases in meaning, but many of these studies have used measures that are heavily confounded with depression, making it difficult to interpret the meaning of findings about meaning (Johnson & Robinson, 2008). Among minority group members, religious involvement and ethnic identity may both be involved in reducing the likelihood of SUDs, but further work is needed in this area (Herd & Grube, 1996). Additional potential mediators of the relationship between R/S and SUDs include sanctification of the body (Mahoney et al., 2005), self-regulation, use of religious coping, alcohol-related God locus of control (Murray, Goggin, & Malcarne, 2006), self-esteem (Belcher, 2006), self-efficacy, helping behavior, and use of specific R/S practices. In addition, the relationship between R/S and both use and abuse may be moderated by other factors, such as gender, race, religious commitment, or denomination (Koenig, 2002; Michalek et al., 2007).

R/S AND TREATMENT OF SUDS

The sections that follow provide a brief overview of important developments in addiction treatment in the 21st century and a discussion of various ways that R/S can be and have been integrated into addiction treatment. Examples include the addition of spiritual components to approaches that were originally entirely secular as well as approaches that focus overtly on spiritual issues.

Addiction Treatment in the 21st Century

Effective treatments for addiction are available but not always widely used (Miller, Wilbourne, & Hettema, 2003; Wilbourne & Miller, 2002) and "no single treatment is appropriate for everyone" (NIDA, 2009, p. 2). Miller and colleagues contend that the range of empirically supported treatments is broad enough that therapists should be encouraged to learn and preferentially employ such approaches, especially when substantial evidence has documented that some techniques are ineffective (e.g., educational lectures and films) or even harmful (e.g., confrontation). Collins et al. (2009) suggested that outcome research also tells us "something fundamental about the nature of human problems and the processes by which change in these problems is most likely to occur" (p. 134). Understanding general principles helps the clinician go beyond treatment manuals in an informed way. Wilbourne and Miller (2002) noted that approaches with substantial evidence of efficacy often "focus on practical skills for effective self-management" (p. 44) or on "enriching the person's life without alcohol" (p. 45). Other important general aspects of treatment include a positive therapeutic relationship, helping create an initial period of abstinence, enhancing motivation for change, "enhancing positive reinforcement for nonuse" (Miller & Carroll, p. 307), "diminishing the rewarding aspects of drug use" (p. 308), and providing alternative positive reinforcement. In less behavioral terms, this translates into helping the client find meaningful social, vocational, recreational, and spiritual activities without drugs.

Motivational interviewing. Among the most important developments in addiction treatment in the past decades were MI (Miller & Rollnick, 2002) and the stages of change (SoC) model (Prochaska & DiClemente, 1984). MI is "a client-centered, directive method for enhancing intrinsic motivation to change by exploring and resolving ambivalence" (Miller & Rollnick, 2002, p. 25). MI assumes that people facing change are often ambivalent. There are costs and benefits to change but also costs and benefits for continuing on the same path. MI involves taking an empathic stance and helping clients articulate and resolve their ambivalence about change. By asking open-ended questions and using reflections, affirmations, and summaries, the therapist attempts to help the client generate his or her own arguments for change. Understanding what the client likes about his or her substance use is crucial and being willing to discuss this openly goes a long way toward dispelling the "baloney sausage" that clients otherwise may be tempted to serve up. Although MI is not a magic bullet, it is a powerful approach with substantial empirical support (Miller & Rollnick, 2002).

Reluctance to admit to having a substance problem is legendary among clients with SUDs. Rather than labeling such resistance as denial, MI treats it as an interpersonal issue, a sign that the client and therapist are working toward different goals. This leads to a more compassionate and effective way of responding. Resistance is not confronted, but bypassed, using variations on reflection and other techniques. One client, referred to me after failing a drug screen, related that he had started to walk in the door of a party, smelled the pot smoke, and left immediately. In short, his "contact buzz" caused him to fail the drug screen. If I had confronted him about the obvious implausibility of his story, we probably would not have gotten far in treatment. Instead, I began by focusing on identifying what he did want, which turned out to be to get back to work and to keep his job. In this way we were able to agree on the tasks and goals of therapy and eventually move on to what he might do with his life that did not involve drugs.

Stages of change. The SoC model was developed to represent how individuals make important changes and the types of interventions that might be most effective at each stage of change (Connors, Donovan, & DiClemente, 2001). Table 15.1 lists the stages of change and examples of techniques proposed as helpful at each stage in the model. Given the recent prominence of MI and the stages of change in the addiction field, future work exploring the relationships between R/S and both MI and the stages of change would be welcome.

Why Should R/S Be a Part of Treatment?

R/S can offer a variety of benefits in treating SUDs. Severe addiction crowds out other goals and aspects of life until the addictive substance or behavior is the central focus (Miller, 1998). When Jung wrote *spiritus contra spiritum* (Kurtz, 1979), he was indicating that both spirituality and addiction can be total life commitments, so an intrinsic spirituality can work against addiction by providing an alternative central unifying force in people's lives, supplying meaning and organizing their goals and priorities (Pargament, 2007).

At the same time, there are also extrinsic benefits associated with R/S. At the mundane level, involvement with an organized religious group can increase individuals' access to a wide variety of social and personal resources (e.g., social support, financial assistance, recreation) that can facilitate a substance-free lifestyle. Clients with more psychosocial resources (e.g., social support, self-efficacy) have a better prognosis in addiction treatment (Miller & Carroll, 2006; Thombs, 2006).

Integrating R/S Into Treatment for SUDs: Levels of Intensity

R/S can be a component of treatment, or they can *be* the treatment. Various options are introduced in this section and more specific examples are provided in subsequent sections. The most basic way that R/S can be a part of SUD treatment occurs when the therapist takes care to address R/S issues as part of a comprehensive approach. This is consistent with the American Psychological Association (APA) definition of evidence-based practice in psychology (EBPP) as considering "patient characteristics, culture, and preferences" (APA Presidential Task Force on Evidence-Based Practice, 2006, p. 273). This will look different in different clients, but it might involve monitoring the client's religious and spiritual functioning, discussing spiritually related goals or values, connecting the client to religious or spiritual resources, helping clients examine their understanding of and comfort with 12-step spirituality, or even trying to help resolve spiritual struggles. At this level, R/S is not the central focus of treatment, but attention is given to how R/S issues affect or are being affected by addiction and related problems. It may be that no special therapeutic techniques are

TABLE 15.1

Stages of Change Model With Sample Interventions

Stage	Description	Example interventions
Precontemplation	Unaware of problem or not thinking about change	Motivational interviewing; exploring goals and values; self-monitoring; providing feedback on health and how client's behavior compares to others
Contemplation	Thinking about change, but may be ambivalent	Motivational interviewing; consciousness raising; discuss past successes and failures
Preparation	Planning to change, but may not be sure how	Offer a menu of options; make an action plan or change plan; sobriety sampling (contract for initial period of abstinence); enhance self-efficacy
Action	Committed to change and taking steps to initiate change	Skills training; 12-step facilitation therapy; involvement in mutual help; contingency management; help restore lifestyle balance
Maintenance	Has made some changes and is attempting to avoid relapse	Stimulus control; self-management; mindfulness-based relapse prevention

involved other than those the therapist typically uses in other areas of the clients' life (e.g., problem solving, cognitive–behavioral interventions). I suggest that this is the minimum level of attention that should be given to R/S for ethical practice in treating SUDs.

For clients in which salience of R/S is high, a second level of integration could be used in which specific R/S elements or practices (forgiveness, prayer, etc.) could be incorporated into treatment. These elements could be added to existing SUD treatments or introduced to address issues unique to a specific client.

A third level of integration would be for the therapist to learn and offer one of several manualized addiction treatment approaches that include spiritual practices or that address spiritual issues (mindfulness-based relapse prevention [MBRP], spiritual self-schema [3-S] therapy, 12-step facilitation [TSF] therapy).

Historically, some groups have viewed religious conversion or spiritual transformation as necessary and sufficient for "curing" addictive behaviors. In this model, R/S effectively is treatment. Even in the 21st century, some programs continue to have a primary focus on religious or spiritual matters. In some faith based programs, religious instruction and activities are the central component of treatment (Johnson & Bennett, 2009). Many, but not all, AA members view the spiritual nature of the program, or even divine intervention, as the primary mechanism for change, and the stated intent of the 12 steps is to affect a spiritual awakening. Regardless of the way that R/S is integrated into treatment, the therapist must collaborate with the client and obtain his or her consent in selecting goals and interventions.

Introducing Discussion of R/S in SUD Treatment

Many individuals in addiction treatment are open to discussion of R/S in treatment or to treatments incorporating spiritual elements, although levels of interest may differ with race, age, and gender (Johnson & Bennett, 2009). In reviewing the literature, Johnson and Bennett (2009) found little evidence that outcomes in R/S-based treatments was related to client levels of R/S. It is not clear whether this is due to such treatments having nonspecific effects or to existing studies including individuals with a fairly narrow range of religious backgrounds. A common stereotype in the clinical literature is that alcoholics are religiously alienated. Robinson, Brower, and Kurtz (2003) found some evidence that alcoholics in a treatment sample identified more with spirituality than with religion. Although more studies are needed, it may still be worthwhile to ask clients for their personal definitions of R/S and to identify which constructs they most identify with.

An important first step in addressing R/S in treatment is to demonstrate to the client a willingness to talk about sacred matters. Taking a religious history (see Chapter 5 in this volume) or asking the client to what extent their R/S life has been affected by their current situation are good ways to introduce the topic. Pargament (2007) has offered a very helpful set of example questions to gather information about sacred pathways, destinations, and struggles. Some of his questions could be used with clients regardless of whether they believe in God. Some examples that might be particularly appropriate for clients with SUDs include, "Where do you find peace? For what are you deeply grateful? What are you striving for in life? What would you like to be able to let go of in your life?" and "When have you felt most deeply and fully alive?" (Pargament, 2007, p. 218). Other questions are likely to be useful with clients who self-identify as being spiritual or religious (e.g., "How has your faith helped you in your current situation?" and "In what ways has your current situation challenged your faith?").

R/S and Specific Treatment Modalities

Training in social or coping skills is a part of a number of empirically supported SUD treatments (Miller et al., 2003). Some skills are related to SUDs (e.g., managing cravings, refusing offers of drugs, etc.), whereas others address broader areas of life functioning (managing emotions, developing relationships, etc.). On the basis of what is known about R/S and coping (Pargament, 2007), a comprehensive approach to improving coping skills should include R/S coping, but there is currently no empirical work on training in R/S coping as part of SUD treatment.

Although forgiveness can be both a secular and a sacred value, and thus occur with or without a R/S context, training in forgiveness can be incorporated into SUD treatment (Lin, Mack, Enright, Krahn, & Baskin, 2004; see Chapter 25 in this volume).

MI lends itself well to integration with R/S due to its emphasis on therapist empathy and helping clients identify discrepancies between their current behavior and important goals or values. Saunders et al. (2007) found that problem drinkers were more likely than nonproblem drinkers to report discrepancies between their actual and ideal levels of R/S functioning, suggesting that increasing awareness of such discrepancies might enhance motivation for change or that working on ways to reduce those discrepancies could be a fruitful focus for treatment. Pargament (2007) noted that the therapeutic relationship can be viewed as a spiritual resource and indicated that "the sacred qualities of the connection between clients and therapists may be among the most critical of therapeutic ingredients" (p. 269). Empathy and acceptance are "fundamental and defining" characteristics of MI (Miller & Rollnick, 2002, p. 37), and they are also consistent with the values of most faiths. In both cases, however, acceptance does not mean approval of all behaviors. Given that MI is at least in part "about changing what a person wants" (Miller & Rolnick, 2002, p. 161), Miller and Rollnick (2002) emphasized the importance of careful consideration of ethics in the practice of MI and offered an entire chapter on the subject that would be important reading for clinicians who wish to integrate MI and R/S in treatment.

Individuals who have an array of sources of positive reinforcement in their lives are at lower risk for SUDs and have a greater likelihood of successful treatment outcomes, so increasing access to positive reinforcement has become an important component of many treatments (Miller & Carroll, 2006). Spiritual emotions (awe, gratitude, joy, etc.) and experiences (peak experiences, awareness of God, etc.) are powerful (Pargament, 2007) and may reduce motivations to use substances. Robinson, Cranford, Webb, and Brower (2007) found that increases in daily spiritual experiences over the course of treatment predicted less likelihood of heavy drinking 6 months after treatment. Involvement in organized religious groups could increase access to rewarding activities across a number of life domains, including, not only the spiritual, but also social, recreational, or other domains. Several interventions related to R/S might increase clients' awareness of the positive aspects of their lives, including interventions to foster gratitude and mindfulness practices (see the section Mindfulness-Based Relapse Prevention later in this chapter).

Contingency management (CM) interventions reinforce engagement in non-drug-related activities by offering vouchers, small prizes, or other reinforcers for participation. Petry, Lewis, and Østvik-White (2008) reported that individuals receiving CM interventions who were involved in religious activities "remained in treatment longer, were abstinent for longer durations, and submitted more substance-negative samples" (p. 408) than those who were not religiously engaged. Furthermore, after discontinuation of CM, some clients continued to use religious activities as a source of personal reinforcement (Petry, Kelley, Brennan, & Sierra, 2008).

Meditation

Meditative practices are often categorized as either concentration-based meditation—meditation involving focus on some word, phrase, or object (e.g., a mantra such as in transcendental meditation [TM]) or mindfulness meditation, in which the emphasis is on nonjudgmental, nonreactive awareness of whatever enters into consciousness (see Volume 1, Chapter 17, this handbook and Chapter 10, this volume). Although a number of early studies supported the efficacy of concentration-based techniques, such as TM, in the treatment for SUDs (Alexander, Robinson, & Rainforth, 1994), recently there has been much more interest in mindfulness practices (Hsu, Grow, & Marlatt, 2008).

Mindfulness meditation involves nonjudgmental awareness of present moment experiences or as Vietnamese Buddhist monk Thich Nhat Hanh (1987) put it, "keeping one's consciousness alive to the present reality" (p. 11). Trainees typically begin by observing their breathing. If their attention wanders, they simply return their focus to their breath without judging or mentally commenting. Other exercises can include body scans, where attention is focused successively on different parts of the body to note pains or other sensations. Mindfulness trains one to have increased awareness of experiences, without automatically acting on urges (e.g., to drink), reacting to thoughts, or otherwise attempting to escape from experience. There is some evidence that not attempting to suppress thoughts, not being judgmental of experiences, and not acting on urges or thoughts explain the effects of mindfulness on alcohol and drug use (Fernandez, Wood, Stein, & Rossi, 2010). Increased present moment awareness may be beneficial by increasing an individual's awareness of pleasant experiences. This aspect of mindfulness is important in programs to reduce binge eating by helping individuals essentially eat less and enjoy it more (Kristeller, Baer, & Quillian-Wolever, 2006).

Bowen et al. (2006) showed that a 10-day intensive meditation retreat in an incarcerated population was associated with reduced substance abuse after release. Such work has led to the development of an eight-session, manualized treatment integrating mindfulness into a relapse-prevention model (Bowen, Chawla, & Marlatt, 2011). Mindfulness is also a component of 3-S therapy (Avants & Margolin, 2004). Both of these approaches are described in the next section, Other Approaches. Although some proponents of mindfulness emphasize that it can be an entirely secular practice, studies in other areas have demonstrated an additive effect of including an explicit R/S focus in meditation-based interventions (Wachholtz & Pargament, 2005). This issue deserves more investigation in the addiction field. Clinicians who wish to integrate mindfulness or other meditation practices into treatment are encouraged to become familiar with such methods through their own practice as well as through workshops, retreats, and published materials.

Other Approaches

A study including spiritual direction (i.e., assisting people on their spiritual journey with the goal of helping them to grow closer to the sacred) in addiction treatment failed to find effects (Miller, Forcehimes, O'Leary, & LaNoue, 2008), but Delany, Forcehimes, Campbell, and Smith (2009) presented a case example of a client for whom prayer, gratitude, and meditation interventions were integrated into treatment with a positive outcome. More studies are needed to help identify which clients might benefit from integrating which spiritual practices into SUD treatment.

MANUALIZED APPROACHES

Several manualized addiction treatment approaches include elements of R/S. MBRP incorporates a secularized mindfulness meditation practice, whereas 3-S therapy and TSF are overtly spiritual.

Mindfulness-Based Relapse Prevention

Relapse prevention is a cognitive–behavioral treatment for addiction that has considerable empirical support (McCrady, 2000). Relapse prevention attempts to help clients achieve a more balanced lifestyle, identify triggers for cravings and risky situations, and develop skills to lower the risk of relapse. The original relapse prevention approach included training in urge surfing, a mindfulness technique for managing cravings and urges to use a substance or engage in an addictive behavior. Urge surfing involves helping the client increase awareness of urges, including recognizing that they come and go with time. By imagining that urges are like a wave and that they can ride the wave, clients learn to observe urges without reacting to them by using. MBRP expands the role of mindfulness skills in the relapse-prevention model (Bowen et al., 2011). MBRP is designed as an eight-session group-based program. The program helps clients realize that sometimes relapse can occur because they operate on "automatic pilot" and fail to notice triggers that could cause relapse. Mindfulness may increase awareness of such triggers. MBRP was initially designed as an aftercare program, so it assumes clients are ready to take action toward change. Although the program strongly supports abstinence, clients are allowed to set their own goals and are not removed from the program if they have a lapse. A return to use is treated as a learning experience rather than a failure. A pilot study produced positive results (Bowen et al., 2009), and hopefully, the availability of a treatment manual (Bowen et al., 2011) will encourage more research.

Spiritual Self-Schema Therapy

3-S therapy (3-S; Avants & Margolin, 2004), a treatment intended to be suitable for all persons of all faiths, is based on social cognitive theory and Buddhist concepts. Clients are explicitly encouraged to integrate their own personal religious and spiritual views into treatment. 3-S therapy attempts to deactivate a client's view of himself or herself as an addict and activate a view of the self as a spiritual being. Use of this approach is appropriate for clients willing to commit to following a personal spiritual path; however, it is not recommended for those clients in active withdrawal. Group and individual treatment manuals are available for an eight-session program. A special 12-session version of the treatment (3-S+) has been developed specifically for drug users who are HIV positive (Margolin et al., 2007). Treatment manuals and training videos are available for both 3-S and 3-S+ (see Spiritual Self-Schema Development Program website: http://info.med.yale.edu/psych/3s/training.html).

Controlled studies suggest that 3-S therapy may be helpful in reducing substance use, increasing spiritual practices and self-perception of spiritual qualities, and decreasing impulsivity (Avants, Beitel, & Margolin, 2005; Margolin et al., 2007). Presently, all of the published research has been conducted by the team that developed the approach, so additional studies by other researchers would be helpful in further establishing the efficacy and generalizability of the approach.

Twelve-Step Facilitation Therapy

TSF therapy is a manualized treatment approach that was evaluated in Project MATCH, a longitudinal, national, multisite study of the efficacy of three treatment approaches for alcoholism (Babor & Del Boca, 2003). TSF includes activities and interventions designed to help a client get involved in a 12-step program and begin to work on the first three steps (Nowinski & Baker, 2003): adopt the view that addiction is a chronic, progressive disease; surrender to a higher power; and get involved in 12-step meetings and activities. Therapists and clients who do not accept some aspects of the 12-step doctrine may not be amenable to this approach, but clinical trials of individual and group versions have shown positive effects on commitment to AA practices. Moreover, treatment outcomes have been similar to other empirically supported interventions (Babor & Del Boca, 2003). TSF was especially helpful in individuals who did not have peer networks that supported abstinence.

R/S AS TREATMENT—FAITH-BASED TREATMENT

Some of the first attempts to "reform" individuals with SUDs were made by religious denominations or socially active groups such as the Salvation Army. Treatment programs that self-identify as faith based (FB) differ widely in the balance between sacred and secular elements (Johnson & Bennett, 2009). FB approaches have been the focus of considerable controversy since the Clinton era, with supporters arguing that FB groups often work with minority groups or populations that otherwise have little access to treatment, and detractors citing concerns over lack of training and credentialing and issues of separation of church and state (Johnson & Bennett, 2009; Ringwald, 2002). Currently, programs that focus on religious education or conversion as a primary component of their approach range from numerous local missions to international organizations, such as Teen Challenge. Teen Challenge was started in 1958 by a Pentecostal minister who wanted to help gang members in New York City. As of 2012, there are more than 200 locations in the United States. The Teen Challenge website lists curricula used in programs, primarily focusing on education in aspects of Christian faith. There are a limited number of studies on explicitly religious programs, such as those conducted by Teen Challenge and the Salvation Army, but the methodological quality of the studies is generally poor, and the evidence for efficacy of these programs is not strong (Johnson & Bennett, 2009). Because several FB programs have cooperated in studies of their programs, however, we may eventually learn more about their efficacy (see Johnson & Bennett, 2009).

Zemore (2008) noted that some spiritually focused interventions, especially if they are explicitly aimed at producing a spiritual transformation, could do damage because "rather than targeting thoughts and behaviors directly related to an addiction, they aim for wide-ranging changes in core belief systems and behaviors—some of which may be harmless or even better left intact" (p. 119).

Zemore's concern seems especially relevant for clients who are successfully conserving their contact with the sacred, in which case an intervention aimed at transformation might do violence to the client's existing faith. Individuals seeking to transform their relationship to the sacred might be more open to programs, such as AA or FB treatment, that hold out the promise of a spiritual awakening. According to Pargament (2007), the spiritually integrated therapist must possess knowledge, openness to, and tolerance of clients' belief systems, self-awareness, and authenticity. Such qualities are essential to minimize the damage Zemore has described.

SPIRITUALITY AND MUTUAL-HELP PROGRAMS

Researchers who study AA tend to refer to such programs as mutual-help rather than self-help because of the emphasis these programs place on service to others (Zemore & Pagano, 2008). AA is the best known mutual-help organization, but a number of other secular and spiritually based programs exist.

Alcoholics Anonymous

AA developed from an early 20th-century Protestant Christian organization known as the Oxford Group, and vestiges of that origin can still be seen in such AA practices as making a personal moral inventory, having a spiritual awakening, and carrying the message to others (Kurtz, 1979; Mercadante, 1996). Although the dropout rate in AA is high, with estimates running from 40% to 80% across different sources, active involvement in AA (actually working the steps as opposed to simply attending meetings) is a good predictor of posttreatment abstinence, especially among individuals who attend AA while in treatment (Tonigan, Toscova, & Miller, 1996). Most studies, however, have examined individuals attending AA while in treatment or individuals in 12-step-based treatments, such as TSF therapy, rather than AA alone. Because of the nature of AA's program, no randomized clinical trials have been conducted other than several investigations of court-ordered AA, which has been shown to be ineffective (Miller et al., 2003). Long-time AA members, with whom I have spoken, are not surprised by this finding. One succinctly stated, "You can't court order a spiritual awakening!"

Around 3% of people in the United States and Canada have attended an AA group sometime during their life (Kaskutis et al., 2008). Minorities seem to be less likely than Whites to attend AA, but once attending, they are no more likely to drop out. Tonigan, Toscova, and Connors (1999) distinguished between the program of AA (i.e., the beliefs and practices of AA as contained in the 12 steps and 12 traditions) and the fellowship of AA (i.e., the group format, group practices, and relationships among members). They identified five core spiritual beliefs in AA: (a) the existence of a higher power; (b) the importance of developing a personal relationship with that higher power; (c) mysticism, specifically the belief that recovery involves personal transformation via divine intervention; (d) the need to renew spiritual commitments and practices (e.g., surrender, prayer) on a daily basis; and (e) interpersonal or intrapersonal discord as a sign that the individual needs to make a course correction or continue to work the steps. Part of the AA view of alcoholism is that it involves "self-will run riot." This is in part why surrender is emphasized in the third step. Research examining what types of individuals benefit more or less from surrender would be helpful. Individuals who use collaborative religious coping (coping with God; Pargament, 1997) might do well in AA. Those with a self-directed religious coping style might resist the concept of surrender. For individuals with a deferring religious coping style (letting God handle things without one's own personal effort), concepts of surrender or "let go and let God" might encourage excessive passivity or limit self-efficacy for change.

Atheists and agnostics are less likely than individuals who believe in God to affiliate with AA, but data from one study showed that when they did, they derived equal benefits (Tonigan, Miller, & Schermer, 2002). Unfortunately, up to this point, research on R/S and AA has been relatively simplistic, generally comparing whether people who are "religious" do better in AA than those who are "not religious." Given the diversity of sacred pathways and destinations in the United States, such research is almost meaningless because it does not study religious or spiritual commitment and experience with any measure of depth. We need research on how specific aspects of R/S (hopefully including constructs that can be readily assessed by clinicians) are related to AA variables (e.g., affiliation or disaffiliation, liking for the program, drinking outcomes).

Studies attempting to identify mediators of the effect of AA involvement on recovery are fairly recent. The existing research provides consistent support for AA as affecting recovery via contributing to enhanced self-efficacy, motivation, and coping skills as well as by providing a nondrinking social network (Kelly, Magill, & Stout, 2009). There is some evidence that helping others may contribute to the efficacy of AA (Zemore & Pagano, 2008). A focus on helping others, however, could become problematic if it leads to overcommitment or poor self-care (Zemore & Pagano, 2008). In a national study of three different alcoholism treatment approaches (Project MATCH), the relationship between AA attendance and outcome was not mediated by having had a spiritual awakening but rather by establishing nondrinking social networks (Babor & Del Boca, 2003). Zemore (2007) reported that increases 12-step attendance over time predicted greater likelihood of abstinence at follow-up and claimed that "this relationship was partially explained by changes in spirituality," p. 76S). However, all but one of the items on the measure of "spirituality" used (having direct experiences of God) involved religious behaviors (believing in God, praying, meditating, attending worship services, reading/studying holy writings). Given that the 12 steps prescribe believing in God, praying, and meditating, the measure was at least partially confounded with AA involvement. In short, outside of the vast testimonial literature, we have essentially no evidence that spirituality mediates the effect of AA. Few studies have attempted to test this model, however, and those that have did not use strong measures of spirituality. Further research with better measures of spirituality is required to more effectively examine the role of the spiritual component of AA.

A review of the empirical literature suggests that for many individuals AA can play an important role in their recovery; however, research does not support requiring such participation. Clinicians should routinely ask about a client's prior experience with AA (if any), including what he or she liked and disliked about the program. Rather than directly suggesting that the client attend AA, clinicians can use the MI strategy of asking for permission to make some suggestions and then offering a menu of options, including AA, and discussing these with the client. Discussion might include exploring the pros and cons of different options as well as a rationale for how specific options might be helpful to the client. If clients express interest in or willingness to attend any mutual-help program, give them information on meeting times and locations and help them make a plan for when they will attend, including how they will get there. Therapists who consider referring clients to AA should become familiar with the program by attending some open meetings and reading some of the standard AA literature (AA, 2002a, 2002b).

Therapists should make it a point to monitor clients' reactions when they elect to attend AA or other mutual-help groups, including asking about what is most and least helpful, what they like and dislike, what could help make it more effective for them, and how they relate to the spiritual content. Zweben (1995) suggested encouraging clients to "shop" for meetings until they find one they like. Some therapists set up a "buddy system," using former patients, colleagues, or other trusted persons who attend AA, and will help provide transportation for newcomers.

Therapists should attend to the level of balance in the clients' lifestyle. When I first began working in addictions, I heard some counselors insist that the only way to recover was "90 meetings in 90 days." Daily 12-step meetings for 3 months might help restore balance and stability to the lives of some clients, but might destroy the lives of others by interfering with work, family, sleep, worship, or adaptive recreation. How can you tell if AA, or any other aspect of treatment, is hurting or helping? Outcome studies have tended to focus on the binary criterion of abstinence, although other measures of drinking behavior have become more common. The goal of AA is not simply to achieve abstinence, however. Rather, it is to transform the life of the individual, suggesting we need more holistic outcome criteria.

Efforts to incorporate religious and spiritual resources in treatment should be carefully monitored, paying close attention to the effects (Pargament, 2007).

Clinicians should be alert for two other potential risks associated with AA. Some AA members maintain that alcoholism is a "primary disease"; in other words, it is not caused by anything else. Others argue that if the person has other problems, taking care of the alcoholism will make the other problems go away. The reality is that many individuals have both an SUD and some other diagnosis, and research suggests that in such cases it is important to treat *both* problems simultaneously (Thombs, 2006). Historically, some AA members have been opposed to the use of medication of any kind, including psychotropics. This viewpoint is not only potentially dangerous to individuals being medicated as part of treatment of a comorbid disorder, it is also unfortunate because over the past two decades immense progress has been made in identifying medications that are helpful in the treatment of addiction (NIDA, 2009).

Other Programs

Although AA and other 12-step fellowships remain the most widely available source of help for individuals facing addiction, other organizations and mutual-help programs have been developed. Some groups have attempted to eliminate the spiritual elements found in AA to create secular programs (e.g., Lifering, Secular Organization for Sobriety), whereas others cater to individuals of specific faiths (e.g., Jewish Alcoholics, Chemically Dependent Persons, and Significant Others; Buddhist Recovery Network; Celebrate Recovery). Space allows mention of only a few such programs here, but Humphreys (2004) has provided a good introduction to numerous addiction-related groups. The organization Faces and Voices of Recovery (2011) maintains a regularly updated online list of spiritual and secular mutual-help resources.

Celebrate Recovery. Celebrate Recovery (2011) is a Christian recovery program founded in 1991 in California, which has its roots in the evangelical tradition. It uses an eight-point program based on the biblical account of Jesus's teaching of the Beatitudes and outlined by the acronym RECOVERY, which is intended to help individuals deal with "hurts, hang-ups, and habits." Although presented as an alternative to AA, examination of the points reveals a close resemblance to the steps of AA, including admission of powerlessness, confession of faults, making amends, and bringing the "good news" to others. No matter the resemblance, growth of Celebrate Recovery has been rapid. Celebrate Recovery meetings have been held in all 50 states and seven other countries (Celebrate Recovery, 2011). There were more than 300 meetings listed in California alone. The regions with the largest number of meetings are the Midwest and the South. Despite its growing popularity, there are as yet no published follow-up studies or other research on Celebrate Recovery.

Spirituality in secular programs. A number of mutual-help programs have arisen either in direct opposition to the spiritual aspects of AA or as a secular alternative, including Secular Organization for Sobriety, SMART Recovery, and Lifering. These "secular" groups may also include individuals who self-identify as religious or spiritual (Bishop, 1995; Niclaus, 2009). Interestingly, some religious clients prefer secular mutual-help groups over AA. For example, Niclaus (2009) included a story from Betty D, who remarked that she had

> tried several 12-step programs but because I am a Christian I could not accept a lot of their ways of doing things and that is when I came across Lifering. I loved it because my faith was not challenged but was accepted. (p. 114)

According to Niclaus, religion and politics are considered "off topic" at Lifering meetings, even though "our membership is about as church going as the average" (p. 81). Few data are available on the efficacy of secular mutual-help programs and the potential role of spirituality in such.

R/S BARRIERS TO TREATMENT

Within specific religious traditions, there can be practices, traditions, or doctrines that can interfere with an individual recognizing an addiction problem, seeking treatment for that problem, or succeeding in recovery. Several such barriers are described in the following sections.

"We Don't Do This"

In denominations that proscribe alcohol use or where there are seemingly low levels of addiction problems, there may be a perception that alcoholism or other addictions "can't happen here." This could reduce the likelihood that others will identify a congregant with an SUD and perhaps even be used as an excuse by individuals trying to minimize their own difficulties. Spiegel and Kravitz (2001) related the story of a Jewish woman in the 1960s who turned to her rabbi for help with her husband's drinking, only to be told that "Jews are not alcoholics, thus she should examine her own behavior to see what she was doing to make [him] drink" (p. 265). They noted that although alcoholism rates are lower among Jewish Americans than in the population at large, great strides have been made in combating the myth that Jews cannot be addicted to alcohol. Nonetheless, clinicians may still wish to ask Jewish clients about this belief. Jewish mutual-help groups are available in 19 states in the United States and in four other countries (JACS, 2011). Spiegel and Kravitz have offered suggestions for Jewish pastoral caregivers working with Jews with SUDs. Many of these suggestions also would be useful to secular clinicians, including using the story of the Jews' slavery in Egypt and Exodus to the Holy Land as a metaphor for "the journey from addiction to recovery" (p. 274).

Stoltzfus (2006) has worked with Christian clients who maintain that Christians cannot become addicted or who are unaware of the level of substance abuse problems in their communities or congregations. To combat this "denial in the church" he advocated more education programs for clergy and congregations to increase awareness of the prevalence of addiction and that treatment stresses personal responsibility. Although there is a paucity of published research on Muslims and alcohol use, some Muslims may also fail to recognize the extent of alcohol problems among members of their faith (Michalek & Trocki, 2006).

Perceived Conflict With the 12-Step Programs

I have worked with clients who were reluctant to attend 12-step meetings because they claimed that AA "puts the Big Book ahead of the Bible." Although some religious congregations host 12-step meetings on their premises, others have various objections to 12-step groups. When a client objects to 12-step participation on religious grounds, there are several options open to the clinician. One option is to seek out meetings that have modified the 12-steps to make them more culturally appropriate for particular subgroups, such as Native Americans (Coyhis, 2000) and Jews (Olitzky & Copans, 1991). If clients are involved with a specific denomination, it may be possible to consult with clergy to verify whether their clients' concerns are correct. Even if it is correct, the clinician might be able to help the client work out some means by which the conflict could be managed, such as the client meeting regularly with a clergy member to discuss what they are learning in their 12-step group or a ritual that sanctifies 12-step program attendance. If mutual-help group participation seems indicated—for example, if most of a client's friends use drugs or alcohol, investigate whether a group specific to the client's faith tradition is available locally, or whether the client may feel more comfortable in a secular group. Some benefits of mutual-help group participation might be available in other groups, such as religious congregations.

Use of Alcohol in Sacraments

Alcohol is used in religious rituals by Jews, Catholics, Episcopalians, and some Lutherans. Clients from these denominations who are trying to remain abstinent may feel cut off from religious participation or believe they are at risk of relapse if they did participate. The simplest way of dealing with this situation is to encourage the client to explore whether nonalcoholic wine or grape juice can be made available at their place of worship. Spiegel and Kravitz (2001) noted that some synagogues have provided white grape juice at services to make it easily distinguishable from red wine. A recent trend in some larger cities in the United States has been the growth of Christian "recovery churches," with services and sacraments geared toward persons in recovery.

Reliance on Faith Healing

Some Christian denominations emphasize to varying degrees that healing is a spiritual process or a result of direct divine intervention. This can create problems when it leads an individual to reject psychosocial treatments or medications, or when it creates guilt or shame in individuals who are told they have not been healed because of their own lack of faith (Stoltzfus, 2006). Some individuals who receive this type of message may leave their congregation, so clinicians may need to work with the religious struggles or disengagement stemming from the experience (see Pargament, 2007).

In some cases, clergy can help counter a client's belief, but other clergy might reinforce the client's self-blame. Stoltzfus (2006) suggested that certain passages from Christian scriptures (e.g., "The Red Sea did not part until Moses struck it with his staff," p. 145) can be used to demonstrate that "God . . . nearly always chooses to work through people" (p. 145). Personal stories and testimony may be particularly useful with some Christian clients in describing experiences of recovery as well as countering false expectations. The experiences of David Wilkerson, the pastor who founded Teen Challenge, provide such an example. Wilkerson expected conversion to put an end to the drug problems in the gang members with whom he was working. When confronted by the reality that the youth typically relapsed, however, he developed a residential program of religious instruction and job training that became Teen Challenge.

CONCLUSION

Empirical research on R/S and substance use and abuse continues to grow; however, much of this published work is limited to Christians in the North America and Western Europe. This literature finds that R/S is consistently inversely related to substance use and abuse; however, less is known about aspects of R/S, such as spiritual struggles, that appear to be positively related to SUDs. Although several mediators of the relationship between R/S and substance use show consistent support (beliefs about substances, social influences, well-being), more empirical research is needed, examining multiple dimensions of R/S as well as examining the use of substances other than alcohol. Longitudinal studies are required to help clarify the relationship between stages of change and stages in spiritual journeys and daily process studies to help identify more short-term connections between R/S behaviors and specific episodes of substance use or nonuse. Finally, future research should place more emphasis on how gender, race, denomination, or other factors might moderate the impact of R/S on substance use and problems.

Hopefully, the clinical literature on R/S and treatment and recovery will continue to develop. The existing evidence suggests that it would be worthwhile to routinely include appropriate measures of R/S in most studies of addiction treatment outcomes. More studies should investigate existing manualized approaches, including assessment of R/S dimensions as mechanisms of change. We know next to nothing about the impact of FB addiction treatment, especially as it occurs at the local, grassroots level. Although there is a growing literature on AA, more sophisticated studies of the spiritual aspects of AA are sorely needed, as are studies of R/S in other mutual-help programs.

Integrating R/S into addiction treatment offers great promise, but it should not be undertaken without familiarity and training in both addiction treatment and spiritually integrated or spiritually oriented therapy. Because no one type of treatment seems to be effective with every client, therapists need to be flexible and sensitive to each client's unique sociocultural and spiritual background and motivation for treatment as well as the factors that help maintain their addiction; such an approach is consistent with evidence-based practice (APA Presidential Task Force on Evidence-Based Practice, 2006). Clinicians wishing to integrate R/S into treatment of SUDs should

1. Legitimize discussion of religious and spiritual issues in therapy.
2. Conceptualize how (if at all) the client's spiritual journey intersects with, parallels, or follows their journey from substance use to substance use disorder to recovery.

3. Recognize the sacred qualities of the client therapist relationship (Pargament, 2007) by demonstrating empathy, respect for the clients' faith, and awareness of one's own spiritual orientation. MI techniques are helpful here.
4. Consider where the client is in the stages of change. Religious values or sacred experiences can be a catalyst for change if they help clients resolve ambivalence.
5. Consider where a client is in their search for the sacred and collaborate with the client to determine where and how the sacred might enter into therapy, ranging from something to occasionally monitor, to incorporating specific practices into therapy, to being the central focus.
6. Consult with or refer to clergy or pastoral care professionals when indicated.
7. Become familiar with local resources, including mutual-help groups, clergy, congregations, and providers of FB social services and help clients connect with these resources as appropriate.
8. Learn a variety of secular and spiritually related addiction treatment techniques, and tailor the treatment plan and interventions to the individual needs of specific clients.
9. Because this field is still evolving, stay up to date through books, journals, workshops, and conferences.

References

Alcoholics Anonymous. (2002a). *Alcoholics anonymous.* New York, NY: Author.

Alcoholics Anonymous. (2002b). *Twelve steps and twelve traditions.* New York, NY: Author.

Alexander, C. N., Robinson, P., & Rainforth, M. (1994). Treating and preventing alcohol, nicotine, and drug abuse through transcendental meditation: A review and statistical meta-analysis. *Alcoholism Treatment Quarterly, 11,* 13–87. doi:10.1300/J020v11n01_02

American Psychological Association Presidential Task Force on Evidence-Based Practice. (2006). Evidence-based practice in psychology. *American Psychologist, 61,* 271–285. doi:10.1037/0003-066X.61.4.271

Avants, S. K., Beitel, M., & Margolin, A. (2005). Making the shift from "addict self" to "spiritual self": results from a stage I study of spiritual self-schema (3-S) therapy for the treatment of addiction and HIV risk behavior. *Mental Health, Religion, and Culture, 8,* 167–177. doi:10.1080/13694670500138924

Avants, S. K., & Margolin, A. (2004). Development of spiritual self-schema (3-S) therapy for the treatment of addictive and HIV risk behavior: A convergence of cognitive and Buddhist psychology. *Journal of Psychotherapy Integration, 14,* 253–289. doi:10.1037/1053-0479.14.3.253

Babor, T. F., & Del Boca, F. K. (Eds.). (2003). *Treatment matching in alcoholism.* Cambridge, England: Cambridge University Press.

Bachman, J. G., O'Malley, P. M., Schulenberg, J. E., Johnston, L. D., Bryant, A. L., & Merline, A. C. (2002). *The decline of substance use in young adulthood: Changes in social activities, roles, and beliefs.* Mahwah, NJ: Erlbaum.

Belcher, J. R. (2006). Protestantism and alcoholism: Spiritual and religious considerations. *Alcoholism Treatment Quarterly, 24,* 21–32. doi:10.1300/J020v24n01_03

Bishop, F. M. (1995). Rational-emotive behavior therapy and two self-help alternatives to the 12-step model. In A. M. Washton (Ed.), *Psychotherapy and substance abuse: A practitioner's handbook* (pp. 141–160). New York, NY: Guilford Press.

Bowen, S., Chawla, N., Collins, S. E., Witkiewitz, K., Hsu, S., Grow, J., . . . Marlatt, G. A. (2009). Mindfulness-based relapse prevention for substance use disorders: A pilot efficacy trial. *Substance Abuse, 30,* 295–305. doi:10.1080/08897070903250084

Bowen, S., Chawla, N., & Marlatt, G. A. (2011). *Mindfulness-based relapse prevention for addictive behaviors: A clinician's guide.* New York, NY: Guilford Press.

Bowen, S., Witkiewitz, K., Dillworth, T. M., Chawla, N., Simpson, T. L., Ostafin, B. D., . . . Marlatt, G. A. (2006). Mindfulness meditation and substance use in an incarcerated population. *Psychology of Addictive Behaviors, 20,* 343–347. doi:10.1037/0893-164X.20.3.343

Burkett, S. R. (1993). Perceived parents' religiosity, friends' drinking, and hellfire: A panel study of adolescent drinking. *Review of Religious Research, 35,* 134–154. doi:10.2307/3511780

Calhoun, F. J. (2007). Developmental research on alcohol and spirituality: What we know and what we don't know. *Southern Medical Journal, 100,* 427–429. doi:10.1097/SMJ.0b013e3180315de4

Celebrate Recovery. (2011). *Celebrate recovery: A Christ centered recovery program.* Retrieved from http://www.celebraterecovery.com

Collins, F. L., Leffingwell, T. R., Callahan, J. L., & Cohen, L. M. (2009). Evidence-based practice. In L. Cohen, F. L. Collins, A. M. Young, D. E. McChargue, & T. R. Leffingwell (Eds.), *The pharmacology and treatment of substance abuse: An evidence based approach* (pp. 129–151). Mahwah, NJ: Erlbaum.

Connors, G. J., Donovan, D. M., & DiClemente, C. C. (2001). *Substance abuse treatment and the stages of change.* New York, NY: Guilford Press.

Coyhis, D. (2000). Culturally specific addiction recovery for Native Americans. In J. Krestan (Ed.), *Bridges to recovery: Addiction, family therapy and multicultural treatment* (pp. 77–114). New York, NY: Free Press.

DeAngelis, T. (2001, June). Substance abuse treatment: An untapped opportunity for practitioners. *Monitor on Psychology, 32.* Retrieved from http://apa.org/monitor/jun01/treatopp.aspx

Delany, H. D., Forcehimes, A. A., Campbell, W. P., & Smith, B. W. (2009). Integrating spirituality into alcohol treatment. *Journal of Clinical Psychology, 65,* 185–198. doi:10.1002/jclp.20566

Donovan, D. M. (2005). Assessment of addictive behaviors for relapse prevention. In D. M. Donovan & G. A. Marlatt (Eds.), *Assessment of addictive behaviors* (pp. 1–48). New York, NY: Guilford Press.

Doweiko, H. E. (2012). *Concepts of chemical dependency* (8th ed.). Belmont, CA: Brooks/Cole.

Drerup, M. L. (2005). Religion, spirituality, and motives for drinking in an adult community sample. *Dissertation Abstracts International, 66*(12). (UMI No. 3199426)

Drerup, M. L., Johnson, T. J., & Bindl, S. (2011). Mediators of the relationship between religiousness/spirituality and alcohol use in an adult community sample. *Addictive Behaviors, 36,* 1317–1320. doi:10.1016/j.addbeh.2011.07.013

Dyslin, C. W. (2008). The power of powerlessness: The role of spiritual surrender and interpersonal confession in the treatment of addictions. *Journal of Psychology and Christianity, 27,* 41–55.

Faces and Voices of Recovery. (2011). *Guide to mutual aid resources.* Retrieved from http://www.facesandvoicesofrecovery.org/resources/support/resources/all.htm

Fernandez, A. C., Wood, M. D., Stein, L. A. R., & Rossi, J. S. (2010). Measuring mindfulness and examining its relationship with alcohol use and negative consequences. *Psychology of Addictive Behaviors, 24,* 608–616. doi:10.1037/a0021742

Galanter, M. (1990). Cults and zealous self-help movements: A psychiatric perspective. *American Journal of Psychiatry, 147,* 543–551.

Galanter, M. (1996). Cults and charismatic group psychology. In E. P. Shafranske (Ed.), *Religion and the clinical practice of psychology* (pp. 269–296). Washington, DC: American Psychological Association. doi:10.1037/10199-010

Gorsuch, R. L. (1995). Religious aspects of substance abuse and recovery. *Journal of Social Issues, 51,* 65–83. doi:10.1111/j.1540-4560.1995.tb01324.x

Herd, D., & Grube, J. (1996). Black identity and drinking in the US: A national study. *Addiction, 91,* 845–857. doi:10.1111/j.1360-0443.1996.tb03579.x

Hsu, S. H., Grow, J., & Marlatt, G. A. (2008). Mindfulness and addiction. In M. Galanter & L. A. Kaskutis (Eds.), *Recent Developments in Alcoholism: Vol. 18. Research on Alcoholics Anonymous and spirituality* (pp. 229–250). New York, NY: Springer.

Humphreys, K. (2004). *Circles of recovery: Self-help organizations for addictions.* Cambridge, England: Cambridge University Press.

JACS. (2011). *Jewish alcoholics, chemically dependent persons and significant others: Local Jewish meetings offering recovery.* Retrieved from http://www.jacsweb.org/directory.php

Johnson, T. J., & Bennett, P. (2009). Faith based programs. In L. Cohen, F. L. Collins, A. M. Young, D. E. McChargue, & T. R. Leffingwell (Eds.), *The pharmacology and treatment of substance abuse: An evidence based approach* (pp. 605–651). Mahwah, NJ: Erlbaum.

Johnson, T. J., Carlisle, R., Sheets, V. L., & Kristeller, J. (2008, February). *Prospective examination of the relationship between religious struggle and alcohol problems in a college sample.* Paper presented at the annual midyear meeting of APA Division 36, The Psychology of Religion, Columbia, MD.

Johnson, T. J., & Robinson, E. A. R. (2008). Issues in measuring spirituality and religiousness in alcohol research. In M. Galanter & L. A. Kaskutis (Eds.), *Recent Developments in Alcoholism: Vol. 18. Research on Alcoholics Anonymous and spirituality* (pp. 167–186). New York, NY: Springer.

Johnson, T. J., Sheets, V. L., & Kristeller, J. (2007, July). *Prospective examination of the relationship between religiousness and alcohol use and problems.* Poster presented at the meeting of the Research Society on Alcoholism, Chicago, IL.

Johnson, T. J., Sheets, V. L., & Kristeller, J. (2008a). Empirical identification of dimensions of religiousness and spirituality. *Mental Health, Religion, and Culture, 11,* 745–767. doi:10.1080/13674670701561209

Johnson, T. J., Sheets, V. L., & Kristeller, J. (2008b). Identifying mediators of the relationship between religiousness/spirituality and alcohol use. *Journal of Studies on Alcohol and Drugs, 69,* 160–170.

Kaskutis, L. A., Ye, Y., Greenfield, T. K., Witbrodt, J., & Bond, J. (2008). Epidemiology of Alcoholics Anonymous participation. In M. Galanter & L. A. Kaskutis (Eds.), *Recent Developments in Alcoholism: Vol. 18. Research on Alcoholics Anonymous and spirituality* (pp. 261–282). New York, NY: Springer.

Kelly, J. F., Magill, M., & Stout, R. L. (2009). How do people recover from alcohol dependence?

A systematic review of the research on mechanisms of behavior change in Alcoholics Anonymous. *Addiction Research and Theory, 17*, 236–259. doi:10.1080/16066350902770458

Kendler, K. S., Liu, X.-Q., Gardner, C. O., McCullough, M. E., Larson, D., & Prescott, C. A. (2003). Dimensions of religiosity and their relationship to lifetime psychiatric and substance use disorders. *American Journal of Psychiatry, 160*, 496–503. doi:10.1176/appi.ajp.160.3.496

Koenig, H. G. (2002). The connection between psychoneuroimmunology and religion. In H. G. Koenig and H. J. Cohen (Eds.), *The link between religion and health: Psychoneuroimmunology and the faith factor* (pp. 11–30). New York, NY: Oxford University Press.

Kristeller, J. L., Baer, R. A., & Quillian-Wolever, R. (2006). Mindfulness based approaches to eating disorders. In R. A. Baer (Ed.), *Mindfulness-based treatment approaches: Clinician's guide to evidence base and applications* (pp. 75–91). San Diego, CA: Elsevier. doi:10.1016/B978-012088519-0/50005-8

Kurtz, E. (1979). Not-God: A history of Alcoholics Anonymous. Center City, MN: Hazelden.

Lin, W. F., Mack, D., Enright, R. D., Krahn, D., & Baskin, T. W. (2004). Effects of forgiveness therapy on anger, mood, and vulnerability to substance use among inpatient substance-dependent clients. *Journal of Consulting and Clinical Psychology, 72*, 1114–1121. doi:10.1037/0022-006X.72.6.1114

Mahoney, A., Carels, R. A., Pargament, K. I., Wachholtz, A., Leeper, L. E., Kaplar, M., & Frutchey, R. (2005). Sanctification of the body and behavioral health patterns of college students. *The International Journal for the Psychology of Religion, 15*, 221–238. doi:10.1207/s15327582ijpr1503_3

Margolin, A., Schuman-Olivier, Z., Beitel, M., Arnold, R. M., Fulwiler, C. E., & Avants, S. K. (2007). A preliminary study of spiritual self-schema (3-S+) therapy for reducing impulsivity in HIV-positive drug users. *Journal of Clinical Psychology, 63*, 979–999. doi:10.1002/jclp.20407

McCrady, B. S. (2000). Alcohol use disorders and the Division 12 Task Force of the American Psychological Association. *Psychology of Addictive Behaviors, 14*, 267–276. doi:10.1037/0893-164X.14.3.267

Mercadante, L. (1996). *Victims and sinners: Spiritual roots of addiction and recovery*. Louisville, KY: Westminster John Knox Press.

Michalak, L., & Trocki, K. (2006). Alcohol and Islam: An overview. *Contemporary Drug Problems, 33*, 523–562.

Michalak, L., Trocki, K., & Bond, J. (2007). Religion and alcohol in the U.S. National Alcohol Survey: How important is religion for abstention and drinking? *Drug and Alcohol Dependence, 87*, 268–280. doi:10.1016/j.drugalcdep.2006.07.013

Miller, W. R. (1998). Researching the spiritual dimensions of alcohol and other drug problems. *Addiction, 93*, 979–990. doi:10.1046/j.1360-0443.1998.9379793.x

Miller, W. R., & Carroll, K. M. (2006). Drawing the scene together: Ten principles, ten recommendations. In W. R. Miller & K. M. Carroll (Eds.), *Rethinking substance abuse: What the science shows and what we should do about it* (pp. 293–311). New York, NY: Guilford Press.

Miller, W. R., Forcehimes, A., O'Leary, M. J., & LaNoue, M. D. (2008). Spiritual direction in addiction treatment: Two clinical trials. *Journal of Substance Abuse Treatment, 35*, 434–442. doi:10.1016/j.jsat.2008.02.004

Miller, W. R., & Rollnick, S. J. (2002). *Motivational interviewing: Preparing people for change*. New York, NY: Guilford Press.

Miller, W. R., Wilbourne, P. L., & Hettema, J. E. (2003). What works? A summary of alcohol treatment outcome research. In R. K. Hester & W. R. Miller (Eds.), *Handbook of alcoholism treatment approaches: Effective alternatives* (3rd ed., pp. 13–63). Boston, MA: Allyn & Bacon.

Mullen, K., Williams, R., & Hunt, K. (1996). Irish descent, religion, and alcohol and tobacco use. *Addiction, 91*, 243–254. doi:10.1111/j.1360-0443.1996.tb03185.x

Murray, T. S., Goggin, K., & Malcarne, V. L. (2006). Development and validation of the alcohol-related God locus of control scale. *Addictive Behaviors, 31*, 553–558. doi:10.1016/j.addbeh.2005.12.023

Myers, P. L. (1991). Cult and cult-like pathways out of adolescent addiction. *Journal of Adolescent Chemical Dependency, 1*, 115–137. doi:10.1300/J272v01n04_06

National Center on Addiction and Substance Abuse at Columbia University. (2001). *So help me God: Substance abuse, religion and spirituality* (A CASA White Paper). New York, NY: Author.

National Institute on Drug Abuse. (2006). *Research report series: MDMA (ecstasy) abuse* (NIH Publication No. 06–4728). Washington, DC: National Institute on Drug Abuse, U.S. Department of Health and Human Services, National Institutes of Health.

National Institute on Drug Abuse. (2009). *Principles of drug addiction treatment: A research-based guide*, 2nd ed. (NIH Publication No. 09–4180). Washington, DC: National Institute on Drug Abuse, U.S. Department of Health and Human Services, National Institutes of Health.

Nelson, J. B. (2004). *Thirst: God and the alcoholic experience*. Louisville, KY: Westminster John Knox Press.

Nhat Hanh, T. (1987). *The miracle of mindfulness: An introduction to the practice of meditation*. Boston, MA: Beacon Press.

Niclaus, M. (2009). *Empowering your sober self: The Lifering approach to addiction recovery*. San Francisco, CA: Jossey-Bass.

Nowinski, J., & Baker, S. (2003). *The twelve-step facilitation handbook: A systematic approach to recovery from substance dependence*. Center City, MN: Hazelden.

O'Brien, C. (2011). Addiction and dependence in DSM-V. *Addiction, 106*, 866–867. doi:10.1111/j.1360-0443.2010.03144.x

Olitzky, K. M., & Copans, S. A. (1991). *Twelve Jewish steps to recovery: A personal guide to turning from alcoholism and other addictions*. Woodstock, VT: Jewish Lights.

Pargament, K. I. (1997). *The psychology of religious coping*. New York, NY: Guilford Press.

Pargament, K. I. (2007). *Spiritually integrated psychotherapy: Understanding and addressing the sacred*. New York, NY: Guilford Press.

Petry, N. M., Kelley, L., Brennan, M., & Sierra, S. (2008). What happens when contingency Management treatment ends? A tale of two clients. *American Journal on Addictions, 17*, 241–244. doi:10.1080/10550490802019923

Petry, N. M., Lewis, M. W., Østvik-White, E. M. (2008). Participation in religious activities during contingency management interventions is associated with substance use treatment outcomes. *American Journal on Addictions, 17*, 408–413. doi:10.1080/10550490802268512

Prochaska, J. O., & DiClemente, C. C. (1984). *The transtheoretical approach: Crossing the traditional boundaries of therapy*. Malabar, FL: Krieger.

Ringwald, C. (2002). *The soul of recovery*. New York, NY: Oxford University Press.

Rivers, P. C. (1994). *Alcohol and human behavior*. Englewood Cliffs, NJ: Prentice-Hall.

Robinson, E. A. R., Brower, K. J., & Kurtz, E. (2003). Life-changing experiences, spirituality, and religiousness of persons entering treatment for alcohol problems. *Alcoholism Treatment Quarterly, 21*, 3–16. doi:10.1300/J020v21n04_02

Robinson, E. A. R., Cranford, J. A., Webb, J. R., & Brower, K. J. (2007). Six-month changes in spirituality, religiousness, and heavy drinking in a treatment-seeking sample. *Journal of Studies on Alcohol and Drugs, 68*, 282–290.

Saunders, S. M., Lucas, V., & Kuras, L. (2007). Measuring the discrepancy between current and ideal spiritual and religious functioning in problem drinkers. *Psychology of Addictive Behaviors, 21*, 404–408. doi:10.1037/0893-164X.21.3.404

Spiegel, M. C., & Kravitz, Y. (2001). Confronting addiction. In D. A. Friedman (Ed.), *Jewish pastoral care* (pp. 264–285). Woodstock, VT: Jewish Lights.

Stoltzfus, K. M. (2006). An elephant in the sanctuary: Denial and resistance in addicted Christians and their churches. *Social Work and Christianity, 33*, 141–163.

Sylvan, R. (2005). *Trance formation: The spiritual and religious dimensions of global rave culture*. New York, NY: Routledge.

Thombs, D. L. (2006). *Introduction to addictive behaviors* (3rd ed.). New York, NY: Guilford Press.

Tonigan, J. S., Miller, W. R., & Schermer, C. (2002). Atheists, agnostics and Alcoholics Anonymous. *Journal of Studies on Alcohol, 63*, 534–541.

Tonigan, J. S., Toscova, R., & Miller, W. R. (1996). Meta-analysis of the literature on Alcoholics Anonymous: Sample and study characteristics moderate findings. *Journal of Studies on Alcohol, 57*, 65–72.

Tonigan, J. S., Toscova, R. T., & Connors, G. J. (1999). Spirituality and the 12-step programs: A guide for clinicians. In W. R. Miller (Ed.), *Integrating spirituality into treatment: Resources for practitioners* (pp. 111–131). Washington, DC: American Psychological Association. doi:10.1037/10327-006

Turner, S. (2006). *The Gospel according to the Beatles*. Louisville, KY: Westminster John Knox Press.

Wachholtz, A. B., & Pargament, K. I. (2005). Is spirituality a critical ingredient of meditation? Comparing the effects of spiritual meditation, secular meditation, and relaxation on spiritual, psychological, cardiac, and pain outcomes. *Journal of Behavioral Medicine, 28*, 369–384. doi:10.1007/s10865-005-9008-5

Weir, E. (2000). Raves: A review of the culture, the drugs, and the prevention of harm. *Canadian Medical Association Journal, 162*, 1843–1848.

Wilbourne, P. L., & Miller, W. R. (2002). Treatments for alcoholism: Older and wiser? *Alcoholism Treatment Quarterly, 20*, 41–59. doi:10.1300/J020v20n03_03

Zemore, S. E. (2007). A role for spiritual change in the benefits of 12-step involvement. *Alcoholism: Clinical and Experimental Research, 31*, 76S–79S.

Zemore, S. E. (2008). An overview of spirituality in AA (and recovery). In M. Galanter & L. A. Kaskutis (Eds.), *Recent Developments in Alcoholism: Vol. 18. Research on Alcoholics Anonymous and spirituality* (pp. 111–123). New York, NY: Springer. doi:10.1007/978-0-387-77725-2_7

Zemore, S. E., & Pagano, M. E. (2008). Kickbacks from helping others: Health and recovery. In M. Galanter & L. A. Kaskutis (Eds.), *Recent Developments in Alcoholism: Vol. 18. Research on Alcoholics Anonymous and spirituality* (pp. 141–166). New York, NY: Springer.

Zweben, J. E. (1995). Integrating psychotherapy and 12-step approaches. In A. M. Washton (Ed.), *Psychotherapy and substance abuse* (pp. 124–140). New York, NY: Guilford Press.

Chapter 16

RELIGIOUSNESS AND SPIRITUALITY IN THE ETIOLOGY AND TREATMENT OF EATING DISORDERS

P. Scott Richards, Sarah L. Weinberger-Litman, Sara Susov, and Michael E. Berrett

Historically, the topics of religiousness and spirituality have received little attention in the eating disorders field. According to a systematic review of two prestigious eating disorder journals, only about 2% of empirical studies published from 1993 to 2004 included a measure of religiousness or spirituality (Richards & Bartz, 2005). Furthermore, most scholarly books about eating disorders have given scant attention to the possible role of religiousness or spirituality in etiology and treatment. Finally, the most recent eating disorder practice guideline monograph published by the American Psychiatric Association (2006) gives only cursory attention to these topics (Berrett, Hardman, & Richards, 2010).

Fortunately the neglect of religiousness and spirituality in the eating disorders field appears to be waning as a growing number of studies on this topic have been published recently in professional journals as well as several books and book chapters, all of which are discussed in this chapter. Also, according to an exhaustive Internet search, more than 40% of eating disorder facilities in North America now advertise that they address patients' spiritual needs in their treatment programs (Susov & Richards, 2010).

We hope that this chapter will help stimulate further theory, research, and effective practice in this important domain. We begin by providing brief background information about eating disorders, followed by a review of theoretical and empirical evidence that religiousness and spirituality may play a role in the etiology of eating disorders. We also review studies that indicate that religiousness and spirituality may play an important part in eating disorder treatment and recovery. We discuss recent clinical literature that provides insight and guidelines into how to implement spiritual perspectives and interventions during treatment. We conclude by offering some recommendations for future research, training, and practice.

Consistent with the integrative paradigm of this handbook, we use the term *religiousness* in this chapter to refer to beliefs, practices, relationships, or experiences having to do with the sacred that are explicitly and historically rooted in established institutionalized systems (see Volume 1, Chapter 1, this handbook). Many eating disorder patients, similar to the general public, are affiliated with a specific religious denomination, and their beliefs about the sacred are directly grounded in the teachings of their denomination. We use the term *spirituality* to refer to beliefs, practices, relationships, or experiences having to do with the sacred that are not necessarily linked to established institutionalized systems (see Volume 1, Chapter 1, this handbook). Other eating disorder patients have never been, or no longer are, affiliated with a formal religious denomination, but nevertheless they regard themselves as spiritually inclined with interests in the sacred or divine. In this chapter, we frequently use both terms together because we wish to include both types of patients and both ways of understanding and approaching the sacred. Finally, for the sake of brevity, we abbreviate the words *eating disorder* (ED) and *eating disorders* (EDs) where appropriate throughout the remainder of the chapter.

DOI: 10.1037/14046-016
APA Handbook of Psychology, Religion, and Spirituality: Vol. 2. An Applied Psychology of Religion and Spirituality, K. I. Pargament (Editor-in-Chief)

BACKGROUND INFORMATION ON EATING DISORDERS

The rates of EDs in the United States, Europe, and other industrial nations have increased in recent decades with an estimated 5 million Americans alone suffering from an ED. EDs disproportionately affect women (Hudson, Hiripi, Pope, & Kessler, 2007) and are the third most common form of chronic illness among adolescent and young adult women in the United States (Gordon, 2000). EDs are recognized as multifaceted and complex illnesses with biological, genetic, psychological, and sociocultural factors all contributing to their etiology and course (Fairburn, Cooper, Shafran, & Wilson, 2008; Klein & Walsh, 2004). The extent to which these factors interact is not well understood (Klein & Walsh, 2004).

The *Diagnostic and Statistical Manual of Mental Disorders* (4th ed., text revision; *DSM–IV–TR*; American Psychiatric Association, 2000) currently recognizes three distinct EDs: anorexia nervosa (AN); bulimia nervosa (BN); and a residual category, eating disorder not otherwise specified (EDNOS). Binge eating disorder (BED) is listed as a diagnosis for further study. Each ED has distinct diagnostic criteria, but they all share overlapping core features of psychopathology, primarily a preoccupation with weight and shape and an overvaluation of oneself on the basis of one's weight and shape (American Psychiatric Association, 2000; Fairburn et al., 2008). The fear of gaining weight is more extreme and excessive thinness is more often achieved in AN; however, all ED sufferers show an undue concern about thinness (body shape and weight; American Psychiatric Association, 2000).

Unique features of AN include an intense fear of gaining weight, a refusal to maintain a minimally acceptable body weight (below 85% of ideal body weight), and amenorrhea in postpubertal women (American Psychiatric Association, 2000). AN has the highest mortality of any psychiatric disorder, with an estimated 10% to 20% of those with the disorder eventually dying of medical complications or suicide (Fairburn et al., 2008; Klein & Walsh, 2004).

BN is characterized by recurrent episodes of eating objectively large quantities of food while feeling a loss of control over one's eating (i.e., bingeing), followed by extreme weight loss behavior or purging such as vomiting, laxative abuse, or excessive exercising (American Psychiatric Association, 2000). Although the medical consequences of BN are typically less severe than those of AN, many individuals with BN exhibit electrolyte imbalances, cardiac disturbances, and gastrointestinal problems that are sometimes fatal (Fairburn et al., 2008).

EDNOS is the most common diagnostic category and is often reserved for those not meeting full criteria for either AN or BN or for those exhibiting mixed symptoms of both BN and AN, but it does not necessarily imply lesser clinical severity (Fairburn et al., 2008; Klein & Walsh, 2004). It is quite common for individuals to cycle through the various ED diagnostic categories depending on the stage of their illness (Fairburn et al., 2008).

BED is currently subsumed under the heading of EDNOS, but it will be assigned its own diagnostic category in subsequent editions of the *DSM*. BED is thought to be somewhat distinct from the other three categories in onset and course (Fairburn et al., 2008). It is characterized by recurrent episodes of binge eating without the compensatory weight loss strategies seen in BN (Fairburn et al., 2008). We were unable to locate any studies that have examined the relations between BED and religiousness or spirituality.

EATING DISORDERS AND THE CONNECTION TO RELIGION AND SPIRITUALITY

There are both theoretical and empirical reasons to hypothesize that religious and spiritual influences may play a role in the etiology of EDs. In the sections that follow, we review theoretical literature that articulates this connection and discuss empirical studies relevant to the question.

Historical Background

Throughout history, women have chosen control over their bodies, including the denial of food, as a way to express both their autonomy and their religious devotion (Bell, 1985; Bemporad, 1996;

Brumberg, 2000; Bynum, 1987; Vandereycken & Van Deth, 1994). Numerous scholars have argued that by 21st-century diagnostic standards, the earliest documented cases of EDs are fasting saints who denied themselves food as a means of becoming closer to God (Bell, 1985; Bemporad, 1996; Brumberg, 2000; Bynum, 1987; Vandereycken & Van Deth, 1994). Many of these "holy anorexics" (Bell, 1985) were admired for their sacrifices and were declared saints by the church. It is notable that many of these women also engaged in forms of self-mortification and other ascetic practices (Bell, 1985; Bemporad, 1996; Brumberg, 2000; Bynum, 1987; Vandereycken & Van Deth, 1994).

Self-starvation as a religious testimony among pious women became particularly pronounced in the late Middle Ages and early Renaissance (Bemporad, 1996). One of the earliest of these cases is that of St. Wilgefortis (c. 8th century C.E.), whose name means "strong virgin" in Latin, who was the daughter of the king of Portugal (Bell, 1985; Bemporad, 1996). Wilgefortis took an early vow of chastity, and when her marriage was arranged, she refused to eat, became emaciated, and grew hair all over her body (a common late stage sign of AN), and the proposal was withdrawn. She was crucified by her father and came to be known as the saint who liberated women from their prescribed roles and the immense burden of sexuality (Bemporad, 1996).

Perhaps the most well known of these fasting saints was Catherine of Siena (1347–1380), who would become a model for holy fasters. Rampling (1985) argued that the case of Catherine and her religious asceticism included many behaviors and clinical manifestations observed in contemporary EDs. Around age 12, her parents began looking for a suitable husband for Catherine; she took a vow of virginity and became intensely religious, horrified at the idea of being married (Bemporad, 1996; Rampling, 1985). She soon became unable to eat more than a handful of herbs each day and when forced to eat would purge with a twig (Bynum, 1987). According to her biographer, eating caused her greater suffering than starving, and she would sometimes force herself to eat large amounts of food as means of punishing herself further (Rampling, 1985). She was renowned for her devotion and boundless energies to the ill and impoverished. Catherine died of starvation at the age of 32.

After the medieval period, the phenomenon of surviving on little (or no) food for religious purposes remained common but was seen mainly in adolescent girls and younger women. The ability to survive without any or with very little food was considered miraculous and a testament to the sanctity of these women, and their actions and became known as *anorexia mirabilis*, a miraculous loss of appetite (Brumberg, 2000; Bynum, 1987). Especially in Western Europe, several cases of fasting girls were documented. This severe restriction of food was a reflection of the ascetic and austere lifestyle characteristic of many women as a way of espousing their religious faith and devotion (Brumberg, 2000). It was not until 1689 that Richard Morton first described this phenomenon as an illness of a hysterical nature, and it was Sir William Gull that finally named this condition *anorexia nervosa* in 1874 (Brumberg, 2000).

Food Restriction as a Pathway to Salvation

Caution is needed to avoid pathologizing or equating the anorexic behavior patterns in medieval times with those in modern times because the cultural context was radically different historically. Ancient and medieval women used food restriction as a means of control because there was little else in their lives that they could control (Brumberg, 2000; Bynum, 1987). Many fasting saints sought power through control of their bodies in a patriarchal society in which a complete denial of physical needs and a life devoted to God was the only way to avoid a forced marriage, or to gain control over other undesirable life circumstances (Bell, 1985). In addition, medieval women did not exhibit the pathological fear of fatness or pursuit of excessive thinness characteristic of modern-day women with EDs, although their pursuit of holiness as an expression of power was an all-consuming endeavor, much like the pursuit of extreme thinness is all consuming for modern-day women with EDs (Bell, 1985; Lelwica, 2010). Thus, in ancient and medieval times, religious holiness offered women a pathway to control, power, salvation, and admiration, which they gained through asceticism and fasting.

As pointed out by several scholars, one cannot help but notice some similarities between the "holy anorexia" and "anorexia mirabilis" of the medieval and Victorian eras and EDs seen in the 21st century; for example, asceticism, denial of or ambivalence about sexuality, extreme pursuit of selected cultural ideals, and seeking control and power through food restriction (Bell, 1985; Brumberg, 2000; Bynum, 1987; Huline-Dickens, 2000; Lelwica, 1999; Vandereycken & Van Deth, 1994). Modern-day women with EDs also struggle for control and autonomy in a world that is often still experienced as dominating and patriarchal (Huline-Dickens, 2000; Maine, 2009; Maine & Bunnell, 2010). Women with EDs in the 21st century pursue extreme thinness in a culture in which thinness is sanctified and venerated (Lelwica, 1999, 2010). Thinness offers the hope of power and success in a world in which the female body is objectified and sexualized and in which aberrant thinness is epitomized in the media as the ultimate form of female beauty (Lelwica, 1999; Maine & Bunnell, 2010; Maine & Kelly, 2005). Thus, in contemporary Western society, the pursuit of extreme thinness is a prominent way for women to elicit admiration, try to exert control over their lives, and seek happiness, goals that a minority of women reach for through restricting and purging. The pursuit of excessive thinness has replaced religious holiness as a secular pathway to salvation.

Eating Disorders as a Spiritual Hunger

Several scholars have recently theorized that the pursuit of pathological thinness manifested in modern-day women with EDs represents a misguided quest to resolve spiritual hunger, or in other words, to satisfy unmet spiritual needs (Emmett, 2009; Lelwica, 1999, 2010; Richards, Hardman, & Berrett, 2007). According to this perspective, EDs are a spiritual problem and the resolution of ED sufferers' spiritual struggles are an essential part of the recovery process.

Hardman, Berrett, and Richards (2003; see also Richards et al., 2007) suggested that ED patients relentlessly pursue thinness as a solution to painful life events and emotions instead of reaching out to others and to God. They conceptualized EDs as a futile attempt to construct meaning and find identity, success, love, and happiness. They hypothesized that ED patients may adhere to a number of false beliefs; namely, that the ED will (a) give them control of their life and emotions, (b) effectively communicate their pain and suffering, (c) make them exceptional, (d) prove that that they are bad and unworthy, (e) make them perfect, (f) give them comfort and safety from pain, (g) give them a sense of identity, (h) compensate or atone for their past, (i) allow them to avoid personal responsibility for life, and (j) give them approval from others. When women place their faith in an ED rather than in their family, friends, and God, this leads to emotional and spiritual estrangement from those who could help them the most. As their relationship with God and with family and friends deteriorate, they rely ever more exclusively on their ED as a way of coping with pain and problems (Richards et al., 2007). This also undermines their spiritual values and identity and contributes to feelings of spiritual unworthiness, shame, and self-alienation (Hardman et al., 2003; Richards et al., 2007).

Emmett (2009) conceptualized EDs from an existential psychospiritual perspective, referring to them as "stark manifestations of spiritual disharmony" (p. 19). He explained that

> my exposure to the intriguing connection between eating disorders and psychospiritual dysfunction came during an intake with the first eating-disordered person I had ever encountered. "I absolutely worship my bulimia," Janna said in passing, and at that very moment, I glimpsed the all-consuming emotional straitjacket of alienation, shame, powerlessness, and despair inherent in eating disorders. Sufferers are harshly self-critical, cut off from compassionate feelings for both themselves and their fellow human beings, while their ability to be vulnerable and truthful is often seriously compromised. (pp. 19–20)

He suggested that treatment involves creating an environment in which "a sort of psychospiritual CPR (cardiopulmonary resuscitation) on the deadened heart of the sufferer can be caringly and faithfully performed" (Emmett, 2009, p. 20).

Lelwica (2010) also conceptualized EDs as a spiritual problem and argued that traditional religious values have been replaced by the "religion of thinness," which she described as a "secular faith with a loosely organized set of rituals, symbols, stories, images, and beliefs" that give contemporary women (a) an ultimate concern or purpose, (b) myths to believe in regarding the rewards of thinness, (c) iconographic imagery to which to aspire, (d) rituals to organize daily life, (e) moral rules and vocabulary to judge self and others, (f) a community of women with the same objectives, and (g) the promise of salvation (Lelwica, 2010, pp. 37–38). Lelwica suggested that whereas people have traditionally turned to religious or spiritual traditions to provide meaning and content in their lives, the decline of these traditional values created the need for a replacement for their natural "spiritual hungers." Some may be disappointed in certain religious traditions for their rigid or patriarchal structures and as a result need to look elsewhere. She argued that as the role of religion has decreased in people's lives, the pursuit of thinness has become almost a bona fide religion in and of itself. Furthermore, the false promises of salvation through thinness leads to the constant pursuit of an unattainable standard that leaves one devoid of any capacity for spiritual nourishment (Lelwica, 2010).

In a recent self-help book written for women, Roth (2010) explored the relationship between food and women's deepest, core beliefs about such issues as love, fear, anger, meaning, transformation, and God. She argued that women both overeat and diet for the same underlying reasons—spiritual hunger—and the need to get back in touch with their true spiritual nature.

Contemporary Empirical Research About Religious Etiological Influences

Although relatively little empirical research exists on the role of religious and spiritual influences on ED development and course, preliminary evidence links some dimensions of religiousness and spirituality to ED prevalence and symptoms. Several tentative conclusions appear warranted at the present time: (a) Religious rationales may be used to justify anorexic behaviors, (b) religious orientation may be predictive of ED symptoms, (c) secure attachment to God is negatively associated with ED risk factors, and (d) religious affiliation may predict the severity of ED symptoms.

Religious justifications for anorexic behaviors. In a study of members of an ED self-help group (Joughin, Crisp, Halek, & Humphrey, 1992), women with the lowest body mass index and highest level of AN symptoms were most like to say that religion was very important to them. Furthermore, several studies provide evidence that women with AN may use religious rationales to justify their anorexic behaviors.

Morgan, Marsden, and Lacey (2000) presented four cases of women with EDs. Two patients used religious themes to justify their anorexic behaviors, while two also used starvation as a conscious way of suppressing physical and sexual urges that they deemed inappropriate on religious grounds. Dancyger et al. (2002) compared eight Orthodox Jewish girls (four were ultra-Orthodox and four were modern Orthodox) with 72 non-Orthodox Jewish patients in a day treatment program. They concluded that several of the ultra-Orthodox young women in the program felt threatened by the possibility of an early marriage, and this became a factor in their refusal to reach their goal weight. Some patients also used religious rationales for refusing food (e.g., religious fasting, needing Kosher foods).

Marsden, Karagianni, and Morgan (2007) employed structured interviews conducted with ED inpatients who said religion was important to them. Most participants considered their restricted eating behaviors as a form of moral control. Furthermore, their efforts at self-denial were an attempt to combat negative self-images, which were often conflated with religious themes of shame, guilt, and self-hatred. For some, their ED represented a form of salvation or had religious significance. Graham, Spencer, and Andersen (1991) noted a reduction in religious activities that may contain food, such as communion, weddings, or holiday celebrations among those suffering from an ED. They concluded that their withdrawal from communal religious rituals not only increased feelings of guilt and sinfulness among patients for whom religion played a central role in their lives but also removed them from the spiritual benefits and community support of religious life that could potentially aid in recovery.

Garrett (1996) interviewed 32 people diagnosed with anorexia who participated in group treatment about their self-starvation and recovery. She found that participants referred to anorexia as a misguided spiritual quest and, for many of them, recovery involved rediscovery of the self. She concluded that the women "regarded anorexia nervosa as a distorted form of spirituality and a misguided way of life, even when they were engaged in it" (Garrett, 1996, p. 1493).

Religious orientation and ED symptoms. Several empirical studies have investigated the role of religious orientation or devoutness in the development and progression of EDs. In the study of members of the ED self-help group mentioned earlier (Joughin et al., 1992), women with tendencies toward BN reported a lower importance of religion compared with patients with AN symptoms. The researchers hypothesized that those with bulimic tendencies may feel estranged from God or religious practice because their eating behaviors may symbolize a form of "giving in" to sin or gluttony through overindulgence.

M. H. Smith, Richards, and Maglio (2004) found a positive association between an extrinsic religious orientation and disordered eating and body dissatisfaction among inpatients being treated for bulimia in a subsample of undergraduates who had scored within the clinical range on a measure of disordered eating. Intrinsic religious orientation was not associated with level of ED symptoms. In addition, in a large nonclinical sample of women, an extrinsic orientation was found to be predictive of greater levels of bulimic symptoms and drive for thinness (M. H. Smith et al., 2004). Higher levels of extrinsic religiosity also increased the strength of the relationship between family dysfunction and ED symptoms.

In a nonclinical sample of young adult Jewish women, an extrinsic religious orientation was associated with higher levels of disordered eating and body dissatisfaction, whereas an intrinsic religious orientation was associated with lower scores on these measures (Weinberger-Litman, Rabin, Fogel, & Mensinger, 2008). Furthermore, an extrinsic religious orientation was also associated with higher levels of additional risk factors for the development of EDs, such as thin-ideal internalization (Weinberger-Litman, 2007). Finally, Kendler et al. (2003) conducted a large-scale epidemiological study using a measure of religiosity that closely resembled the construct of an intrinsic religious orientation and found that higher religiosity was tied to a lower tendency toward bulimic symptoms

Taken together, this body of research suggests that individuals who engage in religious activities because of social pressures and for self-serving and utilitarian purposes (i.e., extrinsic religious orientation; Allport & Ross, 1967) may be more vulnerable to exhibiting ED symptoms. In contrast, pursuing religious activities for inherent spiritual purposes (i.e., intrinsic religious orientation) appears to be unrelated to or associated with fewer ED symptoms.

Attachment to God and ED risk factors. Homan and Boyatzis (2010) studied a college sample of religiously devout women and found that those with a secure attachment to God experienced less pressure to be thin and had lower levels of thin-ideal internalization, body dissatisfaction, and dieting behavior than those with a more anxious attachment to God. Moreover, a secure attachment to God attenuated the association between thin-ideal internalization and body dissatisfaction. It was also found that pressure to be thin and the internalization of the thin ideal was longitudinally predictive of body dissatisfaction only in women with an anxious, less secure attachment to God.

Religious affiliation and ED symptoms. Several studies have investigated whether certain religious groups are more likely to develop EDs. Some have reported no differences in ED prevalence among different religious groups (Garfinkel & Garner, 1982), whereas others have reported higher rates among Catholics, Baptists, Methodists, and Jews (Oomen, 2000; Sykes, Gross, & Subishin, 1986).

Research on Jewish women illustrates the mixed results yielded by relying on religious affiliation versus other measures of religiousness. A study of a large nationally representative sample reported that Jewish women were more likely than other denominations to overestimate their body weight, which may imply greater levels of body dissatisfaction and weight control behavior, although this was not measured directly (Kim, 2007). Additionally, a study of Canadian high school students found higher rates of disordered eating among Jewish female adolescents compared with their non-Jewish counterparts (Pinhas, Heinmaa, Bryden, Bradley, & Toner, 2008). Conflicting results emerge, however, in studies on levels of religious observance among Jewish women. In a study of high school girls in Israel, greater levels of observance were also associated with lower levels of ED psychopathology (Latzer, Orna, & Gefen, 2007). Other studies, however, have failed to find significant differences between Orthodox versus non-Orthodox women (Pinhas et al., 2008). Furthermore, Weinberger-Litman (2007) found that the level of disordered eating among Jewish women did not differ by level of religious observance but only as a function of religious orientation (intrinsic or extrinsic).

Limited research has been conducted on other religious groups. Oomen (2000) found that women that identified as Methodist reported higher levels of disordered eating than other denominations. Moreover, Mormon women had lower levels of disordered eating than Baptist, Catholic, and Methodist women. Mormon women also reported being more intrinsic in their religious orientation.

As has been emphasized in the integrative paradigm of this handbook, religiousness and spirituality are complex, multidimensional phenomena. EDs are also multifaceted, and so it should not be surprising to find that the relations observed between them and religiousness and spirituality are complex. The small amount of research to date offers some preliminary insights and provides ample incentive for further empirical investigation of what role religion and spirituality may play in ED etiology and course.

ROLE OF RELIGIOUSNESS AND SPIRITUALITY IN TREATMENT AND RECOVERY

In the sections that follow we discuss scholarly and clinical literature that provides insight into how spiritual perspectives and interventions can be integrated ethically and effectively into ED treatment to promote patients' healing and recovery. We describe research findings that support the conclusion that patients' religiousness and spirituality are important resources in treatment and may help facilitate recovery from eating disorders, and we review strategies and interventions for integrating spirituality into treatment.

Empirical Evidence That Faith and Spirituality Facilitate Recovery

Several survey and interview studies with patients and former patients indicate that many women regard spirituality as crucial resources in their treatment and recovery from EDs. For example, Mitchell, Erlander, Pyle, and Fletcher (1990) surveyed former patients diagnosed with bulimia and reported that that "the single most common write-in answer as to what factors have been helpful in their recovery had to do with religion in the form of faith, pastoral counseling, or prayer" (p. 589). In a study of 372 former ED patients, 59% said that "spiritual pursuits" had been helpful, and 35% said that Overeaters Anonymous, a 12-step spiritual program, had been helpful (Hall & Cohn, 1992). Rorty, Yager, and Rossotto (1993) interviewed 40 women who had recovered from BN and found that approximately 40% of them had participated in a 12-step program and felt the "spiritual aspects" of the program were helpful. Others had sought out and found other forms of spiritual guidance helpful.

Marsden et al. (2007) interviewed 11 patients at St. George's inpatient ED unit in London, England, to examine relationships between EDs, religion, and treatment. Several participants experienced psychological and religious maturation as treatment progressed. Initially, some patients viewed starvation as a form of atonement, but they later came to see it as being against God's will and used their beliefs as a source of spiritual comfort to aid them in recovery. The authors concluded that for "patients with strong religious faith, spiritual practice is helpful in recovery, and spiritual maturation goes hand in hand with positive psychological changes" (Marsden et al., 2007, p. 11).

Richards et al. (2008) surveyed 36 women who had successfully completed ED inpatient treatment and asked them open-ended questions about the role of spirituality in their treatment and recovery.

Most patients reported that their spirituality gave them purpose and meaning, expanded their sense of identity and worth, helped them experience feelings of forgiveness toward self and others, and improved their relationships with God, family, and others. Many of the patients also indicated that it was their faith and spirituality that sustained them during their most difficult challenges.

Several quantitative studies also provide some support for the conclusion that attending to religious and spiritual issues facilitates recovery. For example, F. T. Smith, Richards, Fischer, and Hardman (2003) quantitatively examined the correlation between growth in spiritual well-being and other positive treatment outcomes in a sample of 251 women who received inpatient treatment for their EDs. They found that improvements in spiritual well-being were significantly associated with positive gains in attitudes about eating and body shape as well as healthier psychological functioning.

Richards, Berrett, Hardman, and Eggett (2006) compared the effectiveness of a spirituality group for 122 women in an inpatient treatment using a randomized, control group design. At the conclusion of treatment, patients in the spirituality group reported less psychological disturbance and ED symptoms, and greater spiritual well-being compared with patients in cognitive and emotional support groups. On weekly outcome measures, the patients in the spirituality group also tended to improve more quickly during the first 4 weeks of treatment than the other groups. In another experimental study, researchers found that college women who read theistically centered positive body affirmations before being exposed to images of ultrathin models had higher levels of body esteem after exposure than those in a control group (Boyatzis, Kline, & Backof, 2007).

Several published case studies also indicate that attending to issues of religiousness and spirituality during treatment is essential with some patients and can contribute to positive outcomes (Hardman, Berrett, & Richards, 2004; Morgan et al., 2000; Richards, Smith, Berrett, O'Grady, & Bartz, 2009). For example, Morgan et al. (2000) presented four cases of women with EDs for whom religion was relevant to treatment. The first woman displayed punitive religious devotions, which eventually turned into AN. She responded to behavioral therapy, and her religious beliefs became more sustaining than punitive. The second woman used religious arguments to justify low weight, and the clinical team was unsure how to challenge these arguments. A pastoral counselor who enjoyed religious credibility with the patient helped her recognize which of her religious arguments were nondoctrinal. The third woman saw psychodynamic therapy as a challenge to her faith, and as a result she did not make full use of the treatment. The fourth woman was a nun who was overwhelmed by guilt and starved herself in expiation (atonement for sin), which led to the development of anorexia. Through psychotherapy, she was able to make sense of her experiences and restore her weight, albeit at the loss of her religious faith.

Hardman et al. (2004) described their work with a 19-year-old Mormon woman diagnosed with AN and major depression. In addition to mainstream medical and psychological interventions, the psychotherapist helped the patient explore her religious beliefs and personal spirituality through discussions during individual therapy sessions and during a spirituality group. The patient was also given opportunities for solo times, which she used for prayer, contemplation, journaling, and reading sacred writings. On several of these occasions, the patient reported having spiritual experiences that reassured her of God's love and acceptance and that affirmed her goodness and spiritual worthiness. Treatment helped the patient reexamine, challenge, and modify her negative self-perceptions, overcome her depression, and cease her eating disordered behavior.

Richards et al. (2009) described a 23-year-old Episcopal woman who received inpatient treatment for EDNOS and a substance abuse problem. The patient said religion was important to her but that she had felt ostracized from peers in her religious community during her teen years. She also said she felt undeserving of God's love and care. During inpatient treatment, which included medical and psychological interventions, the patient reexamined her negative perceptions about God and her negative spiritual identity, and her God-image and self-image became more positive. She eventually was able to overcome her feelings of unworthiness and her fears about reaching out to God and to members of her religious community. She also became more confident about listening to spiritual impressions and trusting her heart and personal values. By the time of discharge, her ED and psychiatric symptoms had improved significantly, although further outpatient treatment was still needed.

INCORPORATING SPIRITUALITY INTO ED TREATMENT PROGRAMS

Increasing numbers of ED treatment facilities now regard spirituality as important in treatment. Susov and Richards (2010) conducted an exhaustive Internet search to determine how many ED treatment facilities advertise on the Internet that they address issues of spirituality in their treatment programs. Of the 150 ED treatment programs identified in the Internet search, 64 (42.7%) indicated that religious or spiritual issues are addressed in some way in their programs (Susov & Richards, 2010). Follow-up phone calls to these 64 ED treatment facilities were made to solicit more detailed information about how they include spirituality in treatment. Of the 64 treatment centers, 43.8% indicated that they use yoga, 36.9% offer a spirituality group, 21.5% offer 12-step groups, 13.9% teach meditation, 10.8% teach mindfulness, and 30.8% incorporate spirituality in some other manner.

GROWTH IN CLINICAL LITERATURE ABOUT SPIRITUALITY AND EDS

Growing numbers of ED practitioner-scholars have published clinical literature that provides insights and guidelines about how to incorporate spiritual perspectives into the treatment of ED patients. Table 16.1 summarizes many of the recent contributions about spirituality and ED treatment, and illustrates that a variety of frameworks have been proposed, including feminist, metaphorical, narrative, theistic, integrative–medical, Protestant Christian, and 12-step approaches. These writers also describe a wide variety of spiritual interventions and practices they have found helpful in the treatment of EDs.

Johnston (1996) explored EDs from a feminist and metaphorical perspective, suggesting that underlying an obsessive desire for thinness may be the belief that the only pathway to success and happiness in our society is by denying the feminine side of one's being (e.g., the emotional, intuitive, receptive, cooperative, circular). She strongly affirmed the importance of intuitive, spiritual ways of being and knowing in healing and recovery from ED. The book describes many practices that can assist women in nurturing and recovery their feminine, intuitive capacities, including connecting to one's heart, cultivating a state of receptivity, and taking time each day to be still and focus on being instead of doing; letting thoughts and feelings enter awareness without judgment; honoring one's emotions; keeping a journal of hunches, insights, and impulses; and trusting and following one's intuitions.

Manley and Leichner (2003) have offered a treatment that combines narrative, feminist, cognitive, and spiritual perspectives. They suggested that a focus on spirituality may be life-affirming for the adolescent and enable her to recognize that suicide has no place in her own personal ethical framework. They reason that a spirituality group may empower adolescents to discover and implement in their lives the values that are of great personal significance to them.

Maine (2009) has proposed a feminist–integrative approach in which "psychoeducation about the mental, emotional, spiritual, and medical effects of starvation and other ED symptoms is essential" (p. 13). In this approach, she has encouraged women to be media and cultural critics and to learn to monitor and change their thinking. She also described the *body myth*, which is the false belief that "the answer to life's meaning and challenges lies in our body's appearance" and that "our self-worth (and our worth to others) is (and ought to be) based on how we look, what we weigh, and what we eat" (Maine & Kelly, 2005, p. 2). She also affirmed the importance of spirituality and recommended a number of spiritual practices, including creating quiet time for reflection, mindfulness meditation, pondering "the legacy" one wishes to leave, seeking for balance in one's life (rest, rejuvenate, relax), clarifying one's values and priorities, learning to breathe fully, and developing a new relationship with one's body and food (learning to love one's body; Maine & Kelly, 2005).

TABLE 16.1

Spiritual Approaches for Treating Eating Disorder Patients

Conceptual framework	Author(s)	Role of spirituality in recovery	Spiritual interventions
Feminist, metaphorical	Johnston	Reclaiming one's feminine, intuitive capacities facilitates recovery.	Connecting to one's heart; cultivating a state of receptivity; being still; focusing on being instead of doing; mindfulness; honoring one's emotions; keeping a journal of hunches and insights; testing and following one's intuitions
Narrative, feminist, cognitive, spiritual	Manley and Leichner	Spirituality can empower adolescents to discover and implement values of personal significance.	Spirituality group; motivational work
Feminist, integrative	Maine	Spirituality is one part of a healthy, more complete and balance approach to living that can help women clarify their values and nurture their faith.	Quiet time for reflection; mindfulness meditation; seeking balance; pondering the legacy one wishes to leave; clarifying one's values and priorities; learning to breath fully; learning to love one's body
Feminist, spiritual	Lelwica	Spirituality can help women reject the dogma that having a perfect body will give them health, happiness, and well-being and instead find meaning and purpose through a connection to the sacred.	Mindfulness; cultural criticism; developing an embodied ethics of eating; building nourishing relationships; accepting one's self and body; experiencing and accepting pain and suffering; extending compassion to self and others
Theistic, integrative, multidisciplinary	Berrett, Hardman, and Richards	Reclaiming one's sense of spirituality and placing faith in a higher power and the love of significant others rather than in the false promises of the ED can empower patients with a sense of hope, purpose, and spiritual worth which motivates and facilitates physical and emotional healing and growth.	Learn to "listen to one's heart"; solo times for contemplation, prayer, and spiritual journaling; reading sacred writings; spirituality and 12-step groups; service; forgiveness; art therapy; spiritual mindedness; giving and receiving gifts of love; living in a principled manner; spiritual assessments
Integrative medical (body-mind-spirit)	Ross; Wingate	Getting in touch with the deeper urges of the soul or spirit and with their spiritual longings can help patients find their passion in life and bring renewed vigor for and purpose in life.	Buddhist prayer; guided imagery; hypnosis, mindfulness meditation; progressive relaxation; yoga; bodywork therapies; practicing gratitude; forgiveness; nurturing inspiration and awe; enjoying art; serving others; going to church; relationships with pets; supplements and herbs
Psychospiritual, existential	Emmett	Spirituality can help patients reclaim the self and restore a healing sense of wholeness and holiness.	Facilitating psychospiritual literacy; conducting a spiritual assessment; psychospiritual restructuring; encouraging authenticity; affirming spiritual worthiness; sowing seeds of faith, hope, and love
Protestant Christian	Cumella, Eberly, and Wall	Spiritual healing and growth is necessary for physical, psychological, and social recovery and growth.	Spiritual assessment; classes to explore spiritual issues; daily attendance at chapel; songs of praise and worship; Celebrate Recovery groups; Christian 12-step groups
12-step, theistic	Johnson and Sansone; Yeary	Faith in and reliance on a higher power rather than self is essential for overcoming addictive eating disordered behaviors.	Group support; confession; restitution; seeking forgiveness from God and others; prayers of petition and invocation; meditation; service to others

Richards, Hardman, and Berrett (2007) have proposed a theistic, spiritual approach for treating women with EDs (see also Berrett, Hardman, & Richards, 2010; Hardman et al., 2003, 2004; Richards, Smith, Berrett, O'Grady, & Bartz, 2009). In this approach, they described common spiritual issues they observed while working with ED patients, including negative images or perceptions of God, feelings of spiritual unworthiness and shame, fear of abandonment by God, guilt /or lack of acceptance of sexuality, reduced capacity to love and serve, difficulty surrendering and having faith, and dishonesty and deception (Richards et al., 2007). They suggested that many ED patients place their faith in the false pursuit of extreme thinness rather than reaching out to others and to God for help in coping with painful life events and emotions. Their overarching therapeutic goal is to help patients give up their worship of the ED so that they can open their hearts to reconnecting with God and with significant others (Hardman et al., 2003). They offered recommendations for how therapists can establish a spiritually safe therapeutic environment, conduct a religious–spiritual assessment, and implement spiritual interventions as part of treatment. These interventions encompass spirituality and 12-step groups, solo times for reflection, contemplation and prayer, reading sacred writings, spiritual journaling, creating opportunities for service, and referrals to religious leaders for spiritual direction. They also described six spiritual pathways that lead to healing and recovery (Berrett et al., 2010).

Ross (2007, 2009) has described an integrative medical approach to treating EDs that "takes into account the whole person: body, mind, and spiritual, including all aspects of lifestyle" (Ross, 2007, p. 3, Introduction). She discussed a number of mainstream treatment approaches, including medical, nutritional, and psychological ones (e.g., dialectical behavior therapy; stress management) as well as complementary and alternative (mind–body) approaches, including Buddhist prayer, guided imagery, hypnosis, mindfulness meditation, progressive relaxation, yoga, bodywork therapies, gratitude, forgiveness, and inspiration and awe (e.g., reading inspiring literature, finding awe in nature, listening to inspirational music, serving others, keeping a journal, going to church). Wingate (2009) also proposed an integrative medical approach, which she has described as "a commitment to knowing and treating the patient as a whole person, embedded in, and influenced by, a particular social context" (p. 63). She affirmed the importance of attending to patients' spiritual issues and described a number of spiritual interventions she has used during treatment, including yoga, meditation, supplements and herbs, and relationships with pets.

Cumella, Eberly, and Wall (2008) have developed a Protestant Christian treatment approach based on a biopsychosocial–spiritual model that integrates medical, psychological, and social strategies of treatment. Their treatment philosophy is grounded in the view that humans are "unified, indivisible beings," composed of a "body, soul, spirit, and interpersonal relations" and all people have vulnerabilities created by the "fallen or broken condition of the world" (Cumella et al., 2008, pp. 27–28). Prospective patients are "informed that they will be exposed to expressions of biblical Christianity, and they explicitly consent to this prior to admission" (p. 215). The treatment staff conducts a spiritual assessment of all patients to find out how they perceive God and to identify other spiritual issues with which they may be struggling (e.g., shame and judgment, spiritual wellness, past spiritual experiences, religious abuse). A number of structured spiritual interventions are included in the treatment program, including classes to explore spiritual issues, daily attendance at chapel (which includes a devotional message and songs of spiritual praise and worship), and groups called Celebrate Recovery and 12 Steps for Christians.

Emmett (2009) described an existential psychospiritual perspective of EDs that assumes that they are manifestations of spiritual disharmony. He sought to address the "fundamental existential struggle to reclaim the self and restore a healing sense of wholeness and holiness" (p. 20). He also described a variety of spiritual interventions he has used with ED patients, including facilitating psychospiritual literacy, conducting a spiritual assessment, psychospiritual bibliotherapy, psychospiritual restructuring (redirecting one's heart, mind, and spirit vis-à-vis relationship to oneself, others, and the divine), encouraging authenticity, affirming spiritual worthiness, and "sowing seeds of faith, hope, and love" (p. 32). All of this takes place within a psychospiritual therapeutic relationship that is characterized by loving acceptance and spiritual openness and self-disclosure.

Lelwica (2010) explored the *religion of thinness* and the spiritual roots of ED sufferers' obsession with thinness, which includes the false belief that "by achieving the perfect body we will achieve the health, happiness, and well-being we've been looking for" (p. 38). She described a number of self-help strategies and spiritual practices to assist those who struggle with disordered eating, including mindfulness, cultural criticism, developing an embodied ethics of eating, building nourishing relationships, developing acceptance of one's self and body, "touching" (experiencing and accepting) our pain and suffering, extending compassion to self and others, strengthening our connection to the sacred and to that which give our lives meaning and purpose, praying, and playing.

Several professionals have described how they use 12-step groups in the treatment of EDs (e.g., Johnson & Sansone, 1993; Wasson & Jackson, 2004; Yeary, 1987). The 12-step approach assumes that to recover from addictions, people must humble themselves before God, or their higher power, and acknowledge that they are powerless to overcome their addiction on their own. Religious and spiritual practices that may be used to facilitate the recovery process in 12-step programs for ED patients include confession, making restitution, seeking forgiveness from God and others, prayers of petition and invocation, meditation, and service to others.

Several other articles and books provide valuable additional perspectives about why and how clinicians integrate spiritual perspectives into their work with ED patients. For example, Newmark (2001) described how she incorporates spiritual direction and counseling into her work as a registered dietician working with ED patients. Costin (2002), a marriage and family psychotherapist, also described her spiritual approach for treating EDs, which involves teaching "soul lessons" to patients to help instill in them "a sense of connectedness to a greater purpose than his or her individual life" (p. 11). Finally, Sesan (2009) described the role of forgiveness in healing from EDs and wrote that "recovery from an ED is about opening up to life, the good and the bad, and living with a more open heart" (p. 235).

In this section, we have surveyed the diverse ways that experienced clinicians have begun to incorporate religion and spirituality into the treatment of EDs. More than 40% of ED treatment programs mention in their marketing materials that they address religious or spiritual issues (Susov & Richards, 2010). Remarkably, other than case studies, scarce controlled research has been conducted to evaluate the effectiveness or efficacy of various spiritually integrated methods for the treatment of EDs (Richards et al., 2007). We hope that this chapter will encourage clinical researchers and funding sources to expand the evidence base for the integration of religion and spirituality for EDs in the upcoming decades.

CONCLUSION

Much more empirical and scholarly work is needed if the role of religion and spirituality in ED etiology, treatment, and recovery is to be more fully understood. The American Psychiatric Association's (2006) recommendations concerning future research directions about EDs almost completely ignore the need for more research about religion, spirituality, and EDs. We hope that researchers and practitioners with interests in EDs and spirituality will collaborate and use their creativity and resources to advance the scholarship in this neglected domain.

As scholars further explore the relationship between EDs and religiousness and spirituality, we hope they will keep in mind the American Psychological Association's (2006) recent task force report and policy statement about evidence-based practice. This report strongly affirms the value of various quantitative and qualitative research methodologies, as well as clinical experience and expertise, in seeking to develop an evidence base for best practice with various psychological disorders. We think a methodologically pluralistic approach to developing an evidence base concerning the role and efficacy of religious and spiritual perspectives and interventions in treating EDs holds much promise (Richards & Worthington, 2010).

The theoretical, empirical, and clinical literature reviewed in this chapter collectively provides strong support for the conclusion that religiousness and spirituality are important in the etiology and treatment of EDs. We encourage ED professionals to seek training in religious and spiritual aspects of diversity and treatment so that they are prepared to work sensitively and ethically with the religious and spiritual issues of their ED patients. The best ED treatment is multimodal and multidisciplinary and addressing the religious and spiritual dimensions is often an extremely important aspect of treatment and recovery (Richards et al., 2007). Attending to religious and spiritual aspects of recovery requires patience, kindness, and in-depth emotional and spiritual work (Richards et al., 2007). Despite the challenges, ED professionals who address religious and spiritual issues and draw on the resources of their patients' faith and spirituality will advance in their ability to facilitate healing and recovery.

References

Allport, G. W., & Ross, J. M. (1967). Personal religious orientation and prejudice. *Journal of Personality and Social Psychology, 5*, 432–443. doi:10.1037/h0021212

American Psychiatric Association. (2000). *Diagnostic and statistical manual of mental disorders* (4th ed., text revision.). Washington, DC: Author.

American Psychiatric Association. (2006). *Practice guideline for the treatment of patients with eating disorders* (3rd ed.). Arlington, VA: Author.

American Psychological Association. (2006). Evidence-based practice in psychology. *American Psychologist, 61*, 271–285. doi:10.1037/0003-066X.61.4.271

Bell, R. M. (1985). *Holy anorexia.* Chicago, IL: University of Chicago Press.

Bemporad, J. R. (1996). Self-starvation through the ages: Reflections on the pre-history of anorexia nervosa. *International Journal of Eating Disorders, 19*, 217–237. doi:10.1002/(SICI)1098-108X(199604)19:3<217::AID-EAT1>3.0.CO;2-P

Berrett, M. E., Hardman, R. K., & Richards, P. S. (2010). The role of spirituality in eating disorder treatment and recovery. In M. Maine, B. H. McGilley, & D. W. Bunnell (Eds.), *Special issues in the treatment of eating disorders: Bridging the gaps* (pp. 367–385). Maryland Heights, MO: Elsevier. doi:10.1016/B978-0-12-375668-8.10022-1

Boyatzis, C. J., Kline, S., & Backof, S. (2007). Experimental evidence that theistic-religious body affirmations improve women's body image. *Journal for the Scientific Study of Religion, 46*, 553–564. doi:10.1111/j.1468-5906.2007.00377.x

Brumberg, J. J. (2000). *Fasting girls: The history of anorexia nervosa.* New York, NY: Vintage.

Bynum, C. W. (1987). *Holy feast and holy fast: The significance of food to medieval women.* Los Angeles: University of California Press.

Costin, C. (2002). Soul lessons: Finding the meaning of life. *Eating Disorders Today, 1*(2), 1, 11.

Cumella, E. J., Eberly, M. C., & Wall, A. D. (2008). *Eating disorders: A handbook of Christian treatment.* Nashville, TN: Remuda Ranch.

Dancyger, I., Fornari, V., Fisher, M., Schneider, M., Frank, S., Wisostky, W., . . . Charitou, M. (2002). Cultural factors in Orthodox Jewish adolescents treated in day program for eating disorders. *International Journal of Adolescent Medicine and Health, 14*, 317–328. doi:10.1515/IJAMH.2002.14.4.317

Emmett, S. (2009). Wholeness and holiness: A psycho-spiritual perspective. In M. Maine, W. N. Davis, & J. Shure (Eds.), *Effective clinical practice in the treatment of eating disorders: The heart of the matter* (pp. 19–33). New York, NY: Routledge.

Fairburn, C. G., Cooper, Z., Shafran, R., & Wilson, G. T. (2008). Eating disorders: A transdiagnostic protocol. In D. H. Barlow (Ed.), *Clinical handbook of psychological disorders: A step-by-step treatment manual* (4th ed., pp. 578–614). New York, NY: Guilford Press.

Garfinkel, P. E., & Garner, D. M. (1982). *Anorexia nervosa: A multidimensional perspective.* New York, NY: Brunner/Mazel.

Garrett, C. J. (1996). Recovery from anorexia nervosa: A Durkheimian interpretation. *Social Science and Medicine, 43*, 1489–1506. doi:10.1016/0277-9536(96)00088-3

Gordon, R. A. (2000). *Eating disorders: Anatomy of a social epidemic* (2nd ed.). Malden, MA: Blackwell.

Graham, M. A., Spencer, W., & Andersen, A. E. (1991). Altered religious practice in patients with eating disorders. *International Journal of Eating Disorders, 10*, 239–243. doi:10.1002/1098-108X(199103)10:2<239::AID-EAT2260100215>3.0.CO;2-4

Hall, L., & Cohn, L. (1992). *Bulimia: A guide to recovery.* Carlsbad, CA: Gurze Books.

Hardman, R. K., Berrett, M. E., & Richards, P. S. (2003). Spirituality and ten false pursuits of eating disorders: Implications for counselors. *Counseling and Values, 48*, 67–78. doi:10.1002/j.2161-007X.2003.tb00276.x

Hardman, R. K., Berrett, M. E., & Richards, P. S. (2004). A theistic inpatient treatment approach for eating disorder patients: A case report. In P. S. Richards & A. E. Bergin (Eds.), *Casebook for a spiritual strategy in counseling and psychotherapy* (pp. 55–73). Washington, DC: American Psychological Association. doi:10.1037/10652-003

Homan, K. J., & Boyatzis, C. J. (2010). The protective role of attachment to God against eating disorder risk factors: Concurrent and prospective evidence. *Eating Disorders, 18*, 239–258. doi:10.1080/10640261003719534

Hudson, J. I., Hiripi, E., Pope, H. G., & Kessler, R. C. (2007). The prevalence and correlates of eating disorders in the National Comorbidity Survey replication. *Biological Psychiatry, 61*, 348–358. doi:10.1016/j.biopsych.2006.03.040

Huline-Dickens, S. (2000). Anorexia nervosa: Some connections with the religious attitude. *British Journal of Medical Psychology, 73*, 67–76. doi:10.1348/000711200160309

Johnson, C. L., & Sansone, R. A. (1993). Integrating the Twelve-Step approach with traditional psychotherapy for the treatment of eating disorders. *International Journal of Eating Disorders, 14*, 121–134. doi:10.1002/1098-108X(199309)14:2<121::AID-EAT2260140202>3.0.CO;2-N

Johnston, A. (1996). *Eating in the light of the moon: How women can transform their relationships with food through myths, metaphors and storytelling*. Carlsbad, CA: Gurze Books.

Joughin, N., Crisp, A. H., Halek, C., & Humphrey, H. (1992). Religious belief and anorexia nervosa. *International Journal of Eating Disorders, 12*, 397–406. doi:10.1002/1098-108X(199212)12:4<397::AID-EAT2260120407>3.0.CO;2-2

Kendler, K. S., Liu, X., Garndner, C. O., McCullough, M. E., Larson, D., & Prescott, C. A. (2003). Dimensions of religiosity and their relationship to lifetime psychiatric and substance use disorders. *American Journal of Psychiatry, 160*, 496–503. doi:10.1176/appi.ajp.160.3.496

Kim, K. H. (2007). Religion, weight perception, and weight control behavior. *Eating Behaviors, 8*, 121–131. doi:10.1016/j.eatbeh.2006.03.001

Klein, D. A., & Walsh, B. T. (2004). Eating disorders: Clinical features and pathophysiology. *Physiology and Behavior, 81*, 359–374. doi:10.1016/j.physbeh.2004.02.009

Latzer, Y., Orna, T., & Gefen, S. (2007). Level of religiosity and disordered eating psychopathology among modern-orthodox Jewish adolescent girls in Israel. *International Journal of Adolescent Medicine and Health, 19*, 511–522. doi:10.1515/IJAMH.2007.19.4.511

Lelwica, M. M. (1999). *Starving for salvation*. New York, NY: Oxford University Press.

Lelwica, M. M. (2010). *The religion of thinness*. Carlsbad, CA: Gurze Books.

Maine, M. (2009). Beyond the medical model: A feminist frame for eating disorders. In M. Maine, W. N. Davis, & J. Shure (Eds.), *Effective clinical practice in the treatment of eating disorders: The heart of the matter* (pp. 3–17). New York, NY: Routledge.

Maine, M., & Bunnell, D. W. (2010). A perfect biopsychosocial storm. In M. Maine, B. H. McGilley, & D. W. Bunnell (Eds.), *Special issues in the treatment of eating disorders: Bridging the gaps* (pp. 3–16). Maryland Heights, MO: Elsevier. doi:10.1016/B978-0-12-375668-8.10001-4

Maine, M., & Kelly, J. (2005). *The body myth: Adult women and the pressure to be perfect*. Hoboken, NJ: Wiley.

Manley, R. S., & Leichner, P. (2003). Anguish and despair in adolescents with eating disorders: Helping to manage suicidal ideation and impulses. *Crisis: The Journal of Crisis Intervention and Suicide Prevention, 24*, 32–36.

Marsden, P., Karagianni, E., & Morgan, J. F. (2007). Spirituality and clinical care in eating disorders: A qualitative study. *International Journal of Eating Disorders, 40*, 7–12. doi:10.1002/eat.20333

Mitchell, J. E., Erlander, M., Pyle, R. L., & Fletcher, L. A. (1990). Eating disorders, religious practices and pastoral counseling. *International Journal of Eating Disorders, 9*, 589–593. doi:10.1002/1098-108X(199009)9:5<589::AID-EAT2260090517>3.0.CO;2-Z

Morgan, J. F., Marsden, P., & Lacey, J. H. (2000). "Spiritual starvation?" A case series concerning Christianity and eating disorders. *International Journal of Eating Disorders, 28*, 476–480. doi:10.1002/1098-108X(200012)28:4<476::AID-EAT19>3.0.CO;2-T

Newmark, G. R. (2001). Spirituality in eating disorder treatment. *Healthy Weight Journal, Sept./Oct.*, 76–77.

Oomen, J. S. (2000). Religiosity and eating attitudes among college women ages 18–30. *Dissertation Abstracts International: Section B. Sciences and Engineering, 61*(1), 188.

Pinhas, L., Heinmaa, M., Bryden, P., Bradley, S., & Toner, B. (2008). Disordered eating in Jewish adolescent girls. *Canadian Journal of Psychiatry, 53*, 601–608.

Rampling, D. (1985). Ascetic ideals and anorexia nervosa. *Journal of Psychiatric Research, 19*, 89–94. doi:10.1016/0022-3956(85)90003-2

Richards, P. S., & Bartz, J. (2005). *Systematic review of religion and spirituality in eating disorder research, theory, and practice*. Center for Change, Orem, UT. Unpublished manuscript.

Richards, P. S., Berrett, M. E., Hardman, R. K., & Eggett, D. L. (2006). Comparative efficacy of spirituality, cognitive, and emotional support groups for treating eating disorder inpatients. *Eating Disorders, 14*, 401–415. doi:10.1080/10640260600952548

Richards, P. S., Hardman, R. K., & Berrett, M. E. (2007). *Spiritual approaches in the treatment of women with eating disorders*. Washington, DC: American Psychological Association. doi:10.1037/11489-000

Richards, P. S., O'Grady, K. A., Berrett, M. E., Hardman, R. K., Bartz, J. D., Johnson, J., & Olson, M. (2008, May). *Exploring the role of spirituality in treatment and recovery from eating disorders: A qualitative survey study*. Paper presented at the Academy of Eating Disorders International Conference on Eating Disorders, "Bridging Science and Practice: Prospects and Challenges," Seattle, WA.

Richards, P. S., Smith, M. H., Berrett, M. E., O'Grady, K. A., & Bartz, J. D. (2009). A theistic spiritual treatment approach for women with eating disorders. *Journal of Clinical Psychology, 65*, 172–184. doi:10.1002/jclp.20564

Richards, P. S., & Worthington, E. L., Jr. (2010). The need for evidence-based spiritually-oriented psychotherapies. *Professional Psychology: Research and Practice, 41*, 363–370. doi:10.1037/a0019469

Rorty, M., Yager, J., & Rossotto, E. (1993). Why and how do women recover from bulimia nervosa? The subjective appraisals of forty women recovered for a year or more. *International Journal of Eating Disorders, 14*, 249–260. doi:10.1002/1098-108X(199311)14:3<249::AID-EAT2260140303>3.0.CO;2-O

Ross, C. C. (2007). *Healing body, mind and spirit: An integrative medicine approach to the treatment of eating disorders*. Denver, CO: Outskirts Press.

Ross, C. C. (2009). *The binge eating and compulsive overeating workbook: An integrated approach to overcoming disordered eating*. Oakland, CA: New Harbinger.

Roth, G. (2010). *Women, food and God: An unexpected path to almost everything*. New York, NY: Scribner.

Sesan, R. (2009). Forgiveness: The final frontier in recovery from an eating disorder. In M. Maine, W. N. Davis, & J. Shure (Eds.), *Effective clinical practice in the treatment of eating disorders: The heart of the matter* (pp. 235–248). New York, NY: Routledge.

Smith, F. T., Richards, P. S., Fischer, L., & Hardman, R. K. (2003). Intrinsic religiousness and spiritual well-being as predictors of treatment outcome among women with eating disorders. *Eating Disorders, 11*, 15–26. doi:10.1080/10640260390167456-2199

Smith, M. H., Richards, P. S., & Maglio, C. J. (2004). Examining the relationship between religious orientation and eating disturbances. *Eating Behaviors, 5*, 171–180. doi:10.1016/S1471-0153(03)00064-3

Susov, S., & Richards, P. S. (2010, April). *The role of spirituality in eating disorder treatment programs: An Internet survey of contemporary clinical practice*. Poster presented at the semi-annual convention of the Association of Mormon Counselors and Psychotherapists, Salt Lake City, UT.

Sykes, D. K., Gross, M., & Subishin, S. (1986). Preliminary findings of demographic variables in patients suffering from anorexia and bulimia nervosa. *International Journal of Psychosomatics, 33*, 27–30.

Vandereycken, W., & Van Deth, R. (1994). *From fasting saints to anorexic girls*. New York: New York University Press.

Wasson, D. H., & Jackson, M. (2004). An analysis of the role of Overeaters Anonymous in women's recovery from bulimia nervosa. *Eating Disorders, 12*, 337–356. doi:10.1080/10640260490521442

Weinberger-Litman, S. L. (2007). The influence of religious orientation, spiritual well-being, educational setting, and social comparison on body image and eating disturbance in Jewish women. *Dissertation Abstracts International, 68*(10), 7008.

Weinberger-Litman, S. L., Rabin, L. A., Fogel, J., & Mensinger, J. L. (2008). The influence of religious orientation and spiritual well-being on body dissatisfaction and disordered eating in a sample of Jewish women. *International Journal of Child and Adolescent Health, 1*, 373–387.

Wingate, B. (2009). Holistic integrative psychiatry and the treatment of eating disorders. In M. Maine, W. N. Davis, & J. Shure (Eds.), *Effective clinical practice in the treatment of eating disorders: The heart of the matter* (pp. 63–77). New York, NY: Routledge.

Yeary, J. (1987). The use of Overeaters Anonymous in the treatment of eating disorders. *Journal of Psychoactive Drugs, 19*, 303–309. doi:10.1080/02791072.1987.10472417

Chapter 17

SPIRITUALITY, RELIGION, AND SEXUAL TRAUMA: INTEGRATING RESEARCH, THEORY, AND CLINICAL PRACTICE

Nichole A. Murray-Swank and Lynn C. Waelde

In the aftermath of violence,
  when the inner sanctum of being has been desecrated,
  we may be blessed with the presence of companions,
  who venture with us into the innermost sanctum,
  empowering us,
  so that we can take on the gods who reign there,
  cast them out,
  and consecrate again this holiest of places,
  God within us.

(Doehring, 1993, p. iii)

GH[1] was a 22-year-old female Christian client who was raped by a stranger as an adolescent. She grew up in a moderately religious Presbyterian home and maintained an active spiritual life before the traumatic assault. She participated in a Bible study group for young adults as well as numerous social justice initiatives. After the rape, she initially turned to her religion for comfort and support. She sought connection from her faith community and prayed every morning. As time progressed, however, she began to feel confused and disillusioned as feelings of abandonment and anger emerged. At one session she arrived with a letter she wrote to God:

> Dear God, I don't understand how you can do this? I believed in you; I trusted you. "Why have you forsaken me?" I try to tell myself to have faith, to believe, to remember Jesus on the cross. But, I can't keep feeling this pain. Why is there such pain and tragedy? I feel as though you never answer me. I feel abandoned by you.

Although not always articulated so directly, this clinical presentation rings true for many survivors of sexual trauma as they raise "ultimate questions" about suffering, violation, trust, abandonment, and betrayal. Overall, this case example highlights the complex relationship between spirituality, religion, and sexual trauma. Numerous survivors turn to spiritual and religious resources for healing and hope. Spiritual beliefs and practices can provide support, comfort, meaning, and resilience in a survivor's life. Others, or even the same individuals, struggle with spiritual doubts and fears as well as feelings of anger, abandonment, and disconnection. Survivors raise questions about God and the divine and wrestle with their religious and spiritual beliefs. In this chapter, we explore the multifaceted role that spirituality and religion play in the lives of survivors of sexual trauma, considering both Western and Eastern spiritual perspectives.

We start with a targeted empirical review of the relationships between spirituality, religion, and sexual trauma. In this chapter, we focus mostly on spirituality; however, we also include an emphasis on institutional religion when relevant (for a comprehensive comparison of the broad domains of

[1]For the cases presented in this chapter, a pseudonym is used, and identifying details have been altered for purposes of confidentiality. All examples in this chapter are drawn from sexual trauma clients and research participants of Nichole A. Murray-Swank.

DOI: 10.1037/14046-017
APA Handbook of Psychology, Religion, and Spirituality: Vol. 2. An Applied Psychology of Religion and Spirituality, K. I. Pargament (Editor-in-Chief)

spirituality and religion, see Volume 1, Chapter 1, this handbook). Next, we highlight research on a manualized, spiritually integrative program for sexual abuse survivors. We then turn to a broader foundation for clinical intervention and consider theoretical frameworks and various strategies for integrating spirituality in sexual trauma work, illustrating our concepts with a case example. Finally, we focus on meditation and mindfulness in sexual trauma work.

REVIEW OF EMPIRICAL WORK ON SPIRITUALITY, RELIGION, AND SEXUAL TRAUMA

A female client who experienced repeated instances of rape by her older brother declared, "I prayed and prayed for it to stop. God never answered me, just left me there. He didn't answer me at all. He wasn't there for me, just complete pain and isolation."[2] Another survivor of childhood incest, after reflecting on her spiritual beliefs, commented, "God was the only one there for me all those years. I completely relied on that." She experienced sexual abuse by her father between the ages of 6 and 10 and felt spiritually connected and supported by God even as a young child facing painful trauma. Yet another survivor stated, "I no longer believe in God. I can't believe in a God who doesn't protect innocent children." These clinical examples mirror the empirical research literature on spirituality, religion, and sexual trauma. Many survivors turn to spiritual beliefs and practices for support, healing, and connection; survivors also frequently experience profound spiritual struggles or religious questions and doubts. And still others turn away completely. Walker, Reid, O'Neill, and Brown (2009) described how frequently survivors are "somewhere in between" (p. 130) as they attempt to reconcile their trauma with religious and spiritual worldviews. Therapeutically, helping survivors confront spiritual struggles, draw from spiritual resources, and resolve this "in-between" space can facilitate trauma recovery and lead to psychological and spiritual well-being.

SPIRITUAL DECLINE AND STRUGGLES IN RESPONSE TO SEXUAL TRAUMA

In a review of 34 retrospective studies of adult survivors of childhood abuse, Walker et al. (2009) found that participants more often recalled experiencing a *decrease* rather than *increase* in religion and spirituality after childhood abuse. Several studies highlight that sexual trauma tends to lead to decreased spiritual well-being, less stability in religious practices and beliefs, increased spiritual injury, and more negative images of God (e.g., Chibnall, Wolf, & Duckro, 1998; Kane, Cheston, & Greer, 1993; Lawson, Drebing, Berg, Vincellette, & Penk, 1998; Pritt, 1998).

When compared with nonabused samples, sexual abuse survivors often report being less religious and experiencing more spiritual struggles than nonsurvivors. For example, in a sample of Jewish women, survivors of sexual trauma were less religious than a control sample (Ben-Ezra et al., 2010). In this study, 47% in the sexual assault group became more secularized after sexual trauma, whereas only 8% became more religious. In other research, Hall (1995) found that abused, outpatient female Christian clients were less likely to report a sense of God's grace and love, an ability to discern God's will, and an ability to be religiously involved than nonabused, clinical and nonabused, nonclinical women. Rossetti (1995) demonstrated that female survivors of sexual abuse reported a more negative relationship with God than nonabused participants, and this relationship was particularly difficult if the perpetrator was a religious leader. Finally, Fallot and Heckman (2005) found that survivors of abuse used more negative religious coping (e.g., felt punished and abandoned by God) than a comparison randomized national sample.

Focusing specifically on male survivors of childhood abuse, Lawson et al. (1998) found that all forms of abuse (emotional, physical, and sexual) were associated with increased spiritual injury; sexual abuse also contributed a significant amount of variance in spiritual injury after the effects of emotional abuse and physical abuse had been partialled out. Spiritual injury and betrayal were also common themes in a national sample of male and female

[2]All quotes used in this chapter are drawn from sexual trauma clients and research participants of Nichole A. Murray-Swank.

survivors of clergy sexual abuse (Murray-Swank, 2010). In this study, the majority of participants strongly endorsed such responses as, "Wondered whether my church had abandoned me" (71%), "Questioned God's love for me" (56%), and "Wondered whether God had abandoned me" (53%) (Murray-Swank, 2010). Additionally, open-ended questions about religious and spiritual changes yielded several thematic responses: a movement away from organized religion, a sense of spiritual betrayal, a loss of trust in religious authority, and spiritual struggles and wounds. In general, the empirical literature paints a picture of sexual trauma leading to less religiousness, increased spiritual struggles, and decreased spiritual well-being across genders and diverse spiritual traditions.

Furthermore, the increased spiritual struggles experienced by sexual trauma survivors are associated with increased psychological difficulties. For example, in a study of spirituality and coping among survivors of childhood sexual abuse, spiritual discontent (e.g., anger at God) was related to increased depression after controlling for age, income, type of abuse, perceived impact of the abuse, and other cognitive appraisals about the trauma (e.g., controllability, perceived threat; Gall, 2006). For female survivors with comorbid substance abuse and mental health disorders, negative forms of spiritual coping were related to posttraumatic symptoms and psychological distress (Fallot & Heckman, 2005). Similarly, for survivors of clergy sexual abuse, negative religious coping methods were related to increased posttraumatic stress disorder (PTSD) and psychological distress, above and beyond negative affect and attributions surrounding the abuse, and important demographic variables, such as income (Murray-Swank, 2010). Spiritual struggles among survivors of sexual trauma are tied to increased psychological distress and posttraumatic stress reactions.

SPIRITUAL RESOURCES, COPING, AND GROWTH IN RESPONSE TO SEXUAL TRAUMA

Despite the increased spiritual struggles that can result from sexual trauma, many survivors also turn to spirituality as a beneficial resource to cope with trauma. Spiritual beliefs and practices can provide support, hope, meaning, connection, a sense of transcendence, and evoke healing emotions (e.g., feelings of compassion, love, joy) when stressful life events occur (e.g., Pargament, 1997). Griffith (2010) wrote how spiritual and religious beliefs and practices can promote resilience or "the capacity to endure hardship or to emerge from adversities in some way stronger than before" (p. 84). Overall, ample research literature indicates that survivors of sexual trauma frequently turn to spirituality and religion to cope as well as experience a sense of spiritual growth and change afterward.

For example, in adult women sexually abused as children, religion and spirituality emerged as aspects of resiliency (Valentine & Feinauer, 1993). The survivors commented that religion provided them with a support network, helped them to create meaning and purpose, and helped to free them from feelings of blame and guilt. In a qualitative study of both male and female survivors of sexual violence, participants described *spiritual connecting*, particularly to a God or a higher power, as the most salient aspect of their spiritual experiences (Knapik, Martsolf, Draucker, & Strickland, 2010). In another study, Ahrens, Abeling, Ahmad, and Hinman (2010) found that female rape survivors reported high levels of spiritually based coping (e.g., "experienced God's love and care") when coping with their sexual assault, and turned to their beliefs to find meaning and support. Spiritually based coping was even more likely among African American survivors. In Fallot and Heckman's (2005) study of female trauma survivors with co-occurring mental health and substance use disorders, participants reported a higher prevalence of positive religious coping (e.g., "I think about how my life is part of a larger spiritual force") than negative religious coping (e.g., "I wonder whether God has abandoned me"). In addition, the trauma survivors used more positive religious coping than did a randomized national sample; there were no ethnic differences in this study. Similarly, although male veterans abused as children demonstrated increased spiritual injury, they also reported increased frequency of prayer and spiritual experiences than nonabused participants (Lawson et al., 1998).

Some survivors also often seem to experience a sense of spiritual growth after sexual assault occurs. For example, in a sample of women with recent sexual assault experiences, the survivors indicated a significantly increased role for spirituality in their lives (Kennedy, Davis, & Taylor, 1998). Similarly, Frazier and Berman (2008) discussed how 47% of respondents indicated positive changes in spiritual well-being as a result of their rape experiences. In survivors of clergy sexual abuse, one primary qualitative theme involved a sense of "spiritual transformation: increased depth, empowerment, and inner knowing" (Murray-Swank, 2011, p. 2). For example, survivors wrote: "It made me look for substance in what I believe in"; "I have a deeper more active spiritual awareness"; and "I think I have matured—I developed a belief that God may not take care of me the way I like, he does not swoop down and fix things even when we are praying, but he can take our brokenness and create strength" (Murray-Swank, 2011, p. 3).

In terms of psychological health and well-being, positive forms of spirituality and religious coping are typically helpful to survivors of sexual trauma. For example, frequency of private prayer, self-reported spirituality, frequency of meditation, and positive religious coping were associated with posttraumatic growth (e.g., personal strength, improved relationships with others) for survivors of clergy sexual abuse (Murray-Swank, 2010). In addition, a sense of prayer fulfillment (e.g., "In the quiet of my prayers and/or meditations, I find a sense of wholeness"; Piedmont, 1999) predicted both posttraumatic growth and satisfaction with life, above and beyond positive religious coping, prayer, meditation, and self-reported spirituality. Thus, the sense of *fulfillment in prayer and meditation* appeared to be particularly helpful in coping with clergy sexual abuse and in fostering general life satisfaction. In a sample of rape survivors, positive religious coping was also associated with increased posttraumatic growth among White women (Ahrens et al., 2010). Gall (2006) likewise demonstrated that seeking spiritual support, active spiritual surrender, and religious forgiveness were associated with less angry and depressed moods among childhood sexual abuse survivors. Rooted in an Eastern perspective, Kimbrough, Magyari, Langenberg, Chesney, and Berman (2010) found that mindfulness-based stress reduction helped decrease psychological distress and PTSD and increase mindfulness in child sexual abuse survivors.

PREDICTING RELIGIOUS AND SPIRITUAL REACTIONS TO TRAUMA

What makes one survivor rely on God or practice prayer or meditation as a source of support following sexual trauma, another (or even the same individual) to feel abandonment and disconnection, and many others to turn away completely from religion or spirituality after sexual trauma? Researchers have started to examine such complex questions. For example, Fallot and Heckman (2005) found that those forced to have sex as children as well as those with an increased frequency of abuse experiences reported higher levels of negative religious coping. Gall (2006) demonstrated that a greater perceived impact of childhood abuse and an increased number of perpetrators were related to spiritual discontent. Falsetti, Resick, and Davis (2003) found that people who developed PTSD were more likely to report religious changes after their first or only traumatic event (30% reported becoming less religious; 20% more religious). In a sample of Jewish women, feeling stigmatized was associated with a change toward more secular beliefs (Ben-Ezra et al., 2010). In our research with survivors of clergy sexual abuse, perpetration by a trusted religious or spiritual leader was particularly destructive to a person's spiritual life. In their review of childhood abuse, Walker et al. (2009) discussed how abuse by a father or father figure can be particularly problematic. Thus, the type of abuse, type of perpetrator, frequency and severity of abuse, age and timing of abuse, and emotional impact are all important aspects in understanding how the spiritual lives of sexual trauma survivors unfold.

The research literature highlights how both utilizing spirituality as a resource in recovery as well as addressing spiritual struggles represent key considerations in working with survivors of sexual trauma. More specifically, although positive forms of spirituality have been related to growth and life satisfaction, negative forms of spiritual coping (such as feeling abandoned by, angry at, or punished by God) have been robustly linked with a variety of problematic outcomes and psychological difficulties (including PTSD, depression, and anxiety). Therefore, the empirical literature underscores the need for focused clinical attention on spiritual struggles in therapy with sexual trauma survivors as well as attention to spirituality and religion as powerful sources of meaning, resilience, and connection. We turn next to research on one promising manualized clinical intervention that was specifically developed to do just this.

SOLACE FOR THE SOUL: A SPIRITUALLY BASED, MANUALIZED INTERVENTION FOR SEXUAL TRAUMA

The treatment manual *Solace for the Soul: A Journey Towards Wholeness* (Murray-Swank, 2003) outlines a program that was specifically designed to integrate spirituality in sexual trauma work, including both a focus on addressing spiritual struggles as well as on facilitating a sense of spiritual connection and well-being. The innovative Solace for the Soul intervention incorporates the principles of a client-centered, pluralistic, and integrative approach, even as it reflects a theistic worldview. Thus, clients with a belief in a divine other or higher spiritual force can benefit from this therapy.

Broadly, the eight sessions in the Solace for the Soul intervention target six themes: images of God and spiritual journeys, spiritual struggles and negative spiritual coping, fostering a sense of spiritual connection, spirituality and letting go of shame, spirituality and the body, and spirituality and sexual wholeness (see Table 17.1). Therapists aim to address spiritual struggles resulting from sexual trauma (e.g., abandonment, anger, shame, disconnection) as well as facilitate spiritual connection (e.g., with God and with others). The intervention incorporates discussion and spiritual exploration, spiritual meditation and prayer, journaling, and spiritual rituals. Overall, it focuses on hope, growth, change, and connection.

More specifically, in Session 1, clients gain information about the program, discuss goals, and explore areas of personal strength, beauty, and wholeness. For example, clients read an adaptation of the spiritual poem "The Weaver" (Foote, 1994) and reflect on aspects of the poem such as, "Out of the torn places, I reclaim wholeness. Out of the broken places, I reclaim strength" (p. 17). They write their responses to and discuss the following questions: "In what areas of my life do I desire wholeness? In what areas am I called to regain strength?" Therapists guide clients in a spiritual light visualization to end the session.

Session 2 focuses on clients' images of God and spiritual journeys. Clients chart their spiritual journeys, including spiritual high points and low points. In addition, clients describe who God is to them, explain how this has changed for them, and explore various images and descriptions of God. At the end of the session, clients participate in spiritual visualization exercises, such as imaging God's love as a waterfall within and God as a spirit of freedom. Clients continue this work at home in between sessions.

In Session 3, clients begin the process of addressing spiritual struggles surrounding their experiences of sexual abuse. Clients reflect on times they have felt abandonment, anger at God, or spiritual disconnection. If clients have not experienced times of spiritual struggle, they reflect on spiritual questions they have. They engage in a process of two-way journaling to God, in which they write a letter to God, and then "listen" for a reply and write the words or images they "hear." Therapists review other ways to express spiritual struggles, and normalize that it is okay to struggle, feel anger, and have spiritual doubts and questions. The intervention encourages exploration and expression of struggles to facilitate new insights and integration.

Session 4 focuses on enhancing a sense of spiritual connection with God and with others (the "Vertical" and the "Horizontal"). Clients reflect on times they have felt the presence of God or experienced a sense of spiritual connection in their lives, and they explore various ways to connect in a spiritual way (e.g., imagery, prayer, loving relationships). At the end of the session, clients are guided through a spiritual imagery exercise of divine light, followed by a loving kindness meditation.

TABLE 17.1

Solace for The Soul: A Journey Toward Wholeness

Session number	Session content
Session 1: Solace for the soul	Gain information about program Discuss goals Identify areas of strength and wholeness
Session 2: Who is my God?	Map spiritual journeys Explore current images of God Explore varied images of God (e.g., God as a spirit of freedom; God's love as a waterfall within)
Session 3: God, where are You?	Reflect on and express spiritual struggles (e.g., abandonment and anger at God) Two-way journaling to God Coping with spiritual struggles
Session 4: Spiritual connection	Enhance a sense of spiritual connection with God and others Loving kindness meditation
Session 5: Letting go of shame	Explore distorted cognitions about the self Reduce shame-based views Use spiritual affirmations and rituals to reduce feelings of shame
Session 6: God's beautiful creation	Restore healthy connection to body Reduce body disparagement and loathing Use spiritual affirmations to counter negative thoughts about the body
Session 7: Restoring sexual wholeness	Increase ability to say no in sexuality Decrease sexual dysfunction Use spiritual affirmations and exercises to separate the abuse from the positive nature of sexuality Enhance sacredness in sexuality
Session 8: Moving forward	Solidify progress Plan for future areas of growth

Note. From "Solace for the Soul: Evaluating a Spiritually Integrated Counseling Intervention for Sexual Abuse," by N. A. Murray-Swank & K. I. Pargament, 2008, *Counselling and Spirituality, 27,* p. 161. Copyright 2008 by Saint Paul University. Reprinted with permission.

Session 5 raises the issue of shame, focusing on the "lies of shame," such as "I am worthless; damaged; inadequate; unlovable; at fault." Clients explore such distorted cognitions about the self and use spiritual affirmations (e.g., "I am sacred; lovable; strong") and rituals to reduce shame-based views. For example, clients engage in a spiritual ritual called "the shame basket" in which they write out the shame-based messages they carry, rip them up, and place them in a basket full of sticks and symbols of dryness. A guided reflection is used to facilitate letting go of the messages of shame, and a rose is used to represent the spirit of beauty within.

In Sessions 6 and 7, clients explore messages and experiences of the impact of sexual abuse on their bodies and sexuality. Spiritual affirmations, cognitive restructuring, and journal reflections are used to reduce sexual dysfunction and body disparagement (e.g., body loathing). For example, clients consider the ways that sexual abuse shaped their thoughts about sex (e.g., "sex is shameful"; "sex is frightening") and consider alternate spiritual affirmations about sex (e.g., "sex is respectful"; "sex is sacred"). A primary goal of these sessions is to separate the abuse experiences from positive experiences of the body and sexuality.

Finally, Session 8 focuses on future directions and solidifying progress made in the spiritually integrated intervention. A spiritual ritual is used to highlight the strengths, courage, growth, transformation, and vibrancy of clients as well as to connect them with other survivors of sexual trauma.

In research on the Solace for the Soul program, female survivors of sexual abuse with diverse spiritual beliefs experienced significant decreases in psychological distress (e.g., depression and anxiety) and trauma symptoms across the course of intervention and at 1- to 2-month follow-up (Murray-Swank & Pargament, 2008). Additionally, in a single-case interrupted time-series design, clients with spiritual struggles demonstrated increases in positive religious coping, spiritual well-being, and positive images of God (Murray-Swank & Pargament, 2005). From a qualitative perspective, clients reported an enhanced sense of spiritual connection and hope as well as psychological wholeness and well-being.

Solace for the Soul represents one of the first attempts to empirically evaluate a spiritually integrative treatment program for sexual abuse clients. Although the initial studies were small, current work is focused on larger randomized controlled studies to evaluate the effectiveness of this approach. Solace for the Soul offers one manualized approach with research support for working specifically with spiritual and religious themes in sexual abuse therapy. We turn next to a broader clinical dialogue about integrating spirituality and religion in practice with sexual trauma survivors.

SPIRITUALLY BASED CLINICAL WORK WITH SURVIVORS OF SEXUAL TRAUMA

In the sections that follow, we focus on spiritually based practice with survivors of sexual trauma. We describe our clinical foundation and approach, discuss core spiritual themes, and offer a framework for therapeutic change in the spiritual and psychological lives of survivors of sexual trauma. Finally, we illustrate this process with a case example.

Foundational Principles: Client Centered, Pluralistic, and Integrative

Sexual trauma results in an intense experience of disempowerment, and clients with sexual trauma histories frequently encounter fears about safety and trust. Therefore, a validating, nonjudgmental therapeutic relationship forms the essential backdrop for working with survivors of sexual trauma, no matter what the particular clinical or spiritual orientation of the therapist may be. Sexual trauma involves a violation of physical, emotional, and spiritual boundaries; thus, the importance of an empathic, trusting therapeutic presence cannot be emphasized enough. It is from this platform of a safe relationship that we consider working with the spiritual themes in sexual trauma therapy.

Additionally, we maintain a client-centered, pluralistic–constructivist, diversity-oriented approach for spiritually integrative work. Zinnbauer and Pargament (2000) discussed the pluralist and constructivist approaches as well suited to working with diverse clients. They described a pluralist approach as one in which therapists "recognize the existence of a religious or spiritual absolute reality but allow for multiple interpretations and paths towards it" (p. 167) and a constructivist approach as one that "recognizes the ability of individuals to construct their own personal meanings and realities" (Zinnbauer & Pargament, 2000, p. 166). Therefore, a therapist does not have to be spiritual or religious to work effectively with clients. Overall, we respect the diversity of traditions, spiritual perspectives, and religious paths (or lack of) in both therapists' and clients' lives. In addition, Pargament (2007) recommended four essential qualities in a "spiritually integrated therapist" (p. 190): knowledge, openness and tolerance, self-awareness, and authenticity. Finally, we utilize an integrative therapeutic approach, mainly drawing from cognitive–behavioral, emotion-focused, and existential theories of psychotherapy. We also consider meditation and mindfulness as therapeutic avenues for sexual trauma work.

Four Substantive Themes in Spiritually Based Sexual Trauma Work

McCann and colleagues (McCann & Pearlman, 1990; McCann, Sakheim, & Abrahamson, 1988) discussed five fundamental psychological needs or schemas that can become disrupted in trauma: safety, dependency or trust, power, esteem, and intimacy. Cognitive processing therapy (CPT), a widely used and researched psychological model for working with trauma, also emphasizes these five key themes in sexual abuse therapy (e.g., Resick & Schnicke, 1996). The same core themes are evident in the spiritual realm, as survivors frequently voice difficulties and questions in these areas after sexual trauma: spiritual safety and trust, spiritual power and control, spiritual self-esteem, and spiritual intimacy and

TABLE 17.2

Core Spiritual Themes in Sexual Trauma Therapy

Spiritual themes	Some core spiritual questions	Sexual abuse examples
Spiritual safety and trust	Can God be trusted?	"It shattered my trust in God and it has taken years to get that back."
	Is the universe a safe place?	"I am afraid. I no longer trust God or anyone for that matter."
	Can I count on spirit?	
	Is there a divine order?	
Spiritual power and control	Who's in charge?	"I no longer believe in the power of God to protect living beings."
	Does God intervene?	"I can't understand how God would let this happen to an innocent child."
	What about evil forces?	
	Who protects the innocent?	
	Who is in control?	
Spiritual self-esteem	Am I good?	"I lived with shame for decades. Felt that God was disgusted with me because I was molested and raped."
	Am I lovable?	"I no longer feel like a part of the body of Christ, rather like a leg that has been amputated because I committed the most awful of sins."
	Am I of divine worth?	
	Am I sinful?	
	Am I evil?	
	Am I worthy?	
Spiritual intimacy and connection	Have I been abandoned?	"It's very hard for me to pray and feel close to God."
	Have I been betrayed?	"I feel completely lost and abandoned by God."
	Am I all alone?	
	Why do I feel so spiritually disconnected?	
	How can I connect spiritually?	

Note. These themes were adapted from the five themes (safety, dependency/trust, power, esteem, and intimacy) in McCann et al.'s (1988) theory of adaptation to trauma and Cognitive Processing Therapy (e.g., Resick & Schnicke, 1996). We translated the themes to incorporate a spiritual perspective.

connection (see Table 17.2). Notably, we have found that a sense of safety and trust are intimately related in the spiritual realm and therefore have merged these into one category (see Table 17.2). In addition, although Resick, Monson, and Chard (2008) briefly mentioned how religious and moral questions may arise in CPT (McCann et al., 1988; Resick & Schnicke, 1996), these experts on trauma do not specifically integrate spirituality into the themes of their model for working with trauma survivors. In this chapter, we specifically translated the key themes highlighted in the CPT model (i.e., safety, dependency/trust, power, esteem, and intimacy) into a spiritual framework (i.e., spiritual safety and trust, spiritual power and control, spiritual self-esteem, and spiritual intimacy and connection; see Table 17.2). We believe that focusing on these four core spiritual themes can help organize a therapist's thinking when working in the spiritual realm.

Spiritual safety and trust. Many survivors of sexual trauma confront deep questions about spiritual safety in the world. For example, the experience of sexual trauma may shatter a client's belief in a God that protects from harm and call into question basic spiritual safety. Survivors may ask questions: Is God safe? Is the Universe a safe place? In the research we have conducted on sexual abuse survivors, many commented on a basic loss of spiritual safety. One survivor wrote about how her spirituality has been affected by sexual abuse: "I have struggled so much with this. I have experienced shame and fear of God. I struggle with believing he will protect me. I am afraid." Fear, confusion, and a lack of safety can result from sexual trauma.

In a related vein, survivors struggle with spiritual trust: Can I trust God? If I can't trust the divine, whom can I trust? Numerous survivors of sexual trauma that we have counseled have discussed concerns about spiritual trust. One survivor of clergy sexual abuse declared how her abuse "shattered my trust in God and it has taken years to get that back." In the words of another survivor: "I have a hard time turning to the spiritual, trusting God, praying, and feeling loved by God." Also, survivors struggle with spiritual trust in others. In a research study we conducted on survivors of clergy sexual abuse, a sense of betrayal and lack of trust in others, particularly faith communities, represented a primary concern (Murray-Swank, 2011). Overall, regaining or finding a new sense of spiritual safety and trust can be an important goal in psychotherapy.

Spiritual power and control. Sexual trauma clients may also specifically call into question the power of God. A client survivor of childhood incest asked God: "Where were you when I prayed for it to stop?" Another sexual trauma survivor wrote: "I can't understand how God would let this happen to an innocent child." In both cases, the survivors were questioning the role of power and control. In so many words, they wonder, "Who is in charge? If God is in charge and all-powerful, why did this happen? Did the devil cause this? How can bad things happen to innocent children? How can a father rape his own child? If God is in charge, and this happened, either something is wrong with me, or something is wrong with God. A good, loving God would not allow such suffering of the innocent." Helping clients arrive at acceptable and useful answers to questions about the power of God, or other spiritual deities, as well as the power of the self and others, can be important in sexual trauma therapy.

Spiritual self-esteem. Survivors often question themselves after sexual trauma, frequently experiencing self-blame and feelings of shame. It is common to encounter clients who enter therapy with the idea that they are bad, damaged, evil, sinful, or deserving of punishment. A client survivor of sexual abuse by her stepfather asked, "What did *I* do to deserve this?" A survivor of clergy sexual abuse declared, "I felt that God was disgusted with me because I was molested and raped." Another survivor of sexual abuse wondered, "What did I do in past lives to deserve this type of karma?" Working with spiritual self-esteem is important in psychotherapy.

Many spiritual traditions emphasize a loving, good core to the human person. Western traditions frequently draw attention to how individuals contain a divine spark or how they are created in God's image. Eastern traditions speak of one's Buddha nature, Inner Self, True Nature, or a sense of Basic Goodness. Thus, helping clients affirm their spiritual goodness and worth can powerfully counter messages of blame and shame that are elicited by sexual trauma.

Spiritual intimacy and connection. Many survivors of sexual trauma turn to spirituality for support, healing, and connection. Sexual trauma, however, can interfere with intimacy at many levels. Spiritually speaking, although some survivors may maintain a strong connection with the divine, many others feels disconnected, abandoned, or betrayed. One survivor of clergy sexual abuse stated, "I feel betrayed by God." Another survivor of childhood incest declared, "I have been completely cast off by God, forgotten about." Many survivors feel angry with, abandoned by, or disconnected from God or a sense of transcendence. Frequently, survivors may experience conflicting spiritual emotions, at times feeling close and connected, at other times feeling distant, angry, or neglected as they cope with the aftermath of sexual trauma.

In general, numerous sexual trauma survivors long for a sense of spiritual connection and support. Pargament, Koenig, and Perez (2000) described how seeking spiritual comfort and intimacy are two primary functions of religion. Kirkpatrick (2005) described one's attachment to God as a central attachment relationship in human functioning. The perceived loss of this attachment relationship results in grief, suffering, and anxiety. Overall, clients may raise questions of spiritual intimacy and support. Where is God in my pain and suffering? How can I connect to a sense of ultimacy and transcendence? How can I seek spiritual comfort and solace? How can I seek assistance and guidance from God? Addressing these types of questions, and facilitating a sense of spiritual connection, can assist clients in their search for recovery and healing.

Spiritual sticking points. In addition to the core themes of safety and trust, power and control, self-esteem, and intimacy, CPT emphasizes "stuck points" (Resick & Schnicke, 1996; Resick et al., 2008). Stuck points are "inadequately processed conflicts between prior schemata and the new information (that is, the rape)" (Resick & Schnicke, 1996, p. 18). We also have found that clients frequently have "spiritual sticking points." For example, I (Nichole) worked with a 57-year-old survivor of sexual abuse by her stepfather. For 30 years, and through numerous years of psychotherapy, she had been angry at God and felt abandoned by God. Her spiritual sticking point was that "God should have stopped the abuse." In working together, we explored this belief fully: Does God stop bad things from happening? We discussed her thoughts on free will and other beliefs she held (God is all-powerful). As we worked with expressing her anger at God, she also unearthed years of unexpressed grief and sadness. She felt alienated and alone. Working through her spiritual sticking point was central to her recovery. This client desired a connection with God, and as she began to shift blame from God to her stepfather, she began to feel a closeness with God, and also a renewed intimacy with others in her life. It was as if her tensions with God had kept her constricted in all of her relationships.

A myriad of spiritual sticking points plague the lives of sexual trauma survivors. They can be related to the core themes we discussed earlier. For example, a client survivor of clergy sexual abuse spoke about the spiritual impact of his experiences: "I continually believe that I am evil and full of sin that I must atone for." The spiritual sticking point for some might be feelings of spiritual unworthiness, spiritual shame, or a feeling that punishment was deserved. For others, the sticking point could be that God should have intervened or feelings of abandonment. Identifying spiritual sticking points is a critical step in the process of psychotherapy. We illustrate this in the case example later in this chapter.

A Note About Theology and Spiritual Integration

In the intervention and spiritual themes we have discussed, it becomes impossible to avoid questions of theology. Psychotherapists are typically not trained in theology, yet clients bring forth theological questions and concerns. In general, we support the use of a client-centered, pluralistic approach that appreciates the diversity of expressions of spirituality, theology, and religion. Doehring (2006) described a capacity for "theological empathy" or the "ability to stand in the shoes of someone theologically different from us and appreciate how her theology can be a 'home' for her in troubled, challenging times" (p. 118). In addition, she recommended paying attention to both clients' "embedded," or underlying theological assumptions as well as their "deliberative," or consciously thought out, theologies (Doehring, 2006, p. 112).

Most broadly, we encourage therapists to gain knowledge and familiarity with diverse spiritual traditions and worldviews. It is impossible, however, to fully know all belief systems or even the specifics of one client's spiritual world. Therefore, we recommend a process of *collaborative exploration* with clients to determine whether spiritual and theological beliefs, practices, and questions seem helpful or harmful to clients in their quests for wholeness and healing (see also Chapter 4 in this volume). In his book, *Religion That Heals, Religion That Harms*, Griffith (2010) discussed how religion and spirituality can help people live with resilience. His discussion of "Existential Postures of Resilience and Vulnerability" offers one fruitful way of discerning whether a certain spiritual or theological belief is helpful or harmful (see Exhibit 17.1). For example, does the theological worldview appear to provide a sense of coherence in the client's life, a feeling of communion and connection, or a sense of hope? Does the belief or practice promote a sense of agency, purpose, and commitment? Does the client feel more courage or gratitude? Or does the specific theological viewpoint lead to confusion, isolation, despair, helplessness, meaninglessness, indifference, cowardice, or resentment (Griffith, 2010; see also Exhibit 17.1)?

Additionally, in his book *Spiritually Integrated Psychotherapy*, Pargament (2007) described aspects

Exhibit 17.1
Griffith's Existential Postures of Resilience and Vulnerability

Vulnerability	Resilience
Confusion	Coherence
Isolation	Communion
Despair	Hope
Helplessness	Agency
Meaninglessness	Purpose
Indifference	Commitment
Cowardice	Courage
Resentment	Gratitude

Note. From *Religion That Heals, Religion That Harms: A Guide for Clinical Practice* (p. 84), by J. L. Griffith, 2010, New York, NY: Guilford Press. Copyright 2010 by Guilford Press. Reprinted with permission.

of a "well-integrated spirituality" that can be helpful when working in the theological realm:

> At its best, spirituality is defined by pathways that are broad and deep, responsive to life's situations, nurtured by the larger social context, capable of flexibility and continuity, and oriented toward a sacred destination that is large enough to encompass the full range of human potential and luminous enough to provide the individual with a powerful guiding vision (p. 136).

Murray-Swank and Pargament (2011) echoed these qualities of spiritual integration, discussing how therapists can pay attention to whether a certain worldview provides the client with a significant transcendent vision to strive toward that can encompass difficult life changes and even traumatic events. In addition, therapists can ascertain whether the spiritual worldview is flexible, capable of change, offers balance, promotes growth, and brings out the best in people (Murray-Swank & Pargament, 2011; Pargament, 2007).

When working with the spiritual and theological world of trauma survivors, we listen for whether a survivor's worldview is large enough and flexible enough to encompass the sexual trauma. We pay attention to whether a spiritual orienting system is broad and deep enough to encounter the numerous changes in recovery from sexual trauma. We explore whether the theological worldview offers a transcendent guiding vision that allows for both change and growth (Murray-Swank & Pargament, 2011; Pargament, 2007). Last, we assess whether a survivor's spiritual beliefs and practices appear to be moving him or her in the direction of resilience factors, such as coherence and connection, agency and purpose, commitment and courage, and gratitude and hope (Griffith, 2010; see also Exhibit 17.1).

Three Phases of Spiritually Based Sexual Trauma Work

From the foundation of a client-centered, integrative orientation, a one-size-fits-all approach is not appropriate for sexual trauma work. Instead we offer a general framework that can guide the process of change within the complex spiritual and religious world of survivors. As mentioned, we incorporate elements of cognitive therapy, emotion-focused trauma therapy, and existential theory in our spiritually integrative work with sexual trauma survivors.

Three key phases guide our psychotherapeutic work: *spiritual exploration, spiritual processing, and spiritual integration* (see Table 17.3). These phases are not linear or categorically distinct in practice; we present them as a way to conceptualize and organize a therapist's thinking and intervention. More specifically, in the spiritual exploration phase, therapists work to identify spiritual themes and assess spiritual sticking points, as described previously. For example, does the client utilize spirituality or religion as a coping resource? What types of beliefs and practices appear to be helpful or harmful? Is the client facing spiritual struggles, or encountering questions about spiritual safety and trust, spiritual power and control, spiritual self-esteem, or spiritual connection and intimacy? Is the client feeling abandoned by God, angry, or disconnected? What particular spiritual sticking point(s) seem relevant?

In the spiritual processing phase, the bulk of therapy, we attend to both cognitions and emotions (see Table 17.3). Cognitively, if a client has a spiritual sticking point, we look for ways to become "unstuck." Often clients hold numerous beliefs in their spiritual worldview, and they become narrow

TABLE 17.3

Clinical Phases of Spiritually Based Sexual Trauma Work

Phase	Therapeutic process	Examples
Spiritual exploration	Identify existing spiritual and religious resources	Supportive beliefs
		Prayer
		Relationship with God or the divine
		Meditation
		Spiritual or faith communities
	Identify spiritual themes and struggles	Spiritual safety and trust
		Spiritual power and control
		Spiritual self-esteem
		Spiritual intimacy and connection
	Assess spiritual sticking points	I am being punished
		I am undeserving of God's love
		God abandoned me
		Bad things shouldn't happen to good people
Spiritual processing	Work through spiritual sticking points and other problematic beliefs	Identification of problematic beliefs
		Socratic questioning
		Challenging beliefs worksheets
		Spiritual maps of beliefs
	Access, accept, experience, and express core spiritual emotions such as abandonment, anger, isolation, and fear as well as gratitude, joy, and presence	Empathic responding
		Emotional validation and normalization
		Moment to moment emotions in therapy room
		Experiential exercises
		Spiritual imagery
		Art and creative expression
	Build coping resources for painful emotions that are acceptance based (versus avoidance based)	Emotional awareness and regulation
		Mindfulness
		Two-way journaling to God
		Imagery
Spiritual Integration	Accommodation of new insights	Encourage integration of new insights (assimilation or transformation)
	Acceptance and letting go of emotions	Support acceptance of and experiencing emotions, and then letting go without "staying stuck"
		Transformation of emotions
	Seeking spiritual connection	Pay attention to forms of the sacred that the client finds supportive and facilitate this connection
		Connection with communities, if this would be helpful
	Building resilience factors	Encourage and validate sources of spiritual meaning, hope, courage, and strength
		Listen for gratitude and joy
	Fostering integration characteristics	Are the spiritual and religious worldviews:
		Flexible and adaptive?
		Have breadth and depth?
		Do they offer coherence, connection, balance, stability, vision, and purpose?
		Do they promote growth?

and rigid about one or two key beliefs. For example, if a client is thinking that he was abandoned by God, we listen for the beliefs that underlie this. For example, does the client believe that an all-powerful God should have stopped the sexual abuse? Does the client believe that God comforts people in pain? Many people who cry out in abandonment want comfort, support, and presence. Therefore, we may work specifically with the client's beliefs about spiritual power and control as well as spiritual intimacy and connection. We may use cognitive techniques, such as identifying problematic thinking, using Socratic questioning, or completing a challenging beliefs worksheet (e.g., Resick & Schnicke, 1996; Resick et al., 2008).

Working with thoughts and beliefs can be powerful in helping clients in the midst of spiritual struggles. We have repeatedly witnessed how expanding or transforming a belief can lead to well-being. For example, several clients that the first author worked with shifted beliefs from an abandoning God to a God who allows free will and supports people in the midst of suffering. This opened the doorway to connection and support, instead of despair and pain. Additionally, clients often come into therapy feeling bad. They feel alone, isolated, sad, abandoned, betrayed, in pain, hopeless, fearful, or anxious. They also feel spiritually alone, abandoned, angry, despairing, and fearful. Therefore, we also draw from an emotion-focused approach to help clients process core spiritual emotions, neither denying or being overwhelmed by negative spiritual emotions that are part of their experience.

From an emotion-focused perspective, trauma can lead to "affective disruptions," such as underregulation or overcontrol of emotions that are "at the heart of disturbances stemming from trauma" (Paivio & Pascual-Leone, 2010, p. 26). Advanced empathic responding from the therapist is one primary intervention used throughout therapy, and the relationship itself represents a key mechanism of change (Paivio & Pascual-Leone, 2010). In addition, emotion-focused trauma therapy (EFTT) offers four primary ways of working with emotions: increasing awareness of feelings and emotional arousal, regulation and learning to manage intense feelings, reflection and the development of new emotional insights, and transformation and supporting adaptive emotions (Paivio & Pascual-Leone, 2010). EFTT emphasizes the overcoming of avoidance, the evoking of affective experience, and the promotion of experiential awareness (Fosha, Paivio, Gleiser, & Ford, 2009). As Fosha et al. (2009) wrote: "Living a life of vitality, resilience, and human connectedness in the face of adversity requires ready access to emotional experience" (p. 286).

Overall, the ability to *access, accept, experience,* and *express* difficult spiritual emotions can facilitate recovery from sexual trauma. We explore this process more fully in the case example. As with many challenging emotions, clients may want to avoid certain feelings such as spiritual despair, anger, shame, or abandonment. Sometimes certain spiritual communities may avoid challenging spiritual emotions and doubts. This avoidance, however, can perpetuate the chronic nature of spiritual struggles and lead to psychological decline. Therefore, we gently encourage the expression of spiritual emotions through a variety of means, such as facilitating expressions of moment-to-moment emotions in the therapy room, using experiential exercises, practicing guided spiritual imagery, teaching two-way journaling to God (if relevant), encouraging mindfulness practices, and engaging in discussion. We also help clients develop approach-based coping methods at home, such as continued two-way journaling, use of imagery exercises, and mindfulness practice. As therapists, we continually express empathy and validation, normalize painful feelings, stay present and attuned, and provide a container for difficult core spiritual emotions.

Last, from an existential point of view, we listen for and support sources of connection, meaning, hope, and resilience. In the spiritual integration phase, we encourage the accommodation of new insights, the acceptance of and letting go of emotions, and the facilitation of connection with the self, the divine, and others. Additionally, therapists pay close attention to emerging or existing resilience factors, such as spiritual meaning, agency and purpose, courage and strength, and gratitude and joy (e.g., Griffith, 2010; see Exhibit 17.1). We also consider the spiritual integration characteristics we presented. For example, does the client's spirituality offer a guiding vision that is flexible, adaptable, and large enough to accommodate the experience of sexual trauma (e.g., Pargament, 2007, p. 136)? Does the client hold spiritual beliefs that demonstrate both breadth and depth? Does the client have a spiritual orienting system that is coherent and offers a sense of connection, stability, hope, and courage?

The therapeutic phases of spiritual exploration, spiritual processing, and spiritual integration represent a dynamic, fluid process that can facilitate both psychological and spiritual recovery from sexual trauma. We turn next to a case example to illustrate this process more fully.

Case Example: Uncovering Themes and Phases of Spiritually Based Work—God Hates Me and Spiritual Shame

On the outside, JP looked like she "had it all together," as she described it. A 42-year-old married professional businesswoman, she was bright, successful, and competent. On the inside, JP continually thought of taking her own life, secret ruminations that she disclosed to no one outside of therapy, including her husband. JP was sexually abused as a child by her stepfather starting at the age of 4 and continuing until age 10. She believed that her mother knew of the abuse but was too afraid to confront the stepfather because of his violent temper and because her mother was afraid to be alone.

When JP entered therapy with me (Nichole), we focused first on building a trusting relationship. JP continually felt insecure in the relationship, and I continually provided validation and empathy, normalized her concerns, addressed questions without defensiveness, and offered a nonjudgmental, safe space. Over time, her trust in the therapy relationship developed.

Even though I cannot describe the entire therapy process, I want to highlight some key aspects and turning points in our work together. As part of the spiritual exploration phase, we identified spiritual themes and struggles, and I listened for spiritual sticking points (see Table 17.3). To facilitate this process, JP completed a "Lies of Shame Exercise" in which she considered what the voice of sexual abuse told her. As a visual client, JP drew a "map of shame." In the center circle of this map, she wrote in black ink: "God hates me." She depicted other circles emanating from this center circle: "I don't deserve God's love," "I deserve punishment," "I am bad at the core of me," "I am ugly," and "I deserve to die." This map provided a poignant visual depiction of her problematic spiritual self-esteem and deep sense of spiritual shame.

As we worked with her spiritual shame (spiritual processing), we focused on her center circle "God hates me" (spiritual sticking point). As sessions progressed, I attempted to gently challenge the belief that she is undeserving of God's love and that God hated her. JP declared, "But you don't understand, I really am bad."

From an emotion-focused perspective, shame is a difficult core emotion to work with because people feeling shame want to hide and cover up their inner sense of badness. Shame desperately fears exposure, yet silence and secrecy breed further shame. Therefore, I continually commented on her courage, and we directly discussed how shame grows in silence. One session, JP came in and asked, "Is it okay if we turn the lights down?" We turned on a lamp in the room that gave off a softer light and turned off the overhead lights. She then asked, "Is it okay if I turn my chair away from you?" I replied that it was, and she sat in the darkened room with her chair, face, body, and eyes turned away from me. These were such powerful behavioral demonstrations of shame. She proceeded, "I need to tell you something." I encouraged her that she could. She started to cry and said, "When I was a kid, I was at my friend's house and she had a little brother." She cried even harder: "I wanted to do sexual things with him."

JP did not act on her desires. For 30 years, however, she felt intense shame and felt that God hated her, that she deserved punishment, and that she deserved to die because of having these thoughts. She considered taking her own life and had made several attempts throughout the years. She voiced that "God could never look at such an ugly creature." After JP disclosed this painful memory, I normalized her experience, I supported her, and I did not judge her:

> Your sexual abuse had just ended. You endured years of abuse, where boundaries were confusing. Your own developing sexuality was intertwined with abuse that was painful and harmful. Your sexual feelings were confusing to you. And, also, you did not act on those feelings. What courage and strength that took. Some survivors of abuse do act on their confusion. It took a lot of courage to come in here and say that. A lot of strength.

For JP, this session represented a dramatic turning point. She had exposed a spiritual secret that had been eating away at her for decades. As she accessed, experienced, and expressed her core spiritual shame, she found doorways of connection that started to open for her. For example, she subsequently asked if we could bring in her husband to share her experiences. I knew her husband was supportive of her, and we did this. It was a powerful session when her husband came in and enveloped her in love, affection, and support. She also felt that she could start to connect with God again. Toward this end, she wrote a poignant journal entry about a withered tree that still had roots and was alive. And, perhaps most important, although she continued to struggle with depression, she did not feel like she deserved to die or be punished. Therefore, her suicidal ideations decreased.

JP was able to address her spiritual sticking point of "God hates me" by accessing her core spiritual emotion of shame, exposing this, and accommodating a new insight that her early history of sexual abuse created confusing sexual feelings and thoughts. She began the process of spiritual integration as we began to focus on her strengths, her resilience in the face of sexual trauma, and her basic sense of goodness. She actively sought avenues of spiritual connection and formed a warm and nurturing connection with a minister. We collaborated with her minister to create a spiritual ritual that acknowledged her sense of strength, connection, and spiritual goodness. JP's integration process included the building of spiritual connection in many ways, creating a strong positive sense of spiritual self-esteem, and recognizing her resilience in the face of trauma.

We turn next to two other ways clients can build inner strength and resilience, spiritual connection, and integration in sexual trauma therapy.

Two Techniques Especially Helpful for Spiritually Based Sexual Trauma Work: Meditation and Mindfulness

Thus far, we have considered how practitioners can understand and address specific spiritual and religious content in sexual trauma survivors lives. In this section, we focus on two treatment techniques that we have found especially useful in working with these clients—meditation and mindfulness. These types of interventions do not target the *content* of thoughts and feelings. Instead, these approaches focus on a person's *relationship* with one's thoughts, feelings, and sensations. Therapists help clients accept the trauma and their feelings and thoughts about it; however, the goal is to facilitate more present moment awareness. Thus, a therapist encourages a client shift from a focus on the past (e.g., thinking about the trauma or intrusive images) or worry about the future (e.g., fear of triggers, new traumas, danger) to the present moment. A large part of the treatment consists of teaching clients mindfulness exercises both to cognitively defuse from thoughts and feelings (e.g., "I am not my thoughts or feelings") and to maintain a present moment awareness that brings clarity of mind, a sense of well-being and peace even in the midst of turmoil, and an experience of transcendence.

From a spiritual perspective, various forms of meditation and meditative practices are found across the world's religions (e.g., Buddhism, Hinduism, contemplative Christianity; see Volume 1, Chapter 17, this handbook). Although the traditions vary in the forms and beliefs about the nature of transcendent reality, meditation is commonly practiced as a way to connect to a spiritual dimension of life. Often a person connects to something larger than the self or ego, such as God within, Awakened Mind, the Inner Self, or Buddha-nature. For example, Lama Surya Das (1997) wrote: "For Buddhism is less a theology or a religion than a promise that certain meditative practices can effectively show us how to awaken our Buddha-nature and liberate us from suffering and confusion" (p. 17). Writing about Vedanta, Frawley (2000) stated: "Vedanta is a simple philosophy. It states that our True self, what it calls the *Atman*, is God" (p. 4). He continued, "True meditation requires not dwelling in the present moment, but dwelling in presence. Presence is Being, which is in all things, in all time and beyond" (Frawley, 2000, p. 54). In a similar way, Thomas Keating, a Christian monk, wrote about centering prayer: "Deeper still, or more 'centered,' is the Divine Indwelling where the divine energy is present as the source of our being and inspiration at every moment" (Keating, 2009, p. 29). He wrote about Christian-centering prayer as a way to access this presence. In general, meditative practices allow people to tap into sources of the sacred, often by moving beyond the mind, thoughts, and emotions and entering a space of transcendence.

As mentioned, meditation practices are found across diverse spiritual traditions and form a central component of many Eastern spiritual traditions (e.g., Buddhism, Hinduism). Thus far, psychological therapy models emphasizing meditation and mindfulness techniques have drawn on Eastern spiritual practices for inspiration, particularly psychological models that directly integrate Buddhism with psychology (see Volume 1, Chapter 35, this handbook). For example, a main component of dialectical behavior therapy (e.g., Linehan, 1993), a widely used model for sexual abuse survivors, involves building the core skill of mindfulness. In addition, acceptance and commitment therapy has focused on increasing mindful awareness, such as maintaining contact with the present moment and defusing from thoughts and feelings, with trauma survivors (e.g., Walser & Westrup, 2007). These types of therapeutic approaches have gained increasing popularity among psychologists and mental health professionals (see Chapter 10 in this volume). We turn next to a more detailed discussion of meditation in sexual trauma work.

How to integrate meditation into sexual trauma work. Meditation as applied to sexual trauma therapy aims to help the client maintain present focused awareness so that distressing memories, thoughts, feelings, and sensations can be experienced and processed rather than avoided, fragmented, and dissociated. Meditation may directly address the symptoms of hyperarousal, reexperiencing, and avoidance that are characteristic of posttraumatic reactions (for a review, see Waelde, 2008). Breath-focused meditation practice may directly reduce hyperarousal through physiological mechanisms (Ospina et al., 2007) and promote better emotion regulation (Arch & Craske, 2006). With reduced hyperarousal, clients should be better able to tolerate trauma reminders and less motivated to avoid trauma-related material. As clients develop the capacity to engage in trauma material without being overwhelmed by distress, they begin to reclaim parts of their experience that have been ignored and dissociated from awareness. The capacity to maintain present focused awareness is facilitated by letting go of trauma-related distress as it arises, which fosters a sense of wholeness and self-mastery and a renewed (or new) sense of connection to the sacred.

Meditation to support psychotherapy. Therapists can supplement their work with sexual trauma clients by integrating mindfulness and meditation practices into sessions. Many therapists have found it helpful to use a brief period of meditation at the start of therapy sessions to reduce the anxiety that many survivors experience when they anticipate confronting their trauma in therapy. Very often, clients experience these brief meditations as calming and relaxing. The practice can be as simple as taking 5 min to pay attention to the quality of the breath. Clients can notice if their breathing is slow or fast and the sound and feel of the breath, and they can pay attention to where the breath seems to be going or not going. For example, does the breathing seem to stop in the chest or is the breathing a deeper "belly breath"? These brief meditation periods help to orient clients to the therapy session and serve as a useful self-check about their physical, mental, and emotional states as they begin the session.

As the meditation practice develops, clients become aware that their thoughts and feelings, however painful, are not permanent. With this realization comes a sense of mastery because the client is no longer at the mercy of trauma triggers but has gained the capacity to stay in the present even in the face of disturbing reminders. With practice, even the most potent reminders become less disturbing. For many people, this experience speaks of real freedom and peace and leads to a natural sense of connection with the sacred.

Monitoring response to meditation. Using brief meditations in the early phase of treatment will give the therapist an opportunity to assess how the client responds to meditation practice. The therapist should watch the client during the practice for signs of distress, such as quickened breath pace or shaking and should be prepared to ask the client at any point in the practice about how she is feeling. It is useful to check in with the client after every period of practice to find out about his or her experience of the meditation (e.g., "How did the practice go?"). This check-in yields information about the client's condition and about how well a particular practice matches the client's capacities and needs. If the client says that the practice did not work, it is important to begin by asking about her experience of the practice, rather than by clarifying the instructions. In many cases, a particular practice may not suit a client. For example, clients who have panic attacks may feel more anxious in response to instructions to change the pace or depth of breathing (Conrad et al., 2007).

The therapist also can try different types of meditation instruction to see which work best for the client. For example, clients who are very ruminative may have difficulty with less structured meditation practices because they may find that their rumination becomes unbearable when they try to sit quietly. Likewise, some clients respond better to breath-focused imagery rather than simply watching the breath. A recent study of meditation homework adherence that pooled data from two studies with traumatized participants found that a technique involving breath-focused imagery to release tension was used to a greater degree than other mindfulness and imagery techniques (Waelde et al., 2008).

Therapeutic meditation should not be a one-size-fits-all process. Each client comes into therapy with particular strengths and vulnerabilities, so the meditation instruction should be individualized to match the client. Two issues common to sexually traumatized clients include prominent reexperiencing and dissociation symptoms, both of which can make meditation difficult and require a tailored instructional approach. For example, with sexually abused clients with intrusive reexperiencing or flashbacks, the therapist can provide additional structure (a) by verbally guiding the client through the meditation practice and (b) by providing additional structure in the types of practices that are taught. Clients who dissociate can be encouraged to notice discontinuities in their attention and develop their motivation for maintaining present moment awareness. The therapist should demonstrate a sense of respect for the survival value of dissociation yet should gently challenge the client's avoidance (for a review of strategies for integrating meditation with clients who are dealing with reexperiencing and dissociation, see Waelde, 2004, 2008).

We offer meditation as a potential avenue for increased spiritual awareness, connection, and well-being. Many clients and therapists, however, concentrate specifically on the psychological aspects of meditation, such as focused awareness and attention, relaxation, symptom reduction, and emotion regulation. Overall, some clients may use meditation alongside their religious traditions, others may focus on meditation as their primary spiritual path, and yet others will utilize meditation and mindfulness solely for psychological recovery. Our client-centered, pluralistic, diversity-oriented approach offers a valuable framework to guide the integration of meditation into psychotherapy.

FUTURE DIRECTIONS

The role of spirituality and religion in the lives of survivors of sexual trauma is multifaceted and complex. Current research is diving more deeply into what specific types of spiritual beliefs and practices facilitate well-being, growth, and recovery from sexual trauma, and what factors potentially lead to struggle and decline. It is important to continue to examine the diverse beliefs, practices, and spiritual needs and concerns of sexual trauma survivors. Also, a continued focus on what moderates the complicated relationships between sexual trauma and spiritual growth and decline across time, in both children and adults, can provide a useful platform for clinical intervention. Clinical intervention studies can help refine effective clinical strategies for addressing core spiritual themes and working with spiritual struggles in therapy, considering the efficacy of both Western and Eastern spiritually based interventions and practices.

Finally, increased attention to training students and therapists in the integration of spirituality, religion, trauma, and meditation practices is warranted. Training of therapists, counselors, psychological, social workers, and other care providers can focus on both an increased sensitivity to spirituality and religion in the therapy process as well as specifically learning how to help sexual trauma survivors utilize spiritual resources and address spiritual and religious struggles. Trained therapists are well poised to facilitate the complex recovery process in sexual trauma survivors, assisting both psychological and spiritual well-being and health.

CONCLUSION

In this chapter, we have reviewed the research literature and offered clinical interventions and strategies for working with spirituality, religion, and sexual trauma. We have proposed ways to help facilitate recovery and well-being, considering both Western and Eastern spiritual perspectives. Additionally, we believe that one of the greatest gifts therapists can give survivors of sexual trauma is *presence*, walking alongside clients in their painful and potentially dark descent into violation at the deepest of levels. In the opening quote, Doehring (1993) mentioned the importance of "companions" who "empower" and help survivors "consecrate," or connect with the sacred (or sacredness), again. Helping survivors of sexual trauma address spiritual struggles and facilitate spiritual connection, meaning, and presence can foster both psychological and spiritual well-being, integration, and wholeness. Therapists can serve as companions in spiritual darkness; can offer hope and connection; and can witness resilience, transformation, and transcendence.

References

Ahrens, C. E., Abeling, S., Ahmad, S., & Hinman, J. (2010). Spirituality and well-being: The relationship between religious coping and recovery from sexual assault. *Journal of Interpersonal Violence, 25*, 1242–1263. doi:10.1177/0886260509340533

Arch, J. J., & Craske, M. G. (2006). Mechanisms of mindfulness: Emotion regulation following a focused breathing induction. *Behaviour Research and Therapy, 44*, 1849–1858. doi:10.1016/j.brat.2005.12.007

Ben-Ezra, M., Palgi, Y., Sternberg, D., Berkley, D., Eldar, H., Glidai, Y., . . . Shrira, A. (2010). Losing my religion: A preliminary study of changes in belief pattern after sexual assault. *Traumatology, 16*, 7–13. doi:10.1177/1534765609358465

Chibnall, J. T., Wolf, A., & Duckro, P. N. (1998). A national survey of sexual trauma experiences of catholic nuns. *Review of Religious Research, 40*, 142–167. doi:10.2307/3512299

Conrad, A., Müller, A., Doberenz, S., Kim, S., Meuret, A. E., Wollburg, E., & Roth, W. T. (2007). Psychophysiological effects of breathing instructions for stress management. *Applied Psychophysiology and Biofeedback, 32*, 89–98. doi:10.1007/s10484-007-9034-x

Doehring, C. (1993). *Internal desecration: Traumatization and representations of God.* Lanham, MD: University Press of America.

Doehring, C. (2006). *The practice of pastoral care: A postmodern approach.* Louisville, KY: Westminster John Knox Press.

Fallot, R. D., & Heckman, J. P. (2005). Religious/spiritual coping among women survivors with mental health and substance use disorders. *Journal of Behavioral Health Services and Research, 32,* 215–226. doi:10.1007/BF02287268

Falsetti, S. A., Resick, P. A., & Davis, J. L. (2003). Changes in religious beliefs following trauma. *Journal of Traumatic Stress, 16,* 391–398. doi:10.1023/A:1024422220163

Foote, C. (1994). *Survivor prayers: Talking with God about childhood sexual abuse.* Louisville, KY: Westminster John Knox Press.

Fosha, D., Paivio, S. C., Gleiser, K., & Ford, J. D. (2009). Experiential and emotion-focused therapy. In C. A. Courtois & J. D. Ford (Eds.), *Treating complex traumatic stress disorders: An evidence-based guide* (pp. 286–311). New York, NY: Guilford Press.

Frawley, D. (2000). *Vedantic meditation: Lighting the flame of awareness.* Berkeley, CA: North Atlantic Books.

Frazier, P. A., & Berman, M. I. (2008). Posttraumatic growth following sexual assault. In P. A. Linley (Ed.), *Trauma, recovery, and growth: Positive psychological perspectives on posttraumatic stress* (pp. 161–181). Hoboken, NJ: Wiley.

Gall, T. L. (2006). Spirituality and coping with life stress among adult survivors of childhood sexual abuse. *Child Abuse and Neglect, 30,* 829–844. doi:10.1016/j.chiabu.2006.01.003

Griffith, J. L. (2010). *Religion that heals, religion that harms: A guide for clinical practice.* New York, NY: Guilford Press.

Hall, T. A. (1995). Spiritual effects of childhood sexual abuse in adult Christian women. *Journal of Psychology and Theology, 23,* 129–134.

Kane, D., Cheston, S. E., & Greer, J. (1993). Perceptions of God by survivors of childhood sexual abuse: An exploratory study in an underresearched area. *Journal of Psychology and Theology, 21,* 228–237.

Keating, T. (2009). *Intimacy with God: An introduction to centering prayer.* New York, NY: Crossroad.

Kennedy, J. E., Davis, R. C., & Taylor, B. G. (1998). Changes in spirituality and well-being among victims of sexual assault. *Journal for the Scientific Study of Religion, 37,* 322–328. doi:10.2307/1387531

Kimbrough, E., Magyari, T., Langenberg, P., Chesney, M., & Berman, B. (2010). Mindfulness intervention for child abuse survivors. *Journal of Clinical Psychology, 66,* 17–33. doi:10.10002/jclp.20624

Kirkpatrick, L. A. (2005). *Attachment, evolution, and the psychology of religion.* New York, NY: Guilford Press.

Knapik, G. P., Martsolf, D. S., Draucker, C. B., & Strickland, K. D. (2010). Attributes of spirituality described by survivors of sexual violence. *Qualitative Report, 15,* 644–657. Retrieved from http://www.nova.edu/ssss/QR/QR15-3/knapik.pdf

Lama Surya Das. (1997). *Awakening the Buddha within: Eight steps to enlightenment.* New York, NY: Broadway Books.

Lawson, R., Drebing, C., Berg, G., Vincellette, A., & Penk, W. (1998). The long term impact of child abuse on religious behavior and spirituality in men. *Child Abuse and Neglect, 22,* 369–380. doi:10.1016/S0145-2134(98)00003-9

Linehan, M. M. (1993). *Cognitive–behavioral treatment of borderline personality disorder.* New York, NY: Guilford Press.

McCann, I. L., & Pearlman, L. A. (1990). *Psychological trauma and the adult survivor: Theory, therapy, and transformation.* New York, NY: Brunner/Mazel.

McCann, I. L., Sakheim, D. K., & Abrahamson, D. J. (1988). Trauma and victimization: A model of psychological adaptation. *The Counseling Psychologist, 16,* 531–594. doi:10.1177/0011000088164002

Murray-Swank, N. A. (2003). *Solace for the soul: A journey towards wholeness. Treatment manual for female survivors of sexual abuse.* Baltimore, MD: Loyola University.

Murray-Swank, N. A. (2010, November). *Spirituality, religion, and PTSD among survivors of clergy sexual abuse.* Paper presented at the meeting of the International Society for Traumatic Stress Studies, Montreal, Quebec, Canada.

Murray-Swank, N. A. (2011). *Trauma and transformation: The spiritual and religious impact of sexual abuse by clergy and church professionals.* Manuscript submitted for publication.

Murray-Swank, N. A., & Pargament, K. I. (2005). God, where are you? Evaluating a spiritually-integrated intervention for sexual abuse. *Mental Health, Religion, and Culture, 8,* 191–203. doi:10.1080/13694670500138866

Murray-Swank, N. A., & Pargament, K. I. (2008). Solace for the soul: Evaluating a spiritually-integrated counselling intervention for sexual abuse. *Counselling and Spirituality, 27,* 157–174.

Murray-Swank, N. A., & Pargament, K. I. (2011). Seeking the sacred: The assessment of spirituality in the therapy process. In J. D. Aten, M. R. McMinn, & E. L. Worthington (Eds.), *Spiritually oriented interventions for counseling and psychotherapy* (pp. 107–135). Washington, DC: American Psychological Association.

Ospina, M. B., Bond, T. K., Karkhaneh, M., Tjosvold, L., Vandermeer, B., Liang, Y., . . . Klassen, T. P. (2007, June). *Meditation practices for health: State of the research* (Evidence Report/Technology Assessment

No. 155; prepared by the University of Alberta Evidence-based Practice Center under Contract No. 290–02-0023; AHRQ Publication No. 07-E010). Rockville, MD: Agency for Healthcare Research and Quality.

Paivio, S. C., & Pascual-Leone, A. (2010). *Emotion-focused therapy for complex trauma: An integrative approach.* Washington, DC: American Psychological Association. doi:10.1037/12077-000

Pargament, K. I. (1997). *The psychology of religion and coping: Theory, research, and practice.* New York, NY: Guilford Press.

Pargament, K. I. (2007). *Spiritually integrated psychotherapy: Understanding and addressing the sacred.* New York, NY: Guilford Press.

Pargament, K. I., Koenig, H. G., & Perez, L. (2000). The many methods of religious coping: Development and initial validation of the RCOPE. *Journal of Clinical Psychology, 56,* 519–543. doi:10.1002/(SICI)1097-4679(200004)56:4<519::AID-JCLP6>3.0.CO;2-1

Piedmont, R. L. (1999). Does spirituality represent that sixth factor of personality? Spiritual transcendence and the five factor model. *Journal of Personality, 67,* 985–1013. doi:10.1111/1467-6494.00080

Pritt, A. F. (1998). Spiritual correlates of reported sexual abuse among Mormon women. *Journal for the Scientific Study of Religion, 37,* 273–285. doi:10.2307/1387527

Resick, P. A., Monson, C. M., & Chard, K. M. (2008). *Cognitive processing therapy: Veteran/military version.* Washington, DC: U.S. Department of Veterans Affairs.

Resick, P. A., & Schnicke, M. K. (1996). *Cognitive processing therapy for rape victims: A treatment manual.* Newbury Park, CA: Sage.

Rossetti, S. J. (1995). The impact of child sexual abuse on attitudes toward God and the Catholic Church. *Child Abuse and Neglect, 19,* 1469–1481. doi:10.1016/0145-2134(95)00100-1

Valentine, L., & Feinauer, L. L. (1993). Resilience factors associated with female survivors of childhood sexual abuse. *American Journal of Family Therapy, 21,* 216–224. doi:10.1080/01926189308250920

Waelde, L. C. (2004). Dissociation and meditation. *Journal of Trauma and Dissociation, 5,* 147–162. doi:10.1300/J229v05n02_08

Waelde, L. C. (2008). Meditation. In G. Reyes, J. Elhai, & J. Ford (Eds.), *Encyclopedia of psychological trauma* (pp. 419–421). Hoboken, NJ: Wiley.

Waelde, L. C., Uddo, M., Estupinian, G., Mortensen, M. J., Kukreja, S., Spannring, J., & Zief, A. (2008, November). *Meditation homework adherence in PTSD treatment.* Paper presented at the meeting of the International Society for Traumatic Stress Studies, Chicago, IL.

Walker, D. F., Reid, H. W., O'Neill, T. O., & Brown, L. (2009). Changes in personal religion/spirituality during and after childhood abuse: A review and synthesis. *Psychological Trauma: Theory, Research, Practice, and Policy, 1,* 130–145. doi:10.1037/a0016211

Walser, R., & Westrup, D. (2007). *Acceptance and commitment therapy for the treatment of post-traumatic stress disorder and trauma-related problems: A practitioner's guide to using mindfulness and acceptance strategies.* Oakland, CA: New Harbinger.

Zinnbauer, B. J., & Pargament, K. I. (2000). Working with the sacred: Four approaches to religious and spiritual issues in counseling. *Journal of Counseling and Development, 78,* 162–171. doi:10.1002/j.1556-6676.2000.tb02574.x

CHAPTER 18

THE PSYCHOLOGY OF CONTEMPORARY RELIGIOUS VIOLENCE: A MULTIDIMENSIONAL APPROACH

James W. Jones

Throughout the centuries, religion has played a major role in fomenting political violence and promoting terrorism. Humanity's most horrific acts have been done in the name of humanity's highest ideals. Yet religions also have played a significant role in restraining violence and promoting reconciliation. The psychology of religion should seek to understand these paradoxes (Jones, 2002; Nepstad, 2004; Silberman, Higgins, & Dweck, 2005).

Virtually all contemporary students of ethnopolitical violence and terrorism agree that they are multidetermined, multidimensional phenomena (e.g., see Reich, 1998; see also Volume 1, Chapter 26, this handbook). Only an interdisciplinary analysis can hold any hope of understanding of such violence. Even within psychology, as we will see shortly, social psychologists, political psychologists, clinicians, and many others have conducted research and offered analyses of these movements. In addition, within the psychology of religion, there is a general agreement that religion, too, is multidimensional, multileveled, and multidetermined. If psychologists of religion have learned nothing else in the more than 100 years of the discipline's existence, they have learned that religion is far too complex to be viewed through a single lens (Wulff, 1991; see also Volume 1, Chapters 1 and 3, this handbook). Combining these two lines of agreement underscores a serious concern: Understanding, even psychologically, a phenomenon like religion's role in movements of ethnopolitical violence and terrorism is a complicated task. This chapter reviews some of the many different psychological approaches to understanding religion's role in political violence and terrorism. But it is only a review. There is not space to analyze any of these theories in depth. This chapter concludes with some of the practical applications of this material and the implications for further research. And this chapter illustrates some of the reasons why the multidisciplinary, integrative paradigm outlined in the introduction to this handbook (see Volume 1, Chapter 1, this handbook) represents exactly the type of approach that is necessary to study and understand religious violence.

PSYCHOPATHOLOGY?

Virtually all studies of those involved in acts of ethnopolitical violence and terrorism have concluded that the most extraordinary acts of inhumanity are committed by ordinary people. No serious contemporary study has found any evidence for diagnosable psychopathology in those who commit acts of terror and atrocity (e.g., see the review in Horgan, 2005). After reviewing all the literature on the perpetrators of genocide, the social psychologist James Waller concluded that all the evidence supports "the reality of the propensity of ordinary people to commit extraordinary evil" (Waller, 2002, p. 121; see also Volume 1, Chapter 26, this handbook). He could find no evidence that the actual perpetrators of large-scale atrocities, taken as a whole, displayed any particular psychopathology or character disorder (for a similar conclusion, see also Atran, 2003; Horgan, 2005; Post, 1984; Reich, 1998; Victoroff, 2005).

DOI: 10.1037/14046-018
APA Handbook of Psychology, Religion, and Spirituality: Vol. 2. An Applied Psychology of Religion and Spirituality, K. I. Pargament (Editor-in-Chief)

PSYCHOLOGICAL PERSPECTIVES ON ETHNOPOLITICAL VIOLENCE

The psychiatrist Jerrold Post has organized violent political groups into three categories (Post, 2007; Post, Ruby, & Shaw, 2002): "nationalist separatist" groups, such as the Palestinian Liberation Organization and the Irish Republican Army (IRA); "social revolutionary" groups, such as the Red Brigades in Italy, the Shining Path in Peru, and the Fuerzas Armadas Revolucionarias de Colombia in Columbia; and "religious extremist terrorism," which includes all violent religious fundamentalist movements, regardless of religious tradition. Each type has its own particular character. The first expresses devotion to a national (or sometimes ethnic) identity. Such groups often retell a history of national or ethnic grievance—seeking to correct injustices experienced by previous generations. Rather than carrying intergenerational continuity, the second type represents intergenerational conflict—rebelling against the parental generation. This category represents the extremist members of the New Left in the 1970s and 1970s. Few of these organizations are still active in the 21st century, although the violence-prone groups within the animal rights and ecological movements may represent more contemporary examples of this category. The third group is motivated by religious commitments. Post has stressed that political violence is a group activity that cannot be understood by looking for individual pathologies. Rather political violence must be seen as a function of a "collective identity." The group dynamic that Post has emphasized most is the role of the leader in these violent movements. His 2007 book is organized as a series of chapters, each devoted to a particular group, with each chapter containing brief biographical studies of their various leaders.

Such a structure reveals Post's (2007) basic point. Those who commit violence in the name of a political or religious ideology "have subordinated their individual identity to the collective identity, so that what serves the group, organization, or network is of primary importance" (Post, 2007, p. 8). Such subordination to the group gives leaders almost limitless powers to shape the behavior of members. So for Post, understanding the psychology of the leader gives us crucial insights into the motivations of the group. For example, Post claimed that the September 11 hijackers were

> true believers who had subordinated their individuality to the group. They had uncritically accepted the directions of the destructive charismatic leader of the organization, Osama bin Laden, and what he declared to be moral was moral and indeed was a sacred obligation. (Post, 2007, p. 193)

What follows is a brief biography of bin Laden, emphasizing his distant, if not nonexistent, relationship with his father, who arbitrarily divorced his mother and then died when Osama was 10 years old. Post found the same pattern of little or no relationship with fathers in many of the "charismatic" leaders of violent groups, including, for example, Abdullah Ocalan of the Kurdistan Workers Party (Post, 2007, pp. 70–71) and Abimael Guzman of the Shinning Path (Post, 2007, p. 131). Such a childhood history, Post asserted, can produce "an intensely narcissistic personality" (Post et al., 2002, pp. 85–86; Post, 2007, p. 75), externally confident and inspiring but vulnerable at the core. Post finds this dynamic of narcissistic leaders and needy followers key to the psychology of violent political and religious movements (Post et al., 2002, p. 87; Robins & Post, 1997).

Charismatic leadership, which Post took as an essential characteristic of violence-prone political and religious groups, is not simply an individual trait but is rather "a property of a social system, a fit between leaders with particular characteristics and a wounded fellowship at a moment of crisis" (Post et al., 2002, p. 87). Charisma is an interaction effect because "a leader is not formed until he encounters his followers" (Post, 2007, p. 195). Followers give charismatic leaders absolute allegiance and accept uncritically the leader's teachings and instructions. Because the leader sets the tone and direction for the group, whether or not a political or religious movement turns violent "depends on the disposition of the leader" (Post et al., 2002, p. 88). If the leader endorses and preaches violence, there is every likelihood the movement will engage in murder and terror.

Like Post, Vamik Volkan has spent decades studying ethnic and political violence (Volkan, 1997). Like Post, he has focused on the centrality of group behavior in ethnopolitical violence. For him, the nature of what he terms the large group is central to understanding ethnopolitical conflict. A large group—a nation, a racial, or ethnic group—is characterized by a common history and shared values. In addition, such groups organize their identity around two factors: what Volkan calls the group's "chosen trauma" and what he calls the group's "chosen glory" (Volkan, 1997, p. 48). *Chosen trauma* refers to the "collective memory" of a catastrophe from the past, experienced by the group's forbearers. *Chosen* describes how the large group organizes its self-definition around an injustice or wrong done to its ancestors. Thus, the group's identity becomes bound with the intergenerational transmission of trauma. Making a past trauma central to group identity requires that the trauma be reevoked in each succeeding generation through rituals, stories, beliefs, and ideologies that developed in relation to this ancestral wrong. These evoke certain feelings and attitudes in later generations and nurture and reinforce the large group's identity as a wronged party (Volkan, 1997, pp. 81–82). The idea of the chosen trauma points to a sense of group humiliation. And there is much research connecting humiliation and violence (Gilligan, 1996; W. Miller, 1993; Stern, 2003).

Large groups also nurture memories of past successes and triumphs. These ancestral memories Volkan has called the "chosen glory" (1997, p. 48). Usually the "chosen glory" contains memories of "deserved victories over another group." Like the chosen trauma, the chosen glory is a psychological constellation of affects, cognitions, and inducements to action. When reevoked, these complex "mental representations" of a historical event induce feelings of triumph and grandiosity. These feelings, too, create group cohesion.

Both the chosen trauma and the chosen glory are psychologically complex. More than simply memories, they are "a shared mental representation of the event, which includes realistic information, fantasized expectations, intense feelings, and defenses against unacceptable thoughts" (Volkan, 1997, p. 48). Around a kernel of historical truth can be woven a complicated web of desire and fantasy that soon becomes central to the group's identity. The chosen glory serves to potentiate group pride and self-esteem. The chosen trauma also contributes to the large group's self-defined character and may power a wish for redress and revenge and even be a motivation for violent actions.

Volkan (1997) has suggested that those individuals most susceptible to being recruited into campaigns for ethnopolitical violence have had some personal experience of victimization or trauma in their own history and become mobilized as they identify with injury to the larger ethnic or national group. Such vulnerable individuals regress to a position of almost total dependency on the group and its leader. For Volkan, understanding this relationship of the member to the group and to the leader is key to understanding the psychology of group violence. Volkan has suggested that leaders of violent nationalistic and religious groups come from troubled families, often with missing or unavailable parents. Such leaders seek to create a "family" in which they become the parent and so attempt to make up for a deficiency in their early experience. They soon begin to abuse their "family members," however, as they were abused as children. Thus rage develops within the "family." Such leaders and groups attract people without secure identities who regressively depend on the leader and the group for their identity.

For Volkan (1997), the psychology of identity thus helps explain group violence: The large group is prone to violence because its identity is formed around the chosen trauma and its members are prone to violence because their identities are the result of dependence on a leader and a group. In Volkan's view, such total dependence breeds a rage that may be masochistically turned against the self (committing suicide as did Heaven's Gate and the Solar Temple or martyrdom operations) or sadistically turned against outsiders (unrestricted warfare). In addition, violent tendencies are exacerbated when the group on which the individual depends appears threatened. Threats to the group are easily translated into threats against the self, which depends on the group for its psychological existence (Volkan, 2004).

Volkan (1997) also pointed to the reciprocal, interaction effects between a violent group and those outside it. Even before they turn violent, such groups often evoke fear and anger on the part of those around them. Sometimes this is the result of the group's deviant activities and sometimes it is simply the result of the outsider's fear of those who are different. This cycle of mutually increasing suspicion and mistrust almost always ends in catastrophe as it feeds the group's incipient paranoia about the outside world. This clearly happened with Aum Shinrykio in Japan (Jones, 2008; Reader, 2000); the Branch Dividians in Waco, Texas (Wessinger, 2000); and the People's Temple in Guyana (Kimball, 2002).

The political psychologist Clark McCauley has made the same point in relation to terrorism: The terrorist and their opponents should be understood as two parts of a single, reciprocal system. McCauley (2006) wrote, "Understanding terrorist behavior means understanding the interactions between terrorist attacks and state responses. These form a dynamic of violence and counterviolence that must be seen as a whole, as a pattern" (p. 52). Terrorists act in part in the hope of provoking a disproportionate counterresponse that will generate support for the terrorists and undermine support for the counterterrorists. McCauley called this "jujitsu politics; using the enemy's strength to mobilize against the enemy" (p. 49). In a 2006 article, he applied this model particularly to al-Qaeda and the reciprocal actions and reactions of al-Qaeda and United States after September 11.

Volkan (1997) also discussed violence-prone groups organized around religion, not ethnic or national identity. He distinguished "regressive" and "nonregressive" forms of religion. Paralleling D. W. Winnicott's theory of transitional objects, Volkan said that people require "moments of rest" (like Winnicott's transitional space) in which they can let go of compulsive reality-testing and indulge in creativity and fantasy through art, literature, music, and religion (Volkan, 2004). For Volkan, like Winnicott, this function of religion is a normal developmental process throughout the life cycle. According to Volkan, however, individuals whose parent–child bond was not secure, or who were raised in an excessively religious environment, use religion in a regressive way. That is they use religion to blot out and deny rationality and reality rather than as a means of imaginatively transforming reality while remaining in touch with it. Denying reality in this way leaves the person vulnerable to leaders who magnify and reinforce their fears and anxieties.

Volkan (1997) sought to combine individual explanations with theories of group process to explain ethnopolitical and religiously motivated violence. Psychodynamic theories describe some of the factors that make an individual vulnerable to the messages of violence-prone groups (Jones, 2006, 2008). But a purely individual approach is not sufficient because these groups also possess significant common characteristics that shape the behavior of their members and increase their likelihood of turning violent—for example, their absolutist approach to a sacred text, idealized leader, need to demonize their opponents, and strict boundaries around the group (Eidelson & Eidelson, 2003; Kimball, 2002).

Although Post (2007) and Volkan (1997) have emphasized the influence of leaders, the psychiatrist Marc Sageman has argued for the *lack* of hierarchical leaders and leadership in contemporary violence-prone religious movements, as the title of his 2008 book, *Leaderless Jihad*, implies. Focusing primarily on terrorist groups with a global agenda, rather than those with strictly local, nationalistic aims, he found that most recruits were grown men (not impressionable teenagers). They feel alienated from their societies but have long term bonds with each other, forged in naturally occurring groups like sports leagues, religious communities, kinship networks, or online chat rooms.

Sageman (2008) described four factors that lead a group to violence. First, there is moral outrage, especially regarding the current treatment of their ethnic, national, or religious community. Sageman emphasized the importance of a moral vision in the turn toward violence: both a sense of moral outrage about the treatment of their community and the wish to build a better, more just world. Second, there is an ideology or framework of interpretation that claims to explain the source of their group's mistreatment, usually by blaming some other group. Third, Sageman pointed to a resonance between the person's own experience, often the humiliation and alienation they feel in their societies, and the mistreatment they feel their group is undergoing. Making a connection between this general sense of outrage and some immediate personal experience of humiliation is an important catalyst in the turn toward violence. Fourth, there is a network that forms along ordinary lines of friendship, kinship, and common interests. Sageman claimed that no top-down recruitment or charismatic leadership is necessary. Such groups "self-radicalize." Already reliant on their friends and bonded together, they turn to one another, withdrawing more and more from the larger community. Gradually the group "radicalizes" together. Ideology and outrage are not enough, sustained violent action almost always requires a group for mobilization.

APPLYING PSYCHOLOGICAL RESEARCH TO ETHNOPOLITICAL VIOLENCE

The two most widely cited social–psychological experiments in the literature of violent group behavior are Milgram's (1974) obedience to authority and Zimbardo's (Zimbardo, Maslach, & Haney, 2000) prison experiments. In the early 1960s, Stanley Milgram recruited a cohort of 40 ordinary men from New Haven and found that the majority of them were willing to inflict what they thought were increasingly severe shocks on a subject as a punishment for wrong answers to questions. Even when the subject portrayed signs of severe distress or cried out, 65% of the participants were willing to inflict what they were told was a near-fatal shock to the subject in obedience to the experimenter's commands. Significantly less than half the participants were willing to defy the experimenter at all. Over the years, Milgram's findings have been replicated time and time again in a variety of different settings and countries. In every variation of the experiment, at least some participants were fully compliant with the experimenter's orders (Blass, 2000; Milgram, 1974). Proximity was an important variable here. The closer the participants were to the "victim" physically (seeing him, hearing his screams, etc.), the more likely they were to protest and even to disobey. So the capacity to empathize with victims or potential victims may be an important factor in countering blind obedience (Eisenberg, Valiente, & Champion, 2004).

In 1971, at Stanford University, Philip Zimbardo recruited a cohort of typical college male undergraduates and randomly assigned one group to play the role of prisoners and the other to play the role of prison guards. He set them up in a mock prison setting. Anyone with noticeable psychological problems was screened out; only those most mature and stable participated. Given the random assignments, both groups were basically similar. Within days, a third of those assigned to be guards became increasingly cruel, sadistic, and tyrannical toward the prisoners, whom they knew were really just fellow undergraduates like themselves. This finding dramatically demonstrated how easy it is to elicit cruel and sadistic behavior even from those not otherwise inclined or socialized in that direction. In the mock prison, this brutality escalated so rapidly that the 2-week long experiment was stopped completely after 6 days (Zimbardo et al., 2000).

Although often cited as analogues for intergroup violence and terrorism, there are significant differences between these experimental conditions and campaigns of terrorism and ethnopolitical warfare. There is more to such acts of violence than obedience (A. Miller, 2004). Many other factors like the demonizing of the opponent, the fascination with violence, and the sacralizing of one's cause play crucial roles in political violence and terrorism. And there are almost always economic, political, or cultural conflicts associated with ethnopolitical and religiously sponsored killing. Both experiments, however, strongly suggest that ordinary people, with no particular history of violence, can be relatively easily recruited into roles in which they are willing and able to inflict severe pain on their fellow human beings.

James Waller (2002) offered a model of four social–psychological factors that allow ordinary people to become perpetrators of atrocities (see also Volume 1, Chapter 26, this handbook). Two are so-called dispositional factors and refer to characteristics of the perpetrators themselves. The first is "our ancestral shadow," which, based on evolutionary psychology, refers to certain genetic predispositions, such as tendencies toward ethnocentrism, xenophobia, and the drive for social dominance. Under the right circumstances, these traits can make us susceptible to committing vicious deeds.

Waller's (2002) second dispositional factor points to the ways in which the individual is shaped by culture. Among the significant "cultural belief systems" are religious beliefs about the role of authority that may generate an external locus of control as well as about the dichotomy between the in-group and out-group and the demonizing of those considered outside the true fold.

The third factor in his model, a situational factor, is "a culture of cruelty." This involves the individual, already predisposed in this way by his genetic inheritance and his religious and cultural training, to be directly trained as a killer. Through escalating commitments (in which an individual is gradually introduced and desensitized to more heinous acts) and a ritual initiation, the individual's conscience is gradually numbed or repressed when inside a culture of violence. Initiation into such violent groups allows for a diffusion of responsibility, creates an ethos of "deindividuation" in which individuals can act with anonymity, and makes them subject to an almost irresistible peer pressure. The result is what Waller has called the "merger of role and person" in which a culture of cruelty comes to overwhelm and subsumes the individual and his conscience.

Waller's (2002) fourth factor concerns the victim experiencing a "social death." As a prelude to genocide and terrorism, potential victims are dehumanized, labeled as beyond the pale of human compassion and empathy. Potential victims are often blamed for their victimization.

Along this line, Albert Bandura (1998, 2004) has written at length about the role of what he has called "moral disengagement" by which individuals become desensitized to the heinousness of their actions. The vast majority of people who participate in ethnopolitical violence and terrorism are normal, nonpsychopathological people with inhibitions against killing other human beings, which have to be overcome for normal people to become terrorists and killers. According to Bandura, some of the mechanisms by which a human being's tendencies toward empathy and compassion are "disengaged" are as follows: the "redefinition of harmful conduct as morally justified," "sanitizing language," "diffusion of responsibility within a group," "minimizing the harm done," and "dehumanizing the victims and blaming them for the harm done to them." Bandura emphasized that people need a moral justification before they will engage in reprehensible actions. He argued that "the conversion of socialized people into dedicated fighters is achieved not by altering their personality structures, aggressive drives, or moral standards. Rather it is accomplished by cognitively redefining the morality of killing" (Bandura, 2004, p. 124). Bandura pointed out that "religion has a long and bloody history" as one of the major vehicles for providing that moral justification of mass bloodshed (Bandura, 2004, p. 125).

In addition, group activities provide a diffusion of agency so that no one has to feel the burden of responsibility for a terrible act. Dehumanization of the victim is, as Waller (2002) and others pointed out, another crucial mechanism by which wide-scale violence becomes normalized. Bandura (2004) also emphasized that all of these social–psychological processes happen gradually. Individuals and groups may not set out to become violent but may gradually evolve in that direction—the course followed by Aum Shinrykio, for example (Jones, 2008; Reader, 2000). For Bandura, these cognitive–psychological processes describe the conversion of formerly quiet and peaceful people into dedicated killers.

THE LIMITS OF SOCIAL INFLUENCE THEORIES

Most recently published, psychologically oriented articles on ethnopolitical violence and terrorism focus primarily on the group processes and induction procedures by which individuals are recruited to perform such actions (Atran, 2003; Moghaddam, 2005; Moghaddam & Marsella, 2004; Post, Sprinzak, & Denny, 2003). The stated assumption of this literature is that group dynamics alone can explain the transformation of a normal individual into one who kills for a cause (Zimbardo, 2004). Milgram's (1974) and Zimbardo's (Zimbardo et al., 2000) classic experiments and the commonly asserted finding that terrorist do not seem to exhibit any common personality or psychopathological traits appear to point in that direction.

Not every member of a society from which political violence and terrorism arise joins a violent group, and not every member of a violent cell actually engages in a violent operation, nor did every subject in Milgram's (1974) experiments comply with the experimenter's demands. So it seems most prudent to conclude with Victoroff (2005), who wrote, after an extensive review of the literature, that "terrorist behavior is probably *always* determined by a combination of . . . factors . . . the much-cited claim that no individual factors identify those at risk for becoming terrorists is based on completely inadequate research" (p. 34; see also Tobeña, 2004).

Also, these social influence and social process models apply best to tight-knit groups in which there is a structured process of recruitment, initiation, training, and eventual deployment (this is the kind of process described by Horgan and most of the essays in Reich's, 1998, collection and that of Moghaddam & Marsalla, 2004). Here the type of group dynamics that Bandura, Milgram, Zimbardo, Horgan, and others emphasize are certainly strong factors. Although this certainly applies to the IRA, the Red Brigades, and other such groups, we have already mentioned Sageman's (2008) finding that contemporary religious terrorism is more likely the result of rapidly evolving "leaderless groups" or "self-starters" in which there is little overt recruitment and much of the training is done over the Internet or in small cliques (Atran, 2008). Current examples, such as the formation of radical jihadist cliques in Europe or the Army of God in America, suggest that commitment to a violent group happens without the heavy hand of a group leader or trainer, but rather through reading religious literature on one's own, listening to sermons on tape or over the Internet, and having discussions with friends (e.g., see Atran, 2008; Khosrokhavar, 2005; Sageman, 2008). In such loose confederations of the like-minded, classical models of social influence may lose some of their explanatory power.

PSYCHODYNAMIC THEORIES OF ETHNOPOLITICAL VIOLENCE AND TERROR

Psychoanalytic thinking about group psychology and its potential for violence begins with Freud's (1921/1955), "Group Psychology and the Analysis of the Ego." Freud claimed that groups arose when the members identify with the leader and assume the leader's ego in place of their own. The leader then takes over the functions of the individual's ego and the leader's thoughts and wishes replace those of the individual, including the norms of the individual's own conscience. This ego-loss on the part of the members explains, for Freud, why groups appear to regress, act irrationality, and are easily manipulated by a strong leader. Thus, group members behave in ways they would never do if acting alone, including resorting to violence.

The contemporary U.S. psychoanalyst, Otto Kernberg (1998) has argued that this "mass psychology" arises from a vulnerable individual's fear of abandonment that causes such a person to relinquish their autonomy and lose their personal boundaries by joining a large group. For both Freud (1921/1955) and Kernberg, group membership represents a regression to an earlier psychological state. For Kernberg, the individual returns to the psychological organization that characterized early life, especially earlier, more dependent forms of object relations and more primitive impulses and defenses. Because groups are composed of individuals and because the individual members are regressed, the group as a whole almost always regresses to states of extreme dependency or paranoid suspicion. Dependency and paranoia can each generate rage and so both lead inevitably to a group filled with what Kernberg has called "primitive aggression." For Kernberg, this regressive tendency, and the aggression that accompanies it, are inherent in the nature of mass psychology. Groups are inclined toward violence because they are inclined toward dependency and paranoia, which are almost always associated with violent tendencies, a point similar to that made by Volkan (1997), as discussed.

For Freud (1921/1955) and Kernberg (1998) the psychology of the group is really the sum of the individual psychologies of the members. The perceived individual psychological dynamics are then generalized and attributed to the group. Group processes appears to posses no particular psychological dynamics of their own. There does not seem to be any unique psychological structure that results from the organizational dynamics of the collective body beyond that supplied by the individual members. This is in large part because Freud and Kernberg attributed to the group categories and constructs derived from work with individuals, including processes like regression, projection, and primitive aggression. All of this tends to make group membership appear necessarily immature and pathological.

Such theorizing calls attention to the potential for violence often found in groups and the widely reported phenomenon that people do things when they get caught up in a group enthusiasm that they later regret and are even bewildered by. In addition, this psychoanalytic approach theorizes the relationship between the leader and the group to which other nonpsychoanalytic writers have also called attention. Members often do idealize the group leader and are willing to follow the leader in his (most destructive charismatic leaders are men) descent into apocalyptic violence and self-destruction as the examples of the People's Temple, the Branch Dividians, the Solar Temple, and Aum Shinrikyo amply demonstrate.

Heinz Kohut's (1977) theory of the origins of violence emphasizes the role of a person's sense of self and any threats to it. An important aspect of Kohut's theorizing for the psychology of religion is the way he has shown that beliefs, institutions, and ideals can become a part of that sense of self. Then we become dependent on them to maintain that sense of self. A threat to a cherished belief, ideal, of institution can feel like as much (if not more) of a threat than a direct physical threat. Kohut (1977) suggested that "destructive rage, in particular, is always motivated by an injury to the self" (p. 117). The injury that evokes this destructive rage can be a direct threat, or more commonly, it can be a threat to some ideal, ideology, or institution on which the individual depends for his or her identity and self-esteem. If a person's identity and sense of self-worth are inextricably bound to an identification with a religious, political, ethnic, or professional community and its beliefs, when these beliefs are threatened, Kohut has said, these individuals feel threatened at their most basic level as human beings. Then one responds with what he called "narcissistic rage" (Kohut, 1972, p. 379). The main characteristic of such rage is that "those who are in the grip of narcissistic rage show total lack of empathy toward to offender" (Kohut, 1972, p. 386). Such total lack of empathy is one of the most striking traits frequently seen in those who commit violence in the name of some ideal.

Kohut (1972) distinguished such narcissistic rage from ordinary aggression by its totalistic qualities and complete lack of empathy. Here there is a limitless, insatiable quality to the desire for revenge, like that seen in the apocalyptic fanatics who want to purge the world of all evil-doers, sinners, and nonbelievers. In contrast to normal aggression or even a normal desire for revenge, narcissistic rage "in its typical forms is an utter disregard for reasonable limitations and a boundless wish to redress an injury and to obtain revenge" (Kohut, 1972, p. 382). Although some religiously motivated terrorists may employ violence purely tactically in the pursuit of limited and achievable political goals, others dream of complete purification and the apocalyptic eradication of all unholy people. Such totalistic schemes of divine vengeance reek of narcissistic rage born of threats to cherished beliefs and institutions. These totalistic dreams of vengeance on the unrighteous do not necessarily coincide with a loss of cognitive functioning. Devotees motivated by narcissistic rage can still fly planes, make sophisticated bombs, and author brilliantly rhetorical texts in the service of their visions of terror.

Religions almost always idealize and sanctify some ideas, beliefs, institutions, books, codes of conduct, or various leaders (Jones, 2002). The idealized, sanctified religious object becomes a "self-object" in Kohut's (1972) sense. The devotees have made that religious object a part of their sense of self and it has become a part of their identity. Pargament and his colleagues have conducted a series of studies on the psychological impact of considering an activity as sacred or sanctified (reviewed in Pargament & Mahoney, 2005). Studying such common activities as being married (Mahoney, Pargament, Murray-Swank, & Murray-Swank, 2003), parenting, having a sexual relationship (Murray-Swank, Pargament, & Mahoney, 2000), engaging in environmental activism (Tarakeshwar, Swank, Pargament, & Mahoney,

2001), they found that those who denote a facet of life as sacred place a higher priority on that aspect of life, invest more energy in it, and derive more meaning from it than happens with things not denoted as sacred. So denoting something as sacred appears to have significant emotional and behavioral consequences, maybe even if that something is the jihad or ending abortion and turning America into a biblical theocracy, or restoring the boundaries of biblical Israel, or purifying the Hindu homeland, or converting the Tamils to Buddhism.

Another aspect of the process of sanctification is that people universally seek to conserve and protect those aspects of life considered sacred. And it is reasonable to suggest that when that universal search for significance involves the sacred, the individual and the group become even more psychologically invested in preserving and protecting it than they would with more secular goals. Study, ritual, spiritual discipline, deepening commitment to coreligionists are common ways to preserve and protect those aspects of life considered sacred. Perhaps violent action and terror are additional ones.

But this process of sanctification can set us up for narcissistic rage. Pargament and his colleagues investigated exactly that possibility in a study of what they call "desecration" (the opposite of sanctification), which involves the perceived violation of something held sacred (Pargament, Magyar, Benore, & Mahoney, 2005). As distinct from "sacred loss" involving the loss of something held sacred (a belief, commitment, or object), which usually leads to depression, the desecration of something held sacred most likely leads to rage. Although posttraumatic growth and increased self-reported spiritual development often follows sacred loss, psychospiritual development most often goes in the opposite direction following the desecration of something held sacred. The desecration of something held sacred is most often experienced as a significant trauma bringing with it intense emotional distress. Desecration is usually associated with decreased mental health and increased anger. In another study, Pargament, Trevino, Mahoney, and Silberman (2007) found that Christians who believed that Jews were responsible for Jesus' crucifixion and other desecrations of Christian values displayed higher than average levels of anti-Semitism. Even when all other predictors of anti-Semitism were controlled for, belief that Jews desecrated Christian values was a robust predictor of anti-Semitism. Such results fit neatly with Kohut's (1972) model of narcissistic rage.

From the perspective of self-psychology, the U.S. historian Charles Strozier and the psychiatrist David Terman have argued in a series of essays for the centrality of paranoia in the relationship between religion and violence (Strozier, Terman, Jones, & Boyd, 2010). In their essays, paranoia is not a psychosis or other mental disorder but rather is a way of experiencing the self and the world characterized by hostility and feelings of victimization that are blamed on an out-group. Psychologically, a very short distance separates creating a despised other from fomenting a violent apocalyptic crusade against them. Individuals who see the world in this way find that the proclamations of a violent religious ideology make sense to them. From this self-psychological perspective, shame and humiliation give rise to paranoia and apocalyptic fantasies in individuals and in groups. Humiliation represents the collapse of an idealization and a threat to the sense of self, evoking a search for someone to blame and punish for this loss.

Thus, paranoia requires an out-group that is responsible for the humiliation the subject is experiencing. This apocalypticism inevitably constitutes an evil other who carries the evil that rules the world until history's climatic battle (Strozier, 1994; Strozier et al., 2010). Such an analysis accounts for the dichotomizing of the world into totally opposed camps of the completely pure and righteous against demonic and evil enemies. The world of the violent religious partisan is a world at war, a war of good against evil. This kind of theorizing recognizes that, in contrast to terrorist groups who focus on nationalist concerns, contemporary terrorism is often marked by an apocalyptic theology that requires its own psychological analysis.

RELIGIOUS TERRORISM

Turning to the more specific topic of religiously motivated terrorism, we find the same kind of research profile noted in relation to the more general question of ethnopolitical violence. Again there is general agreement that religiously motivated terrorism is a multidetermined, multidimensional issue that requires a broad interdisciplinary approach to understanding. This type of integrative approach, however, is often missing from the work of many authors who seem to imply that their approach really is the only correct one.

Most of the current social science articles on religious terrorism are written either by social psychologists who focus on the dynamics of leadership, recruitment, induction and training, and deployment or by politically oriented social scientists who select a group's political or quasipolitical agendas for emphasis. The same social–cognitive processes noted earlier in reference to large-scale ethnopolitical violence are also referenced in relation to religious terrorism. Post (2007) referred earlier to bin Laden as the charismatic leader of the September 11 cell whose members subordinated their identities to al-Qaeda. In their statements, these groups often refer, in ways similar to what Volkan (1997) has described for much larger groups, to the chosen trauma that propels their grievances and the chosen triumph they seek to recapture. The "moral disengagement" that Bandura (1998, 2004) wrote about is clearly required to commit acts of large scale terror. Sageman's (2008) work focused on social network analysis and the various interconnections among the members of globalized terror cells.

Along the same line, there is the wide-ranging work of Scott Atran who has interviewed terrorists from around the world and who approaches the material primarily from the standpoint of evolutionary psychology. In a 2008 article entitled "Who Becomes a Terrorist Today?" Atran endorsed Sageman's conclusion that contemporary terror "networks are also built up around friendship and kinship but members are more marginal relative to surrounding society" (Atran, 2008, no page number). Looking at the formation of terrorist networks from an evolutionary perspective, Atran concluded that current terrorists

> kill and die for faith and friendship, which is the foundation of all social and political union, that is, all enduring human associations of non-kin: shared faith reigns in self-interest and makes social life possible; friendship allows genetically unrelated individuals to cooperate to compete. (Atran, 2008; see also Atran, 2002)

The implication is that terrorist groups are no different psychologically from any other human group. The same inherited traits that drive other social forms of social bonding also drive religiously motivated terror cells. They can be understood with exactly the same tools of analysis used for all human communities.

Such analyses are a necessary approach to understanding religious violence. But are they sufficient for a full understanding? They say nothing about individual motivations beyond the common human needs for belonging, adventure and a meaningful life. I certainly agree with Horgan (2005) that "explanations of terrorism in terms of personality traits are insufficient alone in trying to understand why some people become terrorists and others do not" (p. 76). No explanation is *sufficient alone* to explain that—that much should be clear by now. But it does not follow that individual factors play no role. There remains the fact that some people have "a greater openness to increased engagement than others" with terrorist groups (Horgan, 2005, p. 101). Hafez (2006) raised precisely this question when he asked, "Why do some religious frames resonate with people whereas others fail to gain adherents?" (p. 169).

A careful study of writings, websites, speeches, interviews, and videos produced by religiously motivated terrorists reveals that certain themes seem common to most religiously sponsored terrorists: teachings and texts that evoke shame and humiliation; the demand for submission to an overly idealized but humiliating institution, text, leader, or deity; a patriarchal religious milieu; an impatience with ambiguity and an inability to tolerate ambivalence that lead to a splitting of the world into polarized all-good and totally evil camps and the demonizing of the other; a drive for total purification and perfection; narcissistic rage and a fascination with violence and violent imagery; doctrines that link violence and purification; and the repression of sexuality (Jones, 2008; Silberman et al., 2005). These constructs and images, embodied in the narratives of religious terrorists, regardless of tradition, are full of psychological content.

From a clinical, psychodynamic perspective it is not coincidence that such themes often occur together. Something within certain individuals may predispose them to be attracted to and to accept a religion characterized by an apocalyptic view of the world and the splitting of humanity into all good and all bad camps, leading to prejudice and crusades against outsiders (Jones, 2006, 2008). For example, psychoanalytic theory provides an account—grounded in clinical experience—of the genesis of the need to divide the world into rigidly polarized, warring camps that many commentators find lie at the heart of religious fanaticism. One solution to overpowering guilt or shame appears in the pursuit of perfection and absolute purity that pacifies a demanding conscience or rids the self of self-hatred and self-loathing. In both cases, the pure cannot tolerate the impure, the holy cannot tolerate the unholy. Thus, the apocalyptic scenarios of Asahara (Lifton, 2000) and the *Left Behind* series so popular in U.S. apocalyptic Christian circles (Jones, 2008, 2010), as well as bin Laden's pronouncements, conclude with a vision of the future in which all the impure and unrighteous have been eliminated and the pure and holy can return to a paradise without complication or ambiguity or any sign remaining of the unrighteous and impure ones. Purification of oneself and the world comes to mean destroying impurity rather than transforming it, creating a perfectly clean, antiseptic, sterilized existence.

In addition, terrorist religions are "totalizing" religions: They make absolute claims upon their devotees. Here, too, there is a psychology—the psychology of the need for something absolute, certain, infallible. This partly reflects the psychological need to overly idealize the objects of one's commitments and devotion. A devotee may demonstrate their devotion to an overly idealized object by committing extreme acts of violence and murder. Such totalistic visions erase all doubt and ambiguity and provide a claim of absolute certainty. The themes of splitting the world into completely pure and totally evil groups and the inability to tolerate ambivalence and ambiguity are connected. Totalistic visions promise the eradication of all ambivalence and ambiguity.

Research into the personality correlates of certain types of religion support these general conclusions. For example, research on authoritarianism and religion finds strong correlations between prejudices, the belief that my religion is the only true religion, and what researchers call *right-wing authoritarianism,* which involves submission to external authorities and the demand for submission from others, support for very punitive measures in law enforcement and childrearing, and a rigid adherence to conventional norms and expectations and hostility toward those who deviate from them (Altemeyer & Hunsberger, 2005). These traits characterize fanatical and violence-prone religions regardless of tradition. There is also research that suggests, at least for religiously committed populations, that punitive and wrathful images of God are associated with external locus of control, anxiety and depression, lack of empathy, and less mature interpersonal relations (Brokaw & Edwards, 1994; Spear, 1994; Tisdale, 1997). Thus, it makes theoretical as well as empirical sense that a person who envisions God as wrathful and punitive—as do those who hold the kind of apocalyptic vision affirmed by many religious terrorists—would be inclined toward a more rigid dichotomizing of the world and less capacity for empathy, traits that characterize many religiously motivated terrorists.

IMPLICATIONS FOR PRACTICE

There are at least two practical implications from these studies of religious violence. First are the warning signs: Although predicting violent behavior is rarely successful in any context, the salient themes discovered in violence-prone groups across traditions suggest some possible factors that might serve as warning signs that a religious group has a high potential for violence: (a) profound experiences of shame and humiliation either generated by social conditions outside the group and potentiated by it or generated from within the group; (b) splitting humanity into all-good and all-evil camps and the demonizing of the other; (c) a wrathful, punitive idealized deity or leader, especially a leader who preaches violence; (d) a conviction that purification requires the shedding of blood; and (e) often a fascination with violence.

Second are responses to religiously motivated violence, and especially religious terrorism: Commenting on his interviews with jihadists around the world, Atran (2006) spoke of them as "yearning for a sense of community and a deeper meaning in life" (p. 135). These are the same desires that motivated young Japanese to join Aum Shinrikyo and that motivate religious converts around the world, whether contemporary U.S. intellectuals embracing Buddhism or a New Age spirituality, or anomic suburbanites joining far-right megachurches, or students in the flocking to cults (Galanter, 1989). Interviews with and statements by jihadists, soldiers in the Army of God, and settlers in the occupied Palestinian territories make it clear that the lure of such movements is not simply the lure of revenge or rage but rather the lure of spiritual renewal, moral seriousness, and a meaningful life (Atran, 2006; Jones, 2008; Stern, 2003). If we do not understand the spirituality that motivates the many contemporary terrorists and the power of religious convictions to reorient and give meaning to people's lives, we will never counter them effectively. If part of their attraction is the attraction of personal transformation and spiritual renewal, then a crucial part of our response must be the articulation of an equally powerful alternative religious and moral vision (some rudimentary suggestions for such a response can be found in the concluding chapters of Jones, 2002, 2008).

FUTURE RESEARCH

The motivations for violence, both personal and ethnopolitical, are so multidetermined and the psychological processes involved in religion so complex that there is always room for more research from within every psychological subdiscipline. We must not forget that religion may mute and transform humiliation and aggression rather than reinforce them, as the Dalai Lama is trying to do with the Tibetans under Chinese occupation, as Martin Luther King Jr. attempted to do with the humiliation of African Americans in the face of U.S. racism, and as Gandhi tried with Indians under British colonial domination. Clearly, a different psychology—a different view of the divine, a rejection of splitting and dichotomizing, a conscious muting or transformation of aggression—is at work in those who seek to transform humiliation and aggression rather than magnify them. Ironically, much more research has gone into studying religion's role in violence than religion's role in peacemaking and reconciliation. This is a crucial frontier area for psychological research.

Some attempts have begun (e.g., see Nepstad, 2004; Silberman, 2005; Silberman et al., 2005). Silberman et al. (2005), for example, listed four ways that religion can facilitate peacemaking and reconciliation: All religions contain values that promote peace; all religions contain teachings that support activism for peace and reconciliation; all religions contain rules that prescribe peaceful intergroup relations; and all religions have rituals and practices of forgiveness and reconciliation. Although such descriptive analysis (for other examples, see also Nepstad, 2004) is a good start, it says little about the distinctively psychological processes that either promote or interfere with the enacting of these aspects of the various religions.

For example, a ferocious lack of empathy characterizes terrorists (Jones, 2008) and research has shown that the ability to empathize with a victim mutes the use of violence (Eisenberg, Valiente, & Champion, 2004). Research is needed into the psychological factors that can move those feeling humiliated away from violence and that work to encourage compassion and empathy for the other, even when the other is a source of social or economic humiliation.

Along with empathy, the past decade has seen a burgeoning (to put it mildly) field of research on the topic of forgiveness (for reviews, see McCullough, Pargament, & Thoresen, 2000; McCullough, Root, Tabak, & Witvliet, 2009; Worthington, 2006). Although most of this research refers to interpersonal conflict, there have been some empirical studies that relate forgiveness to reconciliation in intergroup conflicts (for typical examples, see Myers, Hewstone, & Cairns, 2009; Staub, Pearlman, Gubin, & Hagengimana, 2005). Reviewing the research on this complex set of relationships between religion and forgiveness and forgiveness and conflict resolution is far beyond the scope of this chapter except to note that this too is a promising area for further research.

CONCLUSION

This chapter has emphasized the need for a multimethod approach to religion's role in ethnopolitical conflict and terrorism. This work requires exactly the kind of multilevel, multideterminant, multidimensional paradigm that is the foundation of this handbook. Making progress both in understanding religion's role in fostering group conflict and in responding to it demands the capacity to integrate many different disciplines and levels of analysis. Although researchers often attend primarily either to group process theories and network analysis or to individual-focused models that look at personal motivations, traits, and vulnerabilities, most agree that studying both individual and group dynamics is necessary for a comprehensive understanding. There are other points of agreement: that individual psychopathology is rarely an explanation; that the experience of humiliation is often a precursor to violence; that religiously motivated terrorist groups share common themes regardless of tradition; that previously the leader–follower dynamic appeared crucial for turning a group violent but understanding contemporary, "leaderless" groups may require different models; and that understanding the psychology of apocalyptic theologies is important.

Taken together the studies reviewed in this chapter suggest that religions give rise to violence when they emphasize shame and humiliation, when they dichotomize the world into warring camps of the all-good against the totally evil, when they demonize those with whom they disagree and foment crusades against them, when they advocate violence and blood sacrifice as the primary means of purification, when their devotees seek to placate or be unified with a punitive and humiliating idealized figure or institution, when they offer theological justifications for violent acts, and when they promote prejudice and authoritarian behavior.

In addition, I would suggest (Jones, 2008) that universal religious themes such as purification or the search for reunion with the source of life or the longing for personal meaning and transformation—the classic instigators of spiritual search and religious conversion—can become subsumed into destructive psychological motivations, such as an apocalyptic dichotomizing of the world into all-good, all-evil camps, or the drive to connect with and appease a humiliating or persecuting idealized other. The result is the psychological preconditions for religiously sponsored terrorism and violence, and it is the combination of these powerful psychological motivations and spiritual desires that gives the rhetoric of religious violence its appeal and power.

All of this illustrates the paradox of religion. Religion can bring into people's lives a sense of hope, meaning, and purpose so necessary to human flourishing. Religion can inspire great works of art, music, and literature. Religion can give rise to powerful movements for social justice and experiences of personal transformation. Here religion can do great good and enrich human life. Religion also strengthens feelings of shame and humiliation and the longing for revenge. Religion also plays on people's needs for submission and authority. Religion also inculcates prejudices and the splitting of the world into a battle between the completely pure and the irredeemably evil. Here religion does great mischief and brings calamity on the human species.

A complete psychology of religion must include the psychology of religious violence. Such psychological processes as shame and humiliation, splitting and seeing the world in black-and-white terms along with the inability to tolerate ambivalence, the dynamic of projection, and demonizing the other all contribute to violence and terror apart from religion. But the history and psychology of religion make clear that such dynamics are not only central to the evocation of violence but also lay close to the heart of much religious experience. By demanding submission to a deity, text, institution, group, or teacher that is experienced as wrathful, punitive, or rejecting, religions inevitably evoke or increase feelings of shame and humiliation that are major psychological causes of violent actions. By continually holding before the devotee an overly idealized institution, book, or leader, religions set up the psychodynamic basis for splitting and bifurcating experience. By teaching devotees that some groups are inferior, evil, satanic, or condemned by God, religions encourage the demonizing of others and their "social death," making their slaughter seem inconsequential, justified, or even required. For these reasons, any turn to violence is not accidental but rather is close to the heart of much of the religious life.

References

Altemeyer, B., & Hunsberger, B. (2005). Fundamentalism and authoritarianism. In R. Paloutzian & C. Park (Eds.), *Handbook of the psychology of religion and spirituality* (pp. 378–393). New York, NY: Guilford Press.

Atran, S. (2002). *In Gods we trust.* New York, NY: Oxford University Press.

Atran, S. (2003). Genesis of suicide terrorism. *Science, 299,* 1534–1539. doi:10.1126/science.1078854

Atran, S. (2006). The moral logic and growth of suicide terrorism. *Washington Quarterly, 29,* 127–147. doi:10.1162/wash.2006.29.2.127

Atran, S. (2008). Who becomes a terrorist today? *Perspectives on Terrorism,* 2(5). Retrieved from http://www.terrorismanalysis.com

Bandura, A. (1998). Mechanisms of moral disengagement. In W. Reich (Ed.), *Origins of terrorism* (pp. 161–190). Washington, DC: Woodrow Wilson Center Press.

Bandura, A. (2004). The role of selective moral disengagement in terrorism and counterterrorism. In F. M. Moghaddam & A. Marsella (Eds.), *Understanding terrorism: Psychosocial roots, consequences, and interventions* (pp. 121–150). Washington, DC: American Psychological Association.

Blass, T. (Ed.). (2000). *Obedience to authority.* Mahwah, NJ: Erlbaum.

Brokaw, B., & Edwards, K. (1994). There is a relationship of god image to level of object relations development. *Journal of Psychology and Theology,* 22, 352–371.

Eidelson, R. J., & Eidelson, J. (2003). Dangerous ideas: Five beliefs that propel groups towards conflict. *American Psychologist, 58,* 182–192. doi:10.1037/0003-066X.58.3.182

Eisenberg, N., Valiente, C., & Champion, C. (2004). Empathy-related responding. In A. Miller (Ed.), *The social psychology of good and evil* (pp. 386–415). New York, NY: Guilford Press.

Freud, S. (1955). Group psychology and the analysis of the ego. In James Strachey (Ed.), *Standard edition of the complete psychological works of Sigmund Freud* (Vol. 18, pp. 67–143). London, England: Hogarth Press. (Original work published in 1921)

Galanter, M. (1989). *Cults: Faith, healing, and coercion.* New York, NY: Oxford University Press.

Gilligan, J. (1996). *Violence.* New York, NY: Random House.

Hafez, M. (2006). Rationality, culture, and structure in the making of suicide bombers. *Studies in Conflict and Terrorism, 29,* 165–185.

Horgan, J. (2005). *The psychology of terrorism.* London, England: Routledge.

Jones, J. (2002). *Terror and transformation: The ambiguity of religion in psychoanalytic perspective.* London, England; New York, NY: Routledge.

Jones, J. (2006). Why does religion turn violent? A psychoanalytic exploration of religious terrorism. *Psychoanalytic Review, 93,* 167–190. doi:10.1521/prev.2006.93.2.167

Jones, J. (2008). *Blood that cries out from the earth: The psychology of religious terrorism.* New York, NY: Oxford University Press. doi:10.1093/acprof:oso/9780195335972.001.0001

Jones, J. (2010). Eternal warfare: Violence on the mind on American apocalyptic Christianity. In C. Strozier, D. Terman, J. Jones, & K. Boyd (Eds.), *The fundamentalist mindset* (pp. 91–103). New York, NY: Oxford University Press. doi:10.1093/acprof:oso/9780195379655.003.0009

Kernberg, O. (1998). *Ideology, conflict, and leadership in groups and organizations.* New Haven, CT: Yale University Press.

Khosrokhavar, F. (2005). *Suicide bombers: Allah's new martyrs* (D. Macey, Trans). London, England: Pluto Press.

Kimball, C. (2002). *When religion becomes evil.* San Francisco, CA: Harper.

Kohut, H. (1972). Thoughts on narcissism and narcissistic rage. *Psychoanalytic Study of the Child, 27,* 360–400.

Kohut, H. (1977). *The restoration of the self.* Madison, CT: International Universities Press.

Lifton, R. (2000). *Destroying the world to save it.* New York, NY: Henry Holt-Owl Books.

Mahoney, A., Pargament, K., Murray-Swank, A., & Murray-Swank, N. (2003). Religion and the sanctification of family relationships. *Review of Religious Research, 44,* 220–236. doi:10.2307/3512384

McCauley, C. (2006). Jujitsu politics: Terrorism and responses to terrorism. In P. Kimmel & C. Stout (Eds.), *Collateral damage* (pp. 45–65). Westport, CT: Praeger.

McCullough, M., Pargament, K., & Thoresen, C. (2000). *Forgiveness: Theory research and practice.* New York, NY: Guilford Press.

McCullough, M., Root, C., Tabak, B., & Witvliet, C. (2009). Forgiveness. In S. Lopez & C. Snyder (Eds.), *The Oxford handbook of positive psychology* (pp. 427–435). New York, NY: Oxford University Press.

Milgram, S. (1974). *Obedience to authority.* New York, NY: Harper & Row.

Miller, A. (2004). What can the Milgram obedience experiments tell us about the Holocaust? In A. Miller (Ed.), *The social psychology of good and evil* (pp. 193–239). New York, NY: Guilford Press.

Miller, W. (1993). *Humiliation and other essays on honor, social discomfort, and violence.* Ithaca, NY: Cornell University Press.

Moghaddam, F. M. (2005). The staircase to terrorism: A psychological exploration. *American Psychologist, 60,* 161–169. doi:10.1037/0003-066X.60.2.161

Moghaddam, F. M., & Marsella, A. (2004). *Understanding terrorism: Psychosocial roots, consequences, and interventions.* Washington, DC: American Psychological Association.

Murray-Swank, N., Pargament, K., & Mahoney, A. (2000, August). *The sanctification of sexuality in loving relationships.* Paper presented at the 108th Annual Convention of the American Psychological Association, Washington, DC.

Myers, E., Hewstone, M., & Cairns, E. (2009). Impact of conflict on mental health in Northern Ireland: The mediating role of forgiveness and collective guilt. *Political Psychology, 30,* 269–290. doi:10.1111/j.1467-9221.2008.00691.x

Nepstad, S. (2004). Religion, violence, and peacemaking. *Journal for the Scientific Study of Religion, 43,* 297–301. doi:10.1111/j.1468-5906.2004.00235.x

Pargament, K., Magyar, G., Benore, E., & Mahoney, A. (2005). Sacrilege: A study of loss and desecration. *Journal for the Scientific Study of Religion, 44,* 59–78. doi:10.1111/j.1468-5906.2005.00265.x

Pargament, K., & Mahoney, A. (2005). Sacred matters: Sanctification as a vital topic for the psychology of religion. *The International Journal for the Psychology of Religion, 15,* 179–198. doi:10.1207/s15327582ijpr1503_1

Pargament, K., Trevino, K., Mahoney, A., & Silberman, I. (2007). They killed our Lord: The persecution of Jews as desecrators of Christianity as a predictor of anti-Semitism. *Journal for the Scientific Study of Religion, 46,* 143–158. doi:10.1111/j.1468-5906.2007.00347.x

Post, J. (1984). Notes on a psychodynamic theory of terrorist behavior. *Terrorism, 7,* 241–256. doi:10.1080/10576108408435577

Post, J. (1998). Terrorist psycho-logic. In W. Reich (Ed.), *Origins of terrorism* (pp. 25–42). Washington, DC: Woodrow Wilson Center Press.

Post, J. (2007). *The mind of the terrorist.* New York, NY: Palgrave Macmillan.

Post, J., Ruby, K., & Shaw, F. (2002). The radical group in context. *Studies in Conflict and Terrorism, 25,* 73–100. doi:10.1080/10576100275350246б

Post, J., Sprinzak, E., & Denny, L. (2003). The terrorists in their own words: Interviews with 35 incarcerated Middle Eastern terrorists. *Terrorism and Political Violence, 15,* 171–184. doi:10.1080/09546550312331293007

Reader, I. (2000). *Religious violence in contemporary Japan: The case of Aum Shinrikyo.* London, England: Curzon Press.

Reich, W. (Ed.). (1998). *Origins of terrorism.* Washington, DC: Woodrow Wilson Center Press.

Robins, R., & Post, J. (1997). *Political paranoia: The psychopolitics of hatred.* New Haven, CT: Yale University Press.

Sageman, M. (2008). *Leaderless jihad.* Philadelphia: University of Pennsylvania Press.

Silberman, I. (2005). Religious violence, terrorism, and peace. In R. Paloutzian & C. Park (Eds.), *Handbook of the psychology of religion and spirituality* (pp. 529–549). New York, NY: Guilford Press.

Silberman, I., Higgins, E., & Dweck, C. (2005). Religion and world change: Violence, terrorism versus peace. *Journal of Social Issues, 61,* 761–784. doi:10.1111/j.1540-4560.2005.00431.x

Spear, K. (1994). *Conscious and pre-conscious God representations: An object relations perspective.* Unpublished doctoral dissertation, Fuller Theological Seminary, Pasadena, CA.

Staub, E., Pearlman, L., Gubin, A., & Hagengimana, A. (2005). Healing, reconciliation, forgiving and the prevention of violence after genocide and mass killing. *Journal of Social and Clinical Psychology, 24,* 297–334. doi:10.1521/jscp.24.3.297.65617

Stern, J. (2003). *Terror in the name of God.* New York, NY: Ecco Press.

Strozier, C. (1994). *Apocalypse: On the psychology of fundamentalism in America.* Boston, MA: Beacon Press.

Strozier, C., Terman, D., Jones, J., & Boyd, K. (2010). *The fundamentalist mindset.* New York, NY: Oxford University Press. doi:10.1093/acprof:oso/9780195379655.001.0001

Tarakeshwar, N., Swank, A., Pargament, K., & Mahoney, A. (2001). The sanctification of nature and theological conservatism. *Review of Religious Research, 42,* 387–404. doi:10.2307/3512131

Tisdale, T. (1997). *A comparison of Jewish, Muslim, and Protestant faith groups on the relationship between level of object relations development and experience of God and self.* Unpublished doctoral dissertation, Rosemead Graduate School, LaMirada, CA.

Tobeña, A. (2004). Individual factors in suicide terrorists: A reply to S. Atran. *Science, 304*, 47–49. doi:10.1126/science.304.5667.47

Victoroff, J. (2005). The mind of the terrorist: A review and critique of psychological approaches. *Journal of Conflict Resolution, 49*, 3–42. doi:10.1177/0022002704272040

Volkan, V. (1997). *Bloodlines: From ethnic pride to ethnic terrorism.* New York, NY: Farrar, Straus, and Giroux.

Volkan, V. (2004). *Blind trust: Large groups and their leaders in times of crises and terror.* Charlottesville, VA: Pitchstone.

Waller, J. (2002). *Becoming evil.* New York, NY: Oxford University Press.

Wessinger, C. (2000). *How the millennium comes violently.* New York, NY: Seven Bridges Press.

Worthington, E. (2006). *Forgiveness and reconciliation: Theory and application.* New York, NY: Routledge.

Wulff, D. (1991). *Psychology of religion.* New York, NY: Wiley.

Zimbardo, P. (2004). A situationalist perspective on the psychology of evil. In A. Miller (Ed.), *The social psychology of good and evil* (pp. 21–50). New York, NY: Guilford Press.

Zimbardo, P., Maslach, C., & Haney, C. (2000). Reflections on the Stanford prison experiment. In T. Blass (Ed.), *Obedience to authority* (pp. 193–237). Mahwah, NJ: Erlbaum.

Chapter 19

RELIGIOUS AND SPIRITUAL DIMENSIONS OF TRAUMATIC VIOLENCE

Roger D. Fallot and Andrea K. Blanch

Events of the past decade, including the terrorist attacks on September 11, clergy sexual abuse scandals, high-profile violence against women and minority groups, and ongoing combat in many areas of the world have focused attention on the prevalence and impact of traumatic violent events. Simultaneously, people's frequent "turn to religion" (Schuster et al., 2007) after such events has raised many questions about the place of spirituality and religion in relation to trauma. This chapter will explore (a) our working definition of trauma in the context of interpersonal violence and the impact of interpersonal trauma on psychological well-being; (b) spirituality and religion in the aftermath of trauma, including the place of spiritual and religious resources in trauma recovery and healing; and (c) the relationships between religious contexts and interpersonal violence, including the impact of religious abuse and the role of religious involvement in violence prevention. We will conclude with some recommendations for developing trauma-informed services and communities that reflect knowledge about religion, spirituality, violence, and trauma recovery.

INTERPERSONAL VIOLENCE AND TRAUMA: DEFINITION AND CONSEQUENCES

To understand the importance of spirituality and religion in the context of interpersonal violence, it is first necessary to define trauma and to describe some of its common consequences.

Definitional Issues

Although virtually all traumatic events are relevant to the discussion of the relation between trauma and religion or spirituality, we will focus on the often-devastating experience of violence. Interpersonal violence takes many forms and can occur in many contexts. In childhood and adolescence, physical, sexual, and emotional abuse are common as are experiences of bullying and peer and gang violence (Finkelhor, 2011). Community-based surveys report that many adults have experienced physical and sexual assaults (Kessler, Sonnega, Bromet, Hughes, & Nelson, 1995). Violence occurs in the home and family (including intimate partner violence); on the streets; in institutions, such as schools, faith communities, and jails; in human trafficking; in terrorism and torture; in refugee settings; and in combat. Violence may be embedded in historical trauma, such as that experienced over generations by African Americans, Native Americans, women, and other groups, including those identified primarily by their religious affiliation. People experience violence both directly and indirectly, as witnesses to violence perpetrated on others. Finally, violence may occur in a single incident or be repeated and prolonged.

Virtually all of these forms of violence constitute potentially traumatic events. Whether or not they become "psychologically traumatic" depends on the impact they have on the individual. Definitions of psychological trauma therefore have often been two-sided, drawing on both "objective" and "subjective" indicators. For example, Calhoun and Tedeschi (2006) stated that traumatically stressful or "seismic"

DOI: 10.1037/14046-019
APA Handbook of Psychology, Religion, and Spirituality: Vol. 2. An Applied Psychology of Religion and Spirituality, K. I. Pargament (Editor-in-Chief)

events have the unique capacity to disrupt personal narratives, to divide one's experience into a "before and after" (pp. 8–9). For the purposes of this chapter, we consider psychologically traumatic those experiences of violence that overwhelm a person's internal and external resources for positive coping. By placing additional weight on the individual's experience, this definition takes seriously the tremendous range of events that might be traumatizing (or retraumatizing) for a particular person, especially on the basis of their histories of previous exposure to adversity. Because people intentionally commit acts of interpersonal violence—in contrast to those potentially traumatic events that we think of as "natural"—violence frequently has unique contextual meanings. One example is "betrayal trauma," in which those who have relational or caretaking responsibilities use their power abusively (Freyd, 1998).

Consequences of Traumatic Events

Studies of the *negative* impact of psychological trauma have often centered on posttraumatic stress disorder (PTSD). The consequences of trauma, however, especially of repeated violent victimization, extend well beyond PTSD and its three hallmark symptoms of arousal, reexperiencing, and avoidance. The negative effects of exposure to trauma include depression, anger or hostility, generalized anxiety, interpersonal difficulties, substance abuse, and physical health problems. The Adverse Childhood Experiences Study has provided extensive documentation of the risks associated with childhood trauma: mental health problems (depression, suicidality, hallucinations), substance use (smoking, intravenous [IV] drug use, alcoholism), impaired work performance, physical health problems (liver disease, heart disease—after controlling for the usual predisposing factors), and mortality, among others (Felitti & Anda, 2010). The strength of these relationships is noteworthy. For example, population-attributable risk results indicate that 54% of current depression and 58% of suicide attempts in women can be attributed to adverse childhood experiences (Felitti & Anda, 2010). Although the PTSD literature has been very helpful in addressing single-incident traumas and their neurobiological and psychological impact, PTSD alone cannot adequately reflect response to the kinds of multiple, repeated adversities to which many people, especially children, are exposed.

In spite of the challenges faced by those who are exposed to violence, trauma may ultimately lead to *positive* changes, such as those summarized as posttraumatic growth (PTG; Tedeschi & Calhoun, 1996). Calhoun and Tedeschi (2006) described several psychosocial domains that characterize their understanding of PTG. First, trauma survivors may develop a stronger sense of self, as those who have survived horrific events and simultaneously may acknowledge the strength it took to do so. Second, individuals may report that accompanying this renewed sense of self is an openness to new possibilities and new goals for the future. For example, many survivors describe a sense of mission, a plan to ensure others' safety and well-being that grows out of seeing clearly their own vulnerability and strength. In a related way, persons sometimes report that their exposure to trauma has left them with greater compassion for other people in general, especially for those who suffer. Enhanced empathy is one marker of stress-related growth.

Although it is important for researchers and practitioners to attend to processes of PTG or "growth following adversity" (Joseph & Linley, 2008), these concepts may have limited applicability to the experiences of some individuals and groups. For example, those who have been abused repeatedly in childhood may not have had the time to develop the coherent sense of self, with well-established assumptive worlds, presumed in most PTG studies (cf. Janoff-Bulman, 2006). Many survivors of childhood abuse and neglect face the primary challenge of forming a valued sense of self, with necessary personal and social skills, rather than transforming an already established self. PTG may be more useful in understanding responses to single traumatic events, such as a violent assault in youth or adulthood; concepts such as recovery and healing may be more helpful in understanding responses to repeated and prolonged exposure to violence (for a discussion of self-healing, see the section Spirituality in Interventions Designed to Facilitate Trauma Recovery and Growth later in this chapter). Though "recovery" does not necessarily entail a return to pretrauma levels of well-being or functioning, it does mean that the recovering person is assimilating and working through the trauma in a way that offers hope for a chosen and positive life course.

RECIPROCAL RELATIONSHIPS: RELIGION AND SPIRITUALITY AFTER TRAUMA

Attempts to describe the complex biological, psychological, and interpersonal sequelae of trauma raise important questions about the relation of trauma to spirituality and religion. For example, van der Kolk (2005) has argued persuasively for the inclusion of "developmental trauma disorder" as a particularly needed diagnostic category. While acknowledging the resilience of many children exposed to chronic childhood abuse or neglect, he described the often broad-ranging impact of such maltreatment, including altered schemas of the world in general, increased skepticism and distrust of others, and a sense of lost recourse to social justice. In discussing the effects of such experiences on adults, Herman (1992) also outlined the need for an alternative descriptor, "complex PTSD." Among the frequent characteristic adaptations to prolonged coercive control and abuse in either childhood or adulthood, in addition to alterations in consciousness and changed perceptions of self and others, are "alterations in systems of meaning," including a "loss of sustaining faith" and a "sense of hopelessness and despair" (Herman, 1992, p. 121). In a similar way, Briere and Rickards (2007) reported that the impact of childhood emotional and sexual maltreatment may lead to disturbed "self-capacities," including problems with identity, interpersonal relationships, and affect regulation. Spirituality and religion have much to contribute to understanding this whole-person impact of trauma.

There are serious methodological flaws in much of the research examining the impact of trauma on religious or spiritual beliefs and behaviors. Many studies examining this issue are based on convenience sampling of specialized groups, and most have not controlled for background factors that might predispose individuals to abuse or to religiousness (Bierman, 2005). Two recent reviews, however, provide convincing evidence that the experience of interpersonal trauma affects subsequent measures of religious beliefs and behaviors (Chen & Koenig, 2006; Walker, Reid, O'Neill, & Brown, 2009). In a review of 34 studies of child abuse and later measures of spirituality and religiosity, with a total of more than 19,000 participants, Walker et al. (2009) found that 14 studies showed a decline of religiousness, 12 showed a combination of growth and decline, and seven gave preliminary indications that religiousness or spirituality can moderate the development of posttraumatic symptoms. Similarly, in a review of 11 cross-sectional studies of the impact of trauma on religion and spirituality, Chen and Koenig (2006) found three studies reporting a negative relationship between trauma and religiousness, four reporting a positive relationship, and three reporting mixed associations. Some of this variability is almost certainly due to the use of different measures of religious and spiritual beliefs and behavior. The 11 studies reviewed by Chen and Koenig (2006) had 10 different operational definitions of spirituality and religion, including spiritual beliefs, well-being, and coping; religious faith, beliefs, and coping; beliefs in the afterlife and reincarnation; intrinsic religious orientation; and change in religious faith.

Trauma can affect religion or spirituality *negatively*, undermining the belief in a benevolent God or a meaningful universe, or limiting the individual's ability to "be intimate" with God (Bilich, Bonfiglio, & Carlson, 2000). Research indicates that trauma may affect an individual's image of God, their religious beliefs and faith, and their religious practice. Doehring (1993) found that trauma history in cases of severe trauma or complex PTSD was associated with negative images of God. Falsetti, Resick, and Davis (2003) reported a relationship between PTSD and a loss of religious beliefs following the first traumatic event. Fontana and Rosenheck (2004) found that in a group of war veterans in treatment for PTSD, the experience of killing others and failing to prevent death weakened religious faith, both directly and as mediated by feelings of guilt. Elliott (1994) reported that religious practice decreased for conservative Christian women professionals after they were sexually abused (particularly after abuse within the immediate family); however, religious practice increased for agnostics, atheists, and adherents of other faiths.

Gender also appears to play a role. Ganzevoort (2002) suggested that for sexually abused boys, aspects of masculine gender identity contribute to a negative or even dysfunctional posttraumatic spirituality. Gender may also interact with the perpetrator of the trauma because abuse by fathers but not by mothers has a negative impact on religiosity (Ganzevoort, 2006). Bierman (2005) suggested that this finding may reflect the Jewish and Christian traditions of explicitly viewing God as a "father," leading the victim to see all higher powers as potentially abusive.

In addition to trauma's negative effects on religion and spirituality, trauma recovery may in turn be adversely affected by specific religious or spiritual concerns. Certain *styles* of religious and spiritual believing, like experiencing "spiritual struggles" (Exline & Rose, 2005; see also Volume 1, Chapter 25, this handbook) and "negative religious coping" (e.g., Pargament, 1997) seem especially problematic. For example, Pargament, Smith, Koenig, and Perez (1998) have described the ways in which negative religious coping (involving punishing or abandoning God (re)appraisals, spiritual and interpersonal religious discontent, and demonic reappraisals, among others) is related to more mental health problems following trauma exposure. Exline (2002) described several of the potential difficulties in the religious life, "stumbling blocks" that may interfere with the individual's achieving more positive outcomes. In a multisite study of women abuse survivors with co-occurring mental health and substance use problems, Fallot and Heckman (2005) found that negative religious coping was related to a number of trauma-related and other mental health symptoms. Using very different methods and a much broader sampling of the population, Newberg and Waldman (2009) reported that meditating on negative God images, including "ruminating" on God-related problems, has distinctive and possibly negative effects on the brain, resulting in a more reactive and often-irritable mood state. The picture is consistent: Coping with trauma in ways that focus on the difficulties one experiences with God or the sacred is associated with more problematic mental health outcomes.

In contrast to these deleterious effects of trauma on religion or spirituality, for decades, trauma survivors have also spoken eloquently about the *positive* ways in which their trauma experiences have helped them to gain spiritual wisdom and strength. The literature on posttraumatic growth explicitly addresses this possibility: "It is in the realm of existential and, for some persons, spiritual and religious matters, that the most significant PTG may be experienced" (Calhoun & Tedeschi, 2006, p. 6). Research suggests that even severe forms of interpersonal trauma may strengthen people's religious beliefs and practices. Başoğlu et al. (2005) found that compared with controls, people who had survived war in the former Yugoslavia (with at least one war-related stressor) had stronger faith in God. Similarly, survivors of torture had more posttraumatic growth and practiced their religion more than survivors of "general trauma" (Kira et al., 2006). In some cases, trauma may lead people to separate themselves from formal religious practices while maintaining a "sense of the mystical" in their lives and turning to a more personal form of spirituality (Bierman, 2005). Calhoun and Tedeschi (2006) noted that PTG frequently involves a "changed philosophy of life" (p. 6), including enhanced appreciation for life in general and a reordering of particular life priorities (e.g., devoting more time to family and less to work). Survivors frequently frame such changes in spiritual or religious language. In a long-term follow-up (average of 16 years postassault) study of women sexual assault survivors, 56% reported a greater appreciation of life and 47% noted increased spiritual well-being (Frazier & Berman, 2008). Kennedy, Davis, and Taylor (1998) found that 60% of the women sampled 9 to 24 months after a sexual assault reported increased spirituality, whereas 20% reported decreased spirituality. Positive changes in one's spiritual life are thus not uncommon among survivors of violence.

Just as trauma can have positive effects on one's spiritual well-being, a significant body of evidence supports the potentially reciprocal value of spirituality and religion in trauma recovery. For example, positive religious coping (including spiritual support-seeking, collaborating with God in dealing with the stressor, and benevolent religious reappraisal) has been related to more sanguine mental health outcomes (Pargament, 2010; see also Volume 1, Chapter 19, this handbook). Newberg and Waldman (2009) summarized their own research and a wide range of other projects in the book *How God Changes Your Brain*. Drawing on studies of transcendental meditation, prayer, and other spiritual activities, they reported that thinking about a loving and caring God while in a meditative state facilitates a calm, peaceful, and attentive state of mind. Although believing more strongly in a particular meditative content may deepen this effect, Newberg and Waldman found very similar patterns of brain responses in Christian contemplatives and Buddhist practitioners. They concluded that the "ritual techniques of breathing, staying relaxed, and focusing one's attention upon a concept that evokes comfort, compassion, or a spiritual sense of peace" (Newberg & Waldman, 2009, p. 48) is key to achieving this sense of calm.

Specific coping strategies people use after a traumatic experience may affect the impact of trauma on religion and spirituality and help to account for this mixed pattern of positive and negative consequences, Furthermore, these distinct ways of responding to trauma may help to explain the positive and negative roles of spirituality and religion in trauma recovery. As Pargament et al. (1998) have demonstrated, positive and negative religious coping are both common responses to traumatic events and have quite different impacts on the aftermath of trauma (Pargament et al., 1998; Pargament, Desai, & McConnell, 2006). Krumrei, Mahoney, and Pargament (2009) described three different spiritual responses to divorce: Appraising the event as a sacred loss and desecration, engaging in adaptive spiritual coping, and experiencing spiritual struggles. J. I. Harris et al. (2008) noted two similar coping responses in a sample of church-going self-identified trauma survivors: seeking spiritual support and religious strain. Trauma that is malicious and intentional (as in sexual abuse) may be far more devastating to an individual's sense of a benevolent universe than an unintended tragedy, and may directly affect the choice of religious coping strategy, the resultant change in religious or spiritual beliefs or behaviors, and spirituality's place in trauma recovery.

Some authors have suggested that the complicated relationship between trauma and religion or spirituality is directly attributable to the meaning-making process over time. Trauma may initially destroy existing structures of meaning, including religious beliefs, but later attempts to reconstruct a sense of meaning may actually spur the individual to higher levels of faith or spiritual development (Bierman, 2005). In a review of 23 studies, Schaefer, Blazer, and Koenig (2008) found preliminary indications that the impact of trauma on religion or spirituality changes depending on time after the event, suggesting that people go through a process of interpreting and reinterpreting their experience and its relationship to their religious beliefs. Religious beliefs may provide a framework and tools for reappraising circumstances and events, restoring a sense of well-being, or even catalyzing a process of PTG (see Shaw, Joseph, & Linley, 2005; see also Volume 1, Chapters 8 and 19, this handbook).

SPIRITUALITY IN INTERVENTIONS DESIGNED TO FACILITATE TRAUMA RECOVERY AND GROWTH

The relationship between religion and traumatic stress is thus a complicated one; the literature sometimes appears to support the value of spiritual responses to trauma and at other times reports that religion or spirituality undermines recovery. The broad question (i.e., Does religion or spirituality assist or impede trauma recovery?) is better reframed in more specific terms: For whom, drawing on what particular expressions of religion or spirituality, at what points in the recovery process, and on the basis of what outcomes, is religion or spirituality more likely to be helpful or harmful? Although the early stages of research in this area, characterized largely by cross-sectional and correlational studies with a plethora of measures, do not permit clear answers to these questions, clinicians and researchers have begun to describe ways to maximize the positive role spirituality and religion may play in healing from trauma.

Individual Psychotherapies

In the past decade, several comprehensive models for integrating spirituality and religion into psychotherapy have been developed (Pargament, 2007; Plante, 2009; Richards & Bergin, 2005). Practitioners interested in the application of these approaches to individual work with trauma survivors are encouraged to familiarize themselves with the many options available for appropriately bringing discussions of spirituality and religion into the therapy relationship. Pargament (2007) provided an especially rich array of examples that involve potentially traumatic events and the many ways people have found to cope with them spiritually or religiously. Recognizing the possible negative as well as positive outcomes related to the use of spiritual coping techniques, he has offered a thoughtful way to assess spirituality (implicitly and explicitly) early in the relationship.

Because there is much overlap between such "integrative" psychotherapies in general and those that may be helpful to trauma survivors, we address two themes in individual work that are especially salient for trauma recovery: narrative and self-healing. The first theme focuses on narrative approaches to understanding and (re)forming a sense of self. Many theologians, psychologists and physicians have placed central importance on the stories that give shape and structure to individual lives. Narrative approaches are particularly appropriate for efforts to grapple with the complexities of religion, spirituality, and trauma responses. Spiritual and religious elements frequently play a significant part in both larger individual life stories ("macronarratives") and smaller life episodes ("micronarratives"; Neimeyer, 2004). In addition, they constitute key elements of most *cultural* understandings and thus remind us of the importance of the cultural contexts in which violent trauma is experienced and interpreted. These cultural and subcultural narratives, and their religious or spiritual expressions, then may offer significant resources for, and obstacles to, recovery and healing. Cultural narratives provide guidelines for constructing meaningful, coherent, and self-strengthening personal stories, and these cultural parameters are likely to be as diverse as the societies and historical eras that they reflect (Pals & McAdams, 2004).

For example, "being delivered" emerged as a key theme in one grounded theory study of the responses of men and women survivors of sexual violence (Knapik, Martsolf, & Drucker, 2008). The concept of "being delivered" refers to survivors' sense of being "rescued, saved, or set free from the effects of sexual violence by a spiritual being or power" (Knapik et al., 2008, p. 335); it draws heavily on liberation and freedom motifs in U.S. culture and Jewish and Christian religious history. Similarly, in another study, women survivors of sexual abuse reported that their sense of God as a companion or friend offered them a needed resource for recovery:

> One [woman] talked about the necessity of having a "working relationship" with God. In contrast to some other relationships, she noted that she had always felt capable of standing up to God. "God had to prove to *me* He was real. I wasn't going to confess without proof." Another woman described her prayer conversations with God in this way: "I make a joke with God. I fuss with Him if it doesn't work out—like Job." (Fallot, 1997, p. 344)

The friend- or companion-God was discussed alongside the all-powerful God in these women's stories; distinctive God images existed comfortably with each other and had complementary roles to play in support of recovery.

The first lessons to be drawn from a narrative approach are to listen carefully to the spontaneous stories that survivors tell about their experiences, and to put them in historical and sociocultural context. Neimeyer (2004) described three distinct kinds of "narrative disruptions" especially likely to emerge in response to trauma: disorganized narratives flooded with overwhelming images; dissociated narratives that are compartmentalized both internally and interpersonally; and dominant narratives that prescribe an individual's identity and are enforced socially, politically, or culturally. It is not difficult to weave spiritual and religious resources into Neimeyer's account of how these narratives can be reconstructed in therapeutic relationships. Disorganized narratives may respond well to meditation or guided imagery (Newberg & Waldman, 2009), both of which may be supplemented with spiritual content that is meaningful to the survivor. Dissociated narratives may be particularly responsive to a faith community that is accepting and affirming of all parts of the individual's story. A woman abuse survivor, for example, reported the incredible impact of finding herself actively valued by church members even though her substance abuse and other ways of coping with the violence in her life had distanced her from friends and family (Fallot, 1997). Dominant narratives that require challenging (e.g., "real men are never victims") can be engaged by exploring alternative stories (e.g., of religious figures who persevered in spite of the violence done to them). All of these alternative narratives must be rooted in, and accessible to, the experience of the individual survivor and her or his culture. Images of potentially life-transforming events, especially those in which positive changes occur in spite of rather than because of the event, are part of most Western religious traditions. By attending to the content, style, tone, and emphases of the stories of trauma survivors, the therapist may gain greater access to implicit or explicit spiritual resources to facilitate healing.

The second main theme for clinicians to consider in working with trauma survivors is the possibility of "self-healing" (Mollica, 2006). Drawing on his extensive experience with refugees around the world, Mollica (2006) focused repeatedly on what he considers a fundamental capacity of human beings: "After violence occurs, a self-healing process is immediately activated, transforming, through physical and mental responses, the damage that has occurred to the psychological and social self" (p. 94). Consistent with many narrative concepts, a primary path to recovery is through the telling of the trauma story to a listener who is able to be helpful, not through interpretations or advice, but though empathic engagement with the experienced reality of the storyteller. Mollica's fully told "trauma story" has four parts: (a) a factual recounting of what happened; (b) the cultural meaning of the trauma; (c) an opportunity to "look behind the curtain," or gain perspective, including appropriate distance from the intensity of the trauma and wisdom; and (d) a telling of the story to an enthusiastically immersed listener who is willing to learn from the storyteller.

Most important for the purposes of this chapter is Mollica's (2006) conviction that spirituality, along with altruism and work, are key factors in healing from violent trauma. He described vividly some of the ways in which spiritual activities, on both a personal and community level, can facilitate the self-healing process. For example, the commitment to pursuing a spiritual "discipline," such as prayer, meditation, or reading holy writings, engages the individual's capacity to control often-uncontrolled affective states and to make meaning of the violent events. Preserving adaptive spiritual resources or finding new relationships to previously held spiritual beliefs and activities may both be part of trauma healing. Mollica's work focuses on the place of culture as the bearer of spiritual and religious beliefs and rituals and on the capacity of people to discover unknown strengths within themselves, other people, and the divine or sacred in coming to terms with horrifically destructive life events. The model of "therapist as listener and learner" is a helpful reminder of the value of this stance and of the importance of validating the survivor's story of recovery.

Group Therapies

Group therapies for responding to trauma have proliferated in recent years and several explicitly encourage the exploration or use of spiritual and religious recovery resources. Pargament (2007) has compiled a list of manualized spiritually integrative therapies, most of which are primarily offered in-group settings. Only one of these, Solace for the Soul (Murray-Swank & Pargament, 2005) has a primary goal of facilitating recovery from violence, in this case, sexual abuse (see Chapter 17 in this volume). Several of the group interventions, however, address populations that have been traumatized or that are likely to have extensive trauma histories. For example, one addresses the needs of women with HIV and another focuses on addiction and HIV risk behavior; both of these groups have very high rates of trauma exposure.

Bowland's (2008; Bowland, Edmond, & Fallot, 2012) recent research provides an instructive example of the potential effectiveness of this kind of group approach to spirituality. She conducted a small ($N = 43$) randomized controlled trial of a manualized 11-session group model designed to

> address the ways in which participants' religious or spiritual experiences have been, and may be, related to trauma and recovery. It does not prescribe a particular spiritual path nor does it require a specific set of practices. Rather, it invites group members to reflect on their own spiritual journeys, to examine common trauma-related concerns, and to consider ways in which spirituality may offer them strength for coping with the impact of trauma. (Fallot & the Spirituality Workgroup, 2001–2004, p. 2)

Each of the sessions has a specific topic, goals, questions for discussion, and an experiential exercise. The session topics include, among others, "What It Means To Be Spiritual," "Spiritual Gifts," "Spiritual Coping Strategies," "Anger," Shame and Guilt," "Forgiveness and Letting Go," and "Hope and Vision."

Bowland's study (2008) included women (55 and older) who had histories of interpersonal trauma (childhood physical or sexual abuse, intimate partner violence, or sexual assault). Postgroup interviews revealed that the spirituality group participants had significantly lower depressive symptoms, anxiety, and physical symptoms and higher spiritual well-being than a group of wait-list controls. Posttraumatic stress symptoms and spiritual distress also dropped significantly in the spirituality group. These gains were sustained at 3-month follow-up.

These findings need to be contextualized by returning to the questions of for whom and at what point in recovery such interventions may be helpful. The participants were all women who, in spite of their histories of trauma exposure, were not currently in crisis nor were they participating in psychotherapy of another sort. They were all part of the Christian tradition; all had at least mild trauma-related symptoms and self-reported spiritual struggles related to their abuse experiences; and all indicated that they might benefit from participating in a "group discussing religious and spiritual issues in recovery." In short, the women participants were selected appropriately—that is, they "fit" well with the stated goals of the group, including motivation to join. One of the key lessons for practitioners is that a careful assessment of potential group members' backgrounds (psychological and spiritual or religious), current functioning (e.g., level of support needed), and current situations (e.g., dangerous relationships) is essential to constituting an effective group.

The voices of survivors in Bowland's study provide a glimpse of the ways in which group discussions may be helpful. "Vicki" had experienced domestic violence and had also been raped by a man in her workplace. She said, "I still need to forgive myself for not struggling when I was raped at gunpoint. My early religious understanding of the virgin saints was that they died rather than suffer violation." Her work on minimizing self-blame and on forgiving herself may plausibly be related to her very significant decrease in depressive symptoms. Women who made the greatest improvements generated more positive responses to the group in their postsession journals (Bowland, Evearitt, Sharma, & Linfield, 2010). These qualitative reports included comments indicating social support ("It is a great group and [I] want to talk more with them and share with each other") and spiritual support ("It is becoming a resource, but I am having to create my own version of God that is very different from my childhood version"). In addition, participants reported the value of self-efficacy, hopeful recognition of problems, and receiving helpful information ("Interesting speculation on 'original sin.' I thought about a book I read on original blessing and like the idea of a loving and gracious God").

We have described the findings of this group study in greater detail not because of its uniqueness but because we have found such comments characteristic of discussions that frequently occur among survivors of interpersonal violence. Telling and retelling the trauma story—frequently, in small, manageable bits and pieces, and in the presence of supportive others—can enable survivors to conserve, rework, and discover spiritual and religious resources that facilitate healing.

TRAUMA AND INSTITUTIONAL POWER: THE IMPACT OF RELIGIOUS ABUSE

No chapter on trauma and religion or spirituality can ignore the issue of abuse of power within organized religious communities. Since 1983, when allegations of child sexual abuse were filed in Louisiana against a local Catholic priest (Frawley-O'Dea, 2007), repeated sexual abuse scandals have rocked institutional religion in the United States and around the globe. In addition to the Catholic church, sexual abuse of minors has been reported in the Australian Anglican church (Parkinson et al., 2009) and among Protestant ministers, Jewish rabbis, Islamic clerics, Buddhist monks, and Hare Krishna officials (Fogler, Shipard, Rowe, Jensen, & Clarke, 2008; Frawley-O'Dea, 2007). Unwanted sexual advances of religious leaders toward women congregants are also common across religious traditions (Chaves & Garland, 2009).

Any consideration of the role of religion and spirituality in trauma healing must begin with the recognition that some religious leaders are perpetrators and some religious structures may be seen as enabling abuse. Religious abuse has unique characteristics that deserve discussion, and any attempt to position religious and spiritual authorities as healers must reflect awareness of the potential for retraumatization for those who have experienced religious abuse.

Nature and Extent of the Problem

On the basis of data from the John Jay College of Criminal Justice (2004), it is estimated that between 1950 and 2004, at least 5,214 Roman Catholic priests were credibly accused of sexually abusing a minor—4.75% of the priesthood in the United States. These numbers are probably low for several reasons, including the reluctance of victims to report abuse: Studies indicate that up to a third of female victims and a higher percentage of males never disclose. In fact, Roman Catholic church experts estimate that 6% to 12% of the 50,000 priests in the United States have engaged in illegal sex with children under the age of 16 (Leyden-Rubenstein, 2002). Rates of abuse within the Catholic church are similar nationwide, with little variation between geographic regions or between urban and rural dioceses. Although the rate of sexual abuse in other faith traditions has not been as thoroughly researched as in the Catholic church, initial research suggests that Protestant churches are receiving equivalent numbers of child sexual abuse allegations (Clayton, 2002) and that Protestant and Catholic churches have similar rates of child sexual abuse among clergy (Jenkins, 1996). The lack of accountability within the church hierarchy has also been problematic. Frawley-O'Dea cited a report in 2002 that two thirds of all presiding Bishops had allowed accused priests to continue working in ministry and noted that "the cover up is the scandal" (p. 10).

Clergy sexual abuse is similar in many ways to sexual abuse of minors by coaches, scoutmasters, teachers, and other youth leaders. It is opportunistic, exploiting access to vulnerable and impressionable youth, and it is based on the misuse of authority and influence. Clergy abuse, however, also involves a misuse of spiritual power, and it involves fear, awe, and respect for clergy on the basis of religious faith and training—a factor that has been referred to as "religious duress." Religious duress can seriously impede a person's ability to perceive and evaluate abusive actions, and can lead to confusion, numbness, and inability to take action (Benkert & Doyle, 2009). In many ways, clergy abuse resembles incest—the betrayal of a trusted authority figure who is generally presumed to be loving and to have the youth's best interests at heart. Clinical observations suggest that the victim may also experience a crisis of faith, feeling that his or her actions have betrayed God (Gartner, 2004).

Consequences of Clergy Abuse

These dynamics can cause serious relational problems, including a distrust of authority figures, a tendency to see relationships in hierarchical, exploitative terms, distancing and isolation, and a general fear of forming relationships (Gartner, 2004). In addition, the lack of accountability for authorities in faith communities can create a sense of powerlessness and lack of worth—as if the community values clergy and institutional survival above the victims—and a sensitivity to all forms of impunity. Clergy sexual abuse can also have a profound impact on the relationship between the faith community and both the victim and the perpetrator.

Often, religious communities deny the abuse, attempt to cover it up, or blame the victim. As Fogler et al. (2008) pointed out, "It is certainly easier to condemn a single "deviant"/outgroup member than to question the goodness of the clergyman who represents the entire religious community" (pp. 317–318). Attitudes toward abusive clergy on the part of the religious community may be profoundly ambivalent and polarized, ranging from outright denial of the abuse to extreme demands for punishment of the clergy. Finally, people who have experienced religious-related abuse or exploitation or who have challenged the authoritarian structures of their religion may be shunned or scapegoated. Shunning may serve the faith community by strengthening the boundaries between internal conformity to norms and external behavior, but it can have devastating effects on the individual (Stark & Bainbridge, 1996).

Other Forms of Religious Trauma

The hierarchical and authoritarian structure of many organized religions represents a potential source of structural domination and oppression that may contribute to complex PTSD (Herman, 1992). Several authors have commented on theological constructs that can be distorted to become abusive. For example, the concept of "surrender" to God or a higher power can become mindless submission to destructive authority, forgiveness can be used to overlook or excuse abuse, and in some Christian traditions, suffering itself can be "valorized" (Frawley-O'Dea, 2007).

There is also much speculation about whether specific religious theologies can contribute to domestic violence and child abuse. Empirically speaking, according to research done on national or community samples, men and women who frequently attend religious services are about half as likely as nonattenders to perpetrate physical aggression against intimate partners, according to both partners (see review by Mahoney, 2010). Likewise, more frequent attenders also report less often being a victim of partner aggression in marital, cohabiting, or dating relationships. Furthermore, higher parental religious attendance substantially decreases the occurrence or potential of physical abuse (Mahoney, 2010). Thus, higher religious attendance appears to lower the risk of the occurrence of intimate violence in the general population (Mahoney, 2010). Yet scarce research exists on the role of religion within at-risk or dysfunctional families where intervention is needed because family violence has occurred or is very likely to occur (Mahoney, 2010). Qualitative research with female survivors indicates that some abusers use religious grounds to rationalize their abuse. Others may act without consequences because they are part of a fundamentalist religious group that endorses their position of power (Ganzevoort, 2006). Some victims may be consumed by a "sacred silence" on the issue or encouraged to remain in abusive situations to "save the family" (Nason-Clark, 2004).

Bottoms, Nielsen, Murray, and Filipas (2003) examined the long-term outcomes of child abuse justified in religious terms, using a retrospective design and a convenience sample of college students. They concluded that religion-related abuse has significantly more negative implications for victims' long-term psychological well-being than abuse that is not religion-related (Bottoms et al., 2003). Like other forms of abuse, the severity of the impact of abuse perpetrated under the guise of religion increases with the number and combination of abuse experiences (Goodman, Bottoms, Redlich, Shaver, & Diviak, 1998).

In contrast, for some victims and survivors, spirituality can sustain, heal, and even empower them to leave their abusers. In other cases, religious involvement may play a role in reducing the risk of violence. For example, religious perpetrators are more likely to stop battering when they attend programs with religious involvement and are more likely to complete batterers' programs when they are referred by clergy rather than by a judge (Nason-Clark, 2004). Ellison, Bartkowski, and Anderson (1999) found that regular attenders at religious services are less likely to be abusive to their partners. The mutual accountability of individual members of the faith community, in contrast to the ignoring of leaders' perpetration, may be one factor in this protective pattern (Nason-Clark, 2004).

IMPLICATIONS FOR CLINICAL PRACTICE

Psychologists interested in working at the interface of spirituality, religion, and trauma recovery may need to expand their awareness of the roles clergy and faith communities often play in response to interpersonal violence. As Weaver, Koenig, and Ochberg (1996) noted nearly 15 years ago, there is a clear need for collaboration among mental health and religious professionals, not least because of the fact that clergy are often among the first to respond in the aftermath of trauma (see also Chapter 26 in this volume). In addition, although research on the role of religious involvement in healing and preventing family violence is in its infancy, it is worth further exploration. Currently, as Nason-Clark (2004) pointed out, the "religious contours" of family violence often create a gap between "steeple" and "shelter," with secular professionals urging victims to leave the situation—and their faith—behind, and faith leaders reluctant to refer parishioners to outside help. More cooperation between these sectors could be fruitful.

Clinicians should also assume that they may see victims of religious trauma in their practices, whether or not they identify the trauma as such. Most forms of religious abuse have several things in common that the clinician needs to be alert to, including attributions of divine or absolute authority, a formal or informal hierarchy that reinforces the power of the perpetrator, theological justification for surrender, overt and subtle forms of retribution and control, and a cloak of secrecy. In addition to people who have themselves experienced religious abuse, members of victim's families, church communities, and the general public may experience vicarious trauma through the media and through the disruption of normal church functioning.

The primary responsibility of a therapist working with trauma survivors is to be trauma-informed, and in particular, to be aware of any aspect of the therapeutic environment that could potentially "trigger" (i.e., cause potentially overwhelming responses based on the original trauma for) survivors' self-protective responses. Because the therapeutic relationship can be seen as mirroring the pastoral relationship, with the therapist holding both knowledge and authority not available to the client, it is critical that practitioners be familiar with the specific ways in which religious authority has been misused, the steps taken (or not taken) by institutional religion to address these abuses, and the implications for trauma healing.

The implications for the clinical setting are clear. Individuals often view religious and spiritual leaders as holding the key to salvation, imbued with divine authority. In many cases, therapists have replaced clergy as "confessors," and transference of authority issues are likely.

Retraumatization of clients can occur from two different sources. First, the structure of the clinical relationship, the organized clinical setting, or the profession of psychology itself can potentially replicate conditions of the original abuse. For example, any trappings or invocation of authority (e.g., calling the therapist "Doctor") or accoutrements of power (e.g., wearing a white coat or having a diploma on the wall) can echo the organized hierarchical structure of religion, as can references to knowledge that is inaccessible to the "layperson" or allegiance to an "inner circle" with more power than those on the outside. Similarly, any instance of professional misconduct, regardless of how close or distant from the specific clinical setting, holds the potential to be retraumatizing. Minimizing accounts of misconduct, maintaining uncritical professional loyalty, or projecting blame onto others can trigger memories of clerical misconduct and impunity. An individual who has been abused and silenced by an authority figure can misconstrue as secrecy even the rules of confidentiality that apply to the therapeutic context, if the rules are applied in a rigid way.

Explicit introduction of religious or spiritual material into the clinical environment is also, of course, fraught with potential for retraumatization. The use of sacred texts, practices, symbols, or theological constructs may trigger survivors of religious abuse, as may working directly with clergy or spiritual leaders or being in an environment with incense, candles, stained glass windows, or organ music. Clinicians who seek to build a religious or spiritual component into their practice must be vigilant in examining both environment and behavior to avoid retraumatizing individuals who have been affected by abuse involving religion or spirituality—or, indeed, any abuse of power within an organized institutional setting.

Psychologists have devoted most of their clinical and research efforts at understanding the reality of trauma at an individual or family level. Increasing evidence, however, points to the necessity of interrupting the cycle of violence at larger social and political levels as well (Bloom & Reichert, 1998). Consequently, a commitment to social justice is a necessary and ethical response to interpersonal violence.

Mollica's (2006) work with refugees highlights a similar theme. He has reduced his trauma story model to four questions that can be asked of anyone recovering from traumatic violence:

> (a) What traumatic events have happened? (b) How are your body and mind repairing the injuries sustained from these events? (c) What have you done in your daily life to help yourself recover? (d) What *justice* do you require *from your society* [emphasis added] to support your personal healing? (p. 243)

Questions that place individual concerns in this larger context of justice-seeking are distinctly different from the kinds of questions most practitioners routinely ask of the people they see in therapy. As a trauma-informed intervention, they invite the survivor to allocate responsibility for their situation in a realistic way. Given most survivors' tendencies toward shame, humiliation, and self-blame, this is a helpful and ultimately empowering way to frame the issue of accountability. Although these questions are posed to individuals, they also point beyond the individual to the social and political realities that lie behind violence. Because social justice is a central value and goal of many religious traditions, seeking justice is a spiritual as well as a moral or ethical injunction for believers in these faith communities. As Rye and Pargament (2002) found in a study of spiritual and secular models of forgiveness, it is often difficult to separate these worlds into neat compartments of religious and nonreligious. In a similar way, individuals disposed to see justice as an inherently social as well as a religious or spiritual concern will bring that understanding to their recovery. The challenge for psychotherapists working with these individuals is to understand empathically not only their spiritual orientation but also the larger social connections such an expansive spirituality entails.

TRAUMA-INFORMED FAITH COMMUNITIES

Researchers and practitioners have begun to broaden conceptualizations of how trauma survivors may experience recovery, growth, and healing. "Trauma-specific" interventions directly focus on an individual's experience of trauma and are designed to facilitate recovery and healing. Individual therapies (e.g., prolonged exposure, cognitive processing therapy) and group interventions (Trauma Recovery and Empowerment Model, Beyond Trauma, Seeking Safety, ATRIUM, TARGET) are in this sense "trauma-specific" interventions. By contrast, any human service—or any larger community—can be "trauma-informed" when it develops a culture of understanding trauma, its impact, and diverse paths to recovery (M. Harris & Fallot, 2001). A trauma-informed culture becomes more hospitable and engaging for trauma survivors; prevents further (re) traumatization, and builds on such core values as safety, trustworthiness, choice, collaboration, and empowerment (Fallot & Harris, 2008). Trauma-informed care may be thought of as a "values-based" approach similar to a recovery orientation (Farkas, Gagne, Anthony, & Chamberlin, 2005), offering a context supportive of trauma-specific, evidence-based practices. But, because of its expansive purview, trauma-informed care may readily engage larger communities, including faith communities (Day, Vermilyea, Wilkerson, & Giller, 2006). Discussion of the relationships between spirituality and religion and trauma needs to take into account this broader perspective.

The idea of "trauma-informed" faith communities is of particular importance, not only to creating safe and healing environments for survivors but also to preventing abuse in religious contexts. Many of the same factors that make religious trauma so pernicious also make religious healing powerful. Clergy, chaplains, and pastoral counselors may offer "trauma-specific" counseling that explicitly employs the metaphors, rituals, music, art, and other spiritual resources of their traditions. For example, Sigmund (2003) described some ways in which chaplains have worked in collaboration with mental health professionals in a Veterans Administration (VA) hospital serving veterans with PTSD (see also Chapter 29 in this volume). Some religious and faith leaders have begun to harness their own tools to promote trauma healing. Keepin, Brix, and Dwyer (2007) reported on a program of reconciliation between women and men designed to confront gender injustice and abuse and to promote new forms of healing and intimacy between the sexes. The intervention, which is a direct application of spiritual practices from a spectrum of religious traditions, has been used throughout the United States as well as in India and South Africa (Keepin et al., 2007).

The basic trauma-informed values of safety, trustworthiness, choice, collaboration, and empowerment represent antidotes to the toxic effects of violence in people's lives. Faith communities, as fully as mental health and substance abuse services, schools, shelters, and other human service settings, may find creative ways to maximize the expression of such values in every activity, relationship, and physical environment sponsored by the community. For example, establishing a safe and trustworthy context, a true "sanctuary," for all of those involved in the community has emerged as a clear priority in the aftermath of clergy sexual abuse scandals.

One promising model for such an approach is found in Risking Connection in Faith Communities, a curriculum for developing trauma-sensitive relationships in religious settings (Day et al., 2006). Reflecting its theistic roots, this paradigm is interfaith in its language, images, and examples. Although weighted toward the Jewish and Christian traditions, it nonetheless reflects an invitation to people of all faiths to participate in strengthening communities of care for trauma survivors. The training manual adapts an earlier and more general Risking Connection curriculum that was based solidly in constructivist self-development theory and a thorough understanding of trauma's complexities (Saakvitne, Gamble, Pearlman, & Lev, 2000). A growing awareness of the challenges and opportunities in responding helpfully to trauma survivors makes this approach to training leaders of faith communities in the key relational dynamics of traumatic abuse an especially valuable resource. Under headings like "Trauma Can Lead to Spiritual Distress," "Spirituality Can Promote Healing," and "Recovery From Trauma Can Lead to Spiritual Growth," this work brings numerous rich examples of the ways in which faith leaders may develop a fuller understanding of trauma's psychological and spiritual impact and facilitate healing among those they serve. The closing section on Healing Communities is particularly salient in terms of creating a welcoming, safe, and hospitable setting for trauma survivors to engage or reengage with religious beliefs and practices. "How Faith Communities Can Promote Healing" includes discussions of the community as a "secure base" in which self-capacities and beliefs can be healed.

SUMMARY AND RECOMMENDATIONS

The complexities of this field raise questions that do not lend themselves to easy answers. It is clear that interpersonal abuse and violent victimization have tremendously negative consequences in most people's lives. It is also true, however, that as people come to terms with the violence in their lives, healing and recovery are possible, and the posttraumatic process may even be described as growthful. The extent to which such "growth" is related to traditional measures of mental health (e.g., fewer "symptoms") is not clear. Therefore, in terms of implications for therapy, close attention to *individual* understandings of interpersonal violence, in their *cultural context*, is extremely important. Both personal and cultural narratives frequently involve spiritual and religious elements in coping with trauma. Yet these same spiritual and religious factors may either facilitate or undermine the healing and recovery process. There is some evidence that providing a safe group setting in which individuals can explore their spiritual resources for recovery is effective in alleviating both psychological and spiritual distress. In addition, the larger contexts, including faith communities, that shape people's responses to trauma need to be "trauma-informed."

Since 2001, both federal and state governments have made a commitment to establishing and supporting linkages with faith-based organizations, demonstrating recognition of the potentially mutually enriching relationships among trauma-informed care, spirituality, and faith communities. The Center for Mental Health Services (CMHS) of the Substance Abuse and Mental Health Services Agency (SAMHSA) has begun to build bridges with religious and faith communities. In 2002, CMHS convened a 2-day facilitated dialogue among consumers of mental health services and representatives of a variety of diverse faith traditions and community organizations. In 2009, CMHS/SAMHSA, in cooperation with the Office of Refugee Resettlement, sponsored a 2-day "listening session" with representatives from the world's major religious traditions. The meeting explored what the world's religions have to offer people who are suffering, ways in which they can and do assist in trauma healing, and suggestions for closer cooperation between religious and mental health providers. Plans are currently under way to conduct a series of related activities over the next 5 years.

The preliminary status of most of the research in this area indicates that there is still much work to be done. For example, the relationships between psychological and spiritual trauma remain unclear as do the relationships of both of these experiences to PTG or distress. Factors that are known to affect the psychological domain (e.g., age at first abuse, severity of exposure, relationship to abuser) may not affect the person's spirituality in identical ways, leading to spiritual responses to trauma that differ markedly from psychological ones. Developmental differences (childhood vs. adult), types of trauma exposure (prolonged vs. single incident), and the trajectories of healing need to be studied longitudinally, so that initial responses to trauma are distinguished from long-term responses. Finally, both clinicians and researchers need to understand the embeddedness of spiritual and religious resources in specific cultural contexts. People's "turn to religion" in response to violent trauma, and the corresponding therapeutic interventions that integrate spirituality, each call for the sort of multimethod studies that combine the best of quantitative and qualitative research.

References

Başoğlu, M., Livanou, M., Crnobarić, M., Franciskovič, T., Suljić, E., Durić, D., & Vranesić, M. (2005). Psychiatric and cognitive effects of war in former Yugoslavia. *JAMA, 294*, 580–590. doi:10.1001/jama.294.5.580

Benkert, M., & Doyle, T. P. (2009). Clericalism, religious abuse and its psychological impact on victims of clergy sexual abuse. *Pastoral Psychology, 58*, 223–238. doi:10.1007/s11089-008-0188-0

Bierman, A. (2005). The effects of childhood maltreatment on adult religiosity and spirituality: Rejecting God the Father because of abusive fathers? *Journal for the Scientific Study of Religion, 44*, 349–359. doi:10.1111/j.1468-5906.2005.00290.x

Bilich, M., Bonfiglio, S., & Carlson, S. (2000). *Shared grace: Therapists and clergy working together*. New York, NY: Haworth Press.

Bloom, S. L., & Reichert, M. (1998). *Bearing witness: Violence and collective responsibility*. Binghamton, NY: Haworth Press.

Bottoms, B. L., Nielsen, M., Murray, R., & Filipas, H. (2003). Religion-related child physical abuse. Characteristics and psychological outcomes. *Journal of Aggression, Maltreatment, and Trauma, 8*, 87–114. doi:10.1300/J146v08n01_04

Bowland, S. (2008). *Evaluation of a psycho-social-spiritual intervention with older women survivors of interpersonal trauma* (Unpublished doctoral dissertation). George Warren Brown School of Social Work, Washington University, St. Louis, MO.

Bowland, S., Edmond, T., & Fallot, R. D. (2012). Evaluation of a spiritually focused intervention with older trauma survivors. *Social Work, 57*, 73–82. doi:10.1093/sw/swr001

Bowland, S., Eveaitt, A., Sharma, S., & Linfield, K. J. (2010, March). *Documenting older women survivors' religious/spiritual struggles and resiliency*. Presented at the spring meeting of Division 36 of the American Psychological Association, Columbia, MD.

Briere, J., & Rickards, S. (2007). Self-awareness, affect regulation, and relatedness: Differential sequels of childhood versus adult victimization experiences. *Journal of Nervous and Mental Disease, 195*, 497–503. doi:10.1097/NMD.0b013e31803044e2

Calhoun, L. G., & Tedeschi, R. G. (2006). The foundations of posttraumatic growth: An expanded framework. In L. G. Calhoun & R. G. Tedeschi (Eds.), *Handbook of posttraumatic growth: Research and practice* (pp. 3–23). New York, NY: Psychology Press.

Chaves, M., & Garland, D. (2009). The prevalence of clergy sexual advances towards adults in their congregations. *Journal for the Scientific Study of Religion, 48*, 817–824. doi:10.1111/j.1468-5906.2009.01482.x

Chen, Y. Y., & Koenig, H. G. (2006). Traumatic stress and religion: Is there a relationship? A review of empirical findings. *Journal of Religion and Health, 45*, 371–381. doi:10.1007/s10943-006-9040-y

Clayton, M. (2002, April 5). Sex abuse spans spectrum of churches. *Christian Science Monitor*, p. 1.

Day, J. H., Vermilyea, E., Wilkerson, J., & Giller, E. (2006). *Risking connection in faith communities: A training curriculum for faith leaders supporting trauma survivors.* Baltimore, MD: Sidran Institute Press.

Doehring, C. (1993). *Internal desecration: Traumatization and representations of God.* Lanham, MD: University Press of America.

Elliott, D. M. (1994). The impact of Christian faith on the prevalence and sequelae of sexual abuse. *Journal of Interpersonal Violence*, *9*, 95–108. doi:10.1177/088626094009001006

Ellison, C. G., Bartkowski, J. P., & Anderson, K. L. (1999). Are there religious variations in domestic violence? *Journal of Family Issues*, *20*, 87–113. doi:10.1177/019251399020001005

Exline, J. J. (2002). Stumbling blocks on the religious road: Fractured relationships, nagging vices, and the inner struggle to believe. *Psychological Inquiry*, *13*, 182–189. doi:10.1207/S15327965PLI1303_03

Exline, J. J., & Rose, E. (2005). Religious and spiritual struggles. In R. F. Paloutzian & C. L. Park (Eds.), *Handbook of the psychology of religion and spirituality* (pp. 315–330). New York, NY: Guilford Press.

Fallot, R. D. (1997). Spirituality in trauma recovery. In M. Harris & C. L. Landis (Eds.), *Sexual abuse in the lives of women diagnosed with severe mental illness* (pp. 337–355). Amsterdam, The Netherlands: Harwood Academic.

Fallot, R. D., & Harris, M. (2008). Trauma-informed services. In G. Reyes, J. D. Elhai, & J. D. Ford (Eds.), *The encyclopedia of psychological trauma* (pp. 660–662). Hoboken, NJ: Wiley.

Fallot, R. D., & Heckman, J. (2005). Religious/spiritual coping among women trauma survivors with mental health and substance use disorders. *Journal of Behavioral Health Services and Research*, *32*, 215–226. doi:10.1007/BF02287268

Fallot, R. D., & the Spirituality Workgroup. (2001–2004). *Spirituality and trauma recovery: A group approach* (Unpublished working paper). Washington, DC: Community Connections & Lutheran Social Services.

Falsetti, S. A., Resick, P. A., & Davis, J. L. (2003). Changes in religious beliefs following trauma. *Journal of Traumatic Stress*, *16*, 391–398. doi:10.1023/A:1024422220163

Farkas, M., Gagne, C., Anthony, W., & Chamberlin, J. (2005). Implementing recovery oriented evidence based programs: Identifying the critical dimensions. *Community Mental Health Journal*, *41*, 141–158. doi:10.1007/s10597-005-2649-6

Felitti, V., & Anda, R. F. (2010). The relationship of adverse childhood experiences to adult medical disease, psychiatric disorders, and sexual behavior: Implications for healthcare. In R. Lanius, E. Vermetten, & C. Pain (Eds.), *The hidden epidemic: The impact of early life trauma on health and disease* (pp. 77–87). Cambridge, England: Cambridge University Press. doi:10.1017/CBO9780511777042.010

Finkelhor, D. (2011). Prevalence of child victimization, abuse, crime, and violence exposure. In J. W. White, M. P. Koss, & A. E. Kazdin (Eds.), *Violence against women and children: Vol. 1. Mapping the terrain* (pp. 9–29). Washington, DC: American Psychological Association.

Fogler, J. M., Shipard, J. C., Rowe, E., Jensen, J., & Clarke, S. (2008). A theoretical foundation for understanding clergy-perpetrated sexual abuse. *Journal of Child Sexual Abuse*, *17*, 301–328. doi:10.1080/10538710802329874

Fontana, A., & Rosenheck, R. (2004). Trauma, change in strength of religious faith, and mental health service use among veterans treated for PTSD. *Journal of Nervous and Mental Disease, 192*, 579–584. doi:10.1097/01.nmd.0000138224.17375.55

Frawley-O'Dea, M. G. (2007). *Perversion of power: Sexual abuse in the Catholic Church.* Nashville, TN: Vanderbilt University Press.

Frazier, P. A., & Berman, M. I. (2008). Posttraumatic growth following sexual assault. In S. Joseph & P. A. Linley (Eds.), *Trauma, recovery, and growth: Positive psychological perspectives on posttraumatic stress* (pp. 161–181). Hoboken, NJ: Wiley.

Freyd, J. (1998). *Betrayal trauma: The logic of forgetting childhood abuse.* Cambridge, England: Harvard University Press.

Ganzevoort, R. R. (2002). Common themes and structures in male victims' stories of religion and sexual abuse. *Mental Health, Religion, and Culture*, *5*, 313–325. doi:10.1080/13674670210130045

Ganzevoort, R. R. (2006, May). *Masculinity and posttraumatic spirituality*. Paper presented at the international colloquium on Christian Religious Education in Coping with Sexual Abuse, Montreal, Quebec, Canada.

Gartner, R. R. (2004). Predatory priests: Sexually abusing fathers. *Studies in Gender and Sexuality*, *5*, 31–56. doi:10.1080/15240650509349239

Goodman, G. S., Bottoms, B. L., Redlich, A., Shaver, P. R., & Diviak, K. R. (1998). Correlates of multiple forms of victimization in religion-related child abuse cases. *Journal of Aggression, Maltreatment, and Trauma*, *2*, 273–295. doi:10.1300/J146v02n01_15

Harris, J. I., Erbes, C. R., Engdahl, B. E., Olson, R. H. A., Winskowski, A. M., & McMahill, J. (2008). Christian religious functioning and trauma outcomes. *Journal of Clinical Psychology*, *64*, 17–29. doi:10.1002/jclp.20427

Harris, M., & Fallot, R. D. (Eds.). (2001). *Using trauma theory to design service systems.* San Francisco, CA: Jossey-Bass.

Herman, J. L. (1992). *Trauma and recovery.* New York, NY: Basic Books.

Janoff-Bulman, R. (2006). Schema-change perspectives on posttraumatic growth. In L. G. Calhoun & R. G. Tedeschi (Eds.), *Handbook of posttraumatic growth: Research and practice* (pp. 81–99). Mahwah, NJ: Erlbaum.

Jenkins, P. (1996). *Pedophiles and priests.* New York, NY: Oxford University Press.

John Jay College of Criminal Justice. (2004). *The nature and scope of the problem of sexual abuse of minors by Catholic priests and deacons in the United States.* Washington, DC: U.S. Conference of Catholic Bishops.

Joseph, S., & Linley, P. (Eds.). (2008). *Trauma, recovery, and growth: Positive psychological perspectives on posttraumatic stress.* Hoboken, NJ: Wiley. doi:10.1002/9781118269718

Keepin, W., Brix, C., & Dwyer, M. (2007). *Divine duality: The power of reconciliation between women and men.* Prescott, AZ: Hohm Press.

Kennedy, J. E., Davis, R. C., & Taylor, B. G. (1998). Changes in spirituality and well-being among victims of sexual assault. *Journal for the Scientific Study of Religion, 37,* 322–328. doi:10.2307/1387531

Kessler, R. C., Sonnega, A., Bromet, E., Hughes, M., & Nelson, C. B. (1995). Posttraumatic stress disorder in the National Comorbidity Survey. *Archives of General Psychiatry, 52,* 1048–1060. doi:10.1001/archpsyc.1995.03950240066012

Kira, I. A., Templin, T., Lewandowski, L., Clifford, D., Wiencek, P., Hammad, A., . . . Al-Haidar, A. (2006). The effects of torture: Two community studies. *Peace and Conflict: Journal of Peace Psychology, 12,* 205–228. doi:10.1207/s15327949pac1203_1

Knapik, G. P., Martsolf, D., & Drucker, C. (2008). Being delivered: Spirituality in survivors of sexual violence. *Issues in Mental Health Nursing, 29,* 335–350. doi:10.1080/01612840801904274

Krumrei, E. J., Mahoney, A., & Pargament, K. I. (2009). Divorce and the divine: The role of spirituality in adjustment to divorce. *Journal of Marriage and Family, 71,* 373–383. doi:10.1111/j.1741-3737.2009.00605.x

Leyden-Rubenstein, L. (2002). Treating child survivors of clergy sexual abuse. *Annals of the American Psychotherapy Association, 5*(6), 32.

Mahoney, A. (2010). Religion in families, 1999–2009: A relational spirituality framework. *Journal of Marriage and Family, 72,* 805–827. doi:10.1111/j.1741-3737.2010.00732.x

Mollica, R. F. (2006). *Healing invisible wounds: Paths to hope and recovery in a violent world.* Orlando, FL: Harcourt.

Murray-Swank, N., & Pargament, K. (2005). God, where are you? Evaluating a spiritually-integrated intervention for sexual abuse. *Mental Health, Religion, and Culture, 8,* 191–203. doi:10.1080/13694670500138866

Nason-Clark, N. (2004). When terror strikes at home: The interface between religion and domestic violence. *Journal for the Scientific Study of Religion, 43,* 303–310. doi:10.1111/j.1468-5906.2004.00236.x

Neimeyer, R. A. (2004). Fostering posttraumatic growth: A narrative elaboration. *Psychological Inquiry, 15,* 53–59.

Newberg, A., & Waldman, M. R. (2009). *How God changes your brain.* New York, NY: Ballantine Books.

Pals, J. L., & McAdams, D. (2004). The transformed self: A narrative understanding of posttraumatic growth. *Psychological Inquiry, 15,* 65–69.

Pargament, K. I. (1997). *The psychology of religion and coping: Theory, research, practice.* New York, NY: Guilford Press.

Pargament, K. I. (2007). *Spiritually integrated psychotherapy: Understanding and addressing the sacred.* New York, NY: Guilford Press.

Pargament, K. I. (2010). Religion and coping: The current state of knowledge. In S. Folkman (Ed.), *Handbook of stress, health and coping* (pp. 269–288). New York, NY: Oxford University Press.

Pargament, K. I., Desai, K. M., & McConnell, K. M. (2006). Spirituality: A pathway to posttraumatic growth or decline? In L. G. Calhoun & R. G. Tedeschi (Eds.), *Handbook of posttraumatic growth: Research and practice* (pp. 121–137): Mahwah, NJ: Erlbaum.

Pargament, K. I., Smith, B. W., Koenig, H. G., & Perez, L. (1998). Patterns of positive and negative religious coping with major life stressors. *Journal for the Scientific Study of Religion, 37,* 710–724. doi:10.2307/1388152

Parkinson, P., Oates, K., & Jayakody, A. (2009). *Study of reported child sexual abuse in the Anglican Church.* Unpublished document.

Plante, T. G. (2009). *Spiritual practices in psychotherapy: Thirteen practices for enhancing psychological health.* Washington, DC: American Psychological Association. doi:10.1037/11872-000

Richards, P. S., & Bergin, A. E. (2005). *A spiritual strategy for counseling and psychotherapy* (2nd ed.). Washington, DC: American Psychological Association. doi:10.1037/11214-000

Rye, M. S., & Pargament, K. I. (2002). Forgiveness and romantic relationships in college: Can it heal the wounded heart? *Journal of Clinical Psychology*, *58*, 419–441. doi:10.1002/jclp.1153

Saakvitne, K., Gamble, S., Pearlman, L. A., & Lev, B. T. (2000). *Risking connection: A training curriculum for working with survivors of childhood abuse.* Baltimore, MD: Sidran Institute Press.

Schaefer, F. C., Blazer, D. G., & Koenig, H. G. (2008). Religious and spiritual factors and the consequences of trauma: A review and model of the interrelationship. *International Journal of Psychiatry in Medicine*, *38*, 507–524. doi:10.2190/PM.38.4.i

Schuster, M. A., Stein, B. D., Jaycox, L. H., Collins, R. L., Marshall, G. N., Elliott, M. N., . . . Berry, S. H. (2007). A national survey of stress reactions after the September 11, 2001, terrorist attacks. In B. Trappler (Ed.), *Modern terrorism and psychological trauma* (pp. 25–38). New York, NY: Gordian Knot Books/ Richard Altschuler.

Shaw, A., Joseph, S., & Linley, P. A. (2005). Religion, spirituality and posttraumatic growth: A systematic review. *Mental Health, Religion, and Culture*, *8*, 1–11. doi:10.1080/1367467032000157981

Sigmund, J. A. (2003). Spirituality and trauma: The role of clergy in the treatment of posttraumatic stress disorder. *Journal of Religion and Health*, *42*, 221–229. doi:10.1023/A:1024839601896

Stark, R., & Bainbridge, W. S. (1996). *A theory of religion.* New Brunswick, NJ: Rutgers University Press.

Tedeschi, R. G., & Calhoun, L. G. (1996). The posttraumatic growth inventory: Measuring the positive legacy of trauma. *Journal of Traumatic Stress*, *9*, 455–471. doi:10.1002/jts.2490090305

van der Kolk, B. (2005). Developmental trauma disorder. *Psychiatric Annals*, *35*, 401–408.

Walker, D. F., Reid, H. W., O'Neill, T., & Brown, L. (2009). Changes in personal religion/spirituality during and after childhood abuse: A review and synthesis. *Psychological Trauma: Theory, Research, Practice, and Policy*, *1*, 130–145. doi:10.1037/a0016211

Weaver, A. J., Koenig, H., & Ochberg, F. (1996). Posttraumatic stress, mental health professionals, and the clergy: A need for collaboration, training, and research. *Journal of Traumatic Stress*, *9*, 847–856. doi:10.1002/jts.2490090412

CHAPTER 20

AN APPLIED INTEGRATIVE APPROACH TO EXPLORING HOW RELIGION AND SPIRITUALITY CONTRIBUTE TO OR COUNTERACT PREJUDICE AND DISCRIMINATION

Carrie Doehring

In the following three case examples, consider the ways that religion and spirituality contribute to and counteract prejudice.

Case Example 1

Janice initiated marital counseling because of escalating conflict between her husband Bill and their 18-year-old daughter Suzy. Janice disagreed with how Bill was handling this conflict. At the dinner table, whenever Bill made derogatory remarks about the Latino men who worked in his lawn care business, Suzy heatedly challenged him: How could he say he was a Christian and be so prejudiced? Bill argued that he had to lay down the law with his employees because they were lazy. Being a strict boss was part of his Christian work ethic. Suzy said she was against racism and wanted to be part of a summer outreach to illegal immigrants on the Mexican–American border. Bill had forbidden her to go. Bill agreed to marriage counseling if they could find a Christian marriage counselor who held religious views similar to his: Someone who could help them live out biblical mandates to be strong parents.

Case Example 2

Samantha, a supervising psychologist at a campus-based clinic, consulted with a colleague who specialized in organizational diversity training. She was troubled by remarks made by other supervisors about an international practicum student, Eunjoo Cho, a woman from Korea, who had the lowest caseload at the clinic.

At a recent supervisory meeting there was an extensive discussion about whether Eunjoo's quiet demeanor and her accent were making it "hard for her to retain clients." Samantha was beginning to question whether subtle forms of racism and sexism might be influencing the way she and her colleagues identified aspects of Eunjoo's identity as the problem. These questions distressed her because she was committed to valuing social justice and antiracism as part of her Jewish beliefs.

Case Example 3

Jasmine is an African American 24-year-old woman who joined the Army after her college graduation. During her college years she was part of a woman's group in her community of faith that used African-centered spiritual practices to cope with all kinds of stress, including racism. She has been deployed in Afghanistan as a chaplain's assistant.

DOI: 10.1037/14046-020
APA Handbook of Psychology, Religion, and Spirituality: Vol. 2. An Applied Psychology of Religion and Spirituality, K. I. Pargament (Editor-in-Chief)

During her deployment she hoped to draw upon her undergraduate major in religious studies and use her spiritual practices in her work. She also wanted to explore a vocation for ministry.

She recently went to the psychologist at her base with symptoms of anxiety and depression. She described how angry she is with Roy, another chaplain's assistant, who has made her life miserable by constantly questioning her appearance—her fitted uniform, styled hair, fingernail polish and make-up. He attributes her popularity among the soldiers who stop by the chaplain's office to the way she "dolls herself up." Roy comes from a Christian denomination that does not ordain women. He uses biblical texts to question how a "sexy babe" like her can even think about Christian ministry. Jasmine is bitter and disillusioned about her naive hope that she could not only survive but thrive during her deployment by being a spiritually strong team member of the chaplain's office. Now she can't even pray, is experiencing religious struggles, and hates going on duty.

As these three examples illustrate, the ways that religion and spirituality contribute to and counteract prejudice are complex and multifaceted. In Case Example 1, Bill's religious paternalism contributes to the way he makes his daughter the problem and not his racism. He hopes he can find a counselor whose religious beliefs will support his paternalism. In Case Example 2, Samantha's religious commitment to social justice counteracts possible prejudice by raising questions about how Eunjoo's supervisors focus on her accent and demeanor as the problem. In Case Example 3, Jasmine's spiritual practices, which helped her cope with racism in the past, seem to have failed her in the face of religiously oriented sexual harassment. In these scenarios, people seek help. How will their clinicians address the complex ways that religion, spirituality, and prejudice are related?

To address this complexity, clinicians need to draw on an integrated paradigm for the psychology of religion and spirituality (see Volume 1, Chapter 1, this handbook). Using this paradigm, clinicians assume that religion and spirituality are multidimensional, "made up of a myriad of thoughts, feelings, actions, experiences, relationships, and physiological responses" (Volume 1, Chapter 1, this handbook, p. 5) and hence are related to prejudice in a variety of life-enhancing, life-limiting, and destructive ways. Although some clinicians might be inclined to focus on religion as contributing to prejudice and spirituality rather than as counteracting prejudice, "the critical question is not *whether* religion and spirituality are good or bad [when it comes to prejudice], but rather *when, how,* and *why* they take constructive or destructive forms" (Volume 1, Chapter 1, this handbook, p. 7).

In this chapter, I explore the ways religion and spirituality contribute to or counteract prejudice using an integrated paradigm that strives to engage

- psychological, cultural, religious, and theological theories about prejudice, religion, and spirituality;
- psychological research on religion and spirituality;
- social psychological research on prejudice and discrimination; and
- clinical, supervisory, and educational interventions with persons and organizations who are prejudiced, who discriminate, or who are targets of prejudice and discrimination.

The purpose of this chapter is to *apply* this integrated psychological paradigm of religion, spirituality, and prejudice to the practices of clinical care and supervision. In this way, research findings and theories about religion, spirituality, and prejudice will be brought into conversation with practices of care and supervision in ways that take into account the complex psychological roles of religion and spirituality in the well-being of persons, families, and communities. The ultimate goal is to twofold: (a) to challenge the ways religion and spirituality psychologically contribute to prejudice and (b) to enhance spiritually integrated psychological change processes that counteract prejudice. In this way, counselors, supervisors, and teachers can be part of social transformation that opposes religiously linked prejudice.

I begin with definitions of three types of prejudice, illustrating how clinicians can identify the role of religion and spirituality in each type of prejudice. Next, I review research on the relationship between prejudice and people's religious worldviews or orientations. I highlight the clinical need to assess when religion becomes "toxic" because of right-wing authoritarianism. I turn to research and education programs that counteract prejudice to highlight how clinicians, supervisees, and clients can implement religious and spiritual humanitarian values to counteract their tendencies toward prejudice. I briefly consider how organizational antiprejudice interventions can incorporate religion and spirituality by using an applied integrative paradigm for the psychology of religion and spirituality. Finally, I look at how this paradigm can be used by clinicians working with clients who are targets of prejudice and discrimination. Clinical narrative threads are woven throughout this chapter because of my focus on applying an integrative paradigm. I return to the opening examples to keep addressing the "So what?" question of how an integrated paradigm for understanding the psychology of religion, spirituality, and prejudice is relevant in the practices of clinical care and supervision.

DEFINING PREJUDICE, STEREOTYPING, AND DISCRIMINATION

Stereotyping is

> perceiving and treating others as representative of some group to which, on the basis of superficial appearance alone, one assumes they belong, and in the belief that they possess the psychological traits which one believes to characterise [*sic*] members of that group. (Richards, 2008, p. 238)

Social psychologists define *prejudice* as prejudgment that associates aspects of someone's appearance or accent with stereotypes about gender, age, race (as a social or cultural and not a biological category), or other aspects of social identity. Although stereotypes and prejudice can be positive, in this chapter, I will focus on negative stereotypes and prejudice. There are various types of prejudice. Prejudice can affirm one's own group (*self-affirming prejudice* or *in-group favoritism*), express hostility or hatred toward a targeted group (*hate prejudice*; see Chapter 18 in this volume), or protect one's group from threats (*threat prejudice*; Brewer, 2007). *Discrimination* is prejudice put into action: rejecting or excluding people who are targets of prejudice from access to the social privileges enjoyed by those in the majority. These terms can be elaborated and illustrated by returning to the opening examples.

Religion and Self-Affirming Prejudice

Religious beliefs may be used to justify self-affirming prejudice, often in subtle, self-righteous ways. According to Silberman, Higgins, and Dweck (2005),

> Religions often contain values and ideas that may facilitate prejudice, discrimination, and violence by encouraging the consciousness of belonging to a select and privileged community, and by emphasizing the "otherness" of those who do not follow the tenets of the religion. (p. 774)

In Case Example 2, the supervisors comprise a select and privileged group within the clinic. As such, they may not recognize the ways that Eunjoo's demeanor and accent make her "other." They may be expressing a self-affirming form of prejudice. They might, for example, believe that if only Eunjoo and other international students could speak English without an accent and act assertively like their supervisors do, they would be able to retain clients. These supervisors probably hold strong liberal beliefs about being fair and nondiscriminatory. These progressive beliefs make it harder for them to question their attitude toward Eunjoo. This lack of reflection, along with the belief that they are not prejudiced, may paradoxically contribute to self-affirming prejudice. On the other hand, religious beliefs have prompted Samantha to feel uneasy and to question whether she is living according to Jewish beliefs of being hospitable and looking after those who are marginalized. Her religious value of social justice make her aware of the subtle ways that Eunjoo's "otherness" may marginalize her.

Religion and Threat Prejudice

Threat prejudice may be a "response to sacred values under threat and, in part, as a way of defending against these threats" (Pargament, Trevino, Mahoney, & Silberman, 2007, p. 147; see also Stephan & Renfro, 2002). For example, Christians who see Jews as a threat—even as desecrators of Christianity—are more likely to have anti-Semitic attitudes (Pargament et al., 2007, p. 155). In this same study, people affirming the Christian value of love were less likely to be prejudiced against Jews. On the other hand, Pargament et al. (2007) found that negative religious coping, including beliefs that Jews are being punished by God, was tied to greater conflict with Jews and greater anti-Semitism. In a similar study, Abu-Raiya, Pargament, Mahoney, and Trevino (2008) found that Christians who view Muslims as desecrating Christianity and use negative religious coping (including beliefs that God is punishing Muslims) are more likely to hold anti-Muslim attitudes. Christians using positive religious coping, including an emphasis on Christian love and a valuing of Islamic spirituality, had lower anti-Muslim beliefs (Abu-Raiya et al., 2008).

When clinicians ask questions about how clients are using religion in positive and negative ways to cope with stress, they can assess how religious coping contributes to or counteracts threat prejudice. For example, in Case Example 1, Bill may feel threatened by his dependence on his employees (threat prejudice) because without them, he could not successfully run his business. He may be using religion in negative ways to cope with the stress of being dependent on his Latino employees. He may hold embedded beliefs that the success of his business is a consequence of both hard work and being blessed by God. Conversely, the hardships experienced by his Latino employees may signify that they have not worked as hard or been as blessed by God. This negative religious coping contributes to threat prejudice. If he were to examine these beliefs in spiritually integrated counseling (Pargament, 2007), then he might be able to use religion in positive ways to cope with the stress of running a business. A therapist could explore Bill's fears and whether he could collaboratively work with God to feel more hopeful about his business and thus less threatened by his reliance on his employees. Alternatively, life-enhancing spiritual practices could be explored, like expressing gratitude for moments when work goes well and taking in the beauty of nature when working outdoors. These interventions may help Bill draw on his religion in positive ways that alleviate prejudice toward his employees.

Religion and Hate Prejudice

Threats to one's religious beliefs are often experienced as particularly dangerous and may provoke violent reactions that combine hate and threat prejudice (Silberman et al., 2005). Religious beliefs can easily be used to fuel hate prejudice, as Appleby (2000) noted: "The facile invocation of religious symbols and stories can exacerbate ethnic tensions and foster a social climate conducive to riots, mob violence, or the random beatings and killings known as hate crimes" (p. 119). An example of hate prejudice is the increase in hate crimes toward those identified as Muslim after the September 11, 2001, terrorist attacks (Sheridan, 2006). This kind of prejudice is evident in Case Example 1. Suzy accuses her father of making derogatory remarks about his Latino employees, remarks that express hostility if not hatred (hate prejudice). His authoritarian religious beliefs about needing to be a "strong" boss and father, and his need for a Christian counselor who supports his authoritarianism, reinforce both threat and hostile forms of prejudice.

As terror management theorists propose, the more people use their religious worldview and values to ward off their terror of death, the more aggressively they will challenge groups that threaten their worldviews, sometimes going so far as to experience such groups as evil (see Greenberg, Landau, Kosloff, & Solomon, 2009; Jones, 2002; see also Volume 1, Chapter 5, this handbook). Case Example 3 captures some of the complex ways religion contributes to hate prejudice. Roy believes that women should not seek ordination; he may also believe that women sexually tempt men to sin. Being deployed in Afghanistan may provoke a terror of death for both Roy and Jasmine. Roy may react by challenging Jasmine for all of the ways she threatens his worldviews; indeed, he may see her as evil. The terror of death that Jasmine may experience in Afghanistan will be compounded by having someone on her team who is no longer "watching her back" but rather is ready to stab her in the back. Jasmine experiences Roy's hate prejudice as both life and soul threatening. She feels like Roy is desecrating a sacred part of herself: her spiritual practices and religious vocation.

These research findings and illustrations can help clinicians begin to conceptualize and thus assess the ways that their clients' religion may contribute to or counteract self-affirming, threat, and hate prejudice. To elaborate on the complex ways that religion, spirituality, and prejudice are related, I will summarize research on how prejudice is related to one's worldview and, specifically, one's religious orientation. Using this research, clinicians and supervisors can identify which religious orientations will likely contribute to or counteract prejudice. They can assess whether right-wing authoritarianism—the "toxic" element of religious orientations that makes religious people prejudiced—is part of a client's or supervisee's worldview.

EMPIRICAL RESEARCH ON HOW RELIGIOUS ORIENTATIONS CONTRIBUTE TO PREJUDICE

Allport (1954/1979, 1966) was the first psychologist to explore the relationship between prejudice and two kinds of religious orientations: an intrinsic motivation for religion that is personally meaningful and an extrinsic motivation for religion that has external benefits (Allport & Ross, 1967). Initial empirical studies supported Allport's theory that an extrinsic religious orientation correlates with higher levels of prejudice, whereas an intrinsic religious orientation is associated with lower levels of prejudice (Batson, Schoenrade, & Ventis, 1993). Subsequent ways of conceptualizing intrinsic and extrinsic religious orientations included a third orientation of religion as a quest that values searching and questioning (Batson & Schoenrade, 1991a, 1991b; Batson et al., 1993). Extensive research has also focused on a fourth orientation, fundamentalism, which is characterized as inflexible, close-minded convictions that one's religious beliefs are absolutely true and must be followed. A fundamentalist orientation involves an attitude toward one's beliefs and not the content of one's beliefs, and thus it can be used to describe any set of beliefs that are absolute and rigid (Altemeyer & Hunsberger, 1992). Clinicians may well find it daunting to use this extensive research on prejudice and religious orientation within an applied integrative paradigm for the psychology of religion and spirituality. Several meta-analyses provide helpful overviews. In a meta-analysis of 16 North American studies between 1990 and 2005 that used measures of religious orientation (intrinsic, extrinsic, quest, and religious fundamentalism) and prejudice, Hunsberger and Jackson (2005) found that the relationship between religious orientations and prejudice depends on whether particular kinds of prejudice, such as racism, are proscribed (i.e., explicitly opposed by one's religious tradition or community) or nonproscribed (i.e., either endorsed or implicitly encouraged, such as heterosexism or benevolent sexism). In the 39 studies Hunsberger and Jackson (2005) analyzed that looked at religious fundamentalism, they found that fundamentalism was positively correlated with prejudice against sexual minority persons, Communists, women, and religious out-groups, but it was not as clearly correlated across the board with prejudice toward racial minority persons (Batson et al., 1993; Hunsberger & Jackson, 2005). What is it about fundamentalist religious attitudes that make them more likely to contribute to prejudice? This is an important question for clinicians and one that has been recently researched.

Research on Fundamentalism, Right-Wing Authoritarianism, and Prejudice

Initial empirical research demonstrated that both religious fundamentalism and right-wing authoritarianism (RWA) are positively correlated with prejudice (Altemeyer & Hunsberger, 1992; Hunsberger, Owusu, & Duck, 1999; Laythe, Finkel, Bringle, & Kirkpatrick, 2002). RWA has three components: submitting oneself to established authority, aggression toward out-groups or deviants identified by the established authority, and conformity to traditions (conventionalism; Altemeyer, 1996, 2003). When Altemeyer and Hunsberger (1992) separated RWA from religious fundamentalism, they found, first, that prejudice was no longer correlated with religious fundamentalism, and, second, that RWA was still significantly related to prejudice. Discussing similar findings, Laythe, Finkel, and Kirkpatrick (2001) proposed that religious fundamentalism might consist of two components: (a) RWA (which shapes the rigid and absolute way in which beliefs are held), which contributes to prejudice, and (b) Christian belief content, which does not contribute to prejudice. These findings were corroborated by Rowatt and Franklin (2004).

These findings suggest that clinicians will need to assess and address the toxic role of RWA with clients whose religious beliefs contribute to prejudice. There is no research on how self-affirming, hate, or threat prejudice are related to these three components of RWA (i.e., submitting oneself to established authority, aggression toward out-groups or deviants identified by the established authority, and conventionalism). Clinicians could make some guesses about this. Using religion to support aggression, especially toward religious out-groups or deviants, may foster both hate and threat prejudice. For example, in the first scenario, Bill's religious paternalism includes being aggressive toward his Latino employees. If his religious orientation includes RWA, he might defer to anti-immigration political and media authorities that view Latino immigrants as out-groups (the second component of RWA). Bill seems to hold these sentiments: He views employees as lazy and, perhaps, deviant.

Another component of RWA, conformity toward traditions, could contribute toward self-affirming prejudice as well as prejudice that protects one's religious tradition. This aspect of RWA may be part of Case Example 3, if Roy feels the need to conform to a religious tradition that identifies women as sexual temptresses and unsuitable for ordained ministry. An Army psychologist counseling Jasmine might decide with her permission to consult with the chaplain's office about helping team members explore moral dilemmas generated by conflicts between their religious beliefs and their duties of providing spiritual care (e.g., to gay or lesbian soldiers). This intervention might help team members talk about what it is like when their religious beliefs and values are at odds with military policies against discrimination on the basis of gender, race, and sexual orientation. Team members can be encouraged to explore overarching common values, like teamwork, spiritual care, and compassion, all of which support the mission of the military. Open dialogue will encourage team members to challenge the way that beliefs and behaviors like Roy's sexism undermine their common mission. Group work permits Jasmine to contribute to these discussions before using other channels to confront Roy.

Research on the "toxic" role of RWA helps clinicians evaluate whether a client's religious fundamentalism is contributing to prejudice. In spiritually integrated therapy (Pargament, 2007), clinicians can help clients identify beliefs, for example, in a loving God, that counteract their tendencies toward RWA and, hence, toward prejudice. Remembering that a client's religious faith is dynamic, not static, clinicians can use the metaphor of religion and spirituality as a journey with pathways and destinations (Pargament, 2007; see also Volume 1, Chapter 1, this handbook). In the first scenario, a clinician could ally herself with Bill by empathizing with his goals to protect his daughter and his business. Then she could explore the origins of his hate and threat prejudice and also the religious journey that has made him value the destinations of being a "strong" father and boss. This exploration of his journey would help Bill feel understood. Then she could question whether Bill has other religious beliefs that offer alternative pathways to meet his goal of having strong relationships with his daughter and employees. For example, he could identify the ways that he, Janice, their church community and God have worked together to make Suzy who she is. If he can experience the way he has collaborated with God in raising Suzy, he might be able to religiously cope with his fears about her safety by collaborating with a loving God who wants to let Suzy go her own way. Similarly, Bill could be asked to talk about the ways he tries to be a good boss with each of his employees as individuals. This conversation could encourage

Bill to become more intentional about living out his values of being a good boss by attending to his employees as unique persons and not as representatives of a group. These conversations would focus on positive aspects of his roles as father and boss in ways that reduce his religious paternalism and hostility.

Research on Religion, Cognitive Reasoning, and Prejudice

Recent research on prejudice and religious fundamentalism has focused on the role of cognitive reasoning styles in the relationship of religion and prejudice. Hunsberger and Jackson (2005) suggest that people endorsing religious fundamentalism use less complex ways of thinking about their belief systems, and they also may think convergently by making information fit into preexisting religious schema (Hunsberger, Alisat, Pancer, & Pratt, 1996). In contrast, those using a quest orientation are more likely to use critical-thinking skills to question and reconstruct religious beliefs when experiences or information challenges these beliefs (McFarland & Warren, 1992).

Another line of research with similar findings has focused on the relation between racism and whether people hold literal or symbolically oriented beliefs. This research uses the Post-Critical Belief Scale (Duriez, Fontaine, & Hutsebaut, 2000) developed to measure two distinctive features of religious beliefs: whether people believe in a transcendent reality and whether such beliefs are interpreted in literal or symbolic ways (Wulff, 1997). For example, fundamentalist Christians usually believe that Mary, the mother of Jesus, was a virgin who conceived by the power of the Holy Spirit. In contrast to this literal belief in the immaculate conception, Christians who approach doctrine in more symbolic ways might question whether the gospel stories about the birth of Jesus were told by early Christians because in their historical context, extraordinary prophets and religious leaders were thought to have extraordinary birth narratives. Research on whether beliefs in a transcendent reality are literal or symbolic is particularly significant for an integrated psychological paradigm of religion, spirituality, and prejudice because this research attempts to operationalize a distinctive aspect of religious worldviews: literal or symbolic religious interpretations. In investigating the relationships between prejudice and literal or symbolic beliefs in a transcendent reality in three samples drawn from Flanders (Belgium), Duriez (2004) found that beliefs or lack of beliefs in a transcendent reality were not related to racism. In contrast, the more people interpreted religious beliefs literally, the more likely they were to endorse items on a racism scale. This relationship remained significant even after controlling for right-wing authoritarianism. Duriez concluded that "the danger of religious fundamentalism (RF) does not lie in religion as such but in the cognitive style that is applied when processing religious issues" (Duriez, 2004, p. 187).

These research findings suggest that clinicians may need to assess whether clients, supervisees, or students are using less complex cognitive styles when they draw on religious beliefs or worldviews to understand differences between themselves and others. When prompted to think in more complex ways about beliefs, people may be able to let go of simplistic or literal interpretations of religious beliefs that may have helped them cope in the past and to develop more multilayered religious insights that help them navigate difficult situations. For example, in Case Example 1, Bill and Janice's marriage counselor could ask them whether being married and being parents have sacred meanings for them (Mahoney, Pargament, Murray-Swank, & Murray-Swank, 2003). She could invite them to explore their goals in marriage and parenthood and how they are trying to reach their goals. Bill's parental goal is to protect Suzy through prohibiting and arguing with her because he fears that Suzy will put herself in a dangerous situation and not be suspicious of those who might harm her. His marital goal is to provide a united front as parents, which means not arguing with each other. Because Janice is the one who wanted to pursue marriage counseling, she may well have a goal of open communication in her marriage and with Suzy. The counselor can invite them to elaborate on the sacred dimensions of their goals as a couple and as parents. She will listen closely for whether there are other spiritual goals besides protecting Suzy and whether there are other ways to reach these sacred goals besides Janice backing up Bill, and Bill taking the lead as a husband and father, in prohibiting his daughter from her pursuits and in arguing with her about their conflicting beliefs. Exploring the pros and cons of these sacred goals and methods may foster open communication. New and more complex meanings about their spiritual goals and methods as parents and a couple may emerge. For example, participating in counseling might persuade Bill to consider open communication as a spiritual parental goal. By inviting them to use spiritual ways of coping with stressful parental and marital moments, such as prayer, they may become more open to collaborating with each other and with God, which in turn can lead to more flexibility, closeness, and compassion.

Although this case study could go in many different directions, the exploration of marital and parental spiritual goals and methods will help the counselor assess how religious beliefs and practices are contributing to these problems and, in this case, to Bill's prejudice. Additionally, it will help the counselor determine whether religious beliefs can become a resource if clients are more intentional about seeking spiritual integration as parents and couples (for an elaboration of how to assess and work with spirituality in family counseling, see Mahoney, LeRoy, Kusner, Padgett, & Grimes, 2013).

COUNTERACTING PREJUDICE BY IMPLEMENTING RELIGIOUS OR SPIRITUAL VALUES

Having explored how religion and spirituality psychologically contribute to prejudice, I turn in the sections that follow to an examination of how religious beliefs and values along with spiritual practices can be used intentionally in personal, communal, and cultural ways to counteract prejudice.

Research on Automatic Activation of Prejudice

Clinicians can help clients, supervisees, and students implement religious or spiritual values to counteract the automatic activation of prejudice by drawing on recent studies on this unconscious process. Researchers use the term *automatic activation of prejudice* to refer to people's immediate reactions to others being shaped by stereotypes in ways outside of their conscious awareness. Social psychologists have recently started using neuroimaging to understand the specific brain mechanisms of automatic activation of prejudice, focusing on the amygdala, a part of the brain that responds to the emotional intensity of a stimulus (Amodio & Lieberman, 2009; Anderson et al., 2003; Cunningham, Nezlet, & Banaji, 2004). In one such study, Cunningham et al. (2004) had White participants view Black and White faces using a neuroimaging method (an event-related functional magnetic resonance imaging). They found that the amygdala is more active when Black faces rather than White faces are presented subliminally for brief time periods (30 ms). When the time period is extended to 525 ms, then there is greater activation of the prefrontal cortex, suggesting that higher order cognitive processing may be offsetting automatic activation of stereotypes. Such research supports distinctions made by social psychologists between implicit stereotype-based prejudice associated with amygdala activity that occurs outside of awareness versus prejudice and discrimination that engages semantic processing involving the prefrontal cortex. The latter process occurs when people either marshal beliefs to justify or rationalize prejudice or are internally motivated to counteract feelings and thoughts recognized to be discriminatory.

Laboratory-based research has demonstrated that guilt can play a positive role in motivating people to counteract prejudice. In a complex study by Amodio, Devine, and Harmon-Jones (2007), research participants were told that their neurological responses to a multiracial series of faces were anti-Black. Participants who reported feeling guilty about these responses were subsequently more likely to interact with a Black member of the research team. The authors concluded that guilt is a complex social emotion that can play a dynamic role in motivating people to change (Amodio et al., 2007, p. 529). One can easily imagine how a healthy sense of guilt could be fostered when clinicians explore religious and spiritual values that focus less on individual shortcomings (understood theologically as personal sin) and more on all humans falling short in treating every person with dignity and respect (understood theologically as collective sin). For example, in Case Example 2 (the scenario with the supervisors), Samantha seems to be initially motivated by guilt when she feels uneasy about how the supervisory group focuses on Eunjoo as the problem. Consultation may help her see the complex and paradoxical ways that self-righteousness, whether rooted in liberal or conservative religious beliefs, can play into self-affirming prejudice toward Eunjoo. Samantha's sense of religious responsibility to correct this wrong may become even more nuanced when she realizes that she and the other supervisors in a secular context use unspoken cultural group norms that judge those, like Eunjoo, who are different. When these unspoken group norms, whether rooted in secular or religious beliefs, contribute to self-affirming prejudice, they are part of systemic racism and sexism, which, theologically speaking, is a form of collective wrongdoing. This nuanced appreciation for collective wrongdoing and guilt will help Samantha in multiple ways, especially as she empathically rather than judgmentally approaches her colleagues and invites them to explore what is going on.

As this and other research indicates, to counteract automatically activated prejudice, people must first become aware of these automatically activated stereotypes; second, they must be personally motivated to counteract prejudice; and third, they must practice how to respond intentionally in nonprejudicial ways (Devine & Sharp, 2009). In helping students and supervisees prevent prejudice, clinicians can assess whether they are internally or externally motivated (Devine, Brodish, & Vance, 2005; Plant & Devine, 1998). Internal motivation includes a desire to put egalitarian or humanitarian values into practice. External motivation comes from the desire to conform to societal expectations by not appearing prejudiced. In one research study, those with high internal motivation to live out egalitarian values showed very little stereotype activation compared with those who lacked such values and goals (Moskowitz, Gollwitzer, Wasel, & Schaal, 1999). Clinicians, supervisors, teachers, and consultants can help people clarify their values and decide whether they want to draw on religiously or spiritually based humanitarian convictions to show compassion and not prejudice (van der Slik & Konig, 2006).

The Role of Religion and Spirituality in Organizational Interventions

Diversity training has become a very popular form of prejudice reduction in hundreds of educational, business, government, and health organizations. In a recent comprehensive review of 985 published and unpublished reports written by academics and nonacademics about interventions and programs designed to reduce prejudice, Paluck and Green (2009) described the array of such prejudice-reducing interventions, which includes "multicultural education, anti-bias instruction more generally, workplace diversity initiatives, dialogue groups, cooperative learning, moral and values education, intergroup contact, peace education, media interventions, reading interventions, intercultural and sensitivity training, [and] cognitive training" (Paluck & Green, 2009, p. 341). They evaluated the methodological rigor used in tracking the outcomes of such interventions and found that nearly two thirds of these studies are nonexperimental. They do not use random assignment and control groups and thus cannot demonstrate empirically that their programs made a significant difference in reducing prejudice. More alarming is their finding that "entire genres of prejudice-reduction interventions, including moral education, organizational diversity training, advertising, and cultural competence in the health and law enforcement professions, have never been tested" (Paluck & Green, 2009, p. 356). Other surveys and evaluative reviews of the range of interventions for prejudice reduction (Aboud & Levy, 2000; Pedersen, Walker, & Wise, 2005; Pettigrew & Tropp, 2005; Price et al., 2005) all highlight the need for organizational interventions based on laboratory research and outcome studies. This paucity of outcome studies is challenging for clinicians designing group interventions for reducing prejudice among students and supervisees.

This chapter has reviewed a number of research findings that could be utilized to design religiously oriented prejudice reduction interventions with the following features:

- Exploring motivation to change. When people can find religious and spiritual reasons for reducing prejudice, they are more likely to be intrinsically rather than extrinsically motivated to change.

- Making use of healthy guilt about automatic prejudice. Research on positive and negative religious coping suggests that healthy guilt may incorporate beliefs in a compassionate loving God, unlike guilt based on beliefs in a punitive God or beliefs that suffering is a consequence of wrongdoing. Healthy guilt about prejudice will be more likely to motivate people to recognize when they experience automatic activation of prejudice and counteract such prejudice as a way of living out beliefs in love and compassion, beliefs that are part of their religion and spirituality.
- Using religious and spiritual role models, men tors, and peers who promote nonprejudiced responses and intergroup contact. Use of role models, mentors, and peers has been found to be effective in both laboratory and field research (McAlister, Ama, Barroso, Peters, & Kelder, 2000; Nagda, Kim, & Truelove, 2004; see also Volume 1, Chapter 10, this handbook); they would likely be even more effective when they explicitly incorporate their religious and spiritual beliefs and practices into counteracting prejudice.
- Using media and stories of cooperation that emulate religious, spiritual, and humanitarian values. Media and reading interventions, especially those portraying people similar to readers interacting positively with those different from themselves, are effective in reducing prejudice and are grounded in theories about extended contact and the persuasive power of stories that can communicate norms, deepen empathy, and facilitate perspective taking (Paluck & Green, 2009, p. 356).
- Clarifying religious, spiritual, and humanitarian values, including injunctions such as the golden rule ("love your neighbor as yourself"). Exploration of values can help people shift from literal to more symbolic interpretations of their beliefs, sacred texts, and religious symbols. Symbolic interpretations are more likely to reduce prejudice because they support complex rather than simple reasoning (Duriez, 2004; Duriez, Fontaine, & Hutsebaut, 2000).
- Exploring spiritual and religious practices like prayer and meditation that help one regulate one's immediate reactions. Spiritual and religious practices that enhance positive rather than negative religious coping will help people experience love and compassion.

These suggestions for how to incorporate aspects of religion and spirituality into organizational interventions for counteracting prejudice highlight both the complexity and the potential of applying an integrative psychological approach to religion, spirituality, and prejudice.

Religious and Spiritual Practices That Help Victims Counteract Prejudice

Since the 1980s, psychologists have studied how people who are targets of prejudice cope with stigma and discrimination (for a review, see Crocker, Major, & Steele, 1998). Extensive research (summarized by Major, 2006) demonstrates that there is tremendous variability in how stigmatized groups cope with and respond to stigma. Within the past decade, research has begun to explore how religion facilitates coping with the stress of prejudice, discrimination, and stigma. Most of this research has been done with African Americans and uses a variety of ways to measure spirituality and religion that is specific to African Americans and Canadians as well as Black South Africans (see Volume 1, Chapter 30, this handbook). Pargament (1997) noted that groups, such as African Americans, who have less access to secular resources and power in society often report that religion is a particularly helpful resource, as is demonstrated in these studies of spirituality, religion, and racism.

Several studies use Utsey and colleague's (Utsey, Adams, & Bolden, 2000; Utsey, Brown, & Bolden, 2004) African-centered epistemological framework for understanding and measuring four dimensions of coping behavior: (a) cognitive–emotional debriefing; (b) spiritual-centered coping, such as connecting with spiritual elements in the universe; (c) collective coping; and (d) ritual-centered coping using African cultural practices that honor ancestors and deities and that celebrate events using rituals, such as lighting candles and burning incense. African American women experiencing stress generated by institutional racism used cognitive–emotional debriefing coping, spiritual-centered coping, and collective coping (Lewis-Coles & Constantine, 2006). In a study of Black Canadians, Joseph and Kuo (2009) found that spiritual-centered coping strategies were the most frequently used ways of responding to interpersonal and institutional discrimination. In a study of Black South African women using the Black Women's Spirituality and Religiosity Measure (Mattis, 1995), Copeland-Linder (2006) found that engagement in formal religion (e.g., church membership and attendance) buffered the effects of racism and work stress on physical health. The author noted that the women used prayer to gain perspective on problems and life purpose, which reduced the impact of racism stress and work-related stress on depressive symptoms. In a qualitative study of 196 African American women, Shorter-Gooden (2004) found that they coped with racism and sexism by using strategies that included self-affirming worldviews or belief systems; prayer; and connection to their heritage, to African and African American culture, and particularly to their ancestors. Bowen-Reid and Harrell (2002) used the 25-item spirituality scale designed by Jagers, Boykin, and Smith (1994) to measure spirituality from an Afrocultural perspective. They found that Afrocultural spirituality moderated or buffered the relationship between perceived racial stress and psychological health outcomes among those who seem to internalize racist stress. The more one group of African American men used religious coping, the more they were able to forgive racial discrimination (Hammond, Banks, & Mattis, 2006). Religious services have been found to moderate the relationship between daily experiences of chronic racial discrimination and negative affect for mid-life African Americans (Bierman, 2006). A national longitudinal survey demonstrated that African Americans who gain guidance in daily living from religious practices like prayer and devotions, and who attended religious services, were less likely to experience psychological distress in response to racist encounters (Ellison, Musick, & Henderson, 2008). Drawing on the work of Pargament and others on experiences of violation or desecration (Pargament, Magyar, & Murray-Swank, 2005), the authors suggested that racist encounters may represent a kind of desecration or violation of one's soul and that religious practices and attendance may moderate the distress of soul-violating experiences of racism.

This review of research on how religion and spirituality can reduce the effects of racism highlights the value of exploring religious and spiritual coping that is especially relevant and meaningful for minorities. Yet few research studies have been conducted with racial and ethnic groups other than African Americans. One exception is a study of American Indians in the upper Midwest United States, which found that participation in various aspects of native culture (powwow participation, tribal language fluency and use, and others) moderated the relationship between perceived discrimination and depression (Whitbeck, McMorris, Hoyt, Stubben, & LaFramboise, 2002). Although clinically oriented literature on minority groups occasionally describes the benefits of religion and spirituality for coping with prejudice, empirical studies are needed on ethnically meaningful religious coping. This arena of research, theory, and practice would benefit greatly from use of an interdisciplinary integrative approach that engages (a) the psychology of religious coping; (b) social psychological research on the effects of prejudice, discrimination, and stigma; and (c) psychologies and theologies of liberation.

Psychologists writing about the relationships among racism, religion, and spirituality have argued for a psychology of liberation (Adams, 2008) that draws on an African worldview (for a summary, see Hunter & Lewis-Coles, 2004), womanist spirituality (Williams & Wiggins, 2010), and Native American spirituality (Duran, Firehammer, & Gonzalez, 2008). Psychologists can also draw on cross-disciplinary perspectives on psychologies and theologies of liberation written by African American practical theologians like Ashby (2003) and Watkins Ali (1999). Fontenot's (2002) research on sexual minorities and religious coping illustrates the richness of a cross-disciplinary approach (see Volume 1, Chapter 34, this handbook). Fontenot found that those who replaced traditional heterosexist religious symbols with nontraditional religious symbols or those who rejected heterosexist religious symbols and used a self-directing style of religious coping experienced lower degrees of psychological well-being. Conversely, sexual minority persons who reconstructed religious symbols traditionally associated with heterosexist religious beliefs and used a collaborative style of religious coping experienced higher degrees of psychological well-being. For example, David, portrayed in the documentary *Trembling Before God* (Dubowski, 1993), returns to a rabbi in Jerusalem who 25 years earlier had counseled him to remain true to his Orthodox Jewish faith by using adversive techniques to inflict physical pain whenever he felt sexual desire for a man. David confronts this learned spiritual teacher with the torment he suffered in following his counsel and how he now affirms both his Orthodox Jewish and gay identity. Then he goes to the Wailing Wall with his partner to tearfully lament the suffering he has endured as a gay Orthodox Jew. He stays in his tradition, lives in a committed relationship, and has a collaborative relationship with a God who hears his lament. Fontenot's research illustrates the need for theologically informed empirical measures of specific beliefs and practices that help people cope with discrimination in religious, spiritual, and psychological ways.

Given the array of psychological and theological perspectives on various kinds of populations that experience stigma, prejudice, and discrimination (gender and sexual minorities, ethical and racial minorities, people with disabilities, mental illness, HIV and AIDS, people of lower socioeconomic classes, people with weight problems, the elderly), there is enormous potential for exploring relationships among discrimination, prejudice, and religious and spiritual coping. As Pargament's (2007) writing on spiritually integrated psychotherapy has illustrated, there needs to be more direct dialogue between researchers and practitioners—both clinical and spiritual—on the complex role of religion and spirituality in the health and well-being of persons, especially those who cope with stigma, prejudice, and discrimination.

In this chapter, I have attempted to explore the ways religion and spirituality contribute to or counteract prejudice, using an integrated paradigm that draws on cross-disciplinary theories about prejudice, religion, and spirituality; psychological research on religion, spirituality, prejudice, and discrimination; and clinical practice. By continually returning to clinical scenarios, I have illustrated both the challenges and potential of applying an integrated psychological paradigm of religion, spirituality, and prejudice. Finding ways to help people draw on their religion and spirituality to counteract prejudice within themselves and when they are targets of prejudice is profoundly important. To do this complex work and do it well, we need the kind of applied integrated paradigm described in this chapter and throughout this volume. In addition, we need to do our own work. We need to recognize when we experience automatic psychological activation of stereotypes, and we need to explore how our journeys—existential, spiritual, or religious—motivate us to do the personal and professional work of counteracting prejudice.

References

Aboud, F. E., & Levy, S. R. (2000). Interventions to reduce prejudice and discrimination in children and adolescents. In S. Oskamp (Ed.), *Reducing prejudice and discrimination* (pp. 269–293). Mahwah, NJ: Erlbaum.

Abu-Raiya, H. A., Pargament, K. I., Mahoney, A., & Trevino, K. (2008). When Muslims are perceived as a religious threat: Examining the connection between desecration, religious coping, and anti-Muslim attitudes. *Basic and Applied Social Psychology, 30,* 311–325.

Adams, G. (2008). Commemorating *Brown*: Psychology as a force for liberation. In G. Adams, M. Biernat, N. R. Branscombe, C. S. Crandall, & L. S. Wrightsman (Eds.), *Commemorating Brown: The social psychology of racism and discrimination* (pp. 3–23). Washington, DC: American Psychological Association. doi:10.1037/11681-001

Allport, G. W. (1954/1979). *The nature of prejudice.* Cambridge, MA: Perseus Books.

Allport, G. W. (1966). The religious context of prejudice. *Journal for the Scientific Study of Religion, 5,* 448–451. doi:10.2307/1384172

Allport, G. W., & Ross, J. M. (1967). Personal religious orientation and prejudice. *Journal of Personality and Social Psychology, 5,* 432–443. doi:10.1037/h0021212

Altemeyer, B. (1996). *The authoritarian specter.* Cambridge, MA: Harvard University Press.

Altemeyer, B. (2003). Why do religious fundamentalists tend to be prejudiced? *The International Journal for the Psychology of Religion, 13,* 17–28. doi:10.1207/S15327582IJPR1301_03

Altemeyer, B., & Hunsberger, B. (1992). Authoritarianism, religious fundamentalism, quest, and prejudice. *The International Journal for the Psychology of Religion, 2*, 113–133. doi:10.1207/s15327582ijpr0202_5

Amodio, D. M., Devine, P. G., & Harmon-Jones, E. (2007). A dynamic model of guilt implications for motivation and self-regulation in the context of prejudice. *Psychological Science, 18*, 524–530. doi:10.1111/j.1467-9280.2007.01933.x

Amodio, D. M., & Lieberman, M. D. (2009). Pictures in our heads: Contributions of fMRI to the study of prejudice and stereotyping. In T. D. Nelson (Ed.), *Handbook of prejudice, stereotyping, and discrimination* (pp. 347–365). New York, NY: Psychological Press.

Anderson, A. K., Christoff, K., Stappen, I., Panitz, D., Ghahremani, D. G., Glover, G., . . . Sobel, N. (2003). Dissociated neural representations of intensity and valence in human olfaction. *Nature Neuroscience, 6*, 196–202. doi:10.1038/nn1001

Appleby, R. S. (2000). *The ambivalence of the sacred: Religion, violence and reconciliation*. Lanham, MD: Rowman & Littlefield.

Ashby, H., Jr. (2003). *Our home is over Jordan: A Black pastoral theology*. St. Louis, MO: Chalice Press.

Batson, C. D., & Schoenrade, P. A. (1991a). Measuring religion as quest: I. Validity concerns. *Journal for the Scientific Study of Religion, 30*, 416–429. doi:10.2307/1387277

Batson, C. D., & Schoenrade, P. A. (1991b). Measuring religion as quest: II. Reliability concerns. *Journal for the Scientific Study of Religion, 30*, 430–447. doi:10.2307/1387278

Batson, C. D., Schoenrade, P., & Ventis, W. L. (1993). *Religion and the individual: A social psychological perspective*. New York, NY: Oxford University Press.

Bierman, A. (2006). Does religion buffer the effects of discrimination on mental health? Differing effects by race. *Journal for the Scientific Study of Religion, 45*, 551–565. doi:10.1111/j.1468-5906.2006.00327.x

Bowen-Reid, T. L., & Harrell, J. P. (2002). Racist experiences and health outcomes: An examination of spirituality as a buffer. *Journal of Black Psychology, 28*, 18–36. doi:10.1177/0095798402028001002

Brewer, M. B. (2007). The social psychology of intergroup relations: Social categorization, ingroup bias, and outgroup prejudice. In A. W. Kruglanski & E. T. Higgins (Eds.), *Social psychology: Handbook of basic principles* (pp. 695–715). New York, NY: Guilford Press.

Copeland-Linder, N. (2006). Stress among Black women in a South African township: The threat role of religion. *Journal of Community Psychology, 34*, 577–599. doi:10.1002/jcop.20116

Crocker, J., Major, B., & Steele, C. (1998). Social stigma. In D. Gilbert, S. Y. Fiske, & G. Lindzey (Eds.), *Handbook of social psychology* (4th ed., pp. 504–553). Boston, MA: McGraw-Hill.

Cunningham, W. A., Nezlek, J. B., & Banaji, M. R. (2004). Implicit and explicit ethnocentrism: Revisiting the ideologies of prejudice. *Personality and Social Psychology Bulletin, 30*, 1332–1346. doi:10.1177/0146167204264654

Devine, P. G., Brodish, A. B., & Vance, S. L. (2005). Self-regulatory processes in interracial interactions: The role of internal and external motivation to respond without prejudice. In J. P. Forgas, K. D. Williams, & S. M. Laham (Eds.), *Social motivation: Conscious and unconscious processes* (pp. 249–273). New York, NY: Cambridge University Press.

Devine, P. G., & Sharp, L. B. (2009). Automaticity and control in stereotyping and prejudice. In T. D. Nelson (Ed.), *Handbook of prejudice, stereotyping, and discrimination* (pp. 61–87). New York, NY: Psychological Press.

Dubowski, S. S. (Producer/Director). (1993). *Trembling before G–d* [Motion picture]. United States: New York Video.

Duran, E., Firehammer, J., & Gonzalez, J. (2008). Liberation psychology as the path toward healing cultural wounds. *Journal of Counseling and Development, 86*, 288–295. doi:10.1002/j.1556-6678.2008.tb00511.x

Duriez, B. (2004). A research note on the relation between religiosity and racism: The importance of the way in which religious contents are being processed. *The International Journal for the Psychology of Religion, 14*, 177–191. doi:10.1207/s15327582ijpr1403_3

Duriez, B., Fontaine, J. R., & Hutsebaut, D. (2000). A further elaboration of the Post-Critical Belief Scale: Evidence for the existence of four different approaches to religion in Flanders-Belgium. *Psychologica Belgica, 40*, 153–181.

Ellison, C. G., Musick, M. A., & Henderson, A. K. (2008). Balm in Gilead: Racism, religious involvement, and psychological distress among African-American adults. *Journal for the Scientific Study of Religion, 47*, 291–309. doi:10.1111/j.1468-5906.2008.00408.x

Fontenot, E. (2002). The use of religious resources in response to anti-homosexual religious attitudes and behaviors. *Dissertation Abstracts International: Section B. Sciences and Engineering, 62*, 5961.

Greenberg, J., Landau, M., Kosloff, S., & Solomon, S. (2009). How our dreams of death transcendence breed prejudice, stereotyping, and conflict: Terror management theory. In T. D. Nelson (Ed.), *Handbook of prejudice, stereotyping, and discrimination* (pp. 309–332). New York, NY: Psychological Press.

Hammond, W. P., Banks, K. H., & Mattis, J. S. (2006). Masculine ideology and forgiveness of racial discrimination among African American men: Direct and interactive relationships. *Sex Roles, 55*, 679–692. doi:10.1007/s11199-006-9123-y

Hunsberger, B., Alisat, S., Pancer, S. M., & Pratt, M. (1996). Religious fundamentalism and religious doubts: Content, connections, and complexity of thinking. *The International Journal for the Psychology of Religion, 6*, 201–220. doi:10.1207/s15327582ijpr0603_7

Hunsberger, B., & Jackson L. M. (2005). Religion, meaning, and prejudice. *Journal of Social Issues, 61*, 807–826. doi:10.1111/j.1540-4560.2005.00433.x

Hunsberger, B., Owusu, V., & Duck, R. (1999). Religion and prejudice in Ghana and Canada: Religious fundamentalism, right-wing authoritarianism, and attitudes toward homosexuals and women. *The International Journal for the Psychology of Religion, 9*, 181–194. doi:10.1207/s15327582ijpr0903_2

Hunter, C. D., & Lewis-Coles, M. E. (2004). Coping with racism: A spirit-based psychological perspective. In J. L. Chin (Ed.), *The psychology of prejudice and discrimination: Racism in America* (Vol. 1., pp. 207–222). Westport, CT: Praeger.

Jagers, R. J., Boykin, A. W., & Smith, T. D. (1994). *A measure of spirituality from an Afrocultural perspective.* Unpublished manuscript.

Jones, J. (2002). *Terror and transformation: The ambiguity of religion in psychoanalytic perspective.* New York, NY: Brunner-Routledge.

Joseph, J., & Kuo, B. C. (2009). Black Canadians' coping responses to racial discrimination. *Journal of Black Psychology, 35*, 78–101. doi:10.1177/0095798408323384

Laythe, B., Finkel, D. G., Bringle, R. B., & Kirkpatrick, L. A. (2002). Religious fundamentalism as a predictor of prejudice: A two-component model. *Journal for the Scientific Study of Religion, 41*, 623–635. doi:10.1111/1468-5906.00142

Laythe, B., Finkel, D. G., & Kirkpatrick, L. A. (2001). Predicting prejudice from religious fundamentalism and right-wing authoritarianism. *Journal for the Scientific Study of Religion, 40*, 1–10. doi:10.1111/0021-8294.00033

Lewis-Coles, M. E., & Constantine, M. G. (2006). Racism-related stress, Africultural coping, and religious problem-solving among African Americans. *Cultural Diversity and Ethnic Minority Psychology, 12*, 433–443. doi:10.1037/1099-9809.12.3.433

Mahoney, A., LeRoy, M., Kusner, K., Padgett, E., & Grimes, L. (2013). Addressing parental spirituality as part of the problem and solution in family psychotherapy. In D. F. Walker & W. Hathaway (Eds.), *Spiritually oriented interventions in child and adolescent psychotherapy.* Washington, DC: American Psychological Association.

Mahoney, A., Pargament, K. I., Murray-Swank, A., & Murray-Swank, N. (2003). Religion and the sanctification of family relationships. *Review of Religious Research, 44*, 220–236. doi:10.2307/3512384

Major, B. (2006). New perspectives on stigma and psychological well-being, In S. Levin & C. van Laar (Eds.), *Stigma and group inequality: Social psychological perspectives* (pp. 193–210). Mahwah, NJ: Erlbaum.

Mattis, J. S. (1995). *Workings of the spirit: Spirituality, meaning construction and coping in the lives of Black women.* Unpublished doctoral dissertation, University of Michigan, Ann Arbor.

McAlister, A., Ama, E., Barroso, C., Peters, R. J., & Kelder, S. (2000). Promoting tolerance and moral engagement through peer modeling. *Cultural Diversity and Ethnic Minority Psychology, 6*, 363 373. doi:10.1037/1099-9809.6.4.363

McFarland, S. G., & Warren, J. C., Jr. (1992). Religious orientations and selective exposure among fundamentalist Christians. *Journal for the Scientific Study of Religion, 31*, 163–174. doi:10.2307/1387006

Moskowitz, G. B., Gollwitzer, P. M., Wasel, W., & Schaal, B. (1999). Preconscious control of stereotype activation through chronic egalitarian goals. *Journal of Personality and Social Psychology, 77*, 167–184. doi:10.1037/0022-3514.77.1.167

Nagda, B., Kim, C., & Truelove, Y. (2004). Learning about difference: learning with others, learning to transgress. *Journal of Social Issues, 60*, 195–214. doi:10.1111/j.0022-4537.2004.00106.x

Paluck, E. L., & Green, D. P. (2009). Prejudice reduction: What works? A review and assessment of research and practice. *Annual Review of Psychology, 60*, 339–367. doi:10.1146/annurev.psych.60.110707.163607

Pargament, K. I. (1997). *The psychology of religion and coping: Theory, research, practice.* New York, NY: Guilford Press.

Pargament, K. I. (2007). *Spiritually integrated psychotherapy: Understanding and addressing the sacred.* New York, NY: Guilford Press.

Pargament, K. I., Magyar, G. M., & Murray-Swank, N. (2005). The sacred and the search for significance: Religion as a unique process. *Journal of Social Issues, 61*, 665–687. doi:10.1111/j.1540-4560.2005.00426.x

Pargament, K. I., Trevino, K., Mahoney, A., & Silberman, I. (2007). They killed our Lord: The perception of Jews as desecrators of Christianity as a predictor of anti-Semitism. *Journal for the Scientific Study of Religion, 46*, 143–158. doi:10.1111/j.1468-5906.2007.00347.x

Pedersen, A., Walker, I., & Wise, M. (2005). "Talk does not cook rice": Beyond antiracism rhetoric to strategies for social action. *Australian Psychologist, 40*, 20–30. doi:10.1080/00050060512331317290

Pettigrew, T. F., & Tropp, L. (2005). Allport's intergroup contact hypothesis: Its history and influence. In J. Dovidio, P. Glick, & L. A. Rudman (Eds.), *On the nature of prejudice: Fifty years after Allport* (pp. 262–277). Malden, MA: Blackwell.

Plant, E. A., & Devine, P. G. (1998). Internal and external motivation to respond without prejudice. *Journal of Personality and Social Psychology, 75*, 811–832. doi:10.1037/0022-3514.75.3.811

Price, E. G., Beach, M. C., Gary, T. L., Robinson, K. A., Gozu, A., & Palacio, A. (2005). A systematic review of the methodological rigor of studies evaluating cultural competence training of health professionals. *Academic Medicine, 80*, 578–586. doi:10.1097/00001888-200506000-00013

Richards, G. (2008). *Psychology: The key concepts.* Hoboken, NJ: Routledge.

Rowatt, W. C., & Franklin, L. M. (2004). Christian orthodoxy, religious fundamentalism, and right-wing authoritarianism as predictors of implicit racial prejudice. *The International Journal for the Psychology of Religion, 14*, 125–138. doi:10.1207/s15327582ijpr1402_4

Sheridan, L. P. (2006). Islamophobia pre- and post-September 11th, 2001. *Journal of Interpersonal Violence, 21*, 317–336. doi:10.1177/0886260505282885

Shorter-Gooden, K. (2004). Multiple resistance strategies: How African American women cope with racism and sexism. *Journal of Black Psychology, 30*, 406–425. doi:10.1177/0095798404266050

Silberman, I., Higgins, E. T., & Dweck, C. S. (2005). Religion and world change: Violence and terrorism versus peace. *Journal of Social Issues, 61*, 761–784. doi:10.1111/j.1540-4560.2005.00431.x

Stephan, W. G., & Renfro, C. L. (2002). The role of threats in intergroup relations. In D. Mackie & E. R. Smith (Eds.), *From prejudice to intergroup emotions* (pp. 191–208). New York, NY: Psychology Press.

Utsey, S. O., Adams, E. P., & Bolden, M. (2000). Development and initial validation of the Africultural Coping Systems Inventory. *Journal of Black Psychology, 26*, 194–215. doi:10.1177/0095798400026002005

Utsey, S. O., Brown, C., & Bolden, M. (2004). Testing the structural invariance of the Africultural Coping Systems Inventory across three samples of African descent populations. *Educational and Psychological Measurement, 64*, 185–195. doi:10.1177/0013164403258461

van der Slik, F. W. P., & Konig, R. P. (2006). Orthodox, humanitarian, and science-inspired belief in relation to prejudice against Jews, Muslims, and ethnic minorities: The content of one's belief does matter. *The International Journal for the Psychology of Religion, 16*, 113–126. doi:10.1207/s15327582ijpr1602_3

Watkins Ali, C. (1999). *Survival and liberation: Pastoral theology in African American context.* St. Louis, MO: Chalice Press.

Whitbeck, L. B., McMorris, B. A., Hoyt, D. R., Stubben, J. D., & LaFramboise, T. (2002). Perceived discrimination, traditional practices, and depressive symptoms among American Indians in the upper Midwest. *Journal of Health and Social Behavior, 43*, 400–418. doi:10.2307/3090234

Williams, C. B., & Wiggins, M. (2010). Womanist spirituality as a response to the racism-sexism double bind in African American women. *Counseling and Values, 54*, 175–186. doi:10.1002/j.2161-007X.2010.tb00015.x

Wulff, D. M. (1997). *Psychology of religion: Classic and contemporary views* (2nd ed.). New York, NY: Wiley.

CHAPTER 21

THE INTERFACE AMONG SPIRITUALITY, RELIGION, AND ILLNESS IN FAMILIES OF CHILDREN WITH SPECIAL HEALTH CARE NEEDS

Sian Cotton, Michael S. Yi, and Jerren C. Weekes

In the following fictionalized case example, Ebony and her family represent one instance of the approximately 13 million children and adolescents under the age of 18 in the United States who are living with a chronic illness or a special health care need (Newacheck et al., 1998).

> **Case Example 1: Ebony**
> Ebony is a 5-year-old African American girl who was diagnosed at 6 months of age with sickle cell disease (SCD). As a result of her condition, Ebony has started to receive blood transfusions to help address the anemia. She experiences fatigue and recurrent pain in her legs and arms. Ebony says that her mom gives her massages and medicine to help her feel better. When asked about other things that make her feel better, Ebony drew a picture of God and said that He helps her smile and makes her feel better when she hurts. She said that her mother prays that her pain will go away, which sometimes helps. Ebony's parents consider themselves to be religious people who go to church every week and are very involved in their faith community. Her mother prays that Ebony will not have pain or have to be hospitalized again, and she regularly asks her church prayer group to pray for her sick daughter. Ebony's mom, though burdened by her child's illness, often tries to see how God might be strengthening her in this difficult situation.

Although Ebony is in many ways like any other 5-year-old girl, she and her family must find ways to cope with repeated hospitalizations, daily medication regimes, and the unpredictable course of this life-shortening and painful disease. Among other sources of comfort and strength, Ebony's family relies on their faith and religious beliefs to cope. To help practitioners and researchers appreciate the various roles that faith can potentially play in families such as Ebony's, this chapter reviews theory, research, and practice on ways that religion and spirituality could potentially reduce or intensify distress in the lives of youth who have special health care needs.

We begin by outlining definitions of key constructs. Although we use the phrase *special health care needs* to encompass medical illnesses, developmental disabilities, and mental health issues, most of the related research focuses on medical illnesses and developmental disabilities with limited research addressing youth with psychiatric diagnoses (Mahoney, 2010). We use the terms *religiousness* and *spirituality* to refer to both traditionally based (religiousness linked to an established faith system or institution) and nontraditionally based (spirituality not necessarily linked to faith system or institution) beliefs, practices, relationships, or experiences having to do with the sacred. We refer the reader to

We acknowledge Sara Pendleton for sharing the protocol for a previous study. This protocol served as a basis for some of the material presented in this chapter.

DOI: 10.1037/14046-021
APA Handbook of Psychology, Religion, and Spirituality: Vol. 2. An Applied Psychology of Religion and Spirituality, K. I. Pargament (Editor-in-Chief)

the introduction of this handbook (see Volume 1) for a more thorough discussion of the meanings of the terms *religiousness* and *spirituality* used throughout the handbook's chapters.

In this chapter, we initially discuss relevant theoretical models and empirical studies. We then translate available findings into practical examples of how religiousness and spirituality can be integrated into clinical work with children with special health care needs (CSHCN) and their families, using hypothetical case examples to illustrate key points. Because the family system plays essential roles in children's adaptation to illness, we also discuss the effect religiousness and spirituality may have on parents and caregivers. Given the extensive body of research on family functioning in coping with CSHCN, we refer the reader to the work of Kazak, Rourke, and Crump (2003) for a summary of this literature, restricting ourselves to reviewing general models of coping with CSHCN (Wallander, Thompson, & Alriksson-Schmidt, 2003) because this provides a context to consider where religiousness and spirituality may fit best conceptually into the broader field. In addition, we briefly review Pargament's (1997) seminal work on models of religious coping and specifically how they apply to families with CSHCN. Before concluding, we highlight various unanswered key questions, limitations of previous work, methodological challenges inherent in this type of research, and suggestions for strengthening future work. We conclude with recommendations to advance research and practice on the interface between religiousness, spirituality, and CSHCN.

CHILDREN WITH SPECIAL HEALTH CARE NEEDS

Medical advances in the past few decades have significantly improved life expectancy for CSHCN, a population defined by the Department of Health and Human Services Maternal and Child Health Bureau as "those who have or are at increased risk for a chronic physical, developmental, behavioral, or emotional condition and who also require health and related services of a type or amount beyond that required by children generally" (McPherson et al., 1998). In this chapter, we discuss religiousness and spirituality as they relate to CSHCN across this wide spectrum of chronic conditions—and use the terms *CSHCN* and *children with chronic conditions* interchangeably. In addition, because of the lack of literature in this area overall, the majority of examples focus on children with chronic physical health conditions—although much of the information presented will be applicable regardless of actual chronic condition.

Because of advances in medical technologies and therapeutics, many patients even with previously life-shortening physical conditions, such as SCD, major congenital heart disease, or cystic fibrosis, are living well into their adult years. Greater than 90% of patients born with a chronic physical illness or a disabling physical condition can now be expected to live into adulthood (Blum, 1995). As a result of those advances, there has been a substantial increase in the overall prevalence of CSHCN, with estimates in the range of 13% to 19% or approximately 10 million or more children (Newacheck et al., 1998). Moreover, the prevalence of CSHCN increases with age. On the basis of a number of national survey data, the age-based prevalence of CSHCN has been estimated to be in the range of 11% in children 0 to 5 years of age, 20% in those 6 to 11 years of age, and approximately 24% in children 12 to 17 years of age (Newacheck et al., 1998). These estimates encompass any physical, developmental, or psychological dimensions that may put a child's health at risk as defined by the Maternal Child Health Bureau; however, those dimensions do not necessarily map explicitly onto the American Psychiatric Association's (2000) *Diagnostic and Statistical Manual of Mental Disorders* Axis I mental health diagnoses.

Models of Coping With Special Health Care Needs

Because of the increasing population of children and adolescents with special health care needs, individual and environmental factors that may buffer patients and their families from poorer outcomes in the context of a chronic condition have been examined. Protective factors, such as greater self-esteem, positive coping, and better family competence, may help ameliorate the negative effects of childhood chronic illness (Wallander et al., 2003). Existing models of adaptation to chronic physical illness provide a framework by which children may develop resilience against, or vulnerability to, poorer outcomes in the face of difficulties such as trauma or illness. For example, Moos, Tsu, and Schaefer (1977) described physical illness as a life crisis, in which several factors, such as one's personal characteristics, historical or past experiences, and current structural and social environment, are viewed within the context of the physical condition or disability. Furthermore, these factors may influence adaption to the life crisis in both positive and negative ways. Although Moos's model does not specifically address religiousness and spirituality, one could imagine, for example, how a religious congregation (structural and social environment) might provide integral support, or lack of support, in relation to a child's new diagnosis or repeated hospitalizations because of a medical condition. This positive or negative response from the religious community could influence how the family and child adapt to the experience of the special health care need.

Of critical importance to understanding the adaptation of a child to a special health care condition is consideration of the coping techniques, family dynamics, and overall structure of the child's family. One model that uses a family systems perspective is Thompson and Gustafson's (1996) transactional stress and coping model. In this model, the chronic medical condition is a major stressor to the individual and his or her family, and certain adaptive mechanisms (e.g., family dynamics, coping) can explain connections or "transactions" between the illness and the outcomes beyond those explained by the illness and structural factors (e.g., social class).

In summary, evidence indicates that personal, family, and socioenvironmental characteristics increase the risk for or protection against maladaptive outcomes in CSHCN. This biopsychosocial perspective incorporates the individual's ability to cope with and adapt to illness in the context of biologic and physiologic processes related to health and disease but also emphasizes the importance of psychology, behavior, the family, and the social context. The growing evidence of the links between religiousness, spirituality, and health calls, however, for an even broader, biopsychosocial–spiritual perspective on health and illness (Sulmasy, 2002).

Religious and Spiritual Coping for CSHCN and Their Families

Religiousness and spirituality are important to individuals in the United States whether or not they have a special health care need. For instance, most adults believe that our national well-being depends in part on the spiritual well-being of individuals and communities (Gallup Organization, 2006). National surveys of adolescents and young adults have similar findings, with 95% reporting belief in God, more than 85% responding that spirituality or religion is important to them, and more than 50% reporting that they attend religious services regularly (Smith & Denton, 2005).

Religiousness or spirituality is particularly important to parents of children with a special health care need. The experience of parenting a child with a chronic illness has been described as "exhausting" and a time of "chronic sorrow" (Gravelle, 1997). Although some parents do describe the experience as a positive one in which they were able to find meaning (Gravelle, 1997) or learn that they could cope with anything (Rando, 1983), the stressors and worries often take a toll on even the most resourceful of families. Many turn to their religiousness or spirituality in trying times such as these. The next sections delineate ways in which religiousness and spirituality can facilitate and sometimes undermine adaptation and successful coping in CSHCN and their families. We first begin with definitions of religious coping.

DEFINING RELIGIOUS COPING

In Pargament's (1997) seminal work, he defined *religious coping* as the search for significance under stress, in ways related to the sacred. Restated, religious and spiritual coping focuses on how individuals or families use religion and spirituality to deal with a stressor, such as a chronic illness. Religion can be used to gain control of a situation, gain comfort, or derive meaning in difficult situations (Pargament, 1997; Pargament, Koenig, & Perez, 2000). Pendleton, Cavalli, Pargament, and Nasr (2002) have described additional developmentally relevant coping strategies for children with cystic fibrosis that while similar to Pargament's strategies, differ in their child-focused language (e.g., belief in God's intervention). Although little empirical work has yet to exhaustively delineate religious coping in CSHCN and their families, some studies described in the next section help us to understand how parents and children may be relying on and even undermined by religion in times of distress.

When Families Turn to Religion for Support

Religiousness and spirituality may offer many families with CSHCN a source of strength and comfort in often-difficult and sometimes devastating situations. Particularly under those conditions, patients and families may increase spiritual or religious practices such as prayer and religious attendance for several reasons. For many, serious illness and trauma raises existential issues regarding the meaning of life and death. As patients seek explanations for their illness and health, they may believe that their health course and ultimate outcomes are beyond their means to control (Pargament & Hahn, 1986). Some of the ways in which religiousness or spirituality may facilitate adaption could be through the following: (a) promoting positive personal health and lifestyle behaviors, (b) improving psychological resources (e.g., self-efficacy), (c) enhancing a sense of belonging and meaning, and (d) and increasing access to interpersonal supports (George, Ellison, & Larson, 2002). Studies of positive effects of religiousness and spirituality on adaptation in light of medical or physical illness, developmental disability, and mental health conditions are described in the following paragraphs.

Regarding medical illnesses, the majority of the studies that have been conducted on this subject, which are relatively few compared with the adult literature, suggest that parents and children or adolescents often use religiousness or spirituality, usually prayer, to cope with chronic health conditions. A few examples of these studies include the following:

- child's cancer diagnosis (Beltrão, Vasconcelos, Pontes, & Albuquerque, 2007; Nicholas et al., 2009; Schneider & Mannell, 2006),
- adolescents with sickle cell disease and their parents (Cotton et al., 2009),
- children with cystic fibrosis (Pendleton et al., 2002),
- Brazilian mothers of children with HIV (da Silva, Rocha, Davim, & Torres, 2008), and
- African American female caregivers of children with asthma (Sterling & Peterson, 2003).

Many of these studies found that spirituality was one of the most common coping mechanisms that parents or children used to manage their illness. The majority of studies have been with parents or caregivers and have found that parents report using chaplaincy services as a support system (Nottage, 2005), believed that God was their most important coping mechanism (Beltrão et al., 2007), and turned to religion or faith as a source of strength (da Silva et al., 2008). Only a handful of studies have reported on children and adolescents' own use of religiousness or spirituality to cope with an illness. In one such study, 35% of African American adolescents with sickle cell disease reported using prayer once or more a day to manage symptoms (Cotton et al., 2009). In a qualitative study of religious coping in children (ages 5 to 10) with cystic fibrosis, Pendleton et al. (2002) reported on a 7-year-old who said that Jesus "helps me get better when I am sick" (p. 3). Less well understood, however, is whether the use of religious coping by CSHCN and their families actually relates to better health outcomes (Zehnder, Prchal, Vollrath, & Landolt, 2006), although many anecdotally report this positive impact.

Regarding developmental disabilities, most of the research has been on families of children living with autism. Positive outcomes, particularly enhanced optimism and overall well-being, have been found among parents of children with autism who report using religion to cope (Ekas, Thomas, Shivers, & Shivers, 2009). Literature also notes that parents of children with autism may increase their use of religious coping over time (Gray, 2006). In a sample of 45 parents of children with autism, use of positive religious coping was associated with better religious outcomes such as spiritual growth (Tarakeshwar & Pargament, 2001). Rogers-Dulan (1998) studied 52 African American caregivers who had a child with mental retardation and found, for the most part, that religious experiences were a source of strength for the families. In addition, greater religiousness in one's personal and family life as well as church support were both related to better adjustment (Rogers-Dulan, 1998).

Religious coping in psychiatric child and adolescent populations has received even less attention (Mahoney, Pendleton, & Ihrke, 2006). In a study of 266 children with attention deficit hyperactivity disorder (ADHD), 63% of parents reported using religion as a self-care strategy to control their child's ADHD symptoms (Bussing, Koro-Ljungberg, Williamson, Gary, & Garvan, 2006). This study, however, also found that parents' reliance on religion (e.g., increased church attendance, participation in rituals, advice from congregation and church leaders) was associated with higher levels of caregiver strain; this could be a case of reverse causality in which stressed caregivers turned to religion for support. Dew, Daniel, Goldston, and Koenig (2008) prospectively followed a sample of 12- to 18-year-olds ($N = 145$) being treated at two psychiatric outpatient clinics. Even when controlling for social support, they found that forgiveness, negative religious support, loss of faith, and negative religious coping were related to increased depressive symptoms in adolescents. In addition, longitudinally, loss of faith predicted less improvement in depressive symptoms scores over 6 months. Thus, although studies focused on physical illnesses imply that religiousness and spirituality tend to facilitate positive child or parent adjustment, the limited studies conducted on psychiatric populations highlight that the reverse scenario is also possible. We turn next to ways that religious or spiritual issues can become burdensome and even detrimental to the coping process.

When Families With CSHCN Have Spiritual Struggles

Negative religious coping or spiritual struggles in relation to CSHCN can take several forms, such as parents who may experience their child's illness as a punishment from God or an adolescent who feels that God gave her a disability because He is angry at her (see Volume 1, Chapter 25, this handbook). In adults, greater endorsement of negative religious coping has been associated with poorer health outcomes, such as higher depression and lower quality of life (Pargament, Koenig, Tarakeshwar, & Hahn, 2004). Unfortunately, very little research currently exists on spiritual struggles within families of CSHCN. In an initial exploration of this topic in medical samples, children who used negative religious coping were more likely to experience the following during hospitalization and 1-month follow-up: poorer adjustment, poorer perception about their adjustment, more difficulty managing asthma symptoms, continued concern about quality of life with asthma, and increased anxiety (Benore, Pargament, & Pendleton, 2008). Not only did the negative consequences of the spiritual struggles persist over time, but also they predicted unique amounts of variance in children's adjustment after accounting for other types of secular coping.

Regarding developmental disabilities, a study of 45 parents of children with autism found that negative religious coping was associated with greater depressive affect and poorer religious outcomes (e.g., closeness to God; Tarakeshwar & Pargament, 2001). In addition, although 40% of parents interviewed stated that they looked to clergy or church members for support, 30% of parents felt they were "abandoned by their church or were dissatisfied with the clergy" (Tarakeshwar & Pargament, 2001, p. 255); another 25% expressed spiritual discontent. For example, one mother said, "If there is a God looking out for us, He certainly is cruel" (Tarakeshwar & Pargament, 2001, p. 255). And another parent said, "My spirituality has created more stress for me because I cannot take my son to church anymore. My husband stays home to look after him. This separates our family" (Tarakeshwar & Pargament, 2001, p. 255).

To date, very few studies have empirically assessed issues of spiritual struggles in children or adolescents with mental health issues (Grossoehme, 2008). This is ironic, however, because there are many spiritual support groups that currently are being implemented as key parts of inpatient psychiatric units for children (Grossoehme & Gerbetz, 2004). Dew et al. (2008) found that adolescents' depressive symptoms were related to feeling abandoned or punished by God, feeling unsupported by one's religious community, and experiencing a lack of forgiveness by God in 117 psychiatric outpatients ages 12 to 18. In another study of 48 young adults with schizophrenia or bipolar disorder (Phillips & Stein, 2007), the belief that mental illness was a punishment from God was associated with lower levels of psychological well-being, higher levels of a sense of personal loss, and greater psychological distress. Taken together, these studies highlight the possible negative influences that religious beliefs (e.g., child's illness seen as a punishment from God) may have on CSHCN if not addressed.

When the Illness Experience Affects Religiosity and Spirituality

In general, researchers have primarily focused on ways that religion may help or hinder family members' psychological and medical adjustment when faced with major illnesses or disabilities. Yet the reverse direction of influence is also possible and important for researchers to understand. Namely, acute or chronic illnesses may foster spiritual growth or decline. For example, parents of children with life-threatening illnesses have described sudden moments of spiritual insight and meaning triggered by coping with their child's shortened life (Raingruber & Milstein, 2007), attaining new levels of depth in their spiritual journey in the process of caring for their ill child (Nicholas et al., 2009), and increasing their faith since their child's diagnosis (Elkin et al., 2007). Studies on how an illness experience affects a child's or adolescent's sense of spirituality are lacking.

Other times, caring for a CSHCN or living with a chronic condition may negatively affect a caregivers' or child's religious or spiritual lives. Although these data are largely drawn from adult samples, religious stigma or religious doubts may negatively affect well-being (McConnell, Pargament, Ellison, & Flannelly, 2006). For example, if a parent or a child views the illness or life crisis as a punishment from the divine, this may exacerbate feelings of guilt and other negative emotions rather than facilitate coping with illness, resulting in less spiritual and religious connectedness even in the face of need (Steele & Davies, 2006).

In sum, clinicians working with CSHCN and their families should realize that the illness experience may affect religiousness and spirituality positively and negatively, particularly in the context of initial diagnosis, life-threatening conditions, and end-of-life concerns. For example, families of children with chronic medical illnesses may become more spiritual or religious because they are seeking clearer explanations for their circumstances, or they may believe their future road is beyond their control. Conversely, certain aspects of religion and the value systems they represent (e.g., sense of retribution) may exacerbate feelings of guilt and other maladaptive mechanisms rather than facilitate coping, resulting in less spiritual or religious connectedness. The remainder of this chapter focuses on clinical implications of empirical findings on the double-sided coin of religion and spirituality for families of CSHCN.

IMPLICATIONS OF INTEGRATING RELIGION AND SPIRITUALITY INTO THE CLINICAL CARE OF CSHCN

Controlled research is scarce on what effect actually addressing religiousness and spirituality with CSHCN has on patient and family outcomes. Nevertheless, plenty of literature offers clinical suggestions and techniques for addressing these issues with children. The relevant literature is discussed in the following sections. We now turn to the initial step of assessment, which is screening for the relevance of religiousness and spirituality in children's and families' lives.

Screening for Religious and Spiritual Needs in CSHCN

As indicated, religiousness and spirituality can serve as a source of great strength for some families and alternatively can be a source of distress and alienation for others. Although training in identifying and addressing spiritual needs varies greatly by discipline, clinicians should, at a minimum, be able to identify when religiousness and spirituality is an important area that should be addressed more fully within a health care context. With these basic skills, clinicians can help CSHCN and their family members articulate spiritual concerns and issues, access spiritual resources, and obtain referrals in a time of need. Spiritual screening may be warranted across a variety of health care settings (see Koenig, 2007). In addition, referral to a chaplain or spiritual care provider for children or their families experiencing a mental health or spiritual crisis may be warranted (Koenig, 2007). Others have suggested that a religious community may be a source of social support or may even provide respite care or information about other families facing similar challenges (Tarakeshwar & Pargament, 2001).

One relatively simple way to begin addressing these issues is with the use of spiritual screening tools, such as the FICA and the HOPE (see Chapter 5 in this volume). Screening questions to probe for the relevance of religious coping could easily be integrated within one of these tools. Fitchett and Risk (2009) recently published a protocol for screening for spiritual struggles in an acute medical rehabilitation unit. This protocol can be adopted for use in a pediatric subspecialty or primary care setting, or a mental health care facility, where such questions could be asked as, "Is your religion or spirituality important to you as you cope with your illness?" and, if yes, "How much strength and comfort do you get from your religion or spirituality now?" (Fitchett & Risk, 2009). These screening tools could have the benefits of triaging busy pediatric pastoral care providers and potentially increasing family satisfaction by addressing spiritual needs. The questions, however, are just preliminary screens and additional questions that involve taking a spiritual history or asking what religious coping strategies are being used may be warranted. The fictional case example of Jackie illustrates this point.

Case Example 2: Jackie

Jackie is a 15-year-old girl who has been diagnosed with acute lymphocytic leukemia (ALL). Since her diagnosis, she has undergone several chemotherapy treatments and has experienced multiple side effects (e.g., nausea, pain, hair loss). Jackie dislikes receiving medical treatments and refuses to take her medication or attend clinic visits. Per the recommendation of Jackie's doctor, her parents have taken her to a health psychologist for help. During the initial evaluation, Jackie tells the therapist that she hates "being different" from the other teens at her school. She wishes that she was never diagnosed and thinks it may be a punishment from God. After further probing, she tells her psychologist that although she is a religious person, she feels that God doesn't care about her or hear her.

Taking a Spiritual or Religious History

Particularly because Jackie has introduced the topic of God and religion in therapy, her therapist or provider should gather a spiritual history. As indicated, however, even if she had not brought up God directly, a provider could still inquire about whether Jackie has ever used religion or spirituality to manage stress in the past as a probe. Initiating questions about a client and family's spiritual history is important because it allows a provider to (a) understand how religion or spirituality may be used by family members to cope effectively or ineffectively (e.g., relieve or exacerbate stress) and (b) understand how the clients' and parents' beliefs affect future health care decisions and health outcomes (Koenig, 2007). Thus, in addition to addressing how Jackie's religiousness and spirituality affects her condition, it is also important to assess her parents' religious and spiritual beliefs because Jackie should be understood within the context of her family unit (Hart & Schneider, 1997). Furthermore, her parents may be experiencing their own spiritual distress, which may contribute to the distress that Jackie is facing (Hart & Schneider, 1997).

Tools such as the FICA and HOPE can be used as a spiritual screening for children or adolescents and parents. It is important to be sensitive to phrasing and developmentally appropriate word usage when adapting these tools to younger children. Along with considering terminology, Jackie's level of cognitive and moral functioning should be kept in mind. How does she understand the terms religion and spirituality? What abstract concept of faith does she have? Cognitive functioning and level of abstract thinking should be considered because they directly influence a child or adolescent's ability to comprehend spirituality and God (Fulton & Moore, 1995). Formal testing with the use of measures such as the FICA and HOPE in clinical settings, and determining whether such testing affects outcomes, would be beneficial.

Assessing for Religious and Spiritual Coping Methods

At a minimum, providers such as psychologists and physicians should work in tandem with pastoral care providers and chaplains in hospital settings to help families access spiritual resources and resolve spiritual crises that may be brought about by an illness experience. Another step would be to conduct spiritually focused dialogues with CSHCN and their families, without necessarily offering specific theological solutions. Simply asking questions about the use of religiousness and spirituality to cope with the illness can be a very useful intervention unto itself. The goal of this is to bring to light the spiritual resources that may not have been accessed yet as well as the spiritual struggles that may not have been recognized. Again, although we do not have empirical evidence as to what impact this type of dialogue might have on families, we do know that some families say they want to be able to discuss these issues, and we do have a solid conceptual framework from Pargament (1997) on a range of religious coping methods to assess. Exhibit 21.1 presents questions that could be asked to elicit specific positive or negative religious coping methods. These questions are based on conversations with a child at least 12 years old who has abstract reasoning capabilities, and the questions would need to be developmentally modified for a younger child. Similarly, the same set of questions could be tailored to parents or guardians regarding their own experiences. In addition to these questions and dialogues, further interventions or modalities that draw on spiritual resources or that address spiritual problems and struggles can be used (Pargament, 2007).

Eliciting Spiritual Discussions Using Specific Modalities

Although not formally evaluated with research, art mediums (e.g., therapeutic drawing) are another modality to consider when assessing children's concepts of spirituality as they relate to being a CSHCN. Art drawings may help children express their positive and negative spiritual experiences in relation to their illness, especially because they may not be able to articulate these thoughts. For example, with Jackie, a direction such as, "Draw a picture of you and God or a higher power before and after you got sick" could be given to gain a more complete understanding of how she conceptualizes and experiences

Exhibit 21.1
Religious and Spiritual Coping Methods and Corresponding Assessment Questions

Sample religious and spiritual coping methods	Sample questions
Benevolent R/S reappraisal	"Do you think there is a reason why God makes some people sick and some people well?"
Collaborative R/S coping	"Can you talk to God about your illness so that He can help you?"
Petitionary R/S coping	"In your prayers, do you ever ask God to take away your illness and make you better?"
Ritual response	"Do you ever go to church/temple/mosque when you are not feeling well to try and make yourself better?"
Pleading	"Do you ever beg God to make you better or ask for a miracle to help heal you?"
Discontent with God	"Do you ever feel that you are angry at God because of your illness?"
Belief in God's intervention	"Do you think that God will make you well when you are sick?"

Note. This list can be adapted for use with children at earlier developmental stages and does not represent an exhaustive list of religious coping methods (see, e.g., Pargament, 1997; Pendleton et al., 2002). Words such as *God* or *church* need to be tailored so as to be appropriate for the child's or family's religious tradition.

God's role in her illness (Cotton, Grossoehme, & McGrady, 2012; Pendleton et al., 2002). Art activities can be used to facilitate nonverbal communication and establish rapport in a safe, fun, and accessible way for children.

Practitioners also could use metaphors with Jackie to reintroduce the issue of her disconnect or lack of communication with God. It might be helpful to start with metaphor questions most related to something the teen or child has interest in, such as cell phones, texting, or instant messaging (Hoogestraat & Hayunga, 2006). Hoogestraat and Hayunga (2006) recommended the following interesting questions: "Do you talk on the phone . . . or use instant messenger? How do you talk to God or a higher power? Is God always online? Are there times when there are delays in God's response?" (p. 103). In addition to the use of metaphors, role-playing (Levenson & Herman, 1991) may help the practitioner to understand a child or adolescent's concept of God as well as God's role in and view of his or her illness (e.g., role-playing conversations with God). This practice, however, not yet been evaluated with clinical research.

It may be helpful to address any negative cognitive thoughts that Jackie may have that relate to her spiritual beliefs (e.g., blaming God) as they likely contribute to her dissatisfaction and distress. The exploration and reshaping of negative cognitions has consistently been related to better outcomes for adolescents experiencing recurrent thoughts associated with depressive and anxiety symptoms (Harrington, Whitaker, Shoebridge, & Campbell, 1998; Kendall & Gosch, 1994). For example, a provider or parent could ask Jackie to examine the evidence for and against the likelihood that God made her ill as a form of punishment (see Chapter 8 in this volume). Likewise, if Jackie engages in negative comparisons (e.g., "My friend was sick but God healed her quickly. I've been sick for a long time and I'm still not better"), it may be helpful to explore her notion that God "plays favorites," giving better treatment to some over others, possibly through the use of narrative therapy approaches (Freedman & Combs, 1996).

Of note, practitioners could use all of these aforementioned techniques to talk directly to parents and guardians about their own use of religious or spiritual coping when their child faces a chronic illness. In addition, addressing parents' religious issues offers a respectful way to attend to the entire family's religious and spiritual issues. If parents are encouraged to deal with their own religious and spiritual concerns, they may then be better equipped to make decisions about how they would like their children's religious and spiritual issues to be addressed. Although this certainly raises ethical and moral issues beyond the scope of this chapter, we believe that transparent and collaborative discussions about parent and child spiritual perspectives will be helpful. Furthermore, although most of the modalities described are at the individual or family level, group intervention is also a possibility.

Although there are multiple examples of adult spiritually based group interventions for chronic illness (Tarakeshwar, Pearce, & Sikkema, 2005), we were able to locate only one that has been applied to CSHCN. In a 2008 article, Farrell, Cope, Cooper, and Mathias described the adaptation of Montessori techniques, as used to teach children about religion and spirituality (Berryman, 2002), to create a "spiritually-based intervention" for CSHCN, entitled "Godly Play." This intervention helps children consider existential issues and may be particularly useful with younger children. "Godly Play" consists of instructors telling biblical stories to children with the use of specially designed props to help them visually internalize the message of the story. Children are then encouraged to retell interesting aspects of the story with the use of art, props, figures, or music. Working with children who were hospitalized for various medical conditions, Farrell et al. used "Godly Play" as the foundation for their spiritual intervention. Compared with children in the control group (who simply received a fairytale book), children in the intervention group had significant decreases in anxiety and depressive symptoms, and an increase in spirituality (i.e., closeness with God; Farrell et al., 2008).

POTENTIAL EFFECTS OF ADDRESSING SPIRITUALITY WITH CSHCN

Although the effects of having discussions about religious coping with CSHCN have not been empirically documented, many such discussions are already taking place, primarily by pastoral care services within hospitals. Discussions such as these could have various effects on children and parents: (a) They could make children and parents feel comforted or understood when their religiousness and spirituality is considered within the context of the disease as a positive resource; (b) they could cause children and parents distress or even pain if their religious beliefs are somehow in conflict with the illness or condition, or if a child or parent feels punished by the disease itself or in conflict with each others' perspectives; or (c) they could have both or neither of these effects. Cautious clinical judgment should be used when exploring these issues with CSHCN and ongoing feedback should be elicited about how the child or parent is responding to the discussion.

Recommendations for Parents

In addition to paying attention to their own spiritual and religious needs, parents of CSHCN can strive to understand how their child's religious or spiritual perspectives may be related to their child's distress. Parents should be attuned to possible signs of spiritual distress in their children. Fulton and Moore (1995) described potential signs of child spiritual distress, including crying, nightmares, excessive questions surrounding God, and illness, anger, and withdrawal from normal peer or familial interactions. Because many of these behaviors overlap with symptoms of depression, parents should consult a health care provider to clarify the possible sources and solutions of distress. Hufton (2006) gave the following suggestions for alleviating children's spiritual distress: soothing music; relevant biblical or religious readings that speak to God's comfort, love, care, and healing power; or therapeutic drawings related to spiritual themes. For example, a therapeutic drawing exercise could have family members or the child draw a challenge they are currently facing (e.g., health issues or chronic illness), draw a picture of how the problem would look if it were resolved, and draw any obstacle that would prevent the family from resolving the issue (McDonnell, Cerridwen, & Carney, 2006). This activity is meant to stimulate discussion about the struggles experienced by both the caregivers and children and could be modified to include spiritual themes (McDonnell et al., 2006).

Additionally, Prest and Robinson (2006) suggested that families and adolescents could be helped to cope with chronic or terminal illness by family discussions centering on a deeper understanding of spiritual distress and a renewed sense of hope or connection. A sample discussion question could include, "How has your illness or family member's illness changed your faith, your sense of spirituality, and your connection to the world around you?" Prest and Robinson also suggested that parents share their own feelings and spiritual struggles as they relate to their child's illness to facilitate mutual understanding, openness, and connection.

Multicultural Considerations

All of the potential interventions and studies we have reviewed need to be considered within a multicultural context as we live in a diverse world, an ever expanding religious and cultural landscape (see Volume 1, Chapter 2, this handbook). For example, although 78% of the people in the United States are Christians, a shift is taking place in which the number of Americans identifying as Protestant or Catholic is declining, and the number of people of other faiths (e.g., Muslim, Buddhist, Hindu) is increasing (Pew Forum on Religion & Public Life, 2008). Although a notable percentage of non-Christians exist within the United States, the percentage of non-Christians is significantly larger internationally. As such, a major limitation of work in this area is the focus on largely Western samples of people who are theists. It is important, however, to remain attuned to religious differences and attend to religious diversity (Walsh, 2009) when considering interventions with clients who have differing beliefs, experiences, and worldviews. In fact, the *Ethical Principles of Psychologists and Code of Conduct* (the Ethics Code; American Psychological Association [APA], 2002) states that in addition to patient's unique factors like ethnicity, gender, and sexual orientation, we are to "be aware of and respect culture . . . religious/spiritual factors" when working with members of such groups. Thus, the ideas presented in this chapter, though based largely within the Western theistic context, can and should be adapted for use in other religious traditions.

Readings by Koenig (2007), Pargament (2007), and Sperry and Shafranske (2005) may be helpful for those interested in applying these concepts when working with CSHCN from various religious and cultural backgrounds. Several of these sources combine helpful cultural and religious information with clinical practice and highlight specific religious beliefs and practices that clinicians should be aware of to provide culturally and religiously relevant care. For example, although psalms and religious scriptures have been used as tools for coping with medical illness among Christians, these methods could be adapted by replacing the psalms with revered text from the Qur'an (see Volume 1, Chapter 38, this handbook). We urge readers to consider how these proposed interventions and previous studies could be applied to a wide variety of children and families with CSHCN when tailored to their particular religious belief systems.

Future Directions

The role of religiousness and spirituality as it relates to caring for families of CSHCN is ripe for further investigation. Although there is a large and growing body of literature examining the role religiousness and spirituality play in the lives of adults living with chronic or terminal illness, much less is known about how the families of children and adolescents living with medical conditions access spiritual and religious resources to cope. Furthermore, there is a lack of empirically based information regarding how clinicians should assess and engage families' religiousness and spirituality to facilitate coping with a CSHCN. Elements to study, as they pertain to health care, include spiritual screening or taking a spiritual history, engaging in spiritually focused dialogues, administrating and evaluating spiritually based interventions, and exploring how clinicians and their families may engage external sources of spiritual resources such as congregations and ministers or spiritual leaders. Data increasingly show that patients are interested in discussing such topics (Cotton et al., 2010; MacLean et al., 2003) and are using religious coping in the context of illness (Benore et al., 2008; Cotton et al., 2009). As such, it is critical that we study how to most effectively intervene to meet the spiritual needs and manage spiritual crises of CSHCN and their families.

Many unanswered and exciting questions remain regarding religiousness and spirituality with CSHCN and their families. For example, would cognitive–behavioral therapy (CBT) enhanced with religious language tailored to a child's or parent's faith belief system improve health-related quality of life or decrease pain or depressive symptoms any more so than traditional CBT? Would systematically screening for spiritual struggles on a cancer inpatient unit or an outpatient mental health unit improve outcomes for pediatric populations and their families? What are adolescents' and children's preferences for having their religious or spiritual needs addressed in the medical context? How does the experience of an illness or disability affect a child's or parent's own faith and use of religion to cope? These questions reflect only part of the uncharted territory regarding the interface between religiousness, spirituality, and CSHCN.

CONCLUSION

In this chapter, we have reviewed theory, research, and practice on the role that religiousness and spirituality play in families of children and adolescents who have special health care needs. Overall, the literature supports the notion that many families utilize religion and spirituality to cope with the demands and difficulties of having a CSHCN. This often includes prayer and viewing the illness as an opportunity to find a deeper meaning or purpose in life. Many, however, also experience spiritual struggles in the face of CSHCN, either feeling that the illness is a punishment from God or that they have been abandoned by God in a time of great need. Often, the illness is an opportunity for spiritual and personal growth on the part of the parent, although at times the opposite is true, and a loss of faith is experienced. A variety of techniques to incorporate spiritual issues in the context of therapy or the medical setting with a CSHCN were presented, although few have been empirically evaluated.

Several limitations of previous work are important to consider. First, very few of the studies discussed in this chapter have asked children or adolescents how religiousness or spirituality fits into their own coping process or experience of their illness; this body of research has focused almost exclusively on parents' perspectives. Second, because the vast majority of previous studies have been cross-sectional in design, we know little about how religiousness or spirituality develops over time for children and their parents in the context of a CSHCN. In addition, with small sample sizes, studies are limited in their power to detect relationships between key religious or spiritual variables and clinically relevant outcomes. Finally, although many tools for spiritual assessments and clinical interactions have been developed, virtually no clinical trials empirically examine how health might be affected by addressing religiousness or spirituality with CSHCN and their families using such tools.

Understandably, numerous challenges are involved in assessing spirituality in the context of CSHCN, including, but not limited to, the following: complexities of measurement of religious and spiritual variables; human protection issues surrounding the interface between religion, health care settings, and children; and incorporating religious diversity in creative ways that utilize the religious landscape and language of the child and parent. Given the range of research methodologies available—including qualitative interviews and other such modalities as art or narratives, quantitative surveys, and advanced statistical methods—the possibilities for additional informative research to advance clinical practice are abundant.

The case examples of Ebony and Jackie are just a sampling of what many CSHCN and their families struggle with daily. Whether their faith provides solid ground to stand on or reason for questioning and anger, a clinician's job is to "enter into the worldview of the patient" (Koenig, 2007, p. 50). It is our duty to explore the place where religiousness and spirituality intersect with the challenges of living as a child or with a child with a special health care need.

References

American Psychiatric Association. (2000). *Diagnostic and statistical manual of mental disorders* (4th ed., text revision). Washington, DC: Author.

American Psychological Association. (2002). *Ethical principles of psychologists and code of conduct*. Retrieved from http://www.apa.org/ethics/code/index.aspx#

Beltrão, M. R., Vasconcelos, M. G., Pontes, C. M., & Albuquerque, M. C. (2007). Childhood cancer: Maternal perceptions and strategies for coping with diagnosis. *Jornal de Pediatria, 83,* 562–566. doi:10.2223/JPED.1723

Benore, E., Pargament, K. I., & Pendleton, S. M. (2008). An initial examination of religious coping in children with asthma. *The International Journal for the Psychology of Religion, 18,* 267–290. doi:10.1080/10508610802229197

Berryman, J. W. (2002). *The complete guide to Godly play* (Vols. 1–4). Denver, CO: Learning the Good News.

Blum, R. W. (1995). Transition to adult health care: Setting the stage. *Journal of Adolescent Health, 17,* 3–5. doi:10.1016/1054-139X(95)00073-2

Bussing, R., Koro-Ljungberg, M. E., Williamson, P., Gary, F. A., & Garvan, C. W. (2006). What "Dr. Mom" ordered: A community-based exploratory study of parental self-care responses to children's ADHD symptoms. *Social Science and Medicine, 63,* 871–882. doi:10.1016/j.socscimed.2006.03.014

Cotton, S., Grossoehme, D., & McGrady, M. (2012). Religious coping and the use of prayer in children with sickle cell disease. *Journal of Pediatric Hematology/Oncology, 58,* 244–249. doi:10.1002/pbc.23038

Cotton, S., Grossoehme, D., Rosenthal, S. L., McGrady, M. E., Roberts, Y. H., Hines, J., . . . Tsevat, J. (2009). Religious/spiritual coping in adolescents with sickle cell disease: A pilot study. *Journal of Pediatric Hematology/Oncology*, *31*, 313–318. doi:10.1097/MPH.0b013e31819e40e3

Cotton, S., Weekes, J. C., McGrady, M. E., Rosenthal, S. L., Yi, M. S., Pargament, K. I., . . . Tsevat, J. (2010). Spirituality and religiosity in urban adolescents with asthma. *Journal of Religion and Health*. (Online advance publication) doi:10.1007/s10943-010-9408-x

da Silva, R. A., Rocha, V. M., Davim, R. M., & Torres, G. V. (2008). Ways of coping with AIDS: Opinion of mothers with HIV children. *Revista Latino-Americana de Enfermagem, 16,* 260–265. doi:10.1590/S0104-11692008000200014

Dew, R. E., Daniel, S. S., Goldston, D. B., & Koenig, H. G. (2008). Religion, spirituality, and depression in adolescent psychiatric outpatients. *Journal of Nervous and Mental Disease, 196,* 247–251. doi:10.1097/NMD.0b013e3181663002

Ekas, N. V., Thomas, L., Shivers, W., & Shivers, S. (2009). Religiosity, spirituality, and socioemotional functioning in mothers of children with autism spectrum disorder. *Journal of Autism and Developmental Disorders, 39,* 706–719. doi:10.1007/s10803-008-0673-4

Elkin, T. D., Jensen, S. A., McNeil, L., Gilbert, M. E., Pullen, J., & McComb, L. (2007). Religiosity and coping in mothers of children diagnosed with cancer: An exploratory analysis. *Journal of Pediatric Oncology Nursing, 24*, 274–278. doi:10.1177/1043454207305285

Farrell, J., Cope, S. B., Cooper, J. H., & Mathias, L. (2008). Godly play: An intervention for improving physical, emotional, and spiritual responses of chronically ill hospitalized children. *Journal of Pastoral Care and Counseling, 62*, 261–271.

Fitchett, G., & Risk, J. L. (2009). Screening for spiritual struggles. *Journal of Pastoral Care and Counseling, 63*, 1–12.

Freedman, J., & Combs, G. (1996). *Narrative therapy: The social construction of preferred realities.* New York, NY: Norton.

Fulton, R. A. B., & Moore, C. M. (1995). Spiritual care of the school aged child with a chronic condition. *Journal of Pediatric Nursing, 10*, 224–231. doi:10.1016/S0882-5963(05)80019-3

Gallup Organization. (2006). *The spiritual state of the union: The role of spiritual commitment in the United States.* Retrieved from http://www.spiritualenterprise.org/archive/opinion/Final_Gallup_Report.pdf

George, L. K., Ellison, C. G., & Larson, D. B. (2002). Explaining the relationship between religious involvement and health. *Psychological Inquiry, 13*, 190–200. doi:10.1207/S15327965PLI1303_04

Gravelle, A. M. (1997). Caring for a child with a progressive illness during the complex chronic phase: Parents' experience of facing adversity. *Journal of Advanced Nursing, 25*, 738–745. doi:10.1046/j.1365-2648.1997.1997025738.x

Gray, D. E. (2006). Coping over time: The parents of children with autism. *Journal of Intellectual Disability Research, 50*, 970–976. doi:10.1111/j.1365-2788.2006.00933.x

Grossoehme, D. H. (2008). Development of a spiritual screening tool for children and adolescents. *Journal of Pastoral Care and Counseling, 62*, 71–85.

Grossoehme, D. H., & Gerbetz, L. (2004). Adolescent perceptions of meaningfulness of inpatient psychiatric hospitalization. *Clinical Child Psychology and Psychiatry, 9*, 589–596. doi:10.1177/1359104504046162

Harrington, R., Whitaker, J., Shoebridge, P., & Campbell, F. (1998). Systematic review of efficacy of cognitive behavior therapies in childhood and adolescent depressive disorder. *British Medical Journal, 316*, 1559–1563. doi:10.1136/bmj.316.7144.1559

Hart, D., & Schneider, D. (1997). Spiritual care for children with cancer. *Seminars in Oncology Nursing, 13*, 263–270. doi:10.1016/S0749-2081(97)80023-X

Hoogestraat, T. L., & Hayunga, H. G. (2006). Cell phones, the Internet, and God? Online with adolescent spirituality. In K. B. Helmeke & C. F. Sori (Eds.), *The therapist's notebook for integrating spirituality in counseling* (Vol. 2, pp. 101–108). Binghamton, NY: Haworth Press.

Hufton, E. (2006). Parting gifts: The spiritual needs of children. *Journal of Child Health Care, 10*, 240–250. doi:10.1177/1367493506066484

Kazak, A. E., Rourke, M. T., & Crump, T. A. (2003). Family and other systems in pediatric psychology. In M. C. Roberts (Ed.), *Handbook of pediatric psychology* (3rd ed., pp. 159–175). New York, NY: Guilford Press.

Kendall, P. C., & Gosch, E. A. (1994). Cognitive-Behavioral interventions. In T. H. Ollendick, N. J. King, & W. Yule (Eds.), *International handbook of phobic and anxiety disorders in children and adolescents* (pp. 415–438). New York, NY: Springer.

Koenig, H. G. (2007). *Spirituality in patient care: Why, how, when, and what.* West Conshohocken, PA: Templeton Foundation Press.

Levenson, R. L., & Herman, J. (1991). The use of role-playing as a technique in the psychotherapy of children. *Psychotherapy: Theory, Research, Practice, Training, 28*, 660–666. doi:10.1037/0033-3204.28.4.660

MacLean, C. D., Susi, B., Phifer, N., Schultz, M. D., Bynum, D., Franco, M., . . . Cykert, S. (2003). Patient preference for physician discussion and practice of spirituality. *Journal of General Internal Medicine, 18*, 38–43. doi:10.1046/j.1525-1497.2003.20403.x

Mahoney, A. (2010). Religion in families, 1999–2009: A relational spirituality framework. *Journal of Marriage and Family, 72*, 805–827. doi:10.1111/j.1741-3737.2010.00732.x

Mahoney, A., Pendleton, S. M., & Ihrke, H. (2006). Religious coping by children and adolescents: Unexplored territory in the realm of spiritual development. In E. C. Roehlkepartain, P. E. King, L. Wagener, & P. L. Benson (Eds.), *The handbook of spiritual development in childhood and adolescence* (pp. 341–354). Thousand Oaks, CA: Sage.

McConnell, K. M., Pargament, K. I., Ellison, C. G., & Flannelly, K. J. (2006). Examining the links between spiritual struggles and symptoms of psychopathology in a national sample. *Journal of Clinical Psychology, 62*, 1469–1484. doi:10.1002/jclp.20325

McDonnell, K. A., Cerridwen, H. A., & Carney, S. A. (2006). Using creative arts techniques to address spirituality with caregivers in group counseling. In K. B. Helmeke & C. F. Sori (Eds.), *The therapist's notebook for integrating spirituality in counseling* (Vol. 2, pp. 243–253). Binghamton, NY: Haworth Press.

McPherson, M., Arango, P., Fox, H., Lauver, C., McManus, M., Newacheck, P. W., . . . Strickland, B. (1998). A new definition of children with special health care needs. *Pediatrics, 102*, 137–139. doi:10.1542/peds.102.1.137

Moos, R. H., Tsu, V. D., & Schaefer, J. A. (Eds.). (1977). *Coping with physical illness*. New York, NY: Plenum Medical. doi:10.1007/978-1-4684-2256-6

Newacheck, P. W., Strickland, B., Shonkoff, J. P., Perrin, J. M., McPherson, M., McManus, M., . . . Arango, P. (1998). An epidemiologic profile of children with special health care needs. *Pediatrics, 102*, 117–123. doi:10.1542/peds.102.1.117

Nicholas, D. B., Gearing, R. E., McNeill, T., Fung, K., Lucchetta, S., & Selkirk, E. K. (2009). Experiences and resistance strategies utilized by fathers of children with cancer. *Social Work in Health Care, 48*, 260–275. doi:10.1080/00981380802591734

Nottage, S. L. (2005). Parents' use of nonmedical support services in the neonatal intensive care unit. *Issues in Comprehensive Pediatric Nursing, 28*, 257–273. doi:10.1080/01460860500396922

Pargament, K. I. (1997). *The psychology of religion and coping: Theory, research, and practice*. New York, NY: Guilford Press.

Pargament, K. I. (2007). *Spiritually integrated psychotherapy: Understanding and addressing the sacred*. New York, NY: Guilford Press.

Pargament, K. I., & Hahn, J. (1986). God and the just world: Casual coping attributions in health situations. *Journal for the Scientific Study of Religion, 25*, 193–207. doi:10.2307/1385476

Pargament, K. I., Koenig, H. G., & Perez, L. M. (2000). The many methods of religious coping: Development and initial validation of the RCOPE. *Journal of Clinical Psychology, 56*, 519–543. doi:10.1002/(SICI)1097-4679(200004)56:4<519::AID-JCLP6>3.0.CO;2-1

Pargament, K. I., Koenig, H. G., Tarakeshwar, N., & Hahn, J. (2004). Religious coping methods as predictors of psychological, physical, and spiritual outcomes among medically ill elderly patients: A two-year longitudinal study. *Journal of Health Psychology, 9*, 713–730. doi:10.1177/1359105304045366

Pendleton, S. M., Cavalli, K. S., Pargament, K. I., & Nasr, S. Z. (2002). Religious/Spiritual coping in childhood cystic fibrosis: A qualitative study. *Pediatrics, 109*, e8. doi:10.1542/peds.109.1.e8

Phillips, R. E., III, & Stein, C. H. (2007). God's will, God's punishment, or God's limitation? Religious coping strategies reported by young adults living with serious mental illness. *Journal of Clinical Psychology, 63*, 529–540. doi:10.1002/jclp.20364

Prest, L. A., & Robinson, W. D. (2006). Exploring spirituality within the crucible of illness and healing. In K. B. Helmeke & C. F. Sori (Eds.), *The therapist's notebook for integrating spirituality in counseling* (Vol. 2, pp. 191–201). Binghamton, NY: Haworth Press.

Raingruber, B., & Milstein, J. (2007). Searching for circles of meaning and using spiritual experiences to help parents of infants with life-threatening illness cope. *Journal of Holistic Nursing, 25*, 39–49. doi:10.1177/0898010106289859

Rando, T. A. (1983). An investigation of grief and adaptation in parents whose children have died from cancer. *Journal of Pediatric Psychology, 8*, 3–20. doi:10.1093/jpepsy/8.1.3

Rogers-Dulan, J. (1998). Religious connectedness among urban African American families who have a child with disabilities. *Mental Retardation, 36*, 91–103. doi:10.1352/0047-6765(1998)036<0091:RCAUAA>2.0.CO;2

Schneider, M. A., & Mannell, R. C. (2006). Beacon in the storm: An exploration of the spirituality and faith of parents whose children have cancer. *Issues in Comprehensive Pediatric Nursing, 29*, 3–24. doi:10.1080/01460860500523731

Smith, C. L., & Denton, M. L. (2005). *Soul searching: The religious and religious lives of American teenagers*. New York, NY: Oxford University Press.

Sperry, L., & Shafranske, E. P. (Eds.). (2005). *Spiritually oriented psychotherapy*. Washington, DC: American Psychological Association. doi:10.1037/10886-000

Steele, R., & Davies, B. (2006). Impact on parents when a child has a progressive, life-threatening illness. *International Journal of Palliative Nursing, 12*, 576–585.

Sterling, Y. M., & Peterson, J. W. (2003). Characteristics of African American women caregivers of children with asthma. *American Journal of Maternal Child Nursing, 28*, 32–38. doi:10.1097/00005721-200301000-00008

Sulmasy, D. P. (2002). A biopsychosocial-spiritual model for the care of patients at the end of life. *The Gerontologist, 42*(Suppl. 3), 24–33. doi:10.1093/geront/42.suppl_3.24

Tarakeshwar, N., & Pargament, K. I. (2001). Religious coping in families of children with autism. *Focus on Autism and Other Developmental Disabilities, 16*, 247–260. doi:10.1177/108835760101600408

Tarakeshwar, N., Pearce, M. J., & Sikkema, K. (2005). Development and implementation of a spiritual coping group intervention for adults living with HIV/AIDS: A pilot study. *Mental Health, Religion, and Culture, 8*, 179–190. doi:10.1080/13694670500138908

Pew Forum on Religion & Public Life. (2008). *U.S. religious landscape survey religious affiliation: Diverse and dynamic*. Retrieved from http://religions.pewforum.org/pdf/report-religious-landscape-study-full.pdf

Thompson, R. J., & Gustafson, K. E. (1996). *Adaptation to chronic child illness*. Washington, DC: American Psychological Association. doi:10.1037/10188-000

Wallander, J. L., Thompson, R. J., Jr., & Alriksson-Schmidt, A. (2003). Psychosocial adjustment of children with chronic physical conditions. In M. C. Roberts (Ed.), *Handbook of pediatric psychology* (3rd ed., pp. 141–158). New York, NY: Guilford Press.

Walsh, F. (2009). Integrating spirituality in family therapy: Wellsprings for health, healing, and resilience. In F. Walsh (Ed.), *Spiritual resources in family therapy* (2nd ed., pp. 31–61). New York, NY: Guilford Press.

Zehnder, D., Prchal, A., Vollrath, M., & Landolt, M. A. (2006). Prospective study of the effectiveness of coping in pediatric patients. *Child Psychiatry and Human Development, 36*, 351–368. doi:10.1007/s10578-005-0007-0

CHAPTER 22

SPIRITUAL AND RELIGIOUS PROBLEMS: INTEGRATING THEORY AND CLINICAL PRACTICE

Aaron Murray-Swank and Nichole A. Murray-Swank

John[1] was urgently referred to psychotherapy from our emergency service at the medical center. As we sat down to talk, the cause of John's current problems was quickly apparent. John was experiencing intense urges to harm a man that he recently met. He learned that this man was convicted of a crime, which triggered memories of a previous experience during which John's family was traumatized by a shooting in his community. John had gone as far as considering how and when he could shoot this man he recently met. With chilling intensity, John explained how this man personified evil. John was also a veteran of the Vietnam War, and experienced chronic, untreated symptoms of posttraumatic stress disorder (PTSD) as well as some cognitive problems and difficulty with impulsivity resulting from a traumatic brain injury.

As I asked him questions to assess the situation, John talked of his inner "spiritual warfare." He poignantly used religious terms and images to describe his situation. John identified himself as a Catholic. Although he struggled to fit in and participate in a religious community, his religious and spiritual beliefs were personally important to him and were integral to how he approached the world. John described being a tortured soul, noting the importance of his spiritual life and his relationship with God. He talked of his struggle with the "evil and demons" he personally experienced and the need for "divine justice," which fueled his homicidal thoughts. John viewed the perpetrator of the crime as a scourge on society and part of a larger pattern of social decay, in which the "evil" elements of society threatened what was most sacred to him, his family. When asked why he had chosen to seek help, he talked of his spiritual responsibility to be a good father and husband, which appeared to be one of the primary motivators to restrain his rage. In providing services to John, many issues needed to be addressed: the acute and pressing safety issues, his untreated PTSD, his problems with emotional regulation and impulsivity. One of the most remarkable aspects of our first conversation was the spiritual problem he presented. He had experienced many horrible events in his life and the life of his family, driving him to feel that he was literally engaged in a spiritual war with evil forces. This was leading him to the edge of taking another human life. At the same time, his spiritual belief system appeared to be restraining his behavior. Although there were clearly important psychological issues going on, John largely expressed his problems in spiritual terms.

John's case is a dramatic example of a spiritual problem in a clinical setting. Spiritual problems, however, may present in a variety of forms for practitioners: a client experiencing distress related to a religious conversion, a client struggling with religious obsessions and compulsions, a sexual abuse survivor who feels intense alienation from God, or a college student struggling with a loss of faith.

This chapter focuses on the role of psychology in helping people come to terms with spiritual problems. We begin by providing a rationale for why

[1]For cases presented in this chapter, pseudonyms are used, and identifying details have been altered for confidentiality.

DOI: 10.1037/14046-022
APA Handbook of Psychology, Religion, and Spirituality: Vol. 2. An Applied Psychology of Religion and Spirituality, K. I. Pargament (Editor-in-Chief)

psychologists should be equipped to address spiritual problems in clinical practice. Next, we review literature on spiritual problems and prominent models for working with spiritual problems in clinical practice. We discuss interventions that flow from these models and broader psychological and spiritual interventions for spiritual problems. Finally, we consider some unique challenges of addressing spiritual problems in practice, and directions for future clinical, research, and training needs in this area of practice.

In our chapter, the terms *religious* and *religious problems* are used to encompass phenomena and problems associated with institutional religion and religious practices. We use the terms *spiritual* and *spiritual problems* when focusing on beliefs, practices, and experiences having to do with the sacred that are not necessarily linked to established institutionalized systems (see Volume 1, Chapter 1, this handbook).

RATIONALE FOR ADDRESSING RELIGIOUS AND SPIRITUAL PROBLEMS

Traditionally, there has not been a strong emphasis on addressing religious and spiritual problems among mental health practitioners. Clients often present with spiritual problems as a prominent concern, however. Although systematic investigations of the frequency of spiritual problems are limited, existing data suggest that it is relatively common for psychologists to encounter spiritual problems in their practice. For example, in a survey of psychologists who were members of the American Psychological Association (APA), Shafranske and Maloney (1990) found that on average, psychologists reported that at least one in six clients presented with problems directly related to religion or spirituality. In a survey of 5,472 university students, Johnson and Hayes (2003) reported that approximately 25% of students reported considerable distress related to spiritual concerns. In sum, from both client and clinician perspectives, it appears that spiritual problems are relatively common.

We propose that mental health practitioners have an important role to play in addressing spiritual problems. This is underscored by the *Ethical Principles of Psychologists and Code of Conduct* (the Ethics Code; APA, 2002), which states that

> psychologists are aware of and respect cultural, individual, and role differences, including those based on age, gender, gender identity, race, ethnicity, culture, national origin, *religion* [emphasis added], sexual orientation, disability, language, and socioeconomic status and consider these factors when working with members of such groups.

Religion and spirituality are similar to other areas of diversity that are woven into the fabric of the lives of individuals, families, and communities with whom psychologists work. Thus, psychologists should routinely assess the religious and spiritual dimension of clients' lives, similar to the manner in which psychologists seek to understand issues of culture, gender, sexual orientation, or disability status among clients.

Fortunately, increasing attention has focused on identifying core competencies in assessing and working with spiritual issues and problems. Hathaway and Ripley (2009) have spearheaded efforts within APA Division 36 (Society for the Psychology of Religion and Spirituality) in this regard. In 2005, an ad hoc committee within Division 36 generated preliminary practice guidelines, focusing on assessment, intervention, and diversity considerations for psychologists working with religious and spiritual issues. These preliminary guidelines, derived from expert consensus and application of ethical principles, have been published in a recent text on spirituality and psychotherapy (Hathaway & Ripley, 2009). These practice guidelines focus on three general areas: religious or spiritual assessment, religious or spiritual interventions, and religious or spiritual issues in multicultural and diversity practice. Although preliminary, this work represents the current best practice guidelines and current standard of care for the clinician addressing spiritual problems in practice.

In another vein, Pargament (2007) provided a pragmatic and empirical foundation for addressing spirituality as part of psychotherapy on the basis of four propositions: spirituality can be part of the solution, spirituality can be part of the problem, spirituality cannot be separated from psychotherapy, and people want spiritually sensitive help. Although other chapters in this handbook review research on spirituality as a resource, our attention will focus more sharply on situations in which spirituality is identified as part of the problem.

DEFINING RELIGIOUS AND SPIRITUAL PROBLEMS

For much of the 20th century history, spiritual problems were generally either ignored by traditional mental health practitioners or assumed to be related to some other form of psychopathology (e.g., religious delusions in psychotic processes). During the past few decades, a new view has emerged within the field. This paradigm highlights the importance of religion and spirituality among clients, and views spiritual problems as an important, legitimate, and necessary area of focus for practitioners.

One milestone reflective of this shift in the mental health field was the inclusion of Religious and Spiritual Problem as a diagnostic category in the *Diagnostic and Statistical Manual of Mental Disorders* (4th ed., text revision; *DSM–IV–TR*; American Psychiatric Association, 2000). This new diagnostic category was introduced in 1994 (Lukoff, Lu, & Turner, 1998). The *DSM–IV–TR* defines a Religious or Spiritual Problem (V62.89) in the following way:

> This category can be used when the focus of clinical attention is a religious or spiritual problem. Examples include distressing experiences that involve loss or questioning of faith, problems associated with conversion to a new faith, or questioning of spiritual values that may not necessarily be related to an organized church or religious institution. (American Psychiatric Association, 2000, p. 741)

Currently, the diagnostic category Religious or Spiritual Problem is being reviewed and refined for the upcoming fifth edition of the *DSM* (Peteet, Lu, & Narrow, 2011).

The recognition of spiritual problems as a legitimate area of clinical attention is a significant step forward, but a pressing challenge for practitioners is to develop a comprehensive and scientifically informed knowledge base about religious and spiritual problems that may be the focus of clinical attention. Before we can adequately address religious and spiritual problems, we need to have some way of defining and understanding them. In this chapter, we define a religious or spiritual (R/S) problem as "a problem involving aspects of religious or spiritual belief, experience, or practice, as indicated by an individual's distress or impairment in functioning." This definition is intentionally broad, to capture the wide range of phenomenon that reflect religious and spiritual problems, which we will discuss in further detail in the next section.

CONCEPTUAL MODELS OF RELIGIOUS AND SPIRITUAL PROBLEMS

We now review some prominent perspectives on spiritual problems in the literature (see also Chapter 4 in this volume). In this review, we will describe each theory or description of spiritual problems and provide examples of clinical interventions that flow from the theory.

Pargament: Spiritually Integrated Psychotherapy

One framework for understanding spiritual problems is provided by Pargament's (2007) work on spiritually integrated psychotherapy. Pargament's model focuses on how individuals discover, conserve, and transform their experience of the sacred in their lives. The sacred refers to the individuals' experience of God, the divine, or some transcendent reality as well as aspects of life that take on divine character and significance. In this model, the sacred is conceptualized as the core of spirituality.

According to this theory, people generally seek to conserve, or hold on to, the sacred in their lives. This is especially the case when people encounter life stressors, tragedies, and losses. Examples of conservational methods of spiritual coping include seeking spiritual support from various sources (e.g., God, clergy, other individuals in the spiritual community) and making benevolent spiritual reappraisals, such as redefining a stressor through a spiritual understanding. At times, the individuals' understanding and experience of the sacred is challenged, which can result in spiritual struggle. During these times, conservation may no longer be a compelling method of coping. This can prompt another type of spiritual coping, one more focused on transforming the sacred. Whereas conservational coping focuses on holding onto and enhancing one's existing relationship to the sacred, transformational spiritual coping involves a fundamental change or shift in the individual's relationship with the sacred.

In addition to processes of conservation and transformation, other concepts in Pargament's (2007) theory are destinations and pathways in the search for the sacred. Destinations are the ends that are sought (e.g., closeness to God, spiritual understanding, spiritual connection with other people), whereas pathways are the means by which individuals seek their spiritual destinations (e.g., prayer, meditation, participation in a spiritual community).

With regard to spiritual problems, a key idea is that individuals can move toward greater integration or disintegration in their spiritual journeys. In the following passage, Pargament (2007) contrasted spiritual integration and spiritual disintegration:

> A well-integrated spirituality is defined not by a specific belief, practice, emotion, or relationship, but by the degree to which the individual's spiritual pathways and destinations work together in synchrony with each other. At its best, spirituality is defined by pathways that are broad and deep, responsive to life's situations, nurtured by a larger social context, capable of flexibility and continuity, and oriented towards a Sacred destination that is large enough to encompass the full range of human potential and luminous enough to provide the individual with a powerful guiding vision. *At its worst, spirituality is dis-integrated, defined by pathways that lack scope and depth, fail to meet the challenges and demands of life events, clash and collide with the surrounding social system, change and shift too easily or not at all, and misdirect the individual in pursuit of spiritual value* [emphasis added]. (p. 236)

Within this model, spiritual problems are conceptualized as problems of disintegration, either in the spiritual destinations that the individual is seeking or in the pathways that are used to seek the sacred.

Along these lines, Pargament (2007) delineated two broad categories of spiritual problems: problems of spiritual destinations and problems of spiritual pathways (see Table 22.1 for description and examples). In problems of spiritual destinations, the individual's concept and experience of the sacred is limited, resulting in negative consequences. Problems of spiritual destinations include problems of small gods, problems of false gods, and problems of sacred clashes within the self. For example, addictions can represent a problem of false gods, in which objects or experiences unable to hold the sacred become a consuming focus of worship (e.g., drugs, alcohol, sex). One of the strengths of Pargament's framework is that it outlines specific intervention strategies that flow from the theoretical understanding of the problem. In addressing problems of false gods, the strategies include the steps of naming false Gods, identifying the underlying spiritual yearning, letting go of false Gods, and practicing altered perceptions of the sacred.

Problems of spiritual pathways include problems of breadth and depth, problems of fit, and problems of continuity and change. In problems of spiritual pathways, the primary disintegration involves the path the individual is taking to pursue the sacred. The case example of John can be conceptualized, at least in part, as a problem of fit. John's image of the sacred included concepts of divine justice. It was this concept—combined with his current circumstances of encountering a perpetrator—that led him to consider murder as a way to preserve and protect his sacred notion of divine justice. His dilemma reflects a problem of fit between the pathways he was considering (i.e., seeking retribution by harming the perpetrator) and his ultimate spiritual destination (i.e., seeking justice, being a loving father and husband). It was clear that the pathway John was considering was disproportionate to his destination, and it was also likely to interfere with other valued goals, such as being a loving father and husband.

TABLE 22.1

Types of Religious and Spiritual Problems

Theory of religious or spiritual problem	Category of religious or spiritual problem	Subtype of religious or spiritual problem	Description and example(s)
Pargament, *Spiritually Integrated Psychotherapy* (2007)	Problems of spiritual destinations	Problems of small gods	Holding a limited view of the range and depth of the sacred, which contributes to poorly integrated spirituality. For example, holding a narrow image of a punishing or exclusionary God, resulting in distress and dysfunction.
		Problems of false gods	The problem of idolatry, when an object "substitutes" for the sacred. For example, using alcohol or drugs to fill a spiritual vacuum.
		Problems of sacred clashes within	Includes ambivalence toward the sacred, self-degradation in relation to the sacred, demonization of self and others, and internal sacred wars. For example, holding conflicting images of the sacred, resulting in distress and dysfunction.
	Problems of spiritual pathways	Problems of breadth and depth	Spirituality is not well integrated or lacking depth. For example, religion or spirituality is compartmentalized in the life of the individual.
		Problems of fit	*Between spiritual pathways and destinations*: Disconnect between what is sought and the pathway to achieve it. ■ Spiritual extremism: Using extreme means to achieve spiritual goals (e.g., religious violence). ■ Spiritual hypocrisy: Misusing spiritual pathways to reach non-spiritual or antispiritual ends. For example, a religious leader who abuses or manipulates followers. *Between spiritual pathways and situations*: Poor fit between the particular spiritual pathway the person is taking and the situation. For example, using prayer but not seeking medical treatment for a treatable medical problem. *Between the individual and the social context*: Disharmony between the individual's spiritual pathways and the social context. For example, being in a religious or spiritual community in which one feels ostracized or rejected, leading to distress and dysfunction.
		Problems of continuity and change	Difficulty navigating the dialectic between continuity and change in religious and spiritual life. For example, ineffective clinging to fixed beliefs in the face of new challenges.
Griffith, *Religion That Harms, Religion That Heals* (2010)	"When religious life propels suffering"	Clinical problems from insecure attachments	Disturbance in relationship with God as an attachment figure. For example, feeling unworthy of God's love (anxious attachment), sense of distance from God (dismissive avoidant), or fearing punishment from God (fearful avoidant).
		Clinical problems from social hierarchy, peer affiliation, and reciprocal altruism	Group expectations supersede individual needs in a way that results in harmful behaviors. For example, denying needed medical treatment to a child on the basis of religious beliefs.
		Clinical problems from peer affiliation, kin recognition, and social exchange	Problems resulting from social processes that create a powerful identification with an in-group and exclude members of an out-group. For example, religion provides justification and motivation for violence because of in-group and out-group processes.

(*Continued*)

TABLE 22.1 (*Continued*)

Types of Religious and Spiritual Problems

Theory of religious or spiritual problem	Category of religious or spiritual problem	Subtype of religious or spiritual problem	Description and example(s)
	"When mental illness infiltrates religious life"	Religion distorted by a mood disorder	Religious and spiritual life is distorted by themes of depression, such as excessive and inappropriate guilt regarding sin, or themes of mania, such as grandiosity about one's spiritual experience. In extreme cases, religion can interact with the disorder to contribute to suicidal behavior.
		Religion disorganized by psychosis	Expression of religious and spiritual life is disorganized by psychotic symptoms such as delusions and hallucinations. This should be distinguished from experiences within religious and spiritual life that may resemble psychotic symptoms (e.g., mystical experiences, kundalini awakening).
		Religion shrunken by an anxiety disorder	Religious and spiritual life becomes constricted by themes of anxiety and fear. For example, experiencing frequent and persistent obsessions about one's sins, and engaging in religious rituals to neutralize this anxiety.

John's problem also could be considered a problem of "small gods," in the sense that he came into therapy narrowly focused on one aspect of God (a God of justice and revenge) but had lost sight of other aspects of his experience of God. In working with John, it proved beneficial to address his spiritual problem by helping him see this problem of fit and broadening his spiritual experience beyond his "small god," which was narrowly focused on revenge. The following dialogue provides an example of what this looked like in session:

Therapist: So, there is one part of you that feels very angry and wants to take matters into your own hands with this guy. However, it also seems there is another, maybe even deeper part of you that wants something else . . .

John: I just can't get it out of my head, I'm totally thinking about him all the time. I'm here talking to you because I'm afraid of what I might do.

Therapist: I can tell this is a real struggle for you. We were talking about how your spiritual beliefs are an important part of this. How would harming his guy fit with who you want to be spiritually?

John: I know it's probably not the way to go, but I'm really at my wits end. I mean, there has to be some justice here! Everything in our society is falling apart. To tell you the truth, the only thing holding me back the other day was thinking of what would happen to my daughter if I did something stupid. I don't want to put her through that.

Therapist: Your daughter is deeply important to you. You talked earlier about being a "spiritual father" and "protector" for her. Can you tell me more about what that means to you?

John: I just want to be a "normal dad," to be there for her. It is a man's role to be a spiritual father, a role model . . .

Therapist: What does it mean to be a "normal dad" and a spiritual father and role model?

John: For her not to be afraid of me, or embarrassed of me. To just spend time with her. For her to know I'm there for her.

Therapist: Can you tell me about a time you experienced this, the feeling that you were there for her?

John: I can remember a time when we took a trip camping together and spent a lot of time together, just doing stuff outside. Me and her. That was before everything happened with the shooting . . .

Therapist: You have made this contrast between this part of you who wants to seek revenge, and this part of you who wants to be there for your daughter, as a spiritual father and role model. This seems like a difficult conflict that goes on inside for you.

John: Obviously, my daughter is most important—it is just hard to see and remember when I get triggered by all the bad stuff . . .

Therapist: I'm wondering if we can put a plan together to help you apply what we have talked about—how to connect with the importance of your spiritual role as a father—especially in times when you get triggered with these feelings.

John and I worked together to devise a plan, making a concrete list of things he could do in coping with his situation. This included things like bringing thoughts of his daughter to mind and developing coping statements that reminded him of his deepest spiritual values. Our work also included simple breathing and grounding techniques, some of which incorporated practices from his spiritual tradition (e.g., saying the Lord's Prayer). This work targeted the problem of small gods by broadening his experience to include other sacred strivings, and it also addressed the problem of fit by bringing his pathways and destinations into better alignment. Over the next several weeks, John kept the plan in his wallet, and he reported that this list was helpful to ground him in what was ultimately most important to him and to give him specific coping techniques to deal with his situation.

John's case probably is not "typical," but we believe it illustrates several important points relevant to addressing religious and spiritual problems. First, and probably most important, the clinician took the spiritual dimension of John's problem seriously, and made it clear to the client that this was an important aspect of the therapy. It could have been tempting to reduce his problem to some more fundamental psychological issue: intrapsychic conflicts, PTSD, cognitive rigidity, and impulsivity. Although these psychological issues were present and important, they were not given primacy over the religious and spiritual dimensions of his problems. This approach went a long way toward forming a collaborative relationship with John.

Second, this example illustrates several strategies suggested by Pargament (2007) for addressing problems of spiritual pathways. For example, making the spiritual conflict explicit helped John see that his pathways and destinations were inconsistent. Of note, John's fantasies of "enacting justice" were imbued with sacred meaning for John. This is an illustration of the potential dark side of sacred strivings. They were only part of the picture, however, albeit one to which John was devoting significant time and energy. By seeing the spiritual conflict and clarifying and connecting with his spiritual destinations, John was able to broaden and deepen his spiritual pathways. He was able to put this into practice through specific activities, such as focusing on other sacred strivings (i.e., to be a "spiritual father") and using spiritual practices (i.e., prayer).

Griffith: Religion That Harms, Religion That Heals

Another framework for conceptualizing religious and spiritual problems is offered by Griffith (2010) in his text *Religion That Heals, Religion That Harms: A Guide for Clinical Practice*. Griffith's theory is based on a sociobiological perspective on religion and how sociobiological processes intersect with religious life in problematic ways. Griffith has described six sociobiological processes—attachment, peer affiliation, kin recognition, social hierarchy, social exchange, and reciprocal altruism—which are hard-wired in human biology and social experience. In Griffith's theory, religious and spiritual problems occur when these processes go awry to produce behavior and experiences that are harmful for individuals and society. Griffith's theory offers a unique contribution to the literature on religious and spiritual problems, particularly by addressing harmful and clinically important aspects of religion within a novel conceptual framework.

As outlined in Table 22.1, Griffith's theory considers religious and spiritual problems in two broad categories: problems "when religious life propels suffering" and problems "when mental illness infiltrates religious life." There are three types of problems within the former category, including (a) clinical problems from insecure attachments; (b) clinical problems from social hierarchy, peer affiliation, and reciprocal altruism; and (c) clinical problems from peer affiliation, kin recognition, and social exchange.

Although the complexities of the sociobiological processes are beyond the scope of this chapter, we will briefly describe the key features of each of these types of religious and spiritual problems.

When Religious Life Propels Suffering

Clinical problems from insecure attachments. Attachment processes are a fundamental way in which human beings feel safe and connected to others in the world. Researchers have used the concept of attachment relationships to understand God as a relational figure in individual's lives (e.g., Kirkpatrick, 2005; see Volume 1, Chapter 7, this handbook). Clinical problems from insecure attachments arise from an emotionally problematic connection with God. As detailed in Table 22.1, these include problems of anxious attachment, dismissive avoidant attachment, and fearful avoidant attachment with God.

Clinical problems from social hierarchy, peer affiliation, and reciprocal altruism. Social processes of social hierarchy (following leaders and institutional structures), peer affiliation (establishing connection with other peers), and reciprocal altruism (performing and receiving altruistic acts between members of a community) are very important in religious and spiritual life. They help religious and spiritual groups form strong communities that provide a powerful source of support and connection. Problems arise, however, when these social processes promote harmful behaviors by subjugating individuals' needs to the larger group. Griffith (2010) cited the example of Wesley Parker, an 11-year-old boy with diabetes who died when his parents withheld insulin following their experience with an evangelist preacher at a religious revival. In this case, the evangelist encouraged church members to place their faith in God that they would be physically healed. Wesley felt that he was healed from his diabetes and was encouraged by his religious social network to forgo his medical treatment. The resulting social processes within Wesley's family and church community contributed to his tragic death.

Clinical problems from peer affiliation, kin recognition, and social exchange. In this type of problem, peer affiliation, kin recognition (recognizing members of one's own race/religion/culture), and social exchange processes (members of a group taking care of each other) create a powerful "in-group" among religious and spiritual communities. Problems result when others are defined as an "out-group" and then are subject to oppression, discrimination, or violence. The protypical example of this type of religious or spiritual problem is religiously motivated acts of violence and aggression.

When Mental Illness Infiltrates Religious Life

The second broad category of problems occurs when symptoms of mental illness influence religious beliefs and experience. Within this category, Griffith (2010) considered the different ways in which different forms of psychiatric illness may negatively interact with religious and spiritual experiences. Specific subtypes of problems discussed include those related to mood disorders, psychotic disorders, and anxiety disorders (see Table 22.1 for examples). As we will see shortly, one of the particular challenges in dealing with these types of problems is disentangling the complex interplay between the psychiatric disorder and the individuals' religion or spirituality.

Griffith (2010) outlined an assessment and intervention strategy for working with religious and spiritual problems. The heart of the intervention strategy is creating a context in which positive aspects of the individuals' spirituality can emerge, and the influence of the harmful sociobiological processes is minimized. Griffith offered the useful concept of "whole person-relatedness" as a therapeutic stance of the clinician. He described this as "opening oneself and responding fully to the other as a person" (Griffith, 2010, p. 29), demonstrating keen interest in understanding the experience of the other person, and putting aside distinctions about social categories. Whole person-relatedness creates a context in which dialogue and reflection about religious and spiritual problems is possible.

Another component in Griffith's (2010) therapeutic approach is helping the client identify the personal elements of adaptive spirituality within the context of their religious life. In this vein, Griffith's framework contrasted eight common "existential postures of vulnerability" versus "existential postures of resilience": confusion versus coherence, isolation versus communion, despair versus hope, helplessness versus agency, meaninglessness versus purpose, indifference versus commitment, cowardice versus courage, and resentment versus gratitude. In his text, Griffith outlined ways for clinicians to help clients enhance resilience in their religious and spiritual lives. The goal of this work is to broaden elements of spirituality that foster growth and healing in the face of religious and spiritual problems. Griffith tied the rationale for this line of intervention back to his sociobiological theory:

> When personal spirituality strengthens, the religious world of sociobiology does not disappear. However, it is domesticated to serve the well-being of individual persons. The role of sociobiological religion is transformed. Personal spirituality tends to recruit secure attachment styles rather than anxious or avoidant ones. Social hierarchy and peer affiliation processes are refocused to attend first to the needs of individual members of religious groups rather than group missions. (p. 141)

The clinical example of John discussed earlier in the chapter can be viewed through the lens of Griffith's (2010) theory. John's spiritual problem involved the identification and demonization of an out-group (e.g., those who had committed crimes and thus threatened his family). Religious feeling and imagery served as a factor that amplified his violent fantasies and impulses when he personally encountered a member of this out-group. In his situation, PTSD also intensified his perception of threat and heightened the intensity of his emotion regarding the situation. His PTSD interacted with his religious belief system and his strong identification of an out-group, resulting in the strong urges toward violence that drove him to seek help.

Therapeutically, it was essential to work with John from a stance of whole person-relatedness, acknowledging and entering into his perspective and experience. From the perspective of Griffith's (2010) theory, this type of therapeutic relationship diminished the effects of sociobiological processes driving the urge toward violence and created an alternate context in which dialogue and reflection about his situation was possible. Another component of the therapy was helping John come in contact with another part of his personal spiritual convictions, which involved his connection with his daughter and family. In Griffith's terminology, this was locating his personal spirituality though existential inquiry of what was most deeply important to him. It was this mobilization of this dimension of his personal spirituality that ultimately helped him weather his storm of emotions.

Lukoff: Religious and Spiritual Problems in Transpersonal Psychology

From a transpersonal psychology perspective, psychologist David Lukoff has done extensive work in describing a range of religious and spiritual problems. Currently, Lukoff's (Lukoff, Lu, & Turner, 1998) typology includes separate categories of religious problems and spiritual problems. Religious problems include loss or questioning of faith; changes in religious membership, practice, or beliefs; new religious movements and cults; and religious problems associated with life-threatening and terminal illness. Spiritual problems include difficulties associated with mystical experiences, near-death experiences, problems related to meditation and spiritual practice, psychic experiences, visionary experiences shamanic experiences, alien encounter experiences, and possession experiences. Although some of these topics are outside of mainstream psychology (e.g., alien encounter and possession experiences), Lukoff's typology provides a broad sweep of different types of religious and spiritual problems that have been described in this literature.

A distinct aspect of Lukoff's theory is that it provides guidance for working with spiritual problems that have been termed *spiritual emergencies*. Lukoff et al. (1998) have cited the definition of Grof and Grof, who define spiritual emergencies as follows:

> Crises when the process of growth and change becomes chaotic and overwhelming. Individuals experiencing such

> episodes may feel that their sense of identity is breaking down, their old values no longer hold true, and that the very ground beneath their personal realities is radically shifting. In many cases, new realms of mystical and spiritual experiences enter their lives suddenly and dramatically, resulting in fear and confusion. They may feel tremendous anxiety, have difficulty coping with their daily lives, jobs, and relationships, and maybe even fear for their own sanity. (p. 28)

In their review of this literature, Lukoff et al. (1998) and Lukoff, Lu, and Yang (2010) offered a more detailed description of the different types of spiritual problems and emergencies as well as recommendations for helping people with these types of problems. For example, they provided an example cited in Kornfield (1993) of a young man who was engaged in intensive meditation practice and experienced an explosive energy, leading to erratic verbal outbursts and activity as well as an inability to sleep. In this case, the meditation teacher addressed this spiritual problem by making several recommendations to the young man: taking a break from meditation practice, making dietary changes to eat more "grounding" foods, increasing physical and outdoor activity, taking soothing baths, and gradually and carefully reintroducing meditation practice after his mental and emotional state had stabilized. Additionally, Lukoff et al. (1998) offered the following guidance for working with such spiritual emergencies in practice: providing information to clients about spiritual emergencies and normalizing the experience, using art therapy to allow expression of emotions and experiences, and consulting with spiritual teachers with expertise in the specific type of spiritual problem.

Hathaway: Clinically Significant Religious Impairment

Hathaway's work on clinically significant religious impairment (CSRI) introduced a novel construct into the literature on religious and spiritual problems. The concept of CSRI is that psychological disorders may result in impairment in the religious or spiritual life of the individual, and that this impairment is important to address in the treatment of psychological and spiritual problems. Hathaway, Scott, and Garver (2004) have defined CSRI as "a reduced ability to perform religious/spiritual activities, achieve religious/spiritual goals, or experience religious/spiritual states because of a psychological disorder" (p. 97). For example, Hathaway and Barkley (2003) further delineated specific types of CSRI that may be linked to attention-deficit/hyperactivity disorder, including problems in the area of spiritual focus, socialization into religious traditions, internalization of faith, stability of faith, and issues with religious and spiritual alienation. One of the advantages of this construct is that it explicitly highlights the religious and spiritual problems that can result as a consequence of psychological disorders and helps clinicians identify specific areas for intervention.

The CSRI construct reminds us that the relationship between psychological problems and spiritual distress is likely bidirectional. This interplay between psychological disorders and spiritual problems is an important issue, and one that deserves further attention in the research literature. For example, Pargament (2007) suggested the possibility that specific types of psychological problems might be related to specific types of spiritual problems, pointing to literature that has linked such disorders as depression and anxiety with particular forms of spiritual distress. As Pargament noted, learning about such patterns would be clinically useful, as it would help devise specific treatment strategies, tailored to particular constellations of psychological and spiritual problems.

WAYS TO ADDRESS RELIGIOUS AND SPIRITUAL PROBLEMS

As discussed in this chapter, a number of models offer ways to conceptualize and intervene with religious and spiritual problems. In this next section, we will consider several ways of working with religious and spiritual problems in the clinical setting, including psychological interventions for spiritual problems, spiritual interventions for spiritual problems, and collaborating and consulting with religious professionals.

Psychological Interventions for Religious and Spiritual Problems

Clinicians must convey basic therapeutic postures of respect, empathy, and openness to the clients' experience. Although these are nonspecific factors common to nearly all psychotherapies, it is particularly crucial in the realm of religious and spiritual problems. Simple listening and acceptance can be a powerful intervention. Clients may experience layers of shame around religious and spiritual problems. Providing a nonjudgmental and accepting space in which to explore religious and spiritual concerns can be very healing.

Elsewhere, we have presented a broad model of working with spiritual struggles that includes five key therapeutic tasks: assess, normalize, express, create meaning, and seek connection (Murray-Swank & Murray-Swank, 2012). This basic approach can be integrated within psychotherapy from a broad range of theoretical orientations (e.g., cognitive–behavioral, psychodynamic, humanistic–existential). With regard to assessment, several helpful frameworks have been proposed to guide this process, and we refer the interested reader to this body of work (see Murray-Swank & Pargament, 2012; Pargament, 2007; Plante, 2009; also see Chapter 5 in this volume). We next briefly comment on each of the other components of this approach.

Normalizing religious and spiritual problems can be a very helpful first step. Religious and spiritual traditions contain stories of many epic figures who experienced struggle (see Volume 1, Chapter 10, this handbook). For example, Job wrestled with the problem of suffering in the Hebrew Bible, Buddha struggled under the Bodhi tree in the path toward his enlightenment, Arjuna experienced internal warfare on the battlefield in the *Bhagavad Gita*, and Muhammad the prophet struggled with a range of challenges of Arab tribal society in the seventh century. In our clinical experience, we have found that it can be helpful for clients to draw on examples within their own religious or spiritual tradition when they are experiencing religious and spiritual struggles.

Expressing the problem involves helping the client verbalize and identify the religious or spiritual problem as well as processing their associated emotions. For example, the first author once treated a client for longstanding obsessive–compulsive disorder (OCD), with prominent themes of sexual obsessions and extensive repetition of rituals to neutralize his associated anxiety. During one session, Jason told me that he had gone to his priest and asked about these sexual thoughts. He related that the priest had told him that his sexual thoughts were sinful. This idea that ran counter to the approach we were following in therapy, which focused on helping Jason accept these thoughts without acting on them or engaging in rituals. I encouraged Jason to share his thoughts and feelings about what his priest had said. Jason shared how he struggled with "whether to believe religion or psychology" and expressed his emotions of guilt and confusion around this issue. After exploring this struggle, I tried to clarify the problem and create a context to work with the religious problem:

> As we have been working your OCD, it has become clear that there are significant spiritual dimensions to your problem. Your religious tradition and priest have defined these obsessive thoughts that you experience as sinful. In addition to feeling psychologically stuck, you also feel spiritually stuck. I'm wondering if we can figure out how to work on this spiritual dimension of your problem?

This comment opened up a fruitful avenue for discussion with Jason. We generated and pursued several lines of intervention. With Jason's permission, I consulted with his priest and discussed the treatment process for Jason's OCD from a psychological perspective. Jason also sought out the medical center chaplain to discuss his concerns, read religious books that addressed this particular issue, and broadened his prayer life. He reported that these resources and practices gave him a broader perspective on his problems with OCD and helped him feel less distressed about the content of his thoughts.

For many clients experiencing religious and spiritual problems, it is helpful to use interventions that facilitate emotional expression. For example, elsewhere we have described the use of a "spiritually based empty chair technique" in the process of therapy with a survivor of childhood sexual abuse who was experiencing spiritual struggles (Murray-Swank & Murray-Swank, 2012). This intervention involved having the client imagine that God was present in the chair across from her and encouraging the client to express her feelings toward God regarding the abuse and subsequent struggles. Other examples of techniques to encourage emotional expression include letter-writing, two-way journaling with God, and the use of therapeutic tasks involving artistic expression.

An extensive body of work indicates that religion and spirituality can be helpful in providing meaning in the face of the struggles and challenges of life (Slattery & Park, 2012; see also Volume 1, Chapter 8, this handbook). In working with religious and spiritual problems, clinicians can explore how clients understand or make sense of their problems and can draw on religious and spiritual resources to facilitate more adaptive ways of making meaning. For example, a client might be struggling to make sense of a traumatic event or experience, a diagnosis of terminal illness, or a painful divorce. Clinically, it can be very helpful to identify how the particular situation "violates" their assumptions of how the world works and thus identify where the client is "stuck" in making meaning of their situation. As discussed, the facilitation of "existential postures of resilience" can provide a framework for working with issues of meaning embedded in religious and spiritual problems (e.g., Griffith, 2010). Therapeutic interventions from a diverse range of theoretical perspectives (e.g., cognitive, psychodynamic, existential–humanistic) can facilitate meaning making for clients in this domain.

Part of the power of religion and spirituality lies in how they connect people to each other, a deeper sense of self, and transcendent realities in life. In working with religious and spiritual problems, therapists can help clients access adaptive forms of religious and spiritual connection. For example, therapists can help clients connect with personally relevant sacred forms and images (e.g., God, Allah, Jesus, Shiva, nature). Imagery exercises can be used with clients to facilitate this process. Some clients may find connection in communities of religious or spiritual support (such as church, synagogue, mosque, or sangha communities), whereas others might connect more with inner resources (such as an inner self, spiritual center, heart or inner wisdom).

Manualized Psychospiritual Interventions for Religious and Spiritual Problems

Several promising manualized psychospritual interventions have been developed to help clients address religious and spiritual problems. For example, the second author developed and evaluated the Solace for the Soul program to address common spiritual struggles following sexual abuse, including themes such as spiritual disconnection, abandonment and anger at God, and feelings of spiritual shame (Murray-Swank & Pargament, 2005; see Chapter 17 in this volume). Harris et al. (2011) have developed Building Spiritual Strength, an eight-session program for veterans who have experienced trauma during their military service, and found positive outcomes in reducing trauma symptoms in a pilot study of the program. In another vein, interventions have been developed to address religious and spiritual struggles that may be associated with medical problems, such as cancer (Recreating Your Life: During and After Cancer; Cole, 2005) and HIV/AIDS (Tarakeshwar, Pearce, & Sikkema, 2005). Although further research evaluation is need, these manual-based programs have begun to offer some promising, research-based interventions for working with religious and spiritual problems in a range of clinical populations.

Religious and Spiritual Interventions

For many mental health professionals, the domain of religious and spiritual problems is somewhat new territory. Religious and spiritual traditions, however, have developed a range of well-worn pathways for people facing problems and struggles. Plante (2009) has provided a helpful overview of 13 spiritual and religious "tools" that are commonly found across traditions: (a) meditating; (b) praying; (c) having vocation, meaning, purpose, or calling in life; (d) accepting self and others (even with faults); (e) maintaining ethical values and behaviors; (f) being part of something larger and greater than oneself; (g) emphasizing forgiveness, gratitude, love, kindness, and compassion; (h) practicing volunteerism and charity; (i) participating in ritual and community support; (j) emphasizing social justice; (k) having spiritual models; (l) using bibliotherapy; and (m) emphasizing the sacredness of life. Obviously, this is a wide-ranging set of concepts and practices, and not all of these "tools" would be relevant to a particular religious or spiritual problem. It is helpful, however, to explore and draw on relevant resources within the client's own tradition when working with religious and spiritual problems.

Collaboration and Consultation With Religious and Spiritual Professionals

We have argued that mental health professionals can and should address spiritual problems, but this role is distinct from that of a spiritual leader or teacher (see Chapter 11 in this volume). In most traditions, religious and spiritual leaders have a set of specific roles and functions that are formally legitimated by the respective tradition (e.g., defining and articulating teachings or doctrine, performing formal rituals or ceremonies, absolving or pardoning sins). For some types of spiritual problems and issues, the client's needs may be better addressed by a religious or spiritual leader. For example, the first author of this chapter recently worked with a man from a Hindu background in psychotherapy. One aspect of the therapy for his anxiety-related problems was helping him reconnect with meditative practices in his tradition. One session, he raised some specific questions about the meditation practice and his experiences in meditation. I chose to direct him to a spiritual teacher in his tradition to address this particular issue.

In many cases, it may be beneficial to collaborate with religious and spiritual leaders in providing treatment. This is consistent with the Ethics Code guideline that "psychologists consult with, refer to, or cooperate with other professionals to the extent needed to serve the best interests of those with whom they work" (APA, 2002, p. 1062). On the basis of their research on such collaboration, McMinn et al. (2003) provided a helpful framework that makes a distinction between basic and advanced competencies in collaborating with religious professionals. Basic competencies, which McMinn et al. defined as essential for all psychologists, refer to the skills of respect and communication with clients about their religion and spirituality. More advanced competencies, which are relevant to psychologists who explicitly address religious and spiritual issues in therapy, require a deeper base of knowledge and expertise about working with such issues, and an ability to attend to and skillfully work with values and value differences in the therapeutic relationship.

In another vein, Plante (2009; see Chapter 26 in this volume) offered several key principles to guide therapists interested in collaboration with religious leaders, including (a) maintaining mutual respect and reciprocity, (b) understanding the faith tradition, (c) using a shared language, (d) avoiding jargon, (e) appreciating clergy stressors, and (f) respecting boundary issues. In addition to collaborating in providing services, it is important to remember that religious and spiritual leaders can be a valuable source of consultation for mental health professionals. The insight and expertise of such professionals can illuminate clients' problems, spiritual background, and context in novel and important ways.

Challenges and Complexities of Addressing Religious and Spiritual Problems in Treatment

Dealing with the interconnection between psychiatric disorders and religious or spiritual problems. One particular challenge of working with religious and spiritual problems involves the overlap between symptoms of psychiatric disorders and experiences that are associated with religious and spiritual problems. For example, one client, Sarah, came to the first author for therapy because she had begun to experience an expansive sense of connection with the universe, along with increased energy, decreased need for sleep, and engagement in her spiritual practice of contemplative prayer. Her family and friends had expressed concern about this shift, prompting her to seek therapy. On one hand, I respected the validity of her spiritual experiences and communicated this to her. On the other hand, I observed that many of the features of her presentation were consistent with symptoms of a manic episode, and I did not want to neglect any underlying psychiatric illness. Sarah's presentation illustrates a common dilemma for practitioners trying to assess the interconnection between psychological and spiritual problems.

Griffith (2010) offered a helpful set of considerations for clinicians in making this determination. First, it can be useful to assess whether the onset of the experience corresponded to any identifiable event or stressor and to consider whether the response is a proportional and understandable reaction. Reactions and experiences that are more out of proportion to the situation may be more likely to suggest the presence of a psychiatric disorder. Second, attending to the client's thought processes can be a helpful clue to assess for the presence of a psychiatric illness. As Griffith noted, psychiatric illness is characterized by abnormal forms of cognition, including "disjunctures of logic in the smooth flow of thoughts, an absence of awareness for other people's thoughts and feelings, and nonmodulated thoughts or emotions that dominate a person's mental life to excess" (p. 188). It is important to observe the client's thought processes in the session and assess their level of awareness and ability to regulate their experience outside of the session. Third, Griffith recommended assessing for associated symptoms of a psychiatric disorder, considering any history of a psychiatric disorder or the presence of risk factors. For example, in Sarah's case, it could have been helpful to assess for other possible mania symptoms (e.g., other goal-directed activities, increase in impulsive behaviors without regard for consequences, racing thoughts), explore her history to see whether there was any history of mood problems, and ask about family history of mood disorders. In assessing all of these considerations, collateral information from family members, friends, and members of the clients' religious and spiritual community can be invaluable in fully understanding the dimensions of the client's problems.

The distinction between psychiatric disorders and religious and spiritual problems is not an either–or proposition. A client can be diagnosed with a psychiatric disorder and also have a religious and spiritual problem (that even sometimes overlaps with symptoms of their disorder). For example, it is possible that Sarah could have bipolar disorder and also be experiencing a spiritual problem that could be a focus of treatment alongside any medication or therapy treatments for her psychiatric condition.

Ethical considerations. The mental health professional working with religious and spiritual problems must consider a range of important ethical issues. Chapter 3 in this volume as well as other texts on spiritually integrated psychotherapy provide comprehensive and helpful discussions of ethical issues and dilemmas when addressing the religious and spiritual dimension of client's lives (see also Hathaway & Ripley, 2009; Richards & Bergin, 2005). We briefly comment on the ethical issue of boundaries of competence because this is a particularly important consideration for clinicians who encounter clients with religious and spiritual problems in their clinical practice.

Standard 2.01b of the Ethics Code (APA, 2002) focuses on the importance of Boundaries of Competence in the context of religious and spiritual issues:

> Where scientific or professional knowledge in the discipline of psychology establishes that an understanding of factors associated with . . . religion . . . is essential for effective implementation of their services . . . psychologists have or obtain the training, experience, consultation, or supervision necessary to ensure the competence of their services, or they make appropriate referrals. (p. 5)

Personal religious spiritual experience and knowledge are not sufficient to prepare clinicians to address spiritual problems in their professional practice. Professional knowledge, skills, and competencies are needed. Fortunately, there is an expanding base of training resources for clinicians to develop specific competencies in working with spiritual issues in therapy (e.g., texts, professional conferences, formal training programs). In his helpful discussion of developing competencies in spiritually integrated psychotherapy, Pargament (2007) argued for the importance of knowledge, experiential learning, and therapist self-awareness in this domain of practice. Despite the expansion of training resources, there is a limited base of scientific knowledge about religious and spiritual problems in psychotherapy. Thus, the determination of how and when to implement interventions for religious and spiritual problems, and assessing one's competence to do so, may be difficult. Personal reflection guided by ethical principles, consultation, and supervision may all be helpful in making these determinations.

FUTURE DIRECTIONS FOR CLINICAL PRACTICE, TRAINING, AND RESEARCH

In this chapter, we have argued that religious and spiritual problems represent an important but often-neglected area in clinical practice. Fortunately, this area is receiving increasing attention in the professional literature. To produce culturally competent practitioners, it is critical for mental health professionals to integrate formal training into graduate education that teaches aspiring professionals how to recognize and work with religious and spiritual problems. Once training is completed, practicing clinicians may benefit from continuing education as well as regular consultation with colleagues around the challenges inherent in this domain of practice.

Several areas of research could help inform applied efforts to address religious and spiritual problems. Systematic investigations of the prevalence and types of religious and spiritual problems that clients present to therapists in different real-world settings would be helpful. Furthermore, developing a greater understanding of client's preferences about the place of spiritual problems in therapy would be useful. Post and Wade (2009) provided a helpful review of seven studies that have examined client's views about spirituality in therapy. Overall, they concluded that many clients are interested in broaching religious and spiritual issues in therapy, although this may vary depending on religious background and other characteristics of the client (e.g., level of conservatism, age, gender). Further studies could specifically assess clients' views about whether they would like to address religious and spiritual problems in therapy and could investigate whether these preferences vary across different types of clients and types of problems.

In terms of *how* to address spiritual problems, further clinical research on specific interventions or intervention approaches is needed. One significant challenge in this area of research is the balance between standardizing particular interventions for study and developing strategies that are flexible enough to be adapted to a range of individual spiritual problems and religious or spiritual backgrounds. This challenge is not unique to spiritual problems; indeed, this is a tension that exists in the larger field of psychotherapy research. We propose that this is not an either–or proposition, but rather that research should attend both to developing and testing specific manualized interventions and to studying the process of treating spiritual problems in naturalistic settings. This is consistent with the approach recommended by the APA Presidential Task Force on Evidence-Based Practice (2006), which emphasizes using a range of research methodologies relevant to evidence-based practice in psychology (e.g., randomized clinical trials, effectiveness studies, single-case designs, examining expert practitioners). Efforts should be made to conduct research across diverse populations, in terms of religious and spiritual backgrounds as well as other relevant characteristics (e.g., racial or ethnic background, socioeconomic status).

In this chapter, we have argued that mental health professionals have an important role to play in addressing religious and spiritual problems. Many challenges are inherent in this endeavor. At the same time, we believe that this task creates a unique opportunity for dialogue among practitioners, researchers, clergy and spiritual leaders, and others who are interested in assisting people who are experiencing these types of problems. Ultimately, an approach to religious and spiritual problems must be informed by solid psychological science, clinical expertise regarding psychotherapy, and the accumulated wisdom of spiritual traditions. We believe that such an approach can lead to important strides forward in helping individuals who experience difficulty and distress in their religious and spiritual journeys.

References

American Psychiatric Association. (2000). *Diagnostic and statistical manual of mental disorders* (4th ed., text revision). Washington, DC: Author.

American Psychological Association. (2002). Ethical principles of psychologists and code of conduct. *American Psychologist, 57*, 1060–1073. doi:10.1037/0003-066X.57.12.1060

American Psychological Association Presidential Task Force on Evidence-Based Practice. (2006). Evidence-based practice in psychology. *American Psychologist, 61*, 271–285. doi:10.1037/0003-066X.61.4.271

Cole, B. S. (2005). Spiritually-focused psychotherapy for people diagnosed with cancer: A pilot outcome study. *Mental Health, Religion, and Culture, 8*, 217–226. doi:10.1080/13694670500138916

Griffith, J. L. (2010). *Religion that heals, religion that harms: A guide for clinical practice.* New York, NY: Guilford Press.

Harris, J. I., Erbes, C. R., Engdahl, B. E., Murray-Swank, N. A., Grace, D., Ogden, H., . . . Le, T. (2011). The effectiveness of a trauma focused spiritually integrated intervention for veterans exposed to trauma. *Journal of Clinical Psychology, 67*, 425–438. doi:10.1002/jclp.20777

Hathaway, W. L., & Barkley, R. A. (2003). Self-regulation, ADHD, and child religiousness. *Journal of Psychology and Christianity, 22*, 101–114.

Hathaway, W. L., & Ripley, J. S. (2009). Ethical concerns around spirituality and religion in clinical practice. In J. D. Aten & M. M. Leach (Eds.), *Spirituality and the therapeutic process: A comprehensive resource from intake to termination* (pp. 25–52). Washington, DC: American Psychological Association. doi:10.1037/11853-002

Hathaway, W. L., Scott, S. Y., & Garver, S. A. (2004). Assessing religious/spiritual functioning: A neglected domain in clinical practice? *Professional Psychology: Research and Practice, 35*, 97–104. doi:10.1037/0735-7028.35.1.97

Johnson, C. V., & Hayes, J. A. (2003). Troubled spirits: Prevalence and predictors of religious and spiritual concerns among university students and counseling center clients. *Journal of Counseling Psychology, 50*, 409–419. doi:10.1037/0022-0167.50.4.409

Kirkpatrick, L. A. (2005). *Attachment, evolution, and the psychology of religion.* New York, NY: Guilford Press.

Kornfield, J. (1993). *A path with heart: A guide through the perils and promises of spiritual life.* New York, NY: Bantam.

Lukoff, D., Lu, F., & Turner, R. T. (1998). From spiritual emergency to spiritual problem: The transpersonal roots of the new DSM-IV category. *Journal of Humanistic Psychology, 38*, 21–50. doi:10.1177/00221678980382003

Lukoff, D., Lu. F., & Yang, P. (2010). *DSM–IV* religious and spiritual problems. In J. Peteet & F. Lu (Eds.), *Religious and spiritual considerations in psychiatric diagnosis: A research agenda for* DSM–V (pp. 187–214). Washington, DC: American Psychiatric Association Press.

McMinn, M. R., Aikins, D. C., & Lish, R. A. (2003). Basic and advanced competence in working with clergy: Survey findings and implications. *Professional Psychology: Research and Practice, 34*, 197–202. doi:10.1037/0735-7028.34.2.197

Murray-Swank, N. A., & Murray-Swank, A. B. (2012). Navigating the storm: Helping clients in the midst of spiritual struggles. In J. D. Aten, K. A. O'Grady, & E. L. Worthington Jr. (Eds.), *The psychology of religion and spirituality for clinicians: Using research in your practice* (pp. 217–244). New York, NY: Brunner-Routledge.

Murray-Swank, N. A., & Pargament, K. I. (2005). God, where are you? Evaluating a spiritually-integrated intervention for sexual abuse. *Mental Health, Religion, and Culture, 8*, 191–203. doi:10.1080/13694670500138866

Murray-Swank, N. A., & Pargament, K. I. (2012). Seeking the sacred: The assessment of spirituality in the therapy process. In J. D. Aten, M. R. McMinn, & E. L. Worthington Jr. (Eds.), *Spiritually oriented interventions for counseling and psychotherapy* (pp. 107–135). Washington, DC: American Psychological Association. doi:10.1037/12313-005

Pargament, K. I. (2007). *Spiritually integrated psychotherapy: Understanding and addressing the sacred.* New York, NY: Guilford Press.

Peteet, J. R., Lu, F., & Narrow, W. E. (2011). *Religious and spiritual issues in psychiatric diagnosis: A research agenda for DSM-V.* Arlington, VA: American Psychiatric Association.

Plante, T. G. (2009). *Spiritual practices in psychotherapy: Thirteen tools for enhancing psychological health.* Washington, DC: American Psychological Association. doi:10.1037/11872-000

Post, B. C., & Wade, N. G. (2009). Religion and spirituality in psychotherapy: A practice-friendly review of the research. *Journal of Clinical Psychology, 65*, 131–146. doi:10.1002/jclp.20563

Richards, P. S., & Bergin, A. E. (2005). *A spiritual strategy for counseling and psychotherapy.* Washington, DC: American Psychological Association. doi:10.1037/11214-000

Shafranske, E. P., & Maloney, H. N. (1990). Clinical psychologists' religious and spiritual orientation and their practice of psychotherapy. *Psychotherapy: Theory, Research, Practice, Training, 27*, 72–78. doi:10.1037/0033-3204.27.1.72

Slattery, J. M., & Park, C. L. (2012). Meaning making and spiritually oriented interventions. In J. D. Aten, M. R. McMinn, & E. L. Worthington Jr. (Eds.), *Spiritually oriented interventions for counseling and psychotherapy* (pp. 15–40). Washington, DC: American Psychological Association. doi:10.1037/12313-001

Tarakeshwar, N., Pearce, M. J., & Sikkema, K. J. (2005). Development and implementation of a spiritual coping group intervention for adults living with HIV/AIDS: A pilot study. *Mental Health, Religion, and Culture, 8*, 179–190. doi:10.1080/13694670500138908

CHAPTER 23

FAITH AND HEALTH BEHAVIOR: THE ROLE OF THE AFRICAN AMERICAN CHURCH IN HEALTH PROMOTION AND DISEASE PREVENTION

Marlyn Allicock, Ken Resnicow, Elizabeth Gerken Hooten, and Marci K. Campbell

Recent trends in health promotion and disease prevention have moved toward community-based interventions rather than just addressing individual-level risk factors. Individual-level approaches to health promotion, although important, tend to obscure the role of social and environmental conditions in health and disease. From an ecological perspective, the potential to change individual risk behaviors is considered within the social and cultural context in which it occurs (McLeroy, Bibeau, Steckler, & Glanz, 1988; Stokols, 2000). Community-based interventions, thus, are aimed at entire populations, usually a geographically defined place or setting, and attempt to change disease risk and health behavior. Health promotion efforts at the community level can originate as researcher-driven initiatives or with the active engagement and influence of community members in all aspects of the intervention process (Hatch, Moss, Saran, Presley-Cantrell, & Mallory, 1993; Israel, Schulz, Parker, & Becker, 1998). Research in community settings acknowledges the importance of interpersonal behaviors, organizational climate, community resources, and policy effects as having important implications for health.

Faith-based organizations are promising settings within communities that can have a unique role in the delivery of such community-based interventions. Religious organizations and places of worship are important because (a) at the community level, they are often among the most important structures and established institutions, and over time, they have withstood natural disasters, political oppression, and conflict, which has led to their legitimacy and credibility; (b) they shape cultural norms and have the ability to promote positive and supportive community norms and to promote and increase awareness about social issues; (c) they have an established structure in which people convene on a regular basis and can be used to deliver health promotion programs and facilitate information sharing among its congregants; (d) the faith tenets of most faith-based organizations promote health, living, and healing; and (e) they have access to people of many backgrounds and can facilitate participation from marginalized or hard-to-reach populations that traditional health care systems cannot reach (Goldmon & Roberson, 2004; see also Chapter 32 in this volume).

The ways in which community-based health promotion efforts have involved religion and religious institutions have varied. For instance, secular interventions in which the program is devoid of religious content and designed to be delivered in religious or other organizations have been used (Ma et al., 2009; Winett, Anderson, Wojcik, Winett, & Bowden, 2007). Others have used religious-based interventions delivered within a secular context such as hospitals (Fitzgibbon et al., 2005) or via community-wide events (Griffith, Pichon, Campbell, & Allen, 2010). Finally, other programs couple religious-based interventions in a religious institutional context (Campbell et al., 2004; Holt, Roberts, et al., 2009; Resnicow et al., 2002).

Strong evidence has accumulated for the efficacy of promoting health behavior changes, through religious institutions, particularly for dietary behavior.

DOI: 10.1037/14046-023
APA Handbook of Psychology, Religion, and Spirituality: Vol. 2. An Applied Psychology of Religion and Spirituality, K. I. Pargament (Editor-in-Chief)

The Black Churches United for Better Health project, for example, demonstrated significant dietary impact (0.85 serving daily fruit and vegetable [F&V] increase) from a multilevel intervention that included 11 different types of activities (Campbell, Demark-Wahnefried, et al., 1999; Campbell et al., 2000). The Eat for Life study (Resnicow et al., 2001) also demonstrated increased F&V consumption (approximately 1.2 serving increase) from an intervention in Black churches utilizing a combination of self-help materials and motivational interviewing (MI) telephone counseling. Most recently, the Eating for a Healthy Life project conducted in predominantly White religious organizations in the Seattle area reduced dietary fat consumption using a 9-month dietary intervention package that included an advisory board, interpersonal support, social activities, healthy eating sessions, dietary change mailings, motivational messages, and print advertisements (Bowen et al., 2004; Bowen, Beresford, et al., 2009). Other faith-based behavior-change programs have improved smoking cessation (Schorling et al., 1997; Voorhees et al., 1996), diabetes self-management (Samuel-Hodge et al., 2009), physical activity (Winett et al., 2007), nutrition (Campbell, Demark-Wahnefried, et al., 1999, Campbell et al., 2004; Resnicow et al., 2000), cardiovascular health (Yanek, Becker, Moy, Gittelsohn, & Koffman, 2001), and weight loss (Kennedy et al., 2005; McNabb, Quinn, Kerver, Cook, & Karrison, 1997). Studies have shown positive impacts using a variety of strategies, including educational sessions, awareness raising, screening programs, environmental support, lay health advisors, and individual change strategies, such as tailored messages and MI counseling (Campbell et al., 2000; Campbell, Resnicow, Carr, Wang, & Williams, 2007; Resnicow et al., 2001).

This chapter reviews health promotion efforts that have been conducted through and with religious organizations. We address challenges involved in the development of spiritually integrated prevention programs and provide examples of efficacious collaborations with faith-based organizations. The final section provides recommendations to improve faith-based partnerships. Although faith-based intervention programs have been implemented with persons of different faith and ethnic backgrounds, this chapter will focus on African American churches because much of the work in this area has been conducted within these religious institutions and communities. Also, minority populations continue to experience disproportionately high rates of many diseases, including cancer, cardiovascular disease, diabetes, and HIV/AIDS (Office of Minority Health and Health Disparities, 2010), therefore community interventions aimed at these groups are of particular importance. Although efforts to reduce behaviors that increase the risk for chronic diseases have enjoyed some success in recent decades, such as a reduction in smoking rates, much work remains to close disparity gaps and to improve overall population health. One useful way to deliver behavior change messages and programs to minority communities is through their religious organizations.

Research involving faith-based institutions has used both *religiosity* and *spirituality* to define work in this sphere. For clarity, we have chosen the language of religion to refer to the work referenced here. Consistent with the integrative paradigm of this handbook, we use *religion* or *religiosity* to mean any beliefs, practices, relationships, or experiences having to do with the sacred that are explicitly and historically rooted in established institutionalized systems[1] (e.g., churches, synagogues, and mosques) and to describe the psychological, social, or physical functions of beliefs, practices, relationships, participation, frequency of religious service attendance, or experiences having to do with the sacred that may influence health behaviors. We describe faith-based interventions in which researchers collaborate with members of religious groups and incorporate religious messages and use religious themes to motivate behavior change. The studies discussed in this chapter largely involve Christian churches in the United States, but faith-based health promotion also can be conducted in other denominations, religions, and cultures (Black, 1997; Castro et al., 1995; Hansen, 2005; Welsh, Sauaia, Jacobellis, Min, & Byers, 2005).

[1]We use *faith-based institution* to refer to the full variety of religious institutions.

THE NATURE OF RELIGIOUS AND HEALTH PROFESSIONAL PARTNERSHIPS

The determinants of health and illness are multifaceted and involve interaction among biological, social, and cultural factors. Before the 1970s, the medical treatment of disease was the dominant focus for improving population health (Stokols, 2000). Over time, there has been a gradual shift in recognizing that the patterns of health and illness were not just confined to individual-level biological and psychological factors but also that health behaviors and health status are determined by economic, political, environmental, social, and sociocultural factors. For example, the attributes of communities in which people live, work, and play influence social norms, determine access to resources and information, and shape policies—each of which impact wellness. Such a perspective, referred to as the *social ecological paradigm* (Stokols, 1992; Stokols, Allen, & Bellingham, 1996), emphasizes a more integrative approach to addressing health by recognizing the joint and dynamic influence of individual behavior and the environmental context, rather than focusing exclusively on either health determining factor. The intent is to go beyond the individual to include the social and cultural factors that clearly or subtly affect behavior. Acknowledgment of the joint interplay between individual, cultural, and environmental factors is a core tenet for addressing behavior change through community approaches. Comprehensive community-based approaches, including those in which interventions are delivered within religious institutions, address multiple levels of health determinants and have the potential to (a) influence individual knowledge, attitudes, and behavior; (b) create institutional and organizational support for intervention programs; and (c) modify the environment to support health behavior initiation and maintenance or prohibit unhealthy behaviors (Farquhar, 1978; Green, Richard, & Potvin 1996; Rothman, 1969; Stokols, Allen, & Bellingham, 1996; Stone, 1991).

Furthermore, the conceptualization of health as more than just the physical domain, as one that includes a religious dimension as well as the recognition of the interrelation between religion and health, supports the argument for faith-based health promotion partnerships. There has long been recognition that faith-based institutions can serve an important function in health promotion (Eng, Hatch, & Callan, 1985). For example, a study conducted in Alameda County by Berkman and Syme (1979) examined the efficacy of churches as sites for health promotion. They found church attendance to be a significant positive predictor of health status in numerous studies. In addition, they reported that churches demonstrated a high receptivity for becoming health-promotion sites in their communities (Berkman & Syme, 1979). Such partnership efforts to leverage the resources and institutional capacity provided by faith communities are expanding.

Recently, presidential initiatives have recognized and emphasized the expansion of faith-based partnerships for health care in the United States. During the administrations of Presidents Bill Clinton and George W. Bush, the federal government endorsed the role of faith institutions with charitable choice legislation that reduced barriers for faith institutions to compete for federal funding to implement effective programs (Federal Register, 2001; Wineburg, Coleman, Boddie, & Cnaan, 2008). In 2009, President Obama launched the White House Office of Faith-Based and Neighborhood Partnerships to help build the capacity of faith institutions to address pressing health and social needs (Dubois, 2009). In addition, local and state health departments, university-based research groups, parish nurses, and hospitals have collaborated with religious organizations (Zahner & Corrado, 2004). There has also been a shift in pastoral theology in some denominations to infuse a more community-centric view in ministry, in contrast to focusing only on the individual–clergy relationship (Dunlap 2009; Patton, 1993). These developments at national as well as local levels have expanded opportunities to enhance collaborations for health promotion with religious institutions.

Although recent developments in federal policy are certainly important, it is useful as well to examine the nature of the involvement of faith institutions in health activities over time. Partnering with faith communities to promote health is not a new concept. Public health professionals have worked for more than 30 years in multiple ways using faith communities as the setting for delivering services, providing faith-based programming, and collaborating with outside groups (DeHaven, Hunter, Wilder, Walton, & Berry, 2004).

An important and overarching distinction emerges out of a review of that history. Distinctions must be made between health programs conducted *through* churches versus those conducted *with* churches. Work done through faith institutions refers to programs in which the church is a venue for health promotion delivered by outsiders, such as researchers. One example is a study in which the church is simply a place for recruiting individuals to participate in a particular program or research study that is done elsewhere. In a second example, the church might serve as a site for program delivery, where, for example, health education sessions are offered after religious services. A further distinction at this level is the absence or presence of religious content. For example, Winett's health promotion intervention (Winett et al., 2007) was conducted in churches, but it was largely devoid of faith-based messages. The second category, work done with churches, involves faith-based partnerships along the lines of community-based participatory research principles. Lasater, Becker, Hill, and Gans (1997) described faith-based partnerships in which professionals work in formal collaborations with faith-based organizations to promote health. Intervention approaches may emphasize partnerships with churches to design and implement programs to train church volunteers as lay health educators to implement a researcher-derived protocol. Other faith-based interventions emphasize content in which religious or spiritual themes, including the use of scriptures and religious texts, are integrated with health messages to motivate congregants.

AFRICAN AMERICAN FAITH INSTITUTIONS AND HEALTH PROMOTION TO REDUCE DISPARITIES

The majority of faith-based health promotion programs and research has been conducted with African American congregations, largely driven by a health disparities agenda (DeHaven et al., 2004). In the United States, health disparities are described as the persistent gaps between the health status of minorities and nonminorities (U.S. Department of Health and Human Services, 2010). Proposed efforts to eliminate health disparities include using science and knowledge as a basis for developing policies and programs for diseases prevention and health promotion directed at at-risk populations. For that reason, active engagement with minority populations is required—in light of their increased health risks. Compelling health disparities, particularly for African Americans, together with the unique role the African American church serves within this population, have motivated the formation of numerous health promotion partnerships.

Several historical, social, and cultural aspects of African American churches make them appealing for collaboration. The African American church has a long and rich history as the center of spiritual, social, and political life for many African Americans, often to a larger extent than for other groups (see Volume 1, Chapter 30, this handbook). Black churches are often among the most visible, respected, and credible "agencies" in the community, and as such, the legitimacy of public health efforts that partner with them may be considerably enhanced; similarly, distrust on the part of many African Americans toward public health and medical agencies and practitioners may be reduced (Baskin, Resnicow, & Campbell, 2001; Lincoln & Mamiya, 1990). Historically, Black churches have included health as a component of their overall mission (Lasater et al., 1997; Lasater, Wells, Carleton, & Elder, 1986; Thomas, Quinn, Billingsley, & Caldwell, 1994). Many larger churches have a health ministry or similar group that conducts health programs for their members or their communities. The church, as a religious organization, also offers the potential for recruiting African Americans from the entire socioeconomic spectrum, often including segments of the population that are sometimes viewed as "hard to reach" by health care systems. Churches can provide an excellent venue for recruiting and retaining study participants. Between 70% and 80% of African Americans report belonging to a church and most have been members of the same church for many years. One limitation of working in Black churches, however, is that such studies exclude nonchurchgoers who may differ in such factors as gender, age, and socioeconomic status. Additionally, churches possess innate "social capital," that is, members of the congregation who are doctors, nurses, teachers, social workers, and other professionals who are willing to devote their time to improve the health of their fellow congregants. Finally, the African American church can serve as a viable dissemination channel for health promotion efforts. Existing infrastructure, such as health ministries and a community-outreach orientation often found in churches, further make them ideal settings in which to conduct health programs. A growing literature exists indicating that faith-based programs can improve health outcomes (DeHaven, Hunter, Wilder, Walton, & Berry, 2004). We turn now to an example of a faith-based program developed for African American churchgoers that includes religious content and relies on church members to deliver the intervention.

BODY AND SOUL: AN EXEMPLARY FAITH-BASED HEALTH PROMOTION PROGRAM FOR AFRICAN AMERICANS

The Body and Soul program is an example of dissemination of an evidence-based, faith-based program (Resnicow et al., 2004). It is of particular importance to our discussion, because it is the only faith-based program to date that has gone through each of the research phases of efficacy, effectiveness, and dissemination.

Body and Soul: A Celebration of Healthy Living is a church-based nutrition program for African Americans (Resnicow et al., 2004). It originated as a collaborative effort among the National Cancer Institute (NCI), the American Cancer Society (ACS), and two university research groups, which previously had conducted independent efficacy studies of similar nutrition interventions among African American church members (Campbell, Bernhardt, et al., 1999; Campbell et al., 2000; Campbell, Resnicow, et al., 2007; Resnicow et al., 2000, 2001). In each of these efficacy studies, an increase in F&V consumption of approximately one serving daily was reported. These findings led NCI and ACS to spearhead the development of a composite program, subsequently named Body and Soul.

Body and Soul has four components or "pillars": pastoral leadership and support, educational activities, church environmental changes, and peer counseling. The first pillar emphasizes pastors as organizational and spiritual leaders of their churches and encourages them to support the program by delivering messages about healthy eating and living in their sermons and by supporting the church in its efforts to provide healthier foods. Pastors can model healthy behaviors for their congregations. Pastoral support involves pastors explaining to church members the ways in which the program reflects the mission of the church and the links between physical health and spiritual well-being. The second pillar, education, includes group activities and promotional events that inform congregants of the benefits of including fruits and vegetables in one's diet. Churches select from various suggested activities on the basis of their own resources. The third pillar is a church environment that supports healthy eating by giving church members the opportunity to eat fruits and vegetables at church functions and events. The final pillar, peer counseling, is a program of individual counseling about eating a healthy diet, done by church members with other church members. Peer counselors are trained via videos and an interactive group workshop, both based on MI skills (Miller & Rollnick, 1991). Members who are interested in receiving peer counseling sign up to talk with a trained volunteer over the phone or in person. The church member and peer counselor talk about how eating healthier relates to their life goals and personal values, including religious beliefs (e.g., the body as God's temple). Together, the church member and peer counselor come up with an action plan for eating more fruits and vegetables.

The impact of Body and Soul was tested in a cluster-randomized effectiveness trial of 16 churches recruited by ACS from three geographic areas: mid-Atlantic, Southeast, and California (Resnicow et al., 2004). The primary outcome was F&V intake, measured with two types of food frequency questionnaires at baseline and at 6-month follow-up. At the 6-month follow-up, intervention participants showed significantly greater F&V intake relative to controls. Statistically significant positive changes in fat intake, motivation to eat F&V, social support, and efficacy to eat F&V were also observed. Process evaluation also showed that greater frequency of intervention exposure was associated with higher F&V intake. The results suggested that research-based interventions, delivered collaboratively by community volunteers and a voluntary health agency, can be effectively implemented under real-world conditions. Body and Soul then was adopted for national dissemination by NCI and underwent further adaptations such as converting the peer counseling training previously done by a professional trainer in a live format to a video-based training program using a church lay member as facilitator (Allicock et al., 2010). Materials were created jointly by NCI and the leaders of the original research studies and were made available free of charge online via NCI's Cancer Control Planet.

The next phase of research was to determine how churches were using the disseminated program without any researcher involvement, and if the impact on F&V intake was sustained in the dissemination phase. Allicock et al. (2012) conducted a randomized controlled trial of 16 churches (not involved in the Body and Soul Effectiveness study) that requested the Body and Soul program from NCI. Churches were randomized to either the early or the delayed or control intervention. Churches in the early intervention arm, led by the church coordinator and the church's Body and Soul planning team, began implementing the program over a 6-month intervention period. A 6-month follow-up survey was administered to church participants at the end of the intervention period. The delayed intervention churches served as the control group and initiated the program after completing the 6-month follow-up. At 6-month follow-up, the adjusted mean F&V intake was slightly greater for intervention participants compared with control participants, but the difference was not statistically significant (Allicock et al., 2012). Process measures, however, showed that greater program recall and exposure were associated with higher F&V intake. The variable "Recall of talking with a peer counselor" was associated with significantly greater F&V intake. Added resources, training, quality control, and technical assistance may be required to achieve significant public health impact. Suboptimal program implementation may explain the lack of effect on dietary change. For example, process evaluation showed that only half of the 16 churches implemented the peer-counseling component fully (Allicock et al., 2010).

The Body and Soul program represents a unique effort to improve health outcomes of African American congregants. At this point of dissemination, however, there was no longer any researcher involvement, and no formal mechanism for technical assistance currently exists. Our research suggests that without such support and technical assistance, churches may not implement the program as intended. Further investigation at the dissemination phase is needed to identify the following: (a) factors to promote intervention fidelity, (b) appropriate supports for program implementers, (c) implementation barriers and facilitators, and (d) implementation environments. Such research will facilitate an understanding of best practices for disseminating evidence-based programs. Major issues include whether programs are highly prescriptive (i.e., requiring rigid implementation in a specific manner for outcome effects versus allowing for flexibility and variability in its implementation), how to balance scientific rigor with the values and resources of the faith community, and how to enhance the engagement of program implementers to ensure sufficient program fidelity while allowing expected variability among churches (Campbell, Hudson, et al., 2007; Faridi et al., 2010; Minkler, 2004). At the dissemination phase, when there is no researcher involvement, churches are free to adopt and implement the program at the levels they desire, based on resources such as time and funding, and within their own time frame. As such, it can be expected that there will be dilution of program effects. A program that is characterized by intervention components that are specific and simple can promote greater adherence in its implementation. Similarly, the quality of the program delivery (e.g., whether implementers are simply going through the motions or delivering the program with care and thoughtfulness) can affect outcomes. Finally, participant (those delivering and receiving the program) responsiveness regarding the relevance and acceptance of the program can promote program engagement. Therefore, factors such as the intervention complexity, quality of the delivery, and participant and implementer responsiveness are important factors to be considered to enhance adherence to program implementation and thus increase potential for successful outcomes.

Body and Soul is the first of its kind to follow a community-based program through the phases of efficacy testing, effectiveness trial, and dissemination research. Early evaluations of the disseminated program indicate a greater need to focus on improving factors important for successful uptake with church communities adopting the program. The evaluation highlighted some important factors that researchers seeking to disseminate similar community-level programs should consider if they are to experience greater success.

FAITH-BASED INITIATIVES AMONG OTHER MINORITY GROUPS

Although other minority ethnic cultural groups such as Latinos and Native Americans experience significant disparities in health and well-being, fewer faith-based programs among these groups have been reported in the literature. Given the centrality religion plays in many communities, implementation of health promotion programs is suitable in a variety of faith denominations. Religious communities such as churches are settings in which many Latinos share meaning from life experiences and practice cultural traditions such as baptism, first communion, and *quinceañera* (Falicov, 1996; see also Volume 1, Chapter 33, this handbook). Others note that Latino churches play a central role in Latino communities, particularly among less acculturated, Spanish-speaking women (Castro et al., 1995). Researchers and health care professionals are increasingly recognizing the importance of spirituality in health, illness, and well-being across a variety of populations. The changing demographics of the United States where there is increasing influx of immigrant populations, most notably Hispanics, have shifted the focus to reaching minority populations with health screenings and health educations. The evidence is beginning to suggest that faith-based health programs provide crucial links between immigrant populations and mainstream health care (Orr & May, 2000). There is indication that among Latinos (Derose, Duan, & Fox, 2002; Zahuranec et al., 2008) and Samoans (Aitaoto, Braun, Dang, & So'a, 2007), there is willingness to participate in church-based health promotion and that these programs can be efficacious (Duan et al., 2000; Lopez & Castro, 2006; Sauaia et al., 2007).

THE CHALLENGES OF RELIGIOUS AND HEALTH PROFESSIONAL PARTNERSHIPS

Although faith communities represent particularly important venues for health promotion, challenges to implementing programs and conducting research exist (Campbell, Hudson, et al., 2007; Chatters, Levin, & Ellison, 1998). Potential challenges are found within the realm of the religious institution itself (or Church; e.g., issues related to church doctrine, separation of church and state) or that of the research partner (e.g., researcher's personal spiritual beliefs, research program design).

Church-Related Issues

How and whether health is prioritized can influence participation in health promotion and adoption of healthy behaviors. Some faith tenets explicitly espouse health. For example, Seventh-day Adventists (SDAs) believe that not only the church but also the individual Christian is a temple for the indwelling of the Holy Spirit. Therefore, practicing good health habits protects the "the command center of their body temples, the mind, the dwelling place of the Spirit of Christ" (Ministerial Association, 1988). SDAs almost completely abstain from the use of tobacco and alcohol and, to a lesser extent, from consuming coffee, tea, fish, and meat. Regular physical activity and nutritious diets are emphasized. Research studies show that SDAs are less likely than the general population to develop almost any of the major diseases (Koenig, McCullough, & Larson, 2001). Similarly, religious tenets of the Nation of Islam have informed its emphasis on healthy diets and a lifestyle of sobriety (Raboteau, 1986). Health and faith practices may take into consideration a combination of faith healing and scientific medicine. For example, the Pentecostal Church gives equal importance to faith healing (including the use of intercessory prayer and the laying on of hands) as it does to the role of sanctification, or growing in holiness, which requires members to refrain from health-inhibiting use of tobacco, alcohol, and narcotics (Wimberly, 2001). These religious doctrines are compatible with health and wellness promotion and thus can be a mutual starting point for health promotion partnerships.

On the other hand, religious doctrines may pose barriers to health promotion efforts. Organ donation and transplantation is a prime example in which beliefs about the death and the human body vary by religion. In Islam, the concept and definition of brain death is highly debated, and it is forbidden to violate the human body whether living or death. Altruism, however, is a highly regarded principle and saving life is emphasized in the Qur'an. Yet many individuals in the faith are reluctant regarding deceased donations (Einollahi, 2008). Because of ongoing uncertainties regarding this matter, Muslims may seek advice from their local imam whose decision is respected. It is suggested that education in organ donation be targeted at individuals who are most influential in the community and to use the month of Ramadan with its emphasis on altruism to foster organ donation among this community (Najafizadeh et al., 2010). Similarly, in Judaism, there is uncertainty over the definitions of death, and the lack of a unified interpretation (Oliver, Woywodt, Ahmed, & Saif, 2011) can lead to hesitancy to become organ donor. Many Jewish scholars, however, agree that these concerns are overridden by the need to save lives (*pikuack nefesh*). In Tibetan Buddhism, preserving the physical integrity of the dead body is not necessarily a priority, but the belief that the spiritual consciousness may remain in the body for several days after breathing has ceased and that any interference might disturb the person's next rebirth is a crucial tenet within this religious group (Sugunasiri, 1990). As such, organ donation is not permissible. For African Americans, in general, religiosity is negatively correlated with organ donation willingness (Davidson & Devney, 1991; Hall et al., 1991; Plawecki, Freiberg, & Palwecki, 1989). In some studies, African Americans express spiritual concerns that the body should remain whole (Spigner et al., 1999), and body integrity has been shown to be negatively correlated with African Americans' willingness to donate organs (Rubens & Oleckno, 1998; Spigner et al., 1999). Researchers and practitioners attempting to conduct health promotion interventions should manifest cultural sensitivity regarding religious doctrines of religious communities and institutions.

A second church-related issue relevant to health promotion is religious versus scientific values. Where substantial evidence finds a connection between religion and physical and mental health, potential conflicts exist between the values and beliefs held by religious institutions and its members and those held within the scientific community. This can be found, for example, in religious versus scientific (or secular) views of homosexuality in relation to HIV. During the beginning of the HIV/AIDS crisis in the African American community, the African American church was slow to respond to this health issue (Cohen, 1999; Francis & Liverpool, 2009). One possible reason for the delayed response is the difficulty of discussing the behaviors that increase a person's risk of contracting HIV/AIDS and religious doctrines regarding homosexual behaviors. Some Black churches' responses to gay relationships have been described as ranging from hostile to silent (Ward, 2005). This potential "cultural clash" between science and religion may lead to mistrust and misunderstanding (Chatters et al., 1998) and further create barriers leading to lost opportunities to effectively respond to health crises. If the HIV/AIDS epidemic is regarded as not only a sexual or moral issue but also a health issue, faith-based organizations can be important partners in disseminating accurate but sensitive information (Coyne-Beasley & Schoenback, 2000).

Also, the issue of separation of church and state may muddy the waters for partnership. Although churches may be truly interested in promoting health, religious leaders may choose not to participate in health promotion programs funded by the government if there is financial reporting or potential auditing involved (Campbell, Hudson, et al., 2007). Thus, a clear understanding of the roles of each partner and of the program details is useful before entering into partnership to avoid potential conflicts.

Research-Related Issues

The issue of religious differences between research program staff and the church may also come into play in health promotion partnerships. Conflicts may arise if research team members are unfamiliar or uncomfortable with church norms and beliefs, and those who have differing religious orientations may face personal and project dilemmas (Campbell, Hudson, et al., 2007). In working with communities of faith, respect and sensitivity for church norms and customs must be observed. Discomfort may arise when deciding whether and to what extent to participate in a religious worship service (e.g., what to wear, how much to put in the collection plate, whether to join in prayer, sing, take communion, praise, etc.). Other problematic issues may be opposing views about issues such as homosexuality and abortion. Local pastors and church leaders can help to increase knowledge and comfort with church customs and expectations and reduce anxiety for the research team by providing an orientation about church's missions, values, and culture (Campbell, Hudson, et al., 2007). Openness and a sincere demeanor usually result in researcher acceptance and welcome by the church, regardless of personal beliefs or other religious affiliations.

A common issue relevant to participation in community-based research is that of the research design. Careful consideration should be paid to whether a particular research approach may discourage churches from participating in research (Campbell, Hudson, et al., 2007). For example, is it unethical to recruit comparison churches that receive no intervention or a delayed intervention? The first option may be driven more by the needs of the researchers than the community. The latter option, while offering similar benefits, may leave participants frustrated with the time lapse and risks potential dropout. One solution is to offer the control group a test intervention or another program not related to the research study question. For example, in the Body and Soul evaluation study, which employed a randomized delayed design, churches in the delayed arm often expressed frustration at having to wait 6 months before implementing the program. On the basis of the lessons learned from the Body and Soul evaluation, we have designed newer studies offering the control group an evidence-based program instead of a nonintervention condition. In a Centers for Disease Control and Prevention (CDC) grant intervention churches received a cancer-screening intervention and comparison churches received the Body and Soul intervention (CDC, 2005). This solution was more acceptable to the church communities (Flint, Michigan; and Raleigh, Durham, and Greensboro, North Carolina) than a no-intervention or delayed-intervention design. Both interventions include community participation and peer-counseling training for church members regarding the respective health behavior change. This model seems to be more acceptable and allows for greater participation, enthusiasm, and study engagement overall. In addition, we can compare changes in screening versus changes in F&V intake, gather more information on outcomes, conduct intervention fidelity checks, and enhance our Body and Soul evaluation using the comparison churches.

RELIGIOUS CONTENT OF HEALTH PROMOTION INTERVENTIONS

As discussed earlier, religious institutions may be used as a venue for participant recruitment or delivery of a health promotion program, or they may be active partners in developing programs. The content of the programs may or may not include religious content. The extent to which spiritual and religious content is featured in programs is an important consideration, however. The discussion that follows illustrates factors relevant to the use of religious content. These include potential ethical concerns, multicultural sensitivity to the targeted populations, role of the message source for delivering the religious content, and religious content as the intervention and impact on program outcomes.

Ethics and Religious Content

Public health practitioners and researchers are governed by a code of ethics that acknowledges individual autonomy, self-determination, and informed consent (Association for the Advancement of Health Education, 1994). The use of religious content (e.g., scriptures) may be perceived as coercive when used as a tool to deliver persuasive health messages. Particular scriptures may be thought of as a way to use fear to persuade health promotion behaviors—for example, I Corinthians 3:16, 17:

> Know ye not that ye are the temple of God, and that the Spirit of God dwelleth in you? If any man defile the temple of God, him shall God destroy; for the temple of God is holy, which temple ye are.

On the other hand, a scriptural passage such as III John 2 may be perceived as noncoercive: "Beloved, I wish above all things that thou mayest prosper and be in health, even as thy soul prospereth." Careful attention should be paid to how messages are crafted. From a theoretical perspective, such as self-determination theory, such messages may be viewed as controlled motivation, which has been shown to be less effective than autonomous motivation (Ryan, Lynch, Vansteenkiste, & Deci, 2011; Williams, Freedman, & Deci, 1998; Williams, Niemiec, Patrick, Ryan, & Deci, 2009). To avoid the appearance that scripture is being used to manipulate congregants toward a desired outcome and to avoid errors in creating religious-oriented content, pastors or a pastoral advisory board can be asked to write or review intervention content and messages. In this way, researchers can be assured that the messages fit with the congregation's values and practices.

Religious Content Reflects Multicultural Sensitivity

A prevailing view of health promotion practice is that health promotion, like health care, must be practiced with cultural sensitivity. Cultural sensitivity is shown when social and cultural characteristics of the target population inform and are incorporated into the work intended for specific groups. Thus, health information that does not correspond with an individual's beliefs or practices can be interpreted as insensitive and maladaptive (Kagawa-Singer, 1994). Given that religion and spirituality play a major role among African Americans, programs that integrate religiously based content may be more culturally appropriate. This, however, is not always the case, and it is important to conduct formative research with target audiences to determine whether such content is desired, and in what format.

The effort to promote cultural sensitivity with the use of religious or spiritual messages, biblical texts, and prayer is not intended to increase the religiosity or spirituality of congregants. Rather, the focus is to maximize the degree to which the intervention fits with the cultural belief systems of the target population (Holt, Roberts, et al., 2009). This requires a collaborative partnership with churches in intervention design and delivery (Campbell, Hudson, et al., 2007). For example, the Eat for Life trial, a multicomponent intervention to increase F&V consumption among African Americans, used an advisory board composed of local pastors and opinion leaders from the local faith community to assist with the development of health messages using religious themes (Resnicow et al., 2000). As part of the intervention, a video was developed that used biblical and spiritual themes to motivate healthy eating. The advisory board was instrumental in providing feedback and ideas for the video script, guidance for editing the video, and input for the project name and logo to enhance cultural appropriateness of the intervention materials.

Message Source of Religious Content

Findings from Black Churches United for Better Health, a church-based intervention aimed at increasing consumption of F&V for cancer prevention (Campbell, Demark-Wahnefried, et al., 1999) suggested that the source of religious content matters. A substudy was conducted to understand more about the importance of message source in tailoring communications for an African American church population (Campbell, Bernhardt, et al., 1999). Concern about source credibility had arisen from formative research focus groups for the study that revealed substantial skepticism and distrust of research stemming from the historical legacy of the Tuskegee experiments (Thomas & Quinn, 1991). But focus group participants indicated confidence in the Bible and scripture to provide health guidance. On the basis of these findings, tailored newsletters were introduced and endorsed by either the participant's pastor or by nutrition experts (Campbell, Bernhardt, et al., 1999). The newsletters using pastor-source messages featured a cover message from the pastor of the participant's church, addressing why he or she believed it was important for parishioners to eat more F&V. In addition, each pastor provided his or her photograph and a Five-a-Day "grace" or prayer. Graphics were tailored to spiritual versus secular audiences. The expert-source messages, on the other hand, provided cover information about why researchers believe it is important to eat five a day and (in place of the pastor photo) the NCI Five-a-Day for Better Health logo. Both newsletters were identical in terms of individually tailored behavioral construct feedback information. Churches were then randomized to receive either the spiritual-oriented or the expert-oriented tailored newsletters. Results showed that compared with those reading expert-source newsletters, participants who read the pastor-source newsletters rated them as more trustworthy (53.6% vs. 63.5%, $p < .05$) and as having a greater impact on their intention to eat more F&V (45% vs. 58%, $p = .02$). Results from this substudy did not reveal whether differences in these communication mediators led to the observed differences in dietary behavior at 2-year follow-up because the intervention included multiple components that most likely contributed to the overall improvement in the intervention churches (Campbell et al., 2000). The findings, however, suggest a need for more research studying variations in communication elements, such as message source and cultural orientation to better design tailored communications to address health disparities.

Religious Content as Intervention

Several studies highlight ways in which religious content has been used to promote health with congregants. These studies illustrate the use of religious versus secular messages, degree of religious information, and the impact of the programs. Voorhees et al. (1996) used sermons, testimony in church services, and a stop-smoking booklet to provide smoking-cessation messages. Others (Yanek et al., 2001) have included scriptures in health messages and have used group prayer, aerobics set to gospel music, and a newsletter from the pastor on diet and physical activity. The Healthy Body/Healthy Spirit trial included a video, gospel-based audio walking tape, a cookbook, and a physical activity guide (Resnicow et al., 2002, 2005). Healthy Body/Healthy Spirit was a multicomponent intervention to increase F&V consumption and physical activity (PA), delivered through Black churches. Sixteen churches were randomly assigned to three intervention conditions. At baseline, 1,056 individuals were recruited across the 16 churches, of which 906 (86%) were assessed at 1-year follow-up. Group 1 received standard educational materials, Group 2 received culturally targeted self-help nutrition and PA materials, and Group 3 received the Group 2 intervention as well as four telephone counseling calls based on MI. At 1-year follow-up, Groups 2 and 3 showed significant changes in both F&V intake and PA. Changes were somewhat larger for F&V. For F&V, but not for PA, there was a clear additive effect for the MI intervention.

RELIGIOUS VERSUS SECULAR CONTENT

As explained, the use of relevant religious themes and scriptures within intervention programs is one way to ensure cultural relevance and may be useful for improving program effectiveness. Holt and colleagues (Holt, Lee, & Wright, 2008; Holt, Roberts, et al., 2009) have tested religious themes versus secular themes for breast and prostate cancer prevention programs in African American churches. In one study, Holt, Wynn, et al. (2009) evaluated a spiritually based prostate cancer screening intervention for African American men who attend church to determine its efficacy for increasing informed decision making. Churches were randomized to receive either the spiritually based or the nonspiritual intervention. The intervention consisted of an educational session led by a trained community health advisor (CHA) from each church. Each session was conducted in a "Sunday school" fashion in which the CHA taught the session material (the lesson) to the class at church, using printed materials as a guide just as Sunday school teachers use their lesson or the Bible as a guide. The materials consisted of a 16-page full-color booklet with information on prostate cancer risk, incidence, development, symptoms, screening, and treatment. The materials contained spiritual content along with wellness and prostate information. The nonspiritual intervention was identical in all ways as the spiritual intervention except that the content did not include spiritual themes or scripture. Trained CHAs, also African American male church members, led an educational session and distributed educational print materials. Participants completed baseline and immediate follow-up surveys to assess the intervention impact on study outcomes. Results showed that the spiritually based intervention appeared to be more effective in increasing knowledge, and men read more of their materials in the spiritually based group than in the nonspiritual group.

Another study (Holt et al., 2008) compared the communication effectiveness of a spiritually based approach to breast cancer early detection education with a secular approach, using a cognitive response analysis. A total of 108 women from six Alabama churches were randomly assigned by church to receive a spiritually based or secular education booklet discussing breast cancer early detection. After reading the booklets, participants were asked to complete a thought-listing task based on the elaboration likelihood model (Petty & Cacioppo, 1981), writing down any thoughts they experienced and rating them as positive, negative, or neutral. Compared with the secular booklet, the spiritually based booklet resulted in significantly more thoughts involving personal connection, self-assessment, and spiritually based responses. These results suggest that a spiritually based approach to breast cancer awareness may be more effective than the secular approach, causing women to process the message more actively and stimulating central route processing (i.e., a cognitive process that requires more thought to scrutinize the merits of the message).

Although religious content has been shown to be beneficial in health promotion programs, it should not necessarily be prescribed as an automatic program feature. Religious content includes the use of scriptures, prayers, songs, and testimony incorporated into health messages and activities derived from the beliefs, values, and mission of the faith-based organization. Within faith-based institutions, there may be substantial diversity about the need for and appropriateness of religious content. It should not be assumed that all participating church members hold the same preferences for religious and spiritual content regarding health information.

PRACTICAL ILLUSTRATION

The ACTS (Action through Churches in Time to Save Lives) of Wellness study encourages colorectal cancer screening, healthy eating, and physical activity among African Americans (CDC, 2005). Nineteen African American churches in North Carolina and Michigan were randomized to intervention and control conditions. Intervention churches receive four personalized, tailored newsletters, motivational calls, and a variable number of targeted videos about colorectal cancer prevention and physical activity (one video for the church and one for each participant out of compliance with colorectal cancer screening). Formative focus groups for this project evaluated previously developed materials as well as proposed messages and graphic content for the tailored newsletters, and results indicated that participants had discrete preferences about the delivery of health information in a religious context. Some focus group members had a very strong preference for secular delivery of health information, feeling that their pastor was not medically trained and should limit exhortations to motivational ones to "be healthy" (e.g., to care for the body as a temple). Therefore, newsletters were developed with two different sets of graphic content and themes, one religious (e.g., photographs of an open Bible, praying hands, a church) and one secular (e.g., photographs of people gardening, walking). On the baseline survey, a question asked participants' preference for "health information to be received from a reliable source and tied to (or separate from) your spiritual or religious preference." The secular version of the newsletter did not include biblical quotes or prayers. On the baseline survey, 705 participants chose the secular option and 228 chose the religious one (Campbell et al., 2010). Without this information, providing religious content to participants who had a clear preference for nonreligious content could have cause a mismatch. Such a mismatch could reduce participants' perceptions of intervention relevance and trustworthiness and accuracy.

SUMMARY

A substantial body of research (mostly, although not exclusively, from African American churches) indicates an important role of faith organizations for promoting healthy behavior change. Although individuals are responsible for instituting and maintaining the lifestyle changes necessary to reduce risk and improve health, individual behavior is determined to a large extent by social environment (e.g., community norms and values, regulations, and policies). Practitioners and researchers have come to recognize the limitations of just focusing on the individual level and have moved toward approaches that take into account cultural and environmental influences. Working with religious organizations offers opportunities to address not only individual level factors but also the environmental and cultural influences on health. Researchers have used religious institutions as a way to access research participants. Additionally, to address the complexities of the multiple influences on health, cultural and faith aspects of religious organizations have been incorporated into research interventions to influence health behaviors. The literature to date suggests that religious organizations and health professionals can collaborate to implement successful health promotion programs across diverse health behaviors. Additionally, studies have provided guidance about how best to work with religious partners for health promotion (Ammerman et al., 2003; Campbell, Hudson, et al., 2007; Goldmon & Roberson, 2004; Peterson et al., 2002). These recommendations are provided in the next section.

RECOMMENDATIONS TO PROMOTE PREVENTIVE EFFORTS WITH FAITH-BASED ORGANIZATIONS

Researchers (Ammerman et al., 2003; Campbell, Hudson, et al., 2007; Goldmon & Roberson, 2004; Peterson et al., 2002) have provided suggestions for improving faith-based and public health collaborations. These include (a) understanding the faith partner, (b) building trust and credibility, (c) ensuring the transparency of roles, and (d) promoting program sustainability.

Understanding the Faith Partner

To engage in research that is culturally and spiritually appropriate, keen attention should be paid to learning about the faith partner to ensure that the research design is appropriate and the messages and strategies are effective as well as to augment the working relationship throughout the process. Formative research and discussions with congregants and key informants are critical to learn about the church theology, leadership structure, social teachings, and behavior. It should not be assumed that because two churches are of the same denomination they operate similarly. There is much diversity even within denominations regarding doctrine, policies, and leadership structures that dictate the way worship is conducted, the order of service, and the understanding and exhibition of faith. For example, there are many denominations under the umbrella of the Baptist church, and each vein varies in its beliefs and worship. It is, therefore, imperative for the researcher to have a working knowledge of the doctrinal beliefs, polity, leadership, and organizational structures of the faith partner to ensure successful engagement. Attending church services, observing the church community's behavior, and reading church bulletins and denomination materials are all useful in learning about the church culture and values. Enlisting the support of a key stakeholder such as the pastor or another congregant to serve as the "cultural mediator" (Hatch & Derthick, 1992) is also important for understanding informal power structures, values, and mores.

Building Trust and Credibility

Mistrust of medical research may play a role in whether and how churches engage with researchers. Historical wrongs, such as the legacy of Tuskegee (Thomas & Quinn, 1991), demand that researchers pay attention to developing a culture of trust, respect, and credibility to increase the likelihood that churches will serve as equal partners in the process. Part of building trust involves ensuring that the research program does not conflict with the church's core values. Several steps can be taken to nurture a culture of trust. For example, key church leaders can be involved even at the grant-writing stage to shape the research, allowing them to voice concerns about health and research, competing priorities, and discuss potential program benefits. It is also essential that members of the research team attend and participate in church services, meetings to discuss the program, and other church-sponsored events. The act of showing up conveys a sense of commitment and is also an opportunity to learn more about the faith partner's perspective and culture. Baskin, Resnicow, and Campbell (2001) also emphasized the use of culturally competent research staff to ensure that the cultural and ethnic strengths and assets of the faith community are respected. The use of culturally competent research staff goes beyond simply matching race and ethnicity of staff to the faith-based partner. It also involves a willingness to understand the church's values, customs, and cultural norms without manipulation or trivialization of the church's beliefs.

Ensuring Transparency of Research Roles

To build a sustainable partnership, a clear understanding of research roles is needed. Churches and research institutions may not have similar perspectives on how best to address an issue of mutual concern; thus, it is important that all aspects of the research process be crystal clear. A memorandum of understanding is one way to recognize the voluntary nature of the partnership and also to provide an exit strategy if aspects of the agreement are not fulfilled or if other circumstances arise. An advisory board including both public health professionals and key church leaders can review program content and procedures (Hatch, Cunningham, Woods, & Snipes, 1986). Additionally, share budgets with church partners to provide a sense of who is getting what and how much is going to research versus service components.

Promoting Program Sustainability

A legitimate concern of faith institutions is that research can be a one-way process, in which the researchers collect their data and then leave. Even when research projects offer benefits to congregation members, those benefits may not be readily perceived or may be overshadowed by other pressing concerns, such as underemployment or discrimination (Campbell, Hudson, et al., 2007). When church members are involved from the beginning, long-term needs can be identified and strategies for transferring ownership of the project can be instituted. Carefully considering how to build community capacity is a step toward ensuring that something is left behind. For example, research projects may choose to hire and train church members to serve on different aspects of the project (conducting focus groups, assisting with participant recruitment, conducting interviews). Program materials and equipment may be donated to churches for future use. Researchers can help churches identify other sources of funding to continue the program once the research phase is completed (Campbell, Hudson, et al., 2007).

THE ROLE OF PSYCHOLOGY IN FAITH- AND COMMUNITY-BASED HEALTH PROMOTION PROGRAMS

This chapter describes a public health orientation regarding faith-based initiatives conducted at the community level. As with any public health intervention, however, there are many ways that psychologists can contribute to the design, implementation, and evaluation of such programs. For example, behavioral and health psychologists can help elucidate the mechanisms through which faith-based interventions work (e.g., social support, social norms, and optimism) as well as how church involvement in general promotes better emotional and behavioral health. This can include applying theoretical models as well as measurement expertise. Psychologists can also enhance these efforts by providing training to lay counselors as well as shaping messages contained in self-help motivational interventions. Expertise in research design can help elucidate those components of religion- and faith-based interventions that are generic to all religions as opposed to unique factors associated with specific religions or subsects. Although the emphasis in this chapter has been on the positive impact of religion- and faith-based intervention, psychologists can also help examine potential deleterious effects of religious involvement and faith-based interventions.

IMPLICATIONS AND CONCLUSIONS

Enhancing health and well-being through prevention in the context of faith communities is becoming a more widespread and successful approach for health interventions. Several research gaps and opportunities for improvement exist, however. To date, health promotion programs in faith communities have addressed a multiplicity of topics, with varying levels of spiritual and religious content and varying levels of success. In some instances, changes have been significant, although most interventions have been evaluated for relatively short-term outcomes. Less is known about the sustained effects of programs and whether they are maintained after the grant funding ends.

Also, there are limitations associated with problem-specific approaches, because of the multiplicity of health concerns that most people face, either for themselves or for their families, across the life span. For example, focusing exclusively on cancer screening runs the risk of omitting the importance of diabetes management and vice versa. The focus of health efforts in the context of faith organizations should move toward a more comprehensive and long-term view of the relationship among knowledge, beliefs, and behavior and the collective impact these have on health outcomes.

In addition to supporting congregants' spiritual health and reinforcing behavioral beliefs that help ensure spiritual well-being, emphasis on mental and physical health should be echoed and supported in instruction (e.g., church education across the life span, sermons, bulletin inserts), church policy (e.g., guidelines for food at church functions or exercise or stretching at church meetings, etc.), and community program development (e.g., transportation programs for older congregants to assist with access to health care, development of lay health advisor programs in which youth and young adults provide help and guidance to older congregants, or provision of church facilities for clinical services open to all in the community). In addition, concern for the spiritual, physical, and mental well-being of church staff and leadership must be supported for leadership to model health stewardship to congregants. Within the organizational frame of many churches, these activities fall under stated objectives related to compassionate pastoral care and local, domestic mission initiatives in which tenets of service and witness hold sway (Carter-Edwards, Jallah, Goldmon, Roberson, & Hoyo, 2006).

Historically, churches have served as a resource for the sick and their families, not only in terms of supplication for healing but also in terms of basic social support (food, shelter, caring, etc.). In addition, tenets in many faith traditions encourage healthy behaviors (abstinence from alcohol, tobacco, caffeine, etc.) as well as certain prescriptions regarding foods that are acceptable. A critical third element of a healthy faith community is literacy regarding health promotion and maintenance as well as resources, such as health ministries, that can sustain health promotion efforts across the life span. Health literacy in the broadest sense could provide the foundational frame for providing the specific knowledge that would help people to be better stewards of their own health and that of their families.

Whereas an empirically based approach to disease incidence and prevalence is one tool for identifying priorities, it is not the only one that is valid. Community-identified priorities also must be acknowledged and addressed. Clinical and faith concerns can converge to build health literacy and healthier lifestyles across the life span. Community-based participatory research and intervention efforts provide a reasonable context in which to initiate this type of comprehensive, long-term endeavor. The challenge remains shifting the rubric of success from short-term behavioral change to a long-term view of behavioral maintenance and a healthier congregation overall.

Future research focused on the development of faith-based prevention programs must attend to sustainability. Longitudinal data and data evaluating sustainability are missing in the work that has occurred to date. For the most part, after intervention programs have concluded, information about program maintenance is absent. Some research (Bopp et al., 2007), however, has indicated that church members continue to participate in health programs that persist after the research phase ends. There is a need for more assessment of the organizational capacity of faith communities to sustain programs. Organizational capacity specifically includes resources (e.g., collective knowledge, attitudes, beliefs, expertise) as well as physical assets (e.g., buildings, grounds, church vans) within a congregation or at a denominational level to make it possible to include wellness, health literacy, and health service facilitation in programming (Carter-Edwards et al., 2012). Combined with development of long-term community partnerships (e.g., work with health departments, hospitals, clinics, institutions of higher education, or other resources external to the church per se), programs will likely have a greater chance of initial success as well as sustained application across time. Another important issue is that of dissemination. Successful programs and key findings often are not adequately disseminated to the target populations that need them. Others have noted (Bowen, Sorensen, et al., 2009) that systematic research on dissemination of public health promotion programs is still in its infancy, making it imperative to begin to examine relevant elements such as channels for dissemination, support for program implementers, and factors that determine program readiness and eligibility for dissemination. These issues, too, are relevant for religious organizations involved in health promotion for which, to date, very little research regarding the evaluation of programs disseminated to religious organizations has been conducted.

The research literature provides burgeoning evidence that African American faith communities have an important role to play in improving the health status of their congregants and reducing health disparities (Chatters, Levin, & Ellison, 1998; Eng, Hatch, & Callan, 1985; Lincoln & Mamiya, 1990). There are still challenges related to successful engagement and maintenance of health promotion programs in this arena. Future research should home in on the particular impacts of interventions with faith organizations aimed at closing the disparity gap. Although the focus of this chapter has been on work within African American faith communities (primarily Christian), faith-based health preventive and promotion interventions can be extended to other mainline religious institutions. As with African American faith communities, understanding the context in which these interventions take place is an important factor for potential success in health promotion efforts.

Finally, an emerging disjuncture between religion or spirituality and health promotion is threatening to impair the ability of public health professionals to work in faith-based cultural contexts. A recent study conducted by Duke University researchers (Koenig et al., 2010) found that fewer than half of the schools of public health in the United States have any curricular content on religion or spirituality and health. In this same survey, schools of nursing consistently led in recognizing the need for the inclusion of religion and health curricular content, followed closely by schools of medicine, although this content was usually a part of broader course topics (e.g., medicine in society) and unlikely to be part of a required, dedicated course on the topic (Koenig et al., 2010). The divide between what is taught and the growing need to address health promotion programs in the context of faith communities requires attention, not only in what is taught in schools of public health but also what may be found in other helping professions (e.g., medicine, nursing, social work, pharmacy, physical therapy, psychology). Research that addresses these gaps will help to define the next phase of research using faith-based partnerships.

References

Aitaoto, N., Braun, K. L., Dang, K. L., & So'a, T. (2007). Cultural considerations in developing church-based programs to reduce cancer health disparities among Samoans. *Ethnicity and Health, 12*, 381–400. doi:10.1080/13557850701300707

Allicock, M., Campbell, M. K., Valle, C. G., Carr, C., Resnicow, K., & Gizlice, Z. (2012). Evaluating the dissemination of Body & Soul, an evidence-based fruit and vegetable intake intervention: Challenges for dissemination and implementation research. *Journal of Nutrition Education and Behavior*. Advance online publication. PMID: 22406012

Allicock, M., Campbell, M., Valle, C., Barlow, J., Carr, C., Meier, A., & Gizlice, Z. (2010). Evaluating the implementation of peer counseling in a church-based dietary intervention for African Americans. *Patient Education and Counseling, 81*, 37–42. doi:10.1016/j.pec.2009.11.018

Ammerman, A., Corbie-Smith, G., St George, D. M., Washington, C., Weathers, B., & Jackson-Christian, B. (2003). Research expectations among African American church leaders in the PRAISE! project: A randomized trial guided by community-based participatory research. *American Journal of Public Health, 93*, 1720–1727. doi:10.2105/AJPH.93.10.1720

Association for the Advancement of Health Education. (1994). Code of ethics for health educators. *Journal of Health Education, 25*, 197–200.

Baskin, M. L., Resnicow, K., & Campbell, M. K. (2001). Conducting health interventions in Black churches:

A model for building effective partnerships. *Ethnicity and Disease*, *11*, 823–833.

Berkman, L. F., & Syme, S. L. (1979). Social networks, host resistance and mortality: A nine year follow-up of Alameda County residents. *American Journal of Epidemiology*, *109*, 186–204.

Black, B. (1997). HIV/AIDS and the Church: Kenyan religious leaders become partners in prevention. *Aidscaptions*, *4*(1), 23–26.

Bopp, M., Lattimore, D., Wilcox, S., Laken, M., McClorin, L., Swinton, R., . . . Bryant, D. (2007). Understanding physical activity participation in members of an African American church: A qualitative study. *Health Education Research*, *22*, 815–826. doi:10.1093/her/cyl149

Bowen, D. J., Beresford, S. A., Christensen, C. L., Kuniyuki, A. A., McLerran, D., Feng, Z., . . . Satia, J. (2009). Effects of a multilevel dietary intervention in religious organizations. *American Journal of Health Promotion*, *24*, 15–22. doi:10.4278/ajhp.07030823

Bowen, D. J., Beresford, S. A., Vu, T., Feng, Z., Tinker, L., Hart, A., Jr., . . . Campbell, M. K. (2004). Baseline data and design for a randomized intervention study of dietary change in religious organizations. *Preventive Medicine*, *39*, 602–611. doi:10.1016/j.ypmed.2004.02.021

Bowen, D. J., Sorensen, G., Weiner, B. J., Campbell, M., Emmons, K., & Melvin, C. (2009). Dissemination research in cancer control: Where are we and where should we go? *Cancer Causes and Control*, *20*, 473–485. doi:10.1007/s10552-009-9308-0

Campbell, M. K., Allicock, M., Carr, C., & Resnicow, K. (2010). *Health behaviors for cancer prevention in urban African American churches.* Unpublished manuscript.

Campbell, M. K., Bernhardt, J. M., Waldmiller, M., Jackson, B., Potenziani, D., Weathers, B., & Demissie, S. (1999). Varying the message source in computer-tailored nutrition education. *Patient Education and Counseling*, *36*, 157–169. doi:10.1016/S0738-3991(98)00132-3

Campbell, M. K., Demark-Wahnefried, W., Symons, M., Kalsbeek, W. D., Dodds, J., Cowan, A., . . . McClelland, J. W. (1999). Fruit and vegetable consumption and prevention of cancer: The Black Churches United for Better Health project. *American Journal of Public Health*, *89*, 1390–1396. doi:10.2105/AJPH.89.9.1390

Campbell, M. K., Hudson, M. A., Resnicow, K., Blakeney, N., Paxton, A., & Baskin, M. (2007). Church-based health promotion interventions: Evidence and lessons learned. *Annual Review of Public Health*, *28*, 213–234. doi:10.1146/annurev.publhealth.28.021406.144016

Campbell, M. K., James, A., Hudson, M. A., Carr, C., Jackson, E., Oates, V., . . . Tessaro, I. (2004). Improving multiple behaviors for colorectal cancer prevention among African American church members. *Health Psychology*, *23*, 492–502. doi:10.1037/0278-6133.23.5.492

Campbell, M. K., Motsinger, B. M., Ingram, A., Jewell, D., Makarushka, C., Beatty, B., . . . Demark-Wahnefried, W. (2000). The North Carolina Black Churches United for Better Health Project: Intervention and process evaluation. *Health Education and Behavior*, *27*, 241–253. doi:10.1177/109019810002700210

Campbell, M. K., Resnicow, K., Carr, C., Wang, T., & Williams, A. (2007). Process evaluation of an effective church based diet intervention: Body and Soul. *Health Education and Behavior*, *34*, 864–880. doi:10.1177/1090198106292020

Carter-Edwards. L., Hooten, E. G., Bruce, M. A., Toms, F., Lloyd, C. L., & Ellison, C. (2012). Pilgrimage to wellness: An exploratory report of rural African American clergy perceptions of church health promotion capacity. *Journal of Prevention and Intervention in the Community*, *40*, 194–207.

Carter-Edwards, L., Jallah, Y. B., Goldmon, M. V., Roberson, J. T., Jr., & Hoyo, C. (2006). Key attributes of health ministries in African American churches: An exploratory survey. *North Carolina Medical Journal*, *67*, 345–350.

Castro, F. G., Elder, J., Coe, K., Tafoya-Barraza, H. M., Moratto, S., Campbell, N., & Talavera, G. (1995). Mobilizing churches for health promotion in Latino communities: Companeros en la Salud. *Journal of the National Cancer Institute*, *18*, 127–135.

Centers for Disease Control and Prevention. (2005). *Increasing colorectal cancer screening in urban African American Communities via Churches (more informally called ACTS of Wellness)* (Special Interest Project, Cooperative Agreement U48/DP000059). Washington, DC: Author.

Chatters, L. M., Levin, J. S., & Ellison, C. G. (1998). Public health and health education in faith communities. *Health Education and Behavior*, *25*, 689–699. doi:10.1177/109019819802500602

Cohen, C. J. (1999). *The boundaries of blackness: AIDS and the breakdown of Black politics.* Chicago, IL: University of Chicago Press.

Coyne-Beasley, T., & Schoenback, V. J. (2000). The African-American church: A potential forum for adolescent comprehensive sexuality education. *Journal of Adolescent Health*, *26*, 289–294. doi:10.1016/S1054-139X(99)00097-X

Davidson, M. N., & Devney, P. (1991). Attitudinal barriers to organ donation among Black Americans. *Transplantation Proceedings*, *23*, 2531–2532.

DeHaven, M. J., Hunter, I. B., Wilder, L., Walton, J. W., & Berry, J. (2004). Health programs in faith-based organizations: Are they effective? *American Journal of Public Health*, *94*, 1030–1036. doi:10.2105/AJPH.94.6.1030

Derose, K. P., Duan, N., & Fox, S. A. (2002). Women's receptivity to church-based mobile mammography. *Journal of Health Care for the Poor and Underserved*, *13*, 199–213.

Duan, N., Fox, S. A., Derose, K. P., & Carson, S. (2000). Maintaining mammography adherence through telephone counseling in a church-based trial. *American Journal of Public Health*, *90*, 1468–1471. doi:10.2105/AJPH.90.9.1468

Dubois, J. (2009). *Inside the Federal Centers for Faith-Based and Neighborhood Partnerships*. Retrieved from http://www.whitehouse.gov/blog/2009/11/17/inside-federal-centers-faith-based-and-neighborhood-partnerships

Dunlap, S. J. (2009). *Caring cultures: How congregations respond to the sick*. Waco, TX: Baylor University Press.

Einollahi, B. (2008). Cadaveric kidney transplantation in Iran: Behind the Middle Eastern countries? *Iranian Journal of Kidney Diseases*, *2*, 55–56.

Eng, E., Hatch, J., & Callan, A. (1985). Institutionalizing social support through the church and into the community. *Health Education Quarterly*, *12*, 81–92. doi:10.1177/109019818501200107

Falicov, C. (1996). Mexican families. In M. McGoldrick, J. Giordano, & J. K. Pearce (Eds.), *Ethnicity and family therapy* (pp. 169–182). New York, NY: Guilford Press.

Faridi, Z., Shuval, K., Yanchou Njike, V., Katz, J. A., Jennings, G., Williams, M., & Katz, D. L. (2010). Partners reducing effects of diabetes (PREDICT): A diabetes prevention physical activity and dietary intervention through African-American churches. *Health Education Research*, *25*, 306–315. doi:10.1093/her/cyp005

Farquhar, J. W. (1978). The community-based model of life style intervention trials. *American Journal of Epidemiology*, *108*, 103–111.

Federal Register. (2001). Executive Order 13198—Agency responsibilities with respect to faith-based and community initiatives. Executive Order 13199—Establishment of White House office of faith-based and community initiatives. *Presidential Documents, 66*(21). Retrieved from http://frwebgate.access.gpo.gov/cgi-bin/getdoc.cgi?dbname=2001_register&docid=fr31ja01-115.pdf

Fitzgibbon, M. L., Stolley, M. R., Ganschow, P., Schiffer, L., Wells, A., Simon, N., & Dyer, A. (2005). Results of a faith-based weight loss intervention for Black women. *Journal of the National Medical Association*, *97*, 1393–1402.

Francis, S. A., & Liverpool, J. (2009). A review of faith-based HIV prevention programs. *Journal of Religion and Health*, *48*, 6–15. doi:10.1007/s10943-008-9171-4

Goldmon, M. V., & Roberson, J. T., Jr. (2004). Churches, academic institutions, and public health: Partnerships to eliminate health disparities. *North Carolina Medical Journal*, *65*, 368–372.

Green, L. W., Richard, L., & Potvin, L. (1996). Ecological foundations of health promotion. *American Journal of Health Promotion, 10*, 270–281. doi:10.4278/0890-1171-10.4.270

Griffith, D. M., Pichon, L. C., Campbell, B., & Allen, J. O. (2010). Your Blessed Health: A faith-based CBPR approach to addressing HIV/AIDS among African Americans. *AIDS Education and Prevention*, *22*, 203–217. doi:10.1521/aeap.2010.22.3.203

Hall, L. E., Callender, C. O., Yeager, C. L., Barber, J. B., Jr., Dunston, G. M., & Pinn-Wiggins, V. W. (1991). Organ donation in Blacks: The next frontier. *Transplantation Proceedings*, *23*, 2500–2504.

Hansen, H. (2005). Isla evangelista—A story of church and state: Puerto Rico's faith-based initiatives in drug treatment. *Culture, Medicine, and Psychiatry*, *29*, 433–456. doi:10.1007/s11013-006-9002-6

Hatch, J., Cunningham, A. C., Woods, W. W., & Snipes, F. C. (1986). The Fitness Through Churches project: Description of a community-based cardiovascular health promotion intervention. *Hygiene*, *5*(3), 9–12.

Hatch, J., & Derthick, S. (1992). Empowering Black churches for health promotion. *Health Values*, *16*(5), 3–9.

Hatch, J., Moss, N., Saran, A., Presley-Cantrell, L., & Mallory, C. (1993). Community research: Partnership in Black communities. *American Journal of Preventive Medicine*, *9*(Suppl.), 27–31.

Holt, C. L., Lee, C., & Wright, K. (2008). A spirituality based approach to breast cancer awareness: Cognitive response analysis of communication effectiveness. *Health Communication*, *23*, 13–22. doi:10.1080/10410230701626919

Holt, C. L., Roberts, C., Scarinci, I., Wiley, S. R., Eloubeidi, M., Crowther, M., . . . Coughlin, S. S. (2009). Development of a spiritually based educational program to increase colorectal cancer screening among African American men and women. *Health Communication*, *24*, 400–412. doi:10.1080/10410230903023451

Holt, C. L., Wynn, T. A., Litaker, M. S., Southward, P., Jeames, S., & Schulz, E. (2009). A comparison of a spiritually based and non-spiritually based educational intervention for informed decision making for prostate cancer screening among church-attending African-American men. *Urologic Nursing*, *29*, 249–258.

Israel, B. A., Schulz, A. J., Parker, E. A., & Becker, A. B. (1998). Review of community-based research: Assessing partnership approaches to improve public health. *Annual Review of Public Health, 19*, 173–202. doi:10.1146/annurev.publhealth.19.1.173

Kagawa-Singer, M. (1994). Cross-cultural views of disability. *Rehabilitation Nursing, 19*, 362–365.

Kennedy, B. M., Paeratakul, S., Champagne, C. M., Ryan, D. H., Harsha, D. W., McGee, B., . . . Bogle, M. L. (2005). A pilot church-based weight loss program for African-American adults using church members as health educators: A comparison of individual and group intervention. *Ethnicity and Disease, 15*, 373–378.

Koenig, H. G., McCullough, M. E., & Larson, D. B. (2001). *Handbook of religion and health.* New York, NY: Oxford University Press. doi:10.1093/acprof:oso/9780195118667.001.0001

Koenig, H. G., Meador, K. G., Hooten, E. G., & Lindsay-Calkins, E. (2010). *Spirituality and health in education and research* (Preliminary Report of a National Survey of Schools of Medicine, Nursing and Public Health, March 2009). Unpublished manuscript.

Lasater, T. M., Becker, D. M., Hill, M. N., & Gans, K. M. (1997). Synthesis of findings and issues from religious-based cardiovascular disease prevention trials. *Annals of Epidemiology, 7*, s47–s53.

Lasater, T. M., Wells, B. L., Carleton, R. A., & Elder, J. P. (1986). The role of churches in disease prevention research studies. *Public Health Reports, 101*(2), 125–131.

Lincoln, C. E., & Mamiya, L. H. (1990). *The Black church in the African American experience.* Durham, NC: Duke University Press.

Lopez, V. A., & Castro, F. G. (2006). Participation and program outcomes in a church-based cancer prevention program for Hispanic women. *Journal of Community Health, 31*, 343–362. doi:10.1007/s10900-006-9016-6

Ma, G. X., Shive, S., Tan, Y., Gao, W., Rhee, J., Park, M., . . . Toubbeh, J. I. (2009). Community-based colorectal cancer intervention in underserved Korean Americans. *Cancer Epidemiology, 33*, 381–386. doi:10.1016/j.canep.2009.10.001

McLeroy, K. R., Bibeau, D., Steckler, A., & Glanz, K. (1988). An ecological perspective on health promotion programs. *Health Education Quarterly, 15*, 351–377. doi:10.1177/109019818801500401

McNabb, W., Quinn, M., Kerver, J., Cook, S., & Karrison, T. (1997). The PATHWAYS church-based weight loss program for urban African-American women at risk for diabetes. *Diabetes Care, 20*, 1518–1523. doi:10.2337/diacare.20.10.1518

Miller, W. R., & Rollnick, S. (1991). *Motivational interviewing: Preparing people to change addictive behavior.* New York, NY: Guilford Press.

Ministerial Association. (1988). *Seventh-day Adventists believe . . . A biblical exposition of 27 fundamental doctrines.* Hagerstown, MD: Review & Herald.

Minkler, M. (2004). Ethical challenges for the "outside" researcher in community-based participatory research. *Health Education and Behavior, 31*, 684–697. doi:10.1177/1090198104269566

Najafizadeh, K., Ghorbani, F., Hamidinia, S., Emamhadi, M. A., Moinfar, M. A., Ghobadi, O., & Assari, S. (2010). Holy month of Ramadan and increase in organ donation willingness. *Saudi Journal of Kidney Diseases and Transplantation, 21*, 443–446.

Office of Minority Health and Health Disparities. (2010). *Disease burden and risk factors.* Retrieved from http://www.cdc.goc/omhd?AMH/dbrf.htm

Oliver, M., Woywodt, A., Ahmed, A., & Saif, I. (2011). Organ donation, transplantation and religion. *Nephrology, Dialysis, Transplantation, 26*, 437–444. doi:10.1093/ndt/gfq628

Orr, J., & May, S. (2000). *Religion and health services in Los Angeles: Reconfiguring the terrain.* Los Angeles, CA: Center for Religion and Civic Culture, University of Southern California. Retrieved from http://crcc.usc.edu/docs/healthandfaith.pdf

Patton, J. (1993). *Pastoral care in context: An introduction to pastoral care.* Louisville, KY: Westminster John Knox.

Peterson, J., Atwood, J. R., & Yates, B. (2002). Key elements for church-based health promotion programs: Outcome-based literature review. *Public Health Nursing, 19*, 401–411. doi:10.1046/j.1525-1446.2002.19602.x

Petty, R. E., & Cacioppo, J. T. (1981). *Attitudes and persuasion: Classic and contemporary approaches.* Dubuque, IA: William C. Brown.

Plawecki, H. M., Freiberg, G., & Palwecki, J. A. (1989). Increasing organ donation in the Black community. *Nephrology Nursing Journal, 16*, 321–324.

Raboteau, A. J. (1986). The Afro-American traditions. In R. L. Numbers & D. W. Amundsen (Eds.), *Caring and curing: Health and medicine in the Western religions traditions* (pp. 539–562). Baltimore, MD: Johns Hopkins University Press.

Resnicow, K., Campbell, M. K., Carr, C., McCarty, F., Wang, T., Periasamy, S., . . . Stables, G. (2004). Body and Soul. A dietary intervention conducted through African-American churches. *American Journal of Preventive Medicine, 27*, 97–105. doi:10.1016/j.amepre.2004.04.009

Resnicow, K., Jackson, A., Blissett, D., Wang, T., McCarty, F., Rahotep, S., & Perasamy, S. (2005). Results of the healthy body health spirit trial. *Health Psychology, 24*, 339–348. doi:10.1037/0278-6133.24.4.339

Resnicow, K., Jackson, A., Braithwaite, R., DiIorio, C., Blisset, D., Rahotep, S., & Perasamy, S. (2002). Healthy body/healthy spirit: A church-based nutrition and physical activity intervention. *Health Education Research, 17*, 562–573. doi:10.1093/her/17.5.562

Resnicow, K., Jackson, A., Wang, T., De, A. K., McCarty, F., Dudley, W. N., & Baranowski, T. (2001). A motivational interviewing intervention to increase fruit and vegetable intake through Black churches: Results of the Eat for Life trial. *American Journal of Public Health, 91*, 1686–1693. doi:10.2105/AJPH.91.10.1686

Resnicow, K., Wallace, D. C., Jackson, A., Digirolamo, A., Odom, E., Wang, T., . . . Baranowski, T. (2000). Dietary change through African American churches: Baseline results and program description of the Eat for Life trial. *Journal of Cancer Education, 15*, 156–163.

Rothman, J. (1969). An analysis of goals and roles in community organization practice. In R. M. Kramer & H. Specht (Eds.), *Readings in community organization practice* (pp. 260–268). Englewood Cliffs, NJ: Prentice-Hall.

Rubens, A. J., & Oleckno, W. A. (1998). Knowledge, attitudes and behaviors of college students regarding organ and tissue donation and implications for increasing organ/tissue donors. *College Student Journal, 32*, 167–178.

Ryan, R. M., Lynch, M. F., Vansteenkiste, M., & Deci, E. L. (2011). Motivation and autonomy in counseling, psychotherapy, and behavior change: A look at theory and practice. *The Counseling Psychologist, 39*, 193–260.

Samuel-Hodge, C. D., Keyserling, T. C., Park, S., Johnston, L. F., Gizlice, Z., & Bangdiwala, S. I. (2009). A randomized trial of a church-based diabetes self-management program for African Americans with type 2 diabetes. *The Diabetes Educator, 35*, 439–454. doi:10.1177/0145721709333270

Sauaia, A., Min, S. J., Lack, D., Apodaca, C., Osuna, D., Stowe, A., . . . Byers, T. (2007). Church-based breast cancer screening education: Impact of two approaches on Latinas enrolled in public and private health insurance plans. *Preventing Chronic Disease, 4*(4), A99.

Schorling, J. B., Roach, J., Siegel, M., Baturka, N., Hunt, D. E., Guterbock, T. M., & Stewart, H. L. (1997). A trial of church-based smoking cessation interventions for rural African Americans. *Preventive Medicine, 26*, 92–101. doi:10.1006/pmed.1996.9988

Spigner, C., Weaver, M., Pineda, M., Rabun, K., French, L., Taylor, L., & Allen, M. D. (1999). Race/ethnic-based opinions on organ donation and transplantation among teens: Preliminary results. *Transplantation Proceedings, 31*, 1347–1348. doi:10.1016/S0041-1345(98)02022-3

Stokols, D. (1992). Establishing and maintaining healthy environments: Toward a social ecology of health promotion. *American Psychologist, 47*, 6–22. doi:10.1037/0003-066X.47.1.6

Stokols, D. (2000). The social ecological paradigm of wellness promotion. In M. Schneider Jamner & D. Stokols (Eds.), *Promoting human wellness: New frontiers for research, practice and policy* (pp. 21–37). Berkeley: University of California Press.

Stokols, D., Allen, J., & Bellingham, R. L. (1996). The social ecology of health promotion: Implications for research and practice. *American Journal of Health Promotion, 10*, 247–251. doi:10.4278/0890-1171-10.4.247

Stone, E. J. (1991). Comparison of NHLBI community-based cardiovascular research studies. *Journal of Health Education, 22*, 134–136.

Sugunasiri, S. H. (1990). The Buddhist view concerning the dead body. *Transplantation Proceedings, 22*, 947–949.

Thomas, S. B., & Quinn, S. C. (1991). The Tuskegee syphilis study, 1932 to 1972: Implication for HIV education and AIDS risk education programs in the Black community. *American Journal of Public Health, 81*, 1498–1505. doi:10.2105/AJPH.81.11.1498

Thomas, S. B., Quinn, S. C., Billingsley, A., & Caldwell, C. (1994). The characteristics of northern Black churches with community health outreach programs. *American Journal of Public Health, 84*, 575–579. doi:10.2105/AJPH.84.4.575

U.S. Department of Health and Human Services. (2010). *Healthy people 2010: With understanding and improving health and objectives for improving health* (2nd ed.). Washington, DC: U.S. Government Printing Office.

Voorhees, C. C., Stillman, F. A., Swank, R. T., Heagerty, P. J., Levine, D. M., & Becker, D. M. (1996). Heart, body, and soul: Impact of church-based smoking cessation interventions on readiness to quit. *Preventive Medicine, 25*, 277–285. doi:10.1006/pmed.1996.0057

Ward, E. G. (2005). Homophobia, hypermasculinity, and the US Black church. *Culture, Health, and Sexuality, 7*, 493–504. doi:10.1080/13691050500151248

Welsh, A. L., Sauaia, A., Jacobellis, J., Min, S. J., Byers, T. (2005). The effect of two church-based interventions on breast cancer screening rates among Medicaid-insured Latinas. *Preventing Chronic Disease, 2*(4), A7.

Williams, G. C., Freedman, Z. R., & Deci, E. L. (1998). Supporting autonomy to motivate patients with diabetes for glucose control. *Diabetes Care, 21*, 1644–1651. doi:10.2337/diacare.21.10.1644

Williams, G. C., Niemiec, C. P., Patrick, H., Ryan, R. M., & Deci, E. L. (2009). The importance of supporting autonomy and perceived competence in facilitating long-term tobacco abstinence. *Annals of Behavioral Medicine, 37*, 315–324. doi:10.1007/s12160-009-9090-y

Wimberly, A. E. S. (2001). The role of Black faith communities in fostering health. In R. L. Braithwaite & S. E. Taylor (Eds.), *Health issues in the Black community* (2nd ed., pp. 129–150). San Francisco, CA: Jossey-Bass.

Winett, R. A., Anderson, E. S., Wojcik, J. R., Winett, S. G., & Bowden, T. (2007). Guide to health: Nutrition and physical activity outcomes of a group-randomized trial of an Internet-based intervention in churches. *Annals of Behavioral Medicine, 33*, 251–261. doi:10.1007/BF02879907

Wineburg, R. J., Coleman, B. L., Boddie, S. C., & Cnaan, R. A. (2008). Leveling the playing field: Epitomizing devolution through faith-based organizations. *Journal of Sociology and Social Welfare, 35*, 17–42.

Yanek, L. R., Becker, D. M., Moy, T. F., Gittelsohn, J., & Koffman, D. M. (2001). Project Joy: Faith based cardiovascular health promotion for African American women. *Public Health Reports, 116*(Suppl. 1), 68–81. doi:10.1093/phr/116.S1.68

Zahner, S. J., & Corrado, S. M. (2004). Local health department partnerships with faith-based organizations. *Journal of Public Health Management and Practice, 10*, 258–265.

Zahuranec, D. B., Morgenstern, L. B., Garcia, N. M., Conley, K. M., Lisabeth, L. D., Rank, G. S., . . . Brown, D. L. (2008). Stroke health and risk education (SHARE) pilot project: Feasibility and need for church-based stroke health promotion in a bi-ethnic community. *Stroke, 39*, 1583–1585. doi:10.1161/STROKEAHA.107.503557

CHAPTER 24

CAN RELIGION AND SPIRITUALITY ENHANCE PREVENTION PROGRAMS FOR COUPLES?

Frank D. Fincham and Steven R. H. Beach

An estimated 5.6 billion people (84% of the world's population) profess some religious faith (Adherents.com, 2011). Belief in God and prayer are also commonplace; in the United States, for instance, 92% of people believe in God (Pew Forum on Religion and Public Life, 2008), and approximately 90% pray at least occasionally (McCullough & Larson, 1999; see also Volume 1, Chapter 16, this handbook). Notwithstanding these facts, social scientists have tended to keep "their distance from religion and spirituality" (Hill & Pargament, 2003, p. 65), and this is especially true regarding the role of religious and spiritual resources in the prevention of couple and family problems or best practices for the promotion of couple and family strengths (Mahoney, 2010; see also Volume 1, Chapter 20, this handbook). This chapter addresses this omission by examining how religion and spirituality influences marital relationships. We focus in particular on colloquial, petitionary prayer to illustrate how specific religious and spiritual practices may be helpful in the prevention of marital distress and in strengthening marital relationships.

CONCEPTUAL HYGIENE

In turning to our task, we need to be clear about the overarching constructs of religion and spirituality and the more specific construct of prayer. As reflected throughout this handbook, it has become increasingly common to distinguish religion from spirituality (for more complete discussion, see Volume 1, Chapter 1, this handbook). Specifically, religion is often used to refer to a more formalized set of ideological commitments associated with a group (i.e., an organized system of beliefs, rituals, and cumulative traditions within a faith community), whereas spirituality is often used to refer to the personal and more subjective side of religious experience (e.g., Carlson, Kirkpatrick, Hecker, & Killmer, 2002; Worthington & Aten, 2009). Although spirituality means different things to different people, between two thirds and three fourths of Americans consider themselves to be both spiritual and religious (Marler & Hadaway, 2002).

According to Mahoney (2010), most research relating to religion and the family (79% of marital studies and 76% of parenting studies over the past decade) uses one or two items to measure religious variables (e.g., affiliation, attendance, self-rated importance, Biblical conservatism). Although such studies generally show that religiosity is related to several positive outcomes in family relationships, they provide little information about what specific, modifiable aspects of religious behavior and spirituality are associated with such outcomes. Consequently, it is difficult to determine whether specific religious behaviors have a causal connection to these outcomes, or whether the association is due primarily to self-selection or correlated third variables. In line with these concerns, several studies have reported self-selection bias to be problematic for making inferences from the current research

This chapter was made possible by Department of Health And Human Services Administration for Children and Families Grant No. 90FE0022/01 awarded to Frank D. Fincham and by a grant from the John Templeton Foundation.

DOI: 10.1037/14046-024
APA Handbook of Psychology, Religion, and Spirituality: Vol. 2. An Applied Psychology of Religion and Spirituality, K. I. Pargament (Editor-in-Chief)

findings on religiosity (e.g., Koenig, McCullough, & Larson, 2001). Others have highlighted the potential impact of the more expansive social networks found among religious participants and the social support they provide as potentially responsible for outcomes attributed to religiosity (Ellison & George, 1994; Taylor, Chatters, & Levin, 2004). Compounding the difficulty of using existing research to guide practical decision making, the global item(s) used show small effect sizes. For example, those who attend religious services frequently are less likely to divorce than nonattenders, but the average effect size is only $r = .125$ (Mahoney et al., 2001). As Mahoney (2010) so aptly noted, "A central challenge in moving ahead is to develop conceptual models that go beyond a reliance on global religious indices to clarify what about religion matters, for better or worse, in family life" (p. 806). Responding to this challenge will require more concrete behavioral specification of referents, and the introduction of experimental methods to complement the survey research methods that have dominated research in the area to date.

One specific behavior with great salience and potential practical importance is prayer. Like religion and spirituality, however, prayer has many potential referents and it behooves us to be clear about our usage of this term. William James (1902), a founding father of modern psychology, defined prayer as "every kind of inward communion or conversation with the power recognized as divine" (p. 464). Certainly this definition fits well for the Abrahamic faiths (i.e., Judaism, Christianity, and Islam), and appears to have strong parallels in other religious traditions (e.g., Hinduism), including those that are less theist or even nontheist (e.g., Buddhism, Shinto, New Age). Some have even argued, "if prayer is regarded as every kind of communication with the power recognized (by the pray-er) as divine, then, arguably, all individuals pray to some degree" (Breslin & Lewis, 2008, p. 10).

Several different types of prayer have been identified. One taxonomy offered by Poloma and Gallup (1991) identified ritual prayer (recited through reading a text or from memory), petitionary prayer (includes requests to meet specific material needs), colloquial prayer (use of everyday conversational language to communicate with the divine, ultimate power, etc.), and meditative prayer (being in the presence of the divine, thinking about the divine). Many other taxonomies of prayer exist, but it suffices for our purposes to simply note that researchers will need to be clear when describing the effects of prayer because the impact of ritual or meditative prayer could be quite different from the impact of petitionary or colloquial prayer. The focus of our own research on prayer, reviewed later, is colloquial, petitionary prayer, a form of prayer that invokes the deity's help in response to specific needs, using the individual's own language rather than a set or "memorized" prayer. We focus attention on this form of prayer because it may be a response to ongoing stressors and life events, and because of its ability to serve as a point of connection with family members, but this should not be taken to imply that other forms of prayer (e.g., meditative or ritual) are a less valuable focus of future research attention or that other forms of religious and spiritual activity should be ignored by researchers.

REVIEW OF THEORETICAL WORK THAT LINKS RELIGION AND SPIRITUALITY TO MARITAL AND FAMILY OUTCOMES

Early on, James (1902) sought to understand why humans were religious and what practical benefits spirituality brought them. Both psychology and religion, James observed, converged on the view that humans can be transformed by forces beyond their normal consciousness. As a result, he argued that intense, religious experiences should be studied because they provide a microscope of the mind by showing us in enlarged form, normal psychological processes. Although theoretical analyses offered by subsequent psychologists, such as Maslow and Erikson, placed greater attention on the relationship between religion and mental health, the focus on the individual remained. Allport (1950), who helped shape social psychology, paid attention to how humans use religion in different ways but, ironically, retained a focus on the individual. Each of these scholars provided influential contributions that are considered classics in the psychology of religion, but they offer little when it comes to understanding religion and family functioning. Indeed,

Parke (2001) noted that research on religion "is rarely represented in the scientific journals devoted to family issues" (p. 555). This state of affairs is beginning to change, however. Recently a theoretical framework relating specific aspects of religion and spirituality to family relationships has emerged, as has one relating prayer to intimate relationships in general. We now turn to briefly review each of these theoretical developments.

Relational Spirituality

Mahoney (2010) has developed a relational spirituality framework to "help stimulate in-depth questions that have or could be asked about religion's unique role in family life" (p. 807; also see Volume 1, Chapter 20, this handbook). Defining *spirituality* as "the search for the sacred" and *religion* as a "a search for significance in ways related to the sacred" (Pargament, 1997, p. 34), Mahoney has identified three avenues through which religion and spirituality can be integrated into family relationships, namely, (a) family member(s)' individual relationship with the divine, (b) imbuing family relationships with sacred properties, and (c) family member(s)' relationships with broader religious communities. These three sets of mechanisms are portrayed as ones that can operate at any of three stages of family relationships, including their formation (creation and structuring of relationships), maintenance (conserving the relationship), and transformation (changes in the structure or processes of distressed relationships).

Mahoney (2010) has argued that a family member may draw on his or her felt connection to the divine to determine goals for family relationships and how to deal with obstacles thwarting such goals. She has noted that most religions offer theological directives about the deity's wishes about family relationships and the conduct of family life. Accordingly, a person may rely on his or her relationship with the deity in forming and maintaining relationships as well as in coping with relationship problems.

In addition, a family relationship may itself be experienced as an expression or vehicle of spirituality. For example, people may perceive a family relationship as having sacred qualities (e.g., see it as sacred, holy) or see it as a manifestation of God (e.g., an expression of God's will or infused with God's presence). This mechanism relating spirituality to family relationships, labeled *sanctification,* has already spawned a productive line of research (see Mahoney, Pargament, & Hernandez, in press; Pargament & Mahoney, 2005; see also Volume 1, Chapter 14, this handbook). Alternatively, family members may engage in behaviors together that substantively center on spiritual issues, such as engaging in religious rituals or intimate spiritual dialogues; these pathways presumably could deepen both an individual family member's felt connection to the divine and the sense that the relationship itself possesses a distinctive spiritual dimension that may not apply to other relationships.

Finally, a person's search for the sacred can take place in a spiritual community that influences and supports various aspects of family life. Certainly highly religious couples report that their religious community supports faith practices that, in turn, help maintain their views of the spiritual nature of marriage and parenting (e.g., Dollahite & Marks, 2009). Some faith communities may provide access to resources that can be obtained via involvement in secular groups, such as integrating into a broader community, facilitating access to recreational or social service organizations, and providing general social support. Such tangible provisions may lead researchers to ask whether the unique feature of a spiritual or faith community, its concern with the sacred, affects family life above and beyond effects found in supportive secular groups of like-minded people. This question is clearly a difficult one to address at the level of research design, and this may account for the lack of studies on this topic. Nonetheless, at a conceptual level, it is quite possible that the spiritual beliefs and practices related to family life that are encouraged and reinforced by faith communities have unique effects on the family relationships of its members, effects that go beyond family-strengthening activities of secular organizations, and it would be useful to better understand such effects.

Mahoney (2010) has offered an interesting construct (i.e., relational spirituality) and has identified potential mechanisms through which it may operate at various stages of family life. Her goal in doing so was, in part, to develop a framework for summarizing the literature on religion in families and to identify questions for future research. It succeeds in achieving both goals, leaving the ongoing task of providing greater specificity and detail for each of the pathways to flesh out testable theoretical propositions. The same can probably be said about the goal theory framework outlined in the next section. Accordingly, after the presentation of the goal theory framework, we offer a three-pronged, specific model consistent with Mahoney's general framework.

Goal Theory Framework Applied to the Role of Religion and Spirituality in Marriage

One possible mechanism linking spiritual and religious behavior to couple outcomes involves motivational processes. As suggested by Mahoney (2010), spiritual and religious activity has an impact on an individual's goals (see also Volume 1, Part I, this handbook). Choice of goals and thereby the intention and willingness to engage in particular behaviors could result in behavioral changes with the potential to support or undermine the relationship. For example, Dudley and Kosinski (1990) have suggested that spiritual activities may help couples to more often "think of the needs of others, be more loving and forgiving, treat each other with respect, and resolve conflict" (p. 82). If correct, this suggests that there may be multiple motivational processes that potentially connect spiritual and religious activities to relationship outcomes (see also the theoretical chapters in Volume 1, this handbook: Chapters 6, 7, 10, 14, 20, 23, and 24).

Fincham and Beach (1999) noted that motivational processes of the sort that may be influenced by prayer, or other religious and spiritual activities, may change the course of relationship conflict as well as enhance recovery from negative interactions that have already occurred. Specifically, they hypothesize that when couples perceive a conflict of interest, they may switch from the cooperative goals they typically profess to a set of emergent goals that are highly adversarial in nature. Spouses locked in conflict may find themselves focused on "getting their own way" or "not losing an argument." In this motivational state, knowing how to reach cooperative solutions may not produce a positive outcome. That is, although they are focused on getting their own way, partners may engage in negative behaviors toward each other even when they "know better." This dynamic was captured by Wile (1993) in his observation that "it is impossible to make I-statements when you are in the 'hating my partner, wanting revenge, feeling stung and wanting to sting back' state of mind" (p. 2). Indeed, the rapidly escalating chains of increasingly negative behavior that can result from such a state of mind have been documented as the behavioral signature of a distressed relationship (see Fincham, 2003).

Beach, Fincham, Hurt, McNair, and Stanley (2008) have argued that prayer for a relationship partner's well-being (Agape-focused prayer that might, e.g., ask God to do good things for the partner, envelope the partner in God's love, etc.), when utilized in the context of a conflict of interest, could provide a specific mechanism that allows cooperative goals to regain their dominance, replacing revenge-oriented or competition-oriented ones. Likewise, privately praying for the partner's well-being when a conflict occurs may also have the added advantage of providing what can be considered (the ultimate form of) "social support" and assurance of "attachment security" by reaffirming a connection to a dependable attachment figure and thus decreasing the impact of negative partner behavior. The cycle by which goals may be transformed from cooperative to win–lose and back again is shown in Figure 24.1.

The regular (private) practice of prayer for the partner's well-being, even in absence of an active conflict, is hypothesized to chronically prime a range of prosocial motives, setting the stage for other positive relationship outcomes. Praying benevolently for the partner necessarily involves "joining" with the partner vis-à-vis the deity and is thereby likely to promote a greater sense of couple identity, closeness, and relationship satisfaction. For some, praying privately in this way may lead him or her to view the relationship as sacred or increase the salience of this view if already held. Importantly,

FIGURE 24.1. Goal theory model illustrating role of prayer in reestablishing cooperative goals in context of conflict.

such prayer, in addition to being self-reinforcing, is likely to be supported by the spiritual community and, in this way, be sustained by natural reinforcers.

Additional mechanisms that may occur whenever a religious or spiritual activity helps focus attention on God's love for the partner, and one's own wishes to be a vehicle of God's love, can also operate in the context of benevolent (i.e., Agape focused) prayer for the partner. Specifically, praying for God to bless, protect, and guide one's partner may prime awareness of God's love for one's partner. Focusing on God's love for the partner, in turn, would be expected to facilitate the propensity to forgive and exit from negative cycles of interaction with the partner that might otherwise become self-maintaining. Because greater forgiveness is associated with a variety of indicators of positive relationship functioning, including relationship satisfaction (e.g., Fincham & Beach, 2007), increased commitment (e.g., Tsang, McCullough, & Fincham, 2006), and effective conflict resolution (Fincham, Beach, & Davila, 2007; see Fincham, 2009, for review), practicing religious or spiritual behaviors that enhance forgiveness should lead to increased relationship satisfaction over time.

Similarly, we would expect an impact of certain religious and spiritual practices, and particularly prayer, on gratitude. Specifically, prayer that highlights God's blessings and asks for them to continue may prime a response of gratitude for God's beneficence. Supporting this expectation, several studies have found a relationship between religiosity and gratitude (e.g., Adler & Fagley, 2005), and most religions promote gratitude (Emmons & Crumpler, 2000), including the practice of thanking God in prayer. Indeed, in a prototype study of prayer (Lambert, Graham, & Fincham, 2011), participants were asked to list the characteristics or attributes that come to mind when they thought of prayer. Of 219 attributes, "thanking" was the second most frequently mentioned feature, next only to "God." Accordingly, we might anticipate that gratitude would be a likely component of naturally occurring prayers. Because gratitude has been linked to greater prosocial behavior and social bonds (Emmons & Shelton, 2002; McCullough & Tsang, 2004) as well as lower levels of psychopathology (e.g., posttraumatic stress disorder; Masingale et al., 2001), there is a foundation for viewing this as an effect with substantial potential to influence family relationships in a positive manner. Thus, prayer may prime spouses to experience increased gratitude for their partner's positive characteristics as well as for their relationship.

Religious and spiritual activity, such as prayer, may also directly foster some goals or decrease the attractiveness of other goals. Intentions (i.e., conscious goal states) directly influence behavioral choices and are themselves influenced by beliefs about what significant others would think of one's behavior (see Gibbons, Gerrard, & Lane, 2003). Because spiritual activities often may highlight the mandates of a particularly important significant other (God), they have the potential to bring behavioral intentions under pressure to conform to the belief that if God loves one's partner, then the individual should also be loving toward him or her. If so, there could be downstream effects on behaviors toward one's partner across a range of settings. For example, praying benevolently for one's mate or partner could strongly decrease behaviors likely to negatively affect the relationship, such as infidelity and substance abuse (see Fincham, Lambert, & Beach, 2010). To the extent that various spiritual and religious activities make salient the view of important others, this increased salience should influence subsequent behavioral intentions. Similarly, constructive motivations may be enhanced by spiritual and religious activity that primes "implemental intentions" (i.e., plans or means of achieving desired goals), thereby influencing future behavior (Gollwitzer & Moskowitz, 1996). As a result, there is considerable potential for spiritual and religious activity to influence motivation, intentions, and implemental intentions, enhancing relationship-promoting intentions as well as the probability of following through on those intentions.

A final factor potentially linking religious and spiritual behavior to positive relationship outcomes is the extent to which they promote a positive relational context and view of the partner, reinforce general promarriage attitudes and commitment to marriage, and foster the sense of the couple as "we" as opposed to two individuals. Several studies have shown a positive effect of religious involvement on relationship quality for married couples (e.g., Wolfinger & Wilcox, 2008), potentially reflecting both the direct effects of increased social support of norms and values of marriage and relationship-enhancing behaviors (e.g., partner forgiveness) as well as indirect effects, such as fostering increased individual psychological well-being and temperance (Wolfinger & Wilcox, 2008). To the extent that promarriage attitudes fostered by various forms of religious engagement and activity generate trust between partners, they should also encourage greater spousal investment in the marriage (Edin & Kefalas, 2005).

WHAT PARTICULAR SPIRITUAL AND RELIGIOUS ACTIVITIES ARE MOST PROMISING FROM THE STANDPOINT OF INTERVENTION?

Mahoney's (2010) framework suggests that it may be important to examine specific behaviors at each of three general levels (dyadic, community, and individual). The foregoing overview has made it clear that at all three levels, there could be many forms of religious and spiritual activity with the potential to influence relevant mechanisms as well as long-term marital outcomes of interest. Although many religious and spiritual activities may have an impact on relationship outcomes, empirical research is more likely to advance from specific hypotheses (even when wrong). Accordingly, we offer three specific sets of behavior that seem potentially within reach of preventive intervention (i.e., may be malleable) and also seem to have a good empirical foundation for positing effects on relationship functioning. Accordingly, in the spirit of hypothesis generation, we offer a model that highlights these three sets of behavior (see Figure 24.2).

First, we suggest that colloquial, intercessory prayer in which partners pray to God for their partner's well-being is a malleable spiritual activity of particular potential importance for the marital dyad. This activity involves individuals relying on a felt connection to God to pray for their partner with or without their partner's awareness and has been the focus of much of our recent research. When this behavior occurs on a purely private basis, it represents an individual level of activity although, as illustrated, it may have major implications for dyadic functioning. Some spouses, however, may overtly pray together for one another, a dyadic spiritual activity. Second, a focus on meditative prayer regarding one's own connection to the divine and study of scripture that encourages the self to engage in unselfish love and forgiveness may prove to have an impact of relationship functioning (see Volume 1, Chapter 17, this handbook and Chapter 10, this volume). Meditative prayer would appear to have the potential to increase distress tolerance and positive mental health outcomes as well as enhance positive self-control, resulting indirectly in positive relationship outcomes. Scripture addressing unselfish love also would seem to have the potential to influence goals and behavior through a variety of relationship mechanisms. Finally, at the level of the religious community, we suggest that joint religious activities may be of particular interest and worthy of future investigation. We have found that among the groups studied to date, frequency of religious attendance by husbands tends to be lower than that for wives; to the extent that wives are attending services without their husbands, or their spouses attend different services, increased joint attendance may offer some potential relationship benefits. Decreasing

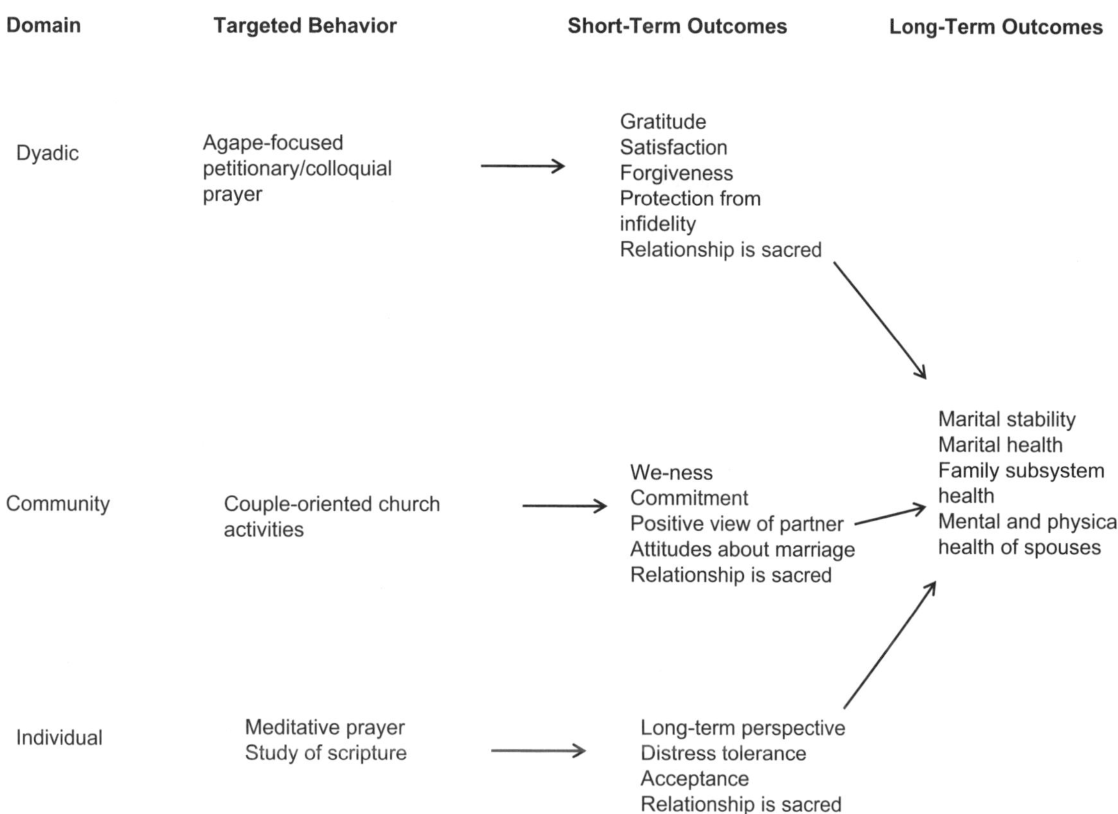

FIGURE 24.2. A model to test specific effects of spiritual and religious behavior on marital outcome.

rates of religious homogamy in couples in the United States (Bisin, Topa, & Verdier, 2004) may pose obstacles to joint attendance at religious services for some couples.

We suggest that each of these sets of behavior could be examined empirically to test the proposed relationships. To the extent that effects are consistent with the model, each set of behaviors could serve as a potential target for intervention to strengthen marital relationships. In each case, we suggest that increases in these behaviors should lead to short-term positive outcomes that are beneficial to the couple. Changes in these short-term outcomes should mediate the impact of behavior change on long-term marital outcomes, such as increased marital stability, healthier functioning of the relationship, enhanced functioning of family subsystems such as coparenting and parent–child relationships, as well as improved mental and physical health outcomes of spouses.

The deceptively simple heuristic model presented in Figure 24.2 implies that there are at least three, and perhaps many more, relatively simple targets for change efforts within the broad domain of spiritual and religious activities and behaviors, each with the potential to produce substantial short- and long-term impacts on positive couple outcomes. These include increasing the extent to which couples (a) engage in prayer focused on requesting good outcomes for the partner (Agape-focused intercessory prayer); (b) engage in joint organized religious activities (i.e., attending services together and being involved together in various other religious activities jointly); and (c) engage in personal meditative prayer and scriptural study to increase distress tolerance and acceptance in the relationship while also encouraging a broader, forgiving, long-term perspective. Each of these targets has the advantage of being potentially additive to other intervention approaches and each may address some of the limitations that have been noted for skill-based interventions of the sort that have dominated the prevention area.

We turn now to brief reviews of background research as well as our own basic research on prayer and relationship outcomes. The program of research we describe provides a template for the sort of empirical work we propose for each of the areas in Figure 24.2. As will be clear, our initial work on prayer supports the potential for intervention to encourage religious and spiritual activity with beneficial effects on marital outcomes.

EMPIRICAL STUDIES THAT ADDRESS THE CONNECTIONS AMONG RELIGION, SPIRITUALITY, AND FAMILY OUTCOMES

In the absence of relevant, prior studies in the field of prevention, we draw on related basic research linking spirituality and religion to marital outcomes. Because Mahoney (2010; Mahoney et al., 2001) has provided comprehensive reviews of research on religion in families, here we highlight only those findings that are particularly relevant to prevention and that provide a foundation for our research on prayer.

Some scholars have concluded that "religion plays a role in maintaining positive relationships within nuclear families" (Mattis & Jagers, 2001, p. 526). Although such sweeping claims are largely true, they require qualification to be completely accurate. For example, earlier research has reliably shown that religiosity covaries with marital satisfaction, but some recent studies limit this effect to a single sex, showing that only husband church attendance predicts later satisfaction (e.g., Wilcox & Wolfinger, 2008; Wolfinger & Wilcox, 2008). A dyadic approach focusing on spousal similarity and shared spiritual rituals may be more consistently associated with marital satisfaction (Myers, 2006). Because husband religious attendance tends to be lower than wife religious attendance, even among couples who are both members of the same church or religious group, the practical significance of individual and dyadic approaches may be the same: Increased religious attendance by husbands may be helpful to marital relationships because it will often result in couples benefiting from increased positive couple activities.

Even more critical to prevention is what accounts for the religiosity–marital satisfaction association. As our theoretical analysis suggests, reduced marital conflict, or better management of conflict when it occurs, is one such candidate. Overall religiousness is either unrelated or slightly inversely related to conflict (Curtis & Ellison, 2002; Mahoney et al., 2001). Several descriptive and qualitative studies, however, highlight the importance of prayer for coping effectively with conflict and marital problems when such issues occur. Studying more than 20 denominations in the United States, Abbott, Berry, and Meredith (1990) found that 63% of respondents reported frequently asking for help from God for family difficulties. Butler et al. (2002) found that 31% of respondents almost always, and 42% sometimes, prayed during marital conflict. In their qualitative study, Marsh and Dallos (2001) found that religious practices such as prayer helped couples to manage their anger during marital conflict. Finally, couples in a recent study reported that prayer alleviated tension and facilitated open communication during conflict situations (Lambert & Dollahite, 2006). Such findings are consistent with a national survey showing that most Americans (90.4% of African Americans and 66.7% of non-Hispanic Whites) say that prayer is very important when coping with stress, a response that is higher among married than never married respondents (Chatters, Taylor, Jackson, & Lincoln, 2008).

In light of these descriptive findings and the absence of research on the impact of prayer on relationships, we began a program of research on this topic. Using participants in dating relationships, the program of research began by documenting that prayer predicted later relationship satisfaction and not vice versa. Moreover, prayer for the partner, and not prayer in general, accounted for unique variance in satisfaction over and beyond positive and negative dyadic behavior (Fincham, Beach, Lambert, Stillman, & Braithwaite, 2008). Although promising, the correlational nature of the data limited our confidence in making causal inferences, and hence we embarked on a program of research in which documented associations were followed by experimental studies. Given our earlier observations regarding prayer and forgiveness, we next established that prayer for the partner leads to reports of increased forgiveness, using as control conditions, general prayer, and engaging in positive thoughts about the partner (Lambert, Fincham, Stillman,

Graham, & Beach, 2010). Consistent with our predictions, we also showed that the impact of prayer for the partner on forgiveness was mediated by increased selfless concern for the partner. Because the limits of self-report are well known, we went on to show that prayer following a transgression in the laboratory, compared with a control activity, led to more cooperation in a subsequent computer game. Furthermore, in another study, we tested whether partners of participants who prayed over the course of 4 weeks would report the participants as more forgiving. Apparently, prayer has a strong enough effect on participants' forgiving behavior to be perceived by the partners (Lambert, Fincham, DeWall, Pond, & Beach, in press). It should be noted, however, that whether the impact of forgiveness is positive or negative depends on the relational context in which it occurs (e.g., presence vs. absence of abuse; see McNulty & Fincham, 2012). But the impact of prayer is not limited to forgiveness.

In another set of studies, we also documented that prayer for the partner leads to greater gratitude (Lambert et al., 2009). This is important for all the reasons discussed thus far. A fifth series of studies, demonstrated that prayer influences satisfaction with sacrificing for the relationship. In one of these studies, we videotaped participants after a month-long prayer intervention. They were asked to "please describe something you have given up, or would be willing to give up, for your partner or for your relationship." Responses were coded by a group of five trained research assistants, blind to study hypotheses and the condition to which the participant was assigned. Observer responses showed that those randomly assigned to the prayer condition were rated as more satisfied with sacrifice than those who had daily recalled positive partner characteristics but had not been asked to pray (Lambert, Fincham, & Stanley, in press). Clearly such findings show that prayer has a number of effects on relationship processes, but does it also protect against risk factors?

A critical risk factor for relationships is infidelity, as extramarital affairs are the leading cause of divorce across 160 cultures. In a recent set of studies, we were able to show that prayer for the partner also decreased infidelity (Fincham et al., 2010). Moreover, relationship sanctification mediated this effect. Again, in one of the studies in this series, we were able to show that those who were randomly assigned to pray were rated differently by trained research assistant coders, blind to study hypotheses and the condition to which the participant was assigned. Specifically they were rated as more committed to the relationship, which helps explain why there was less cheating during this period when taking into account baseline rates of cheating (Fincham et al., 2010). This replicates a finding in our initial correlational studies in which we found that commitment mediated the association between prayer and relationship satisfaction. Finally, in view of the association between casual sex and alcohol, we also investigated the role of prayer in alcohol use. After establishing that an association exists between prayer frequency and alcohol use, we conducted two experimental studies both of which showed that daily prayer for 4 weeks decreased the amount of alcohol use by about half (Lambert, Fincham, Marks, & Stillman, 2010). Interestingly, both partner-directed prayer and general prayer decreased alcohol use.

Although numerous other relationship outcomes and the mechanisms whereby prayer influences them remain to be identified, the foregoing is sufficient to illustrate the potential power of specific spiritual behaviors as candidates for inclusion in prevention and enhancement programs. Before turning to evidence relating to their efficacy, we briefly clarify our approach to prevention.

A CLOSER LOOK AT PREVENTION AND THE FOUNDATIONS OF OUR APPROACH TO IT

The approach that we offer is informed by an integrated prevention and treatment perspective that focuses on enhancing strengths as well reducing problems for people at risk. We explicitly acknowledge the importance of context and the value of attending to cultural and structural factors that maintain risk behavior or support strengths. For example, as noted, facilitating forgiveness may be easier for someone embedded in a social network that encourages forgiveness. A comprehensive marital enrichment, prevention, and treatment model therefore needs to encompass change in participation in a broader community as well as dyadic activities and potentially relevant individual behavior.

A second premise is that programs should be developed with the goal of moving them into the community, consulting with local stakeholders, and evaluating community-based intervention efforts. In the present context, this is particularly important because many potential beneficiaries of marital enrichment and prevention are likely to be reached through natural community groups (e.g., religious organizations). Third, persons who might benefit from marital programs may not have the financial resources to obtain professional help or be located in areas served by mental health care providers. This problem is particularly acute in low-income and disadvantaged areas. Therefore, interventions should be designed to reach people in a variety of settings (including rural and geographically isolated settings) and be culturally viable for use in these settings. Thus, at a minimum, the intervention should involve familiar terminology and easy access that fits naturally in the community.

Finally, we operate from the premise that any attempt to provide enrichment, prevention, and treatment services should represent best practice in terms of what is currently known scientifically about processes leading to lasting, healthy relationships. A corollary is that any intervention must lend itself to evaluation, for without evaluation no program can be assumed to be effective. The notion that "something is better than nothing" is simply misguided, no matter how well intentioned, and as Bergin (1963) has reminded us, anything that has the potential to help also has the potential to harm.

LEVELS OF PREVENTIVE INTERVENTIONS

In the literature on prevention programs, distinctions are drawn among levels of intervention. Researchers distinguish among *universal* preventive measures, considered desirable for everyone in the population; *selective* preventive measures, considered desirable for subgroups of the population at higher than average risk; and *indicated* preventive measures, considered desirable for individuals who are known to be at high risk (Mrazek & Haggerty, 1994). In universal prevention, benefits outweigh the minimal costs and risks for everyone. In contrast, indicated interventions are not minimal in cost (e.g., time, effort). This reflects the fact that recipients of an indicated prevention may be experiencing some (subclinical) level of distress.

In offering intervention to African American couples in the Southeast, we found that a range of couples chose to participate. Some were motivated by a desire to affirm their commitment to each other, whereas others appeared to be motivated by a recently experienced transgression or problem in the relationship. As such, the data set we now turn to reflects all three levels of prevention, but it does not apply to those who need couple counseling for marital dysfunction (sometimes characterized as secondary prevention).

INITIAL EFFICACY EVIDENCE: PROGRAM FOR STRONG AFRICAN AMERICAN MARRIAGES

To examine the potential of adding spirituality to skills training, we examined a prayer-focused version (PFP) of the Prevention and Relationship Enhancement Program (PREP), a widely used prevention program for couples. PFP is offered to groups and includes all the basic components of PREP as well as a strong focus on private, intercessory prayer for the partner. Because the vast majority of African Americans self-identify as Protestant (78%; Pew Forum on Religion and Public Life, 2009), we utilized prayers reflective of African American Protestant traditions in our examples. The full report can be found in Beach et al. (2011).

Participants in PFP were given examples of prayers and encouraged to generate their own prayers for the well-being of their partner. In addition to video footage about communication, problem solving, and couples' activities, participants were given a conceptual framework for the use of colloquial, intercessory prayer for their partner and given specific encouragement to pray for good things to happen to their partners. All prayers were introduced as being in keeping with the higher order goal of "helping you to be a vehicle of God's love in your relationship." In addition, participants were encouraged to pray on their partner's behalf regarding their partner's needs and aspirations (Beach et al., 2008) and not to focus on nonconstructive themes, including retribution or "praying for God to change my mate." Discussion of prayer occurred throughout the program, and prayer was used to introduce and conclude all segments of the PREP instructional materials.

There were two comparison conditions: an information-only control group and a standard PREP comparison condition (CS-PREP). Couples in the control group were provided with the book *12 Hours to a Great Marriage* (Markman et al., 2004) at the conclusion of their baseline assessment. All couples were assigned to a condition on the basis of a block randomization schedule. Data were collected before the start of the intervention, again following completion of the program, at 6-month follow-up, and at 12-month follow-up.

A main effect showed improved marital outcomes over time. In addition, the anticipated group by time interaction was also significant, reflecting significantly greater change, for the intervention groups than the control group. There was no change overall for those in the information-only control condition, but a comparable level of overall change for those couples assigned to the two treatment conditions. These findings are shown in Figure 24.3.

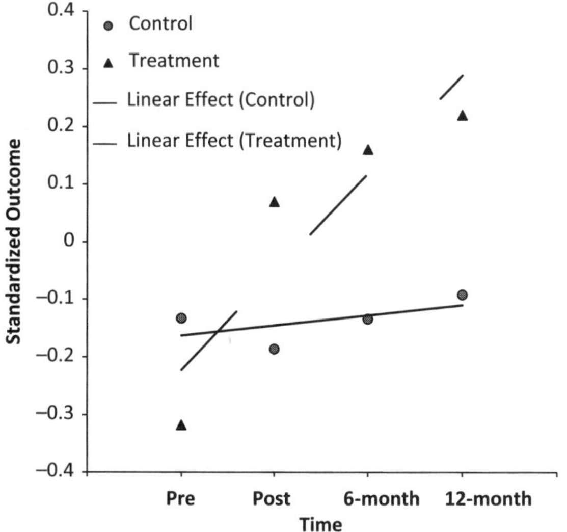

FIGURE 24.3. Outcomes averaged across husbands and wives for PREP and control group.

Because there was no reliable change as a function of time in the control group, we removed the control group to examine sex differences in response to the two active treatments, yielding a significant three-way interaction of sex, condition, and time. To explicate the three-way interaction, we compared response to CS-PREP and PFP separately for husbands and wives. For husbands, there was a significant main effect of time only, indicating an equivalent positive response to intervention for both active intervention conditions. For wives, however, in addition to the significant main effect of time, there was also a significant interaction of group with time. Specifically, wives began at similar starting points but showed differing outcome patterns over time depending on the intervention. In particular, there was significantly greater change from baseline to posttest in PFP than in CS-PREP for wives, indicating a more rapid initial change process in PFP that resulted in marginally better outcome even at 12-month follow-up.

In sum, a program that included prayer was as efficacious for husbands as a program focused only on traditional PREP material. For wives, the addition of prayer appeared to result in a more efficacious program, particularly in terms of its immediate effects from baseline to posttest. In addition, both interventions were more efficacious than the control condition. Participants indicated a high level of satisfaction with both formats and with the inclusion of a focus on spirituality and prayer. Although the mechanism of action is not known, it is possible that the enhanced response of wives to the PFP condition reflects a better fit to their needs, given that they were, on average, more involved in church activities than were husbands. Given initial evidence for enhanced efficacy, the question arises as to whether there is potential for dissemination of the program.

DISSEMINATION

Religiously and spiritually infused interventions have two great advantages. First, they may provide some advantages with regard to efficacy for some groups of people (e.g., the highly religious) or in some targeted areas (e.g., forgiveness). Second, they have the potential to enhance dissemination of effective marital enhancement and intervention. In our work with Program for Strong African American Marriages (ProSAAM), we found that dissemination was a particularly important issue in working with African American couples, who often are skeptical of the benefits to be derived from mental health services; therefore, they are unlikely to seek out or advocate for such services in their communities (Brody, Stoneman, & Flor, 1996; Murry & Brody, 2004). As a result, establishing trust and making the program culturally relevant was essential to effective program delivery. We suspect that similar issues may be common in many groups with strong religious commitments (see Chapters 26 and 32 in this volume).

We discovered early on from focus groups with community members drawn from the communities we hoped to serve that success was more likely if we worked through churches and with the blessing of local pastors. As one focus group member said,

> You've got to work with the churches. The churches are key. That's where it all begins for most married people . . . ya know, in the church. That's where we not only begin our marriages, but it's where we come to learn more about how to stay married and be husbands and wives.

Another group member noted, "You're going to need someone to endorse the program because marriages are so personal . . . bottom line, it's a real incentive to us if the pastor endorses it." The focus groups gave us a strong and consistent message that we should have community pastors evaluate the program and endorse it from the pulpit before we offered it to congregation members. When using spiritual and religious components to strengthen marital enrichment, prevention, and treatment, it will be useful and perhaps essential to have strong partnerships with local religious groups.

As a consequence of our focus group experiences, we developed a packet of materials designed to introduce ProSAAM to pastors and pulpit associates. We used the packets to connect with local churches and congregations (Hurt et al., 2008). One successful means of introducing ourselves to the community was to hold a reception for area pastors that we called An Evening of P.R.A.I.S.E.—prayer, recruitment, advertisement, information, sponsorship, and endorsement, the six ways in which we asked pastors to support ProSAAM. The reception featured a catered meal and a presentation that introduced church officials and their spouses to ProSAAM. After the presentation, we answered questions, took suggestions for ways to improve the program, and met with each church official individually to discuss the formation of partnerships with them and their congregations. The reception's success was grounded in the fact that it was culturally appropriate for our context, it gave us the opportunity to make clear to the clergy that we valued their input and desired their feedback, and it allowed us to tell pastors how important they were in the broad scheme of the program. The pastors, many of whom knew each another, appreciated the opportunity to socialize while learning about an exciting program that used prayer and skills to enhance marriages. After establishing partnerships with clergy, program staff were often invited and sometimes requested to attend church meetings, Bible studies, worship services, and other church events to meet, network with, and inform congregations about ProSAAM and to recruit couples into the program.

One consequence of direct contact with pastors was their excitement about the program and their pledges to support the program. They told us that strong churches begin with strong families and that they had seen the negative impact on the church and on church-families of weak or broken marital bonds. As a consequence, they were strongly motivated to strengthen marriage within the African American community and were enthusiastic about the role of prayer in building better marriages. We also found that the pastors of many smaller churches were eager to offer a marriage ministry for their congregation and welcomed ProSAAM as an effective step toward meeting their goals. This suggests that there is considerable potential for religious organizations to work as full partners with prevention scientists, and this collaboration can result in more effective dissemination when religious and spiritual activities with direct marital relevance are not separated from other marital enhancement activities, such as communication skills training.

Generalizing to Other Groups and Regions

Our experience is consistent with research by Stanley et al. (2001), in that religious organizations appear to be excellent partners for preventive intervention programs because (a) they can provide access to couples; (b) they have a structure and approach that is consistent with educational models; (c) they provide deep connections with communities, particularly hard-to-reach underserved populations and minorities; and (d) they are strongly supportive of programs to strengthen healthy marriages. Their experiences suggest that religious leaders can play a potent role in many communities across the United States. Religious organizations may offer secular prevention programs, however, and secular organizations may offer programs with a spiritual component.

Potential Challenges to Utilizing Spiritual and Religious Behavior to Enhance Relationship Outcomes

Before utilizing primary interventions that focus on change in spiritual and religious behavior, it is important to ask whether spiritually or religiously infused marital enrichment models can have an effect on well-established patterns of spiritual or religious behavior—and whether such changes would be tolerated by participants. The evidence we reviewed above suggests that the answer to these questions is yes. With regard to prayer, we found that before their participation in the program, many of the participants prayed regularly and prayed for their spouses but did not systematically pray for good things to happen for their spouses. The couples particularly valued the direction and focus provided by the program with regard to their prayers for their spouses. As a consequence, they reported praying somewhat differently for the partners after the program than before it. The key appears to be that they did not experience this shift in their prayer activity as a change in their spiritual or religious behavior or as a change in any fundamental religious or spiritual commitments. Rather, it was experienced as a natural extension of their preexisting commitments and religious sentiments. That is, the program was not experienced as suggesting change in their spiritual or religious behavior—it was viewed as empowering participants to fulfill their religious and spiritual goals and objectives more effectively.

Is it Ethical for Prevention Scientists to Pick Scripture and Provide Sample Prayers for Participants?

A potential challenge to implementing spiritually or religiously infused marital enrichment is the assumption that the melding of religious and spiritual activities with other marital enrichment activities can be accomplished without violating couples' religious self-determination or overstepping the appropriate boundaries of prevention science (see Chapter 3 in this volume). This represents both an ethical as well as a practical challenge. In addition to providing sample prayers that emphasize God's love (see Appendix 24.1), we often supplemented the suggested prayers with particular verses of scripture to resonate with key aspects of the prayer. Often these were Agape-related verses (i.e., those reflecting selfless love), such as "Love is patient, love is kind. It does not envy, it does not boast, it is not proud. It is not rude, it is not self-seeking, it is not easily angered, it keeps no record of wrongs" (1 Corinthians 13:4–5). But the suggested scripture also included many other verses dealing with relationships, such as those encouraging perseverance, kindness, and the value of marriage. One may wonder if this approach rests on a theologically sound foundation and whether it has the potential to create greater polarization in some contexts. In our view, meditation on sacred texts (part of the third pathway in Figure 24.2) should be tailored in an idiographic manner to support the objectives of the intervention and to fit the beliefs of the couple. That is, the program designer's role is not to decide what beliefs, or scripture, or activities to accept and what to ignore, it is to help the couple identify resources that are already in their repertoire that may be helpful as they move forward together in the development of a more fulfilling marital relationship. Specifically, we suggest that program designers stay focused on enhancing marital relationships and not try to introduce new beliefs or make religious choices for the couple. In our own work, it has been the construct of Agape that has proven most useful and versatile in facilitating marital interactions. This is the "content" that we emphasize and that often guides our choice of scripture. In the sample prayers we give to couples, the focus is on living an

Agape-filled life with one's partner. The purpose of inviting the deity into one's relationship is to promote Agape and be a vehicle of Agape. The use of scripture is often similarly motivated by the search for inspiration related to Agape. We have concluded, however, that it is more important for prevention scientists working with religious clients to be knowledgeable, respectful, and sensitive than it is for them to be "expert." That is, to the extent that the prevention scientist is merely offering a template that the couple may find useful as they incorporate their own religious resources into strengthening their relationship, we hope that many potential problems with religiously and spiritually infused prevention approaches may be sidestepped.

Other Opportunities

It is possible that providing opportunities for religiously and spiritually infused marital enhancement that includes prayer may have positive systemic consequences that go well beyond the immediate effect of a particular intervention approach. Marks (2008) has suggested that as community-based marital intervention programs become more faith-friendly, it will be easier for pastoral counselors to work with clinicians on their more difficult or complex cases. This has the potential to enhance treatment outcomes in addition to outcomes of psycho-educational prevention efforts, such as those discussed in this chapter. It is also possible that greater couple-level engagement in church activities could combat a different affliction of modern couples. As noted in a recent book detailing extensive analyses of how marriages have changed in the past 20 years, married couples are increasingly isolated and uninvolved with others as couples (Amato, Booth, Johnson, & Rogers, 2007). These trends are associated with declining marital quality, and the only context in which they found this trend not to hold was among those religiously involved.

Some Caveats

We do not mean to imply that all prayer is likely to be helpful to couples in preventing future problems or responding to ongoing issues, and we should be alert to potential conditions for which prayer, or types of prayer, may have negative effects. For example, praying for the personal strength to endure the partner's transgressions seems likely to be counterproductive in some circumstances and might even increase risk in some contexts, such as for spouses in abusive marriages. Similarly, asking for divine retribution for a partner's failings could potentially focus an individual's attention on the shortcomings of his or her partner, supporting a ruminative, blaming process. Likewise, prayer requests that focus on changing the partner or the way the partner behaves toward the self would seem to have the potential to reinforce a lack of accommodation and decrease propensity toward forgiveness, again leading to less positive relationship outcomes. These concerns, at a minimum, point to the possibility of adverse effects of prayer or other religious and spiritual activities under some circumstances.

Another potential area of concern that deserves attention in the application of prayer is the issue of gender equality in decision making. One spouse's support of the life goals of the other spouse is associated with greater marital satisfaction (Brunstein, Dangelmayer, & Schultheiss, 1996). Also, Amato et al. (2007) have shown that decision-making equality is one of the strongest correlates of positive marital quality—not only for wives but also for husbands. This suggests that, at least in the United States, equality in decision making is a feature of contemporary marriages that stabilizes or improves marital quality (Brunstein et al., 1996). To the extent that increased prayer or other religious and spiritual activity were to decrease support for partner life goals, or decrease perceived equality or decision-making equality, these could potentially diminish or undermine the beneficial effects of prayer activity on other key aspects of marital interaction. Accordingly, it is important for researchers to remain alert to both positive and negative effects of spiritual and religious activity as the field develops.

FUTURE RESEARCH AGENDA

To advance the field, several lines of basic and applied research are needed. At the basic research level, it is clear that much work is needed to understand fully the extent to which prayer for the partner affects relationship outcomes. In addition, the identification of mechanisms of this impact is still preliminary. Thus far, data show that commitment, selfless concern, and sanctification can mediate the effect of prayer on relationships. But other potential mechanisms, such as a broader time perspective, forgiveness, and activating the view of a particularly important significant other (e.g., a deity), have yet to be investigated. Finally, it is worth noting that there has not been any research on the boundary conditions under which the documented effects occur.

Deepening the current line of prayer research is, however, only a small part of the picture, as illustrated in Figure 24.2. For each of the other two targeted behaviors in Figure 24.2, one can imagine the kind of research program begun for Agape-focused prayer. First, researchers must establish an association between the behaviors of interest (e.g., meditative prayer, study of scripture, couple-oriented religious activities) and relationship outcomes, attempting to isolate the key element(s) of the behavior that are important. Once established, the search for mechanism begins and is followed by documentation of factors that might moderate the effects or create boundary conditions for the observed effects. Then the implications for intervention are spelled out, an intervention program is developed, and its efficacy is tested. This becomes an iterative process as one cycles back to the first stage informed by the intervention findings.

At the applied level, it is clear that research has barely begun. Although the findings of the ProSAAM efficacy trial are encouraging, much work needs to be done in isolating the active components of the program and in identifying what mediates their effects. In particular, it would be helpful to better understand the observed sex effect. As with virtually all marital prevention programs, much work remains to determine how to bolster effect sizes and to improve maintenance of intervention gains. Here, we believe that spiritually and religiously informed programs have a potential edge because gains may be naturally reinforced by the individual's ongoing spiritual and religious commitment and by the religious community within which he or she is situated.

CONCLUSION

We have covered a great deal of ground. In doing so, we hope to have convinced scientists and practitioners of the potential value of faith-informed prevention in appropriate contexts. We attempted to do so not only by offering data to illustrate the efficacy of one such intervention but also by outlining basic research that supports targeting a specific spiritual behavior, prayer. There are difficult judgment calls to be made when targeting spiritual and religious behaviors for intervention and not all scientists will be comfortable with having to deal with them. Such concerns are less evident in conducting basic research on the role such behaviors play in marital and family relationships. Given the large number of families that profess a religious faith and the central role such faith can play in their lives, it is clear that behavioral scientists cannot avoid the study of spiritual and religious behavior. To do otherwise would institutionalize an incomplete picture of marriage and families found in the professional literature and constitute a grave disservice to those we seek to help.

APPENDIX 24.1: EXAMPLE PRAYER USED IN PROGRAM FOR STRONG AFRICAN AMERICAN MARRIAGES

Dear Lord,

I come to you because you love us. I know you care deeply about the two of us and our relationship to each other. I look to you for a perspective that can let us see with new eyes and hear with new ears. I understand that if we see each other from your perspective, we will make better choices and cement our relationship to a foundation that will not be shaken. I know that you are the rightful ruler of life and I pledge to treat my wife/husband with love in accordance with your will and your example.

When opportunities arise for me to express my love for [spouse's name], I will be ready to make that opportunity a reality, not a missed chance. I will set my intentions so that I identify ahead of time the different ways I can be the vehicle of your love. I will practice your deep acceptance and perfect it in my actions toward my partner. I will engage in prayer for [spouse's name] on a regular basis and will ask for good things for [spouse's name]. I will also ask for the strength, patience, forgiveness, and love I need to be a good partner—now and in the long run.

We know we are not perfect. Our flaws are often all too painfully clear. Help us forgive and be forgiven. I know there is no power greater than the power of repentance followed by forgiveness. I will seek your strength as a shield against temptations large and small. I ask you to protect and watch over the trust in our relationship so that it can grow as we work to support and sustain each other.

When difficult times come, please help me listen and be supportive. With your help, I can be delivered from impulses that might lead us to harm. Help us reach out and touch each other in love—never in anger.

I know it is in your power to make each of us a source of your love. I know that you can help us show love more fully than we have before.

Let our marriage be a testament to your love and power to transform the world. Forever. Amen.

References

Abbott, D. A., Berry, M., & Meredith W. H. (1990). Religious belief and practice: A potential asset in helping families. *Family Relations, 39*, 443–448.

Adherents.com. (2011). *Major religions of the world ranked by number of adherents.* Retrieved from http://www.adherents.com/Religions_By_Adherents.html

Adler, M. G., & Fagley, N. S. (2005). Appreciation: Individual differences in finding value and meaning as a unique predictor of subjective well-being. *Journal of Personality, 73*, 79–114. doi:10.1111/j.1467-6494.2004.00305.x

Allport, G. W. (1950). *The individual and his religion.* New York, NY: Macmillan.

Amato, P. R., Booth, A., Johnson, D. R., & Rogers, S. J. (2007). *Alone together.* Cambridge, MA: Harvard University Press.

Beach, S. R. H., Fincham, F. D., Hurt, T., McNair, L. M., & Stanley, S. M. (2008). Prayer and marital intervention: A conceptual framework. *Journal of Social and Clinical Psychology*, 27, 641–669. doi:10.1521/jscp.2008.27.7.641

Beach, S. R. H., Hurt, T. R., Fincham, F. D., Kameron, J., Franklin, K. J., McNair, L. M., & Stanley, S. M. (2011). Enhancing marital enrichment through spirituality: Efficacy data for prayer-focused relationship enhancement. *Psychology of Religion and Spirituality*, 3, 201–216.

Bergin, A. E. (1963). The effects of psychotherapy: Negative results revisited. *Journal of Counseling Psychology, 10*, 244–250. doi:10.1037/h0043353

Bisin, A., Topa, G., & Verdier, T. (2004). Religious intermarriage and socialization in the United States. *Journal of Political Economy, 112*, 615–664. doi:10.1086/383101

Breslin, M. J., & Lewis, C. A. (2008). Theoretical models of the nature of prayer and health: A review. *Mental Health, Religion, and Culture, 11*, 9–21. doi:10.1080/13674670701491449

Brody, G. H., Stoneman, Z., & Flor, D. (1996). Parental religiosity, family processes, and youth competence in rural, two-parent African American families. *Developmental Psychology, 32*, 696–706. doi:10.1037/0012-1649.32.4.696

Brunstein, J. C., Dangelmayer, G., & Schultheiss, O. C. (1996). Personal goals and social support in close relationships: Effects on relationship mood and marital satisfaction. *Journal of Personality and Social Psychology, 71*, 1006–1019. doi:10.1037/0022-3514.71.5.1006

Butler, M. H., Stout, J. A., & Gardner, B. C. (2002). Prayer as a conflict resolution ritual: Clinical implications of religious couples' report of relationship softening, healing perspective, and change responsibility. *American Journal of Family Therapy, 30*, 19–37. doi:10.1080/019261802753455624

Carlson, T. D., Kirkpatrick, D., Hecker, L., & Killmer, M. (2002). Religion, spirituality, and marriage and family therapy: A study of family therapists' beliefs about the appropriateness of addressing religious and spiritual issues in therapy. *American Journal of Family Therapy, 30*, 157–171. doi:10.1080/019261802753573867

Chatters, L. M., Taylor, R. J., Jackson, J. S., & Lincoln, K. D. (2008). Religious coping among African Americans, Caribbean Blacks and non-Hispanic Whites. *Journal of Community Psychology, 36*, 371–386. doi:10.1002/jcop.20202

Curtis, K. T., & Ellison, C. G. (2002). Religious heterogamy and marital conflict—Findings from the National Survey of Families and Households. *Journal of Family Issues, 23*, 551–576. doi:10.1177/0192513X02023004005

Dollahite, D. C., & Marks, L. D. (2009). A conceptual model of family and religious processes in highly religious families. *Review of Religious Research, 50*, 373–391.

Dudley, M. G., & Kosinski, F. A. (1990). Religiosity and marital satisfaction: A research note. *Review of Religious Research, 32*, 78–86.

Edin, K., & Kefalas, K. (2005). *Promises I can keep: Why poor women put motherhood before marriage.* Berkeley: University of California Press.

Ellison, C. G., & George, L. K. (1994). Religious involvement, social ties, and social support in a southeastern community. *Journal for the Scientific Study of Religion, 33*, 46–61. doi:10.2307/1386636

Emmons, R. A., & Crumpler, C. A. (2000). Gratitude as human strength: Appraising the evidence. *Journal of Social and Clinical Psychology, 19*, 56–69. doi:10.1521/jscp.2000.19.1.56

Emmons, R. A., & Shelton, C. M. (2002). Gratitude and the science of positive psychology. In C. R. Snyder & S. J. Lopez (Eds.), *The positive psychology handbook* (pp. 459–471). Oxford, England: Oxford University Press.

Fincham, F. D. (2003). Marital conflict: Correlates, structure and context. *Current Directions in Psychological Science, 12*, 23–27. doi:10.1111/1467-8721.01215

Fincham, F. D. (2009). Forgiveness: Integral to a science of close relationships? In M. Mikulincer & P. Shaver (Eds.), *Prosocial motives, emotions, and behavior: The better angels of our nature* (pp. 347–365). Washington, DC: American Psychological Association.

Fincham, F. D., & Beach, S. R. (1999). Marital conflict: Implications for working with couples. *Annual Review of Psychology, 50*, 47–77. doi:10.1146/annurev.psych.50.1.47

Fincham, F. D., & Beach, S. R. H. (2007). Forgiveness and marital quality: Precursor or consequence in well-established relationships. *Journal of Positive Psychology*, 2, 260–268. doi:10.1080/17439760701552360

Fincham, F. D., Beach, S. R. H., & Davila, J. (2007). Longitudinal relations between forgiveness and conflict resolution in marriage. *Journal of Family Psychology, 21*, 542–545. doi:10.1037/0893-3200.21.3.542

Fincham, F. D., Beach, S. R. H., Lambert, N., Stillman, T., & Braithwaite, S. R. (2008). Spiritual behaviors and relationship satisfaction: A critical analysis of the role of prayer. *Journal of Social and Clinical Psychology, 27*, 362–388. doi:10.1521/jscp.2008.27.4.362

Fincham, F. D., Lambert, N. M., & Beach, S. R. H. (2010). Faith and unfaithfulness: Can praying for your partner reduce infidelity? *Journal of Personality and Social Psychology, 99*, 649–659. doi:10.1037/a0019628

Gibbons, F. X., Gerrard, M., & Lane, D. J. (2003). A social reaction model of adolescent health risk. Social psychological foundations of health and illness. In J. Suls & K. A. Wallston (Eds.), *Social psychological foundations of health and illness* (pp. 107–136). Malden, MA: Blackwell. doi:10.1002/9780470753552.ch5

Gollwitzer, P. M., & Moskowitz, G. B. (1996). Goal effects on action and cognition. In A. W. Kruglanski & E. T. Higgins (Eds.), *Social psychology: Handbook of basic principles* (pp. 361–399). New York, NY: Guilford Press.

Hill, P. C., & Pargament, K. I. (2003). Advances in the conceptualization and measurement of religion and spirituality. *American Psychologist, 58*, 64–74. doi:10.1037/0003-066X.58.1.64

Hurt, T. R., Franklin, K. J., Beach, S. R. H., Murry, V. B., Brody, G. H., McNair, L. D., & Fincham, F. D. (2008). Dissemination of couple interventions among African American populations: Experiences from ProSAAM. *The Behavior Therapist, 31*, 17–19.

James, W. (1902). *The varieties of religious experience: A study in human nature.* New York, NY: Random House.

Koenig, H. G., McCullough, M. E., & Larson, D. B. (2001). *Handbook of religion and health.* New York, NY: Oxford University Press. doi:10.1093/acprof:oso/9780195118667.001.0001

Lambert, N. M., & Dollahite, D. C. (2006). How religiosity helps couples prevent, resolve, and overcome marital conflict. *Family Relations, 55*, 439–449. doi:10.1111/j.1741-3729.2006.00413.x

Lambert, N. M., Fincham, F. D., Braithwaite, S. R., Graham, S., & Beach, S. R. H. (2009). Can prayer increase gratitude? *Psychology of Religion and Spirituality, 1*, 139–149. doi:10.1037/a0016731

Lambert, N. M., Fincham, F. D., DeWall, C. N., Pond, R. S., & Beach, S. R. H. (in press). Shifting toward cooperative goals: How partner-focused prayer facilitates fogiveness. *Personal Relationships.*

Lambert, N. M., Fincham, F. D., Marks, L. D., & Stillman, T. F. (2010). Invocations and intoxication: Does prayer decrease alcohol consumption? *Psychology of Addictive Behaviors, 24*, 209–219. doi:10.1037/a0018746

Lambert, N. M., Fincham, F. D., & Stanley, S. (in press). Prayer and satisfaction with sacrifice in close relationships. *Journal of Social and Personal Relationships.*

Lambert, N. M., Fincham, F. D., Stillman, T. F., Graham, S. M., & Beach, S. R. M. (2010). Motivating change in relationships: Can prayer increase forgiveness? *Psychological Science, 21*, 126–132. doi:10.1177/0956797609355634

Lambert, N. M., Graham, S. M., & Fincham, F. D. (2011). Understanding the layperson's perception of prayer: A prototype analysis of prayer. *Psychology of Religion and Spirituality, 3*, 55–65. doi:10.1037/a0021596

Mahoney, A. (2010). Religion in families, 1999–2009: A relational spirituality framework. *Journal of Marriage and Family, 72*, 805–827. doi:10.1111/j.1741-3737.2010.00732.x

Mahoney, A., Pargament, K. I., & Hernandez, K. M. (in press). Heaven on earth: Beneficial effects of sanctification for individual and interpersonal well-being. In S. David, I. Boniwell, & A. C. Ayers (Eds.), *Oxford handbook of happiness.* New York, NY: Oxford University Press.

Mahoney, A., Pargament, K. I., Swank, A., & Tarakeshwar, N. (2001). Religion in the home in the 1980s and 1990s: A meta-analytic review and conceptual analysis of religion, marriage, and parenting. *Journal of Family Psychology, 15,* 559–596. doi:10.1037/0893-3200.15.4.559

Markman, H. J., Whitton, S. W., Kline, G. H., Stanley, S. M., Thompson, H., St. Peters, M., . . . Cordova, A. (2004). Use of an empirically based marriage education program by religious organizations: Results of a dissemination trial. *Family Relations, 53,* 504–512. doi:10.1111/j.0197-6664.2004.00059.x

Marks, L. D. (2008). Prayer and marital intervention: Asking for Divine help or professional trouble? *Journal of Social and Clinical Psychology, 27,* 678–685. doi:10.1521/jscp.2008.27.7.678

Marler, P. L., & Hadaway, C. K. (2002). "Being religious" or "being spiritual" in America: A zero-sum proposition? *Journal for the Scientific Study of Religion, 41,* 289–300. doi:10.1111/1468-5906.00117

Marsh, R., & Dallos, R. (2001). Religious beliefs and practices and Catholic couples' management of anger and conflict. *Clinical Psychology and Psychotherapy, 7,* 22–36. doi:10.1002/(SICI)1099-0879(200002)7:1<22::AID-CPP217>3.0.CO;2-R

Masingale, A. M., Schoonover, S., Kraft, S., Burton, R., Waring, S., Fouad, B., . . . Witkins, P. (2001, December). *Gratitude and posttraumatic symptomatology in a college sample.* Paper presented at the convention of the International Society for Traumatic Stress Studies, New Orleans, LA.

Mattis, J., & Jagers, R. (2001). A relational framework for the study of religiosity and spirituality in the lives of African-Americans. *Journal of Community Psychology, 29,* 519–539. doi:10.1002/jcop.1034

McCullough, M. E., & Larson, D. B. (1999). Prayer. In W. R. Miller (Ed.), *Integrating spirituality into treatment: Resources for practitioners* (pp. 85–110). Washington, DC: American Psychological Association. doi:10.1037/10327-005

McCullough, M. E., & Tsang, J.-A. (2004). Parent of the virtues? The prosocial contours of gratitude. In R. A. Emmons & M. E. McCullough (Eds.), *The psychology of gratitude* (pp. 123–141). New York, NY: Oxford University Press. doi:10.1093/acprof:oso/9780195150100.003.0007

McNulty, J., & Fincham, F. D. (2012). Beyond positive psychology? Toward a contextual view of psychological processes and well-being. *American Psychologist, 67,* 101–110. doi:10.1037/a0024572

Mrazek, P. J., & Haggerty, R. J. (Eds.). (1994). *Reducing risks for mental disorders: Frontiers for preventive intervention research.* Washington, DC: National Academies Press.

Murry, V. M., & Brody, G. H. (2004). Partnering with community stakeholders: Engaging rural African American families in basic research and the Strong African American Families preventive intervention program. *Journal of Marital and Family Therapy, 30,* 271–283. doi:10.1111/j.1752-0606.2004.tb01240.x

Myers, S. M. (2006). Religious homogamy and marital quality: Historical and generational patterns, 1980–1997. *Journal of Marriage and Family, 68,* 292–304. doi:10.1111/j.1741-3737.2006.00253.x

Pargament, K. I. (1997). *The psychology of religion and coping: Theory, research, practice.* New York, NY: Guilford Press.

Pargament, K. I., & Mahoney, A. (2005). Sacred matters: Sanctification as vital topic for the psychology of religion. *The International Journal for the Psychology of Religion, 15,* 179–198. doi:10.1207/s15327582ijpr1503_1

Parke, R. D. (2001). Introduction to the special section on families and religion: A call for a recommitment by researchers, practitioners, and policymakers. *Journal of Family Psychology, 15,* 555–558. doi:10.1037/0893-3200.15.4.555

Pew Forum on Religion and Public Life. (2008). *U.S. religious landscape survey.* Retrieved from http://religions.pewforum.org/pdf/report-religious-landscape-study-full.pdf

Pew Forum on Religion and Public Life. (2009). *A religious portrait of African Americans.* Retrieved from http://pewforum.org/docs/?DocID=389

Poloma, M., & Gallup, G. (1991). *Varieties of prayer: A survey report.* Philadelphia, PA: Trinity Press International.

Stanley, S. M., Markman, H. J., Prado, L. M., OlmosGallo, P. A., Tonelli, L., St. Peters, M., . . . Whitton, S. W. (2001). Community-based premarital prevention: Clergy and lay leaders on the frontlines. *Family Relations, 50,* 67–84. doi:10.1111/j.1741-3729.2001.00067.x

Taylor, R. J., Chatters, L. M., & Levin, T. S. (2004). *Religion in the lives of African Americans.* Thousand Oaks, CA: Sage.

Tsang, J., McCullough, M., & Fincham, F. D. (2006). Forgiveness and the psychological dimension of reconciliation: A longitudinal analysis. *Journal of Social and Clinical Psychology, 25,* 404–428.

Wilcox, W. B., & Wolfinger, N. H. (2008). Living and loving "decent": Religion and relationship quality among urban parents. *Social Science Research, 37*, 828–843. doi:10.1016/j.ssresearch.2007.11.001

Wile, D. B. (1993). *After the fight: A night in the life of a couple*. New York, NY: Guilford Press.

Wolfinger, N. H., & Wilcox, W. B. (2008). Happily ever after? Religion, marital status, gender and relationship quality in urban families. *Social Forces, 86*, 1311–1337. doi:10.1353/sof.0.0023

Worthington, E. L., & Aten, J. D. (2009). Psychotherapy with religious and spiritual clients: An overview. *Journal of Clinical Psychology, 65*, 123–130. doi:10.1002/jclp.20561

CHAPTER 25

THE ROLE OF RELIGION AND SPIRITUALITY IN POSITIVE PSYCHOLOGY INTERVENTIONS

Mark S. Rye, Nathaniel G. Wade, Amanda M. Fleri, and Julia E. M. Kidwell

Researchers have developed and evaluated the effectiveness of a variety of positive psychology interventions. Unlike traditional clinical interventions that focus on the alleviation of psychopathology, positive psychology interventions are concerned with the development of human strengths and virtues. Although many of the virtues promoted in positive psychology interventions are grounded in religious and spiritual teachings, programs developed by psychologists seldom incorporate these teachings. Consequently, participants who maintain strong religious and spiritual beliefs are often presented with strategies for promoting virtues that do not fully incorporate key aspects of their worldview. The purpose of this chapter is to discuss ways of reconnecting religious and spiritual concepts to positive psychology interventions so that they are more consistent with practices and beliefs that many people hold sacred.

SCOPE OF THE CHAPTER

This chapter focuses on the following four virtues: hope, gratitude, forgiveness, and self-compassion. We selected these virtues because (a) they are each the focus of empirically validated interventions and (b) they historically have been intricately linked with diverse religious traditions. For each virtue, we first consider whether psychological theories are generally compatible with varying religious or spiritual perspectives. Subsequently, we describe examples of interventions that promote each virtue, paying particular attention to programs that incorporate religious or spiritual beliefs and practices. We focus on interventions developed for adults, even though a few positive psychology interventions have been created for children (e.g., Buchanan, 2008; Froh, Kashdan, Ozimkowski, & Miller, 2009). Positive psychology interventions for children are often administered through public schools where integration of religious and spiritual content can be problematic. After describing interventions for adults, we summarize various methods for incorporating religious and spiritual concepts into positive psychology interventions and examine possible advantages and pitfalls that can accompany the inclusion of these concepts. Finally, we offer suggestions for advancing research on the role of religion and spirituality in positive psychology interventions.

Our examination of religious perspectives on each virtue focuses on the major monotheistic religions (i.e., Judaism, Christianity, and Islam) and the nontheistic tradition of Buddhism. We selected these religions because clinicians in the West are most likely to encounter clients from these traditions, and it is useful to consider how positive psychology interventions could be adapted to incorporate either theistic or nontheistic ideas. There is considerable diversity within each religious tradition, however, and one must be cautious about generalizing to all adherents. Our goal is simply to examine how participants from various religious backgrounds might experience positive psychology interventions that promote each of the virtues. Clinicians and researchers would be wise to view these ideas as working hypotheses because the best way to

DOI: 10.1037/14046-025
APA Handbook of Psychology, Religion, and Spirituality: Vol. 2. An Applied Psychology of Religion and Spirituality, K. I. Pargament (Editor-in-Chief)

learn about how someone from a particular religious tradition will experience a positive psychology intervention is to ask him or her. Moreover, the lens through which we approach this task is that of social scientists, not religious scholars. Many of the concepts we examine in this chapter can apply to individuals who consider themselves spiritual but who do not belong to an organized religious group. With these cautions in mind, we begin our examination of positive psychology interventions with the virtue of hope.

THE PROMOTION OF HOPE

Before considering how religion and spirituality can be integrated into hope interventions, it is important to consider whether psychological theories of hope are consistent with religious and spiritual perspectives. One of the most comprehensive and widely cited psychological theories of hope, developed by Snyder et al. (1991), conceptualizes hope as the perception that one's goals can be achieved. According to this model, hope will only be experienced if goal identification is accompanied by both pathways and agency. Pathways are the perceived means by which an individual is able to achieve his or her goals. Agency involves the desire to reach a goal, the perception that one can take steps toward reaching goals, and the belief that one can persevere until the goals are attained (Snyder, 2000). Although hope can be influenced by past and present experiences, the focus of hope is on future events.

Religious and Spiritual Views on Hope

Hope theory is generally consistent with the theologies of the major monotheistic religions (i.e., Judaism, Christianity, Islam). All three monotheistic traditions advocate placing hope in God for attaining spiritual goals and for meeting practical needs. The celebrations of Passover, Easter, and Ramadan are often viewed as hopeful reminders of God's love. References to hope can be found in sacred scriptures of the monotheistic traditions. For instance, Psalm 39:7 (Revised Standard Version) states, "And now, Lord, for what do I wait? My hope is in thee." In the Christian New Testament, references to hope frequently appear in letters attributed to Paul. In 1 Corinthians 13:7, Paul referred to hope as being a natural consequence of love. In Romans 5:3–5, Paul wrote, "More than that, we rejoice in our sufferings, knowing that suffering produces endurance, and endurance produces character, and character produces hope, and hope does not disappoint us." Similarly, the Qur'an provides references to hopefulness (4:105), and urges adherents to guard against despair (15:55–56).

Hope is often expressed in monotheistic religions through prayer. Although many different forms of prayer exist (Poloma & Gallup, 1991; for a review, see Volume 1, Chapter 16, this handbook), petitionary prayer is commonly used by Jews, Christians, and Muslims to ask God to meet a specific need or desire. The person who is praying often has a clearly defined goal in mind and believes that one (and sometimes the only) pathway to reaching the goal is through divine assistance. Divine assistance may be requested to increase one's motivation (agency) to achieve a goal. The assumption behind petitionary prayer is that God intervenes in the affairs of humans and can grant wishes that will improve one's future.

In contrast, to the extent that one's goals are for private fulfillment, hope theory is less consistent with some Buddhist traditions. Although there are many forms of Buddhism, they commonly embrace the Four Noble Truths taught by the Buddha. The Four Noble truths recognize that suffering (*dukkha*) is caused by the desire for private fulfillment (*tanha*) (Smith, 1995). Goal setting, as promoted by positive psychology interventions, could be viewed as encouraging desire for private fulfillment. Pema Chödrön (1997), a Tibetan Buddhist, wrote, "Hope and fear come from a sense of poverty. . . . We hold on to hope, and hope robs us of the present moment" (p. 41). Chödrön explained that the Tibetan word for hope (*rewa*) and the word for fear (*dokpa*) are often combined (*re-dok*) because the presence of one always signifies the presence of the other. Chödrön even suggested that from a Buddhist perspective, "abandon hope" is a helpful affirmation.

The future-oriented emotion of hope may be viewed as being inconsistent with meditation as commonly practiced within Buddhist traditions. Although some practitioners of theistic religious traditions also embrace meditation, they sometimes combine this practice with forms of prayer that are connected with hope. The essence of Buddhist forms of meditation is to fully experience the present moment (Trungpa, 1996). Many forms of Buddhist meditation begin with the instruction to focus on one's breath. Whenever the practitioner's thoughts stray and begin to focus on the past or the future, he or she is instructed to observe the thought but then consciously return one's focus to the breath and the experience of the present moment (Trungpa, 1996). When one is fully engaged in experiencing the present moment, it is not possible to set goals for the future. Researchers and clinicians need to be aware that a hope intervention may not match with the worldview of some Buddhist participants. With this caution in mind, we now review hope intervention outcome studies, which generally omit religious and spiritual concepts.

Hope Interventions

Several hope interventions have been designed for people with serious medical problems (see Table 25.1). For instance, Duggleby et al. (2007) studied the effectiveness of the Living With Hope Program, which is designed to foster hope and increase the quality of life for older adults suffering from cancer. Terminally ill cancer patients ($N = 60$) who were more than 60 years old were recruited from palliative home care programs in Canada. Participants were randomly assigned to either a treatment group or a wait-list control group. Participants in the treatment group viewed a film about hope and subsequently chose from among a variety of hope-related activities to work on during the following week. The option selected most frequently involved collecting songs, poems, and stories related to hope. Other participants chose to write a letter to someone on the topic of hope. Another option was

TABLE 25.1

Examples of Studies Evaluating Hope Interventions

Study	*N*	Target population	Study design and findings	Explicit religious content
Berg, Snyder, and Hamilton (2008)	172	University students	Randomly assigned participants to: 1. Hope intervention 2. No-treatment control ■ Participants in hope intervention experienced higher pain tolerance and more awareness of pain compared with control.	None
Boucher (2002)	100	Chemotherapy patients	Randomly assigned participants to: 1. Hope intervention 2. No-treatment control ■ No significant treatment effects were found.	None
Cheavens, Feldman, Gum, Michael, and Snyder (2006)	32	Adults from the community	Randomly assigned participants to: 1. Hope intervention 2. No-treatment wait-list control ■ Participants in hope intervention experienced increased hope, life meaning, and self-esteem, and decreased anxiety and depressive symptoms compared with control.	None
Duggleby et al. (2007)	60	Older adults with cancer	Randomly assigned participants to: 1. Hope intervention 2. No-treatment wait-list control ■ Participants in hope intervention improved on hope and quality of life compared with control.	None

for participants to write about their own life or collect materials about their life that provided them with hope and comfort. On average, participants spent 4.3 hr on the hope activities during the week. All participants completed quantitative measures at pretest and posttest and intervention participants also completed qualitative measures. Results from both quantitative and qualitative analyses found that the program increased hope and quality of life for participants in the treatment group more than participants in the wait-list control group.

Another hope intervention for cancer patients was delivered via telephone (Boucher, 2002). Participants ($N = 100$), who were recruited from a cancer clinic over the course of 2 years, were randomly assigned to either a treatment or a comparison group. Those assigned to the intervention condition received three structured phone calls from a nurse during the course of chemotherapy treatment. During the phone conversations, which lasted 10 to 15 min, the nurse asked participants how they were being affected by chemotherapy and reviewed and monitored patient goals. The nurse encouraged participants to think about their supportive relationships and to maintain contact with their social support network during treatment. Participants also received education about preventing side effects from chemotherapy. In contrast, nonnurse staff members at the clinic spent 2 to 5 min on three occasions calling participants in the control group to remind them about their next appointment. Measurements of hope, symptom distress, and emotional distress were obtained before the start of chemotherapy and four additional times during treatment. Contrary to hypotheses, participants assigned to the intervention did not show greater increases in hope or more reductions in symptom distress than comparison participants.

Other hope interventions have been designed for the general adult population. For instance, Cheavens, Feldman, Gum, Michael, and Snyder (2006) evaluated the effects of an eight-session intervention to promote hope. Participants, who were recruited from newspaper advertisements and flyers, were randomly assigned to a treatment group or a wait-list control group. The intervention consisted of eight group sessions lasting 2 hr each. Advanced doctoral students in clinical psychology led groups of between four and eight participants each. During the first half hour of each session, the group discussed homework and reviewed events from the previous week. This was followed by 20 min of working on psychoeducational skills and 50 min of discussing how to apply the skills to one's life. The last few minutes of each session focused on the homework assignment for the following week. Techniques employed for fostering hope included letter writing, starting "hope collections," and storytelling. Participants completed surveys at pretest and again immediately following the intervention. Results from both quantitative and qualitative data found that the program increased hope (as measured by agency thinking), life meaning, and self-esteem, and decreased anxiety and depressive symptoms.

One study examined how a hope intervention affected pain tolerance (Berg, Snyder, & Hamilton, 2008). University students were eligible to participate if they scored below the median on a measure of trait hope. Participants ($N = 172$) were randomly assigned to either a hope intervention condition or a comparison condition. The hope intervention lasted approximately 16 min. The first component involved guided imagery in which participants imagined a goal that they wanted, considered how they could enhance motivation to pursue this goal, and visualized strategies for pursuing this goal. Following the guided imagery, participants had a conversation with the experimenter about what they had imagined. The experimenter subsequently provided participants with a list of strategies for promoting goal setting, generating methods of reaching goals, and increasing motivation for achieving goals. Finally, participants were given a worksheet on which they wrote about a time when they had successfully achieved a goal. In contrast, participants in the control condition spent about 15 min reading a book on home organization. Pain tolerance was measured by the amount of time that passed before participants withdrew their hand from a bin of ice water. Results showed that participants assigned to the hope intervention had higher pain tolerance than participants assigned to the control condition. Interestingly, intervention participants also reported experiencing more pain. The authors suggested that the intervention might have caused participants to pay more attention to the pain, even though they were better able to tolerate it.

Summary of the Role of Religion and Spirituality in Hope Interventions

Several of the studies described thus far showed program benefits, such as increased hope, increased pain tolerance, better perceived quality of life, increased sense of meaning, and improved self-esteem (Berg et al., 2008; Cheavens et al., 2006; Duggleby et al., 2007). One of the studies failed to find any benefits from a hope intervention (Boucher, 2002). In spite of the mixed findings, some of these studies suggest that hope interventions hold promise for improving the lives of participants.

Consistent with hope theory, these interventions encouraged participants to identify and work toward goals, and some required participants to complete homework assignments related to hope. None of these hope interventions, however, explicitly incorporated religious ideas. This is striking because several of the interventions were designed to help individuals with cancer or other serious medical problems. Many individuals faced with medical crises rely on religious coping and believe that their religious faith helps them to cope (for review, see Pargament, 1997). Believing that one's religion is helpful during times of crisis does not necessarily make it true. An important question that researchers should be asking is whether hope interventions that incorporate religious and spiritual components are more beneficial than hope interventions that exclude these components. If so, under what conditions are religious interventions more helpful? Are they ever less helpful? Not only have these questions not been asked but also, as shown from the review, hope interventions generally omit references to religion. How might the content of a religiously or spiritually integrated hope intervention differ from secular interventions? Using Snyder et al.'s (1991) hope theory as a reference point, we examine ways in which religion or spirituality might contribute to goal selection, agency, and pathways.

Religion or spirituality and goal selection. Religious participants may wish to set goals that enhance their spiritual life and that are consistent with their faith tradition. For instance, the goals of cancer patients in a religiously or spirituality integrated hope intervention might involve strengthening a sense of connection to the divine, relinquishing control over the outcomes of medical treatment, and becoming more loving toward others. Participants from monotheistic traditions are likely to be concerned whether the goal they have selected is consistent with the will of God and may rely on prayer, scripture reading, or consultation with religious leaders to help discern this. As noted, some Buddhist participants may view personal goals as a source of suffering and therefore a hope intervention focused on personal goal setting may not fit with their worldview.

Religious and spiritual pathways. Once individuals have identified goals, it sometimes can be difficult to identify means by which the goal might be achieved. Individuals from a monotheistic religious background who are having difficulty perceiving a means for achieving their goals may look to God to reveal a pathway. In group interventions, participants could be provided with an opportunity to discuss how they have drawn on their faith in the past to achieve challenging goals. Weekly homework assignments on hope could encourage participants to incorporate spiritual strategies such as prayer or reading and reflecting on scriptures. For instance, many Christians take comfort from Philippians 4:13, which states, "I can do all things in him [Christ] who strengthens me." Religious participants who wish to work together with God to find a pathway to reach goals employ what Pargament (1997) has termed *collaborative religious coping*. Individuals who look to God to find the pathway without taking steps on their own are engaging in what Pargament has termed *deferring religious coping*. Regardless of their religious coping approach, facilitators of hope interventions could encourage monotheistic religious participants to consider how their faith tradition might provide insight into pathways for reaching goals.

Religion or spirituality and agency. Some participants in hope interventions may wish to draw on their faith tradition to enhance motivation for goal attainment. Homework assignments for hope interventions could ask participants to identify various ways in which their faith tradition could strengthen their motivation to achieve a goal. They also could consider religious role models from scriptures or within their religious community who could inspire them to persevere to achieve goals even in the face of obstacles (see Volume 1, Chapter 10, this handbook). Individuals who are part of a healthy and supportive religious community may be aided by religious social support in their quest to achieve goals. By helping religious participants consider how they could draw on their religious community as a source of support and inspiration when striving toward goals, intervention leaders can help participants develop a stronger sense of connection with others. Individuals who have limited contact with a religious or spiritual community might consider whether they could connect and find support through computer-based technologies, such as chatrooms, social networking sites, or e-mail exchanges.

While hope involves the desire to reach goals in the future, gratitude recognizes blessings that already have been bestowed or currently are being experienced. We now turn our attention to the promotion of gratitude.

THE PROMOTION OF GRATITUDE

Gratitude involves acknowledgment of the goodness in one's life and a recognition that the source of this goodness lies at least partially outside of oneself (Emmons, 2007; see also Volume 1, Chapter 23, this handbook). Gratitude is frequently conceptualized in psychological literature as an emotion connected to morality. For instance, Buck (2004) defined gratitude as "a higher level moral emotion involving a constellation of interpersonal/situational contingencies, including the acknowledgement that (a) one has received benefits and (b) one's power is limited" (p. 101). McCullough and Tsang (2004) described gratitude as a prosocial moral emotion that serves as (a) a moral barometer because it indicates when an interpersonal transaction is perceived as beneficial and (b) a moral motivator because it inspires one to behave in a prosocial manner. The emotion of gratitude can be either a state or a trait (Wood, Maltby, Stewart, Linley, & Joseph, 2008) and the object of gratitude can be people, animals, nature, life experiences, or God (Emmons & McCullough, 2003).

Religious and Spiritual Views on Gratitude

Gratitude is deeply valued and promoted by the major monotheistic religions. According to Jewish theology, gratitude toward God motivates people to obey God's commandments (Schimmel, 2004). Schimmel noted that Jews believe God provides rewards to those who express gratitude. Moreover, gratitude is a theme in the Hebrew Bible, the rabbinic biblical exegeses of Talmud and Midrash, and the Passover Seder ceremony (Schimmel, 2004). Gratitude is also a central theme within Christianity and is often a focus of prayer. Jesus is portrayed on multiple occasions as giving thanks (Matthew 15:36; Matthew 26:27), and gratitude is a frequent theme in letters attributed to the Apostle Paul. For instance, in 1 Thessalonians 5:18, Paul urges Christians to give thanks in all circumstances and connects this with the will of God and Jesus. Within Islam, one of the 99 names of God is The Grateful (Ash-Shakoor; "An Explanation of the Perfect Names," n.d.). Prayer, which is one of the five pillars of the Islamic faith, often focuses on gratitude toward God (Smith, 1995). The Qur'an explains that fasting during the holy month of Ramadan is a way of expressing gratitude to God (2:181) and believers are frequently encouraged to express thanksgiving toward God (e.g., 16:115). Moreover, on several occasions, the tendency for humans to be ungrateful is mentioned (e.g., 17:69).

Although gratitude is often connected to the divine in monotheistic religions, it is also an important concept in Buddhism. Emmons (2007) noted that the Nichiren Buddhist tradition teaches that gratitude is owed to all living beings, one's parents, and the three jewels (Buddha, dharma, sangha). Theravada Buddhist histories (*vamsas*) are replete with references to gratitude (Berkwitz, 2003). Thich Nhat Hanh (1995), a Buddhist monk from the Zen tradition, described the importance of practicing gratitude in all aspects of life as follows:

> Every time we eat a meal, gratitude is our practice. We are grateful for being

> together as a community. We are grateful that we have food to eat, and we really enjoy the food and the presence of each other. We feel grateful throughout the meal and throughout the day, and we express this by being fully aware of the food and living every moment deeply. This is how I try to express my gratitude to all of life. (p. 26)

Given that gratitude is central to both theistic and nontheistic religions, it is worth considering the possible role of religious teachings in gratitude interventions. The gratitude interventions reviewed in the next section, however, generally exclude religious content.

Gratitude Interventions

Several studies have evaluated gratitude interventions (see Table 25.2). For example, Emmons and McCullough (2003) conducted three studies that examined the effects of journal-based gratitude interventions on mental health. In Study 1, undergraduates (N = 192) were randomly assigned to one of the following three conditions: gratitude, hassles, or neutral life events. All participants kept a weekly journal for 10 weeks and were instructed to list up to five things that they were grateful for (gratitude condition), five things that they were hassled by (hassle condition), or five events that they were affected by (neutral condition). Over the course of 9 weeks, participants completed ratings of well-being, physical symptoms, reactions to receiving help, gratitude, and affect. Results showed that participants in the gratitude intervention improved more on ratings of life as a whole, had more optimistic expectations for the coming week, and reported fewer symptoms of physical illness than participants in the other conditions. In Study 2, undergraduates (N = 157) were randomly assigned to one of the following three conditions: gratitude, hassles, or social comparison. Participants were instructed to keep daily journals for 2 weeks on what they were grateful for (gratitude condition), what they were hassled by (hassles condition), or how their lives compared with others (social comparison condition). Participants completed measures each day concerning affect, health behaviors, and prosocial behaviors. Participants assigned to the gratitude condition showed greater positive affect and were more likely to report helping someone than participants in the other conditions. The third study examined the effect of a gratitude intervention on adults with neuromuscular diseases. Participants were assigned to a gratitude condition, in which they kept a gratitude journal for 21 days, or a control condition, in which participants only completed study measures. Participants completed measures of affect, well-being, health, and daily living skills. Observer reports of well-being were also collected from each participant's significant other. Participants in the gratitude condition showed enhanced subjective life appraisal and positive affect, and reduced negative affect. The observer reports corroborated the improvements in well-being.

Another study that evaluated a journal-based gratitude intervention was conducted by Sheldon and Lyubomirsky (2006). Undergraduate introductory psychology students (N = 67) were randomly assigned to one of the following conditions: gratitude intervention, best possible selves intervention, or control. The gratitude intervention was modeled from Emmons and McCullough (2003) and involved keeping a gratitude journal for 4 weeks. Participants in the best possible selves condition were asked to visualize and write about their conceptualization of their best possible selves for 4 weeks. Participants in the control condition were instructed to think about their day. Participants completed online measures of affect and motivation for completing the assigned exercises at pretest, posttest, and follow-up. Results showed that both intervention conditions improved in positive affect compared with the control condition. Participants in the best possible selves intervention improved more than the control condition on motivation for completing the assigned exercises, whereas there was no difference between participants in the gratitude and control conditions.

As part of a series of studies examining the relationship between gratitude and mood, Watkins, Woodward, Stone, and Kolts (2003) evaluated the effectiveness of both journal-based gratitude interventions and interventions that incorporated alternate techniques. The first two studies evaluated the

TABLE 25.2

Examples of Studies Evaluating Gratitude Interventions

Study	*N*	Target population	Study design and findings	Explicit religious content
Emmons and McCullough (2003), Study 1	192	Undergraduates	Randomly assigned participants to: 1. Gratitude intervention 2. Hassle condition 3. Neutral control condition ■ Participants in gratitude intervention experienced increased ratings of life and optimistic expectations and decreased symptoms of physical illness compared with controls.	None
Emmons and McCullough (2003), Study 2	157	Undergraduates	Randomly assigned participants to: 1. Gratitude intervention 2. Hassle condition 3. Social comparison condition ■ Participants in gratitude intervention improved on positive affect and helping behavior compared with controls.	None
Emmons and McCullough (2003), Study 3	65	Adults with neuromuscular diseases	Randomly assigned participants to: 1. Gratitude intervention 2. No-treatment control ■ Participants in gratitude intervention experienced increased subjective life appraisal, positive affect, and observed well-being and decreased negative affect compared with controls.	None
McIntosh (2008)	161	Undergraduates	Randomly assigned participants to: 1. Gratitude intervention 2. Mindfulness-based gratitude intervention 3. Control condition ■ Participants in gratitude interventions experienced increased positive affect and decreased negative affect compared with controls.	No explicit references to religion; however, religiously based mindfulness techniques could be integrated into meditation practice
Sheldon and Lyubomirsky (2006)	67	Undergraduates	Randomly assigned participants to: 1. Gratitude intervention 2. Best possible selves intervention 3. Control condition ■ Participants in both interventions improved on positive affect compared with controls and participants in best possible selves intervention improved on motivation compared with controls.	None
Watkins, Woodward, Stone, and Kolts (2003), Study 3	104	Undergraduates	Randomly assigned participants to: 1. Gratitude intervention 2. No-treatment control ■ Participants in gratitude intervention experienced decreased negative affect compared with controls.	None

(*Continued*)

TABLE 25.2 (*Continued*)

Examples of Studies Evaluating Gratitude Interventions

Study	N	Target population	Study design and findings	Explicit religious content
Watkins, Woodward, Stone, and Kolts (2003), Study 4	157	Undergraduates	Randomly assigned participants to: 1. Gratitude, thinking intervention 2. Gratitude, essay intervention 3. Gratitude, letter intervention 4. Control condition ■ Participants in gratitude interventions improved on positive affect (grateful thinking showing the most improvement) compared with controls.	None

psychometric properties of a gratitude measure and will not be described here. In the third study, undergraduate psychology students ($N = 104$) were randomly assigned to one of two conditions. In the gratitude condition, participants reflected for 5 min on events that occurred during the summer for which they were grateful. In the comparison condition, participants reflected for 5 min on activities that they had hoped to participate in but did not. Participants completed measures immediately after the intervention on gratitude, depression, and life satisfaction. Participants in the gratitude condition showed lower negative affect than those assigned to the control condition. In Study 4, undergraduate participants ($N = 157$) were randomly assigned to one of four conditions. Participants assigned to the grateful thinking condition spent 5 min thinking about a person for whom they were grateful. Participants assigned to the grateful essay condition were instructed to spend 5 min writing about someone for whom they were grateful. Those assigned to the letter writing condition were instructed to write a letter expressing gratitude. Researchers told participants that they would mail the letter but instead returned it at the conclusion of the study. Finally, participants assigned to the control condition wrote about the layout of their living room. Participants completed measures of positive and negative affect and other mood measures at pretest and posttest. Participants in all of the gratitude interventions showed greater increases in positive affect than those in comparison conditions. Interestingly, the grateful thinking condition showed the greatest improvement in positive mood.

McIntosh (2008) developed a brief gratitude intervention that incorporates mindfulness techniques. Participants consisted of undergraduate psychology students ($N = 161$) who were randomly assigned to a gratitude intervention, a mindfulness-based gratitude intervention, or a control condition. Participants in the gratitude intervention were asked to spend 5 min making a list of what they were grateful for. In the mindfulness-based intervention, participants were initially instructed to think about something for which they were grateful. They subsequently wrote down a few words about whatever came to mind and then vividly imagined and considered the feelings or emotions that were prompted by what they were grateful for. This process was repeated for 5 min. In the control condition, participants wrote about how their dorm or living room was set up. All participants completed measures of gratitude, social desirability, relaxation states, affect, and empathy at pretest and again immediately following the intervention. Participants in both gratitude conditions showed increased positive affect and decreased negative affect as compared with those in the control group. No differences were found, however, on outcome measures when comparing the gratitude induction with the mindfulness-based gratitude induction.

Summary of the Role of Religion and Spirituality in Gratitude Interventions

As noted, studies using randomized controlled methodologies have shown that gratitude interventions have positive benefits, such as reduced negative affect, enhanced positive feelings, and improved well-being (Emmons & McCullough, 2003; Sheldon & Lyubomirsky, 2006; Watkins et al., 2003). The gratitude interventions described above do not explicitly incorporate religious or spiritual ideas, although none of them would preclude participants from expressing gratitude in ways connected to their faith. Although the mindfulness-based gratitude intervention tested by McIntosh (2008) was not specifically tied to a religious perspective, it could easily be adapted for religious practitioners who value meditation or contemplative prayer. We next examine some ways in which gratitude interventions might incorporate religious and spiritual practices.

Gratitude and prayer or meditation. Although not a direct test of a gratitude intervention, a study by Lambert, Fincham, Braithwaite, Graham, and Beach (2009) concerning the effects of prayer on gratitude is relevant to the present discussion (see Chapter 24 in this volume). In the fourth of a series of studies, they recruited undergraduates ($N = 104$) who were involved in a romantic relationship and who had prayed in the past. Participants were randomly assigned to a partner prayer condition, a general prayer condition, a daily activities condition, or a positive thoughts condition. Participants in the partner prayer condition were instructed to pray for their romantic partner's well-being at least once a day for 4 weeks. Participants submitted a record of their prayers online. Participants in the general prayer condition were given similar instructions but could pray about anything that they wished. Participants assigned to the daily activities condition were instructed to think about and record their activities during the day for 4 weeks. Those participants assigned to the positive thoughts condition were instructed to think positive thoughts about their partner daily for 4 weeks. Participants completed measures of gratitude, religiosity, social desirability, and prayer at pretest and posttest. Results showed that participants in the prayer conditions improved more on gratitude than those in the control condition, even though participants were not instructed to incorporate gratitude into the prayers. Future research should compare the effects of prayer focused on gratitude with other forms of prayer.

Gratitude-focused prayers in positive psychology interventions can be performed alone or in the presence of groups. With respect to solitary prayer, participants could be encouraged to spend time at the end of each day thanking God for blessings that occurred during the day. An important component of this exercise is developing a daily routine in which gratitude is actively focused on. Prayers of thanksgiving can be offered in the context of communal prayer. Communal prayer, when spoken out loud, allows one to state what one is grateful for in the presence of others and also to hear what others are thankful for. This process may allow individuals who are praying together to model and reinforce the cultivation of a grateful attitude. Examples of situations in which gratitude focused communal prayer might be practiced include families who pray before meals or groups who have gathered to study scripture and to pray.

Religious individuals from nontheistic traditions and theistic traditions that value contemplative approaches may appreciate the opportunity to strengthen their grateful outlook through meditation. The first study to compare a mindfulness-based gratitude intervention (McIntosh, 2008) with one that excluded mindfulness techniques showed no differences in effectiveness. This study, however, used a brief mindfulness induction as opposed to longer meditation sessions modeled after Buddhist practice. In any event, religious individuals often incorporate gratitude into prayer and meditation and therefore they might be particularly appreciative of homework assignments that encourage such expressions of gratitude. Time could be set aside during interventions for participants to engage in guided meditations focusing on gratitude. Alternatively, participants could engage in gratitude meditations on their own outside of intervention sessions. Some participants may find it useful to listen to a recorded guided meditation, whereas others may prefer meditating on their own in silence.

Other suggestions for connecting gratitude and religion or spirituality. For interventions involving journaling, monotheistic participants could be prompted to consider how they are grateful toward God. This could be accomplished through daily journaling or by encouraging participants from theistic religious perspectives to write a letter to God. Interestingly, Krause (2006) found that gratitude toward God might buffer the effects of stress on older adults, although this has not yet been tested in the context of a specific intervention to promote gratitude. Through journaling or letter writing, participants could be prompted to consider how the blessings they have received have affected their spiritual life. Another approach would be to prompt religious participants to consider how their religious role models have expressed gratitude. Moreover, religious rituals and holy days can be viewed as opportunities to contemplate gratitude.

In addition to focusing on the blessings that one has received, positive psychology interventions have been developed to help individuals cope with severe transgressions committed by others in the past. In the next section, we discuss the promotion of forgiveness.

THE PROMOTION OF FORGIVENESS

Of the various definitions that have been proposed for forgiveness (for review, see Wade & Worthington, 2005), most involve letting go of anger toward an offender and replacing it with more positive emotions, such as benevolence, empathy, compassion, or love. Unlike reconciliation, forgiveness does not require one to maintain a relationship with the offender (Freedman, 1998). Moreover, forgiveness is not the same as condoning, denying, excusing, forgetting, or pardoning offenses (McCullough, Pargament, & Thoresen, 2000).

One of the broadest theories related to forgiveness was developed by McCullough (2008). McCullough has argued that desires for and acts of revenge evolved as an adaptive behavior to protect humans and their social groups from violence, aggression, and other forms of injustice. Likewise, forgiveness also emerged as an adaptive individual and social response to keep relationships and communities together even in the face of injustice, interpersonal injuries, or violence. McCullough argued that forgiveness is a natural human instinct that is activated in certain social situations. Specifically, humans are more likely to forgive when offenders apologize or offer restitution, when people experience a sense of fairness or justice in their world, and when they are not under consistent threat of violence, aggression, or oppression.

One hypothesis that is particularly useful in a therapeutic setting and in light of positive psychology is Worthington and Wade's (1999) distinction between forgiveness and unforgiveness. Worthington and Wade posited that forgiveness is not just the simple reduction of unforgiveness. To illustrate this, they suggested several ways that people who have been hurt might deal with their unforgiving feelings and motivations other than by forgiving. For example, individuals who have been hurt or wronged might seek justice, turn their vengefulness over to a higher power who they believe will exact revenge or balance the scales of justice, or simply deny or minimize the hurt. In these cases, forgiveness has not been invoked, and yet the person may no longer carry the anger and bitterness of unforgiveness. Instead of simply reducing something negative, Worthington and Wade (1999) have argued that forgiveness necessarily involves the active promotion of a positive human strength, which is in line with the idea of forgiveness being a virtue. Thus, forgiveness can be a prosocial choice in response to a hurt, which is facilitated by positive emotions, such as empathy or compassion.

Worthington, Witvliet, Pietrini, and Miller (2007) further developed this idea by describing two types of forgiveness: decisional forgiveness and emotional forgiveness. *Decisional forgiveness* occurs when a victim of an offense makes a choice or decision to forgive their offender and engages in deliberate, behavioral-based efforts to forego unforgiving thoughts, feelings, and behaviors. For example, a person hurt by a spouse could decide to forgive and to treat the spouse in a respectful manner while refraining from entertaining feelings of anger. This decision, however, does not necessarily mean the person has developed positive feelings toward the spouse. *Emotional forgiveness,* in contrast, involves the development of positive feelings toward the offender that might include compassion, empathy, mercy, and love. Some individuals who have been wronged will engage in both decisional and emotional forgiveness. In both forms of forgiveness, something other than the mere reduction in unforgiveness is occurring; individuals hurt by others are responding with a positive prosocial response that attempts to resolve the hurt without creating more pain or conflict.

Religious and Spiritual Views on Forgiveness

Forgiveness is a virtue that is extolled by both monotheistic and nontheistic religious traditions (Rye et al., 2000). For instance, Jewish traditions place great importance on forgiveness as a vital element of faith (Dorff, 1998; Rye et al., 2000). According to Judaism, the extension of forgiveness to another person, in essence, removes a debt and wipes clear the offender's record of wrongdoings. Like Christians and Muslims, Jews believe that because God is forgiving toward humans, as demonstrated in the Torah (e.g., Exodus 34:6, Psalms 145:17, and Deuteronomy 11:22), humans must also forgive each other. Rye et al. (2000) wrote, "It is not only God's forgiveness that occupies this central place in Judaism, but also human forgiveness" (p. 30). Furthermore, the Jewish faith proposes that after genuine contrition is offered and the offender has made amends for his or her actions, it is the victim's duty to extend forgiveness (Dorff, 2003).

Christian traditions also express a strong belief in the value of forgiving others for their transgressions (Marty, 1998; Rye et al., 2000; Worthington, Berry, & Parrott, 2001). According to Christian beliefs, forgiveness relates to Christ's death on the cross for the salvation of the world. In his death, Christ forgave all persons of their transgressions and provided them with salvation despite any previous offenses they had committed. Christians believe that people are mandated to forgive others because they are forgiven by God (e.g., Luke 23:34, Matthew 6:12, and Mark 11:25; Beals, 1998; Rye et al., 2000). Beals (1998) explained, "God's forgiving love in Christ remains freely offered to sinners and it seasons and sustains the lives of Christians . . . we become forgiven to be forgiving" (p. 123) and furthermore, "when we know we are forgiven by God for Christ's sake, we become moved to forgive others" (p. 125). Christianity, therefore, proposes that to imitate Christ's forgiveness of people, humans must also extend forgiveness to their offenders (Rye et al., 2000).

Similarly, Islamic traditions believe that for true forgiveness to occur, an individual must be forgiven not only by others (interpersonal forgiveness) but also by Allah. According to Islamic beliefs, Allah is a compassionate and merciful God who forgives all who honestly repent of their sins (Siddiqi, 2004). Because Allah extends grace, mercy, and forgiveness to humans, it is vital that people also extend this forgiveness to others. Furthermore, forgiveness between individuals is the basis for many Islamic beliefs. Numerous verses in the Qur'an mention the importance of forgiveness (24:22; 39:53; 42:25) and emphasize offering forgiveness to others as Allah has first modeled forgiveness toward humans. Last, the Qur'an states that those who forgive others will in turn receive rewards from Allah (42:40).

The wide variety of languages and conceptual diversity found in Buddhist traditions can make it difficult to find equivalents for Western moral categories, such as forgiveness (Rye et al., 2000). With this caution in mind, the Buddhist concept of forgiveness could be viewed as a combination of compassion and forbearance (Rye et al., 2000). In Buddhist traditions, forgiveness is thought to be the opposite of resentment and represents the absence of anger toward an offender (Tsang, McCullough, & Hoyt, 2005). When one is resentful, he or she may act unjustly toward others. To prevent this, Buddhists encourage a two-part forgiveness process (Farrer-Halls, 2000). First, to truly embrace forgiveness, victims must reduce and eventually release desires or plans for retribution or revenge against their offender. Second, victims must alter their feelings and emotions toward their offender. Specifically, they must strive to release anger and resentment they feel toward the offender. According to Buddhist beliefs, forgiveness does not encompass only one of these elements (e.g., not avenging an offense but continuing to experience intense anger); instead, forgiveness occurs only when both elements are present (no retaliatory behavior and a reduction of anger).

In addition, Buddhists believe that the world is "fundamentally unjust" but that through karma the balance of justice in the world is maintained (Rye et al., 2000, p. 27). Karma, the belief that everything we do has a direct influence on our future, either in this life or upon reincarnation, is an essential part of Buddhist traditions (Farrer-Halls, 2000). Positive actions can enable one to reap future rewards, whereas negative actions can result in future punishment. Therefore, if a Buddhist chooses not to forgive, he or she will likely reap negative repercussions later in life or in a future life (Farrer-Halls, 2000). Essentially, forgiveness is considered a moral quality that promotes balance, relationship harmony, and positive karma.

Forgiveness Interventions

Numerous studies have documented the efficacy of interventions to promote forgiveness (see Volume 1, Chapter 23, this handbook). Because it is not possible to review all of them in this chapter, we have limited the scope to providing examples of interventions that have been empirically tested and show some significant promise for promoting forgiveness (see Table 25.3). In addition, we describe both interventions that have explicitly incorporated religious and spiritual elements and those that have not.

Forgiveness interventions without religious or spiritual elements. One of the first empirically tested forgiveness intervention models was developed by Enright and his colleagues (Enright & the Human Development Study Group, 1991). The Enright model is organized into four phases and is designed to promote forgiveness. The first phase, called the *uncovering phase*, is aimed at examining psychological defenses that may prevent an individual from recalling a hurt, coping with anger toward an offender, developing an awareness of shame due to an offense, and gaining insight about the role of the hurt in one's life. The *decision phase* focuses on committing to forgiveness and encouraging clients to embrace the possibility of forgiving their offender. In the *work phase*, clients are asked to consider the offense from the offender's viewpoint and discuss the importance of empathizing with their offender. Finally, in the *outcome phase*, the meaning of forgiveness is reviewed and the personal nature of forgiveness is emphasized. At this stage, clients begin to experience true forgiveness wherein their behaviors, thoughts, and feelings toward the offender shift to become more positive.

The Enright model (Enright & the Human Development Study Group, 1991) has been tested in several different clinical trials for people suffering from incest, emotional abuse, parental neglect, and other hurts (Wade, Worthington, & Meyer, 2005). In one of the earliest tests of the model, Hebl and Enright (1993) offered the treatment to elderly women seeking to forgive an interpersonal offense. Hebl and Enright randomly assigned women ($N = 24$) to either the forgiveness intervention condition, which was based on Enright's forgiveness model, or the comparison discussion condition. Participants completed pretest and posttest measures of self-esteem, depression, and anxiety. Participants only completed posttest measures of forgiveness because the researchers did not want pretest measures of forgiveness to influence the content of discussions among control group participants. Participants in the forgiveness condition reported greater forgiveness of a specific offense and willingness to forgive than those assigned to the comparison condition.

Other studies evaluating Enright's forgiveness intervention have also demonstrated beneficial program effects. Freedman and Enright (1996), for example, randomly assigned 12 female incest survivors to a forgiveness intervention condition or a wait-list control condition. The intervention consisted of weekly 60-min individual sessions for an average of 14.3 months. Participants completed measures of forgiveness and mental health at multiple pretest and posttest administrations. Results showed that participants in the intervention condition reported greater increase in hope and forgiveness, and greater reductions in anxiety and depression than those in the control condition.

Another study examining the effectiveness of Enright's forgiveness model was conducted by Reed and Enright (2006). Female participants ($N = 20$) who had experienced emotional abuse in a prior relationship were randomly assigned to either a forgiveness intervention condition or a comparison condition that focused on anger validation, assertiveness training, and interpersonal skills. The mean intervention time was approximately 8 months. Participants completed measures of forgiveness and

TABLE 25.3

Examples of Studies Evaluating Forgiveness Interventions

Study	N	Target population	Study design and findings	Explicit religious content
Freedman and Enright (1996)	12	Female incest survivors	Randomly assigned participants to: 1. Forgiveness intervention 2. No-treatment wait-list control ■ Participants in forgiveness intervention increased on hope and forgiveness and decreased on anxiety and depression compared with controls.	None
Hebl and Enright (1993)	24	Elderly women	Randomly assigned participants to: 1. Forgiveness intervention 2. Control condition ■ Participants in forgiveness intervention improved on forgiveness of a specific offense and willingness to forgive compared with controls.	None
Lampton, Oliver, Worthington, and Berry (2005)	65	Christian undergraduates	Pseudo-randomly assigned participants to: 1. Christian-based REACH forgiveness intervention 2. No-treatment wait-list control ■ Participants in forgiveness intervention increased on positive thoughts and feelings toward offender and decreased on revenge and avoidance compared with controls.	Christian-based intervention used scripture passages, worship music, and discussions about biblical framework for forgiveness and Christ as a forgiveness model
McCullough, Worthington, and Rachal (1997)	134	Undergraduates	Randomly assigned participants to: 1. REACH intervention 2. No empathy REACH intervention 3. No-treatment wait-list control ■ Participants in REACH intervention improved on forgiveness and affective empathy compared with no-empathy REACH intervention and controls.	None
Reed and Enright (2006)	20	Females who had experienced emotional abuse in a prior relationship	Randomly assigned participants to: 1. Forgiveness intervention 2. Control condition ■ Participants in forgiveness intervention increased on self-esteem, forgiveness, sense of meaning, and environmental mastery and decreased on depression, anxiety, and posttraumatic stress symptoms compared with controls.	None
Rye and Pargament (2002)	58	College women who had experienced romantic hurt	Randomly assigned participants to: 1. Secular forgiveness intervention 2. Religious forgiveness intervention 3. No-treatment wait-list control ■ Participants in forgiveness interventions improved on forgiveness and well-being compared with controls.	Religious forgiveness intervention used religious discussions, prayer, and scripture passages

(*Continued*)

TABLE 25.3 (*Continued*)

Examples of Studies Evaluating Forgiveness Interventions

Study	N	Target population	Study design and findings	Explicit religious content
Rye et al. (2005)	149	Divorced individuals	Randomly assigned participants to: 1. Secular forgiveness intervention 2. Religious forgiveness intervention 3. No-treatment wait-list control ■ Participants in forgiveness interventions improved on forgiveness of an ex-spouse and understanding of forgiveness compared with controls, and participants in the secular condition also decreased on depressive symptoms compared with controls.	Religious forgiveness intervention used scripture passages, prayer, and discussions about religious support and role models
Stratton, Dean, Nonneman, Bode, and Worthington (2008)	114	Christian undergraduates	Randomly assigned participants to: 1. REACH workshop condition 2. Essay-writing condition 3. REACH workshop and essay condition 4. No-treatment control ■ Participants in REACH workshop and essay condition improved on positive responses toward offender compared with other conditions in the short term, but in the long-term, no significant difference was found between the REACH workshop condition and REACH workshop plus essay condition.	Essay and workshop and essay conditions included writing about the role of religious beliefs in personal forgiveness process along with standard REACH Christian-based elements

mental health at pretest, posttest, and follow-up. The study found that participants in the forgiveness condition reported significantly larger reductions in depression, anxiety, and posttraumatic stress symptoms and larger increases in self-esteem, forgiveness, and sense of meaning and environmental mastery as compared with participants in the comparison condition.

Another forgiveness intervention model that has been extensively studied is Worthington's (2001) REACH model. This model was originally conceived as a broad, secular intervention but was later adapted to include Christian concepts, imagery, and symbols. The model includes five steps, with each of the main components represented in the acronym REACH. The first step provides individuals with an opportunity to recall (R) the offense. Second, clients complete exercises to help them empathize (E) with their offender. For example, clients are asked to consider possible situational factors that may have encouraged the offending person's actions. During the third step, clients consider forgiveness as an altruistic (A) gift. During this step, individuals recall when they have received the gift of forgiveness from others and the gratitude they may have felt. Next, clients are encouraged to commit (C) to forgiving their offender when they are ready to extend forgiveness. Finally, clients hold (H) onto forgiveness through specific "relapse prevention" strategies, such as telling others about their decision to forgive and reminding themselves that they have chosen to forgive their offender and move forward with their life.

The REACH model has been tested in multiple clinical outcome studies. Most of these studies have investigated the use of the REACH model in a group setting in which participants have experienced different kinds of hurts (e.g., sexual infidelity, betrayals, or parental abuse) and have found that the forgiveness treatment is effective for promoting forgiveness for a specific offense (Wade et al., 2005). For instance, McCullough, Worthington, and Rachal

(1997) compared the REACH model to a version of the treatment that did not include one of the main theoretical components (building empathy for the offender). Undergraduate volunteers ($N = 134$), with a variety of interpersonal hurts, were randomly assigned to one of two treatment conditions or a wait-list control group. One treatment condition utilized each of the five REACH steps, whereas the other treatment condition did not include the empathy component of the REACH model. Participants completed measures of affective empathy, cognitive empathy, and forgiveness at pretest, posttest, and follow-up. The full REACH intervention promoted forgiveness and affective empathy better than either the partial REACH intervention or the comparison group. This study suggests that developing empathy for one's offender may be a key element in the forgiveness process.

Forgiveness interventions including religious or spiritual elements. One of the first studies to test the explicit integration of religious or spiritual elements into a forgiveness intervention was conducted by Rye and Pargament (2002). Rye and Pargament randomly assigned college women ($N = 58$) who had experienced wrongdoing in a romantic relationship to one of the following conditions: secular forgiveness intervention, religiously tailored intervention, or no-intervention comparison. The interventions consisted of a variety of discussions and activities designed to facilitate forgiveness and incorporated some of the strategies used in the Worthington (2001) and Enright and the Human Development Study Group (1991) models. Participants in the secular intervention received many of the same basic components as participants in the religiously integrated condition (e.g., discussed emotions following wrongdoing, learned cognitive–behavioral strategies for coping with negative emotions, learned about the definition and steps involved in forgiveness, learned how to avoid obstacles to forgiveness) but were not encouraged to draw on their faith. In contrast, the religiously tailored intervention encouraged participants to actively draw on their faith to forgive and included elements such as weighing the impact of the offense on one's spiritual life, discussing religious role models for forgiveness, discussing theological justifications for forgiveness, considering how prayer might facilitate forgiveness, and reading religious passages. Participants completed pretest, posttest, and follow-up measures of forgiveness and mental health. Results showed that participants in both intervention conditions improved more than those in the comparison condition on forgiveness and well-being. No differences were found between the secular and religiously integrated interventions. Interestingly, participants in both intervention conditions reported relying on religiously based strategies when trying to forgive.

A similar study by Rye et al. (2005) compared the effectiveness of secular and religiously integrated forgiveness interventions for divorced individuals. Participants ($N = 149$) were randomly assigned to a secular condition, a religiously integrated condition, or to a wait-list comparison condition. Similar to the interventions described in Rye and Pargament (2002), the religiously integrated condition encouraged participants to draw on their faith by discussing religious sources of support for forgiveness, considering how prayer might facilitate forgiveness, reading scripture passages, and examining religious role models for forgiveness. In contrast, religious ideas were not introduced in the secular condition, but the remainder of the program content was similar (e.g., processing emotions related to wrongdoing, making an inventory of one's grudges, discussing how attributions about the offender's behavior affect one's response to the offender, discussing strategies for facilitating forgiveness, and presenting research on the possible benefits of forgiveness). Participants completed pretest, posttest, and follow-up measures of forgiveness and mental health. Results showed that participants assigned to both intervention conditions improved more than comparison participants on forgiveness of an ex-spouse and understanding of forgiveness. Participants in the secular condition also showed a greater decrease in depressive symptoms than comparison participants. In addition, the authors examined the relationship between participant religiosity and the effectiveness of the two interventions and found no special benefits or additional forgiveness gains made by highly religious individuals in the religious condition. Similar to Rye and Pargament (2002), participants in both intervention conditions reported using religious strategies when working on forgiveness, although it is unclear whether these strategies were responsible for beneficial program effects.

As stated, Worthington's (2001) REACH model has been adapted to incorporate religious elements (Worthington, Scherer, et al., 2007). This adaptation involved integrating Christian religious scriptures, concepts, imagery, and symbols into the intervention. For example, participants were encouraged to imagine themselves holding their hurt in their hands. Then, when they felt ready, they imagined releasing the hurt into God's care and allowing God to take the hurt from them and send them a blessing in return. Several studies have documented the efficacy of this Christian-integrated REACH program for college students (Lampton, Oliver, Worthington, & Berry, 2005; Stratton, Dean, Nonneman, Bode, & Worthington, 2008) and adults in the Philippines (Worthington et al., 2010).

For example, Lampton et al. (2005) examined the efficacy of Worthington's REACH intervention when applied to Christian college students. Students from a Christian university ($N = 65$) had the choice of participating in one of two study conditions: a Christian-based REACH forgiveness condition or a wait-list control condition. The results of this study should be interpreted with caution given the lack of random assignment. The intervention not only included the traditional REACH steps as outlined by Worthington (2001) but also incorporated Christian elements, such as considering the biblical framework of forgiveness, listening to Christian worship music, reading scriptural references pertaining to forgiveness, and reflecting on Christ as a forgiveness model. Participants completed pretest and posttest questionnaires measuring trait forgiveness, revenge, avoidance, and positive emotions associated with forgiveness. Although there were no intervention effects on trait forgiveness over time, participants in the Christian-based REACH condition reported greater reductions in revenge and avoidance and greater increases in positive thoughts and feelings toward the offender as compared with those in the wait-list condition. Because this study did not include a nonreligious forgiveness group, it is not possible to ascertain whether the religious components of the program were responsible for the beneficial effects.

An additional test of this type of intervention involved randomly assigning Christian college students ($N = 114$) to one of four conditions: Christian-based REACH workshop, religiously enhanced essay writing, Christian-based REACH workshop plus religiously enhanced essay, or no treatment (Stratton et al., 2008). Participants assigned to the REACH condition received the Christian-based REACH intervention, whereas those assigned to the REACH plus essay condition completed the intervention and wrote an essay detailing their unique story of forgiveness. The essay included a narrative of the transgression, their decision to forgive, the experience of forgiving, and the role their religious beliefs played in the forgiveness process. Participants assigned to the essay condition only wrote the essay. Participants completed pretest, posttest, and follow-up measures assessing state and trait forgiveness and positive emotions associated with a specific offender. Results indicated that students in the workshop plus essay condition reported greater improvement on positive responses toward an offender than participants in the other conditions. The authors concluded that the workshop plus writing condition enhanced the immediate effects of the intervention but that, over time, the findings were no different than participants in the intervention-only condition. The lack of a treatment condition without religious content makes it difficult to assess the effectiveness of the religious components of the program.

Summary of the Role of Religion and Spirituality in Forgiveness Interventions

As shown, studies have demonstrated that forgiveness interventions can increase forgiveness (Freedman & Enright, 1996; Hebl & Enright, 1993; Lampton et al., 2005; McCullough et al., 1997; Rye & Pargament, 2002; Rye et al., 2005; Stratton et al., 2008) and improve mental health (Freedman & Enright, 1996; Reed & Enright, 2006; Rye & Pargament, 2002; Rye et al., 2005). Several studies have also shown that religiously based forgiveness interventions can be beneficial relative to no intervention (Lampton et al., 2005; Rye & Pargament, 2002; Rye et al., 2005; Stratton et al., 2008), but no evidence has been found that interventions that incorporate religious ideas are more effective than forgiveness interventions that exclude religion. In addition, the interventions that incorporated religious content were largely rooted in mainstream Protestant Christian perspectives and studies are needed to examine the effectiveness of interventions that incorporate ideas from other forms of Christianity and non-Christian traditions. We next summarize some ways that religious and spiritual practices can be incorporated into forgiveness interventions.

Making sense of the offender's actions from a religious or spiritual framework. After being wronged, victims often develop a narrative to explain the meaning behind the offender's actions. Individuals with a religious or spiritual perspective may construct this narrative using foundational concepts of their faith tradition. For instance, many Buddhists might focus on the interconnectedness between the offender and themselves. From this viewpoint, attacking the offender in retribution will cause suffering to both oneself and the offender. The desire to help all sentient beings overcome suffering may provide a powerful motivation for some Buddhist participants to refrain from responding through retaliation. Practitioners of both non-theistic and monotheistic traditions may wish to view the offender's actions as a consequence of the offender's own suffering. Furthermore, the monotheistic religions posit that God is loving and that all human beings fall short of God's expectations. Understanding one's capacity to fall short of God's expectations may make it easier for some religious individuals to experience empathy toward an offender and to avoid demonizing the offender.

Facilitating forgiveness through prayer. There are several published accounts of individuals who, after being wronged, relied on prayer to help them to forgive. For instance, Corrie Ten Boom (2006) described how she was able to forgive her guard at the Nazi prison camp only after she prayed to God for assistance. Gerald Jampolsky (1999) similarly wrote about how he gained strength to forgive his ex-wife by asking for God's help. In addition to published anecdotal reports, research has revealed that prayer is an important component to the forgiveness process for many religious individuals (Kidwell et al., 2010). McMinn et al. (2008) studied how a group of Christians affiliated with an evangelical Christian university connected prayer with forgiveness of an offender. When asked to identify the most important aspects of the process they went through when forgiving an offender, 54% mentioned prayer. Many other participants subsequently mentioned prayer when prompted to elaborate on any additional spiritual disciplines that they found helpful when forgiving.

In addition to showing that religious participants often use prayer when forgiving, research has found that prayer can lead to increased forgiveness. For example, two studies by Lambert, Fincham, Stillman, Graham, and Beach (2010) showed that participants instructed to pray for an offender increased on forgiveness more than participants assigned to engage in other tasks. The first study revealed that participants assigned to pray for a romantic partner increased willingness to forgive him or her more than participants who were asked to describe their partner's physical characteristics. The second study demonstrated that participants assigned to pray for a close friend reported higher levels of forgiveness toward the friend than participants assigned to pray (undirected) or to think positive thoughts about the friend. On the basis of this research, individuals developing forgiveness interventions for religious or spiritual participants may wish to consider possible ways of incorporating prayer into the program.

Prayer is an important component of previously published religiously based forgiveness interventions. For instance, the religious version of the Rye et al. (2005) forgiveness intervention for divorced individuals incorporated prayer in several ways. During one session, group leaders asked participants to engage in silent prayer or meditation for 15 min. Participants were also assigned a homework assignment in which they were encouraged to engage in prayer or meditation throughout the week to help them through the forgiveness process. These approaches to integrating prayer into group forgiveness interventions may be especially helpful because they allow participants from diverse religious or spiritual perspectives to pray or reflect in whatever way is meaningful to them. Similarly, prayer is a basic component of the religiously based REACH model. It is used throughout the various steps, in the form of clients praying for themselves, their offenders, or the process of forgiveness. The REACH model provides specific opportunities for participants to pray, if they desire to do so, as a group aloud or silently to themselves within the group.

Looking to religious role models for inspiration. A significant element of the Christian REACH intervention is the opportunity for participants to learn about biblical role models of forgiveness. Christ is presented as a model of divine forgiveness in numerous Bible passages (such as Luke 15:11–32; Matthew 6:12, 14–15, and Matthew 19:21–25), and many clients find it helpful to reflect on times Christ was able to empathize with (and ultimately offer forgiveness) to those who ridiculed him and eventually crucified him. In addition, some clients may find it helpful to consider Christ as a model of altruism throughout the forgiveness process. Specifically, participants discuss how Christ was able to unselfishly give forgiveness as a gift to others and recognized the fact that nearly everyone, at one time or another, will need to give or offer forgiveness. Many Christian clients may find strength in drawing on Christ's example of forgiveness.

Regardless of whether forgiveness interventions include or exclude religious or spiritual content, most promote feelings of compassion toward an offender. Psychological theories and interventions, however, also have been developed to promote a sense of compassion toward oneself. Examples of self-compassion interventions are described in the next section, but most of these interventions do not explicitly incorporate religious or spiritual content.

THE PROMOTION OF SELF-COMPASSION

Neff (2003) posited that self-compassion involves three components. First, self-compassion involves expressing kindness toward oneself and viewing one's shortcomings with a nonjudgmental attitude. Second, self-compassion involves connecting one's experience of suffering with that of the collective human experience. Neff (2008) wrote, "Self-compassionate individuals recognize that pain and imperfection are an inevitable part of the human experience, something that we all go through instead of an isolated occurrence that happens to 'me' alone." (p. 95). Third, self-compassion requires that one become mindful of suffering without becoming attached or making it a central aspect of one's identity. Neff (2003) explained that self-compassion is not based in feelings of superiority but rather a realization that humans are equal and interconnected. Self-compassion does not imply that one can engage in harmful behavior with impunity but instead encourages making amends while maintaining an attitude of gentleness toward oneself. Unlike those experiencing self-pity, individuals with self-compassion do not exaggerate their own pain, become attached to their pain experience, or view their pain as being disconnected from the experience of others (Neff, 2003). Unlike self-esteem, self-compassion does not involve comparing how one's own performance matches with others (Neff, 2008).

Religious and Spiritual Views of Self-Compassion

Although self-compassion is consistent with the theology of many religions, psychologists have generally emphasized its role within Buddhism. The Dalai Lama (1997) noted that compassion is the foundation of the dharma and the basis for human happiness. Kornfield (2002) attributed the following quote to the Buddha:

> You can search throughout the entire universe for someone who is more deserving of your love and affection than you are yourself, and that person is not to be found anywhere. You, yourself, as much as anybody in the entire universe, deserve your love and affection. (p. 101)

The basis of self-compassion in monotheistic religions lies in the assertion that God is compassionate toward humans and that humans are expected to imitate God. Within the Judeo-Christian tradition, the assertion that you should love your neighbor as yourself (Leviticus 19:18) could be interpreted as a call for both self-compassion and compassion toward others.

Self-Compassion Interventions

Several studies have evaluated interventions that promote self-compassion (see Table 25.4). For instance, one study evaluated the effects of compassionate mind training (Kelly, Zuroff, & Shapira, 2009). Participants ($N = 75$) who suffered from facial acne were recruited using online classified and newspaper ads. Participants were assigned to a self-soothing intervention condition, an attack-resisting intervention condition, or a control condition. Participants in both of the intervention conditions were seated in front of a computer with an attached mirror and were shown a PowerPoint slideshow. Participants were prompted by the slides to engage in imagery followed by instructions for completing a measure related to their distress concerning their acne. They were provided with the rationale behind the intervention and were given exercises to work on during the following 2 weeks. Participants assigned to the self-soothing condition were presented with slides adapted from compassionate mind training that discussed the importance of engaging in compassionate self-talk. Participants were instructed to visualize themselves in a compassionate way and describe the image in writing. Finally, participants were instructed to engage in compassionate imagery and repeat their compassionate self-statements three times a day for the next 2 weeks. In contrast, participants assigned to the attack-resisting intervention viewed a slideshow that focused on how self-criticism causes distress. Activities involving imagery, letter writing, and self-statements encouraged participants to view themselves as confident and resilient. Participants were instructed to repeat these images and self-statements three times a day over the next 2 weeks. Participants in the control condition received no intervention. Participants completed measures of depression, shame, and severity of acne problems at pretest and 2-week posttest. Results showed that compared with the control condition, participants in the self-soothing intervention experienced reduced shame

TABLE 25.4

Examples of Studies Evaluating Self-Compassion Interventions

Study	*N*	Target population	Study design and findings	Explicit religious content
Kelly, Zuroff, and Shapira (2009)	75	Young adults with facial acne	Randomly assigned participants to: 1. Self-soothing intervention 2. Attack-resisting intervention 3. No-treatment control ■ Participants in intervention conditions experienced decreased shame and skin complaints compared with controls, and participants in attack-resisting intervention also experienced decreased depression compared with controls.	Mindfulness exercises that were not explicitly tied to religion
Kirkpatrick (2005)	80	University students	Randomly assigned participants to: 1. Self-compassion intervention 2. No-treatment control ■ No significant effects were found.	None
Weibel (2007)	71	Undergraduates	Randomly assigned participants to: 1. Loving-kindness intervention 2. No-treatment control ■ Participants in loving-kindness intervention improved on self-compassion and compassionate love at posttest compared with controls and experienced increased self-compassion and decreased anxiety at 2-month follow-up compared with controls.	Loving-kindness intervention used formal training in meditation consistent with Tibetan Buddhist practice

and skin complaints, whereas participants in the attack-resisting intervention experienced reduced shame, skin complaints, and depression.

Another intervention for facilitating self-compassion incorporated a Gestalt two-chair technique to mediate resolution between judged and critical parts of the self (Kirkpatrick, 2005). University students ($N = 80$) were assigned to an intervention or a control condition. For the intervention condition, therapists asked participants to think about a situation in which they had been critical of themselves. After elaborating on the "critical voice," participants were asked to identify thoughts that countered the criticism. After participants had visualized the situation, the therapist introduced them to a two-chair intervention, in which one chair represented the voice of self-criticism and the other chair represented the response to the criticism. The therapist subsequently discussed the experience with participants. In contrast, participants in the control condition received no intervention. Participants completed online measures at pretest, posttest, and follow-up of self-compassion and mental health. Contrary to hypotheses, results showed no intervention effects on self-compassion or mental health.

Another study examined the influence of a loving-kindness intervention on compassion of self and others in undergraduates (Weibel, 2007). Participants ($N = 71$) were randomly assigned to an intervention or a control condition. Participants in the intervention condition, who met in groups of 10 to 12 participants, attended four weekly meditation groups that lasted 90 min each. The intervention consisted of group discussion and practicing mindfulness and loving-kindness meditations consistent with Tibetan Buddhist practice. In addition, participants were instructed to meditate between meeting times and to keep track of their meditation practice in diary entries. Participants assigned to the control group did not receive an intervention. All participants completed measures of self-compassion, compassionate love, and trait anxiety at pretest, posttest, and 2-month follow-up. Results showed that at posttest, participants in the intervention group improved significantly more than control group participants on self-compassion and compassionate love. At follow-up, intervention participants improved more on self-compassion and showed decreased anxiety compared with control participants.

Summary of the Role of Religion and Spirituality in Self-Compassion Interventions

Studies evaluating self-compassion interventions suggest they can increase self-compassion (Weibel, 2007), improve mental health (Kelly et al., 2009; Weibel, 2007), and reduce complaints about a physical condition (Kelly et al., 2009). One study found no beneficial effects of a self-compassion intervention (Kirkpatrick, 2005). Although the findings across studies are mixed, studies showing positive outcomes from self-compassion programs suggest that they may be a useful means of reducing suffering.

Many of the self-compassion interventions utilized mindfulness techniques without explicitly mentioning Buddhist meditation practices. In fact, Gilbert and Procter (2006) noted that compassionate mind training is rooted in social mentality theory (i.e., individuals create different role relationships that activate various physiological processes) rather than Buddhism. In contrast, Weibel (2007) provided instruction on meditation techniques consistent with Tibetan Buddhist practice. More research is needed on how traditional Buddhist meditation practices could enhance the effectiveness of self-compassion interventions. For instance, researchers could compare outcomes after randomly assigning participants to a self-compassion intervention that incorporates traditional Buddhist meditation practices or a self-compassion intervention that excludes traditional Buddhist meditation practices. Self-compassion interventions could be adapted for religious participants from theistic backgrounds. Examples of how self-compassion interventions could be adapted to include religious or spiritual concepts are described in the following section.

Connecting self-compassion with theistic religious and spiritual perspectives. Individuals from religious or spiritual traditions that emphasize God as being compassionate could reflect on how this idea pertains to them. Homework assignments in self-compassion interventions could encourage participants to imagine "seeing themselves" through the eyes of God rather than the self-critical lens they currently are applying. Gestalt "empty-chair" exercises could be used in cases in which participants are instructed to speak to themselves in the same way that they would imagine a spiritual teacher might speak to them. Participants who are having difficulty letting go of negative self-talk might consider imagining themselves surrendering this perspective to God. Interventions could incorporate religiously based rituals designed to help individuals let go of their negative thought patterns in ways that are connected to the sacred.

Connecting self-compassion with nontheistic religious and spiritual perspectives. Individuals from a nontheistic religious perspective may appreciate making self-compassion the focus of meditative practices. Guided or silent meditations could be incorporated into group self-compassion intervention sessions. Alternatively, leaders of self-compassion interventions could encourage participants to listen to audio-recorded guided meditations on self-compassion as a homework assignment. Participants could be asked to read books that provide instruction on self-compassion meditation. For instance, Kornfield (2002), in his book entitled *The Art of Forgiveness, Lovingkindness, and Peace*, described a meditation on self-compassion in which he encourages people to recite the phrases, "May I be held in compassion. May I be free from pain and sorrow. May I be at peace" (p. 126). Germer's (2009) *The Mindful Path to Self-Compassion* is another example of a book with practical suggestions for meditating on self-compassion

SUMMARY OF THE ROLE OF RELIGION AND SPIRITUALITY IN POSITIVE PSYCHOLOGY INTERVENTIONS

As shown by the review, the number of positive psychology interventions that explicitly incorporate religious ideas varies depending on which virtue is being promoted. The virtue with the most research on religiously based interventions is forgiveness. This partly may be due to the fact that forgiveness intervention research has been conducted for the past 2 decades, whereas researchers have only more recently begun to develop and evaluate interventions for the other virtues. Even the majority of published forgiveness interventions, however, do not include explicit religious references. For example, on the basis of a meta-analysis of forgiveness intervention studies conducted in 2005, only two out of 49 interventions included in the study (4.1%) incorporated explicit religious or spiritual elements (Wade et al., 2005).

Religiously integrated hope interventions have not yet appeared in the literature and therefore little is known about whether religious ideas could enhance their effectiveness. Most gratitude interventions have similarly omitted explicit references to religious ideas, although preliminary research has examined the possible role of mindfulness and prayer. Although the self-compassion interventions use mindfulness techniques, they generally do not incorporate training in more formal meditation techniques, such as would be encountered within many Buddhist traditions. Overall, research on the role of religion and spirituality in positive psychology interventions is still at an early stage.

Possible Advantages of Incorporating Religious or Spiritual Content Into Positive Psychology Interventions

Why might researchers and clinicians want to incorporate religious or spiritual ideas into the content of positive psychology interventions? The most important reason would be if religious or spiritually integrated positive psychology interventions were more effective than secular interventions. This has not been proven, however, and the question is rarely a focus of intervention outcome studies. As noted in this chapter, a few studies have shown that when directly compared, religiously integrated and secular interventions have similar outcomes (e.g., Rye & Pargament, 2002; Rye et al., 2005). Other studies have found positive outcomes from interventions that incorporate religious ideas (e.g., Lampton et al., 2005; Stratton et al., 2008; Worthington et al., 2010). Moreover, there is evidence that religious practices such as prayer can promote gratitude (Lambert et al., 2009) and forgiveness (Kidwell, Wade, & Blaedel, 2010; see also Volume 1, Chapter 23, this handbook). Research also has found that some participants draw on their religious beliefs in positive psychology interventions even if not explicitly encouraged by the intervention (Rye & Pargament, 2002; Rye et al., 2005). This raises the question of whether positive psychology interventions can ever be characterized as purely secular. Because many individuals who participate in positive psychology interventions have been exposed to ideas about the virtue from their religious faith, it seems natural that these ideas would influence how they experience the intervention. The most useful question might be whether there are any advantages to explicitly introducing religious and spiritual ideas into positive psychology interventions.

In theory, there are several reasons why explicit introduction of religious and spiritual content into positive psychology interventions might be useful. First, psychologists generally strive to work with clients from within the framework of their clients' existing worldviews. This facilitates the development of rapport, makes it more likely that people will remain in therapy, and helps psychologists to avoid imposing their own belief system on clients. Thus, for religious and spiritual participants, it might make sense to adapt positive psychology interventions so as to be more consistent with their perspectives. Second, some religious participants regard their faith tradition as the only legitimate path to truth, and they may be distrustful of any attempt to disconnect a virtue from the teachings of their faith tradition. Third, religious and spiritually integrated interventions may be especially pertinent when individuals are faced with the limits of their personal control. This idea was emphasized by Pargament (1997), who wrote,

> Religion complements nonreligious coping, with its emphasis on personal control, by offering responses to the limits of personal powers. Perhaps that is why the powers of the sacred become most compelling for many when human powers are put to their greatest test. (p. 310)

Fourth, some individuals may make greater investments and perceive greater benefits in objects or activities that are considered to be sacred (Mahoney, Rye, & Pargament, 2005; see also Volume 1, Chapter 14, this handbook). Pargament and Mahoney (2005) noted that theistic sanctification involves connecting objects, events, or activities to the divine. Sanctification, however, also can occur in nontheistic perspectives, in which a connection is made with that which is transcendent, timeless, of ultimate value, or everlasting. When developing positive psychology interventions, it is important to consider the possible impact of desecration. Desecration occurs when a perceived connection between the human and the divine or transcendent is destroyed (Mahoney et al., 2005). For instance, when an offender commits an act that is perceived as a desecration, it may make it more difficult to forgive. Positive psychology interventions could encourage participants who perceive desecration to rely on their faith to reconnect to the sacred and move toward emotional healing. A summary of possible strategies for helping participants connect their religious and spiritual beliefs to positive psychology interventions are described in the sections that follow.

The role of prayer and meditation. Because prayer is such a common practice among adherents of theistic religions, participants might appreciate having the opportunity to pray in connection with positive psychology interventions. As discussed, in hope interventions, prayer might be used to help participants identify goals, seek divine assistance to find the means for reaching goals, and request divine support and perseverance when encountering difficulties along the way. Because many adherents to theistic religions already incorporate gratitude into their prayer lives, they might be interested in homework assignments that involve prayer. Similarly, prayer could be connected to forgiveness interventions. Participants may wish to pray for the offender or pray for strength while undertaking the process of forgiveness. Prayer could be used to assist individuals who wish to let go of self-judgment and enhance self-compassion.

Practitioners of Buddhism or monotheistic contemplative traditions might be especially receptive to the incorporation of meditation practices into positive psychology interventions (see Volume 1,

Chapters 17 and 35, this handbook). In addition, psychotherapists from a variety of theoretical orientations are beginning to recognize ways in which mindfulness practices can enhance treatment (see Chapter 10 in this volume). As noted, the future orientation of hope might not match well with the present focus emphasis of mindfulness meditation. Mindfulness techniques, however, could be adapted to help individuals enhance gratitude, forgiveness, and self-compassion.

The role of scripture reading. Adherents from both theistic and nontheistic religions often are inspired by the sacred scriptures of their tradition. As noted, the virtues of hope, gratitude, forgiveness, and self-compassion are frequently encouraged in religious scriptures. Moreover, scriptures offer comfort and support for individuals who are facing challenging circumstances. For instance, an individual who has been deeply wronged by an offender and who wishes to forgive might view it as a nearly impossible task given the depth of the wrongdoing that has taken place. Similarly, an offender may be having difficulty with self-compassion because he or she has committed an egregious transgression. Scriptures often provide role models of individuals who have cultivated each virtue. Scriptures also can provide support when encountering challenges. When working with clients who are from the same religious background, religious scriptures could be discussed during the interventions or included in homework assignments. An option when working with participants from different religious backgrounds is to design homework assignments in which they seek out scriptures from their own religious tradition.

The role of religious community. Regardless of whether one practices a theistic or a nontheistic religion, one's religious community is often highly valued and may be perceived as a source of support. The Buddhist community, called *sangha*, is deeply valued and considered to be one of the three jewels of Buddhism (Dalai Lama, 1997). Many Jews, Christians, and Muslims similarly value the support and encouragement they receive from their religious community. Positive psychology interventions could encourage religious participants to obtain support from their religious community when trying to cultivate virtues. Researchers might consider implementing and evaluating positive psychology interventions at the congregational level of analysis. For instance, researchers could compare outcomes between congregations in which sermons focus heavily on virtues such as forgiveness, gratitude, and hope versus congregations in which sermons focus on other topics.

Possible Disadvantages to Explicitly Incorporating Religious or Spiritual Content Into Positive Psychology Interventions

Although there may be benefits to incorporating religious teachings into positive psychology interventions, challenges and pitfalls can arise. For instance, incorporating religious content into positive psychology interventions for children is problematic unless it is delivered in the context of a religious community in which parents have fully consented to the intervention content. Religiously integrated positive psychology interventions for adults also can pose challenges, particularly if the intervention is delivered in a group format. In a group, it can be difficult to incorporate religious content in a way that matches the faith perspectives of all group members, even when they are all from a similar religious background. This problem is compounded when participants come from a variety of different faith traditions. Psychologists need to be sensitive to the fact that some participants have had negative experiences in the past in religious communities and may have encountered judgmental and shaming attitudes. Moreover, some nonreligious participants would be comfortable participating in a religious or spiritually based intervention, whereas others would not. It is important that participants are fully informed of the program content before deciding whether they wish to sign up and have the option to decline to participate if religious components make them uncomfortable. Psychologists also need to be aware that some forms of spiritual coping promoted by religious communities may be harmful, such as negative religious framing (e.g., interpreting events as a sign of God's punishment; Pargament, 2011; see also Volume 1, Chapter 25, this handbook). Finally, psychologists who are unfamiliar with the basic practices of religious participants risk presenting religious material in a way that does not meet their needs or may even be perceived as offensive. Consultations with religious clergy or psychologists who are trained to work with particular religious populations could minimize this possibility.

SUGGESTIONS FOR FUTURE RESEARCH

Although researchers have made progress on understanding how religion can play a role in positive psychology interventions, there is more work to be done. Are there some conditions under which religiously integrated forgiveness interventions are more effective? To what extent are participants in positive psychology intervention drawing on religious coping strategies irrespective of program content? Would religious participants be more inclined to participate in positive psychology interventions and more devoted to completing intervention exercises if the virtues were explicitly connected to the sacred? Under what conditions might the inclusion of religious content be harmful or problematic? Hopefully, researchers will begin to examine some of these questions as research on positive psychology interventions continues to advance.

References

An explanation of the perfect names and attributes of Allah. (n.d.). Retrieved from http://www.jannah.org/articles/names.html

Beals, I. A. (1998). *A theology of forgiveness: Towards a paradigm of racial justice.* San Francisco, CA: Christian Universities Press.

Berg, C. J., Snyder, C. R., & Hamilton, N. (2008). The effectiveness of a hope intervention in coping with cold pressor pain. *Journal of Health Psychology, 13,* 804–809. doi:10.1177/1359105308093864

Berkwitz, S. C. (2003). History and gratitude in Theravada Buddhism. *Journal of the American Academy of Religion American Academy of Religion, 71,* 579–604. doi:10.1093/jaarel/lfg078

Boom, C. T. (2006). *The hiding place: 35th anniversary edition.* Grand Rapids, MI: Baker.

Boucher, J. E. (2002). Telephone intervention: Hope for cancer patients. *Dissertation Abstracts International: Section B. Sciences and Engineering, 63*(1), 174.

Buchanan, C. L. (2008). Making hope happen for students receiving special education services. *Dissertation Abstracts International: Section B. Sciences and Engineering, 69*(3), 1943.

Buck, R. (2004). The gratitude of exchange and the gratitude of caring: A developmental-interactionist perspective of moral emotion. In R. A. Emmons & M. E. McCullough (Eds.), *The psychology of gratitude* (pp. 100–122). New York, NY: Oxford University Press. doi:10.1093/acprof:oso/9780195150100.003.0006

Cheavens, J. S., Feldman, D. B., Gum, A., Michael, S. T., & Snyder, C. R. (2006). Hope therapy in a community sample: A pilot investigation. *Social Indicators Research, 77,* 61–78. doi:10.1007/s11205-005-5553-0

Chödrön, P. (1997). *When things fall apart: Heart advice for difficult times.* Boston, MA: Shambhala.

Dalai Lama. (1997). *The four noble truths.* London, England: Thorsons.

Dorff, E. N. (1998). The elements of forgiveness: A Jewish approach. In E. L. Worthington Jr. (Ed.), *Dimensions of forgiveness: Psychological research and theological perspectives* (pp. 29–55). Philadelphia, PA: Templeton Foundation Press.

Dorff, E. N. (2003). *Love your neighbor and yourself: A Jewish approach to modern personal ethics.* Philadelphia, PA: Jewish Publication Society.

Duggleby, W. D., Degner, L., Williams, A., Wright, K., Cooper, D., Popkin, D., & Holtslander, L. (2007). Living with hope: Initial evaluation of a psychosocial hope intervention for older palliative home care patients. *Journal of Pain and Symptom Management, 33,* 247–257. doi:10.1016/j.jpainsymman.2006.09.013

Emmons, R. A. (2007). *Thanks! How the new science of gratitude can make you happier.* Boston, MA: Houghton Mifflin.

Emmons, R. A., & McCullough, M. E. (2003). Counting blessings versus burdens: An experimental investigation of gratitude and subjective well-being in daily life. *Journal of Personality and Social Psychology, 84,* 377–389. doi:10.1037/0022-3514.84.2.377

Enright, R. D., & the Human Development Study Group. (1991). The moral development of forgiveness. In W. M. Kurtines & J. L. Gewirtz (Eds.), *Handbook of moral behavior and development: Vol. 1. Theory* (pp. 123–152). Hillsdale, England: Erlbaum.

Farrer-Halls, G. (2000). *The illustrated encyclopedia of Buddhist wisdom: A complete introduction to the principles and practices of Buddhism.* Wheaton, IL: Quest Books.

Freedman, S. (1998). Forgiveness and reconciliation: The importance of understanding how they differ. *Counseling and Values, 42,* 200–216. doi:10.1002/j.2161-007X.1998.tb00426.x

Freedman, S. R., & Enright, R. D. (1996). Forgiveness as an intervention goal with incest survivors. *Journal of Consulting and Clinical Psychology, 64*, 983–992. doi:10.1037/0022-006X.64.5.983

Froh, J. J., Kashdan, T. B., Ozimkowski, K. M., & Miller, N. (2009). Who benefits the most from a gratitude intervention in children and adolescents? Examining positive affect as a moderator. *Journal of Positive Psychology, 4*, 408–422. doi:10.1080/17439760902992464

Germer, C. K. (2009). *The mindful path to self-compassion: Freeing yourself from destructive thoughts and emotions*. New York, NY: Guilford Press.

Gilbert, P., & Procter, S. (2006). Compassionate mind training for people with high shame and self-criticism: Overview and pilot study of a group therapy approach. *Clinical Psychology and Psychotherapy, 13*, 353–379. doi:10.1002/cpp.507

Hanh, T. N. (1995). *Living Buddha, Living Christ*. New York, NY: Riverhead Books.

Hebl, J. H., & Enright, R. D. (1993). Forgiveness as a psychotherapeutic goal with elderly females. *Psychotherapy: Theory, Research, Practice, Training, 30*, 658–667. doi:10.1037/0033-3204.30.4.658

Jampolsky, G. G. (1999). *Forgiveness: The greatest healer of all*. Hillsboro, OR: Beyond Words.

Kelly, A. C., Zuroff, D. C., & Shapira, L. B. (2009). Soothing oneself and resisting self-attacks: The treatment of two intrapersonal deficits in depression vulnerability. *Cognitive Therapy and Research, 33*, 301–313. doi:10.1007/s10608-008-9202-1

Kidwell, J. E., Wade, N. G., & Blaedel, E. (2010). *Understanding forgiveness in the lives of religious people: The role of sacred and secular elements*. Manuscript submitted for publication.

Kirkpatrick, K. L. (2005). Enhancing self-compassion using a Gestalt two-chair intervention. *Dissertation Abstracts International: Section B. Sciences and Engineering, 66*(12), 6927.

Kornfield, J. (2002). *The art of forgiveness, lovingkindness, and peace*. New York, NY: Bantam Books.

Krause, N. (2006). Gratitude toward God, stress, and health in late life. *Research on Aging, 28*, 163–183. doi:10.1177/0164027505284048

Lambert, N. M., Fincham, F. D., Braithwaite, S. R., Graham, S. M., & Beach, S. R. H. (2009). Can prayer increase gratitude? *Psychology of Religion and Spirituality, 1*, 139–149. doi:10.1037/a0016731

Lambert, N. M., Fincham, F. D., Stillman, T. F., Graham, S. M., & Beach, S. R. H. (2010). Motivating change in relationships: Can prayer increase forgiveness? *Psychological Science*. doi:10.1177/0956797609355634

Lampton, C., Oliver, G. J., Worthington, E. L., Jr., & Berry, J. W. (2005). Helping Christian college students become more forgiving: An intervention study to promote forgiveness as part of a program to shape Christian character. *Journal of Psychology and Theology, 33*, 278–290.

Mahoney, A., Rye, M. S., & Pargament, K. I. (2005). When the sacred is violated: Desecration as a unique challenge to forgiveness. In E. L. Worthington Jr. (Ed.), *Handbook of forgiveness* (pp. 57–71). New York, NY: Routledge.

Marty, M. E. (1998). The ethos of Christian forgiveness. In E. L. Worthington Jr. (Ed.), *Dimensions of forgiveness: Psychological research and theological perspectives* (pp. 9–28). Philadelphia, PA: Templeton Foundation Press.

McCullough, M. E. (2008). *Beyond revenge: The evolution of the forgiveness instinct*. San Francisco, CA: Jossey-Bass.

McCullough, M. E., Pargament, K. I., & Thoresen, C. E. (2000). The psychology of forgiveness: History, conceptual issues, and overview. In M. E. McCullough, K. I. Pargament, & C. E. Thoresen (Eds.), *Forgiveness: Theory, research, and practice* (pp. 1–14). New York, NY: Guilford Press.

McCullough, M. E., & Tsang, J.-A. (2004). Parent of the virtues? The prosocial contours of gratitude. In R. A. Emmons & M. E. McCullough (Eds.), *The psychology of gratitude* (pp. 123–141). New York, NY: Oxford University Press. doi:10.1093/acprof:oso/9780195150100.003.0007

McCullough, M. E., Worthington, E. L., Jr., & Rachal, K. C. (1997). Interpersonal forgiving in close relationships. *Journal of Personality and Social Psychology, 73*, 321–336. doi:10.1037/0022-3514.73.2.321

McIntosh, E. M. (2008). Noticing and appreciating the sunny side of life: Exploration of a novel gratitude intervention that utilizes mindfulness techniques. *Dissertation Abstracts International: Section B. Sciences and Engineering, 69*(1), 688.

McMinn, M. R., Fervida, H., Louwerse, K. A., Pop, J. L., Thompson, R. D., Trihub, B. L., & McLeod-Harrison, S. (2008). Forgiveness and prayer. *Journal of Psychology and Christianity, 27*, 101–109.

Neff, K. (2003). Self-compassion: An alternative conceptualization of a healthy attitude toward oneself. *Self and Identity, 2*, 85–101. doi:10.1080/15298860309032

Neff, K. D. (2008). Self-compassion: Moving beyond the pitfalls of a separate self-concept. In H. A. Wayment, & J. J. Bauer (Eds.), *Transcending self-interest: Psychological explorations of the quiet ego* (pp. 95–105). Washington, DC: American Psychological Association. doi:10.1037/11771-009

Pargament, K. I. (1997). *The psychology of religion and coping: Theory, research, practice*. New York, NY: Guilford Press.

Pargament, K. I. (2011). Religion and coping: The current state of knowledge. In S. Folkman (Ed.), *The handbook of coping* (pp. 269–288). New York, NY: Oxford University Press.

Pargament, K. I., & Mahoney, A. (2005). Sacred matters: Sanctification as a vital topic for the psychology of religion. *The International Journal for the Psychology of Religion, 15*, 179–198. doi:10.1207/s15327582ijpr1503_1

Poloma, M. M., & Gallup, G. H. (1991). *Varieties of prayer: A survey report.* Philadelphia, PA: Trinity Press.

Reed, G. L., & Enright, R. D. (2006). The effects of forgiveness therapy on depression, anxiety, and post-traumatic stress for women after spousal emotional abuse. *Journal of Consulting and Clinical Psychology, 74*, 920–929. doi:10.1037/0022-006X.74.5.920

Rye, M. S., & Pargament, K. I. (2002). Forgiveness and romantic relationships in college: Can it heal the wounded heart? *Journal of Clinical Psychology, 58*, 419–441. doi:10.1002/jclp.1153

Rye, M. S., Pargament, K. I., Ali, M. A., Beck, G. L., Dorff, E. N., & Hallisey, C.. . . Williams, J. G. (2000). Religious perspectives on forgiveness. In M. E. McCullough, K. I. Pargament, & C. E. Thoresen (Eds.), *Forgiveness: Theory, research, and practice* (pp. 17–40). New York, NY: Guilford Press.

Rye, M. S., Pargament, K. I., Pan, W., Yingling, D. W., Shogren, K. A., & Ito, M. (2005). Can group interventions facilitate forgiveness of an ex-spouse? A randomized clinical trial. *Journal of Consulting and Clinical Psychology, 73*, 880–892. doi:10.1037/0022-006X.73.5.880

Schimmel, S. (2004). Gratitude in Judaism. In R. A. Emmons & M. E. McCullough (Eds.), *The psychology of gratitude* (pp. 37–57). New York, NY: Oxford University Press. doi:10.1093/acprof:oso/9780195150100.003.0003

Sheldon, K. M., & Lyubomirsky, S. (2006). How to increase and sustain positive emotion: The effects of expressing gratitude and visualizing best possible selves. *Journal of Positive Psychology, 1*, 73–82. doi:10.1080/17439760500510676

Siddiqi, M. (2004). *Forgiveness: An Islamic perspective.* Retrieved from http://www.islamawareness.net/Repentance/perspective.html

Smith, H. (1995). *The illustrated world's religions: A guide to our wisdom traditions.* New York, NY: HarperCollins.

Snyder, C. R. (2000). Hypothesis: There is hope. In C. R. Snyder (Ed.), *Handbook of hope: Theory, measures, and applications* (pp. 3–21). San Diego, CA: Academic Press. doi:10.1016/B978-012654050-5/50003-8

Snyder, C. R., Harris, C., Anderson, J. R., Holleran, S. A., Irving, L. M., Sigmon, S. T., . . . Harney, P. (1991). The will and the ways: Development and validation of an individual-differences measure of hope. *Journal of Personality and Social Psychology, 60*, 570–585. doi:10.1037/0022-3514.60.4.570

Stratton, S. P., Dean, J. B., Nonneman, A. J., Bode, R. A., & Worthington, E. L., Jr. (2008). Forgiveness interventions as spiritual development strategies: Comparing forgiveness workshop training, expressive writing about forgiveness, and retested controls. *Journal of Psychology and Christianity, 27*, 347–357.

Trungpa, C. (1996). *Meditation in action.* Boston, MA: Shambhala.

Tsang, J.-A., McCullough, M. E., & Hoyt, W. T. (2005). Psychometric and rationalization accounts of the religion-forgiveness discrepancy. *Journal of Social Issues, 61*, 785–805. doi:10.1111/j.1540-4560.2005.00432.x

Wade, N. G., & Worthington, E. L., Jr. (2005). In search of a common core: A content analysis of interventions to promote forgiveness. *Psychotherapy: Theory, Research, Practice, Training, 42*, 160–177. doi:10.1037/0033-3204.42.2.160

Wade, N. G., Worthington, E. L., Jr., & Meyer, J. E. (2005). But do they work? A meta-analysis of group interventions to promote forgiveness. In E. L. Worthington Jr. (Ed.), *Handbook of forgiveness* (pp. 423–439). New York, NY: Routledge.

Watkins, P. C., Woodward, K., Stone, T., & Kolts, R. L. (2003). Gratitude and happiness: Development of a measure of gratitude, and relationships with subjective well-being. *Social Behavior and Personality, 31*, 431–451. doi:10.2224/sbp.2003.31.5.431

Weibel, D. T. (2007). A loving-kindness intervention: Boosting compassion for self and others. *Dissertation Abstracts International: Section B. Sciences and Engineering, 68*(12), 8418.

Wood, A. M., Maltby, J., Stewart, N., Linley, P. A., & Joseph, S. (2008). A social–cognitive model of trait and state levels of gratitude. *Emotion, 8*, 281–290. doi:10.1037/1528-3542.8.2.281

Worthington, E. L., Jr. (2001). *Five steps to forgiveness: The art and science of forgiving.* New York, NY: Crown.

Worthington, E. L., Jr., Berry, J. W., & Parrott, L., III. (2001). Unforgiveness, forgiveness, religion, and health. In T. G. Plante & A. C. Sherman (Eds.), *Faith and health: Psychological perspectives* (pp. 107–138). New York, NY: Guilford Press.

Worthington, E. L., Jr., Hunter, J. L., Sharp, C. B., Hook, J. N., Van Tongeren, D. R., Davis, D. E., . . . Monforte-Milton, M. (2010). A psychoeducational intervention to promote forgiveness in Christians in the Philippines. *Journal of Mental Health Counseling, 32*, 75–93.

Worthington, E. L., Jr., Scherer, M., Hook, J. N., Davis, D. E., Gartner, A. L., Campana, K. L., & Sharp, C. B. (2007). Adapting a secular forgiveness intervention to include religion and spirituality. *Counselling and Spirituality, 26*, 171–186.

Worthington, E. L., Jr., & Wade, N. G. (1999). The psychology of unforgiveness and forgiveness and implications for clinical practice. *Journal of Social and Clinical Psychology, 18*, 385–418. doi:10.1521/jscp.1999.18.4.385

Worthington, E. L., Jr., Witvliet, C. V. O., Pietrini, P., & Miller, A. J. (2007). Forgiveness, health, and well-being: A review of evidence for emotional versus decisional forgiveness, dispositional forgivingness, and reduced unforgiveness. *Journal of Behavioral Medicine, 30*, 291–302. doi:10.1007/s10865-007-9105-8

PART IV

RELIGION AND SPIRITUALITY APPLIED TO SPECIFIC CONTEXTS

CHAPTER 26

CONSULTATION WITH RELIGIOUS INSTITUTIONS

Thomas G. Plante

One might assume that there is a large literature of high-quality published books, chapters, empirical articles, and reviews about clergy–psychology collaboration and consultation. After all, most Americans (as well as others around the globe) describe themselves as being religiously identified and engaged as well as affiliated with a particular religious tradition. In fact, in each year for the past half century, about 40% of Americans state that they have attended a religious service during the past week (Gallup, 2002). Only 6% of Americans report not being affiliated with a religious or spiritual tradition (Gallup, 2002). More than 80% maintain that they would like to increase and nurture their spiritual development as well (Myers, 2000). So, most clients of psychologists surely must be actively engaged with religious traditions and clergy members. Yet surprisingly little has been published on clergy–psychology (or clergy–mental health professional in general) collaboration and consultation (e.g., Kloos & Moore, 2000; McMinn & Dominquez, 2005; Milstein, Manierre, Susman, & Bruce, 2008; Plante, 1999, 2009; Tyler, Pargament, & Gatz, 1983; Weaver, Flannelly, Flannelly, & Oppenheimer, 2003). In fact, only one scholarly book has been written specifically on this topic as of this date (McMinn & Dominquez, 2005), and most professional articles and chapters that have been published in this area are descriptive rather than empirical. It is odd that so little has been published on this important topic. Why might this be?

Although it is impossible to fully understand all of the factors and motives that have resulted in such a lack of professional literature on clergy–psychology collaboration, several important matters should be taken into consideration that perhaps shed light on this surprising state of affairs. First, although most Americans are religious and spiritual, most psychologists are not. Delaney, Miller, and Bisono (2007) reported that psychologists are "more than twice as likely to claim no religion, three times more likely to describe religion as unimportant in their lives, and five times more likely to deny belief in God" (p. 542) compared with the general population. Although 94% of Americans are affiliated with a religion tradition, only 33% of psychologists are according to research conducted by Shafranske (2000; see also Chapter 2 in this volume). Second, psychologists generally obtain no training in spiritual and religious matters or on consultation with clergy (Plante, 2009; see also Chapters 2 and 33 in this volume). For example, it is incredible that 68% of all internship training directors reported that they "*never* foresee religious/spiritual training being offered in their [APA-accredited clinical internship training] program" (Russell & Yarhouse, 2006, p. 434). This is especially surprising because 66% of medical schools report offering spiritual and religious diversity training (Puchalski, 2004). Thus, compared with the general population, psychologists are much less interested in and engaged by spiritual and religious matters, and they receive no training in the area. Much has been written about the relationship between psychology and religion over the years and why psychologists are less likely to be attentive to religious and spiritual matters both personally and professionally (e.g., Delaney et al., 2007; Pargament, 2007; Plante, 2009; Russell & Yarhouse,

DOI: 10.1037/14046-026
APA Handbook of Psychology, Religion, and Spirituality: Vol. 2. An Applied Psychology of Religion and Spirituality, K. I. Pargament (Editor-in-Chief)

2006; see also Chapter 2 in this volume) and is not be repeated here.

Education about religion and spirituality is critical for practitioners interested in this area, however, because consultation between religious institutions, clergy, and psychologists is unique. Psychologists consult with a variety of organizations, such as for-profit and nonprofit companies, public and private schools, athletic teams, and organizations, and much has been published about psychologists consulting with organizations broadly defined (e.g., Dougherty, 2004; Peltier, 2010; Wallace & Hall, 1996). In fact, Dougherty (2004) categorized six typical consultation roles for psychologists that include acting as an expert, trainer–educator, advocate, collaborator, fact finder, and process specialist, with details and guidance available for each of these roles. Yet unlike consultation with secular organizations, consultation with religious organizations addresses intimate details on how people should or should not live their lives, discusses what they should believe or not believe in, offers perspectives on this life and an afterlife, and raises all sorts of issues not attended to in most organizations. Clergy, for example, are not simply employees of an institution. Often, they are held to very high standards of behavior, and employment laws often do not apply to clergy. For example, in the Roman Catholic tradition, the Church can demand celibacy, obedience, and poverty of their clergy, which does not occur among almost all other institutions and organizations. Psychologists consulting with religious organizations need to be mindful of the unique situation they are in as well as the lack of quality research and writing available on this topic.

A PERSONAL REFLECTION

During the past 25 years I have worked closely with the Roman Catholic Church and, more recently, the Episcopal Church in the United States and Canada as a practicing clinical psychologist and as a psychology professor at Santa Clara University (a Roman Catholic and Jesuit university in the San Francisco Bay Area). These collaborative efforts have mostly involved four issues. First, I conduct psychological screening evaluations of applicants to ordained ministry for those who wish to become priests, deacons, and religious brothers or sisters through a wide range of religious orders and dioceses. These screening evaluations include conducting clinical interviews, administering psychological tests, and consulting with religious superiors such as bishops, vocation and formation directors, religious order provincials, and seminary rectors and presidents to help them determine whether applicants to ministry are psychologically healthy or pose any significant risks to themselves or others (e.g., alcoholism, pedophilia or other sexual disturbance, personality disorders). Second, I evaluate, treat, and consult with clergy who have found themselves in significant distress because of a variety of psychological, behavioral, or relational issues. These may include depression, anxiety, sexual indiscretions, alcohol or other substance abuse problems, impulse-control troubles, and conflicts with congregants or religious superiors. Third, Roman Catholic and Episcopal clergy often refer troubled congregants to my practice. Perhaps because they know that I work closely with these denominations and am an active and engaged Roman Catholic myself, they believe that I will understand their theological perspectives on a variety of moral and behavioral topics and will respect the religious traditions, structures, and beliefs that often are very important not only to clergy members but also to many congregants. Fourth, I serve on several local and national review boards, including as a member and vice chair of the National Review Board of the U.S. Council of Catholic Bishops (USCCB). In this role, I regularly consult on the Roman Catholic Church's efforts to ensure that all children, youth, and vulnerable others are safe within the Roman Catholic Church; that clergy applicants are appropriately and competently screened for psychological and behavior problems; and that clergy showing any risks for harming others are quickly removed from ministry, evaluated, and treated, if necessary.

Over several decades, my part-time clinical practice has become almost exclusively involved with these four issues pertaining to collaboration and consultation with these religious institutions. I did not set out to specialize in consultation with the Roman Catholic and Episcopal Churches. In fact, my plans were to specialize in behavioral medicine. Although I worked in the behavioral medicine area for several years, more and more requests for consultation with religious institutions emerged over time. I believe my practice changed, in part, because few psychologists are interested in close ongoing collaboration with religious institutions. Furthermore, as noted, few psychologists have any graduate or postgraduate training in religious issues and religious diversity. Because there is no clear advanced educational pathway to this type of consultation, those interested in this field must work hard to find their own way to obtain appropriate training and experience. Finally, in my experience, it appears that few psychologists are actively engaged with the major religious traditions. For example, although more than 90% of Americans reports that religion is important in their lives, less than 50% of psychologists do (Gallup, 2002; Shafranske, 2000). So, although I would like to think that so many clergy and religious institutions seek my services because they are of such high quality and are so useful, I may be busy with this kind of work simply because I am one of the only shops in town.

This is an unfortunate state of affairs. In many ways, clergy and religious institutions can benefit from ongoing and close collaboration with psychologists. Also, psychologists can often benefit from ongoing and close collaboration with clergy and religious institutions. It can be a win–win situation for both parties. With these issues in mind, the purpose of this chapter is to discuss what we know about psychological consultation with religious institutions and what principles may be most helpful in this type of work. Typical problems and conflicts are highlighted as well. Finally, I call for more research and writing about the collaboration between psychological and religious communities and institutions.

THREE TYPICAL PRACTICAL APPLICATIONS OF CONSULTATION BETWEEN PSYCHOLOGISTS AND RELIGIOUS INSTITUTIONS

To develop a sense of typical collaboration and consultation between psychologists and the religious community, let us examine several practical illustrations of this important work. These and all of the case examples in this chapter are real, but details have been altered to ensure confidentiality.

Case Example 1

Rabbi Janet is the head rabbi at a local Reform Jewish temple and has been worried about some of the teens in her congregation. The local public high school has had several suicides in recent months, including a Jewish student from a nearby temple. Rabbi Janet asked Dr. A, a psychologist who is also a member of the congregation, if she could consult with her to better care for the teens in the Jewish community and to develop a plan to identify at-risk youths. Dr. A met with the education staff and other rabbis at the temple to learn about their concerns in more detail. She then worked with them to develop a multifaceted program to help identify at-risk youths and provide programming for better managing stress and depression for teens in the congregation as well as a program for concerned parents. The staff also provided names and contact information for teens who appear to be severely stressed or who might experience suicidal ideation so that they would have someone to call day or night 7 days per week. Dr. A also developed a list of professionals in the community for private referrals.

In this example, Rabbi Janet used the expertise of a member of her congregation, a psychologist, to help her better serve the needs of the teens and parents in her religious community. Dr. A was careful to offer helpful consultation and had the advantage of knowing a great deal about not only psychology and professional mental health education and intervention services but also the congregation because she had been a member of the temple for many years. Dr. A avoided potentially exploitive dual relationships by not treating individual congregants in her temple herself but instead by securing an appropriate list of professionals in the local community who she believed could serve individual clients well.

Rabbi Janet was grateful to have a trusted professional psychologist available for consultation so that the temple could do all that they could to help their congregation and assist those who might be at risk for self-harm.

Case Example 2

Father Mark is highly stressed as a Roman Catholic priest working in a local parish. The parish is a large one and is very diverse ethnically and socioeconomically. He is confronted with many people in his parish who come to him for spiritual direction and guidance but who appear to have severe problems with marital and family relationships, job stress, alcohol troubles, and suicidal impulses. One of his congregants was killed in a domestic violence conflict that shook Fr. Mark to the core because he had counseled the victim just a few weeks earlier. Fr. Mark freely admits that he does not have the expertise to help those with such serious mental health issues. He consults with Dr. B, a local psychologist who works with many parishioners, to help him figure out how to respond to those who seek his care. Although Roman Catholic himself, Dr. B is not a member of this particular church parish. He evaluates, treats, and consults with many of the parishioners that Fr. Mark refers to him. He also meets with Fr. Mark periodically to consult with him about how he, as a priest and pastoral counselor, can better assist his congregation. Dr. B has provided Fr. Mark with other referral contacts who can help with specialty services, such as drug and alcohol abuse treatment, child protection services, and neuropsychological evaluation services. Dr. B also has recommended particular books and conferences that congregants might benefit from as well as community resources. Additionally, Fr. Mark feels relieved that he can call Dr. B at any time to consult on congregants he is worried about or who he believes need mental health services.

In this example, Fr. Mark feels overwhelmed with the mental health needs of his large and diverse parish. Although he can provide spiritual and pastoral support, he knows that he can get in over his head quickly when it comes to significant psychological, behavioral, and relationship problems and feels relieved that he can consult with a trusted professional psychologist who understands and appreciates his church and religious traditions. Because Dr. B is not a member of Fr. Mark's parish, he feels that he does not need to worry about potentially exploitive dual relationships and can readily refer congregants in need of mental health services and consultation to Dr. B (assuming that they have concerns within the training and competence of Dr. B). Fr. Mark also feels that Dr. B can be an excellent resource when questions and issues emerge about mental health–related, child protection, and substance abuse issues.

Case Example 3

Elizabeth is highly engaged with her Episcopal church. She has served on the vestry, helps with the food pantry program, and has been involved with prison ministry for many years. Now that she is planning to retire from her administrative job at the local hospital, she is interested in the deaconate program wishing to become an ordained minister in the church. After an interview with her local bishop, she was referred to Dr. C, a clinical psychologist who does a great deal of work with the church, for a psychological screening evaluation to determine whether she is psychologically suitable for ordained ministry. Dr. C reviews her autobiographical information and resume, conducts a clinical interview, and administers several psychological tests (e.g., Minnesota Multiphasic Personality Inventory; Sixteen Personality Factors Questionnaire; Millon Clinical Multiaxial Inventory; Forer Sentence

> Completion). He then provides Elizabeth with feedback and sends a confidential written evaluation summary report to the bishop. Dr. C does not tell the bishop whether he should accept Elizabeth in the deaconate formation training program, but he does provide a summary of her psychological and personality functioning and identifies potential risk factors that the bishop should consider.

In this example, Dr. C provides a psychological screening evaluation for a local Episcopal bishop to help him determine the suitability of applicants to ordained ministry in the church. Anyone who has the public trust, such as an ordained minister, could violate that trust and harm others. Thus, the bishop (as well as many religious superiors in various religious institutions and communities) consults with a psychologist to evaluate the clergy applicant for psychological or behavioral dysfunctions that might result in harm to others. These also include risk factors for potential psychiatric troubles as well as alcoholism, sex offending, impulse-control disorders, and personality disorders. The bishop also appreciates being able to ask Dr. C questions about how to best manage psychological and behavioral issues that emerge among ordained clergy or those in formation and to secure consultation services as needed.

WHAT CAN WE LEARN FROM THESE THREE EXAMPLES?

These three case examples are fairly typical for psychologists who collaborate with clergy and religious institutions. Clergy often confront congregants with serious psychosocial stressors or significant behavioral, relational, or psychological conflicts, issues, and crises. Other than immediate family members and perhaps very close friends, clergy are typically the frontline professionals to whom people turn times of need, including psychological, emotional, and relational crises (McMinn & Dominquez, 2005; Plante, 1999, 2009). Religious institutions must select applicants to ministry who can be trusted with others, especially vulnerable others such as children, the disabled, elderly, and those from poor, oppressed, and marginalized backgrounds. Thus, those experiencing certain significant behavioral or psychological dysfunction (e.g., sex offenders) should be screened out of working as trusted ordained ministers. Clergy usually readily acknowledge that their seminary training did not prepare them very well to deal with the complex mental health and behavioral problems with which they are often confronted during the course of their pastoral work. Although clergy obtain a good deal of pastoral counseling training while in seminary formation, they usually do not secure the kind of training needed to become licensed mental health professionals. Furthermore, their training rarely includes material related to major psychopathology. Thus, having readily available consultation with psychologists (and other mental health professionals) can be invaluable to their ministry. This important relationship, however, is not just a one-way street with only clergy benefiting from psychological expertise.

Psychologists and other mental health professionals can greatly benefit by closely working with clergy, too. For example, they can make further gains with their religious clients when clergy have been appropriately consulted. Clergy can help psychologists better understand the context of their religious community, beliefs, and traditions and the role that their faith community and practices plays in their client's lives. They can learn how religious and spiritual perspectives and rituals can be integrated into their efforts to help their clients manage their psychological, behavioral, and family troubles and concerns. They can coordinate clinical care with clergy members especially because faith-based social services offer so many community services, such as food pantries, soup kitchens, health clinics, immigration counseling, and legal services. They can help psychologists develop a deeper appreciation of how spiritual and religious approaches can be used to answer challenging life questions and place life's challenges into a broader context and perspective. Clergy can teach psychologists a great deal about the benefits and sometimes pitfalls of religious and spiritual engagement. Thus, there is much to be gained from mutual consultation (McMinn & Dominquez, 2005; Plante, 1999, 2009).

ETHICAL MANDATES

Being attentive to religious and spiritual matters, skilled in consultation with religious professionals, and sensitive to religious diversity is also a mandated ethical concern. The *Ethical Principles of Psychologists and Code of Conduct* (the Ethics Code; American Psychological Association [APA], 2002), which is the current and most updated version of the Ethics Code for the APA and its members, states that

> psychologists are aware of and respect cultural, individual, and role differences, including those based on age, gender, gender identity, race, ethnicity, culture, national origin, religion, sexual orientation, disability, language, and socioeconomic status and consider these factors when working with members of such groups. (p. 1064)

Therefore, being "aware of and respect(ful)" of religious issues is now encouraged by the Ethics Code in the same manner that psychologists must be aware of and respectful of other diversity issues.

Additionally, psychologists must be responsible and competent. One could argue that just as it is appropriate and responsible to consult with colleagues in other relevant fields that affect our client services such as medicine, law, and education, psychologists should consult with clergy as needed. Typically, mental health professionals feel comfortable consulting with physicians, attorneys, school teachers, and guidance counselors, among others who might be working with their clients. Multidisciplinary collaboration and consultation is likely to be more of the norm rather than the exception. Furthermore, the APA (2002) Ethics Code states that "when indicated and professionally appropriate, psychologists cooperate with other professionals in order to serve their clients/patients effectively and appropriately" (Section 3.09) and that they "consult with, refer to, or cooperate with other professionals and institutions to the extent needed to serve the best interest of those with whom they work" (Principle B). Thus, it is expected that psychologists will consult with colleagues and professionals (including institutions) as needed. These guidelines and expectations include clergy and religious institutions as well.

MANAGING A SUCCESSFUL CONSULTATIVE PROFESSIONAL RELATIONSHIP WITH CLERGY

McMinn and several colleagues (Chaddock & McMinn, 1999; McMinn et al., 1998, 2003) have offered some of the few empirical studies in this area. They completed a national interview survey project with both clergy and psychologists to better understand the elements and nature of their consultation relationship and experiences with one another. After carefully evaluating their data, McMinn and Dominquez (2005) provided some principles to best nurture the consultation relationship between psychologists and clergy. These include highlighting (a) the relationship, (b) communication, (c) respect, (d) common values and goals, (e) complementary expertise, (f) psychological and spiritual mindfulness, and (g) trust. Their useful and empirically evaluated principles focus on the need to develop a respectful, trusting, collaborative, and collegial relationship in which participants are able to articulate common goals and values. Other researchers have also underscored the need for mutual trust, respect, and understanding (e.g., Weaver et al., 2003). Both psychologists and clergy must have a significant degree of spiritual and psychological mindfulness as well as a willingness to come together in collaboration to help clients seeking their respective services.

What is meant by spiritual and religious mindfulness? Although psychologists generally receive little if any training on spirituality and religion during the course of their graduate and postgraduate training (unless they specifically seek it out), they must develop a sensitivity to and appreciation for spiritual and religious matters to work successfully and collaboratively with clergy as well as religiously engaged clients. Perhaps they regularly read and study in this area, consult with colleagues actively engaged with spiritual and religious issues and clients, and secure what training and experiences are available to them through workshops, courses, and ongoing peer supervision. There is a wide literature regarding the psychology of religion and spirituality, and psychologists can well educate themselves in this literature though journal and book reading and engagement with appropriate organizations that specialize in this area (e.g., APA Division 36 [Society for the Psychology of Religion and Spirituality]). Informal and more formal mentoring and consultation with experts is available as well through these organizations and listservs too. In fact, both psychologists and clergy can be found as members of Division 36 and related organizations.

Similarly, although clergy generally receive little training in psychology (unless they seek it out) they too must learn to have an appreciation for and sensitivity to psychological and behavioral factors and issues to work successfully with psychologists and other mental health professionals. They might seek additional training, reading, and consultation to better understand the psychological and behavioral factors and influences on their congregants and others with whom they work.

McMinn et al. (2003) further outlined both basic and advanced consultation relationships; basic services highlight communication, respect, and shared goals and more advanced consultation focuses on spiritual and psychological mindfulness as well as the development and nurturance of mutual trust. Therefore, a successful collaborative and consultative relationship between psychology and clergy must be one that develops the kind of mutual respect and trust in any ongoing professional collegial relationship with common values and goals and at least some appreciation for the skills that are offered by each other. Although McMinn et al. offered advice that is useful for any potential collaborative relationship (e.g., with legal, medical, educational, athletic professionals), what makes working with clergy unique and special is the religious and spiritual foundation of the collaboration work. Ancient traditions, practices, and reflections on some of the biggest life questions provide the context within which the collaborative relationship unfolds. Religious traditions and their representative clergy offer thoughtful reflections and advice on most of the troubles affecting people who may seek services of a psychologist. Because the majority of people are engaged with their religious and spiritual tradition and do consult with clergy about life troubles and decisions, psychologists must be aware of and thoughtful about engaging with those so influenced by these traditions and communities. Although it may sound fairly easy to follow these useful principles offered by McMinn et al., several conflicts and problems frequently emerge in clergy and psychology consultation.

THREE COMMON PROBLEMS AND CONFLICTS WITH PSYCHOLOGY–CLERGY CONSULTATION

Conflicts and problems with consultation usually fall into one of the following three categories: (a) conflicts regarding values and goals, (b) confidentiality, and (c) boundary issues. Although these conflicts are likely found within any organizational consultation relationship, they may take distinctive forms in consultative work with religious institutions and clergy.

Conflicts Regarding Values and Goals

Psychologists may have goals of evaluation and treatment that directly conflict with the goals supported by clergy and the particular religious community and tradition involved. This may be the case with certain values as well. For example, a psychologist might be working with a client toward separation and divorce when a spouse is physically, sexually, or emotionally abusive, whereas a member of the clergy, acting as a pastoral counselor or spiritual director, might insist that divorce is not an option. Or perhaps a long-time marital couple without any particular traumas or major conflicts within the marriage have gradually grown apart and seek divorce to pursue other adult relationships and personal growth. The psychologist might support the divorce to maximize client happiness and personal development, whereas the clergy member may not. Another example might include the understanding by a psychologist that marital partners should have equal say about family matters, whereas a clergy person might insist that the man may dominate a woman in a relationship because of religious traditions, customs, and beliefs. A psychologist might help a pregnant teen learn about possible options for her pregnancy, including abortion, whereas a member of the clergy might insist that abortion is never an option regardless of the circumstances of the pregnancy and parties involved. A variation on this theme might include the engagement of a young couple in premarital sexual activity. A psychologist might expect that premarital sexual activity or masturbation is normal among young adults or those in their late teens, whereas a clergy member may see both premarital sex and masturbation as sins to be avoided. Therefore, there may be many ways that psychological treatment goals and values could directly conflict with those of clergy. These conflicts can be devastating for clients who are pulled in two opposite directions by psychologists and clergy. Unlike the likely issues found among most secular institutions, many of the conflicts that emerge in consultation with religious organizations can involve highly intimate and personal behaviors, such as sexual expression.

It is critical for psychologists and clergy to discuss these potential value and goal conflicts in advance to minimize the possible damage they might cause for clients. For example, clients might be conflicted and confused when their psychologist supports one course of action that is not supported by their clergy member (e.g., divorce, abortion, sexual expression outside of marriage). Certainly, psychologists and clergy may not always agree on a course of action for their client–congregant. Sometimes agreeing to disagree in a respectful manner is the best that one can hope for when these conflicts are unavoidable and undeniable. Psychologists and clergy may not always be on the same page, but they can work respectfully together anyway.

One challenging and contemporary example that I regularly experience in my work with the Roman Catholic Church is the issue of homosexual men pursuing ordained ministry in the priesthood. The Roman Catholic Church has made it clear that homosexual men are not invited to enter seminary and become priests (see Congregation for Catholic Education, 2005, for details). The church has a variety of reasons for this policy, which are beyond the scope of this chapter to detail. Interested readers may wish to read about this issue in more depth elsewhere (for details, see Coleman, 2004; Congregation for Catholic Education, 2005; Plante, 2004). Additionally, women and married men are not invited to become Roman Catholic priests either. The church can rather easily screen out women and married men for seminary without the need for psychological services. They cannot, however, as easily screen out homosexual men. Psychologists, working in concert with the APA (2002) Ethics Code and other policy documents, are forbidden to discriminate on the basis of race, ethnicity, gender, and sexual orientation and yet are asked to participate in the church's efforts to ensure that only celibate heterosexual men enter seminary. This conflict is also complicated by the fact that somewhere between 25% and 45% of Catholic priests are homosexual (Plante, 2007a, 2007b) and that many church leaders privately do not agree with this Vatican policy (Coleman, 2004).

Psychologists asked to conduct psychological screening evaluations for the Roman Catholic Church (including myself) must do so in a manner that is consistent with professional ethics yet respectful of religious diversity and the perspectives of the Roman Catholic church (Plante, 2007a, 2007b). One way to manage this possible dilemma is to not include comments about sexual orientation in the psychological evaluation reports but rather focus on the results of the psychological testing, clinical interview, and the assessment of potential risk factors, such as any history of psychiatric disturbance, impulse-control disorders, and sexual disorders. This may collude with a "don't ask, don't tell" policy, but there may be no way to resolve some dilemmas that emerge with church policies and procedures. Perhaps an important goal is to discuss this dilemma with church officials to develop an evaluation plan that is consistent with psychological professional ethics yet still respectful of the policies of the church (Plante, 2007a). For example, because Vatican policy clearly prohibits men with homosexual orientations from entering seminary, psychologists ethically should not be used to "out" homosexuals for the church. The APA (2002) Ethics Code certainly does not apply to nor likely interest the Vatican. Psychologists may wish to assist the church in screening psychological healthy applicants to the clergy and identifying those at risk of harming others (e.g., sex offenders) but not be put in the position of identifying the sexual orientation of applicants. Certainly this issue may bring up conflicts for the psychologist doing evaluations as well as for homosexual applicants who believe that they are called to the priesthood and can manage sexual impulses in the seminary as ordained priests. The acceptability (and discrimination) regarding homosexuality is a potentially conflictual issue unique to particular religious institutions and is unlikely to occur with consultations for secular institutions that must follow antidiscrimination laws. The following example may help the reader better appreciate the challenges of clergy–psychologist collaboration and consultation when there may be a conflict of goals and values.

Case Example 4

Dr. D is providing psychotherapy services to Dawn, a 15-year-old pregnant high school freshman. Her parents are conservative Roman Catholics who are terribly upset about the pregnancy. Their parish priest was emotionally supportive when they consulted with him, and he strongly encouraged them to consider adoption as the best path for Dawn to follow. He mentioned that abortion is never an option, period. Dawn, however, would like to have an abortion and does not want to bring the child to term. Her boyfriend and his family, who are more secular and nonpracticing Roman Catholics, agree with the abortion option as well. Dr. D listens carefully to the family's concerns, and they discuss both the advantages and the disadvantages of abortion. With the family's permission, Dr. D and the parish priest discuss the situation in detail and, although respectful of each other's point of view, maintain opposing views on abortion as a possible solution to the dilemma. Dr. D and the priest communicate to the family that although they respect and appreciate each point of view, they must respectfully disagree about the abortion option. They explain to the family why they have the views that they do and hope that the family can make a decisions that is helpful to them even when the professionals involved have differing perspectives.

In this common example, Dr. D and the parish priest thoughtfully and respectfully consult with each other about abortion as a possible solution for Dawn have to agree to disagree about abortion being a viable option for her. They maintain opposing goals and values about abortion as a possibility to the challenge of an unwanted teenage pregnancy. In the end, Dawn and her parents must weigh various points of view and decide for themselves how best to proceed. They do, however, appreciate that the psychologist and priest consulted with each other and tried to find common ground in their recommendations. Although a consensus of opinion did not emerge through this consultation, the process of the consultation and discussion assisted the family in thinking through the issues for themselves more thoughtfully before making a difficult decision.

Confidentiality

Any time multiple persons and disciplines are involved in consultation, confidentiality may be compromised in one way or another. Different disciplines often have different points of view about the terms and limits of confidentiality. Often, psychologists are highly vigilant and restrictive about confidentiality, and this rigorous attention to and protection of confidential material may frustrate other professionals during consultation. Therefore, it is very important that the expectations and understanding about confidentiality are carefully considered and articulated (perhaps both orally and in writing) with clients as well as consulting professionals such as clergy who are engaged in collaboration with psychologists.

For example, in my consultation work with religious institutions, I must make very clear to all parties when conducting evaluations that the resulting information and report will be submitted to a religious superior, such as a bishop, provincial, or formation and vocation director. The person being evaluated must fully understand this and agree to these terms before an evaluation can be conducted. In treatment with clergy or congregants referred by clergy, confidentiality must be understood and maintained as well so that those who are receiving professional psychological services know that what they say in treatment will not get back to the referring clergy member without their oral and written permission. The following case example underscores the challenges of managing confidentiality in clergy–psychologist consultation.

Case Example 5

Dr. E, a psychologist, provides couples counseling for those in marital distress. One of his clients is a well-known and popular politician who has engaged in marital infidelity with several women. The couple and their children are also active in a local Presbyterian church that is one of the largest and more active churches in the community. The couple has met with their pastor regarding their marital distress who referred them to Dr. E. Dr. E maintains strict confidentiality in accordance with ethical and legal guidelines. With appropriate permission from the couple, the pastor and Dr. E consult with each other about how they can work together to help the family. The pastor later mentions the marital infidelity troubles to several people who also work at the church, including his administrative assistant and choir director. Within a few days, local media report in the newspapers that the couple are having marital problems and are seeking professional counseling to help work them out. Dr. E is mentioned in the article by name and several reporters call Dr. E for comment. Dr. E refuses to comment on the case and situation and then speaks with the pastor about confidentiality issues. Dr. E then approaches the couple to inform them that he did not violate confidentiality and to work through their upset with the pastor regarding letting others know of their marital troubles.

Routine office gossip can easily compromise professional confidentiality. Although psychologists are likely to be attentive to professional confidentiality, other professionals including clergy, administrative assistants, choir directors, and youth ministers may maintain different views on confidentiality within a particular religious community and tradition. Psychologists cannot control the behavior of other professionals and cannot be responsible for the kind of breach that occurred in the Case Example 5. They can, however, discuss expectations about confidentiality with those with whom they work in a respectful and professional manner to try and maximize the chances that others will agree with the confidentiality arrangements and expectations that the psychologist endorses. This could be accomplished both orally and in writing.

Boundary Issues

As in most organizations and social environments, clergy typically use the professional services of those they know and trust. Why go to a stranger for most services when you can go to a friend or trusted acquaintance? For example, clergy often get to know the members of their congregations very well and thus naturally feel more comfortable referring to professionals from within the ranks of their own church community. So, it is common to have church congregants obtain all sorts of professional and personal services from fellow members of their church community. This is often true for dentists, plumbers, doctors, lawyers, accountants, and other professionals and service workers alike. Therefore, psychologists who happen to be congregants of a particular faith community are very likely to receive professional referrals, including consultation requests from clergy within their own faith tradition and community. If a clergy member is concerned about the family functioning or mental health of a congregant, it is easy to spend a few minutes after Church services or a committee meeting talking to a psychologist who happens to be at these services and events who the clergy member may know and trust well. This situation creates many challenging boundary concerns that must be thoughtfully considered. Problematic and exploitive dual relationships can unfold quickly. The psychologist likely wants to help his or her faith community and clergy but also wants to avoid problematic boundary violations as well. Again, a case example illustrates these boundary concerns.

Case Example 6

Through her participation in volunteer, social, and liturgical activities at her local Jewish temple, Dr. F has come to know the rabbi there. Dr. F has become a member of the board of the directors of the temple and has become well acquainted with members of the local Jewish community. Because Dr. F is also a skilled psychologist and a warm, friendly, and engaging person, people tend to be drawn to her and perceive her as the Jewish community's "shrink." The rabbi relies on her for diverse consultations about many issues that she experiences with members of the Jewish community. Dr. F was initially honored to be thought of as such an important resource and "go-to" person in the community. Yet, her life has become more complicated now that the rabbi wants to discuss her troubles with congregants who are Dr. F's friends. Dr. F also now finds that some of her current and past clients are on the same committees on which she serves.

When clergy members depend on the expertise of psychologists who are members of their religious communities, boundary issues and conflicts will emerge and emerge quickly. There is no avoiding it. However, psychologists have to anticipate these potential boundary challenges and manage them in a way to avoid potentially exploitative dual relationships. They might consider, for example, avoiding treating fellow congregants unless there is a highly compelling reason to do so, such as when they are the only competent professional with a particular and unique skill set in rural environments. Psychologists must be attentive to the possibility of exploitative dual relationships yet still be respectful and thoughtful of the desire of clergy to refer cases to them and consult with them about fellow congregants.

THREE PRINCIPLES FOR SUCCESS IN CLERGY–PSYCHOLOGIST CONSULTATION

Psychologists should be mindful of several critical principles when consulting with clergy and religious institutions to increase the odds of successful collaboration. This section highlights what perhaps are the three most important principles: (a) mutual respect and reciprocity, (b) understanding and appreciating the faith tradition, and (c) requesting and securing corrective feedback.

Mutual Respect and Reciprocity

Although it might appear obvious that that consultation between clergy and psychologists must be based on mutual respect and reciprocity, there are too many instances in which consultation and collaboration is destroyed by a lack of respect and lack of reciprocity. For example, too often psychologists (as well as other mental health professionals) find particular religious tradition's policies, procedures, beliefs, and structures to be unacceptable, odd, and just plain wrong. For example, many feel that the Roman Catholic's insistence that only heterosexual celibate men should be priests, thus excluding women, homosexuals, and married persons, is archaic. Some also feel that the prohibition on eating pork products and insistence on following kosher dietary laws by Jews is rather odd. Regardless of what a psychologist might think about the policies, procedures, perspectives, and beliefs of religious traditions and the individuals within these traditions, it is critical that they work toward respect and reciprocity when working with clergy and religious institutions. Sadly, some psychologists and other professionals behave in a manner that suggests that they have all of the answers, and the clergy or religious institution has little to offer the consultation relationship. Psychologists and other professionals can sometimes act in a paternalistic manner toward religious groups. In fact, recent survey research has provided evidence that mental health professionals are perceived as being arrogant with clergy by not seeing them as professionals who offer much to the consultation relationship (McMinn et al., 2003). McMinn et al. (2003) reported that 13% of clergy in their survey described experiences with psychologists that were not respectful. For example, one clergy stated, "I felt like he had no respect for what I could bring to the issue," and added,

> The psychologist seemed to project an attitude that he was the professional and I was just a simple preacher. He thought he knew best and did not need or want my input and would not care to develop any professional relationship. (McMinn et al., 2003, p. 199)

Mutual respect and reciprocity is fundamental for any consultation relationship. Additionally, it is expected from the Ethics Code as well (APA, 2002). Collaboration must rest on a belief in the professional relationship as a partnership of equals, with each participant offering an important and beneficial piece to the collaborative puzzle. A spirit of learning from each other, working as a team, and mutual respect and reciprocity has to permeate all communications and engagement (McMinn & Dominquez, 2005; Plante, 2009). The following example illustrates this important principle.

> **Case Example 7**
>
> Dr. G and Rabbi B closely consult with each other on a regular basis concerning family crises that typically occur before a wedding or a bris (ritual circumcision). Dr. G focuses her clinical practice on families and couples, whereas Rabbi B manages a large urban temple that includes numerous interfaith couples and families. Rabbi B has observed that frequently the non-Jewish members of the family or extended family are conflicted about the upcoming ceremony. Periodically, the conflicts turn into a family crisis when families or couples wonder whether they should cancel the event. Sometimes extended family members increase the crisis when important persons in the family adamantly refuse to attend the ceremony event or are protesting it. Rabbi B is grateful for Dr G's skill and expertise and appreciates that they can work together to help solve many of these crises. Because Dr. G is Jewish and in an interfaith family as well, she enjoys being able to help and finds this work meaningful and important. Dr. G and Rabbi B work closely and collaboratively together in a respectful and reciprocal manner.

Understanding and Appreciating the Faith Tradition

Although psychologists cannot be expected to be experts on religion or on all of the various religious and spiritual traditions, they must have a solid working understanding of the faith traditions with which they work. They must be conversant in the history, beliefs, customs, and diversity of perspectives held within these faith communities. They need to know enough to be effective in their services and avoid insensitive, disrespectful, and false assumptions. If the psychologist is a knowledgeable and engaged member of a particular tradition and thus has significant personal experiences with a certain religious group, then it may be a natural fit to consult with clergy from that religious tradition and from those traditions that may be similar. Of course, being a member of a religious tradition and community does not make one an expert, and thus psychologists who are engaged with their religious and spiritual traditions need to be sure that they are competent to offer services that go beyond their membership in a congregation. Dr. G in Case Example 7 is a good example. If psychologists know nothing about the faith group that they are being asked to consult with, they need to make that clearly known to the clergy from that community to determine whether they are the appropriate persons to do this work or whether another referral to a more appropriate psychologist is necessary.

Many religious traditions and communities can be highly complex in terms of their theology, traditions, dogmas, customs, and worldviews, and the diversity among subgroups can be overwhelming. Therefore, it is critical for psychologists to closely monitor their areas of competence and skills obtaining appropriate consultation themselves to ensure competent and responsible professional service.

Additionally, there is a wide literature now available regarding the psychology of religion and spirituality. It would be important for psychologists working in this field to be mindful of this literature, read the professional journals available, consult with colleagues engaged in this field, and attend conventions and workshops that are frequently offered as well. Let us consider two case examples highlighting this point.

Case Example 8

Dr. H is both a psychologist as well as a Mormon bishop. In addition to his doctoral degree in counseling psychology, he has a divinity degree. He regularly consults with Mormons in his local community, focusing his work on family and couples issues. Naturally, he is well aware of Mormon beliefs and traditions and finds that this information and familiarity provides him with a clearer understanding of the issues that Mormon couples and families experience. He also regularly consults with other Mormon bishops and church elders in a large geographic and multistate region and assists with marriage preparation and family education programming offered by the church.

Case Example 9

Dr. I is a practicing psychologist as well as a deacon in her local Episcopal church. During midlife after her children were grown, she decided to attend divinity school given her interests in her faith tradition, which ultimately led to her ordination as a deacon. She is active in the homeless community and ran a soup kitchen and food pantry early in her career. She regularly consults with the local bishop and vocation committees about strategies to screen and select church leaders and ordained ministers. She also helps with policies and procedures to ensure that those who work with children are appropriately screened and trained. Additionally, when psychiatric or family crises emerge in her diocese, clergy, including the local bishop, feel that they can count on her to guide them.

In these two case examples, the psychologists are actively engaged in their respective religious traditions (in these particular cases, they are ordained ministers), and their comfort with and understanding of their religious traditions and communities can be put to good use in their professional work as psychologists. The consultation fit is comfortable and natural for them. Of course, they need to be mindful of the possibilities of dual relationships in their work. Unforeseen consequences and awkward moments are possible when religiously and spiritually engaged psychologists active within their faith communities see clients from the same communities.

Requesting and Securing Corrective Feedback

It is always important to secure ongoing corrective feedback that can better ensure that the collaborative consultation working relationship is effective and that all parties (e.g., clergy, religious institutions, psychologist, congregants, and clients) are indeed getting what they hoped from the collaborative professional relationship. Typically, unless professionals directly requests feedback, they will not obtain the information needed to foster an effective and satisfying collaborative consultative relationship. Often, clergy and members of religious institutions are very polite, and thus negative feedback is given silently by having referrals withheld and consultation requests atrophy. It is critical that psychologists solicit corrective feedback and, perhaps even more important, that they are willing to adjust their services, policies, and professional practices to the feedback that they receive. Ensuring that the clients' consultation needs are being addressed and met will increase the quality (and quantity) of satisfying professional consultations with clergy and religious groups.

Case Example 10

Dr. J always informs his clergy and religious institution clients that he wants to ensure that their needs are being adequately met regarding their collaborative consultation work and that he would appreciate any feedback about his services. He frequently and routinely uses a brief client satisfaction questionnaire, includes a statement about feedback with each report and invoice sent out, and informally asks for feedback during meetings. Dr. J usually receives feedback and tries to respond nondefensively. He adjusts his professional services and practices to accommodate to the helpful feedback.

CONSULTATION WITH RELIGIOUS INSTITUTIONS REGARDING POLICIES, PROCEDURES, AND SYSTEMS IMPROVEMENT

Psychologists often consult with clergy and religious institutions on policies, procedures, and systems improvement in addition to consultation regarding individual clients, congregants, or clergy applicants as discussed throughout this chapter thus far. Psychologists and religious institutions often work closely together to develop programs for premarital preparation, marital communication, and intervention (e.g., Sullivan & Karney, 2008), child development programming, parenting issues, and other matters (McMinn & Dominquez, 2005).

Because most of my experience in this area involved the Roman Catholic Church and policies and procedures regarding clergy sexual abuse, I will highlight this area as an illustration of religious institution consultation that seeks to result in systems-wide improvements that are national and international in scope.

Following the clergy sexual abuse crisis in the Roman Catholic Church beginning in 2002, many steps were taken to safeguard children. Now all Catholic diocese across the United States as well as most of the religious order (e.g., Jesuit, Franciscan, Carmelite) provincial offices have local review boards that include psychologists as well as other appropriate professionals (e.g., attorneys, social workers, probation and law enforcement officers, canon lawyers, child advocates) to assist the church in developing policies and procedures for child safety. According to these policies, all church workers (clergy and nonclergy alike) are appropriately screened and evaluated before working with children. Also, all church workers (most especially ordained ministers such as priests) who are accused of sexual misbehavior are now immediately withdrawn from ministry, evaluated and treated as needed, and do not return to active ministry with the public unless they were cleared by appropriate child protection, legal, and mental health professionals. Additionally, these professionals are now asked to provide victims with services offered and paid for by the church (USCCB, 2002).

In addition to these local review boards, the USCCB, representing all of the Catholic dioceses throughout the United States, created a national review board. The board's purpose is to help develop policies and procedures to keep children safe in the church as well as to see that offending priests or other ordained ministers (e.g., deacon) are permanently removed from ministry if they have harmed a child. The highest ranking female at the Federal Bureau of Investigation was selected to be the first executive director of the office that manages this review board. As a psychologist who specialized in clergy abuse and the evaluation of applicants to the clergy, I currently serve as a member and vice chairperson of the national review board. Several other psychologists are also members of the board as well.

Psychologists work with the USCCB to assist the national church in developing policies and procedures so that the dioceses throughout the United States adequately train their employees, clergy, volunteers, and congregants (including children and parents) in child protection and safety through programs that are specifically designed for each population. Psychologists also help in developing guidelines to evaluate applicants to ordained ministry, evaluating and treating possible sex offending clergy, and establishing additional policies and procedures that are articulated in documents produced by the USCCB (2002). In doing so, psychologists work closely with the highest level of the administrative structure of the Catholic Church in the United States through the USCCB, drawing on the best available science and practice of psychology to increase the safety of children and vulnerable others in the church. Child safety in the Catholic Church includes a wide variety of new programs, policies, and procedures that are beyond the scope of this chapter to detail. They include, for example, safe environment training for all adult volunteers and employees of Catholic institutions, a zero-tolerance policy for any clergy or church worker with a credible accusation of child abuse or maltreatment, and complete psychological and legal background checks for all those interested in ordained ministry. Interested readers should review related documents from the USCCB (2002) for additional details.

PROMISING AREAS FOR FUTURE RESEARCH AND PRACTICE

As mentioned, there is a surprising lack of quality research concerning clergy–psychology consultation. Therefore, much work needs to be done in this area. It is important to develop a better understanding of those practices and programs that currently are working well. Thus, those psychologists who practice in this area should be encouraged to publish their experiences and what data they do have in quality professional outlets. Additionally, survey research from clergy and religious institutions concerning their experience of collaboration with psychology could better inform our work. Psychologists who regularly interact with clergy and religious institutions may wish to collaborate and compare notes themselves. It appears that most professionals engage in these efforts in isolation from each other. There are no professional organizations and conferences that bring these professionals together for ongoing collaboration or discussion. Informal collaboration is what generally occurs.

The clergy–psychology consultation relationship certainly has many rewards and challenges. Religious institutions provide an important and often-critical context for the lives of many people and also represent a mechanism for outreach to people with a variety of concerns and issues relevant to the professional practice of psychology. Additionally, many people would not seek psychological consultation or services of any kind on their own but perhaps would be open to services offered through their religious institutions or endorsed by their religious leaders. Religious leaders such as clergy are usually at the front lines of most of the challenges that people face and typically benefit from ongoing consultation with psychologists. Psychologists also have much to learn from the wisdom offered by clergy. Overall, consultation between clergy and psychologists can be a win–win situation, which both parties find to be satisfying and meaningful.

References

American Psychological Association. (2002). Ethical principles of psychologists and code of conduct. *American Psychologist, 57*, 1060–1073. doi:10.1037/0003-066X.57.12.1060

Chaddock, T. P., & McMinn, M. R. (1999). Values affecting collaboration among psychologists and evangelical clergy. *Journal of Psychology and Theology, 27*, 319–328.

Coleman, G. (2004). Clergy sexual abuse and homosexuality. In T. G. Plante (Ed.), *Sin against the innocents: Sexual abuse by priests and the role of the Catholic Church* (pp. 73–84). Westport, CT: Praeger/Greenwood.

Congregation for Catholic Education. (2005). *Instruction concerning the criteria for the discernment of vocations with regard to persons with homosexual tendencies in view of their admission to the seminary and to holy orders*. Vatican City, Italy: Author.

Delaney, H. D., Miller, W. R., & Bisono, A. M. (2007). Religiosity and spirituality among psychologists: A survey of clinician members of the American Psychological Association. *Professional Psychology: Research and Practice, 38*, 538–546. doi:10.1037/0735-7028.38.5.538

Dougherty, A. M. (2004). *Consultation: Practice and perspectives in school and community settings* (4th ed.). Pacific Grove, CA: Brooks/Cole.

Gallup, G. H., Jr. (2002). *The Gallup poll: Public opinion 2001*. Wilmington, DE: Scholarly.

Kloos, B., & Moore, T. (2000). The prospect and purpose of locating community research and action in religious settings. *Journal of Community Psychology, 28*, 119–137.

McMinn, M. R., Aikins, D. C., & Lish, R. A. (2003). Basic and advanced competence in collaborating with clergy: Survey findings and implications. *Professional Psychology: Research and Practice, 34*, 197–202. doi:10.1037/0735-7028.34.2.197

McMinn, M. R., Chaddock, T. P., Edwards, L. C., Lim, R. K. B., & Campbell, C. D. (1998). Psychologists collaborating with clergy: Survey findings and implications. *Professional Psychology: Research and Practice, 29*, 564–570. doi:10.1037/0735-7028.29.6.564

McMinn, M. R., & Dominquez, A. W. (2005). *Psychology and the church*. Hauppauge, NY: Nova Science.

Milstein, G., Manierre, A., Susman, V. L., & Bruce, M. L. (2008). Implementation of a program to improve the continuity of mental health care through clergy outreach and professional engagement (C. O. P. E.). *Professional Psychology: Research and Practice, 39*, 218–228. doi:10.1037/0735-7028.39.2.218

Myers, D. (2000). *The American paradox: Spiritual hunger in a land of plenty*. New Haven, CT: Yale University Press.

Pargament, K. I. (2007). *Spiritually integrated psychotherapy: Understanding and addressing the sacred*. New York, NY: Guilford Press.

Peltier, B. (2010). *The psychology of executive coaching: Theory and application* (2nd ed.). New York, NY: Routledge.

Plante, T. G. (1999). A collaborative relationship between professional psychology and the Roman Catholic Church: A Case study and suggested principles for success. *Professional Psychology: Research and Practice, 30*, 541–546. doi:10.1037/0735-7028.30.6.541

Plante, T. G. (Ed.). (2004). *Sin against the innocents: Sexual abuse by priests and the role of the Catholic Church*. Westport, CT: Praeger/Greenwood.

Plante, T. G. (2007a). Ethical considerations for psychologists screening applicants for the priesthood in the Catholic Church: Implications of the Vatican instruction on homosexuality. *Ethics and Behavior, 17*, 131–136. doi:10.1080/10508420701378073

Plante, T. G. (2007b). Homosexual applicants to the priesthood: How many and are they psychologically healthy? *Pastoral Psychology, 55*, 495–498. doi:10.1007/s11089-006-0051-0

Plante, T. G. (2009). *Spiritual practices in psychotherapy: Thirteen tools for enhancing psychological health*. Washington, DC: American Psychological Association. doi:10.1037/11872-000

Puchalski, C. (2004). Spirituality in health: The role of spirituality in critical care. *Critical Care Clinics, 20*, 487–504. doi:10.1016/j.ccc.2004.03.007

Russell, S. R., & Yarhouse, M. A. (2006). Religion/spirituality within APA-accredited psychology predoctoral internships. *Professional Psychology: Research and Practice, 37*, 430–436. doi:10.1037/0735-7028.37.4.430

Shafranske, E. P. (2000). Religious involvement and professional practices of psychiatrists and other mental health professionals. *Psychiatric Annals, 30*, 525–532.

Sullivan, K. T., & Karney, B. R. (2008). Incorporating religious practice in marital interventions: To pray or not to pray? *Journal of Social and Clinical Psychology, 27*, 670–677. doi:10.1521/jscp.2008.27.7.670

Tyler, F. B., Pargament, K. I., & Gatz, M. (1983). The resource collaborator role: A model for interactions involving psychologists. *American Psychologist, 38*, 388–398. doi:10.1037/0003-066X.38.4.388

U.S. Council of Catholic Bishops. (2002). *Charter for the protection of children and young people*. Washington, DC: Author.

Wallace, W. A., & Hall, D. L. (1996). *Psychological consultation: Perspectives and applications*. Pacific Grove, CA: Brooks/Cole.

Weaver, A. J., Flannelly, K. J., Flannelly, L. T., & Oppenheimer, J. T. (2003). Collaboration between clergy and mental health professionals: A review of professional health care journals from 1980 through 1999. *Counseling and Values, 47*, 162–171. doi:10.1002/j.2161-007X.2003.tb00263.x

Chapter 27

ADDRESSING RELIGION AND SPIRITUALITY IN HEALTH CARE SYSTEMS

Michelle J. Pearce

The integration of religion and spirituality and health care is not a new concept. Modern-day health care systems began with the efforts of the Eastern Orthodox Christian church in 370 C.E. There was no need for discussion on how to most appropriately integrate religion and health because the two were seen as naturally coexisting. Indeed, many of the health care providers were priests and monks. Illness was understood in spiritual terms until the 17th century, when the mind–body dualism proposed by Descartes became the prevailing model of health. At that time, illness began to be understood in biological, material terms. It was not until the past few decades that the spirit was once again seen as relevant to medicine and health care. Proponents of a holistic understanding of health argue that health is more than proper biological functioning; it is the existence of right relationships between all facets of being: biological, emotional, mental, social, and spiritual (Sulmasy, 2002). Healing, in this context, means attending to the disrupted relationships within and between each of these dimensions.

This holistic understanding of health mirrors the public's demand for more than diagnoses, prescriptions, and medical interventions from their doctors and health care systems. Patients want to be cared for, and caring is increasingly understood to result from the emotional connection between the patient and the physician, not just the mending of the body. One of the ways in which this emotional and relational connection is formed is by attending to the nonbiological or nonmaterial dimensions of being, such as the spiritual. Within the holistic model of health, attending to the spiritual dimension of patients may mean helping patients come to terms with questions of pain and suffering, creating meaning and purpose, and attending to ways in which illness has affected the patients' spiritual relationships and identity.

Psychologists play an important role in the holistic care model and in the management of health and physical illness. The major contributors to mortality in the Western world are chronic diseases, such as heart disease, obesity, and diabetes. Chronic diseases are related to lifestyle and health behaviors and account for 75% of total health care expenditures (Centers for Disease Control and Prevention [CDC], 2010). Indeed, behavior is the primary determinant of overall health status (Alto, 1995). One of the strengths psychologists bring to the health care setting is their expertise in predicting and managing behavior. Furthermore, research has shown that behavioral medicine interventions for a number of health problems are cost saving, improve clinical outcomes, and reduce high-risk health behaviors (e.g., Friedman, Sobel, Myers, Caudill, & Benson, 1995). Therefore, the contribution of psychologists in the health care setting, through collaboration and the integration of psychological knowledge and techniques, is an increasingly important part of holistic care.

The chapter is divided into four main sections. The first part of this chapter presents and elaborates on the many ways in which religion and spirituality are relevant to health care. In the second section, several programmatic spiritual interventions for

DOI: 10.1037/14046-027
APA Handbook of Psychology, Religion, and Spirituality: Vol. 2. An Applied Psychology of Religion and Spirituality, K. I. Pargament (Editor-in-Chief)

patients and providers implemented within the health care setting are reviewed as examples of best practices. A discussion of the opportunities for psychologists within these contexts follows. The third section discusses the particular challenges associated with the integration of religion and spirituality in health care systems. The chapter concludes with clinical- and research-based recommendations to advance integrative work in health care systems. Although distinctions have been made in the literature between the concepts of religion and spirituality (for an extended discussion, see Volume 1, Chapter 1, this handbook), the terms are combined in this chapter (i.e., *religion/spirituality*, abbreviated hereafter as R/S) because both concepts are relevant to much of the content discussed. When research is reviewed that specifically studied only one of the two concepts, that term is used rather than R/S.

RELEVANCE OF R/S IN HEALTH CARE

Numerous researchers and clinicians have addressed the question of whether R/S should be part of the clinical encounter. Proponents argue that it should be, asserting that regardless of whether practitioners consider themselves religious or spiritual people, R/S shapes many individuals' worldview, values, morals, decision making, and framework for meaning and purpose, and, for some, R/S provides a sense of identity or essence. These proponents argue that the separation of R/S and health care is illusionary because neither patients nor physicians leave their faith traditions, moral commitments, and worldview behind when they step into the physician's office (Curlin & Hall, 2005). In contrast, critics argue against addressing R/S in the clinical encounter, asserting that to do so wastes precious clinical time, invades privacy, threatens patient autonomy, crosses professional boundaries, trivializes religion, and could be perceived as coercion or proselytism, resulting in potential harm to patients (Sloan, Bagiella, & Powell, 1999).

After reviewing the current literature in this area, it seems clear that whether R/S should be part of the clinical encounter is no longer the right question to be asking. Rather, the literature supports the notion that R/S is and will be a part of the clinical encounter whether or not it is acknowledged. As such, this chapter will argue that it is important to understand how R/S influences the participation of patients and providers, including psychologists, in the health care system, and what the most appropriate and effective ways are to address and manage R/S issues at the patient, programmatic, and systemic levels. There are at least seven reasons why R/S is important and relevant to the provision of health care.

Individual R/S Is Related to Health

The first is that individuals' R/S beliefs and practices are related to their health, well-being, and use of health services. Specifically, many empirical studies have documented a relationship between R/S and greater self-esteem, social support, life satisfaction, happiness, hope, quality of life, optimism, adaptation to bereavement, and meaning as well as less anxiety, depression, loneliness, substance abuse, and suicide (Koenig, McCullough, & Larson, 2001). Other studies show that religious attendance is associated with reduced mortality (e.g., Hummer, Rogers, Nam, & Ellison, 1999) and that religious involvement is associated with better disability outcomes and lower use of hospital services by medically ill adults and bereaved caregivers (Pearce et al., 2002).

R/S Is Important to Many Americans

Second, R/S is an important part of many American's lives. A recent national Gallup poll revealed that 96% of Americans believe in God; 44% have attended church, synagogue, or temple in the past week; and 84% reported that spirituality is "very" to "somewhat" important to them (Princeton Religion Research Center, 2005). Consideration should be given to the role of R/S in health care if for no other reason than it is relevant and important to a majority of the population.

R/S Is a Resource to Cope With Illness

A third reason why R/S is relevant to health care is that many people turn to R/S to cope with illness, and the R/S coping strategies they choose can affect their health and mortality. People often respond to stress in terms of R/S language, attitudes, practices, and sources of spiritual support (Pargament, 1997).

R/S beliefs and practices can have a positive influence on patients' and caregivers' attitudes, hope, optimism, and quality of life and can provide a helpful narrative framework for meaning and purpose (e.g., Pargament, Koenig, Tarakeshwar, & Hahn, 2001; Pearce, Singer, & Prigerson, 2006; see also Chapters 8 and 19, this volume). One study revealed that 90% of medical patients reported that spiritual beliefs and practices are important ways of coping and understanding illness (Koenig, 1998). Other research suggests that patients who have a deep sense of meaning and purpose in life may be better able to cope with illness and live longer (Pargament, 1997). Older adults who indicate that religion is very important to them are also more likely to report that they are very satisfied with their health care, even after controlling for demographic, social, and health variables (Benjamins, 2006).

For some, the onset of illness may result in the questioning of one's faith. Research has shown that a significant minority of patients and their caregivers experience an R/S struggle, such as questioning God's benevolence and sovereignty, feeling punished by the divine, and expressing disappointment in faith community members (Pargament et al., 2001; Pearce et al., 2006; see also Volume 1, Chapter 25, this handbook). R/S struggles are associated with anxiety, depression, poorer quality of life and physical health, and even greater mortality over a 2-year period (Pargament et al., 2001). In contrast, other studies have shown that for some, R/S struggles can be related to stress-related and spiritual growth (Tarakeshwar & Pargament, 2001).

Beliefs Influence Medical Decision Making and Adherence

A fourth reason R/S is relevant to health care is that patients' and providers' R/S beliefs and practices influence their medical decision making, including decisions about end-of-life issues, medication use, birth control, vaccinations, and blood transfusions. In a study of 177 pulmonary clinic outpatients, 45% reported that their religious beliefs would influence their medical decision making if they became seriously ill (Ehman, Ott, Short, Ciampa, & Hansen-Flaschen, 1999). In another study of cancer patients, the patients' religiosity was associated with greater desire for life-sustaining interventions (Balboni et al., 2007). Physicians' R/S beliefs also influence the type of care they provide. For example, physicians with higher levels of religious beliefs are less likely to endorse and assist patients with morally controversial procedures, such as assisted suicide (e.g., Meier et al., 1998).

Medical adherence is also influenced by R/S beliefs. One study found that adherence rates were 2.6 times higher among patients whose physicians took the time to gain a holistic understanding of them than among patients whose physicians did not (Safran et al., 1998). A physician who inquires about spiritual issues is demonstrating to the patient that she cares about him as a whole person. This increases trust and satisfaction with care, which is related to a greater likelihood of following medical advice (Thom, Ribisl, Stewart, Luke, & Stanford Trust Study Physicians, 1999) and less health service use (Hall & Dornan, 1990). In addition, engagement in health behaviors is associated with the commitment to a faith practice. For example, those who report greater religiousness tend also to report less cigarette, alcohol, and drug use, and less premarital sexual activity (Donahue & Benson, 1995).

Patients Want Their Physicians to Address R/S Issues

A fifth reason supporting integration is the fact that 41% to 94% of patients *want* their physicians to address R/S issues in their health care encounters (Daaleman & Nease, 1994; Ehman et al., 1999; MacLean et al., 2003). In a national Gallup survey (Gallup Organization, 2002), 70% of adults surveyed reported that it was very to somewhat important to have a physician who is spiritually attuned to them. Although this percentage is highest for those who are the most religious, even 45% of nonreligious patients reported a desire for their physicians to make a polite inquiry regarding their spiritual beliefs (Moadel et al., 1999).

Patient desire is not matched by physician behavior, however. For example, a survey of 921 patients and family members in residency training sites and a private group practice in northeastern Ohio found that 83% of patients wanted their physicians to ask about spiritual beliefs in at least some circumstances, but only 9% had ever had their physicians make such an inquiry (McCord et al., 2004). Patients' desire for physician inquiry depends on the severity of the illness setting and the intensity of the interaction. A number of studies indicate that people voice a greater desire to discuss spiritual issues at the end of life (e.g., Ehman et al., 1999; McCord et al., 2004). MacLean et al. (2003) found that patients' desire decreased when the intensity of the interaction moved from simple discussion of spiritual issues (33% agree) to silent prayer (28%) to physician prayer with a patient (19%).

Patients and Health Care Providers Have R/S Needs

A sixth reason for the importance of the integration of R/S and health care is that both patients and health care workers report having spiritual needs (e.g., Balboni et al., 2007; Pearce, Coan, Herndon, Koenig, & Abernethy, 2012). Patients particularly report having spiritual needs when facing serious and terminal medical illness. For example, in a survey study by Fitchett, Burton, and Sivan (1997), more than three quarters of the surveyed hospitalized psychiatric and medical inpatients reported three or more spiritual needs. Some research has shown that meeting patients' spiritual needs is related to greater positive health outcomes, quality of life (e.g., Balboni et al., 2007; Daaleman, Williams, Hamilton, & Zimmerman, 2008), and satisfaction with care (Pearce et al., 2012).

Addressing R/S Is Required

Finally, the integration of R/S and health care is relevant and important because numerous medical guidelines, regulations, codes of ethics, and criteria for institutional accreditation (e.g., Institute of Medicine, National Hospice and Palliative Care Organization, International Council of Nurses; see also the Joint Commission on Accreditation of Healthcare Organizations [Joint Commission], 2001) now require health care providers to address patients' spirituality and spiritual needs. For example, the Joint Commission, a major health care accrediting agency, now mandates spiritual assessment, documented in the medical record, of each patient in a number of settings, including hospitals, homecare organizations, long-term care facilities, and certain behavioral health care organizations (Joint Commission, 2001). In 1998 the American College of Physicians concluded in a consensus conference that it is the physician's responsibility to be attentive to all dimensions of their patients' suffering, including psychosocial, spiritual, and existential suffering (Lo, Quill, & Tulsky, 1999). The guidelines for the American Psychiatric Association state that professionals are to respect patients' beliefs and rituals without enforcing a diagnosis or using treatment that is at odds with the patients' morality. Furthermore, psychologists and psychiatrists are ethically mandated to exhibit spiritual competency, which is a form of cultural competency. The World Health Organization (WHO) also has stated that spirituality is a key dimension of quality of life (WHO, 2003). Clearly, there are a variety of ways in which R/S intersects and influences health and health care, including the interpretation of symptoms, adherence to treatment, choice of coping strategies, and the types of desires and needs patients have when they are ill.

Despite the well-supported reasons explored thus far and health care providers' general agreement that they should be attentive to and respectful of religious commitments, physicians and nurses are often reluctant to do so (Ellis, Vinson, & Ewigman, 1999), as are psychologists (Kaut, 2002), and these health care providers feel less responsible for spiritual distress compared with other types of distress (Kristeller, Zumbrun, & Schilling, 1999). Moreover, physicians and nurses infrequently make referrals to chaplains (Sulmasy, Geller, Levine, & Faden, 1992). One study of advanced cancer patients revealed that patients had spiritual needs, but that for the majority of these patients, these needs were not being met by their religious communities or the medical system (Balboni et al., 2007). The reasons providers give for not addressing spiritual issues include fear of projecting their own beliefs, lack of time or training, difficulty identifying patients' desires, assumption that patients will self-refer, lack of provider's own religious belief, and being overburdened with competing demands (Ellis et al., 1999; S. G. Post, Puchalski, & Larson, 2000). Among those who agree that R/S should be integrated in the health care setting, there is little consensus on how providers should inquire about or address religious concerns.

REVIEW OF INTEGRATIVE CLINICAL APPLICATION AND BEST PRACTICES

Integration of R/S at the Systemic Level of Health Care

Lest too bleak a picture be painted regarding the current state of integration, a number of subspecialties in medicine, including nursing; oncology; hospice and palliative care; and, more recently, psychiatry have emphasized the integration of R/S into clinical practice. Over the past few decades, a burgeoning of research and clinical interest has emerged for the integration of R/S in psychotherapy. Numerous texts and articles have been written outlining the various ways R/S influences therapists, clients, and treatment methods as well as the development of spiritually based mental health treatments (for reviews, see B. C. Post & Wade, 2009). Little research has been conducted within the field of psychology on the integration and application of R/S in medical health care settings, despite the fact that ample research documents the relationship between R/S and physical health. A few researchers have made a compelling case for the role psychologists can and should play in palliative care (Kaut, 2002; Moss & Dobson, 2006). One potential contributing factor to this deficit of research may be the fact that psychology students and interns receive minimal education and training in R/S diversity and interventions (Hage, Hopson, Siegel, Payton, & DeFanti, 2006). In addition, psychologists tend to be less religious than the population they serve (see Chapter 2 in this volume). In a recent survey, 48% of psychologists reported that religion was not very important in their life, compared with only 15% of the public surveyed (Delaney, Miller, & Bisono, 2007).

Programmatic Innovations of R/S in Health Care

A few empirical studies in the past decade have explored programmatic spiritually oriented innovations in health care organizations for both patients and health care providers. The most promising of these innovations are reviewed as well as their impact on patients and providers. This section begins with a general overview of the assessment of R/S needs in health care settings, which is seen by some as a powerful intervention in and of itself, communicating to the patient that his or her spiritual identity and needs are important and respected (Koenig, 2002). Although the "best practices" in programmatic spiritual innovations in health care settings have not been conducted by or involved psychologists, the opportunities that exist for psychologists will be explored.

Spiritual history and assessment instruments. The Joint Commission (2001) has mandated that all hospitalized patients receive a spiritual assessment and has recommended that at minimum this assessment should consider important R/S beliefs and practices and denominational affiliation. This initial assessment can be part of the social history and is used to determine whether further assessment or intervention is needed. Spiritual assessment helps to identify what patients value and why, what motivates them, and who is part of their support system (Koenig, 2002). It has been recommended that inquiries emphasize the functional nature of patients' R/S beliefs and practices rather than focusing on the content of their worldview. Psychologists can play an important role in taking a R/S history. Psychologists often are afforded more time to spend with patients. As such, they are well positioned to develop a trusting relationship in a safe atmosphere, which provides the foundation for sharing deeply personal information, such as one's R/S.

A number of brief assessment tools with catchy acronyms have been created to help health care providers better understand the role R/S plays in their patients' lives and their experience of illness. The HOPE assessment tool queries about sources of *hope*, the role of *organized* religion, the patient's *personal* spirituality and practices, and the *effects* of spirituality on care and decision making (Anandarajah & Hight, 2001). The FICA assessment tool is used to inquire about *faith* and beliefs, the *importance* of spirituality, the spiritual *community* of support, and how the patient wishes these issues to be *addressed* (S. G. Post et al., 2000). R/S struggles and challenges also need to be assessed and addressed. One study found that 15% of the medical patients queried reported having moderate to high levels of religious struggle and that this was associated with higher levels of depression and emotional distress (Fitchett et al., 2004). Some have cautioned against too readily trying to ameliorate R/S distress, citing evidence that spiritual crises often result in the development, not the destruction, of faith (Walter, 1997).

Depending on what information is gleaned from the initial assessment, health care providers can pursue a number of different options depending on their level of comfort and training. Some will not wish to pursue anything other than taking the spiritual history and making a referral to a chaplain, clergy, or pastoral counselor, should the need arise. Indeed, the primary role of providers is to listen, support, validate, and encourage (Koenig, 2002). Other providers may feel comfortable with additional actions, such as linking the patient with R/S support (e.g., members of their faith community), providing R/S resources (e.g., spiritual literature such as the Bible or Qur'an, rosary beads, religious programming), encouraging spiritual practices and rituals (e.g., scripture reading, prayer, meditation, music, nature walks), helping the patient to draw strength and comfort from their beliefs, and engaging in silent prayer (Hodge, 2004). If it becomes apparent that R/S is not relevant to the patient, the inquiry can change to address sources of meaning and purpose, coping strategies, hope, resilience, gratitude, and social resources (Koenig, 2002), all of which are topics with which psychologists are familiar and comfortable discussing.

The act of practitioners praying openly for or with patients on their behalf is likely the most controversial spiritual intervention. Some believe that health care providers should never pray with their patients (Lawrence, 2002; Sloan et al., 1999). Others think it is appropriate in some cases, such as when the provider has beliefs similar to the patient's beliefs or when a thorough spiritual history has been taken revealing that the patient desires prayer (Koenig, 2002). Much has been written on psychologists' use of prayer and other explicit R/S strategies in psychotherapy, although not in medicine; some psychologists endorse and even encourage the use of these practices (e.g., Richards & Bergin, 2005; Tan, 1996), whereas others argue these practices are questionable and detrimental (McMinn, 1996). Studies have reported that a wide range of patients (from 28% to 67%) have a positive attitude toward physicians praying with their patients (Oyama & Koenig, 1998). When providers decide to pray for their patients, who are aware of their efforts, it is advised that the prayer be short, supportive, comforting, and consistent with the beliefs of the patient (Koenig, 2002).

R/S intervention for patients. A handful of studies have addressed ways that integrating R/S into patient care may affect medical outcomes for those obtaining primary care, palliative care, and oncology services. Patient outcomes have included satisfaction with care, mental health, sense of meaning, physical symptoms, spiritual well-being, quality of life, and health care utilization. For instance, in a study of 90 outpatients with advanced congestive heart failure, those who received services from palliative medicine consultation teams that included spiritual support by a chaplain reported more improvement in dyspnea, anxiety, and spiritual well-being as well as a decrease in primary care and urgent care visits relative to a control group (Rabow, Dibble, Pantilat, & McPhee, 2004). Because the multidisciplinary intervention also included advance care planning, family caregiving training, and psychosocial support, however, it is unclear whether the chaplain visits embedded in the intervention were directly related to outcomes or only indirectly related through other elements of the comprehensive care.

In another study, 69 patients with life-threatening medical conditions participated in a 12-month intervention group focused on acknowledging the central role of R/S in the process of dying and coping and on equipping patients with strategies for living well despite their illness (Miller, Chibnall, Videen, & Duckro, 2005). Intervention patients reported significantly fewer depressive symptoms and feelings of meaninglessness and better spiritual well-being than did control patients. The authors concluded that medical care that supports the spiritual dimension of patients' health improves the spiritual and emotional well-being of patients at the end of life.

A randomized-controlled trial of 137 family practice patients demonstrated that 90% of patients accepted their physician's offer to briefly pray for them. This offer did not have a significant short-term impact on patient satisfaction scores (Mann et al., 2005). Patients were primarily African American females, a more religious subset of the general population (Levin, Taylor, & Chatters, 1994), and thus the generalizability of these results is unknown.

In another intervention study, oncologists engaged in a brief (i.e., 5–7 min) and broadly focused semistructured exploration of R/S concerns with 118 patients and offered R/S resources, such as a chaplain visit or support group, if indicated (Kristeller, Rhodes, Cripe, & Sheets, 2005). The intervention did not require the oncologists, who were of differing religious faiths (i.e., Christian, Hindu, Sikh), to have specific knowledge or R/S training, and 85% rated themselves as comfortable during the inquiry. Seventy-six percent of the patients found the inquiry useful, and after 3 weeks, they reported decreased depressive symptoms, greater improvement in quality of life, and more satisfaction with the care provided by their oncologist than patients who did not receive the brief R/S inquiry. Thus, raising spiritual issues with patients can be done sensitively, effectively, and in a time-sensitive manner, and doing so improves the doctor–patient relationship and the patients' well-being.

R/S interventions for health care professionals. Several studies have investigated ways in which spiritual care training and provision affect health care professionals, including physicians, nurses, staff, and medical students. These studies examined the impact on mental health, empathy, compassion for self and the dying, competency in providing spiritual care, work satisfaction, work-related stress, and spiritual well-being.

Those who provide care for the dying must confront suffering and death on a daily basis. Although it can be a rewarding experience, the risk of burnout and job-related stress is heightened because these providers must face their own mortality and grapple with existential issues. Inquiring about and attending to the spiritual issues of their patients may benefit health care providers by allowing them the opportunity to connect with their patients at a different, more intimate level. Qualitative research among family medicine residents revealed almost unanimous agreement that discussing spiritual issues contributes to better health and physician–patient relationships (Olson, Sandor, Sierpina, Vanderpool, & Dayao, 2006). A study of 215 hospice team members found that job satisfaction was significantly related to transforming and integrating one's spirituality at work. Spirituality without integration and application did not have a direct impact on job satisfaction (Clark et al., 2007). Weaver, Flannelly, and Flannelly (2001) found that delivering spiritual care caused nurses to consider their own spirituality and become more self-aware, which can increase sensitivity to their patients' spiritual needs (Sawatzky & Pesut, 2005).

Several studies have examined ways in which spiritually based interventions affect health care professionals' coping skills and mental health. Wasner, Longhorn, and Borasio (2005) offered a 3.5-day spiritual care training for palliative care professionals aimed at helping them to better recognize and compassionately respond to suffering and death. They found that 6 months after the training, participants reported significant improvements in self-perceived compassion for the dying, compassion for oneself, satisfaction with work, reduction in work-related stress, and spiritual well-being.

In a randomized controlled trial, spiritual passage meditation was investigated as a means to reduce perceived stress among health care professionals (Oman, Hedberg, & Thoresen, 2006). Participants in the intervention attended an 8-week group training on passage meditation, which involved memorizing and silently repeating to oneself a passage from a major spiritual tradition. Follow-up at 19 weeks revealed that participants in the intervention group ($n = 27$) reported a reduction in stress and improvement in mental health compared with those in the wait-list control group ($n = 31$). Interestingly, treatment effects were larger among those who were the least and the most spiritual. Study limitations include small sample size, lack of a comparison stress management group, and lack of information on participants' prior meditation experience.

In light of these initial findings, it is easy to imagine the role that practicing psychologists could be playing in the integration of R/S in the medical health care system. Psychologists are well trained and competent in diagnostic assessment and evaluation, program development and evaluation, clinical work, and consultation. They must be skillful in creating and maintaining a therapeutic relationship; thinking critically; making decisions; perceiving subtle changes in affect, behavior, and body language; understanding relationships and human nature from a holistic perspective; and discussing sensitive topics.

Each of these areas of competence and specific clinical skills lend themselves to integrative work in spirituality. Just as physicians are encouraged to take a spiritual history, psychologists also could play an important role on the health care team, exploring in greater depth the biopsychosocial–spiritual aspects of patients' health and illness experience. Indeed, this is often the standard practice for clinical assessments (see Chapter 5 in this volume). Psychologists can collaborate with other health care professionals to provide additional information about patients' spiritual beliefs and spiritual needs; help make appropriate referrals; involve religious community resources; encourage forgiveness; intervene through various empirically validated spiritually oriented techniques, such as meditation and mindfulness; lead spiritual coping or mind-body skills groups (e.g., Tarakeshwar, Pearce, & Sikkema, 2005); and provide more extensive inpatient or outpatient counseling around spiritual and existential issues (Martinez, Smith, & Barlow, 2007). Additionally, psychologists can play an important part in medical professionals' training, helping them to better understand the role of R/S at both the individual and systemic level of health care.

CHALLENGES AND ETHICAL ISSUES OF INTEGRATING R/S AND HEALTH CARE

The third section of this chapter will discuss the challenges of integrating R/S in health care systems, including ethical issues, barriers, and special considerations.

Different Approaches to Spiritual Care

The type of spiritual care provided to patients depends on the health care providers' spiritual care approach or model. Problems arise when the provider's approach differs from the patient's spiritual care philosophy and desired approach. Several models of spiritual care have been articulated. For example, Walter's (1997) has identified three approaches to spiritual care. The first approach relegates all spiritual care to the religious community. The second approach calls the chaplain to address R/S needs. The third approach creates a multidisciplinary team in which all members are responsible for some appropriate level of spiritual care, defined as helping the patient in their search for meaning. Walter argued that the third approach is the most appropriate for holistic care and can be taken regardless of staff and patient R/S.

Potential Harmful Impact on Patients

Not all derive strength and comfort from R/S. Those who interpret their illness as their own moral failure or lack of belief suffer from the added burden of guilt and shame and question whether they are less deserving of good health. To this end, health care providers need to be cautious about implying a causal relationship between lack of R/S beliefs and practices and illness. Nor are all the effects of R/S on health positive. At times, religion can result in rigid, intolerant, and judgmental beliefs and persecutory actions. Many believe, however, that it is not the role of the health care provider to determine which beliefs are healthy and which are not (Lawrence, 2002). Some providers have been concerned that patients will rely on R/S instead of medical care or refuse medical intervention because of certain religious beliefs. Research suggests that this happens in very few cases. Most patients who have religious beliefs and engage in religious practices rely on both their faith and medicine when ill (Koenig, 2002).

Providers also need to be aware that spiritual needs and desired care differ according the specific faith tradition of the patient. For example, devout followers of Islam are expected to dress and behave in a modest manner. As such, they can find health and personal care assessments from opposite-gender professionals distressing. In addition, O'Connor and Vandenberg (2005) found that the further a religious belief was from mainstream religious beliefs (e.g., Christianity), the higher the rating of pathology it was assigned by mental health professionals. Thus, professionals need to be cautious of making poorer clinical judgments regarding patients who hold religious beliefs that are unfamiliar to them.

Although research has not yet examined or reported negative consequences of taking a spiritual history or attending to spiritual needs, there is the potential for harm. This includes offending and alienating patients who are of a different or no religious faith, creating anxiety that death is imminent (e.g., last rites), evoking guilt for not being religious enough, or uncovering spiritual issues without having the resources to adequately address them (Koenig, 2002). In a few exceptional cases, patients have sued health care providers for dealing with R/S in a perceived insensitive manner.

Descriptive Versus Prescriptive R/S Care

Another debate within the literature is whether R/S in clinical practice should be descriptive, with a focus on providing spiritual support to patients, or whether it should be prescriptive, implying that providers influence, intervene, and at times work to directly change the R/S of their patients. Pesut and Sawatzky (2006) have asserted that a prescriptive approach is ethically problematic because spirituality does not have a normative standard or common language, and as such, objective judgments cannot be made about the spiritual condition of a patient. Other critics of the intentional integration of R/S in the clinical encounter have argued that to inquire or intervene in the area of R/S is intrusive, is inappropriate, crosses professional boundaries, could be perceived as coercive or as proselytism, and denigrates both medicine and religion (Sloan et al., 1999). The decision to act on the information gleaned from a spiritual assessment can be ethically complex, and health care providers are right to feel reluctant to delve into issues without clear ethical guidelines as to what actions may or may not be taken. There are times, however, when faith stances are clearly problematic and require intervention on the part of the health care provider, such as when a patient claims to hear a voice from God telling the individual to kill himself or others. When encountering a situation like this, safety trumps all concerns of making "objective judgments" or being "coercive" in regard to the patient's spiritual beliefs. Professional clinical practice standards and ethical guidelines, along with good common sense, provide appropriate ways of dealing with these types of life-threatening situations.

Competency and Vulnerability

Two other areas of concern are the competency of the provider and the vulnerability of the patient. Health care providers are mandated to do no harm and are required to practice only within their area of expertise. Appropriate boundaries must be set and respected. Health care providers are not trained theologians or priests, and as such, they are not equipped to give spiritual advice or counsel. Instead, they need to seek the good of the patient and ensure that they have access to resources that can meet these needs. Curlin and Hall (2005) have argued that the most appropriate way to understand the discussion of R/S is as a "form of philosophical discourse about ultimate human concerns" (p. 370) in which the provider engages with the patient in an "ethic of friendship" with a desire for their good, rather than conceptualizing the dialogue as a therapeutic technique. To respect and protect patients' wishes and autonomy, patients must give consent for all actions beyond the spiritual assessment and support (Koenig, 2002). Even referrals to and provider communication with chaplain or clergy cannot occur without obtaining informed consent.

In our attempt to integrate R/S with health care, we need to be careful to avoid "reinventing the wheel." Chaplains, clergy, and pastoral counselors are specifically trained to meet the R/S needs of patients. For example, to be certified by the Association of Professional Chaplains, an individual has to receive 4 years of college, 3 years of divinity school, 1 to 4 years of clinical pastoral education, and 1,625 hr of clinical supervision (Danylchuk, 1992). Unfortunately, research suggests that chaplains are not called on as frequently as may be necessary. In one study, physicians, nurses, and social workers felt it was important to refer patients to chaplains for end-of-life issues, but they thought it less important to refer patients for unresolved grief, chronic anxiety, or demoralization (Galek, Flannelly, Koenig, & Fogg, 2007). Psychologists, who are now gaining further training in spiritually integrated assessments and treatments, are increasingly becoming another important, specifically trained resource to help meet the R/S needs of patients.

Funding for Spiritual Care

The United States was founded on the belief of a necessary separation between church and state. As such, formalized attention to and practice of R/S has been largely removed from public domains, including health care. This makes funding for spiritually based programs within health care settings a complicated issue. Eastern healing methods that focus on individual strengths, ability to participate in one's healing process, and acceptance of suffering as a part of life (e.g., yoga, mindfulness) seem more accepted within the secular medical settings than do traditional religious methods (e.g., prayer, reading scriptures, worship). Funding may be more readily provided for these types of spiritual care interventions.

One-Size-Fits-All Mentality

There are a multitude of religions, definitions of spirituality, and ways of being religious and spiritual. Even within one church, each member has his of her own way of relating to the transcendent and understanding and evaluating that which is sacred. It is simplistic and incorrect to assume a "one-size-fits-all" approach when it comes to R/S and the ways in which these beliefs intersect and influence health care. In an attempt to please and include all in the use of our language, understanding of patients, and provision of care, we risk alienating and dissatisfying all. Shuman and Meador (2003) and others have argued for the careful attention to the particularities of faith beliefs and practices as well as the particularities of those who hold these beliefs and engage in these practices.

RECOMMENDATIONS FOR ADVANCEMENT OF INTEGRATIVE CARE

In conclusion, a number of clinical- and research-based recommendations to advance integrative work in health care systems are presented.

Clinical Recommendations and Guidelines for Integrative Care

After reviewing the literature in this area, at least seven guidelines appear to help psychologists and other health care providers, as well as researchers, most appropriately and effectively integrate R/S in health care. First, it is important to understand that R/S is a way of being in the world, not an isolated aspect of an individual. R/S will be present in the health care encounter whether acknowledged or not. As this chapter has reviewed, there are many good reasons why it should be acknowledged.

Second, it is important to understand the role of R/S in health and the practice of holistic medicine. Care cannot be holistic without attention to the spiritual. The value of R/S is not in its effects on health. For most, R/S is not a *thing* that is *used* as merely a utilitarian tool. Rather, R/S is something one embraces, participates in, and holds as sacred (Curlin & Hall, 2005). There is no research showing that engaging in R/S for the purpose of becoming healthier actually results in better health (Koenig, 2002).

Third, it is vital that providers know their patients not just their bodies and illnesses. Patients' beliefs, assumptions, expectations, values, and narrative frameworks influence the way they perceive illness, understand treatment, and adhere to medical advice, and perhaps even how their body responds to intervention. When providers do not know their patients' religious worldviews or are not willing to enter into these worldviews, it is more likely that the provider will feel frustrated or offended by their patients' beliefs and decisions regarding their health and treatment. Providers should work to keep the patient from having to make a choice between angering God or angering their provider by choosing to follow a religious doctrine rather than the professional's medical advice (Koenig, 2002).

Fourth, providers need to understand the context in which they practice. How R/S is talked about, understood, and practiced varies across individuals and groups. Research has demonstrated correlates, such as ethnicity, socioeconomic status, and region of the country, for various markers of faith (e.g., attendance, prayer, importance). For example, the language used may differ depending on geographic location. One is more likely to hear patients talk about their *religion* in the "Bible belt," and of their *spirituality* in the Northeast. Research has shown that women, ethnic minorities, and the elderly are more likely to endorse being religious and to engage in religious practices (Levin et al., 1994). This does not mean that providers should make sweeping generalizations on the basis of sociodemographic factors. Rather, having an awareness of the empirical findings can facilitate and guide appropriate inquiry and provision of resources.

Fifth, it is important that providers know themselves and their limitations. The risk of mutual misunderstanding is greater when providers and patients have fundamental differences in worldview. Being aware of one's belief system, prejudices, formative spiritual experiences, biases, and limitations helps providers to better avoid misunderstandings and protects patients from the projection of physician beliefs and agendas.

Sixth, providers need to know what they are required to do so they may provide culturally and spiritually competent care, as described by the jurisdictions and organizations under whose authority they practice (e.g., American Psychological Association, Institute of Medicine, National Hospice and Palliative Care Organization, nursing regulations; see also Joint Commission, 2001). As a caveat, it is understood that spiritual competence is a lifelong process and providers are at different places along the continuum in regard to various R/S groups. It is not necessary, or feasible, to be trained in the specifics of all R/S perspectives. Competent spiritual care also includes strictly avoiding all forms of religious coercion and proselytism.

Seventh, providers need to educate themselves on ways to appropriately assess and address R/S issues with their patients. Providers need an empathetic understanding of spiritual worldviews as well as treatment strategies that are appropriate, relevant, and sensitive to patients' spiritual views. Again, addressing spiritual issues does not mean that spiritual issues need to be "taken on" (Sloan et al., 1999). Patients do not expect or desire their provider to be their primary spiritual advisor (Hart, Kohlwes, Deyo, Rhodes, & Bowen, 2003). Spiritually competent care includes, and often involves, referral to chaplains and clergy.

Recommendations for Research on Integrative Care

Much research to date has focused on why R/S is relevant and important in the health care setting. Much less research has investigated how R/S can be appropriately and effectively integrated into the clinical practice of medicine, not to mention how this can be done effectively by psychologists and others in the mental health field. More studies like Kristeller et al.'s (2005) brief, structured interview on spiritual concerns for oncologists can provide information on the feasibility of providing spiritual care, the practical application of care, the receptivity of patients, and the influence this type of care has on outcomes.

More information is also needed on how to create a streamlined process in which all relevant health care personnel are involved in the spiritual care of patients. Gordon and Mitchell (2004) have argued that spiritual care is too nebulous to be captured by standard spiritual assessment tools used at specific set points. Rather, they argued that spiritual care should be an ongoing, coordinated approach, such that each member of a health care team provides spiritual care at their level of training and competency. Further research may demonstrate this to be an effective model for the delivery of spiritual care in medical systems.

Individuals offering spiritual care often become recipients of care (Jenkins, 2002). More research on the impact of the delivery of specific types of spiritual care on a variety of provider outcomes, such as well-being, job satisfaction, and job turnover, may help to lessen the reluctance of some professionals to provide spiritual care for their patients.

Some assert that medical professionals should be trained to see themselves as an integral part of the therapeutic intervention, rather than seeing a potential cure as stemming only from medicine (Olson et al., 2006). This raises interesting questions in the context of spiritual care, such as, "Does matching providers and patients on the basis of a shared faith tradition have an impact on patient and provider outcomes?" and "Does treatment and the patient–provider relationship differ for believing versus nonbelieving patients and providers?" To address such questions, one needs to better define the roles of mental health providers, physicians, nurses, family, friends, and pastoral care; know more about what these individuals believe and are capable of doing; and understand what is most effective for patients (Sulmasy, 2002). Klitzman and Daya (2005) suggested that future research ask not whether providers and patients differ in religious beliefs but rather in what ways, why, and with what implications.

Milstein (2008) asserted that spiritual interventions should be studied within the context of a strong theoretical model of health, such as exploring the relationship between spirituality and internal resources (e.g., sense of control and meaning), external resources (e.g., social support), grief reactions, family functioning, and perceptions. He recommended studying the effects of spiritual interventions by a simple case-control experimental design. For example, patients and their families can complete assessment instruments before and after an intervention. Results can then be compared with those of control patients and families.

The use of standardized assessment instruments that are specifically crafted to capture the spiritual dimension of health are also needed. To this end, Katerndahl and Oyiriaru (2007) developed and validated the Biopsychosociospiritual Inventory to provide a holistic assessment of the impact of disease and its treatment on five domains of health: functional status, physical, psychological, social, and spiritual. The authors suggested that the use of this scale may aid in the understanding of various clinically relevant health outcomes (e.g., health care utilization, quality of life), provide a more holistic picture of a patient's functioning, and emphasize the need to address spiritual issues along with other more standard medical factors and areas of functioning.

CONCLUSION

This chapter has argued that R/S is an integral component of the provision and receipt of holistic care. Because individual worldviews cannot be "turned off," R/S will be part of the clinical encounter whether or not it is acknowledged. Research demonstrates that R/S underlies and shapes the nature of the relationship professionals have with their patients and influences patients' and providers' understanding of illness, treatment, adherence, coping, and type of support systems. As such, R/S needs to be addressed with respect and sensitivity. Professionals must avoid imposing their own belief system or lack of belief on their patients. Not all patients find comfort or strength in R/S. For some, illness is a time of intense spiritual questioning and struggle; it is important to create a safe sharing environment so that spiritual concerns and distress can be addressed as well.

It seems that the best approach is one of curiosity and sincere interest. With this mind-set, providers allow their patients to guide them into a fuller understanding of their worldviews. Spiritual care does not necessarily mean taking more time, but rather it is a communication of respect and is expressed in the form of a relationship. It also seems clear that spiritual care does not rest with just one member or division of health care. Instead, patients need an interdisciplinary spiritual care team in which each member plays a role in providing spiritually competent care. Hospital chaplains have the most training in this area and should be the ones who provide more in-depth counseling. Other specifically trained professionals include clergy, culturally based healers, pastoral counselors, parish nurses, and some psychologists. In addition, R/S communities can be important support systems for patients. The author agrees with others in this field that, above all, we must use wisdom and respect as we continue to seek how to best address and integrate R/S into health care.

References

Alto, W. A. (1995). Prevention in practice. *Primary Care, 22*, 543–554.

Anandarajah, G., & Hight, E. (2001). Spirituality and medical practice: Using the HOPE questions as a practical tool for spiritual assessment. *American Family Physician, 63*, 81–89.

Balboni, T. A., Vanderwerker, L. C., Block, S. D., Paulk, M. E., Lathan, C. S., Peteet, J. R., & Prigerson, H. G. (2007). Religiousness and spiritual support among advanced cancer patients and associations with end-of-life treatment preferences and quality of life. *Journal of Clinical Oncology, 25*, 555–560. doi:10.1200/JCO.2006.07.9046

Benjamins, M. R. (2006). Does religion influence patient satisfaction? *American Journal of Health Behavior, 30*, 85–91. doi:10.5993/AJHB.30.1.8

Centers for Disease Control and Prevention. (2010). *Partnership to fight chronic disease.* Retrieved from http://www.cdc.gov/nccdphp/overview.htm

Clark, L., Leedy, S., McDonald, L., Muller, B., Lamb, C., Mendez, T., . . . Schonwetter, R. (2007). Spirituality and job satisfaction among hospice interdisciplinary team members. *Journal of Palliative Medicine, 10*, 1321–1328. doi:10.1089/jpm.2007.0035

Curlin, F. A., & Hall, D. E. (2005). Strangers or friends? A proposal for a new spirituality-in-medicine ethic. *Journal of General Internal Medicine, 20*, 370–374. doi:10.1111/j.1525-1497.2005.04110.x

Daaleman, T. P., & Nease, D. E. (1994). Patient attitudes regarding physician inquiry into spiritual and religious issues. *Journal of Family Practice, 39*, 564–568.

Daaleman, T. P., Williams, C. S., Hamilton, V. L., & Zimmerman, S. (2008). Spiritual care at the end of life in long-term care. *Medical Care, 46*, 85–91. doi:10.1097/MLR.0b013e3181468b5d

Danylchuk, L. S. (1992). The pastoral counselor as mental health professional: A comparison of the training of AAPC fellow pastoral counselors and licensed clinical social workers. *Journal of Pastoral Care, 46*, 382–391.

Delaney, H. D., Miller, W. R., & Bisono, A. M. (2007). Religiosity and spirituality among psychologists: A survey of clinician members of the American psychological association. *Professional Psychology: Research and Practice, 38*, 538–546. doi:10.1037/0735-7028.38.5.538

Donahue, M. J., & Benson, P. L. (1995). Religion and the well-being of adolescents. *Journal of Social Issues, 51*, 145–160. doi:10.1111/j.1540-4560.1995.tb01328.x

Ehman, J. W., Ott, B., Short, T., Ciampa, R., & Hansen-Flaschen, J. (1999). Do patients want physicians to inquire about their spiritual or religious beliefs if they become gravely ill? *Archives of Internal Medicine, 159*, 1803–1806. doi:10.1001/archinte.159.15.1803

Ellis, M. R., Vinson, D. C., & Ewigman, B. (1999). Addressing spiritual concerns of patients. *Journal of Family Practice, 48*, 105–109.

Fitchett, G., Burton, L. A., & Sivan, A. B. (1997). The religious needs and resources of psychiatric patients. *Journal of Nervous and Mental Disease, 185*, 320–326. doi:10.1097/00005053-199705000-00006

Fitchett, G., Murphy, P. E., Kim, J., Gibbons, J. L., Cameron, J. R., & Davis, J. (2004). Religious struggle: Prevalence, correlates and mental health risks in diabetic, congestive heart failure, and oncology patients. *International Journal of Psychiatry in Medicine, 34*, 179–196. doi:10.2190/UCJ9-DP4M-9C0X-835M

Friedman, R., Sobel, D., Myers, P., Caudill, M., & Benson, H. (1995). Behavioral medicine, clinical health psychology, and cost offset. *Health Psychology, 14*, 509–518. doi:10.1037/0278-6133.14.6.509

Galek, K., Flannelly, K. J., Koenig, H. G., & Fogg, S. L. (2007). Referrals to chaplains: The role of religion and spirituality in healthcare settings. *Mental Health, Religion, and Culture, 10*, 363–377. doi:10.1080/13674670600757064

Gallup Organization. (2002). *Religion in America, 2002*. Princeton, NJ: Author.

Gordon, T., & Mitchell, D. (2004). A competency model for the assessment and delivery of spiritual care. *Palliative Medicine, 18*, 646–651. doi:10.1191/0269216304pm936oa

Hage, S., Hopson, A., Siegel, M., Payton, G., & DeFanti, E. (2006). Multicultural training in spirituality: An interdisciplinary review. *Counseling and Values, 50*, 217–234. doi:10.1002/j.2161-007X.2006.tb00058.x

Hall, J. A., & Dornan, M. C. (1990). Patient sociodemographic characteristics as predictors of satisfaction with medical care: A meta-analysis. *Social Science and Medicine, 30*, 811–818.

Hart, A., Kohlwes, R., Deyo, R., Rhodes, L., & Bowen, D. (2003). Hospice patients' attitudes regarding spiritual discussion with their doctors. *American Journal of Hospice and Palliative Care, 20*, 135–139. doi:10.1177/104990910302000212

Hodge, D. R. (2004). Spirituality and people with mental illness: Developing spiritual competency in assessment and intervention. *Families in Society, 85*, 36–44.

Hummer, R. A., Rogers, R. G., Nam, C. B., & Ellison, C. G. (1999). Religious involvement and U.S. adult mortality. *Demography, 36*, 273–285. doi:10.2307/2648114

Jenkins, B. (2002). Offering spiritual care. In B. Rumbold (Ed.), *Spirituality and palliative care: Social and pastoral perspectives* (pp. 116–129). South Melbourne, Australia: Oxford University Press.

Joint Commission on Accreditation of Healthcare Organizations. (2001, July 31). *Spiritual assessment*. Retrieved from http://www.jointcommission.org/Accreditation/Programs/Hospitals/Standards/FAQs/Provision+of+Care/Assessment/Spiritual_Assessment.htm

Katerndahl, D., & Oyiriaru, D. (2007). Assessing the biopsychosocialspiritual model in primary care: Development of the Biopsychosocialspiritual Inventory (BioPSSI). *International Journal of Psychiatry in Medicine, 37*, 393–414. doi:10.2190/PM.37.4.d

Kaut, K. P. (2002). Religion, spirituality, and existentialism near the end of life. *American Behavioral Scientist, 46*, 220–234. doi:10.1177/000276402236675

Klitzman, R. L., & Daya, S. (2005). Challenges and changes in spirituality among doctors who become patients. *Social Science and Medicine, 61*, 2396–2406. doi:10.1016/j.socscimed.2005.04.031

Koenig, H. G. (1998). Religious beliefs and practices of hospitalized medically older adults. *International Journal of Geriatric Psychiatry, 13*, 213–224. doi:10.1002/(SICI)1099-1166(199804)13:4<213::AID-GPS755>3.0.CO;2-5

Koenig, H. G. (2002). *Spirituality in patient care: Why, how, when, and what*. Philadelphia, PA: Templeton Foundation Press.

Koenig, H. G., McCullough, M., & Larson, D. B. (2001). *Handbook of religion and health*. New York, NY: Oxford University Press. doi:10.1093/acprof:oso/9780195118667.001.0001

Kristeller, J. L., Rhodes, M., Cripe, L. D., & Sheets, V. (2005). Oncologist assisted spiritual intervention study (OASIS): patient acceptability and initial evidence of effects. *International Journal of Psychiatry in Medicine, 35*, 329–347. doi:10.2190/8AE4-F01C-60M0-85C8

Kristeller, J. L., Zumbrun, C., & Schilling, R. (1999). 'I would if I could'" how oncologists and oncology nurses address spiritual distress in cancer patients. *Psycho-Oncology, 8*, 451–458. doi:10.1002/(SICI)1099-1611(199909/10)8:5<451::AID-PON422>3.0.CO;2-3

Lawrence, R. J. (2002). The witches' brew of spirituality and medicine. *Annals of Behavioral Medicine, 24*, 74–76. doi:10.1207/S15324796ABM2401_09

Levin, J. S., Taylor, R. J., & Chatters, L. M. (1994). Race and gender differences in religiosity among older adults: Findings from four national surveys. *The Journals of Gerontology, Series B: Psychological Sciences and Social Sciences, 49*, S137–S145.

Lo, B., Quill, T., & Tulsky, J. (1999). Discussing palliative care with patients: ACP-ASIM End of Life Consensus Panel. *Annals of Internal Medicine, 130*, 744–749.

MacLean, C. D., Susi, B., Phifer, N., Schultz, L., Bynum, D., Franco, M., . . . Cykert, S. (2003). Religion and spirituality in the medical encounter: Results from a multi-center patient survey. *Journal of General Internal Medicine, 18*, 38–43.

Mann, J. R., McKay, S., Daniels, D., Lamar, C. S., Witherspoon, P. W., Stanek, M. K., & Larimore, W. L. (2005). Physician-offered prayer and patient satisfaction. *International Journal of Psychiatry in Medicine, 35*, 161–170. doi:10.2190/2B0Q-2GW0-80L9-N3TK

Martinez, J. S., Smith, T. B., & Barlow, S. H. (2007). Spiritual interventions in psychotherapy: Evaluations by highly religious clients. *Journal of Clinical Psychology, 63*, 943–960. doi:10.1002/jclp.20399

McCord, G., Gilchrist, V., Grossman, S. D., King, B. D., McCormick, K. F., Oprandi, A. M., . . . Srivastava, M. (2004). Discussing spirituality with patients: A rational and ethical approach. *Annals of Family Medicine*, 2, 356–361. doi:10.1370/afm.71

McMinn, M. R. (1996). *Psychology, theology, and spirituality in Christian counseling*. Wheaton, IL: Tyndale House.

Meier, D. E., Emmons, C. A., Wallenstein, S., Quill, T. Morrison, R. S., & Cassel, C. K. (1998). A national survey of physician-assisted suicide and euthanasia in the United States. *New England Journal of Medicine, 338*, 1193–1201. doi:10.1056/NEJM199804233381706

Miller, D. K., Chibnall, J., Videen, S., & Duckro, P. (2005). Supportive-affective group experience for persons with life-threatening illness: Reducing spiritual, psychological, and death-related distress in dying patients. *Journal of Palliative Medicine, 8*, 333–343. doi:10.1089/jpm.2005.8.333

Milstein, J. M. (2008). Introducing spirituality in medical care: Transition from hopelessness to wholeness. *JAMA, 299*, 2440–2441. doi:10.1001/jama.299.20.2440

Moadel, A., Morgan, D., Fatone, A., Grennan, J., Carter, J., Laruffa, G., . . . Dutcher, J. (1999). Seeking meaning and hope: Self-reported spiritual and existential needs among an ethnically-diverse cancer patient population. *Psycho-Oncology*, 8, 378–385. doi:10.1002/(SICI)1099-1611(199909/10)8:5<378::AID-PON406>3.0.CO;2-A

Moss, E. L., & Dobson, K. S. (2006). Psychology, spirituality, and end-of-life care: An ethical integration? *Canadian Psychology, 47*, 284–299. doi:10.1037/co2006019

O'Connor, S., & Vandenberg, B. (2005). Psychosis or faith? Clinicians' assessment of religious beliefs. *Journal of Consulting and Clinical Psychology, 73*, 610–616. doi:10.1037/0022-006X.73.4.610

Olson, M. M., Sandor, M. K., Sierpina, V. S., Vanderpool, H. Y., & Dayao, P. (2006). Mind, body, and spirit: Family physicians' beliefs, attitudes, and practices regarding the integration of patient spirituality into medical care. *Journal of Religion and Health, 45*, 234–247. doi:10.1007/s10943-006-9020-2

Oman, D., Hedberg, J., & Thoresen, C. E. (2006). Passage meditation reduces perceived stress in health professionals: A randomized, controlled trial. *Journal of Consulting and Clinical Psychology, 74*, 714–719. doi:10.1037/0022-006X.74.4.714

Oyama, O., & Koenig, H. G. (1998). Religious beliefs and practices in family medicine. *Archives of Family Medicine, 7*, 431–435. doi:10.1001/archfami.7.5.431

Pargament, K. I. (1997). *The psychology of religion and coping: Theory, research, practice*. New York, NY: Guilford Press.

Pargament, K. I., Koenig, H. G., Tarakeshwar, N., & Hahn, J. (2001). Religious struggle as a predictor of mortality among medically ill elderly patients: A 2-year longitudinal study. *Archives of Internal Medicine, 161*, 1881–1885. doi:10.1001/archinte.161.15.1881

Pearce, M. J., Chen, J., Silverman, G. K., Kasl, S. V., Rosenheck, R., & Prigerson, H. G. (2002). Religious coping, health, and health service use among bereaved adults. *International Journal of Psychiatry in Medicine*, 32, 179–199. doi:10.2190/UNE0-EFAN-XPNJ-9N3G

Pearce, M. J., Coan, A., Herndon, J. E., Koenig, H., G., & Abernethy, A. (2012). Unmet spiritual care needs impact emotional and spiritual well-being in advanced cancer patients. *Supportive Care in Cancer*. Advance online publication. doi: 10.10071500520-011-1335-1

Pearce, M. J., Singer, J., & Prigerson, H. G. (2006). Religious coping among caregivers of terminally ill cancer patients: Main effects and psychosocial mediators. *Journal of Health Psychology*, *11*, 743–759. doi:10.1177/1359105306066629

Pesut, B., & Sawatzky, R. (2006). To describe or prescribe: Assumptions underlying a prescriptive nursing process approach to spiritual care. *Nursing Inquiry*, *13*, 127–134. doi:10.1111/j.1440-1800.2006.00315.x

Post, B. C., & Wade, N. G. (2009). Religion and spirituality in psychotherapy: A practice friendly review of research. *Journal of Clinical Psychology*, *65*, 131–146. doi:10.1002/jclp.20563

Post, S. G., Puchalski, C. M., & Larson, D. B. (2000). Physicians and patient spirituality: Professional boundaries, competency, and ethics. *Annals of Internal Medicine*, *132*, 578–583.

Princeton Religion Research Center. (2005). *The Gallup poll: Public opinion 2005*. Princeton, NJ: Gallup Organization.

Rabow, M. W., Dibble, S. L., Pantilat, S. Z., & McPhee, S. J. (2004). The comprehensive care team: A controlled trial of outpatient palliative medicine consultation. *Archives of Internal Medicine*, *164*, 83–91. doi:10.1001/archinte.164.1.83

Richards, P. S., & Bergin, A. E. (2005). *A spiritual strategy for counseling and psychotherapy* (2nd ed.). Washington, DC: American Psychological Association. doi:10.1037/11214-000

Safran, D. G., Taira, D. A., Rogers, W. H., Kosinski, M., Ware, J. E., & Tarlov, A. R. (1998). Linking primary care performance to outcomes of care. *Journal of Family Practice*, *47*, 213–220.

Sawatzky, R., & Pesut, B. (2005). Attributes of spiritual care in nursing practice. *Journal of Holistic Nursing*, *23*, 19–33. doi:10.1177/0898010104272010

Shuman, J. J., & Meador, K. M. (2003). *Heal thyself: Spirituality, medicine, and the distortion of Christianity*. Oxford, England: Oxford University Press.

Sloan, R. P., Bagiella, E., & Powell, T. (1999). Religion, spirituality and medicine. *Lancet*, *353*, 664–667. doi:10.1016/S0140-6736(98)07376-0

Sulmasy, D. P. (2002). A biopsychosocial-spiritual model for the care of patients at the end of life. *The Gerontologist*, *42*, 24–33. doi:10.1093/geront/42.suppl_3.24

Sulmasy, D. P., Geller, G., Levine, D. M., & Faden, R. (1992). The quality of mercy: Caring for patients with 'do not resuscitate' orders. *JAMA*, *267*, 682–686. doi:10.1001/jama.1992.03480050086030

Tan, S. (1996). Religion in clinical practice: Implicit and explicit integration. In E. P. Shafranske (Ed.), *Religion and the clinical practice of psychology* (pp. 365–387). Washington, DC: American Psychological Association. doi:10.1037/10199-013

Tarakeshwar, N., & Pargament, K. I. (2001). Religious coping in families of children with autism. *Focus on Autism and Other Developmental Disabilities*, *16*, 247–260. doi:10.1177/108835760101600408

Tarakeshwar, N., Pearce, M. J., & Sikkema, K. J. (2005). Implementation of a spiritual coping group intervention for adults living with HIV/AIDS: A pilot study. *Mental Health, Religion, and Culture*, *8*, 179–190. doi:10.1080/13694670500138908

Thom, D. H., Ribisl, K. M., Stewart, A. L., Luke, D. A., & Stanford Trust Study Physicians. (1999). Further validation and reliability testing of the trust in physician scale. *Medical Care*, *37*, 510–517. doi:10.1097/00005650-199905000-00010

Walter, T. (1997). The ideology and organization of spiritual care: Three approaches. *Palliative Medicine*, *11*, 21–30. doi:10.1177/026921639701100103

Wasner, M., Longhorn, C., & Borasio, G. D. (2005). Effects of spiritual care training for palliative care professionals. *Palliative Medicine*, *19*, 99–104. doi:10.1191/0269216305pm995oa

Weaver, A. J., Flannelly, L., & Flannelly, K. J. (2001). A review of research on religious and spiritual variables in two primary gerontological nursing journals 1991 to 1997. *Journal of Gerontological Nursing*, *27*, 47–54.

World Heath Organization. (2003). *WHO definition of palliative care*. Retrieved from http://www.who.int/cancer/palliative/definition/en

CHAPTER 28

ADDRESSING RELIGION AND SPIRITUALITY IN CORRECTIONAL SETTINGS: THE ROLE OF FAITH-BASED PRISON PROGRAMS

Byron R. Johnson

It is not a new idea that the life of even the worst prisoner can be transformed. Religious practitioners have preached this message as long as prisons have existed. In recent years, however, there has been considerable interest going beyond traditional prison ministry to establishing faith-based prison programs, dorms, or even entire faith-based prisons. One of the rationales for the emphasis on faith-based prison interventions is the common criticism that traditional prison programs simply are not effective in rehabilitating inmates or helping former prisoners become law-abiding citizens once they are released back into society. There is now preliminary empirical evidence showing participation in faith-based programs is associated with reductions in recidivism. If participation in relatively small doses of religious programs can have a beneficial effect on inmates, what might be the effect of a more extensive faith-based prison program? Drawing largely from the experience of several faith-based prison programs, a much more intensive religious intervention has been implemented in several prisons in the United States and around the world. This chapter summarizes initial evidence on the role of religion and spirituality within the correctional environment and the influence of a uniquely faith-based approach to offender treatment and aftercare. Other religious and spiritual issues are relevant to correctional settings (e.g., religiously based preventive programs), but most of the work in this area has focused on faith-based programs among prisoners.

BACKGROUND: HISTORY, PHILOSOPHY, AND TREATMENT

The United States had a total prison population of 319,598 in 1980 (Bureau of Justice Statistics, 2009). As a result of various law enforcement strategies, changes in sentencing guidelines, and especially efforts linked to the War on Drugs, a record number of offenders entered the criminal justice system during the 1980s and 1990s. Not surprisingly, a dramatic correctional buildup accompanied these developments. To adequately keep pace with the number of offenders that ultimately would be sentenced after entering the criminal system, it became necessary to significantly expand the number of state and federal prisons. Consequently, the prison population rose dramatically over the next 2 decades, and by 2000, the total prison population increased by more than 400% and reached a total of 1,316,333 prisoners—an increase of approximately 1 million prisoners in just 20 years. By year-end 2008, prisons in the United States held a total of 1,610,446 prisoners (Bureau of Justice Statistics, 2009).

As might be expected, a significant percentage of prisoners during this correctional buildup were convicted of drug-related crimes (Lo & Stephens, 2000; Peters, Greenbaum, Edens, Carter, & Ortiz, 1998), and the obvious link between drugs and crime is well documented (e.g., Ball, Shaffer, & Nurco, 1983; Davis & Lurigio, 1996; Tonry & Wilson, 1990; Wish & Johnson, 1986). Consider that surveys of prisoners find that 45% to 56% of inmates reported drug use in the month prior to their offense.

DOI: 10.1037/14046-028
APA Handbook of Psychology, Religion, and Spirituality: Vol. 2. An Applied Psychology of Religion and Spirituality, K. I. Pargament (Editor-in-Chief)

According to the Bureau of Justice Statistics (1999), 75% of state prisoners may be characterized as alcohol- or drug-involved offenders. As bleak as these findings happen to be, perhaps the most striking statistic is that barely 1 in 10 prisoners participated in some kind of drug treatment program while incarcerated (Bureau of Justice Statistics, 1999). Considering the fact there are so many drug-involved inmates, a logical question to ask is why such a small percentage of prisoners receive treatment.

For more than 200 years, U.S. prisons have been designed for incapacitating convicted offenders. As a correctional philosophy, incapacitation suggests criminals cannot harm society during the time they are removed from it. Any doubt this view is dominant would be erased by asking any prison worker—from guard to warden—the main purpose of prisons. Correctional facilities are tasked with the primary objective of keeping convicted offenders isolated from society and thereby protecting the public. Public safety is the unmistakable goal. This recognition is not meant to imply that correctional employees are generally opposed to the idea of rehabilitation or that prisons do not have purposes beyond incapacitation. Rather, it is the recognition that rehabilitation is seen as a secondary or peripheral correctional objective, at best. Correctional administrators see the value in having prisoners participating in treatment programs; they simply do not have the resources necessary to fund them.

America's earliest prisons did not have rehabilitation programs as we understand them in the 21st century. It would be more than 100 before anything resembling a systematic rehabilitation model was to be put forward as a serious policy recommendation. And although it is not uncommon to find examples of drug treatment programs or even sex offender intervention units in contemporary prisons, it is the case that the vast majority of prisons do not provide treatment programs for most prisoners. U.S. prisons have never operated from a therapeutic perspective or model. Law-and-order crime policies have consistently trumped those favoring offender treatment models (Cullen, 2002), and it is highly unlikely this will change.

Although scholars, advocates, practitioners, and others continue to debate the purpose of prisons, a tour of contemporary prisons reveals that priorities remain focused on running clean, well-managed facilities with low levels of violent behavior. In terms of programmatic features, most prisons have several things in common. These programs include the General Educational Development (GED) test, adult basic educational offerings, and institutional work. Prisoners are expected to work while incarcerated, and most of these prison jobs are very basic, such as laundry, kitchen detail, or floor cleaning. Although some prisons have vocational training programs preparing offenders for skilled jobs, such programs tend to be rare.

Because a significant percentage of prisoners are school dropouts, many can benefit from participating in adult basic education or obtaining a high school diploma. These programs, however, should not be viewed as a proxy for specific offender treatment or rehabilitation programs. In sum, most prisons offer basic education and work opportunities, but they do not provide counseling or offender treatment programs to most prisoners. Control, security, and public safety remain the primary focus of prison management, and inmate treatment has taken and likely always will take a backseat to custody and security issues. Evidence of this fact is that treatment programs are the first things to be cut when correctional budgets are forced to shrink.

Treatment programs represent the exception rather than the rule in U.S. prisons, but they do exist. Furthermore, many of these programs have been the subject of evaluation research. Consequently, it is possible to give an empirical answer to the question, "What works in reducing recidivism?" The question of whether treatment programs are effective was initially addressed in Robert Martinson's (1974) widely cited study, "What Works? Questions and Answers About Prison Reform." This study, or at least many of the subsequent interpretations of it, seemed to emphatically answer this question in the negative—nothing works (Martinson, 1974). Subsequent research, however, has more accurately answered the question this way: Some programs do reduce recidivism for some offenders in some settings (Sherman et al., 1997). Over the past 2 decades, there have been a number of studies systematically evaluating the effectiveness of various correctional treatment programs in reducing recidivism. These research reviews drew similar conclusions about what is effective in reducing recidivism following release from prison. Rehabilitation programs that were most efficacious included at least one of the following components: (a) academic skills training, (b) vocational skills training, (c) cognitive skills programs, and (d) drug abuse treatment. The amount of recidivism reduction when compared with prisoners not receiving program interventions, however, tends to be rather small (Petersilia, 2003).

MacKenzie (2006) completed the most exhaustive review to date of the evaluation literature on treatment programs and interventions. The 284 evaluations MacKenzie reviewed were scored for quality of the research methods utilized. MacKenzie's meta-analysis of the research on correctional interventions revealed that some programs were effective and others were not in reducing recidivism. The following correctional interventions did not reduce recidivism:

- life skills education,
- correctional industries,
- psychosocial sex offender treatment,
- domestic violence treatment using a feminist perspective,
- boot camps, and
- scared straight programs.

Among the reasons suggested as to why these interventions may be ineffective is that these programs (a) tend to focus on punishment, deterrence, or control instead of rehabilitation or (b) emphasize the formation of ties or bonds without first changing the individual's thought process.

What can we conclude, therefore, about offender treatment and prisoner rehabilitation programs? First, various interventions can be successful in reducing recidivism. A common element among in each of the effective interventions is a rehabilitation component. MacKenzie (2006) found that none of the effective programs were based on a control or deterrent philosophy. In fact, cognitive–behavioral therapy has become more commonplace in recent years within correctional settings. These therapies encompass interventions focusing on human change through demonstrated behavioral outcomes. In essence, changes in how individuals perceive and think about their lives are subsequently linked to changes in behavior (Dobson & Khatri, 2000). The assumption is that cognitions affect behavior. Stated differently, people can monitor and alter their cognitive activity, and these changes in cognitions can lead to changes in behavior. Thus, therapy emphasizes this connection between cognition and behavior (Dobson & Craig, 1996). In therapy, offenders are made aware of their dysfunctional behaviors and their maladaptive thought processes, and they are encouraged to change the way they think (Proportion, Fabian, & Robinson, 1991). The effects of cognitive–behavioral approaches to treatment have been a regular theme in reviews of rehabilitation research (Andrews et al., 1990; Cullen & Gendreau, 1989; Gendreau & Ross, 1987; Lipsey, 1992). These reviews of juvenile correctional treatment programs indicate cognitive–behavioral treatment tends to be more effective than other types of correctional treatment (Andrews et al., 1990; Lipsey, 1992). Cognitive–behavioral therapies assert that criminals think differently than noncriminals either because they have dysfunctional information processing and coping skills or a lower level of moral development.

Second, although most prisons do have education and work programs, most correctional facilities do not employ full-time treatment staff. For example, more than 200,000 heroin addicts are incarcerated every year in the United States, but many prisons still lack appropriate treatment for opiate addiction. Nunn et al. (2009) conducted a nationwide survey of prisons and found only half of the nation's prison systems offer opiate replacement therapy through methadone and buprenorphine treatments, even though these drug treatments are recognized to be more effective than drug-free or abstinence methods. The researchers also addressed heroin addicts released from prison, more than half of whom relapse within a month of their discharge.

THE LINK BETWEEN RELIGION AND CRIME REDUCTION

In a recent paper, we reported the results of the most comprehensive assessment to date of the religion–crime literature by reviewing 269 studies published between 1944 and 2010 (Johnson & Jang, 2010). In this systematic review, we examined the type of study (e.g., cross-sectional, prospective cohort, retrospective, experimental, case control, descriptive), the sampling method (e.g., random, probability, systematic sampling, convenience or purposive sample), the number of subjects in the sample, population (e.g., children, adolescents, high school students, college students, adults), location, religious variables included in the analysis (e.g., religious attendance, scripture study, subjective religiosity, religious commitment, religious belief, religious experience), controls, and findings (e.g., no association, mixed evidence, beneficial association, harmful association).

The results of the review confirm that the vast majority of the studies report prosocial effects of religion and religious involvement on various measures of crime and delinquency. Approximately 91% of the studies (244 of 269) find an inverse or beneficial relationship between religion and some measure of crime or delinquency (i.e., increasing religiosity is associated with lower crime and delinquency). Only 9% of the studies (23 of 269) found no association or reported mixed findings, whereas only two studies from this systematic review of the literature found that religion was positively associated with a harmful outcome. In sum, we found religion to be a robust variable that tends to be associated with the lowered likelihood of crime or delinquency (Johnson & Jang, 2010). Also, the vast majority of studies document the importance of religious influences in protecting from harmful outcomes as well as promoting beneficial and prosocial outcomes. The weight of this evidence is especially important in light of the fact that religion has been the "forgotten factor" for many researchers and research initiatives (Johnson, 2009). The review documents that the methodological quality of the studies has generally improved over time. Although the majority of the studies are cross-sectional, more powerful longitudinal and randomized studies tend to follow the same pattern—that is, increasing religiosity tends to be associated with declines in measures of deviance. It is also important to acknowledge that a systematic review does not carry the same weight as a meta-analysis, in which effect sizes for individual studies are considered in the overall assessment of research literature under consideration.

This review of the literature identifies major deficits in two research areas. Despite the increasing significance of the life-course perspective, research on religion and crime continues to be mostly nondevelopmental. For example, we know little about the long-term influence of childhood involvement in religion on adolescent and adult criminality as well as religiosity, and few studies have examined reciprocal relationships between religion and crime over time (Jang, Bader, & Johnson, 2008). Also, we need to learn more about the relevance of religion to desistance research (i.e., focusing on factors that help persistent offenders become crime free), and potential "turning point" effects (e.g., events that trigger dramatic changes in behavior) stemming from religious conversions or spiritual transformations among offenders, for which we have only preliminary evidence (Clear & Sumter, 2002; Giordano, Longmore, Schroeder, & Seffrin, 2008; Johnson, 2003, 2004, 2009; Kerley, Allison, & Graham, 2006; Kerley & Copes, 2009).

A second area requiring more research is the subject of resiliency given that the potential links between resilient and prosocial behavior are clearly understudied. For example, we know that youth living in disorganized communities, are at particular risk for a number of problem behaviors, including crime and drug use. At the same time, we know that residents from disorganized communities who participate in religious activities are less likely to be involved in deviant activities (Jang & Johnson, 2001; Johnson, Jang, Larson, & Li, 2001; Johnson, Jang, Li, & Larson, 2000; Johnson, Larson, Li, & Jang, 2000). Richard Freeman (1986), an economist at Harvard University, found this effect when he studied young, Black males residing in housing projects in Boston, Chicago, and Philadelphia. Freeman found that church attendance was a significant protective factor and significantly reduced the likelihood crime and delinquency.

These findings suggest the religiously committed are "resilient" to the negative consequences of living in communities typified by disadvantage, but we do not have sufficient research to answer why this might be the case. Religious involvement may provide networks of support that help individuals internalize values that encourage behavior that emphasizes concern for others' welfare (Johnson, Larson, Jang, & Li, 2000). Such processes may contribute to the acquisition of positive attributes that engender a greater sense of empathy toward others and, in turn, may reduce the likeliness of committing acts that harm others. Similarly, if individuals become involved in deviant behavior, it may be possible that participation in specific kinds of religious activity can help steer them back to a course of less deviant behavior and away from potential career criminal paths (see Volume 1, Chapter 6, this handbook).

THE ROLE OF RELIGION IN PRISONS

The belief that the life of even the worst prisoner can be reformed is not new. Religionists have always preached this message in our prisons. In fact, America's first prisons drew heavily on the notion that religious commitment was linked to moral behavior. Crime was widely considered to be the result of an individual's moral poverty and required an appropriate response—"let the punishment fit the crime." Deterrence as a perspective has been and remains a guiding philosophy not only for corrections but also for law enforcement as well as the courts.

Historically, incarceration was meant to cause prisoners to recognize their moral failings and hopefully turn to God. Intensive religious instruction and training became central to the fabric and philosophy of the prison movement in early America (Morris & Rothman, 1998).

Some 200 years later, the U.S. correctional system has grown and changed in many dramatic ways. From prison architecture to philosophical approaches regarding inmate, classification, treatment, and management, the 21st-century U.S. correctional system bears little resemblance to those from 2 centuries ago. Perhaps the only constant linking 21st-century prisons to 19th-century prisons is religion. The prominent role religion continues to play in contemporary correctional settings cannot be denied by even the most casual of observers.

Every day thousands of faith-motivated volunteers frequent prisons, jails, halfway houses, reformatories, and other correctional facilities across the country. In fact, the sheer volume of religious volunteers represents perhaps the only offender-based intervention that has kept pace with the unprecedented growth in the prison population over the past 3 decades. From religious instruction, Bible studies, and worship services, to mentoring and a host of other areas, faith-motivated volunteers continue to bring their religion and spirituality into correctional facilities across the country. There is another common theme among the vast majority of religious volunteers—they tend not only to be Christian but also evangelical in orientation. Although prisoners obviously follow different kinds of religion, this does not change the fact that religious programs in most prisons are populated by faith-motivated volunteers who are Christian. More than 20 years of studying prisons of all custody levels and locales confirms the obvious—that the bulk of volunteers are people of faith (Johnson, 2011). An intriguing area of study would be to examine why non-Christian volunteers and nonevangelical groups are so underrepresented in reaching out to inmates in correctional institutions.

As noted, rehabilitation programs in some prisons have been linked to modest reductions in postrelease recidivism. Moreover, when comparing effective to ineffective programs, an interesting difference emerges. Almost all of the effective programs focused on individual-level change (e.g., thinking, reasoning, empathy, problem solving). Interestingly, these findings run counter to sociological perspectives that have had a major influence on research within criminology. For instance, there is a significant research literature emphasizing the importance of ties and bonds to social institutions and the resulting relationships between these ties and bonds and desistence from criminal activity. On the basis of meta-analyses of correctional interventions, however, MacKenzie (2006) proposed that individual-level changes must occur before changes in ties or bonds to social institutions can be formed. Otherwise, it is unlikely that these important social ties and bonds will become strong and ultimately capable of preventing crime.

A dilemma facing the field of corrections is that individual-level change is needed to ensure that ex-prisoners have the best chance to connect with social institutions that can help them lead crime-free lives, but rehabilitation programs (designed to target individual-level change) are not prevalent in U.S. prisons. Faith-based programs are present in all prisons, however, and there is a growing body of empirical evidence linking religiosity to crime reduction. These observations lead to the question, "Might faith-based prison programs, especially those led by volunteers, play a more meaningful role in offender rehabilitation by facilitating individual-level change?"

Faith-based organizations like Prison Fellowship (PF) reach out to prisoners, ex-prisoners, and their families because they believe faith to be a critical ingredient in offender rehabilitation. At the core of PF's mission is the premise that crime is fundamentally a moral and spiritual problem requiring a moral and spiritual solution. PF identifies itself as a non-profit, volunteer-reliant ministry whose mission is "to seek the transformation of prisoners and their reconciliation to God, family, and community through the power and truth of Jesus Christ" (PF, 2012). PF is the largest organized prison ministry in the United States. According to PF's most recent annual report, the ministry is supported by the efforts of more than 300,000 volunteers. Some 200,000 prisoners per month, participate in either Bible studies or seminars led by PF-trained volunteers in more than 1,300 of the country's 1,850 state and federal correctional facilities (PF, 2002).

In fact, this is nothing new because some of the earliest prisons in the United States also were formed on the basis of the belief that crime represented a moral and spiritual problem and that prisoners needed religion to be reformed. Consequently, intensive religious instruction and training was integral in some of America's earliest prisons. PF and many other prison ministries (e.g., Kairos, Champions for Life) still believe faith is the missing ingredient in offender rehabilitation as well as helping ex-prisoners to lead a crime-free life. These faith-based organizations offer prisoners a variety of in-prison programs. Through seminars, Bible studies, and other programs, inmates are taught how to build a relationship with God, manage anger, strengthen families, set goals, and prepare for life beyond prison. Weekly Bible studies usually last 1 hr, and 1- to 3-day seminars might be offered several times a year at a particular prison. The level of prisoner exposure to such religious programs, on an annual basis, may be a maximum of 50 hr of Bible study and several days of intensive seminars—a relatively modest correctional intervention.

In spite of such modest interventions, there is preliminary evidence that regular participation in volunteer-led Bible studies is associated with reductions in recidivism (Johnson, Larson, & Pitts, 1997). In a more recent study tracking the same prisoners for an additional 7 years, regular participation in volunteer-led Bible studies remained significantly linked to lower rates of recidivism for 2 years and even 3 years postrelease (Johnson, 2004). To observe a significant effect over a 2- or 3-year postrelease period is noteworthy even for a major intervention, but it is even more compelling considering the relatively minor intervention of volunteer-led Bible studies over the course of 1 year before release from prison. Quasi-experimental designs, like the one utilized in this study, can never eliminate the possibility of selection bias. On the other hand, publications collecting data by using rigorous matching techniques are increasingly common in the research literature. If participation in relatively small doses of religious programs can have a measurable and beneficial effect on inmates, what would be the consequence of substantially increasing the amount and type of faith-based prison programs? Considering the plethora of religious programs in prisons, it makes sense to rigorously examine the question of whether faith-based prison programs should be considered allies in addressing the civic goal of reducing recidivism.

TEXAS LAUNCHES THE FIRST FAITH-BASED PRISON

In the mid-1990s, PF undertook an unusual correctional experiment. PF's plan was to launch a program replacing occasional volunteer efforts with a completely faith-based approach to prison programs. The ultimate goal was to reform prisoners as well the prison culture. Charles Colson, founder of PF pitched this idea of a faith-based program to the Texas Department of Criminal Justice (TDCJ) in January 1996. The concept described a program with a distinctly Christian orientation: the InnerChange

Freedom Initiative (IFI) Pre-Release Program, as it was originally called (later, "Pre-Release Program" was dropped from the name), was launched in April 1997.

After responding to a competitive grant solicitation from TDCJ, PF was awarded a contract to provide a faith-based prison program. The collaboration between TDCJ and PF represented a first for Texas, if not the country. According to PF, the IFI is different from other prison ministries in that it represents the first full-scale attempt to offer religious programs in a prison environment virtually around the clock. The IFI promotes adult basic education, vocational training, life skills, mentoring, and aftercare, while linking each of these components in a setting permeated by faith. IFI is a "faith-saturated" prison program whose mission is to "create and maintain a prison environment that fosters respect for God's law and rights of others, and to encourage the spiritual and moral regeneration of prisoners" (Johnson & Larson, 2003, p. 8). According to the IFI promotional material, the program is a "revolutionary, Christ-centered, Bible-based prison program supporting prison inmates through their spiritual and moral transformation beginning while incarcerated and continuing after release" (Johnson & Larson, 2003, p. 8).

Anchored in biblical teaching, life-skills education, and group accountability, IFI established a three-phase program involving prisoners in 16 to 24 months of in-prison biblical programs and 6 to 12 months of additional programs while on parole. Phase I provides a spiritual and moral foundation on which the rest of the program is based. Phase II tests the inmate's value system in real-life settings in hopes of preparing him for life after prison. Commonly referred to as *aftercare*, Phase III is the reentry component of IFI and is designed to help assimilate the inmate back into the community through productive and supportive relationships with family, local churches, and the workplace.

Phase I is designed to transform the criminal thinking process and establish a new foundation for growth. Six months into Phase I, IFI participants are supposed to be matched with a mentor. Mentors are Christian men from the Houston community who meet with IFI prisoners one on one for a minimum of 2 hr per week.

Phase II of the IFI program lasts 6 to 12 months and seeks to continue the education, work, and support group aspect of the program. The main difference in Phase II is that IFI participants are allowed to perform community service work during the day at off-site locations, such as Habitat for Humanity. IFI members in Phase II continue with Christian-based education, Bible study courses, mentoring, and support groups, but with a special emphasis on leadership issues. Because IFI encourages spiritual growth, it is expected that in Phase II participants will begin to take on leadership roles within the program. Evening programs are also offered to IFI participants throughout the week with support groups focusing on a different topic each night, including personal faith, mentoring, substance abuse, family/crime victims, and community Bible study. Additionally, intensive spiritual weekend retreats are offered periodically through Kairos, another nationally recognized prison ministry.

Phase III of IFI, the aftercare component of the faith-based program, lasts for an additional 6 to 12 months. The mission of the aftercare program is to assist participants in their reentry into society by helping with housing and employment referrals, facilitating the mentoring relationship, and making connections between the offender and local church communities that will provide a nurturing environment to continue the former prisoner's spiritual growth. Aftercare workers recruit churches and volunteers to assist in the mentoring of IFI participants and to help with other critical reentry needs, such as housing, transportation, and employment.

DOES PARTICIPATION IN IFI REDUCE RECIDIVISM?

The evaluation approach combined both a quantitative and a qualitative study (Johnson, 2003). The quantitative aspect of the independent evaluation essentially focused on recidivism outcomes, namely arrest and incarceration of former IFI participants. The qualitative component, however, relied largely on observational work and field interviews. This approach helped to document the workings of the faith-based prison program, the spiritual changes in the participants as well as the prison environment, and the experiences of IFI participants following release from prison.

Findings presented in Table 28.1 compare the measures of recidivism between the total sample of IFI participants and each of the three comparison groups. As can be seen, 36.2% of IFI participants were arrested during the 2-year period following release. Similarly, 35% of the matched group (prisoners selected from the record of inmates released during the evaluation period who met program selection criteria but did not enter the program), 34.9% of the screened group (prisoners selected from the record of inmates released during the evaluation period who met program selection criteria and were screened as eligible but did not volunteer or were not selected for program participation), and 29.3% of the volunteered group (prisoners selected from the records of inmates released during the evaluation period who actually volunteered for the IFI program but did not participate either because they did not have a minimum-out custody classification, their remaining sentence was not between the required length to be considered, or they were not planning to return to the Houston area following release) were arrested during the 2-year follow-up period. Likewise, there was little difference between IFI members (24.3%) and the matched group (20.3%), the screened group (22.3%), and the volunteered group (19.1%) in terms of the percentage of former prisoners who were once again incarcerated in the 2-year postrelease period. Table 28.1 also presents the recidivism findings comparing IFI participants with various comparison groups. As mentioned, there was no difference between the total IFI sample and the matched group on either measure of recidivism. Simply stated, participation in the IFI program was not related to recidivism reduction. Many of the IFI participants were paroled early by TDCJ and did not have the benefit of staying in the program. As one might expect, program graduates were much less likely than IFI participants who did not complete the program to be arrested within the 2-year tracking period (17.3% vs. 50%). In a similar pattern, IFI graduates were significantly less likely to be incarcerated within 2 years of release than those IFI members not completing the program (8% vs. 36.3%).

IFI program graduates had significantly lower rates of arrest than the matched group (17.3% vs. 35%) or either of the two comparison groups: the screened group (34.9%) and the volunteered group (29.3%). Similarly, those completing the

TABLE 28.1

Results of IFI Texas 2-Year Recidivism Analysis

	Full sample ($N = 1{,}931$)		IFI Sample ($n = 177$)		IFI graduates ($n = 75$)		IFI noncompleters ($n = 102$)	
	(1a) IFI vs. (2a) match group		(1b) IFI graduates vs. (3b) noncompleters		(1c) < 16 months vs. (3c) > 16 months		(1d) < 16 months vs. (3d) > 16 months	
Recidivism type	**(1a)**	**(2a)**	**(1b)**	**(3b)**	**(1c)**	**(3c)**	**(1c)**	**(3c)**
Arrest								
Percent arrested	36.2%	35.0%	17.3%	50.0%	15.0%	20.0%	46.5%	68.8%
No. arrested	64	614	13	51	6	7	40	11
Sample size	177	1,754	75	102	40	35	86	16
Chi-square	0.09, $p = .76$		19.98, $p < .0001$		0.33, $p < .5652$		2.67, $p < .1023$	
Incarceration								
Percent incarcerated	24.3%	20.3%	8.0%	36.3%	5.0%	11.4%	34.9%	43.8%
No. incarcerated	43	356	6	37	2	4	30	7
Sample size	177	1,754	75	102	40	35	86	16
Chi-square	1.57, $p = .21$		18.79, $p < .0001$		1.05, $p < .3059$		0.46, $p < .4982$	

Note. All tests used the Pearson χ^2 statistic with 1 degree of freedom for a 2 × 2 table.

IFI program had significantly lower rates of incarceration than the matched group (8% vs. 20.3%), the screened group (22.3%), and the volunteered group (19.1%). The fact that IFI graduates were significantly less likely to be either arrested or incarcerated during the 2-year period following release from prison represents initial evidence that program completion of this faith-based initiative is associated with lower rates of recidivism of former prisoners. The IFI has now spread to a number of different states, and the Minnesota Department of Correction has completed an outcome evaluation of the effects of IFI on recidivism among 732 offenders released from Minnesota prisons between 2003 and 2009. The average follow-up period for the 732 offenders was a little more than 3 years. Participation in IFI significantly decreased the risk of recidivism by 26% for rearrest, 35% for reconviction, and 40% for new offense reincarceration (Duwe & King, 2012).

Duwe and King (2012) suggested the recidivism reductions were due not only to the fact that Inner Change promotes a prosocial, crime-free lifestyle but because InnerChange attempts to mitigate the recidivism risk of those who participate by emphasizing education and reduction of criminal thinking and chemical dependency. Similar to effective therapeutic communities, IFI participants live in a separate housing unit and receive a continuum of care that links the delivery of programs in the prison institution to those in the community. Moreover, the authors concluded that IFI expands offender social support networks by providing them with mentors and connecting them with faith communities after their release from prison. The findings suggest that fait-based correctional programs can work but only if they apply what is known about effective correctional programs (Duwe & King, 2012).

DISCUSSION OF THE RECIDIVISM FINDINGS

Petersilia (2003) identified several major prisoner reintegration practices in need of correctional reform. First, Petersilia argued that it is necessary to alter the in-prison experience and essentially change the prison environment from one fostering antisocial behavior to one promoting prosocial behavior. This shift in philosophy would call for fundamentally changing the prison culture so as to teach skills and values that more closely resemble those found in society at large. Second, it is critical that relevant criminal justice authorities revise postrelease services and supervision and target those with high-need and high-risk profiles. In other words, provide closer supervision and assistance to those most likely to recidivate. Third, there is a need to seek out and foster collaborations with community organizations and thereby enhance mechanisms of informal social control. Stated differently, there is a need to establish partnerships that will provide a network of critically needed social support to newly released offenders facing a series of reintegration obstacles.

Interestingly, IFI incorporates all three of these correctional reforms. This faith-based program not only attempts to transform prisoners but also attempts to change the prison culture from one that often promotes antisocial behavior to one that is both conducive to and promotes prosocial behavior. Additionally, IFI provides critically needed aftercare services to prisoners following release from prison. Employment and housing are two of the main areas in which IFI aftercare workers provide invaluable assistance. Petersilia (2003) also has noted that it is important to prioritize risk and provide extra close supervision and assistance to those most likely to get in trouble. This is exactly the role IFI aftercare workers assumed as most prudent for them to play. Indeed, IFI aftercare staff place a great deal of their energies on parolees on their "critical care" list. Central to this process of aftercare is the role of IFI mentors—an asset missing from many prisoner reentry initiatives.

Finally, IFI made a concerted effort to partner with both parole officials and congregations throughout the Houston area. Collaborating with parole officials has been important because it has allowed both parole officers and IFI aftercare workers to pool their resources in supervising parolees. Partnerships with churches have made it possible to recruit scores of volunteers who teach a wide variety of classes in the IFI program. Similarly, these congregations have been the places IFI has targeted for recruiting mentors and, indeed, entire congregations to agree to work with both prisoners and former prisoners. Without the partnership with these faith-based organizations, IFI would not exist.

Petersilia (2003) claimed that promising in-prison and postprison programs exist that help ex-convicts lead law-abiding lives. She argued that community-based organizations, local businesses, and faith-based organizations are showing themselves to be critical partners in assisting offenders with the transition back into society. The key word in this observation, however, is the reference to *promising* rather than *proven* programs. The IFI study contributes preliminary but important evidence that a faith-based program combining education, work, life-skills, mentoring, and aftercare has the potential to influence the prisoner reentry process in a paradigm-shifting way. For example, these findings should provide insights for how faith-based organizations can be involved in the development of similar programs but that those programs should be based in the communities that will eventually be home to the 700,000 inmates leaving prison each year. From job training to housing, and life-skills counseling to mentoring, former prisoners need continued assistance postincarceration if they are to lead crime-free lives. Otherwise, as decades of research now confirm, the majority will return to prison for new crimes or technical violations while on parole (Travis, 2005).

CONNECTING SPIRITUAL TRANSFORMATION TO PRISONER REHABILITATION

Several observations from interviews with prisoners, staff, and volunteers are worth noting. Almost without exception, IFI participants indicated they had grown spiritually since coming to IFI. Interestingly, although many indicated they were Christians and had been involved in chaplaincy (i.e., religious programs in other prisons) before IFI, most indicated they had not experienced a spiritual transformation until entering the IFI program. This is a very important point that may be consistent with PF's belief that the level or intensity of involvement is the critical factor in the spiritual transformation of prisoners. Many of the prisoners indicated that they had become believers during their youth, but they quickly followed a different path after leaving church during adolescence. Furthermore, they indicated that the IFI program had caused them to reevaluate their lives and brought them back to God.

Focus groups with prisoners entering IFI seem to support PF's contention that length of time in the program would be associated with spiritual growth. Interviews revealed that the newest IFI members were much more likely to respond negatively to the program. A common set of criticisms consistently emerged from some of the new IFI participants. For example, some felt the IFI environment was negative, resulting from enforcement of program rules, and that staff displayed favoritism, especially in the selection of IFI leaders. The "leaders" were referred to by new IFI participants as "show ponies" or "poster boys" who were "faking it." After having been in the program for several months, however, focus groups revealed that most members thought the environment was positive and that there were many opportunities for positive change in IFI. Most realized that positive and negative aspects exist, but the newest program participants seemed to be most likely to dwell on the more restrictive aspects of the IFI environment. The newest groups had much more of a negative assessment of IFI staff. New members complained not only about staff favoritism but also about what they perceived as the constant changing of rules. On the other hand, members who had been in the program for at least 3 months generally reported having positive experiences with the staff and claimed IFI staff affirmed and supported them. Finally, IFI members diverged regarding their views on correctional officers. IFI participants new to the program often felt that correctional officers and other TDCJ staff were harsh or tried to provoke them. With more time in the program, however, these same members felt that TDCJ staff tended to treat them in a more positive way than correctional staff in other prisons where they had served time. Clearly, the IFI program, inmates, staff, environment, and correctional officers did not change noticeably from overly negative to positive. It is possible that staff and officers became more positive to participants as they progressed through the program. The more likely explanation, however, is that these IFI participants were the ones who had changed and, as a result, tended to have more positive feedback all around. These observations are consistent with the idea that spiritual transformation is a developmental process.

OBSERVATIONS OF SPIRITUAL TRANSFORMATION

Over the course of 6 years, I conducted hundreds of in-depth interviews with prisoners in multiple settings. These interviews were not structured and were conducted simply to report on how they were doing and what reactions, if any, they had to the IFI program (Johnson, 2011). Content analysis of these interviews with prisoners revealed five distinct spiritual transformation themes. Furthermore, spiritual transformation not only corresponds to but also can be seen as providing the impetus for various characteristics and attributes that are often associated with prisoner rehabilitation. What follows is a brief discussion of how these spiritual transformation themes are consistent with elements thought to be essential in achieving rehabilitation.

Theme 1: I'm Not Who I Used to Be

Theme 1 is important because it carries a recognition on the part of the offender that his previous behavior was justifiably unacceptable to society. In fact, the person they have become is now able to condemn their previous behavior because the new person appreciates and promotes prosocial rather than antisocial behavior. This spiritual theme is important and potentially powerful because it allows many prisoners to reconcile their troubled past and move forward.

Theme 2: Spiritual Growth

This growth is critical because it suggests that the person understands they are very much a work in progress. Although many report they have made a great deal of progress in putting their life back together, most acknowledge they still have a long way to go. They are quite surprised and encouraged about their own spiritual growth, and this progress is confirmed and validated by staff, volunteers, and mentors—further strengthening their resolve to continue this path of spiritual development. Particular events like being "born again," or the recognition that God and others actually love and care for them, appear to be critically important turning points in their spiritual development.

Theme 3: God Versus the Prison Code

Adopting a God code is particularly significant because many correctional staff already concede that the penitentiary mentality or prison code is so pervasive and strong as to move the inmate beyond the possibility of reform or rehabilitation. As stated, the prison code runs counter to the various components of offender rehabilitation programs. To be able to successfully oppose or even reverse the influence of the prison code is a remarkable achievement. This evaluation provides a number of observations confirming that the IFI environment successfully opposed if not reversed the prison environment.

Theme 4: Positive Outlook on Life

A positive outlook is important because it reflects a paradigm shift for many offenders from a cynical outlook to an outlook on life typified by hope and purpose. Following release from prison, many former prisoners relapse or commit new crimes because of minor setbacks with a friend, family member, or employer. Instead of being fatalistic about their circumstances and perhaps making bad decisions, a positive outlook can help them to be resilient in the face of adversity. Believing that their life now has meaning and knowing that they are loved and accepted by God, a mentor, and others, they are much more likely to view their life and circumstances in a positive rather than negative or hopeless way.

Theme 5: The Need to Give Back to Society

The need to give back is something many seemed to feel strongly about. They simply report feeling compelled to give back, to make a contribution to society in a way that improves the situation of others, especially others who come from similar backgrounds and experiences as their own. In sum, all five spiritual transformation themes reflect behavior and attitudes consistent with those one would hope for in achieving offender rehabilitation.

In general, face-to-face interviews offer subjective evidence that many of the IFI members had made spiritual progress. In free-flowing conversation, inmates responded in ways indicating their lives had changed as a result of their involvement in IFI. The parallels between markers of spiritual development and rehabilitation are intriguing. The relationship between spiritual transformation and rehabilitation is, unfortunately, a grossly understudied topic, but it is one that may yield important and practical insights for offender treatment both inside and outside correctional institutions (see Volume 1, Chapter 22, this handbook).

MENTORING MATTERS

Focus groups with IFI participants confirmed the many struggles they face following release from prison. In addition, these same focus groups highlighted the centrality of mentors and spiritual growth in succeeding on parole. The men in these focus groups shared how the IFI program had helped them in a number of ways—from bringing them to salvation, to preparing them for the outside, to resolving their questions about God. The group shared that they had been transformed during their time in the IFI program and that the spiritual growth had been invaluable to them on the outside. The men shared how through IFI they had discovered a new way to live and a new way to look at things. The program also helped some men to realize that people on the outside do care about them, rather than believing that society as a whole had rejected them. Some said that they learned how to be a leader at IFI, how to be held accountable, and even how to accept responsibility for their words and deeds. These attributes seemed to be helpful during the difficult transition back into society.

Following release from prison, IFI participants did not see much of each other aside from the mandated support group meetings. For most, these meetings were beneficial times of sharing trials and encouraging one another. Without exception, the parolees indicated that they missed the fellowship they enjoyed with the other IFI participants while in prison and wished it were possible to get together more often and support each other. This is where the significance of mentors becomes magnified. Without the constant support from others in the program, the mentoring relationship, if it is active and productive, can make the difference in achieving successful reintegration.

Ex-prisoners have indicated that the time immediately following release from prison is a honeymoon of sorts for many of them. But this honeymoon period dissipates as trials and responsibilities arrive, thus making it more difficult to keep God as a priority in their life. Such trials include temptations from old friends, fatigue, employment difficulties, transportation problems, adjustments to a new environment (e.g., finding their way around again), and "little things" like impatience, relational issues with family members and friends, and financial struggles.

Interviews with and observations of IFI participants (pre- and postrelease), IFI staff, TDCJ employees, and mentors provide insights that help to explain the success as well as failure of IFI participants following release from prison. First, as noted, five spiritual transformation themes emerged from the ongoing interviews with IFI participants. Although prisoners may identify a single point in time when they had a conversion experience, spiritual transformation is best viewed as an ongoing process shaped by the faith-based environment and program curriculum. Additionally, each of these spiritual transformation themes seem to be consistent with characteristics associated with offender rehabilitation. Stated differently, it would appear that markers of spiritual transformation and rehabilitation are quite similar and may well overlap. Indeed, it may be that markers of spiritual transformation and rehabilitation are mutually reinforcing.

Second, mentoring matters for prisoners and especially ex-prisoners. Furthermore, it is important that mentoring be continuous throughout the period of incarceration. Mentors should be matched with inmates as soon as possible rather than waiting for a length of time to be eligible for a mentor. This is particularly true for ex-prisoners during reentry into the community following release from prison.

Finally, because mentors are natural role models for prisoners, it makes sense that they also facilitate the spiritual development of prisoners and bolster the postrelease decision making of ex-prisoners.

Third, severing ties to a mentor makes the reentry process much more difficult to successfully navigate. If ex-prisoners fail to remain connected to mentors, they are much more likely to take a downward spiral typified by a lack of accountability, isolation, and ultimately, recidivism. Fourth, failure to connect with congregations in an intentional way prevents IFI participants from receiving a host of important social and spiritual supports they were accustomed to receiving while in prison, thus making them prone to an increasingly fatalistic attitude, eventually leading to a return to criminal behavior.

LINKING SPIRITUAL TRANSFORMATION TO CHANGE OVER THE LIFE COURSE

Sheldon and Eleanor Glueck conducted one of the most well-known delinquency studies of all time, described in their classic book *Unraveling Juvenile Delinquency* (1950), in which they studied, among other things, 500 troubled boys raised in Boston who had already been involved in delinquent behavior and had been put into reform school. The Gluecks collected extensive records about the boys and tracked them through adolescence. Many years later, Robert Sampson and John Laub, two leading criminologists, found all of the original files from the Glueck's research and followed up with the original respondents to see how they were doing now that they were around 60 years of age. Sampson and Laub (1995) found that some of the troubled boys, as one might expect, remained in trouble with the law for the rest of their lives. Others, however, lived normal lives and had no legal problems. In an important book, Sampson and Laub (1993) examined not only why troubled kids remained in trouble, but more important, they focused on how so many of these troubled youth actually turned out well.

Sampson and Laub (1993, 1995) discovered that the troubled kids who stayed out of trouble experienced some sort of a turning point or event that was pivotal in bringing them out of a criminal lifestyle and into a more conventional or law-abiding pattern of behavior. These turning points, for example, could be getting a job, marriage, or becoming a parent. For others, going into military service proved to be a turning point by perhaps providing the discipline and structure they were lacking. Likewise, the demands and responsibility that tend to come with employment, marriage, or raising a family likely provided the stability and purpose that are part and parcel of looking out for the welfare of others—while staying out of trouble. In other words, life-course theory suggests people can and do change. Just because people start out on the wrong track does not mean that they are destined to stay on the wrong track the rest of their lives.

Essentially, Sampson and Laub (1993, 1995), as well as other life-course theorists, have agreed that having ties or bonds to social institutions (marriage, family, employment, etc.) significantly influences behavior over the course of a lifetime (Horney, Osgood, & Marshall-Ineke, 1995; MacKenzie, Browning, Priu, Skroban, & Smith, 1998; MacKenzie & Li, 2002). These theorists, however, have had precious little to say about the factors that lead to the changes in ties or bonds. Stated differently, scholars have been reluctant to discuss how changes within the individual during adulthood may lead to the formation of these important social bonds.

Recently, however, several scholars have acknowledged that changes in the individual must take place before that person is ready to develop ties and bonds to social institutions. In other words, the individual must change if the bond is to form. According to MacKenzie (2006),

> To get along with family, keep a job, support children, or form strong, positive ties with other institutions, the person must change in cognitive reasoning, attitude toward drug use, anti-social attitudes, reading level, or vocation skills. A focus on individual change is critical to our understanding of what works in corrections. (p. 337)

Giordano, Cernkovich, and Rudolph (2002) have called this kind of change *cognitive transformation*. For them, these cognitive transformations are essential before a person is able to sustain a new way of life. In this way religion can be viewed not only as a source of external control over an individual's conduct but also as a catalyst for new definitions and a cognitive blueprint for how one is to proceed as a changed individual (Giordano, Longmore, Schroeder, & Seffrin, 2008; see also Volume 1, Chapters 14 and 22, this handbook). This process of change is facilitated by a spiritual or faith factor, whether through an affiliation with a religious congregation, or based more on personal spiritual experiences, or both. This process makes possible the development of a new and more favorable identity to replace the old one associated with any or all of the following: failure, violence, abuse, addiction, heartbreak, and guilt (Heimer & Matsueda, 1997; Maruna, 2001).

This is why religious conversions and spiritual transformations are important. These religious experiences are turning points or events in the lives of offenders. These religious experiences allow offenders to build a new foundation and to start their lives over. As Maruna (2001) argued, getting a chance to rewrite one's own narrative can be a powerful and redemptive thing, giving ex-prisoners the hope and purpose they need to start a new and prosocial life, while at the same time coming to grips with the antisocial life they have left behind (Maruna, 2001). Along these same lines, a number of restorative justice programs are interested in bringing crime victims and offenders face to face. These programs, many of which are faith based, exist to bring closure and emotional healing to an experience that has never been reconciled. For example, victim–offender mediation programs, also known as victim–offender reconciliation programs, follow a restorative justice approach that brings offenders face to face with the victims of their crimes with the assistance of a trained mediator, usually a community volunteer. Crime is personalized as offenders learn the human consequences of their actions, and victims (who may be ignored by the criminal justice system) have the opportunity to speak their minds and their feelings to the one who most ought to hear them, contributing to the healing process of the victim. Offenders take meaningful responsibility for their actions by mediating a restitution agreement with the victim, to restore the victims' losses, in whatever ways that may be possible. Restitution may be monetary or symbolic; it may consist of work for the victim, community service, or anything else that creates a sense of justice between the victim and the offender.

Petersilia (2003) has identified several major prisoner reintegration practices in need of correctional reform. First, she argued it is necessary to alter the in-prison experience and essentially change the prison environment from one fostering antisocial behavior to one promoting prosocial behavior. Second, it is critical that relevant criminal justice authorities revise postrelease services and supervision while targeting those with high-need and high-risk profiles. Third, there is a need to seek out and foster collaborations with community organizations and thereby enhance mechanisms of informal social control. Stated differently, Petersilia argued there is a need to establish partnerships that will provide a network of critically needed social support to newly released offenders facing a series of reintegration obstacles. Faith-based prison programs often incorporate all three of these correctional reforms.

Beyond attempting to transform prisoners, faith-based programs attempt to change the prison culture itself from one that often condones antisocial behavior to one that is both conducive to and promotes prosocial behavior. Additionally, faith-based programs can provide critical transitional and aftercare services to prisoners when they eventually return to society. Finally, as faith-based groups seek to partner with secular and government agencies the possibility for pooling resources to benefit programs for prisoners and ex-prisoners increases dramatically. Partnerships with religious congregations and faith-based organizations have made it possible to recruit and train thousands of volunteers who assist in offering classes and far-ranging resources. Similarly, volunteer-rich churches have been the places targeted for recruiting mentors and, indeed, entire congregations to work with prisoners and ex-prisoners.

Petersilia (2003) noted that promising in-prison and postprison programs exist to help ex-convicts lead law-abiding lives and that community-based organizations, local businesses, and faith-based organizations are showing themselves to be critical partners in assisting offenders with the transition back into society. Preliminary evidence suggests faith communities may be able to accomplish what prisons have been unable to achieve. By combining education, work, life skills, counseling, mentoring, and aftercare, faith-based efforts have the potential to influence the prison environment in a paradigm-shifting way, thereby facilitating the process of inmate treatment and rehabilitation. As has been discussed earlier, the relationship between spiritual transformation and rehabilitation is a grossly understudied topic. This is unfortunate because this research may yield important and practical insights for how to provide offender treatment both inside and outside correctional institutions. This chapter has elaborated on how these two topics may be mutually reinforcing and how faith-based organizations (along with the human and spiritual capital they can wield) may yet become valued partners to U.S. corrections and provide future approaches to offender treatment and rehabilitation.

Every year, hundreds of thousands of prisoners participate in religious services and interact with faith-motivated volunteers and mentors. Many of these offenders will have religious conversions. In and of itself, this may not mean a great deal to criminologists, correctional practitioners, or policymakers, but faith-based reentry and aftercare programs have the potential to build on these religious conversions. In the life course, conversions should not be viewed cynically as "jailhouse religion," but rather as the opportunity to connect these converts to volunteers and faith-based networks that may facilitate and nurture spiritual transformation. This is exactly why the most effective programs helping offenders may be those that intentionally link spiritual transformation to other support networks, especially those that are faith motivated and faith friendly.

References

Andrews, D. A., Zinger, I., Hoge, R. D., Bonta, J., Gendreau, P., & Cullen, F. T. (1990). Does correctional treatment work? A clinically relevant and psychologically informed meta-analysis. *Criminology, 28*, 369–397.

Ball, J. C., Shaffer, J., & Nurco, D. (1983). Day to day criminality of heroin addicts in Baltimore: A study of offense rates. *Drug and Alcohol Dependence, 12*, 119–142. doi:10.1016/0376-8716(83)90037-6

Bureau of Justice Statistics. (1999). *Substance abuse and treatment, state and federal prisoners, 1997*. Washington, DC: U.S. Department of Justice.

Bureau of Justice Statistics. (2009). *Total correctional population, 2008*. Washington, DC: U.S. Department of Justice.

Clear, T., & Sumter, M. (2002). Prisoner, prison, and religion: Religion and adjustment to prison. *Journal of Offender Rehabilitation, 35*, 127–159.

Cullen, F. (2002). Rehabilitation and treatment programs. In J. Q. Wilson & J. Petersilia (Eds.), *Crime: Public policies for crime control* (pp. 253–289). Oakland, CA: ICS Press.

Cullen, F., & Gendreau, P. (1989). The effectiveness of correctional rehabilitation: Reconsidering the "nothing works" debate. In L. Goodstein & D. L. MacKensie (Eds.), *The American prison: Issues in research policy* (pp. 23–44). New York, NY: Plenum Press.

Davis, R. C., & Lurigio, A. J. (1996). *Fighting back: Neighborhood antidrug strategies*. Thousand Oaks, CA: Sage.

Dobson, K. S., & Craig, K. D. (1996). *Advances in cognitive behavioral therapy*. Newbury Park, CA: Sage.

Dobson, K. S., & Khatr, N. (2000). Cognitive therapy: Looking backward, looking forward. *Journal of Clinical Psychology, 56*, 907–923. doi:10.1002/1097-4679(200007)56:7<907::AID-JCLP9>3.0.CO;2-I

Duwe, G., & King, M. (2012). Can faith-based correctional programs work? An outcome evaluation of the InnerChange Freedom Initiative in Minnesota. *International Journal of Offender Therapy and Comparative Criminology, 20*, 1–9.

Freeman, R. B. (1986). Who escapes? The relation of churchgoing and other background factors to the socioeconomic performance of Black male youth from inner-city tracts. In R. B. Freeman & H. J. Holzer (Eds.), *The Black youth employment crisis* (pp. 353–376). Chicago, IL: University of Chicago Press.

Gendreau, P., & Ross, R. R. (1987). Revivification or rehabilitation: Evidence from the 1980s. *Justice Quarterly, 4*, 349–407.

Giordano, P. C., Cernkovich, S. A., & Rudolph, J. L. (2002). Gender, crime, and desistance: Toward a theory of cognitive transformation. *American Journal of Sociology, 107*, 990–1064. doi:10.1086/343191

Giordano, P. C., Longmore, M. A., Schroeder, R. D., & Seffrin, P. M. (2008). A life-course perspective on spirituality and desistance from crime. *Criminology, 46*, 99–132. doi:10.1111/j.1745-9125.2008.00104.x

Glueck, S., & Glueck, E. (1950). *Unraveling juvenile delinquency*. New York, NY: Commonwealth Fund.

Heimer, K., & Matsueda, R. L. (1997). A symbolic interactionist theory of motivation and deviance: Interpreting psychological research. In D. W. Osgood (Ed.), *Nebraska Symposium on Motivation: Vol. 44. Motivation and delinquency* (pp. 223–276). Lincoln: University of Nebraska Press.

Horney, J., W. D. Osgood, & H. Marshall-Ineke. (1995). Criminal careers in the short-term: Intra-individual variability in crime and its relation to local life circumstances. *American Sociological Review, 60*, 655–673.

Jang, S. J., Bader, C. D., & Johnson, B. R. (2008). The cumulative advantage of religiosity in preventing drug use. *Journal of Drug Issues, 38*, 771–798. doi:10.1177/002204260803800306

Jang, S. J., & Johnson, B .R. (2001). Neighborhood disorder, individual religiosity, and adolescent use of illicit drugs: A test of multilevel hypotheses. *Criminology, 39*, 109–144. doi:10.1111/j.1745-9125.2001.tb00918.x

Johnson, B. R. (2004). Religious programs and recidivism among former inmates in prison fellowship programs: A long-term follow-up study. *Justice Quarterly, 21*, 329–354. doi:10.1080/07418820400095831

Johnson, B. R. (2009). The role of religious institutions in responding to crime and delinquency. In P. B. Clarke (Ed.), *The Oxford handbook of the sociology of religion* (pp. 857–875). New York, NY: Oxford University Press.

Johnson, B. R. (2011). *More God, less crime: Why religion matters and how it could matter more*. Conshohocken, PA: Templeton Press.

Johnson, B. R., & Jang, S. J. (2001). Neighborhood disorder, individual religiosity, and adolescent drug use: A test of multilevel hypotheses. *Criminology, 39*, 501–535.

Johnson, B. R., & Jang, S. J. (2010, November). *Crime and religion: Assessing the role of the faith factor*. Paper presented at the annual meeting of the American Society of Criminology, San Francisco, CA.

Johnson, B. R., Jang, S. J., Larson, D. B., & Li, S. D. (2001). Does adolescent religious commitment matter? A reexamination of the effects of religiosity on delinquency. *Journal of Research in Crime and Delinquency, 38*, 22–44. doi:10.1177/002242780 1038001002

Johnson, B. R., Jang, S. J., Li, S. D., & Larson, D. B. (2000). The invisible institution and Black youth crime: The church as an agency of local social control. *Journal of Youth and Adolescence, 29*, 479–498. doi:10.1023/A:1005114610839

Johnson, B. R., & Larson, D. B. (2003). *The InnerChange freedom initiative: Evaluating a faith-based prison program*. Retrieved from http://www.baylorisr.org/wp-content/uploads/ISR_Innerchange_Free1.pdf

Johnson, B. R., Larson, D. B., Jang, S. J., & Li, S. D. (2000). The "invisible institution" and Black youth crime: The church as an agency of local social control. *Journal of Youth and Adolescence, 29*, 479–498.

Johnson, B. R., Larson, D. B., Li, S. D., & Jang, S. J. (2000). Escaping from the crime of inner cities: Church attendance and religious salience among disadvantaged youth. *Justice Quarterly, 17*, 377–391. doi:10.1080/07418820000096371

Johnson, B. R., Larson, D. B., & Pitts, T. G. (1997). Religious programs, institutional adjustment, and recidivism among former inmates in prison fellowship programs. *Justice Quarterly, 14*, 145–166. doi:10.1080/07418829700093251

Kerley, K. R., Allison, M. C., & Graham, R. D. (2006). Investigating the impact of religiosity on emotional and behavioral coping in prison. *Journal of Criminal Justice, 29*, 71–96.

Kerley, K. R., & Copes, H. (2009). "Keepin' my mind right": Identity maintenance and religious social support in the prison context. *International Journal of Offender Therapy and Comparative Criminology, 53*, 228–244. doi:10.1177/0306624X08315019

Lipsey, M. W. (1992). Juvenile delinquency treatment: A meta-analytic inquiry into the variability of effects. In T. D. Cook, H. Cooper, D. S. Cordray, H. Hartmann, L. V. Hedges, R. J. Light, . . . F. Mosteller (Eds.), *Meta-analysis for explanation: A casebook* (pp. 83–127). New York, NY: Russell Sage Foundation.

Lo, C. C., & Stephens, R. C. (2000). Drugs and prisoners: Treatment needs on entering prison. *American Journal of Drug and Alcohol Abuse, 26*, 229–245. doi:10.1081/ADA-100100602

MacKenzie, D. L. (2006). *What works in corrections: Reducing the criminal activities of offenders and delinquents*. New York, NY: Cambridge University Press. doi:10.1017/CBO9780511499470

MacKenzie, D. L., Browning, K., Priu, H., Skroban, S., & Smith, D. (1998). *Probationer compliance with conditions of supervision* (Unpublished report.). Washington, DC: National Institute of Justice, U.S. Department of Justice.

MacKenzie, D. L., & Li, S. D. (2002). The impact of formal and informal social controls on the criminal activities of probationers. *Journal of Research in Crime and Delinquency, 39*, 243–276.

Martinson, R. (1974). What works? Questions and answers about prison reform. *Public Interest, 35*, 22–35.

Maruna, S. (2001). *Making good: How ex-offenders reform and reclaim their lives.* Washington, DC: American Psychological Association. doi:10.1037/10430-000

Morris, N., & Rothman, D. J. (1998). *The Oxford history of the prison: The practice of punishment in Western society.* New York, NY: Oxford University Press.

Nunn, A., Zaller, N., Dickman, S., Trimbur, C., Nijhawan, A., & Rich, J. (2009). Methadone and buprenorphine prescribing and referral practices in U.S. prisons: Results from a nationwide survey. *Drug and Alcohol Dependence, 105,* 83–88. doi:10.1016/j.drugalcdep.2009.06.015

Peters, R. H., Greenbaum, P. E., Edens, J. F., Carter, C. R., & Ortiz, M. N. (1998). Prevalence of DSM-IV substance abuse and dependence disorders among prison inmates. *American Journal of Drug and Alcohol Abuse, 24,* 573–587. doi:10.3109/0095299980 9019608

Petersilia, J. (2003). *When prisoners come home: Parole and prisoner reentry.* New York, NY: Oxford University Press.

Prison Fellowship. (2002). *Annual report, fiscal year 2001–2002.* Lansdowne, VA: Author.

Prison Fellowship. (2012). *Mission, vision, and values statements.* Retrieved from http://www.prisonfellowship.org/about/mision-vision-values

Proportion, F. J., Fabian, E. A., & Robinson, D. (1991). *Focusing on successful reintegration: Cognitive skills training for offenders.* Ottawa, Ontario, Canada: Research and Statistics Branch, Correctional Service of Canada.

Sampson, R. J., & Laub, J. H. (1993). *Crime in the making: Pathways and turning points through life.* Cambridge, MA: Harvard University Press.

Sampson, R. J., & Laub, J. H. (1995). Crime and deviance over the life course: The salience of adult social bonds. *American Sociological Review, 55,* 609–627. doi:10.2307/2095859

Sherman, L. W., Gottfredson, D., MacKenzie, D., Eck, J., Reuter, P., & Bushway, S. (1997). *Preventing crime: What works, what doesn't, what's promising.* Washington, DC: U.S. Department of Justice.

Tonry, M., & Wilson, J. E. (1990). *Drugs and crime.* Chicago, IL: University of Chicago Press.

Travis, J. (2005). *But they all come back: Facing the challenges of prisoner reentry.* Washington, DC: Urban Institute Press.

Wish, E. P., & Johnson, B. D. (1986). The impact of substance abuse on criminal careers. In A. Blumstein, J. Cohen, J. A. Roth, & C. A. Visher (Eds.), *Criminal careers and career criminals* (Vol. 2, pp. 54–59). Washington, DC: National Academies Press.

CHAPTER 29

ADDRESSING RELIGION AND SPIRITUALITY IN MILITARY SETTINGS AND VETERANS' SERVICES

David W. Foy, Kent D. Drescher, and Mark W. Smith

Over the more than 230-year history of the U.S. military dating back to the Revolutionary War, the spiritual needs of soldiers, sailors, and marines in military service have been recognized. From the beginning, chaplains have served on active duty and have been integral spiritual support providers to U.S. service members in all branches of the military. Similarly, the chaplaincy has been a vital professional service within the organization of the Veterans Administration (VA) since its founding. Other health and mental health care providers, including psychologists, are also concerned with the spiritual well-being of current and former military personnel. It is the aim of this chapter to examine key relationships between spirituality and aspects of military service that are manifest while members are in active service as well as those found among veterans after their discharge from active duty. We illustrate many of our points with work we have conducted with the U.S. Navy and Marines, although this work will be relevant to other military branches.

In turn we examine the following: historical perspectives on chaplaincy in both the U.S. Navy and the VA; how religion and spirituality may affect mental health and coping of active-duty personnel and veterans; how military involvement may affect religious and spiritual life; the roles of religion and spirituality in dealing with the unique demands of life-threatening combat experiences, particularly the possible role of spirituality as a buffer to the development of posttraumatic stress disorder (PTSD) and as a resource for positive adaptation; and spiritually based interventions for active-duty military personnel, veterans, and their families. We briefly discuss how spiritual and mental health care providers may experience challenges to their own spiritual well-being. In conclusion, we identify key areas for progress and make recommendations for ways to advance knowledge and practice in the area of military service and spirituality.

HISTORICAL PERSPECTIVES ON CHAPLAINCY IN THE MILITARY AND VA

Chaplains have a long and respected tradition as primary providers of religious and spiritual care to military personnel and their families. As follows, we present a brief history of chaplaincy to provide a context for psychologists and other mental health professionals to understand the roles their military and VA colleagues serve.

Military and Navy Perspectives

Since 1775, approximately 25,000 Army chaplains have served as religious and spiritual leaders for more than 25 million soldiers and their families. Whether assigned to military installations, deployed combat units, or service schools and military hospitals, chaplains are always present with their soldiers in war and in peace. Army chaplains have served in more than 270 major wars and combat engagements. Some 400 Army chaplains have been killed in battle, and six have been awarded the Medal of Honor. Currently, more than 2,800 chaplains are serving on active duty, representing more than 130 different religious organizations. More than

DOI: 10.1037/14046-029
APA Handbook of Psychology, Religion, and Spirituality: Vol. 2. An Applied Psychology of Religion and Spirituality, K. I. Pargament (Editor-in-Chief)

800 chaplains and chaplain assistants are currently mobilized or deployed in support of contingency operations throughout the world (U.S. Army, 2011).

In 1949, the U.S. Army Air Corps became what is now the U.S. Air Force and developed its own chaplaincy. Currently, there are more than 500 active-duty Air Force chaplains and nearly 600 in service with the Reserves and Air National Guard. Although each chaplain is endorsed by his or her own religious denomination and remains faithful to its tenets, chaplains also offer broad based ministry to meet the diverse pastoral needs of a pluralistic military community. Active duty and Reserve chaplains are responsible for supporting free exercise of religion for all service members and their families (U.S. Air Force, 2011).

The U.S. Navy Chaplain Corps was established on November 28, 1775. The first Navy chaplain is believed to have been a Harvard-educated Congregational minister, Rev. Benjamin Balch, whose father had been a British Royal Navy Chaplain in King George's War in 1745. Rev. Balch had already fought at Lexington as a minuteman and served briefly as an Army chaplain at the siege of Boston. He served on two frigates, earning the nickname "the fightin' Parson," for his aggressive "ministry" during sea battles aboard the *Alliance* (Dickerson, 2005). After winning independence, and without the ability to tax under the Articles of Confederation, the U.S. Congress could not afford to maintain a Navy, and the *Alliance* was the last ship sold in 1785. Even the army dwindled to about 700 men. At that point, the only naval force the fledgling country had was the Revenue Cutter Service, which eventually became the U.S. Coast Guard.

The Department of the Navy was created on April 30, 1798, as authorized by the U.S. Constitution 13 years earlier, to deal with the rising threat of Barbary pirates and the French Navy on U.S. merchant ships (Naval Historical Center, n.d.). Then, in 1799, Rev. Balch's son, Rev. William Balch, became the first commissioned chaplain in the new department. By the start of the Civil War, there were 24 chaplains serving the Navy. During the following years, chaplains were given relative rank, uniforms, and a staff corps device to identify them as one of the professional corps who supported the officers of the line. By World War I, there were 203 chaplains, with 13 serving with the U.S. Marine Corps. But in 1939 the number of chaplains in the Navy was down to 94, and numbers higher than 200 were not seen again until just after the start of World War II. Before World War II was over, there were more than 2,800 chaplains on active duty in the Navy. In the past 25 years, the number has dropped from about 1,200 to 840, with around 600 in Navy assignments, 200 serving with the Marines, and 40 with the U.S. Coast Guard.

General Order No. 456 (U.S. Navy Department, 1919) specified "that every possible assistance and encouragement [is] to be given our chaplains" for their work "to provide the officers and men with rest and recreation so essential to efficiency." The work of chaplains began as a provision for the free exercise of religious faith for those serving their country, but it has always encompassed many other avenues perceived as necessary for the care of service members. Chaplains were the teachers onboard Navy ships, providing basic education as well as junior officer training. Navy chaplains also successfully lobbied for the end of the flogging of sailors in 1850 and the end of the serving of grog aboard vessels in 1872 (Zeiger, 2009). They were early advisors to their commanders, with Chaplain John Brown Frazier standing alongside Commodore George Dewey on the bridge of the cruiser *Olympia* during the famed Battle of Manila Bay in 1898 (Dickerson, 2005). Although these tasks were natural to most chaplains, it is only in recent years that the Navy Chaplain Corps has been able to quantify their four core capabilities to meet commanders' requirements. These include providing religious services, facilitating the religious needs of other faith groups, caring for all members of the command and their families, and advising the command (Office of Public Affairs, Navy Chief of Chaplains, 2007).

Before 1841, ordination was not a requirement to be a chaplain; some were procured for teaching abilities only, and others were appointed from the ship's company. After 1841, however, both ordination and good moral character were required by General Regulations. For the first 80 years, Methodists and Episcopalians dominated the ranks of chaplains, but later, other Christian denominations grew to a majority and eventually rabbis, imams, and Buddhist chaplains were added so that 21st-century Navy chaplains represent more than 100 faith groups (Dickerson, 2005).

In 1906, the secretary of the Navy appointed a board of chaplains that established the office of the Chief of Chaplains in 1917. By this time, the board had required that all chaplains be graduates of both college and seminary, along with formal endorsement by a religious denomination (Osborne, 2007). With the large increase in the numbers of chaplains needed for World War II, there came a need to coordinate their training for service in the fleet, so the Navy Chaplains School was established in 1942. The school was decommissioned in 1945, but it was reestablished in 1951 at the outbreak of hostilities in Korea. The school continues to this day, having recently moved from Newport, Rhode Island, to Fort Jackson, South Carolina, as part of a move to centralize the training of all armed services' chaplains at one site (Naval Chaplaincy School and Center, n.d.). The training of Navy chaplains continues throughout their careers through required annual professional development training courses and optional training workshops, in addition to personal education goals pursued by chaplains on their own. In recent years, the current authors have contributed to these education opportunities for the Navy Chaplain Corps by developing professional training curricula and leading many seminars.

VA Perspectives

Chaplain services for war veterans began with the order signed by Abraham Lincoln in 1865 that established the first National Homes for disabled Civil War soldiers. Chaplains were paid $1,500 per year and forage for one horse to provide services to these disabled soldiers. In 1930, an act of Congress consolidated all the National Soldier's Homes under the control of the VA, and part-time local clergy served in chaplaincy roles in the hospitals.

The year 1945 is often seen as the formal beginning of chaplaincy within the VA. Rev. Crawford W. Brown was appointed to be the first chief of a national chaplaincy service "to assure beneficiaries the best possible spiritual guidance, religious services, etc." (U.S. Department of Veterans Affairs, 2010). At the end of that year, VA administrator Gen. Omar Bradley authorized placement of full-time and part-time chaplains in all VA Hospitals, and 125 chaplains were proposed to provide a chaplain for each VA Hospital of 500 beds or more. The following year (1946), the first chaplains' conference was held in Washington, DC. VA projections called for 195 full-time chaplains and anticipated a need for 600 full-time chaplains by 1960. Currently, nearly 1,000 chaplains are working in the VA system (U.S. Department of Veterans Affairs, 2010).

As time passed, increasing attention was paid to the training and qualifications for VA chaplains. In 1964, a chaplain school was created at the VA in St. Louis, Missouri. By 1966, new chaplains were required to complete up to 13 weeks at the chaplain training school, after which they would receive a permanent assignment to a VA field station. In 1986, a new national chaplain training facility was opened in its present location at the Veterans Affairs Medical Center in Hampton, Virginia. In 1988, the VA authorized the first VA clinical pastoral education (CPE) programs. In 1998, the VA issued new qualification requirements for VA chaplains: A minimum of two units of CPE or its equivalent is required (U.S. Department of Veterans Affairs, 2010).

With the post–Vietnam War increase in mental health services for veterans, there was a corresponding increase in hospital-based outpatient services as well as movement toward community-based clinics that provide both primary care and mental health services. These clinics, along with community-based Vet Centers provide care closer to where the veterans live. Traditionally, VA chaplains have provided hospital-based ("bedside") spiritual support for physically ill and dying veterans. In recent years, approximately 300,000 veterans from the wars in Iraq and Afghanistan have entered the VA system, and approximately 96% of those new veterans have been served in outpatient settings. Thus, a prominent challenge currently faced by the VA chaplain service is to identify and adapt best practice models for meeting the pastoral care needs of these new veterans.

SPIRITUALITY, MENTAL HEALTH, AND COPING IN ACTIVE DUTY MEMBERS AND VETERANS

Research findings from studies about combat, PTSD, and spirituality demonstrate that spirituality may enhance or diminish health and well-being. Moreover, combat may leave spirituality strengthened, weakened, or unchanged. On the positive side, spirituality may help combat veterans achieve adversarial or posttraumatic growth that could lead to benefits, such as increased resilience in the face of future life challenges, increased meaning or purpose, and strengthened capacity to utilize positive coping resources amid crises (Fontana & Rosenheck, 2004; Pargament et al., 1998). An early study (Green, Lindy, & Grace, 1988) found increased religious coping and positive attempts to assign meaning to war-zone events by combat veterans. In a study of female veterans, women who reported experiences of military sexual assault had significantly poorer overall mental health and higher levels of depression when compared with veterans who did not report being assaulted (Chang, Skinner, & Boehmer, 2001). Results also showed that more frequent religious participation was associated with lower depression and higher overall mental health scores among the sexually assaulted women, consistent with a buffering effect for religious participation on mental health.

Religion and spirituality, however, have also been associated with more problematic outcomes. Surviving combat trauma may be associated with a shift to more negative beliefs about the safety, goodness, and meaningfulness of the world (Janoff-Bulman, 1992); negative views of one's relationship with God, such as beliefs that God is punishing or abandoning the individual; loss of core spiritual values; and estrangement from or questioning one's spiritual identity (e.g., Decker, 1993; Drescher & Foy, 1995; Falsetti et al., 2003).

In our study of veterans in residential treatment for PTSD, spiritual distress (i.e., abandoning faith during combat and afterward, difficulty reconciling war-zone events with faith) was found in a high percentage of military veterans (Drescher & Foy, 1995). Several more recent studies have identified both positive and negative associations between spirituality and combat trauma or related PTSD. Witvliet, Phillips, Feldman, and Beckham (2004) identified two dimensions of spirituality, that is, lack of forgiveness and religious coping (both positive and negative) were associated with PTSD and depression severity among veterans in outpatient treatment for PTSD. Relatedly, Fontana and Rosenheck (2004) found significant correlations between specific types of combat trauma, loss of religious faith, and increased utilization of VA mental health services among veterans in treatment for combat-related PTSD. Specific combat experiences (killing others, failure to save the wounded, etc.) were directly and indirectly (mediated by guilt) associated with reduction in comfort derived from religious faith. Both guilt and reduced comfort from religious faith were shown to be associated with increased use of VA services.

What are some implications of these findings for those tasked with providing mental and spiritual health services to active-duty service members and veterans with combat exposure? Clergy as well as health and mental health service providers, need to be aware that for a sizeable minority, combat exposure may lead to serious spiritual questioning and, at times, a loss of faith. Spiritual tensions that arise for many combat returnees attempting to come to terms with their war-zone experiences may reduce their use of spiritual resources to cope with reentry and may be associated with increased psychiatric symptoms and higher medical service utilization. Accordingly, staying alert for signs of "negative religious coping/spiritual struggles" or negative attributions about God (e.g., God has abandoned me, God is persecuting or punishing me; Pargament et al., 1998; see also Volume 1, Chapter 25, this handbook) is important because these can be associated with more severe PTSD and depression. Difficulties with forgiveness, hostility, and guilt also may be associated with more severe problems (Drescher & Foy, 2008).

POSTDEPLOYMENT INTERVIEWS OF MARINES ON SPIRITUALITY, RELIGION, AND THE MILITARY

This section focuses in detail on one study of the role of spirituality among Marines facing military deployment and combat. One of the authors (Mark W. Smith) conducted postdeployment interviews with more than 500 Marines upon their recent return from combat tours of duty in Iraq, and his summary of key observations regarding spirituality and combat in the first 200 of those interviews has been described (cf. Drescher, Smith, & Foy, 2007). This section presents an update that includes observations from more than 300 additional interviews. All interviewees were Marine officers or senior enlisted noncommissioned officers, ranked E-7 or higher.

Positive Effects of Spirituality

The organizing question for the first portion of the interview was "How does spirituality and religion help an individual's life in military service?" Many of the Marines reported that their faith provided them with a *sense of meaning to life*, a sense of their own place in the world. "Everything happens for a reason" is a common comment expressed in these interviews. Having a belief that there was ultimate goodness in the world, and that that goodness was worth fighting for, sustained many and kept them going. As some Marines stated, "God is love," "God promised to be with us," and "God will not let evil triumph." For some it was a *sense of justice and rightness* that could be achieved. "Sometimes we are God's hands to make things right." Even more significant for many was the thought that there was a *divine Goodness, God, who has a plan for the ultimate defeat of evil* in the world. For example, one Marine said, "I know who's really in charge. It may not always look like it, but I know who ultimately decides, and He won't abandon us." This perspective allowed many Marines to see God as protecting them from injury at times, as well as keeping them safe even if they were to be wounded or killed, because there is an *ultimate victory in an eternal sense*. This was a source of peace for many.

Marines also described the strength and comfort they derived from their faith and religious practices. Some talked of Bible study groups that reinforced this thinking, and many mentioned that they gained strength in the moment from physically carrying a Bible or wearing a cross or saint's medal. Many mentioned the spiritual *practice of prayer in the moment of greatest need*—often as a quick, desperate prayer in a critical dangerous moment—and some even reported dropping to their knees to pray just the instant before having to respond in dramatic battle or evasion. In fact, prayer was the most commonly mentioned source of support and was often described as the practice that also most helped them with the memories of combat.

Other Marines talked about *encouraging words from those professing faith*. A number spoke of eliciting support from a chaplain not necessarily by arranging an appointment but by deliberately engaging in surface banter and counting on the chaplain to impart some spiritual encouragement. Although they were a little embarrassed by this approach, it seemed important to avoid direct requests for help but rather to be within earshot to receive it. Marines who were involved in firefights and dramatic rescues also gained support during downtimes by talking about what had happened. After-action reviews were greatly appreciated, but there were conflicting views about chaplains' participation in them. Although some expressed a stronger desire to have chaplains at those events to add encouragement, others only wanted members of the intimate battle team present in those discussions. More generally, several felt that along with all the medical and psychological screenings, there needed to be more time with the chaplains.

Many interviewees reported that their strong sense of God being with them, and being available in prayer, was a significant part of what kept them going, gave them peace in turmoil, and connected them with higher purposes and a broader community of support. Among those interviewed there were a few who, even at that early point, clearly needed some form of psychological intervention. Among those needing referral for more extensive mental health services, one of the most frequent comments made was "not feeling human anymore" or "feeling more like an animal." Overall, these interviews demonstrated that many of these combat-experienced Marines value their spirituality as a vital coping resource.

Impact of Combat on Religion and Spirituality

Although combat experiences can stimulate some service members toward positive spiritual growth, others suffer setbacks in their spirituality. The possibility of spiritual harm or injury has been recognized among branches of the U.S. military, For example the Navy and Marine Corps have identified a particular kind of negative change in spirituality, *moral injury*, as an expected consequence of combat for a sizeable minority of participants, along with PTSD, grief, and operational fatigue. In general terms, moral injury refers to damage or harm to one's moral center, or compass, as a consequence of direct and indirect experiences in the war zone (Drescher & Foy, 2008; Litz et al., 2009).

To examine the full range of effects of military life on spirituality, Marine interviewees also responded to the following question: "How does military life affect religion and spirituality for Marines deployed to Iraq?" Most of the Marines expressed that their spirituality was important to them and that combat deployment presented an opportunity for growth ("My faith was tested in ways I did not expect, and it made me a more mature Christian"). Although many reported they had, in fact, grown spiritually, a few reported being angry with God after the horrors they had experienced ("I can't believe in a God who would let this happen"). Some expressed fear that they would "never get better, never be the same as before" and were particularly worried that they might never regain a sense of compassion after having to numb themselves emotionally while serving in the war zone. As some said, "I will never be the same"; "The crap that goes on back here, the shit people complain about, just doesn't seem to matter anymore."

Some of the effects of service on the faith of Marines were evidenced in decisions to behave differently and to change their practices. The most common decision reported by those of nominal faith was a desire to deepen their own faith, both in reflection and study, and in developing practices related to their faith. Almost all expressed the conviction that life was more precious now, and they needed to make intentional efforts to treasure those they love and live life to the fullest. Some felt they needed to not only think more about their faith but also live it out fully in their lives, by praying more, studying more, going to church more, and sharing their faith more directly with their comrades in service. Many noted that the faith of fellow service members around them inspired and sustained them, and this led them to pray in more significant ways when they particularly needed help. Many also reported that they found themselves more emotional when attending church services—finding it helpful but also much more meaningful than it had been before their combat experiences. A number of them—perhaps reflecting the scripture quoted in the memorial ceremonies for fallen comrades—mentioned the significance of giving up one's life for a friend, as Christians believe Christ had done for humanity.

SPIRITUALLY BASED INTERVENTIONS FOR ACTIVE DUTY MILITARY PERSONNEL, VETERANS, AND FAMILIES

Spiritual fitness of all active-duty service members has been emphasized as an essential element of overall health by the Office of the Chairman of Joint Chiefs of Staff. A recent conference of military and civilian experts convened by that office was tasked with the goal of setting the right conditions to promote fitness among service members in all branches of service. Conferees defined *health* as follows: "A state of complete physical, mental, social, and spiritual well-being and not merely the absence of disease or infirmity" (Institute for Alternative Futures, 2009, p 2). Additionally, *spiritual fitness* was defined as

> development of positive and helpful beliefs, practices and connecting expressions of the human spirit. "Human spirit" refers to the essential core of the individual, the deepest part of the self, and includes the essential capacities for autonomy, self-awareness, and creativity, as well as the ability to love and be loved and to appreciate beauty and language. (Institute for Alternative Futures, 2009, p. 13)

U.S. Navy Chaplain Programs of Spiritual Care for Operational Stress

Warrior Transition. Warrior Transition is a term that evolved early in the various unit efforts to assist service members returning from Operation Iraqi Freedom and Operation Enduring Freedom, which later evolved into an official title for specific standardized programs. Increasingly over the years, predeployment training for Navy and Marine Corps has included an operational stress component, often taught by the ship's or battalion's docs (a term used for both enlisted corpsmen and physicians), but frequently also by the chaplain if that chaplain had some stress management experience. Often, in fact, the chaplain, as an experienced "preacher" was the primary teacher even when a physician was available. With the advent of the wars in Iraq and Afghanistan, chaplains in the Marines took the lead in developing Warrior Transition programs. These were typically a series of large group briefs before deployment, just before redeployment (return home), and after return home. The goal was to help those trained, experienced, and deployed in war to transition back to home. Although there was some consistency, each chaplain leading the briefs tended to develop his or her own special flavor or format. In the Marine Corps in 2006 and beyond, these briefs came to be more standardized but were developed with input from psychiatrists and chaplains returning from Iraq and Afghanistan. There are now a series of nine briefs for before deployment, just before or after returning home, and several months after return home, which are targeted at three groups: leaders, warriors, and family members. Although still subject to interpretation by individual commanders and chaplains, some of the basics of each presentation are required by the commandant of the Marine Corps. Elements of these briefs have been adopted by Navy and other Department of Defense (DoD) services. The cycle includes specific goals for each point—broad information on stress and "how to recover" in predeployment, "how to make the transition" on return, and "how are we doing?" postdeployment. These efforts originated by chaplains providing spiritual care but became line programs as the need was more fully recognized by leadership.

Warrior Transition II. Warrior Transition II (WTII) is a specific, standardized, brief self-evaluative program developed exclusively for Marines returning from combat deployment. WTII is conducted within 3 to 6 months postdeployment and offers each service member an opportunity to self-evaluate current functioning in eight critical life spheres: relationships, work function, public behavior, substance use and abuse, money and finances, physical and mental health, life roles, and spirituality. In each sphere, participants consider behaviors they see in themselves while noting whether they fall under the columns of "Doing okay," "Need a little work," or "Need some help." The spiritual sphere not only includes worship attendance and value but also includes items like the ability to express love or compassion, appreciate beauty, or have a sense of meaning to life. Participants screen their own behaviors to determine whether self-help or professional help is indicated. They are given information about many resources for each area so the member can self-help or self-refer, as needed (Warrior Transition, version 2, n.d.).

Chaplain's Religious Enrichment Development Operation. Chaplain's Religious Enrichment Development Operation (CREDO) is a retreat program designed to encourage sailors and Marines to live a more intentionally thoughtful life and work on their spirituality. There are personal growth retreats, marriage enrichment retreats, and a number of specialty retreats and training events. A number of these programs are aimed specifically at warrior preparation and transition. As many as 10,000 people attend these retreats every year, with up to a thousand of them each year specifically aimed at the stress of war experience, including events for family members. Although the transition programs tend to focus on stress management and recovery, the CREDO programs emphasize a "generic" spirituality, aiming to increase awareness of spirituality without specifying what the source should be. The goal is to examine what is important to each individual, who then can decide how to be more intentional in living out that value, without being pressured to adopt a specific religion. The program encourages awareness of the spiritual nature of humans; employs some spiritual practices, such as meditation (prayer), giving to others, and communal support and expressions; and encourages participants to explore their own understanding of these practices within the spiritual traditions they call their own.

Current Spiritually Based VA Programs

In response to the growing body of literature that supports a positive relationship between healthy spirituality and both physical and mental health, health care accreditation bodies have begun to mandate that health facilities address spirituality as a part of holistic care services. In 2001, the Joint Commission on Accreditation of Healthcare Organizations (the Joint Commission) implemented a change in standards requiring spiritual assessment as a part of a larger multidisciplinary patient assessment. Minimally, the assessment should include three areas: (a) denomination or faith tradition, (b) significant spiritual beliefs, and (c) important spiritual practices (Hodge, 2006).

The Joint Commission is not designated a particular discipline to perform the assessment, but the VA Chaplaincy has been mandated to perform spiritual assessment on all patients seen, although patients can refuse. The VA Chaplaincy is moving toward the development of more standard systemwide guidelines for these assessments. Incorporating spirituality into care is not without obstacles. Groups opposing religious involvement in government-funded programs have at times voiced opposition and even filed legal challenges to the activities of both VA and DoD chaplains. There is a fine balance between the constitutional proscription of government establishment of religion, and the rights of deployed military service members and veterans confined in hospital beds to freely access religious and spiritual care consistent with their traditions. Although lawsuits filed in recent years have found in support of the appropriateness of chaplain activities, chaplain leadership in both DoD and VA are vigilant to ensure that their respective chaplain providers are well trained and provide services appropriately within the constraints of law.

Twelve-step programs. The longest-standing spiritually based intervention in the VA system would likely be Alcoholics Anonymous (AA), a 12-step program for individuals engaged in substance use treatment and recovery. AA is a self-help approach to recovery from alcoholism that proscribes 12 behavioral steps, 11 of which explicitly refer to the importance of God or a higher power to recovery (see Chapter 15 in this volume). The 12th step of AA states that as a result of working through the 12 steps, one will have a "spiritual awakening." In the late 1990s, a randomized clinical efficacy trial of alcohol dependence treatments called Project MATCH compared three treatments: 12-step facilitation, cognitive–behavioral therapy, and motivation enhancement treatment. The study found positive outcomes for all treatments with few differences across groups but noted higher 12-month abstinence rates among those in the 12-step facilitation group (Project MATCH Research Group, 1997). Although it is not clear that AA-defined spirituality has a direct effect on reducing drinking, there is evidence that spirituality helps sustain AA involvement that, in turn, is associated with sustained abstinence (Tonigan, 2007). Somewhat surprisingly, the benefits of AA involvement appear not to be dependent on religious belief (i.e., atheists, agnostics receive equal benefit; Tonigan, Miller, & Schermer, 2002). Effectiveness studies in the VA have confirmed the Project Match findings within the VA population (Donovan, 1999; Moos, Finney, Ouimette, & Suchinsky, 1999), and it appears that advocacy of AA involvement will continue to be an integral element of substance abuse recovery, along with other empirically based treatments in both outpatient and inpatient VA settings.

Mindfulness and acceptance interventions. In recent years, several additional spiritually based mental health interventions incorporating mindfulness and acceptance have begun to be evaluated and utilized within the VA system. Although it may be debated whether present-day mindfulness and acceptance techniques should be considered to be "spiritually based" (see Chapter 10 in this volume), these techniques find their roots in Eastern meditative and Western Christian contemplative spiritual traditions that originated many hundreds of years ago and predate the modern science of positive psychology that has appropriated them. On this basis, the authors of this chapter have chosen to include them among spiritually based interventions. Mindfulness has been described as a process involving "the self-regulation of attention so that it is maintained on immediate experience, thereby allowing for increased recognition of mental events in the present moment" (Bishop et al., 2004, p. 232). It also involves "adopting a particular orientation toward one's experiences in the present moment, an orientation that is characterized by curiosity, openness, and acceptance" (Bishop et al., 2004, p. 232; see also Chapter 10 in this volume).

One treatment utilizing mindfulness that is being widely disseminated throughout the VA system is acceptance and commitment therapy (ACT). ACT (Hayes, Strosahl, & Wilson, 1999) is a behavior therapy that incorporates spiritually based mindfulness and acceptance techniques to help individuals reduce experiential avoidance. The mindfulness and other techniques used in ACT are directed at decreasing the client's use of avoidance or escape strategies in coping with unwanted inner experiences and at increasing their acceptance of, or willingness to experience, these private events while engaging in previously avoided behavioral action. ACT is not focused only on symptom reduction as an outcome, but rather there is an attempt to increase clients' ability to maintain commitments to change behavior in ways that reflect their personal values. The ACT treatment approach includes exercises that address forgiveness, identification, and pursuit of core (and for many individuals, spiritual) values, and engagement in meaningful life activities. The VA Office of Mental Health Services has initiated training programs to teach mental health providers in VA how to use a number of research-based treatments. ACT currently is being disseminated by the VA as an empirically based treatment for anxiety and depression. There also has been a published article describing the use of ACT for PTSD (Orsillo & Batten, 2005).

Another treatment utilizing mindfulness in use in the VA is dialectical behavior therapy (DBT; Linehan et al., 2006). DBT has been evaluated in several randomized clinical trials as a treatment for women who meet criteria for borderline personality disorder (BPD). Overall, outcome data support the efficacy of DBT as a treatment for women with BPD, which has been designated as an "empirically supported" treatment by the American Psychological Association's clinical psychology division. A clinical trial with female veterans with BPD was conducted in 2001 (Koons et al., 2001) and ongoing VA research continues.

Two additional interventions, mindfulness-based stress reduction and mindfulness-based cognitive therapy, are also being actively evaluated for VA use with ongoing randomized trials. A search on http://www.ClinicalTrials.gov using the terms *mindfulness* and *veterans* identified more than 10 current mindfulness-based intervention studies that currently are approved and funded in VA locations.

Mantrum repetition. Another spiritual practice that has been utilized as an intervention for war veterans is mantrum repetition (see Volume 1, Chapter 17, this handbook). This practice has roots in both Western and Eastern spiritual traditions. In the West it is called *holy name repetition* and in the east *mantrum repetition*. Although mindfulness is a technique in which practitioners place their attention on present experience, usually with a focus on breathing, the use of a mantra provides a word or phrase as way of shifting and maintaining attentional focus. Bormann and Oman (2007) provided a useful chapter describing the techniques and use for health care. A successful pilot study of an eight-session group-based intervention with veterans was conducted (Bormann et al., 2005) that yielded improvements in a number of significant outcomes in PTSD outpatients. A second, two-group, pre- and postfeasibility trial of a similar six-session group intervention was conducted (Bormann, Thorp, Wetherell, & Golshan, 2008) that found significant improvement on all measured variables with effect sizes ranging from small (PTSD symptom interview) to medium (anger and spiritual well-being) to large (distress, quality of life enjoyment, mindfulness, and PTSD checklist). Additional domains of spirituality and interventions on the horizon that are being evaluated for veterans include yoga for chronic pain (Groessi, Weingart, Aschbacher, Pada, & Baxi, 2008), relational forgiveness (Solomon, Dekel, & Zerach, 2009), and gratitude (Kashdan et al., 2006).

Spirituality and trauma group. Although full empirical validation of interventions for alleviating adverse spiritual consequences of combat is presently lacking, there is ongoing development and research on promising spiritually based interventions (cf. Harris et al., 2011). Our personal research efforts have been geared toward developing a module for group treatment to promote reexamination and reintegration of personal spirituality among those suffering from combat-related PTSD. The spirituality and trauma (ST) group was developed to meet the needs of veterans in residential treatment for PTSD following military combat exposure. This manualized eight-session group treatment has been run in PTSD residential treatment programs since 2001. It was designed as an adjunct to other empirically supported PTSD treatments, not as a primary PTSD treatment. It utilizes brief didactic presentations by facilitators, member-to-member interactions, as well as large and small group discussion. Descriptions of the groups' development and thoughts about its application to additional trauma populations are available (Drescher, 2006; Drescher et al., 2004, 2007).

Group-based therapies like the ST offer the possibility of increased social support for survivors of trauma as well as other individuals with similar experiences to be able to wrestle with these existential questions. This is especially important because avoidance and isolation are primary features of PTSD. Group-based trauma treatment that allows for discussion of and reflection on spiritual questions and concerns and integrates these with standard mental health approaches would seem to be a useful clinical approach.

The ST group shares some characteristics with more traditional present-centered treatments. Specifically, clients are asked to keep their focus on here-and-now concerns. As a result of this present-centered focus, the therapeutic work can be client directed. The group sessions do not focus on the details of past traumatic events, but rather how the impact of the events is being experienced in the present. The model views an individual's spiritual background and history as aspects of their life that may affect and be affected by traumatic events and the direct symptoms of trauma. The tension or "dissonance" created between the experience of trauma and the individual's pretrauma beliefs, values, and expectations generate the motivation to pursue change in the aftermath of the events.

These group sessions differ slightly from many present-centered therapeutic approaches in that they address specific themes. They devote focused attention on particular spiritual and existential issues that might or might not arise naturally in a present-centered group. These sessions are specifically designed to address concerns that clients may not have resources to voice, and that clinicians frequently do not have background, experience, or training to address.

The ST group attempts to utilize some therapeutic styles and models of other treatment approaches. Murphy and colleagues (2002) has developed a group treatment approach to addressing a broad array of PTSD issues by enhancing client motivation to change. This treatment is conceptually focused on literature describing the stages of change and the techniques of motivational interviewing. Consistent with these approaches, the ST group invites facilitators to incorporate a similar therapeutic stance in addressing the spiritual–existential impact of trauma. First, it attempts to create a collaborative and friendly relationship between facilitators and clients. It communicates that clients are responsible for their decisions and for choosing to pursue growth and change and that facilitators avoid prescribing specific methods or techniques. The group seeks to help participants identify discrepancies between what they experience currently and what they want for their future to build motivation and energy for change. Even when it comes to defining spirituality, every attempt is made to create so broad a space that everyone can locate themselves within it according to their own personal definition.

The ST group has several overarching goals. One goal is to encourage client consideration of the role that a healthy vital spirituality might play as a healing resource in coping with traumatic events. This may involve strengthening and deepening group members' present spiritual or religious understandings and practices. It may involve reconnection with their own religious or spiritual roots and traditions from childhood. It may also involve searching out and exploring new avenues of spiritual experience and expression that are more immediately relevant to the members' recent experiences. Group activities are selected to express both diversity and the inherent value of a wide variety of spiritual experiences.

Another goal of this intervention is to help facilitate cognitive processing of the meaning associated with traumatic events and the personal significance individuals might attach to them. This includes identification of cognitive distortions (i.e., inappropriate survivor guilt, including self-blame), helping members begin to reframe or restructure their understandings in ways that are more healthy and adaptive. It also includes helping individuals find personal explanations for the difficult existential questions of "why" and "how" these events have occurred. It facilitates the shared feedback and reflections from other group members about the meanings they associate with these prior stressful and traumatic experiences.

A third primary goal of the group intervention is to increase perceived social support and to encourage the development of a healthy family and community support system. Support for trauma survivors varies considerably depending on the type and context of the trauma experience. Solitary survivors of a personal violation may live the aftermath of trauma in fear, distrustful, and alone. In contrast, whole communities may rally and provide support for survivors in the immediate aftermath of disasters. Soldiers, sailors, marines, and air force personnel may return from war zones to parades and fanfare in communities located near military installations or may return home individually welcomed only by family and a few friends in other locations. Over time, however, as people continue with their own day-to-day struggles of life, even an enhanced sense of community may fade. A good network of support may allow a trauma survivor to feel less alone and more capable of obtaining necessary resources. The intended outcome of these interventions and group sessions is to increase hope, to decrease anger and hostility, and to decrease the intensity of feelings of grief and loss, while enhancing the individual's sense of purpose and the meaningfulness of life.

The ST group provides a facilitator's manual to provide group leaders with clinical strategies and guidelines for implementing the group treatment. The facilitator's manual details the eight-session group intervention using a predominantly present-centered motivation enhancement approach. The eight session themes include the following:

1. Defining spirituality. For the ST group, a definition of spirituality is used that directly addresses a primary problem area for many trauma survivors, that is, disconnection and isolation. Defining spirituality as "connecting to something outside the self" frees each individual to define that connection for him- or herself. The group helps individuals examine how personal disconnection might be changed as a part of their recovery. Engaging in a discussion of what an individual sees as core elements of a personal definition of spirituality can be useful in helping that person realize that he or she can actually reconsider views or teachings learned in childhood. For clients for whom loss of faith has been a consequence of traumatic experience, it can sometimes be difficult to see themselves from a perspective that includes spirituality. One such client, a rancher from a Western state, was quite vocal week after week, insisting during group that he had lost all spirituality in the war and that the group was not relevant to him. Toward the end of the eight sessions, he approached one of the facilitators outside of group and shared a poem he had written. The poem described the sense of awe and wonder that he experienced while sitting astride a horse watching the sun rise over the mountaintops. He concluded the poem with words to the effect of "if that's what it means to have spirituality, then I guess I've had it all along."
2. Building connections. By defining spirituality as connection, the group encourages trauma survivors to increase the number and quality of their social supports both within and beyond the group. Spiritual communities frequently provide both emotional and instrumental supports for their members.
3. Spiritual practices. Spiritual activities are described as both inward and outward. A variety of inward experiential exercises involving meditation, breathing, guided imagery, and silent prayer can be useful in addressing PTSD issues of anxiety and hyperarousal. From an outward perspective, spiritual practices include service and work on behalf of others. Most spiritual traditions encourage service as a form of spiritual practice. One direct benefit of service is engagement in the lives of others, which for a person suffering from PTSD counters the tendency toward social isolation and withdrawal.

4. Theodicy—the "why" question. The term *theodicy* comes from the Latin *théos díe*, meaning justification of God. Many trauma survivors, along with their families and friends, experience a lifelong process of making sense of their experiences. Group interaction around these issues can be particularly helpful; simply discussing the issue and hearing differing viewpoints voiced by other participants can be of value to those who are seemingly "stuck" in negative ways of viewing their situation.
5. Forgiveness of self. Thoresen, Harris, and Luskin (2000) defined *forgiveness* as "the decision to reduce negative thoughts, affect, and behavior, such as blame and anger, toward an offender or hurtful situation, and to begin to gain better understanding of the offense and the offender" (p. 255). Depending on the type and contextual circumstance of the trauma, guilt and self-blame may be experienced by survivors. Many veterans in particular carry with them extremely negative and distorted beliefs, such as guilt, shame, or self-blame related to the trauma, which affect their perceptions of personal worth and value, their motivation to pursue treatment, and their hope for successfully recovering from their experiences. Finding ways to view their traumatic experiences through a less distorted lens can be extremely important for those recovering from PTSD.
6. Forgiveness of others. *Forgiveness* can be a word frequently associated with "should statements." Clients frequently have been told by parents or religious authorities that they "should" forgive others. Upon hearing in group that forgiveness was the topic of the day's session, one client angrily raised his hand and stated, "Do you mean to tell me that I need to forgive my father who beat the crap out of me frequently during my childhood?" The facilitator clarified that he had not said that, and he reemphasized that forgiveness from the perspective of the ST group is a choice that an individual may make to relieve his or her present experience of suffering, or to let go of resentment and bitterness, but that no one is suggesting that he or she "should" do that. The client is free to evaluate forgiveness as an option and to reject it or embrace it as he or she chooses.
7. Values. Values are the ideas and beliefs that individuals hold as good, as important, and as worthy of time and energy. When speaking with veterans, the things they frequently mention as valuing the most include a sense of belonging, self-respect, inner harmony, freedom, family security, health, and enjoying life. A crucial question for each participant attempting to move forward into health is the degree to which perceived values are reflected in day-to-day behavior.
8. Making and finding meaning. Traditional ways that individuals attempt to find meaning in traumatic events include at least two things—finding benefit and making sense out of the event (Davis, Nolen-Hoeksema, & Larson, 1998)—both of which can be problematic. A recent review of the role of spirituality in adjustment to bereavement noted studies that suggest that meaning making is a mechanism that mediates the relationship between spirituality and positive adjustment (Wortmann & Park, 2008; see also Volume 1, Chapter 8, this handbook). The ST group also looks at the sense of meaning that one derives from outside the self (i.e., from one's personal support system). In this context, we talk about finding meaning by "being meaningful" or by creating a life in which one "matters" to other people.

Although no controlled trials of the ST group have been conducted, anecdotal comments from graduates who have returned to visit have frequently been supportive of the utility of the group. Individuals who had been alienated from their religious or spiritual traditions have reported that they subsequently began meaningfully attending church services with family members again. Others have commented on the benefits they have received in terms of meaning and self-worth through volunteering in veteran or community activities.

CAREGIVING CHALLENGES FOR PROVIDER SPIRITUAL WELL-BEING

Chaplains and mental health professionals, whether serving on active duty in the military or as civilian employees of the VA, are subject to vicarious trauma or compassion fatigue in the line of duty when they bear witness to the tragic personal stories of combat survival from their service recipients (Bride & Figley, 2009). In addition, they may be at greater risk for occupational burnout and other familiar mental health consequences, such as PTSD, depression, and addiction. Factors increasing risk for vicarious trauma include relative inexperience in providing trauma services, high proportion of trauma clients on caseload, and personal history of trauma exposure, especially during childhood (Bride & Figley, 2009). Accordingly, to optimize the quality of their professional services and their own professional durability, providers need to be aware of these risks and manage them.

A key aspect of personal risk management involves maintaining healthy self-care practices. In our professional training seminars during 2008 with Navy chaplains and other military health and mental health caregivers, we informally surveyed more than 300 attendees about their self-care practices. Best practices, reported anonymously in this group, included not smoking, abstinence or drinking in moderation, healthy sexuality, finding meaning in one's work, and maintaining a sense of humor. Among the same respondents, worst practices were not taking vacations, spending insufficient time with friends, unhealthy sleep, perfectionism, and inadequate stress control. Aspects of self-care involving spirituality that were particularly subject to neglect were time in reflection, spiritual practices (e.g., prayer, music, meditation), and faith community involvement. Thus, among active-duty military spiritual care providers, maintaining personal spirituality as a coping resource is challenging. Although reports from controlled trials are lacking, an example of a formal 4-day seminar to promote positive self-care among active-duty Canadian chaplains has been provided by Zimmerman and Weber (2000). Broad topics included in the seminar are PTSD, vicarious traumatization, coping techniques, spirituality, self-care, and family issues. Within the spirituality component, a spiritual direction exercise and a nondenominational closing ritual are used to address making meaning of deployment experiences (Zimmerman & Weber, 2000).

CARE FOR THE CAREGIVER

CREDO has a program addressing the needs of chaplains and medical personnel that has involved more than 400 individuals in the past 3 years. Many senior chaplains and Marine Corps Counseling Centers have also conducted Care for the Caregiver retreats and seminars of their own creation. These programs recognize the fact that chaplains, and medical workers, often not only are secondary victims but also have first-level exposure. They travel and live in the same dangerous environment, and they listen to and care for all who are affected by traumatic and long-term operational stress exposure. But as the "healers" for their unit, they often feel they have no one to whom they can turn when they are injured. Retreats for caregivers, and specifically for chaplains, often include the same kinds of brainstorming exercises as used for warriors, "How have you changed?" and "What do you need to recover?" They also involve exercises meant to help chaplains remember their sense of calling to religious ministry and begin to decide how that calling may have changed in light of their war-time experiences. Chaplains are encouraged to spend time in prayer and meditation and to read their scriptures. Journaling opportunities are often included and allow chaplains to share struggles they may fear facing in other contexts. The concept of pastoral mentors is encouraged so that chaplains will seek trusted colleagues in whom they can confide. In these retreats, many chaplains have reported that their faith has been challenged, that they suffer from spiritual burnout, and that their faith practices have changed because of their experiences (Drescher et al., 2007).

RECOMMENDATIONS FOR ADVANCING KNOWLEDGE ABOUT SPIRITUALITY AND MILITARY SERVICE

Psychologists and other mental health providers working with veterans or active-duty service members need to be aware of the complex interface between spirituality and combat-related trauma. Although spirituality is increasingly seen as an integral coping resource for many service members and veterans, the concept of moral injury is less well recognized. Although the inclusion of moral injury as an expectable consequence of combat exposure is part of current Navy and Marine Corps doctrine, the empirical foundation documenting the relationship between combat and changes in spirituality has not yet been fully developed. Clearly, more research is needed to identify the range of morally injurious experiences and the spiritual and psychological reactions that arise after them. This research could be more fully integrated with studies of spiritual struggle in the psychology of religion and spirituality (e.g., Pargament et al., 2005; see also Volume 1, Chapter 25, this handbook).

Risk and resiliency factors that foster coping resources and render combatants more or less susceptible to moral injury also need to be identified. Early interventions for those who are negatively affected need to be developed. Ideally, the Warrior Transition and CREDO programs in current use among active-duty sailors and marines will be more rigorously evaluated and improved accordingly. Evaluation of the spiritual fitness component within the Army's Comprehensive Soldier Fitness program is also needed (Pargament & Sweeney, 2011). In a VA context, it is important to identify specific techniques that chaplains can use for moral injury that will interface with existing empirically supported treatments for PTSD.

Whether or not mental health providers are themselves religious, it is important for them to respect that many of their clients hold worldviews that are inseparable from their spirituality. Psychologists and other mental health professionals can improve their knowledge and skills in addressing their clients' spiritual concerns by becoming familiar with the various religious heritages represented among military service members. In addition, those providing psychological care related to military trauma need to stay abreast of expanding literature on spirituality and trauma. In particular, new research on moral injury (Drescher et al., 2011) and spiritual struggle (Pargament, Murray-Swank, Magyar, & Ano, 2005) and recommended interventions for spiritually based problems by psychologists (Litz et al., 2009) are important innovations for psychological care. They are also examples of key advances in the applied psychology of religion. Furthermore, as the role of spirituality in military trauma and its treatment continues to find its place in mental health and chaplaincy, psychologists will be called on to develop expertise, in addition to respect and understanding, in integrating spiritual resources in psychotherapy. Broad-based efforts to enhance the education and training of psychologists to be sensitive to religion and spirituality and skilled in performing treatments that integrate religious and spiritual resources will better prepare clinicians to address the needs of military personnel, their families, and veterans.

References

Bishop, S. R., Lau, M., Shapiro, S., Carlson, L., Anderson, N. D., Carmody, J., . . . Devins, G. (2004). Mindfulness: A proposed operational definition. *Clinical Psychology: Science and Practice, 11*, 230–241. doi:10.1093/clipsy.bph077

Bormann, J. E., & Oman, D. (2007). Mantram or holy name repetition: Health benefits from a portable spiritual practice. In T. G. Plante & C. E. Thoresen (Eds.), *Spirit, science, and health: How the spiritual mind fuels physical wellness* (pp. 94–112). Westport, CT: Praeger.

Bormann, J. E., Smith, T. L., Becker, S., Gershwin, M., Pada, L., Grudzinski, A. H., & Nurmi, E. A. (2005). Efficacy of frequent mantram repetition on stress, quality of life, and spiritual well-being in veterans: A pilot study. *Journal of Holistic Nursing, 23*, 395–414. doi:10.1177/0898010105278929

Bormann, J. E., Thorp, S., Wetherell, J. L., & Golshan, S. (2008). A spiritually based group intervention for combat veterans with posttraumatic stress disorder: Feasibility study. *Journal of Holistic Nursing, 26*, 109–116. doi:10.1177/0898010107311276

Bride, B. E., & Figley, C. R. (2009). Secondary trauma and military veteran caregivers. *Smith College Studies in Social Work, 79*, 314–329. doi:10.1080/00377310903130357

Chang, B.-H., Skinner, K. M., & Boehmer, U. (2001). Religion and mental health among women veterans with sexual assault experience. *International Journal of Psychiatry in Medicine, 31*, 77–95. doi:10.2190/0NQA-YAJ9-W0AM-YB3P

Davis, C. G., Nolen-Hoeksema, S., & Larson, J. (1998). Making sense of loss and benefiting from the experience: Two construals of meaning. *Journal of Personality and Social Psychology, 75*, 561–574. doi:10.1037/0022-3514.75.2.561

Decker, L. R. (1993). Beliefs, post-traumatic stress disorder, and mysticism. *Journal of Humanistic Psychology, 33*, 15–32. doi:10.1177/00221678930334003

Dickerson, B. J. (2005, October 27). The Navy Chaplain Corps: 230 years of service to God and country. *Marine Corps News*. Retrieved from http://www.freerepublic.com/focus/f-news/1510766/posts

Donovan, D. M. (1999). Efficacy and effectiveness: Complementary findings from two multisite trials evaluating outcomes of alcohol treatments differing in theoretical orientations. *Alcoholism: Clinical and Experimental Research*, *23*, 564–572. doi:10.1111/j.1530-0277.1999.tb04154.x

Drescher, K. D. (2006). Spirituality in the face of terrorist disasters. In L. A. Schein, H. I. Spitz, G. M. Burlingame, & P. R. Muskin (Eds.), *Psychological effects of catastrophic disasters: Group approaches to treatment* (pp. 335–381). New York, NY: Haworth Press.

Drescher, K. D., & Foy, D. W. (1995). Spirituality and trauma treatment: Suggestions for including spirituality as a coping resource. *NCPTSD Clinical Quarterly*, *5*, 4–5.

Drescher, K. D., & Foy, D. W. (2008). When they come home: Posttraumatic stress, moral injury, and spiritual consequences for veterans. *Reflective Practice: Formation and Supervision in Ministry*, *28*, 85–102.

Drescher, K. D., Foy, D. W., Kelly, C., Leshner, A., Schutz, K., & Litz, B. T. (2011). An exploration of the viability and usefulness of the construct of moral injury in war veterans. *Traumatology*, *17*, 8–13. doi:10.1177/1534765610395615

Drescher, K. D., Ramirez, G., Leoni, J. J., Romesser, J. M., Sornborger, J., & Foy, D. W. (2004). Spirituality and trauma: Development of a group therapy module. *GROUP: Journal of the Eastern Group Psychotherapy Society*, *28*(4), 71–87.

Drescher, K. D., Smith, M. W., & Foy, D. W. (2007). Spirituality and readjustment following war-zone experiences. In C. R. Figley & W. P. Nash (Eds.), *Combat stress injury: Theory, research, and management* (pp. 295–310). New York, NY: Routledge.

Falsetti, S. A., Resick, P. A., & Davis, J. L. (2003). Changes in religious beliefs following trauma. *Journal of Traumatic Stress*, *16*, 391–398. doi:10.1023/A:1024422220163

Fontana, A., & Rosenheck, R. (2004). Trauma, change in strength of religious faith, and mental health service use among veterans treated for PTSD. *Journal of Nervous and Mental Disease*, *192*, 579–584. doi:10.1097/01.nmd.0000138224.17375.55

Green, B. L., Lindy, J. D., & Grace, M. C. (1988). Long-term coping with combat stress. *Journal of Traumatic Stress*, *1*, 399–412. doi:10.1002/jts.2490010403

Groessi, E. J., Weingart, K. R., Aschbacher, K., Pada, L., & Baxi, S. (2008). Yoga for veterans with chronic low-back pain. *Journal of Alternative and Complementary Medicine*, *14*, 1123–1129. doi:10.1089/acm.2008.0020

Harris, J. I., Erbes, C. R., Engdahl, B. E., Thuras, P., Murray-Swank, N., Grace, D., . . . Le, T. (2011). The effectiveness of a trauma-focused spiritually integrated intervention for veterans exposed to trauma. *Journal of Clinical Psychology*, *67*, 425–438. doi:10.1002/jclp.20777

Hayes, S. C., Strosahl, K. D., & Wilson, K. G. (1999). *Acceptance and commitment therapy: An experiential approach to behavior change.* New York, NY: Guilford Press.

Hodge, D. R. (2006). A template for spiritual assessment: A review of the JCAHO requirements and guidelines for implementation. *Social Work*, *51*, 317–326. doi:10.1093/sw/51.4.317

Institute for Alternative Futures. (2009). *Total fitness for the 21st century*. Retrieved from http://www.altfutures.com/pubs/govt

Janoff-Bulman, R. (1992). *Shattered assumptions: Towards a new psychology of trauma.* New York, NY: Free Press.

Kashdan, T. B., Uswatte, G., & Julian, T. (2006). Gratitude and hedonic and eudaimonic well-being in Vietnam war veterans. *Behaviour Research and Therapy*, *44*, 177–199. doi:10.1016/j.brat.2005.01.005

Koons, C. R., Robins, C. J., Lindsey Tweed, J., Lynch, T. R., Gonzalez, A. M., Morse, J. Q., . . . Bastion, L. A. (2001). Efficacy of dialectical behavior therapy in women veterans with borderline personality disorder. *Behavior Therapy*, *32*, 371–390. doi:10.1016/S0005-7894(01)80009-5

Linehan, M. M., Comtois, K., Murray, A. M., Brown, M. Z., Gallop, R. J., Heard, H. L., . . . Lindenboim, N. (2006). Two-year randomized controlled trial and follow-up of dialectical behavior therapy vs therapy by experts for suicidal behaviors and borderline personality disorder. *Archives of General Psychiatry*, *63*, 757–766. doi:10.1001/archpsyc.63.7.757

Litz, B. T., Stein, N., Delaney, E., Lebowitz, L., Nash, W. P., Silva, C., & Maguen, S. (2009). Moral injury and moral repair in war veterans: A preliminary model and intervention strategy. *Clinical Psychology Review*, *29*, 695–706. doi:10.1016/j.cpr.2009.07.003

Moos, R. H., Finney, J. W., Ouimette, P. C., & Suchinsky, R. T. (1999). A comparative evaluation of substance abuse treatment: Treatment orientation: Amount of care, and 1-year outcomes. *Alcoholism: Clinical and Experimental Research*, *23*, 529–536. doi:10.1111/j.1530-0277.1999.tb04149.x

Murphy, R. T., Rosen, C. R., Cameron, R. P., & Thompson, K. E. (2002). Development of a group treatment for enhancing motivation to change PTSD symptoms. *Cognitive and Behavioral Practice*, *9*, 308–316. doi:10.1016/S1077-7229(02)80025-6

Naval Chaplaincy School and Center. (n.d.). *Naval chaplains school history*. Retrieved from https://www.netc.navy.mil/centers/chaplain/History

Naval Historical Center. (n.d.). *The reestablishment of the Navy, 1787–1801: Historical overview and select bibliography*. Retrieved from http://www.history.navy.mil/biblio/biblio4/biblio4a.htm

Office of Public Affairs, Navy Chief of Chaplains. (2007). Navy Chaplains Corps aligns for future. *Navy NewsStand*. Retrieved from http://www.globalsecurity.org/military/library/news/2007/08/mil-070817-nns10.htm

Orsillo, S. M., & Batten, S. V. (2005). Acceptance and commitment therapy in the treatment of posttraumatic stress disorder. *Behavior Modification, 29*, 95–129. doi:10.1177/0145445504270876

Osborne, J. (2007, April 17). Ceremony establishes naval chaplains school. *Naval Personnel Development Command Public Affairs*. Retrieved from http://www.navy.mil/submit/display.asp?story_id=28908

Pargament, K. I., Murray-Swank, N., Magyar, G., & Ano, G. (2005). Spiritual struggle: A phenomenon of interest in psychology and religion. In W. R. Miller and H. Delaney (Eds.), *Judeo-Christian perspectives on psychology: Human nature, motivation, and change* (pp. 245–268). Washington, DC: American Psychological Association.

Pargament, K. I., & Sweeney, P. J. (2011). Building spiritual fitness in the Army: An innovative approach to a vital aspect of human development. *American Psychologist, 66*, 58–64. doi:10.1037/a0021657

Pargament, K. I., Zinnbauer, B. J., Scott, A. B., Butter, E. M., Zerowin, J., & Stanik, P. (1998). Red flags and religious coping: Identifying some religious warning signs among people in crisis. *Journal of Clinical Psychology, 54*, 77–89. doi:10.1002/(SICI)1097-4679(199801)54:1<77::AID-JCLP9>3.0.CO;2-R

Project MATCH Research Group. (1997). Matching alcohol treatments to client heterogeneity: Project MATCH posttreatment drinking outcomes. *Journal of Studies on Alcohol, 58*, 7–29.

Solomon, Z., Dekel, R., & Zerach, G. (2009). Posttraumatic stress disorder and marital adjustment: The mediating role of forgiveness. *Family Process, 48*, 546–558. doi:10.1111/j.1545-5300.2009.01301.x

Thoresen, C., Harris, A., & Luskin, F. (2000). Forgiveness and health: An unanswered question. In M. McCullough, K. Pargament, & C. Thoresen (Eds.), *Forgiveness: Theory, research, and practice* (p. 254–280). New York, NY: Guilford Press.

Tonigan, J. S. (2007). Spirituality and Alcoholics Anonymous. *Southern Medical Journal, 100*, 437–440. doi:10.1097/SMJ.0b013e31803171ef

Tonigan, J. S., Miller, W. R., & Schermer, C. (2002). Atheists, agnostics, and Alcoholics Anonymous. *Journal of Studies on Alcohol, 63*, 534–541.

U.S. Air Force. (2011). *History of Air Force chaplaincy*. Retrieved from http://www.usafhc.af.mil/howtobecomeachaplain

U.S. Army. (2011). *History of Army chaplaincy*. Retrieved from http:/www.army.mil/info/organization/chaplaincy

U.S. Department of Veterans Affairs. (2010). *History of VA chaplaincy*. Retrieved from http://www1.va.gov/CHAPLAIN/components/History_of_VA_Chaplaincy.asp

U.S. Navy Department. (1919, March 15). *General order No. 456*. Washington, DC: Author.

Witvliet, C. V. O., Phillips, K. A., Feldman, M. E., & Beckham, J. C. (2004). Posttraumatic mental and physical health correlates of forgiveness and religious coping in military veterans. *Journal of Traumatic Stress, 17*, 269–273. doi:10.1023/B:JOTS.0000029270.47848.e5

Wortmann, J. H., & Park, C. L. (2008). Religion and spirituality in adjustment following bereavement: An integrative review. *Death Studies, 32*, 703–736. doi:10.1080/07481180802289507

Zeiger, H. (2009). Why does the U.S. military have chaplains? *Pepperdine Public Policy Review*. Retrieved from http://publicpolicy.pepperdine.edu/policy-review/2009v2/why-does-us-military-have-chaplains.htm

Zimmerman, G., & Weber, W. (2000). Care for the caregivers: A program for Canadian military chaplains after serving in NATO and United Nations peacekeeping missions in the 1990s. *Military Medicine, 165*, 687–690.

CHAPTER 30

ADDRESSING RELIGION AND SPIRITUALITY IN EDUCATIONAL SETTINGS

Alyssa Bryant Rockenbach and Tyler Townsend

The religious and spiritual dynamics present in educational settings have a long and intricate history and have gained renewed attention among education scholars and practitioners in recent years, introducing unique challenges and possibilities. On the side of challenge, some question the appropriateness of infusing religion and spirituality in the educational sphere—particularly in public education—given concerns about breaching the separation of church and state. Moreover, the sheer diversity of religious and spiritual beliefs and values sets the stage for intergroup conflict and power imbalances between majority and minority worldviews. On the side of possibility, religion and spirituality can provide a compelling opportunity in educational contexts for growth in self-understanding, well-being, acceptance of diverse others, and religious literacy.

In light of the challenges and possibilities, this chapter seeks to identify best practices for harnessing religion and spirituality for the benefit of students, teachers, faculty, and other stakeholders in education. Aligned with this handbook's "integrative paradigm," this chapter considers religion and spirituality in education from multiple and interrelated frames of reference, including the historical, empirical, theoretical, and practical. Our intent is to provide (a) a summative overview of the ways in which religion and spirituality have been integrated in education in past and present eras; (b) a portrait of the religious and spiritual inclinations of those served by educational institutions, namely children and young adults; (c) an empirical and theoretical rationale for the inclusion of religious and spiritual dimensions in educational settings (along with acknowledgment of justified concerns); (d) practical solutions for integrating religion and spirituality in education based on exemplary approaches adopted across a spectrum of contexts; (e) reflection on the roles of psychologists and educators; and (f) recommendations for future effectiveness.

Given that the handbook's integrative paradigm characterizes religion and spirituality as multidimensional phenomena, the definitions that undergird our approach to the chapter are correspondingly complex and drawn from current educational literature. Scholars who have joined the discourse on religion and spirituality in education define these concepts in myriad ways, and the range of descriptors often associated with the terms reveals their inherent multidimensionality (Astin et al., 2005; Chickering, Dalton, & Stamm, 2006). As historical and current trends attest, the concepts *religion* and *spirituality* are both relevant to education and are discussed in tandem throughout this chapter. The definitions of these terms in educational settings generally mirror the meanings set forth in this handbook. Understanding the rich language used by educators to express the diverse meanings of religion and spirituality establishes a framework for explicating the educational purposes behind their efforts and evaluating the effectiveness of their practices.

Stamm (2006a) explained that religion "encompass[es] the complexity of beliefs and practices delineated by established denominational institutions and framed through defined doctrines, theology, and historical narratives or myths accounting

DOI: 10.1037/14046-030
APA Handbook of Psychology, Religion, and Spirituality: Vol. 2. An Applied Psychology of Religion and Spirituality, K. I. Pargament (Editor-in-Chief)

for the establishment of these doctrines and practices" (p. 37). For our purposes, we agree that the institutional domain is a critical aspect of religion; however, to this we add that the religious experience can be intensely personal. The degree to which a person adheres to the standard beliefs and practices of a particular organized religious tradition or community is self-determined. Whereas some individuals model their lives on specific religious doctrines and principles, others may distance themselves from denominational specificity yet still encounter the "religious" dimension of life on a regular basis.

In the education literature, Love and Talbot's (1999) landmark synthesis of numerous and varied definitions of spirituality resulted in five key elements that serve as the basis of our understanding of spirituality throughout this chapter:

- seeking personal authenticity, genuineness, and wholeness;
- transcending the self;
- developing connectedness to self and others;
- deriving meaning, purpose, and direction in life; and
- exploring and relating to the transcendent.

Love and Talbot's (1999) definition was developed primarily to inform educators and practitioners in higher education. The movement toward holistic learning in primary and secondary education uses a somewhat different (though related) language to urge nurturing the whole person, including "the intellectual, emotional, physical, social, aesthetic, and spiritual" (J. P. Miller, 2005, p. 2). Holistic education, of which spirituality is a critical component, has been encouraged in postsecondary contexts as well, most notably in the field of college student affairs (American Council on Education, 1949). The spiritual development component of holistic education, suggested Kessler (2005), is composed of multiple domains as varied as "longing for silence and solitude," "hunger for joy and delight," "creative drive," and "deep connection" (pp. 103–104). Another common catchphrase in education is the notion of "character," that is, "a window into personality, a constellation of attitudes, values, ethical considerations, and behavioral patterns that represent what people believe and value, how they think, and what they do" (Kuh & Umbach, 2004, p. 37). Although spirituality is distinct from character, the two concepts overlap in their mutual emphasis on self-knowledge, personal values, and ethical beliefs and behaviors. Beyond Love and Talbot's five components of spirituality and the multivalent language used in primary, secondary, and postsecondary education, spirituality necessarily involves the sacred, or those aspects of life that are set apart from the ordinary and associated with the divine or the transcendent (Pargament & Mahoney, 2005). With an understanding of key definitions, we turn now to another foundational issue: historical patterns in the integration of religion and spirituality in education.

HISTORICAL TRENDS IN EDUCATION'S INCLUSION OF RELIGION AND SPIRITUALITY

Religion and spirituality have played a vital role in education settings for centuries. The integration of religion and spirituality in education is a fluid phenomenon that is influenced by changes in social norms and contexts. Philosophical shifts over time have transformed the ways that spirituality and religion have been manifest in education from one historical era to the next. When U.S. educational institutions emerged in the colonial era, nine colonial colleges, which would later evolve into our current higher education system, were firmly rooted in Protestant Christian values and each claimed a specific and regionally determined denominational association (Stamm, 2006b). Although compulsory precollege educational opportunities did not present themselves until much later, young men seeking a formal education attended the colonial colleges and were introduced to a classical curriculum steeped in Christian moral philosophy. Many of these students aspired to ministerial roles (Cohen, 1998; Hart, 1999), although from the outset students were prepared for careers in public service and the professions as well (Cohen, 1998; Stamm, 2006b).

According to standard historical accounts, higher education became increasingly "secularized" after the Civil War as modern science developed and as naturalism, positivism, and empiricism assumed positions of prominence in the philosophical foundation of the academy (Hart, 1999). Two trends converged to ensure the gradual movement away from denominational allegiances, the rise of the U.S. research university, and fundamental changes in the purposes and pursuits of higher education. First, the German university model, brought to the United States by American scholars studying abroad, infused burgeoning U.S. universities with values and practices attuned to the advancement of knowledge through empirical research, graduate training in specialized academic disciplines, and faculty professionalization (Cohen, 1998). Second, the denominational hold on higher education was simultaneously deteriorating, paradoxically by its own hand. Liberal Protestantism, with its open idealism, accommodated modernist and progressive ideologies, which further facilitated the turn toward science and ironically led to the demise of the Protestant monolith and the rise of a new secular establishment (Marsden, 1994). Stamm (2006b) summarized the turning tide in higher education:

> Whereas nineteenth-century colleges and universities had the express purpose of promoting the intellectual and character development of their students through moral philosophy and required participation in religious services, the new universities being established after World War I stressed research, disciplinary specialization, and a diverse curriculum. (pp. 77–78)

Despite traditional historical speculation that the emergence of the modern university secularized U.S. higher education, the secularization thesis is not uncontested, as three examples testify. First, Hart (1999) posited that "the modern American University was not as hostile to religion as older histories argue, nor was religion marginal to the ethos of the new research university" (p. 11). In tracing the history of religious studies as an academic discipline, Hart demonstrated that religious studies came to be recognized as an established discipline in the heyday of the modern research university, between 1925 and 1965.

Second, beginning shortly after World War II, postmodern criticism raised new intellectual challenges to counter modern assumptions that religion and spirituality were irrelevant to contemporary education. In fact, postmodern currents in the present era have created an optimal environment conducive to the inclusion of spiritual dimensions in education (Love, 2000). Love (2000) explained,

> Postmodernism rejects the assumption that through reason we will be able to achieve agreement about the nature of truth. . . . Postmodernism rather than trying to replace one set of truths with another instead encourages multiple voices and multiple perspectives.

In short, postmodernism allows for the reemergence in education of the religious—and now spiritual—realms of life. What modernism cast as untenable, unscientific, and beyond the scope of legitimate knowledge, postmodernism welcomed as part of the plurality of possible truths. The "epistemological uncertainty" wrought by postmodernism created "opportunities for rethinking the place of faith in the academy" (Wuthnow, 2008, p. 35).

A third example that further challenges the thesis of secularization rests on more recent evidence. Cherry, DeBerg, and Porterfield (2001) have contended on the basis on their empirical study that religion is very much alive on college and university campuses with the "ethos of decentered, diverse, religiously tolerant institutions of higher education [serving as] a breeding ground for vital religious practice and teaching" (p. 295). Their examination of four distinct institutions revealed a trend toward voluntary religion and pluralism. Spirituality has also become more apparent in society at large. Increasingly, "the approach to religious experience as spiritual searching or quest is now pervasive throughout American society" (Stamm, 2006b, p. 69). Stamm (2006b) asserted that spiritual seeking rather than religious dogma has become paramount, a trend that we discuss in greater detail in the next section as it pertains to youth in educational settings.

CURRENT RESEARCH ON RELIGION AND SPIRITUALITY AMONG YOUNG ADULTS

Several large-scale national and international studies inform us about the ways in which young people approach and integrate religion and spirituality in their lives. These studies are significant because they effectively take the pulse of the generation of students currently learning in our schools, colleges, and universities. We begin with the studies focused on younger samples before summarizing research pertaining to college-age young adults.

According to a multicountry study conducted by the Center for Spiritual Development in Childhood and Adolescence (2008), the majority (93%) of youth between the ages of 12 and 25 tend to believe there is a spiritual dimension to life, and as many as one third of youth perceive themselves as "pretty" or "very" spiritual. In the sample of more than 7,000 participants, variations by country were apparent, but, overall, youth were inclined to report that their spirituality has increased over time and to view religion and spirituality in a positive light. The majority of youth divulged that they are both religious *and* spiritual, with just under a quarter claiming to be spiritual but not religious. Young people mentioned nature, music, service, and spending time alone most often as helping to nurture their spirituality, with other potential sources of spiritual support—mentors, school, and religious activities—mentioned less frequently.

Whereas the aforementioned study centered on the spiritual inclinations of youth, Smith and Denton's (2005) investigation of the religious and spiritual lives of U.S. teenagers illuminated many of the religious trends apparent in the 13- to 17-year-old population using data from the National Study of Youth and Religion (NSYR). According to their findings, religion is significant among U.S. teenagers and many participate in the congregations in which their families raised them. Although religion is important in their lives, many teens struggle to articulate their beliefs in a definitive and focused manner. Teenage religiosity is conventional and rarely involves seeking or questing; many are content to simply follow the lead of their parents rather than rebelling. Taken together, Smith and Denton have contended that teenage religiosity tends toward moralistic therapeutic deism, a philosophy that is increasingly prevalent in religious congregations in the United States and defined as living a happy life by being a good, moral person; enjoying religion's therapeutic benefits and attaining a subjective well-being; and believing that God exists and created the world but keeps a safe distance from human affairs.

Smith and Snell (2009) have revealed what becomes of the NSYR cohort of teenagers as they transition to early adulthood (defined as 18 to 23 years of age). They identified the religious changes and continuities evident in early adulthood and the factors that shape patterns of religious commitment. The findings cast younger adults in the United States as considerably less religious than older adults, but this generational distinction must be qualified by the fact that emerging adults are not appreciably less religious than they were as teenagers. The overarching message expressed by Smith and Snell is that "religious change happens"—specifically, religious disaffiliation—but these changes are offset by "a larger amount of religious continuity" (p. 108). Several factors make a significant difference in determining religious outcomes, namely personal prayer and religious experiences, the importance of faith, parental religious commitment, and religious doubts. Moreover, higher levels of religious engagement and commitment are associated with positive life outcomes.

Like Smith and Denton (2005) and Smith and Snell (2009), Pearce and Denton (2011) used the NSYR data to explore religiosity among U.S. adolescents and identified five prevailing profiles: abiders, atheists, assenters, avoiders, and adapters. *Abiders* express a high degree of conventional religiosity in terms of their engagement in traditional and institutionally affiliated religious practice, sense of closeness to God, and the value they place on religion in their lives. By contrast, *atheists* are defined by their rejection of religion and consistent patterns of nonreligiousness. The other three profiles appear to fall along a continuum between abiders and atheists. *Assenters* are moderately religious, but they do not display the high level of commitment and practice exhibited by abiders. Instead, assenters typically believe in God and engage in some religious practice, but they do not treat religious faith as a central facet of their lives. *Adapters* show some similarity to assenters in terms of their moderate approach to religion. They, however, exhibit high levels of personal religiosity (e.g., prayer, importance of faith in their lives, sense of closeness to God) at the same time that they are less consistent in their engagement with institutional religious practice (e.g., religious service attendance) than abiders. Adapters' religious expression involves commitment to helping others and thinking about the meaning of life more so than the other profiles. *Avoiders* are almost entirely disengaged from religious belief and practice and have little connection to religion through the social networks to which they belong.

Shedding light on trends among people in their 20s and 30s, Wuthnow (2007) provided a comprehensive account of the post–baby boomer generation and described young adults of this era as "tinkerers" or "bricoleurs" when it comes to religion and spirituality. The tendency toward spiritual tinkering, which reflects the pluralistic society in which we live, involves an individualized and improvised piecing together of one's religious faith or worldview. Wuthnow explained, "Hardly anybody comes up with a truly innovative approach to life's enduring spiritual questions, but hardly anybody simply mimics the path someone else has taken either" (p. 14). Importantly, Wuthnow's study of post–baby boomers revealed a trend similar to that uncovered among younger adults in the study conducted by the Center for Spiritual Development in Childhood and Adolescence (2008). That is, the prevailing pattern is "not spirituality or religion, but spirituality and religion" (Wuthnow, 2007, p. 134). Although it has become popular to brand this generation as "spiritual but not religious," empirical assessments show that only about one sixth to one third of the post–baby boomer generation can be characterized as such.

Unlike Wuthnow (2007, 2008) who considered the population at large, a recent national study longitudinally examined college students' religious and spiritual inclinations from the first through the third year of college. As students enter college, they report holding certain expectations of their institutions:

> About two-thirds consider it "essential" or "very important" that their college enhance their self-understanding (69%), prepare them for responsible citizenship (67%), develop their personal values (67%), and provide for their emotional development (63%). Moreover, nearly half (48%) say that it is "essential" or "very important" that college encourage their personal expression of spirituality. (Astin et al., 2005, p. 6)

Astin et al. (2005) reported that 42% of entering 1st-year college students feel "secure" in their religious and spiritual beliefs, whereas another 23% are "seeking," 15% are "conflicted," 10% are "doubting," and 15% are "not interested." In other words, close to half of young adults matriculating into colleges and universities are facing critical—potentially transforming—phases in their spirituality as they seek, doubt, and feel conflicted. With respect to change over time, students become less religiously engaged during the first 3 years of college (Astin, Astin, & Lindholm, 2010; Bryant, Choi, & Yasuno, 2003), but they exhibit growth along several dimensions that the researchers characterized as "spiritual," including quest (searching for meaning and purpose), equanimity (feeling peaceful and centered even during hardships), ethic of caring (relating compassionately to others), and ecumenical worldview (being open to others of different faiths and life philosophies; Astin et al., 2010). These findings provide an interesting contrast to those articulated by Smith and Denton (2005). The conventionality and unquestioning adherence to parents' religious and spiritual beliefs and values appears to diminish once young adults encounter new challenges in college.

Supplementing international and national survey data, Nash and Bradley (2008) offered personal observations of college student spirituality and religiosity derived from their experiences as coteachers of a seminar on religious pluralism. Specifically, Nash and Bradley put forth a compelling and in-depth five-part typology to capture the varieties of religious and spiritual seeking that are manifested in the diverse spiritual narratives of the young U.S. adults with whom they interacted in college classes. The five categories into which these narratives are sorted within the typology are not expressly linked to any particular religious perspective, although some religions or worldviews resonate with a particular narrative more so than the others.

Orthodox believers hold to certain absolute and revealed truths found in "a particular book, institution, prophet, or movement" (Nash & Bradley, 2008, p. 138). Orthodox believers perceive as their mission communicating truth to others in hopes that nonbelievers will be convinced of its validity.

Mainline believers seek to balance traditional religious doctrine with their unique and individualized approach to interpreting sacred texts and worshiping God. Accordingly, students who speak from this perspective readily acknowledge the traditional doctrines and rituals they espouse and practice, but they put their own special "twist" on some of these traditional beliefs and practices, and it is this special twist that mainliners typically describe as their own spirituality (Nash & Bradley, 2008, p. 140).

Spiritual seekers are on a journey, and many have not found a home in traditional or mainline religion. Several strands—including *wounded seekers* (who experienced harm in past religious communities or who struggle to reconcile the problems of suffering and evil with a good and loving God), *mystical seekers* (who seek calm and mindfulness in alternative or personal spiritualities), and *social justice seekers* (who seek to build the kingdom of God here and now through activism)—make up this narrative, reflecting its eclecticism.

In place of supernatural explanations of the world and reality, *spiritual humanists* embrace a naturalistic philosophy of life along with "a belief that consciousness does not survive death . . . and a conviction that human beings alone have the power and responsibility to solve their own problems without assistance from any mythical, superhuman beings" (Nash & Bradley, 2008, p. 143). Students identifying with this narrative typically relate to existential humanism (valuing individual freedom and authenticity as central to their spirituality) or a spirituality of scientific empiricism (seeking scientific evidence to support or refute theistic claims).

Lastly, *spiritual skeptics* are "methodological questioners, wonderers, challengers, and doubters" (Nash & Bradley, 2008, p. 146). Among students who fall within this narrative are militant atheists, postmodern doubters, spiritual pluralists, and apatheists (who are completely indifferent to religion and whether there is a God).

On the whole, these studies point to a general openness toward religion and spirituality on the part of this generation of young people. Young adults have an interest in the sacred dimensions of life and appear to become increasingly committed to exploring their spiritual and religious curiosities in their late teens and twenties, typically in conjunction with their college years. The findings from large-scale studies reveal overarching patterns and offer a "big picture" perspective. Even so, the nuanced orientations to religion and spirituality illustrated by the Nash and Bradley (2008) typology supply further detail, reminding us that if the religious and spiritual journeys of young adults are not uniform and predictable, neither should our educational programs and interventions assume a one-size-fits-all approach in response to students' needs.

INTEGRATION OF RELIGION AND SPIRITUALITY IN EDUCATION: THE RATIONALE

Integrating religion and spirituality in education rests on several justifications. The first justification has to do with the disproportionate weight given to rational, material, and cognitive factors in our educational systems and the negative implications of such imbalances, particularly given the goals and purposes we claim to value across educational tiers. Astin (2004) articulated one of the foremost arguments for placing spirituality at the center of liberal education. He made the case that uneven attention to the "exterior" dimensions of education compared with the "interior" dimensions has undermined a central premise of liberal education: knowing the self. In other words, an emphasis on students' test scores, grades, degree attainment, and career success (the "exterior") has resulted in "neglect [of] our 'inner' development—the sphere of values and beliefs, emotional maturity, moral development, spirituality, and self-understanding" (Astin, 2004, p. 34). Astin has contended that imbalances in our educational system, along with minimal effort to nurture individual and collective self-awareness, undermine our ability to solve the global problems of our time.

In a similar vein, Lantieri (2001b) has asked teachers, principals, and parents what they would seek to teach the children of the world were they to have the power to shape education. Typically, the responses revolve around several central goals for educating children: demonstrating that they are loved, encouraging them to find a sense of purpose, teaching them tolerance and compassion, and fostering their interconnectedness with other people and the natural world. Ironically, "no present system of public education in our country attends consciously to and systematically to what we clearly feel matters most" (Lantieri, 2001b, p. 11). In short, if we are serious about the values and purposes often associated with education, innovative endeavors to integrate spirituality and religion in education have merit.

A second justification for addressing religion and spirituality in education concerns the needs and expectations of students. According to a number of primary, secondary, and postsecondary educators and scholars (Astin et al., 2005; Chickering et al., 2006; Eisler, 2005; Kessler, 2005; Parks, 2000), learners across the life span hunger for wholeness, connectedness, and meaning. They come to educational settings primed with existential questions and curiosities, interested in spirituality, and prepared to cultivate the affective domain of their lives alongside the cognitive domain. Spiritual development, variously referred to as inner development (Seifert & Holman-Harmon, 2009) or faith development (Fowler, 1981), is considered by some to be a human universal. To ignore this aspect of life is synonymous with ignoring part of what it means to be human. Moreover, because spiritual development is associated with other benefits, namely well-being and physical health (Benson & Roehlkepartain, 2008), we can expect that cultivating spiritual and religious development and self-awareness will enhance other key areas of students' lives as well.

A third line of reasoning purports that infusing spirituality and religion in education fosters cultural sensitivity and awareness, understanding of others, and appreciation of pluralism (Bellous, 2006; Benson & Roehlkepartain, 2008; de Souza, 2008; Tisdell, 2003). Educational practice that encourages authentic engagement across differences entails "promot[ing], among students, the traits of resilience, connectedness, compassion and meaning; and increas[ing] their chances of becoming more productive and affirmed community members in a global society that is besieged by divisiveness, violence and terrorism" (de Souza, 2006, p. 165). When dialogue about spirituality and religion is stifled, students miss an important opportunity to learn about and develop sensitivities toward the core attributes, beliefs, values, and practices of people who differ from them. Arguably, the global problems that Astin (2004) feared cannot be overcome without infusing spirituality in education are linked to the serious discord stemming from an inability to understand and relate compassionately to "the other."

Also connected to the third justification is the concept of culturally responsive teaching (Tisdell, 2008), which necessitates attending to the role of spirituality and religion, as both are intrinsic to the knowledge construction process of many cultural groups. Enlightenment principles and notions of church–state separation may be taken-for-granted elements of U.S. society, but they do not reflect the cultural experiences of many students of color for whom "cutting off the spiritual from the academic seems more foreign than it may seem to their white Euro-American peers" (Tisdell, 2008, p. 153). In light of our nation's exceptionally diverse educational systems, integration of religion and spirituality marks an important step toward ensuring that learners find inclusive space where they can holistically express the many facets of their identities.

Taken together, the foundational purposes of spirituality and religion in education ideally involve elevating the importance of inner development for the good of individuals and communities. Moreover, the integration of religion and spirituality in education is based largely on several objectives: affirming the long-standing aims that have been central to our educational systems; enhancing students' development as self-aware, compassionate, and pluralistically competent global citizens; addressing students' spiritual yearnings; and fostering interconnectedness among members of diverse educational, local, national, and global communities.

Although the scholars who have articulated rationales for integrating spirituality in education speak from the distinct educational contexts in which they are situated—including early childhood, secondary, and postsecondary contexts—the justifications they provide show that attention to religion and spirituality in education has the potential to benefit learners across the life span. In light of the evidence presented earlier that spirituality and religion are relevant in the lives of children, adolescents, and young adults, objectives to promote compassion, pluralistic competence, global citizenship, and interconnectedness are worthwhile aims for individuals of all stages of development.

CONCERNS ABOUT RELIGION AND SPIRITUALITY IN EDUCATION

Despite sound justification for attending to religion and spirituality in educational settings, several legal and ethical concerns remain. Should parents, educators, administrators, counselors, psychologists, and student services providers broach issues of spirituality and religion in educational contexts? Although the empirical evidence and intuitive rationale presented in the last section suggest an affirmative response to this question, in this section, we present some of the counterpoints and strategies to address them.

The legal ramifications of addressing religion and spirituality in education present a potentially daunting challenge. Constitutional provisions in the First Amendment that protect the free exercise of religion and simultaneously prevent government establishment of religion raise questions about the appropriateness of religion and spirituality in the public educational domain (Chickering, 2006b; Clark, 2001; Lowery, 2007). The notion of separation of church and state stems directly from the First Amendment to the Constitution of the United States, which widely "protects public school children from the imposition of any particular worldview or religious practices . . . [and] at the same time . . . protects the rights of our children to *freely express their own beliefs*" (Kessler, 2000, p. xiv). In both K–12 and higher education contexts, a number of issues have been brought before the courts: discussion of religion and spirituality in the classroom; academic freedom of faculty; student-led religious activities and organizations on campus; and prayer in colleges, universities, and schools (Lowery, 2005, 2007). Because these issues and associated court cases are discussed in detail by others (Kaplin & Lee, 2009; Lowery, 2005, 2007), we offer a few examples to highlight the complexities as well as the differences among various educational settings.

The establishment clause of the First Amendment requires that public institutions maintain a neutral position on religion (Kaplin & Lee, 2009). For example, the Supreme Court's decision in the case of *School District of Abingdon Township v. Schempp* (1963) prohibited school-sponsored Bible reading in public schools. The implication of this ruling for counselors, educators, and administrators is the need to distinguish between teaching religion and teaching *about* religion, the latter of which is consistent with the First Amendment. The challenge, of course, is that the line between the two approaches can become blurred whenever the personal perspectives of teachers and administrators enter the educational discourse. Educators and practitioners are not objective conduits of information; they come to educational settings with their own set of values, ideological inclinations, and religious and spiritual worldviews. Arguably, a truly unbiased presentation of "the facts" whether in the classroom or in cocurricular situations cannot be accomplished with ease. Moreover, attempts at sterile objectivity may come across as inauthentic in the eyes of students. Finding innovative ways to teach *about* religion and spirituality (in place of teaching students to embrace particular religious or spiritual beliefs and practices) is essential per landmark court decisions. Finding appropriate and effective strategies to acknowledge and relay the subjectivities of educators and practitioners whenever spirituality and religion are part of the conversation is also important.

Although the establishment clause disallows public institutions' entanglement with religion and requires religious neutrality, the free speech and exercise clauses of the First Amendment enable students to express themselves religiously and spirituality through noncoercive student-led campus activities (Kaplin & Lee, 2009). One form of religious expression, prayer, is often viewed as a tangible manifestation of one's spirituality and has been the subject of many court cases over the past 5 decades. Supreme Court rulings have consistently determined "that prayers at public events such as graduation or football games are unconstitutional in the context of K–12 public education, even when led by students" (Lowery, 2005, p. 17). Court decisions regarding prayer have been handled differently in higher education settings, however. The courts have stressed that a younger audience is more impressionable and therefore warrants more protection from religious observance in the public school context, even when participation is not explicitly mandatory (Lowery, 2005). Showing a broader acceptance of religious expression in higher education, appellate courts in *Tanford v. Brand* (1997) and *Chaudhuri v. Tennessee* (1997) have allowed prayers as invocations during graduation ceremonies (Lowery, 2005). Yet, the court system's decision in 2002 against the student-led traditional mealtime prayer at Virginia Military Institute has further confused the practical discernment of one student's right to exercise her or his religion and another student's right to avoid a setting in which the institution is perceived as favoring a particular view of spirituality or religion. In this case, the court stopped the prayer activity, citing as coercive the military academy's mandatory mealtime participation requirement (Lowery, 2005).

Moving from legal to ethical concerns, the issues of diversity and power are related and noteworthy. Given the somewhat-elusive meaning of spirituality and spiritual development, critics of movements to integrate spirituality and religion in education contend that presumed definitions may reflect the interests of the majority and inadequately account for diverse perspectives and experiences (Watson, 2000). Similarly, individuals with the authority to define spirituality for others run the risk of indoctrinating those without the power to articulate spiritual meanings on their own accord (Marples, 2006). Both of these ethical concerns have legal ramifications at their extreme, but can be guided by the discussion of legal issues. To counter these problems, multiple definitions of what it means to be a "religious" or "spiritual" person should be developed with diverse worldviews and faith traditions in mind. Members of educational communities—including students, parents, teachers and faculty, and administrators with minority and majority perspectives—should work together to collectively establish definitions and processes for integrating religion and spirituality in their respective settings.

Given the tensions emanating from the legal and ethical realities that spirituality and religion bring to education, three distinct responses come to mind. First, erring on the side of church–state separation is the choice to fully secularize the educational experience (an option relevant only in public and private, nonreligious educational settings). The second approach is to fully embrace spirituality and religion as integral components of students' lives and learning, despite the potential legal and ethical issues. The third option, which we perceive as preferable to the first two approaches, is to remain vigilant about legal and ethical dilemmas while adopting practices that draw on the religious and spiritual dimensions of students' lives.

The first option, to fully secularize the educational experience, seems on the surface to be the "safe" response to complex legal and ethical concerns and may simplify decision making. Very few practitioners, however, find it satisfactory or even possible given Constitutional protections of free speech and exercise of religion (Kaplin & Lee, 2009). Lewy and Betty (2007, p. 325) argued that excluding these components from education is "unfair" to students because religion is a fundamental part of life for most people. And spirituality mostly reaches children through the religion to which they are being exposed. Not to discuss religion in the classroom is to give the impression that it is unimportant and that smart people and role models (their teachers) do not engage in it. Full-scale secularization of education promotes the idea that one can stand behind what L. Miller and Athan (2007) called "the veil of so-called professional neutrality . . . like the Wizard of Oz" (pp. 18–19).

The second option, to integrate spirituality and religion in education without limitations, involves assuming that spiritual or religious elements are inherent in every individual. The fallacy of religious and spiritual homogeneity embedded in this approach has the potential to devalue the worldviews and meaning-making processes of students who do not identify as explicitly religious or spiritual while privileging those who do. Moreover, in public settings, such an approach may violate legal mandates regarding religious neutrality.

The third option, to remain vigilant about legal and ethical dilemmas while adopting practices that draw on the religious and spiritual dimensions of students' lives, provides a promising middle ground in which the spiritual, religious, and existential realms of experience—the "interior" life (Astin, 2004)—are welcomed into an open educational forum that prizes holism as well as pluralism. The next section of the chapter speaks to how this third option may be accomplished in educational practice.

RELIGION AND SPIRITUALITY IN EDUCATIONAL PRACTICE

Educational practices that incorporate religion and spirituality are evident across all levels of education. Although the specific practices vary according to the developmental readiness of learners, generally they tend to align with one of five categories, all with the common thread of interconnectedness that is so central to religion and spirituality: connecting to the self, connecting to the natural world, connecting to diverse others in pluralistic community, connecting to others through service and social justice, and connecting to spiritual support networks. In this section, we define each category of practice and provide examples to illustrate how each practice might be implemented across different educational settings.

Before we describe the categories of practice, we offer a few reflections on the prevalence of these practices and the factors that support and detract from their implementation. The integration of religion and spirituality in higher education has become increasingly evident in recent years primarily because of the growing interest in these issues among college students (Astin et al., 2005) and the long-standing holistic aims of liberal education and college student personnel work (American Council on Education, 1949; Astin, 2004; Cohen, 1998). Examples of spiritual or religious practices in public K–12 education are somewhat less common by comparison (although the conversation is ongoing and evolving), and we speculate that concerns about church-state separation, children's impressionability, and standardization efforts leave little room in the curriculum for addressing spirituality (Lantieri, 2001a). Beyond the United States, other countries appear to be taking steps to address the spiritualities and religious diversity of children and adolescents. For example, in the United Kingdom, the 1988 Education Reform Act affirms spiritual development as one of many developmental purposes of education, but in the United States there appear to be few large-scale, organized efforts to this end.

Turning now to the five categories of practice, the first category, *connecting to the self*, involves practices that encourage learners to explore and convey who they are at the core. Whether within or beyond the classroom, these educational initiatives are designed to help students (or teachers, faculty, and staff) discern purpose and calling, find meaning, develop contemplative practices, and express emotion and creativity. The Passages Program, developed by Rachael Kessler (2000, 2001), is a curriculum intended for public and private school settings that is based on "a set of principles and practices for working with adolescents that integrates heart, spirit, and community with a strong academic component" (Kessler, 2001, p. 109). The approach is designed in response to the seven gateways to the soul of young people, including "the search for meaning and purpose, the longing for silence and solitude, the urge for transcendence, the hunger for joy and delight, the creative drive, the call for initiation, and the yearning for deep connection" (Kessler, 2001, p. 111). The program assumes many forms depending on the context, but Kessler encouraged a combination of methodologies to enact Passages: play, symbols and metaphors, the arts, opportunities to pose important life questions, the council process (a structured form of conversation in which participants speak uninterrupted and without immediate response from others), silence, and reflection.

Nurturing teachers is another critical component of practices within this category. Courage to Teach focuses on nourishing the spiritual needs of K–12 teachers, administrators, and counselors who work in public school settings (Hare, Jackson, & Jackson, 2000; Palmer, Jackson, Jackson, & Sluyter, 2001). Retreat groups of 20 to 30 people meet quarterly over a 2-year period to seek inner renewal through six fundamentals that serve as the basis of approach: "framing evocative questions, welcoming silence, working with paradox, identifying birthright gifts, using poetry and teaching stories, and practicing the clearness committee" (a practice used in the Quaker tradition to achieve clarity on an issue or dilemma; Palmer et al., 2001, p. 137). Evaluations of Courage to Teach have affirmed the program's capacity to rejuvenate educators and their passion for teaching. Retreat participants report better teaching practices and connection to students as well as improvements in reflective habits, collegiality, leadership ability, and mindfulness (Palmer et al., 2001).

The second category of practice, connecting to the natural world, reflects the premise that being outdoors encourages young people to engage their inner lives. Affirming this principle, the National Study of College Students' Search for Meaning and Purpose found that more than 60% of 1st-year college students in 2004 reported having had a spiritual experience "while witnessing the beauty and harmony of nature" (Astin et al., 2005, p. 4). Outdoor adventure programs are vital educational practices that connect students to the natural world, thereby enhancing such character strengths as self-efficacy, self-concept, and self-actualization (Hanna, 1995). Roerden (2001) described a summer marine biology program, Ocean Matters, in which high school students from around the world come together for a 5-week course involving ecological exploration of the Caribbean coral reef. Roerden explained that the study of marine science on which the group embarks inevitably invokes significant questions and reflections on life meaning and purpose. To encourage meaningful outcomes to unfold in outdoor programs, Roerden recommended pedagogies that blend sensory engagement; knowing and feeling; solitude and community; and rituals, myths, art, and reflection.

The third category of practice, connecting to diverse others in pluralistic community, consists of educational opportunities to experience interconnectedness that stems from deep and active engagement with diversity (Eck, 1993). Coursework and activities designed to enhance religious literacy; to promote discussions on religious and worldview differences and commonalities; and to generate understanding, acceptance, and appreciation of religious and cultural pluralism fall within this category. A number of programs have been implemented in higher education to accommodate students' needs in these areas, although there are indications that some attention has been given to honoring diverse religious traditions in primary and secondary schools, even if these initiatives are lesser known (Lewy & Betty, 2007).

The Wellesley College model of religious and spiritual life, known as Beyond Tolerance, is one exemplar that reflects the pluralism category of practice. The college's Multifaith Student Council created a performance-piece in the late 1990s using drama, music, song, dance, and ritual to portray their collective efforts and challenges in building a multifaith community. The performance piece was presented at the 1998 "EDUCATION as *Transformation*" conference, a landmark gathering on religious pluralism in higher education, and is available to educators on video in conjunction with a campus religious diversity manual to guide similar initiatives at colleges and universities.

In another recent development, the Ford Foundation initiated Difficult Dialogues: Promoting Pluralism and Academic Freedom on Campus in 2005 with the intent to generate conversations around challenging topics—including religious diversity—at 43 institutions across the country (Schwartz, 2007). The innovative approaches that campuses have put into practice consist of faculty development and curriculum enrichment in the areas of religious diversity and conflict (Arizona State University), faculty seminars devoted to topics at the intersection of religion and academic freedom (Barnard College), and student dialogue groups on religion and roundtables on the connection between faith and community service (University of Michigan, Ann Arbor; Schwartz, 2007).

To foster the sort of outcomes anticipated as a result of initiatives such as Beyond Tolerance and Difficult Dialogues, "moral conversation" offers a valuable framework for dialogue on religious pluralism in the higher education context (Nash, 2001). The framework has provided guidance to faculty in classroom settings and to student affairs practitioners in cocurricular programming. The essential premise of moral conversation "emphasize[s] the fundamental worth and dignity of each participant in the exchange" (Nash, 2001, p. 174) and consists of six principles that invite participants to (a) be aware that declarations of beliefs are not the equivalent of moral conversation; (b) begin with initial respect for all views; (c) find the truth in what they oppose and the error in what they espouse; (d) avoid either-or, all-or-nothing thinking; (e) realize that with religion we live not in reality itself but in stories about reality; and (f) recognize the liberal–postmodern leaning of moral conversation (Nash, 2001).

Connecting to others through service and social justice represents a fourth category of spiritually infused educational practice and includes curricular and cocurricular occasions for students, faculty, and staff to understand and apply humanitarian values through service learning, volunteer work, and other justice-oriented projects. Chickering (2006a) cited the evidence garnered by Astin and colleagues in stating that among "pedagogical practices calling for behaviors that are consistent with our desired outcomes concerning spiritual growth and strengthening authenticity, purpose, and meaning . . . perhaps the most powerful is service learning" (p. 135). Likewise, Cherry et al. (2001) affirmed that there are "significant connections between personal spirituality and volunteer social service" (Cherry et al., 2001, p. 279). Recent initiatives at two California institutions illustrate the intentional associations that educators are drawing between spirituality and service learning. Educators at the University of San Diego, a Roman Catholic institution, are working to integrate reflective practices (e.g., journaling, storytelling, evocative questions, dialogue, and art) as key components of service-learning courses (Elliott, Quinn, & Nayve, 2009). Linking spirituality and service is not merely within the purview of private education; in fact, Six Billion Paths, a course at UC Berkeley, encourages students to explore the relationship between their "daily actions and their contributions to peace-building and service for social change" (Lin, Louie, Voorhees, Wolf, & Yoshida, 2009, p. 1). Students in the course are introduced to theory on conflict resolution, service opportunities, and the practice of reflection, and many become more inclined "to relate to the larger communities in which they live and feel like they have a voice and place to make a difference" (Lin, Louie, Voorhees, Wolf, & Yoshida, 2009, p. 1). Representing a merging of categories (service and pluralism), Keen (2000) described the E Pluribus Unum conference, which brings together recent high school graduates who identify as Catholic, Protestant, or Jewish "to afford each group an opportunity to learn more about their own traditions, particularly how these support community service and interreligious collaboration on issues of social justice" (p. 208). Beyond the higher education context, Louie-Badua and Wolf (2008) noted that service work is an "effective vehicle" for developing children's spirituality (p. 91).

The fifth and final category, connecting to spiritual support networks, involves providing space for members of educational communities to wrestle with existential questions, spiritual struggles, and stressful life experiences through coursework; cocurricular programming; retreats; and mentoring relationships with teachers, staff, counselors, and peers. At the precollege level, research in Australia has revealed the implications of curricula geared toward helping children and adolescents deal with grief and loss (Rowling, 1996, 2008). Rowling (1996) concluded that in addition to promoting spiritual development, including "loss and grief in the curriculum can serve both to intervene to support grieving young people and act in a preventative way, by information exchange and positive attitude formation for handling experiences" (p. 281).

An intervention intended for college students provides support for another set of challenges that young adults routinely face: spiritual struggles. Developed and piloted by researchers at Bowling Green State University, Winding Road frames spiritual struggles as an important and normal part of human development (Gear et al., 2008; Gear, Krumrei, & Pargament, 2009). The intervention is designed to help students normalize their spiritual struggles, recognize the diversity of struggles with which people contend, define their own spiritual path, and foster a "spirituality that is flexible, integrated, and differentiated" (Gear et al., 2009, p. 1). Students representing diverse religious backgrounds and types of struggle met in group sessions with trained therapists for 9 weeks. The sessions included a wide range of activities: experiential exercises, discussion, written reflection, reading, and music, which together emphasized acceptance of struggles, the positive aspects of struggling, reformulation of conceptions of God, and living in ways consistent with one's personal values. According to Gear et al. (2009),

> Following the program, students reported experiencing fewer spiritual struggles. Perhaps more importantly, they experienced fewer self-stigmatizing views of spiritual struggles. The program also was successful in raising awareness of the fact that struggles are a normal aspect of spiritual development and growth. (p. 3)

Winding Road's success at a public university suggests that spiritual interventions are possible regardless of the type of institution.

This section has highlighted the variety of programs and practices that educational leaders may implement for the express purpose of nurturing the inner lives of students, teachers, and staff. Many questions remain regarding the effectiveness of these diverse initiatives in promoting intended outcomes. The programs certainly have intuitive appeal, leading us to suspect that participants of all ages may benefit from exposure to such innovative practices. Nonetheless, with the exception of Courage to Teach (Hare et al., 2000; Palmer et al., 2001) and Winding Road (Gear et al., 2009), both of which appear to foster spiritual development, we were unable to find explicit evidence of program effectiveness for the other initiatives we have described, which points to an imperative need for further evaluation and assessment of these endeavors and others like them. We turn now to a discussion of roles that leaders may assume to make a difference in their particular educational settings.

ROLES FOR EDUCATORS AND PRACTITIONERS

Psychologists, counselors, educators, and administrators all have invaluable roles to assume with respect to integrating religion and spirituality in educational contexts. We suggest five roles to provide definition and direction to educational leaders: collaborator, model, historian, pioneer, and researcher.

Foremost among the various roles is that of *collaborator* in fostering students' religious and spiritual wellness. Oftentimes, resources for students are available in compartmentalized spaces across campus, rather than in a single "one-stop-shop" location. By partnering with teachers, campus or local clergy, and campus-based or community religious organizations, practitioners can help to establish a multifaceted support network for students (Weinstein, Parker, & Archer, 2002). Opportunities for religious and spiritual enrichment may exist in other spaces not explicitly devoted to these purposes, such as centers focused on community service projects or student organizations and centers focused on gender; sexual orientation; and race, ethnicity, and culture. Remaining cognizant of these spaces and establishing relationships with those who oversee them will enable practitioners to encourage students to draw on the constellation of resources available.

The second role, *model*, involves exemplifying authenticity, wholeness, and self-awareness and, by serving as an example, encouraging others to do likewise. Educators and counselors who merely teach or speak about spirituality without embodying spiritual qualities may be less effective in conveying their message to students. The spiritual journeys of teachers or counselors will be evident in their demeanor, the questions they pose, and the educational opportunities they offer students (Bandura, 2003; see also Volume 1, Chapter 10, this handbook). When students witness congruence between espoused values and behaviors in the lives of the adults who lead and teach in their schools and colleges, they will be motivated to cultivate meaning and purpose in their own lives.

The role of *historian* entails maintaining a repository of information on the role of spirituality and religion in a given educational setting. Understanding the historical context of the school, college, or university is critical to enacting successful programs and effective policies—and avoiding decisions that simply replicate past mistakes. Historians also understand the larger national and international historical context and use this information to shape the local educational environment within which they work. A broad-based knowledge of the history of spirituality and religion in education can be used to generate a rationale for action or an innovative approach to problems informed by long-standing educational philosophies or models that continue to have enduring utility.

A *pioneer*, the fourth role, leads the way into new territory. Religion and spirituality may be taboo and concealed in many educational settings. The pioneer finds ways to open the conversation, bringing matters of the inner life into focus. The pioneer exercises creativity to fashion interventions that will work well in the context at hand. Many of the practices described earlier are building blocks of the pioneer's efforts: engagement with diversity, preservation and access to the natural world, promotion of the arts, sustained individual and community reflection, and service work and social justice. With hopefulness about the possibilities and promise of tending to the inner life, the pioneer sets forth a vision for prioritizing meaning, purpose, and spirituality and calls the educational community to action.

Finally, the *researcher* role involves attending to the empirical exploration of religion and spirituality in early, secondary, and postsecondary education. Recent scholarship in multiple disciplines has succeeded in illuminating the nuances of religious and spiritual phenomena among children, adolescents, and young adults. Several large-scale longitudinal studies have made compelling contributions to the knowledge base with the examination of spiritual and religious development—and the factors that facilitate or impede development. As expressed in the section on educational practice, the wide range of initiatives that integrate religion and spirituality in education require the attention of researchers to gauge the effectiveness of these innovations. Moreover, research that assesses the impact of spirituality on educational and life outcomes (e.g., academic success, satisfaction, emotional well-being) is emerging (Astin et al., 2010) and should continue to be a priority among those in the researcher role.

CONCLUSION: RECOMMENDATIONS TO ENHANCE THE EFFECTIVENESS OF RELIGIOUS AND SPIRITUAL INITIATIVES IN EDUCATION

The future of spirituality and religion in education depends on further attention to context, integration, and assessment. Because educational settings serve diverse age-groups and populations and exist within both public and private sectors, remaining mindful of context will guide practice in effective directions. Likewise, connecting spiritual programs to the mission and goals of schools, colleges, and universities will ensure that initiatives are seamlessly integrated within institutional environments, and utilizing and transforming existing programs can be more effective than add-on programs that lack an integral place in the institution. Finally, research and assessment are critical (Chickering & Mentkowski, 2006). Many questions remain about the ways that initiatives related to religion and spirituality affect students—are they accomplishing their intended purposes? Programs that yield desired developmental outcomes among learners will likely garner the support of members of the educational community. Thus, gathering evidence based on empirical investigation will solidify the foundation on which innovative practice rests.

References

American Council on Education. (1949). *The student personnel point of view*. Washington, DC: Author.

Astin, A. W. (2004). Why spirituality deserves a central place in liberal education. *Liberal Education, 90*(2), 34–41.

Astin, A. W., Astin, H. S., & Lindholm, J. A. (2010). *Cultivating the spirit: How college can enhance students' inner lives*. San Francisco, CA: Jossey-Bass.

Astin, A. W., Astin, H. S., Lindholm, J. A., Bryant, A. N., Szelényi, K., & Calderone, S. (2005). *The spiritual life of college students: A national study of college students' search for meaning and purpose*. Los Angeles, CA: Higher Education Research Institute, UCLA.

Bandura, A. (2003). On the psychosocial impact and mechanisms of spiritual modeling. *The International Journal for the Psychology of Religion, 13*, 167–173. doi:10.1207/S15327582IJPR1303_02

Bellous, J. (2006). Five classroom activities for sustaining a spiritual environment. *International Journal of*

Children's Spirituality, 11, 99–111. doi:10.1080/13644360500504389

Benson, P. L., & Roehlkepartain, E. C. (2008). Spiritual development: A missing priority in youth development. *New Directions for Youth Development, 118*, 13–28. doi:10.1002/yd.253

Bryant, A. N., Choi, J. Y., & Yasuno, M. (2003). Understanding the religious and spiritual dimensions of students' lives in the first year of college. *Journal of College Student Development, 44*, 723–745. doi:10.1353/csd.2003.0063

Center for Spiritual Development in Childhood and Adolescence. (2008). *With their own voices: A global exploration of how today's young people experience and think about spiritual development* [Press release]. Minneapolis, MN: Search Institute.

Chaudhuri V. Tennessee, 130 F. 3d 232 (6th Cir. 1997).

Cherry, C., DeBerg, B. A., & Porterfield, A. (2001). *Religion on campus*. Chapel Hill: University of North Carolina Press.

Chickering, A. W. (2006a). Curricular content and powerful pedagogy. In A. W. Chickering, J. C. Dalton, & L. Stamm (Eds.), *Encouraging authenticity and spirituality in higher education* (pp. 113–144). San Francisco, CA: Jossey-Bass.

Chickering, A. W. (2006b). Policy issues: Legislative and institutional. In A. W. Chickering, J. C. Dalton, & L. Stamm (Eds.), *Encouraging authenticity and spirituality in higher education* (pp. 97–112). San Francisco, CA: Jossey-Bass.

Chickering, A. W., Dalton, J. C., & Stamm, L. (Eds.). (2006). *Encouraging authenticity and spirituality in higher education*. San Francisco, CA: Jossey-Bass.

Chickering, A. W., & Mentkowski, M. (2006). Assessing ineffable outcomes. In A. W. Chickering, J. C. Dalton, & L. Stamm (Eds.), *Encouraging authenticity and spirituality in higher education* (pp. 220–242). San Francisco, CA: Jossey-Bass.

Clark, R. T. (2001). The law and spirituality: How the law supports and limits expression of spirituality on the college campus. *New Directions for Student Services, 95*, 37–46. doi:10.1002/ss.21

Cohen, A. M. (1998). *The shaping of American higher education: Emergence and growth of the contemporary system*. San Francisco, CA: Jossey-Bass.

de Souza, M. (2006). Educating for hope, compassion, and meaning in a divisive and intolerant world. *International Journal of Children's Spirituality, 11*, 165–175. doi:10.1080/13644360500504488

de Souza, M. (2008). Education for transformation: Meeting students' needs in changing contemporary contexts. *International Journal of Children's Spirituality, 13*, 27–37. doi:10.1080/13644360701834817

Eck, D. L. (1993). *Encountering God: A spiritual journey from Bozeman to Banaras*. Boston, MA: Beacon Press.

Eisler, R. (2005). Tomorrow's children: Education for a partnership world. In J. P. Miller, S. Karsten, D. Denton, D. Orr, & I. C. Kates (Eds.), *Holistic learning and spirituality in education* (pp. 47–67). Albany: State University of New York Press.

Elliott, E., Quinn, B., & Nayve, C. (2009). The art of spiritual reflection: Applications for service-learning and civic engagement on campus. *Spirituality in Higher Education Newsletter, 5*(1), 1–7.

Fowler, J. W. (1981). *Stages of faith: The psychology of human development and the quest for meaning*. San Francisco, CA: Harper & Row.

Gear, M. R., Faigin, C. A., Gibbel, M. R., Krumrei, E., Oemig, C., McCarthy, S. K., & Pargament, K. I. (2008). The Winding Road: A promising approach to addressing the spiritual struggles of college students. *Spirituality in Higher Education Newsletter, 4*(4), 1–8.

Gear, M. R., Krumrei, E. J., & Pargament, K. I. (2009). Development of a spiritually-sensitive intervention for college students experiencing spiritual struggles: Winding Road. *Journal of College and Character, 10*(4), 1–5. doi:10.2202/1940-1639.1048

Hanna, G. (1995). Wilderness-related environmental outcomes of adventure and ecology education programming. *Journal of Environmental Education, 27*, 21–32. doi:10.1080/00958964.1995.9941968

Hare, S. Z., Jackson, M., & Jackson, R. (2000). Teacher formation: Identity, integrity, and the heart of a teacher. In V. H. Kazanjian & P. L. Laurence (Eds.), *Education as transformation: Religious pluralism, spirituality, and a new vision of higher education in America* (pp. 275–284). New York, NY: Peter Lang.

Hart, D. G. (1999). *The university gets religion: Religious studies in American higher education*. Baltimore, MD: Johns Hopkins University Press.

Kaplin, W. A., & Lee, B. A. (2009). *A legal guide for student affairs professionals* (2nd ed.). San Francisco, CA: Jossey-Bass. doi:10.1002/9781118269565

Keen, J. P. (2000). Appreciative engagement of diversity: E Pluribus Unum and the education as transformation project. In V. H. Kazanjian & P. L. Laurence (Eds.), *Education as transformation: Religious pluralism, spirituality, and a new vision of higher education in America* (pp. 207–212). New York, NY: Peter Lang.

Kessler, R. (2000). *The soul of education: Helping students find connection, compassion, and character at school*. Alexandria, VA: Association for Supervision and Curriculum Development.

Kessler, R. (2001). Souls of students, souls of teachers: Welcoming the inner life to school. In L. Lantieri (Ed.), *Schools with spirit: Nurturing the inner lives of children and teachers* (pp. 107–131). Boston, MA: Beacon Press.

Kessler, R. (2005). Nourishing adolescents' spirituality. In J. P. Miller, S. Karsten, D. Denton, D. Orr, & I. C. Kates (Eds.), *Holistic learning and spirituality in education* (pp. 101–107). Albany: State University of New York Press.

Kuh, G. D., & Umbach, P. D. (2004). College and character: Insights from the National Survey of Student Engagement. *New Directions for Institutional Research, 122*, 37–54. doi:10.1002/ir.108

Lantieri, L. (2001a). Epilogue: The challenge of creating schools that are divided no more. In L. Lantieri (Ed.), *Schools with spirit: Nurturing the inner lives of children and teachers* (pp. 164–171). Boston, MA: Beacon Press.

Lantieri, L. (2001b). A vision of schools with spirit. In L. Lantieri (Ed.), *Schools with spirit: Nurturing the inner lives of children and teachers* (pp. 7–20). Boston, MA: Beacon Press.

Lewy, S., & Betty, S. (2007). How to expose fourth and fifth graders to religion and spirituality in a public school classroom. *International Journal of Children's Spirituality, 12*, 325–330. doi:10.1080/13644360701714993

Lin, A., Louie, L., Voorhees, M., Wolf, M., & Yoshida, K. (2009). Listening, reflecting, and collaborating: A look from inside the creation of a peace and service course. *Spirituality in Higher Education Newsletter, 5*(2), 1–10.

Louie-Badua, L. J., & Wolf, M. (2008). The spiritual nature of service-learning. *New Directions for Youth Development, 118*, 91–95. doi:10.1002/yd.260

Love, P. G. (2000). Spirituality comes to college. *Spirituality on Campus.* Retrieved from http://www.collegevalues.org/spirit.cfm?id=187&a=1

Love, P. G., & Talbot, D. (1999). Defining spiritual development: A missing consideration for student affairs. *NASPA Journal, 37*, 361–375.

Lowery, J. W. (2005). What higher education law says about spirituality. *New Directions for Teaching and Learning, 104*, 15–22. doi:10.1002/tl.208

Lowery, J. W. (2007). Spirituality and higher education law. In B. W. Speck & S. L. Hoppe (Eds.), *Searching for spirituality in higher education* (pp. 53–67). New York, NY: Peter Lang.

Marples, R. (2006). Against (the use of the term) "spiritual education." *International Journal of Children's Spirituality, 11*, 293–306. doi:10.1080/13644360600797313

Marsden, G. M. (1994). *The soul of the American university: From Protestant establishment to established nonbelief.* New York, NY: Oxford University Press.

Miller, J. P. (2005). Introduction: Holistic learning. In J. P. Miller, S. Karsten, D. Denton, D. Orr, & I. C. Kates (Eds.), *Holistic learning and spirituality in education* (pp. 1–6). Albany: State University of New York Press.

Miller, L., & Athan, A. (2007). Spiritual awareness pedagogy: The classroom as spiritual reality. *International Journal of Children's Spirituality, 12*, 17–35. doi:10.1080/13644360701266085

Nash, R. (2001). *Religious pluralism in the academy: Opening the dialogue.* New York, NY: Peter Lang.

Nash, R., & Bradley, D. L. (2008). The different spiritualities of the students we teach. In D. Jacobsen & R. H. Jacobsen (Eds.), *The American university in a postsecular age* (pp. 135–150). New York, NY: Oxford University Press. doi:10.1093/acprof:oso/9780195323443.003.0011

Palmer, P. J., Jackson, M., Jackson, R., & Sluyter, D. (2001). The courage to teach: A program for teacher renewal. In L. Lantieri (Ed.), *Schools with spirit: Nurturing the inner lives of children and teachers* (pp. 132–147). Boston, MA: Beacon Press.

Pargament, K. I., & Mahoney, A. (2005). Sacred matters: Sanctification as a vital topic for the psychology of religion. *The International Journal for the Psychology of Religion, 15*, 179–198. doi:10.1207/s15327582ijpr1503_1

Parks, S. D. (2000). *Big questions, worthy dreams: Mentoring young adults in their search for meaning, purpose, and faith.* San Francisco, CA: Jossey-Bass.

Pearce, L., & Denton, M. L. (2011). *A faith of their own: Stability and change in the religiosity of America's adolescents.* New York, NY: Oxford University Press.

Roerden, L. P. (2001). Lessons of the wild. In L. Lantieri (Ed.), *Schools with spirit: Nurturing the inner lives of children and teachers* (pp. 53–76). Boston, MA: Beacon Press.

Rowling, L. (1996). Learning about life: Teaching about loss. In R. Best (Ed.), *Education, spirituality, and the whole child* (pp. 271–284). London, England: Cassell.

Rowling, L. (2008). Linking spirituality, school communities, grief and well-being. *International Journal of Children's Spirituality, 13*, 241–251. doi:10.1080/13644360802236482

School District of Abingdon Township v. Schempp, 374, U. S. 203 (1963).

Schwartz, L. M. (2007). Pluralism projects in action: A report on the difficult dialogues initiative. *Spirituality in Higher Education Newsletter, 3*(4), 1–4.

Seifert, T. A., & Holman-Harmon, N. (2009). Practical applications for student affairs professionals' work in facilitating students' inner development. *New Directions for Student Services, 125*, 13–21. doi:10.1002/ss.303

Smith, C., & Denton, M. L. (2005). *Soul searching: The religious and spiritual lives of American teenagers.* New York, NY: Oxford University Press.

Smith, C., & Snell, P. (2009). *Souls in transition: The religious and spiritual lives of emerging adults.* New York, NY: Oxford University Press.

Stamm, L. (2006a). The dynamics of spirituality and the religious experience. In A. W. Chickering, J. C. Dalton, & L. Stamm (Eds.), *Encouraging authenticity and spirituality in higher education* (pp. 37–65). San Francisco, CA: Jossey-Bass.

Stamm, L. (2006b). The influence of religion and spirituality in shaping American higher education. In A. W. Chickering, J. C. Dalton, & L. Stamm (Eds.), *Encouraging authenticity and spirituality in higher education* (pp. 66–91). San Francisco, CA: Jossey-Bass.

Tanford v. Brand, 104, F.3d 982 (7th cir. 1997).

Tisdell, E. J. (2003). *Exploring spirituality and culture in adult and higher education.* San Francisco, CA: Jossey-Bass.

Tisdell, E. J. (2008). Spirituality, diversity, and learner-centered teaching. In D. Jacobsen & R. H. Jacobsen (Eds.), *The American university in a postsecular age* (pp. 151–166). New York, NY: Oxford University Press. doi:10.1093/acprof:oso/9780195323443.003.0012

Watson, J. (2000). Whose model of spirituality should be used in the spiritual development of school children? *International Journal of Children's Spirituality, 5,* 91–101. doi:10.1080/713670894

Weinstein, C. M., Parker, J., & Archer, J., Jr. (2002). College counselor attitudes toward spiritual and religious issues and practices in counseling. *Journal of College Counseling, 5,* 164–174. doi:10.1002/j.2161-1882.2002.tb00218.x

Wuthnow, R. (2007). *After the baby boomers: How twenty- and thirty-somethings are shaping the future of American religion.* Princeton, NJ: Princeton University Press.

Wuthnow, R. (2008). Can faith be more than a sideshow in the contemporary academy? In D. Jacobsen & R. H. Jacobsen (Eds.), *The American university in a postsecular age* (pp. 31–44). New York, NY: Oxford University Press. doi:10.1093/acprof:oso/9780195323443.003.0004

Chapter 31

ADDRESSING RELIGION AND SPIRITUALITY IN THE WORKPLACE

Stephen T. Carroll

The U.S. Bureau of Labor Statistics' "Time Use Survey" for 2009 reports that employed Americans ages 25 to 54 who live in households with children under the age of 18 spend on an average workday 8.8 hr working, 7.6 hr sleeping, 2.6 hr engaging in leisure and sports activities, and 1.3 hr caring for others, including children (U.S. Bureau of Labor Statistics, 2010). For these Americans, work consumes the majority of their day; it takes up the biggest slice of their daily pie graph. Is it any wonder, then, that work is a topic of great interest these days? There is, of course, much focus on the dearth of work during economic downturns, as seen in many articles reporting on the lack of work for 2010 U.S. college graduates (Greenhouse, 2010) and on job retraining for U.S. workers who have seen their jobs shipped overseas (Luo, 2009). Perhaps paradoxically, however, there is also a renewed focus on discerning the type of employment that will lead not only to financial stability and general job satisfaction but also to broader life fulfillment. Interest in this topic is evident even from the magazines displayed at the checkout line in the grocery store, where the November 2010 cover of *O* (*The Oprah Magazine*) challenged readers to ask themselves, "What's Your True Calling? An Easy-Does-It Guide to Finding (and Fulfilling) Your Life's Purpose."

Life's calling is a weighty issue to contemplate in the checkout line. And what does it mean, anyway, in this day and age? The *Oprah* article leads with the premise that "there is the thing you do for a living and then the thing you were born to do; [but how do you] make them one and the same[?]" (DiBenedetto, 2010, p. 171). As this example suggests, work can have a deeper meaning to it, a meaning that may carry with it religious or spiritual significance. This is not a new idea, however.

Starting with the Reformation, and continuing with the growth of capitalism, the concept of work in the modern Western world has evolved from representing a mere means for daily survival to an activity with complex meaning and significance, even a reflection of a person's religious and social status (Giddens, 1985). Because many people spend the majority of their week working, the intersection of faith and work can provide critical insights about psychosocial and organizational functioning. Reinhold (1996) saw religion and spirituality as a positive influence on work. He proposed, "being committed to 'something' about your work prolongs your ability to stay working and increases the likelihood that you will remain healthy and energized" (p. 136). On the other hand, a person's religion or spirituality could potentially prompt negative behaviors and attitudes in relation to his or her work.

Employees, employers, and psychologists may have much to gain by a clearer understanding of how religiousness and spirituality affect behavior in workplace settings. Employees would benefit from learning how their religiosity or spirituality affects their behaviors in workplace settings, for example, what motivates them, and how they cope with stress. Employers would benefit from discerning how an organization's increased sensitivity to and accommodation of religious and spiritual issues can lead to increased productivity and job satisfaction.

DOI: 10.1037/14046-031
APA Handbook of Psychology, Religion, and Spirituality: Vol. 2. An Applied Psychology of Religion and Spirituality, K. I. Pargament (Editor-in-Chief)

And psychologists would greatly benefit from a clearer insight into how a person's spirituality or religiosity affects their attitudes toward work, and whether those attitudes promote healthy growth, or rationalize avoidance of other personal issues.

In fact, psychologists have begun to substantiate links between religion and spirituality and the workplace behaviors and attitudes of employees and managers, using quantitative and qualitative analyses in fields ranging from business to education to nonprofit service agencies (Brooks & Matthews, 2000; Sagie, 1993; Serow, 1994; Sikorska-Simmons, 2005; Steger et al., 2010). This chapter discusses the role of religion and spirituality in workplace settings by charting historical and religious institutional influences on the interface between religion, spirituality, and the workplace; presenting an overview of empirical research in this area addressing employees' performance and personal adjustment; presenting an overview of research on the role of religion and spirituality at the organizational level; and highlighting areas for future research. In doing so, the chapter utilizes the handbook's "integrative paradigm" to investigate the effects of religion and spirituality on occupational environments by examining the multidimensional and multilevel implications of religion and spirituality on people's working lives. The integrative approach is essential to this examination because individuals do not pursue their religion or spirituality in isolation; rather, they are influenced by social and cultural forces in their families, communities, and work settings. The "integrative paradigm" presents an effective means to assess the full range of psychological implications of religion and spirituality in the workplace because employees can, and often do, incorporate a broad spectrum of personal beliefs and practices into their work (see Volume 1, Chapter 1, this handbook). The studies discussed in this chapter analyzed "work" that was based on the traditional employer–employee model in the formal labor market sector, which is generally considered to include only those enterprises that are organized and registered under the laws of the country in which they operate and subsequently are subject to the labor and business laws that govern such enterprises (Fields, 2005). Therefore, although work performed in the informal labor market sector, which encompasses unpaid domestic and household labor, is equally important to the concepts described here, this chapter focuses primarily on traditional employer–employee relationships typically found in the formal labor market sector.

HISTORICAL AND RELIGIOUS INSTITUTIONAL INFLUENCES ON THE INTERFACE OF SPIRITUALITY AND THE WORKPLACE

Religious institutions, economists, and theologians have long been interested in the interface between religion and spirituality and the workplace. The Papacy of the Catholic Church imposed a centralized and hierarchical influence over all aspects of Western society, including work, until the Protestant Reformation. For 1,500 years the leadership of the Catholic Church, under the auspices of the magisterium interpreting God's will, dictated the guidelines by which believers could integrate spirituality into their lives and work. The Reformation changed this existing paradigm to one in which the believer could determine whether his or her actions, such as work, were pleasing to God through signs such as his or her continued prosperity. The Reformation's influence over religious, cultural, and economic values significantly changed how many Christians approached the practice of sanctifying their work (Armstrong, 1993; Giddens, 1985).

Protestant teachings about faith and work also coincided with the initial growth of capitalism in Europe. In the early 20th century, Max Weber, the German economist and sociologist, theorized that the relationship between religion and capitalism was an outgrowth of the beliefs of Puritan groups during the Reformation. Weber summarized that since these Puritan groups considered the accumulation of wealth to be an indication that a person was part of the holy elect, work was more than a means of providing for individual and family survival (Giddens, 1985). The idea that God would base an individual's eligibility for eternal salvation on his job performance was a significant change in Christian theology. The notion of an individual having a *calling*—the Protestant ideal that God has a plan and purpose for each believer who is required to satisfy his or her obligation to be saved—built upon this premise. Giddens proposed that the Protestant concept of calling was "the highest form of moral obligation of the individual to fulfill his or her duty in world affairs" (p. 183). This concept of obligation was especially present in Calvin's doctrine of predestination, which proposed that only some humans are chosen to be saved and spared damnation.

The Calvinists and later descendants of the Puritan movements believed that professional advancement and the accumulation of wealth were confirmation that their calling was being successfully fulfilled. For a person to truly be part of the elect, believers could accumulate wealth and power, but they had to remain sober, proficient, and avoid using their blessings to self-indulgent ends. The Puritan work ethic provided endless inspiration for the dedication of work to God; workers were perpetually motivated because they could not ever fully know during their lives whether they were a member of the elect and could only seek signs from God (this rationale represents the basis for the modern workaholic, except that the Puritan goal was primarily religious). The Reformation thus presented converts with a compelling doctrine from which they could legitimize their economic prosperity. Moreover, the Protestant notion of calling had a significant historical influence on the development of the spiritualization of work because it oriented people to perceive their professional lives as essential to receiving eternal life. Later in the 19th century, the influence of Calvinism grew in the United States where parts of the population became less religious but embraced a nationalist adaptation of "the Puritan work ethic and to its Calvinist notion of election, seeing Americans as a 'chosen nation' whose flag and ideals have a semi divine purpose" (Armstrong, 1993, p. 279). The simultaneous developments of capitalism and Calvinism in Western societies were also responsible for a major paradigm shift in the manner in which people conceptualized their religion and spirituality with work.

In the early 20th century, theologians Karl Rahner and Paul Tillich addressed the challenges of living and working in industrial societies and contrasted this with the role of spirituality in people's daily lives. Rahner's and Tillich's writings presented the intriguing question of whether spirituality and religion have measureable effects on people's daily experiences, although their analyses primarily focused on the experiences of White males in middle to upper economic classes. Tillich (1956) observed that modern industrial societies since the 18th century had attempted to place "God alongside the world without man's permission to interfere with it, because every interference would disturb man's technical and business calculations; the universe had been left to man as its master" (p. 42). Tillich proposed that the continued exclusion of God from people's professional lives was unnatural and counterproductive because the absence of spirituality intensified the pursuit of self-interest. Tillich suggested that employment was complemented by spirituality because it fostered concern for family, colleagues, and the broader community.

Similarly, Rahner offered a modern perspective on the Jesuit principle of "finding God in all things," especially work. Egan (1998) suggested that "Rahner's 'theology of everyday things' presented a model for how God's mysteries unfold for believers who seek to integrate their spirituality into ordinary daily activities such as work" (p. 2). Rahner presented an innovative perspective that spiritual people could experience God's revelations whether at work or play, rest or religious services. Rahner's teachings thus presented a theological framework for the inclusion of spirituality into daily life, even in a society that was facing increased tension between the time spent at work and time with family. Tillich and Rahner proposed challenging questions that would fuel the intellectual debate of whether spirituality possesses any measurable effect on people's daily lives.

The contemplation of the role of religion and spirituality in workplace settings has not been limited to the past century of scholarship. The fundamental aspects of integrating one's faith into daily work are considered in the sacred texts of many world religions and spiritual traditions. Throughout human history, holy writings such as the Bible, the Qur'an, and the Bhagavad Gita have instructed followers to apply their beliefs to all areas of daily life, especially their work. These sacred texts suggest strategies that people across the globe have utilized for centuries to integrate religion or spirituality into their daily labor. The Hebrew scriptures, for example, identify many situations in which God calls a prophet to dedicate his work to God even when that individual feels unworthy or unequipped to fulfill God's request. Moses is perhaps the best illustration of this premise. Judeo-Christian art portrays Moses as an imposing and charismatic prophet who fearlessly leads his people. Moses is depicted less frequently as the reluctant man in exile who resists God's call because of a speech impairment. God tells Moses that if he dedicates his work and life to God, then God will provide the wisdom and resources necessary for Moses to succeed. Moses was required to completely change his professional and private life to devote his work to God.

The Hebrew scriptures also present the integration of faith and work within the context of God's covenant. This covenantal relationship requires believers such as Moses to subject all aspects of their lives to God's will, with the promise that God will provide for them in return. Jewish leaders such as Moses were called from their ordinary lives to perform extraordinary deeds, thus requiring them to dedicate their work toward a specific higher goal. And yet, not everyone in the Hebrew scriptures had such a calling. Traditional figures like Moses exemplify a model whereby only a select few individuals are called by God to fulfill their God-given mission and serve in turn as religious leaders for other believers. In the Christian scriptures, Peter spent his life as a faithful Jew working as a fisherman. Jesus called Peter to a different vocation with the invitation, "Follow me and I will make you fishers of men; immediately, they left their nets and followed him" (Matthew 4:19–20). This passage offers an example of a Jesus beckoning a disciple to a sacred path in life, although for Peter to fulfill this calling, he had to drastically alter both his occupation and his cultural environment. Brown (1997) suggested that Peter was a model for all Christians, as a person of fluctuating faith who required Jesus' constant encouragement to gradually integrate his beliefs into daily activities such as work, relationships, and worship. The Christian scriptures thus offer models, such as Peter, to show that people could either pursue their current work as a means to fulfill spiritual purposes or commit to a more extreme occupational change such as the ministry. Moses and Peter are two important examples in the Judeo-Christian tradition of imperfect individuals who learned to gradually integrate their faith and work.

Non-Western writings and practices have also underscored the relationship between faith and labor. The earliest Islamic teachings, for example, stressed that a devout Muslim must consistently dedicate words in the form of prayer (*salat*) and actions such as alms-giving (*zakat*) to adhere to the Five Pillars of Faith, the sacred beliefs central to Islam (see Volume 1, Chapter 38, this handbook). These two Pillars—prayer and alms-giving—formed the basis of Mohammed's teachings that instruct Muslims how to conduct their professional lives. The Qur'an teaches that all prosperity comes from Allah, and accordingly, requires that Muslims seeking to devote their work to Allah "should not stockpile wealth [and] build private fortunes [but] . . . share the wealth of society fairly by giving a regular proportion of one's wealth to the poor" (Armstrong, 1993, p. 143).

The notion of dedicating work to God is not a concept exclusive to monotheistic religions. Ancient Eastern spiritual traditions such as Buddhism and Hinduism teach that dedicating daily activities like work will further followers' path to enlightenment. For example, Buddha or Gotama taught his followers that they must cultivate positive attitudes and loving kindness in all their daily activities and not simply avoid the "five prohibitions" or unhelpful (*akusala*) activities (violence, lying, stealing, intoxication, and sex). Gotama challenged his followers to apply the Noble Eightfold Path to all aspects of daily living, which consists of cultivating the right speech, right action, and right livelihood (Armstrong, 1993). He taught that right livelihood required consistent application of the Noble Eightfold Path to a person's professional and personal life. The followers of Buddha were required, whether king or peasant, to incorporate these teachings into their work, which ranged from simple daily tasks to complicated affairs of state (see Volume 1, Chapter 35, this handbook). Similarly, Hinduism teaches that the meaning of work transcends the traditional concept of labor as a means of providing basic needs (see Volume 1, Chapter 36, this handbook). The *Bhagavad Gita*, one of Hinduism's most sacred writings, challenges followers in all social classes to approach their work with compassion and selflessness with the goal of alleviating the suffering of others, thus furthering their path to enlightenment. In the Bhagavad Gita (3:3–4), Sri Krishna, an incarnation of God, instructs Arjuna, the spiritual seeker, that enlightenment requires two paths: "jnana yoga, the contemplative path of spiritual wisdom, and karma yoga, the active path of selfless service." This ancient premise of selfless service emphasizes the integration of spiritual practices into daily responsibilities, such as work. This teaching encourages followers to engage their communities and the infusion of jnana and karma yoga into tasks of daily living (Easwaran, 1985). The Hindu teachings in the Bhagavad Gita posit that perfection of spiritual nature is achieved through attention to others, not the self. This Hindu approach of infusing work with spiritual qualities was grounded in the practice of serving the needy in their communities.

The Eastern traditions of Buddhism and Hinduism stress that believers will learn the spiritual wisdom necessary to integrate their faith and work through personal meditation, whereas the Judeo-Christian traditions emphasizes communal worship. Advances in global travel and access to the Internet have helped to expose religious scholars from East and West to different religious texts and teachings that identify similar themes regarding the integration of faith and work. The various spiritual perspectives on work that these religions have promoted over the centuries raise intriguing questions for social scientists examining the influence of an individual's religion and spirituality on his or her work.

RESEARCH ON THE ROLE OF RELIGION AND SPIRITUALITY FOR EMPLOYEES

This section summarizes the development of research on religion and spirituality in the workplace, with a particular focus on one topic that is receiving increased attention—*calling*—a term that overlaps with psychologically grounded work on the construct of sanctification, a process in which an aspect of life, such as work, is perceived as having spiritual significance and character (Carroll, 2008; Hernandez, Mahoney, & Pargament, 2011; Oates, 2008; Pargament & Mahoney, 2005). This section also considers the influence of religion and spirituality on individuals coping with the stresses associated with work over a range of occupational settings.

Positive Roles of Religion and Spirituality for Employees

Research on calling. Psychologists have begun to examine the concept of *calling* in studies of religion and spirituality in the workplace. In these studies, this concept takes on a deep, expansive meaning. As D. T. Hall and Chandler (2005) explained, a *calling* is "work that a person perceives as his or her purpose in life" (p. 160). Dik and Duffy (2009) proposed the multiple components of *calling* as

> a transcendent summons, experienced as originating beyond the self, to approach a particular life role (in this case work) in a manner oriented toward demonstrating or deriving a sense of purpose or meaningfulness and that holds other-oriented values and goals as primary sources of motivation. (p. 427)

The development of the construct of sanctification, which focuses on the implications of religion and spirituality for areas of daily functioning, including work, was an important development for researchers studying the concept of calling. *Sanctification* has been defined as "the process through which aspects of life are perceived as having divine character and significance" (Pargament & Mahoney, 2005, p. 183). Mahoney et al. (1999) noted that people can sanctify various objects in their lives theistically and nontheistically. Theistic sanctification is assessed through the Manifestation of God subscale, which measures the degree to which people "perceive an object being a manifestation of one's images, beliefs, or experience of God" (p. 222). This process is more common among members of faith traditions that stress a higher power involved with the world (God, Holy Spirit, Buddha, or Allah). Nontheistic sanctification is measured through the

Sacred Qualities subscale (Mahoney et al., 1999). This scale allows "people to perceive an object as having spiritual character and significance by attributing qualities like transcendence (e.g., holy, heavenly, miraculous), ultimate value, purpose (e.g., blessed, sacred), and timelessness (e.g., everlasting, eternal) without reference to a specific deity" (p. 222). These sanctification scales, adapted to the workplace, have been used recently to assess the construct of calling. These studies have provided insights into the implications of religion and spirituality for employment behaviors and attitudes, such as job satisfaction, organizational commitment, and turnover intention (Carroll, 2008; Walker, Jones, Wuensch, Shahnaz, & Cope, 2008). We turn now to this literature. For the purpose of reviewing comparable studies, I use the terms *calling* and *sanctification of work* interchangeably.

Studies have generally shown a positive relationship between calling and job satisfaction (Duffy, Dik, & Steger, 2011; Serow, 1994; Sikorska-Simmons, 2005; Wrzesniewski, McCauley, Rozin, & Schwartz, 1997). Serow (1994) examined the role of *calling* among a target group of teachers. The results showed that teachers who felt called to their jobs were more likely to make personal sacrifices and devote extra time to their job. Likewise, a survey of office workers who were asked to define their work as a job, a career, or a calling demonstrated that respondents who perceived their work as a calling reported significantly higher levels of job satisfaction than those respondents who viewed their work as a job or career (Wrzesniewski et al., 1997). A more recent study determined that employees working at a university who perceived their job as a calling had increased career commitment (Duffy et al., 2011). The results of this study indicated that career commitment fully mediated the relationship between calling and job satisfaction, and partially mediated the relationship between calling with organizational commitment and withdrawal intentions. These findings suggest that "experiencing a calling to a particular career is likely to lead to one to become committed to a line of work, find a specific job that allows one to fulfill that commitment, and in turn be happier with, and committed, to a specific job" (Duffy et al., 2011, p. 216).

Carroll (2008) extended studies of calling to other work-related outcomes. Using a large national sample, he found that the sanctification of work scale was a significant predictor of job satisfaction, turnover intention, and organizational commitment after controlling for the Big Five theory of personality traits (Costa & McCrae, 1992). The sanctification of work also predicted the largest amount of variance in job satisfaction relative to the other outcome measures of organizational commitment and turnover intention. Similar results were obtained by Walker et al. (2008), who examined people working in a range of professional environments and found that the sanctification of work correlated with positive outcomes on comparable work-related behaviors after controlling for demographic variables and general religiosity. This study did not control for personality factors or the propensity for spiritual transcendence. The findings of these studies point to the value of using the sanctification of work scale when assessing the role of religion and spirituality in work-related issues, such as career decisions or coping skills. These studies have demonstrated significant relationships between religion and spirituality and established employment constructs, such as turnover intention, organizational commitment, and job satisfaction.

Through a combination of quantitative and qualitative approaches, Oates, Hall, and Anderson (2005) explored the relationship between the spirituality of mothers employed in higher education and their ability to cope with the stress of fulfilling their dual roles as parent and employee. Utilizing a grounded theory analytic strategy, Oates et al. (2005) concluded that the participants' sanctification of work helped people cope with interrole conflict "through a sense of certitude, collaboration, and a context of purpose that developed out of viewing one's work as a calling" (p. 214). In a follow-up quantitative study, Oates (2008) found that individuals reporting a higher degree of calling to their occupations tended to experience fewer conflicts between their professional and parental responsibilities. These studies exemplify the complementary benefits of utilizing qualitative and quantitative approaches to more fully investigate the interactions of religion and spirituality in the workplace.

Research on religion, spirituality, and occupational stress. A number of studies have examined links between religion, spirituality, and work-related outcomes among people dealing with stressful occupations. Sikorska-Simmons (2005) examined whether religiosity had a relationship to job satisfaction and organizational commitment among health care staff and administrators working at multiple assisted living facilities. The study's results indicated that the health care staff's self reported strong religious orientations to their daily lives were highly correlated with job satisfaction and organizational commitment. These findings were similar to earlier studies, such as Connecticut Mutual Life Insurance Company (1981) and Sagie (1993), which indicated that strong religiosity was associated with higher organizational commitment and lower turnover intention, although the studies noted that other factors specific to each employee, such as education and ethnicity, required additional consideration. Hellman (2008) surveyed a group of Jewish female executives at Fortune 1000 companies by utilizing a quantitative inventory from a similar study (Monson, 1987) to assess the participants' integration of their religious beliefs into their professional, family, and community settings. Respondents with higher participation in activities at their synagogue and adherence to daily religious rituals (observance of Sabbath rituals such as no driving or recitation of Hebrew prayers) reported that such religious involvement provided emotional sustenance to counteract their work-related stress (Hellman, 2008). These highly successful executives also viewed their high religious involvement as assets in their career advancement. They felt that the fellowship experienced at their synagogues helped them cope with the challenges of working in male-dominated office environments. These results substantiate a relationship between workers' religious beliefs and work-related outcomes, such as job satisfaction and organizational commitment.

Studies have demonstrated that religion and spirituality can affect job satisfaction, burnout, and the desire to look for a new job for employees in highly stressful jobs. For example, one study revealed that palliative care nurses who did not receive sufficient training to help them address the emotional and spiritual needs of patients and their families were under substantial stress (Power & Sharp, 1988). In a similar investigation of palliative care workers, Wasner, Longaker, Fegg, Johannes, and Gian (2005) examined whether nurses who attended stress management classes that introduced nondenominational spiritual practices, such as meditation, journaling, and controlled breathing, experienced decreased work-related stress. The findings showed that nurses often have little training on the religious and spiritual issues of their patients and families who are struggling with end-of-life issues. Furthermore, the spiritual care program increased the nurses' job satisfaction and reduced work-related stress. The findings suggested that spiritual care courses can improve overall patient care and reduce the frequency of burnout among palliative care nurses.

Brooks and Matthews (2000) identified benefits of spirituality for counselors involved in the taxing work of treating clients with addictions. Counselors who were actively involved in daily spiritual practices demonstrated improved scores on the spiritual well-being scale (C. W. Ellison, 1983). Higher spiritual well-being scores, in turn, strongly correlated with reduced burnout. These findings suggest that spirituality might help workers proactively address job-related stresses. Along these lines, medical schools have begun providing future physicians with basic training in religious and spiritual issues. Puchalski, Larson, and Lu (2001) reported that in 1992 only three of 125 U.S. medical schools had academic courses regarding spiritual issues and patient treatment, but 7 years later, 72 of 125 schools had added the topic to their curriculum, a tacit acknowledgment that comprehensive religious and spiritual training for medical professionals can help reduce stress and burnout when dealing with end-of-life issues (Wasner et al., 2005).

The relationship between religion and spirituality and work-related outcomes among individuals in stressful occupations can also be studied through qualitative research methods. Qualitative research methods offer respondents greater opportunities to explain the impact of their religious or spiritual beliefs and practices on specific occupational tasks and stressors. Dlugos and Friedlander (2001) found that psychologists who reported high levels of spiritual commitment were more likely to report higher job satisfaction, more effective balance between home and job responsibilities, and lower burnout. Mittal, Rosen, and Leana (2009) examined the work-related factors that led direct care health professionals to remain in or leave a particular job. This qualitative study utilized focus groups working in acute care and hospice settings to identify the impact of lack of respect, inadequate management, work and family conflicts, and caregiver stress, on retention or turnover. The results indicated that direct care workers with a more active faith life were more likely to remain 3 years or longer in this line of work (Mittal et al., 2009). These same participants reported that integrating religion or spirituality into their work responsibilities helped them cope with challenging job conditions. Many participants identified prayer as an essential resource for them to better serve their patients. One participant specified the positive benefits of integrating her spirituality into the job: "I pray a lot. Through my job, as well as otherwise . . . it gets me through the night shift" (Mittal et al., 2009, p. 629). The results from these studies demonstrate the potential benefits of further utilizing qualitative methods to obtain expanded employee feedback with increased emotional depth regarding the role of religion and spirituality in the workplace.

Research on the Negative Role of Religion and Spirituality for Employees

Although it is well documented that religion and spirituality are utilized as primary means of dealing in a positive way with daily adversities, ranging from a patient's death to a reduction of work hours (Sikorska-Simmons, 2005; Wasner et al., 2005), less is known about how religious or spiritual struggles can adversely affect workers. Research has started to reveal the depth of the cognitive, emotional, and spiritual struggles that can occur for people who integrate their religious and spiritual beliefs into their jobs (Oates et al., 2005). For example, one series of studies examined the challenges faced by women who attempted to balance their religious or spiritual beliefs with their parental and professional roles (Elvin-Nowak, 1999; Polasky & Holahan, 1998). Role conflicts among these women produced feelings of guilt and insecurity that could lead to decreasing psychological and physical health. Negative implications can coexist with positive implications. For example, in the studies discussing Christian women working in academia and Jewish female executives in Fortune 1000 companies, participants reported emotional pressures related to the tension between the modern workplace and arcane religious expectations for women (Hellman, 2008; Oates, 2008; Oates et al., 2005). The participants in both studies reported psychological stress from the daily adjustments between work and home, and persistent, emotional exhaustion from attempting to reconcile demanding career responsibilities with conservative religious ideals dictating that women are primarily responsible for home and family. Both sets of working mothers in the studies reported that their male colleagues created stress because they expected their female colleagues to provide emotional support around the office when staff members were struggling with personal issues. The working mothers reported that their emotional exhaustion was magnified when they were expected to provide the same emotional support for family members (Hellman, 2008; Oates, 2008; Oates et al., 2005). The female professionals in these studies indicated that their religiosity provided an essential resource for them to manage the psychological stress of their dual roles of providing emotional support at home and the office. These initial findings are intriguing because they suggest significant adverse psychological implications when conflicts develop between working women's career advancement and traditional religious roles.

Additional research has examined the possible adverse consequences on employment behaviors and attitudes when individuals experience spiritual or religious struggles. It is understandable that a person's spiritual and religious struggles can significantly affect his or her job performance, because most people cannot check their emotions at the door of their workplace. Exline and Bright (2011) summarized the growing body of research that has identified the relationship between spiritual or religious struggles and decreases in work-related outcomes, such as productivity, as well as employee psychological well-being, such as depression, physiological indicators of stress, and higher mortality rates (Ai et al., 2009; Pargament et al., 2001). The authors noted that when an employee is "questioning [his or her] own deeply held beliefs," such conflicts might result in employee "anxiety, disorientation, or loss," which ultimately might lead to a positive personal outcome but also might, at least in the short term, manifest itself through poor job performance (Exline & Bright, 2011, p. 135). Furthermore, Exline and Bright suggested that highly sensitive religious or spiritual individuals could become less productive if they have increasing moral conflicts regarding their firm's business practices. Individuals with strong religiosity or spirituality could possibly enhance their productivity if they proactively seek employment with firms that share similar ethical or moral principles (Exline & Bright, 2011). Additional research will need to assess the longitudinal impact of spiritual and religious struggles to determine whether workers become more or less productive after they have resolved their questions of belief.

Further research is needed to examine the potential adverse implications of religion and spirituality in the workplace. Such research would help psychologists to better understand, for example, if and why an individual may perceive the loss of a sanctified job as a religious or spiritual failure, and if and why the worker's anticipated loss of a sanctified job might intensify maladaptive coping with unemployment (Carroll, Stewart-Sicking, & Thompson, 2010). Future research could examine the psychological implications of situations when religion is used to manipulate workers into accepting substandard job conditions or unjust mistreatment from supervisors. A recent report by the Southern Poverty Law Center (Bauer & Ramirez, 2010) found that 80% of women farmworkers of Mexican descent had experienced sexual harassment and substandard workplace conditions while working in the California Central Valley (Waugh, 2010). Research examining the effect of these workers' religiosity or spirituality on their work lives could clarify whether religion or spirituality either contributed to their acceptance of mistreatment or empowered them to deal more actively with their working conditions.

Future Considerations for Examining the Role of Religion and Spirituality for Employees

Over the past 20 years, research has identified the broad implications of religion and spirituality in the workplace. Additional research is needed to expand the investigation of the positive and negative effects of religion and spirituality on productivity in workplace settings, particularly those employment situations that could cause psychological distress. Studies of high-stress occupations, such as health care professions, have shown that management could potentially utilize the deep religious commitments of some nursing staff as a means to rationalize unjust working conditions and lower pay for the betterment of patient care (Sikorska-Simmons, 2005; Wasner et al., 2005). From an employer perspective, workers who express a strong sense of calling could possess unrealistic expectations regarding the organizations' standards for employees' workplace attitudes and behaviors (Bunderson & Thompson, 2009). From an employee perspective, Duffy et al. (2011) indicated that job seekers should be aware of "the 'dark side' of having a calling; namely, if one ends up in job that does not fit with one's calling, it may lead to lower levels of workplace well-being" (p. 216). These studies show the relevance of assessing both the positive and negative implications of religion and spirituality in workplace settings. The utilization of an integrative research model would contribute to a deeper understanding of the possible influences of workers' personal beliefs and practices on the full range of psychological functioning in workplace settings.

Toward this end, it is important to develop instruments that can simultaneously assess the potential positive and negative implications of religion and spirituality for occupational behaviors and attitudes (see Volume 1, Chapter 3, this handbook). Several relevant measures of religion and spirituality have been developed for the positive end of the continuum, such as the spiritual well-being scale (Bufford et al., 1991; C. W. Ellison, 1983), the spiritual transcendence scale (Piedmont, 2001), and the multidimensional scale of religion and spirituality (Idler et al., 2003). More recently, instruments such as the Faith at Work Scale have been developed to specifically identify the positive and negative effects of religiousness on the daily job functioning of workers involved in Christian institutions (Lynn & Naughton, 2009). As discussed earlier, the sanctification of work scale offers a way to assess the degree employees view their jobs as having spiritual significance and meaning, including those who do and do not believe in a particular deity (Carroll, 2008; Walker et al., 2008).

Researchers must continue to develop constructs that are inclusive of individuals who believe their work has sacred qualities, but who express their beliefs in an alternative manner from traditional religions (Pargament & Mahoney, 2005). Carroll (2008) identified participants who self-reported their work as possessing sacred qualities but did not associate themselves with traditional religious groups. In fact, almost 5% of participants who viewed their work as highly sacred chose "Other, Atheist, or None" for their religious affiliation. More research could be devoted to better understanding the factors that motivated these respondents to say that they viewed their work as a sacred endeavor and how these individuals conceptualized the sanctification of work outside the context of a theistic or organized religious framework. Perhaps some people can sanctify their work while not otherwise viewing their identities as involving religion or spirituality. Future studies should examine whether some people sanctify their work because their occupation provides them with a general sense of meaning or satisfaction rather genuinely imbuing work with religious or spiritual characteristics (Steger, Pickering, Shin, & Dik, 2010).

Social scientists must also develop constructs to assess the broad range of religious and spiritual beliefs that could emerge in the increasingly diverse 21st-century workplace. Cash and Gray (2000) cautioned that research in this area must guard against biases that might limit the occupational analysis by overemphasizing comparisons to Western religious traditions. Furthermore, the authors proposed that companies and industries facing increased globalization must create business strategies that improve tolerance and sensitivity toward Eastern spiritual and culture practices. The majority of the research in this field has concentrated on conservative Christian denominations and how they conceptualize calling in careers and the implications for calling primarily on working males in heterosexual relationships (Dik & Steger, 2008; Duffy et al., 2011; C. G. Ellison & Bartkowski, 2002). In the 21st-century marketplace, successful businesses will need to incorporate an understanding of non-Western religious and spiritual traditions to enhance effective working relationships with international firms. For example, important psychological insights might develop from a comparative study of U.S. employees who are Christian working in Muslim societies versus the experiences of Muslims from the Middle East working in the United States. Future empirical research should consider evaluating the experiences of employees working for international firms who relocate to new countries in which they become a religious minority group.

RESEARCH ON THE ROLE OF RELIGION AND SPIRITUALITY AT THE ORGANIZATIONAL LEVEL

The previous section summarized the implications of religion and spirituality for individual employee behaviors. In this section, we consider the implications of religion and spirituality at the organizational level.

Organizational Leadership and Spirituality

The previous sections have discussed the effects of religiosity or spirituality on daily work behaviors, but it is also important to acknowledge that religion and spirituality have the potential to influence the leadership strategies of organizations. The initial research in this area suggests that religion and spirituality have influence on the organizational level to some degree. Fry and Slocum (2008) proposed that successful modern business leaders must develop new organizational models that increase ethical leadership, employee well-being, sustainability, and social responsibility, while maintaining profits and revenue growth. Spiritual leadership theory represents one such initiative, designed on the basis of "the fundamental needs of both leader and follower for spiritual well-being through calling and membership, to create vision and value congruence across the individual, empowered team, and organizational levels" (Fry & Cohen, 2009, p. 269). A series of studies have identified the relationship of the spiritual leadership model (SLM) to improved work-related outcomes when these SLM strategies were implemented in more than 100 organizations (samples ranging from 10 to more than 1,000), including schools, military units, cities, police, and for-profit companies. The SLM is designed operationally to "comprise the values, attitudes, and behaviors that are necessary to intrinsically motivate one's self and others so they have sense of spiritual well-being through calling and membership" (Fry & Cohen, 2009, p. 269). For example, the SLM strategies were tested in a longitudinal study of a U.S. Army squadron in which 189 soldiers were assessed at the start of training and 5 months later at completion (Fry, Vitucci, & Cedillo, 2005). The soldiers were assessed with quantitative surveys measuring whether the spiritual leadership dimensions of vision (an organization's purpose), hope/faith (commitment to fulfill an organization's purpose), altruistic love (mutual concern for the personal and the collective growth of the organization), meaning/calling (considering the compatibility of personal beliefs with the organization), and membership (validation that each member feels respected and valued by the organization) influenced their levels of organizational commitment and productivity. The participants utilized a Likert scale when responding to survey items, such as for the meaning/calling dimension, which inquired whether the respondents valued their work responsibilities as personally fulfilling. Regarding the hope/faith dimension, the respondents were asked whether they were motivated to exceed their required job responsibilities because they believed in the organization's principles and practices (Fry et al., 2005). The results of the hierarchical regression analyses indicated that "the Meaning/Calling and organizational commitment relationship was negligible, and that Membership accounted for over twice as much variance for unit productivity as did Meaning/Calling" (Fry et al., 2005, p. 858). Companion studies demonstrated similar results. Spiritual leadership strategies produced significant positive effects on employee life satisfaction, organizational commitment, productivity, and sales growth (Fry et al., 2005; Fry & Matherly, 2006; Fry & Slocum, 2008; Malone & Fry, 2003).

The SLM provides the leaders of organizations an innovative approach to simultaneously cultivate a shared sense of mission and membership among managers and employees while enhancing productivity and loyalty to the organization. Nevertheless, questions arise as to whether the SLM dimensions tap into spirituality or assess positive psychology constructs that are not necessarily linked to the sacred. Furthermore, the findings are limited by the lack of a longitudinal research design that measures differences in annual organizational outcomes, the need to examine possible adverse consequences on employees supervised under the spiritual leadership theory, and the fact that participants in this research were homogenous, primarily American and Christian. Future field research must replicate these initial findings with more diverse samples that reflect the globalization of organizations in the 21st century.

There is limited empirical research on the practical implications of religion and spirituality for organizational leadership. To stimulate work in this area, a number of individuals from varied backgrounds—experienced leaders of labor unions, and financial, education, and nonprofit organizations—agreed to be interviewed for this chapter to give their perspectives on the effects of religion and spirituality in the workplace from a leadership and management perspective. These highly experienced professionals provided their insights regarding the benefits and limitations of integrating religion and spirituality into the workplace and offered several practical recommendations to improve education and increase public awareness about the effect of religion and spirituality on employment behaviors and attitudes.

Ethical Leadership

It could be expected that a personal lodestar, such as religion or spirituality, could help business leaders avoid the temptation to take ethical shortcuts with business strategies. Another difficult question is how much of an influence religion or spirituality plays in the global marketplace. Charles I. Clough was the chief global strategist for Merrill Lynch for 13 years and is currently the chairman of Clough Capital Partners, L.P., which manages equity portfolios, hedge funds, and mutual funds for individuals and organizations through investment in public equity markets across the globe. Clough has also served as an ordained deacon in the Archdiocese of Boston since 1986. In an interview, Clough stated his personal belief that although religion and spirituality may indirectly inform the ethics of individuals who work in the financial sector, Wall Street is always driven by the profit margin. For example, recent moves by financial firms to strengthen their ethical standards consistent with virtues heralded by religious institutions were prompted not by personal ethics but by a number of prominent investment scandals: Firms know they will lose customers quickly if they are perceived as having questionable ethical practices, customers do not want their money tied up in firms that may be under investigation, and current financial customers have a heightened sensitivity about ethical practices and will move their money if a firm is implicated in any sort of scandal.

Regarding his own career development, Clough stated that "my personal faith and role as a deacon provided me a consistent reminder to not let myself be defined by my occupation" (personal communication, November 26, 2010). He believes that religion and prayer provide him with the clarity to not cross the line into unethical behavior, which is of utmost importance because the temptations are always present and attractive. Clough concluded that religion was essential for him to maintain consistent ethical boundaries as well as to maintain the distinction between his personal and professional life. Empirical research is needed to provide a more systematic test of whether religion in fact reduces the likelihood of ethical transgressions among business leaders.

Optimizing Organizational–Employee Match

Although organizations are constantly developing strategies to improve productivity and reduce job turnover, firms that do not proactively and clearly communicate their organization's mission to prospective and current employees may be missing out on an important opportunity to ensure an effective match between the employers' needs and the employees' expectations. This communication becomes even more essential when the institution is founded on religious or spiritual principles that play an active role in its operations, as we learn in the following scenario.

Reverend Father Scott Pilarz, SJ, has served as president of the University of Scranton for the past 6 years, and became president of Marquette University in July 2011. Father Pilarz observed (personal communication, October 10, 2010) that university administrators can enhance employee job satisfaction and organizational commitment if new employees are thoroughly informed about the institution's religiously based mission during the recruitment and orientation periods. For example, over a 3-year period, the University of Scranton experienced a major faculty transition. Father Pilarz emphasized the strategic implications of educating new employees about the institution's mission. At the University of Scranton, the institution's core principles of learning, faith, and service are highlighted during the hiring process to ensure that new employees are ready to support the university's strategic goals. Father Pilarz stated that organizations can positively influence employee productivity and morale when the institution's mission is integrated into all phases of professional development programs. To this end, the University of Scranton created a new orientation program, in which he played an active role, to emphasize to new employees the importance of integrating the university's mission into the daily operations of the university. These strategies might also prevent future conflict because the employer has encouraged the job applicant to proactively consider whether the employment relationship, particularly given the religious foundation of the institution, will be successful.[1]

Scientific research is needed to substantiate whether and how businesses can utilize religion and spirituality in the workplace to promote the development of ethics training. Even though many

[1]Employers must be careful to heed the legal constraints imposed by Title VII of the Civil Rights Act of 1964, which prohibits most employers from considering an applicant or employee's religion when making hiring, firing, and other decisions affecting the terms and conditions of employment as well as other federal and state laws prohibiting employment discrimination on the basis of religion.

businesspersons, such as Clough, might separate their personal religious or spiritual beliefs from their work, their religiosity or spirituality might play an indirect role in helping them adhere to ethical business practices. This expanding field of calling research could provide resources to organizations considering the development of spiritually integrated ethics training. Father Pilarz's scenario suggests that there may be benefits for workers and management when expectations for business practices are clearly communicated at the beginning of the employment relationship, particularly if an organization has a religious or spiritual affiliation.

ROLE OF RELIGION AND SPIRITUALITY IN THE LABOR FORCE

Religion and spirituality could affect the strategies of union leaders for organizing workers in manufacturing, retail, or service industries. Again, there is little empirical study of how this process might unfold. Some anecdotal reports are suggestive, however. One person who regularly observes the intersection of personal beliefs and labor markets is Chris Chafe, who has worked in national union organizations for 20 years. Chafe led several organizing campaigns in the southeastern United States and currently serves as president of the Clean Economy Center, a consulting group that promotes the expansion of green jobs. Chafe observed (personal communication, September 26, 2010) that labor organizing represents a unique area of occupational functioning in which religion is a dominant factor. In the southeastern United States, religion is at the forefront of all union organizing because it is a significant resource for people in working communities, particularly factory and agricultural workers, who often encounter adversity in the form of layoffs, health problems, or financial struggles. For these workers, religious faith represents a pillar of strength, facilitates coping with setbacks, and inspires motivation for change. Chafe commented that an organizing campaign's success often depends on obtaining the support of local religious leaders and inviting their active participation in the negotiating process. Because religion is the dominant lens through which most issues are seen, it is imperative for union leadership to respect and work with the local religious leaders, and learn about local religious customs, before initiating an organizing campaign.

Religion is an essential factor in the future growth of labor organizing because it represents a core component of how new immigrant workers cope with stressful occupational realities. Minimal research currently exists on the ways that new immigrant groups who adhere to non-Judeo-Christian traditions (e.g., Islam, Hinduism) cope with job stress. For the past 15 years, Kim Bobo has directed the Interfaith Worker Justice Center (IWJ) in Chicago, a nonprofit organization that advocates for workers' rights through the creation of partnerships between religious congregations and union members and that increases public awareness about low-income workers by training community organizers, holding educational conferences, and coordinating political action campaigns with union leaders. Bobo suggested (personal communication, November 18, 2010) that the IWJ's mission is interfaith because most major faith traditions teach that "work is a sacred act." She believes that religious communities and union leaders share in the mission to promote dignified, safe, and equitable working conditions for low-income laborers. The IWJ's Labor in Pulpits program has trained speakers and sent them to more than 1,000 religious congregations to discuss labor and social justice issues. Through its Seminary Summer Program, IWJ coordinates internships for ministers and rabbis to work with union officials on advocacy campaigns. Bobo believes that these outreach programs promote collaboration between religious communities and union leadership to more effectively advocate for issues of common interest. Furthermore, she maintains that the facilitation promoted by the IWJ has helped to improve mutual understanding between union leaders and their members regarding religious and cultural issues. In one recent example, the IWJ facilitated discussions between local imams and business leaders that resulted in the accommodation of female Muslim workers' head coverings and established breaks that would coincide with times for daily prayers. She emphasized that future research should examine the implications of religion for improvements in the medical and mental health services for new immigrant workers, such as Muslims.

With the increased globalization of companies, manufacturing firms have witnessed increasing religious diversity in their workforces, which has enhanced the efforts to develop greater tolerance and respect within the workplace for new religious groups. Another person witnessing the changing influences of religion and spirituality in the workplace is Harris Raynor, who has worked for 30 years with labor unions in the southern United States. Raynor is currently the vice president for the Southern Region Workers United, part of the Service Employees International Union (SEIU). Raynor believes that the U.S. labor force is experiencing significant changes in its religious and spiritual diversity (personal communication, December 21, 2010). In the 1970s, union members were primarily Christian and had only a small Jewish component. In the 21st century, union members come from diverse backgrounds. This changing demographic has prompted manufacturers and labor unions to adapt their work practices to accommodate a steadily increasing number of non-Western faith traditions, such as Islam, Hinduism, and Buddhism. Raynor stressed that employers and union leadership will need increased adaptability and improved communication because of globalization and the rapidly changing demographics in the U.S. labor force.

Like Bobo, Raynor stressed that unions and management must pay careful attention to religious and spiritual issues. For example, a few years ago his union requested that a large corporation provide an additional paid religious holiday to acknowledge the diverse religious backgrounds of a new workforce that included Vietnamese (Taoism), Somali (Muslim), and Indian (Hinduism). During the negotiations, a rank-and-file Christian member of the bargaining committee suggested that the company could observe a "Diversity Day," which would allow employees to take a paid holiday to observe a religious holiday of their choosing. This suggestion became standard policy in all of the company's distribution centers, which employed almost 15,000 workers. Also at the suggestion of the union, the company cafeteria also started offering some alternative food choices to allow employees to adhere to basic religious dietary restrictions. This is an important example of employers and employees collaborating on religious issues to promote their mutual economic survival. Employers are more willing to consider adapting personnel policies to demonstrate sensitivity to their employees' religious or spiritual traditions to sustain the productivity and morale of their workforce. The union leadership's responsiveness to the religious and spiritual concerns of its increasingly diverse membership helps to sustain the recruitment of new members.

ROLE OF RELIGION AND SPIRITUALITY IN SUSTAINING AND MOTIVATING EMPLOYEES IN NONPROFIT ORGANIZATIONS

Because nonprofit agencies lack the resources of for-profit entities, they often rely on the religion or spirituality of their employees to encourage innovation and commitment to the organization. This assertion has not been tested through systematic empirical research, but some anecdotal reports are relevant. Kathleen Haser has worked for more than 25 years in nonprofit leadership with the Jesuit Volunteer Corps (JVC), an organization of lay volunteers who commit 1 or 2 years of service, domestically and internationally, by working and living in impoverished communities. Haser stated (personal communication, November 4, 2010) that she has witnessed a gradual transition among the volunteers' personal beliefs over this period of time. Over the past 10 years, she has seen more volunteers associating their motivation for service out of their sense of personal spirituality, rather than fulfilling a sense of obligation to the doctrines of a particular religious denomination. The same observation applies to the nonprofit service agencies, which have become more ecumenical and less religiously exclusive when attempting to serve local needs. More nonprofits have been willing to collaborate with publically funded agencies to improve the consistency and quality of client care. For example, the Times Square Hotel, which was created in 1994 to establish stable housing opportunities for individuals transitioning out of homelessness in New York City, was created through a partnership of religious organizations, private foundations, and government agencies.

Domestic JVC volunteers work full time in a range of challenging direct service occupations that assist veterans, homeless families, the elderly, and individuals with severe physical and mental health conditions. Haser stated that JVC's Spiritual Development Program, which offers individual mentoring, group discussions, and retreats, complements the career training received at the job site. Haser suggested that these spiritual growth opportunities "provide volunteers the additional emotional and spiritual resources to remain effective in often stressful and challenging work settings" (personal communication, November 4, 2010). Haser recognized that volunteers could experience increased job-related stress if managers at faith-based agencies utilize religious teachings to rationalize the exploitation of young volunteers by requiring them to perform more hours or duties than those of other staff. Similarly, a volunteer could have intensified feelings of frustration if he or she felt the agency's leadership was acting inconsistently with its mission and was not maximizing its resources for the clients. Haser concluded that religion and spirituality have provided the volunteers with the awareness and resilience necessary to "achieve more good with less material resources."

To expand our understanding of the practical implications suggested in these scenarios, future research will need to examine the links between religion, spirituality, and relevant, current work related outcomes. For example, a recent study examined the relationship between religion, spirituality, and career adaptability (Duffy & Blustein, 2005). Individuals with high scores on the religious motivation scale (Gorsuch & McPherson, 1989) and the spiritual assessment inventory (T. W. Hall & Edwards, 1996) reported greater self-confidence to make career decisions and more openness to a broad range of career options. The researchers concluded that strong religious or spiritual beliefs provided the participants with the stability and support necessary to make proactive and constructive deliberations about the kinds of jobs that would allow them to balance their professional and spiritual growth (Duffy & Blustein, 2005). These findings are consistent with Haser's observation that young adult JVC volunteers with strong religious or spiritual awareness performed well in extremely stressful jobs despite their inexperience and that young workers who were religiously or spiritually inclined reported that their beliefs fueled them with meaning, purpose, and a source of coping. This research suggests that religion and spirituality have important psychological implications throughout the employment process, from finding employment to actual job performance.

FUTURE DIRECTION

Social scientists should be alert to the practical implications of religion and spirituality for business outcomes. The growing body of research in this field holds practical implications for employees, employers, and faith communities. For example, Hellman (2008) proposed that corporations would benefit by improving their understanding of their workers' religious or spiritual practices and by adapting their workplace policies to reflect greater sensitivity to those practices, which would particularly benefit the companies' religious minorities. Religious leaders could improve awareness within their faith communities of the possibility of religious doctrines being used to rationalize or accept discriminatory employment practices in hiring or promotions. These collaborative strategies could reduce work-related stress and improve productivity. Findings of this kind should be of interest not only to employees and religious communities but also to employers and organizations.

For business leaders to consider partnering in future research, they must see the practical significance of this kind of scholarship. To create a constructive dialogue with business leaders, psychologists should emphasize research models that examine outcomes familiar to businesspersons, such as job satisfaction, organizational commitment, and turnover intention. A combination of quantitative and qualitative methods could best advance our understanding of the practical effects of religion and spirituality on daily work functioning and career development. Research studies will need to address topics relevant to modern business environments, such as psychosocial functioning, communication, and group dynamics. Ultimately, the successful expansion of research examining the role of spirituality and religion in the workplace will require collaboration between social scientists and members of the business community. Such a coordinated effort will help to determine with greater accuracy how spirituality and religion might uniquely affect different employment environments.

This chapter is only an initial examination of the current psychological research measuring the effect of religion and spirituality in the modern-day workplace. There is still a great deal to be explored in this area, and if the existing studies are any indication of what future studies might reveal, much more to be learned. If psychology can develop a better understanding of this area of human functioning, it might unlock important insights not only for mental health practitioners but also for employees and employers, making this area of research truly unique.

References

Armstrong, K. (1993). *A history of God.* New York, NY: Ballantine Press.

Bauer, M., & Ramirez, M. (2010). *Injustices on our plates: Immigrant women in the U.S. food industry.* Montgomery, AL: Southern Poverty Law Center. Retrieved from http://www.splcenter.org/foodreport

Brooks, C., & Matthews, C. (2000). The relationship among substance abuse counselors' spiritual well-being and values. *Journal of Addictions and Offender Counseling, 21*, 23–33. doi:10.1002/j.2161-1874.2000.tb00149.x

Brown, R. (1997). *An introduction to the New Testament.* New York, NY: Doubleday.

Bufford, R., Paloutzian, R., & Ellison, C. (1991). Norms for the spiritual well-being scale. *Journal of Psychology and Theology, 19*, 56–70.

Bunderson, J. S., & Thompson, J. A. (2009). The call of the wild: Zookeepers, callings, and the dual edges of meaningful work. *Administrative Science Quarterly, 54*, 32–57. doi:10.2189/asqu.2009.54.1.32

Carroll, S. T. (2008). The role of the sanctification of work, religion, and spirituality as predictors of work-related outcomes for individuals working at religiously affiliated institutions. *Dissertation Abstracts International: Section B. Sciences and Engineering, 69*(6), 3887.

Carroll, S. T., Stewart-Sicking, J. A., & Thompson, B. J. (2010). *Sanctification of work: Assessing the role of spirituality in employment behaviors.* Unpublished manuscript.

Cash, K., & Gray, G. (2000). A framework for accommodating religion and spirituality in the workplace. *Academy of Management Perspectives, 14*, 124–133. doi:10.5465/AME.2000.4468072

Connecticut Mutual Life Insurance Company. (1981). *Report on American values in the 1980s: The impact of belief.* Hartford, CT: Author.

Costa, P. T., & McCrae, R. R. (1992). *NEO PI/FFI Manual Supplement.* Odessa, FL: Assessment Resources.

DiBenedetto, C. (2010, November). What is your true calling? *Oprah Magazine, 11*(11), 170–185.

Dik, B. J., & Duffy, R. D. (2009). Calling and vocation at work: Definitions and prospects for research and practice. *The Counseling Psychologist, 37*, 424–450. doi:10.1177/0011000008316430

Dik, B. J., & Steger, M. (2008). Randomized trial of a calling-infused career workshop. *Journal of Vocational Behavior, 73*, 203–211. doi:10.1016/j.jvb.2008.04.001

Dlugos, R., & Friedlander, M. (2001). Passionately committed psychotherapists: A qualitative study of their experience. *Professional Psychology: Research and Practice, 32*, 298–304. doi:10.1037/0735-7028.32.3.298

Duffy, R. D., & Blustein, D. L. (2005). The relationship between spirituality, religiousness, and career adaptability. *Journal of Vocational Behavior, 67*, 429–440. doi:10.1016/j.jvb.2004.09.003

Duffy, R. D., Dik, B. J., & Steger, M. F. (2011). Calling and work-related outcomes: Career commitment as a mediator. *Journal of Vocational Behavior, 78*, 210–218. doi:10.1016/j.jvb.2010.09.013

Easwaran, E. (1985). *The Bhagavad Gita: Translated for the modern reader.* Tomales, CA: Nilgiri Press.

Egan, H. D. (1998). *Karl Rahner: The mystic of everyday life.* New York, NY: Crossroads.

Ellison, C. G., & Bartkowski, J. P. (2002). Conservative Protestantism and the division of household labor among married couples. *Journal of Family Issues, 23*, 950–985. doi:10.1177/019251302237299

Ellison, C. W. (1983). Spiritual well-being: Conceptualization and measurement. *Journal of Psychology and Theology, 11*, 330–340.

Elvin-Nowak, Y. (1999). The meaning of guilt: A phenomenological description of employed mothers' experiences of guilt. *Scandinavian Journal of Psychology, 40*, 73–83. doi:10.1111/1467-9450.00100

Exline, J. J., & Bright, D. S. (2011). Spiritual and religious struggles in the workplace. *Journal of Management, Spirituality, and Religion, 8*, 123–142. doi:10.1080/14766086.2011.581812

Fields, G. S. (2005). *A guide to multisector labor market models.* Washington, DC: World Bank, Social Protection Unit, Human Development Network.

Fry, L. W., & Cohen, M. P. (2009). Spiritual leadership as a paradigm for organizational transformation. *Journal of Business Ethics, 84*, 265–278. doi:10.1007/s10551-008-9695-2

Fry, L. W., & Matherly, L. L. (2006, October). *Spiritual leadership as an integrating paradigm for positive leadership development.* Paper presented at the International Gallup Leadership Summit, Washington, DC.

Fry, L. W., & Slocum, J. (2008). Maximizing the triple bottom line through a strategic scorecard business model of spiritual leadership. *Organizational Dynamics, 37,* 86–96. doi:10.1016/j.orgdyn.2007.11.004

Fry, L. W., Vitucci, S., & Cedillo, M. (2005). Spiritual leadership and army transformation: Theory, measurement, and establishing a baseline. *Leadership Quarterly, 16,* 835–862. doi:10.1016/j.leaqua.2005.07.012

Giddens, A. (1985). An introduction to Weber. In M. Weber, *The Protestant ethic and the spirit of capitalism* (pp. vii–xxvi). London, England: Unwin.

Gorsuch, R. L., & McPherson, S. E. (1989). Intrinsic/extrinsic measurement: I/E-Revised and single-item scales. *Journal for the Scientific Study of Religion, 28,* 348–354. doi:10.2307/1386745

Greenhouse, S. (2010, May, 24). Glimmers of hope for grads. *New York Times.* Retrieved from http://www.nytimes.com/2010/05/25/business/economy/25gradjobs.html

Hall, D. T., & Chandler, D. E. (2005). Psychological success: When the career is a calling. *Journal of Organizational Behavior, 26,* 155–176.

Hall, T. W., & Edwards, K. J. (1996). The initial development and factor analysis of the spiritual assessment inventory. *Journal of Psychology and Theology, 24,* 233–246.

Hellman, Y. (2008). A profile of Jewish women executives in corporate America. *Dissertation Abstracts International: Section A. Humanities and Social Sciences, 68*(12), 5131.

Hernandez, K. M., Mahoney, A., & Pargament, K. I. (2011). Sanctification of sexuality: Implications for newlyweds' marital and sexual quality. *Journal of Family Psychology, 25,* 775–780. doi:10.1037/a0025103

Idler, E. L., Musick, M. A., Ellison, C. G., Krause, N., & Pargament, K. I. (2003). Measuring multiple dimensions of religion and spirituality for health research: Conceptual background and findings from the General Social Survey. *Research on Aging, 25,* 327–365. doi:10.1177/0164027503025004001

Luo, M. (2009, July 5). Job retraining may fall short of high hopes. *New York Times.* Retrieved from http://www.nytimes.com/2009/07/06/us/06retrain.html

Lynn, M. L., & Naughton, M. J. (2009). Faith at Work Scale: Justification, development, and validation of a measure of Judeo-Christian religion in the workplace. *Journal of Business Ethics, 85,* 227–243. doi:10.1007/s10551-008-9767-3

Mahoney, A. M., Pargament, K. I., Jewell, T., Swank, A. B., Scott, E., Emery, E., & Rye, M. (1999). Marriage and the spiritual realm: The role of proximal and distal religious constructs in marital functioning. *Journal of Family Psychology, 13,* 321–338. doi:10.1037/0893-3200.13.3.321

Malone, P. F., & Fry, L. W. (2003, August). *Transforming schools through spiritual leadership: A field experiment.* Paper presented at the Annual Meeting of the Academy of Management, Seattle, WA.

Mittal, V., Rosen, J., & Leana, C. (2009). A dual-driver model of retention and turnover in the direct care workforce. *The Gerontologist, 49,* 623–634. doi:10.1093/geront/gnp054

Monson, R. G. (1987). *Jewish women on the way up: The challenge of family, career, and community.* New York, NY: American Jewish Council.

Oates, K. (2008). Calling and conflict: A quantitative study of interrole conflict and the sanctification of work and mothering. *Dissertation Abstracts International: Section B. Sciences and Engineering, 68*(9), 6326.

Oates, K., Hall, E., & Anderson, T. (2005). Calling and conflict: A qualitative exploration of interrole conflict and the Sanctification of work in Christian mothers in academia. *Journal of Psychology and Religion, 33,* 210–223. doi:0091-6471/410-730

Pargament, K. I., & Mahoney, A. (2005). Sacred matters: Sanctification as a vital topic for the psychology of religion. *The International Journal for the Psychology of Religion, 15,* 179–198. doi:10.1207/s15327582ijpr1503_1

Piedmont, R. L. (2001). Spiritual transcendence and the scientific study of Spirituality. *Journal of Rehabilitation, 67,* 4–14.

Polasky, L. J., & Holahan, C. K. (1998). Maternal self-discrepancies, interrole conflict, and negative affect among married professional women with children. *Journal of Family Psychology, 12,* 388–401. doi:10.1037/0893-3200.12.3.388

Power, K. G., & Sharp, G. R. (1988). A comparison of sources of nursing stress and job satisfaction among mental handicap and hospice nursing staff. *Journal of Advanced Nursing, 13,* 726–732. doi:10.1111/j.1365-2648.1988.tb00563.x

Puchalski, C., Larson, D., & Lu, F. (2001). Spirituality in psychiatry residency training programs. *International Review of Psychiatry, 13,* 131–138. doi:10.1080/09540260120037371

Reinhold, B. (1996). *Toxic work: How to overcome stress, burnout, overload, and revitalize your career.* New York, NY: Penguin.

Sagie, A. (1993). Measure of religiosity and work obligations among Israeli youth. *Journal of Social Psychology, 133,* 529–537. doi:10.1080/00224545.1993.9712178

Serow, R. (1994). Called to teach: A study of highly motivated preservice teachers. *Journal of Research and Development in Education, 27,* 65–72.

Sikorska-Simmons, E. (2005). Religiosity and work-related attitudes among paraprofessionals and professional staff in assisted living. *Journal of Religion, Spirituality, and Aging, 18*. doi:10.1300/J496v18n01_05

Steger, M., Pickering, N. K., Shin, J. Y., & Dik, B. J. (2010). Calling in work. *Journal of Career Assessment, 18*, 82–96. doi:10.1177/1069072709350905

Tillich, P. (1956). *The dynamics of faith*. New York, NY: Harper.

U.S. Bureau of Labor Statistics. (2010). Time use on average work day. Table A-1. *American Time Use Survey*. Retrieved from http://www.bls.gov/tus/charts

Walker, A., Jones, M., Wuensch, K., Shahnaz, A., & Cope, J. (2008). Sanctifying work: Effects on satisfaction, commitment, and intent to leave. *The International Journal for the Psychology of Religion, 18*, 132–145. doi:10.1080/10508610701879480

Wasner, M., Longaker, C., Fegg, M., Johannes, B., & Gian, D. (2005). Effects of spiritual care training for palliative care professionals. *Palliative Medicine, 19*, 99–104. doi:10.1191/0269216305pm995oa

Waugh, I. M. (2010). Examining the sexual harassment experiences of Mexican immigrant farmworking women. *Violence Against Women, 16*, 237–261. doi:10.1177/1077801209360857

Wrzesniewski, A., McCauley, C. R., Rozin, P., & Schwartz, B. (1997). Jobs, careers, and callings: People's relations to their work. *Journal of Research in Personality, 31*, 21–33. doi:10.1006/jrpe.1997.2162

CHAPTER 32

ADDRESSING RELIGION AND PSYCHOLOGY IN COMMUNITIES: THE CONGREGATION AS INTERVENTION SITE, COMMUNITY RESOURCE, AND COMMUNITY INFLUENCE

Kenneth I. Maton, Mariano R. Sto. Domingo, and Anna M. L. Westin

Psychologists have focused relatively little attention on religion in the community context; rather their focus has been on the individual believer or on the congregation apart from the surrounding community. Yet, congregations are influenced by, and in turn influence, the communities in which they are located. Consistent with the integrative paradigm that guides this handbook, the current chapter brings together available practice-based, theoretical, and empirical work that addresses the role of the congregation in community context. Three important roles of the congregation will be addressed: the congregation as intervention site, community resource, and community influence (see Table 32.1).

In terms of the congregation as a site of intervention for psychologists, the chapter focuses on congregation-based physical health and mental health programs and on congregational development efforts. As a community resource, we examine the contribution of congregations to community-based human services programs, their religious outreach programs for troubled individuals, and their role in community development. Finally, with regards to the congregation as a community influence, we focus on the contribution of congregations to local issue advocacy, electoral politics, and social movements. In some cases, a given project or initiative may simultaneously represent more than one of the three domains. Nonetheless, we distinguish the three roles to most clearly explain the distinctive practice, theory, and research associated with each one.

In each domain, we highlight the contributions that psychologists have made to date. Given the relatively limited amount of work done by psychologists in the religion and community area, however, the chapter expands beyond psychology to encompass allied disciplines as well. When information is available, we distinguish between interventions that incorporate explicit religious language or religious practice and those that do not. Also, although the positive potential of the congregation as intervention site, community resource, and community influence is emphasized, negative features and challenges, including proselytizing, restricted hiring, and problematic perspectives on human rights are discussed as well. Finally, for this chapter, we have chosen the language of religiousness (for a complete discussion, see Volume 1, Chapter 1, this handbook) because congregations, with associated religious belief systems and member relationships, represent established, institutionalized systems.

CONGREGATION AS SITE OF INTERVENTION

Congregations can fruitfully be viewed as potential sites for a variety of interventions conducted by psychologists. Of special note are interventions that focus on congregations composed of low-income,

DOI: 10.1037/14046-032
APA Handbook of Psychology, Religion, and Spirituality: Vol. 2. An Applied Psychology of Religion and Spirituality, K. I. Pargament (Editor-in-Chief)

TABLE 32.1

The Congregation in Community Context

Characteristic	Congregation as Site for intervention	Congregation as Community resource	Congregation as Community influence
Defining feature	Access to subgroups of citizens at risk or in need	Extensive human and financial resources	Source of political, social, and cultural influence
Action focus	Congregation-based physical health and mental health programs Congregational development	Community-based human service programs Religious outreach Community development	Local issue advocacy Electoral politics Social movements
Potential outcome	Individual well-being Community incidence and prevalence rates	Quality of community life	Economic, social, and political empowerment
Role of congregation member	Recipient	Volunteer	Change agent
Role of practitioner	Program developer Consultant Evaluator	Program developer Consultant Evaluator	Organizer Collaborator Consultant Evaluator
Sample theories	Socioecological model Social cognitive theory	Social capital Social learning theory	Empowering community settings Social capital Resource mobilization
Case example	Stephen Series	Amachi Initiative	Camden Community Housing Campaign

ethnic minority, and immigrant population members—residents who often have less access to traditional health and mental health services. In congregation-focused interventions, congregational members serve in the role of service recipient and sometimes as peer helpers as well. Potential roles for psychologists (and allied professionals) in such collaborations include program developer, consultant, and program evaluator. Although working with congregations has long been taboo in psychology, such collaborations appear to be increasing in frequency, perhaps reflecting the increased recognition that religious culture is central to the identity of most Americans (e.g., Barnes & Curtis, 2009).

Three primary targets for work in this area include physical health promotion, mental health promotion, and congregational development. Some of the programs described in this chapter are secular, developed with the goal to be transported into a wide variety of settings, of which the congregation is only one (i.e., "faith-placed" interventions). Others were developed solely for congregations and explicitly incorporate religious language or practice (i.e., "faith-based" interventions). Still others do not indicate whether or not they incorporate religious content.

Key outcomes of interest are as follows: personal well-being at the congregation member level, congregational vitality and wellness at the congregation level, and changes in problem prevalence and incidence rates at the community level. Unfortunately, little work has been done to evaluate systematically success in achieving these outcomes or to link theory and research to practice. Most of the programs presented in this chapter, then, are best looked at as promising rather than as evidence based because they have not yet been supported by rigorous research. Nonetheless, individuals rate the services they receive from congregations as being more effective and trustworthy than those received from other organizations in the community (Wuthnow, Hackett, & Hsu, 2004).

Programs Addressing Physical Health

Perhaps most well-researched and supported in the congregational domain are prevention, promotion, and intervention programs related to physical health. These include programs that target cancer (e.g.,

Lopez & Castro, 2006), diabetes (e.g., Samuel-Hodge et al., 2009), heart disease (e.g., Yanek, Becker, Moy, Gittelsohn, & Koffman, 2001), HIV/AIDS (e.g., Agate et al., 2005), and weight loss (e.g., Kennedy et al., 2005). According to DeHaven, Hunter, Wilder, Walton, and Berry (2004), approximately 25% of such health programs are developed from within the congregation and are faith based, whereas 40% come from outside the congregation and are faith placed. The remaining 35% are developed through collaborations between the congregation and those outside the congregation. Significant positive outcomes have been found in programs from all three of these categories (DeHaven et al., 2004). Furthermore, many health promotion programs focus on underserved populations; thus, congregations may be particularly well suited to address the health disparities that currently plague the nation (Barnes & Curtis, 2009; Francis & Liverpool, 2009).

The socioecological model explains why congregations are viewed as particularly promising target populations for social scientists and community practitioners interested in health promotion (Campbell et al., 2007). Congregations have the potential to influence health-related behavior change across multiple levels, including individual, interpersonal, community, and policy contexts. The Black Churches United for Better Health (BCUBH) program targets fruit and vegetable consumption among African Americans and presents an example of a multilevel health promotion initiative based on the socioecological model. Specifically, the project included components of individualized tailored feedback, social support, churchwide events and education, pastor support, and community coalitions and activities (Campbell et al., 2000). In addition, religious themes were incorporated into sermons and other communication on the basis of information gathered from focus groups with congregation members and interviews with pastors. BCUBH led to a significant increase in fruit and vegetable intake among congregants, and these positive findings were sustained at the 2-year follow-up (Campbell et al., 1999).

Many different disciplines have contributed to health promotion programs to date, including public health, and to a lesser extent, psychology. In several cases, randomized controlled trials have been conducted on promising programs, including Body & Soul, a program focused on diet-related behavior change among members of African American congregations developed by health psychologist Kenneth Resnicow and public health researcher Marci Campbell. Body & Soul incorporates pastor involvement in program-related activities, tailored religious messages, and policy adoption of the target foods for church events. Outcomes as well as a process evaluation of the program are detailed in Chapter 23 in this volume.

Another example of a successful program targeting health behavior is Guide to Health (GTH), developed by psychologist Richard Winett and implemented in rural churches in southwest Virginia. GTH is an individually tailored secular Internet intervention. It was implemented both with and without church-based supports to examine the additional influence of congregational settings on behavior change related to nutrition and physical activity (Winett, Anderson, Wojcik, Winett, & Bowden, 2007). The intervention produced positive nutrition changes at posttest compared with the control group (waitlist), but only the intervention with church-based supports produced changes in nutrition and physical activity at follow-up as well as posttest. The findings indicate that secular interventions (i.e., without spiritually integrated messages) can be successfully implemented within congregations. Social cognitive theory (SCT; Bandura, 1997) was used to explain why the socially mediated intervention was the most effective—that is, the church-based supports simultaneously targeted individual self-regulation of behavior and increased social support for behavior change.

Sternberg, Munschauer, Carrow, and Sternberg (2006) have offered a useful review of congregation-based cardiovascular health promotion programs. Although they did not distinguish between programs that did and did not incorporate religious content, they identified six themes underlying program success, including faith support, secular support, partnership, faith organization capabilities, secular organization capabilities, and caring intervention. Regarding faith support, it was found that congregations contribute to extended support for cardiovascular health through pastors, family members, peers, volunteers, and setting. It also appears that secular support, including outside expertise and funding, is crucial for success. Given the involvement of both congregations and secular partners, collaboration becomes highly important, as does the capabilities of both congregations (i.e., education, training, social contracting) and secular organizations (i.e., spiritual and cultural awareness). Finally, care and trust need to be established through highly involved professionals, along with the participation of the community throughout the program process (e.g., through community-based participatory research).

Programs Addressing Mental Health

A review of the literature revealed a limited number of interventions developed by psychologists that address the mental health needs of congregation members. The programs described in this section focus on peer helping, disaster mental health, and prevention of suicide. An example of an intervention program that was conceived within the church and includes explicit religious content is the Stephen Series. The Stephen Series is a national peer-helping ("Christian Care") initiative, which was developed by pastor and clinical psychologist Kenneth Haugk in 1975. It incorporates Christian faith through both religious language and practice, and it is described in more detail in Case Example 1.

Several other initiatives are in the early stages of development or implementation. The Church Disaster Mental Health Project (CDMH; see http://www.churchdisasterhelp.org) was developed in part on the basis of research by psychologist Jamie Aten and colleagues. The researchers interviewed African American pastors about mental health needs of members in their congregations (and the surrounding community) following Hurricane Katrina (Aten, Topping, Denney, & Bayne, 2010). CDMH aims to provide secular education and outreach to pastors and other church leaders, who in turn can help identify mental health needs following a disaster, provide care and support, improve access to professional mental health services, and promote community self-care following the disaster. No outcome information is currently available.

A still-untested model for implementing youth suicide prevention programs in African American churches, HAVEN, was developed by clinical psychologist and minister Sherry Molock and colleagues through the use of community-based participatory research (Molock, Matlin, Barksdale, Puri, & Lyles, 2008). In this model, pastors or other congregational members, preferably young adults, serve as gatekeepers and connect at-risk adolescents to mental health services via lay helpers that coordinate referral information. To ensure the affordability, accessibility, quality of care, and cultural appropriateness of the referral sources, referrals are made using a mental health resource directory developed specifically for the congregation. Finally, a community education component, focusing on the identification of risk and protective factors for suicide and depression, is instituted by clergy or lay leaders as part of regular congregational activities (e.g., sermons, Sunday school). The HAVEN model was developed to be consistent with the religious values of the Black church.

To date, collaboration between congregations and psychologists related to mental health appears to be scarce, perhaps reflecting in part their distinct conceptualizations of the cause and treatment of mental health problems (Blank, Mahmood, Fox, & Guterbock, 2002; see Chapters 4 and 26 in this volume). Hopefully, over time, more programs will be developed that bring together existing theory, research, and practice, contributing to the development of an integrative paradigm.

Congregational Development

Another important area in which psychologists can collaborate with congregations is congregational development through psychological consultation. Congregations of all sizes may encounter challenges with regards to meeting the needs of congregation members, conflict among members or between members and clergy, rapid growth or decline, and achieving congregational goals (Dominguez & McMinn, 2005; Pargament et al., 1991). Psychologists can assist congregational development by collaborating with key leaders and members to assess congregational needs and resources, to clarify goals and future directions, and to develop strategies and programs to resolve identified problems or improve functioning in various domains.

One published account of congregational development is provided by community psychologists Paul Dokecki and Robert Newbrough, who, in collaboration with theologian and religious educator Robert O'Gorman, served as consultants on the request of a Roman Catholic pastor who wanted to give new life to his "fragmented and stagnant" parish (Dokecki, Newbrough, & O'Gorman, 2001). The team used pastoral theology and action research methods to promote community development in the parish over a period of more than 10 years. First, they conducted a needs assessment in the parish and helped clarify its goals. Then they met with the pastor, the parish's leadership team, and small groups of parish members to develop strategies to promote parish community development. Finally, they focused again on the overall parish community and on how awareness (through self-study and feedback) as well as psychological sense of community (through small groups) had improved (or failed to improve) the parish community. Unfortunately, explicit outcomes of the intervention were not reported.

In the Congregation Development Program, Pargament et al. (1991) partnered with congregations, who conducted their own needs assessment of strengths and weaknesses through validated surveys. The surveys were analyzed by psychologists, who then worked with the congregation to make sense of the findings and plan for change. The work through this data-based consultation effort suggested four distinct process stages for working with congregations: entry, assessment, intervention, and evaluation and termination. Of particular interest to any type of collaboration is the entry stage. In some cases, psychologists may be contacted by congregations, but commonly, congregations are unaware of the range of services provided by psychologists (Pargament et al., 1991). More frequently, then, the psychologist may try to engage the congregation, which may be difficult because of mistrust. Emphasis is placed on clarifying expectations, determining readiness, and building a collaborative working relationship. The stages of assessment, intervention, evaluation, and termination may vary widely depending on the type of partnership being built. Likely relevant to all collaborations, however, are the key aspects of shared goal setting, identification of strengths and weaknesses, dealing with resistance, and accountability on the part of the consultant to resolve problems before the consulting relationship is terminated (Pargament et al., 1991).

Published accounts of congregational development collaborations appear promising, although findings are often qualitative and informal rather than quantitative and formal. For example, interactive needs assessment provided through data-based consultation in more than 50 diverse congregations across the country appear to have been well received as evaluated by informal qualitative reports (Pargament et al., 1991). When consulting with congregations, it is important to maintain a keen cultural sensitivity to the religious nature of the setting to ensure that the services provided are not inconsistent with or threatening to members' religious beliefs, values, and goals. Future work in this area would benefit from more systematic evaluation as well as integrated development of theory, research, and action (see also Chapter 26 in this volume).

Case Example 1: The Stephen Series

The Stephen Series is a comprehensive system for training, supervising, and organizing congregation members with the goal of providing quality Christian care in the congregation (or the surrounding community) to individuals experiencing bereavement, terminal illness, divorce, or other major life changes or crises (Stephen Ministries, 2010). Christian care involves lay support through active listening and emotional support along with helping people experience Jesus, find meaning, and connect to a loving religious community. Recognizing that there were more congregation members in need of assistance than he could handle on his own, Rev. Haugk trained nine members of his congregation to provide care under his supervision.

The ministry was successful, and over the next several years, Rev. Haugk trained members in other congregations to provide the same services. Unfortunately, without Rev. Haugk present, the congregations were unable to receive appropriate supervision, train new caregivers, or expand their services. To resolve these problems, Rev. Haugk decided that it would be more efficient to train Stephen Leaders, selected congregation members, who would return to their home congregations to train and supervise other congregation members. The infrastructure added by the Stephen Leaders component helped transform the Stephen Series from a relatively isolated ministry to a widely implemented, national endeavor.

Once congregations enroll in the Stephen Series, Stephen Ministries St. Louis provides training for a selected congregation member to become a Stephen Leader. This Stephen Leader then returns to the congregation to recruit, train, and supervise several Stephen Ministers. The Stephen Leader also is in charge of matching Stephen Ministers with congregation members in need who want help. Stephen Ministers then meet with the congregation member once a week for as long as their service is needed. Both Stephen Ministers and Stephen Leaders are encouraged to seek continuing education and ongoing support.

In 2009, there were reported to be more than 10,000 congregations, representing more than 150 different Christian denominations, enrolled in the Stephen Series. More than 55,000 individuals have been trained as Stephen Leaders, and more than 500,000 congregation members have been trained as Stephen Ministers. These Stephen Ministers have provided confidential one-on-one care to millions of people in and around their congregation. Clearly, the Stephen Series, and similar programs using a peer-based model, have the potential to provide benefits on a broad scale, consistent with the socioecological model. Unfortunately, given the absence of empirical outcome data, the nature and extent of the benefits of the program are not known at this time.

Although the congregation as site for intervention holds promise, there are also potential barriers, challenges, and negative consequences of such collaborations that warrant attention. For example, in the case of Stephen Series, the lack of infrastructure early in the development threatened the maintenance and expansion of the program. Similar issues likely are also faced in instances in which psychologists bring a program to a congregation and then leave, without ensuring that the appropriate infrastructure and ongoing support is available. By providing ongoing support, or ensuring that the congregation has the resources to sustain a program, such problems can potentially be prevented.

CONGREGATION AS A COMMUNITY RESOURCE

Given the strong emphasis of most religions on reaching out to and helping individuals in need beyond their own members (i.e., in the surrounding community), congregations represent a vital community resource, providing substantial amounts of money, volunteers, and programming to vulnerable citizens. Of note, while charitable giving in general decreased by 2% in 2008 because of the recession, contributions to religious organizations increased by 5.5% that same year (Giving USA, 2009). In addition, Americans who volunteer are more likely to do so for a religious organization than for any other type of organization, a pattern that is true across racial groups (Ramakrishnan, 2006).

The community-based services that congregations provide and contribute to are wide-ranging in scope, including but not limited to mentoring programs, health promotion, treatment for drug and alcohol abuse, food pantries, language training for immigrants, refugee resettlement, neighborhood crime prevention, and provision of low-income housing. There is also a wide range in the structure of congregational outreach, ranging from efforts initiated by a single congregation, to collaborative partnerships with other congregations, to congregational partnerships with local or national faith-based organizations—that is, nonprofit entities that themselves have some level of faith-based affiliation (e.g., Catholic Charities; Salvation Army; see Cnaan & Boddie, 2006; Green, 2007; Wuthnow et al., 2004).

A social science theory that is often applied to congregations as community resources is social capital theory (e.g., Foley & Hoge, 2007; Schneider, 2006). Putnam (2001) noted that "faith communities in which people worship together are arguably the single most important repository of social capital in America" (p. 66). Social capital generally denotes any facet of social relations that enable individuals to pursue shared goals (Smidt, 2003). An important aspect of social capital is resources, which includes people who connect with others and solve problems (Bourdieu, 1983). This broad theoretical conception aside, it is not clear, in most cases, whether the faith-based organizations that developed the programs described thus far have drawn on existing social science theory or research to guide their efforts.

In this section, we divide the community-based contributions of congregations into three areas: community-based services, religious outreach to troubled individuals, and community development initiatives. In each domain, we found only occasional instances in which psychologists (or other social scientists) were involved, whether as program developer, evaluator, consultant, or applied researcher. A concern related to faith-based initiatives in each domain, especially when government funding is involved, is the separation of church and state—that is, the possibility that congregational volunteers or staff will influence the religious beliefs of program recipients (Garringer, 2003; Maton, Dodgen, Sto. Domingo, & Larsen, 2005). Also of note, although many have called for research comparing the distinctive nature of faith-based versus secular community-based programs—and their relative effectiveness—with few exceptions quality research to date is lacking (Boddie & Cnaan, 2006; Hula, Jackson-Elmoore, & Reese, 2007).

Community-Based Services

Helping individuals in the community has long been a priority for religion. Thus, congregations contribute to a multitude of human service and social service initiatives, often called social or outreach ministries, serving the entire range of human needs, for individuals of all ages and living situations. Here we limit attention to two areas for which some level of involvement of psychologists or other social scientists was found: mentoring programs for youth, and illness prevention and health promotion programs. Not all programs explicitly lay out the religious rationale or content of their work, but when available, they are included in the following project descriptions.

Faith-based mentoring programs for youth have become increasingly popular in recent years, in part because of enhanced federal funding (e.g., Akers, Lane, & Lanza-Kaduce, 2008; Bauldry, 2006). Congregations are viewed as an especially viable source of mentors, because the mentors are expected to be motivated by religious faith and to receive ongoing support from their congregation. One national mentoring program, Amachi, initiated by social scientist John Dilulio for children with an incarcerated parent, is described in detail in Case Example 2. Another interesting statewide program that includes a mentoring component is the Faith- and Community-Based Juvenile Detention Treatment Initiative for youth in residential juvenile correctional facilities in Florida. The program combines psychological (cognitive–behavioral) components with religious features. The latter include recruitment of faith-based mentors, sponsorship and facilitation of religiously oriented volunteer work (such as conducting worship services in correctional facilities by volunteers other than the mentors), and provision of the services of chaplains in juvenile facilities. Of note, in specific response to issues related to the separation of church and state, mentors are instructed not to discuss faith and religion when dealing with their mentees unless the latter ask questions, and the youth are given the option to choose secular mentors if they want. Also, chaplains are cautioned not to try to convert the youth to any particular faith (Lane & Lanza-Kaduce, 2007).

One interesting aspect of the program is its underpinnings in social learning theory (Akers et al., 2008), particularly its emphasis on the influence of peer reference groups. The theory implies that when participants adopt peer reference groups that are religiously centered, group-level standards of morality deter negative behavior and reinforce positive ones (see Volume 1, Chapter 10, this handbook). Preliminary findings indicate that faith-based mentors appear to maintain longer term relationships with their mentees than mentors recruited from secular settings. Outcome findings for mentees are not yet available.

Congregation-supported illness prevention and health promotion programs focused on citizens in the larger community represent another domain of community-based programs in which psychologists and members of allied disciplines have been involved (e.g., DeHaven et al., 2004; Fox, Stein, Gonzalez, Farrenkopf, & Dellinger, 1998; Francis & Liverpool, 2009). These programs differ from the programs described in the first section of the chapter in that the primary focus is to make a difference in the lives of community members, as opposed to focusing only on congregation members. For example, a program that involves collaboration between churches and public health officials, Churches United to Stop HIV (CUSH), was designed to prevent HIV in minority communities (Agate et al., 2005). CUSH has provided training to more than 2,850 faith leaders, HIV prevention education services to 32,000 individuals, and counseling and testing for more than 825 participants. It does not appear that explicit religious content is incorporated into the program. Agate et al. attributed the magnitude of service provision primarily to the influence of large centers of worship with considerable infrastructure and resources, but they noted that smaller storefront churches were still important, helping to reach people at higher risk for HIV. Unfortunately, outcome data are not available.

Religious Outreach to Troubled Individuals

A number of faith-based programs explicitly focus on religious conversion as central to their outreach to troubled individuals in the community (Johnson, Larson, & Pitts, 1997; Maton & Wells, 1995). One such program is Teen Challenge, an evangelical Christian recovery program that primarily serves drug and alcohol abusers. This residential therapeutic program, formed in 1958 by David Wilkerson, a pastor of the Assemblies of God, involves several months of intensive "discipleship" and evangelization meant to cure the clients of compulsive deviant behavior and related problems, replacing them with "a meaningful Christian life." According to websites promoting the program, Teen Challenge has been highly successful in changing the lives of troubled teens, citing data from an unpublished dissertation (Bicknese, 1999). The controversial nature of the program, along with criticism of major methodological weaknesses in the dissertation study cited to support program effectiveness (e.g., Zanis & Cnaan, 2006), have been highlighted in the national media (e.g., Goodstein, 2001).

Another target population for religious programming is prisoners (see also Chapter 28 in this volume). One well-known program in this area is the Prison Fellowship (PF), a conservative, transdenominational Christian organization that ministers to incarcerated men and women, ex-prisoners, crime victims, and their families through Bible studies and seminars. Its basic premise is that prisoners are first and foremost in need of spiritual transformation, and the intervention is structured accordingly. According to the program, this can be attained by "reconciliation to God, family and community through the power and truth of Jesus Christ" (Prison Fellowship, 2012). The program was founded in 1976 by Charles Colson (Nixon aide, incarcerated in 1974 for Watergate-related charges) and is largely volunteer-driven. Studies showed that PF participants with a high rate of participation (i.e., attendance in 10 or more Bible studies) had a significantly lower rate of recidivism compared with a matched group of non-PF participants (Johnson, 2002; Johnson, Larson, & Pitts, 1997), although the effect diminishes over time (Johnson, 2004).

Community Development

Community development has been defined as "asset building that improves the quality of life among residents of low to moderate income neighborhoods" (Ferguson & Dickens, 1999). It represents an important arena of involvement of multiple religious organizations, such as Baptist, Presbyterian, and Methodist churches, especially concerning housing and community economic development (Hula, Jackson-Elmoore, & Reese, 2008). Another area of focus includes efforts to enhance the fabric of relationships within the community.

In terms of housing and real estate community development, the percentage of community development corporations that were religiously based increased from 14% in 1998 to 25% in 2005 (National Congress for Community Economic Development, 1999, 2006). Activities include development of transitional housing for homeless families, housing units for senior citizens, and row houses in central cities affordable to low-income families. The most well-known faith-based housing program is Habitat for Humanity, an ecumenical Christian housing ministry that addresses poverty by building houses together with families in need. According to Chaves (2004), supplying volunteers to Habitat for Humanity is the most common form of participation in housing development by congregational members. This is perhaps explained by the organization's inclusivity in its volunteer recruitment efforts, as its website notes, "We invite people of all faiths to join our mission to build and renovate simple, decent, affordable houses" (Habitat for Humanity, 2010). Congregations are encouraged to contribute money, volunteers, and prayer and to engage the larger community. To date, the organization has built more than 350,000 houses around the world, providing more than 1.75 million people in 3,000 communities with safe, decent, affordable shelter.

In terms of enhancing the quality of relationships within communities, one notable ecumenical initiative is the Ten Point Coalition in Boston. The program was conceived in 1992 as a result of the escalating violence in Boston neighborhoods and the acknowledged opportunity for congregations and faith-based agencies to work collaboratively to reduce youth violence and help youth develop more positive and productive lifestyles. A study of the program indicated a large drop in homicide rate (80%) in the 40 communities served by churches where the program was established (Berrien, McRoberts, & Winship, 2000). The authors attributed the decrease in crime primarily to the "bridging" activities of the pastors who worked to enhance communication and trust between the police and local community residents.

Case Example 2: The Amachi Initiative

An example of a successful collaboration between secular and religious organizations is the Amachi initiative, a mentorship program for children with one or more parents in prison. The Amachi initiative is responsible for building partnerships with churches, evaluating results of the program, communicating those results to stakeholders, and connecting with funding sources. Pastors and ministers at local churches identify qualified mentors and provide ongoing information about matches to Public/Private Ventures (P/PV, a national nonprofit organization aiming to improve the effectiveness of social policies and programs; Jucovy, 2003). Although all mentors are recruited through churches, most activities engaged in by mentors and mentees are secular in nature—for example, playing sports, doing schoolwork, or just hanging out. According to one report, in a typical month, 16% to 21% of mentor–mentee pairs attend church services or other church activities, an indication that religious activities are an option but not a program emphasis or requirement. The national mentoring program Big Brothers and Big Sisters (BBBS) provides infrastructure, screening, matching, and training of mentors identified by the churches. Congregations have allowed access to motivated mentors who likely would have been difficult to recruit otherwise; Amachi and BBBS have provided the expertise and infrastructure needed to enable evidence-based and sustained implementation.

The program was originally conceived in 1998 by social scientist John DiIulio, who at the time was the director of the Center for Research on Religion and Urban Civil Society at the University of Pennsylvania and board member of P/PV. DiIulio was aware that there were more than 20,000 children in Philadelphia with at least one parent in prison and that children of prisoners were 5 times more likely to themselves become incarcerated compared with other children in poor urban neighborhoods (Husock, 2003). Dilulio believed that a diverse range of religious groups would be best able to promote change in the poor, African American communities where the rate of crime and incarceration was the highest. His research and ideas, along with the organizational plan provided by Gary Walker, president of P/PV, lay the foundation for the Amachi initiative (Husock, 2003).

To promote effective implementation of the Amachi program, P/PV hired W. Wilson Goode, the former African American mayor of Philadelphia and recently ordained Baptist minister, in September 2000. Goode was passionate about the Amachi initiative because his father had been in prison during his childhood; he believed that his own congregation had played a central role in supporting him during that difficult time (Husock, 2003). Goode appeared well-situated to bridge the gap between P/PV and local churches in poor, high-crime neighborhoods in Philadelphia. In his presentations to pastors, he talked about the theological foundation of Amachi, citing Isaiah, who had a vision for a troubled city: "Your people will rebuild the ancient ruins and will raise up age-old foundations; you will be called Repairer of Broken Walls, Restorer of Streets with Dwellings" (Isaiah 58:12, quoted by Jucovy, 2003). Initially, Goode helped established partnerships with 42 churches, each committed to finding 10 caring adult volunteers (Jucovy, 2003). By 2003, 542 mentors had been matched with 700 children of prisoners (Husock, 2003).

Preliminary research suggests that Amachi has been valuable. Visiting prisoners and helping their children are activities that appealed to the religious sensibilities of congregations and fit their mission to serve people in the larger community (Jucovy, 2003). Churches have recruited mentors that have stayed committed to meeting with youth for an average of 7.3 hr a month for at least 1 year (Farley, 2004). Both mentors and caregivers have reported an increase in youth's self-confidence, academic performance, behavior in school, and future orientation (Farley, 2004). The Office of Juvenile Justice and Delinquency Prevention (OJJDP) provided funding support for the national expansion of Amachi starting in 2003. Amachi has now expanded to 250 programs in 48 states, serving more than 100,000 children of prisoners (Amachi, 2010). A large-scale randomized trial of the Amachi program is currently in progress.

Collaboration between secular groups and faith-based institutions appears to hold great potential. For example, in the case of Amachi, 82% of program volunteers were African American, whereas only about 15% to 20% of volunteers in most mentoring programs are ethnic minorities (Farley, 2004). The Amachi initiative thus provides a meaningful lesson about the power of using congregations to reach volunteer populations that otherwise would be difficult to recruit. In addition, having an established secular organization provide infrastructure and expertise to churches, which likely lack the capacity for implementing an initiative of this type on their own, also appears crucial. Finally, having a strong, effective, and engaging project leader accepted and respected by secular and faith-based partners appears to have been central to both initial engagement and ongoing program success. In terms of challenges, some churches and pastors believe that mentoring children of incarcerated parents is the role of government and that the church's prophetic mission might be contaminated by federal funding (Jucovy, 2003). More generally, the incorporation of religious meaning and in some cases religious practice (e.g., PF, Teen Challenge, Ten Point Coalition) may be seen as problematic by potential service recipients who do not believe that the best, or the only, means of improving their lives is through religious belief and redemption (Wuthnow, 2004).

CONGREGATION AS COMMUNITY INFLUENCE

Citizens within congregations of diverse orientations can be viewed as potential sources of influence on the community and larger society (Charlton, 2007; Pargament & Maton, 2000). This may be especially important for those citizens who have limited economic and political influence through other means, including ethnic minority, immigrant, and lower income individuals. Mechanisms of potential congregational influence include local issue advocacy, electoral politics, and involvement in larger social movements. Psychologists and allied social scientists and community practitioners can potentially play important roles as researchers, expert resources, collaborators, program developers, consultants, and program evaluators.

Local Issue Advocacy

Local issue advocacy can be pursued by congregations in many ways, including mobilization of members to sign petitions, send e-mails to local officials, lobby fellow citizens, or participate in protest demonstrations (Barnes, 2005; Chaves, 2004; Schneider, 2006). One influential means of asserting local influence that has greatly increased in frequency in recent decades is faith-based community organizing (Swarts, 2008; Wood, 2003). National organizations involved in this work include Gamaliel Foundation (named after a Biblical figure), Industrial Areas Foundation (initiated by well-known organizer Saul Alinksy), and Pacific Institute for Community Organization (founded by a Jesuit priest).

Local efforts generally focus on issues affecting low-income families and neighborhoods. Faith-based community organizing is facilitated by a small number of professional organizers who connect with congregations in a community. The organizers identify, train, and work closely with lay leaders from these congregations. The lay leaders and organizers hold numerous individual meetings (i.e., "one-on-ones") with congregational members and local citizens, and on the basis of what they learn, identify key concerns that appear to be widely shared. Ultimately, public officials are confronted, often in carefully arranged public meetings attended by a large number of congregational members, and are asked to take specific actions to address the local problem. Clergy support is critical to congregational member involvement, and a combination of public confrontation and behind-the-scenes relationship building and negotiation with officials is often critical for effective action. Reference to religious values (e.g., helping the poor, serving God) and use of public prayer are included throughout advocacy campaigns to motivate members to initiate and sustain advocacy efforts (Wood, 2003).

Researchers from a range of disciplines have documented the success and processes of faith-based community organizing. Results of local issue advocacy include the passage of living-wage legislation, funding for neighborhood revitalization, public education reform, public works infrastructure, youth development programming, and health insurance (Gold, Simon, Mundell, & Brown, 2004; Swarts, 2008; Wood & Warren, 2002). Interestingly, according to Kleidman (2008), local and national affiliates have engaged a number of social science researchers "in policy projects, in research based on their concerns, in speaking and writing to help popularize organizing, and in helping to lead a variety of conversations within organizing networks" (p. 34).

Various theoretical models have been applied to understanding the success of faith-based community organizing, including social capital (e.g., Wood & Warren, 2002) and empowering community settings (Maton, 2008). The social capital perspective, described in the section Congregation as a Community Resource, emphasizes the critical contribution of the "bonding" and "bridging" social ties provided by congregations to the success of faith-based organizing efforts. Empowering community settings theory posits that faith-based community organizing efforts are most likely to achieve success when (a) the faith-based rationale for action inspires change, is strengths-based, and focuses beyond the self (i.e., serving God by contributing to social justice); (b) the organizing activities are engaging, involve active learning, and are of high quality; (c) the effort is characterized by a sense of community, caring relationships, and a multifaceted support system; (d) roles for lay leaders and members are accessible, numerous, and bidirectional; (e) leadership is talented, shared, and committed; and (f) organizational learning and change occur because of an ongoing learning orientation, mechanisms to bridge groups differing in ethnicity and religious beliefs, and multiple linkages to external resources (including research experts).

Electoral Politics

Many congregations seek to enhance electoral politics, both local and national, using a range of strategies (Brown, 2006; Djupe & Gilbert, 2009; Wald & Calhoun-Brown, 2007). The 1998 National Congregational Study, for example, indicated that 26% of congregations informed congregants at worship services about opportunities for political activity; 17% distributed voter guides; 9% worked to get people to vote; 7% discussed politics; and 6% and 4%, respectively, had an elected government official, or someone running for office, as a visiting speaker (Chaves, 2004). Overall, 40% of congregations participated in at least one electoral political activity. Jewish and mainline Protestant congregations were most likely to initiate discussion groups and to invite elected officials or candidates for office to speak to the congregation. Black Protestant congregations most frequently focused on getting people registered to vote, and Conservative and evangelical White Protestant congregations most frequently distributed voter guides—with 70% of these voter guides identifying politicians supportive of Christian Right issues.

Social capital and resource mobilization theories have been applied by scholars to understand the value and use of these congregational electoral politics strategies (Brown, 2006; Djupe & Gilbert, 2009; Wald & Calhoun-Brown, 2007). Social capital theory emphasizes the preexisting social connections within the congregation as crucial facilitators of member political influence and activity (Schneider, 2006). Resource mobilization theory, in turn, helps to explain the reality that congregations with greater resources (e.g., members, income, clergy leadership, civic ties) are more likely to be involved in political activities (Beyerlein & Chaves, 2003). It also helps to explain the finding that Black congregations are more involved in voter registration efforts—because of the heightened social–political expectations of African American congregants and the relatively low resource cost of voter registration programs (Brown, 2006).

Social Movements

Throughout American history, religious organizations have been central players in major social movements, including abolitionists, women's Christian temperance, civil rights, new Christian right, and environmental movements (J. E. Williams, 2002). Religious communities appear to be uniquely situated to provide inspiration, people, ideas, and cultural and organizational resources—all of which are necessary to mobilize and sustain the mass involvement of citizens necessary for bringing about fundamental social changes. Depending on the nature of the social movement and the religious values involved (i.e., prolife movement, "sanctity of life"; civil rights movement, "repairing the world"; gay rights movement, "we are all God's children"), the goals and outcomes will vary in terms of their consistency with the values and goals of organized psychology and of individual psychologists.

Research on religious social movements has been guided by multiple theoretical orientations, including cultural and resource mobilization perspectives. The cultural perspective emphasizes the issue-framing and motivational contribution of religion to social movements (J. E. Williams, 2002). As summarized by J. E. Williams (2002),

> religious ideas and beliefs can reveal aspects of the world to be unjust or immoral, can provide the identity that people draw on when they are urged to get active on an issue, and can give them a sense of agency because it convinces them that their action matters. (p. 317)

The resource mobilization perspective emphasizes the importance of local religious resources in contributing to social movements (Morris, 1984; J. E. Williams, 2002), including meeting places, leadership (i.e., clergy), capacity to raise funds, relationships among cocongregants, and ties to local community institutions.

One emerging religious social movement, religious environmentalism, is of special note because of the wide diversity of religious groups involved worldwide, including Buddhists, Christians, Muslims, Jews, and Hindus (e.g., Gottlieb, 2006). Interestingly, 56% of Americans ascribe to the view that we should preserve the environment "because it is God's creation" (Biodiversity Project, 2002). Many religious groups have taken policy positions related to the importance of "stewardship" of the planet's natural resources. Movement actions have ranged from civil disobedience (e.g., Christian protests at the Department of Energy) to advocacy campaigns on such topics as climate change to the creation and distribution of ecoreligious resources for religious education (Gottlieb, 2006). Furthermore, major religious organizations have joined together to pursue this work, both nationally and internationally. For example, in the United States, the National Religious Partnership for the Environment is composed of the U.S. Conference of Catholic Bishops, the National Council of Churches of Christ, the Coalition on Environment and Jewish Life, and the Evangelical Environmental Network, together serving more than 100 million Americans. Finally, scholars from various disciplines have helped to promote and advance religious environmentalism as a social movement (e.g., Gottlieb, 2006), and interdisciplinary efforts have emerged that center on the role of religions in contributing to meaningful environmental change. The Yale Forum on Religion and Ecology, for example, involves scholars from environmental science, economics, religion, ethics, and public policy.

Potential Congregation Member and Community-Level Outcomes

Outside of case study accounts, little empirical research has been conducted specifically examining outcomes of congregation-based issue advocacy, electoral politics activity, and social movement involvement. Potential congregational member outcomes of involvement in such efforts include psychological, civic, and political empowerment (Maton, 2008). Potential community-level outcomes vary depending on the nature of the focal issue. In many cases, when progressive causes are involved, potential outcomes include reductions in social, economic, and political inequality and, more generally, enhanced quality of life (Christens, Hanlin, & Speer, 2007; Wald & Calhoun-Brown, 2007; R. H. Williams, 2003). When the issues reflect conservative ideologies, outcomes may be controversial for many psychologists, particularly concerning issues related to rights of groups historically lacking power in society, including sexual minorities, immigrant populations, ethnic minorities, and women (e.g., abortion, gay marriage, legal status for immigrants).

Case Example 3: The Camden Community Housing Campaign

Community psychologist Paul Speer contributed to a successful faith-based community organization attempt in the 1990s to influence policy in Camden, NJ, working with Camden Community Churches Organized for People (CCOP; affiliated with Pacific Institute for Community Organizing; Speer et al., 2003). At the time, CCOP was composed of two staff organizers and approximately 60 active lay leaders from 18 member congregations. CCOP staff and leaders conducted more than 600 one-on-one conversations with Camden residents, designed to reconnect individuals, facilitate dialogue, and reveal shared community experiences. A major theme that emerged was concern over the elevated levels of violent crime and the realization that vacant houses were repeatedly the locations for violent drug dealing. CCOP then held approximately 20 research meetings with groups, including the local police, the housing authority, community development officials, bankers, and elected officials with knowledge of crime and housing. It became clear that no person or organization within the city had knowledge of the extent of vacant housing, and officials did not see a link between vacant housing and drug crime. Leaders of CCOP next met with the mayor of Camden. The mayor indicated that vacant housing was not a pressing problem and that financial limitations made interventions unrealistic.

CCOP then drew on a relationship with a research center at Rutgers University (the Center for Social and Community Development [CSCD]), directed by community psychologist Paul Speer. Upon CCOP's request, CSCD, using a geographical information system (GIS), examined the association between violent crime and vacant housing. A strong association was found. The researchers presented their findings to CCOP leaders in a series of meetings over 6 weeks. CCOP then repeated their earlier attempt to influence the Mayor, this time through a public meeting—an "action" in CCOP language—attended by approximately 1,000 of its members. In the meeting, CCOP presented the CSCD data, including the GIS maps. The maps, along with case study narratives obtained in the one-to-one interviews, were reported to have had a powerful effect on those attending the meeting, including CCOP members, public officials, and the media.

CCOP then demanded that the mayor convene an ongoing series of public planning meetings, jointly sponsored by himself and CCOP to study the problem of Camden's vacant housing. The mayor agreed, and for a year and a half, CCOP, the mayor, CSCD, and an array of municipal agencies and organizations examined the vacant housing–drug crime relationship. This process was enhanced by the publication in Camden's major daily newspaper of a series of stories about vacant housing. These stories included interviews with CCOP leaders, the group's research-based analysis, and the maps generated by CCOP leaders and CSCD.

The process became formally known as the Camden Community Housing Campaign. Concrete results included an inventory conducted by the Camden Fire Department of all vacant houses in Camden (just over 3,300), a new competitive bidding process to lower demolition costs dramatically (from as much as $30,000 to $8,000 per vacant house), a 40% reduction in fees at landfills for debris dumped from demolished vacant houses, and more effective processes to board up vacant housing. Furthermore, CCOP met with the New Jersey governor who was supportive of the group's efforts. Over a 6-month period, CCOP obtained $3 million from state and local sources to support the Camden Community Housing Campaign.

After 2 years, CSCD analyzed results of the Camden Community Housing Campaign. To conservatively estimate the effect of CCOP's housing campaign, the citywide drop in drug crime during that period (assuming this drop was in no way related to CCOP's efforts) was subtracted from the drop in drug crime in blocks where vacant houses were significantly affected (two or more boarded up or demolished). The analysis attributed a 25% drop in drug crime in those areas where CCOP's Housing Campaign was targeted.

CSCD's role in the CCOP initiative underscores the potential contribution psychologists can make to faith-based initiatives to bring about positive change. Mutual respect between the parties involved, open communication, and investment of the time and effort necessary to forge productive collaboration exemplify this particular initiative. Of note, Speer et al. (2003) emphasized that their work was centered in an action research approach and that "rather than emphasizing its expertise, the Center shared the knowledge it had and understood the knowledge and power CCOP had" (p. 401). Although differences in perspectives and priorities should lead to care on the part of psychologists when partnering with faith-based groups, this case study reveals that positive outcomes can ensue when values and goals related to important problems are shared.

CHALLENGES FACED, BEST PRACTICES, AND CONCERNS FOR THE FIELD

Two key challenges to effective collaboration between psychologists and congregations, relevant to all three domains discussed in this chapter, are mutual distrust and stereotypes. These stem in part from differing worldviews and in part from limited contact (Barnes & Curtis, 2009; Maton et al., 2005). Worldview differences between religion and psychology include contrasting views of people (spiritual or moral vs. biopsychosocial perspectives), attributes considered important (knowledge of scriptures or discernment vs. research knowledge or practical skills), bases of knowledge (received tradition vs. research findings), and values and goals (spiritual growth vs. emotional well-being). These differences notwithstanding, there are clearly areas of common ground and purpose, as illustrated by the collaborative initiatives described in this chapter. Over time, with increased contact and positive engagement, mutual distrust and stereotypes can be expected to erode, potentially replaced by mutual respect for what religion and psychology have to offer each other. For community members, such collaborations have the potential to reduce barriers related to financial resources, logistics (e.g., access to services, referral procedures) and stigma.

In terms of best practices, a common theme voiced in the literature is the importance of collaborative working relationships (e.g., Lane & Lanza-Kaduce, 2007; Molock et al., 2008; Sternberg et al., 2006). Concrete strategies to enhance such relationships include involvement of religious partners in projects early in their design, time committed to personal relationship development, careful attention to differences in language and terminology, and open communication (Benes, Walsh, McMinn, Dominguez, & Aikins, 2000; Pargament et al., 1991; Sternberg et al., 2006). Furthermore, psychologists building viable partnerships need to be equipped not only with expertise in their areas of research and practice but more generally with cultural sensitivity, interpersonal skills, and an understanding of the organizational culture and structure of congregations (e.g., Pargament et al., 1991).

Some of the interventions reviewed in this chapter, in each domain, explicitly incorporated religious content (e.g., language) or practices (e.g., prayer), whereas others did not. It is possible that each is associated with distinct advantages and distinct challenges. For example, integration of religious content or practice may facilitate development of partnerships between psychologists and congregations and may enhance cultural sensitivity, program participation, and program impact within congregations by building on the religious beliefs and experiences of members. A distinct challenge, however, perhaps especially for psychologists who do not share the religious beliefs of the congregations with which they are working, is the additional time and effort involved in collaboration and program development. It is also possible that the potential for iatrogenic effects is greater in such programs, for example, for congregational members who interpret their inability to benefit from a given intervention program as a personal religious failing on their part.

For interventions that do not incorporate religious content, it may be more difficult for psychologists to establish viable partnerships with congregations and to gain high levels of congregational member participation. Conversely, out in the community, purely secular interventions conducted by congregations are less likely to antagonize nonbelievers and have the potential to be more broadly applicable (e.g., to community members of different religious faiths or who are nonreligious). An example of the latter type of intervention was the decision to remove explicit Christian content from the original manuscript that became Alcoholics Anonymous (AA's) Big Book, which contains AA's 12-step program, before its public release (Boorstein, 2010). Research is needed to establish the conditions under which different types and levels of integration of religious content and practice affect the development, implementation, sustainability, and impact of interventions.

The positive potential of religion emphasized in this chapter notwithstanding, major concerns exist. The potential for religion to cause harm, as revealed throughout the course of history, is great (e.g., religion-inspired wars, violence, prejudice, oppression, child sexual abuse, and resistance to social change). Congregations, and their members, may contribute actively or passively to such outcomes in multiple ways (e.g., economically, politically, and socially). Psychologists have a special responsibility to work to minimize potential negative effects on community members (American Psychological Association, 2002; Maton et al., 2005) through research, practice, and advocacy. In terms of research, special attention must be paid to assessing the anticipated and unanticipated outcomes, whether they are negative or positive. The development and implementation of programs need to be attended to as well (Lane & Lanza-Kaduce, 2007). In community practice collaborations, psychologists need to help ensure that appropriate safeguards are included, for example, related to religious discrimination in project staff hired, proselytization of community service recipients, appropriate relationships with vulnerable populations (e.g., children), and appropriate standards of care for services provided. In terms of advocacy, organized psychology must remain a voice for social justice, and one that bears witness to the negative influences of existing policies, practices, and programs in the religious domain.

IMPLICATIONS FOR THE INTEGRATIVE PARADIGM

The integration of theory, research, and practice in the community domain has primarily been limited to a small number of congregation-based physical health promotion programs (see Chapter 23 in this volume). Researchers and practitioners involved in these efforts have drawn from established behavior change theories in the areas of focus, designed theory-based programs often incorporating relevant religious content, collaborated with congregations to both develop and implement the programs, and evaluated the process and outcomes of such efforts. For other initiatives, including some reviewed in this chapter, psychologists and those from allied disciplines have not been involved in initial program development, and it is not clear whether available theory and research were drawn on. Furthermore, most programs have not been rigorously evaluated, if evaluated at all. Ideally, future efforts will use a wide range of applicable theories and related research to guide the design of interventions, and increasing numbers of psychologists will collaborate with congregations or faith-based organizations as well as with members of other disciplines, to design, implement, contribute to, and evaluate initiatives.

Even in cases in which psychologists are not involved in the design and implementation of projects, and psychological theory is not used to guide initial program development, evaluation research has an important role to play. Evaluation efforts not only serve the public good by demonstrating the extent of program effectiveness but also contribute important knowledge to future program refinement and development as well as to related theory development. Consistent with the integrative paradigm, ideally, such research will encompass multiple levels of outcomes, both potential positive and negative effects, theory-based intervening variables, and the processes of implementation and collaboration.

CONCLUSION

Congregations represent highly prevalent and important settings in U.S. communities. For those concerned with community betterment, congregations simultaneously represent a site for intervention, providing access to citizens in need; a community resource, possessing extensive human and financial resources; and an important community influence, representing a vital source of political, cultural, and social power. Psychology practitioners and researchers have important contributions to make in each of these domains, in collaboration with congregations, each other, and members of allied disciplines. In future work, we hopefully will learn from and build on the initiatives described in this chapter, both in terms of enhancing religion's positive potential and in limiting its negative potential. In the process, we will be contributing in important ways to theory, research, and practice and to the betterment of our communities and society.

References

Agate, L. L., Cato-Watson, D., Mullins, J. M., Scott, G. S., Rolle, V., Markland, D., & Roach, D. L. (2005). Churches United to Stop HIV (CUSH): A faith-based HIV prevention initiative. *Journal of the National Medical Association*, 97(7, Suppl.), 60S–63S.

Akers, R., Lane, J., & Lanza-Kaduce, L. (2008). Faith-based mentoring and restorative justice: Overlapping theoretical, empirical, and philosophical backgrounds. In H. V. Miller (Ed.), *Restorative justice: From theory to practice. Sociology of crime, law, and deviance* (Vol. 2, pp. 136–166). Bingley, England: Elsevier.

Amachi. (2010). *Amachi updates.* Retrieved from http://www.amachimentoring.org

American Psychological Association. (2002). *Ethical principles of psychologists and code of conduct.* Retrieved from http://www.apa.org/ethics/code/code.pdf

Aten, J. D., Topping, S., Denney, R. M., & Bayne, T. G. (2010). Collaborating with African-American churches to overcome minority disaster mental health disparities: What mental health professionals can learn from Hurricane Katrina. *Professional Psychology: Research and Practice, 41*, 167–173. doi:10.1037/a0018116

Bandura, A. (1997). *Self-efficacy: The exercise of control.* New York, NY: Freeman.

Barnes, P. A., & Curtis, A. B. (2009). A national examination of partnerships among local health departments and faith communities in the United States. *Journal of Public Health Management and Practice, 15*, 253–263.

Barnes, S. L. (2005). Black church culture and community action. *Social Forces, 84*, 967–994. doi:10.1353/sof.2006.0003

Bauldry, S. (2006). *Positive support: Mentoring and depression among high-risk youth.* Retrieved from http://www.ppv.org/ppv/publications/assets/202_publication.pdf

Benes, K. M., Walsh, J. M., McMinn, M. R., Dominguez, A. W., & Aikins, D. C. (2000). Psychology and the church: An exemplar of psychology-clergy collaboration. *Professional Psychology: Research and Practice, 31*, 515–520. doi:10.1037/0735-7028.31.5.515

Berrien, J., McRoberts, O., & Winship, C. (2000). Religion and the Boston miracle: The effect of Black ministry on youth violence. In M. J. Bane, B. Coffin, & R. Thiemann (Eds.), *Who will provide? The changing role of religion in American social welfare* (pp. 266–285). Boulder, CO: Westview.

Beyerlein, K., & Chaves, M. (2003). The political activities of religious activities in the United States. *Journal for the Scientific Study of Religion, 42*, 229–246. doi:10.1111/1468-5906.00175

Bicknese, A. (1999). *The Teen Challenge drug treatment program in comparative perspective.* Evanston, IL: Northwestern University.

Biodiversity Project. (2002). *Americans and biodiversity: New perspectives in 2002.* Washington, DC: Beldon, Russonello, & Stuart.

Blank, M. B., Mahmood, M., Fox, J. C., & Guterbock, T. (2002). Alternative mental health services: The role of the Black church in the south. *American Journal of Public Health, 92*, 1668–1672. doi:10.2105/AJPH.92.10.1668

Boddie, S. C., & Cnaan, R. A. (2006). Concluding remarks: Common findings and challenges. *Journal of Religion and Spirituality in Social Work, 25*, 287–291.

Boorstein, M. (2010, September 22). AA original manuscript reveals debate on religion. *Washington Post*, p. A3.

Bourdieu, P. (1983). Forms of capital. In J. C. Richards (Ed.), *Handbook of theory and research for the sociology of education* (pp. 241–258). New York, NY: Greenwood Press.

Brown, R. K. (2006). Racial differences in congregation-based political activism. *Social Forces, 84*, 1581–1604. doi:10.1353/sof.2006.0045

Campbell, M. K., Denmark-Wahnefried, W., Symons, M., Kalsbeek, W. D., Dodds, J., Cowan, A., & McClelland, J. W. (1999). Fruit and vegetable consumption and the prevention of cancer: The Black Churches United for Better Health project. *American Journal of Public Health, 89*, 1390–1396. doi:10.2105/AJPH.89.9.1390

Campbell, M. K., Hudson, M. A., Resnicow, K., Blakeney, N., Pzxton, A., & Baskin, M. (2007). Church-based health promotion interventions: Evidence and lessons learned. *Annual Review of Public Health, 28*, 213–234. doi:10.1146/annurev.publhealth.28.021406.144016

Campbell, M. K., Motsinger, B. M., Ingram, A., Jewell, D., Makarushka, C., Beatty, B., & Denmark-Wahnefried, W. (2000). The North Carolina Black Churches United for Better Health Project: Intervention and process evaluation. *Health Education and Behavior, 27*, 241–253. doi:10.1177/109019810002700210

Charlton, J. (2007). Congregations and communities. In R. A. Cnaan & C. Milofsky (Eds.), *Handbook of community movements and local organizations* (pp. 267–280). New York, NY: Springer.

Chaves, M. (2004). *Congregations in America.* Cambridge, MA: Harvard University Press.

Christens, B. D., Hanlin, C. E., & Speer, P. W. (2007). Getting the social organism thinking: Strategy for systems change. *American Journal of Community Psychology, 39*, 229–238. doi:10.1007/s10464-007-9119-y

Cnaan, R. A., & Boddie, S. C. (2006). Setting the context: Assessing the effectiveness of faith-based social services. *Journal of Religion and Spirituality in Social Work, 25*, 5–18. doi:10.1300/J377v25n03_02

DeHaven, M. J., Hunter, I. B., Wilder, L., Walton, J. W., & Berry, J. (2004). Health programs in faith-based organizations: Are they effective? *American Journal of Public Health, 94*, 1030–1036. doi:10.2105/AJPH.94.6.1030

Djupe, P. A., & Gilbert, C. P. (2009). *The political influence of churches*. New York, NY: Cambridge University Press.

Dokecki, P. R., Newbrough, J. R., & O'Gorman, R. T. (2001). Toward a community-oriented action research framework for spirituality: Community psychological and theological perspectives. *Journal of Community Psychology, 29*, 497–518. doi:10.1002/jcop.1033

Dominguez, A. W., & McMinn, M. R. (2005). Collaboration through research: The multi-method church-based assessment process. In A. W. Dominguez & M. R. McMinn (Eds.), *Psychology and the church* (pp. 105–112). Hauppauge, NY: Nova Science.

Farley, C. (2004). *Amachi in brief*. Retrieved from http://www.ppv.org/ppv/publications/assets/167_publication.pdf

Ferguson, R. F., & Dickens, W. T. (Eds.). (1999). *Urban problems and community development*. Washington, DC: Brookings Institution Press.

Foley, M. W., & Hoge, D. R. (2007). *Religion and the new immigrants: How faith communities form our newest citizens*. New York, NY: Oxford University Press.

Fox, S. A., Stein, J. A., Gonzalez, R. E., Farrenkopf, M., & Dellinger, A. (1998). A trial to increase mammography utilization among Los Angeles Hispanic women. *Journal of Health Care for the Poor and Underserved, 9*, 309–321.

Francis, S. A., & Liverpool, J. (2009). A review of faith-based HIV prevention programs. *Journal of Religion and Health, 48*, 6–15. doi:10.1007/s10943-008-9171-4

Garringer, M. (2003). Making a difference in the spirit of kinship. *National Mentoring Center Bulletin, 12*, 3–4, 13–14. Retrieved from http://educationnorthwest.org/webfm_send/213

Giving USA. (2009). *The annual report on philanthropy for the year 2008*. Retrieved from http://www.charitablegift.org/docs/Annual-Report.pdf

Gold, E., Simon, E., Mundell, L., & Brown, C. (2004). Bringing community into the school reform picture. *Nonprofit and Voluntary Sector Quarterly, 33*, 54S–76S. doi:10.1177/0899764004265439

Goodstein, L. (2001, April 24). Church based projects lack data on results. *New York Times*. Retrieved from http://www.nytimes.com/2001/04/24/politics/24FAIT.html

Gottlieb, R. S. (2006). *A greener faith: Religious environmentalism and our planet's future*. New York, NY: Oxford University Press.

Green, J. C. (2007). *American congregations and social service programs: Results of a survey*. Retrieved from http://www.pewtrusts.org/uploadedFiles/wwwpew trustsorg/Reports/Religion_in_public_life/American%20Congregations%20Report1.pdf

Habitat for Humanity. (2010). *Church relations: Your church and Habitat*. Retrieved from http://www.habitat.org/cr

Hula, R. C., Jackson-Elmoore, C., & Reese, L. A. (2007). Mixing God's work and the public business: An exploration of faith-based service delivery. *Review of Policy Research, 24*, 67–89. doi:10.1111/j.1541-1338.2007.00268.x

Hula, R. C., Jackson-Elmoore, C., & Reese, L. A. (2008). *The emerging role of faith-based organizations in the low-income housing market*. Retrieved from http://aspe.hhs.gov/fbci/comp08/Hula.pdf

Husock, H. (2003). *Starting Amachi: The elements and operation of a volunteer-based social program*. Retrieved from http://www.urbanministry.org/files/starting-amachi.pdf

Johnson, B. (2004). Religious programs and recidivism among former inmates in prison fellowship programs: A long-term follow-up study. *Justice Quarterly, 21*, 329–354. doi:10.1080/07418820400095831

Johnson, B. R. (2002). Assessing the impact of religious programs and prison industry on recidivism: An exploratory study. *Texas Journal of Corrections, 28*, 7–11.

Johnson, B. R., Larson, D. B., & Pitts, T. C. (1997). Religious programs, institutional adjustment, and recidivism among former inmates in Prison Fellowship Programs. *Justice Quarterly, 14*, 145–166. doi:10.1080/07418829700093251

Jucovy, L. (2003). *Amachi: Mentoring children of prisoners in Philadelphia*. Retrieved from http://www.ppv.org/ppv/publications/assets/21_publication.pdf

Kennedy, B. M., Paeratakul, S., Champagne, C. M., Ryan, D. H., Harsha, D. W., McGee, B., & Bogle, M. L. (2005). A pilot church-based weight loss program for African-American adults using church members as health educators: A comparison of individual and group intervention. *Ethnicity and Disease, 15*, 373–378.

Kleidman, R. (2008, August). *Relational organizing and the dilemma of participatory democracy*. Paper presented at the annual meeting of the American Sociological Association, Boston, MA. Retrieved from http://allacademic.com/meta/p241351_index.html

Lane, J., & Lanza-Kaduce, L. (2007). Before you open the doors: Ten lessons from Florida's faith and community-based delinquency initiative. *Evaluation Review, 31*, 121–152. doi:10.1177/0193841X06294271

Lopez, V. A., & Castro, F. G. (2006). Participation and program outcomes in a church-based cancer prevention program for Hispanic women. *Journal of Community Health, 31*, 343–362. doi:10.1007/s10900-006-9016-6

Maton, K. I. (2008). Empowering community settings: Agents of individual development, community betterment, and positive social change. *American Journal of Community Psychology, 41*, 4–21. doi:10.1007/s10464-007-9148-6

Maton, K. I., Dodgen, D., Sto. Domingo, M., & Larsen, D. (2005). Religion as a meaning system: Policy implications for the new millennium. *Journal of Social Issues, 61*, 847–867. doi:10.1111/j.1540-4560.2005.00435.x

Maton, K. I., & Wells, E. A. (1995). Religion as a community resource for well-being: Prevention, healing, and empowerment pathways. *Journal of Social Issues, 51*, 177–193. doi:10.1111/j.1540-4560.1995.tb01330.x

Molock, S. D., Matlin, S., Barksdale, C., Puri, R., & Lyles, J. (2008). Developing suicide prevention programs for African American youth in African American churches. *Suicide and Life-Threatening Behavior, 38*, 323–333. doi:10.1521/suli.2008.38.3.323

Morris, A. (1984). *The origins of the civil rights movement: Black communities organizing for change.* New York, NY: Free Press.

National Congress for Community Economic Development. (1999). *Coming of age: Trends and achievements of community-based development organizations.* Washington, DC: Author.

National Congress for Community Economic Development. (2006). *Reaching new heights: Trends and achievements of community-based development organizations, 5th national community development census.* Washington, DC: Author.

Pargament, K. I., Falgout, K., Ensing, D. S., Reilly, B., Silverman, M., Van Haitsma, K., & Warren, R. (1991). The congregation development program: Data-based consultation with churches and synagogues. *Professional Psychology: Research and Practice, 22*, 393–404. doi:10.1037/0735-7028.22.5.393

Pargament, K. I., & Maton, K. I. (2000). Religion in American life: A community psychology perspective. In J. Rappaport & E. Seidman (Eds.), *Handbook of community psychology* (pp. 495–522). New York, NY: Kluwer Academic/Plenum.

Prison Fellowship. (2012). *Mission, vision, and values statements.* Retrieved from http://www.prisonfellowship.org/about/mission-vision-values

Putnam, R. D. (2001). *Bowling alone: The collapse and revival of American community.* New York, NY: Simon & Schuster.

Ramakrishnan, S. K. (2006). Political participation and civic voluntarism. In T. Lee, S. K. Ramakrishnan, & R. Ramírez (Eds.), *Transforming politics, transforming America: The political and civic incorporation of immigrants in the United States* (pp. 31–46). Charlottesville: University of Virginia Press.

Samuel-Hodge, C. D., Keyserling, T. C., Park, S., Johnston, L. F., Gizlice, Z., & Bandiwala, S. I. (2009). A randomized trial of a church-based diabetes self-management program for African Americans with type 2 diabetes. *The Diabetes Educator, 35*, 439–454. doi:10.1177/0145721709333270

Schneider, J. A. (2006). *Social capital and welfare reform: Organizations, congregations, and communities.* New York, NY: Columbia University Press.

Smidt, C. (2003). *Religion as social capital: Producing the common good.* Waco, TX: Baylor.

Speer, P. W., Ontkush, M., Schmitt, B., Raman, P., Jackson, C., Rengert, K., & Peterson, N. A. (2003). The intentional exercise of power: Community organizing in Camden, NJ. *Journal of Community and Applied Social Psychology, 13*, 399–408. doi:10.1002/casp.745

Stephen Ministries. (2010). *Stephen Series media fact sheet.* Retrieved from http://www.stephenministries.org

Sternberg, Z., Munschauer, F. E., III, Carrow, S. S., & Sternberg, E. (2006). Faith-placed cardiovascular health promotion: A framework for contextual and organizational factors underlying program success. *Health Education Research, 22*, 619–629. doi:10.1093/her/cyl124

Swarts, H. J. (2008). *Organizing urban America: Secular and faith-based progressive movements.* Minneapolis: University of Minnesota Press.

Wald, K. D., & Calhoun-Brown, A. (2007). *Religion and politics in the United States* (5th ed.). Oxford, England: Rowman & Littlefield.

Williams, J. E. (2002). Linking beliefs to collective action: Politicized religious beliefs and the civil rights movement. *Sociological Forum, 17*, 203–222. doi:10.1023/A:1016085129064

Williams, R. H. (2003). Religious social movements in the public sphere: Organization ideology, and activism. In M. Dillon (Ed.), *Handbook of the sociology of religion* (pp. 315–330). New York, NY: Cambridge University Press.

Winett, R. A., Anderson, E. S., Wojcik, J. R., Winett, S. G., & Bowden, T. (2007). Guide to health: Nutrition and physical activity outcomes of a group-randomized trial of an Internet-based intervention in churches. *Annals of Behavioral Medicine, 33*, 251–261. doi:10.1007/BF02879907

Wood, R. L. (2003). Religion, faith-based community organizing, and the struggle for justice. In M. Dillon (Ed.), *Handbook of the sociology of religion* (pp. 385–399). New York, NY: Cambridge University Press.

Wood, R. L., & Warren, M. R. (2002). A different face of faith-based politics: Social capital and community organizing in the public arena. *International*

Journal of Sociology and Social Policy, 22, 6–54. doi:10.1108/01443330210790148

Wuthnow, R. (2004). *Saving America: Faith-based services and the future of civil society*. Princeton, NJ: Princeton University Press.

Wuthnow, R., Hackett, C., & Hsu, B. Y. (2004). The effectiveness and trustworthiness of faith-based and other service organizations: A study of recipient's perceptions. *Journal for the Scientific Study of Religion, 43*, 1–17. doi:10.1111/j.1468-5906.2004.00214.x

Yanek, L. R., Becker, D., Moy, T., Gittelsohn, J., & Koffman, D. (2001). Project Joy: Faith-based cardiovascular health promotion for African American women. *Public Health Reports, 116* (Suppl. 1), 68–81. doi:10.1093/phr/116.S1.68

Zanis, D. A., & Cnaan, R. A. (2006). Social service research and religion: Thoughts about how to measure intervention-based impact. *Journal of Religion and Spirituality in Social Work, 25*, 83–104.

Part V

FUTURE DIRECTIONS FOR AN APPLIED PSYCHOLOGY OF RELIGION AND SPIRITUALITY

CHAPTER 33

PATHWAYS TOWARD GRADUATE TRAINING IN THE CLINICAL PSYCHOLOGY OF RELIGION AND SPIRITUALITY: A SPIRITUAL COMPETENCIES MODEL

William Hathaway

Religious adherence and spirituality are prevalent within the general population of North American culture and are widespread among those presenting in clinical settings (Saunders, Miller, & Bright, 2010). Formal training venues to acquire competence to address the religious and spiritual dimensions of clinical care are increasing but are still disproportionately rare (Bartoli, 2007; Russell & Yarhouse, 2006). The pathways to acquire such spiritual practice competencies remain disjointed, with only a few structured to systematically instill targeted knowledge, skills, and attitudes.

WHAT IS THE "CLINICAL PSYCHOLOGY OF RELIGION AND SPIRITUALITY"?

The clinical psychology of religion and spirituality is still in a relatively early stage of development. The phrase "clinical psychology of religion" has not been formally defined but was used at least as early as 1991 by Malony. The topic was the focus of the influential volume titled *Religion and the Clinical Practice of Psychology* edited by Shafranske (1996) in the mid-1990s. Shafranske (2005) subsequently wrote about an "applied psychology of religion" as a domain within clinical and counseling psychology. The second volume of this handbook focuses on "the applied psychology of religion and spirituality," which includes but goes beyond clinical and counseling psychology and psychotherapeutic methods to encompass other subdisciplines and practices of psychology that seek to improve the human condition. In Europe, DeMarinis and Wikström (1996) used the phrase "clinical psychology of religion" to refer to both pastoral and psychology of religion applications pertaining to counseling, whereas Van Uden and Pieper (2003) developed a "clinical psychology of religion" course offered within a interdisciplinary master's program at Tilburg University. Van Uden and Pieper offered the following definition:

> Clinical psychology of religion applies insights from general psychology of religion to the field of the clinical psychologist. Clinical psychology of religion can be defined as that part of the psychology of religion dealing with the relation between religion, worldview and mental health. Like the clinical psychologist, the clinical psychologist of religion deals with psychodiagnostics and psychotherapy, but concentrates on the role religion or worldview plays in mental health problems. (p. 156)

All of these formulations follow the construal of clinical psychology as an applied psychological science. Although this notion conveys some productive ways of thinking about the relationship of science and practice, it suggests a strict basic versus applied science dichotomy that tends to obfuscate some distinct aspects of clinical psychology. Clinical

DOI: 10.1037/14046-033
APA Handbook of Psychology, Religion, and Spirituality: Vol. 2. An Applied Psychology of Religion and Spirituality, K. I. Pargament (Editor-in-Chief)

psychology is not simply the application of psychological science to the practice context. Rather it is also a type of field science, as Witmer (1907) noted when he coined the phrase *clinical psychology*. There is overlap with a pure experimental or laboratory psychology, but clinical psychology also has distinct epistemic strategies, tacit knowledge to be mastered, and praxis virtues. The importance of such a realization was noted as early as 1947 by Hiltner. As a subdomain of clinical psychology, the clinical psychology of religion has the same distinct characteristics of a field science and professional practice domain. Consequently, quality clinical psychology of religion and spirituality will not simply be the application of psychology of religion and spirituality research to a practice setting but also will be characterized by competent clinical practice as it overlaps the religious or spiritual domain. A growing body of research support is emerging that may inform the contour of such competent practice from an evidence-based perspective (Hook et al., 2010).

THE COMPETENCIES PERSPECTIVE IN PROFESSIONAL PSYCHOLOGY

There has been an increasing emphasis on competency training models in recent years in clinical and counseling psychology. In the 1990s, these trends began to increasingly affect guidelines for professional accrediting bodies as well as recommended training models from professional associations (Kenkel & Peterson, 2009). In 2002, an influential Competencies Conference was held in Scottsdale, Arizona, that described various competencies in professional psychology and recommended more comprehensive assessment of their instantiation in training (Kaslow et al., 2004). Borden and McIlvried (2009) emphasized that for training models to effectively inculcate professional competencies, they must adequately assess the "knowledge, skills, and attitudes (KSAs) embodied in the . . . competency areas" (p. 45).

Depending on whether one is engaging a particular practice niche as a generalist or specialist, different levels of types of knowledge, skill, and attitude may be needed to meet the standard of competent practice. Generalist and specialist forms of practice may require specification of different competency levels and assessments. For instance, the prerequisite practice skills for a neuropsychologist to perform a neuropsychological evaluation and for a generalist to conduct a neuropsychological screening are different.

Ideally, effective clinical psychology of religion and spirituality graduate training would inculcate explicit and targeted competencies in its students and assess the extent to which the KSAs indicative of competency attainment have been instilled. It would do so in a manner commensurate with the level of competency that is being targeted. Thus, the competency perspective may help clarify what is desired from a graduate training context in this domain. At present, there is no formal agreement on which KSAs should be targeted in graduate clinical psychology of religion and spirituality training. Still, there is some convergence in the growing literature in this domain that can be productively summarized using a competencies perspective.

The George Washington University Institute of Spirituality and Health (GWish) administers an award program originally launched by David Larson's National Institute for Healthcare Research in 1998 for health care training models that effectively incorporate spirituality. Dozens of GWish awards have now been given leading to an emerging set of KSAs that should characterize such training in health-related programs. Much of the work done in these award-winning programs has extended or refined the model curriculum developed by Larson's National Institute for Healthcare Research in 1997.

Josephson, Peteet, and Tasman (2010) provided an overview of recent efforts in psychiatry to formulate a training model to appropriately engage religion in therapy. They noted that the "psychiatric literature of the past generation either neglected religion or linked it almost entirely with psychopathology" (p. 571). A major impetus to alter this pattern has arisen from the Accreditation Council for Graduate Medical Education's explicit mandate that psychiatry training programs address religious and spiritual issues. This mandate moves the medical community to more intentionally incorporate religious or spiritual considerations in practice as a coping resource, as relevant contributing factors, and as an important meaning-making framework for clients who contend with medical issues. Similar calls have emerged for formal inclusion of religion and spirituality in training of psychiatrists in other countries in recent years.

Josephson et al. (2010) have applied the resulting KSA curricular objectives about religion and spirituality to psychiatric training. Psychiatrists with spiritually competent practice are to possess knowledge sufficient for "understanding the spiritual/religious factors that affect the course and treatment of psychiatric disorders." They are to demonstrate skills "diagnosing, assessing and formulating treatment plans for patients, with an understanding of spiritual/religious experiences." And they are to display a "non-judgmental attitude when eliciting a spiritual history" (Josephson et al., 2010, p. 600).

CLINICAL PSYCHOLOGY OF RELIGION AND SPIRITUALITY COMPETENCIES

A number of clinical psychology of religion and spirituality competencies have been advanced as important skills for practitioners in this domain (Aten & Leach; 2009; Pargament, 2007; Richards & Bergin, 2000, 2005; Saunders, Miller & Bright, 2010; Shafranske, 2005). For instance, acquisition of specialized knowledge, assessment skills, intervention approaches, and multicultural competencies as well as awareness of relevant process and ethical considerations have all been recommended as vital for clinical practice with religious and spiritual issues.

Exhibit 33.1 proposes a list of spiritually focused curriculum and training objectives for professional psychology modeled on those advanced for psychiatry by Josephson et al. (2010). The relevant knowledge competency to be inculcated by training is conceptualized as *understanding clinically relevant spiritual and religious factors*. This competence has less of a psychopathology focus than the psychiatry knowledge competency presented by Josephson et al. because psychological assessment is not limited to psychopathology but also may include assessment of normal-range psychological adjustment, as in career assessments. Competent professional psychology practice with religious or spiritual issues

Exhibit 33.1
Curriculum Objectives for Spiritual Competency in Psychology Training

Knowledge: understanding clinically relevant spiritual/religious factors, including—basic understanding of major faith traditions and their varied, lived forms (Richards & Bergin, 2000); demographics of religious and spiritual beliefs in various populations (Richards & Bergin, 2000); appreciating the multidimensional nature spirituality and religion (Nelson, 2009; Richards & Bergin, 2000); distinguishing the role of spirituality and faith in coping, maladjustment, and adjustment (Pargament, 2007); accurately differentiating pathology indicative of religious and spiritual phenomena from those nonindicative of pathology (Pargament, 2007); possessing awareness of the current evidence base for spiritually oriented or accommodative practice (Hook, Worthington, Davis, Gartner, Jennings, & Hook, 2010); and articulating ethical issues pertinent to clinical practice with religious or spiritual issues (Barnett & Johnson, 2011; Hathaway, 2011).

Skills: diagnosing, assessing, formulating and implementing treatment plans with clinically appropriate incorporation of religious or spiritual features, including—taking an adequate and clinically relevant religious or spiritual history (Richards & Bergin, 2005; Sperry, 2012); adequate consideration of religious or spiritual factors in assessment (Hathaway & Childers, 2013; Richards & Bergin, 2005). discriminating maladaptive and adaptive forms of client religiousness/spirituality (Pargament, 2007) conducting appropriate spiritual or religious interventions (Aten, McMinn, & Worthington, 2011; Plante, 2009); managing clinically problematic biases sufficient to prevent adverse impact on treatment (Wiggins, 2009); and demonstrating ability to work collaboratively with religious professionals (McMinn & Dominguez, 2005).

Attitudes: self-aware, respectful, professional, and scientific attitude toward religious and spiritual issues in practice, including—to respect and take seriously the religious and spiritual beliefs of patients (Hathaway, 2011); awareness of one's own religious or spiritual beliefs, experiences, and views (Wiggins, 2009); and tolerance of challenges arising from navigating multiple domains of diversity that often arise when addressing religious or spiritual issues in practice (Hathaway & Ripley, 2009).

Note. From *Religion and Psychiatry: Beyond Boundaries* (p. 600), by P. J. Verhagen, H. M. van Praag, J. J. Lopez-Ibor Jr., J. L. Cox, and D. Moussaoui (Eds.), 2010, Hoboken, NJ: Wiley-Blackwell. Copyright 2010 by John Wiley & Sons Ltd. Adapted with permission.

will require skills in incorporating religious and spiritual considerations or accommodations in treatment planning, given the predominant role conducting psychotherapy plays in psychological practice. In terms of attitudinal competency, effective training in the clinical psychology of religion and spirituality would instill self-awareness among graduates regarding their personal religious or spiritual views and history and a respectful demeanor toward client spirituality and religiousness without sacrificing graduates' professional and science attitudes.

This summary of the KSAs that reflect competency in the clinical psychology of religion and spirituality is not intended as an exhaustive formulation but rather as a description of the scope of the targeted competencies that are already indicated by the available literature. The training level for these desired competencies may vary based on whether the goal of training is to produce a generalist level of competency that should characterize typical clinical skill, a specialized set of proficiencies for practitioners developing a specialized practice niche with religious and spiritual issues, or an interdisciplinary type of practice that involves full competence both as a clinician and religious counseling professional (Hathaway, 2011). Before proceeding to a discussion of the training contexts in which attainment of these competencies might be pursued, I explore some particular challenges with each competency area.

DOMAIN KNOWLEDGE

An extensive knowledge base relevant to the clinical psychology of religion and spirituality exists despite the relatively few places where this information is consolidated specifically for clinical consumption. Knowledge about the common characteristics of particular faiths, unique forms of spirituality, pathways to obtain such information, the psychological correlates of facets of religiousness, and the emerging literature regarding spiritually oriented clinical practice are examples of some of the relevant knowledge to be mastered in the domain. Although an extensive literature exists in religious studies fields, the relevant literature from the psychology of religion for clinical practice will be most important to include in such preparation, such as the rich research that has emerged on religion and coping (Pargament, 1997, 2007).

Religious studies departments or programs are common at many universities. It is very rare, however, for graduate training programs in psychology or the related mental health professions to offer specific and systematic coverage of religion in their psychologically oriented training programs. Brawer, Handal, Fabricatore, Roberts, and Wada-Johnston (2002) found that more than 80% of training directors at American Psychological Association (APA)-accredited doctoral programs reported having no such training in their curriculum. Until this pattern is remedied, it is likely that students who desire graduate training in the clinical psychology of religion and spirituality will need to seek out either those relatively rare graduate training contexts in which it is present or the unsystematic adjunctive training opportunities outside of their graduate programs.

Religion represents one of the most ubiquitous and polyform facets of human experience. Various encyclopedic listings of religion from a religious studies or sociology of religion perspective illustrate the scope of the domain. J. Gordon Melton's (2009) influential *Encyclopedia of American Religions* described more than 2,500 different religions with adherents in North America. A classic approach to comparative religious studies is to compare the major beliefs, practices, social structures, and values of the different organized faiths (Smith, 1991). Although still relatively infrequent, some scholars have attempted to provide descriptions of the characteristic features of the normative forms of major faiths in clinical publications. In a recent text on counseling and spirituality, Gold (2010) condensed a description of the key beliefs of a number of major faith traditions in the space of several pages. Richards and Bergin (2000) edited a several-hundred-page volume exploring aspects of religious diversity relevant to psychotherapy with coverage of specific faith traditions describing such features as their prevalence and patterns of adherence, beliefs, practices, moral prescriptions and proscriptions, and history. The contributors explored relevant clinical considerations for therapeutic practice with adherents of the described tradition. The text also offers a comparison of the similarities and differences of the "official positions" (Richards & Bergin, 2000, p. 478) of the various religious traditions explored in the text on contemporary moral issues that have particular relevance for therapy, including abortion and birth control, sexuality, marriage and divorce, alcohol and drug use, and suicide and euthanasia. They offered a similar set of reflections regarding the attitudes toward therapy, emic healing traditions, characteristic clinical issues associated with religious tradition, and recommendations for assessment and treatment.

Clinicians who are unfamiliar with a client's particular religious tradition can benefit from information about the paradigmatic or characteristic form of the religion. In addition, clinicians could gain from reading scholarly accounts of common faith traditions in any of the plethora of religious studies texts that are available. In some cases, background reading on less prevalent religions may be advised when those traditions are present in the psychologist's clinical population.

Despite the importance of studying the general characteristics of various faith traditions, this classic approach possesses weaknesses. The psychosocial consequences of a client's religion will be most directly a consequence of their particular spirituality, and this often differs from the official or normative form of a faith tradition that clients profess. Religious studies scholars have placed increasing emphasis on studying lived religion as a highly idiosyncratic and fluid phenomenon in contrast to the more universal and crystalized accounts of the particular traditions that are typical of the comparative religions approach (McGuire, 2008; Sharpe, 2009). For instance, Ellison, Acevedo, and Ramos-Wada (2011) found that Latino evangelicals more strongly oppose same-sex marriage than Latino Catholics despite the conservative official position of Catholicism on this matter. The researchers noted the disparity between the lived form of Catholicism among many Latino Catholics for whom Catholicism is primarily an ethnic identity or among those who identify with progressive forms of Catholicism on other issues and those who are conventionally observant Catholics (e.g., regular mass attendance, prolife attitude on abortion). The authors speculated that Latino evangelicals tend to embrace this identification as a matter of doctrinal and personal choice rather than as part of a cultural identification and thus are more likely to conform to the normative convictions of the faith tradition. It is important to add that empirical studies of members of particular religious traditions illuminate the diversity of practices and beliefs within various faiths as well as key differences between them (see Volume 1, Part IV, this handbook). Consequently, it is important for clinicians to be aware of the varieties of lived religion or spiritualties present among their client population and not merely the major contours of the organized faiths they profess.

SPIRITUALLY ORIENTED PRACTICE SKILLS

There is now a growing literature on assessment approaches that focus on the contributions of religion and spirituality to psychological functioning (see Chapter 5 in this volume) and spiritually oriented treatment (see Parts II and III in this volume). Although religious and spiritual issues may be viewed as highly salient to the clinical situation by many clients, most psychologists do not routinely assess religious or spiritual issues in practice (Hathaway, Scott, & Garver, 2004). When such assessment is done, it is frequently as part of a diagnostic formulation considering whether some aspect of client religiousness is indicative of a clinical issue. The introduction of the Religious or Spiritual Problem V-Code in the *Diagnostic and Statistical Manual of Mental* Disorders (4th ed., text revision; *DSM–IV–TR*; American Psychiatric Association, 2000) represented an attempt to promote a nonpathological focus on religious or spiritual concerns in treatment. Evidence indicates, however, that the V-Code is used infrequently and that religious or spiritual concerns remain a neglected area of diagnostic consideration. There is little formal incentive in currently influential psychopathology nosologies to routinely evaluate religious or spiritual issues during assessment.

Some efforts have been made to alter this pattern. Peteet, Lu, and Narrow (2011) have advanced a research agenda for the fifth edition of the *DSM* that identifies religious or spiritual issues that should be considered in the context of psychiatric disorders, such as with major depression or the anxiety disorders. In addition to diagnostic considerations, it is important to assess the role of religion and spirituality more generally in psychological functioning, for example, in offering frameworks for meaning, forms of coping, supportive communities of faith, or prompting spiritual struggles. In addition, in Hathaway (2003) I have argued that religious and spiritual functioning represents a significant domain of functioning that could be adversely affected by psychological disorders. Rather than focusing on problematic forms of religion and spirituality as symptomatic of pathology, this proposal suggests that religious and spiritual functioning be assessed as a potential domain that could be impaired by pathology just as a clinician would assess adverse impacts on occupational or social adjustment across a spectrum of presenting problems. So construed, every clinical situation could present with a religious footprint, and thus religious and spiritual assessment should be a routine area of assessment.

Despite these efforts at encouraging more routine consideration of clinically relevant religious or spiritual issues in practice, very few clinicians have received formal training in how to assess these issues in a clinically appropriate and relevant manner. Furthermore, most religious or spiritual measures have not been developed for clinical use or with clinical norms. Hathaway and Childers (2013) have provided an example of a religious measure developed specifically for clinically relevant use. Using a child case, they illustrate how such tools may be useful in diagnostic assessment, treatment planning, and outcome assessment. Unless such clinically relevant religious and spiritual measures are developed and promulgated, it will not be surprising if the domain continues to be underassessed in practice.

There is a small but growing literature on religiously accommodative treatment, particularly utilizing cognitive therapies (Hook et al., 2010; see Chapter 8 in this volume). Expanding resources also describe with concrete examples how to engage in spiritually oriented practice in clinically appropriate ways (Aten & Leach, 2009; Aten, McMinn, & Worthington, 2011; Nelson, 2009; Pargament, 2007; Plante, 2009; Richards & Bergin, 2005; Sperry & Shafranske, 2005). Evaluative studies indicate that religiously accommodative forms of treatment (i.e., standard approaches to treatment that include religious elements specific to a particular religious tradition) yield comparable or better outcomes when contrasted with nonaccommodative or standard forms of treatment. Additionally, accommodative treatments may produce significantly better spiritual or religious outcomes, such as perceived increased closeness to God (see Chapter 34 in this volume). There is also an a body of research on the use of spiritually integrated treatments that are appropriate for people from a range of religious traditions or for those who may not adhere to any particular religion (Pargament, 2007). The use of meditative interventions, forgiveness protocols, or the fostering of resiliency-bolstering virtues such as gratitude provide examples of such spiritually integrated treatments (Coelho, Canter, & Ernst, 2007; Emmons & McCullough, 2004; Plante, 2009).

Yet researchers must address some challenges before religiously accommodative or spiritually integrated treatments can become a standard approach to therapy. As Hook et al. (2010) have noted, there is no standard form such accommodation takes, making it difficult to build a strong evidentiary base or to disseminate the treatment approaches in training contexts. To the extent that the approaches utilize religious and spiritual techniques, they might take varied forms, such as the therapeutic use of prayer, scriptural bibliotherapy, or God-image work. This lack of standardization of currently researched religiously accommodative treatments makes it difficult to disseminate these interventions to therapists. Some influential approaches of spiritually integrated treatments, such as those associated with the mindfulness therapies, offer promise in this regard (Coelho et al., 2007).

SPIRITUALITY AND RELIGION-COMPATIBLE ATTITUDES

The long-standing prevalence of an anti- or irreligious attitude in contemporary psychology has been well documented elsewhere (Sperry & Shafranske,

2005; Wiggins, 2009; see also Chapter 2 in this volume). Although there is evidence of increased engagement of the religious and spiritual domain in psychological literature, it remains a relatively infrequent focus in clinical practice. Propst (1988) found that clinicians who do not share the religious tradition or convictions of a client could utilize a religiously accommodative cognitive therapy protocol to produce clinical outcomes at least equal to those of therapists who are religiously matched to the client. Such a treatment does not require therapists to buy into the client's faith tradition but rather merely that they engage the client's faith in a respectful and productive manner.

Such research offers incentive for psychologists who may not be personally religious to consider spiritually oriented treatment approaches with suitably disposed clients, but another multicultural competence issue may arise with religious clients. Religious diversity may also create tensions with other diversity domains. Evolving gender roles may be odds with gender-based role expectations in certain conventional religions (see Volume 1, Chapter 20, this handbook). Conventionally religious attitudes about homosexual behavior may present an obstacle to affirmative responses to sexual minorities (see Volume 1, Chapter 34, this handbook).

How can psychologists manage such diversity domain conflicts? Mintz and Bieschke (2009) have proposed a model training values statement that provides guidance on how to navigate such situations respectfully. To the extent that psychology training contexts tend to favor more progressive values about sexual identity, divorce, abortion, or other areas in which tensions with conventional religious traditions may arise, there is a risk for psychologists to model a dismissive attitude toward more conservative religious values or faith commitments. The challenge is for training contexts to mitigate such biases by modeling respectful and inclusive attitudes toward all areas of diversity and by illustrating how to deal with the tensions that arise when such conflicts occur (see Chapter 3 in this volume). Savage (2011) has provided a model of how to navigate tensions between pluralistic value systems inherent in much of professional practice and conventional Muslim religious mores. She has demonstrated positive outcomes in promoting more pluralistic as opposed to "radicalized" values among Muslim participants in a training program titled Being Muslim, Being British. The program is premised on the notion that promoting more complex and integrative thinking about value conflicts helps participants resolve these tensions in a way that makes more room for divergent values while maintaining congruence with one's prior faith tradition.

TRAINING PATHWAYS FOR THE CLINICAL PSYCHOLOGY OF RELIGION AND SPIRITUALITY

The *Ethical Principles of Psychologists and Code of Conduct* (the Ethics Code; APA, 2010) and the *Guidelines and Principles for Accreditation* (APA, 2009) indicate that at least some ability to practice competently when encountering religious and spiritual issues should be an entry-level skill instilled by all professional training programs. Yet as noted, there is evidence that most graduate training contexts for professional psychologists are not providing systematic training aimed at achieving this goal (Brawer et al., 2002; Russell & Yarhouse, 2006). There is even some evidence that applicants with explicit religious or spiritual identifications or interests seeking to enter graduate training for professional psychology may encounter negative attitudes or actions toward those interests by the training programs. For instance, Gartner (1986) found that graduate programs in psychology were less likely to offer admission to student's whose applications expressed religious adherence and participation than identical applications minus the mentions of religiousness.

Despite the modal unenthusiastic posture toward the clinical psychology of religion and spirituality among most training programs, there is a growing set of graduate training options in this domain. Exhibit 33.2 provides a list of training programs falling into each of the distinct training types. These include faith-identified professional psychology programs that specialize in the clinical psychology of religion and spirituality from a particular faith tradition or related group of traditions (Johnson, Campbell, & Dykstra, 1997), nonsectarian religiously

Exhibit 33.2
Examples of Graduate Training Programs Relevant to the Clinical Psychology of Religion and Spirituality

Faith-Identified "Integrative" Doctoral Programs
Azusa Pacific University
Biola University (Rosemead)
Fuller Theological Seminary
George Fox University
Institute for Psychological Science
Regent University
Seattle Pacific University
Wheaton College
Religiously Associated Doctoral Programs
Baylor University
Brigham Young University
Loma Linda University
Pepperdine University

Nonsectarian Spiritually Oriented Doctoral Programs
Institute for Transpersonal Psychology
Saybrook Graduate School
Standard Doctoral Programs With Clinical Psychology of Religion and Spirituality Niches
Boston University
Bowling Green State University
Columbia University
Forest Institute
Georgia Southern University
Indiana State University
University of California, Davis
University of Connecticut
University of Denver
Virginia Commonwealth University

associated programs, nonsectarian spiritually oriented programs, and the presence of psychologists with expertise in the clinical psychology of religion and spirituality who can serve as mentors in secular programs.

Faith-Identified Programs

The faith-identified programs typically offer extensive and intensive training in spiritually focused training. Although they often may provide more training in dealing with a religiously diverse client population than most psychology doctoral programs and are typically APA-accredited, they assume their institution's explicit, underlying religious worldview. In terms of the proposed spiritual competency objectives for graduate psychology training, faith-identified programs provide extensive opportunities to pursue the relevant KSA objectives throughout the preinternship experience.

The eight programs listed in Exhibit 33.2 all share a goal of explicitly integrating professional psychology training with a distinctive Christian worldview. Some of the host institutions for these programs are identified more closely with particular forms of Christian adherence, such as evangelical forms of Protestant Christianity. Many include faculty from the spectrum of Christian traditions. Exhibit 33.2 contains only doctoral programs that have this explicit faith integrative goal in training. Dozens of masters-based programs pursue a similarly explicitly integrative training goal. Evangel University, an integrative program at an institution affiliated with the Assemblies of God, offers a masters of science degree in clinical psychology that has a good reputation for masters-level psychology training. Despite the solid example of programs such as the one at Evangel, there is considerable variability in the quality of professional training between the faith-identified master's programs, perhaps in part because they do not typically have to satisfy professional accreditation standards.

Although the particular Christian traditions vary (e.g., Catholic, evangelical, neocharismatic, varied Protestant) in these programs, they share a common vision of engaging all of psychology training from their faith-based education mission. Some of the frequent strategies utilized to achieve this goal include the hiring of faculty who share the faith perspectives and mission of the programs or host institutions, recruiting students who desire training consonant with the faith-based mission (some of the settings require students to sign a statement of religious faith whereas others do not), augmentation of standard psychology curriculum with theological or spiritual courses, mentorship in clinical psychology of religion and spirituality research and practice, frequent inclusion of religious or spiritual content and topics within the standard psychology coursework, and the incorporation of spiritual formation components that foster spiritual growth and awareness from a Christian perspective. Extensive coverage of spiritual-oriented clinical practice occurs in these settings.

One might suspect that the Christian emphasis within these programs could create a myopic clinical psychology of religion and spirituality competence that is delimited to the Christian domain. Although the majority of the faith-integrative instruction reflects a religiously conservative or conventional Christian tradition, these programs also offer more exposure to non-Christian religious or spiritual issues than is common in psychology training. A number of the programs require coursework in the psychology of religion that includes coverage of psychological research on multiple faith traditions.

Faculty and students from such programs are sometimes met with suspicion by other members of the profession. For instance, students from the faith-based programs have been asked questions on internship interviews about whether they received training in standard assessment or treatment approaches and whether they could work with someone who does not share his or her faith. Consequently, a substantial amount of discussion occurs in these programs regarding how to navigate the tensions that arise from particular and explicit faith identification with other professional roles and areas of diversity.

Are these programs successful in inculcating such multicultural competency? Graduates from these programs have successfully entered the field and functioned as professional practitioners in the spectrum of practice contexts since Fuller opened the first integrative doctoral program in 1965. Seven of the programs are APA accredited and have satisfied APA's Commission on Accreditation (CoA), having met the same expectations all other APA-accredited programs are held to.

Still, some have criticized a number of these programs for invoking the CoA's *Guidelines and Principles for Accreditation of Programs in Professional Psychology* (G&P) controversial footnote 4 (APA, 2009). It is beyond the scope of this article to fully explore the controversy, but some general points will be made to inform readers about the implications for graduate training. The CoA's G&P require educational environments to value diversity both in their construction and training foci. Footnote 4 recognizes that religious preferences may be used in admissions, retention, and hiring to the extent allowed by the U.S. Constitution. The programs must make such preferences known to applicants and typically do so through various published statements on program websites, brochures, applications, and other materials. In addition, the faith-based programs tend to require members of their communities (faculty, students, and staff) to agree to a code of conduct.

The conduct codes may prohibit certain behaviors that are viewed as contrary to tenets of the faith communities, such as alcohol use, pornography, or extramarital sex. Some specifically prohibit homosexual behavior. Although these programs do not exclude applicants based on sexual orientation, the conventionally religious proscription of homosexual behavior is viewed as problematic by the footnote 4 detractors. For those who find themselves outside of the footnote 4 preferred categories, the accommodation of such preferences with regard to homosexuality or religious belief represents an accommodation of institutionalized prejudices and discriminatory practices.

From the perspective of footnote 4 programs, such policies are intended to make possible a community of spiritually likeminded psychologists and trainees who can work on the instantiation of a professional and scientific psychology within their particular religious forms of life. Such religiously congruent academic communities reflect the constitutionally protected liberties essential to the exploration and actualization of their life visions.

None of this is understood to be grounds to ill prepare students for professional practice in psychology. Footnote 4 programs argue that they are able to train students to effectively work with clients who differ from the therapist on religious or spiritual grounds as well as to work with clients for whom religion and spirituality are not personally salient. These programs also note that their graduates are frequently able to gain access to conventional religious communities that may be either unwilling or slow to engage secular providers, thus allowing a more diverse practice scope within psychology than would exist without the faith-identified programs.

Regardless of what one thinks about the CoA's G&P footnote 4, the general intent of the faith-identified programs is to explore the overlap of professional psychology training and a particular faith tradition (or related set of traditions). This means that a student who did not share this goal probably would be asked to invest a great deal of work engaged in training that may not be relevant to his or her interests or career goals than would be the case in other types of programs. Thus, it makes sense for students who would not share the mission of the faith-identified programs to pursue other training options.

A special issue of the *Journal of Psychology and Christianity* provided additional information to guide students in deciding whether to seek admissions to a faith-identified program. Faculty from six of the eight faith-identified programs described their approach to clinical training with a particular focus on how their distinctive faith mission played a role. The editors of the special issue noted that

> graduates from the programs . . . are prepared to work within a particular faith context as psychologists; however, because they receive adequate breadth and depth of psychological training these graduates should also be competent to work with those who do not share their particular faith values. (McMinn & Hill, 2011, p. 99)

Some common themes are evident across the program self-descriptions. The programs report making explicit and intentional integration of faith and training, note that a religious practice competency transfers to other forms of diversity competency, comment about the varied and nonuniform way faculty members within each program carry out integration, describe the engagement of clinical integration in both didactic and applied settings, and discuss targeted inculcation of a religious and spiritual practice competency as a form of multiculturally competent practice (Cimbora, 2011; Graham-Howard & Scott, 2011; Olson, Johnson, Ripley, & Hathaway, 2011; Simpson, 2011).

Religiously Associated Programs

There are a small number of programs operating in religiously associated university settings whose faculties include competent psychologists of religion. These settings are quite varied. Some are housed in religiously affiliated institutions, such as Baylor University or Brigham Young University, and yet they are operated similarly to standard training program housed in secular settings. Because these programs do not impose a preference based on faith compatibility, they function in their admissions and training context in a *nonsectarian* manner even when a particular faith tradition is associated with the institution (e.g., the Latter-day Saints in the case of Brigham Young University). Some of the programs do formally acknowledge the faith-affiliated training mission of their institutions and report some level of integral engagement of spiritual concerns or issues in training, but published course descriptions and clinical training sequences do not reflect an explicit integrative focus. The presence of accomplished psychology of religion researchers on the faculty provide a potential resource for individualized mentoring in the clinical psychology of religion and spirituality within a supportive departmental environment. These settings typically have numerous spiritual development resources on campus, although the resources may be tied to the particular faith background of the institution.

Nonsectarian Spiritually Oriented Doctoral Programs

A few doctoral programs in psychology are offered in training contexts that emphasize humanistic or transpersonal psychology. Examples of programs in this category include the Saybrook Graduate College of Psychology and Humanistic Studies and the Institute for Transpersonal Psychology (ITP). The curriculum in both settings offers students numerous opportunities to explore spirituality from a humanistic and transpersonal perspective. These programs have specific coursework and training opportunities in which explicit engagement with spiritual issues occurs.

The transpersonal approach is not widely accepted in professional psychology and may not comport well with conventionally religious clients. In recent years, however, ITP has been developing a spiritually oriented doctoral program in clinical psychology that engages the clinical psychology of religion and spirituality more generally than from a purely transpersonal approach. This program appears to be emerging as one of the first spiritually oriented training programs outside of a faith-identified training context.

Standard Doctoral Programs With Religious and Spiritual Niches

The last training option, attending a standard secular program that contains faculty with a clinical psychology of religion and spirituality niche, offers the student the opportunity to be mentored in the area while going through a common training pathway. With just a few exceptions, such areas of expertise will be a result of the interests of the faculty member and not an area of training to which the program has made an intentional commitment. Consequently, students will need to ascertain whether any such mentors might be present in these programs, the stability of the training niche, what opportunities would be available for the student with the mentor should they enter the program, and how this training will be incorporated into the overall educative experience.

Despite the lack of formal integration of these spiritually oriented niches into the overall program or department missions, for whatever reason, the spiritually oriented niches that have emerged in these standard settings frequently have become known for their quality. Factors contributing to this may include the varied academic specializations in psychology and related disciplines that can be engaged in such settings. It is not uncommon for research teams in these settings to include students from nonclinical domains of psychology or even from related disciplines.

Unfortunately, there is no single source that maintains a current list of programs that afford training in the clinical psychology of religion and spirituality competencies. The APA publishes a yearly description of training programs called *Graduate Study in Psychology* (e.g., APA, 2012) that may include self-identifications of programs with this training niche. Students can identify such programs by examining whose faculty are regularly publishing and presenting on relevant topics for APA's Division 36 (Society for the Psychology of Religion and Spirituality) or in other appropriate venues.

Predoctoral Internship and Postdoctoral Fellowships

Professional training relevant to the clinical psychology of religion and spirituality can be pursued at the internship and postdoctoral level. The Association of Psychology Postdoctoral and Internship Centers coordinates the matching process for the doctoral internships for most graduate programs in professional psychology. Its online directory allows applicants to search for sites that have either a major or minor specialty in religion and spirituality. A search of directory in July 2011, revealed 21 internship sites that report a "major" specialty in this domain. These sites are listed in Exhibit 33.3. Twelve of these sites were APA accredited. The search also produced 251 sites that report a "minor" specialty in the area, which accounts for approximately 37% of the internships in the directory as of that date. Similarly, 18 of the 127 postdoctoral training sites reported a specialty in the domain (see Exhibit 33.3).

Because of the diversity in these training contexts and the lack of any commonly accepted rubric for competency in the clinical psychology of religion and spirituality, the specific form that such niche training may take is likely to be unpredictable. Some programs provide highly structured didactics, opportunities to participate in ongoing research programs, and supervised training in explicit spiritually oriented practice. Others provide much less structured coverage of the domain. Some recommendations are offered in the next section to help the potential intern or fellow assess the nature of the training that may be available.

Continuing Education

The last set of training options involves the continuing education process. There is now a rapidly growing body of continuing education offerings, professional texts, training videos, and other resources that address the clinical psychology of religion and spirituality. These resources are of variable quality but some outstanding options exist. Beginning and intermediate workshops in various clinical psychology of religion and spirituality topics have been regular staples on the continuing education program during the APA annual convention for

Exhibit 33.3
Pre- and Postdoctoral Training Sites Reporting Religion or Spirituality Specialty

Predoctoral Internship Programs
Brigham Young University
Chicago Area Christian Training Consortium
Christian Psychotherapy Services
Danielsen Institute at Boston University
Eden Counseling Center
Gouverneur Healthcare Services
Kids Peace National Center
Loma Linda University Medical Center
Meier Clinic, Wheaton, IL
Millard Health Centre
Nebraska Internship Consortium in Professional Psychology
Philhaven Hospital
Pine Rest Christian Mental Health Services
San Jose State University Counseling Services
St. Antony's Point, Inc.
Standing Rock Psychology Internship Program
The Catholic University of America
The Central Virginia Consortium for Clinical Psychology
University of Florida
University of Utah
VA Eastern Kansas (Leavenworth/Topeka) Healthcare System
Wright State University

Postdoctoral Programs
Arizona Psychology Training Consortium
Arizona State University Counseling and Consultation
Counseling and Psychiatric Services, University of Georgia
Duquesne University Counseling Center
Emory University School of Medicine
Emory University Student Counseling Center
Kaiser Permanente Central Bay Area Training Consortium
Kaiser Permanente West Bay Consortium
Loyola Marymount University
Nebraska Mental Health Centers and Nebraska Comprehensive Health Care
Norwich University
St. Louis University School of Medicine, Department of Family and Community Medicine
University of Louisville, School of Medicine
University of Michigan Counseling and Psychological Services
University of Rochester University Counseling Center
University of Southern California, Student Affairs Division
VA Pacific Islands Health Care System
VA Palo Alto Health Care System

more than a decade. Such workshops are also popular continuing education offerings at numerous other venues.

RECOMMENDATIONS FOR THE FUTURE OF CLINICAL PSYCHOLOGY OF RELIGION AND SPIRITUALITY TRAINING

Apart from the faith-identified training contexts, the alternative training pathways do not tend to have systematic and targeted objectives for the inculcation of the KSAs suggested in this chapter as characteristic of a spiritual practice competency. Opportunities are available, however, in many of these alternative settings for the proactive student to obtain substantial develop of these competencies.

Just as the GWish awards program has encouraged the formulation of spirituality and health training curriculum in medicine, some recognition and dissemination process for a clinical psychology of religion and spirituality training model would facilitate development in the area. It would be helpful if APA and other entities that advocate for and influence professional psychology could follow medicine's lead and call for the inclusion of religious and spiritual competency development in graduate psychology training to become a more routine part of such training programs.

Saunders, Miller, and Bright (2010) have described a variety of levels of engaging spirituality in practice. Although some forms of engagement would require a high level of competency in the domain (e.g., "spiritually integrative psychotherapy"; Saunders et al., 2010, p. 355), they argued that all psychologists should at least be prepared to engage in "spiritually conscious care." They defined this care as "assessing . . . [spiritual and religious beliefs and practices] . . . in a respectful and sensitive manner to determine their salience to the patient and the patient's problems" (Saunders et al., 2010, p. 355). This care also involves the assessment of the extent to which client religiousness and spirituality might be a resource in treatment.

There appear to be training practice niches that are currently capable of fostering more advanced and specialized spiritual practice competencies in their trainees. Yet these are relatively few in number and several are offered in settings that are preferentially oriented to particular faith traditions (Bartoli, 2007). At present, a clinician who is a novice in this domain will frequently need to acquire spiritual practice competencies through professional readings, by attending continuing education workshops, and perhaps by seeking out consultative mentorships with other professionals who already have specialized in their practice with religious and spiritual issues. Depending on one's goals, interdisciplinary training can be pursued to enhance one's general knowledge about religious and spiritual forms of life, to foster skills in specific forms of religiously accommodative treatments, or to gain skills at providing spiritually integrative treatments for religiously diverse client populations. Training in religious accommodative practice can be found at faith-identified professional meetings, such as those offered by the Christian Association of Psychological Studies in North America or the Christian Counselors Association of Australia and in publications such as the *Journal of Muslim Mental Health*. Numerous workshops in mindfulness approaches are now being offered in a wide variety of continuing education settings.

Students who are enrolled in standard training programs may also benefit from augmenting this optional development with internship or postdoctoral experiences in settings that place some emphasis on religion and spirituality. Because such field settings may have no standardized expectations, it will be important to anyone interested in this option to carefully explore the concrete meaning of the self-described emphasis on religion and spirituality at a site.

Programs historically have neglected coverage of religious and spiritual practice competencies in the curriculum. When such coverage occurs, the most frequently reported context for the training is found in clinical supervision. This suggests that spiritual issues are more likely to be explored in response to a student query or client presentation. It is time for greater program-initiated coverage of religious and spiritual practice competency. This is not likely to occur unless programs make it an intentional priority to do so. Training programs can utilize curriculum reviews and mapping to identify those places where coverage of religious or spiritual practice competency should be intentionally included. If these programs are unsure how to pursue this, conducting this review in consultation with psychologists with a recognized religious or spiritual practice competency is advisable. At minimum, this topic should be given focused attention within multicultural psychology coursework. Yet a strategy of integrating across the curriculum is more likely to alter the culture of pedagogical neglect that currently exists in professional training programs with regard to this competency. Given the prevalence of religious and spiritual issues, it is time for program faculty and administrators to take a more proactive approach to the systematic inclusion of such issues in the training sequence.

References

American Psychiatric Association. (2000). *Diagnostic and statistical manual of mental disorders* (4th ed., text revision). Washington, DC: Author.

American Psychological Association. (2009). *Guidelines and principles for accreditation of programs in professional psychology*. Washington, DC: Author.

American Psychological Association. (2010). *Ethical principles of psychologists and code of conduct (2002, amended June 1, 2010)*. Retrieved from http://www.apa.org/ethics/code/index.aspx

American Psychological Association (2012). *Graduate study in psychology: 2012 edition*. Washington, DC: Author.

Aten, J. D., & Leach, M. M. (Eds.). (2009). *Spirituality and the therapeutic process: A comprehensive resource from intake to termination*. Washington, DC: American Psychological Association. doi:10.1037/11853-000

Aten, J. D., McMinn, M. R., & Worthington, E. L., Jr. (Eds.). (2011). *Spiritually oriented interventions for counseling and psychotherapy*. Washington, DC: American Psychological Association. doi:10.1037/12313-000

Barnett, J. E., & Johnson, W. B. (2011). Integrating spirituality and religion in psychotherapy: Persistent dilemmas, ethical issues, and a proposed decision-making process. *Ethics and Behavior, 21*, 147–164. doi:10.1080/10508422.2011.551471

Bartoli, E. (2007). Religious & spiritual issues in psychotherapy practice: Training the trainer. *Psychotherapy: Theory, Research, Practice, Training, 44*, 54–65. doi:10.1037/0033-3204.44.1.54

Borden, K. A., & McIlvried, E. J. (2009). Applying the competency model to professional psychology education, training, and assessment: Mission Bay and beyond. In M. B. Kenkel & R. L. Peterson (Eds.), *Competency-based education for professional psychology* (pp. 43–53). Washington, DC: American Psychological Association.

Brawer, P. A., Handal, P. J., Fabricatore, A. N., Roberts, R., & Wajda-Johnston, V. A. (2002). Training and education in religion/spirituality within APA-accredited clinical psychology programs. *Professional Psychology: Research and Practice, 33*, 203–206. doi:10.1037/0735-7028.33.2.203

Cimbora, D. M. (2011). Clinical training at an explicitly integrative program: Rosemead School of Psychology. *Journal of Psychology and Christianity, 30*, 137–147.

Coelho, H. F., Canter, P. H., & Ernst, E. (2007). Mindfulness-Based cognitive therapy: Evaluating current evidence and informing future research. *Journal of Consulting and Clinical Psychology, 75*, 1000–1005. doi:10.1037/0022-006X.75.6.1000

DeMarinis, V., & Wikström, O. (Eds.). (1996). *Clinical psychology of religion: Emerging cultural and multi-cultural questions from European and North American voices.* Stockholm, Sweden: Swedish Council for Planning and Coordination of Research.

Ellison, C. G., Acevedo, G. A., & Ramos-Wada, A. I. (2011). Religion and attitudes toward same-sex marriage among U.S. Latinos. *Social Science Quarterly, 92*, 35–56. doi:10.1111/j.1540-6237.2011.00756.x

Emmons, R. A., & McCullough, M. E. (Eds.). (2004). *The psychology of gratitude.* New York, NY: Oxford University Press. doi:10.1093/acprof:oso/9780195150100.001.0001

Gartner, J. D. (1986). Antireligious prejudice in admissions to doctoral programs in clinical psychology. *Professional Psychology: Research and Practice, 17*, 473–475. doi:10.1037/0735-7028.17.5.473

Gold, J. M. (2010). *Counseling and spirituality: Integrating spiritual and clinical orientations.* Upper Saddle River, NJ: Pearson.

Graham-Howard, M. L., & Scott, S. T. (2011). Inter-disciplinary integration in clinical training: The Azusa Pacific University Graduate Program. *Journal of Psychology and Christianity, 30*, 101–107.

Hathaway, W. L. (2003). Clinically significant religious impairment. *Mental Health, Religion, and Culture, 6*, 113–129.

Hathaway, W. L. (2011). Ethical guidelines for using spiritually oriented interventions. In J. D. Aten, M. R. McMinn, & E. L. Worthington Jr. (Eds.), *Spiritually oriented interventions for counseling and psychotherapy* (pp. 65–81). Washington, DC: American Psychological Association. doi:10.1037/12313-003

Hathaway, W. L., & Childers, J. (2013). Assessment of religious functioning in clinical child psychology. In D. F. Walker & W. L. Hathaway (Eds.), *Spiritual interventions in child and adolescent psychotherapy.* Washington, DC: American Psychological Association.

Hathaway, W. L., & Ripley, J. R. (2009). Ethical concerns around spirituality and religion in clinical practice. In J. D. Aten & M. M. Leach (Eds.), *Spirituality and the therapeutic process: A Comprehensive resource from intake to termination* (pp. 25–52). Washington, DC: American Psychological Association. doi:10.1037/11853-002

Hathaway, W. L., Scott, S., & Garver, S. (2004). Assessing religious/spiritual functioning: A neglected domain of practice? *Professional Psychology: Research and Practice, 35*, 97–104. doi:10.1037/0735-7028.35.1.97

Hiltner, S. (1947). *Religion and health.* New York, NY: Macmillan.

Hook, J. N., Worthington, E. L., Jr., Davis, D. E., Gartner, A. L., Jennings, J., & Hook, J. P. (2010). Empirically supported religious and spiritual therapies. *Journal of Clinical Psychology, 66*, 46–72.

Johnson, W. B., Campbell, C. D., & Dykstra, M. L. (1997). Professional training in religious institutions: Articulating models and outcomes. *Journal of Psychology and Theology, 25*, 260–271.

Josephson, A. M., Peteet, J. R., & Tasman, A. (2010). Religion and the training of psychotherapists. In P. J. Verhagen, H. M. van Praag, J. J. Lopez-Ibor Jr., J. L. Cox, & D. Moussaoui (Eds.), *Religion and psychiatry: Beyond boundaries* (pp. 571–586). Hoboken, NJ: Wiley-Blackwell.

Kaslow, N. J., Borden, K. A., Collins, F. L., Jr., Forrest, L., Illfelder-Kaye, J., Nelson, P. D., . . . Willmuth, M. E. (2004). Competencies Conference: Future directions in education and credentialing in professional psychology. *Journal of Clinical Psychology, 60*, 699–712. doi:10.1002/jclp.20016

Kenkel, M. B., & Peterson, R. L. (2009). *Competency-based education for professional psychology.* Washington, DC: American Psychological Association.

Malony, H. N. (Ed.). (1991). *The psychology of religion: Personalities, problems, possibilities.* Grand Rapids, MI: Baker Book House.

McGuire, M. B. (2008). *Lived religion: Faith and practice in everyday life.* New York, NY: Oxford University Press.

McMinn, M. R., & Domiguez, A. W. (2005). *Psychology and the church.* New York, NY: Nova.

McMinn, M. R., & Hill, P. C. (2011). Clinical training in explicitly Christian doctoral programs: Introduction to the special issue. *Journal of Psychology and Christianity, 30*, 99–100.

Melton, J. G. (2009). *Encyclopedia of American religions.* New York, NY: Gale.

Mintz, L. B., & Bieschke, K. J. (2009). Counseling psychology model training values statement addressing diversity: Development and introduction to the major contribution. *The Counseling Psychologist, 37*, 634–640. doi:10.1177/0011000009331923

Nelson, J. M. (2009). *Psychology, religion, and spirituality*. New York, NY: Springer. doi:10.1007/978-0-387-87573-6

Olson, L., Johnson, J. L., Ripley, J., & Hathaway, W. (2011). Clinical training in integrative Christian doctoral programs: The Regent University example. *Journal of Psychology and Christianity, 30*, 128–136.

Pargament, K. I. (1997). *The psychology of religion and coping: Theory, research, and practice*. New York, NY: Guilford Press.

Pargament, K. I. (2007). *Spiritually integrated psychotherapy: Understanding and addressing the sacred*. New York, NY: Guilford Press.

Plante, T. G. (2009). *Spiritual practices in psychotherapy: Thirteen tools for enhancing psychological health*. Washington, DC: American Psychological Association. doi:10.1037/11872-000

Propst, L. R. (1988). *Psychotherapy in a religious framework: Spirituality in the emotional healing process*. New York, NY: Human Sciences Press.

Richards, P. S., & Bergin, A. E. (Eds.). (2000). *Handbook of psychotherapy and religious diversity*. Washington, DC: American Psychological Association. doi:10.1037/10347-000

Richards, P. S., & Bergin, A. E. (2005). *A spiritual strategy for counseling and psychotherapy* (2nd ed.). Washington, DC: American Psychological Association. doi:10.1037/11214-000

Russell, S. R., & Yarhouse, M. A. (2006). Training in religion/spirituality within APA-accredited psychology pre-doctoral internships. *Professional Psychology: Research and Practice, 37*, 430–436. doi:10.1037/0735-7028.37.4.430

Saunders, S. M., Miller, M. L., & Bright, M. M. (2010). Spiritually conscious psychological care. *Professional Psychology: Research and Practice, 41*, 355–362. doi:10.1037/a0020953

Savage, S. (2011). Four lessons for the study of fundamentalism and psychology of religion. *Journal of Strategic Security, 4*, 131–150. doi:10.5038/1944-0472.4.4.6

Shafranske, E. P. (Ed.). (1996). *Religion and the clinical practice of psychology*. Washington, DC: American Psychological Association. doi:10.1037/10199-000

Shafranske, E. P. (2005). The psychology of religion in clinical and counseling psychology. In R. F. Paloutzian & C. L. Park (Eds.), *Handbook of the psychology of religion and spirituality* (pp. 496–514). New York, NY: Guilford Press.

Sharpe, E. J. (2009). *Comparative religion: A history*. London, England: Duckworth.

Simpson, S. W. (2011). Creating "reflective practitioners": Clinical training at Fuller Theological Seminary's School of Psychology. *Journal of Psychology and Christianity, 30*, 108–113.

Smith, H. (1991). *The world's religions*. New York, NY: HarperCollins.

Sperry, L. (2012). *Spirituality in clinical practice: Theory and practice of spiritually oriented psychotherapy* (2nd ed.). New York, NY: Routledge.

Sperry, L., & Shafranske, E. P. (Eds.). (2005). *Spiritually oriented psychotherapy*. Washington, DC: American Psychological Association. doi:10.1037/10886-000

Van Uden, M., & Pieper, J. (2003). Clinical psychology of religion: A training model. *Archive for the Psychology of Religion, 25*, 155–164.

Wiggins, M. I. (2009). Therapist self-awareness of spirituality. In J. D. Aten & M. L. Leach (Eds.), *Spirituality and the therapeutic process: A comprehensive resource from intake to termination* (pp. 53–74). Washington, DC: American Psychological Association.

Witmer, L. (1907). Clinical psychology. *Psychological Clinic, 1*, 1–9.

CHAPTER 34

CONDUCTING EMPIRICAL RESEARCH ON RELIGIOUSLY ACCOMMODATIVE INTERVENTIONS

Everett L. Worthington Jr., Joshua N. Hook, Don E. Davis, Aubrey L. Gartner, and David J. Jennings II

Available evidence from the past 2 decades indicates that highly committed religious people, especially those affiliated with more conservative branches of their religious tradition, often request religiously accommodative interventions (RAIs; Worthington, Kurusu, McCullough, & Sandage, 1996) or spiritually accommodative interventions (SAIs). Two assumptions on the part of clients appear to underline these requests. First, these clients believe they have a right to have a value-consonant approach to psychotherapy that does not undermine their faith. Second, they believe that such an approach to treatment will produce at least equivalent and perhaps better psychological and spiritual outcomes. It has proved challenging, however, to create a base of scientific research that accommodating secular treatments to religious clients is unequivocally beneficial (Worthington, Hook, Davis, & McDaniel, 2011).

In this chapter, we first define and provide a historical overview about the emergence of RAIs. We then describe the challenges of conducting research on the development, evaluation, and dissemination of treatments that have been accommodated from secular treatments to map onto certain religious beliefs, values, and practices promoted by major religions. Second, we describe and evaluate the extant research on RAIs. The focus of this chapter is mostly on randomized clinical trial (RCT) research with explicitly religious accommodation. However, some SAIs (generally those that advocate spiritual practices, values, or beliefs not identified with a particular religion) do exist (see Worthington et al., 2011). Furthermore, most systematic research on RAIs has been conducted on Christian clients, many of whom identify with evangelical or more conservative wings of Christianity, although some studies have been conducted on clients who affiliate with Islam, Buddhism, and general religion or spirituality. Third, on the basis of the challenges and status of the current research, we offer concrete suggestions for conducting research on religiously accommodative treatments. Most extant research has focused on Christians, who are more likely represented in samples drawn from the United States, and it has especially sampled religious subcultures in which people hold moderate to conservative Christian beliefs. Despite this relatively limited set of studies, we believe the issues we discuss generalize to the study of accommodation to other spiritual and religious worldviews.

DEFINITION AND HISTORICAL OVERVIEW OF RELIGIOUSLY ACCOMMODATIVE INTERVENTIONS

In the sections that follow, we define *religiously accommodative interventions.* We then discuss an admittedly selective history of their use.

Definition

We define RAIs as those interventions that modify an existing secular treatment to include methods and goals that reflect certain values, beliefs, or practices promoted by religious institutions or psychological treatments created specifically for use with

DOI: 10.1037/14046-034
APA Handbook of Psychology, Religion, and Spirituality: Vol. 2. An Applied Psychology of Religion and Spirituality, K. I. Pargament (Editor-in-Chief)

people who belong to specific religious or spiritual subgroups (Worthington et al., 2011). For example, besides using behavioral techniques such as exposure to reduce anxiety, an RAI might integrate methods such as prayer, use of scriptures, or religious imagery. Besides pursuing psychological goals, such as reducing depression, an RAI might also work toward spiritual goals such as living in greater alignment with one's spiritual or religious values, beliefs, or practices.

Origins of Religious and Secular Interventions

Secular treatments. Historically, early secular psychotherapeutic treatments formed around the approach of a single theorist. Some psychotherapist–theoreticians started with a theory that held a certain worldview, assumptions of human nature, conceptualization of the cause of problems, and understandings of change processes. These psychotherapist–theoreticians developed psychotherapeutic techniques consistent with the theory's conceptualizations (e.g., Freud's psychoanalytic theory). Other psychotherapists were likely natural and intuitive helpers. They refined their methods and theoretical approaches as they gained experience. Later, they articulated what they were doing and wrote their theory—worldviews, assumptions, and mechanisms of change—that accorded with their intuitively developed methods (e.g., Rogers's humanistic theory). Still other psychotherapist–theoreticians began with basic science and based their approach to psychotherapy on research-based theory and findings (e.g., various applications of Skinner's behavioral theory). Regardless of how the treatment formed initially, the founding theorist was the driving force behind its proliferation.

RAIs. RAIs did not originate similarly to secular treatments (Worthington, 2010). Instead of being driven by an articulate practitioner, RAIs arose from the demands of religious clients who wanted treatments that were tailored more closely to their specific religious goals, beliefs and values, and to the methods used by clergy in their religious settings. Mostly, these were evangelical Christians whose religious values were theologically conservative but who were open to psychotherapy. Thus, Christian practitioners who had been trained in a variety of secular psychotherapeutic frameworks integrated religious techniques and language into their existing approach. Most psychotherapists, of course, held values, beliefs, and religious practices that were similar to their Christian evangelical clients. Typically, the integrations of religion into the secular methods became routinized in practice only if practitioners had many clients with similar values, beliefs, and practices to the psychotherapists. Thus, much early research on RAIs simply surveyed practitioners about which religious or ecclesiastical techniques they employed in psychotherapy (e.g., Ball & Goodyear, 1991; Richards & Potts, 1995; Shafranske, 2000, 2001; Shafranske & Malony, 1990). Those surveys consistently showed that about 30% to 90% of practitioners incorporated religious interventions into their practices. Generally, psychotherapists who were personally religious were more likely to use religious interventions than did psychotherapists who were less religious (Hook & Worthington, 2009; Richards & Bergin, 2004, 2005; Shafranske, 1996; Sperry & Shafranske, 2005; Worthington et al., 1996).

As we observed, many of the first RAIs were accommodated to Christian evangelical theologies. Such theologies emphasized beliefs and worldviews—that is, cognitive constructs—and rational reasoning approaches. It therefore seemed a natural "marriage" to accommodate religion into cognitive therapy (CT) and cognitive–behavioral therapy (CBT) methods. Of course, the content of religious beliefs often differed dramatically with early secular CTs (like early versions of rational emotive therapy; Ellis, 1962), but cognitive methods involving self-talk, beliefs, and rational disputation of maladaptive beliefs were easily able to support beliefs of evangelical Christians with high religious commitment. Later interventions included Muslim-accommodative CBT (Razali, Aminah, & Khan, 2002) and Jewish-accommodated psychotherapy (Rosmarin, Pargament, Pirutinsky, & Mahoney, 2010). The importance that CBT accords to beliefs, thoughts, and values makes CBT ideal for adaptations by incorporating particular religious content instead of nonreligious content.

Virtually all RAIs followed the procedures of the secular psychotherapy they were adapting—such as teaching the cognitive paradigm for CT or CBT. In those approaches, cognitions, not situations, are said to affect emotions or maladaptive behaviors; thus to reduce maladaptive emotions or behaviors, one can systematically change any of a variety of cognitive processes. The content of the cognition in the RAIs, however, was explicitly religious (i.e., use a Christian understanding of sin or of forgiveness; use a Muslim understanding of justice or fairness). Although the secular approaches were standardized from one use to another, the ways that the approaches were religiously accommodated across different uses were often quite different from each other. This has remained the hallmark of RAIs. They typically follow standardized secular treatment protocols. But their religious frameworks, goals, assumptions, and methods are divergent across studies. Thus, Christian CT influenced by the work of Aaron T. Beck might differ widely across practitioners and studies according to the degree and type of religious methods.

CHALLENGES OF DESIGNING RCT RESEARCH ON RAIS

There are many ways to accommodate secular treatments to religious or spiritual clients. These might involve differences in quantity of modifications or in the generality or particularity of the modifications. Methodology of research, other practical considerations, and even (within the United States) the doctrine of separation of church and state can also affect how such accommodation occurs.

Different Perspectives

One problem when designing RCT research on RAIs is that researchers and clients often have different perspectives on religious accommodation. Researchers usually want to create a general treatment that will be effective for a large group of people, such as a "spiritual approach" that works for all spiritual people or a "Jewish approach" that works for all Jewish people. In contrast, religious clients who have most often demanded RAIs want a psychotherapy that aligns closely with their specific religious beliefs. As highlighted, however, the beliefs and values of religious clients may vary widely, even within the same religious community. A client's religious values and beliefs are among the most cherished, strongly held, and deeply defended, especially for those who are highly committed to conservative, moderate, or progressive theological perspectives within their religious tradition. Highly religious clients organize their lives around religious beliefs, values, and practices and may hold to specific beliefs that are difficult to understand by a psychotherapist who is not religious or who is unfamiliar with the client's perspective (Worthington, 1988). One example is the way that clients might treat their sacred texts. For some, the texts are authoritative and literal; for others, authoritative but more metaphorical; and for still others, metaphorical and not authoritative. To a psychotherapist unfamiliar with or even unsympathetic to the client's perspective, the whole issue might seem distracting or irrelevant within the context of therapy. The psychotherapist might value client self-discovery during psychotherapy and not understand why clients might privilege their scriptural interpretation above their own self-discoveries. Highly religious clients often discern when psychotherapists are not sympathetic, however (Worthington et al., 1996). When a psychotherapist fails to respect a client's beliefs, the fallout can strain the working alliance, cause a breach in the relationship, and the client may leave psychotherapy. Thus, RAIs must carefully consider the religious subculture for whom the treatment has been adapted.

Balancing General and Particular

Find the balance. There are many ways to accommodate secular approaches to religious populations. Researchers must recognize precisely who is being targeted so that they (a) will say things that invite religious adherents to trust the treatment approach and (b) not say things that will trigger rejection of the treatment. For example, some psychotherapists may fail to anticipate how some religious language (e.g., *higher power*, *divine spark*, *the sacred*), intended to communicate respect, may actually communicate to some highly committed religious clients that the psychotherapist is *not* a kindred spirit and might lead some to conclude that the psychotherapist might intentionally or unwittingly undermine their faith. Some clients will terminate psychotherapy if they do not trust that the psychotherapist sufficiently understands and respects their particular orientation to their faith. RAIs must therefore be designed to (a) foster value congruence with anticipated clients and (b) not provoke unnecessary conflict or bad feelings that might impair a good working alliance.

Match religious language. Clients rely on language to determine the psychotherapist's relationship with their religious subgroup. For example, clients may view the psychotherapist as a trusted authority within a given in-group; as a knowledgeable, supportive, and respectful out-group member; or as an ignorant, hostile, disrespectful out-group member. For many Christians, the lordship of Jesus is the defining point of Christianity, and the expectation is that a like-minded psychotherapist might at times refer to Jesus as "Lord." Referring to Jesus as "Lord," however, could drive Christians who eschew authority-based language (e.g., some moderate and progressive Christians) and most Jewish, Muslim, Hindu, and Buddhist adherents out of psychotherapy. Part of religiously accommodating an intervention is to match the client's language with enough denomination- or religion-specific terminology to convey that the psychotherapist is an in-group member or at least understands and respects the in-group. There are dangers to trying to use a language system that one does not understand. If the psychotherapist misuses religious terms, the client's confidence in the psychotherapist can be undermined. If the psychotherapist implies (even unintentionally) that he or she is a religious adherent, then the client might ask directly about the implied group membership (e.g., "You sound Muslim. Are you?"). Having to clarify an unwitting claim can weaken the working alliance.

Provide a religious rationale. A major part of religious accommodation is providing a religious rationale that allows clients to draw on their commitment to their religious subgroup to motivate their participation in treatment. As an example, Worthington and his colleagues have developed a secular psychoeducational intervention to promote forgiveness (Worthington, 2006). Individuals learn to reach forgiveness through five steps, with each letter in the word *reach* referring to one of the steps. To accommodate the model for religious adherents who believe in God (Lampton, Oliver, Worthington, & Berry, 2005; Stratton, Dean, Nonneman, Bode, & Worthington, 2008; Worthington et al., 2010), the leader uses the metaphor of building a pillar of concrete to explain how forgiveness involves both actively seeking forgiveness and relying on God's grace. Wooden forms shape the pillar during its formation, but the substance of the pillar is concrete. Accordingly, the five steps of the REACH-forgiveness model (analogous to the wooden forms) prepare and shape a person to receive a more forgiving character, which is poured into the person by God. If successful, the religious rationale conveys to the client that the intervention aligns with, and is not an alternative to, the client's religious beliefs.

Balance secular and religious methods. Clinical researchers must find a balance between the use of secular psychotherapy methods and the use of ecclesiastical methods (i.e., prayer, grounding suggestions in certain interpretations of sacred texts). Some clients may not tolerate any techniques that they recognize as secular (e.g., an empty-chair exercise), whereas others may comfortably accept secular psychotherapy methods, as long as they trust the psychotherapist respects their religious values. Some clients interpret methods intended to be secular as consistent with their religion or spiritual approach, or they simply incorporate their own religious methods in their psychotherapy even though the psychotherapist did not employ them (Rye et al., 2005). To that end, clients may consider any aspect of life to be spiritually important (Pargament & Mahoney, 2005); for instance, they might sacralize marriage, family, or vocation. For example, the lead author of this chapter was supervising an avowedly nonreligious psychotherapist who was doing family therapy with a fundamentalist Christian husband, wife, and unruly daughter. The psychotherapist used problem-solving therapy, the secular approach developed by Haley (1976). Everything was going well. The harmful coalition between wife and daughter had been disrupted successfully, the father had been empowered to parent, joint parenting was being solidified, and the child was responding to direction from both father and mother. Then, as the couple was leaving, only one session away from termination, the wife casually remarked to the psychotherapist, "You seem to believe that the man is head of the wife." In the Christian fundamentalist tradition, the man's "headship" is taken for granted, although it is interpreted differently across denominations. The psychotherapist replied, "No, I believe in an equal husband–wife partnership." The next week, the family did not show for psychotherapy. The psychotherapist phoned repeatedly. When he finally talked to the couple, they informed him that being troubled by his statement about gender roles, they had discussed the issue with their pastor, who had advised them to terminate psychotherapy. Had the psychotherapist recognized that he was being challenged on the basis of religious doctrine held by the clients, he might not have responded directly at first, but instead he might have asked what that might mean to the clients. Or the psychotherapist might have observed that such a belief seems consonant with the beliefs advocated by the clients' church, and then he might have asked whether the treatment was fitting with their religious beliefs and values.

Methodological Issues

Resistance to random assignment. Designing and carrying out *any* controlled efficacy research has many problems associated with it (Kazdin, 1994). Some additional considerations are needed with religious clients or RAIs. One issue is that some highly religious clients may resist being randomly assigned to a comparison treatment (i.e., a secular version of the treatment). Thus, clients for whom accommodation is likely most important (i.e., highly religious clients who are committed to their specific beliefs, values, and practices and who strongly prefer that psychotherapy be tailored to their religion) may be unlikely to participate in RCTs. Likewise, people who do not identify as religious or who might be religious but hold different beliefs, values, and practices from the RAI may resist being randomly assigned to an explicitly religious treatment. These objections make true experimental designs for religious clients that compare an RAI with a secular treatment or different religious treatment difficult. Because random assignment is essential within the logic of RCTs (i.e., it controls extraneous variables), the clinical researcher must select and thoroughly consent participants in RCTs and must state limitations to generalizability in interpreting the findings. The alternative to providing a thorough informed consent will likely be unacceptably high rates of attrition.

Spiritually active components of treatments. Most research on RAIs has tested whether treatments are generally efficacious, but relatively few studies have examined the specific components of treatments that may contribute to outcomes. Researchers need to (a) identify the unique features of various spiritually integrated interventions that distinguish them from nonspiritual intervention models and (b) test whether these specific features add to the strength of treatments beyond typical "secular" interventions. Most of the active ingredients are likely encapsulated in the secular protocol; however, some spiritual elements are worth investigation—for example, religious techniques such as prayer or the use of religious writings offer benefits. Or benefits might occur early in psychotherapy to the degree that accommodation helps to establish a strong psychotherapy alliance.

Matching variables. There are several good candidates for deciding whether clients might benefit from being matched to an RAI or RSI. An obvious one is the client's explicit request. In addition, Worthington (1988) suggested that religious commitment was the best matching variable among religious variables. He theorized that people at least one standard deviation above the mean of religious commitment tended to view the world through a religious lens. Religious commitment is measured generally, and it is considered to be the degree that one integrates his or her religious beliefs, values, and practices (whatever they might be) into his or her daily life. This has received some support (see Worthington et al., 1996; Worthington & Sandage, 2001). Other possible matching variables include specific religious beliefs, practices, denominational similarity, or position on the religious conservatism–liberalism continuum. In recent years, more attention has been paid to measuring spirituality (for a review, see Kapuscinski & Masters, 2010), and matching on spirituality might become increasingly important as measures are refined and if spirituality continues to draw increasing numbers of adherents.

Psychospiritual outcomes. Clinical researchers have rarely measured outcomes other than symptom reduction. Psychospiritual constructs may be important outcomes to consider. For example, in the past, researchers have measured general spiritual well-being (Spiritual Well-being Scale; Ellison & Smith, 1991), specific doctrinal beliefs (e.g., the Shepherd Scale; Bassett et al., 1981), or the degree to which the client values religion or religious constructs (Religious Commitment Inventory—10; Worthington et al., 2003). Many religious and spiritual measures have not been well developed, nor as psychometrically well supported, as measures of psychological functioning. This is due to several factors. First, in RCTs, psychological functioning is of primary concern; however, religious or spiritual functioning has been of concern in a minority of studies. The data base is simply far smaller. Second, many studies target specific religious groups. Hence, many measures were developed to assess particular beliefs (i.e., orthodoxy of religions, doctrinal assent to particular beliefs). Recently, however, several more general—and psychotherapy-relevant—measures of religion and spirituality have been developed and have become a loose canon of measures. These include intrinsic and extrinsic religious motivations, religious commitment, and religious coping (see Hill & Hood, 1999, for measures and summaries of psychometric data; see also Volume 1, Chapter 3, this handbook).

Practical Challenges in Doing RCTs and Using the Findings

A variety of unique methodological concerns have challenged researchers who wish to employ RCTs to test the effectiveness and efficacy of RAIs. In general, RCT research is difficult, time-consuming, and expensive. Few clinical researchers are attracted to outcome research. For many, process research is more manageable. Beyond the sheer difficulty of RCT research, other factors limit the RCT researchers who study RAIs. This section highlights some key pitfalls that have, at times, undermined progress within this literature.

Attraction to conduct outcome research. Few researchers study RAIs. Many of these researchers are themselves loyal to a particular religious subgroup and work at theological seminaries or explicitly religious universities affiliated with a particular branch of Christianity. Researchers at public universities, who face pressures to publish in high-quality outlets and obtain external grant funding, have less often been attracted to conducting research on religious accommodation. In recent years, we believe, RAIs have been increasingly published in higher impact journals. This is particularly likely if an investigation compares two interventions—one secular and the other strictly religiously accommodated. Worthington et al. (2011) meta-analyzed RAIs and found 10 such comparisons published in the past 10 years (but none earlier than that). In addition, given definitive meta-analytic findings that religion affects longevity (McCullough, Hoyt, Larson, Koenig, & Thoresen, 2000), partly by affecting both physical and mental health, granting agencies have been increasingly open to including religious interventions in their funding priorities.

Investment of time needed for research. Outcome research on RAIs is time-consuming. Some members of religious organizations mistrust secular organizations. Thus, sometimes religious clients and religious practitioners refuse to participate in controlled outcome research. Building trust with religious communities requires time and energy. Clinical researchers must devote time to securing buy-in from both practitioners and clients. For example, Wade, Worthington, and Vogel (2007) presented preliminary research at professional conferences and solicited participant religious and secular psychotherapists after describing results from a pilot study and description of the full research design. Furthermore, building buy-in from religious leaders might involve soliciting their critique and suggestions for modifying treatment manuals, procedures, and recruitment strategies.

Use of research in designing RAIs and disseminating findings from RCTs. Some religious practitioners and clients may place greater value on religious authority (e.g., scripture, religious authors) than on scientific authority. Clinicians sensitive to this fact have thus drawn less on basic research in psychology to design RCTs, relative to religious resources, such as certain religious writers, theologians, and church leaders, that fit with the particular religious orientation of most members in their presumed clientele. Furthermore, dissemination of RAIs within religious communities can be difficult. Once RCTs are complete, religious practitioners may not use the treatment, and religiously conservative clients may not care whether a treatment is esteemed within the scientific community. We believe that those who design and test RAIs must engage opinion leaders personally and frame the results of research within the religious framework of the religious community. Opinion leaders such as religious authorities with a broad platform (e.g., megachurch leaders, television personalities, book writers, even local clergy) can do much to promote the acceptability of RAIs within their scope of influence.

Cooperation Between Psychotherapists and Clergy

As we have argued, from a community psychology perspective, a given religious community is unlikely to fully embrace a treatment unless their trusted leaders endorse it (see Chapters 23 and 32 in this volume). Leaders are more likely to endorse a treatment if they are involved in developing it. Historically, however, there has been little cooperation between psychotherapists and clergy. Thus, knowing one might benefit by fostering cooperation between psychotherapists and clergy (or more broadly, opinion leaders in religious subgroups) is not the same as actually fostering it. Meylink and Gorsuch (1988) reviewed research on the relationships between psychotherapists and clergy. They found that about 40% of people who sought help first approached clergy, but fewer than 10% of those help-seekers were referred to mental health professionals. Conversely, psychologists were found virtually never to refer clients to clergy or other religious resources. In recent years, more attention has been paid to promoting a two-way referral flow. Recent models promoting collaboration between clergy and psychologists have drawn on the belief that for clergy and psychotherapists to work well together, they must draw on shared religious values (McMinn & Campbell, 2008; Pargament, 2007; Plante, 2009). These models do not deal with how to promote collaboration of religious leaders and psychologists and other psychotherapists who have limited appreciation of collaboration with religious professionals. We suggest that some highly visible religious leaders are more psychology friendly than others. Clinical researchers must identify such people and seek to establish trusting relationships with them. We believe that such personal relationships are essential to gaining wide cooperation and perhaps collaboration.

Separation of Church and State

Dissemination of both treatments and research on their efficacy has been vigorous in recent years (McHugh & Barlow, 2010). Public health authorities, usually state or federal, have recently earmarked about $2 billion for the dissemination and implementation of mental health treatments in the United States. It is unlikely that much of that money will be available to disseminate and implement RAIs because (a) religious programs are not currently competitive in research support with secular treatments and (b) the tradition of separation of church and state would likely inhibit such dissemination. We believe that the key to public acceptability of RAIs is adequate RCT support. Government agencies also want favored programs to have additional support. First, RCTs with minorities are important to ensure that health and mental health disparities are not being perpetuated, so clinical trials might profitably be done specifically with minority populations. Second, large-scale training programs are a must. Training must be routinized, involving videos, manuals, certification programs, and websites, and must ensure the availability of online, phone, or in-person training, supervision, and consultation. Third, methods of assessment must be built into treatment. They should include assessment of both psychological and religious and spiritual outcomes. For public funding of RAIs, attention must be given to public funding priorities.

Summary of Challenges

There are numerous barriers to building up a research base of RAIs that is comparable in breadth, depth, and sophistication to secular outcome research. In many ways, the infrastructure is stacked against this goal ever becoming a reality. This includes several factors.

- Clients want specifically tailored treatments, but practitioners and scientists want the most generally applicable treatments possible. That difference in perspective limits research by focusing it more narrowly than professionals might believe to be efficient.
- RAIs have historically been more influenced by client-driven concerns (i.e., demand-side pressure) than scientific concerns (i.e., theorist-centered supply-side structure). Namely, practitioners started incorporating religion into psychotherapy for the theologically conservative (mostly evangelical Christian) clientele who demanded it, and later a few researchers started to investigate the practice.
- Having a primarily religious understanding of life affects clients (who resist accepting research-informed findings), practitioners (who often practice in institutions that do not value research), and scientists (who might work in institutions that do not value religion-related research). This limits the use of and research on RAIs.
- Many methodological issues have simply not been clarified. For instance, there is no agreement on the nature of how much and of what kinds of religious accommodations should be considered necessary to qualify a treatment as an RAI. It is not clear why RAIs might be expected to be superior to secular treatments. Measures of spiritual change are numerous and differ, sometimes subtly and sometimes not. It is not clear which measures should be affected in what ways by what religious and spiritual accommodations.
- Political and institutional barriers—like the doctrine of the separation of church and state—create mind-sets that can hamper research on RAIs. With such barriers to designing, conducting, and disseminating high-quality outcome research in RAIs, one might wonder that any have been completed. Yet substantial research has been conducted and important findings have been obtained. We review the current empirical status of the field in the next section.

THE STATUS OF RESEARCH ON RAIs

In the sections that follow, we review the early years of accommodating treatments to religious clients. We then describe the recent reviews of research on religiously or spiritually accommodated treatments.

Early Reviews of the Literature

Before 2010, there were four major reviews of research on RAIs. In 1996, Worthington and his colleagues qualitatively reviewed 148 empirical studies on religion and individual psychotherapy. Only eight were outcome studies. Worthington et al. concluded that religiously oriented cognitive and rational–emotive psychotherapy approaches were efficacious for religious clients, but only slightly more so than were secular approaches. They observed that only a small number of outcome studies had been done on spiritually oriented (rather than religiously oriented) psychotherapies. Furthermore, they suggested that evidence showed that religious clients preferred RAIs to secular ones. Their conclusions, however, were based on research exclusively with Christian evangelical participants.

In 1999, McCullough conducted a meta-analysis of five Christian-oriented cognitive therapies for depression with evangelical clients. He found that they were equally effective as secular treatments at reducing psychological symptoms. In 2001, Worthington and Sandage, in a qualitative review, found that religiously accommodated and secular cognitive and rational–emotive therapies were equally effective for both Christian and Muslim clients with depression and anxiety. Only two studies with Muslims were available.

By 2007, Smith, Bartz, and Richards conducted a meta-analysis on RAIs that included 31 studies. Of those, 15 were religiously accommodated CTs, CBTs, or rational–emotive therapies and 16 were religiously accommodated general psychotherapy studies (i.e., typically psychodynamically flavored interventions). The authors reported a moderate effect size favoring RAIs. Christian and Muslim forms of cognitive and rational–emotive psychotherapy for religious clients were the most consistently supported. In all of these reviews, the authors critiqued the methodological sophistication of studies of RAIs (e.g., small samples, limited number of religions surveyed, analogue designs, etc.).

Current Status of RAIs

In a recent qualitative review, Hook et al. (2010) summarized the status of RAIs regarding their designation as empirically supported RAIs. In general, there was evidence that religiously accommodated psychotherapies were efficacious (i.e., they outperformed a control group or were equivalent to an alternative treatment) and that gains were maintained at follow-up. The number of studies was small, however, and some religiously accommodated psychotherapies had no evidence supporting their efficacy. The evidence for specificity of RAIs was sparse. ("Specificity" is awarded an intervention that consistently betters a known effective intervention.) Thus, in most cases, RAIs performed as well as (but not better than) established secular treatments.

In a recent meta-analysis, Worthington et al. (2011) analyzed 51 samples from 46 studies between 1980 and 2009. Studies compared an RAI or SAI with either a control condition or alternate treatment. Nineteen samples evaluated a Christian intervention, seven evaluated a Muslim intervention, two evaluated a Buddhist intervention, one evaluated a Taoist intervention, one evaluated a Jewish intervention, and 21 evaluated a general religious or spiritual intervention. RAIs and SAIs were treated as those that had been adapted from secular psychotherapies by including religious (or spiritual) material such as religious or spiritual conceptual frameworks, religious stories, quotes from religious texts, and appeals to prayer.

Comparisons on psychological outcomes were made to a control condition (n = 22), to an alternate treatment (n = 29), and to a subset of these studies that used a dismantling design (e.g., similar in theoretical orientation and duration of treatment, but different in the inclusion of specific religious contents; n = 11). Comparisons on spiritual outcomes were made to a control condition (n = 8), an alternate treatment (n = 14), and a subset of these studies that used a dismantling design (e.g., similar in theoretical orientation and duration of treatment, but different in the inclusion of specific religious contents; n = 7). Participants in RAIs outperformed participants in the no-treatment control conditions on both psychological and spiritual outcomes. There was some evidence that participants in RAIs outperformed alternate treatments. When studies were limited to those that used a dismantling design, however, the RAIs outperformed alternate treatments on spiritual but not psychological variables. Again, methodological sophistication of these studies lagged behind state-of-the-art outcome research.

Summary

The six reviews were consistent in concluding that there is support for the efficacy of RAIs. These psychotherapies generally work to reduce psychological symptoms and work about as well as alternate secular psychotherapies. There are mixed findings, however, about whether RAIs offer practical benefits beyond those provided by secular treatments. Each of the six reviews noted methodological weaknesses that need to be corrected in future studies. The most common weaknesses noted included (a) small sample sizes; (b) failure to report attrition; (c) reduced numbers of studies available to review because of failure to randomly assign clients to treatment conditions; (d) no treatment manual or fixed protocol, (e) no treatment fidelity checks; (f) failure to control for psychotherapist effects; (g) failure to perform a long-term follow-up; and (h) failure to include clients from a greater diversity of religious, racial or ethnic, and cultural backgrounds. Several of the reviews also pointed out some methodological strengths of outcome studies in this domain, including the frequent use of (a) experimental designs involving random assignment and control groups, (b) real clients and real psychotherapists in actual treatment settings, and (c) standardized outcome measures.

The methodological limitations of the studies of RAIs or SAIs are not uncommon in general psychotherapy outcome research (Lambert & Bergin, 1994). With the current climate of accountability, continued progress in the quality of outcome studies of RAIs and SAIs is needed. Johnson (1993) described important methodological criteria that psychotherapy outcome researchers should use to evaluate religiously accommodated approaches using experimental studies: (a) treatment manuals or materials, (b) multiple psychotherapists, (c) psychotherapists trained to competence, (d) independent evaluation of psychotherapists' competence, (e) highest evidence of internal validity, (f) verification of treatment integrity, (g) homogeneous samples of clients, (h) clinical samples, (i) multiple measurement modalities, (j) evaluation of the clinical significance of changes, and (k) follow-up assessment.

We suggest that additions to these standard research design considerations are needed if the treatments are RAIs or SAIs. Researchers must additionally (a) identify the psychospiritual goals that the treatment attempts to meet; (b) specify how religious accommodation is accomplished (specificity to a specific religion versus generality, amount of religious accommodation in conceptualization and technique); (c) reveal the degree of self-disclosure of the practitioner's own religious or spiritual beliefs, values, and religious commitment to clients; (d) identify specific religious techniques used; (e) explain the degree of difference from a secular approach from which it is derived; (f) state the specific religious terminology employed (e.g., ways to which God is referred; use of terms such as *crucifixion, five daily prayers,* or holidays like *Yom Kippur*); (g) provide coding manuals on how religious variables are coded; and (h) employ coders who are religiously sophisticated and also trained by researchers who are religiously sophisticated and knowledgeable.

BRINGING RAIs AND SAIs FULLY INTO THE MAINSTREAM

Integration of RAIs and SAIs Into Secular Psychotherapeutic Research

The empirical research on RCTs fit within the current paradigm of secular psychotherapy outcome research. In fact, several RAIs were found to have enough research support to label them empirically supported (Hook et al., 2010). The fairest assessment of the sophistication of the field is this: The existing research integrates theory, research, and practice, yet the ways that the religious constructs are accommodated into secular treatments is poorly specified. Furthermore, there appears to be little literature that represents a conversation between theorists who champion evidence-based religious treatment and practitioners who feed practical questions into the refinement of the theoretical approach. The RAIs that have been studied empirically are connected with the existing secular research. This is generally because most practitioners have been trained in secular research and received licenses to practice using secular approaches. Then, later, religious accommodations were made. Religious and spiritual adaptations have been multidimensional in the sense of the integrative paradigm followed in this handbook (see Volume 1, Chapter 1). Accommodations have included ecclesiastical practices (e.g., prayer, pastoral advice). Adjustments have sought to make approaches consistent with the religious beliefs, values, and worldviews of clients. Religion has been analyzed at multiple levels, including religious spirituality. The spiritual assessments that have accompanied efficacy investigations, however, typically have not employed religious assessments that are as nuanced as the religious measurements that occur in research in the psychology of religion and spirituality (see Hill & Hood, 1999; Hill & Pargament, 2003). Overall, the literature is more focused on whether an intervention works in general than on for whom it works better or worse. Overall, then, although the literature on RAIs and SAIs is integrative in its treatment of religion and spirituality, the literature on RAIs lags behind secular outcome research in the sophistication of research questions addressed, the use of Attribute × Treatment designs, the precise description of treatments (mainly identifying the religious accommodations being tested), and effectiveness and dissemination trials (McHugh & Barlow, 2010).

Generalizability of Religious Research

Effectiveness research is a term used by psychotherapy researchers to apply to how interventions are used in actual practice. This contrasts with the more controlled and constricted RCTs (which is called *efficacy research*). As in secular effectiveness research, there are many challenges and specific problems that arise when psychotherapists attempt to translate narrow, protocol-driven techniques in a laboratory setting (e.g., effectiveness of using of a prayer technique; focus on college students with subclinical distress) into actual clinical practice. Even though psychotherapists may attempt to follow a manual assiduously, in practice, they often deviate based on their clinical judgment. Issues like nonrandom assignment and meeting requirements by third-party payers (e.g., limits on treatments) can yield wide variations from treatment manuals and best practices. Internal validity is typically lower for effectiveness studies than for efficacy studies. In addition, in effectiveness research, the number of self-report or other assessments that psychotherapists use or clients complete can weaken the assessment of the outcomes, moving outcomes farther from objective measures and creating an overreliance on client self-report of clinical judgment of psychotherapists.

The most intriguing example of an effectiveness study to date was conducted by Wade, Worthington, and Vogel (2007). Instead of testing a specifically RAI, they surveyed professional counselors who were identified as Christian counselors ($n = 51$) and their clients ($n = 220$) drawn from six explicitly Christian agencies and one secular agency. They sought to discover (a) what techniques were used in advertised Christian counseling as practiced by those in the field, (b) whether they were effective in terms of client and counselor rated change, and (c) whether matching the religious commitment of clients to their counselors affected outcomes. Wade et al. used general ratings by clients and counselors of change. General ratings were necessary because many types of presenting problems were treated. They found that clients and psychotherapists in Christian psychotherapy generally believed that religiously tailored techniques were appropriate. Clients at Christian agencies reported equally close working relationships to their psychotherapists and equal improvements in their presenting problems over time as did clients at secular agencies. Psychotherapists in Christian agencies used secular techniques as frequently and religious techniques more frequently than did those in secular agencies. Clients with high religious commitment—regardless of secular or explicitly Christian agency—reported more closeness with their psychotherapists and more psychological improvement in RAIs than did clients with low religious commitment.

A variety of elements are missing in effectiveness outcome research to date. First, there are few major controlled studies that have tested an established, evidence-based RAI across a range of actual clinical settings (cf. Markman et al., 2004). Second, there is a need to assess unique elements of treatments that are religious. These are frequently not identified and almost never assessed and related to outcome. Third, there is a need to assess unique mechanisms of change that may bolster the effects of RAIs. For example, if a person prays regularly for God's favor or God's intervention to reduce a symptom, the invocation of God may keep the issue of change on the client's mind, prime spiritual cognition, or imbue the effort with special significance. Such an individual might also engage members of the religious community or other personal supporters to provide social support. Fourth, there is a need to assess both psychological, and religious and spiritual outcomes. Fifth, existing studies typically sample religiously committed clients seeking religiously accommodated services at specifically identified religious psychotherapy sites. They rarely if ever include religious clients seeking services at secular mental health clinics. To complete such research would require counselors at secular sites to be willing to collaborate on such research, and many clinic directors might object, fearing that offering explicitly religious counseling might affect client flow, client expectations, and the reputation of the agency in the community. Sixth, it is difficult in a single study to stratify samples to accurately represent the wide diversity of religious beliefs, attitudes, values, and commitment across Christian denominations (not to mention across different religions) and geographic regions. Such diversity also extends to the interaction between different racial and ethnic backgrounds, and religiousness often is intermixed with other elements of diversity. Overall, effectiveness research on RAIs lags behind secular research even more than is true when considering RCTs.

Sophistication of RCTs Must Increase

Horse-race studies. Almost all of the research to date on RAIs has been aimed at what might be termed a horse-race mentality. At the lowest level or research sophistication, investigators simply document that changes occur from pretreatment to posttreatment (can the "horse" finish the race?). Such pre–post comparisons can be important for pilot studies to test whether an intervention shows enough promise to warrant a more elaborate and expensive study. But such comparisons usually would be considered inadequate for demonstrating clinical efficacy. Beyond that, existing research intends to show that a treatment can "defeat" other "horses"—a no-treatment, placebo, or alternative intervention that is more or less similar to the RAI. At the strictest level of comparison, the RAI is compared with the secular intervention to which religious techniques were added. Future research must go beyond this horse-race approach and evaluate whether RAIs are more (or less) efficacious for certain types of individuals (e.g., those who are more religious).

Funding. Secular efficacy research has moved beyond this horse-race mentality. In secular research, investigators more frequently study which treatment is most effective for which clients for which problems at which time. Typically, such studies require funding from private or public sources. Federal grants typically require pilot data that frankly exceed the sophistication of almost all of the existing RCTs on RAIs. Funding of research on RAIs by private sources has not, to this point, been forthcoming on the scale necessary to study important questions with clinical samples. Lack of research funding can lead to a case of "the rich get richer and the poor get poorer" if changes are not made. Either funding agencies must change (which does not seem likely) or the fund-seeking strategies of investigators must change. Such strategic changes might include the following. RAI researchers could collaborate to (a) do larger studies, (b) use their different strengths (i.e., design, statistics, networking with sites to solicit clients, grant writing, web design, and design of psychotherapist training programs), and (c) test interventions in multiple sites. By collaborating, researchers can produce studies of sufficient quality and size to serve as competitive pilot studies for grant applications.

Interventions across and within religious groups. With the specific religious tailoring of treatments to particular religious subcultures, there is little research that shows how treatments accommodated for one faith tradition might or might not be effective for clients from different world religions or different branches of the same major faith tradition. Muslims or Buddhists would probably not find Christian accommodated treatments acceptable, nor would they likely find Jewish-accommodated CBT acceptable (see Rosmarin et al., 2010). Within religious traditions (e.g., Muslims), however, research is needed on which accommodations might be more broadly acceptable or unacceptable. Most Christian-accommodated CBTs for depression or anxiety have been examined with religiously conservative Christian clients. No studies have investigated how, for example, liberal or mainline Christians might respond to specific accommodations. We already discussed the importance of matching specific religious language used in treatments to the clients' faith tradition, but no research has studied what uses of language and techniques might be broadly acceptable.

The ways studies are done can affect not only outcomes but also availability to practitioners. Interventions that are available online through workbooks or manuals can provide practitioners easy access and can facilitate dissemination. Rosmarin et al. (2010) have made manuals publicly available for Jewish-accommodated treatment for anxiety. Worthington (2012) has made a Christian-accommodated intervention to promote forgiveness available.

General religious interventions. Most religious accommodation has used the beliefs and values of specific religions. That often appeals to theologically conservative religious people. Many mainline and theologically liberal religious people, however, tend to be more broadly accepting of truths culled from different religious traditions and religious truths framed broadly. Pargament (2007), for example, has articulated such an intervention. Richards and Bergin (2005) designed an intervention to appeal to people of religions that are theistic. Both of those psychotherapeutic approaches appeal to different religious groups than, for example, theologically conservative Christian, Muslim, or Jewish adherents. One future experimental avenue would be to randomly assign theologically conservative, moderate, and liberal Muslims (for example) to a general treatment (e.g., Pargament's) or a specifically Muslim-accommodated treatment. In addition, studies are needed that compare mixed religious groups (e.g., each group consisting of Jewish, Muslim, and Christian adherents who attend the group together) with three separate groups aimed at either exclusively Jewish, Muslim, or Christian adherents.

Dissemination. Implementation trials of evidence-based psychological interventions have begun, some on a very large scale, with substantial implications for the science and profession of psychology. But methods to transport treatments to service delivery settings have developed independently without strong evidence for, or even a consensus on, best practices for accomplishing this task or for measuring successful outcomes of training. McHugh and Barlow (2010) reviewed leading efforts at the national, state, and individual treatment development levels to integrate evidence-based interventions into service delivery settings. Effective dissemination involves standardized training materials and procedures for training, certification of competency, and monitoring of implementation over time. Few efforts at dissemination of RAIs exist.

As RAIs have garnered research support for their efficacy, more practitioners—even those who do not embrace the faith commitments—have attended workshops and completed continuing education programs for treating religiously committed clients. We assume that nearly all trained psychotherapists can deliver psychological treatments effectively if they have received good education and training about delivering the treatments and have supervision. Recent surveys, however, show that despite the widespread availability of such training opportunities, few take advantage of them (Bartoli, 2007; Brawer, Handal, Fabricatore, Roberts, & Waida-Johnston, 2002; Russell & Yarhouse, 2006).

The dissemination of RAIs is also hampered by the failure of many training programs in counseling or clinical psychology to treat religion as a diversity variable that demands as much attention as many other diversity variables (Hage, 2006; Worthington et al., 2009). For instance, in a survey of counseling psychology training directors, Schulte, Skinner, and Claiborn (2002) found that only 31% of the programs even discussed spiritual or religious issues.

CONCRETE SUGGESTIONS FOR ENHANCING CLINICAL RESEARCH

Researchers can improve the quality of empirical research on treatments in a variety of ways. They can improve the quality of RCTs, use a variety of non-RCT methods to supplement RCTs, and engage other voices in providing clinical research. In the sections that follow, we provide suggestions for an enhanced research agenda.

Improving the Quality of RCTs

Our evaluation of the research suggests that religious outcome research is not up to the standards of secular outcome research. This manifests in several ways. First, as we have argued, RCTs on RAIs have difficulty using completely crossed treatment-by-attribute designs (because highly religious and overtly nonreligious people refuse to be assigned to value incongruent treatments). Second, several barriers to conducting research on RAIs have resulted in smaller and more limited studies than for secular approaches. Third, the existing measurement of religious and spiritual constructs in RCTs with RAIs often has not been up to the sophistication of measures available in the psychology of religion. Thus, much improvement is needed in conducting RCT research on RAIs. To improve the quality and increase the quantity of RCTs with RAIs, (a) more investigators must be attracted into the field and (b) more collaboration must occur.

The number of investigators is likely to increase in the next 25 years for several reasons. First, the field has gained scientific respectability as acceptance of diversity has increased. Religious diversity is also increasingly recognized. One important bit of evidence occurred with Norcross's (2011) book on relationship factors in psychotherapy. An independent joint task force from American Psychological

Association (APA) Division 12 (Clinical Psychology) and Division 29 (Psychotherapy) evaluated all relationship factors considered by writers in the Norcross volume. Authors conducted meta-analyses and provided summaries of existing research. The evidence by Worthington et al. (2011) was evaluated and religious accommodation was accorded the highest level of endorsement (i.e., demonstrably effective) as a matching variable. Second, the number of investigators is likely to increase because diversity (including religious and spiritual diversity) is increasing as the population changes (Berger et al., 1999). Third, the number of empirically supported RAIs has increased and evidence-based practice makes it likely that even more will reach this status in the next decade (Hook et al., 2010). Thus, both supply-side and demand-side pressures are pushing for more and better RAIs.

More collaboration is needed. To do efficacy research of sufficient size to make an impact, multisite and multidisciplinary teams are necessary. Outcome measures that involve physiological change or report-of-other assessment have been virtually absent in RCTs with RAIs. Larger teams are needed so that there will be expertise to carry out the assessments and analyze the data. Large-scale multisite studies will require collaboration not only among clinical scientists but also between clinical scientists and practitioners, as will dissemination trials.

Diversity of Methods

Non-RCT methods. The RCT is an important method to build confidence in treatment efficacy. Not all important questions have been addressed with RCT research (e.g., for what type of people, with what psychological problems, under what conditions are approaches efficacious?). We support the need for improved RCT research, but we recognize that other (non-RCT) methods of discovering answers might supplement RCT research in answering those questions. The APA's (2005) *Policy Statement on Evidence-Based Practice in Psychology* encourages "the integration of the best available research with clinical expertise in the context of patient characteristics, culture, and preferences" (p. 1). The 2006 report of the APA Presidential Task Force on Evidence-Based Practice (APA, 2006) described best research evidence as follows:

> *Best research evidence* refers to scientific results related to intervention strategies, assessment, clinical problems, and patient populations in laboratory and field settings as well as to clinically relevant results of basic research in psychology and related fields. APA endorses multiple types of research evidence (e.g., efficacy, effectiveness, cost-effectiveness, cost-benefit, epidemiological, treatment utilization) that contributes to effective psychological practice. Multiple research designs contribute to evidence-based practice, and different research designs are better suited to address different types of questions. (p. 274)

The APA (2006) task force described how different types of research designs (including RCTs and meta-analyses) might contribute to evidence-based practice. Those include clinical observation (e.g., individual case studies), systematic case studies, single-case experimental designs, qualitative research, public health and ethnographic research, process-outcome studies, and studies of interventions in naturalistic settings.

Types of non-RCT methods. Richards and Bergin (2005) summarized the defining characteristics of experimental, single-*N*, ethnography, grounded theory, and case study designs. Each has its own strengths and weaknesses and is suited to study different types of questions (for a summary, see Richards & Worthington, 2010).

Single-subject designs can help establish an evidence-base for spiritual psychotherapies. In a *single-subject study*, the client serves as his or her own control. By measuring changes in client symptoms or problems over time, psychotherapists can see the impact of the treatment (Kazdin, 1994). *Discovery-oriented* (Mahrer, 1988) and *change process* (Greenberg, 1986) designs are often more feasible to carry out in clinical settings because they can be less intrusive and ethically problematic than experimental designs. They also can be more clinically relevant. They permit exploration of questions meaningful to psychotherapists (Kazdin, 1994).

From the qualitative research tradition, case study, ethnographic, and grounded theory designs can yield insights into the spiritual nature and processes of psychotherapy and psychotherapeutic change, as viewed from the perspectives of clients and psychotherapists. *Case studies* have a long history in psychology and psychotherapy (Stake, 1994). They can provide qualitative evidence concerning the processes and outcomes of spiritual psychotherapies, although they cannot conclusively rule out threats to internal and external validity. *Ethnographic* and *grounded theory* studies—such as interviewing and participant observation of psychotherapy, clients, and psychotherapists—may provide insight into how clients and psychotherapists perceive spiritually oriented psychotherapies in general, as well as the effects of the various components of such treatment approaches.

Qualitative studies are time-consuming, laborious, and challenging to report given the page limitations of many journals (for a review of qualitative research on religion and spirituality, see Aten & Hernandez, 2005). Many of the methods used for data collection in qualitative research, however, are similar to those used in clinical practice (e.g., unstructured interviews, participant observation, audio-taped conversations, case notes, and diaries; Denzin & Lincoln, 1994). Much of what psychotherapists do in psychotherapy could provide data for qualitative studies. Thus far, qualitative studies have gained little traction relative to quantitative research strategies. Qualitative, ethnographic, naturalistic, and phenomenological methodologies are being used with increasing frequency, which we believe to be advantageous because these approaches hold promise for deepening understanding of the complexities and outcomes of psychotherapy and psychotherapeutic change.

Illustration of a non-RCT method. One example of a non-RCT outcome study is provided by Murray-Swank and Pargament (2005). They evaluated the effectiveness of an eight-session, spiritually integrated intervention for female survivors of sexual abuse with spiritual struggles. An individual psychotherapist conducted manual-driven sessions, using the intervention, Solace for the Soul: A Journey Towards Wholeness. An interrupted time-series design included daily measurements of positive and negative religious coping, spiritual distress, and spiritual self-worth, and measures of spiritual well-being, religious coping, and images of God. Assessments were made pre- and postintervention, and 1 to 2 months later. Clients improved in positive religious coping, spiritual well-being, and positive images of God. In addition, intervention analyses revealed changes in daily use of positive religious coping throughout treatment.

How Can Leaders Help Change the Field?

Leadership is needed to bring about those changes that increase collaboration on RCTs and foster acceptance of non-RCT methods. There are few platforms from which a leader can advocate for changes. Leaders are needed to persuade (a) lay people (i.e., religious opinion leaders and clients) that scientifically tested approaches are valuable and useful; (b) clients to participate in research studies; (c) practitioners to participate in studies, use scientifically supported approaches, and participate in dissemination efforts; (d) religious institutions to modify their reward structures to be more open to valuing psychological theorizing and empirical research; and (e) new researchers to study religious outcomes and develop and test their own theories.

We believe that there is some reason for confidence that the climate is ripe for change. There are numerous examples among book publishers that RAIs provide a base for selling books to secular and religious practitioners. RAIs have proliferated as noted in our review of past reviews. With a fertile field prepared, respected voices are needed that will lead others to sow the seeds needed to grow new crops. We suggest that these voices could probably come from energetic early career and long-established investigators.

Research Agenda

Improvement of individual studies. More investigators must commit to a systematic investigation of treatments. Religious training programs might encourage doctoral students to conduct dissertation research involving clinical trials. Such dissertation research is often not as sophisticated as most published outcome research, which is often team-based, funded, and multisite. The quality of the individual studies must more closely approximate those of secular psychotherapy studies. We suggest, therefore, that collaborators consider team-based studies that extend across laboratories.

Large-scale RCT research. The number of large RCTs and the scale of the research effort must be increased. Secular RCT research is often funded by federal agencies under the R01 mechanism. Such funded research requires, at a minimum, large pilot studies. Those pilot studies are often, themselves, funded by other more limited mechanisms (e.g., K-awards, R21, R26 mechanisms). At present, virtually no research on RAIs approximates the level of sophistication that would be needed for a pilot study for one of these grants. It is no wonder that almost no studies in a recent meta-analysis (Worthington et al., 2011) acknowledged federal support. Large-scale research is necessary to further the field and typically that will mean increased collaboration.

Effectiveness research and dissemination trials. Most researchers despair at the possibility of rigorous experimental controls in effectiveness research. Yet there are ways to exert more control and thus enhance internal validity even on field studies. For example, dismantling designs can be used and random assignment can be employed. For example, suppose Christian CBT was being studied. Two treatment manuals could be created. One uses the entire Christian CBT protocol. The other omits specific techniques from the full protocol (e.g., some combination of prayer, bibliotherapy, references to the Bible, religious imagery). Participating psychotherapists could agree to random assignment of their clients to either full or partial Christian CBT protocol. Perhaps in a large effectiveness trial, multiple manuals could govern treatment (i.e., full, full minus prayer, full minus bibliotherapy, etc.). Or effectiveness could be studied by having psychotherapists and clients agree to have sessions recorded. The "dose"—that is, the number of religious techniques or time spent in each—could be coded and used to determine what techniques and how much of each might contribute to objective psychotherapy outcomes.

Collaboration, cooperation, self-sacrifice, and leadership. Investigators must pool resources and cooperate to conduct a study of sufficient complexity, size, and importance to draw the attention of funding agencies. A coordinated, strategic effort to develop several treatment approaches is needed. To build a base of federally funded projects that investigates RAIs, *collaboration* is needed across researchers so that clinical trials—such as the depression trials (e.g., Rush et al., 1998)—can be conducted at multiple sites. *Cooperation* is needed among institutions to host such studies, invest their resources, and reward such long-term research efforts. *Self-sacrifice* is needed because researchers must agree to investigate treatment approaches that are not necessarily their own so that a research effort of sufficient magnitude to create a large impact can be conducted. *Leadership* is needed to organize such efforts. Leadership requires recruiting participating researchers and institutions, raising private funds, and coordinating a large clinical trial.

CONCLUSION

At the outset of this chapter, we suggested that highly religiously committed (and frequently religiously conservative) clients engage in RAIs because they believe (a) they have a right to it and (b) it will be more effective for them. The first assertion is not an empirical question, but rather it is a question concerning the freedom for clients to choose their own type of treatment. The second assertion is an empirical question that can be answered in meta-analytic reviews (see Worthington et al., 2011). Although the majority of evidence indicates that RAIs work as well as established secular treatments, there is little evidence that these treatments work better than established secular treatments.

Better and more research evidence is needed. There are numerous difficulties in conducting research on RAIs. Many of these difficulties are shared with secular outcome research, but some are unique to research on RAIs. Even with the myriad of difficulties, substantial efficacy research has been produced, although this research is characterized by smaller studies, little replication, few researchers who do programmatic research on one RAI, and little agreement on how religious accommodation has been achieved. For the field to rise to the state-of-the-science standards of the secular field, collaboration, cooperation, self-sacrifice, and leadership are required.

References

American Psychological Association. (2005). *Policy statement on evidence-based practice in psychology.* Washington, DC: Author. Retrieved from http://www.apa.org/practice/ebp.html

American Psychological Association. (2006). Evidence-based practice in psychology. *American Psychologist, 61*, 271–285. doi:10.1037/0003-066X.61.4.271

Aten, J. D., & Hernandez, B. C. (2005). A 25-year review of qualitative research published in spiritually and psychologically oriented journals. *Journal of Psychology and Christianity, 24*, 266–277.

Ball, R. A., & Goodyear, R. K. (1991). Self-reported professional practices of Christian psychologists. *Journal of Psychology and Christianity, 10*, 144–153.

Bartoli, E. (2007). Religious and spiritual issues in psychotherapy practice: Training the trainer. *Psychotherapy: Theory, Research, Practice, Training, 44*, 54–65. doi:10.1037/0033-3204.44.1.54

Bassett, R. L., Saddler, R. D., Kobischen, E. E., Skiff, D. M., Merrill, I. J., Atwater, B. J., & Livermore, P. W. (1981). The Shepherd Scale: Separating the sheep from the goats. *Journal of Psychology and Theology, 9*, 335–351.

Berger, P. L., Sacks, J., Martin, D., Weiming, T., Weigel, G., Davie, G., & An-Naim, A. A. (Eds.). (1999). *The desecularization of the world: Resurgent religion and world politics.* Grand Rapids, MI: Eerdmans.

Brawer, P. A., Handal, P. J., Fabricatore, A. N., Roberts, R., & Waida-Johnston, V. A. (2002). Training and education in religion/spirituality within APA-accredited psychology programs. *Professional Psychology: Research and Practice, 33*, 203–206. doi:10.1037/0735-7028.33.2.203

Denzin, N. K., & Lincoln, Y. S. (Eds.). (1994). *Handbook of qualitative research.* Thousand Oaks, CA: Sage.

Ellis, A. (1962). *Reason and emotion in psychotherapy.* New York, NY: Stuart.

Ellison, C. W., & Smith, J. (1991). Toward an integrative measure of health and well-being. *Journal of Psychology and Theology, 19*, 35–48.

Greenberg, L. S. (1986). Change process research. *Journal of Consulting and Clinical Psychology, 54*, 4–9. doi:10.1037/0022-006X.54.1.4

Hage, S. M. (2006). A closer look at the role of spirituality in psychology training programs. *Professional Psychology: Research and Practice, 37*, 303–310. doi:10.1037/0735-7028.37.3.303

Haley, J. (1976). *Problem-solving therapy.* San Francisco, CA: Jossey-Bass.

Hill, P. C., & Hood, R. W. (1999). *Measures of religiosity.* Birmingham, AL: Religious Education Press.

Hill, P. C., & Pargament, K. I. (2003). Advances in the conceptualization and measurement of religion and spirituality. *American Psychologist, 58*, 64–74. doi:10.1037/0003-066X.58.1.64

Hook, J. N., & Worthington, E. L., Jr. (2009). Christian couple counseling by professional, pastoral, and lay counselors from a Protestant perspective: A nationwide survey. *American Journal of Family Therapy, 37*, 169–183. doi:10.1080/01926180802151760

Hook, J. N., Worthington, E. L., Jr., Davis, D. E., Gartner, A. L., Jennings, D. J., II, & Hook, J. P. (2010). Empirically supported religious and spiritual therapies. *Journal of Clinical Psychology, 66*, 46–72.

Johnson, W. B. (1993). Outcome research and religious psychotherapies: Where are we and where are we going? *Journal of Psychology and Theology, 21*, 297–308.

Kapuscinski, A. N., & Masters, K. S. (2010). The current status of measures of spirituality: A critical review of scale development. *Psychology of Religion and Spirituality*, 2, 191–205. doi:10.1037/a0020498

Kazdin, A. E. (1994). Methodology, design, and evaluation in psychotherapy research. In A. E. Bèrgin & S. L. Garfield (Eds.), *Handbook of psychotherapy and behavior change* (4th ed., pp. 19–71). New York, NY: Wiley.

Lambert, M. J., & Bergin, A. E. (1994). The effectiveness of psychotherapy. In A. E. Bergin & S. L. Garfield (Eds.), *Handbook of psychotherapy and behavior change* (4th ed., pp. 143–189). New York, NY: Wiley.

Lampton, C., Oliver, G. J., Worthington, E. L., Jr., & Berry, J. W. (2005). Helping Christian college students become more forgiving: An intervention study to promote forgiveness as part of a program to shape Christian character. *Journal of Psychology and Theology, 33*, 278–290.

Mahrer, A. R. (1988). Discovery-oriented psychotherapy research: Rationale, aims, and methods. *American Psychologist, 43*, 694–702. doi:10.1037/0003-066X.43.9.694

Markman, H. J., Whitton, S. W., Kline, G. H., Stanley, S. M., Thompson, H., St. Peters, M., . . . Cordova, A. (2004). Use of an empirically based marriage education program by religious organizations: Results of a dissemination trial. *Family Relations, 53*, 504–512. doi:10.1111/j.0197-6664.2004.00059.x

McCullough, M. E. (1999). Research on religion-accommodative counseling: Review and meta-analysis. *Journal of Counseling Psychology, 46*, 92–98. doi:10.1037/0022-0167.46.1.92

McCullough, M. E., Hoyt, W. T., Larson, D. B., Koenig, H. G., & Thoresen, C. (2000). Religious involvement and mortality: A meta-analytic review. *Health Psychology, 19*, 211–222. doi:10.1037/0278-6133.19.3.211

McHugh, R. K., & Barlow, D. H. (2010). The dissemination and implementation of evidence-based psychological treatments: A review of current efforts. *American Psychologist, 65*, 73–84. doi:10.1037/a0018121

McMinn, M. R., & Campbell, C. D. (2008). *Integrative psychotherapy: Toward a comprehensive Christian approach.* Downers Grove, IL: InterVarsity Press.

Meylink, W. D., & Gorsuch, R. L. (1988). Relationship between clergy and psychologists: The empirical data. *Journal of Psychology and Christianity, 7*, 56–72.

Murray-Swank, N. A., & Pargament, K. I. (2005). God, where are you? Evaluating a spiritually-integrated intervention for sexual abuse. *Mental Health, Religion, and Culture, 8*, 191–203. doi:10.1080/13694670500138866

Norcross, J. C. (Ed.). (2011). *Relationships that work* (2nd ed.). New York, NY: Oxford University Press. doi:10.1093/acprof:oso/9780199737208.001.0001

Pargament, K. I. (2007). *Spiritually integrated psychotherapy: Understanding and addressing the sacred.* New York, NY: Guilford Press.

Pargament, K. I., & Mahoney, A. (2005). Sacred matters: Sanctification as a vital topic for the psychology of religion. *The International Journal for the Psychology of Religion, 15*, 179–198. doi:10.1207/s15327582ijpr1503_1

Plante, T. G. (2009). *Spiritual practices in psychotherapy: Thirteen tools for enhancing psychological health.* Washington, DC: American Psychological Association. doi:10.1037/11872-000

Razali, S. M., Aminah, K., & Khan, U. A. (2002). Religious-cultural psychotherapy in the management of anxiety patients. *Transcultural Psychiatry, 39*, 130–136. doi:10.1177/136346150203900106

Richards, P. S., & Bergin, A. E. (Eds.). (2004). *Casebook for a spiritual strategy in counseling and psychotherapy.* Washington, DC: American Psychological Association. doi:10.1037/10652-000

Richards, P. S., & Bergin, A. E. (2005). *A spiritual strategy for counseling and psychotherapy* (2nd ed.). Washington, DC: American Psychological Association. doi:10.1037/11214-000

Richards, P. S., & Potts, R. W. (1995). Using spiritual interventions in psychotherapy: Practices, successes, failures, and ethical concerns of Mormon psychotherapists. *Professional Psychology: Research and Practice, 26*, 163–170. doi:10.1037/0735-7028.26.2.163

Richards, P. S., & Worthington, E. L., Jr. (2010). The need for evidence-based spiritually oriented psychotherapies. *Professional Psychology: Research and Practice, 41*, 363–370. doi:10.1037/a0019469

Rosmarin, D. H., Pargament, K. I., Pirutinsky, S., & Mahoney, A. (2010). A randomized controlled evaluation of a spiritually integrated treatment for subclinical anxiety in the Jewish community, delivered via the Internet. *Journal of Anxiety Disorders, 24*, 799–808. doi:10.1016/j.janxdis.2010.05.014

Rush, A. J., Koran, L. M., Keller, M. B., Markowitz, J. C., Harrison, W. M., Miceli, R. J., . . . Thase, M. E. (1998). The treatment of chronic depression, Part 1: Study design and rationale for evaluating the comparative efficacy of sertraline and imipramine as acute, crossover, continuation, and maintenance phase therapies. *Journal of Clinical Psychiatry, 59*, 589–597. doi:10.4088/JCP.v59n1106

Russell, S. R., & Yarhouse, M. A. (2006). Training in religion/spirituality within APA-accredited psychology predoctoral internships. *Professional Psychology: Research and Practice, 37*, 430–436. doi:10.1037/0735-7028.37.4.430

Rye, M. S., Pargament, K. I., Pan, W., Yingling, D. W., Shogren, K. A., & Ito, M. (2005). Can group interventions facilitate forgiveness of an ex-spouse? A randomized clinical trial. *Journal of Consulting and Clinical Psychology, 73*, 880–892. doi:10.1037/0022-006X.73.5.880

Schulte, D. L., Skinner, T. A., & Claiborn, C. D. (2002). Religious and spiritual issues in counseling psychology training. *The Counseling Psychologist, 30*, 118–134. doi:10.1177/0011000002301009

Shafranske, E. P. (Ed.). (1996). *Religion and clinical practice of psychology.* Washington, DC: American Psychological Association.

Shafranske, E. P. (2000). Religious involvement and professional practices of psychiatrists and other mental health professionals. *Psychiatric Annals, 30*, 525–532.

Shafranske, E. P. (2001). The religious dimension of patient care within rehabilitation medicine: The role of religious attitudes, beliefs, and professional practices. In T. G. Plante & A. C. Sherman (Eds.), *Faith and health: Psychological perspectives* (pp. 311–335). New York, NY: Guilford Press.

Shafranske, E. P., & Malony, H. N. (1990). Clinical psychologists' religious and spiritual orientations and their practice of psychotherapy. *Psychotherapy: Theory, Research, Practice, Training, 27*, 72–78. doi:10.1037/0033-3204.27.1.72

Smith, T. B., Bartz, J. D., & Richards, P. S. (2007). Outcomes of religious and spiritual adaptations to psychotherapy: A meta-analytic review. *Psychotherapy Research, 17*, 643–655. doi:10.1080/10503300701250347

Sperry, L., & Shafranske, E. P. (Eds.). (2005). *Spiritually oriented psychotherapy*. Washington, DC: American Psychological Association. doi:10.1037/10886-000

Stake, R. E. (1994). Case studies. In N. K. Denzin & Y. S. Lincoln (Eds.), *Handbook of qualitative research* (pp. 236–247). Thousand Oaks, CA: Sage.

Stratton, S. P., Dean, J. B., Nonneman, A. J., Bode, R. A., & Worthington, E. L., Jr. (2008). Forgiveness interventions as spiritual development strategies: Comparing forgiveness workshop training, expressive writing about forgiveness, and retested controls. *Journal of Psychology and Christianity, 27*, 347–357.

Wade, N. G., Worthington, E. L., Jr., & Vogel, D. L. (2007). Effectiveness of religiously tailored interventions in Christian therapy. *Psychotherapy Research, 17*, 91–105. doi:10.1080/10503300500497388

Worthington, E. L., Jr. (1988). Understanding the values of religious clients: A model and its application to counseling. *Journal of Counseling Psychology, 35*, 166–174. doi:10.1037/0022-0167.35.2.166

Worthington, E. L., Jr. (2006). *Forgiveness and reconciliation: Theory and application*. New York, NY: Brunner-Routledge.

Worthington, E. L., Jr. (2010). Integration of spirituality and religion into psychotherapy. In J. C. Norcross, G. VandenBos, & D. K. Freedheim (Eds.), *History of psychotherapy* (2nd ed., pp. 533–543). Washington, DC: American Psychological Association.

Worthington, E. L., Jr. (2012). *Forgiveness intervention manuals*. Retrieved from http://www.people.vcu.edu/~eworth

Worthington, E. L., Jr., Hook, J. N., Davis, D. E., & McDaniel, M. A. (2011). Religion and spirituality. In J. Norcross (Ed.), *Psychotherapy relationships that work* (2nd ed., pp. 402–420). New York, NY: Oxford University Press. doi:10.1093/acprof:oso/9780199737208.003.0020

Worthington, E. L., Jr., Hunter, J. L., Sharp, C. B., Hook, J. N., Van Tongeren, D. R., Davis, D. E., . . . Monteforte-Milton, M. (2010). A psychoeducational intervention to promote forgiveness in Christians in the Philippines. *Journal of Mental Health Counseling, 32*, 75–93.

Worthington, E. L., Jr., Kurusu, T. A., McCullough, M. E., & Sandage, S. J. (1996). Empirical research on religion and psychotherapeutic processes and outcomes: A ten-year review and research prospectus. *Psychological Bulletin, 119*, 448–487. doi:10.1037/0033-2909.119.3.448

Worthington, E. L., Jr., & Sandage, S. J. (2001). Religion and spirituality. *Psychotherapy: Theory, Research, Practice, Training, 38*, 473–478. doi:10.1037/0033-3204.38.4.473

Worthington, E. L., Jr., Sandage, S. J., Davis, D. E., Hook, J. N., Miller, A. J., Hall, M. E. L., & Hall, T. W. (2009). Training therapists to address spiritual concerns in clinical practice and research. In J. D. Aten & M. M. Leach (Eds.), *Spirituality and the therapeutic process: A comprehensive resource from intake to termination* (pp. 267–292). Washington, DC: American Psychological Association. doi:10.1037/11853-012

Worthington, E. L., Jr., Wade, N. G., Hight, T. L., Ripley, J. S., McCullough, M. E., Berry, J. W., . . . O'Conner, L. (2003). The Religious Commitment Inventory—10: Development, refinement, and validation of a brief scale for research and counseling. *Journal of Counseling Psychology, 50*, 84–96. doi:10.1037/0022-0167.50.1.84

Index

Volume numbers are printed in boldface type, followed by a colon and the relevant page numbers.